Wondrous Ocean of Eloquence

Shambhala Publications gratefully acknowledges the generous support of Robert H. N. Ho in sponsoring the translation and the Tsadra Foundation in sponsoring the preparation and printing of this book.

Wondrous Ocean of Eloquence

Histories of the Taklung Kagyu Tradition

By Taklung Ngawang Namgyel,
Taklung Trirab Ngawang Tenpai Nyima,
Jedrung Jampel Gyeltsen, and
Kaḥtok Situ Chokyi Gyatso

TRANSLATED BY
Gyurme Dorje

EDITOR'S PREFACE
TO THE TIBETAN EDITION BY
Tharling Jampa Tsering

WITH CONTRIBUTIONS FROM
Phakchok Rinpoche,
John Canti, and Jane Casey

SNOW LION

Snow Lion
An imprint of Shambhala Publications, Inc.
2129 13th Street
Boulder, Colorado 80302
www.shambhala.com

Cover art: Courtesy of the Stephen and Sharon Davies Collection
Cover design: Daniel Urban-Brown

9 8 7 6 5 4 3 2 1

First Edition
Printed in the United States of America

Shambhala Publications makes every effort to print on acid-free, recycled paper.
Snow Lion is distributed worldwide by Penguin Random House, Inc., and its subsidiaries.

LIBRARY OF CONGRESS CATALOGING-IN-PUBLICATION DATA
Names: Ngag-dbang-rnam-rgyal, Stag-lung-pa, 1571–1626, author. | Ngag-dbang-bstan-pa'i-nyi-ma, Stag-lung-pa, author. | Jampel Gyeltsen, Jedrung, author. | Si-tu Paṇ-chen Chos-kyi-'byung-gnas, 1699 or 1700 | Ngag-dbang-rnam-rgyal, Stag-lung-pa, 1571–1626, author. |
Title: Wondrous Ocean of Eloquence: Histories of the Taklung Kagyu tradition / by Taklungpa Ngawang Namgyel, Taklungpa Ngawang Tenpei Nyima Chokyi Jungne, Jedrung Jampel Gyeltsen, Situ Panchen Chökyi Jungne; translated by Gyurme Dorje.
Description: Boulder: Snow Lion, 2025. | Includes bibliographical references and index. |
Identifiers: LCCN 2023053786 | ISBN 9781559395069 (hardcover)
Subjects: LCSH: Stag-lung-pa (Sect)—China—Tibet—History. | Bka'-brgyud-pa lamas—China—Tibet—Biography. | Tibet Autonomous Region (China)—Biography.
Classification: LCC BQ7685.2 .N4313 2025 | DDC 294.3/923—dc23/eng/20240509
LC record available at https://lccn.loc.gov/2023053786

The authorized representative in the EU for product safety and compliance is eucomply OÜ, Pärnu mnt 139b-14, 11317 Tallinn, Estonia, hello@eucompliancepartner.com.

Contents

Foreword by Phakchok Rinpoche

Among the many brave, devoted, and learned masters who brought the sublime Dharma taught by Buddha Śākyamuni to the Snowy Lands of Tibet, the great translator and heart disciple of Mahāsiddha Nāropā (956–1040), Marpa Lotsāwa (1012–1097), stands out. Following in the footsteps of his root guru, Nāropā, and obeying his every command, Marpa received profound teachings that emphasized mahāmudrā meditation and the cultivation of deep devotion through guru yoga. This profound Dharma lineage became renowned as the Kagyu tradition. Its sublime teachings were passed through Jetsun Mila Repa (1040–1123), Gampopa Sonam Rinchen (1079–1153), and Phakmodrupa Dorje Gyelpo (1110–1170) to Taklung Tangpa Tashi Pel (1142–1210). Taklung Tangpa founded the revered Taklung Kagyu tradition in 1180 with the building of Yartang Monastery (Upper Taklung Monastery) in the serene heights of Upper Tibet. Later, the reincarnation of Gampopa and fourth throne holder of Yartang Monastery, Sangye On Drakpa Pel (1251–1296), established a second sanctuary in the tranquil landscape of Lower Tibet, Martang Kham Riwoche (Lower Taklung Monastery), in 1276.

These two main seats (*densa*) of the Taklung Kagyu have upheld and propagated the profound and sublime teachings of this extraordinary lineage in an unbroken chain, like a garland of gold. Reflecting on these extraordinary beginnings inspires great faith and devotion, which are the foundations for receiving blessings and achieving accomplishment (*siddhi*). It is my heartfelt aspiration that all who read this book will be inspired with great faith and devotion, delving deeply into the rich history of the illustrious Taklung Kagyu tradition.

Sarva Maṅgalam
Phakchok Rinpoche
Composed on Guru Rinpoche's Day of the fifth
month of the wood dragon year 2151 (2024)

Note from the Publisher

This multilayered historiographical volume on the political, artistic, architectural, biographical, and spiritual dimensions of the Taklung, a subsect of the Kagyu lineage of Tibetan Buddhism, is unparalleled in its comprehensive treatment of this lesser studied tradition. The four texts translated here tell a complex tale of Tibetan religiopolitical maneuvering in the face of centuries of civil unrest and armed conflict with Central Asian warring dynasties, in the midst of which art, architecture, and Buddhist practice flourished.

Bringing this project to fruition, the final work of the late translator Gyurme Dorje, truly serves an act of cultural preservation. The first and largest of the four texts in this volume is based on a badly damaged and mouse-eaten Tibetan "arrow-length" *pecha* manuscript that was compiled into a readable edition by Tharling Jampa Tsering in the 1990s. His experience retrieving the manuscript from ruins and compiling the critical edition is documented here in the editor's preface to the Tibetan edition of the first two of the four texts translated herein. The two main monastic seats of the lineage, Taklung and Riwoche, were hard hit by the Cultural Revolution, and to publish such a comprehensive history of a relatively minor subsect feels like a just act of resurrection of voices that could easily have disappeared from the history books.

This work is an engaging narrative that displays straightforward historiography on Tibet's real-world struggles (modern warfare, smallpox, leprosy, devious power plays among monastic and political leaders) within a world enlivened by prophecy, miracles, and hidden realms. Tibetan historiography exists in a cosmos enchanted with supramundane actors, multiple infinite world systems, and cosmology entailing cycles of conflict and end-times, which this volume presents at the outset. In Tibetan Buddhism, the authenticity of a tradition or practice is based on maintaining an unbroken lineage. The writing of history is thus not merely a record of events but rather a religious and devotional act of legitimation of a tradition done by scholar-monks. While this work is primarily a compendium of translations of traditional Tibetan historiographical works by and about the scholar-politician-artist monks of the Taklung lineage, it also includes broader lineage analyses of other Kagyu sects, the origins of diverse doctrinal traditions (including Zhije and Chod practice lineages), and the origins of the traditional monastic fields of education.

This massive historiographical work straddles the micro and macro. While detailing the abbatial succession of the tradition's two main monastic seats, Taklung and Riwoche Monasteries, it is also broad and vast in scale, going back to the sixth century B.C.E. in India to include early Indian Buddhist canon formation, moving then to narratives on the Tibetan Kagyu lineage holders (Marpa, Mila Repa, Gampopa), to the twelfth-century founding of the Taklung sect in Tibet, and then all the way through to the early twentieth century, which saw Tibet's first modern military and cultural conflicts both within the country and with Chinese, Mongol, and Gorkha forces.

There are four texts in this volume translated by the late Gyurme Dorje. The first, and central, text, *Wondrous Ocean of Eloquence* by Taklungpa Ngawang Namgyel (1571–1626), was written in 1609. It is a history of the Taklung from the very founding of Buddhism in India through to the author's own lifetime, including an abbatial succession of Taklung Monastery ending with the seventeenth abbot, Taklung Ngawang Namgyel himself. His history of the Taklung begins with a discussion of Buddhist world systems and ends with the civil unrest between the two central Tibetan provinces, U and Tsang, his own prophecy of which factors into his narrative. This history includes the Sakya-Mongol allegiances through the twelfth and thirteenth centuries and the succession of royal dynasties of the Phakmodru, Rinpungpa, and Tsangpa families.

The second text, *Great Divine Drum of Wondrous Renown* by Taklungpa Ngawang Tenpei Nyima Chokyi Jungne (b. 1788) was intended as a supplement to the first work. It was composed in 1824 to extend the abbatial succession of the first work past the lifetime of the first author to include seven more figures, ending with the author's own root teacher.

The third, *A Brief Chronicle of Riwoche, Including Jedrung Tulku Gongma and Gara Lama*, was composed by the twentieth-century Jedrung Jampel Gyeltsen. It is a history (to the year 1935) of Riwoche Monastery, the site of political tension between the central Tibetan government and the Chinese army under the Qing emperor. This narrative centers on the fascinating figure of Gara Lama (1865/76–1936), who was persecuted by both Tibetan and Chinese armies. He was believed by Tibetans to be a Chinese spy and is said to have been the first Tibetan master to teach Tibetan Buddhism within a modern Chinese episteme, though he would eventually fight for Tibetan self-rule and die in a communist prison.

The final supplemental work consists of excerpts from Kaḥtok Situ Chokyi Gyatso's (1880–1923) travelogue to central Tibet, *A Guide to the Sacred Places of Utsang*. It is a snapshot of Taklung Monastery in the early decades of the twentieth century, including elaborate descriptions of chapel architecture, paintings on silk brocade, tooth reliquaries, wall murals, painted scrolls, inventories of scriptures and treatises, and life-size statues of deities, buddhas, and protectors made of bronze, clay, gold, and sandalwood.

Shambhala is honored to be publishing Gyurme Dorje's translation of these histories of the Taklung tradition, which he completed before his passing in February 2020. The draft we received from Gyurme's widow, Xiaohong Dorje, included polished translations of each of the four texts herein. The manuscript was nearly complete, though it was evident that there were still sections Gyurme Dorje wished he could have finalized. The endnotes and references were substantial, but it was clear that he would have included considerably more annotations if he had been able, as there were many places throughout the text where an endnote callout had been placed but the endnote itself was blank. In most cases, these empty endnotes were deleted from the text during the editing process. Shambhala's editorial team made their best efforts to compile the reference list of English, Tibetan, and canonical works based on Gyurme's endnote author-date citations. Editorial notes were inserted for additional clarification and to indicate when Gyurme had marked a passage or term as uncertain. This manuscript was edited with utmost care to remain true to Gyurme's original intentions for the book.

So many have come together to make Gyurme Dorje's impressive and invaluable work a reality, lending their time and expertise to the completion of this project and making their best efforts without the benefit of Gyurme's oversight. John Canti reviewed the final edited manuscript and provides a foreword in honor of Gyurme's life and work. Jane Casey encouraged the project along from the very beginning and provides an introduction to Taklung painting, situating these translations within the larger world of Tibetan Buddhist art. Jane also provided the edited photographs of Taklung art and inscriptions. Phakchok Rinpoche also supported this project and generously provides a foreword, representing the Taklung tradition as it persists today. Jann Ronis at the Buddhist Digital Resource Center facilitated access to Tibetan texts that Gyurme had cited in order to confirm page numbers and reference information for the correct editions. Sangseraima Ujeed reviewed the Chinese and Mongolian terms and names. Robert H. N. Ho sponsored the translation, as did funds from John Eskenazi. The Tsadra Foundation was generous in sponsoring the production of this substantial book with its color images of Taklung art. Finally, Shambhala Publications extends deep gratitude to Xiaohong Dorje for entrusting us with this valuable work, yet another of Gyurme Dorje's exemplary contributions to our understanding of Tibetan Buddhist history, scholarship, and practice.

Shambhala Publications
Boulder, CO
2024

Honoring Gyurme Dorje (1950–2020)

Dr. Gyurme Dorje was one of the most expert and productive translators of Tibetan Buddhist history, philosophy, and practice. He died in February of 2020, in hospital in Dundee, Scotland. His life, personal qualities, and achievements as a translator and scholar are to be celebrated.

Despite his Tibetan name, Gyurme was a Scot. He was born Keith McClellan in Edinburgh but changed his legal name after becoming a Buddhist practitioner. He studied Sanskrit at Edinburgh University and, after obtaining his master's degree in 1971, left Scotland to travel in India and Nepal, where he stayed for most of the 1970s. He was an early Western student of Chatral Rinpoche, Dudjom Rinpoche, Kangyur Rinpoche, and Dilgo Khyentse Rinpoche.

I first met him in the winter of 1973 at Kangyur Rinpoche's monastery in Darjeeling. Gyurme was in retreat doing his preliminary practices in the room below mine in an outbuilding of the monastery. In those days, he lived on almost nothing by way of income. Later in the 1970s, I used to visit him where he lived, very simply, in a series of apartments in Bauddha, near Kathmandu. In 1971, Dudjom Rinpoche asked him to translate his massive *Fundamentals of the Nyingma School.* Gyurme spent years busy on that major task and all the study and research it required, although it was not completed until much later. Extending the project still further, Dudjom Rinpoche asked him in 1980 to produce a translation of his history of the Nyingma school.

In the 1980s, Gyurme returned to the UK, to the School of Oriental and African Studies (SOAS) in London, and studied there for a PhD in Tibetan literature, which he received in 1987. His dissertation included an edited and annotated translation of the *Guhyagarbha Tantra*, along with the important and detailed commentary by Longchenpa, which remains an authoritative reference to the Nyingma tantras. During this time, with the collaboration of Matthew Kapstein, Gyurme completed the projects

Dudjom Rinpoche had requested of him and brought the combined work to publication, along with a mass of research material, as a two-volume set *The Nyingma School of Tibetan Buddhism: Its Fundamentals and History* (Wisdom, 1991). Gyurme also completed in these years his translation of the *Tibetan Book of the Dead*, although the book in its final edited form was only published in 2005 (Penguin Books).

In the 1990s, as a research fellow at SOAS, Gyurme worked for four years with Alak Zenkar Rinpoche on the huge task of translating the content of the *Great Tibetan-Chinese Dictionary* and, indeed adding to that content, to create what was supposed to be the three volume *An Encyclopedic Tibetan-English Dictionary*, though sadly only the first volume (2001) was ever released.

During his years in London at SOAS and afterward, he divided his time between the UK, Nepal, Tibet, and China, and was later based in Chengdu, from where he spent part of the year as a tour guide for groups traveling in Tibet. From 1985 onward, he led over forty expeditions and cultural tours to the Utsang, Kham, Amdo, and Gyarong regions of Tibet, founding in 1989 his own tour company, TransHimalaya. He became a major authority on the sacred places of Tibet. His handbook for travelers in the Footprint series, *Footprint Tibet*, first published in 1996, went to four editions and must rank among the most astonishingly detailed and learned tour guides ever published. Gyurme also authored a *Footprint Bhutan Handbook*, first published in 2004 and now in its second edition.

Gyurme Dorje's work for the 84000 Project, under the aegis of the Padmakara Translation Group, was on two of the major Prajñāpāramitā sūtras, *The Perfection of Wisdom in Ten Thousand Lines* (Toh. 11), published in 2018, and *The Perfection of Wisdom in Twenty-Five Thousand Lines* (Toh. 9), on which he was still working in the final months of his life; it was published posthumously in 2023. These two massive works alone occupy no less than four and a half volumes of the Kangyur. Both texts are extremely dense in technical terms and difficult language, and to translate them Gyurme drew on his deep knowledge of Buddhist phenomenology, psychology, and philosophy.

Meanwhile, Gyurme continued to translate Tibetan texts and write books and articles on a huge range of topics within Tibetan culture, art, medicine, and of course Buddhist thought and practice. Gyurme translated some particularly weighty and impressive works for the Tsadra Foundation. One of my own favorite reference works is his *Indo-Tibetan Classical Learn-*

ing and Buddhist Phenomenology, from book six of the series of Jamgon Kongtrul's *The Treasury of Knowledge* (Snow Lion, 2012). More recently published are two equally massive volumes from the collection by Choying Tobden Dorje, *The Complete Nyingma Tradition from Sūtra to Tantra* (Snow Lion, 2016). His translation of the *Jonang* volume of The Treasury of Precious Instructions was published posthumously (Snow Lion, 2020). In the months before and even during his final illness, he began work on yet another project, a detailed commentary by Khangsar Tenpa'i Wangchuk on Longchenpa's *Treasury of Reality's Expanse*, which has now been completed by the Padmakara Translation Group.

Gyurme was not only a prolific scholar, author, and translator. He was also an unusually kind, courteous, considerate person, a friend to many people, and an experienced Buddhist practitioner. Among the many tributes to him after his passing, Charles Hastings wrote,

> He combined incredible erudition with extraordinary modesty and kindness. His enthusiasm for his work was astonishing. For him it was an immense joy to work on these marvelous texts. I had the privilege of spending a few of his last days with him and his family at the hospital. He was quite serene regarding himself and only concerned for his loved ones, and for all the translations of precious works still to be done!

During his final days, Gyurme received visits and instructions from Kangyur Rinpoche's sons, Jigme Khyentse Rinpoche and Pema Wangyal Rinpoche. He died peacefully in hospital, in the morning of February 5, the anniversary of Kangyur Rinpoche's own passing. He will be sadly missed, fondly remembered, and appreciated—and his writings and translations will continue to inspire us all.

John Canti
2024

Taklung Painting

Over one hundred paintings and approximately eighty small initiation paintings (*tsakli*) associated with Taklung Monastery and its sister monastery Riwoche have come to light in recent decades. These paintings can be associated with the Taklung branch of the Tibetan Kagyu Buddhist tradition because of the inscriptions they bear, though iconographic and stylistic features also help to define the group. The most important literary source for understanding Taklung painting is the history of the Taklung order composed by Taklung Zhabdrung Ngawang Namgyel (1571–1626), the seventeenth abbot of Taklung Monastery, published in part one of this volume (hereafter referred to as *The Doctrinal History of Taklung*).[1] In 2014, Dr. Gyurme Dorje (1950–2020), one of the world's foremost translators of Tibetan Buddhist literature and historical texts, agreed to undertake the task of making an authoritative English translation of *The Doctrinal History of Taklung*.[2] The complete translation was sent to me in the form of Microsoft Word files in August 2019, six months before Gyurme's death. Gyurme's translation provided a rich resource for completing my own lengthy study of chronology in Taklung painting.[3] Indeed, historians are fortunate to have these two significant bodies of evidence with which to explore the Taklung tradition. The text sheds light on the historical figures and iconography represented in the paintings, and the paintings bring to life the names and deeds of the historical figures noted in the text. The text also sheds light on the historical circumstances surrounding some of the inscriptions on the paintings, particularly those connected with Sangye On (1251–1296), interim fourth abbot of Taklung.

The focus of my research has been to establish a reliable foundation for assigning dates to Taklung paintings. Most of these paintings include visual lineages consisting of the succession of historical teachers represented in the top, side, and occasionally the bottom registers of paintings. Narrative scenes in many portraits of the founder of Taklung Monastery, Tashi Pel (1142–1210), include principal structures in the monastery compound, which can be associated with specific dates. A thorough and systematic assessment of these features, along with inscriptions and style, help to create firm chronological designations for these twelfth- to mid-sixteenth-century paintings.

The Taklung painting corpus lends itself to the task of building a chronology. Almost three-quarters of the paintings bear inscriptions with chronological implications. Many paintings are inscribed with more than one inscription of historical interest. Some inscriptions provide firm terminus dates, as with the thirty-nine paintings that bear inscriptions stating that they were consecrated by Onpo Lama Rinpoche—that is, Sangye On, interim abbot of Taklung from 1272 to 1273, who died in 1296. Four paintings have inscriptions recording consecrations by a series of Taklung teachers, ending with Sangye On. Twenty-five paintings have inscriptions invoking the names of a lineage of teachers (including Taklung and Riwoche abbots), the last cited name being the teacher of the person who commissioned the painting. Twenty-three paintings bear inscriptions identifying the central figure of the painting. At least six paintings are inscribed with personalized inscriptions by Sangye On, indicating that they were part of his ritual aspiration to remain connected with his teacher, Sangye Yarjon. Six paintings record Sangye On's profound connection with the *tukdam* (*thugs dam*), the "meditative commitment" (also translated as "high aspiration"), essentially the "spiritual presence" contained in the painting.[4] This large corpus of inscriptions has proven to be crucial for establishing chronology within the Taklung paintings, and the significance of these inscriptions is made clearer by the context established by the group as a whole. Style analysis is also greatly enhanced by the opportunity to observe changes in specific stylistic elements across many works commissioned for the same monastic institutions over several centuries.

The aspiration to establish an accurate chronology for Taklung painting invites these questions: To what extent can this aspiration be achieved? How accurate can one be in assigning dates to these paintings? In brief, one can be as accurate as the evidence allows. Occasionally, one can confidently argue for a precise date, as with the portrait *Phakmodrupa and Drawings of His Feet* (see fig. 1), which can be ascribed a date of c. 1168–1170.[5] In most cases, paintings can be assigned to the tenure of an abbot (or two abbots) with reasonable certainty. Some paintings can be assigned a firm terminus (e.g., 1296, the year Sangye On, who consecrated many of the Taklung paintings, died) or a firm starting point (e.g., the year an abbot who is the subject of a portrait assumed the abbot's chair). Often, chronology is a matter of probabilities and not absolute certainties, as with the portrait of Sangye On, interim abbot at Taklung between 1272 and 1273 (see fig. 2). Inscriptional and iconographic evidence indicates the painting *may have* been made during his brief tenure as abbot at Taklung, but it was *certainly* commissioned between 1272 and his death in 1296.[6] The broader the range of dates one assigns to a painting, the more accurate one is likely to be—but also the less chronologically precise. In my study, I have attempted to strike a balance between precision and accuracy.

All Tibetan paintings are consecrated, but rarely is the name of the consecrator inscribed on a painting. This makes it all the more extraordinary that Sangye On is cited as the consecrator of thirty-nine paintings and as one of several consecrators in four additional paintings. His name also appears in inscriptions on six (possibly seven) paintings in which his name is invoked in the first person ("I, Kīrtiśrīraśmibhadra") in a prayer not to be separated from his teacher Sangye Yarjon (Prajñāguru).[7] And it appears in six paintings that are noted to have been (or to have contained) his *tukdam*. Some paintings bear several of these inscriptions. These unprecedented inscriptions underscore Sangye On's personal connection with forty-five Taklung paintings and are best interpreted in light of the traumatic events surrounding the succession in 1272 of the abbot's seat from his uncle, the third Taklung abbot, Sangye Yarjon (see fig. 3).[8] Although Sangye On became abbot in 1272, his elder cousin Tashi Lama (also known as Maṅgalaguru) assumed the abbatial seat a year later, forcing Sangye On's departure from Taklung and return to his native Kham. The historical records shed scant light on this conflicted transition between Sangye Yarjon and his two nephews, but a rough assessment of the situation can be reconstructed.

The Doctrinal History of Taklung notes that the third abbot, Sangye Yarjon, had promised the abbot's seat to both his nephews: "In 1272 (water male monkey), at the time when Choku Sangye Yarjon was about to pass away into the taintless expanse, he bestowed upon Sangye On the representative artifacts, with which he had a connection and which he was to keep safe. In order that the precious teaching of the lineage of practice might spread, triumph, and long endure in all directions, times, and circumstances, he gave

Sangye On oral advice, made predictions concerning him, and appointed him as regent. He did likewise to his other nephew Maṅgalaguru."[9] Elsewhere in *The Doctrinal History of Taklung*, Sangye Yarjon seems to indicate that Maṅgalaguru was his choice for successor. He says to Lama Phakpa, the National Preceptor to Khubilai Khan, emperor of China: "Once my nephew Tashi Lama [Maṅgalaguru] has taken charge, may you be cognizant of the administration of the patrons and monks of Taklung." Phakpa replies, "Henceforth, I will be cognizant of the administration of Taklung and its short-term and long-term prospects."[10]

The Doctrinal History of Taklung specifies that Sangye Yarjon gave portable objects to Sangye On as part of his inheritance and gave the fixed assets of the monastery to Maṅgalaguru:

> On this occasion, Choku Sangye Yarjon actually saw without obscuration the situations and appearances of all things pertaining to the three times without exception, and so he saw that if the teaching of Taklung were to flourish in both Kham and U, then the three planes of existence would be uninterruptedly covered by the immaculate tradition of the lineage of practice. Consequently, he bestowed upon Venerable Sangye On the separate representative artifacts that he should protect and that were portable, actually entrusting him to teach with the words, "You should take these and firmly plant the sacred and noble wish-granting tree, the teaching of this Kagyu lineage, at glorious Riwoche in the valley of Yisho, and protect the sentient beings who live there from all the feverish torments of physical and mental affliction by dispelling the obscurations that cover the instructions of the oral lineage!" To Tashi Lama, the emanation of Maitreya, he assigned the representational objects of buddha body, speech, and mind that were not portable but fixed like Mount Sumeru, along with the monastic complex of Taklung and its Main Temple, and entrusted him with the teaching, saying, "Hold these, and residing at the Point of Enlightenment, the Adamantine Seat, you should constantly and increasingly illuminate the teaching of the essential meaning for all posterity, uniformly permeating the three worlds with the light of virtuous buddha activity, which is like that of ten million suns!"[11]

The Doctrinal History of Taklung elsewhere reiterates that Sangye Yarjon gave objects to both nephews during the year prior to his death: "He bestowed representative images, manuscripts, and so forth on his two nephews for their respective protection and extensively gave them advice. He appointed them as authentic masters of the Buddhist teaching in Kham and U."[12] This heralded the division between the Taklung traditions of Upper Taklung[13] and Lower Taklung,[14] the former being Taklung Monastery in U and the latter founded by Sangye On in 1277 at Riwoche in Kham.

Despite these statements, uncertainty about the future of Taklung and the particular roles to be played by the two nephews persisted toward the end of Sangye Yarjon's life. Maṅgalaguru apparently tried to clarify the situation:

> On that occasion, [the approaching death of the third abbot, Sangye Yarjon], there were ordinary persons with eyes only for this world who misunderstood the inexhaustible wheel of adornment that is buddha activity and who clamored that the two nephews took their respective inheritances and that their precious predecessor, Sangye Yarjon, had said, "I entrust the teaching to this one! I entrust the teaching to that one!" In order to resolve their doubts, when Rinpoche Sangye Yarjon had no visitors, Rinpoche Tashi Lama (Maṅgalaguru) said to him, "Now that you are alive here, if you did not say that I should be entrusted with the teaching, may this waist of mine become even more decrepit! If what you said is true, may this body of mine become straighter than a plantain tree!" It is said that because Tashi Lama spoke with the power of truth, he insisted on reminding Sangye Yarjon of this pledge a few times, even before he returned from the Yang Gon[15] hermitage to Kadruk. Consequently, his body, decrepit with such chronic ailments, later recovered and became straighter even than the shaft of an arrow.[16]

Aside from the comments about Maṅgalaguru's ill health, thin waist, and stooped posture, the critical point is that Maṅgalaguru appears to have tried to persuade his uncle to make clear to the community that he was to assume the abbot's chair after his uncle's death. Nevertheless, Sangye On assumed the throne while, according to *The Doctrinal History of Taklung*, Maṅgalaguru remained in meditative retreat. After about a year on the throne, Sangye On left Taklung, taking the objects given to him by his teacher. Maṅgalaguru tried to persuade his cousin Sangye On to leave those objects behind at the monastery:

> So, when Venerable Sangye On was requested to assume the lion throne at Taklung, for a while Maṅgalaguru attended to his ascetic discipline, which was pure and blissful in terms of the three isolations of body, speech, and mind. After one year, Venerable Sangye On saw that the time had come for him to train disciples in the east, and he set out for Kham. On that occasion, Tashi Lama seems to have sent a messenger with the request that the separate representative artifacts that were to be protected by Sangye On should be kept here in Taklung. Even later on, he sent another message, which said, "My supreme guide! Lord of our enlightened heritage! You should bring from Taklung Lower Plain the representative objects of buddha body, speech, and mind, along with the library of the profound and vast sacred doctrine, which has many blessings, and come here to this great residence! That will establish an auspicious circumstance for this shared wealth of ours." This also alludes to the report, known in the narrative of the lineage, that Venerable Sangye On himself on one occasion received a prophecy declaring, "The sleeve will be connected to the main part of the costume!"[17]

The Doctrinal History of Taklung notes that an emissary from Sakya, acting on behalf of Maṅgalaguru, also tried to persuade Sangye On to return the objects while he was en route to Kham:

> He then struck camp on the eleventh day of the mouse month. At Ser in Shak, an envoy of the Sakyapa arrived, but owing to Sangye On's conduct of yogic discipline, the envoy was unable to cross the river. Instead, he asked Sangye On to send across some counterfeit representations to placate the people of Taklung, but he did not do so. He denied that request, saying, "From that point on, there would be no confidence in either the relics of Upper or Lower Taklung!" When the envoy repeated that request, he then said, "Lama Rinpoche (Sangye Yarjon) entrusted this seat of the

> Kagyu tradition to me. Wherever I stay, that will be my seat. As long as my life faculties endure, I will not entrust these sacred representations, with which I have a connection and which I am to keep safe, to anyone at all!"[18]

While he was at Riwoche, toward the end of his life, he raised the possibility of returning these objects to Taklung, as well as sending his own students there:

> Then, after some years had passed, Rinpoche Sangye On said, "If I send these sacred representations and the monks to Taklung Upper Plain, I will guide some two hundred yogins, and then if I go to Khawa Karpo or Mount Kailash, I will live a long life and also be of benefit to the Buddhist teaching. My reputation will equal space, and I will have an entourage of five hundred cotton-clad yogins. On the other hand, if I stay here, I will not live long." Thereupon, Gomtsul asked him not to talk in that manner, saying, "Since Lama Rinpoche possesses those sacred representations with which he has a connection, please establish that as the auspicious circumstance for your long life!" Sangye On replied, "If I sustain the pledge concerning those sacred representations with which I have a connection, they will be maintained here, but the merit of sentient beings will be small. It will be greater as a result of not sustaining that pledge!"[19]

Go Lotsāwa Zhonu Pel's fifteenth-century history *The Blue Annals* recounts a slightly different version of the disputed succession. There, Phakpa supports the candidacy of Maṅgalaguru over that of Sangye On. Go Lotsāwa states that while Sangye On assumed the abbotship upon the death of his uncle, he left after one year, compelled to proceed to his native homeland, Kham. The author indicates that Phakpa had supported the older nephew, Maṅgalaguru, for the position of fourth Taklung abbot, and this may have influenced Sangye On's departure.[20]

Whatever the precise dynamics behind the succession of the fourth Taklung abbot, Sangye On left a rich legacy of inscriptions on forty-five surviving Taklung paintings. It is unclear precisely when Sangye On's personalized inscriptions were added to the forty-five paintings. In general, it can be said that the personalized inscriptions citing Sangye On (sometimes along with the name of his teacher Sangye Yarjon) were written on the paintings sometime between 1272, when Sangye On was given objects by his uncle at Taklung, and 1296, the year he died at Riwoche. Sangye On is said to have consecrated all the objects at Taklung during his year as abbot, 1272–1273.[21] Many of the personalized inscriptions were added to already consecrated paintings. Nineteen are paintings commissioned during the tenures of previous abbots, ten paintings were probably created during Sangye On's tenure or lifetime, and sixteen paintings were created sometime during the twelfth to thirteenth centuries, certainly prior to 1297.[22] None of the paintings bearing personalized inscriptions were created after Sangye On's tenure.

Circumstantial evidence suggests that the inscriptions were written at one time or around the same time. The hand of the scribe in nearly all the inscriptions appears to be singular. It is significant that each type of personalized inscription is placed in the same location on the paintings. An inscription stating it was consecrated by Onpo Lama Rinpoche of Taklung and one indicating the painting was consecrated by him and his predecessors both appear along the top edge of the verso (see fig. 4). The inscription stating the painting is or contains the *tukdam* of Sangye On always appears just beneath the throne of the central figure on the obverse and always in gold script (see fig. 5). And the prayer by Sangye On not to be separated from his teacher Sangye Yarjon usually appears in gold script beneath the stūpa-shaped inscriptions (see fig. 6). The regularity of the placement of these inscriptions suggests a clarity of intention. It is tempting to view the inscriptions as Sangye On's way of marking his property—the objects given him by his uncle and those he commissioned as well—at a time when their ownership was contested, possibly before his departure from Taklung in 1273.

The great majority (seventy-seven of ninety-five) of the surviving paintings from the Taklung tradition are portraits of teachers, perhaps a reflection of their pivotal role in their communities. Paintings of Buddhist teachers were a way to maintain the presence of a teacher in his absence. Taklung founder Tashi Pel was aware of the power of such portraits, for it was through seeing a portrait of his teacher Phakmodrupa that he first felt compelled to meet this Buddhist master. As a young man, he traveled to meet a teacher named Geshe Mok in order to receive teachings and empowerments. Ngawang Namgyel writes, "At the very moment when Tashi Pel saw the image of Drogon Rinpoche (Phakmodrupa) on top of Mok's pillow, an uncommon devotion arose, along with extraordinary indications and attributes of spiritual warmth, whereupon he had the thought that he should certainly bow down at the lotus feet of that teacher."[23] A significant number of Taklung portraits are identified by inscriptions. These help to build a picture of the physiognomy of individual masters.

Six painted portraits of Taklung founder Tashi Pel are attributed to his tenure as abbot.[24] All present the central figure with similar iconography and physiognomy: a front-facing enthroned figure with dark hair, the hairline straight across the forehead, and with a light mustache and a trimmed goatee (see fig. 7). He is enthroned and seated within a willow hut, or grass hermitage, itself placed inside a mountain cave. The throne and cave allude to Indian traditions that deem them appropriately lofty settings for deities and revered spiritual figures.[25] The willow hut likely refers to the Jakchil willow hut, which became Tashi Pel's principal residence shortly after he founded Taklung Monastery in 1180.[26] Tashi Pel engages the viewer with a direct gaze. His hands assume a gesture of teaching (*dharmacakra mudrā*) as a rosary of delicate golden beads falls between the fingers and across the palms of both hands. He wears the red robes of an ordained Buddhist monk, his legs folded in a meditation posture, the upward-turned soles of his feet bearing golden wheels (*cakra*), another indication of his transcendent nature (*lakṣaṇa*).[27]

The portrait (fig. 7) includes narrative scenes in the top, side, and bottom registers. In particular, eight vignettes (four in the vertical registers on each side of the central figure) occur in many portraits of the Taklung founder, produced both during and after his lifetime.[28] All eight vignettes depict a "manifestation" of Tashi Pel within willow huts. The manifestations were rooted in Tashi Pel's students' perceptions of their teacher, as noted in historical texts. *The Doctrinal History of Taklung* describes Tashi Pel's students' perceptions of him as a saintly, divine being, some specifically equating him with the Buddha. These perceptions became encoded into a standard iconography of six manifestations represented here (register on viewer's left side of central figure, top to bottom): Māravijaya Buddha, Cakrasaṃvara, Tashi Pel in human form, another image of Māravijaya Buddha. And (in the register on the viewer's right side of central figure, top to bottom): Ṣaḍakṣarī Lokeśvara, Vajravārāhī, another image of Tashi Pel in human form, and another image of Ṣaḍakṣarī Lokeśvara. In this painting, all are depicted within willow huts adorned with gold chains and pendant gems, additionally placed within mountain caves, like the central figure of Tashi Pel.

For Tibetans, a consecrated painting embodies the timeless presence of revered ancestors, enlightened teachers, and powerful gods. But like all works of art, Taklung paintings were created by particular people at specific times. *The Doctrinal History of Taklung* and the large corpus of inscribed paintings from this tradition afford the opportunity to establish a reliable foundation for assigning dates to these paintings. Because the artists who created these works were apparently itinerant and worked for other monasteries as well, a firm foundation for Taklung painting can also help establish a reliable framework for assigning dates to other Tibetan paintings. This immensely valuable translation of *The Doctrinal History of Taklung* by Gyurme Dorje opens doors to the rich history of the Taklung order, providing keys to better understand its doctrinal, social, and artistic traditions.

Jane Casey
New Zealand, 2024

Editor's Preface to the Tibetan Edition of *Wondrous Ocean of Eloquence* and *Great Divine Drum of Wondrous Renown*

There is a purpose and objective behind the publication of this *Wondrous Ocean of Eloquence*—a doctrinal history[1] of the Taklung Kagyu tradition. In general terms, this doctrinal history offers an overview of our outstanding Tibetan cultural development, and in particular it documents the spread of the Kagyu doctrinal approach. But, above all, it establishes many essential points that are hard to find elsewhere, along with the changing circumstances of Tibetan history, in the context of an extensive and detailed account of the Taklung Kagyu tradition. Xylographs were initially carved on the basis of an extant "arrow-length"[2] manuscript, and hundreds of woodblocks were preserved at Taklung. But the print run was small, so this text was not a common resource for anyone's firsthand inspection. It was stacked amid clouds of smoke from butter-lamp and incense offerings on the bookshelves of temples belonging to a few devout persons and the mother and branch monasteries of the Taklung Kagyu tradition. In these circumstances, the transmission of this book almost vanished, as it was consumed by fire and water along with the temples and their sacred contents during the decade of unrest, [the Cultural Revolution]. {2}

The primary source of the present Tibetan publication[3] is that same ancient, worn, and mouse-eaten arrow-length manuscript, all the remaining pages of which have a somewhat incomplete right margin. It was sought, collected, and conserved by the Subcommittee for Materials of Cultural History and Creative Writing[4] of the Lhasa People's Consultative Congress[5] who lent it to us. These pages constituted our primary source. Apart from that, when preparing the present published Tibetan version, to compensate for the lacunae of the right margin of the manuscript, it helped to consult the xylographic version of the eighth part[6] of this doctrinal history, which is preserved even now in the Potala Palace, and a supplement to the biographies of the abbatial succession[7] composed by Ngawang Tashi Chokyi Nyima, the twenty-fifth spiritual and temporal incumbent of the great seminary of Taklung. With the exception of one or two such sources, most of the other relevant works have simply disappeared from view.

First, it is a distinctive feature of the literary style of this doctrinal history that its profound and extensive meanings and poetic words of expression, easy to understand, are related to the genre of poetical doctrinal compositions that uncontrollably impress upon the minds of readers changing historical events and human activities. Unbound by the complex poetic ornaments of synonymics, archaicisms, and the like, it has the power to inspire those with the sharpest minds, those with the dullest, and those in between.

Second, its content, through clear and distinct chapters, sets out the material in an orderly, unconfused, and sensible historical sequence, uninfluenced by the obscure repetition of historical points that is sometimes found in other doctrinal histories. {3} It will, in an exemplary manner, greatly benefit those interested in learning about doctrinal history and historical events since it is easy to understand definitively.

Third, the eighth part, which constitutes the main content of this book, is also a unique reference for those who research the exegetical traditions and distinctions of this uncommon doctrinal approach of the Taklung lineage of spiritual attainment because it exemplifies the combination of history and biography with respect to each individual hierarch who maintained its propagation. Also, incidentally, it is valuable as a reference for historical research because it alludes with precision to the political and economic circumstances of Tibet in the context of each incumbent hierarch, and so it both directly and indirectly sets out the chronology and timeline of the changing periods of mundane political governance through facts that are true and undistorted.

Fourth, above all, the supplement[8] containing the biographies of the individual upholders of the Buddhist teaching—who contributed greatly to the abbatial succession and doctrinal lineage of Taklung from the later life of the aforementioned Zhabdrung Ngawang Namgyel onward—is a work that clearly recounts its story's most profound connections with the unfolding of the civil unrest between U and Tsang. It is thus an indispensable reference tool for understanding the detailed history of the conflicts between the governor of Tsang[9] and the Ganden Palace with regard to political power.[10] {4} That we have managed to rescue the text through the present publication may be seen as a matter of true significance, indicating that Tibet's outstanding cultural heritage is being maintained and preserved.

At this point, the reader should be introduced to some important points regarding the editorial process. As mentioned above, the original source of this Tibetan edition of the doctrinal history was the ancient arrow-length manuscript that is old, tattered, worn, and partly eaten by mice. From that edition, the text up to chapter six (with its lacunae in the right margin) was transcribed by the Literature Study Center of the Tibet Nationalities University, and the lacunae were rectified on the basis of other resource materials[11] that had been mimeographed and that we had in hand. In the case of the main part of the text—that is, chapter eight, titled "A Detailed Exegesis of the Abbatial Succession and Biographies of the Taklung Kagyu Tradition"[12] and its supplement recounting the later abbatial succession, titled *Great Divine Drum of Wondrous Renown*, composed by Taklung Choje Ngawang Tashi Chokyi Nyima—the lacunae were rectified from the Taklung prints available to us, as mentioned above.

Since the authors of the primary text and the supplement that constitute this doctrinal history were perfectly learned, not only in the doctrinal traditions but also in the major and minor fields of Tibetan classical learning, as documented in their own biographies, they were from the beginning faultless in spelling and in terminology. Yet {5} in the course of transcribing, carving, and correcting their writings, the risk of introducing errors was hard to avoid. Above all, there were a great many errors in the extant version of the supplementary biographies, so here for the benefit of readers of the Tibetan text I will describe the notation we have used in this text to indicate editorial corrections and additions.[13]

First, concerning the arrangement of the table of contents,[14] as in the source manuscript of this doctrinal history, there are eleven parts to the text,[15] counting from *ka* to *tha*, with the addition of *oṃ*. The supplementary chapter[16] was not included among these. In addition to the divisions of the part titles indicating the content of the main text, the present edition also separately nests the chapter subdivisions[17] of each part with newly introduced headings, wherever possible, so that the content may be easily searched, as readers now require. For example, in the case of events concerning temples and their sacred contents, the distinctive features of murals and bas-relief sculpture may be separately nested. In the main text, also, within the biographies of each of the lineages of spiritual teachers, the lineages of their disciples may be included within a single biography but nested as separate topics regardless of their length.

Second, concerning the arrangement of the main text and the supplement, the main text of this doctrinal history, composed by Zhabdrung Ngawang Namgyel, has eleven parts, numbered from *ka* to *tha*, with *oṃ* indicating the final part. {6} In the present Tibetan edition, we have placed the supplementary part containing the biographies of the abbatial succession composed by Choje Ngawang Tenpei Nyima [now part two in the English translation] within the alphanumeric sequence, so it precedes the eleventh part indicated by *oṃ*.[18]

Third, concerning the correction of errata, as mentioned above, there are some errors in the original manuscript of this doctrinal history. If we were to mark up the corrections in their entirety, each line of the text would be covered in marks, and we thought that it would not be easy to read. Here, therefore, the most important of these corrections have been inserted within angle brackets preceded by the original error, which is underlined.

Fourth, concerning additions made when the syllables are unclear, these are indicated by square brackets. Since the right margin of the original manuscript of this doctrinal history was eaten by mice, there are random flaws that occur in that margin up to and including the ninth part, and these lacunae have been rectified based on the xylographic print that we used as a separate reference tool.[19] Lacking any separate reference tool for the later parts ten and eleven, here we have similarly enclosed in square brackets our tentative insertions, which accord as far as possible with the context of the preceding and following words.

Fifth, in this doctrinal history there are a few syllables that are indistinct and words that are clearly erroneous but could not be intelligently substituted. In lieu of the brackets, we have placed these within a rectangle. Those words that are hard to understand but not yet corrected are inserted within asterisks to indicate that there are doubts to be resolved. {7}

Sixth, the annotations that ordinarily occur in the original manuscript have been inserted in parentheses to indicate that they are memos not to be mistaken for the words of the text.[20]

In conclusion, though I am feeble in my study of scholarly texts in general, and particularly in the scholarly texts of Tibet, and am of a low standard—and worst of all, I lack any special status as a reader or scribe, not to mention that I am entirely without the courage required to edit a work such as the biographies contained in this doctrinal history, which is profound and extensive in meaning—even so, at the insistence of those responsible for publishing the ancient texts of this cultural heritage, I, like a clod of earth seen as gold, had no choice. Also, at this time when even some minor assistance would facilitate the publishing and distribution of a doctrinal history such as this, I thought to demonstrate my loyalty to those who have maintained our national culture. As an old man responsible for the ascetic discipline of holding lice[21] who merely pretends to be an editor, I must nevertheless make a special request to all those of definitive knowledge to tolerate all my errors.

I should add here, as requested by the publishers of this work,[22] our sincere gratitude to the Subcommittee for Materials of Cultural History and Creative Writing of the Lhasa People's Consultative Congress for lending the original manuscript and the Bureau of the Cultural Relics Department of the Potala Palace[23] who loaned us the original xylographic prints that we used as a separate reference tool.

Tharling Jampa Tsering, 1992
Translated by Gyurme Dorje, 2020

A Brief Introduction to Zhabdrung Ngawang Namgyel and Ngawang Tenpei Nyima

Zhabdrung Ngawang Namgyel, the author of part one of this doctrinal history, was the seventeenth hierarch in the abbatial succession of Taklung Upper Plain. This saintly individual was born in 1571 (iron sheep) during the tenth Tibetan sexagenary cycle at Lhundrub Dzong, which falls within the district of Penyul, revered as the "source of knowledge." His father was the governor Kunga Gyatso, who hailed from the Gazi family, and his mother was Monlam Phuntsok Butri, daughter of the great vajra master Chogyel Rinchen Phuntsok of Drigung, a holder of gnostic mantras. In his infancy, he was given the name Tashi Tobgyel.

It is said that his sole demeanor and manner, starting even from the time he was a child at play, was always that of maintaining, nurturing, and propagating the Buddhist teaching. In his sixth year, in 1576 (fire male mouse), he accompanied his father to the great seminary at Taklung and met for the first time Choje Kunga Tashi, who was the incumbent of the monastic seat[1] during that period. The following year, during the waxing half of the second lunar month, he received the intermediate mendicant vows of the laity,[2] followed by the vows of the novitiate, in the Northern Chamber of the Main Temple of Taklung, and the name Ngawang Namgyel Kunga Zangpo was conferred upon him. {9} Under his tutor, the master Namgyel Chophel, he practiced reading and diligently trained in the regularly recited liturgies associated with Taklung, such that within a short time he perfected them. At the same time, too, when other cycles such as the Drigungpa *Clear Doctrinal Practice of Kudzi*[3] and Sakya Paṇḍita's *Treasure of Precious Eloquence*[4] were recited, he comprehended them simply by listening.

During his ninth year, in the presence of the authentic master Namgyel Rinchen Phuntsok, he received the uncommon profound doctrines, empowerments, and transmissions of the Taklung Kagyu tradition, and in the midst of the monastic congregation,[5] he participated in an elaborate doctrinal discussion based on the transmission of *The Biography of Omniscient Ngagi Wangpo*[6] and *The Guru Yoga of the Profound Path*.[7] Everyone was astonished that from an extremely young age he had become an outstanding and exemplary person of the broadest discernment,[8] and he became an object of homage for devotees. Consequently, Venerable Zhamar Konchok Yenlak especially offered a letter praising him with words that begin,

> May the new-moon days of that incarnation
> Wax in lordship over the three planes of existence,
> Permeating them with the white light of excellent virtue,
> And may he, this gem of the Kagyu lineage, be victorious!

Thereafter, he learned without effort scripts such as Rañjanā and Vartula, as well as the painting of sacred icons. He also trained in and perfected the other major and minor fields of classical learning, including Sanskrit grammar, poetics, and astrology.

In his fifteenth year, in 1585 (wood female bird), he was appointed hierarch of the monastic seat of Taklung, and as he assumed responsibility for maintaining, nurturing, and propagating the Buddhist teaching, {10} his tutor Yongdzin Rinpoche conferred on him the title Pelden Ngawang Chokyi Nyima Jikme Zangpo Chok Tamchele Nampar Gyelweide. Starting from then, combining the two traditions of the spiritual and the temporal, he maintained and nurtured the Buddhist teaching of Taklung and also managed the civil administration of the regency,[9] efficiently maintaining, nurturing, and propagating them in accordance with the tradition of the successive hierarchs who had been his predecessors. By traveling in person to the districts of Upper and Lower Hor, and assuming responsibility for them with physical hardship, he nurtured these nomadic tribes with unsurpassed kindness, reconciling their mutual conflicts, and protected all persons, strong and weak, from all the perilous sufferings arising from the causes of hatred and enmity.

From Yongdzin Rinpoche he received most of the empowerments, transmissions, and pith instructions of the Kagyu tradition in general and the attainment lineage of Taklung in particular. Then, in his nineteenth year, in

1589 (earth female ox), in the Great Lower Hall of the Main Temple of Dorjeden, Taklung Upper Plain, in the presence of the silver image of Maṅgalaśrī Tashi Pel, the lord-protector of the three worlds, named Supreme Auspicious Ornament of the World,[10] he received the precepts of a fully ordained monk from the omniscient Kunga Tashi acting as monastic preceptor in the midst of a gathering of erudite attendants and with Yongdzin Rinpoche alone acting as the master of ceremonies, confessor, and timekeeper.

His loyal activity, so beneficial for the Buddhist teaching in general, caused his reputation for nurturing living beings to spread throughout the land, {11} and among all the dignitaries of Utsang, there were none who did not pay homage to him. During his tenure as hierarch of the monastic seat of Taklung, he efficiently continued the custom of his successive predecessors in restoring the temples of Taklung and their sacred contents and commissioning new ones, and in preserving the local community, the monastic charter, and so forth. Consequently, the way he broadened—to an extent like that of Lake Anavatapta—the dominion of the combined traditions of spiritual and temporal authorities of Taklung was unprecedented even in the time of his successive predecessors. After nurturing the monastic seat for thirty-one years in that manner, in his forty-sixth year, in 1616 (fire male dragon), he entrusted the responsibilities of the monastic seat to his own nephew Ngawang Tashi Pelwa. He continued to be responsible only for the hermitage of Chodzong Namgyel Rabten, and, apart from that, he passed the time in one-pointed meditative stability, combined with the ascetic discipline of renunciation, without ever forgetting his meditative equipoise.

Eventually, however, when here in Tibet the conflict between U, Tsang, and the Mongols drew near, here in Tibet, billowing up like a cloud of smoke, his mind, under the sway of compassion, was unable to bear it, and he traveled many times in person, as well as sending emissaries and so forth, thinking of the well-being of the citizens of Tibet. Although he strove to establish a reconciliation, the minds of unruly and ill-behaved persons were intractable, and the waves of war fiercely surged. Although his labors in this regard were fruitless, when the Mongol forces were turned back by the army of Tsang, the monastic communities of Sera and Drepung were for the most part uneasy about staying in Lhasa and considered going into exile to Amdo. {12} When they reached Taklung, he presented them with his inherited estates, communal tea, and lodgings and nurtured them with kindness, appealing to the king of Tsang on their behalf, and so they were permitted to return home unharmed. In brief, this saintly individual turned his intention solely toward the Buddhist teaching in general, unpolluted by the bias and prejudice of philosophical systems, and so he was a pure practitioner endowed with learning and accomplishment, untainted by the stains of artificial, wrong livelihood, as practiced by those who sell the sacred doctrine out of concern for wealth, profit, respect, major donations, and so forth.

The compositions of this great learned and accomplished master include many volumes of profound and extensive meaning and words of expression that are poetic and magnificent. They are contained in works such as *The Extensive Biography of Taklungpa the Great,*[11] *The Biography Titled Illumination of the Sublime Path,*[12] and his own autobiography titled *Wagon of the Auspicious Mind.*[13] In his thirty-ninth year, in 1609 (earth female bird), he composed this *Doctrinal History Titled Wondrous Ocean of Eloquence: A Narrative of the Wish-Fulfilling Gem of the Lineage.* In addition, he penned innumerable epistles, official documents, aspiration prayers, and so forth.

Relying on activities that were imbued with learning, discipline, and goodness, he fostered, through the kindness of his unsurpassed legacy, the maintaining, nurturing, and propagation of the Buddhist teaching of Tibet and Kham in general and in particular of the Taklung Kagyu tradition. Thereafter, on the sixth day of the fourth lunar month in 1626 (fire male tiger), in his fifty-sixth year, he instructed his attendants in all the future duties that should be undertaken to maintain and nurture the Buddhist teaching, {13} and there, in Taklung, he passed away into the expanse of reality.

This is but a brief account of his life. For details please see the chapter on the biography of the seventeenth hierarch, contained in chapter eight[14] of this doctrinal history.

The supplement titled *Great Divine Drum of Wondrous Renown* [part two of the current volume] contains the biographies of the later abbatial succession of Dorjeden, Taklung Upper Plain, and is distinct from the extensive exegesis of the biographies of the Taklung Kagyu tradition presented in *Wondrous Ocean of Eloquence.* It was composed by the twenty-fifth hierarch of the monastic seat of Taklung Dorjeden, Choje Ngawang Tenpei Nyima, who is also known as Tashi Chokyi Gyeltsen. It seems that a separate, detailed biography of him was written, but at present we have not been able to locate it. The colophon at the end of this text says that he composed this supplement in his thirty-seventh year, in 1824 (wood monkey), which, when clearly investigated, suggests that his natal year was 1788 (earth monkey). It is implicitly indicated in the biographies of this very supplement that the hierarch preceding him, Kyabje Jikme Gocha, was appointed as hierarch during the Tibetan conflict with the Gorkhas at the start of 1791 (iron pig). And since the author's natal year was clearly the earth monkey, one may permissibly establish that this refers to the thirteenth sexagenary cycle—that is, 1788. So if one calculates that the previous hierarch Kyabje Jikme Gocha was in his twenty-eighth year at the time of his appointment, {14} one may know with some degree of certainty that he would have been in his twenty-fifth year at the time when Choje Ngawang Tenpei Nyima was born in 1788 (earth male monkey), during the thirteenth sexagenary cycle. Apart from that, we are unable at present to establish what were the author's family clan social status, anything more of his biography, or how many years he lived.

Tharling Jampa Tsering, 1992
Translated by Gyurme Dorje, 2020

PART ONE

Wondrous Ocean of Eloquence

A Narrative of the Wish-Fulfilling Gem of the Lineage

Taklung Ngawang Namgyel

Verses of Homage

OṂ SVĀSTI
May it be auspicious!

This work, which generates trust and confidence, is titled *Wondrous Ocean of Eloquence: A Narrative of the Wish-Fulfilling Gem of the Lineage.*

I bow my head at the stainless lotus feet of Maṅgalaśrī (Tashi Pel), universal lord, primordial buddha, and embodiment of the five wheels of adornment[1] possessed by all who are accomplished in the precious Kagyu lineage—the expanse of the king of meditative stabilities, in which is elucidated the very same nature of all things.

All the countless lords of enlightened heritage, universal emperors holding sway over the vast and glorious dominion of the sacred doctrine of all the buddhas, have bowed their heads in respectful homage to those who securely wore the adamantine crown of the four buddha bodies and five pristine cognitions,[2] the unobscured pinnacle for actors of supreme courage who voyage across the auspicious ocean of existence and quiescence.

Triumphant in battle over all the demonic forces of Māra, established as foremost in the miraculous emanation of pristine cognition since they surpass all who are exemplary, the Taklungpa's renown blazes forth in this written account.

May those who plant the banner of the four jewel-like cycles[3] of this tradition in the three planes of existence[4] be victorious—elucidating the neverfailing, profound, vast, and illustrious Buddhist teaching of scripture and direct realization!

Homage to the teacher of the matchless Buddhist teaching,
Endowed with the great sun of pristine cognition, which from the
 very first

Vanquished the dark clouds of threefold obscuration,[5]
And the glory that triumphs over the darkness of existence and quiescence! {4}

Homage to the sacred doctrine of the Buddhist teaching,
Composed of the sūtras that embrace the vast earth of virtuous aspiration
And the boundless ocean of the tantra classes,
Eloquently expressed because the thoughts of corporeal beings are subject to external influence!

Homage to the supreme community that maintains the Buddhist teaching,
That can perfectly fulfill the expectations
Of fortunate beings in infinite fields
And bestow the jeweled mass of peace and happiness in its entirety!

Homage to the sun of the Buddhist teaching of definitive meaning,
Its seven horses an infinite threefold collection of words, phrases, and letters
Striding toward Mount Sumeru,[6]
Rejoicing in the diffusion of a hundredfold radiance of pure enlightened activity,
With unfailing splendor of supreme and unchanging bliss, fresh and youthful emptiness in all its finest aspects,
Peerless in manifesting whatever lotus groves might thrill sentient beings embraced by the honey-filled anthers of marvelous good fortune,
Renowned within the Kagyupa tradition as the unfailing transformation of blessing and great pristine cognition!

Homage to the inconceivably secret guides, the Taklungpa,
Who, on the steadfast axis of exceptionally pure chastity,
However the ocean waves of enlightened conduct may fluctuate,
Raise aloft the blazing crest, the wish-granting jewel of the supremely secret two stages,[7]
Until the rebirth process in this field is ended,

And who, emanating from the single buddha body of reality of that protector-lord,
Arise as the five wheels of inexhaustible adornment,
Manifesting as multiplicity—the line of the perfect buddhas of the authentic lineage!

Writer's Pledge

How can one like myself, whose mind resembles a turbid lake,
Express the most wondrous narrative
Of the essential supreme Buddhist teaching and those who uphold it,
Similar to a bee flying through the vast reaches of the sky! {5}

Nonetheless, has not one infinitely small part
Of these marvelous tales fallen upon my ears?
Even if, just for once, I can generate faith on this account,
Why would that not become supremely perfect merit?

This being the case, with intense faith, enthusiasm, and diligence,
Having closely and thoroughly examined
The trustworthy volumes of the ancients,
I shall here begin to write their eloquent exposition.

In this particular sphere of knowledge, the source of all spiritual and temporal well-being is the precious Buddhist teaching of the conquerors, and its joyous resource for disciples of good fortune is exclusively the kindness of the great holy beings, the upholders of the Buddhist teaching who appear throughout time. Moreover, since the path of excellence is produced by the sole power of the inexhaustible wheels of adornment[1]—the utterly pure enlightened activity of the transcendent lord and teacher, the sovereign of the Buddhist teaching himself—those who themselves seek that excellence should first attend correctly and solely upon a qualified spiritual mentor. After carefully considering the words and meanings of the scriptural collections of the Lesser Vehicle and the two systems of the Great Vehicle, which emphasize cause and fruition, and after listening to and impressing upon their minds the historical discussions of the great chariots that compose the

Buddhist teaching of scripture and realization, they should understand the Teacher, the Buddhist teaching, and the upholders of the Buddhist teaching and then earnestly take responsibility for cultivating a devout intelligence.

Furthermore, as it says in the scriptures,

> The sacred doctrine of the Teacher is twofold, {6}
> Embodying scripture and realization.
> The former is grasped and propounded,
> The latter accomplished alone.[2]

The underlying basis thus defined as the Buddhist teaching is the sacred doctrine embodying scripture and realization, and those that take responsibility for studying, reflecting on, and meditating upon it are the upholders of the Buddhist teaching who maintain its lineage. Foremost among these two aspects is the Buddhist teaching of realization, and as Taklung Rinpoche, the omniscient Ngagi Wangpo[3] says,

> Although it is said that the Buddhist teaching of scripture and realization
> May be grasped by means of exegesis and attainment,
> You should know indeed the distinction between these two,
> As the analogy of the outer husk and the essence.
> Therefore, you should rely on the unsurpassed nectar of accomplishment![4]

Also in the stages of meditation leading to clear realization of the definitive meaning, there are three methods: definitive guidance of the explicit teachings that constitute the precious sūtra collection, guidance based on the short path of the most supreme mantra collection, and guidance by means of experiential instructions disgorged[5] by the accomplished masters.

Among these, the last mentioned is composed of pith instructions that include the following: pith instructions on *The King of Meditative Stability*, skillfully revealed by Nāropā and Maitripā, which, like the utterly perfect orb of the moon shining prominently amid the constellations, elucidates the intrinsic sameness of all things, the meaning of the Buddhist teaching composed of all canonical teachings and treatises of the Great Vehicle, headed by *The Sūtra of the King of Meditative Stability*; the pith instruction titled Coemergent Union of the Great Seal,[6] which posits calm meditative stability as supreme and establishes the essential nature of the innate mind; and the Six Doctrines of Glorious Nāropā,[7] which resembles clarified butter from churning the sea of milk of the tantras of unsurpassed union. The latter two are renowned like the sun and moon.

The last mentioned (the Six Doctrines of Glorious Nāropā) consists of the pith instructions that intermingle the three modes of magical display with the three modes of inner radiance—namely, the intermingling of the magical display of daytime appearances with the inner radiance of the path, {7} the intermingling of the magical display of nighttime appearances with the inner radiance of sleep, and the intermingling of the magical display of the intermediate state with the inner radiance of the moment of death. The aforementioned quotation from the venerable great omniscient one Ngagi Wangpo continues as follows:

> Although the traditions of the different practice lineages
> That have appeared in this Land of Snow Mountain Ranges are manifold,
> The one that resembles the full moon amid the constellations
> Is this lineage of glorious Nāropā.[8]

So it was that when Tashi Pel, emanation of the lord-protector, blessed, tathāgata, arhat, genuinely perfect buddha Akṣobhya, infinitely turned the profound and vast doctrinal wheel of perfect realization of the definitive meaning at Taklung, this site for enlightenment, the Adamantine Seat at the center of Tibet, seated upon the precious adamantine lion throne, he definitively revealed the entire profound doctrine of his own meditative commitment[9] in the context of four great principles—namely, the wish-fulfilling gem of the lineage that externally engenders trust, the wish-fulfilling gem of the path of maturational empowerment that internally engenders meditative experience, the wish-fulfilling gem of the path of liberating guidance that secretly introduces the coemergent pristine cognition of coalescence, and the wish-fulfilling gem of the complete supplementary instructions that facilitate the path. The first of these, the wish-fulfilling gem of the lineage, is composed first of both the history of the lineage that engenders trust and second of the profound path of the spiritual mentor that actualizes blessings.

The adamantine words concerning this region in former times that are to be found here have been imparted to the ears of modern-day disciples with good fortune similar to my own, and I, Ngawang Nampar Gyelwa, a mere subject of the line of buddhas of the authentic lineage, have therefore adorned the lake of my mind with the beautiful banks of the flowers of devotion, for I, too, am imbued with faith and enthusiasm.

This eloquently expressed exegesis is composed of eleven parts:

- The first part concerns the presentation of world systems.
- The second explains the deeds of the genuinely perfect Teacher, Buddha Śākyamuni.
- The third describes the compilation of the transmitted teachings and the origins of the three representations of buddha body, speech, and mind.
- The fourth briefly presents the appearance of Buddhism in India through the upholders of the Buddhist teaching.
- The fifth explains in some detail the four descents of the transmitted teachings to Tilopā and the two masters of supreme vision, Tilopā and Nāropā.
- The sixth reveals how the sacred doctrine originated here in Tibet.
- The seventh narrates the lives of the great Tibetan promulgators of the teaching of essential meaning.
- The eighth extensively explains the biographies of the Taklung Kagyu lineage.
- The ninth offers a rough account of the lives of the Kagyu lineage holders in general.
- The tenth alludes to the origins of other diverse doctrinal traditions.
- The eleventh concludes with a reference to the origins of the outer fields of classical learning.

The explicit intent of these eleven parts is to elucidate the narrative of the authentic lineage of blessings that engenders trust and confidence, but implicitly I also wish to relate a brief account of the doctrinal history of the entire Buddhist teaching in a manner that is compatible with the intelligence of disciples of the present day. {9}

1. The Presentation of World Systems

First, the presentation of the world systems, generally speaking, may appear differently since the conquerors do not view the world with any fixation and since a single entity may indeed arise as anything whatsoever—as an impure appearance for sentient beings, as a meditative experience for yogins, as a pure vision for buddhas, and ultimately as something that does not abide anywhere—without those dissimilar appearances being contradictory, for they are in accordance with sentient beings' past actions.

Consequently, when the Buddha taught the doctrinal discourses of the vinaya to those fixated on this world, he delivered and presented them in conformity with the perceptions in the minds of those beings. Similarly, many distinct presentations of the world systems were also taught in the sūtras, tantras, and great treatises, such as the *Kālacakra*, *The Ocean of Ḍākas*,[1] *The Great Bounteousness of the Buddhas*,[2] *The Applications of Mindfulness*,[3] *The Designation of Mundane Phenomena*,[4] the higher phenomenology of *The Compendium of Phenomenology*,[5] and the lower phenomenology.[6] In terms of the definitive meaning, as long as space exists, as many particles as there are on a single atom or the surface of a single hair, these are permeated by as many bodies and fields of the conquerors as there are throughout the three times, such that they are immeasurable and their limits cannot be grasped.

According to such sources, this location of ours is the quintessential Buddha Field Whose Foundation and Center Are Adorned with Flowers,[7] resting upon the thirteenth of the twenty-five vertically stacked anthers of the lotus stem in the alms bowl in the hands of Vairocana Hīmamahāsāgara.[8] The sentient beings of this field are endowed first and foremost with a quality of extremely great forbearance, so it is designated as the World of Enduring Sorrow.[9] {10} Below it there is a maṇḍala of wind, six million one hundred thousand *yojana* in height and immeasurable in width.[10] Above that there is a mass of water, full and overflowing from the continuous rainfall from a great cloud named Golden Yoke[11] and weighed down by the terrain of gold[12] that formed above it.[13] That is to say, the maṇḍala of water is eight hundred thousand yojana in depth, and the terrain of gold above it is three hundred and twenty thousand yojana in thickness.[14] Above that at the center of the ocean filled with water is the four-terraced Mount Sumeru, its eastern face made of silver, the southern one of beryl, the western one of ruby, and the northern one of gold, eighty thousand yojana in breadth and one hundred and sixty thousand yojana in height, half of which is sunk beneath the sea and half rising upward.[15] It lies within seven golden mountain ranges—namely, Yoke-Holder Mountain Range, Plow-Holder Range, Acacia-Covered Range, Range Lovely to Behold, Horse-Ear Range, Perfect Bow Range, and Rim-Holder Range,[16] each one-half the height of the one before and extending outward from Mount Sumeru concentrically. The seven seas between them contain many islands endowed with resources.[17]

Beyond these, in the salt sea, there are three half-moon-shaped islands in the east, three in the south in the triangular shape of a chariot or scapula, three round islands in the west, and three rectangular islands in the north. Their materials correspond to the side of Mount Sumeru on which they are situated, but in this degenerate era of strife, their preciousness has faded and they have the appearance of ordinary earth.[18] The physical forms of the humanlike beings each correspond to their respective island group, as do their different modes of ornament, dress, and resources. Beyond the outer salt ocean is a surrounding ring of iron mountains, like a perimeter wall.[19]

Beneath the southern island known as Jambudvīpa (Rose-Apple Continent) are located the hells and the underworld of anguished spirits.[20] On Cāmaradvīpa (Yak-Tail Island) there are *rākṣasa* cannibal ogres, and on the four main continents and the other peripheral isles apart from Yak-Tail there dwell human beings.[21] {11}

In the caverns of Mount Sumeru are the antigods;[22] on its lower slopes, the gods of the Caturmahārājakāyika realm; and in the sky, the gods of the limitless mansions of the sun, moon, planets, stars, and so forth.[23] On the upper slopes are the many successive orders of protector deities, and at the summit is the actual divine realm of Trāyastriṃśa (The Thirty-Three), where Śakra, mighty lord of the gods, resides in the Mansion of Victory. There is a flat stone resembling a white woolen blanket—the gathering place where the gods hear the excellent law—and there are four parks, the wish-fulfilling coral jasmine tree, and so forth, an infinity of wealth.[24]

In the space above, formed individually like clouds, each with as much space between them as from the ocean upward, are four other god realms: Yāma (Free from Strife), Tuṣita (Joy-Filled), Nirmāṇrata (Delighting in Emanations), and Parinirmitavaśavartin (Mastery over Transformation). The physical forms, lifespans, and resources of the gods there are successively more and more excellent.[25] Everything from these realms downward is termed the world system of desire.[26] Above that are the seventeen abodes of the world system of form,[27] and then the four world systems of formlessness,[28] which reach the Summit of Existence.[29] These realms of form and formlessness are devoid of desire and sustained by meditative stability. The world systems of desire and form each have their sovereigns and so forth, whereas in the world system of formlessness, nothing manifests apart from itself. Among those three world systems, it is said that the beings of the human realm are superior to the gods because three supreme sorts of being—universal emperors, hermit buddhas, and perfect buddhas—make their appearance therein and because all the virtuous and negative actions of human beings have immense potential.[30]

Among the human continents, Uttarakuru (Island of Unpleasant Sound)[31] is a land of material resources, but it lacks the practice of the sacred doctrine. The other three continents are superior to that, being lands where the notion of past actions prevails. And among them, Jambudvīpa itself is especially exalted because it is the place where the perfect buddhas appear.[32] There are many peripheral isles around this Jambudvīpa, including Sumatra,[33] and it also includes the central country, {12} the nation of India, with its sixteen regions and six major cities, a precious continent, resembling a raised canopy of satin brocade.[34] Tartary and Khotan are chariot-shaped lands where all needs and wishes are fulfilled. Mongolia and China are wondrous lands like blossoming lotus flowers, and the nation of Tibet, which resembles a supine ogress, is the land tamed by sublime Avalokiteśvara.[35]

After the worlds that constitute this external environment had taken shape in descending order, a certain god endowed with the second meditative concentration died, transmigrated, and then took birth miraculously in the realm of Mahābrahmā gods. Starting from then, the sentient beings who constitute the living inhabitants of this world came into being in ascending order and filled the abodes of the gods. Then, when a certain deity of the Abhāsvara realm died and transmigrated, he was immediately reborn in Jambudvīpa, and from then on, the miraculously born human beings of Jambudvīpa had an inestimable lifespan, sustained by the food of meditative concentration. Their bodies were formed of light, and through miraculous ability, they could fly through space and so forth. However, they craved nectar, the essence of the earth, and on eating it, their positive attributes deteriorated. Since the essential oils of the earth,[36] the groves of nectarous shoots, uncultivated wild rice, and so on had been previously consumed, they faded and subsequently went into decline.[37]

The sun and moon, planets and stars appeared in space; coarse food gave rise to impure residues; male and female organs were differentiated, along with the four aspects of sexual intercourse;[38] roofed houses were built to conceal embarrassment, and there arose birth by womb. This was called the Third Age.[39] They gathered wild rice and hid it, but there was no immediate recourse to cultivation. Therefore, a wise and kindhearted person divided this wild rice equally and distributed it, such that his own share was cut off, and everyone gave him a little. In this way, he was elevated as a king because his good fortune reigned.[40] {13} The Second Age and the First Age that turned into the Age of Strife were subsequently distinguished due to the appearance of theft, murder, and the telling of lies.

There are also four ages distinguished with reference to the sacred doctrine, the vinaya tradition, in which the phrase "four ages of the past" denotes the Perfect Age of the twelve flawless years of the Buddhist teaching [prior to the testimony of the first defeating act and the three subsequent ages associated with the testimony of the other three defeating acts],[41] coinciding with the initial appearance of the denizens of the Arbuda hell.[42]

There are also four ages distinguished with reference to resources—an explanation derived from the sūtras in which the inception of the Age of Strife is simultaneous with the original appearance of the Buddha of this field, and is posited as a Perfect Age in which all resources were fully present, while the deterioration of lameness is assigned to the Third Age, and so forth.[43] When that Perfect Age turned into the Age of Strife, there were hermit sages, who, disillusioned by it, dwelled in the forests in order to acquire meditative concentration and miraculous abilities; brahmins who were sustained by the poetic verses of the Vedas, and so forth; the royal class (*kṣatriya*) who were sustained by taxation; the mercantile class (*vaiśya*), including tradesmen; the common laboring class (*śudra*), who were sustained by agriculture; and the outcastes (*caṇḍāla*) who survived through defiled activities. The realms of the animals, the anguished spirits, and denizens of the hells also similarly formed their respective hierarchies.[44]

The first king, mentioned above, was initially appointed as the caretaker of the fields, and he was given one-sixth of the produce of those who tilled the fields. He also carefully nurtured everyone equally and was respected by one and all, so he became known as Mahāsammata—the king honored by the multitude. That is to say, he was the first king of the human beings of Jambudvīpa in this Auspicious Eon (Bhadrakalpa).[45]

If you should wonder why this eon is called auspicious, it is because initially, when the world that constitutes the environment was formed, there arose a thousand golden lotuses in the midst of the maṇḍala of water. Seeing these, the gods of the pure abodes knew this to foreshadow the emergence of a thousand buddhas, and they exclaimed, "This eon is indeed auspicious!" So, {14} it became known as the Eon in Which a Thousand Lotuses Are Seen or the Auspicious Eon.[46] {14}

Concluding Verses

As for all things that are naturally pure from the beginning,
Like a flawless crystal ball, interdependent appearances arise
As a mere magical display, with unceasing energy
In the infinite colors of cyclic existence and quiescence.
Whosoever can appraise these colors should know
That they both appear and are fictitious,
And that they are devoid of both truth and falsehood.

May six-legged bees of clear intelligence,
Without attachment, longing, abiding, or rejection,
Suck with skillful analysis the ambrosial nectar
In all the lotus groves that form the entire framework
Of the external environment and its inhabitants.

In this part of the book concerning the general karma of living beings,
With my playful brush that sketches the refined realms of the conquerors,
I have painted in a hundred different colors
The array of the environment and its inhabitants.

Animate and inanimate worlds in myriad different colors—
How fortunate the eye that perceives such wonders!

This completes the first chapter of this book, a presentation of the world systems, from *Wondrous Ocean of Eloquence: A Narrative of the Wish-Fulfilling Gem of the Lineage* compiled by Gelong Ngawang Namgyel.

May it be auspicious! {15}

2. The Deeds of the Teacher {17}

Verses of Homage

OṂ SVĀSTI
May it be auspicious!

Homage to the moon that is the Conqueror,
Beauteous ornament, whose tresses are a source of bliss for the three realms,
Its sphere of major and minor marks waxing from the shoulder of the pure white eastern mountain,
Beautified with the symbolic deer of pristine cognition,
Its doctrinal wheel sends forth a hundred thousand rays of white light,
And its cooling rays of compassion, equanimous to all, cause the nighttime lilies, the liberation of disciples, to bloom.

Among his inconceivable, sky-like enlightened attributes,
The mighty revelation of Lord Buddha's twelve deeds,
Excellently emanated in this field, give rise to marvelous tidings,
And for those who seek liberation,
Even this minute account is like nectar to their ears.

The Life of Buddha Śākyamuni

Second is the explanation of the deeds of the completely perfect Buddha. Generally speaking, in the lineage of King Mahāsammata, there were five early lines of kings and five universal emperors who appeared, the last of whom, Cārumant, nurtured Jambudvīpa.[1] During that time when human beings were capable of a lifespan of forty thousand years, the first buddha of the Auspicious Eon was Krakucchandha. Then, when King Bhandumati[2] nurtured the world and human beings were capable of a lifespan of thirty thousand years, Buddha Kanakamuni appeared. Then, during the reign of King Kṛkī, when the lifespan of human beings was twenty thousand years, Buddha Kāśyapa appeared in the world.

As regards Buddha Śākyamuni, this Teacher of ours, he had set his mind on unsurpassed enlightenment and easily perfected the renunciations and realizations of the path through marvelous loving-kindness, compassion, enthusiasm, and undertakings that far exceeded those of the other bodhisattva heirs of the Conqueror.[3] Countless eons beforehand, he had attained unsurpassable pristine cognition, {18} and yet, because of five hundred former great aspirations to tame living beings who were especially difficult to subdue in the period of the five degenerations[4] when the human beings of Jambudvīpa had a lifespan of one hundred years, he manifested as the bodhisattva heir of the Conqueror Satśvetaketu in the divine paradise of Tuṣita and established assemblies of utterly pure deities in the glory of liberation. Then, he fastened the precious adamantine crown on the head of Venerable Ajita Maitreya, empowering him as his regent, and thereafter turned his enlightened intention toward going to Jambudvīpa. The gods said, "This is not the time because Jambudvīpa is rife with the five degenerations and is malevolent, owing to the ascendancy of eighteen extremist teachers."[5] And he replied, "I will overwhelm and guide all the demonic forces of Māra and extremists, just as the sound of a conch overpowers all the specific sounds of diverse musical instruments!"

He then made five considerations concerning the era (when human beings had a lifespan of one hundred years), the family line, (that of Gautama), the place (the city of Kapilavastu), the father (Śuddhodana), and the mother (Mahāmāyā).[6] Then, in order to inspire higher confidence in those who would rely on the "knower of the world,"[7] he entered his mother's womb in the form of the "king of elephants."[8] He passed ten months within a mansion of exquisite "snake's heart" sandalwood[9] inside the womb, imbued with fragrance, revealing ocean-like doctrinal discourses to infinite bodhisattvas of the ten directions and conferring upon them maturational empowerment and liberating guidance.[10] During that time, also, at the heart of Jambudvīpa, the Tree of Enlightenment sprouted.[11] Two wondrous great signs also occurred.[12]

Finally, during the ascendancy of the constellation Puṣyā [Cancer], in the pleasure garden of Lumbinī, {19} as his mother stood upright, grasping the branch of a fig tree[13] with her limbs stretched out, untainted by the slightest impurity, like a burnished orb of gold, he was born from her right side without hurting her in any way. He was taken up by [Śakra], mighty lord of the gods, and bathed by the *nāga* kings.[14] When he took seven steps in each direction, golden thousand-petal lotuses sprang up at every step, and he vowed a declaration with words of assurance, filling the entire trichiliocosm with an effulgence of light. At that time, eighteen great signs occurred.[15]

On the seventh day, his mother passed away, and he was tended by thirty-two nurses.[16] Four vassal kings,[17] five hundred Śākya youths, eighty thousand maidens, five hundred sets of male and female servants, elephants, horses, buffalo, cattle, and the like were all simultaneously born. All sorts of treasures, jewels and precious substances, spontaneously manifested, and the wealth of kings increased. Consequently, he was given the name Sarvasiddhārtha (All Aims Accomplished). He was also called Śākyamuni (Able Sage of the Śākyas) because he continued to tame all the proud Śākyas, Devadeva (God of Gods) because the *yakṣas* bowed before him, and *Sahasrahastivarcasa (One with the Strength of a Thousand Elephants) because with a single finger he could lift a container of grain that five hundred bulls could not move by force.

Ordinary soothsayers foreordained that he would become either a universal emperor or a buddha, and the hermit sage Araṇa foreordained that he would definitely attain perfect enlightenment.[18] When he went to writing classes, he became a mentor to all the masters, and he demonstrated to them the sixty-four scripts.[19] At the residence of the mathematician Arjuna, to everyone's amazement he could undertake calculations up to and including ten to the power of sixty-two.[20]

The shade of a rose-apple tree did not leave his body, even in the afternoon,[21] {20} and five hermit sages were unable to move through the sky above the prince through their miraculous ability, so his father and those five hermit sages paid homage to him.[22] Yaśodharā was pledged to the royal standard as his consort, and for her he vied in the sixty-four crafts with five hundred powerful Śākya youths who had the proverbial strength of Nārāyaṇa. He eradicated their haughtiness and outshone the entire world. He then married sixty thousand princesses, and Yaśodharā gave birth to the seed of his son.[23]

At the four gates of the palace, he then observed the advantages and disadvantages of an aged person, an ill person, a dead person, and an emanational monk. Encouraged by a symphony of music produced by his queens, he was inspired to seek emancipation from worldly life. His father had tried to guard him with the force of arms, walls, gatehouses, and so forth, but by skillful means he had requested and was granted permission to go outside.[24] Consequently, at midnight, as the lunar mansion Cancer was in the ascendant, he mounted his horse, Kaṇṭhaka.[25] The four great kings of the four directions raised the steed by its feet, while Brahmā and Śakra followed in attendance. Circumambulating the pure abodes of the gods, he traversed the heavens above and alighted in the north, in the country of Kāmarūpa. Once he had sent Kaṇṭhaka and his attendant Candaka[26] back home, he cut off his own hair as a sign of renunciation, and the Viśuddha Stūpa appeared.[27]

A god emanated in the form of a hunter and offered him a saffron robe: he was spontaneously ordained. And then, entering the place where extremists were practicing austerities, he undertook double the hardships that they did, causing them to have faith in him, and he became known as a great religious ascetic. He actualized the sense field of Nothing at All based on the instruction of Ārāḍā and the meditative absorption of the Summit of Existence based on the instruction of Udraka.[28] {21} But he observed that these did not lead to the path of liberation, so he then proceeded to the banks of the Nairañjanā, where he practiced asceticism for six years, overcame sensation and feeling, abandoned the coarse inhalation and exhalation of breath, and remained in the meditative stability called Permeation of Space that no other living creatures, including the gods, had entered. The so-called group of five companions, the first of his entourage, appeared in this place.[29]

According to the yoga tantra of the way of secret mantra, it is explained that he left the frame of his physical body that was practicing austerities in the human realm, and in Akaniṣṭha or at the summit of Mount Sumeru, he attained buddhahood in the body of perfect resource. After turning the doctrinal wheel, he then reentered his physical body while practicing austerities, and displayed the way of attaining buddhahood in the body of emanation.[30] At this point he partook of milk gruel offered by two village girls, Nandā and Nandabalā,[31] made of the seven times purified milk of a thousand buffalo cows, sweetened with the essence of honey, and so forth, and his bodily strength increased.[32]

At that time, the densest area of extensive vegetation and plants in Jambudvīpa was in the environs of the focal point of enlightenment. Sugar cane and other plants exuded their juices, and even the soil here emitted pleasant sounds when touched. Living creatures naturally bowed toward it and took care of the area. The Tree of Enlightenment also was extensive and beautiful, causing the unvirtuous thoughts of all beings to disappear. The bodhisattva advanced with the gait of a lion, endowed with the limitless strength of a great man. He accepted a green grass mat, soft to the touch, from the grass vendor Svastika and proceeded to the focal point of enlightenment. There he assumed his seat in the adamantine posture upon those blades of grass that naturally had a clockwise weave.[33]

With an effulgence of light, {22} he rendered lusterless the domain of Māra, such that when the armed forces of Māra arrived en masse, he was unagitated by their fearsome forms, and he turned their cascades of weapons into a rain of flowers. He transfigured the daughters of Māra who sought to seduce him into old women. When Māra reproached him, saying that there was no causal basis for his proposed attainment of buddhahood, he touched the earth with his right hand, causing the goddess of the earth to raise her torso out of a trembling crevice, and she said, "This is a great man. It is for this reason that I have manifested myself and indeed bear witness to the entire world—that he himself is the transcendent lord Buddha." Immediately after, all the forces of Māra scattered in terror, many of them taking refuge in the Teacher. So it was that, having triumphed in battle over the mighty forces of Māra, he acquired the title Conqueror.[34]

At midnight, he cultivated the four meditative concentrations and, at the conclusion of the fourth, examined the twelve links of dependent origination in ascending and reverse order. Then, having cultivated the three degrees of awareness, when the drum had only just sounded the last watch of the night, with instantaneous wisdom, he attained manifestly perfect buddhahood. Thereupon, all the buddhas of the ten directions offered gifts and praised him, saying, "You have attained buddhahood just as we, ourselves, have attained enlightenment. These attainments may be exemplified by butter and the refined essence of butter!" It is specifically said that, immediately after attaining buddhahood, he ascended into the sky to the height of seven palm trees, maintaining that same adamantine posture.[35]

Seven weeks later, he received the first alms offering from the merchants Trapuṣa and Bhallika, and he consumed and blessed them with auspicious verses, consecrating these offerings in a stone alms bowl that the four great kings had presented.[36] {23} Top-knotted Brahmā, forefather of the world, offered him a thousand-spoked golden wheel, and then, as requested, at Vārāṇasī, on behalf of the five noble companions and a multitude of gods, he turned the doctrinal wheel concerning the four truths three times and in twelve ways.[37] The direct purpose was that the five companions would attain arhatship, and the indirect purpose was that disciples would reverse the grasping of individual personality and be established in the four results. This constituted the first turning of the wheel.[38]

Then again, at Gṛddhrakūṭa (Vulture Peak Mountain), for an assembly of one thousand two hundred and fifty or five thousand monks, nuns, and so forth and an innumerable assembly of one hundred billion trillion bodhisattvas, he turned the doctrinal wheel concerning the absence of defining characteristics, which included *The Transcendent Perfection of Wisdom*. The purpose of this teaching was that those who had resorted to eternalist views might be averted from these and be established in the single modality—emptiness, which is the sole path to be traversed. This constituted the intermediate turning of the wheel.[39]

Furthermore, at Mount Mālaya, at Vaiśālī and elsewhere, on behalf of an assembly of bodhisattvas who had entered upon the entire vehicle, in order to reverse the grasping of the two extremes, he turned the doctrinal wheel concerning the definitive ultimate truth—its purpose being that disciples would be established on the path of the middle way, free from extremes. This constituted the final turning of the wheel.[40]

Following the first turning of the wheel, the group of five close companions were ordained as mendicants, fifty foremost sons of enlightened heritage were established as arhats, and sixty groups of noble companions saw the truth.[41] He converted Kāśyapa of Uruvilvā by miraculous means and established his thousand hermit sage disciples with matted hair in the exhaustion of all contamination.[42] He converted both Upatiṣya Śāradvatiputra and Kolita Maudgalyāyana, {24} along with their retinues, and they respectively became supreme in discriminative awareness and miraculous abilities.[43] Having accepted the Teacher, Mahākāśyapa received the full monastic ordination and became supreme for maintaining the ascetic virtues.[44] Anāthapiṇḍada acquired faith and, on seeing the truth, offered a pleasure garden.[45] Prasenajit was converted by *The Sūtra of Youthful Examples*,[46] and Bimbisāra was established in faith.[47] Then, on meeting his own father Śuddhodana, he established him as one entering the stream to nirvāṇa. Ānanda was ordained as a mendicant and became supreme for retaining what he had heard.[48]

Seven years after attaining buddhahood, the Blessed One benefited his deceased mother, who had been reborn in Trāyastriṃśa and thereafter in Sāṃkāśya. With an array of great miracles, he descended from the god realms.[49] Such were his inexpressible deeds. He overwhelmed six extremist teachers by means of great miracles.[50] In the perception of his disciples of most supreme good fortune, he became equipoised by means of the supreme secret instructions of the tantras in the *bhaga* of the Adamantine Queen, the delightful palace, the sacred and eternal location where the syllables E and VAṂ are indivisible.[51] And there in the guise of Glorious Heruka endowed with seven aspects of union,[52] he revealed the oceanic tantras of the profoundly secret Adamantine Vehicle in a temporal context that never ends. Consequently, he instantaneously established in maturational empowerment and liberating guidance eight hundred million mighty lords of yoga and a host of yoginīs equaling the atoms of thirty-six Mount Sumerus. This precisely constituted the definitive collection of the precious tantras.

Finally, Ānanda became his attendant and he traversed most of the central and northern parts of the country on foot. Though he did not preach there in former times, he did make prophetic declarations concerning Kashmir and Khotan.[53] Later, following in his footsteps, Vajrapāṇi wandered through countless lands and converted them.[54] {25}

When in his eightieth year, Lord Buddha went to the great city of Kuśinagara and lay down on his final bed in the midst of a grove of sal trees. After imparting his final testament, he became equipoised in the four meditative concentrations, the formless absorptions, and the absorption in cessation, in due order and again in reverse order. Then, from the fourth meditative concentration, he passed into final nirvāṇa in the uncontaminated expanse.[55]

His sacred corpse was properly cremated, and the remains, which equaled one orthodox measure, were divided into eight parts, which then became objects of offering throughout the three planes of existence.[56]

Concluding Verses

The illuminating lord, lion of the Śākyas, embodiment of all the pristine cognition of all the conquerors,
Whose thousandfold emanational clouds skillfully appear in the skies of the field of patient endurance,
The great lamp of the inconceivable doctrinal wheel for the three planes of existence,
Protected living beings with his new light, triumphant over the darkness of Māra.

This world, the maṇḍala of darkness,
Hard to tame in an increasing Age of Strife,
Replete with its five degenerations,
Is never abandoned by any of the conquerors.

The guide who is this adamantine sun,
With splendor of kindness, aspiration, and deeds,
Is a mighty light unmatched by the moon and all the stars.

Those who are feeble like me have no power to repay
His utterly inestimable kindness.
Henceforth, forevermore, I bind my body, speech, and mind
In the service of this lord-protector
And vow to correctly engage in study, reflection, and meditation.

This completes the second chapter of this book, an explanation of the deeds of the genuinely perfect Buddha, from *Wondrous Ocean of Eloquence: A Narrative of the Wish-Fulfilling Gem of the Lineage*, compiled by Taklungpa Ngawang Namgyel. {27}

3. The Compilation of the Transmitted Teachings {29}

Verses of Homage

OṂ SVĀSTI
May it be auspicious!

Homage to the compilers of the transmitted teachings
Who polished and excellently refined through chanting
The gems of word and meaning contained in the oceanic doctrinal wheel
And then threaded these as a rosary,
Moving along the string of distinct letters,
And also to the supreme representations of buddha body, speech, and mind—
The peerless fields where even a minute seed of virtue planted with faith
Ripens as the abundant cornucopia of higher rebirth and liberation!

Here I shall describe the manner in which the transmitted teachings of both the Lesser Vehicle and the Great Vehicle were compiled and how the three representations of buddha body, speech, and mind first originated.

The Three Councils

The first council was decreed by the regent Mahākāśyapa for the participation of arhats, who were supreme and unimpeded in divine vision.[1] Entering into the meditative stability that perceives the aims and aspirations of beings,[2] he examined all things up to and including the Summit of Existence, and then he beat the wooden gong,[3] convening together five hundred arhats minus one, as Ānanda was appointed as the water attendant. Setting out, they reached Magadha and summoned King Ajātaśatru, who agreed to offer patronage for the council. He supplied all their resources, and they observed the start of the summer rain retreat (that is, the first day of the month of Śrāvaṇa) in the Banyan Cave. Mahākāśyapa knew that Ānanda above all should be trained and so expelled him, mentioning as a pretext his eight shortcomings.[4] Ānanda went off to the city of Vriji,[5] where he attained arhatship after instructing his own disciples. Then, he returned to the place where the monastic community was residing. {30} Until the termination of the first council, the rules that had applied prior to Lord Buddha's nirvāṇa were still valid. Therefore, the sublime Ānanda was appointed to the assembly on the basis of the rite of the twofold request.[6] Then, five hundred *saṃghāṭī* robes were laid out upon a lion throne, and he took his seat facing toward the focal point of enlightenment. Through recollection, he carefully assembled the entire collection of discourses (*sūtrapiṭaka*) and then said, "That is my transmission. Is your transmission the same?" They replied, "It is so." He then descended from the lion throne.

Similarly, Upāli assembled the collection of discipline (*vinayapiṭaka*). That is to say, he established the vinaya rules in the format of questions and answers, commencing with what constitutes the first precept of training and for whom is it applicable and so forth." Then, Mahākāśyapa assembled the collection of phenomenology (*abhidharmapiṭaka*). The texts of these scriptural collections are each composed of hundreds of thousands of words.[7]

As regards the second council, one hundred and ten years after the Teacher passed into nirvāṇa, during the reign of the king Aśoka, the arhat Yaśaḥ traveled with an entourage of five hundred to the great monastery of Vaiśālī. He knew that the resident monastic community there was engaging in ten transgressions. As it is said,

> (1) Exclamations, (2) celebrating the attainment of arhatship, (3) the deliberate practice of agriculture, (4) the exploring of intoxicants, (5) the misuse of sacred stored salt for seasoning, (6) eating while on the road, (7) eating with two fingers, (8) stirring curd and milk together as an illegal afternoon beverage, (9) using a new mat without an old patch, and (10) handling gold or silver may genuinely be included among the provisional vows.[8]

Yaśaḥ convened an assembly of seven hundred arhats who had all been students of the sublime Ānanda and established through a format of questions and answers that those ten rules should be rejected. They recited the three scriptural collections without addition or omission, and so the seven hundred arhats also said that this was authentic.[9] {31}

As regards the third council, at the time when this Teacher of ours, Lord Buddha, was the brahmin Samudrareṇu in a former life, he made five hundred great prayers of aspiration, including, "After I have passed into nirvāṇa, for the benefit of the disciples, may the Buddhist teaching divide into eighteen!"[10] Also, *The Sūtra of the Prophetic Declaration of the Conqueror Kāśyapa Imparted to King Kṛkī in a Dream* says,

> Your majesty, the dream in which you saw eighteen men pulling on a sheet of cloth means that the teaching of Śākyamuni will be divided into eighteen schools. But the cloth itself, which is liberation, will not be torn asunder![11]

The point is that the arhats strongly adhered to liturgies recited in Prakrit, Apabhraṃśa, and Pāli following the death of the religious king Aśoka. They then gradually aligned themselves with texts on monastic discipline that were different from one another, as they did with the scriptural collection of the discourses, and so forth, which also had extensive oral transmissions. So it was that the Buddhist teaching evolved into eighteen monastic orders.[12]

In order to eliminate schisms in the community and arguments due to disputation concerning whether or not the eighteen orders were canonical, King Kaniṣka offered patronage and a council was convened by five hundred arhats headed by Pūrṇika, five hundred bodhisattvas headed by Vasumitra, and sixteen thousand ordinary scholars. They established that these eighteen monastic orders were canonical, saying that they had been sanctioned in the vinaya, were inherent in the discourses, did not contradict reality, had been founded in accordance with the three principles,[13] emphasized meaning rather than words, and had been differentiated by arhats. In addition, they had originated from the blessings of the buddhas and were absolutely pure because they had been established in accordance with the prophetic declaration contained in the aforementioned sūtra, interpreting the dream of King Kṛkī.[14] {32}

The Eighteen Monastic Orders

As for the four primary orders among these eighteen, the first was the Mūlasarvāstivādin. Their founding monastic preceptor was Rāhulabhadra, the son of the Conqueror, who was of the royal class and was supreme for his devotion to the precepts. Their language was Sanskrit, their saṃghāṭī robes had between twenty-five and twenty-nine patches, and their motifs included a lily, a jewel, and a leaf. This is the only order to have reached Tibet.

The second was the Mahāsaṃghika. Their founding preceptor was Mahākāśyapa who hailed from the brahmin class, and was supreme for maintaining the ascetic virtues. Their language was Prakrit, their saṃghāṭī robes had between twenty-five and twenty-seven patches, and their motif was the conch.

The third was the Sammitīya. Their founding preceptor was Upāli, who hailed from the laboring class and was supreme as an upholder of monastic discipline. Their language was Apabhraṃśa, their saṃghāṭī robes had between twenty-one and twenty-five patches, and their motif was the *socika* flower.

The fourth was the Sthavira. Their founding preceptor was Katyāyana, who hailed from the mercantile class and was supreme for converting the borderlands. Their language was Pāli, and their saṃghāṭī robes and motif are said to resemble those of the Sammitīya.[15]

All of the other suborders were divisions of these four. As has been said,

> All the eighteen orders have indeed been differentiated exclusively owing to the particulars of their views, but they do not differentiate the Teacher.[16]

And,

> Due to the particulars of country, content, and masters,
> Eighteen orders were differentiated.[17]

The Great Vehicle

As regards the Great Vehicle, a million bodhisattva heirs of the Conqueror—headed by Samantabhadra, Mañjuśrī, Vajrapāṇi, and Maitreya—gathered on the mountain called Vimalasvabhāva to the south of the great city of

Rājagṛha, and there they assembled the three scriptural collections. The doctrinal enumerations contained in each of these are inestimable.[18] {32}

The oceanic tantra collections of the way of Secret Mantra {33} were compiled by those who requested them and by hosts of ḍākinīs. They were preserved without degeneration for eternity in places such as the emanational field of Oḍḍiyāna. In general, it is explained that there were many compilers of the transmitted teachings concerning provisional meaning. All the transmitted teachings concerning the somewhat definitive meaning were compiled by Vajrapāṇi—this happened through the power of his own aspiration. As for those concerning the most definitive meaning, their teachers, compilers, and all that is revealed within them are indivisible.[19]

The Origins of the Three Representations

Now I will briefly explain the origin of the representations of buddha body, speech, and mind. King Udrāyaṇa of Roruka presented Bimbisāra with a priceless set of jeweled armor, and, at a loss as to what to give him in return, Bimbisāra consulted the Teacher. With the latter's permission, he had an artist draw an image of the Lord Buddha on cloth, modeled on the reflection of the Teacher that arose in the water when he was seated alongside a bathing pool, and it became known as "the water extract." When he saw this gift and was presented with it, Udrāyaṇa attained realization of the truth, and he acquired the eye of the sacred doctrine.[20] Also, in order to convert Muktikā, daughter of the King of Siṅghala, the artist Veda drew an image on a cotton surface while the Teacher's body was emitting rays of light, and it consequently became known as "the one endowed with rays of light." The moment she saw that gift, the princess beheld the truth.[21] These two were the original icons associated with this Buddhist teaching.

Then, on one occasion, the patrons invited the monastic community for a midday meal, and the Teacher was absent. They noticed the conspicuous absence of his radiant brilliance at the head of the row. At the request of the great householder Anāthapiṇḍada, and with Lord Buddha's consent, many images of the Conqueror were then made. It is said that these constitute the original relief sculptures.[22] {34}

As for the representations of buddha speech, during the intermediate turning of the doctrinal wheel, Śakra inscribed *The Transcendent Perfection of Wisdom* on gold tablets with ink of molten blue beryl. He also inscribed on tablets *The Shoulder Bracelet of the Pinnacle of the Victory Banner*[23] on tablets and attached them to the pinnacle of a victory banner, such that the battle with the antigods was averted. The scriptures of monastic discipline forbid the selling of canonical volumes but permit the selling of heretical, extremist texts. Such remarks establish that the transmitted teachings existed in book form at an early date. It is also said that when the transmitted teachings had been compiled, the compilers committed them to writing in their own lands and in their own respective languages.[24]

As regards the representations of buddha mind, stūpas originated according to their respective circumstances, symbolizing the auspicious nativity, the great enlightenment, the turning of the doctrinal wheel, the subjugation of heretical extremists, the descent from the god realms, the resolution of schisms, and the attainment of nirvāṇa.[25]

In particular, when Brahmā, Śakra, and Rāhula, inspired by contact with the light radiating from the Teacher, requested permission to create representations of the three buddha bodies, Viśvakarman served as the artisan, Maitreya as their sacristan, Vajrapāṇi as their guardian, and the seventy acolytes of glorious Mahākāla agreed to be their protectors.

Brahmā smelted and cast various divine gemstones, and a round stūpa was fashioned that was clear blue in color and the size of his own armspan. Seven circumambulations of it would bring supreme accomplishment. He placed it in Oḍḍiyāna.

Rāhula commissioned an image of the buddha body of perfect resource in the form of Vairocana Hīmamahāsāgara, azure blue in color and in meditative equipoise, fashioned of various nāga jewels, eighty yojana in height. Praying to it caused a shower of uncultivated rice to stream down for twelve days. It was submerged below the navel within the outer ocean, and it was exposed above the navel so as to benefit the living beings of the three planes of existence. {35}

Śakra commissioned an array composed of three statues of the buddha body of emanation, fashioned from five divine jewels, five human jewels, and five hundred and one quartz stones of middling quality. These depicted the Teacher the size of an eight-year-old, a twelve-year-old, and a twenty-five-year-old, respectively. The right hand of each was in the earth-touching gesture, and the left hand in the gesture of meditative equipoise. They had thrones supported by a hundred and eight lions, backrests depicting the twelve deeds, aureoles depicting the thirty-five confession buddhas, and parasols depicting the six buddhas of the past, and so on. When these were arrayed before the Five-Eyed One,[26] diverse rays of light issued from the

Teacher's mouth to fill the entire world, arousing the minds of all buddhas and bodhisattvas, and then returned, permeating the three statues with light and consecrating them, before once again reentering his mouth. Wherever these representations were subsequently placed, they were presented with offerings by countless hosts of bodhisattva heirs and disciples, and the Great Vehicle flourished. Two of the statues in particular, along with one of Avalokiteśvara, were purposefully intended for the conversion of Tibet.

The statue depicting Lord Buddha as a twenty-five-year-old was brought to the god realms, where it was worshipped. The statues depicting him as an eight-year-old and as a twelve-year-old were worshipped in the god realms, in Oḍḍiyāna, in the nāga realms, and at the Adamantine Seat for five hundred years each. Thereafter, during the reign of the Indian king Devapāla, the statue of the twelve-year-old representation, along with its throne, was transported to China, and the statue of the eight-year-old representation to the king of Nepal, where they respectively became objects of offering. During the reign of the religious king Songtsen Gampo, they both reached Tibet, where the statue of the twelve-year-old representation became known as the Jowo of Lhasa and the eight-year-old representation as the Jowo of Ramoche.[27]

According to certain other historical anecdotes, the twelve-year-old statue was commissioned by Maitreya and the eight-year-old statue by King Kṛkī during the era of Buddha Kāśyapa. {36} It is said that when Buddha Kāśyapa consecrated the latter, it was then transformed into a representation of Śākyamuni the size of an eight-year-old.[28]

Almost eighty years after the Teacher had passed into nirvāṇa, the master Śaṅkarasvāmin, who hailed from the brahmin class and was the youngest of three siblings, built a *caitya* with the outer form of a stūpa and the inner form of a *gandhola* shrine near the Tree of Enlightenment, at Vajrāsana. At its heart was a representative image of the Teacher at the age of thirty-five—the age at which he attained manifest buddhahood. It was fashioned of paste, combining white sandalwood powder and various jewels, with eyes of emerald, and it looked exactly like him. Whoever saw it had no choice but to pay homage. Since it was insatiable to behold, observers would forget their inclination to eat and drink, they would experience a long time as a short time, and they could not turn their back toward it. Just by seeing it, illnesses were cured, sorrows forgotten, demonic influences severed, and afflicted mental states pacified. The source of such limitless enlightened attributes, it is renowned like the sun in the sky, as the Mahābodhi of Vajrāsana.[29]

Furthermore, when the transcendent lord Buddha ascended to the god realms, as a field of merit, the king of Vārāṇasī and his entourage commissioned an extremely lifelike sandalwood representation of the Teacher, and it was excellently fashioned. So when the Conqueror descended again from the god realms, it is said that the statue took six steps toward him in greeting, and then with the tip of his finger the Teacher immediately exhorted it to depart for China to benefit living beings, and it departed like a cloud in the sky. Nowadays it is renowned as the Sandalwood Jowo and is seated as a representation on the throne of Jowo Śākyamuni in China.[30] {37}

Later, there were innumerable individuals headed by the religious king Aśoka who constructed icons and caityas.[31]

The Duration of the Buddhist Teaching

Coincidentally, as regards the duration of the Buddhist teaching, according to *The Scriptures of Monastic Discipline*, *The Sūtra of the Auspicious Eon*, *The Shorter Sūtra of Final Nirvāṇa*, and so forth, the foreordained duration of the Buddhist teaching is interpreted as one thousand years. However, this period is one thousand five hundred years according to *Compassion's White Lotus*, two thousand according to *The Sūtra of Candragarbha*, two thousand five hundred according to *The Sūtra of Different Manifestations without Wavering from the Essential Nature of Reality* and so forth, five thousand according to Dāmstrasena's *Commentary on "The Transcendent Perfection of Wisdom in One Hundred Thousand Lines"* and so forth, twenty-one thousand six hundred according to the *Kālacakra*, and up to six hundred "waxing" human lifetimes of the "waxing eon" according to *The Narrative of Nandimitra*[32] and so forth.[33] Since there are a great many opinions exclusively associated with authentic sources such as these, one should refrain from adhering to a single extreme position.

Ultimately, it is through the unvirtuous activities of human beings that their lifespans and resources are diminished. That is to say, when the lifespan shrinks to ten years, people will dress in hairy wool, eat millet, transform their ornaments into weapons, and sustain themselves, in succession, with boxes of hoarded grain, withered bones, rationed spoonfuls, and so forth.[34] Thereafter, famine, sickness, and warfare will be rampant for eons. Then, wearying of this, as they abandon killing each other, life expectancy will increase again to twenty years and so on. As they abandon negative acts and practice virtue, their lifespans will consequently increase to a hundred years, at which time the sixteen elders will arrive in Jambudvīpa.[35] Those with good fortune will be ordained as mendicants, and the teachings of the lord-protector, Lion of the Śākyas, will flourish until human beings have a lifespan of six hundred years. Then, when the lifespan reaches seven hundred years, the sixteen elders will compile all the volumes containing the transmitted teachings of the Teacher and construct caityas of precious gems. Those who circumambulate or make obeisance to them, even the elders of the Lesser Vehicle, will pass into nirvāṇa. {38} This is explained to be the conclusive teaching of Śākyamuni. When the lifespan of this "waxing eon" has increased to eighty thousand years, the deeds of the conquerors will accord with the explanation given in *The Sūtra of the Auspicious Eon*—commencing from the appearance of the perfect buddha Maitreya and the universal emperor Śaṅkha,[36] and so on, and continuing down to the appearance of Adhimukta.[37]

In general, cyclical time is composed of four eons—namely, the eon of formation, the eon of duration, the eon of destruction, and the eon of vacuity—each of which includes twenty intermediate eons. Each period of eighty eons is equivalent to one great eon.[38] Regarding the eon of destruction in particular, *The Treasury of Phenomenology* says,

> There are seven destructions by fire, one by water.
> And then after seven destructions by water have taken place,
> Finally there is the destruction by wind.[39]

This being the case, after this Auspicious Eon, sixty great eons of darkness will pass. Thereafter, in a bright eon known as Mahāmadhura, ten thousand buddhas will appear, and so forth.[40] As long as space endures, they will not come to an end.

Concluding Verses

With breath that can hold in the throat unfailing retention of all scripture,
Able to transform into a crystal flute innumerable words and meanings of precious scripture,
Eloquent musicians amid throngs erudite in scripture—
Immeasurable is the kindness of those compilers of the ocean of scripture!

Since in this Buddhist teaching the expanse without material essence
Can manifest through meritorious actions,
The transmission of undeceiving truth unfailingly arises
Such that perfect enlightenment is manifested upon the invincible seat.

Right it is that those of authentic intelligence
Should enhance like the waxing moon
Their devotion for the compilers
And enthusiasm for those who created the supreme representations! {39}

This completes the third chapter of this book, concerning the compilers of the transmitted teachings—and incidentally, the origins of the representations of buddha body, speech, and mind—from *Wondrous Ocean of Eloquence: A Narrative of the Wish-Fulfilling Gem of the Lineage* compiled by Taklungpa Ngawang Namgyel. {41}

4. The Appearance of Buddhism and Its Upholders in India {43}

Verses of Homage

OṂ SVĀSTI
May it be auspicious!

Illustrious among human beings are all the noble ones,
Who, by their own respective hands,
Can bestow the precious lamp of the Buddhist teaching
Upon all those who seek liberation.

How wondrous are those who assume as their hand emblem
The lamp of the Buddhist teaching
In the supreme abode of unsurpassed pristine cognition,
Who have long quit cyclic existence yet remain within it,
Without tolerating ensnarement by a hundred hardships.

I have faith in scholarly and accomplished captains
Who at will acquire a mass of gems,
Patiently pursuing and extracting those who seek their own and others' benefit
Through the words and meanings of the mighty ocean of sūtra and tantra—
Profound and vast, inestimable in depth,
Depending on wondrous provisions—the raft of study, reflection, and meditation.

Chapter four briefly presents the origins of the Buddhist teaching and the upholders of the Buddhist teaching in India, Land of the Noble Ones.

The Hierarchical Succession

At the outset, with regard to the hierarchical succession of the Buddhist teaching, Mahākāśyapa entrusted the teaching to Ānanda and then passed into nirvāṇa. The latter acted with respect to the Buddhist teaching just as the Teacher himself. Thereafter, Śāṇavāsika, over a five-year period, held a great ceremony on behalf of an entourage of many tens of thousands of arhats, at which Ānanda conferred the mendicant ordination. Intending to pass into nirvāṇa after entrusting the Buddhist teaching to one who had become an arhat endowed with knowledge and liberation, Ānanda then proceeded to the middle of the Ganges, where a hermit sage endowed with miraculous abilities arrived with an entourage of five hundred. There, in midstream, {44} Ānanda materialized an island and conferred upon him the full monastic ordination at midday. At the time when the hermit sage made the formal request for ordination, he attained the fruit of no longer being subject to rebirth, and at the time when the threefold affirmation was made,[1] he attained arhatship and was consequently named Madhyāntika (Midway) or Madhyāhnika (Midday). Ānanda said to him, "I know that you should establish the Buddhist teaching in Kashmir" and then passed into nirvāṇa. Madhyāhnika went to Kashmir where he dried up the lakes, subdued the nāgas, and brought saffron seeds from Gandhamādana Mountain so that they would grow in that land. He caused the Buddhist teaching to flourish supremely. That place, where five hundred arhats always reside, is renowned as Kashmir.[2]

Śāṇavāsika also propagated the activities of the Buddhist teaching, and he entrusted the teaching to Upagupta, who knew the three scriptural collections and had become an arhat. The latter always ensured that the evil Māra would not only be unable to rival him but also be unable to harm the Buddhist teaching. A cavern, twenty-double-arm-spans wide and deep, was filled to the brim with four-inch sticks, one for each of the arhats who were his disciples.[3] On that occasion, he entrusted the Buddhist teaching to Dhītika and then passed into nirvāṇa. The latter entrusted the succession to Kṛṣṇa, and he in turn to Sudarśana. These are said to constitute the seven hierarchs of the Buddhist teaching.[4]

A Commentary on the Sūtra of the Descent to Laṅkā[5] says that Dhītika entrusted the teaching to Micchaka,[6] and then in succession it fell to Buddhānandin, Buddhamitra, Bhikṣu Pārśva, Punyayaśaḥ, Aśvaghoṣa, Nāgārjuna, Āryadeva, Rāhulata, Saṃghānandi, Bhikṣu Arhat, Saṃghayaśaḥ, Kumārata, Śayata, Vasubandhu, Manorhita, Haklenayaśaḥ, and Siṃhabodhi.[7]

The Sixteen Elders

It was the sixteen great elders in particular who nurtured the Buddhist teaching: Aṅgaja at Mount Kailash, Ajita in the Crystal Forest of Hermit Sages, {45} Vanavāsin on the Seven-Leaved Mountain, Mahākālika on Tāmradvīpa, Vajrīputra on Siṅghaladvīpa, Bhadra on an island in the Yamuna River, Kanakavatsa in Kashmir, Kanaka in the western continent of Aparagodānīya, Bhakula in the northern continent of Uttarakuru, Rāhula on the island of Priyaṅku, Kṣudrapanthaka on Vulture Peak, Piṇḍola Bharadvāja in the eastern continent of Pūrvavideha, Panthaka in Trāyastriṃśa, Nāgasena on Mount Urumundu, Gopaka on Mount Bihula, and Abhedya in Himavant. Absolutely all of them were inconceivably great beings, along with the hosts of their retinues, nurturing the sacred doctrine of the Buddhist teaching and teaching the sacred doctrine as long as it endures in the glorious meritorious field of gods and humans.[8]

The Six Ornaments and Their Successors

The six ornaments of Jambudvīpa illuminated like the rising sun the dawn of the teaching of the Great and Lesser Vehicles in the Noble Land of India. Among them were the following. The great being Nāgārjuna, foreordained by the Buddha, was the great promulgator of profound view and mighty lord of the eighth level, elucidating the unique meaning of *The Transcendent Perfection of Wisdom*. Āryadeva, miraculously born from a lotus stem, was a learned authority in all the textual traditions of our own and other (non-Buddhist) traditions, triumphant over the perspectives of opponents. The noble Asaṅga, great promulgator of extensive conduct, was directly instructed by sublime Ajita (Maitreya). He initially acquired the meditative stability called Continuity of the Sacred Doctrine and later the third bodhisattva level known as Illuminating. The accomplished master Vasubandhu, renowned as the second buddha, comprehended the ninety-nine sections of *The Transcendent Perfection of Wisdom in One Hundred Thousand Lines*[9] and was a lamp clarifying the phenomenology of the sacred doctrine. {46} The heroic Dignāga, through the inspiration of the sacred doctrine, outshone negative opponents, conversed directly with Mañjughoṣa, and was supreme in valid cognition, the knowledge of the three vehicles that eradicates the wrong views of others. Dharmakīrti, crown ornament of all logicians, eradicated all Buddhist and non-Buddhist opponents and finally, on the basis of the yoga of Cakrasaṃvara, accomplished the level of a great sky farer in that very lifetime.[10]

To give an approximate list of their students, Buddhapālita was the disciple of master Nāgārjuna who became an authority on the commentaries of *The Transcendent Perfection of Wisdom*. Śāntideva was the grand-disciple of Nāgārjuna who was the subject of seven wonderful episodes and so forth. The fearless Śūra was the disciple of master Āryadeva who simultaneously comprehended all facets of the outer and inner vehicles. Bhāviveka was the master who applied the independent reasoning of the Middle Way to the sūtras. Blessed by Mañjughoṣa in five hundred rebirths, Candrakīrti was the supreme master endowed with signs of spiritual accomplishment—the ability to draw milk from the painting of a cow, to swing his hand through a stone pillar without obstruction, and so forth. Candragomin was favored by sublime Tārā and could question Avalokiteśvara directly concerning the sacred doctrine. Sthiramati, the disciple of Vasubandhu, was learned in phenomenology. Vimuktisena was learned in the transcendent perfection, Guṇaprabha was learned in monastic discipline, and master Śākyaprabha was the disciple of the great master Śāntaprabha and a supreme upholder of monastic discipline. The latter two are called the two supreme ones.[11] {47}

Furthermore, there were an inconceivable number—including Haribhadra, who was learned in elucidating the meaning of the *Mother*—who reached the further shore of their own and others' philosophical systems, mostly based on the perspective of one or other of the two great promulgators, Nāgārjuna and Asaṅga, and who therefore excellently nurtured the Buddhist teaching.[12] It would be difficult to mention them.

The Masters of Secret Mantra

Now, I will approximately mention the foremost of the infinite masters who acquired supreme spiritual accomplishment dependent on the Adamantine Vehicle. All the tantras of the new translations were taught by Heruka, in whom Vajradhara and Vajrayoginī are not differentiated. These were assembled by their compilers and preserved in book form in the doctrinal palace of Dharmajagat in the land of Oḍḍiyāna.[13]

Those who elucidated the tantras were as follows. The great king Indrabhūti was an emanation of Guhyapati (Vajrapāṇi), who transfigured his degenerate physical form in the manner of a snake shedding its skin. He assumed the adamantine body—the body of rainbow light. He wandered from buddha field to buddha field and perfected the coalescence of No More Learning. Glorious Saraha was the crown ornament of all accomplished masters of supreme awareness, whose physical body was intoxicated by the wine bequeathed by the ḍākinī of pristine cognition, whose speech was intoxicated by adamantine songs, and whose mind was intoxicated by the taste of coemergent pristine cognition. The master Nāgārjunagarbha was the one whose activities, with respect to the Buddhist teaching, were those of a second teacher and who will attain buddhahood as the tathāgata named Jñānakāraprabha in the world system called Prasannaprabha (Utterly Radiant Light). Lūipa was the mighty lord of yoga who accomplished the level of adamantine pristine cognition, equal in fortune to all the buddhas, through the yoga of the generation and perfection stages of Cakrasaṃvara. Śavaripā is the immortal sovereign who even now establishes infinite disciples of good fortune in the heart of the supreme vows of all the buddhas through the guise of a hunter on the southern mountain of Śrīparvata. {48} Vajragaṇtapāda was the one who reached the level of Śrīheruka in a single lifetime through the yoga of *The Five Stages of Cakrasaṃvara*,[14] a unique text among the scriptures renowned as the glory of essential intelligence. Virūpa was the glorious protector of the sacred doctrine—a great *paṇḍita* who understood the five fields of classical learning in their entirety, who attained supreme accomplishment through the yoga of Vajranairātmyā, and who, like the mythical creature *śarabha*, terrified all the lion-like heretical extremists through the prowess of his ascetic discipline. Guru Kuddālapāda was the preacher of inconceivable oral instructions who acquired the supreme accomplishment of the Great Seal through the oral instruction of Guhyapati Bhadrapāda. Ḍombhi Heruka attained supreme accomplishment, having been favored by Venerable Vajranairātmyā, and, adorned with serpents and riding a tiger, reveled in space while embracing his consort Ḍombhinī. Kambalapāda attained the supreme level by sleeping for twelve years, during which time his energy channels, winds, and vital essences were transformed into the three indestructible realities of buddha body, speech, and mind. He was named after the robe that he wore at the time when he overwhelmed a host of ḍākinīs and accepted them into his following. Kṛṣṇācārin, clearly foreordained by the Conqueror, attained accomplishment during the intermediate state and actualized the level of supreme eternal bliss. Kukkurāja was debased in physical appearance but profound in mantra, and ultimately he perceived the real nature through the three yogas of the sacred doctrine. He rejoiced in the company of Vajrayoginī, transformed into a dog.[15]

In addition, there were six religious kings in the kingdom of Śambhala in the north.[16] Together with their disciples and grand-disciples, including the Kulika kings (who appeared in the past, who are teaching the sacred doctrine at present, and who will appear in the future[17]), {49} they secured and will secure disciples of good fortune, equal to the atoms of an infinite oceanic field, on the level of an adamantine holder through the nectar of the instructions of the four empowerments and two stages in accordance with the unsurpassed union tantras of the Adamantine Vehicle.

In general, this teaching of the Secret Mantra of the Great Vehicle was first propagated in India in the eastern region by King Prakāśacandra. The tantras of union were extensively propagated by the three men who were skilled therein and so forth.[18] Then, the tantras of skillful means, including the *Guhyasamāja* (*Glorious Secret Assembly*), originated from and were expounded by master Nāgārjuna and his disciples, and they spread through the southern region. After that, the yoginī tantras emerged in the land of Oḍḍiyāna in the western region through glorious Kambalapāda and so forth and then also spread to the central region. Thereafter, the *Kālacakra* and so forth emerged from the land of Śambhala in the north, adorned by commentaries composed by bodhisattvas, and these too flourished in the central region.

It was through the great kindness of master Buddhaguhya and others that the tantras of action and the tantras of conduct were propagated in both India and Tibet in the manner of the tantras of union.[19]

All those masters manifested in a temporal sequence that was based on an oral tradition, so for that reason we cannot evaluate their chronology. Furthermore, there were eighty male accomplished masters, along with four yoginīs endowed with realization and liberation, commencing from the Indian accomplished master Lūipa and continuing down to Vyālipā. The narratives of these eighty-four were collected together by Abhayadatta,[20] along with their respective spiritual songs and commentaries.[21] These were established to be authentic by the compilers of the Tengyur.[22] {50} Their blessings and the transmitted teachings of their scriptures and guidance indeed manifested in India, but surely that was not all. There were others who appeared in the gathering of the same communion circle,[23] whose biographies, as it were, were not properly compiled. Some of them were known in Tibet, and I think it is incorrect to say that they should not be included alongside these eighty-four great accomplished masters. In brief, though there have been many such opportunities to document their lives as well, it has been to no avail. Suffice it to say that to bear witness to them, *The Narrative*[24]—compiled by the great accomplished master Vīraprabhāsvara, translated by Minyak Lotsāwa, and included in the Tengyur—deserves a commentary.

As regards the Secret Mantra tradition known in Tibet as the Ancient Translation (Nyingma) school, although the masters of this tradition, even in India itself, were as numerous as the stars in the sky, if I am to mention just the most important, they include the following: the Teacher Samantabhadra, who constitutes the buddha body of reality;[25] the peaceful and wrathful deities along with the herukas of the Eight Pronouncements, who constitute the buddha body of perfect resource;[26] and Vajradhara, Śākyamuni, Prahevajra, and so forth, who constitute the buddha body of emanation.[27] The compiler of these transmitted teachings was Vajradharma, a peaceful aspect of Vajrapāṇi. There are three lines of transmission—namely, the lineage of the enlightened intention of the conquerors, the lineage of the symbols of the awareness holders, and the lineage of the aural transmission of individuals. In the latter were included the ḍākinī Karmamahendraṇī; Indrabhūti, who mastered the volumes of scripture; Śrīsiṃha, to whom the descent of the transmitted teachings of the Great Perfection fell; Gomadevī, to whom the transmission of the teachings of word and meaning fell; Padmākara, who mastered the creative energy of awareness; Mañjuśrīmitra, who was the awareness holder of buddha body; Nāgārjuna, who was the awareness holder of buddha speech; Hūṃkara, who was the awareness holder of buddha mind; Vimalamitra, who was the awareness holder of buddha attributes; Prabhāhasti, who was the awareness holder of buddha activities; Dhanasaṃskṛta, who was the awareness holder of Mātaraḥ; Śāntigarbha, who was the awareness holder of Vajramantrabhiru; and Rambuguhya, who was the awareness holder of Lokastotrapūjā.[28] {51}

The Patronage of Buddhist Kings

There were patrons who had faith in the Buddhist teaching and benefited it. The religious king Aśoka constructed ten million stūpas that contained essential relics of the Teacher. Moreover, as foreordained in *The Root Tantra of Mañjuśrī*, other royal patrons included Vigataśoka, Vīrasena, Nanda, and so on. After a long interval, there was the Guptan dynasty, composed of the seven Candra kings and so on. After that, there was the dynasty of the seven Pālas, among whom King Gopāla built the monastery of Nālanda. His son, glorious Dharmapāla, built Samudragupta Temple in Kashmir and Somapurī Monastery in the district of Varendra, and his son, Devapāla, built Vikramaśīla. Along with the dynasty of the four Senas and so forth, they all revered the three precious jewels as their teacher and engaged in extensive activities on behalf of the Buddhist teaching.[29]

Concluding Verses

Those supreme scholars, embodying the constellations,
Caused the lilies of scriptural collection to bloom,
And the sun-like masters of supreme accomplishment
Stirred the lotus groves of the tantra collections.
Both of these delight bee-like sentient beings,
Who crave for their elixir of liberation—
Mountain peaks of rivaling and thriving excellence,
Surpassing the three planes of existence.

At this time, amid the beings of the Teaching's final five centuries,
There are those who raise their voices with sincerity
For all classes of disciples who follow with faith and doctrine.
Their intelligence is worthy to behold, like a lucid guide.

This completes the fourth chapter of this book, a brief account of the origin of the Buddhist teaching of India and of those who uphold the teaching, from *Wondrous Ocean of Eloquence: A Narrative of the Wish-Fulfilling Gem of the Lineage* compiled by Taklungpa Ngawang Namgyel. {53}

5. The Four Lineages of Transmitted Teachings and the Two Masters of Supreme Vision {55}

Verses of Homage

OṂ SVĀSTI
May it be auspicious!

Knowing the foremost of the great promulgators of the essential teaching,
I pay homage to Tilopāda, renowned in the three world realms,
In whom are gathered the lineages of the transmitted teachings
Of the lord of enlightened heritage endowed with infinite power,
Vajradhara, indivisibility of bliss and emptiness, glory of existence and quiescence.

Homage too to Jñānasiddhi (Nāropā), lion of speech,
Who acquired the supreme adamantine body, the body of rainbow light,
And furthermore to those named Śavaripā and the sovereign Maitripā, son of the conquerors,
All of whom were masters of accomplishment through the path of the Adamantine Vehicle,
Undifferentiated and indivisible play of the sole buddha body of reality,
Who definitively elucidated the profound view—
The innate pristine cognition of the great seal
And the six branches of indestructible reality—
The short path of meditation that entails mingling, transference, and vital reincarnation.[1]

I rejoice in this essential nectar of good tidings,
The narrative concerning the hierarchs of the Kagyu lineage,
The great vital essence of glorious supreme accomplishment,
Crown jewel of the ocean of supremely fortunate beings,
Like a garland of gems, in whose pure minds
There is a wondrous and inconceivable continuum
Of uninterrupted teaching and study, due to which
Other activities are abandoned, and with the power of unfeigned faith,
A strong potential is actualized.

Fifth, there follows the somewhat detailed explanation of the four lineages of the transmitted teachings and the life stories of the two who were of supreme vision, Tilopā and Nāropā.

The Four Lineages of Transmitted Teachings to Tilopā

In general, the precious Kagyu lineage represents the completely perfect corpus of the authentic teaching, the essence of the supreme conquerors. {56} Furthermore, the actual supreme body of perfect resource—who is mentioned in the sūtras of the Great Vehicle and, according to the unsurpassed way of Secret Mantra, is endowed with the seven aspects of union through his uncommon enlightened attributes—is Mahāvajradhara. On behalf of pure and extraordinary disciples, he is uninterruptedly present in a form embodying the five excellences.[2] From him, Venerable Tilopā, in whom the glorious Cakrasaṃvara manifested as a human reflection, directly received all the uncommon doctrines, such that those individuals of highest acumen rejoiced, whereas those of feeble acumen thought that he lacked a human teacher. In order to dispel these notions, Tilopā attended upon the gurus in the line of the four transmitted teachings. In this regard, although there are a few discrepancies concerning the identification of these transmissions and their sequence in the historical context of the lineages of spiritual teachers who maintained the pith instructions of each suborder of the precious Kagyu lineage, the present account accords with the adamantine words of Tashi Pel, Taklungpa the Great, the sovereign of the Buddhist teaching and universal emperor of the sacred doctrine. That is to say, the mighty lord of yoga, Tilopā, requested the oral instructions on Dream Yoga from Caryāpā, he requested the oral instructions on Illusory Body from Nāgārjuna, he requested the oral instructions on Inner Radiance from Kambalapāda, and he requested the oral instructions on Inner Heat from the ḍākinī Sumatī.[3]

With regard to this account, since diverse and dissimilar narratives are found regarding the aforementioned individual lineage holders even in the biographies of the suborders of the precious Kagyu lineage, at the outset you may wonder how they are expressed here. In the context of the Taklung tradition, the first lineage of the transmitted teachings was from Vajradhara; {57} through King Indrabhūti the Great; Sahajāyoginī, who manifested from the nāga realm;[4] Bhisukalpa, who was a spirit lord of the soil; Saraha the Great; and Nāgārjunapāda; to Venerable Tilopā. This was the line of descent of the transmitted teachings that concerned the *Guhyasamāja Tantra*, the *Tantra of the Four Adamantine Seats*, and the oral instructions of Illusory Body and transference of consciousness from the Six Doctrines.

The second lineage of the transmitted teachings was from Vajradhara, through Jñānaḍākinī, Kukkurāja, and Caryāpā, to Tilopā. This was the line of descent of the transmitted teachings that concerned the *Tantra of Mahāmāya* and the oral instructions of Dream Yoga from the Six Doctrines.

The third lineage of the transmitted teachings was from Vajradhara, through Vajrapāṇi, Ḍombhi Heruka, Vinapavajra,[5] and Kambalapāda, to Tilopā, the supreme "sesame pounder." This was the lineage of the transmitted teachings that concerned all the mother tantras headed by *Cakrasaṃvara* and the oral instructions of Inner Radiance from the Six Doctrines.

The fourth descent of the transmitted teachings was from Vajradhara, through Vajrapāṇi, Anaṅgavajra,[6] Padmavajra,[7] and the ḍāka Kusalibhadra,[8] through to glorious Tilopā. This was the line of descent of the transmitted teachings that concerned *Hevajra*, and the oral instructions of Inner Heat from the Six Doctrines.

Sahajāyoginī

Reference has already been briefly made to the lives of these lineage holders in chapter four, which concerns the narrative of the great promulgators of the Buddhist teaching in India. As for those who were not mentioned therein, regarding Sahajāyoginī, "who had manifested from the nāga realm," after King Indrabhūti the Great had passed away in the manner of a sky farer, the land of Oḍḍiyāna was deserted, and then the great lake of that land was filled with nāgas. The nāgas who frequented it were brought to maturational empowerment by Vajrapāṇi, and gradually they turned into human beings and built a city by the lakeside. Through the experiential cultivation of the Adamantine Vehicle, they acquired spiritual accomplishment, and she is said to have been one among those who turned into spiritual heroes and ḍākinīs—a beautiful girl who was pleasing for the king of that land to behold. {58}

Bhisukalpa

Bhisukalpa had been a spirit lord of the soil. He received ordination as a mendicant at the time when the reigns of the kings of Madhyadeśa were in decline. Although the three scriptural collections had been translated, he had devotion to the Adamantine Vehicle and went to Oḍḍiyāna in accordance with a prophetic declaration given by the ḍākinīs in a dream. In the self-originated temple of Heruka in Oḍḍiyāna, he received empowerment, explication, and further advice on the tantras, and the books were entrusted to him. Also, by having experientially cultivated their meaning, he attained the accomplishment of the Great Seal.[9]

Saraha

The great brahmin Saraha was sublime among the inconceivable masters who attained supreme spiritual accomplishment, dependent on the Adamantine Vehicle, resembling the pinnacle of a victory banner. Three hundred years after the genuinely perfect buddha had passed into nirvāṇa, a brahmin in a place called Rādha, which belonged to Vidarbha in the southern region, had a particularly exalted son. While growing up, he had faith in the Buddhist teaching and was ordained as a mendicant by Rāhulabhadra. The name Rāhulabhadra was also conferred upon him. Perfectly trained in the ocean-like collection of texts, he became an unrivaled paṇḍita and served as the monastic preceptor of glorious Vikramaśīla Monastery. While he was engaged in activities on behalf of the Buddhist teaching, on one occasion when presented with offerings by King Mahāpala, he went into a park for recreation, and there he saw four noble brahmin girls laying out a maṇḍala and performing a communion feast offering. They offered him four different kinds of beer in skull cups, and when he had drunk a little of each, the coemergent pristine cognition of the four delights arose in him.[10] The four brahmin girls actually transformed into the ḍākinīs of the four enlightened families and conferred upon him the four empowerments.[11] Vajraḍākinī said, "Here are your spiritual teachers," and then {59} the bodhisattva Sukhanātha and glorious Hayagrīva appeared in the sky and gave him all the instructions on the instantaneously arising great seal. It is reported that at that time his body was intoxicated with beer, his speech was intoxicated by adamantine songs, and his mind was intoxicated by coemergent pristine cognition. He then went to the market and saw a girl—an arrowsmith who was making an arrow—whereupon all appearances arose as symbolic forms. He took the female arrowsmith as his consort and adopted the appropriate modes of conduct. When the king, the queen, and the populace asked him not to engage in such acts, in response, he liberated them all by chanting *The Spiritual Songs of the Populace*,[12] which emphasizes the buddha body of emanation; *The Spiritual Songs of the Queen*,[13] which emphasizes the buddha body of perfect resource; and *The Spiritual Songs of the King*,[14] which emphasizes the buddha body of reality. Consequently, that land became depopulated, and he then traveled to Śrīparvata. In general, he continued to act on behalf of fortunate living beings in the world for one hundred and eighteen years and then departed in the manner of a sky farer.[15]

Nāgārjuna

His disciple, the second buddha Nāgārjunapāda had been clearly foreordained by the genuinely perfect Buddha in *The Root Tantra of Mañjuśrī*, *The Sūtra of the Descent to Laṅkā*, *The Sublime Sūtra of the Great Cloud in Twelve Thousand Lines*,[16] and so forth. In the land of Vidarbha in the southern region, an excellent brahmin had a son in accordance with divine prophecy. He was shown to a soothsayer who said that although the child exhibited auspicious signs, he might not live out the week. Asked what would help, the soothsayer replied that if a hundred brahmins were invited to a religious feast, he would live for seven months, and if a hundred monks were invited to a religious feast, he could live for seven years, but that beyond that there was no hope. Having done as suggested, as the seventh year was approaching, feeling they could not bear to see the corpse of their son, his parents sent him off, wandering with a servant. {60}

Gradually continuing on his way, he approached the gates of Nālanda where those with knowledge of poetics had formed a line. Thereupon, he listened to the teachings from the brahmin Saraha, who was residing there, and received internal guidance. When he explained his circumstances, the master said that there was a way to help if he could receive ordination as a mendicant. He agreed, and then—after empowerment had been conferred upon him in the maṇḍala of Amitāyus, Subjugator of the Lord of Death—he was made to recite the appropriate incantation (*dhāraṇī*). On the eve of the seventh year, in particular, he recited this throughout the night and, annihilating the Lord of Death, freed himself. From that same preceptor, he was then ordained as a mendicant and eventually received the full monastic ordination. He adroitly trained in all the fields of classical learning and in the Great and Lesser Vehicles in their entirety. He received without exception all the empowerments, tantras, and instructions of the fruitional mantras, headed by the *Guhyasamāja*, and he extensively turned the wheel of the sacred doctrine, refuting those who held wrong views.

On that occasion, when two children came to listen to the sacred doctrine, the entire assembly was permeated by a sweet fragrance. When he asked the reason for this, the children replied, "We are the sons of the nāga king Takṣaka. When we come into the human realm, white sandalwood serves as a protection for us." Then, when they arose in their actual form, he thought that there would be great benefit and said, "May I have this sandalwood?" They replied, "It is the fragrance of our father." And when he asked about that, they said, "If the master were to journey to the realm of the nāgas, it would be offered to him." So it was that he promised to go there. Proceeding to the realm of the nāgas, Nāgārjuna taught the sacred doctrine to the nāga king and his entourage and accepted alms from them. When the nāgas requested him to remain there, he said, "I am looking for clay to build ten million stūpas, and I have come to bring back *The Transcendent Perfection of Wisdom in One Hundred Thousand Lines*. I do not have time to stay." He brought back much clay, along with *The Transcendent Perfection of Wisdom in One Hundred Thousand Lines*, {61} *The Transcendent Perfection of Wisdom in Twenty-Five Thousand Lines*, and so forth. But it is reported that the nāgas were somewhat reluctant to give him the sections that follow on from *The Transcendent Perfection of Wisdom in One Hundred Thousand Lines*. With that clay, the stūpas and so forth were for the most part built with the help of the nāgas, but some were not because he refused to return to the nāga realm.

Nāgārjuna went to Uttarakuru in the north and worked for the benefit of sentient beings. Then, after procuring nectarous elixir, he traveled to Mount Śrīparvata and composed an innumerable number of treatises, making the Buddhist teaching clear like the light of day.

With regard to the name Nāgārjuna that was conferred upon him, *nāga* means "serpentine water spirit" and is rendered as *lu* (*klu*) in Tibetan. He was so called because he was born into the expanse of reality, without abiding in the extremes of eternalism and nihilism, because he owned the treasury of the precious scriptures, and because he possessed the view that burns impurities and is lucidly clear. The word *arjuna* means "virtuous child of Indra" and is rendered as *sidrub* (*srid sgrub*) in Tibetan. He was so called because he nurtured the realm of the sacred doctrine and tamed inimical hosts of miscreants. The *-drub* in "Ludrub" (Klu sgrub, Nāgārjuna) is an abbreviation of *sidrub*. Such is the etymology established in a passage in *Clear Word Commentary*.[17]

Out of great compassion, Nāgārjuna worked for the benefit of the Buddhist teaching and sentient beings for six hundred years, and then, in the end, giving away his head as a donation, he departed for Sukhāvatī.[18]

Caryāpā

As to the master Caryāpā, from whom the second lineage of the transmitted teachings descended to Tilopā, he was born into the mercantile class in Bengal. Glorious Jālandaripā[19] accepted him as a disciple, and he studied all the classes of tantra. Having cultivated the meditative stability of the generation and perfection stages, he asked his teacher for permission to engage in ascetic conduct. Jālandaripā replied, "To engage in ascetic conduct requires an ability to attain the experience of warmth, to eradicate wrong views and take disciples into one's following. Do you have that?" Thereupon, he successfully focused on the magic gaze whereby he could paralyze a tiger, summon an antelope, overpower a water buffalo, and cause fruit to fall down. "Now practice the rite of liberation!" said Jālandaripā.[20] But when he could not do so, the master himself undertook the rite of liberation {62} and then said, "When you engage in ascetic conduct, the deeds pertaining to ordinary consciousness and pristine cognition are identical. You must be able to both slay and resuscitate. So now is not the time to leave!" When he replied that he had to depart by all means, he was told, "In that case, do not go to Devīkoṭa!"

Caryāpā set out with a display of miraculous powers—his feet not touching the ground but one cubit above it, moving through the sky with seven parasols that no one held, and with seven skull drums (*ḍāmaru*) that sounded of their own accord, without a cause. By the banks of the Ganges a leper woman cried out, "Save me!" But he thought, "It is not right that my bone ornaments should be spoiled by puss and blood or that I should be infected by leprosy," and he refused to carry her. He went into the river without sinking. When he had the thought, "I am even stronger than my master!" he sank, but when he had thoughts of devotion, he could pass over it. However, a novice monk in his entourage carried the leper woman, and when they entered into the river, she was transformed into Coemergent Cakrasaṃvara and departed through the sky.

Caryāpā then met someone plowing a field and accepted beer from him but did not consume it. The plowman broke open the stone stopper, and it seemed there were merely a few trickling drops of water. "I will drink," he said but his thirst was not quenched. "You should drink and your thirst will be quenched!" said the plowman. Then he drank, with the result that the beer was endless. The plowman then pointed his index finger toward an ox in the gesture of menace,[21] and it died. "Take it into your following!" he said, but Caryāpā could not resurrect it. The plowman then resurrected it himself.

In an orchard there was a girl taking care of the fruit. When he was about to pluck some, she said, "Make it fall down with your occult power!" He caused the fruit to fall with his magic stare, but the girl then made it stick back with her reverse magic stare. He met someone reading texts who said "You should stay here by all means. This is the milk of yoga!" He asked, "Are you reading?" and the reader replied, "You do not understand reading or speaking!"

Since the activities of Lalitacandra, the king of Bengal, were non-Buddhist and those of his minister, Kalyāṇanātha, were Buddhist,[22] {63} the minister welcomed the master, paid respects, and requested him to consecrate a statue of Mahākāruṇika, the mighty lord of great compassion, in the temple. Reciting *supratiṣṭha* (Let it be consecrated!) and placing flowers on its head, he said, "The consecration is complete." The minister said, "I have no conviction in this," so the master went off, taking the flowers, and the deity also followed him. In remorse, the minister then made another entreaty, whereupon he again placed the flower on its head, and the statue remained there. Furthermore, Caryāpā revealed many magical displays in that place, and when the king and his entourage acquired faith and requested the sacred doctrine, he established all the inhabitants of Bengal as followers of Buddhism.

Then he continued on toward Devīkoṭa, where he succumbed to ill-health due to the obstacles of the ḍākinīs. Since he had incurred the fault of flouting his master's injunction not to go there, he then set out to perform a communion feast offering in the twenty-four sacred lands of India. He said, "Come to fetch medicinal herbs!" and sent his entourage to one particular place. They did so, but on the way back, there were many women bathing at a bathing pool who said, "Will you not bathe?" They said, "We do not have time," but the women said, "The master will recover from his illness!" So they bathed there, and while they were doing so, the bathers carried off the herbal medications they had collected and vanished into space. Coming before the master, they said, "Since now there is an obstacle due to the ḍākinīs, you will not attain nirvāṇa in this lifetime, so you should relinquish this physical body, and you will attain buddhahood during the intermediate state." It was then that he passed away.

Vinapavajra

Vinapavajra, from whom the third lineage of the transmitted teachings descended, belonged to the royal class. He was accepted as a disciple by a master named Aśvottama.[23] He meditated for nine years, during which time he beat a tambura drum and thereby purified mental defilements. The experience of inner radiance arose, as clear as the tip of a butter-lamp flame. {64} After acquiring many enlightened attributes, including the extrasensory powers, he attained the supreme accomplishment of the Great Seal through the oral instructions of the master Ḍombhipa. He then worked extensively for the benefit of sentient beings and departed in that very body in the manner of the sky farers.

Kambalapāda

His disciple was the master Kambalapāda, also known as Indrabhūti the Younger, who ruled over two hundred and fifty thousand villages in a land that belonged to Oḍḍiyāna. He met the master Vinapavajra, after which empowerment was conferred upon him and he was taken into the following. Thinking that there would be obstacles due to his attachment to the kingdom and adherence to the royal class, he wore a blanket of hair from charnel grounds. Kambalapāda declared, "I shall eat only such morsels as come to hand, and on this flat rock before the palace gates, I will fall asleep, practicing one-pointed yoga!" He put this into practice for twelve years and, by doing so, acquired the accomplishment of the Great Seal.

Then, when he went to engage in secret practices in the dark charnel ground of Rauruka, there were only ḍākinīs there, some with thick hair, dark complexions, and old ornaments and others who were the opposite. At that time, one of the ḍākinīs of bright complexion came and handed the master a flower, which he accepted, whereupon her group raised their faces upward and the others looked downcast. Not knowing the reason for this, as he was on his way back, the master's mother, a ḍākinī, arrived and said, "Taking that flower was not a good thing. The ḍākinīs with the dark complexion were Buddhists, and the ones with bright complexion were non-Buddhists. Since they have put their seal on you, three hindrances will come."

"Is there no way out?" he said. "No!" she replied. He asked this repeatedly. "Well then," she said, "there is a lake in the upper reaches of yonder valley. {65} There is an old women there, blinking, thick-lipped, with a goiter and disheveled hair, who whistles, her tresses covered with nits. You should petition her again and again, without fear and without pity. She can offer you a beneficial way out."

Going there, he found the old woman exactly as described and made his request, but she became angry and agitated, beating the ground with her staff, and did not consent to help. Again, he made this entreaty so fervently that he fell unconscious for a while. When he awoke, the lake had transformed into a lotus seat, the woman into Jetsunma Vajravārāhī, her goiter into a sow's head, her nit-covered tresses into bone ornaments, her staff into a *khaṭvāṅga*, and so on. She then imparted instructions that included the releasing of the ḍākinīs' seal and so forth.

Returning to his own residence, Kambalapāda then engaged in meditation. During the first part of the night, the ḍākinīs arrived due to his aforementioned obstacle, but he saw nothing at all. When thoughts arose in his mind, they said, "There is a smell here!" When his mind was equipoised, they said, "There is nothing at all!" At midnight, they said, "His consciousness has vanished into this blanket!" They cut it into bite-size portions and ate it. At dawn, realization of the real nature arose within the master. He acquired fearless confidence and declared, "I am here!" So, the ḍākinīs unleashed a downpour of stones. With his paralyzing magic gaze, the master caused the downpour of stones to freeze in the sky without support. It is said that they remain so even at the present time.

In the morning, he went naked into the presence of the king, who said, "Where has your blanket gone?" He replied, "It's been eaten by your wives." When asked to explain, {66} he said, "It is inside those heretical ḍākinīs!"

While the king hesitated, the master assembled all those women and applied the magic gaze that provokes downfalls, such that they each vomited a piece of the blanket. When these were reassembled, the blanket was not quite complete, so again he summoned those women who had gone to pursue their own interests elsewhere, with the magic gaze that summons. In this way, the blanket was completely restored, as before.

Then, the master expelled the most pernicious of those ḍākinīs through the application of ritual expulsion. As for the remainder, he threaded a ring through their nostrils and held them by his hands above the crown of their heads and tamed them, as they pledged not to harm others. It is said that even nowadays the women of that land wear similar ornaments.

When he attained spiritual accomplishment in this manner, he became known as the master Kambalapāda after the garment that he wore. He taught the sacred doctrine in that land and then departed in the manner of the sky farers in that very body, along with an entourage of seven hundred.

Anaṅgavajra

As regards the master Anaṅgavajra from whom the fourth descent of the transmitted teachings fell, he realized the indestructible reality of desire. Having abandoned the aspects of ejaculation that are associated with afflicted mental states, he attained the supreme accomplishment, indestructible like a vajra. In the land of Oḍḍiyāna in the western region, he worked for the benefit of innumerable sentient beings and was also called Śrīsūkārika (Glorious Swineherd).

Padmavajra

His disciple was Padmavajra who was born into the royal class in the land of Kāñci. Ordained as a mendicant, he became a great paṇḍita, knowledgeable in the five fields of classical learning.[24] At the urging of a ḍākinī, he met the master Anaṅgavajra, who empowered him in an emanational maṇḍala and gave him the tantras and instructions. He then practiced in the company of a low-caste woman for twelve years at Mount Śrīparvata, such that he attained accomplishment. {67} Since he had remained free from harm, even having been burned for many days in a pyre of sandalwood as royal punishment, he became renowned as Saroruhavajra (Lake-Born Vajra). Finally, he departed in the manner of the sky farers.

Sumatī

His disciple was the ḍākinī Kusalabhadrī, who also went by other names such as Sumatī and Śrīmatī. As the sister of King Indrabhūti the Great, she was also known as Lakṣmīnkarā. Endowed with defining characteristics, she was one who had faith in the Buddhist teaching. She entered into the Buddhist teaching after being infected with leprosy, and, by praying to Avalokita, she recovered from the illness. She received instruction from spiritual teachers who had attained accomplishment, headed by the master Saroruhavajra, as well as from buddhas and bodhisattvas, headed by Vajradhara.

Through the practice of secret conduct, she attained accomplishment. At that time, she approached the gates of Jālandaripā, king of the land of Laṅkāpurī, who had previously taken a consort, and she engaged in the ascetic discipline of a mad woman. She taught the sacred doctrine to one of the king's sweepers. Simply on that account, all the people perceived her differently—some saw her as a mad woman, some saw her as a daughter of the gods who was revered by the multitude, her body permeated by light, and some saw her as three identical but different yoginīs. Since all this caused doubt, once, in the marketplace, she cut off her own head with a chopper, transformed it into a skull cup, carried a khaṭvāṅga on her shoulders and danced. Finally, in union with the sweeper, she departed in the manner of a sky farer.

The Two Masters of Supreme Vision: Tilopā and Nāropā

Tilopā

Integrating all the descents of the transmitted teachings that fell through the lineage in that manner, the mighty lord of yoga, Tilopā, was actually blessed by Mahāvajradhara himself. {68} His father was the brahmin Prakāśa and his mother was named Dyutimatī. He was born in the city of Jagora in Zahor in the eastern direction to Bengal. Immediately after his birth, the entire eastern direction was suffused with light.[25]

When he was presented to a soothsayer, he was given the name Prabhāsvara on the basis of the omens of his birth since the soothsayer was not inspired to prophetically declare that he would manifest the various signs of gods, nāgas, yakṣas, universal emperors, or all the buddhas. To care for him there was a woman endowed with thirty-two marks of ugliness who appeared—no one knows from where—and said,

> No matter how well you are nurtured
> There is nowhere on this earth that is without death.
> Rear your buffalo and study letters!
> The ḍākinīs' prophecy will be forthcoming![26]

Heeding her words, he continued to raise buffalo and to read at the foot of an aloewood tree, when that same woman as before appeared and said, "What is your homeland, and who are your parents and sister? What do you say? Why does this tree have no name? What use is raising buffalo and reading letters?" she asked, and, when he answered straightforwardly,[27] showing great scorn she said, "Not so, your country is Oḍḍiyāna in the west. Your father is Cakrasaṃvara, your mother Vajravārāhī, your elder brother Vajradhara, and I am your sister, Sukhadā (She Who Grants Bliss). The tree is the Tree of Enlightenment and the buffalo are meditative experiences. The unwritten aural lineage is in the hands of the ḍākinīs. If you take it, you will become an accomplished master, endowed with prophecies and commitments!"[28]

"By what means should I obtain it?" he asked. "A crystal ladder, jewel bridge, and a key of burdock grass[29] are the three things you will need," she said, and then disappeared.[30] {69}

On returning home, he told his parents of this and gave them all his possessions, saying, "I'm off!" The moment he left, he arrived in Oḍḍiyāna. He approached the area where, surrounded by a perimeter wall and seven moats, the self-originated temple of Heruka is located at the center, with its great treasury of the sacred doctrine. With three magic gazes he overpowered the assembled ḍākinīs indicative of the buddha body of emanation who enact the rites of the devourers, manifesting inconceivable hair-raising miracles. He then set the crystal ladder against the perimeter wall and crossed the moats with the jewel bridge. Reaching the gate, he opened it with the key, slipped inside and overpowered with the three magic gazes the diverse display of miracles manifested by the mundane ḍākinīs, indicative of the buddha body of perfect resource. He made his request to their queen, the ḍākinī of pristine cognition, who is indicative of the buddha body of reality, and obtaining her permission, he entered into the midst of a vast maṇḍala. But when he failed to pay respectful homage to Bhagavatī Jñānaḍākinī therein, the heroes and heroines residing in that place were enraged.[31]

However, Bhagavatī herself purposefully told them, "This is Cakrasaṃvara, father of the buddhas of the three times!" "Why have you come here?" she asked. "I am Pañcapāṇa," he replied, "My sister Sukhadā sent me here to request the unwritten aural lineage."[32] She showed him the three symbols—the sacred icons representing buddha body, the seed syllables representing buddha speech, and the hand emblems representing buddha mind—and he said,

> I request the wish-granting jewel of the lineage
> From the treasury of the icons representing buddha body.
> I request the wish-granting jewel of the path of maturational
> empowerment
> From the treasury of the syllables representing buddha speech.
> I request the wish-granting jewel of the path of liberating guidance
> From the treasury of the hand emblems, representing buddha
> mind.[33] {70}

And she replied,

> The wish-granting jewel of the lineage
> From the treasury of the icons representing buddha body.
> Cannot be opened by those without commitment.
> Bound in the iron shackles of prophetic declarations,
> The wish-granting jewel of the path of maturational
> empowerment
> From the treasury of the syllables representing buddha speech
> Cannot be opened by those who have not been foreordained.
> Bound in the iron shackles of accomplished masters,
> The wish-granting jewel of the path of liberating guidance
> From the treasury of the hand emblems, representing buddha mind,
> Cannot be opened by those without accomplishment.[34]

"As to that," he said, "I have the key to the prophecies of the ḍākinīs," at which the ḍākinīs all burst out laughing like the sound of horses neighing and said,

> Though they look, the blind see no forms.
> Though they listen, the deaf hear no sounds.
> Though they speak, the dumb make no sense.
> Though they run, the lame do not keep up.
> You've been deceived by Māra. It's not true.[35]

To this he replied,

> Since falsehood entails negative speech,
> Those without negativity do not speak words of falsehood
> Because that would be pointless.
> It is because they never speak
> That that is not Māra. The ḍākinīs are true.[36]

And then he continued,

> The secret words of the ḍākinīs are the pledge of buddha mind,
> The lamp of pristine cognition that dispels the darkness of
> fundamental ignorance.
> I have the key to the self-liberating commitment
> Of self-arisen and naturally radiant intrinsic awareness.
>
> As for the nonarising buddha body of reality,
> The nature of mind in which nothing whatsoever arises,
> I have the key to the prophesied meditative experience
> Of the spontaneously present great seal.
>
> The nature of mind is without apprehension,
> Without attentiveness, and without the slightest trace of
> recollection.
> I have the key to the meditative experience of accomplished masters
> Who are endowed with the expanse of reality, the buddha body of
> reality.[37]

Bhagavatī then said, {71}

> Transcendent Lord who is my father,
> Buddha Tilopā, lord-protector of living beings,

Cakrasaṃvara, wheel of perfect bliss—
To you I offer the threefold wish-granting jewel.[38]

Out of compassion and pleased with the offerings that he sought, she granted him the oral instructions of the aural lineage and appointed him custodian of the tantras. Then she said,

Now through miraculous ability,
Prajñābhadra will move unimpededly through space.

The ḍākinīs indicative of the buddha body of emanation and the buddha body of perfect resource, having recognized him as Cakrasaṃvara, tried to postpone his departure, at which he said,

Nāro, Riri, Kasori!
For the benefit of my disciples,
like a bird in the sky, I, the yogin,
Am now leaving for the monastery of Śiromaṇi.[39]

And, as he was on his way, a disembodied voice said,

The commitment is to look into the mirror of your own mind.
Activity is like slashing water with a sword.
The path of maturational empowerment unties the knots of the mind.
The sacraments of commitment bask in the sun of realization.
Secure the lamp of awareness, pristine cognition!
Turn the wheels of the network of energy channels and winds!
Equalize the four external elements in common savor!
Grasp the blissful jewel of buddha speech!
Cultivate the great seal of natural liberation![40]

Such were the words that the incorporeal doctrinal host of ḍākinīs imparted. In reply he said,

Having engaged in the sacred doctrine of incorporeal ḍākinīs
In the shrine of the illusory body,
And then, secured by the bonds of inexpressible speech,
The bird of my inwardly radiant mind takes flight.[41]

So saying, he traveled to the monastery of Odantapurī.[42] There, the news that Tilopā had received the sacred doctrine from the ḍākinī of pristine cognition, the buddha body of reality, in Oḍḍiyāna and had attained accomplishment, permeated all directions. Yogins and paṇḍitas gathered, as many as the stars in the sky, {72} and, having made offerings, asked him who his teacher was. "I have no human teacher," he replied. "My teacher is omniscience."[43]

This master was one who could simultaneously send forth many tens of millions of emanations. When he manifested in one form, as a small boy, the lord-protector Nāgārjuna journeyed to that place and saw him. In order to examine whether he was a worthy recipient for his instructions, he pretended to be unable to cross a small stream. The boy started to carry him, so he could reach the other side, but while they were crossing, as soon as they reached the middle, Nāgārjuna magically transformed the stream into a large river. The boy thought, "I should not wrong this master!" Since he did not appear to have even the slightest regret when sinking, Nāgārjuna observed that he was indeed worthy.

Setting out again, he pretended to play with many other children as kings, ministers, and common people. He said, "Would you like me to be the king?" and they replied, "We like that, but you won't!" However, in consequence of the actions undertaken by the master's noble son and parents, he did become a great king, unrivaled in that land and he would even repel a Tajik army without difficulty. Later, after appointing his son as king, he was ordained as a mendicant at the place called Aśoka Grove, and then he was also called the monk Kālapa.[44] He became a great scholar of the five fields of classical learning and was installed as a monastic preceptor of glorious Nālanda. Whenever he engaged in activities on behalf of the Buddhist teaching, the ḍākinīs of pristine cognition went there and blessed him. In Somapurī temple, he shackled his legs and practiced for twelve years, after which he beheld the meditational deity and obtained control over the gross sense fields of the elements. Thinking to go off and engage in ascetic conduct, he received a prophetic declaration, saying, "Setting out, you will be accepted by Mataṅgi (*ma ta ma ki*) in the Charnel Ground of Terrifying Laughter,[45] {73} and in the marketplace of Pañcapāṇa, you will serve a prostitute and refine your realization."[46]

Going to Pañcapāṇa, he ground sesame seeds and through his experiential cultivation, he grew the realization that actualizes the nature of reality. When the inhabitants of that city beheld him, to some he was surrounded by a mass of fire and fourteen lamps, to some he was seated in the meditative equipoise of a monk in the midst of an aureole of light, and some saw him as a yogin clad in bone ornaments, surrounded by many girls paying homage. They informed his employer, the prostitute Bharimo who went to see for herself, and she saw him seated in the sky in the posture of royal ease, in the midst of an aureole of light, using his pestle and grinding sesame seeds. In remorse, she offered a confession and prayed. He replied, "Now may this pristine cognition of the tantras enter into your heart!" Placing a flower upon the crown of her head, she was liberated at that very moment.[47]

Hearing of this, the king of that land and his entourage arrived to pay him homage, whereupon Tilopā was seated along with Bharimo in the sky by a height of seven palm trees. Based on those demonstrations of the sacred doctrine, starting with the verses that begin "[The coemergent, innate pristine cognition,]/ Which is the essential sesame oil,"[48] the king and his entourage attained the accomplishment of the sky farers through experiential cultivation, and that land became deserted.

There was a king of the southern region named Candradīpa who held a great communion feast offering on behalf of his mother. An inconceivable number of Buddhist and non-Buddhist paṇḍitas and accomplished mastered assembled, but they did not agree as to who should be the leader of the communion. An old woman then said. "My elder brother is now unrivaled!" "Where is he?" they asked. "In Jalandhara he fastened the two big toes of a corpse to the branch of an eaglewood tree with the tail of a horse {74} and, holding it alternately with his two little fingers, he danced in the sky. You should ask him there." The king sent someone to investigate that and it was true, so he then invited him. Also, there was a yogin who said, "I should be the leader of the communion feast offering." So they sat on the teaching throne together. They competed in Sanskrit grammar and logic, and Tilopā was far superior. He drew a maṇḍala in the sky and erased the drawing. He rode on a lion and moved through the sky. He summoned corpses from a charnel ground, and transformed them into the desirable attributes of the senses, and then reversed them back again, and so forth. Again, Tilopā caused the sun and moon to fall, and laid them out as his seat. When his body had reversed back, he emanated innumerable maṇḍalas from each of his pores. He changed these too into other forms, secured multiple forms in a single form, and so forth. By doing so, he could not be rivaled in the slightest. That yogin bowed before him, and was taken into his following. The name Śaktikamati was conferred upon him, and it is said that even now he resides in Oḍḍiyāna in the western direction. Thereupon Tilopā acted as the leader of the communion feast offering and the rivalry was rendered null and void.[49]

Then he said,

> I too attained the Joyful level.
> Through a billion emanations,
> I also went to a hundred buddha fields.
> I also conversed with Nāgārjuna, Āryadeva, and the buddhas.
> I also saw the thousand buddhas.[50]

And,

> Caryāpā, Nāgārjuna, Kambalapāda,
> And Kusalabhadrī are the gurus
> From whom the four lineages of the transmitted teachings fell.
> Enlightened attributes were generated in my mind.[51]

So it was that, in the perspective of disciples of coarse ideation, he also revealed that he did have human teachers.

Moreover, at Nālanda, with a great display of occult power, he defeated learned heretical teachers by debating with the one who was most inimical to the Buddhist teaching. {75} When the latter drew a maṇḍala in the sky, the master could erase it; and when the master drew one, the heretic could not destroy his. The master maintained that magical drawing for seven days, but the heretic found no opportunity to ingress and cause harm. On being encouraged to enter into the Buddhist teaching, he became enraged, brought forth fire from his mouth and sent it toward Tilopā, who magically transformed it into a more intense fire and reversed it. So it was that he eventually paid homage to Tilopā and was taken into his following. He received the name Kālakalyāṇa and, as such, he even now resides at Śītavana.[52]

Also, there was a great illusionist from the southern region who mustered an illusory army and nearly destroyed Bengal, whereupon the master destroyed the illusion. The illusionist was incarcerated, but when he understood the reason, he became devout and was taken into his following. Known as the yogin Satyavacas, he even now resides at Hāhāraurava.[53]

Again, at Laṅkāpurī in the eastern direction, the master emanated as a monkey and a cat and consumed all the beer of a barmaid. Utterly impoverished, she prayed to the master himself, who magically consecrated the beer such that it became inexhaustible, and she experienced many perceptual changes. Taken into the following of Tilopā, she became known as the yoginī Sūryadharā and resides at Sosadvīpa.[54]

Also there was a butcher named Jina, who, one day while cooking the meat of innumerable animals that he had slain, saw himself cooking the flesh of his eldest son. When he had been terrified, Tilopā then brought the boy back to life. Tamed by such miraculous powers, he was taken into the following of Tilopā and named the yogin Śaṅkara. He resides in the land of cannibal ogres.[55] {76}

Also, the master debated with a great paṇḍita who maintained the extremist philosophical system of the Lokāyatika concerning the view that cause and its fruition are fictitious, and emerged victorious, but the extremist said, "If I do not directly perceive cause and its fruition, I will not enter into the Buddhist teaching." Tilopā then actually revealed the terrifying domains of the hells and the excellent realms of the gods. He also revealed lifeless denizens being boiled in molten copper, saying "Those who hold that cause and its fruition do not exist are roasted here!" and beautiful divine girls saying "Those who hold that they do exist come here!" So, the extremist was convinced, and taken into the following of Tilopā. He was named the yogin Nandin, and he resides at Śrīparvata in the southern region.[56]

Again, in Śrīnagara there was an arrogant singer. Tilopā emanated as a singer who was decidedly superior to that one, and tamed him. Taken into his following, he was named Ghoṣavatimūka, and he resides in that very place.[57]

Again, in the city of Pāṭaliputra, he humbled a mighty heretical sorcerer. Whatever the latter did, he could not harm the master, and in addition his own close relative passed away, and so he was distraught. Taken into the following of Tilopā, he became known as the yogin Sūryacandradhara, and he even now resides in the city of Imicikali.[58]

Tilopā also emanated in many forms on behalf of all those engaged in virtuous, negative and neutral actions, and performed even greater virtuous, negative, and neutral actions than they did. When a king named Candrasiṃha requested him to lead a communion feast offering consisting of limitless heroes and yoginīs, he revealed many dissimilar maṇḍalas along with their deities, and when he was asked which one was definitive, he said,

My own body is Hevajra.
My speech is Mahāmāyā. {77}
My mind is Cakrasaṃvara.
My faculties are Guhyasamāja.
My limbs are Red and Black Yamāri.
My appendages are Vajrabhairava.
My energy channels are Catuḥvajrapīṭha.
My winds are Vajramāla.
My vital essences are *Candraguhyatilaka.[59]
My crown protuberance is Buddhakapāla.
My supreme bliss is Buddhasamāyoga.
My total embodiment is Kālacakra.
My pores are inseparable from the body, speech, and mind
Of all the buddhas of the three times.[60]

As regards the disciples on whom he conferred maturational empowerment and liberating guidance, leaving aside the human beings of twelve great lands, he liberated even animals, including birds and ungulates, such that they were innumerable. Finally, he passed away in the manner of the sky farers.

Nāropā

The great Nāropā Jñānasiddhi[61] was a supreme promulgator of the complete corpus of the Buddhist teaching, taken into the following of Tilopā. This great master Nārotapa was born in Kashmir within the best of the eight virtuous familial lines within the brahmin class, which is called Nārotapa.[62] His father was the brahmin king named Śāntivarman, and his mother was Śrīmatī. A soothsayer prophesied that if he remained at home he would rule over the entire earth, but if was ordained as a mendicant, he would be the equal of the buddhas. The name Samantabhadra, or Gaganagarbha, was conferred upon him.[63]

Nāropā spontaneously knew all the fields of classical learning. He attended upon the master Bhīmkalabaṭṭa[64] and others, received lay ordination, and became a paṇḍita. Surrounded by many other paṇḍitas, he taught the sacred doctrine throughout the land. At that time, {78} his father insisted he get married, but he replied, "Tell me if you find an uncomplicated, pure girl named Vimalā who belongs to the enlightened heritage of the Great Vehicle and is the daughter of a non-Buddhist."[65] When a minister was sent out to search, there was a girl named Vimalā, the daughter of a brahmin named Tiṣya, carrying a water pitcher. She saw him and his companions as weary travelers, offered them water, and bid them drink directly from the copper ladle. When she washed it carefully again, the minister knew that she was deeply compassionate, uncomplicated, and very pure. He asked her social class and name, and then, understanding that she was endowed with all the defining characteristics, she was adopted as the queen consort of Nāropā.[66] After staying with her for about one year, he left her.[67] In the monastic estate of Nandanārama, he was ordained as a mendicant by the monastic preceptor Buddhapālita and the master of ceremonies Jñānaprabha. Then, in the temple of Surṇa, in the middle of Triten[68] in Kashmir, he received the full ordination from the monastic preceptor Śrī Dharmakīrti, the master of ceremonies Dharmottara and the confessor Dharmabodhi.[69]

Nāropā then became an upholder of the three scriptural collections and went to Nālanda. From the elder Nāgasena, he received the treatises of Cittamātra, and from Ākāraśāntipa, Sugatigarbha, Jayasena, and others, he received the ocean-like textual traditions of the two branches of the Great Vehicle (that is, sūtra and tantra). Mastering the powers of unforgettable retention, he became a great scholar, unrivaled in all the outer and inner fields of classical learning. He was then known as the elder Śāsanadhara.[70] Then, in the debating college, he tamed all his heretical opponents, who were as proud as elephants, and received the name Vādisiṃha. Since no one among all the factions of his own tradition, or those of other traditions, could dispute with him, {79} he was praised as the glorious Abhayakīrti and honored as the crown jewel among all expositors of the scriptural transmissions and logical reasoning.[71]

Thereupon, Nāropā was appointed as the monastic preceptor of glorious Nālanda. Since he nurtured the Buddhist teaching over a long period of time, it is said that he also became known as the Jinaputra of Nālanda. He composed commentaries including *The Brief Explanation of the Empowerment according to the Kālacakra*,[72] and commentaries on *Hevajra* and *The Subsequent Tantra of the Guhyasamāja*,[73] and he was proclaimed throughout the world as the perfect great paṇḍita Yaśabhadra.[74]

At that time, in the monastery of glorious Nālanda, there were four gatekeepers, or custodians, appointed in the four directions: Ratnākaraśānti in the east; Vagīśvarakīrti, otherwise known as Viṣṇuhāsaśrī, in the south; Prajñākaragupta in the west; glorious Nāropā in the north; and Ratnavajra of Kashmir and Jñānaśrīmitra in the center.[75]

One day, when Venerable Nāropā had passed some time, acting as a great elder, while he was examining many books that lay open all around him, a black shadow fell across him. When he looked up to see who was there, there was a woman with all thirty-seven characteristics of ugliness.[76]

"What's that you're looking at?" she asked. "Do you understand it?" "I do understand it," he replied. "Do you understand the words or do you understand the meaning?" she asked. He said, "I understand the words," and she was delighted. Then he said, "I also understand the meaning," and she was enraged. When he asked why, she said, "There is no one but my elder brother who understands the meaning!" "Well then, I would like to meet him," he said. "Say your prayers and if you have good fortune, you will meet him," she replied and then disappeared.[77]

As for her thirty-seven characteristics of ugliness, {80} outwardly they denoted the thirty-seven flaws of cyclic existence, inwardly they denoted the energy channels and the thirty-seven factors conducive to enlightenment, and secretly they denoted the thirty-seven deities of the maṇḍala.[78] Among these, he understood the meaning of the outer signs, and he said, "I shall go to seek a teacher." When he had abandoned all his possessions, the three masters of the other directions and the pair who functioned as the central pillar requested him to stay, but he refused.[79] To examine whether the prophecy of the ḍākinīs was true or not, he stayed in an isolated forest hermitage. While he was engaged in the meditation and recitation of Hevajra, a voice resounded from the sky, saying,

> The prophecies of the gurus, the buddhas,
> Depends on Cakrasaṃvara![80]

Therefore, he requested instruction on Cakrasaṃvara from a master named Śāntibhadra. In that very place, based on a maṇḍala drawn in vermilion, he recited the seven-syllable mantra of Cakrasaṃvara[81] one hundred thousand times and the earth shook, light blazed, a symphony of music was heard, and the following words resounded:

> In the eastern direction, there resides one called Tilopā,
> The guru, the buddha, who will reveal your objective.

> Since he is your spiritual teacher throughout the three times, go there!
> It is through him that you will accomplish your objective.[82]

Wearing his saṃghāṭī and holding an alms bowl and a staff, he searched and searched exclusively throughout the eastern direction but did not find him. When he grew disheartened, he heard the following words from the heavens:

> Do not revere the demons of indolence,
> But search for the guru, the buddha, and you will find him![83]

So he remained there to continue his search, and not long afterward, at a narrow ravine where rocks and water clashed, he perceived a leper woman who was unbearable to behold and told her to make way, but she said, "If you're in a hurry, step over me. If you are not in a hurry, go around! {81} I am not inclined to step aside." With his religious robe dangling, he covered his nose and stepped across her, whereupon she said, "You with your ritual purity! How will you possibly find a teacher?" and then she vanished.[84]

Again, on the way, there was a female dog, her lower body infested with worms and her upper body afflicted by another ailment. As he stepped across her, she said, "How will the six classes of living beings possibly find the nature of the teacher by searching elsewhere!" and then she vanished. "It's a magical emanation," he thought. "It's useless!"[85]

Again, on the way, he arrived at the realm of a petty king and inquired about Tilopā. "Stay in the palace," he replied. "Take this girl as your queen. Then teach!" The king urged him again, but he was enraged and left the palace, stealing the girl. Subjected to much slander, he was angered and began to undertake rites of sorcery according to Cakrasaṃvara, but at that time she said, "Have you not been deceived by that illusory person?" and she herself then disappeared.[86]

Again on the way, there were two men beating another man repeatedly on the head. He asked them about Tilopā, and they said, "First help us with this, and we will show you!" Since he could not do so, they said, "Without striking egotism on the head . . . ," and then they disappeared.[87]

Again on the way, there were two men throwing another into a mass of fire and burning him alive. He asked them about Tilopā, and they said, "Help us with this!" When he refused, they said, "If you do not burn the firewood of the subject-object dichotomy . . . ," and then they disappeared.

Again, on the way, there were two men cutting out the bowels of a living man with copper knives. He asked them about Tilopā, and they said, "Help us!" When he did not, they said, "Without severing the continuity of cyclic existence . . . ," and then they disappeared.[88] {82}

Again on the way, he saw a man bathing the entrails of another living man in a hot spring. He asked him about Tilopā, and the man replied, "Help me!" When he did not do so, the man continued. He said, "Without cleansing the stains of the mind . . . ," and then he disappeared.[89]

Again, on the way, in an unpleasant valley, he came across a blue man leading a dog, carrying bow and arrows, and hunting a deer. He asked him about Tilopā, and the man replied, "Help me!" When he did not do so, the man said,

> In the mountain of the body, which is egotism,
> I slay the intestines of the deer, which are the subject-object
> dichotomy.
> I am the hunter who wants to kill.
> Tomorrow I will go begging for alms in sacred places.[90]

And then he disappeared.

Again when he reached a large monastic estate, he was welcomed and revered by the monastic community as a great paṇḍita, renowned like the sun and moon. He asked if there was a beggar named Tilopā in their kitchen, but they said, "Throw a handful of lice, and put them in the midst of the fire!" But when he could not do so, they said, "Without killing the sentient beings of the six realms . . . ," and then they disappeared.

Again on the way, there were two venerable old monks plowing a field. He asked him about Tilopā, and they said, "Please teach us the sacred doctrine!" They scooped many fish from the water, and without cooking them, invited him to eat, but when he did not want to do so, they said, "A person fettered by concepts . . . ," and then they vanished.[91]

Again on the way, there was a man who had impaled his own parents on a stake, intending to murder them. He asked him about Tilopā, and he said, "Help me!" But when he could not do so, the man said, "Without slaying your parents, who are the three poisons . . . ," and then he vanished.[92]

Again on the way, there was in a place filled exclusively with one-eyed men, a blind person who could see in a crowded marketplace, {83} a deaf one who could hear, a lame one who could run, and many corpses who were beckoning to him. They were excitedly looking at one another. He asked them about Tilopā, and they said, "There's no point exhausting your body and mind, searching for Tilopā. You should pray with faith and devotion and so forth. Although many signs have been intimated to you, up to now you have not understood them," and then they disappeared.[93]

Then he thought, "I did not recognize that all these were the emanations of the teacher. Now, due to the ripening of my past actions, this has impeded me, and I have not met him. This being the case, I should discard this body and then by whatever means meet him in the next life!" and Nāropā went in search of a razor.[94]

At this point, a blue yogin with bloodshot eyes and round teeth, wearing a turban of red silk and dressed in cotton shorts, arose unsupported in the sky, in the midst of rainbows, and said,

> If you have not found the teacher,
> How will you possibly find the teacher
> By killing the buddhas
> and going to the lower realms!
> Is it not me your evil thoughts desire?[95]

Nāropā paid homage and replied,

> Lord, though I searched for truth
> In things uncertain like clouds in the sky,
> How could I possibly find it!
> Alas! Will you not hold me with your compassion?[96]

Tilopā then said,

> Majestic, undefiled, and worthy vessel,
> You are now a worthy recipient of the oral instructions,
> The wish-granting jewel of the aural lineage,
> The secret essentials of the ḍākinīs![97]

They then went to his abode.

Up until this time, Nāropā had been empowered in the refining of past actions and their ripening, whereupon the objective of cleansing his past actions by means of the water from the ritual vase had been actualized. Then, by whatever means, he presented a maṇḍala offering and prayed, and Tilopā consequently said, "First I shall have to confer empowerment upon you." He placed some embers on a roll of cotton, such that it was incinerated while retaining its shape. {84} "Do you understand this?" he asked, and Nāropā replied, "I understand that the meaning of the empowerment resembles an ember that should incinerate afflicted mental states that resemble the roll of cotton." Tilopā said nothing at all.

In a similar manner, Tilopā then showed him a lump of crystal, placed a wish-granting gem on the crown of his head, and stared at it with an unmoving gaze. He filled a vessel with pure water and bid him to drink it directly. He tied intricate knots eight times and then untied them. He poured a little water into many vessels and finally mixed them together. He made the sealing gesture of the source of phenomena. He drew a vital-essence dot on the palm of his hand. He pointed a finger toward his heart. He smiled. For a while, he said nothing, and then he showed him the trunk of a tree with branches, foliage, and fruit. Then, Tilopā said, "Do you understand the meaning of these symbols?"[98]

In succession, Nāropā replied,

> The lump of crystal purifies my own mindstream.
> The gem is the precious spiritual teacher.
> One should have the immutable faculty of faith and devotion.
> One should drink the fountain of immaculate oral instructions.
> One should undo the intricate knots of the eight worldly concerns.
> The many vessels of water are the common savor.
> The source of phenomena is nonarising.
> All things are the unique buddha body of reality,
> And the buddha body of reality abides as the vital essence itself.
> Reality is ineffable, inconceivable, and indescribable.
> The mute, who does not speak, denotes the extensively spoken teachings.
> The fruit denotes the excellence of the twofold benefit of self and others.[99]

Tilopā then said,

> By undoing the knots of these thirteen symbols,
> You have become a person who knows the symbols.

Worthy recipient of the secrets of the ḍākinīs,
You have now become worthy of the oral instructions
Of the wish-granting gem of Secret Mantra.[100]

Nāropā asked,

Destroying the darkness of attachment to the empowerments
Of water, the crown, and so forth,
I have brought to maturation these thirteen symbols.
Please teach the definitive view!

Tilopā answered,

Watch without watching. {85}
If you see the unrecognized truth
In the unseen disposition,
You will become a naturally liberated yogin, without duality![101]

Nāropā again said,

The precious jewel of my mind,
Relying on the ship of the spiritual teacher,
Perceives the meaning of empowerment
Over the ocean of cyclic existence with its three realms.
This yoga is bliss![102]

But Tilopā replied,

If you are attached to the spiritual teacher who introduces bliss
And to the oral instructions commensurate with the profound
meaning,
That will resemble bondage, the afflicted mental states.
You should not be attached even to the antidote![103]

All these constitute the maturational, causal empowerments. Since Nāropā was skilled in the sacred doctrine of the tantras, in order to cut off his attachment to the stages of public exegesis and to the maṇḍalas of colored sand and so forth, these thirteen symbolic empowerments had to be conferred in that manner. They included three symbols each with respect to the first three empowerments, and four with respect to the fourth empowerment.[104]

Then, Nāropā traversed the levels and the paths by means of twelve great pillars of asceticism. First, without regard for his body or life, in accordance with the command of the spiritual teacher, he jumped from the roof of a particularly tall thirteen-storied pagoda, and broke his limbs, as if they were reeds.[105] Second, entering into the midst of a fiercely blazing sandalwood fire, he was burned to the bone.[106] Third, while he was making a bridge over a river filled with leeches, they covered his body, drained his blood, and he experienced suffering.[107] The forms of austerity in these three acts constitute the ground of purification by means of the vase empowerment, in which the defilements of the body are actually purified. {86} This act of purification stabilized the generation stage of meditation, in which appearances and emptiness are indivisible, and it dispelled the defilements obstructing the body of emanation, the indestructible reality of buddha body.

Fourth, he received an alms bowl full of rice from a place of feasting and offered it to the guru who seemed to enjoy it. Returning to the feast, there was a clay pot similarly filled with vegetable stew, which he carried off. As he ran off, the monks pursued him and just as they were about to catch him, he poured the vegetable stew into the folds of a leaf and handed back the container. He offered the food to the spiritual teacher and asked if it was tasty. Since Tilopā was pleased, he asked if he should bring more. Tilopā gave him a sword and a vase filled with water. "If they chase you," he said, "swing the sword and pour the water from this vase!" Nāropā went back, and there was a full cauldron of vegetable stew. He ladled it up and fled. When they gave chase, he swung the sword in a circle and it turned into an iron hut, blazing with fire, but he got away. When he poured out the water, it turned into a wide flowing river, but the pursuers crossed it by means of a coracle, and they beat him until he could not move.[108] Fifth, when he pursued a mirage-like person, he became exhausted and fainted on the ground.[109] Sixth, his body was pierced through to its core with sharp bamboo stakes.[110] The forms of austerity in these three acts constitute the ground of purification by means of the secret empowerment, in which speech is purified. This act of purification stabilized the yoga of vital energy, and it dispelled the defilements obstructing the body of perfect resource, the indestructible reality of buddha speech.

Seventh, he pulled down the female consort of a minister from her elephant and dragged her about. Beaten by her servants, his body became unrecognizable.[111] Eighth, he pulled down the female consort of a king from her palanquin and then kissed and scratched her. Her servants, who were not amused, beat his body to a quivering pulp.[112] {87} Ninth, he adopted a female consort, but they fell out and he experienced intense suffering. He offered her to the spiritual teacher, who said, "She cares for him!" and then beat Nāropā's penis between two stones.[113] The forms of austerity in these three acts constitute the third empowerment, in which the mental faculty and the vital essences are purified. This act of purification stabilized the realization of the inseparability of bliss and emptiness, and it dispelled the defilements obstructing the body of reality, the indestructible reality of buddha mind.

Tenth, on a wide plain, as commanded, he went in pursuit of a man carrying a heavy load but became exhausted and fainted on the ground.[114] Eleventh, when he was told to prepare a maṇḍala in the middle of a desolate plain, unable to find water or flowers, he sprinkled the site with his own blood and offered it, laying out his sense organs and five limbs as the maṇḍala clusters.[115]

On all these occasions, Nāropā engaged in those austerities, inspired by the injunction of the guru, and just as his consciousness was on the brink of transmigrating, the guru would appear and, after a series of questions and answers, anoint him with his hand, making his body even stronger than before. This was the case in all these early and later episodes.

As for the twelfth, when he requested instruction at a certain point, the guru said, "You never understand, no matter how much I teach!" He kicked Nāropā's heart with his boot and knocked him out. When he recovered consciousness, the entire renunciation and realization of Tilopā had been transferred to him, as if imprinted upon him.[116]

The guru then introduced him to the nature of mind, saying,

> How wonderful! This is the intrinsic awareness, pristine cognition,
> Transcending the pathways of speech,
> Not within perceptual range of the mental faculty.
> I, Tilopā, have nothing else to show you.
> You should know this, expressing yourself by yourself![117]

The forms of austerity in these three acts constitute the ground of purification through which the defilement of fundamental ignorance to be purified in the innate pristine cognition is purified. This act of purification actualized the pristine cognition that is unhindered discernment, and the result of the purification was that it dispelled the defilements obstructing the body of supreme bliss. {88}

During all these austerities, the transmission of the aural lineage was perfected: the wish-fulfilling gem of the lineage during the first austerity; the wish-fulfilling gem of the ordinary instructions during the second austerity; the wish-fulfilling gem of the commitments during the third; the eight instructions of the Six Doctrines, with the addition of resurrection of the dead and the application of the action seal, during the fourth to the eleventh austerities; and the Great Seal during the twelfth austerity.[118]

At that time, when he had excellently acquired all the approaches of the instructions and expositions, the master then purposefully said,

> Having obtained the power of unfailing retention,
> Nāropā has attended upon me through twelve austerities.
> He has my realization.
> Those interested in the welfare of sentient beings of future
> generations
> Should attend upon Nāropā if they want realization.

Tilopā said, "You should now not assume the appearance of a paṇḍita but focus on the essence of spiritual attainment through the ascetic discipline of a yogi." Then he vanished.

Engaging in the conduct of a yogin, Nāropā went about saying only, "I will accept it. I will accept it!" A group of children gave him a sharp knife. Placing it upon his tongue, it melted like butter and he ate it. Imbued with faith, they were granted his blessing and liberated right there.

To test Nāropā, a king set loose a rutting elephant on him, but he slew and then revived it. Imbued with faith, the king requested him to stay there as the household priest and offered him the Princess Jñānadīpī as a consort. He adopted the conduct of a hunter, such that the other court priests and pious attendants had no faith in him and asked him to desist. Once again he slew all the birds in the sky with his magic gaze that caused them to fall and he exposed and slew all those creatures dwelling below the ground with his magic stare that averted them. Through diverse transformations of his physical body, he slew all the creatures dwelling in water and on dry land, {89} such that everyone lost faith in him. They bound him, along with the princess, and set them to burn on a fire of sandalwood, but the couple appeared in the midst of the fire adorned with ornaments and dancing, their bodies shimmering with dew, as they intoned their adamantine spiritual songs. In their dreams, the king and his retinue saw themselves enduring the suffering of the hells for many eons, so they begged forgiveness and were all liberated by his blessing.

While Nāropā was playing with children on the banks of the Ganges, Tilopāda appeared in the sky and delivered *The Gaṅgāma Instruction of the Great Seal,*[119] purposefully speaking, such that Nāropā actualized the conclusive meaning of the Great Seal.

At that time, Riripā and Kosaripā[120] also urged him to act for the benefit of others, and the guru Tilopā placed his hands on his head and made the following prophetic declaration:[121]

> In the monastery of Puṣpahari,
> You should dispel the dark ignorance of the Tibetan
> With the sun of naturally liberated pristine cognition
> And permeate him with the luminosity of pristine cognition![122]

Thereafter, Nāropā once again resumed his role as the guardian of the northern gate at Nālanda. On one occasion, when naked heretics were on the verge of destroying the Buddhist teaching, Nāropā was asked for assistance. Thrones were set up near the gate of the temple for the antagonist, the protagonist, and the adjudicator, and the debate between the two factions commenced. The Buddhist master appeared to be somewhat weaker, but Nāropā knew that this was owing to the sealed injunction of the guru. He prayed, and consequently Tilopāda actually appeared, holding a moist skull. Nāropā made obeisance to him. The heretics accused him of breaching the rules, whereupon Venerable Tilopā exclaimed, "Subdue! Subdue!" He pointed toward a three-storied grand temple of the heretics with the gesture of menace, causing it to completely collapse. They bowed down at the master's feet and were guided into the Buddhist teaching.[123] {90}

Thereafter, Nāropā dwelled at Phulla Vihāra, the Temple Captivated by the Radiance of Flowers, which was so named because even exquisite flowers were outshone by its bouquets. He extensively acted for the welfare of the Buddhist teaching and sentient beings. Finally, he entrusted the common teaching to Jowo Atiśa and the uncommon teaching to the sovereign Lord Marpa.[124] Demonstrating the dissolution of the emanational maṇḍala of the physical body, he departed for the pure realm of the sky farers. At that time, the wondrous signs that appeared were inconceivable. In the place where his sacred corpse was cremated, each month, on the day of his death, there appeared divine offerings, a symphony of music, and a rain of flowers. It is said that this still occurs up to the present day in the common experience of all beings. Furthermore, his body of pristine cognition bestowed further instructions on Venerable Marpa for three months, and finally, welcomed by ḍākinīs, he departed for the realm of the sky farers in that very body.

Nāropā had seven disciples whose renown exceeded his own, namely Ḍombhipa, Śāntipā, Maitripā, Dharipā, Kusulupā, the Kashmiri Jñānākara, and the easterner Jāyaka.[125] There were also paṇḍitas including Śāntibhadra, Śāntivarman, Jowo Smṛti, *Aparājitavajra,[126] Pitopa, and Ratnaśrīmitra.[127] There were four disciples who attended upon him for a long time—namely, Prajñārakṣita, Manakaśrī, Bodhibhadra of Kashmir, and Phamtingwa Dharmamati, who was also known as Phanaguwa. There were innumerable other disciples including the four who pleased him with faith and devotion—namely, the latter's younger brothers, Abhayakīrti, Kālacakrapāda, and Tangchungwa, along with Marpa Lotsāwa.[128]

The Lineage of the Essential Transmitted Teachings of the Great Seal {91}

As intimated previously, this transmission descended from Vajradhara through Sukhanātha, a bodhisattva emanation of Avalokiteśvara; Matiratna, a bodhisattva emanation of Mañjughoṣa; the glorious great brahmin Saraha, who was accepted into the following of both of these; the noble and supreme Nāgārjuna; and the latter's disciple, Śavaripā.[129]

Śavaripā

Once there were three children of a dancer who made their livelihood through song and dance. When they came to beg for alms at Nālanda, Nāgārjunapāda did not regard them as persons of an inferior class but summoned them inside and gave them good food. Establishing them in faith, they sang a song from the *Dohā of Saraha*, and he asked, "Do you know its meaning?" They replied, "We do not understand it, but we sing it with faith." "Do you wish to understand it?" he asked. They were extremely delighted and said, "Yes, we do!" Seeing that they were of good fortune, Nāgārjuna conferred empowerment upon them, and through that blessing an instantaneous realization arose. Śavaripā saw the visage of the bodhisattva Matiratna, who said to him, "You should work for the welfare of living beings through this maturational body of past actions at Śrīparvata, assuming the guise of a hunter!" He resides there even now.[130]

Maitripā

The latter's disciple was lord Maitripā.[131] He had been born in the central land of Madhyadeśa into the royal class. He skillfully mastered all the fields of classical learning and then became a disciple of glorious Nāropā. Ordained as a mendicant by Śāntipā, he became known as Maitri, which is to say, "loving-kindness." As a peerless great paṇḍita, he resided at Vikramaśīla. Once during that time, he minutely partook of the inner sacraments of the meditational deity Vajrayoginī, and when the proctors, including Jowoje (Atiśa), saw him, he was expelled from the monastic community. Described as "a degenerate, for whom it is inappropriate to pass through the gates," he departed without hindrance through the wall. {92} With the River Ganges in front, he sat down on his mat, and grasping his attendant Sakara by the hand, he passed across without sinking. Utterly astonished, Jowo Atiśa, circling in a boat, sought his forgiveness. Maitripā then fasted in front of an image of Khasarpaṇi and obtained a prophecy by way of signs in a dream. Exploring elsewhere, he clearly dreamed of Śavaripā, mighty lord of yogins, with a trident, on Mount Maṇibhaga (Śrīparvat). Befriending a merchant who sailed the seas, they went there.[132]

Arriving at the mountain, they first looked for some fruit to eat. Then they fasted and searched again but found nothing. As Maitripā was preparing to commit suicide, thinking he would receive the guru's advice in the intermediate state, Sakara then saw the dark brown mighty lord of yogins in a maṇḍala of rainbow light, in the middle of a bamboo grove, weighed down with the upper and lower parts of a pig's carcass that he was carrying, and attended by two yoginīs. They called out and prostrated full length before him, and he said, "I have been here from the start, but you simply did not see me, owing to your obscuration." Imbued with faith, an extraordinary meditative stability arose, and Śavaripā taught them *The Meditative Concentration of the Fourfold Seal*,[133] *The Spiritual Song Titled Twenty Verses on the Great Vehicle*,[134] and so forth. Right then and there, Sakara attained liberation and vanished.[135]

Then, again, when the guru pieced a wild boar in the forest with an arrow and killed it, Maitripā became a little lacking in faith. Śavaripā thereupon uttered some verses and vanished like a rainbow. Maitripā again supplicated him and heard him saying, "Since I lacked the good fortune to teach the doctrine through that body of mine that had been ripened by past acts, my emanational body is now present in the low-caste city known as Dhūti in the form of an old novice monk with an entourage of two old novice nuns. Go there!" Thereupon, all his doubts concerning the oral instructions were cleared, {93} and he awoke from sleep. At that moment, as he was suffering due to all the things that he had forgotten, Śavaripā actually appeared in the sky, and said,

> How can there be knowledge
> Of things that are nonarising?
> How can there be forgetting
> Of things that are unceasing?

Instantly, he remembered everything. "You should go to Madhyadeśa!" said the guru. "Accept my likeness as your master, and take fortunate beings into your following!" Maitripā did so, and the eye of unobscured knowledge with respect to all the maṇḍalas of phenomena, abiding and apparent, opened wide. With his fearless lion's roar he overpowered extremists, such as Natikara, who resembled mighty nāgas.

Unique volumes of scripture, such as those of Śavaripā, indeed bypass the deceit established in the writings on debate. Since he was worthy of respect as a great learned and accomplished master, unrivaled upon the earth, Maitripā was appointed as the officiating priest of Vajrāsana. All proud individuals headed by the king of Magadha bowed the gems of their crown ornaments at his lotus feet. He resided at the hermitage of Mount Jvalana and composed *The Twenty-Four Doctrinal Cycles of Nonmentation*[136] and so forth.

His disciples who appeared were inconceivable in number. Among them were four extraordinary disciples—namely, Sahajavajra, who subdued the extremists; Devākaracandra, who was also known as Śunyatāsamādhi; the king Rāmapāla; and Vajrapāṇi, who was also known as the Indian Pāṇi.[137] There were also seven middling disciples, including Abhiyukta, and ten lesser disciples, including Tipupa and Vilamtācārya.[138] {94}

The Lord Marpa Lotsāwa studied under those who were renowned like the sun and moon throughout India and Tibet.

Concluding Verses

In the wide forested valley of the doctrinal wheel
Revealed by the supreme Conqueror,
The ordinary trees of words and concepts
Are endowed with branches, foliage, and fruits of provisional meaning,
And the definitive meaning, which is the mighty lord of wishing trees
Manifestly grants the desire for clear realization in living beings.
But when the reason for this is examined,
In the Great Seal, these are without duality.
Even though beings may be filled like a reed marsh upon the land,
With hoarse speech that adheres, preaches, and attains,
This Great Seal can still point toward buddhahood in the hand.
In the pleasant Land of the Noble Ones,
The two of supreme vision, and Śavaripā,
Father and son, are alone the sons of dawn.

Spreading the news of those who are praised—most praiseworthy owing to the power of enlightened attributes,
Actually buddhas, skilled in devices—other skilled persons are themselves fools in their presence,
Charioteers steering the path of the Adamantine Vehicle, as if converging in the heart of the woods,
These are actually the regents of the Sage—actually indistinguishable from him.

Though well refined at birth, they are masters of modesty in this world, owing to the power of their refinement,
And yet possess the virtuous inspiration to disclose oceanic etymologies—the words and meanings of the scriptures.
Passing day and night in doctrinal activities, they never tire of acting.

And so having compiled this legendary account, without retaining the fruits of this compilation exclusively for his own sake,
In order that limitless beings who have been our mothers may not endure bondage due to hundreds of labors,
To swiftly release them, the guide of the many, Taklungpa, Akṣobhya, lord-protector, {95}

Excellently emanated through the ocean of the Kagyu lineage,
Establishing this ground of emanation—the votive offering of living beings.
Henceforth, throughout the world, the earth, may this Buddhist teaching always be present as an ornament![139]

This completes chapter five of this book, a somewhat extensive account of the biographies of the four lineages of the transmitted teachings, the two of supreme vision and so forth, from *Wondrous Ocean of Eloquence: A Narrative of the Wish-Fulfilling Gem of the Lineage* compiled by Taklungpa Ngawang Namgyel. {97}

6. The Spread of the Sacred Doctrine in Tibet[1] {99}

Verses of Homage

OṂ SVĀSTI
May it be auspicious!

The three ancestral kings are the essence of love, knowledge, and power of all the conquerors[2]—
Noble vases of nectar, sun and moon in human form,
Courageous and steadfast in removing the torments of the four assemblies[3]
Of red-faced Tibetans—
Cast forth from the surging of the ocean waves of glorious Lokeśvara's compassion
To the summit of the three planes of existence.
Knowing this, with intense power of faith,
Those who subsequently rekindled the second lamp of the Buddhist teaching
Are but reflections of those universal emperors of the sacred doctrine,
Whatever their enlightened heritage, and of their noble deeds,
Arising on the mirror of this oceanic field.
May their narratives fill the pools of the mental faculty
With manifold garlands of fresh water lilies—
And therefrom may this essential array be again enhanced
As a beautiful ornament for the ears of the discerning.

Sixth, there is a description of how the sacred doctrine originated in this land of Tibet.

The Land, Peoples, and Early Kings of Tibet

The land of Tibet was originally a habitat for unfortunate beings, covered with water—the highland region of Ngari resembling a reservoir, the moderately high region of Utsang resembling an irrigation channel, and the lower-lying region of Dokham resembling an irrigated field. Seeing that the time had come to discipline that land, sublime Avalokita alighted on the summit of Marpori, in the lower Kyichu region of Uru, and through the blessings of his buddha body, speech, and mind, he caused the water that filled the four horns of Utsang to vanish into the lost river of Kongpo.[4] The other waterways of Ngari and Dokham also dried up naturally. Consequently, the highland region of Ngari became a pasture for wild ungulates, {100} Utsang for beasts of prey, and the lower region of Dokham became an isle for birds. Thereafter, the whole of Tibet became a land of nonhuman spirits, occupied by the ten classes of demons, including yakṣas.[5]

From the union of a bodhisattva simian emanation of sublime Avalokiteśvara and an ogress of the rocks who was an emanation of Tārā, six monkeys who had transmigrated respectively from the six classes of sentient beings were born. This is held to have been the foundation for the separate evolution of the renowned six Tibetan clans.[6] Those six simian offspring originally inhabited the Bird Sanctuary Forest,[7] and after some years they numbered around four hundred. It was from them that the Tibetans multiplied extensively, such that a realm of sentient beings to be tamed was established in Tibet.

Lord Amitābha consecrated this land of Tibet with three attributes—as an abode of the Buddhist teaching, with an abundance of individuals upholding the Buddhist teaching, and with hundreds of millions of precious treasures. Though under the sway of twelve minor kingdoms and forty principalities, the land was constantly endangered by its four frontiers.[8] At that time, a holy emanation of the compassion of sublime Avalokita, descended from the Licchavi race of the Śākyas, alighted from the summit of Lhari Gyangto.[9] Certain fortunate Tibetans found him and invited him to be their ruler. This was Nyatri Tsenpo—the first of the Tibetan kings,[10] who founded the castle of Yumbu Lagang. The lineage of his sons then appeared in succession. Along with him, they are known as the Seven Heavenly Kings Called Tri who moved unimpededly through mountain cliffs, traversed the sky, and finally vanished into rainbow light.[11]

Thereafter, there was the first mortal king Drigum Tsenpo, during whose reign Bon flourished. Of his three sons, Chatri was made the ruler of Kongpo, Jatri of Powo, and Nyatri of Nyangpo.[12] The mother of those three also had a son conceived by the deity Yarlha Shampo who was named Rulekye and is considered to have been the first of Tibet's seven culture heroes.[13] {101} He subdued the usurper minister Longam; made charcoal; extracted gold, silver, copper, and iron; and introduced irrigation, plowing of the fields, and so forth. Jatri was enthroned, and during his reign—as if presaging the later appearance of the mantras, monastic discipline, the discourses, and phenomenology—there arose the tradition of celestial Bon, with its fables and riddles.[14]

Jatri's son was Esho Lek, and his minister was Lhabu Gokar, the son of Rulekye, who is considered the second Tibetan culture hero because he measured agricultural land according to plowed areas and nomadic herds according to animal hides, channeled mountain streams, and irrigated the lower plains that had been unplowed. Altogether, there were six kings called Lek, including his successor, the king Desho Lek.[15] They constructed the palaces known as the six castles of Ching Nga.[16]

Subsequently, there were eight kings called De, commencing with Zanam Zinde,[17] and five kings called Tsen, the first of whom was Tore Longtsen.[18] Until the last mentioned, the queens of the Tibetan kings had been nonhuman goddesses or nāginīs, and their sons had the title of either Divine Prince or Clan Prince. But thenceforth, the kings intermarried with their subjects, such that the divine princes were called Emperor.

The last of the five kings named Tsen was Totori Nyentsen, a manifestation of sublime Samantabhadra. Having reached the age of sixty, while he was residing in the palace at the summit of Yumbu Lagang, there fell from the heavens on to the palace *The Sūtra of the Hundredfold Homage of Renunciation and Fulfillment*[19] and *The Sūtra of the Cornucopia of Avalokiteśvara's Attributes*,[20] inscribed in beryl on golden paper, along with a golden stūpa, a naturally occurring inscription of the six-syllable mantra of precious stone called Seal of the Mudrā, and a mold engraved with the incantation of eleven-faced Cintāmaṇi. These artifacts were accompanied by a shower of flowers, rainbow lights, and a symphony of music, and designated as the Awesome Secret. By offering them prostrations, circumambulations, and elaborate worship, the lifespan of the king was prolonged so that he could live to the age of one hundred and twenty. He then passed away after delivering a final testament to his Tibetan subjects, saying, "You should make offerings to this Awesome Secret, and all your wishes will be fulfilled!" {102} So it was that Tibet acquired the fountainhead of the sacred doctrine.[21]

Lhatotori's son was Trinyen Zungtsen, and then there was Drongnyen Deru. The latter's son was Takri Nyenzik, who had been born blind but whose eyesight was restored through the blessing of making offerings to the Awesome Secret. During his reign, two-thirds of the petty kingdoms that constituted Utsang were gathered under his control. The third Tibetan culture hero, Tridornang, son of Tsunmong, invented weights and measures and implemented the custom of commercial barter between farmers and nomads. The last two kings, Drongnyen Deru and Takri Nyenzik, father and son, are also called the Intervening Teng. The latter's son was the king Namri Songtsen, who adopted medicine and astrology from China and then conquered parts of China and Drugu.[22]

The Reign of Songtsen Gampo

The religious king Songtsen Gampo was born in 617 (fire female ox) at the palace of Jampa Migyurling in Gyama.[23] His father was Namri Songtsen and his mother Driza Tokar. He had a golden complexion, and the hair of his head was bluish black, insatiable to behold. His body was adorned with the major and minor marks, such as wheels on his hands and feet, and the crown of his head was sealed with the face of Amitābha. As soon as he was born, he was empowered by all the buddhas, bodhisattvas recited auspicious verses, and the gods made offerings to him. At that time, there were three different perspectives—the buddhas seeing that Avalokita would demonstrate the twelve deeds of the buddhas in the land of Tibet, the bodhisattvas seeing that Avalokita had emanated as a king and would act for the benefit of living beings, and ordinary Tibetan subjects seeing that an extraordinary divine prince had been born. Those among his inner circle, whose obscurations had been diminished, saw him as eleven-faced Mahākāruṇika, his head adorned with the buddhas of the five enlightened families. {103} He became known as the King with Two Heads because Gar and Tonmi Sambhoṭa, who were both children, told others that they had seen the face of Amitābha. But he was formally given the name Tri Songtsen. Since he "encompassed" all the enlightened attributes and the buddha mind, he was also called Songtsen Gampo.[24]

In his thirteenth year [629 C.E.], the divine prince was offered the kingdom by his father.[25] When he sat upon the precious throne, the deities of empowerment arrived, filling the sky. Nivāraṇaviśkambhin fastened the crown, Samantabhadra bestowed the coronation with water from his vase, and Amitābha placed hands upon his head. At that time, the luminosity of the king's body permeated all the world systems of the ten directions, and from the tip of each ray of light there manifested a field of the buddha body of perfect resource, in each of which the king appeared alongside Vairocana. All these Vairocanas[26] anointed the king's head with their hands, such that from each king multiple lights were diffused, and at the tip of each of these rays of light in turn there appeared the king riding a supreme horse. From these, too, Amitābha was diffused, and from the tip of each of his rays of light, in turn there manifested a field of the buddha body of emanation, in each of which the Conqueror Śākyamuni manifested, alongside each of whom was Songtsen Gampo. Each Munīndra (Śākyamuni) touched the head of the king seated alongside him with his hands, and immediately infinite rays of light were diffused from each of the kings. At the tip of each ray of light in turn there manifested an Avalokita, from each of whom light also was diffused, permeating the sky. At the tip of each of these rays of light in turn there manifested Mahākāruṇika in the form Cintāmaṇi, each of whom also tamed all sentient beings, without exception, through their emanations training each according to need.[27]

Naturally occurring inscriptions of the six-syllable mantra arose on the cliff of Gyere Yartreng. {104} On Marpori, a great palace, awesome and wondrous, was built. The king was offered tribute and gifts at Longtang Castle by the kings of India, China, Byzantium Tartary, Persia, and so forth, and he was also offered caskets of wealth and letters of commendation. Tonmi Sambhoṭa, an emanation of Mañjughoṣa, began to devise a Tibetan script that had not previously existed. Although counted as the fourth of the seven Tibetan culture heroes, he manifestly surpassed all the others and was also the first of the translators. Many scholars were invited from India and Nepal, and Tonmi—along with his disciples, including Dharmakośa and Lhalung Dorje Pel—translated twenty-one sūtras,[28] tantras of Mahākāruṇika, and so forth. By reciting aloud the Awesome Secret, he caused *The Sūtra of the Hundredfold Homage of Renunciation and Fulfillment* and *The Sūtra of the Cornucopia of Avalokiteśvara's Attributes* to appear in Tibetan.[29]

The injunctions of the king were carried out by three hundred senior ministers, and above all by sixteen wise councillors, and the kingdom was securely governed. The fifth Tibetan culture hero, Trizang, the son of

Yangton Nyak, brought dwellings down from the mountains to the valleys and established an urban community at the Castle of Poto.[30]

Then, having unified all his Tibetan subjects, the king wished to establish a great legal code that integrated both temporal and spiritual traditions. He therefore formulated six great codices—namely, the code of Tritse Bumzher, concerning governance; the code of Bumser Tokshachen, concerning weights and measures; the code that served as a model for the nation, based on the five religious laws and sixteen humanitarian laws; the code of the judicial verdict in favor of the status quo requested by Dolon; the code of general law, concerning authoritative verdicts applicable when both parties were guilty; and the code in favor of the domestic treasury applicable when both parties were innocent.[31]

The first of these, the code of Tritse Bumzher, included the six basic articles of governance concerning Tibet:[32] (1) Initially Tibet was separated into five great regions. (2) These were then subdivided into eighteen administrative areas.[33] (3) There were sixty-one military divisions, each composed of one thousand men.[34] (4) There were the divisions of the yeomen, servants, and the servants of servants. (5) There was the central council convened by the king's three maternal uncles (Dro, Chim, and Nanam), along with the minister Ba, who was not a maternal uncle.[35] {105} (6) There were the border-guard posts, manned by three armed divisions.[36]

With the addition of the six great ordinances,[37] the six credentials,[38] the six official seals,[39] the six titles of honor and dishonor,[40] and the six insignia of heroism,[41] alongside the six basic articles of governance, these were collectively called the thirty-six articles of governance concerning Tibet. All are included within the first code.[42]

The second code [that of Bumser Tokshachen] regulated weights and measures—the *dre*, the *sang*, the *phul*, the *zho*, the *se*, the *san*, and so forth.[43]

The third code [serving as a model for the nation] entailed the observance of "fifteen national laws" [divided into five groups of three]. First, there were the three requisite actions—namely, (1) to subdue enemies and establish the kingdom in security, (2) to take domestic responsibilities and maintain attendants and servants, and (3) to practice the sacred doctrine. Second, there were the three actions not to be undertaken—namely, (1) not to explain the doctrine to unworthy recipients, (2) not to sell the secret mantras as property, and (3) not to praise evildoers. Third, there were the three acceptable modes of praise—namely, (1) to praise warriors with the title "tiger," (2) to praise the wise with the title "official," and (3) to praise the good with rewards. Fourth, there were the three modes of disparagement—namely, (1) to disparage cowards with the title "fox," (2) to disparage evildoers with severity, and (3) to disparage criminals with punishment. Fifth, there were the three sorts of people that should not be oppressed—namely, (1) one's biological parents should not be oppressed, (2) one's disciples should not be oppressed, and (3) one's friends should not be oppressed.[44]

This code also included seven major laws: (1) The law prohibiting murder entailed a thousandfold indemnity payment for homicide and a thousandfold indemnity payment for conspiracy to commit murder. (2) The law prohibiting theft entailed, in the case of theft committed against the wealth of the precious jewels, a hundredfold compensation; in the case of royal property, an eightyfold compensation; and in the case of the property of ordinary subjects, an eightfold compensation. (3) The law prohibiting sexual misconduct entailed compensation for adultery and punishment for promiscuity. (4) The law prohibiting falsehood entailed the taking of an oath, having deposed the gods and protectors as a witness. (5) There were restrictions on the use of alcohol. In addition to these five, (6) servants were not to be dismissed and (7) tombs were not to be excavated.[45]

Then, inserted among the laws pertaining to the abandonment of the ten unvirtuous actions, there were the sixteen pure humanitarian laws, which concerned the appropriate maintenance of parents, virtuous ascetics, and brahmins; respect for family elders; the repayment of kindness by children; and the rejection of the deception of others.[46] {106}

Furthermore, one should make offerings faithfully to the precious jewels, one should respect one's parents, one should not cut off those to whom one is grateful, one should not argue with superiors, one should be compatible with those who are noble in lifestyle, one should engage in religion and writing, one should concentrate on adopting virtue and discarding negativity, one should be beneficial without harboring negative thoughts, one should carry out whatever one does in an honest manner, one should be restrained in eating and drinking alcohol, one should repay one's loans and debts in a timely manner, one should abandon fraud in weights and measures and so forth, one should abandon interference in unassigned affairs, one should be hard to change, and one should value oaths and pledges.[47]

The three remaining codes concern judgments of innocence and guilt. That is to say, (4) a verdict could be given simply without embarrassing the dominant party, (5) a verdict could be given in the manner of the brahmin Daṇḍin, when both parties are guilty, and (6) a verdict could be given in the manner of the monk Dvikula, in cases where both parties are innocent.[48]

Since Songtsen Gampo firmly applied such legal codes, heavy as a yoke, that were of benefit to all beings in this life and the next, he ensured that the entire kingdom would become endowed with the sacred doctrine, endowed with the desirable attributes of the senses, and equal to the gods in spiritual and temporal well-being. Even nowadays, the record of these events, when heard, is pleasant, and it sustains a state of mental repose.

Then the king had the thought that he should construct an extraordinarily sublime image of his own meditational deity [Mahākāruṇika] because it would accrue merit and bless his Tibetan subjects. At that time, the gods prophetically declared from the heavens that he should bring to Tibet an image of Avalokita, naturally fashioned of "snake's heart" sandalwood. Immediately, rays of light were diffused from the hair ringlet between the king's eyebrows, {107} and at their extremity there emanated a monk named Ākarmatiśīla.[49] From the ocean shores of the island of Siṅghala, he brought forth an image of eleven-faced Mahākāruṇika with ten principal arms, naturally fashioned of "snake's heart" sandalwood, resplendent and ablaze with blessings. He also brought forth fragments of that same sandalwood, along with a piece of white sandalwood from Potālaka; a full measure of sand and a single bundle of grass from that ocean isle; a wrinkled bone fragment from the seven generations of past buddhas;[50] a fragment from the Tree of Enlightenment, garlands of its flowers, and eight measures of sand from the eight sacred abodes;[51] and a full measure of sand from the Nairañjanā River. These were the ten wondrous objects of worship.

In addition, from inside a sandalwood tree trunk in the midst of a great forest in Nepal there spontaneously appeared five images of standing Mahākāruṇika in the boon-granting gesture. The first four of these were installed, according to their own respective injunctions, in four great towns for the sake of sentient beings. They are known as Sublime Wati, Ukhang, Bhukaṃ, and White Jamali. The last, known as Sublime Lokeśvara, was brought to Lhasa in accordance with its own injunction: "I am going to be the meditational deity of the Tibetan king!" After offering these artifacts into the hands of the king, the emanational monk dissolved into the space between the king's eyebrows.[52]

Then, Songtsen Gampo thought to invite to Tibet the two sacred representations of the Teacher Jowo Śākyamuni, the size of an eight-year-old and a twelve-year-old. He prayed and made offerings to the aforementioned naturally arisen representation of Mahākāruṇika, and consequently two rays of light were diffused from the heart of that image, reaching China and Nepal. He saw that there were two princesses equal in age to himself. Tritsun was the daughter of Amśuvarman, king of Nepal, in the city of Kathmandu, an emanation of the female deity Bhṛkuṭi, skilled in all the treatises. Wencheng Konjo was the daughter of the Chinese emperor Tang Taizong in the region of Chang'an in China, {108} an emanation of Jomo Tārā, skilled in all fields of classical learning. In the morning, he described this as a dream to his ministers and subjects and ordered them to act upon it.[53]

The ministers concurred with one mind and asked the king himself how this should be implemented. He then sent three caskets containing riches and documents to a hundred ministers, headed by Tonmi and Gar, and after praying to Jomo Bhṛkuṭi, he said, "You should set out!" They departed accordingly for Kathmandu and offered gifts and riches to the king of Nepal, who dictated three letters. In response to each of these, the ministers handed over one of the caskets of documents. Knowing therefore that the king of Tibet was endowed with extrasensory powers and infinite miraculous abilities, Amśuvarman became fearful and full of faith. The princess then set out for Tibet, offering a dowry of unimaginable gifts, including the representation of the Teacher in the form Jowo Mikyo Dorje, the size of an eight-year-old; Maitreya in the form Chokhorma; a sandalwood Tārā; and an alms bowl fashioned of beryl. An elaborate festival was held, and she was crowned as supreme queen. Tritsun engaged all the gods, nāgas, and yakṣas in her service, and a palace named Tritse Marpo was constructed on Marpori within a perimeter wall, with nine hundred and ninety-nine rooms—one thousand including the roof. This was unrivaled in the world (Jambudvīpa).[54]

Furthermore, through the splendor of the religious king's onerous and strict injunctions and the devices of skilled ministers headed by Gar Tongtsen,[55] who was an emanation of Vajrapāṇi, the princess Wencheng Konjo set out from China for Tibet,[56] offering a dowry of limitless gifts, including Jowo Rinpoche, the source of spiritual and temporal well-being; {109} many treasure stores of precious jewels; credentials inscribed with layers of gold and turquoise; three hundred and sixty documents concerning the science of elemental divination; twenty thousand ornaments and clothes; countless foodstuffs; a gold amulet inlaid with turquoise;[57] countless sorts of silk cloth; sixty craftsmen; and works of medical science, including the eight methods of examination,[58] the five therapeutic techniques,[59] the six purgative methods,[60] and the four sorts of medicinal compound.[61]

In the perception of people from all four sides, she was seen coming from their own respective directions, and a welcoming reception was held. In the sandy grove by the shore of the Lake of Milk, her chariot sank. The earth quaked, and beasts of burden lay down. Athletic gods and joyful nāgas enthusiastically exerted their strength, but they could not move Jowo Rinpoche. So Wencheng Konjo performed a divination, whereupon she saw that the chariot was pressing down upon a subterranean nāga palace. Entering therein, she made offerings. She was then enthroned as the second exalted queen, and an inconceivably grand festival was held.

At that time, the conquerors saw that infinite rays of light were diffused from the body of Avalokiteśvara, along with those of Bhṛkuṭi and Tārā (that is, the king and his two queens), penetrating all sentient beings, limitless as space, such that they severed the bonds of afflictive mental states and attained the bliss of the adamantine meditative stability. The bodhisattvas saw that these three buddha bodies of emanation had blessed all of Tibet and entered into infinite meditative stabilities. In the perception of ordinary Tibetan subjects, it seemed that they were displaying a mode of conduct in cordial relations with the world.[62]

Furthermore, the king also married Litikmen, the princess of Zhang Zhung; {110} Gyelmotsun, the princess of Ruyong; and Tricham, the princess of Mong. Altogether, he married five queens.[63]

Then the princess Wencheng Konjo performed a geomantic divination and said, "The land of Tibet resembles a supine ogress. You should build a temple to suppress each of her eight principal joints (shoulders, elbows, hips, and knees), as well as the four flat areas (the palms of her hands and the soles of her feet). Since this Milk Plain Lake is the heart blood of the ogress, the gateway to the lower realms, you should raze it and construct a temple. You should suppress the eight geomantic foes[64] with their respective antidotes, and then you should complete the eight-petaled lotus, indicative of earth; the eight-spoked wheel, indicative of heaven; and the eight auspicious symbols,[65] indicative of the cardinal and intermediate directions. Endowed with four kinds of precious gems, indicative of the undiminished four geomantic scrutinies,[66] all enlightened attributes will arise simultaneously!"[67]

Rays of light from the king's heart then penetrated the lake, such that in the middle of the lake a stūpa of light arose. Supported on that, a wall of stone steps was built and roofed over with wood, daubed with the clay of the adamantine nāgas. This was covered with layered bricks upon a base of bronze so that it resembled the adamantine terrain of the world. However, the foundation walls laid above it were destroyed by nonhuman spirits. Thereupon, from the sky there emerged a voice saying that they should first construct an image resembling the king himself. A clay paste made of many particularly sublime materials mixed with sandalwood was placed alongside the king's pillow, and when he fell asleep, the buddhas and bodhisattvas saw sunbeams, like motes of dust, appear and vanish into the clay paste. In the morning when he awoke, there was a naturally arisen image of sublime Avalokiteśvara that had manifested. The three primary faces were white and smiling, indicative of the rites of pacification. Above these were three faces, yellow and laughing, indicative of the rites of enrichment. Above these were two faces, red and grimacing, indicative of the rites of subjugation. Above these were two faces, black and wrathful, indicative of the rites of wrath, {111} and above these was the face of Amitābha, blazing with the major and minor marks. The rest of the image was the same size as the physical body of the king. Among the ten primary hands, the first pair were placed together at the heart. The four remaining right hands were raised upright, holding a rosary, a wheel, the boon-granting gesture, and an image of Amitābha. The four remaining left hands held a white lotus, an anointing vase, an arrow, and a bow. Adorned with jewels and snake ornaments, his chest covered with antelope hide, and with the major and minor marks, it was insatiable to behold. Rays of light from the king's heart were drawn toward that naturally arisen sandalwood image, its relics, and so forth, and, slightly raising the silk sleeves of its arms, they penetrated it, entering its heart in the manner of the being of pristine cognition. It is said that Newar artisans subsequently offered to this image the thirty-eight aspects of the buddha body of perfect resource, and the thousand arms and eyes that are the subsidiary aspects of the buddha body of emanation. They also made the eight bodhisattva images of its entourage, including Lokeśvara. This was the first of the representative images constructed in Tibet. The fiery light rays and wrath emanating from this naturally arisen image of eleven-faced Avalokiteśvara scattered the conspiring mass of demons at Zawatsel[68] and crushed the different geomantic foes of that vicinity.[69]

All the previously recommended temples for the suppression of the terrain were also constructed—the four border-taming temples suppressing the shoulders and hips of the supine ogress, the four further-taming temples suppressing her elbows and knees, and the four district-controlling temples suppressing her hands and feet.[70] In the east were also three temples that ascertained the sun, moon, and planets and two pairs of temples that suppressed each of the fire, water, and wind elements.[71]

When Tradruk, the first of these Tibetan temples, was constructed, the king heard talk about Buddhist mendicants, and he absolutely rejoiced, pledging to offer gold as an act of homage. {112} At that time, the king paid homage to a ragged mendicant beggar and exclaimed "Isn't this most wonderful!" The mendicant then raised the five-pinnacled stūpa of Tradruk on the tip of his finger. The king in turn removed his turban and revealed the head of Amitābha. The mendicant then cut open his own heart and revealed the nineteen deities of *Guhyasamāja*. The king announced that thenceforth respect should be paid to this mendicant who, even though ragged, indeed maintained this guise as a mere token because he had such enlightened attributes.[72]

The king then said, "Construct a temple and a stūpa from the first fruits of the earth and stones for the construction of the Great Temple of Lhasa! All the auspicious circumstances required for Lhasa should be prearranged at Yerpa!" Having consecrated the terrain in this manner, he laid the foundations of the Great Emanational Temple of Lhasa. In order to perfect the roots of virtuous action, the design had a rectangular shape. In order to illustrate the factors conducive to enlightenment, it had charts depicting these thirty-seven factors. In order to illustrate immutable reality, it had *svāstika* motifs in the four corners. In order to demonstrate the ultimate fruition of buddhahood, the center of the design was fashioned in the form of a maṇḍala. The foundations were laid, equivalent in their dimensions to the size of an average ship. The king then emanated an array of five thousand of his own manifestations who constructed the walls, did the carpentry, erected the ceiling, and so forth. The lower floor was finished in two days.[73] In the perception of all the Tibetan subjects, it seemed they heard the voices of many workers shouting in the midst of mist and fog. However, protectors including Śrīdevī and Mahākāla in the form Bhagavat (Lekden)—along with the nāga Nanda, the ogre Dasagrīva of Laṅkā, the yakṣa Kubera, and the *gandharva* Pañcaśikhin—promised to guard the temple, and each did so in their respective forms.[74] The gate faced west toward Nepal. It was known as The Place of the Goat—the temple emanating the four joys.[75]

Having completed the construction of the temple in that manner, the king considered where within it he should install the eleven-faced naturally arisen meditational deity Mahākāruṇika. Inspecting the inner sanctums of the temple, he placed Jowo Akṣobhya within the central inner sanctum, {113} along with the ten deities consisting of Dīpaṃkara and entourage and the two wrathful gatekeepers. He placed the eleven deities consisting of Amitābha and entourage in the sanctum to the right, and he placed Maitreya surrounded by offering deities in the sanctum to the left. He placed the nine deities consisting of Munīndra and entourage in the sanctum to the south. He saw the sacred doctrine spreading everywhere. Since the northern sanctum was extremely beautiful and had no deities, he intended to invite and install the naturally arisen meditational deity Mahākāruṇika and entourage in the morning, but that evening all the deities walked in of their own accord and took their seats there.[76]

When he ordered the artists to paint the murals, those depicting Khasarpaṇi, along with the two isles that ward off the eight great fears and train each according to need, arose of their own accord while the remainder were painted by the artists according to the presentation of *The Hundredfold Udder*.[77]

The princess Tritsun created the other images and the upper story of the Great Temple of Rasa in accordance with the king's considerations. The princess Wencheng Konjo constructed the temple of Ramoche with its "tiger-striped" Chinese roof,[78] and the other three queens each built their own temple. Then, in order to accumulate merit for the Tibetan subjects and enforce previous pledges, the king sent forth five thousand emanations of his own body who built one hundred and eight temples with gates facing east and west, up to and including the last of them, which was Yongdzok Rabga Lhakhang.[79] These, for the most part, filled all the enclaves of Tibet. Mines of precious metals and gems spilled forth, and, in the ubiquitous manner of earth and stones, resources and desirable attributes of the senses were enjoyed, equal to the gods.[80]

Having excellently achieved such works, extensive offerings were arrayed. The king entered upon the maṇḍala, holding a flower with his hands together, and when he uttered a benediction, the conquerors, their bodhisattva heirs, the meditational deities, and doctrinal protectors gathered like dense clouds, as many as the motes of dust in sunbeams, {114} and he was blessed by all buddhas. The bodhisattvas recited prayers of good auspices. The offering deities made their offerings, a rain of flowers fell, a symphony of music resounded, the fragrance of incense arose, and the beings of pristine cognition that filled the sky entered steadfastly and inseparably into the beings of commitment.[81] So it was that an auspicious consecration was spontaneously accomplished.[82]

The Successive Reigns of Gungsong, Mangsong, Dusong, and Tri Detsukten

Tricham, the princess of Mong who was an emanation of Ṣaḍakṣarī, gave birth to the crown prince Gungsong Gungtsen at Draklha Tashikyi Zhelye.[83] An elaborate birthday festival was held. In order to secure the national law of the ten virtuous actions, opponents practicing the ten unvirtuous actions were ostensibly punished in fearsome emanational prisons. And then in order to dispel the doubts of two novice monks from Khotan, the king, with the snap of a finger, made these prisons instantly disappear like a rainbow. Those two monks were brought to maturity in accordance with the sacred doctrine, and they were established on the level of an arhat.[84]

At the age of thirteen [in 641], Gungri Gungtsen acceded to the throne. He reigned for five years and passed away at the age of eighteen [in 646]. His son was Mangsong Mangtsen, but it was his own father who again assumed the governance of the kingdom. In order to promote the excellence of happiness in the land of Tibet, Songtsen Gampo concealed doctrinal treasures near the Vase Pillar in the Great Temple of Lhasa, thereby ensuring that the Buddhist teaching would spread and that the sacred doctrine would be practiced everywhere. He also concealed a treasure of precious gems in the Leaf Pillar, thereby ensuring that precious things would be enjoyed and that the wealth of the borderlands would be gathered at the center. He concealed a treasure of wrathful mantras and occult power in the Snake-Head Pillar, {115} thereby ensuring that foreign armies and obstructing spirits would be pacified. He concealed scrolls concerning the prosperity of cattle in the Lion-Head Pillar, thereby ensuring that milch cattle would flourish. He concealed the gemstone Ratnadeva under the image of Jamabhala,[85] thereby ensuring that ornaments, clothing, grain, and precious metals and gems would increase. He concealed the gemstone called Tiger Meat God in the nāga chapel, thereby ensuring that the harvest would be excellent, rain would fall, and afflictions of the nāgas would be dispelled. He concealed a beryl alms bowl filled with various foods in the yakṣa chapel, thereby ensuring that there would be plenty to eat and drink. He concealed a copper vessel filled with precious gems below the maṇḍala, thereby ensuring that there would be materials for later restorations. Also, he concealed innumerable precious metals and gems in the inner circumambulatory walkway, thereby ensuring that all inauspicious circumstances would be dispelled, harvests would be excellent, and all enlightened attributes would emerge. The king then said, "As long as the Buddhist teaching lasts, may this temple of mine possess all enlightened attributes, like an isle of precious gems. May it always be maintained by beings with diverse forms—by each bodhisattva of the tenth level, by each sublime arhat, by each spiritual hero of supreme accomplishment, and by each ḍākinī of pristine cognition endowed with the appropriate signs!"[86]

To his grandson Mangsong, he taught twenty-one sūtras and tantras pertaining to Mahākāruṇika; exegetical tantras pertaining to the doctrinal wheels; authentic tantras pertaining to the cycle of practice; and the advantages of seeing, hearing, recalling, and touching the Great Temple of Lhasa and of restoring the dikes, and so forth. These, along with the prophecies and testaments that he bestowed, were concealed in the yakṣa chapel and also in the treasure store of Chimphu, and so forth.[87]

The oral instructions that he imparted to the queens, foreign ministers, interior ministers, and subjects, up to and including children, were documented by Tonmi and others, and then concealed. The king's own biography was concealed in the Vase Pillar. {116} He extensively imbued these writings with blessings and aspiration prayers, endowed with the power of truth.[88]

So it was that after the emanational religious king Songtsen Gampo had reigned over the kingdom for a long period of time in accordance with the sacred doctrine, while in his eighty-second year, the array of his physical body demonstrated dissolution into the expanse of reality on the tenth day of Kārtika month in 650 (iron dog).[89] At that time, those of highest acumen saw him being invited by ḍākinīs and departing for Padmadvīpa in the eastern direction. His inner entourage saw the two emanational princesses transform into a white lotus and a blue lily (*utpala*) and then dissolve into the body of the king. The king himself then melted into light, which dissolved into the naturally arisen eleven-faced Mahākāruṇika. In order to instill confidence in the ordinary Tibetan subjects, it was announced that he had fallen ill and died. It is said that a replica of his body was transported in a chariot and placed within a tomb (the Red Mausoleum) at Chongye in Yarlung.[90] Immediately after the king and his two consorts had dissolved into that representational image, light rays were diffused from the heart of the naturally arisen eleven-faced Mahākāruṇika, permeating the entire interior and exterior of the Emanational Temple of Lhasa. The rays of light then penetrated two bronze images depicting Jowo Mikyo Dorje and Maitreya in the form Jampa Chokhor; three clay images with silk fragments[91] depicting Acala, Dīpaṃkara, and Ucchūṣmakrodha; and three mural paintings depicting Bhaiṣajyaguru, the king of medicine, Hayagrīva, and Tārā. These consequently became known as the Eight Deities in Which Rays of Light Were Diffused. From each of their hearts, also, rays of light then emerged, permeating everything inside and outside and giving rise to innumerable virtuous signs. So it was that the secret consecration of the Great Temple of Lhasa itself was spontaneously accomplished.[92]

Mangsong was in his thirteenth year when he acceded to the royal throne [in 650]. He reigned for fifteen years, and died in his twenty-seventh year [in 676].[93] {117} When a Chinese army arrived hear Lhasa, the heart of the image of Ucchūṣmakrodha opened, and the emanational armed forces that emerged from within it repelled the invaders.[94]

Seven days after Mangsong had passed away, Dusong Mangpoje Lungnam Trukgyi Gyelpo[95] was born in the uplands of Drak, and immediately he was appointed king. During his reign, there were seven ministers and subjects of great prowess,[96] and so forth, who appeared. The four borderlands were brought under his control, and regular ancestral offering ceremonies were instated in Lhasa. After reigning for twenty-nine years, he passed away [in 704].[97]

His son Tri Detsukten was born at the Denkar Palace[98] in 698 (earth dog).[99] He built five temples and had many sūtras, medical treatises, and so forth translated, and he founded the Pangtang Palace.[100] He was also called Me Akdzom.[101] When his son, Jangtsa Lhaon[102] was born, the Chinese princess Jincheng Konjo was taken to Tibet to be his consort, but at that time, the prince passed away, so she was crowned as the queen of the father. She extracted the image of Jowo Mikyo Dorje from the southern sanctum of the Great Temple of Lhasa, which has a mirror-shaped door,[103] and established the custom of making offerings in the presence of images. She also introduced the custom of undertaking the roots of virtuous actions on behalf of deceased persons.[104]

The Reign of Tri Songdetsen

The crown prince, an emanation of Mañjughoṣa, was born in 742 (water horse). A rumor was fabricated suggesting that he had been abducted by his father's senior consort Nanamza, [who was his actual mother].[105] The next year, a great festival commemorating the prince's first footsteps was held, during which it is indisputable that he named himself Tri Songdetsen and identified Nanamza as his mother.[106] Before the child had come of age, his father passed away, and immediately [in 755] the prince was appointed to the royal throne and empowered to reign over the entire kingdom. While he was a minor, evil ministers made laws to prohibit the practice of the sacred doctrine. Jowo Rinpoche had been buried in the ground and eventually {118} carried off to Mangyul, such that many inauspicious omens occurred.[107]

When the king had come of age, consideration for the sacred doctrine was born within him, and his enlightened intention was fulfilled by many ministers who upheld the sacred doctrine, such as Go Pema Gungtsen.[108] The evil ministers were punished, and Jowo Rinpoche was escorted back and installed within the southern sanctum. The king then invited the most venerable scholar Śāntarakṣita, who was the son of the king of Zahor in eastern India, and honored him as the jewel upon the crown of his head. When Śāntarakṣita turned the wheel of the sacred doctrine, all the vicious demons and *sin* spirits of Tibet were enraged, and many calamities occurred, including disease and famine. Consequently, in order to safeguard the Tibetan people, the preceptor Śāntarakṣita sojourned for a while in Nepal. As had been foreordained, he requested the second buddha Padmākara—who had been born miraculously from within a lotus, perfected the level of an awareness holder with power over lifespan, and obtained supreme spiritual accomplishment—to eradicate all the arrogant gods and demons of Tibet, headed by the twelve subterranean protectresses, Nyenchen Tanglha and Yarlha Shampo, and to take them into his following. He also requested Padmākara to empty all the ephemeral hells, suppress the adherents of Bon, and enforce compliance with the onerous and strict injunction of the king so that everyone might perfectly complete the construction of a temple.[109]

The foundations of this temple were then laid upon a terrain that resembled a golden vessel filled with saffron. It was modeled on the great monastery of Odantapurī, with a three-storied central temple symbolizing the central Mount Meru, surrounded in each of the four cardinal directions by three temples, representing the four continents and eight subcontinents, with the upper and lower yakṣa temples representing the sun and moon. All the flat surfaces of these buildings were painted with whitewash. On top of the surrounding perimeter wall there were one thousand and eight stūpas, {119} and within the complex there were four stūpas suppressing the elemental spirits in the four directions. Outwardly this design resembled the world system of the four continents, inwardly it was a vast buddha field, and secretly it was a maṇḍala. So it was that they constructed the renowned Samye Monastery—Great Temple of Inconceivable Glory, Unchanging Spontaneously Accomplishment, Great Doctrinal Center Complete with the Thirty-Seven Factors Conducive to Enlightenment[110]—which was unrivaled anywhere in Jambudvīpa.[111]

Representational images, including Śākyamuni in the form Mahābodhi and so forth, which were exclusively actual manifestations of the buddha body of emanation, were excellently created and entrusted to the care of general and specific protectors. Each of the three queens also built their own temples. The entire project was effectively completed within a single year.[112] The king then offered donations of gold and requested them to perform a consecration. The preceptor Bodhisattva (Śāntarakṣita) therefore blessed the site in accordance with *Guhyasamāja* in the form Mañjuvajra, and the master Padmasambhava entered into the meditative stability of the peaceful indestructible expanse according to the primary yoga tantra. Both these masters performed the consecration and undertook the eye-opening ceremony for the representational images eight times, on each of which countless wonders occurred. Lotus stalks grew in the lake of Drakmar Tsomogur,[113] masses of rainbow light converged in the sky, and a rain of flowers fell. At that time, all the people of Tibet gathered together, and it is said that there was an inconceivable festival of song, dance, and amusements that lasted for a full year.[114]

Intelligent boys were then encouraged to train as translators. Twelve monks of the Sarvāstivāda order were invited. With the Bodhisattva Śāntarakṣita acting as monastic preceptor, initially the exceedingly faithful Ba Trizik[115] was ordained as a mendicant, so that he came to possess the five extrasensory powers. He was the first of the Tibetan mendicants. Similarly, the full monastic ordination was then conferred on the Seven Men Who Were Tested, including Ba Trizik, {120} and later the number of novices and fully ordained monks increased greatly.[116]

Many learned *mahāpaṇḍitas* from the central land of India, Zahor, Kashmir, China, and so forth were then invited, and working alongside many translators, they translated most of the Buddhist scriptures that were extant from India, China, Khotan, and so forth. The livelihood of mendicants was provided by the government. Released from the authority of the state, they were consummately venerated. There also appeared an infinite number of holy individuals who were learned in the *tripiṭaka* and endowed with both knowledge and liberation with respect to the purity of the three trainings. And there were countless practitioners who attained the supreme and common accomplishments, including the one hundred and eight accomplished masters in the hills of Yerpa, and the twenty-one accomplished masters at Chuwori.[117]

As requested by the chief minister Go, the king properly established the royal dynastic succession that accorded with worldly convention. He also established the classification of his subjects, the customs of paying homage and addressing noblemen with honorific language, the legends and histories, the methods of positive activity, the virtuous deeds and official credentials instated by his forefathers, and so forth, and he made them universally understood. The king brought two-thirds of Jambudvīpa within his domain. The sixth Tibetan culture hero, Go Trizang Yablhak,[118] determined the rates of compensation for injury and the rates of compensation for homicide, and the seventh, Taktsen Dongzik,[119] introduced the practice of drying summer hay in the winter, and so forth.[120] The edicts of the ruler covered the entire earth impartially, in the manner of sunlight, and the whole of Tibet also enjoyed happiness and engaged with the sacred doctrine.[121]

Then, master Padmākara departed to subdue the ogres of the southwest [in Cāmaradvīpa]. After the preceptor Bodhisattva (Śāntarakṣita) passed into nirvāṇa, a reliquary was constructed for his sacred corpse and the king made offerings to it.[122] {121} He appointed Yeshe Wangpo (Ba Selnang) to preside over the doctrinal tradition in Tibet and extensively promoted the institution of "monastic subjects" on behalf of the three precious jewels, allocating three households among his subjects for each mendicant, and so forth. Shortly thereafter the Chan tradition of Hoshang Mohoyen was propagated, and as had been foreordained by the preceptor (Śāntarakṣita),[123] the master Kamalaśīla eliminated him on the basis of scriptural authority and logical reasoning. It was officially announced that henceforth, in terms of the view, Tibetans should maintain the tradition of Nāgārjuna, in terms of conduct they should train under masters possessing the six transcendent perfections, and in terms of meditation they should experientially cultivate the integration of calm abiding and higher insight. Furthermore, no paṇḍitas should explain the view of Hoshang Mohoyen, no translator should translate it, and no one should practice a doctrine to which the king did not offer patronage.[124]

After entrusting the kingdom to Prince Mune Tsenpo, the religious king Tri Songdetsen passed away in meditation, in his fifty-fifth year [in 796].

The Reigns of Mune Tsenpo, Tri Desongtsen, Relpachen, and Langdarma

Mune Tsenpo established the four great offering ceremonies. On three occasions he sought to equalize the differences between the poor and wealthy Tibetan subjects, but after reigning for one year and nine months, he passed away [in 797].[125]

Subsequently [in 804], the fourth prince Tri Desongtsen acceded to the royal throne. He was also named Senalek Jingyon.[126] He built the Dorjeying Lhakhang[127] at Karchung, where many translators and paṇḍitas translated copious texts of the sacred doctrine. He passed many edicts pledging that the sacred doctrine would never collapse. This king reigned for thirty-two years and passed away in his fifty-fourth year [in 815].[128]

Tri Desongtsen had five sons, among whom the prince Tsangma became a mendicant. The second, Tri Tsukdetsen Relpachen, an emanation of Vajrapāṇi, was born in 806 (fire dog). In his tenth year he acceded to the royal throne.[129] His minister was Drenka Pelyon,[130] and his queen was Chokza {122} Pelgyi Ngangtsul,[131] and so forth. He esteemed the strict legal observance of the ten virtuous actions, and having defeated China, he founded a temple in the Sino-Tibetan borderland. He had the text of his own edicts engraved on three obelisks, proclaiming that China and Tibet resembled the sun and moon in the sky or a nephew and uncle on earth. Henceforth the Chinese and the Tibetans would be happy in their own respective lands![132]

In order to eliminate additions and omissions, the king compiled a catalog of all the texts of the sacred doctrine that had previously been translated. He established them according to the new orthography, and secured all this with three injunctions. He founded thirty seminaries for monastic discipline, exegesis, and meditation, and it is said that the hair of the king's head was made into two dreadlocks, rolls of silk were attached to each of them and stretched out on the right and left, and the two heads of the spiritual community were then asked to be seated upon them.[133] As a support for his meditative commitments, he built the temple of Peme Tashi Gephel[134] at Ushangdo[135] with its sacred representations and nine-storied sanctum that had on top, characterized by nine eaves, a Chinese-style roof with a golden finial that turned like a parasol when stirred by the wind. The tip of the golden finial was equal in height to the turret on the hill to the rear, such that it was unrivaled anywhere in the world.[136]

Triumphant over the four borders, the king brought two-thirds of Jambudvīpa under his sway. But then, the merit of the living beings of Tibet became like a lamp that had run out of oil. Evil ministers conspired covertly to destroy the law of the sacred doctrine, and they exiled Prince Tsangma to Bhutan.[137] They killed the faultless minister Drenka Pelyon and criminally assassinated the king in 841 (iron bird), when he was in his thirty-sixth year.

The governance of the kingdom was then handed to Darma Udumtsen, {123} who intended to destroy the Buddhist teaching completely.[138] The temples apart from those at Lhasa and Samye were mostly despoiled, along with their sacred representations of buddha body, speech, and mind. Diverse ill omens occurred because the best mendicants were killed, the average ones were exiled, and the feeblest were bound into servitude. At that time a great bodhisattva known as Lhalung Pelgyi Dorje, out of concern for the Buddhist teaching and sentient beings, slew the evil king and then fled to Dokham, along with three monks—Mar Śākyamuni, Yo Gejung, and Tsang Rabsel.[139] Bowing to the exceedingly great miracles of the virtuous protector deities, the ministers were afraid. A detailed restoration of the temples was undertaken, and the sacred representations were installed on their respective plinths.

From Osung and Yumten to the Disintegration of the Empire

Osung and Yumten were the two lineal descendants, born to the senior and junior queens.[140] Both were unmistakably of the royal lineage. Pelkhortsen, the son of Lord Osung, erected several temples.[141] The son of his senior queen, in turn, was Kyide Nyima Gon, and the son of his junior queen was Tri Tashi Tsekpa Pel. Both of them journeyed to the highland region of far-west Tibet, where they ruled over the three provinces of Ngari. The son of Tride Yumten was Tride Gonyen. The latter's sons, Tride Rikpagon, Nyima Gon, and so forth, flourished in succession.[142]

The four horns of Utsang were separated from the time of Yumten and Osung, and there were a great many petty rulers in each enclave of the country. Not long afterward, the emanational palace of Rasa Trulnang,[143] {124} along with its sacred representations, dissolved into the expanse of reality. At that time, those of highest acumen saw it being invited by the ḍākinīs and departing for the Akaniṣṭha realm. In the perception of ordinary people, it was seen shrouded with rainbow light, flowing from midstream of a river into an ocean while offerings were made by gods and nāgas. The emanational artifacts of Samye were incinerated by the fire of pristine cognition. Consequently, those who tried to protect these great temples from the ravages of fire and water had immeasurable merits.[144]

The Later Spread of Buddhism

After the Buddhist teaching had disappeared, while Tsang Rabsel, Yo Gejung, and Mar Śākyamuni were staying in meditation at Chuwori, they saw a monk hunting and, on questioning him, understood that the sacred doctrine had disappeared. They packed a load of vinaya texts on to a mule and set out for Qarloq and the Uighur country, thinking to spread the Buddhist teaching in lands where different languages were spoken. But they were not able to propagate it there, and they returned to Beri Salt Lake[145] in southern Dome. While they were staying in meditation at the hermitages of Malung Dorje Drak[146] and Dentik Shelgyi Yang Gon[147] in the basin of the Yellow River, they were seen by a herdsman from the Yellow River area who informed the local people.[148] An aspiring practitioner named Muzu Selbar[149] went to see them, and in faith he asked for ordination as a mendicant. They handed the texts of monastic discipline to him and said, "If you have faith at the sight of these, we will ordain you as a mendicant." On seeing the books out of faith, he burst into tears. Thereupon, with Mar Śākyamuni acting as the monastic preceptor and Yo Gejung acting as the master of ceremonies, he was ordained as a mendicant, and the name that he received from the preceptor and the master of ceremonies was Śākya Gewa Rabsel. {125} Later on, he became renowned as Gongpa Rabsel on account of his most excellent buddha mind. He studied the texts of monastic discipline for fifteen years, and was contacted there in Dome by the Ten Men from Utsang. That is to say, Lume Tsultrim Sherab, Dring Yeshe Yonten, Ba Tsultrim Lodro, Rakshi Tsultrim Jungne, and Sumpa Yeshe Lodro were the five from U; and Loton Dorje Wangchuk, Tsongtsun Sherab Senge, Ngaripa Ogye and his brother,[150] and Bodongwa Upadekar were the five from Tsang. Among them, the first four from U and the first two from Tsang had disciples and grand-disciples from whom the number of ordained mendicants increased. In Tsang, they included the Lo group named after Loton Dorje Wangchuk and the Tsong group named after Tsongtsun Sherab Senge. In U, there was the group named after Lume Tsultrim Sherab and the three named after Dring Yeshe Yonten, Ba Tsultrim Lodro, and Rakshi Tsultrim Jungne. Since each of these groups also had many branches, the teaching of the monastic discipline of the sacred doctrine expanded most excellently. Since the dying embers of the Buddhist teaching were revived from Kham, this lineage was called the Lowland Vinaya tradition.[151]

Separately Ngadak Song Nge[152] invited the paṇḍita Dharmapāla to Tibet. His companions, including the Three Pālas,[153] conferred the full monastic ordination many times. In the presence of Prajñāpāla, Gyelwei Sherab of Zhang Zhung received the full monastic ordination. The lineage that derives from him is called the Highland Vinaya tradition. However, it was not much propagated.[154]

Later, the paṇḍita Śākyaśrī of Kashmir—who had been meritoriously foreordained to practice chastity during the future teaching era of Prakāśa, the seventh buddha of the Auspicious Eon[155]—was invited to Tibet by the faithful, diligent, and learned Trophu Lotsāwa. Initially, he conferred the full monastic ordination on two individuals—Jangchub Pel and Dorje Pel, and stemming from that, the four communities of Śākyaśrī and so forth came about.[156] Subsequently, it was this pure transmission of the monastic vows that increased and expanded in Tibet. {126} Since this is the transmission of the great paṇḍita Śākyaśrī himself, his kindness to Tibet was immeasurable.[157]

The writings of Geshe Dromtonpa mention that the monastic community returned to the central parts of Tibet from Kham in 978 (earth male tiger), seventy-eight years after the Buddhist teaching had disappeared. One should know that the start of the later dissemination of the Buddhist teaching in Tibet necessarily began with that event.[158]

Concluding Verses

Densely exuding camphor, the sandalwood of Avalokiteśvara's
 compassion—
To soothe the torment of affliction in the beings of Tibet (*bhoṭa*),
The royal emperors hailed from the Licchavi race of the Śākyas, of
 divine descent.

As a wonder that permeated the entire world,
With pleasant fragrance sustaining the earth according to the sacred
 doctrine,
All the conquerors' heirs of the buddha fields of the ten directions

Sent forth all their enlightened activities,
And while maintaining these,
The mighty frankincense of the entire Buddhist teaching
Could permeate the wealthy Land of Snows anew.

Courageously attending to the three precious jewels with so much reverence,
Those rulers lived glorious lives.
Where else, apart from space, is there a land such as this
That has such sustaining capacity, without limitation?

Through the causes and fruits of virtuous actions
The Tibetan subjects of that age
Had lain down on degenerate earth
Like a thunderbolt from on high,
And owing to Songtsen, the great and supreme buddha body of emanation,
Who enacted the dance of his twelve deeds on behalf of red-faced Tibetans,
Now I may say I am at rest,
Like the presence of peaceful Śākyasiṃha in a dream.

All the extensive glories of the spiritual wealth of India
Were surpassed by the perfect deeds of Tri Songdetsen,
As a result of which we can maintain this labor,
Scattering flowers of praise upon the great paṇḍitas, mighty lords of speech. {127}

Hearing the good tidings spread by cuckoo mendicants
In the forest of matted hair of Tri Relpachen,
An actual manifestation of Mahābrahmā,
Even now those upholding the saffron victory banner maintain their pride.

Yet like flames dying in an ocean,
Nothing remained of those various material elements,
And the illusion of the mental faculty
Gave rise to phenomenal appearances that were not impossible.[159]

Pulverizing these with the vajra of the holders of gnostic mantras,
The warmth of the sacred doctrine from the nāga lands of Dokham
Then surged upon the terrain of the four horns of Utsang,
And therefrom all that now remains,
This glorious springtime of scripture and realization,
Reveled, owing to the second auspicious feast.

Emaho!
The precious great chariot is endowed with the seven renunciations of the unvirtuous acts of body and speech of living beings, and with the four wheels of faith, diligence, mindfulness, and meditative stability.
And it is endowed with ornamental garlands of magnificent conduct in the mansion of the enlightened mind of pure higher aspiration,
Well distinguished by its jewel crest of towering liberation that confers the swift bliss of the two stages of meditation.
May those who wish for this liberation properly grasp it, more precious than their life, for it is hard to find!

Here, through smiles of effort and virtuous action
That resemble white clouds,
May the mental torments of corporeal beings be dispelled,
And may the peacocks of good fortune be united in supreme joy!

This completes chapter six of this book, a description of how the sacred doctrine originated in this land of Tibet, from *Wondrous Ocean of Eloquence: A Narrative of the Wish-Fulfilling Gem of the Lineage* compiled by Taklungpa Ngawang Namgyel.

Let there be good auspices (*maṅgalam*). {129}

7. The Biographies of the Early Kagyu Lineage Holders in Tibet {131}

Verses of Homage

OM SVĀSTI
May it be auspicious!

The embodiment of Hevajra Heruka, known by Tibetans as Marpa Lotsāwa, is the one of immaculate **intelligence** (*blo gros*),[1] disclosing the definitive secret **of** the **doctrinal** (*chos kyi*) wheel of the glorious and supreme essential vehicle.
Venerable Mila, the embodiment of Guhyasamāja, is the gem who, in this lifetime, surmounted the supreme **victory banner** (*rgyal mtshan*) of the level of coalescence, with steadfast and **adamantine** (*rdo rje*) great fortitude.
Gampopa, the embodiment of Vāgvajra—indestructible reality of buddha speech, is the one with the constant pledge to uphold the most **precious** (*rin chen*) and calm meditative stability, delighting the teacher of gods and humans through **meritorious** (*bsod nams*) activities.
Phakmodrupa, the embodiment of Cakrasaṃvara, lord-protector of living beings, is the one who held the vows of all the buddhas, intermingling the **indestructible reality** (*rdo rje*) of emptiness in all its finest aspects with the **king** (*rgyal po*) of unchanging bliss.[2]

These most marvelous appearances,
An array of adamantine magical emanation,
A single essence with diverse forms,

Incinerated all the degenerate forests of existence and quiescence
With the fire of enlightened activity, quantifiable in its wisdom.[3]
And thereafter, through the great light of innate coalescence,
Their lamp of pristine cognition has illuminated,
For the duration of phenomenal existence,
All traces of darkness, even to the extent of a hair,
Within the sphere of knowable things.

O sentient beings with erudite ears who may analyze this meaning,
It is dependent on my conviction
That I speak of and perpetuate these wonders.

Seventh, there is the narrative of the great Tibetan promulgators of the Kagyu lineage, the Buddhist teaching of quintessential meaning.

Marpa Lotsāwa Chokyi Lodro

Marpa Lotsāwa Chokyi Lodro, the embodiment of Hevajra Heruka, who was a master of the lineage of spiritual attainment, {132} was born in 1012 (water male mouse) at a place called Konchok Topa Tashi Ling Nga,[4] part of Pesar in the Drakbu district of Lhodrak.[5] He belonged to the Marpa clan—his father was Marton Wangchuk Ozer and his mother Gyelmotso, and he was the third of five sons. It is said that they had great wealth and owned land in three places. He was named Chokyi Lodro. In childhood he delighted in beer and quarreling. Due to his extremely bad character, everyone was unhappy. In his twelfth year, he learned writing and reading and mastered them without difficulty. In his fifteenth year, he set out for the residences of Go Khukpa Lhetse and Drokmi. Under Go he studied *Clarifying Lamp*,[6] understood it well, and even composed a text. Under Drokmi he masterfully trained in Sanskrit grammar.

Marpa then considered traveling to India. In Nepal, under Phamtingwa Vijayendra Chiterwa,[7] he studied *Hevajra*, *Catuḥpīṭha*, *Dhūmāṅgārīśrīdevī*,[8] and so forth. He then crossed a poisonous river, and at Lakṣetra in the west, he met glorious Jñānagarbha and requested the cycles of Kriyā and Ubhaya tantra. There, at a communion-feast-offering ceremony, there were four yogins endowed with miraculous abilities who said they were disciples of Nāropā. Simply by hearing that name, faith grew within him. Sendhapa, one of the four, entrusted him to the novice monk Prajñāsiṃha, and the latter escorted him to Nālanda, where an ocean-like number of accomplished paṇḍitas resided, including among them the glorious and unrivaled Nāropā. Their meeting took place at the hermitage of Kanakaparvata[9] near the town of Puṣpahari.[10] Immediately, Nāropā placed hands on the crown of Marpa's head and said,

> In accordance with the guru's prophecy,
> My son, the worthy Marpa Lodro,
> From the northern Land of Snow,
> Has duly arrived to assume the regency.[11] {133}

Their minds were strongly bound together, and Marpa was granted public exegeses and private exegeses along with the pith instructions concerning the root and exegetical tantras of *Hevajra*, and so forth. From his former teacher, glorious Jñānagarbha, he also received all the empowerments, tantras, and pith instructions concerning the *Guhyasamāja*, according to the tradition of sublime Nāgārjuna. Then, Venerable Nāropā appointed three yogins of the charnel grounds to guard him, and, as foreordained, Marpa crossed the expanse of a terrifying lake of poison in half a month. Welcomed there by the doctrinal protectors, he calmed their miraculous disturbances through his prayers and met with master Kukkuripā. The empowerment of *Mahāmāyā* was conferred upon him, he was given the secret name Sukhavajra, and granted all commentaries and pith instructions of *Mahāmāyā* without exception. Thereupon Marpa had a dream in which a beautiful woman placed a vase upon his head, saying she was a messenger of Maitripā. Consequently, an extraordinary meditative experience arose. On the way back, since his vital energy and mind had become pliable, he reached Puṣpahari in the presence of Venerable Nāropā within three days.

Then Marpa visited the temple of Self-Arisen Khasarpaṇi in Bengal, and drank water mixed with milk to alleviate all ailments. In a charnel ground blazing like a mountain of fire, he met with lord Maitripā. Uncontrollable devotion arose within him, he received the empowerments, and the secret name Cittavajra was conferred. He then received *The Litany of the Names of Mañjuśrī*, *The Sacred Songs*,[12] and the Great Seal, and an instantaneous realization arose, equal to space.

Furthermore, through the blessings of his guru, he instantly crossed the lake of poison and requested the *Catuḥpīṭha*[13] from a ḍākinī named Kadalīmañjarī.[14] He was then given the secret name Sukhavajra.

Through the blessings of glorious Nāropā, he then prepared to return to Tibet. {134} One night while he was staying at a place called Liśokara at the Nepal frontier,[15] two ḍākinīs lifted him in a palanquin and he met with the great brahmin Saraha on Śrīparvata in the south. He was blessed by the latter's body, speech, and mind, and Saraha then taught him *The Sacred Doctrine of the Four Syllables.*[16]

Marpa perfected the realization of the meditational deity Cakrasaṃvara, and then arrived in Tibet, where he resided at Drowolung. Ngok Choku Dorje and Tsurton Wangi Dorje met him there and he took them into his following.[17] He then married Lady Dakmema, and so forth. The noble son Dode was born to Dakmema.

Marpa again set out for India via Nepal and met with his teachers—Venerable Nāropā, Maitripā, and so forth. From them he obtained the sacred doctrine that he had previously not received, and they removed the doubts of all those who were listening. In a market street in eastern India, three yoginīs sang an adamantine song, whereby he actualized the meditative stability called Secret Adamantine Lamp, and his mind was filled with unsurpassed and uncontaminated bliss. In the middle of that town, he visited a temple where the sixty-two deities of Cakrasaṃvara were present within the network of energy channels inside the physical frame of the masters Kaṇhapāda and Kambalapāda.[18] It was in the evening of the tenth day of the month, when many ḍākinīs had gathered and were holding a communion feast offering. That evening, twenty-five yogins including Kaṇhapāda,[19] Avadhūtipa, and Śāntipā gathered there practicing ascetic discipline, alongside thirty-seven yoginīs headed by Cuṇḍā. They performed the communion feast offering of Cakrasaṃvara. Vajrasukhī also bestowed the meditative experience of physical bliss upon Venerable Marpa himself, and pristine cognition was generated within him. When morning had broken, the butter lamps were still alight. At that time, when the place was filled with light, the fragrance of perfume wafted, and the earth slightly shook, {135} the spiritual heroes and yoginīs of the twenty-four sacred abodes,[20] filling the entirety of space, spoke their adamantine verses and then returned to their own respective domains.

In general, this great translator Marpa is known to have trained under one hundred and twelve gurus including paṇḍitas and beggar yogins from the east, west, south, and north of India, and from Kashmir, Nepal, and so forth, as well as fifty gurus who were definitive lineage holders, thirteen who definitively changed his perception, and in particular five accomplished masters and two venerable ones without rival. Among them, the two without rival were Nāropā and Maitripā. The five accomplished masters were, in addition to them, Jñānagarbha, Kukuripā, and the ḍākinī Kadalīmañjarī. With regard to the thirteen who definitively changed his perception, he studied the cycles of *Mañjuvajra* under Lalitavajra of glorious Siṅghaladvīpa, *Cakrasaṃvara* under both Kosaripā and Riripā, *Yamāntaka* under black Samayavajra of Oḍiviśa, *Vajrāmṛta* under Jñānākara of Kashmir, *Buddhasamāyoga* under Devākarasiṃha, *Buddhakapāla* under Avijugata, who possessed extrasensory powers, *Catuḥpīṭha* under Phamtingpa, *The Ekajaṭīkalpa*[21] under Sendhapa, *The *Abhidānāmṛta*[22] under glorious Manakaśrī, and *Vajrayoginī* under the ḍākinīs Abhinandanamānasā and Sukhāṅkurā.[23]

When Marpa was about to return to Tibet, in the assembled rows of the thanksgiving feast-offering ceremony, Nāropā placed his hands on Marpa's head and sang a symbolic song, praying that they would meet again.

He was welcomed back in Tibet by Marpa Golek and others. Jetsun Chenpo Mila Repa also met him.[24] As an auspicious circumstance commemorating the perfection of the nine vehicles[25] and the blessings of the lineage, {136} Marpa had him build an octagonal nine-story tower with four truncated corners and a courtyard with a central chapel that resembled blazing gemstones. The consecration was performed in conjunction with the coming of age of his son Marpa Dode.[26]

Marpa then traveled to northern Uru to gather offerings of gold.[27] While performing a concluding rite after conferring empowerments at the residence of Golek, he had a dream in which three ḍākinīs intimated by way of prophecy that he should go again to India.[28] He set out, carrying gold that filled the skull of a sixteen-year-old brahmin girl and other offerings. On the way, he met Atiśa[29] and requested a spiritual connection with him. This was after glorious Nāropā had departed for the realm of the sky farers.[30] When he met the Phamtingwa brothers in Nepal, they said, "Since you are an adamantine disciple with steadfast commitments, and the guru is in his body of pristine cognition, it is certain that you will meet." When he reached the edge of a desolate plain, he was somewhat apprehensive, but in a restful dream a woman dressed in leaves appeared, and she instantly cast off the foliage of a tree trunk. When he felt himself riding upon that, he actually reached the other side of the plain. The woman then said, "In Tibet, is my elder brother Ḍombhi Heruka well?" "I don't know," he replied. "Now he is called Marpa Lotsāwa. Go on your way to India! There will be no obstacles!" And she vanished.

When Marpa reached India, the novice monk Prajñāsiṃha said, "The guru told us to entrust this to you," and he gave him a vajra and bell; a drawing of Hevajra; the volumes of the root tantras of *Cakrasaṃvara*, *Hevajra*, and *Guhyasamāja*; and the handle of a parasol with verses inscribed upon it.[31] Thereupon, he had a great desire to meet the guru, {137} and after performing a month-long communion feast offering, the novice monk said to him,

> I dreamed that on the great plain of desolation,
> I led a blind man and handed him to another,
> Who removed his defective vision
> And showed him the mirror of mind.
> You will certainly meet Nāropā.[32]

Marpa then visited Vajrāsana and so forth. Thereafter, in the presence of each of his gurus, he undertook a month-long communion feast offering, and all the prayers that they made were similar. Glorious Śāntibhadra said,

> I dreamed that the venerable and glorious Nāropā,
> With the gaze of a mighty elephant,
> From the sun and moon within his eyes,
> Sent forth rays of light to Tibet.
> You will certainly meet Nāropā.[33]

The ḍākinī Asthyābharaṇī[34] said,

> I dreamed that conches sounded from three mountain peaks
> And guided you from the confluence of three valleys.
> A lamp burning inside a vase
> Illuminated all of Jambudvīpa.
> You will certainly meet Nāropā.[35]

Lord Maitripā said,

> I dreamed that I fixed a jewel finial atop a victory banner
> And set out, having raised it above the birds that fly;
> A captain was sailing the ship.
> You will certainly meet Nāropā.[36]

Riripā said,

> Just as in the past the brahmin Bhadrika
> Accrued the provisions of merit
> And made aspiration prayers
> On behalf of the Dharmarāja of enlightened heritage,
> Establishing Kalyāṇa and Bhadra as witnesses,
> At this time also you will meet Nāropā.[37]

Kosaripā said,

> In the pure maṇḍala of the moon,
> At immovable Pullahari,
> Nāropā will reveal
> The nature of mind,
> The mirror of the buddha body of reality.[38]

Then, praying with devotion, Marpa went in search of the guru. Consequently, he saw Venerable Nāropā riding a lion, {138} supported by two women dancing momentarily on the sun and moon. While Marpa hesitated, a voice resounded from the sky, saying, "Look for him!"

The footprints of the guru were clearly arrayed on boulders and so forth. Marpa then saw someone in the guise of a yogin, but since he was in two minds, the yogin instantly departed through the forest. Then, when they did meet, Marpa presented a maṇḍala offering of gold, which the guru scattered, before departing who knows where. At that point the gold was again deposited upon that very maṇḍala offering without diminution.

Then, while Marpa was staying in a gorge, Nāropā appeared, cut the skull from a human corpse; disemboweled it; mixed the flesh, brains, and intestines, and so forth; stirred these with a rib as a spoon; and ate them. He was offered a spoonful but could not eat, whereupon Nāropā invisibly departed. Marpa tasted a sliver that had been swept to the side, such that an incomparable savor arose, and he expanded into meditative stability that lasted for a week.

Later, he saw a footprint that had appeared on a crystal rock, and in the middle of a footprint in the earth, there grew the stem of a red lotus. He also saw a handprint arrayed on a large square blue stone, and upon it a vajra of white sandalwood had been fastened, and so forth. Also the nine-deity emanational assemblage of Hevajra was present on the surface of a sandalwood tree. The eight-syllable wheel of Hevajra then appeared in the sand, resembling an upturned flower within the heart of the physical body of a yoginī, clear as crystal. He saw the imprints of the two feet of the guru in a crystal boulder, with combed hairs clearly discernible within and their warmth not yet faded.[39]

Then, when eight months had passed,[40] he actually met Nāropā and offered the golden maṇḍala. The guru's feet struck the ground, and the entire terrain turned to gold. {139} The master and disciple continued traveling together. On the road to Pullahari, ḍākinīs who were possessive of the sacred doctrine revealed all sorts of miracles to Marpa. He asked the master for protection, whereupon Venerable Nāropā placed his hands together at the heart and adopted a prayerful demeanor. Immediately, glorious Tilopā manifested in the sky in front, and with his magical gaze, he paralyzed the ḍākinīs who begged for forgiveness and vanished. Tilopā journeyed on to Pullahari with the master and disciple.[41]

Nāropā then said, "I will arrange a reception for my son who has arrived!" He looked in the sky and a fresh dead fish appeared. "Eat it!" he said, and when Marpa ate it, wondrous representations appeared, including a self-originated crystal image of Vārāhī and a stūpa, as well as limitless sacraments of communion and offering.[42]

When Nāropā conferred an empowerment, they actually met face-to-face with the representational nine deities forming the assemblage of Hevajra, along with the celestial palace that supported them. Emerging from the guru's heart, Sahajā Nairātmyā conferred the vase empowerment. The garland of the eight mantra syllables then emerged from her heart, entered through Marpa's mouth and dissolved into his heart. The guru then actually manifested, upright in the form of Heruka, and from the coalescent union of the male and female, a stream of nectar appeared. Drinking it, all the knots of Marpa's energy channels unraveled, and there arose the experience of radiance and emptiness that resembled a magical display. Padma Ḍākinī then conferred the empowerment of coemergent pristine cognition, such that Marpa's body and mind were filled with uncontaminated bliss, and he remained open for seven days in the continuum of that meditative stability. After that, he was introduced to the fourth empowerment, integrating meditative experience and realization.[43]

When they held a communion feast-offering ceremony in the charnel ground of Sosadvīpa, {140} Marpa saw glorious Nāropā rise up in the form of Cakrasaṃvara in male-female union. Within the maṇḍala of his body there appeared the infinite peaceful and wrathful deities of the way of Secret Mantra. The buddhas of the three times were present in the crown center. White Cakrasaṃvara in male-female union was present in the half-moon of the throat center. The twelve armor-clad male and female warriors were present in the two ears, and Four-Armed Mahākāla was present in the tiger-skirt. He bestowed upon Marpa the oral instructions of the profound Six Doctrines; *The Wish-Fulfilling Gem of the Aural Lineage*;[44] *The Fifteen Cycles of Instruction of the Mind Lineage*;[45] *The Four Scrolls of Essential Direct Guidance*[46] concerning the tantras of *Guhyasamāja*, *Hevajra*, *Catuḥpīṭha*, and *Mahāmāyā*; *The Four Scrolls of Esoteric Instruction*[47] concerning the network of energy channels, winds, energy centers, and so forth; *The Nonduality of Wind and Mind*;[48] *Wish-Fulfilling Gem: Guidance on Mind*;[49] and *The Instructions on Transference and Resurrection*,[50] which are particular attributes of the *Catuḥpīṭha*.

Then, after bestowing *The Hundred and Eightfold Garland of the Meditational Deity Red Lotus*,[51] Nāropā prophetically declared, "You, my son, and I will always be without meeting or parting. Even though the snare of my physical body is destroyed, I will come to welcome you. Later, on the isle of Harikasa, I will be born miraculously from a lotus, and on the southern mountain of Śrīparvata you will meet me, and then you will become one named Abhedaguptavajra (Indivisible Hidden Indestructible Reality). After completing your spiritual practice, you will attain supreme accomplishment, along with your entourage. Since you are appointed as my regent to tame the northern Land of Snows, you should return to Tibet and, for the benefit of sentient beings, turn the doctrinal wheel of the definitive essential meaning through your disciples and grand-disciples as long as the Buddhist teaching prevails. Consequently, you will confer maturational empowerment and liberating guidance on immeasurable disciples."

At that time, the earth, the sky, and all of space were pervaded by a symphony of music, the fragrance of incense, {140} a web of light rays, and a host of offering deities. The guru Nāropā, surrounded by an inconceivable number of heroes and yoginīs, ascended higher and higher and then departed in the manner of a sky farer. The venerable master Marpa fainted out of devotion, and when he awoke, all the torma offerings had been carried off by worldly ḍākinīs and a pack of carnivorous demons. He experienced overwhelming sadness since all his spiritual brothers and sisters had left separately. He continued to pray while staying in a dense acacia forest, whereupon Venerable Nāropā reappeared and sang an adamantine song condensing the Six Doctrines. In this manner, his sorrow was cleared away.

Marpa then approached Lord Maitripā. When the latter conferred empowerment, the fragrance of an exquisite perfume arose, and a lamp filled with merely a digit of pine oil and resin could last for seven days. Heroes and yoginīs of the three planes[52] invisibly intoned the sound of mantra, and when he was taking care of the torma offerings, he saw seven emanational red jackals actually take the tormas and so forth. Maitripā conferred blessings and prophecies upon him.

Marpa then approached glorious Śāntibhadra (Kukkuripā) who cut off the skull from the corpse of a woman that had been brought to the rows of the communion feast offering. Into that the urine of the guru was poured and mixed with the brains. This was then distributed, and, placed directly in front of Marpa, it boiled with fat. When Marpa looked at it, the seed syllables of the mantra of Mahāmāyā were present. He partook of that offering and thereby relished a supreme taste with a hundred flavors. His realization of the three yogas[53] became steady, without increase or decrease.

Marpa then approached glorious Jñānagarbha, but he disregarded a low-caste servant woman who brought him water. {142} Consequently, all the water in the pot became semen, and then, in conjunction with a yogic exercise, that woman secretly caused a stream of *rakta* (blood) to flow from the mouth of the ritual vase. Mixed with the semen, she poured it out, and when he partook of it, the experience of radiance and emptiness arose, resembling a magical display. Looking inside the vase, he beheld the faces of all the deities forming the assemblage of Guhyasamāja. Immediately after that, the guru arrived, introduced the meaning of the four empowerments, and then imparted instructions and subsequent instructions.

Marpa traveled on to Vajrāsana. That evening, there was an almighty noise, coinciding with a rākṣasa offering ceremony. When he looked out the next morning, there was a rākṣasa with a face sixteen handspans in height that had died. The people were afraid and unable to touch it, but Marpa resurrected it and carried it to a grave, such that he became indisputably renowned as an accomplished master.

He gathered together sacred representations that had been blessed and intended to build a stūpa to hold them, but at that moment a self-originated stūpa materialized. He then brought forth masks of the female deities and so forth fashioned of elephant hide. By praying to Maitripā, he averted a bandit who took pleasure in death. An emanational woman gave him a fruit, and on opening it, inside he saw the faces of the fifteen female deities forming the assemblage of Nairātmyā.

When Marpa was staying in Nepal, one night Venerable Maitripā traversed the sky riding a lion. He revealed to Marpa the symbols that can be illustrated by examples and taught him the sacred doctrine that cannot be exemplified. So it was that Marpa realized the meaning that transcends limitation.

Gradually he returned to Lhodrak. One night, he suddenly held a communion feast offering in the presence of female disciples of enlightened heritage, who were actually the nine female deities forming the assemblage of Hevajra, revealing themselves as women in human form. The first fruits of the offering had been exhausted, and there was nothing left but a little dried fish. {143} But at that very moment, the whole room was filled with food, drink, and offering sacraments that had not been previously seen. The earth and the sky were filled with the scent of incense, a symphony of music, songs, and so forth. The room was transformed into a celestial palace, and at its center the guru himself appeared as Hevajra, his wife as Nairātmyā, and the other ladies as the eight female deities, commencing with Gaurī. Countless heroes and yoginīs of the ten directions gathered, and they held a communion feast offering. At dawn the emanations dissolved.

By integrating together the three aspects of illusion,[54] he performed the rite of resurrection many times.[55] When Gyangro Zhangton requested him to perform a communion feast offering, he resurrected the corpse of a pigeon. At a seminary, when he was teaching the *Catuḥpīṭha*, he resurrected the corpse of a sparrow. In Drowolung, he resurrected the corpse of a deer. When he was invited to a teaching on the sacred doctrine, he resurrected the corpse of a lamb. On two occasions, he resurrected the corpse of a female yak that Ngok had offered him. In Lhodrak and Damzhung, he twice resurrected the corpse of a yak. In Jang, he resurrected a sheep and a pigeon that had been presented[56] as an offering to the college. In all these cases, the lama turned into the form of a corpse after undertaking a little meditative stability. Those creatures would rise up and then fly, hover, run, jump, or walk around, and so forth. Then, having achieved his purpose, those creatures would die, and the lama alone would stand up.

That great Lama Marpa opened all the vaults of the sacred doctrine and the oral instructions. He would teach by day and confer the profound empowerment of Nairātmyā while passing the time meditating by night. At dawn he would contemplate the auspicious coincidences of these nocturnal practices {144} and look upon his disciples from the disposition of inner radiance. He foresaw that Ngok would write a commentary on the *Hevajra Tantra*. He foresaw that Tsurton would refine consciousness transference, that Meton would apprehend inner radiance,[57] and that Mila would meditate on Inner Heat. To each of them Marpa granted blessed representations, sacramental substances, manuscripts, and so forth. He said to Ngok, "You should grasp this exegesis of the tantra in the manner of a river!" To Tsurton, he said, "You should accomplish the benefit of others through consciousness transference!" To Meton, he said, "You should grasp inner radiance!" And to Mila, he said, "You should frequent mountain hermitages and experientially cultivate the view and meditation!" He foreordained in dreams that the lineage of attainment would supremely flourish dependent on these four pillars.

On one occasion Marpa emanated in multiple bodies and acted for the benefit of those to be trained in different locations. He transformed his body into diverse meditational deities, and at the time when he performed the communion feast offering, all the sacramental substances were consumed but remained inexhaustible.

Marpa was also the translator of the tantras of the way of Secret Mantra and of many profound and secret doctrines of the generation and perfection stages that rely on them. He composed many treatises including *Authentic Valid Cognition of the Oral Teachings: A Commentary on Difficulties up to the Sixth Chapter of the First Part of the Hevajra Tantra*,[58] *The Sun of the Lesser Hevajra Tantra in One Hundred Thousand Lines*,[59] *The Vitality Tree of Pañjara*,[60] the fourfold scroll, the fifteen scrolls, *The Flowing Stream of Nectar concerning the Six Doctrines*,[61] and *The Esoteric Instructions of Evaṃ*.[62]

Then, on the fifteenth day of the twelfth lunar month in 1097 (female fire ox), in his eighty-sixth year, he told Dakmema that the aggregate of his adamantine body would dissolve. She, his female consort, then turned into a white light and vanished into the lama's heart. The lama entered into meditative equipoise, sitting upright, and immediately a triangular fragment of the skull above the anterior fontanelle of the central channel, along with its hair, flew into the air, about one armspan, {145} and then fell to the ground. Within it there were images of the five enlightened families of Hevajra formed of bone relic. Again, from the crown of his head a moonlike sphere of light shot into space. There was a shower of flowers and a symphony of music that permeated the entire valley of Lhodrak for thirty-seven days without interruption. When the sacred corpse was cremated, representations of buddha body, speech, and mind, along with pearl relics and so forth, extensively appeared. These were extracted by Ngok and installed in a silver reliquary.

The Disciples of Marpa Lotsāwa

This great lama had an infinite number of disciples. Among them were the four spiritual sons—namely, Ngokton Choku Dorje of Zhung, Tsurton Wang Nge of Dol, Meton Tsonpo of Tsangrong, and Marpa Goyak of Tsamlung. Mila Repa of Gungtang was the unique son who attained all-surpassing realization. The four devoted disciples were Lokya Tonpa, Barang Wabachen, Zhang Gyakharwa of Tsangrong, and Shugong Pele of Tamshul. The seven who were incidentally nurtured were Tsangpa Darye of Penyul, Rasang Gompa, Marpa Jazewa, Dampa Lhare of Lhome, Pukyetsek of Yarlung, Gya Tingdzin Zangpo Chingtuwa, and Metson Chung.

Jetsun Mila Repa Dorje Gyeltsen

Mila, the mighty lord of yoga, was the one to whom the oral teachings of Lama Marpa's lineage of attainment descended. He was the greatest of saintly beings, unrivaled in his attainment of the body of pristine cognition, who, in a single lifetime and in a single physical body mastered the uncontaminated adamantine buddha body, the immaculate buddha speech, and the unchanging buddha mind. He was born in 1040 (iron male dragon) at a place called Tsa, which was part of Koron, one of the five small valleys of lower Gungtang.[63] He belonged to the Khyungpo clan, his father was Mila Sherab {146} Gyeltsen, and his mother was Nyangza Kargyen. He was given the name Topaga.[64]

His father suddenly died, and all the family wealth was stolen by his uncle and aunt, such that he was extremely oppressed. Under the translator Len Chung, his hair was tonsured as a novice, and he studied writing, reading, and the cycle of Vajrapāṇi. Then his mother said, "Go to Utsang and train in sorcery! You must destroy these enemies!" So she prepared the necessary provisions. He set out for the residence of Nyak Yungton Trogyel of Yarlung who at that time had a great reputation for sorcery. He studied a little there, but when the requisite signs of success in sorcery did not manifest, he requested not to go home, and so he was instead sent to the residence of Lharje Nubchung in Tsangrong.[65] The latter granted Mila the rites of wrathful mantra in the form of Red and Black-Faced Rāhula, whom he then propitiated. From the fourteenth day, authentic signs of accomplishment arose. Lharje also said, "It is certain that you will have this occult power because the doctrinal protectors are extremely grateful." And he held a thanksgiving ceremony. In his native land, thirty-five of his enemies simultaneously died. He then requested many sacred teachings from Nubchung, including *The Net of Magical Emanation*.[66]

Mila's mother sent a letter saying he should now bring forth a hailstorm, so he returned to the residence of Yungton. The latter granted him *The Rite of Large Hailstone Agitation*,[67] which was of Shaivite origin, and he practiced that. After some fourteen days had passed, the charms made a thunderous rumbling in their pit, there was a flash of lightning, and so forth. Coinciding with that period of stormy weather, Mila returned to his native land with the assistance of a powerful servant of the master, and he caused large hailstones to fall upon the gorges throughout all the valleys.

After that, he returned to the residence of Nubchung. {147} Although his heart was exclusively mindful of the sacred doctrine, he was unable to request teachings, whereupon the lama said, "We have both accrued great negativity. Now it will be best for you to practice the sacred doctrine." He sent Mila to the residence of Dreton Lhaga in Rong, where he studied the Great Perfection and meditated a little but did not develop much aptitude. The lama then said, "Nowadays there is one called Marpa Lotsāwa, a disciple of Venerable Nāropā and Maitripā, who resides at Lhopu Chukhyer. They say that he is one who can introduce the original nature of mind after arranging auspicious circumstances in the physical body. You should go there!"

Mila then set out with faith and great joy, simply through hearing Marpa's name. The night before he was due to arrive, Venerable Marpa saw in a dream a slightly stained vajra fashioned of beryl gems that it seemed his guru Nāropā had given him. He washed it and raised it on top of a victory banner, such that its light permeated all directions.

Mila's perception changed simply on seeing Marpa's face. The field that Marpa had him plow after their initial meeting was later known as the Harmonious Condition. Mila said, "I offer my body, speech, and mind—all three—and I request food, clothing, and the sacred doctrine." Marpa replied, "It has to be one or the other." "Please grant me the sacred doctrine alone!" he requested.

Mila then went begging for alms, and with the first fruits of those provisions, he bought a small copper pot with four handles and offered it to the lama, who said, "This is an auspicious circumstance." In accordance with the lama's orders, he caused severe hailstones to fall upon the Layakpa.[68] Meton Tsonpo of Tsangrong then presented a large subvention, and, on that basis, the lama wished to commission a collection of thirty sūtras and incantations and build a nine-story tower. As an auspicious circumstance that would purify Mila's obscurations, accomplish the four rites of pacification, enrichment, subjugation, and wrath,[69] {148} and reach the pinnacle of the nine vehicles, he said, "Since you are a hard worker, you should build a tower to be named after my son Dode." At first, all by himself, he constructed a round tower on the hillside, but when he had built just two stories, the lama told him to demolish it. Then, he built a semicircular tower and a triangular tower, but he was also told to demolish these. Finally, he was told to build an octagonal nine-story tower with four truncated corners, a finial that resembled blazing gemstones, and a central shrine with a circumambulatory walkway. Mila then laid the foundation of this tower of present-day Sekhar.[70] Once he had finished the seventh story, he was encouraged to build the circumambulatory walkway, but still Marpa did not bestow the sacred doctrine upon him. After carrying earth and rocks continuously, three sores opened on his back, constantly exuding pus, blood, and serum. On the month when others requested empowerment, he squeezed into the room but was expelled from the rows of those receiving the empowerments and beaten severely. Using each minor circumstance as a pretext, Marpa scolded him greatly. He was disappointed seven times, but his faith never waned for an instant. He then sought Lady Dakmema's help to request the sacred doctrine. He let her see the sores on his back, but he was set to work on the annex. Again he labored, such that the wounds were inflamed and aggravated, and the pain became unbearable. At Lady Dakmema's request, he was allowed to rest for some days, and then again, at the lama's insistence, he resumed work. Lady Dakmema, undaunted, sent him to the residence of Ngok Choku Dorje[71] with some blessed representations and a forged letter with the lama's seal. Although Ngok granted him oral instructions, no particular meditative experiences arose because it had not been sanctioned by the lama. He again approached the lama, along with Ngok, on the occasion of the coming-of-age ceremony for Marpa's son Darma Dode, {149} but the lama strongly rebuked Ngok and Lady Dakmema, saying that the exposure of the sacred gifts and the oral instructions was very bad. Mila was in despair, but when Lady Dakmema informed the lama that he was on the verge of committing suicide, Marpa said, "Let him come, since Apho

Tuchen (Old Mister Sorcerer) is now the chief guest to be called!" Since circumstances had changed, Mila approached, wondering if this were true. The lama then said, "Now if I analyze these matters, I am entirely without fault. If I had been able to provoke you nine times to great despair, liberation would have come to you simply by my imparting of the oral instructions. But now you will require great diligence, and thereafter liberation will easily ensue." Joyfully he took Mila into his following, and Mila's happiness was immeasurable. Immediately after that, his hair was tonsured, and the name Dorje Gyeltsen was conferred on him, owing to Marpa's former dream. Marpa then bestowed upon him the vows of refuge and setting of the mind on enlightenment.

At the time when Marpa conferred upon him empowerment in the maṇḍala of Cakrasaṃvara, he said, "That is the maṇḍala of illustrative symbols. This is the maṇḍala of illustrated meaning." Then he pointed toward space, where in the sky Mila saw that maṇḍala of the sixty-two deities forming the assemblage of Cakrasaṃvara was actually present, along with their celestial palace. At the time when the secret name was conferred upon him, the heroes and ḍākinīs of the three planes who filled the sky in unison named him Zhepei Dorje (Indestructible Reality of Laughter). Even when the two higher empowerments were conferred, he manifestly received them. That is to say, during those two empowerments, he beheld the symbolic pristine cognition, so he said that he acquired supreme realization of the nature of mundane phenomena. Starting from then, he received the tantras of *Hevajra*, *Mahāmāyā*, *Catuḥpīṭha*, *Buddhakapāla*, and *Guhyasamāja*, along with the commentaries on those tantras, {150} their empowerments, and means for attainment. He also received maturational empowerment and liberating guidance on the two stages of meditation; the essential cycles that reveal the conclusive truth; and in particular the aural lineage of the ḍākinīs and the distinctive practices of intermingling, consciousness transference, and essential reincarnation.[72]

Marpa filled him to the brim with all the other oral instructions, and then sent him to meditate in the mountain hermitage of Nyanya in Lhodrak.[73] On one occasion, in a dream he saw an appearance of his homeland, so he was saddened. Since he wished to go there, he went to ask for permission, but at that time the sun rose above the tower and above the lama's head through the window. The lama was asleep, and Lady Dakmema was bringing in the morning meal. Alongside his pillow, Mila then offered the spiritual song titled "Going Up to Tsang".[74] The lama said, "If you are to go, I will permit you to do so, but because you arrived here when I was asleep, we will not meet again in the future. Even so, since the sun is rising above the tower and above my head, you will illuminate the Buddhist teaching in general and the teaching of the Kagyu lineage in particular. Since Dakmema is bringing food, this is an auspicious coincidence, suggesting that you will be sustained by meditative stability."[75]

Mila saw that the lama's physical body had infinite attributes of greatness—he could, for example, change into the body of Cakrasaṃvara, Hevajra, Guhyasamāja, and so forth; practice the miraculous consummation of the earth element and so forth; and perform the rites of resurrection. Accordingly, he had actually determined the lama to be a perfect buddha. The lama then said, "I have given the oral instructions to you, and I have given them to others. As the saying goes, 'If these were weighed on the scales, yours would not be much more than thrice theirs.'" With these words, he entrusted the Buddhist teaching to Mila and accompanied him for a short distance as far as Cholha. Placing his hands upon Mila's head, Marpa recited prophecies and benedictions.

Mila then made parting prostrations to Ngok and set out for his native land, {151} where it was as he had seen it in his dream, so he was especially grieved. First he undertook meditation in Kangtsuk Cave, subsisting on the price of his own field.[76] Then he went to Drakar Taso[77] and meditated one-pointedly for three years, subsisting just on the impure residue of flour, which was all that he had, and for six years subsisting on nothing but nettle broth. However, there was no evident benefit. Hearing of his whereabouts, his sister Peta and his betrothed Dzese both offered him a load of roasted barley flour, barley beer, and meat, and due to that, his physical condition underwent some degree of improvement. At that time, he inspected a scroll that the lama Marpa had given him. It was an oral instruction concerning the nonduality of vital energy and mind, and on the basis of that he did make progress. There, he sought the bliss of the physical body through the essential method of the crouching posture.[78] He sought the bliss of verbal articulation through the unraveling of the bondage of the knot of speech, and he sought the bliss of mind through the loosening[79] of the serpentine knot of past actions. By meditating in this manner, he naturally reversed the generative fluid upward, unraveled the knot of the energy channel in the genitals, and mastered the first and second levels. Then, by persevering with this practice for about one year, he unraveled the knot of the energy channel in the navel.[80]

On one occasion, during that period when he was meditating at Lingwei Drak, a miracle associated with the ogress of the rocks occurred.[81] Of this he himself also said, "O lamas! Her rasping sound[82] was the vital breath. Her luminosity was the fire of the descending purgative wind. There was a harsh sensation indicative of these two winds being roughly restrained. Consequently, her circumambulating of me in a clockwise direction indicated that the sensory elements had gathered through the left-side channel. When she nudged me with the point of her elbow and then departed who knows where, this indicated that the potency of the white vital essence above at the crown of the head had descended through the central channel.[83] When she seized my left leg by the big toe, that indicated that the power of the fire of Inner Heat had ignited, such that the generative fluid could be retained without leakage. The interval when she became invisible {152} indicated that it had stabilized at the lower extremity of the central channel."

Then, he journeyed to Drakmar Chonglung and so forth.[84] Thereafter, he went down to undertake a circuit of Tsa, reflecting that a group of six monks and laypeople including Shen Dormo would come that winter to request the sacred doctrine. He went carrying only a few provisions, and that night there was a heavy snowfall. The road could not be opened until the fifth month in late spring. His disciples made offerings there, thinking he had died and with the aim of making meritorious funeral donations. The springtime pastoralists went out, thinking they would find a corpse or skeleton. A watchman saw a snow leopard from Phabongka, and then they saw smoke, heard his voice, and went inside the cave where they saw that his body was radiant and his provisions only slightly depleted, so they knew that he had been sustained by meditative stability, and an unsurpassed faith arose within them. They insisted on inviting him to their home. On the ground where he was welcomed, he trampled over rocks as if they were mud. At that time, he had unraveled the knot of the energy channels at the heart center and mastered the sixth level. He himself said, "Bliss is the descent of the stream of generative essence from above. Bliss is being filled from below with the pure vital essence. Bliss ensues due to the playful encounter of the white and red generative essences in the middle!"

At the time when he stayed in the cave of Zawo Phuk in the uplands of Rala, there was a young boy of that locality in whom faith arose simply at the sight of his face. He attended some sessions of doctrinal teaching and later followed him as a servant, touching his head at the master's feet. Mila bestowed upon him the vows of refuge and setting the mind on enlightenment, along with the empowerment of Cakrasaṃvara and oral instructions on the Great Seal and the Six Doctrines. He was encouraged to meditate, and wore a single cotton robe because the inconceivable warmth of bliss arose within him. He was renowned to all by the name of Rechungpa.[85] {153} Later, he traveled to India, sent by the lama Mila Repa to obtain the four remaining *Doctrinal Cycles of Nirdehaḍākinī*.[86] There, he studied limitless oral instructions under Tebupa,[87] Siddhirajñi, and the Newar Yerangpa. Tebupa sent as a present to Jetsun Chenpo Mila Repa a walking staff of black eaglewood and so forth. During this sojourn in India, Venerable Mila Repa at all times observed Rechungpa within a crystal stūpa. When a heretical teacher offered him many oral instructions that were both harmful and beneficial, the master saw that he had been engulfed by a windstorm. It is said that Rechungpa later had misconceptions and so forth concerning Mila Repa and that these were indeed due to that association with the heretic.[88]

Mila Repa went to welcome him from Peltang. On the way, there was a shower of hailstones, whereupon for shelter the master entered through the artifice of agility into the narrow space within the horn of a yak. Even Rechungpa's hand or head would not fit within it. Since the supreme instructions had been brought forth by the ḍākinīs—and in order to avert Rechungpa's increasing lack of faith because he, Jetsun Mila Repa, had burned the pith instructions of the heretic—Jetsun then revealed the gurus of the root lineage on the crown of his head, a golden stūpa with offering deities upon his tongue, and the nine emanational deities forming the assemblage of Hevajra at his heart. He rode boulders of meteorite as if they were horses, and trampled them like clay. He made them surge up like water, and fired them like an arrow. Finally, making his cotton robe into wings, he flew into the sky and alighted on the summit of Drakmar Chongding.[89] So it was that Rechungpa's faith completely reverted to its original state. He touched his feet at the central emanational head of Jetsun's three buddha bodies and begged forgiveness, such that those former misconceptions vanished and the master and disciple dwelled as before. {154} The lama then prayed, and all nine doctrinal cycles of the ḍākinīs fell to them intact, giving rise to overwhelming faith in Rechungpa, who thereafter attended upon him inseparably.

Furthermore, Mila Repa tamed the supplicant Darma Wangchuk by not sinking in water. He taught a dog and a deer to act like a mother and daughter. Also, at the time when the lamas first stayed in Sengdeng Forest, and specifically at the time when they competed with one another, the array of his body also entered into union with a low-caste girl and gave rise to the first three delights in reliance on that lowly individual. Then, looking into a mirror, he recognized the coemergent delight. He could dissolve into space and dissolve the three appearances in inner radiance.[90]

Again, at the time when he was residing at Chonglung Rock, the array of his physical body could even wear the sun and moon as garments, indicating that he had integrated the blazing and dripping of generative essences within the central channel of the subtle body. The skull of flowers in his hand indicated that he had gathered the nectar of pure essence. The parasol and victory banner on his right and left sides indicated that he had gathered the winds of the right and left channels within the central channel. His riding a lion and departing into the sky indicated that he had drawn the pure essences to the crown of his head. His becoming invisible indicated that his illusory body had entered into inner radiance.

Also, at that time when he resided at Chuwar,[91] the array of his visible physical body transformed into the five winds, manifesting as an ocean indicative of water, a conflagration indicative of fire, a sword indicative of air, a mountain indicative of earth, and a poisonous snake indicative of space.[92] He also sat cross-legged on the point of a spear and transformed into the eleven winds of pristine cognition at the lower end of the central channel.[93] The gem indicated that he had dissolved bliss into the central channel by pursuing the white and red vital essences. On those occasions, he demonstrated the method of reversing upward the vital essences, which could not in the slightest be impeded.[94]

Later, in his seventy-third year, in 1112 (water male dragon), {155} when he was residing at Chuwar without wavering from the meditative equipoise in the disposition where the real nature of all things is inner radiance, as soon as the midnight hour had passed on the evening of the eighth day of the first summer month, certain phenomena manifested as a miraculous sign. This was an auspicious coincidence associated with the refinement of the energy channels and winds of the throat center. That is to say, from the severing of the knots of the energy channels of the five seed syllables—LĀṂ, MĀṂ, PĀṂ, TĀṂ, and VĀṂ—at the throat center, five female carnivore demons manifested. From the severing of the knots of the subsidiary channels that divide therefrom, an army of gods and demons and a host of yakṣas and ogres manifested, brandishing various weapons, and formless beings stretched out their hands.[95] Plants and forests swayed; earth, stones, mountains, and rocks were disturbed; the sky changed; and there were earthquakes and so forth. All these signs indicated that after the severing of the knots, the wind that had entered into the energy channels had separated the chyle and the residue of the elements.[96] When, from that, the elements had been drawn within, there was a red jackal-faced demon dripping blood that gulped an ocean.[97] When this wind entered the central channel, a laughing skeletal woman raised Mount Meru onto her lap. When the chyle and the residue of the white and red generative essences separated, an extremely terrifying female form of Yama clashed the sun and moon together as cymbals. When the refined elements of the minor channels gathered in the central channel, an athletic charcoal-black woman caused the planets and stars to fall to the earth. When, derived from that, he experienced the bliss of melting, a beautiful and smiling goddess acted seductively. From the wind of the earth element, the four directions were encircled by a trench. From the wind of the fire element, the sky was dense with fire. From the wind of the water element, the terrain was filled with water. From the wind of the wind element, the four intermediate directions were guarded by strongmen. When the aforementioned five syllables disintegrated, there was a discordant roaring sound and other such experiences of the elements being absorbed. {156}

Since Mila Repa initially did not recognize these signs, he sang a spiritual song of supplication to the lama Marpa and the deity Cakrasaṃvara and remained equipoised in contemplation. Consequently, those seemingly terrifying phenomena recurred, and he heard an unpleasant song prophesying obstacles. Therefore, he clarified his realization and comprehended the confidence of fearlessness. Singing "The Spiritual Song of Confidence,"[98] he offered gifts of his flesh and blood to those that appeared as gods and demons and explained the sacred doctrine by singing a song of profound meaning, such that they begged for forgiveness and promised to obey him. Paying homage at the feet of Jetsun Mila Repa, they then vanished.

Again, his vital essences became clear, increased in power, and became upwardly stable to some extent, but before he could become attached to that, he blocked the experience of contaminated delight, as a sign of which, the aforementioned five female carnivore demons turned into five worldly ḍākinīs and served him the yogurt of a wild musk deer with a ladle of lapis lazuli. They laid out extensive offerings, each of them offered a common accomplishment, and then they requested the vows that set the mind on supreme enlightenment.

Again, later that same month, those ḍākinīs arrived, assuming the appearance of young girls, and offered him their vital heart mantras. Focusing on the awareness of the female deity Kurukullā, he conferred upon them the vows of the awareness holders. Later still, those ḍākinīs returned and asked him questions. Knowing that they were worthy recipients, he laid out a maṇḍala of their jewels, along with offerings, and conferred on them the blessing of Sahajā. In terms of the view, he established them in the Middle Way. In terms of meditation, he trained them sequentially in the essentials of the generation and perfection stages. In terms of conduct, he differentiated the essentials of the liberating passageways in the intermediate state after death. {157} He entrusted them with the instructions of the aural lineage, the secret oral teachings. Through their offerings of enjoyment, they became mudrās that pleased the guru and facilitated an increase in his experience of self-consecration. Thereupon, the energy center of perfect resource in his throat was filled with pure essence, such that he obtained the realization of the eighth level.[99]

At the time when he bestowed the empowerment of the thirteen-deity assemblage of Cakrasaṃvara on the peerless Gampopa, and so forth, he said, "I, the aged Mila, cannot get up. O vase, you should go yourself and confer the empowerment!" So the ritual vase quickly rose up into the sky and conferred the empowerment.

Rechungpa requested him to consecrate a painting of Vajravārāhī, so he said, "The being of pristine cognition will be present in this being of commitment. It will accept this flower at the feast!" Accordingly, the deity of pristine cognition actually arrived and vanished into the cotton painting. When Rechungpa bowed his head to the painted image, it actually took the flower.

How could the array of such miraculous abilities possibly be explained! Coinciding with these events, the knot of the energy center of his forehead unraveled, such that he became a mighty lord of the tenth level. Finally, he unquestionably became a mighty lord of the twelfth level, and yet it was said that from the perspective of discipline, there were still two remaining levels left to achieve. It is therefore held that he journeyed from this life to the buddha field of Abhirati and was thoroughly purified there. Having lived until his eighty-fourth year, he demonstrated the passing of his physical body at Drin, in 1123 (water female hare).

Even after Mila Repa had passed into nirvāṇa, Rechungpa arrived there at Drin in Chuwar and was manifestly welcomed by him. Afterward, when Rechungpa approached the site of the cremation, the fire ignited of its own accord within the cremation chamber, and in the midst of that, with one hand, Mila Repa pressed down the flames. {158} With the other one, he supported the side of his face while singing a spiritual song. Then, again, his body became a corpse. The sacred bones became a mass of pearl relics, which then disappeared. The offerings of the gods and ḍākinīs could not be embraced by the intellect.

The Disciples of Mila Repa

At the time of his passing, the great accomplished master, Venerable Mila Repa, had four heart sons, eight close sons, six later disciples, and one unequaled lineage holder. The first four were Nyenchung Repa of Gungtang, Ngendzong Repa of Chimlung, Drigom Repa of Tamo, and Sera Repa of Dotra. The second group of eight were Repa Zhiwa-o, Repa Sangye Kyab, Repa Tsayuwa, Repa Dorje Wangchuk, Shengom Repa, Rongchung Repa, Kharchung Repa, and Lengom Repa. The third group of six were Ligor Charuwa, Orton Gedun, Kyoton Shakgu, Dampa Gyakphuwa, Seban Tonchung, and Dreban Tashi. The one constituting the fourth group was the peerless Dakpo Rinpoche (Gampopa).[100]

Gampopa Sonam Rinchen

The one who, here in Tibet, acted as a second Teacher with regard to the teaching of the quintessential meaning is renowned in the world as Jetsun Gampopa the Great. Venerable Marpa said of him, "That wild one will have a disciple. He will be matchless."[101]

In antiquity, he had been the bodhisattva Supuṣpacandra during the time when the tathāgata Ratnapadmacandraviśuddhyabhyudgatarāja[102] was preaching the Buddhist teaching. Then, he subsequently became the bodhisattva Candraprabhakumāra, who in the presence of Śākyamuni pledged to risk his life and uphold *The Sūtra of the King of Meditative Stability* during the degenerate age. {159} At that time, the Teacher had said, "When you uphold the sūtras, I myself will assist you." Lamas say that Candraprabhakumāra later became Venerable Gampopa and that Mahāmuni became glorious Phakmodrupa.[103] There is also a prophetic declaration concerning him that is found in *The Sūtra of Compassion's White Lotus*, which says,

> Ānanda, in the future, after I have passed away, there will appear in the northern region a monk named Jīvaka, who acted above

> all in the service of the conquerors of the past. Having venerated many hundreds of thousands of buddhas, he will plant the roots of virtuous action, engage in the Great Vehicle, become erudite, maintain the scriptural collection of the bodhisattvas, praise the Great Vehicle, and correctly teach the Great Vehicle.[104]

Gampopa's birthplace was Nyelgyi Bunyi, and he was born into the Nyiwa clan in 1079 (earth female sheep).[105] His father was Nyiwa Gyelpo, his mother Shomoza Tsecham, and he was the second of their three sons, named Darma Kyab. Having been instructed many times by masters from India, China, Nepal, and Tibet, he conclusively mastered *The Eight Branches of Medical Science*[106] and brought inconceivable benefit to living beings. He married a lady, and they had two children, a boy and a girl, and he lived as a householder. Even so, he continued to attend upon Geshe Sharawa and others, and he became an erudite person, endowed with the attributes of excellence. In his thirty-second year, his wife and all the children died, so he despaired. He received the three stages of monastic ordination simultaneously from Geshe Shawa Lingpa {160} and was given the name Sonam Rinchen. As an exemplary monk, under that same master, he studied the treasury of monastic discipline and so forth. He also studied *Cakrasaṃvara*, *Vajravārāhī*, and so forth under Geshe Maryulwa Loden Sherab, and *The Sequence of the Path*[107] under Geshe Gyayondak and Nyukrumpa, and he experientially cultivated these practices. He requested pith instructions on meditative concentration from master Jangchub Sempa, and by cultivating these, a meditative stability arose that did not fade for about thirteen days. He always kept to secluded hermitages and devoted himself diligently to contemplation alone.[108]

At that time, Gampopa's mind was inspired by the words of three emanational beggars who made aspiration prayers respectively concerning their desire for food and drink, a rebirth like that of King Tsede,[109] and the renunciation of Venerable Mila. And he resolved to meet Mila.[110] Thereupon, he also experienced portents in his dreams, indicating that his renown would permeate the world and that he would establish innumerable disciples in the maturational empowerments and liberating guidance of the nectar contained in *The Sequence of the Path* of the Kadampas and the oral instructions of the precious Kagyu lineage.

Jetsun the Great Mila Repa also said to his entourage, "Last night, in my dream, there was in my hand a crystal vase full of nectar, from the midst of which a monk appeared and poured it into a silver pot and then went off. This lineage of mine will be maintained not by cotton-clad yogins, but it will be maintained by mendicants." And he also said, "How wonderful will be this gathering of tulkus in my entourage!"[111]

Gampopa then traversed the road in one and a half months at the speed of a donkey and reached Jetsun Mila, who was residing at Trode Tashigang in Chuwar.[112] The lama said, "Cotton-clad yogins should welcome him, playing ḍāmaru drums and thigh-bone trumpets. Upa Tonpa, whoever acts as a go-between when he meets me will not be reborn in the lower realms."[113] {161}

Immediately after they met, Jetsun sang the spiritual song of reception that begins with the words, "That milk of the white lioness of the east."[114] He handed him a leftover skull cup full of barley beer, and Gampopa drank it, such that there was no remainder. In this way, the auspicious coincidence was arranged whereby the lineage would be maintained and the oral instructions perfected. At first, Mila said, "I will confer the blessing of my tradition." He then conferred the four empowerments simultaneously, including those of symbolic relative truth and those of symbolic ultimate truth, relying on a vermilion maṇḍala, and brought him to maturation. Gampopa mentioned all the modes of meditative stability that he had, but Mila said, "Simply through those, you will not progress at all. You should cultivate my oral instruction of the Short Syllable A, Inner Heat, and, as of tomorrow, only now will you come to see the essential nature of mind."[115]

Gampopa then asked him what are the great means[116] for accruing the provisions of merit and so on, and he replied, "Great are those who experientially cultivate the oral instructions revealed by the lama in the appropriate manner. In general, you should be in harmony with those who experientially cultivate meditation. You should act as one who has renounced this life and long-term deliberations. You must be one who does not succumb to the four lapses into emptiness.[117] If you do not determine the fundamental basis of mind, you will experience bliss, radiance, and nonconceptuality, but merely through that you will not pass beyond the three planes of existence. It is vital to follow a lama who holds the lineage. Rest in the disposition of the innate and uncontrived state!"[118]

Having received the instructions concerning Inner Heat, he meditated, and consequently, after seven days, the blissful warmth ignited of its own accord. Exerting himself again, he meditated, and consequently, on the morning of the seventh day, he beheld the faces of the buddhas of the five enlightened families. He mentioned this to the lama, who said, "You have gained control of the five external elements. That is neither negative nor positive." Having applied himself like that for three months, he spun around[119] like the wheel of the trichiliocosm, vomited, and fainted. During the fainting spell, the winds of both the right- and left-side channels entered into the central channel. {162}

One morning, the entire sky was filled with Mahākāruṇika, above each of his heads there was a moon disk, and the vital essence increased in his actual crown center.[120] During one evening session, he perceived the black line indicative of the hells, and consequently, he developed a severe heart and wind disorder, so he shortened his meditation belt and controlled the upward-moving wind. The six classes of the gods of the world system of desire then caused a cascade of nectar to fall down from above, and he was quenched. Without thirst, the vital essences of his right- and left-side channels increased in the energy center of the throat and he blocked the lower opening of the central channel.[121]

One month after he had been given these yogic exercises, his body trembled, became agitated, and shook uncontrollably. His heart center was filled with vital essence, and the sun and moon were both eclipsed by Rāhu, and then Rāhu appeared as a subtle horse tail while the winds of the right- and left-side channels entered into the central channel.[122]

One month after that, he beheld the maṇḍala of red Hevajra, and at the navel center, the blood that derived from his mother increased. He beheld the maṇḍala of skeletal deities in the assemblage of Cakrasaṃvara according to Lūipa, and the emanational energy center of the navel was filled with white vital essence. Within his body, which was the extent of space, he beheld sentient beings of the six classes drinking milk, and some drank what was said to be the milk of the constellations. At all times, there was a sound resembling thunder.[123] Within the inconceivable thousands of minor energy channels of his body, the vital essence was conducted by the vital energy of past actions.[124]

Then, after he had been granted the instructions concerning the supreme Inner Heat, he meditated, and consequently, the valley of Chuwar was filled with smoke. That afternoon, his darkness withered and was dispelled by removing the blockages of a thousand apertures. It seemed that the ends of many channels were joined within the skeleton of his own body, and the harsh wind passed through them.

After one month, he first beheld the seven sibling buddhas of medicine.[125] {163} He was then capable of passing a single day with a single exhalation and inhalation of breath, and when he exhaled, the vision of the buddhas of medicine would vanish. Then, by holding his breath in the afternoon, he beheld the infinite fields of the buddha body of perfect resource. When he was distracted by that and relaxed his breathing, it was late evening. When he held his breath at dawn, he beheld the deeds of Śākyamuni, foremost of the thousand and two buddhas.[126]

Gampopa reported these visions to Mila Repa, who said, "Now, without respite, you have already beheld both the buddha body of perfect resource and the buddha body of emanation. From now on, you are to behold the buddha body of reality, and then you may go off to U. I have cleared those passageways of old. For the passageway of the extrasensory powers that you will now approach,[127] secrecy is important. In general, you should keep secret all enlightened attributes. Since you are endowed with the substantial strength of sharp faculties, you will not be harmed by Māra. Practice one-pointedly, behold the essential nature of mind, and after acquiring stability in that, nurture your group of followers! Since your energy channels and winds are pliable, you will obtain miraculous powers, such as emanation and transformation, and all the supreme and common spiritual accomplishments. Your title will indeed be The Vajra-Holding Monk, Renowned in the World."[128]

One evening at twilight, he undertook the meditation and recitation of the meditational deity. At midnight, he cultivated guru yoga, and at dawn he cultivated breath control, after which he had forty-two wondrous dreams during a single period of sleep. He reported this to Jetsun, who interpreted their symbolic meaning and made the following prophetic declaration:[129]

> (1) Your wearing of a white hat on the head means that the vehicle or the view will be all-embracing. (2) The Chinese silk indicates the profound and subtle reality. (3) The beautiful fur indicates that the philosophical systems will be completely perfect, without intermingling.[130] (4) The vulture feathers indicate the highest view, that of the Great Seal. (5) The shoes indicate the ascent of your conduct. (6) The swelling indicates the spontaneously present fruit of the three buddha bodies. (7) The ring indicates your pure decorum and ethical discipline. {164} (8) The robe indicates

that your own mind is stainless and flawless. (9) The golden belt indicates that you will have unchanging and noble aspirations. (10) The vermilion dot indicates that your great love for the sake of living beings will be effortlessly present. (11) The waistband indicates that you will possess the pristine three vows. (12) The flower ornament indicates that you will guide confident disciples. (13) The felt indicates that you will definitively realize the immaculate buddha body of reality. (14) Your inaction indicates that reality is free from fabrication and contrivance. (15) The ball of yarn indicates that immutable truth. (16) The staff indicates that you will voluntarily be favored by lamas. (17) The enlightened attributes indicate that you will perfect all enlightened attributes, including the seven precious things themselves. (18) The handle indicates that you will bestow the nectar of the aural lineage. (19) The holding of the skull cup in the right hand indicates that you will traverse many buddha fields. (20) The skull cup indicates that all phenomena are essentially emptiness. (21) Its nectarous contents indicate the experience of great bliss. (22) The golden color indicates your complexion is clear, radiant, and unsullied. (23) The drinking bowl indicates that these three—skull, contents, and color—are together. (24) The carrying of it in the left hand indicates that you will be inseparable from meditative experiences. (25) The ornate shoulder bag indicates that whatever appears will arise as the path. (26) The dance steps indicate that you will integrate method and discriminative awareness. (27) The sustenance indicates the fruit of deathless meditative concentration. (28) The antelope hide indicates unwavering and unconfused mindfulness. (29) Its intact head and four hooves indicate that you will guide living beings with compassion. (30) Its use as your seat indicates that emptiness and compassion are inseparable. (31) The pasture indicates that your outer and inner attributes will be extensive. (32) The feeding of calves and lambs indicate that you will fulfill the hopes and wishes of living beings. (33) The herder indicates that you will protect unprotected beings with compassion. (34) The meadow indicates the uncontaminated, coemergent delight. (35) The flowers indicate that the signs of warmth will blaze without limitation. (36) The woman indicates the gathering of the ḍākinīs of pristine cognition. (37)

> The yellow flower indicates the gathering of the monastic community endowed with knowledge and liberation. (38) The lotus seat[131] indicates that your awareness will not abide in phenomenal existence.[132] (39) The fountain indicates that your dominion of the sacred doctrine will flourish. (40) The light indicates that the pure doctrine will appear in Tibet and Kham. (31) The fire indicates the pristine cognition of blissful warmth, the Inner Heat. {165} (42) The rising of the sun and moon in the heart indicates that inner radiance neither comes nor goes.

He continued,

> Now, you should go to U and meditate! You should not associate with people in whom the three poisons flourish. You should act with great care. Be calm and disciplined, with few irritations, and in harmony with all. You should be scrupulously clean, have few conceptual thoughts, and pass your time in silence, sealed off in mountain retreat. Even though you recognize your own mind as the buddha, you should train so as not to abandon the view that the lama is Vajradhara. Even though the accumulations and renunciations are both pure right where they are, you should accumulate the provisions of merit from the smallest upward. Even though the fruits of past actions are pure like space, you should avoid even the slightest negativity. Even though you have experiences that intermingle meditative equipoise and post-meditation, you should experientially cultivate the four-session yoga. Even though you understand that self and others are the same, you should not disparage the sacred doctrine or individual persons![133]

The lama then made prophetic declarations concerning his future monastery and disciples, before escorting him a short distance. Gampopa then set out for U, but Jetsun Mila Repa reappeared and said to the disciples, "Last night, I dreamed that a large vulture flew away from my residence and alighted on the summit of a great mountain. It gathered a large entourage of geese from all directions. Each of these geese even gathered some five hundred servant geese. The entire disposition of the valley turned yellowish on account of the geese. Though I am a yogin, after me many ordained mendicants will follow. That physician is going to be of benefit to sentient beings. I too have acted on behalf of the Buddhist teaching!"

After listening to the parting advice of Jetsun Mila, Gampopa then set out for his own land. {166} He practiced for six years at Sewalung in Nyel[134] and for three years at Gelung, such that there arose within him the extraordinary realization of seeing the essential nature of the original mind as uncontrived. All things became like husk and chaff. He was without thoughts of discovering treasure under the bed of a poor person, or of meeting his former acquaintances, or of arriving in his own house as a guest. He had determined meditation in accordance with the view, and meditation had been entrusted into the hands of its rightful master. Through his devotion to the lama, there arose a perfect certainty with regard to the oral instructions, and henceforth his contemplation was without either increase or decrease.

He had a handheld rosary of twenty-one bodhicitta beads, which he tied by hand to a mountain willow tree and said, "If I have been foreordained by all the buddhas of the three times, may you, this tree, grow from that tree! If I have not been foreordained, may you not grow!" Immediately thereafter, green branches sprouted.

Gampopa then resided for seven years at Olka and visited the snow peak of Ode Gungyel.[135] There, a voice resounded from the sky saying, "When actual disciples are dispersed to the point of vanishing, that is a downfall for bodhisattvas!" Consequently, he traveled to Gampo[136] and considered staying there in a sealed retreat for twelve years, but at that moment a ḍākinī said, "Rather than doing a sealed retreat for twelve years, it would be better to spread the Buddhist teaching for twelve years!" So he engaged in acts of immense benefit for living beings.

The continuous stages of contemplation of this venerable master Gampopa are also elucidated in his own spiritual songs. Accordingly, they consisted of three aspects of the generation stage (namely, Cakrasaṃvara, Satyadvayamukha Bhaṭṭārikā,[137] and Sahajā); three deities that dispel obstacles (namely, Vajrapāṇi in the form Caṇḍamahāroṣaṇa, the fivefold divine assemblage of Hayagrīva, {167} and White Tārā); three deities who perform enlightened activities (namely, Mahākāla in the form Trakṣad,[138] with his sister, Aparājitā, and Ngakdak); three sorts of ritual activities (namely, maṇḍalas, recitations, and torma offerings); three doctrinal practices of four-session meditation (namely, the generation stage, the perfection stage concerning energy channels and winds, and their integration); three doctrinal practices confined to nighttime sessions (namely, inner radiance, consciousness transference, and dreams); three doctrinal practices confined to daytime sessions (namely, impure illusory body, pure illusory body, and the indivisibility of vital energy and mind); and three doctrinal practices of continuous meditation (namely, Mingling, Transference, and Reincarnation; the Great Seal; and Coemergent Union).

Then, worthy recipients of his instructions assembled simultaneously from U, Tsang, and Kham, and not long after, there were many individuals in whom particularly sublime realization, immeasurable refinement of the energy channels and winds, and the six extrasensory powers arose. Furthermore, those in his entourage did not maintain the eight concerns that should not be scrutinized,[139] they persevered with the yogic practices of the crouching posture, they maintained the twelve ascetic virtues,[140] and they focused exclusively on secret practices and mountain retreat.

Gampopa brought forth the water of accomplishment in Zanglung,[141] and his deeds of emanational transformation were countless. On one occasion alone, it is said that he went to the Lhasa area, carried out the preparatory rite of empowerment on the fourteenth day of the lunar month, held the main part of the empowerment on the fifteenth, and held a thanksgiving ceremony on the sixteenth. Meanwhile, at the residence of his patron Gendun Bum, it is said that he carried out a preparatory rite on the fourteenth day, a consecration on the fifteenth, and a thanksgiving ceremony on the sixteenth, after which the group of seven—master and disciples—then departed into the sky. However, the resident monks of Dakpo said that Rinpoche did not go anywhere, {168} that he stayed secretly in retreat on the thirteenth and gave guidance to Tsangpas on the fourteenth, Khampas on the fifteenth, and central Tibetans on the sixteenth. His three attendants said that the lama did not teach the sacred doctrine at all for three months, nor did he eat any food, nor did he go out for recreation, but he remained silent and stayed only in his chamber.

There were signs that he had accomplished the meditative stabilities of the ten total consummations of the elements and the eight sense fields of mastery.[142] When people went into his presence, his body would become invisible. In his chamber, a mass of fire blazed, or it was filled with water. A golden stūpa blazed with rays of light and then was not visible at all, and so forth. Wherever he sat—in sunlight, moonlight, lamplight, and so forth—his body did not cast a shadow. Gampo Loden saw him as the thousand-armed Mahākāruṇika.

Once, when the Venerable One himself was seated in his grass hermitage, an attendant set out in advance, carrying his robe, but before his arrival, the lama had already reached his teaching throne and even accepted tangible offerings.

The lama transformed himself into the form of Munīndra, larger even that Mount Gampori, and was seen entering a room that could hold no more than five people. A thousand monks saw him, in their shared perception, moving this way and that in the sky above the roof of the monastery. When Gargom Karpo requested from him the transmission for the recitation of the thirteen-deity assemblage of Cakrasaṃvara, the lama transformed himself into Cakrasaṃvara with four faces and twelve arms. The mantra syllables, in the form of a red ray of light, emerged from his mouth and dissolved into the heart of that supplicant.

When Kyogom commissioned a complete set of paintings depicting the buddhas of the five families and requested him to perform a speedy consecration, he said, "Burn incense and make a maṇḍala offering!" {169} Then, the lama transformed himself into Śākyamuni, in the aspect Great Enlightenment. From the crown of his head light rays of five colors were diffused, and each of them individually penetrated the corresponding painting. When they were rolled up, they all rumbled, and just when it seemed that parasols, victory banners, streamers, a symphony of music, a rain of flowers, and so forth were emerging from the sky, he said, "If I do a speedy consecration, it's done like that!"

Gyelwa Khyungtsang had a dream in which the entire mountainside of Gampo was filled with caves. In most of these caves, the light rays of a stūpa of precious gems alone were diffused. There were some who said this was a half-finished construction and some who said it was merely a substitute form that had been whitewashed and that these multitudes who paid homage to it were merely officiating priests along with their mundane deities. He went to report this to Gampopa, who cleared his doubts.[143]

The goatherd Gom Kye grew in meditation just by hearing his name. Gyagom Dorje Senge grew in meditation by presenting a maṇḍala offering out of devotion, even though he did not meet him. Namkha Pene and others grew in meditation merely by seeing his face. Dromar Yuwa requested instruction on Inner Heat and the Great Seal. Later he also became a monk, and when he passed away, the smoke from his cremation gathered in rainbows. On one of his vertebrae there was a thumb-size image of Śākyamuni, and the five-colored pearl relics that appeared weighed one *phul* measure.

Once, Lama Gompa asked him, "When the body, appearances, and mind are integrated, how should that properly come about?" Gampopa waved his hand at the pillar in front and demonstrated it passing straight through the pillar, unimpededly as if through a sunbeam, and said, "Body, appearances, and mind are integrated like that." Also when he crossed the Dre Tsangpo, he spread his mat on top of the water and crossed over while counting a rosary with his right hand and making the boon-granting gesture with his left hand.

At the time when he consecrated the deities in the shrine of Tsepo Lhagom, {170} the flowers stuck to the sacred representations of their own accord. He rested the flower container in the sky and suspended his religious robe on the rays of the sun, and so forth. About a hundred people, including Lhagom, saw him as Mahākāruṇika in the form Khasarpaṇi. He went to and fro through walls without impediment and sat in the sky, as in the narrative of Ḍombhi Heruka. Wearing the three religious robes, he stood up, fixed the heels of his feet in space, made the gesture of Vajrakīla in the form Amṛtāñjali on the crown of his head, and stayed there for three days. On the first evening, he appeared to have seven manifestations; on the second evening, fourteen; and on the third evening, multiple manifestations that simply filled his small hut. Then, they all instantly disappeared. For those who requested oral instructions, offered their meditative experiences and realizations, or requested the dispelling of impediments, he would have them arrange tormas and present a maṇḍala offering, and then simply by sitting engaged in yogic exercises, he would teach them whatever they merited without them having to ask.

When the three men from Kham partook a little of the sacramental substances, they became exhilarated and the monastic disciplinarian, hearing of this, expelled all three.[144] Gampopa asked, "What is this that is turning the deities of Gampo and the offering sacraments upside down?" He was told the reason and then said, "If they are not here, I too will not stay!" Carried on the back of a young monk and holding a cane staff in his hand, he set out and met those three at the lower part of the monastery. The lama danced upon the surface of the upper boulder and said, "Come up!" Those three then danced upon the surface of the lower boulder and replied, "We are coming up!" Consequently, both boulders were covered with their footprints.

Finally, when Gampopa was in his seventy-fifth year, in the morning of the fifteenth day of the mid-autumn month in 1153 (water female bird),

{171} he passed into final nirvāṇa. At that time, there was a net of light rays resembling a rainbow tent, the fragrance of incense, a symphony of music, an earthquake, and so forth. When his sacred corpse was cremated on the eighteenth day, the smoke turned into a five-colored rainbow that filled the valley of Dak. There was a shower of blue flowers and all sorts of wondrous signs that are difficult to comprehend. His heart was undamaged, and innumerable pearl relics were retrieved.

It is clearly foreordained in *The Sūtra of the King of Meditative Stability* and in *The Sūtra of Compassion's White Lotus* that in the future, in the world system called Sarvaguṇālaṃkṛta (Ornamented with All Good Qualities), he will become the tathāgata named Vimalaprabha.

The Disciples of Gampopa

The disciples of Venerable Gampopa were limitless. Among them, the four lineage holders were Dakpo Gomtsul,[145] glorious Phakmodrupa, Khampa Use Karmapa Dusum Khyenpa, and Venerable Barompa.[146] The four senior disciples were Shoram Phakpa, Sergong Yeshe Nyingpo, Ramnye Choyung, and Zem Yeshe Nyingpo. The four close sons were Dakpo Duldzin, Jose Layakpa, Kyepo Yeshe Dorje, and Gargom Karpo. The four attendants were Jodan, Lekdze, Jangye, and Seljang.[147]

Phakmodrupa Dorje Gyelpo

Phakmodrupa, the disciple of that venerable and supreme master, whose realization equaled the sky, was appointed to preside over the rows of monks in the entire monastic assembly. When making this announcement, Gampopa extensively praised him, saying, "Spiritual mentor, Great Khampa, you should take your seat at the head of the row." That is to say, he was directly empowered by the command of Gampopa as sovereign of the enlightened heritage of the entire Kagyu lineage. {172} Even as he approached nirvāṇa, Gampopa also said, "Since there is no difference between Geshe Khampa and me, even to the extent of the hundredth of a horsetail hair, you should regard him as such!" His fame permeated the three world systems. If one were to mention just a tiny part of his enlightened attributes, which were as infinite as space, to those of highest acumen he revealed himself to be a perfect buddha, to those of average acumen he revealed himself as a series of saintly beings, and to those of lowest acumen he revealed himself to be a great bodhisattva abiding on the levels since he had been purified through the path followed by ordinary persons of good fortune.[148]

With regard to the first of these three perspectives, he revealed himself to be the tathāgata Krakucchanda, who was the first to appear the morning after the Sage had dried up the lake of phenomenal existence by the thousand suns during this Auspicious Eon. In the Age of Strife, when the five degenerations thrived, he revealed himself as the peerless Śākyasiṃha, the master of this Buddhist teaching endowed with positive enlightened activity that adheres to all sentient beings with the perfect compassion of all the conquerors. In the future, in the world system of the eastern direction named Puṣpābhikīrṇa, he will attain manifestly perfect buddhahood as the transcendent lord Akṣobhyavajra. It is certain that he will extensively turn the doctrinal wheel of the Great Vehicle on behalf of an assembly of bodhisattvas numbering countless billions.

According to the second of these perspectives, despite all that, from the standpoint of disciples to be trained, this lord-protector manifested as the sovereign Mahāvajradhara who foreordained that Guhyapati Vajrapāṇi would take possession of *The Wish-Fulfilling Gem of the Aural Lineage*,[149] which belonged within the Great Library of Oḍḍiyāna. {173} Also, according to *The Garland of Past Lives*,[150] during the teaching period of the buddha *Virāgapadmanetrin (Unattached Lotus Eye), he manifested as the householder Śrīcakra, the monk Kalyāṇmati Dharmaśrībhadra, the "monkey bodhisattva,"[151] the prince Kīrtisiṃha, the minister of King Śaṅkha, and Mahādeva, king of nāgas. In one aspect also, he was present alongside the lords of the three enlightened families when they heard the sacred doctrine from the tathāgata Śākyamuni. And, as had been foreordained in connection with his activities with respect to the Buddhist teaching in the future, he later became the great master Nāgārjunagarbha. At that time, in India, Land of the Sublime Ones, he is said to have simultaneously revealed eight physical manifestations: Pañcapaṇa, who interpreted the secret instructions; Saraha, who penetrated knowledge; Virūpa, who destroyed misconceptions; Dignāga, who parried objections; Indrabhūti, who nurtured a kingdom; Asaṅgakīrti, who interpreted the sūtras; Kambalapāda, who revealed the path of skillful means; and Padmarāja, who tamed the arrogant spirits.

Also, in China, he became the *hoshang* Kara—an erudite and disciplined monk adorned with the conduct of a bodhisattva. And through his four simultaneous emanations, he sustained the Buddhist teaching and living beings in a regal manner: as Indrabhūti in India, Amśuvarman in Nepal, Songtsen Gampo in Tibet, and Tang Gaozong in China.[152]

Furthermore, he was miraculously born in Sukhāvatī in the guise of the buddha body of perfect resource, and on another occasion he appeared in Alakāvatī, where he was the petitioner who received *The Real Nature of the Secrets*[153] from the teacher Mahāvajradhara. {174} He also manifested as the bodhisattvas Matisiṃha and Jñānasiṃha and as the paṇḍita Abhayakīrti.

After these, in the presence of Guhyapati, he became Śīlajvalita, and simultaneously there were three different arrays of his physical body: Gayadhara and Kālacakrapāda the Younger in India and the great yogin Ame Jangchub in Tibet. It was after all that that he took birth as Dewar Shekpa Rinpoche (Phakmodrupa) in person.[154]

According to the third perspective, Phakmodrupa was born in 1110 (iron male tiger) into the We clan at Tikle Takngo Sabkhang in the Mesho valley of the Yangtze.[155] His father was the glorious heruka Wena Adar, and his mother was Royeza Tsune, an emanation of Vajravārāhī. At that time, his mother dreamed that a nine-pronged golden vajra, diffusing light, was placed in her lap, and she was never again tainted with the sufferings of childbirth.[156]

As soon as he was born, the child possessed clear extrasensory powers, recollection of many lives, one-pointed meditative stability, and so forth. In his ninth year, he received the primary mendicant vow in accordance with the Buddhist teaching from the great monastic preceptor Yentub Tsultrim Bar, who was erudite and disciplined, standing on the level of the sublime ones, and the master of ceremonies, Ding Nge Ozer Gyeltsen. The name Dorje Gyelpo was conferred upon him. Without studying, he naturally knew all the fields of classical learning, including writing, leading, medical science, drawing, and so forth. When his preceptor was preparing a silver copy of *The Transcendent Perfection of Wisdom in One Hundred Thousand Lines*, he served as the scribe for one of the volumes and even drew the icon of the deity in the central cartouche.

In all respects, Phakmodrupa was endowed with great courage that could not be deflated, {175} and his charisma increased as he competed in trials of physical prowess. {175} He could carry on his back a large stone that a horse drawn cart could not budge from the middle of a fallow field at his residence and cast it away. When he received the empowerment of profundity from Lama Gyachenmo, he pledged in the rows of the congregation not to drink alcohol. He also studied the sacred doctrine with one named Uring Gyelbar, whom others held to be an ordinary clan chieftain but who he realized was actually a bodhisattva of the tenth level, born with the eye of discernment. Phakmodrupa attended upon some sixteen spiritual guides in Dokham itself. Since he was endowed with the excellence of innate and acquired discriminative awareness, he comprehended the words and meanings of a great many texts and pith instructions, and he became a master who could teach widely to others.[157]

In his twenty-second year, Phakmodrupa intended to travel to Utsang, and at that time he experienced a pure vision in which the wrathful Conqueror Acala's sharp sword of pristine cognition severed the magical portents of obstructing spirits, filled with dark stains, who, he thought, were impeding his journey to Utsang. In U, first he alighted at the residence of Tolung Gyamar and entered a seminary for reading, study, and reflection. Since he was well refined in the ocean of the scriptural collections and their branches, including the monastic discipline of the sacred doctrine, the phenomenology of the Great and Lesser Vehicles, the perspective of *The Transcendent Perfection of Wisdom*, the textual traditions of Madhyamaka concerning freedom from extremes, and the logical science of sophistry and valid cognition, when he explained these, he was the source of ten million eloquent explanations. When he composed texts, he became a great lamp illuminating Buddhist texts. When he debated, he became a vajra that destroyed his opponents, a great paṇḍita free of all rivals.

In his twenty-fifth year, {176} Phakmodrupa formally entered into the Buddhist teaching and received the vows of a fully ordained monk at the great seminary of glorious Zulphu, which was an inexhaustible source for the preaching of scripture and logic. Ja Dulwadzinpa the Great,[158] who was endowed with both steadfastness and learning and stood upon the level of the sublime ones, acted as the monastic preceptor. The great elder Gyamar acted as the master of ceremonies, and the strict monk and great scholar Ar acted as confessor.

Even while residing in that college of dialectics, Phakmodrupa did not interrupt his practice of the four-session yoga. He studied under the great spiritual guide Chapa Chokyi Senge[159] and also under Nyangdren and others. He attended upon certain spiritual guides, such as Yangepa, Dontengpa, and Jayulwa, who were wealthy in learning, discipline, and nobility.[160] He set his mind on supreme enlightenment, and the texts of the Kadampas and the infinite rivers of their instruction flowed into the ocean of his mind.

From Jangdrak Takpa and his nephew Ngok Mune, who were students of Go Lotsāwa and Bari Lotsāwa,[161] he received the empowerments, tantra commentaries, and all the pith instructions, without exception, for *Guhyasamāja* according to the tradition of sublime Nāgārjuna. From Mar Chokyi Gyeltsen, an actual disciple of Purang Lochung, he received all the oral teachings of empowerment, exegesis, and guidance concerning Cakrasaṃvara. From Burgom Nakpo, he listened to all *The Nine Profound Oral Instructions*[162] that derived from Loro Rechungpa. By meditating on these for eight months, his entire body was filled with great bliss.

Traveling to Sakya, he received many tantras, the Path and Its Fruit, and so forth from Sachen Kunga Nyingpo, like a vase being filled to the brim.[163] Sachen delighted in asking questions about the sacred doctrine and was pleased with his correct answers, naming him "The Wise Khampa." {177} Together, the master and disciple meditated in the Dorje Cave, such that the signs of warmth associated with the energy channels and winds excellently arose, and then the lama introduced him to the dawning realization of the path of insight.[164]

Phakmodrupa attended upon the bodhisattva Dawa Gyeltsen, who advised, "You should stay in retreat during the waning half of the month and explain the sacred doctrine during the waxing half of the month. If you cannot confer empowerments and blessings, you should widely study the sacred doctrine that has been excellently taught."[165]

Furthermore, he went to study *The Doctrinal Cycle of Aro*[166] under Drak Karpowa, *The Three Aspects of Dissolution*[167] and so forth under Jim Lotsāwa, and so forth, *The Three Cycles of Kharak*[168] under Nyangom Gopo, *The Eight Distinctions*[169] and so forth under Lama Mangkarwa, and other doctrines under Sangye Nyelchungwa.[170] The last mentioned said to him, "Khampa teacher! Four ḍākinīs with golden ornaments are following you. You will be of benefit to many living beings in the environs of the black mountain of Ngamsho!" Then he conferred upon him the profound instructions of the path of skillful means, along with their practical implementation. Phakmodrupa also met some thirteen yoginī lamas, headed by Machik Zhama.[171]

Khampa Ga Lotsāwa Tutob Wangchuk Zhonu Pel, a disciple of the great scholar Tsāmi Lotsāwa Sangye Drakpa, who had formerly been a monastic preceptor at Vajrāsana in India and subsequently taken birth in the eastern country of Minyak, was indivisible from Cakrasaṃvara, and he carried out the injunctions of Mahākāla.[172] From him Phakmodrupa received the empowerments and tantra commentaries of the *Kālacakra*, along with the Six-Limbed Yoga[173] and so forth, as well as all the anthologies of pith instructions concerning Kākamukha Mahākāla, protector of the Buddhist teaching. These consist of the experiential cultivation of Mahākāla, the natural abiding nature; Mahākāla, the path to be accomplished; and Mahākāla, the spontaneously present result. And they integrate together the streams of three lineages—namely, the lineage of pure teaching derived from the buddhas, {178} the lineage of blessings derived from the ḍākinīs, and the lineage of prophetic declaration derived from spiritual revelations. Phakmodrupa also received the remainder of his teachings from one named Aseng Wangchuk, who was the stem of Secret Mantra. When a slight misconception arose in his mind concerning that teacher, he was refreshed by means of a hundred and eight meditative stabilities.[174]

In brief, under the lamas of U, Tsang and Kham—who were learned in the sacred doctrine, authorities in the great oral instructions, and renowned and accomplished in Tibet, this Land of Snows—Phakmodrupa mastered study, reflection, and meditation as if there were nothing that he did not study and nothing that he did not learn concerning Sanskrit grammar, logic, arts, medicine, the scriptural collections, the tantras, and the pith instructions of maturational empowerment and liberating guidance. Later, whenever intelligent people of that area discussed this, they would assert that even if the anthologies of oral instructions that Lama Phakmodrupa had received were lined up from glorious Phakmodru to glorious Chuwori, they would not be exhausted. That is said, as it were, to have been the actual situation.

So it was that this saintly being resembled Lake Anavatapta, gathering all the rivers of the sacred doctrine without exception. When asked a question and he answered, his intelligence was inexhaustible, like the treasure store of Vaiśravaṇa, a noble tree heavy with the fruit of the pith instructions of the two approaches of the Great Vehicle. Although he had arrived at manifestly perfect buddhahood—the steadfast certainty determining that the isthmus of hesitation and doubt had been crossed and where secret words ascertain that "this cannot be transcended"[175]—despite all that, in order to receive pointed introduction to this solid ground of actual yoga, the real nature of all things where there are no significant questions unanswered, {179} Phakmodrupa went to Gampo in 1151 (iron female sheep) when he was in his forty-second year so that the Kagyu lineage of Lord Marpa would become second to none in the world. He touched the lotus feet of peerless Gampopa the Great, lord of the sacred doctrine. After a few days, Gampopa said to him, "Have you, Khampa Geshe, meditated for years?" "I have meditated for seven years," he replied. "Simply on that basis what reason is there for pride? I have meditated for forty years. How much of the sacred doctrine have you received?" Phakmodrupa related to him his previous studies, and Gampopa replied, "Simply on that basis, what reason is there for pride? The master Nāgārjuna knew the five fields of classical learning and was engaged in purposeful transformation. Apart from that, pride did not arise." They had many profound and extensive conversations like this.[176]

Gampopa held in his hand a ball of barley dough and said, "At those times, what sort of meditative experiences arose?" "The pristine cognition that perceives the path of insight arose," he replied. "Is the path of insight grasped in that?" "It is according to the scriptural authority of the adamantine stanzas of the Path and Its Fruit." "Just kidding, can you grasp the path of insight in that?" "The lama also introduced the path of insight in all sorts of ways." "Wow! Do you truly now grasp the path of insight in that?" "It is the path of insight established by all the meditative experiences of the sūtras, tantras, and pith instructions." "Isn't this barley dough of mine better than that noble path of insight of yours?" Phakmodrupa's mind grew despondent and Gampopa said, "Go over there to that eastern hillside to relax! Once I have finished teaching those people, we should talk."[177] {180} So he went to the eastern hillside and reflected. Those fine experiences of bliss, radiance, and nonconceptuality that he had previously had in all sorts of ways were shredded, and the essential nature of awareness suddenly arose, as if meeting an old acquaintance. All phenomena appeared to resemble outer bark or chaff, and his discriminative awareness too became agile, like a spear twirling in the air. Any status that he might have had in the presence of his former teachers was lost. He stood up after a moment but was unaware of that. After standing up, he went directly into the presence of Gampopa. Without having an opportunity to ask anything, the lama said, "Well then, you have had this sort of experience of the path of insight. I have nothing higher than that to teach. Even so, there is one method of guidance[178] in my own tradition that you should practice." Thereupon, he conferred Coemergent Union of the Great Seal. Phakmodrupa asked him some questions about the perspective of the essential nature, and Gampopa replied, "Geshepa! Since you properly understand the sacred doctrine, I must explain it! You will completely master the profound and extensive doctrines." And he bestowed upon Phakmodrupa all the oral instructions, as if filling a vase to the brim.[179]

At the time when Gampopa passed into nirvāṇa, he said, "Sit here, Geshe Khampa! Since there is not the slightest difference between the two of us, even to the extent of the hundredth part of a hair, you meditators should request oral instructions from him. You should report to him all the doubts that you have to be resolved!"[180]

Then, Phakmodrupa departed to pay his respects one last time to the Sakyapa lama. On the way, while at Nyangro Tsikyi Lhakhang,[181] he had a dream in which he met Venerable Dampa Gyagar Phadampa Sangye, who taught him *The Dream Path of Pacification*.[182] Later, he would actually meet Machik Labdron, who bestowed upon him the Cycle of Profound Severance.[183]

In his forty-ninth year, in 1158 (earth male tiger), {181} at newly founded glorious Phakmodru in the forest of Kuntuzangpo, he took his Adamantine Seat upon the lion throne of the sacred doctrine, whereupon the great drum of his renown reverberated through the entire world, limitless as space. From all directions, countless disciples who had the good fortune to crave a share of the nectar of the definitive meaning gathered like clouds. He also decreed that those who touched his lotus feet should not transgress the habitual conduct of monastic discipline in accordance with the sacred doctrine. He himself was a master of the eloquent ocean of monastic discipline, outstanding for his calm, disciplined, and tranquil demeanor. Because he was a great elder who had perfected the aggregate of ethical discipline, untainted by a speck of negativity, there was no difference even when he slept at night, except for just taking off his shoes. He did not loosen his waistband except when changing his lower robe. An attendant would prepare a clean basin, and he would wash his face with water that was sometimes icy. He did not permit even the slightest mouthful of alcohol or meat to touch his tongue. Also, within the monastery, he did not permit dark seasoning,[184] and at least on one occasion when he ate a meal, unsure whether he had ingested the heat of mountain garlic, he confessed that in the presence of the four assemblies of the monastic community. What else need one say!

Phakmodrupa was established as a great being who—with the quicksilver formed of loving-kindness, compassion, and enlightened mind—could fashion all the iron element of the minds of living beings into the fine gold of the perfect branches of unsurpassed enlightenment because his awareness[185] was unconstrained and never impeded. He was the queen of bees who flirted with ten million configurations of the dance of great bliss that could enjoy honey dripping on the source of great coemergent delight—the immaculate lotus pollen of Dhātvīśvarī. {182} He was the supreme manifestation who presided over and permeated the rank of manifestly perfect enlightenment in the essential nature of the king of meditative stability, where the natural expression of all things diffuses sameness, and whose constant compassion and enlightened activity, an inexhaustible wheel of adornment, reveals the excellent path among living beings as long as phenomenal existence endures.

Phakmodrupa had an inexhaustible omniscient intelligence. Even if one were to ask all the buddhas of the three times over limitless eons questions about the sacred doctrine, at the very moment of asking, and as long as the buddhas continued to ask counter questions about the sacred doctrine, he could respond to their questions. Indeed, on these occasions, he would intermingle the two streams of the Kadam instructions and the Great Seal. In addition, the tradition of glorious Gampopa demonstrates the integration of all things in the twofold essential nature: the great seal that is the abiding nature of reality and the great seal of bliss and emptiness.[186]

As for the details of the disciples who were born from his buddha speech, there were twenty-five great-disciples who were outstanding in renunciation and realization; five hundred who liberated themselves and then raised the parasol for the welfare of others; the group of eight hundred, who were moistened by the nectar of the two accomplishments; and so forth. Illustrated by these, it seemed that even the dust of this great earth was instantaneously brought to maturation and liberation. He properly fulfilled the hopes of the disciples of his lineage, and composed extensive treatises that concerned the quintessence of all the doctrinal wheels with excellent words of expression and excellent meanings and adorned with the constraints of prosody. These are established as progenitors of the later dissemination of the Buddhist teaching. {183}

Phakmodrupa was beheld as the buddhas, bodhisattvas, and meditational deities. He actualized the miraculous abilities of buddha body, speech, and mind. He spoke with the extrasensory powers and could achieve extensive objectives even through a minor auspicious coincidence. How could such activities possibly be explained!

Singularly wonderful was his demonstration of the twelve arrays of his physical body on a single evening when he gave teaching at the request of his regent, the mighty lord of the world, Taklungpa the Great. They were are follows: Through the first array, he received empowerment in the presence of the lords of the three enlightened families through an emanational maṇḍala in Oḍḍiyāna and brought forth many tantras and pith instructions. Through the second array, in Cāritra, he dispersed with the wind of the eon's end the meditative stability of Cakrasaṃvara that had gathered the breath of the ḍākinīs as a mass of diseases. Through the third array, he held a communal feast offering alongside the gurus of the Kagyu lineage at the charnel ground of Tamarauraka in the southwest of India. Through the fourth display, he dispelled the king of the city of Śrīmat (Glorious) in southern India, who had been shrouded by the darkness of heretical views, and established the Buddhist teaching. Through the fifth array, in a small isle to the southeast of Jambudvīpa, he rendered all directions fortunate through the nectar of the instructions of the monk Matirāja. Through the sixth array, in the extreme west of that continent, he brought his own mother from the past to maturation and liberation through marvelous miraculous abilities. Through the seventh array, he actually consecrated the Vajrāsana and placed under oath the protectors of the oral teachings at the monastic seat of his spiritual son, Taklung Tangpa. Through the eighth array, he alleviated the illness of the Chinese emperor Song Xiaozong[187] {184} and turned him away from negative actions.[188] Through the ninth array, in the charnel ground of Haha Gopa, manifesting as Hūṃkara, he paralyzed and subdued elemental spirits through the meditative stability of Cakrasaṃvara. Through the tenth array, in Nepal, with the meditative stability of Hayagrīva, he overwhelmed the viciousness of the protector deities Garnak and Gangkar Shamema. Through the eleventh array, in the south of Kham, with the meditative stability of Vajrapāṇi, he subdued Zing Aten Gyawo, who had been born as a ghost. Through the twelfth array, he resided at Phakmodru itself and revealed all these arrays in a single session in the late evening of the twenty-fifth day of Jyeṣṭha[189] in 1169 (earth female ox). This illustrates his inconceivable emanations of perfect buddhahood.[190]

Finally, in his sixty-first year, on the twenty-fifth day of the month of Kārtika in 1170 (tiger), he said, "I will depart from here for the immaculate buddha field of the eastern direction and become a bodhisattva named Mativimalarāja in the presence of Buddha Akṣobhya and Bhaiṣajyarāja. You should pray to him!" He then passed into nirvāṇa. When the sacred corpse was cremated, the buddhas of the five enlightened families appeared above the cremation chamber and in its four directions. Spiritual heroes and heroines made offerings. The heart, tongue, eyes, and an inconceivable number of pearl relics were retrieved. The earth quaked, a rain of flowers fell, smoke gathered as a rainbow, and there was a symphony of music. The sacred representations were distributed as the disciples' glorious field of merit, and a reliquary was made to represent the buddha body of reality.[191]

The Disciples of Phakmodrupa

Though the array of his disciples were like the constellations in the sky, foremost among them were the four great sons—namely, Kunden Tsangpa Rechung,[192] Zara Kalden Yeshe Senge,[193] the realized yogin Minyak Gomring,[194] and Drubtob {185} Nyakre Sewo.[195] The four perfected sons were Taklungpa, whose liberating career was perfected; Drigungpa, whose auspicious circumstances were perfected; Napuwa, whose realization was perfected; and Puwa, whose discriminative awareness was perfected. The eight supreme ones were Chojedum, Lama Tum, Golphuwa, Yewuwa, Marpa, Lang Senge Gyeltsen, Rechen Samdrub, and Repa Tonrin. The eight attendants were Geshe Shendrongpa, Nyene Jang Ye, Konyer Gomdar, Nepo Gyagom, Gomtson, Sorin, Sengton, and Tonyon. There were also countless meditators, adorned with meditative experiences, including the spiritual guide Gyeltsa, Zhangton Pawa, Chokyi Lama, Geshe Jobum, Bo Dorje Chenpo, Zhangton Khudziripa, Hrewo Gewapel, Tsagyuk Senge, Sangye Nyengom, Nyangom Chenpo, Tsangpa Jose, Yutokpa, Dingchenpa, Tsilungpa, Gazi Gompa, Uyang Konkyab, Ugom Lama, and Takdewa.[196]

Concluding Verses

The translator of essential definitive meaning,
The exemplary one who attained buddhahood in a single life,
The great promulgator of *The King of Meditative Stability*,
And the lord-protector of all living beings, including the gods,[197]
Like the sun and moon in this Rose-Apple Continent,
Are endowed with a hundred thousand light rays of renown,
And their enlightened attributes with four modalities[198] are praised.
Moreover, the taste of this ocean is not a sense object for others
Apart from the tongue of the conquerors.
And yet I have taken a sliver of the precious mountain.
As an exemplary supreme sacrament for dispelling degeneration,
I think that there will be great benefit
When one sees, hears, and recalls
Just this small part of the profound and extensive narratives. {186}

Without blindly exploring my own conceptual fabrications,
To facilitate and benefit those who would inspect all the nuances of history
With the clear eyes of ideation and scrutiny,
I myself have audaciously made this compilation.

Upon the most spacious bedrock of accumulation and refinement,
The gemstone pebbles of higher insight,
Strewn within the wide and vast ocean of calm abiding,
Are recognized by Nāgendra, king of nāgas.
Even though the waves of conceptual thought are agitated,
They dissolve in the expanse of inner radiance, the buddha body of reality,
Causing garlands of spray—
The common savor of cyclic existence and nirvāṇa
That cannot be differentiated in the intrinsic nature—
To crash with laughter.
Though infinite bewildering devices[199] of diverse appearance
Gather and array all sorts of cloud formations in the sky,
From their very appearance, their essential nature is apprehended
To have the intrinsic characteristic of emptiness.
Spacious in the ocean of definitive meaning,
The great seal is within the great perceptual range
Of the mightiest of conquerors of the three times,
Their number inestimable like flocks of seabirds.
The noble wish-granting trees of the four delights—
The uncontaminated supreme inner heat
Derived from the warmth of the active male *caṇḍālī*
And the blissful female *vasudharā*[200]—
Transcend the three planes of existence.
With their thousand branches forming a magical display of appearance and emptiness,
And countless million trillions of young leaves
Integrating the great maṇḍala of adamantine consummate reality and emptiness,
All sorts of variegated flowers arise
From the natural purification of essential bewilderment,
Refining buddha fields that are equal to space,

And then the states and movements of deep sleep are excellently ripened
into the supreme fruit of great inner radiance.
The fragrance of the oral instructions that pursue the sense faculties wafts,
Transforming odors that resort to the impure lower realms,
So that the wondrous wish-granting faculties of the path of liberation
Might protect beings from the torments of the lower realms. {187}

Knowing the Kagyu lineage to be the occult power of Anavatapta nāgas
Who raise the thousand manifestly supreme cobra hoods
Of all the oceans and forests of wish-granting trees, such as these,
I rejoiced in this fresh whirlwind of narrative.

Through the Buddhist teaching, source of the scriptural ocean of the
mighty lords of speech,
Triumphant in battle with the four demonic forces,
And the explanations of the precious treasure of the three trainings
That are a joyful antidote among living beings,
May this noble chariot of the accomplished tradition,
Renowned as the glorious Taklung Kagyu lineage,
Guide to immaculate realms the three planes of existence that fill the sky.

This completes chapter seven of this book, the narrative of the great promulgators of the quintessential Tibetan teaching, from *Wondrous Ocean of Eloquence: A Narrative of the Wish-Fulfilling Gem of the Lineage* compiled by Taklungpa Ngawang Namgyel. {189}

PLATES

Figure 1. Phakmodrupa, flanked by Tashi Pel (?) and Drigungpa, and Drawings of Phakmodrupa's Feet, c. 1168–1170. Distemper on cloth, 55 × 50 cm. approx. Location unknown.

Figure 2. Portrait of Sangye On, interim Fourth Abbot of Taklung and Founder and First Abbot of Riwoche, 1272–1296. Distemper on cloth, 39 × 31 cm. Commissioned for Taklung or Riwoche Monastery. Private collection.

Figure 3. Portrait of Sangye Yarjon, Third Abbot of Taklung, c. 1236–1272. Distemper on cloth, 82 × 63 cm. Commissioned for Taklung Monastery. Private collection.

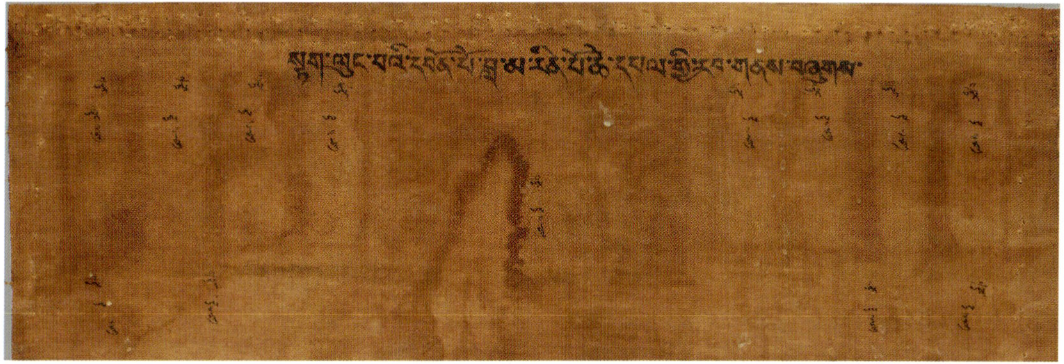

Figure 4. Verso inscription stating the painting was consecrated by Sangye On (1251–1296), interim Fourth Abbot of Taklung and founder and First Abbot of Riwoche. This inscription appears on thirty-nine Taklung paintings: "[In the painting] dwells the consecration of the honorable Onpo Lama Rinpoche of Taklung" (*stag lung pa'i dbon po bla ma rin po che dpal gyi rab gnas bzhugs*).

Figure 5. Inscription in gold script (*dbu can*) stating the painting is the *tukdam* (*thugs dam*, "meditative commitment" or "high aspiration") of Sangye On. This inscription appears just beneath the central figure on six Taklung paintings.

Figure 6. Verso inscription stating the aspiration to remain connected with his teacher by Sangye On. This inscription in gold script (*dbu can*) appears on six (possibly seven) Taklung paintings: "May I, Kīrtiśrīraśmibhadra, being inseparable from the incomparable holy lama Prajñāguru, achieve whatever he commands, and may I have the power to purify the bewilderment of my own mind and act as a guide for living beings" (*mtshungs med bla ma dam pa pradznya 'ghu ru dang// bdag 'ghir ti shri ra smri bha tra //'bral med ci gsung bka' bsgrub cing// rangs sems 'khrul pa dag pa dang// 'gro' ba'i 'dren pa nus par shog//*).

Figure 7. Portrait of Taklung Tangpa Chenpo, First Abbot of Taklung. Central Tibet, c. 1180–1210. Distemper on cloth. 72.2 x 57.2. cm. Private Swiss collection.

8. The Biographies of the Taklung Kagyu Lineage

Verses of Homage

Homage to Maṅgalaśrī,[1] the buddha body of reality!

There now follows a somewhat detailed narrative of the biographies of the glorious Taklung Kagyu lineage.

I pay homage to the lotus feet of the embodiment of the transcendent lord Akṣobhya, who is well known throughout the three planes of existence as the lord-protector Tashi Pel, the natural expression of all the conquerors.

I bow to him—he who formed a garland of **auspicious** (*bkra shis*)[2] white ribbons for the **glory** (*dpal*) of the Buddhist teaching and of living beings, enthroned as a universal monarch of the sacred doctrine in this fortunate place of Taklung, seated upon a well-stacked lion throne within a golden palatial tower, exquisitely fashioned of cyclic existence and quiescence and endowed with the three higher trainings, the two stages of the supremely secret tantras, and enlightened activity imbued with the seven precious things.[3]

Likened to the River Indus, the lineage of profound view and vast conduct,
Endowed with the blessings of experiential cultivation,
And, likened to the River Ganges, the lineage of genuine realization
Both converged in the ocean of the buddha mind of Gampopa Dawo Zhonu.[4]

From the platform of his senior disciples,[5]
It once again cascaded to the ground
Of his venerable enlightened intention, profound and vast,
Forming a pool of ablution,
Purifying the negativity and stains of the three planes of existence.
Within the white beryl barrier of ethical discipline,
Its waters of the generation and perfection stages,
Endowed with eight pure qualities[6]
And adorned with white lotuses of enlightened conduct,
There appeared the joyous springtime row of fortunate water birds.[7]
That is called the Taklung Kagyu lineage.

Its glorious repository of precious gems of the profound doctrine {192}
And those in whose hands it is maintained
Will now be discussed—clarifying to some extent
The Taklung Kagyu traditions of exegesis and attainment.

Prophecies concerning the Sacred Site of Taklung Upper Plain

The transcendent lord Śākyasiṃha is a teacher and master of the Buddhist teaching endowed with the eye of unsurpassed pristine cognition, who definitively knows the ultimate truth, the abiding nature of all maṇḍalas of knowable phenomena throughout the three times without exception and is free from all attachments and impediments with regard to relative truth, as many as there are. He clearly revealed in *The Sūtra of Compassion's White Lotus* the ways in which the location of Dorjeden Pelden Taklung and its mausoleum, containing a tooth relic of the Tathāgata, should be worshipped:

> Ānanda! After I have passed away, in the northern direction there will be a citadel called Jatuka, where the relics of my teeth will be respected, honored, served, and presented with offerings of flowers, garlands, incense, unguents, cymbals, parasols, victory banners, ribbons, ribbons indicative of victory, and so forth, along with robes, silver, gold, and various precious gems. Ānanda! That stūpa of mine will also be adorned with gold.[8]

As for the citadel mentioned here, it denotes this place of Taklung where in antiquity a very large Tibetan nomadic community is said to have settled. Subsequently, this place is revealed to have become a great citadel of joyous doctrine because its inhabitants delighted in the nectar of the sacred doctrine that manifestly understands the definitive meaning. {193} The name Jatuka[9] also denotes the entire land of Tibet that Padmākara, foremost in supreme spiritual accomplishments, had formerly marked out with his feet, where he eradicated all the fierce gods and demons and brought them into his fold, and where he concealed many profound treasures for the sake of the fortunate beings in the future. After consecrating the entire physical environment of Tibet and its inhabitants as a maṇḍala of all the conquerors, he also traveled in this direction of Taklung. At the cliff face of Chilgyi Drago Rawa, he caused a naturally arising stūpa, a representation of buddha mind, to manifest and filled it with many treasures including rites of protective exorcism. On the side of the cliff, a waterfall brought forth a naturally arisen letter A, which is a representation of buddha speech.[10] In the cave of Jutse, he performed a great means for attainment of the peaceful and wrathful deities of *The Net of Magical Emanation*, and he filled the cave with naturally arising features and profound treasures. In the middle of Targyi Lukok, dense with a large forest of pine trees, he bound under an oath of allegiance a venomous water-spirit ogre after opening the semicircular maṇḍala of the rite of subjugation. At Gyawodong, he caused a naturally arising image of Hayagrīva to appear, a representation of buddha body, and he concealed an inconceivable number of treasure doctrines of the generation and perfection stages, as pure as the clarified essence of butter. At that time, the entire region was filled with unbroken forest, like dense rainclouds. Later, when the Podo Dudul Temple and other temples was constructed, it is said that all the wood was taken from there.[11] Moreover, when Kuyal Rinpoche later built the Main Temple, he is said to have cut the huge pillars known as Lupu from Targyi Lukok, and so forth.[12] In brief, it is clearly indicated that this terrain around Taklung was entirely linked by a network of forests.

As for the expression "the relics of my teeth," {194} in general when the sacred corpse of the Teacher Śākyamuni had been cremated, his bone relics multiplied. At that time, among the four tooth relics of that supremely incarnate Buddha, it is explained that the first tooth relic became an object of offering in the Trāyastriṃśa realm. The second tooth relic was kept in the pleasant town of Parvadhara, the third tooth relic in the land of the king of Kaliṅga, and the fourth tooth relic of that supremely sacred being was presented with offerings by the nāga king to the town of Roruka.[13] Among them, the third tooth relic, which had been kept as an object of offering by the king of Kaliṅga, was miraculously taken by the great and illustrious Ga Lotsāwa through his mighty occult power and handed over to glorious Taklung Tangpa the Great.[14]

As for the expression, "Ānanda! My stūpa will be adorned with gold," the supreme incarnation Kuyalwa the Great constructed this reliquary stūpa of great enlightenment, nowadays known as Kumbum Jangma (Northern Reliquary), which radiates vibrantly like a mountain of Jambu gold, and in which he inserted at its core this tooth relic.

As for the expression "the relics of my teeth will be presented with offerings of flowers and so forth," it is clearly stated in the biography that it was above all Choku Sangye Yarjon who, not finding anything equaling, let alone better than, that sacred tooth relic in this land of Tibet, established the definitive Great Offering Ceremony that brings delight, surpassing expectation.[15] Illustrated by this, it is shown that those supreme incarnations who have emerged in the line extending as far as Mahāvajradhara, securing our enlightened heritage, have served this sacred tooth relic continuously, with clouds of offerings, like those conjured by Samantabhadra, not confined to a single occasion but in all circumstances. {195}

The aforementioned quotation from *The Sūtra of Compassion's White Lotus* continues as follows:

> In that delightful region, there will be many beings who become mendicants. Many will maintain ethical discipline, many will possess virtuous attributes, and there will be gatherings of fully ordained monks, hundreds of thousands in number. All of them will pass into nirvāṇa by means of the three vehicles. Do not be sad, because they will cause my teaching to flourish![16]

This definitively foretells that the authentic lineage composed of all the lines of the perfect buddhas will entirely perfect the aggregates of ethical discipline, meditative stability, discriminative awareness, liberation, and the perception of liberating pristine cognition while maintaining a mode of conduct that is pure and chaste. The hidden meaning is that they will continuously appear, endowed with the nectar of supreme spiritual accomplishment that derives from the four empowerments and the two stages of the Adamantine Vehicle, and that their devout disciples will engage with the vital channel of the path of the Great Seal. Attaining success through the teachings of the profound Six Doctrines of Nāropā, from the first generation established on the plains of great bliss until countless billion trillion generations have come forth in this immaculate field, they will pervade all of Jambudvīpa, and in the manner of the sun rising at dawn, they will illuminate the realization of the genuine lineage in which the two streams of the Kadam instructions and the Great Seal are intermingled.

The Abbatial Succession of Taklung Upper Plain

Taklungpa the Great, Tashi Pel, Founder of Taklung

Now I will explain how those foreordained individuals acted on behalf of the Buddhist teaching. {196} The first of those holders of the lineage of attainment to emerge was Taklungpa the Great, Tashi Pel, the peerless and precious lord of the sacred doctrine, embodying the five inexhaustible wheels of adornment, including the body, speech, and mind of all the conquerors whose renown reverberates like a great drumbeat throughout the three world systems. The second buddha and master of indestructible reality, Padmasambhava, also made a clear prediction in these words:

> One called Taklungpa will emerge, maintaining ethical discipline and preserving the teaching of the buddhas with regard to the nature of reality.[17]

As far as the past lives of this lord are concerned, these are mentioned extensively in *The Great Chronicle of the Past Lives of Glorious Phakmodrupa*, precious lord-protector of beings, where it is attested that they shared a former life as father and son.[18]

It is also mentioned in *The Short Biography Titled Melody of the Family Line of Recollection* that at the time of Taklungpa's own nirvāṇa, in response to an entreaty of his main attendants, he said,

> The guide of living beings, lord of the sacred doctrine,
> Glorious Phakmodrupa and I are of the same spiritual lineage.
> There's no need to determine other past lives.[19]

Although he also attested in the presence of his disciples that there were different past lives, here I wish to follow the narrative of those aforementioned accounts since they are most clearly elucidated in the biographies and authentic ancient documents of oral instruction.

In general, while all the tathāgatas of the three times and in particular, the Tathāgata, Arhat, Genuinely Perfect Buddha, and protector Akṣobhyavajra, transcendent lord of the immaculate buddha field of the eastern direction, was turning the wheel of the sacred doctrine of the Great Vehicle uninterruptedly in order to train a billion monks belonging to the community of bodhisattvas, {197} there were manifestations of Mahākāruṇika whose entire training was of a single savor and who were inseparable in their focus. Among them, at that time, Taklungpa the Great had been called by the name of the lord-protector Avalokiteśvara, astonishing in this Auspicious Eon and world of patient endurance among all the conquerors' sons, due to his knowledge, love, and power.

In the great treasury of the sacred doctrine at Oḍḍiyāna, he had been King Indrabhūti the Great, embodiment of pristine cognition, combining the role of an enlightened being through the path of supreme bliss and that of a universal emperor with authority over all those who maintained the gnostic mantras belonging to the holders of the secret repository of the body, speech, and mind of all the conquerors and of those who compiled the transmitted teachings.[20]

He had been the sublime Ānanda, the erudite attendant of the tathāgata Śākyendra, supreme among the hearers of the sacred doctrine and compiler of the entire collection of discourses.

He had been Dharmatāla, the sublime and mighty layman, servant of the great sixteen elders, regents of the Buddha, who alleviated the fever of the afflicted mental states of all sentient beings and was tireless in imparting the liberating nectar of the sacred doctrine.

In Tibet, this Land of Snows, he had been the religious king Songtsen Gampo, who first established the customs associated with the sacred doctrine, having directly introduced a legal code that integrated both temporal and spiritual traditions resembling a golden yoke, and the great maṇḍala of Mahākāruṇika, with its supporting palace and supported deities. {198}

He had been Dromtonpa Gyelwai Jungne, who, starting from this northern region of Uru, covered the entire land of Tibet with fine wish-granting trees—the teaching traditions of the lineage blessed with profound view, extensive conduct, and experiential cultivation.

He had been Jayulwa Chenpo Zhonu-o, who naturally arranged all auspicious events associated with enlightened activities that were exclusively in the service of his teacher—a spiritual adviser, vast in knowledge like space, pervasive in compassion like the earth, and ever authentic. As such, Taklungpa the Great had kindled the lamp of the precious Buddhist teaching throughout the three world systems, sustaining infinite sentient beings.

Here, if those of feeble intelligence harbor doubt, thinking it would be contradictory to claim that King Indrabhūti and sublime Ānanda were emanations of Avalokiteśvara, when all consider them to have been emanations of glorious Vajrapāṇi, I should say a little about that. These bodhisattva beings of the three enlightened families, like divine offerings and donations, are not different in spirit. They are the great generic forms of the body, speech, and mind of all the sugatas of the three times. The adamantine body of the buddhas itself is also the buddha speech and the buddha mind. Therefore, it is appropriate to pay homage to these inconceivable objects of refuge with supremely great devotion, based on the understanding that their intrinsic nature is sameness, and because their bodies emanate at all times, as numerous as the particles of the buddha fields. On the other hand, those who approach them with the intelligence of sophistry, with pride in their own learning, seem to be searching for the bottom of a great ocean with tips of grass. {199}

According to common understanding, the subsequent incarnation of the aforementioned spiritual adviser, Jayulwa Chenpo, was the peerless universal emperor of the sacred doctrine named, according to the virtuous path, Gyelwang Taklungpa the Great, Tashi Pel. He was the lord of the sacred doctrine and the master of the sacred doctrine, manifesting the reflections of the inexhaustible wheels of adornment, which are the three inconceivable mysteries through infinite ways in infinite fields for infinite eons. He was a unique embodiment of understanding and knowledge, combining skillful means and discriminative awareness, the intrinsic nature of the three indestructible realities, the essential nature of the four buddha bodies, and the emanational play of the five pristine cognitions. He frequented lands beyond the seven worlds, revealing the sublime path with its eight branches, proclaiming the scriptures with their nine branches, as the mighty lord overwhelming the ten levels, integrating the twelve aspects and the sixteen aspects of the noble truths, manifestly enlightened in twenty ways, and diffusing the maṇḍala of the hundred enlightened families.[21]

The inner, secret, and definitive biographies of this lord-protector are within the perceptual range of the perfect buddhas alone and since only a portion is within range of the knowledge of the offspring of the Conqueror, the Lord of Secrets, how could we ordinary persons with the narrow vision of this life describe even part of them! Here {200} I have collated and will describe for ease of retention a mere fragment of his outer biography, vast as an ocean, in order to foster the recollection of my own and others' faith.

In Toku Yungang, one of the three upland regions of Dokham,[22] there is a hill called Phuna, resembling eight mountains aligned in rows, where the auspicious gods known as the eight siblings of good fortune reside. Since it is manifestly protected, the place known as Yangsho is filled with great prosperity, happiness, and many heroic, wise, and wealthy persons. There, in a large town called Bongra Tengka,[23] which resembles the opulent palace of the serpent king Phaṇīndra moving above the earth, was a man appropriately named Yonten Zangpo of the Gazi clan, which is a branch of Ba—one of the six Tibetan familial lines—appropriate in that he was a proverbial confluence of merits and enlightened attributes.[24]

He had three sons—the eldest named Dona Dekhyer, the middle one named Dramik Sadeb, and the youngest named Lenka Parko. There were many in the line of the eldest, including Gazi Śākya Zangpo, who became a senior chieftain of Dokham. The youngest was born in his subsequent life as a son of Droje Tsepo. Before he passed away, he turned into a *lhatsen* spirit of astonishing wrath and was then bound under an oath of allegiance by Drogon Phakmodrupa and his disciples, who conferred liberating empowerments and maturational guidance on him and transformed him into a sentinel, upholding the Buddhist teaching.

The middle son had a wild and very generous disposition. He was kind to the lowly, good at keeping promises, and particularly inclined toward the three precious jewels. The local people called him Luge Benlon Barpo because he alone had an authority over Bongra Tengka, which resembled a nāga palace, since he took charge of the Tangkya pilgrimage,[25] and because his prosperity was very great. {201} So it was that in 1142 (water male dog), accompanied by innumerable wondrous and virtuous signs, a son was born to this middle son, who was an embodiment of Śrīheruka, adopting the guise of a householder, and the lady named Bashiza Gesum Tromo, who was an emanation of Vajrayoginī and who was of a holy disposition. Even in demonstrating the ways of childhood, sublime beings, who are naturally arising, disregard the experimental circumstances of growing up, and so he extensively considered the defects of cyclic existence and the advantages of nirvāṇa. He was enthusiastic to enter the portal of the teaching of the supreme Conqueror. But his father disapproved. Even so, due to his excellent mind and the excellence of his perseverance, he conclusively mastered writing, reading, the doctrinal cycle of Vajrakīla, medical science, and so forth. Even though his father and mother beguiled him with many amusements of the senses, his spirit was unmoved, and when he reached his seventeenth year, he left home.

In his eighteenth year, in 1159 (earth female hare year), in the temple of Tangkya, place of the great pilgrimage, he received the precepts of the novitiate, preceded by the lay vows and the intermediate vows of a mendicant from the preceptor and holy elder Gaton Lhakhangpa Sherab Dorje and the master of ceremonies and great disciplinarian Tsarton Gomang in the midst of a full quorum of devout and virtuous monks. The name Tashi Pel was also conferred upon him.[26]

Tashi Pel excellently studied *The Stanzas of the Novitiate* and its commentary. That is to say, he deeply cherished the training in higher ethical discipline. Under master Drakgonpa, a great upholder of the piṭakas, he studied *The Ornament of Clear Realization*, in conjunction with *The Elucidating Commentary*;[27] {202} *The Introduction to the Conduct of a Bodhisattva* and its commentaries; *The Exegesis of the Compendium of Training*; *The Lamp for the Path of Enlightenment*, embellished with its autocommentary; and *The Three Cycles of Spiritual Songs* of the great brahmin Saraha, marked with annotations. He comprehended all their words and meanings conclusively in the expanse of omniscience.

At that time, Tashi Pel had a strong inclination to travel to India, Land of the Sublime Ones and source of the Buddhist teaching. Three times he set out, but he was turned back by his relatives. Not willing to stay at home, he continued to reside at Drakgon in study and reflection.[28] One day, when he went out near the monastery for recreation to alleviate his depression, he saw the local people occupied with the harvest. Under these circumstances there welled up in his mind a pure and higher aspiration that is associated with the enlightened mind of loving-kindness and compassion. When he asked the master about this, he was widely praised, and then he manifestly recovered. One night, when he fell asleep for a short while after midnight, a tall and majestic black woman appeared on a narrow trail where there was no place to pass up or down, and she embraced him around the neck. Thinking that she was the magical emanation of a demonic spirit, he overwhelmed her with the power of his deity visualization, mantra recitation, and meditative stability. Thereupon, she could not begin to obstruct him and said, "You are blessed by thirteen deities!" At that moment, on the ground in front there immediately arose Mount Sumeru, surrounded in its upper regions by a protective circle of vajras and a charnel-ground barrier. At the hub of a crossed vajra, upon lotus and sun cushions, {203} was a celestial palace, complete with all defining characteristics. At its center were the transcendent lord and his consort in union, their essential nature integrating the supreme bliss of skillful means and the emptiness of discriminative awareness. On the prongs of its center were four yoginīs embodying the four applications of mindfulness and four skull vases, indicative of the essential nature of permanence and so forth. At the portals and their intermediate directions were the eight *mātaraḥ*, embodying the purity of the noble eightfold path. These appeared distinctly and perfectly present, in his pure vision of pristine cognition.

When he was staying at Drakgon, a yogin practitioner of Pacification arrived from the highland region, and Geshe Pa Drakgonpa asked him about the essential difficult points in each of the eight parts of *The Transcendent Perfection of Wisdom*. The yogin responded excellently, based on the conviction that arises when all the scriptures, reasoning, and pith instructions converge in the ocean of meditative experience. Thereupon, the master Pa utterly rejoiced, and he along with his students studied *The Three Lamps of Pacification*[29] under that yogin. Since his conduct was one of total renunciation in which attachment was naturally liberated, the yogin set out for Kolti, and at that time Rinpoche Pa saw him off.[30] The yogin presented a skull containing sacraments of commitment, endowed with the appropriate marks. Placing his hands on the crown of Tashi Pel's head, he tugged a protection cord around his neck and then departed, saying, "Keep the commitments in the appropriate manner! Please your teacher with body, speech, and mind and with resources! May you accomplish the sacred doctrine and be liberated from all obstructing demons!"

On one occasion when the master Pa was performing an offering ceremony at Drakgon, while seated in the row of monks, he said, "There is one called glorious Phakmodrupa who nowadays in Utsang {204} holds all doctrines including the scriptural transmissions and realizations, and nurtures the entire congregation. He sent an instruction in the form of a letter to Geshe Mok Cholo, and Geshe Takchenpa received it in turn. After experientially cultivating that instruction, on the day of Geshe Takchenpa's death, when his sacred corpse was cremated, the entire sky was transformed into rainbow colors. Inconceivable pearl relics were brought forth."[31]

Just by hearing the name of Phakmodrupa, inconceivable faith and devotion were born within Tashi Pel. After a short time he went to the residence of Geshe Mok and requested him to give that oral instruction. Mok replied, "Since liberating guidance is given once maturational empowerment has already been conferred, you should go to receive the empowerment!"

Returning to Drakgon, he informed the master Pa, who said, "I will confer it!" Then, Tashi Pel completely received the four empowerments, combining the illustrative symbols and acquired meanings according to *The Six Chapter Glorious Cakrasaṃvara: Conclusive Mystery of the Yoginī*,[32] which embodies the quintessential sixty-two deity maṇḍala of Cakrasaṃvara, and according to the essential nine-deity maṇḍala of Hevajra. He also demonstrated the dramatic spectacle in which the genuine pristine cognition of empowerment arises in the appropriate manner.

Tashi Pel then journeyed again to the residence of Geshe Mok and made his request, whereupon the instructions concerning refuge, setting the mind on enlightenment, the generation stage of the meditational deity, the pith instructions concerning recitation of mantra, the yogic exercises pertaining to the physical body, the methods of settling the mind in reality, the transference of consciousness as a method employed during sleep, and instructions on union with the spiritual teacher were conferred upon him and explained. But, apart from merely mentioning the most important points of experiential cultivation, Geshe Mok did not grant him the essential verses concerning the path of skillful means. However, at the very moment when Tashi Pel saw the image of Drogon Rinpoche (Phakmodrupa) on top of Mok's pillow, {205} an uncommon devotion arose, along with extraordinary indications and attributes of spiritual warmth, whereupon he had the thought that he should certainly bow down at the lotus feet of that teacher.

Tashi Pel postponed setting out for Utsang on four occasions, and consequently he had to remain there in Kham. Altogether he prepared to travel on seven occasions—three to India and four to Utsang. This was to become an auspicious circumstance, ensuring that in the future he would be reborn in Kham in seven successive lives before traveling to U and nurturing enlightened activity in each of them. Relying on the accommodation and sustenance compatible with meditative concentration provided by the preceptor, students, and monastic community at Drakgon, he assumed responsibility for his studies, reflections, and meditations.

In due course, he went to meet one known as Venerable Golphuwa, a learned and venerable master of spiritual attainment, who was an actual disciple of glorious Phakmodrupa. Golphuwa said, "As soon as you arrived, I saw Lama Rinpoche! This is certainly imbued with blessings." In this way, his inclination for traveling to U was revitalized.

Then in isolated hermitages, while he was focusing exclusively on the yoga of genuine mental placement, a limitless exhibition of the gateways to meditative stability was born in his mind. When he was residing at Nyelnge, at the encouragement of one Akhu Sewo, he wrote a treatise titled *Garland of Secret Nectar*,[33] which appears to have been the first of the doctrinal works that he composed.

In 1165 (wood female bird), in his twenty-fourth year, he dreamed that there appeared an extremely large and tall castle, with a many-runged ladder, as white and translucent as crystal. Ascending it, {206} when he had nearly fulfilled his intention to reach the top, he was held up and thought he would have to go back down again, but from above a tall and utterly majestic white man, adorned with ornaments and robes, reached out a hand and pulled him up, so he easily arrived there. It seemed that this was an emanation of Lama Phakmodrupa.[34]

Then, in gratitude, Tashi Pel offered prostrations to his masters as he was about to depart, and on that day when he thought he should travel to U, he set out on the trail with merits and proceeded gradually. When crossing a ford, there was a flood that did not recede, swelling the current for a long time, but somehow the hooves of his horse were steadied on a patch of firm ground, and he easily forded to the far bank. He considered that this was indeed due to the blessing of Phakmodrupa, the lord of living beings.[35]

At Kusamobe, he was met by a patron named Shelpa Trapel, who served him on the way with food, clothing, and other necessities. At first he went to Dokor. At Tongzhe, he befriended one called Churton, who said he was going to Jayul to build a butter-lamp shrine, and he traveled with him for a while. In the company of a physician of Nyenpa, he then reached Nyen via Lungsho.

From lower On, he traveled alone through the narrow gorge of Jang to Tsarong, and after he had covered the rough road, he glimpsed the white earthen walls of Densatil Monastery. At that moment, it was as if he had been sprinkled with nectar. As he was about to enter into Phakmodrupa's grass hermitage, an attendant placed him beside the door saying, "Stay there for a while!" At the command of lord Phakmodrupa, Sengton brought him a leftover wad of butter, a ball of roasted barley, and an excellent brew of tea, which were the ingredients of an easy meal. {207} Tashi Pel consumed them with faith, arranging the auspicious circumstance through which he would become a lineage holder and worthy recipient of all the oral instructions without exception. In the late afternoon he met Phakmodrupa, who inquired, "Are you not tired?" Immediately on hearing these words, he experienced a joy that he had not previously known, similar to that of a monk who has attained the third meditative concentration. He replied in general terms and specifically mentioned that he had been slightly carried away by water at the ford, whereupon the lama said, "At that time, I too was there! Even when I was in Vajrāsana, I had to come wherever you were. I am the teacher who facilitates the development of your meditative experience and realization in all respects, not merely in this life alone."[36]

That evening, when the torma offering was made, the lama said to his attendants, "When this newcomer reached the door, before he actually entered, there was a likeness of the newcomer there that separated from the body of the newcomer and vanished into my heart." This was an intimation of the inconceivably secret magical display of a master and disciple that may be revealed to those requiring training, even after manifestly perfect enlightenment has been attained in the essential nature of the unique buddha body of reality.

Also, on one occasion, he said, gesticulating to his attendant Begom, "Doesn't this newcomer resemble Jayulwa?" Even when there seemed to be a difference in teacher and retinue, Phakmodrupa was making an indirect reference to Taklungpa's past life as the great attendant of Chenga Tsultrim Bar and Rinpoche Pa, who had been known as Jayulwa.[37]

Until that time, the affairs of his attendance were handled by Begom, but starting from that time onward, according to an injunction of Phakmodrupa, lord of living beings himself, it was as when he, Phakmodrupa, had formerly been the great sage Śākyamuni and Rinpoche Taklungwa had been the sublime Ānanda. {208} From that time, they pleased each other with acts of service that were not in the slightest distinguishable, such that throughout the whole country the saying "Like Lama Phakmodrupa and like the attendant Taklung Tangpa" became well known as a proverbial expression of perfect devotion and service.

When almost three months had passed since they met, he thought that if he could maintain his prayers even if his body were now to be fragmented into a hundred pieces, he would certainly survive with happiness. Therefore, he went into the presence of Phakmodrupa and presented a golden maṇḍala, saying, "I request spiritual accomplishment. I do not request any doctrine other than the teachings on union with the spiritual teacher. May my experiential cultivation also be exclusively of devotion!" In this way, with this offering, he somehow expressed the circumstances that arose in his mind. Phakmodrupa replied, "Faith is an action that can restore health! From the time when we first met, our minds have been intermingled as one. On each occasion, you have come as a simple monk, but even among the monks, the best are just equal to you in renunciation and realization. Now, indeed you should offer this maṇḍala and pray! Many sorts of enlightened attributes will arise from within. You will have the perception requisite for apprehending whatever sacred teachings arise. You should act as the master of all my sacred doctrines. To serve the spiritual teacher and act with devotion—that is my oral instruction. Realization arises from within—that is my pith instruction."[38]

Henceforth, even when his teacher uttered a single quatrain of oral instruction, Taklungpa would write it down to facilitate memorization. One day, after the teacher had uttered an oral instruction, {209} he inscribed a memo on the surface of a wall as he went outside for some purpose, and on the way back up, he saw that writing. Starting from then, he could hear the sacred doctrine absolutely without doubt concerning his recall.[39] He could comprehend without error all the words and meanings of all that was spoken only once and acquired mnemonic retention that was as firm as *dhāraṇī* incantations inscribed in stone, unadulterated and immaculate like grains of white rice poured in a glass jar, and carefree, regardless of the occasion, purpose, or exemplar. Such an ability to listen is associated with the sublime arhats who compiled the transmitted teachings of the Conqueror—and the great bodhisattva beings who were the foremost heirs of the Conqueror—but is otherwise hard to manifest.

In general Phakmodrupa, the great lord of living beings, had met with almost a hundred spiritual teachers and advisers of Tsang, U, and Kham, and it was as if there were no doctrines in the way of mantra and the transcendent perfections renowned in Tibet that he did not study. All these had been sealed exclusively with the pith instructions of Dakpo Nyigom Gampopa and excellent preserved in the expanse of his enlightened intention, without the stains of unknowing, and he conferred them upon his senior disciple, this mighty lord of the world, Taklungpa the Great, as if the contents of one vase were poured into another. Therefore, it is impossible to document precisely the full extent of his oceanic studies. Roughly estimated, the most important of these included the Cycle of the Wish-Fulfilling Gem of the Aural Lineage;[40] the Cycle of Coemergent Union of the Great Seal concerning the Abiding Nature;[41] the Cycle of the Six Doctrines of Nāropā concerning the Great Seal of Bliss and Emptiness;[42] the Cycle of the Glorious Nondual Kālacakra Tantra;[43] {210} the Cycle of Quintessential Cakrasaṃvara; the Cycle of Venerable Vajrayoginī;[44] the Cycle of Essential Hevajra;[45] the Cycle of the Four Adamantine Seats Associated with the Protectors of the Transmitted Teachings;[46] the Cycle of Mahāmāyā: The Mother Tantra;[47] the Cycles of the Secret Assembly; and Yamāntaka: The Tantras of Skillful Means;[48] along with their maturational empowerments, liberating guidance, and supporting exegeses on the tantras. In addition, they included the Cycle of Sublime Avalokiteśvara;[49] the Cycle of Tārā: Mother of the Conquerors;[50] the cycles of Sublime Sitātapatrā,[51] Vajrapāṇi,[52] Glorious Hayagrīva,[53] Acala: King of Wrathful Deities,[54] Vajravidāraṇa,[55] Ucchūṣmakrodha,[56] Mañjughoṣa,[57] Amitāyus,[58] Nāgendrarāja,[59] Śabarī,[60] Mārīcī,[61] Uṣṇīṣavijaya,[62] Garuḍa,[63] and Kurukullā;[64] and The Five Classes of Ḍākinī.[65] Furthermore, they also included the cycles of the protector deities headed by Kākamukha Mahākāla, Leader of the Oceanic Protectors of the Buddhist Teaching;[66] Dhūmāṅgārīśrīdevī;[67] Six-Armed Mahākāla: Lord-Protector of Blessings;[68] Kartṛkā: Lord-Protector of Enlightened Attributes;[69] Takṣara: Lord-Protector of Enlightened Activities;[70] the Great King Vaiśravaṇa;[71] Aparājitā;[72] Jambhala;[73] and Gaṇapati.[74] Moreover they also included the Cycle of Torma Offerings,[75] the Cycle concerning Compatible Conditions and Extracting the Essence of Elixir,[76] the Graduated Path of the Vehicle of the Transcendent Perfections,[77] the Hundred and One Details of Random Instruction on the Generation and Perfection Stages of the Way of Mantra,[78] a little-known cycle on the Litany of the Names of Mañjuśrī,[79] and so forth.

In brief, as clarified in the treatise titled *Ornament of the Genuine Appearance of Pristine Cognition*,[80] which was composed by the supreme emanation Sangye Onpo, in general, Tashi Pel completely studied the Seven Treatises of Phenomenology,[81] the Seven Treatises on Valid Cognition,[82] the Six Collections of Reasoning concerning the Middle Way,[83] and the Five Doctrines of Maitreya,[84] along with the empowerments, tantras, and pith instructions of the action, conduct, union, and unsurpassed union classes. {211}

One day, when he went out for recreation on the meadow of Densatil, he became equipoised in *The King of Meditative Stability* in that place, in consequence of which an extraordinary realization the likes of which he had not previously encountered, arose. Aware of this, Phakmodrupa, lord of living beings, arrived there and pointed his staff at his heart, saying, "Our master, Lord Nāropā, has said that one should meditate on the nature of all things as empty and without self and that if from within that disposition, one experiences diverse methods by means of the four immeasurable aspirations, this is the path through which the nonabiding nirvāṇa is attained.

Commencing from that event, Phakmodrupa bestowed the profound and extensive introductions that illustrate the ultimate, fundamental reality, such that Tashi Pel directly saw the actual face of great bliss, intrinsic awareness, the fundamental coemergent pristine cognition of all phenomenal existence and quiescence. All dualistic signs and concepts, subtle and gross, as many as they are, were naturally liberated. He knew that cyclic existence itself is the natural dynamic of the buddha body of reality and that when the abiding modality of the mind is actualized, that is designated as "buddha." Once the conceptual elaborations of hope and doubt, acceptance and rejection, refutation and proof with regard to cyclic existence and nirvāṇa have been calmed, all phenomena, however they arose and however they appeared, manifested as the dynamic of the buddha body of reality and as great luminosity. All mental stains associated with the focus, such as the dichotomy between the object of meditation and the subject of meditation, vanished of their own accord, and the dominion of great nonmeditation, the horizon of meditation, was actualized.

Drogon Phakmodrupa then said to him, "Come here one day, wearing new clothes!" He had him sit upon a large and elevated white throne with a silk cushion, pointed his staff toward his heart, and uttered the following purposeful words: {212} "These profound instructions of my aural lineage are unknown to other monks apart from me, even at Gampo. Here, too, I cannot teach them to anyone but you. You should be their owner. Do not give them to just anyone, but do not let their transmission be interrupted! Do not put into writing the pith instructions of the aural lineage. Do not verbalize the symbolic lineage! Do not sing of your experiential cultivation in public! Do not indulge in the insane methods of virtuous asceticism! By acting in accordance with the words of the buddhas and your spiritual teacher, you will actualize the pristine cognition of the buddha body of reality."

At that time, when he was empowered in accordance with the transmitted teachings as a supreme regent on the lion throne of the sacred doctrine and appointed as a master of the Buddhist teaching, there was no doubt in the perspective of the uncommon disciples that Tashi Pel manifested the inexhaustible, oceanic, emanational play of the empowered heirs of the conquerors, but I dare not write about that here except to describe simply how he appeared from the perspective of ordinary disciples. In that regard, Tashi Pel had three astonishing significant dreams that he reported to Drogon Phakmodrupa. In sequence, these were indications foretelling that he would enjoy the inexhaustible treasure of food and wealth, he would effortlessly perfect the transcendent perfection of generosity and bring the minds of others to maturation and liberation through the profound pith instructions, and he would establish countless assemblies of beings who had attained the three sublime levels[85] and of ordinary persons in provisional and conclusive erudition.

The eighty-four accomplished masters then appeared within the rows of monks who received the communal tea offering at Mangkar Gang—they gave a general teaching, and in particular, they communicated the eight great accomplishments.[86]

In public, Tashi Pel freely instructed others in many profound and secret essential points that were covert, including his personal array of the seven insignia of royal authority, the great tales of his past lives, and the twelve simultaneous projections of his physical body. {213}

In response to the entreaty of Rinpoche Pa, he documented a great many essential pith instructions of maturational empowerment and liberating guidance, which are clearly contained among the Collected Works of Drogon Phakmodrupa.

Again, on a certain occasion, Drogon extensively conferred prophetic declarations, saying, "Even though you depart from here, your disciples and enlightened activities will be immeasurable. Again, there will be an obstacle to your enlightened attributes caused by pride. You should not utilize the material sacraments of your spiritual teacher. Do not obstruct the veneration of pure lands. Do not use the wealth of the monastic community. Do not squander the materials offered by the faithful, indulging in nonsensical talk. Do not impart and entrust the sacred doctrine when there are contagious diseases. Previously, you had to maintain the conduct of a nobleman, but at this point you should be a vajra-holding monk. Since you are naturally inclined toward bountiful conduct, you should receive the complete monastic ordination. On reaching a place that is decreed by your former actions, your enlightened activities will be extensive there. That terrain is also extremely rugged, inhabited by innumerable venomous gods and demons, headed by a *tsen* spirit descended from humans. So it is a place that no one has managed to control, but I have trodden it entirely with my feet and subdued all the gods and demons, and you will take hold of it through my blessings!"[87]

In all, Tashi Pel served Drogon Phakmodrupa for six years. Then, on the twenty-fifth day of the month of Kārtika in 1170 (iron tiger), Drogon Rinpoche passed away. During the funeral ceremony, an immaculate ray of light in the form of a golden vajra was diffused from the heart of the sacred corpse, and it vanished into the heart of the precious Taklung Tangpa. He conclusively presided over the cremation of the sacred corpse, the distribution of the oceanic offering clouds that are the means of fulfilling the enlightened intention of the deceased, {214} the ritual transformation of the sacred bone relics into the buddha body of reality, and so forth.

Then, at the end of that same year, 1170, when he was in his twenty-ninth year, Tashi Pel set out from the great residence of Drogon Phakmodrupa. On the way, in Meldro, he completely received the doctrinal cycle of Chekhawa from a spiritual adviser named Sechil Pub, and he comprehended it.[88] Then, he proceeded to Jayul, where a particularly virtuous inspiration based on the recollection of his past life as Jayulwa, arose. He made extensive offerings there to the representations of buddha body, speech, and mind.

Then, as Drogon Rinpoche had commanded, he intended to depart via Lungsho for Kham. Taking the northern route, he traveled gradually. At the Main Temple of Podo Dudul, where Geshe Zhangton Khangmoche resided, the latter saw just a fraction of Rinpoche's physical attributes of greatness and became extremely devout, offering his respects, and requesting him to stay there as a household priest. Tashi Pel refused but spent the winter at nearby Tango Monastery.[89]

Then, when he intended to move to a mountain hermitage, the geshe informed him that there was an isolated and pleasant place called Sengling.[90] They gradually went in search of it, but it was Rinpoche himself who recognized it well. He was welcomed by the five classes of the ḍākinīs of pristine cognition. On the way through the gorge, an uncouth person broke a vulture bone with his hand—a local custom that pointed toward a pleasant outcome. He made the natural cave at Phabong Karleb into his actual residence. His teaching throne was a natural rock platform. On its right side, {215} there was a natural maṇḍala of Bhaṭṭārikā, as if it were the handiwork of a skilled artist. The platform had a cushion with seven rugs stacked on top, marking the auspicious coincidence of his seven successive journeys, and there were also other signs, such as the renowned boulder depicting someone leading a horse and someone leading a hybrid cow, marking the auspicious coincidence that he would gather the resources of the four frontiers. This was where, later on, the monastic body of Taklung and his attendants would gather.[91]

In that place, Tashi Pel also bound the wrathful *lhatsen* spirit under oath as a protector of the transmitted teachings. The spirit offered him the vital heart mantra that was its natural indication, and he in turn empowered it in the supremely secret maṇḍala. He established it in the oral instructions of maturational empowerment and liberating guidance, and of the generation and perfection stages, and finalized all concluding rites in respect for the Buddhist teaching and those who uphold the Buddhist teaching. He presented it with daily torma offerings and designated its swift messengers, its sharp arrows that guard the Buddhist teaching, and named it Genyen Chenpo.[92]

From the perspective of others, Tashi Pel seemed to reside in that place, engaged in one-pointed practice with the cave entrance plastered off. At that time, he purified the energy channels, generative essences, and winds within the central channel of the subtle body, and the continuum of his mind was filled with a stream of uncontaminated bliss and emptiness. Although the adventitious phenomena of cyclic existence did appear, he beheld them as fictitious appearances, empty of essential nature, an amalgam of subtle wind and mind. Since he was free from the propensities of bewilderment and unimpeded in emanational transformations, he continued to enjoy the oceanic pure lands, and he actually transformed that location, commencing with its environment and inhabitants, into a circle of deities. Even in deep sleep he continued to practice in accordance with the concealed and genuine inner radiance. Liberated from the fetters of birth and death, he perfected the integration of the two truths, such that he could disregard the refinement of the fields of the intermediate state in which those of average and dull acumen engage, and even the transference of consciousness, which has a meditative focus. {216}

He himself said, "The distractions and wanderings of external activities and the rope of the internal subject-object dichotomy have been decisively severed, and in my luminous mind there is no distinction between meditative equipoise and post-meditation."[93] And, "It is said that from great, glorious Tilopā down to me, the lesser monk Tashi Pel, except for the lineage of the sugatas, there have been no obstacles due to ordinary persons."[94] So it was in such isolation that he revealed the way of one-pointed practice and the way in which the actual signs of the levels and path are gradually perfected, dependent thereon. But that accords with the provisional meaning from the perspective of his disciples who required training. As far as the definitive meaning is concerned, it says in his *Memorandum on His Oral Instructions*,[95]

> I uphold the Conqueror of the Three Times:
> Dīpaṃkara, the buddha of the past;
> Śākyaketu, guide of the present;
> And Maitreya, the conqueror of the future![96]

Therefore, once the nature of lord Mahāvajradhara is accomplished, the play of emanations limitlessly arises. How could that possibly be appraised by ordinary persons who would even seek to measure space!

Afterward, someone arrived from Kham to invite him, but instead Tashi Pel set out with him for the glorious glade of Samantabhadra at Phakmodru. He went there to cremate the heart of Venerable Phakmodrupa, lord of living beings, and he performed an act of service by planning the construction of the reliquary stūpa that represents the buddha body of reality. The measurements, design, sacred contents, and consecration were perfectly accomplished.

Once again, he set out and stayed at Sengling itself. At that time, the master Sangye Gompa Tsultrim Sherab went there to pay his respects and request a doctrinal connection.[97] As soon as he met Tashi Pel, {217} he saw his physical body assume the form of glorious Phakmodrupa, and he even heard the intonation of his voice assume the voice of glorious Phakmodrupa. So it was that after determining that the father and son were inseparable, starting from that time onward, he served him inseparably and became the foremost of the attendants who pleased the teacher by means of the three ways of pleasing him.[98]

Then, at the great seminary of glorious Shomara, he properly received the precepts of the full monastic ordination in the midst of a quorum of five from the monastic preceptor Shomarapa—one of the four Zhang, who were the spiritual sons of Geshe Tab Kawachenpo Darma Drak—and an accomplished great elder, who had mastered the three piṭakas of scriptural transmission and the three trainings of clear realization. The erudite Geshe

Marpa Chomtangpa, who was devoted to monastic training and endowed with the nectar of meditative stability, acted as the master of ceremonies, and Geshe Zhangton Gomik, who was authentic and possessed all defining characteristics, acted as confessor.[99] In this way, with mindfulness, awareness, and carefulness, they bestowed upon him the basket of the precious precepts resembling the wish-fulfilling gem.

Tashi Pel deeply cherished the precepts, such that he upheld the victory banner of the monastic robe and became foremost among those who were devoted to the precepts. His title, Taklung Tangpa, Perfect in Ethical Discipline, became renowned throughout the three worlds. Even nowadays, it is undisputedly proven in the common perception of all that by just approaching the statue of this venerable lord, in which the sacred relics of his robe have been inserted, the fragrance of ethical discipline that can dispel all stains of body and mind wafts like the fragrance of the wish-granting tree. {218}

On one occasion, he returned to Densatil, the great monastic seat of Phakmodrupa, to distribute offerings and donations similar to the emanational offerings of Samantabhadra. Then, in his great isolated retreat, he began to make preparations with the intention of going to Kham, whereupon at the exhortation of the gods who delighted in positive virtues, such as the oath-bound Lhei Genyen, all the monks and patrons headed by Geshe Zhang gathered beautiful flowers, and in unison they requested him to stay. So he postponed his travel plans, foreseeing a great objective. Altogether, he resided at the Sengling hermitage for seven years. Since he extensively bestowed the banquet of pith instructions and essential guidance on those who were interested, fortunate disciples congregated there, like bees in a grove of lotuses, and their number multiplied on a daily basis, such that they could not be accommodated at Drakle. He considered moving to another isolated place and went to Taklung, where he stayed for almost three months in a grass hermitage in front of the blessed cave and the small hill. But, thinking that the predicted time for founding Taklung Monastery had not quite arrived, he moved to Sewalung. There, too, his profound and extensive promulgations of the doctrinal wheel and the gathering of his disciples were inconceivable. His attendants began to undertake building works, and he delayed there, teaching the master Sangye Gompa.[100]

At the request of the geshes and great patrons of Dartre, in the last summer month of 1180 (iron male bird), in his thirty-ninth year, he descended to Taklung. {219} This place, as explained above, had been foreordained by the Conqueror, and it had been blessed by the precious master Padmasambhava. When the latter's actual disciple Shelgyi Lhunpo had made it his residence, it was given the name Taklung (Tiger Valley or Birch Valley), due to the array of his miraculous powers. A disciple of Smṛtijñānakīrti named Begom Sangye Yeshe had also attained spiritual accomplishment there. Lord Marpa the Translator had visited and made predictions. Geshe Potowa the Great had even nurtured a community there with many texts and pith instructions. Kharak Gomchung too had also essentialized his spiritual attainments there over a long period of time, and yet the terrain was rough and incapable of being inhabited by anyone at all due to the fierce gods and demons.[101]

Rinpoche Tashi Pel first descended via the hill of Labrang Nakpo, where a raven emanation of Kākamukha Mahākāla, protector of the transmitted teachings, brought him many necessities in its beak. Sojourning in the place where nowadays a grass hermitage stands, he knew that this had been foreordained by the doctrinal protectors. In that location, he built a grass hermitage and some small storerooms. Except when he occasionally spoke words of profound guidance, for the most part he stayed seated exclusively in meditation. Many people arrived there to invite him, headed by his younger brother Lama Da-o from Kham, but he did not break the injunction of Drogon Rinpoche Phakmodrupa.[102]

In order to establish the auspicious circumstances for his enlightened activities, a group of seven, including the master and his disciples, went to the top of Langling Lakha Pass. At his bidding, the attendant Jangseng brought water from a source on the Indo-Tibetan border, and he boiled an excellent brew of tea, saying, "Roll a ball of molasses on this patch of ice and use that! I am going east to Kuyang Gang!" {220} And he sang the sacred song of *The Three Unforgettable Recollections*.[103] That night, he faced toward the east and sat in meditation. In this way, he established the auspicious circumstances for the virtuous enlightened activities of the spiritual and temporal teaching and teachers of the glorious Taklungpa tradition to become widespread and secure throughout the region of Dokham, China, Jang, Mongolia, and so forth, until the present day.[104]

He stayed for a while at Dam Kokhyim, but at the entreaty of most of the monks there, whose monasteries were in the northern direction, and particularly at the joint request of the patrons of Dar, Tre, and Rong, he decided to stay on in the very heart of U, which resembles the sun. Those who had invited him to the east were also ordained as mendicants and applied themselves to exegesis and attainment.

Tashi Pel auspiciously frequented the isolated hermitage of Pargam for approximately three months. In general, it is said that this venerable master had six places of attainment, which were given the name "fortress"—namely, the fortress of Sengling Drakya Dorje, the fortress of Ojo Drakmar Khyung, the fortress of Lang Ngul Mukpo Chong, the fortress of Sewalung Khuyuk Rolwa, the fortress of Uma Drakar Tingdzin, and the fortress of Parti Pargam Namkha.[105]

Afterward, he was sent an invitation on account of a dispute between the communities of Dar and Rong. They completely gave up their dispute, and he established them in mutual friendship, as if they were brothers. To repay his kindness, they invited him to Dar, Tre, and Rong, where he was offered veneration. He imparted inconceivable instructions, turned the wheel of the sacred doctrine, and, for posterity, established all their respective lands and physical resources as his monastic estates in the service of the precious Kagyu lineage.[106] {221}

Then again, Tashi Pel descended to this great plain of Taklung. In his precious grass hermitage with its canopy and in the place called the white storeroom, the yakṣa Aparājitā offered him the spiritual accomplishment of the inexhaustible repository of space. To mark that auspicious circumstance, he savored tea that brewed of its own accord on one occasion, and consequently it was known that for an entire year, this tea could subsequently be consumed without succumbing to food poisoning.

Naktsang Chenmo also said to him, "This is a commune of the world! Since Jangseng seems to be one who knows this, it has been entrusted to him. He has equitably distributed even the tea—from the owner of the monastery on high to the incapacitated blind and destitute below!" To mark the auspicious circumstance of these irregular offerings and donations, he established a threshold without a door.

He then founded the Main Temple, nowadays known as the Ancient Offering Chapel and its representations (images, books, and stūpas)—which are imbued with the blazing splendor of his blessings, as if the reflected images of the row of buddhas had actually manifested there—along with the White Temple of Precious Spiritual and Temporal Well-Being and its annex and the Red Teaching Throne, and these were worthy of homage paid by the world along with the gods.[107]

As for his immediate, daily regimen, just as the bodhisattva Dawa Gyeltsen had instructed glorious Phakmodrupa, he imparted guidance during the first half of the month and practiced retreat during the second half of the month. All the oceanic enlightened activities in which he endlessly engaged—practicing the four-session yoga, instructing the monks, meeting patrons, and so forth—were unceasing, one after another, like the waves of a great ocean. {222} He purposefully said that this very power of blessing, through which there was no difference between him and the actual image of glorious Phakmodrupa, came about naturally through compassion.

After composing *The Prayer Titled Excellent Emergence of Wealth*,[108] he bestowed the oral transmission of *The Precious Source*,[109] which became known as The Reading Transmission of Taklung. The countless images, books, and stūpas representing buddha body, speech, and mind that turned up there from all directions, like a downpour of rain, were installed in the Great Offering Chapel, and since he arrayed an oceanic cloud of offerings, offerings were constantly being made. The outer and inner auspicious circumstances whereby material things fall like rain when attachment is reversed from within occurred, and the resources of Vaiśravaṇa actually manifested. In such ways, he could also observe and comment upon impending disasters.

Since his attendant, the great spiritual being Jangchub Senge, did not squander anything prematurely, they enjoyed extensive offerings and donations. In order to furnish the interior of the temple containing the precious grass hermitage at the great monastic residence of Phakmodru in the forest of glorious Samantabhadra, he prepared sixty measures of salt. On that occasion he offered one measure of salt for each measure of powdered rock that was excavated, and in this way constructed the Great Rock-Cut Temple. The wall on the north side of the Great Temple at Phakmodru was built by Taklungpa. He gave advice to the craftsmen who made all the images, books, and stūpas representing buddha body, speech, and mind, including the two precious images of Phakmodrupa, which are called Meaningful to Behold, and he contributed building materials, clothes for the craftsmen, and their fees.[110]

After completing the consecration ceremony there, he rectified the traditions and his contribution surpassed that of all the disciples at the great monastic residence of Densatil, as he donated seven hundred volumes of scriptures inscribed in blue ink, innumerable volumes inscribed on plain white paper, gold ingots, fifty nuggets of turquoise, sixty bricks of tea, three thousand lengths of brocade silk, {223} many hundreds of hybrid cattle and horses, and two hundred and eighty butter lamps, which burned constantly and were valued at one hundred *sang* of gold in a single night, as well as appropriate supplies of tea and salt, and two hundred fields for the sustenance of those who then lived there, and so forth.[111] He spoke exclusively of the advantages that are always associated with ethical discipline, and established all mendicants in the precious training of keeping vows and avoiding downfalls. *The Tenet concerning the Unique Essential of the Three Vows in the Great Seal* says,[112]

> Purifying natural defects, prohibitions,
> Along with the mundane inadmissible transgressions,[113]
> In the state of luminosity, intrinsic awareness—
> That is the vow of ethical discipline maintained by pious attendants.
> Purifying egotism and malice,
> Possessing the conclusive four immeasurable aspirations,
> Acting for the benefit of others,
> Free from disillusionment with cyclic existence and longing for quiescence—
> That is the vow of ethical discipline maintained by bodhisattvas.
> With one's own mind, nonarising, as king,
> Surrounded by an innate nondual entourage,
> Empty of the inherent existence of the subject-object dichotomy—
> That is the vow of the mantras maintained by awareness holders.[114]

And,

> The outer four elements, planets, stars, and seasons,
> The inner energy channels, letters, winds, mind, and centers,
> And the secret sudden encounter of awareness
> Arise as the wheels of the sacred doctrine, pure in its auspicious circumstance.[115]

Such words roar the lion's roar that outer, inner, and extraneous phenomena are in a common savor in the real nature.[116]

The number of fortunate and saintly persons who beheld him as a buddha and as a bodhisattva was countless. Old Jowo of Tre saw him as Munīndra surrounded by an entourage. The attendants Samten Sherab and Gomdrak both simultaneously {224} saw him reach the teaching throne, preach the sacred doctrine, and meet them at the portico of his grass hermitage. Khyungpo Dawa saw him as Mahākāruṇika. Jose Welchung saw him as the coemergent Cakrasaṃvara. Geshe Meldrowa saw him as Satyadvayamukha Bhaṭṭārikā. Lhopa Drubtob saw him in the form of Drogon Rinpoche himself, indeterminate in size. A disciple of Mokchokpa saw him as Bhaṭṭārikā from the lower part of his costume down to the teaching throne. Dzeden, a master from Tsang, continuously saw him as Śākyamuni. Kangtang Sherab Pel saw him as Mahākāruṇika, and Gomsam saw him for a prolonged period in the form of glorious Phakmodrupa. Such visions were endless.[117]

The categories of his compositions are also most extensive. I have already collated them in the following sections.[118] First, there is the section of wondrous narratives that establish supreme conviction. Second, there is the section of supplication prayers through contentment based on hope, and so forth, through to fervent devotion. Third, there is the section of extensive public teachings that disclose in detail all the sequences of the path, including the three trainings for the sake of such fortunate persons. Fourth, there is the section of rectification of infringements through the observations, offerings, and provisions of the three vows for those who have entered into the sublime monastic community. Fifth, there is the section of verses and epistles that instruct those who believe in terse verbal expressions and meanings. Sixth, there is the section of means for attainment and the generation stage of meditation that instructs fortunate students of the profound and secret Adamantine Vehicle in the first of the two stages, once they have received the maturational empowerments. {225} Seventh, there is the section of the profound essential guidance of the unsurpassed tantras that confer empowerment and liberation. Eighth, there is the section of subtle oral instructions through which those who acquire firmness after experientially cultivating such maturational empowerments and liberating guidance then undertake the twofold benefit of self and others. This division into eight topics accords with the arrangement in the catalog of his Collected Works.

Once, when he stayed near the snow mountain of Nyenchen Tanglha, teaching one of the scriptures titled *Pañcaśikhin*: *King of the Gandharvas*,[119] he sent a letter concerning rituals and so forth, to that great deity, with these words:

Chieftain of deities, with manifold existences,
O king of the world and the sacred doctrine,
Please may you support those who practice the sacred doctrine, in general,
And for us, the master and disciples,
May you act as a sponsor and a patron,
By all your occult forces and abilities whatsoever!
If you act accordingly, you yourself
Will attain the unsurpassed level.[120]

Thereby, in the common perception of all eighteen who were present, the master and disciples, over a period of one month, the deity Nyenchen Tanglha actually arrived there each day, and then made offerings and paid his respects, such that the kindness of the sacred doctrine was conferred upon him. The renowned and powerful mundane protectors who possessed miraculous abilities were also given their injunctions as servants, and the kindness of the teachings was conferred upon them.

When the precious teacher Tashi Pel met glorious Drigungpa the Great, Jikten Gonpo, at On, they had a meeting of minds, and since they knew Tashi Pel was a master of all the oral instructions, in the manner of a vase that had been filled to the brim, Drigungpa asked him for a profound oral instruction that tersely discloses the profound and vast meanings. On that occasion, Tashi Pel spoke as follows:

When Rinpoche is engaged in the preparatory practices,
If he sets the mind on enlightenment
There will be great meritorious power.
When he is engaged in the main practice,
If he cultivates the four immeasurable aspirations,
That will be potently of benefit for sentient beings. {226}
If he is attentive in the appropriate manner,
The light rays of the buddhas will penetrate of their own accord.
If he can similarly express this in words
The blessings of the sacred doctrine will be immediately introduced.
If he cherishes others rather than himself,
The spiritual accomplishments of the monastic community will develop.

If he prays to the spiritual teacher,
That is the root of the Three Precious Jewels.
If he practices from the heart, in accordance with the sacred doctrine,
That is the teaching of the buddhas.
If he cultivates the oral instructions of those who maintain the lineage,
The meaning of all things will be understood.
If he frequents hermitages and experientially cultivates the truth,
His perception will be refreshed.
If he lives alone, by himself,
The creeping plants of attachment and fixation will not reach.
If he observes without conceptual elaboration,
There will be naturally arising pristine cognition.
If he himself abides in the state of nonconceptuality,
Others will gather on the basis of this nonconceptuality.
If he maintains a humble station,
The thoughts "I am great. I am noble!" will not arise.
If he prolongs his pursuit of spiritual attainment,
The fruit will be acquired in this lifetime.
If he dedicates merit for the sake of enlightenment in the future,
His virtuous actions will not become indeterminate.[121]

Accordingly, it is said that Drigungpa became extremely devoted and paid homage to him. Although they were known to be indistinguishable associates, Drigungpa listened to his sacred doctrine and made obeisance to him.[122]

Seeing him to be inseparable from Drogon Rinpoche, some saintly persons genuinely praised his mind, which was identical with the three buddha bodies and the mind of glorious Phakmodrupa, along with his observance of the three vows and his maintaining of the ascetic disciplines of the great hermit sages, and they would pray to him with verses that begin, "Wonderful, marvelous!" Their offerings were adorned with the aspirational prayer that they might be accepted inseparably. That is to say, they respected him because he was indistinguishable from Drogon Phakmodrupa. {227}

The glorious Drukpa Drogon Tsangpa Gyare, who filled beings with the teaching of the lineage of attainment, also sent offerings, eighteen days' march from Ja Gopo. Since he had acquired little success in the cultivation of compassion, he requested an oral instruction that would bring forth the advantages of compassion, whereupon Tashi Pel said, "My child, my child!

I have already refined that!" It is said that he then delivered a profound oral instruction on cultivating compassion, such that Tsangpa Gyare developed it in meditation and became extremely great in compassion.[123]

With regard to Tashi Pel's main disciples, their lives will be explained below in some detail. At the time when he passed into nirvāṇa in this place Taklung, a pure monastic community of approximately five thousand congregated. Those in faraway places were countless. Jambudvīpa—including India, China, Nepal, Lijiang, Minyak, Ngari, Utsang, Dokham, Asura Cave,[124] Oḍḍiyāna, Kashmir, Jalandhara, and Siṅghala—was filled for the most part with his disciples, who were mighty lords of spiritual attainment. Since their disciples and grand-disciples equaled the particles of the great earth, they filled the entire world.

There are extensive remarks concerning his extrasensory powers, exemplified by the pristine cognition that knows the three times without obscuration, and although there are various comments concerning the transformations that he brought about due to auspicious circumstances, those that accrued excellent immediate and long-term outcomes were inconceivable. Indeed, such incidents were indescribable. Although his sacred attributes were mainly concealed, they were exclusively the attributes of the perfect buddhas, and not alien to them. Since these attributes could not be actualized even by those of sharp acumen who were followers of the sacred doctrine or by those of dull acumen who were followers based on faith, the array of his miraculous abilities, surpassing the confines of the intellect, {228} which he extensively revealed even on a daily basis, cannot be completely presented even if one were to speak of them for an eon.

Finally, in his sixty-seventh year, in 1208 (earth male dragon), Tashi Pel appeared slightly unwell. Distinctive rites to secure his life were extensively performed, but from the new year of 1209 (earth female snake), when he was in his sixty-eighth year, his physical strength weakened although he was not very ill. He extensively granted predictions and oral instructions to everyone, in general and in particular. He especially bequeathed the key of the library to the supreme reincarnation of Gyeltsab Tulku and appointed him as regent of the sacred doctrine. During the period of evening tea on the nineteenth day of the eleventh month, he passed away, absorbed in the expanse of supreme ultimate truth, which is the expanse of reality, free from all conceptual elaborations.

On the twenty-fourth day, during the great funeral ceremony, a Bonpo named Monlam Senge approached from the corner of the shrine, holding a precious walking stick and saw the sacred corpse. He had the thought that the interior of the crematorium was rather small to accommodate the sacred corpse, but at that moment the voice of the precious one, Tashi Pel himself, emerged from the sky, saying, "How could that be the case if Sherab Gyeltsen makes it!" The latter performed the rite in accordance with these words, and the sacred corpse fitted easily. When the sacred corpse was cremated, it was instantly consumed by the flames, and the heart, tongue, and eyes, along with innumerable five-colored pearl relics, were retrieved. Even when the place was filled with smoke, there was a downpour of pearl relics. At that very moment, Ngure saw Sahajā. Gazi Gopo saw the hillside permeated with light, {229} and a mantrin saw Rinpoche actually seated amid an aura of light in the sky. Moreover, he was seen in many forms, and even seen as the buddhas of the five families.[125]

On the day that he passed into nirvāṇa, Rinpoche was actually seen to appear to Yorchung Rinchen Pel who was in a group of monks arriving from the uplands of Mong in Taklung. On the day when the sacred corpse was cremated, he was seen seated on the teaching throne of Dzongkar, wearing his hat. The patron Gotruk saw him twice, actually seated within the flames that engulfed the sacred corpse. The wife of that official saw Rinpoche Tashi Pel actually arrive in two embodiments, one displaying the form of Mahākāruṇika, and one with earrings. Dungre saw Bhaṭṭārikā emerge three times from within the smoke and depart into the sky. Anecdotes such as these are indescribable.

I have written this account, roughly integrating the main points explained in the three old manuscript versions of the biography, written respectively by Kuyal Rinpoche, Gompa Tsultrim Pel, and Venerable Tashi Peltsek, along with *The Doctrinal History of Lhorong*, and so forth.

More extensively, there are so many later anecdotes that I have seen and heard, and these are documented in somewhat greater detail in *The Springtime of the Excellently Flourishing Cornucopia of Devout Tales*,[126] which I composed on the basis of the most wonderful, profound, and vast *Great Biography*.[127] Such details should be known from that account.

The Disciples of Taklungpa the Great Tashi Pel

According to a rough account of the emergence of his senior disciples that derives from the old manuscript versions of the biography, it is said that there were eight who equaled him in realization, {230} three disciples who perfected the oral instructions, four heart sons, three who did not have to be asked, eighteen close heirs, and three learned and accomplished masters who were particularly sublime.

First, the eight who equaled him in realization included the supreme emanation Kuyal Rinchen Gonpo, who resided at the main residence and nurtured a congregation of five thousand; Khoyo Khengan, who nurtured seven hundred monks at the imperial court in China; Tokden Bengo, who nurtured five hundred monks in the Sino-Tibetan borderlands; Ago Zhikpo, who nurtured three hundred thousand monks in the kingdom of Lijiang; Venerable Dzagonpa Chenpo, who nurtured seven thousand monks in the lowlands of Yangmuru Chegye; Jamyang Dzase, who nurtured three hundred monks at Gekya in Pubor; Rang Gangpa, who nurtured five hundred monks at Minyak Gangkar; and Jori Repa, who nurtured one thousand two hundred monks at Yulgosho.[128]

Among them, the biography of the supreme emanation Kuyal, who was the regent of the Conqueror Taklungpa, is presented below in detail.[129]

Ago Zhikpo

Ago Zhikpo[130] was born in the part of Puborgang that is nowadays known as Trunglung, as the son of a shepherd and a female butcher.[131] From his seventh year, an understanding of actions, causes, and results and of the definitive meaning naturally arose within him. By acting in the service of a rich man in Lijiang,[132] he understood that he should earnestly achieve what he had to do. By repaying the kindness he had made through his service of Lijiang, he understood that his resources would increase. By hearing the tale of the snake that succumbed to a cat before it could eat a man called Bata, he understood that if he were to repay good with evil, he would be trapped.[133] {231} By seeing an emanational dwarf hunting a deer and carving its flesh, he understood that by acting honestly, he would accomplish all objectives and savor the taste of great bliss, free from the arising, ceasing, and resting of thought.[134] By seeing a girl who could not be disciplined being beaten, he understood that if he took refuge in the precious jewels, he would attain the fruit and that even after entering the portal of the sacred doctrine, if he did not strive to adopt virtuous actions and reject negative actions, and did not keep his commitments in the correct manner, he would experience suffering.[135] Through hearing the framework story of a girl who was a local chieftain, he understood that if he experientially cultivated the doctrine enunciated by his spiritual teacher and did not follow the deceptions of the afflicted mental states, good auspices would emerge in the short term and in the long term.[136]

By explaining cause and effect to his hunter friends, he benefited them somewhat.[137] In lower Pubor, he served a lama named Kyang and received refuge and instruction on setting the mind on enlightenment. From a student of Ga Lotsāwa, named Neljor Nakpo, he received instructions on Cakrasaṃvara and Mahākāla, and he brought forth the signs of realization. In a town, there were five girls who called him to eat, singing a song. By examining that song, he understood that all conditioned phenomena are impermanent, that he should practice, free from activities and without distraction, that he should engage austerely in the conduct of enlightenment, and that even though all things are indeed conclusively identical in supreme bliss, which is reality, and all the doctrinal wheels of the buddhas are methods of guidance for the minds of those to be trained, if oneself is not liberated, one cannot reveal this to others. He partook of the meat and wine they offered, and that evening there arose the pristine cognition of higher insight, like the sun in a cloudless sky. Realizing that these five were ḍākinīs, he requested an empowerment enabling him to see the spiritual teacher as the buddhas, and about thirty times he requested their feast offerings. {232} They replied, "If you go to Taklung and meditate, you can possibly become one who has no regard for the roots of conditioned virtuous actions!" While he was thinking of setting out for Taklung, a singer who was a beggar woman said, "You are not the sort who practices austerities! You are the sort with strong aggression.[138] You should not go to Utsang. Stay for a while at the glorious mountains in the south!"[139]

By staying for five years at a mountain hermitage in the south, he experienced the intermingling of mind and appearances. Again, that previous beggar woman and the four other girls said to him, "You should travel to the east! You will meet the spiritual teacher of your past life!" So he set out and on the way he met the accomplished master Gongkariwa.[140]

At a place called Lemu, he met Garzha Lhuge Chokyi Gyeltsen, an actual student of glorious Taklung Tangpa, and on asking him questions about Utsang, he replied that although Venerable Dakpo, glorious Phakmodrupa, and Rinpoche Taklung Tangpa had assumed different forms for the sake of others, their essential nature is inseparable from the transcendent lord Buddha. Thereupon an immeasurable devotion arose within him. One day, that teacher informed him that he had sent horsemen on three occasions to invite the venerable lord of the doctrine Taklung Tangpa from Kham, after which the latter had composed this treatise and given it to him. He then recited this *Garland of Secret Nectar*[141] once, and immediately on hearing it, Ago Zhikpo acquired a realization equal to space. All his doubts were resolved thereby. Henceforth, he attended upon that teacher, requested the sacred doctrine, and so forth, without the need for conceptual elaborations, such that he became indivisible from the great and glorious Saraha. Although he did not actually meet the precious teachers of the Kagyu lineage, through their kindness he actualized the abiding nature of reality, whereupon he was appointed as a root teacher. {233} For this reason he is indeed counted among the equivalent students of glorious Taklung Tangpa.[142]

Thereupon, Ago Zhikpo received guidance on the path of skillful means from Lama Chokyi Gyeltsen, and by cultivating that, the entire trichiliocosm was transformed into the aggregates of wind, fire, earth, and water. By experiencing such incidental miracles as they arose, from the expanse of miraculous quiescence, the ḍākinī Siṃhavaktrā appeared, her faces colored blue, red, yellow, and black, and she introduced him to pristine cognition. One night, on the fourteenth day of the lunar month, his former consort poured a skull full of nectar upon his head and bumped the container upon his head three times, whereupon all phenomenal existence spun around in the manner of a wheel. When that vision had subsided, the woman then turned into a large human skeleton. It touched his body three times, saying, "Arise! Arise! Arise from the expanse of reality!" Immediately, the room was transformed into a celestial palace. In the center were Cakrasaṃvara and his consort, along with the four yoginīs, the twenty-four black heroes, and the twenty-four white heroines, the four black female gatekeepers, and the four intermediate ones, with half-matching forms [that is, their faces and hair were of different colors]. These yoginīs also transformed into forms of diverse colors with many diverse heads, and moved about, before finally turning into forms with lion heads. While the skeleton woman stirred excrement, urine, and the mixed generative fluids that trickled from the union of the deities inside a moist skull cup, she exhorted them by the syllable PHAṬ, whereupon the heroes and ḍākinīs filled the sky. The skeleton woman vanished into the five Cakrasaṃvara deities in his navel cakra. {234} With dancing movements, she exhorted him, saying, "Proclaim the adamantine verses for the sake of my sixty-four sons, brothers, and sisters and for the seven thousand seven hundred who will come afterward!"[143]

Thereupon, the five deities in the navel cakra sang the following *doha*—the profound and vast adamantine song:

> I am your mother Vajravārāhī, who has gone to bliss.
> When you were in the womb, you were named Vajra—
> You did not have two names.
> Even after your birth,
> I was all those that you met,
> From the rich man of Lijiang
> To Lama Chokyi Gyeltsen![144]

He was introduced to his mind as the buddha, his speech as the sacred doctrine, and his body as the monastic community. Then again, when he had arranged as offerings an assortment of herbs, eight young girls emerged from the heart of the skeleton woman, and they conferred blessing by offering to the central female deity a skull cup full of human flesh and nectar that they had extracted from space. Everyone enjoyed it to satisfaction. All the deities dissolved into one another, and the central male and female consorts dissolved into the crown of his head.[145]

One day, when he had an inconceivable vision of Dvimukhavajravārāhī, he ran toward her, but she turned into a countryside woman.[146] Again, a disembodied voice resonated from the sky, saying "You too are the buddhas of the three times, Vajrāsanapāda, Nāgārjuna, Nāropā, Virūpa, Padmākara, Lūipa, Saraha, Indrabhūti, and Maitripā!" With these words, all deities, mantras, maṇḍalas, and buddha fields were introduced as the nature of reality. And the voice continued, "You previously displayed many past lives: as the monk called glorious Maitreya, alongside the transcendent lord Śākyamuni, and so forth!"[147]

This great natural yogin who had such experiences is known to have nurtured three hundred thousand monks in Jang, Pubor Rabgang, and so forth.[148] {235} His virtuous activities with regard to conditioned phenomena, including the construction of the reliquary stūpa of Lama Chokyi Gyeltsen, are well documented, and in addition, it is said that his residence called Gyelpotsang was later maintained by the line of his paternal relatives.[149]

Jamyang Dzase

Dzam Dzase, also known as Geshe Dzamchenpo, was born in Kham. Traveling to Utsang, he served so many teachers and became a great scholar, learned in many sūtras, tantras, and pith instructions. Once, when he thought about returning to his native place, he stayed overnight at Potseteng. In the morning, he heard the sound of glorious Taklung Tangpa the Great blowing his doctrinal conch and said, "Who is up there?" Clearly informed of these circumstances by those who knew, he said, "I'm going to see." On reaching Chabkedong, he saw Rinpoche taking his seat and teaching the sacred doctrine, the great meditators offering their signs of realization, and the cattle, horses, and sheep that the sponsor Namtangpa had donated glistening in the uplands of Taklung. Thereupon, it seemed in his mind that the meditators, even to the extent of a single marmot with a grassland burrow, accrued such excellence of disciples and resources, and the thought arose, "On reaching Dokham, I too will have resources equal to space!"

Knowing these thoughts in his mind, Rinpoche said to his attendant Jangseng, "While I am seated in the Great Offering Chapel, you should invite the geshe of Chabkedong on yonder hill to come here on horseback with his disciples!" He did as commanded, {236} and so the geshe beheld Rinpoche's body in the form of Avalokita with eleven faces, a thousand arms, and a thousand eyes and said, "This body of yours, Avalokita, is exquisite. May your teacher, wherever that great meditator resides, grant me instruction!" The image replied, "I stand in lieu of this great meditator! Sit here, Geshe, and have some hot water to drink." In a moment, before the geshe could offer prostrations, inquire after his health, or do anything at all, he was suddenly left alone, whereupon Jangseng invited him to sit and offered him hot water to drink. Thereupon, Rinpoche appeared and said, "These resources of mine did not come about through arrogance and pride. They were obtained through the kindness of my precious teacher!" Then, he chanted an extract from *The Melody of the Precious Body*,[150] whereupon the geshe developed intense faith. He divided all his possessions into three parts. One-third he offered to Rinpoche, one-third he donated for humanitarian purposes, and one-third he used to provide for his own spiritual pursuits. After receiving oral instructions, he attained accomplishment by meditating upon them.

Later, he traveled to Kham. In accordance with a prediction of Rinpoche Taklung Tangpa Tashi Pel, he founded the monastery of Paji Dzagol in Pubor Gangchen. In the Main Temple of Taklung, he donated many famous offering sacraments, and his enlightened activity was great. He had innumerable disciples, including Dzamton and Beton. The lineage of his paternal relatives is known to have performed great acts in the service of the teaching by gradually establishing the Buddhist teaching at upper and lower Dza and at Dob, and so forth, in Pubor Gangchung.[151]

Jori Repa

Jori Repa, who was also known as Choje Gopa, was born into the clan of Dong, {237} in a family that had exclusively produced accomplished masters for twelve generations. His father was Jose Gyelbu Lama and his mother Droza Takmo Nyene.[152] In his eighth year, he studied writing, and in his fifteenth year, he received instruction on Vajrakīla. He also received the aural lineage of the Great Perfection according to Aro.[153] In U, he received many doctrinal cycles of Kadam from Geshe Shomarapa. He then went to visit the monastery of Rinpoche Taklung Tangpa and met him. To this student who was like a son, Taklungpa the Great imparted nectar-like oral instructions. He blazed with the candescence of great bliss, and after the teaching, he was given three bundles of candy, which he consumed, experiencing that they possessed eight flavors. He then received the full monastic ordination from Zhangkhang Chenpa.[154]

One day, when Rinpoche was seated on his teaching throne, Jori Repa went into his presence while he was teaching the sacred doctrine and observed the lama's face smiling joyfully, whereupon a sensation of warmth welled up from his navel cakra, gradually filling his body, and the unspoken thought arose, "I am the one who will impart the oral instructions out of devotion to the teacher!" Henceforth, his sensation of bliss and warmth was uninterrupted.[155]

Through the blessing of master Sangye Gompa, he also beheld the visage of Bhaiṣajyaguru.[156] When Rinpoche said to him that the intrinsic nature of mind is nonarising, its emanations unceasing, and its defining characteristics without duality, he simultaneously experienced signs of realization and liberation. When he received an oral instruction on dependent origination, he was told, "You must understand that all things of cyclic existence and nirvāṇa that emerge through the evolving modality of dependent origination naturally arise as their reversal." Thereupon, he transformed dependent origination into the expanse of space. Taklungpa the Great then said, "I have accomplished the benefit of self and others[157] by means of dependent origination. {238} If you understand this, all things whatsoever will arise as dependent origination. You will be mistaken if you seek something else to look for or document."

Jori Repa attended upon Taklungpa the Great for fifteen years, and all the oral instructions were completely conferred upon him.[158] On one occasion, he had a dream in which Rinpoche and his disciples were seated in the midst of a pride of frolicking lion cubs, surrounded by innumerable naturally arisen stūpas. Devotion blazed within him, and he understood this to be an auspicious coincidence that the monastic seat would be established at Taklung. He then requested permission to go to Kham, so Rinpoche advised him as follows: "Stick to the mountains! Cultivate solitude! Cultivate humility! In that way, you will acquire food and resources. Do not confer empowerments or indulge in peripheral offering rites. Strive for the offerings of the precious jewels! By practicing the rain retreat, the lifting of restrictions, the confession ceremony, and so forth in the correct manner here, you will become like me!"[159]

Jori Repa then set out for Kham, where many signs were revealed by heroes and ḍākinīs. He was welcomed by the tsen spirits of Gosho. At Drak Senge, he slept in the presence of a statue of glorious Phakmodrupa, and received predictions concerning the establishment of a monastery, in consequence of which he established the monastery at Rinchen Gang. When he thought of staying instead at Kampo Nenang, a woman appeared and said, "Don't think like that! You should maintain the community here out of gratitude to Taklung Rinpoche. You should bring Markhamgang under your control!"[160]

Taklung Rinpoche sent him a letter from U, saying that he could stay anywhere if there were no strong adverse circumstances, and there would be excellent auspicious coincidences. The nāgas acted as patrons, the inhabitants of Lower Gyade offered him a monastery, and in accordance with the prediction of the two ḍākinīs, his enlightened activities became extensive in the eastern direction.[161] {239}

Lama Gongkariwa said to him, "Since you have met Taklung Tangpa, you have been successful. Many excellent students will come." At Bode, he had a vision of Mahākāruṇika. Then, one day, Taklung Rinpoche appeared in the sky in front of him and revealed the signs of naked awareness. Subsequently, he resided at the mountain of Pelgyiri. Just by seeing his body, ailments and sufferings were alleviated, and when he performed rites of consecration, flowers cascaded upon the representative images, books, and stūpas of their own accord. In conformity with five internal auspicious coincidences, he beheld the meditational deities externally. He experienced many pure visions, prophetic declarations, and emanational transformations. His fame permeated the ten directions. In the regions of Gosho and Bom, he built many monasteries including Lingji.[162]

One night, in a dream, a woman said, "You should make a list of all your property!" Someone offered him a gilded image, wrapped in white silk, and there were heroes and heroines who manifested, as dense as clouds. He knew that all these were indications that he was about to die. His disciples and grand-disciples were innumerable.

Rechen Bom Gonpa

As for the three students of Taklung Tangpa who perfectly obtained the oral instructions, at Draknak in Lato, Venerable Senge Gyeltsen nurtured three hundred monks; in Dokham, Rechen Bom Gonpa nurtured three hundred monks; and in Minyak, in the east, Sumbu Sertsang nurtured countless monks.[163]

Among them, Rechen Bom Gonpa was born in Nyarong, in 1180 (iron mouse), as the son of one Bemushewu Dongtsa. He trained in many of the classical sciences, beginning with writing and astrology. In his twenty-first year, he was ordinated as a mendicant at Gonkar by Lharje Mechopa acting as monastic preceptor and Konchok Senge acting as master of ceremonies. {240} The name Sherab Pel was conferred upon him. He received the blessings of Bhaṭṭārikā and guidance on the path of skillful means from Lama Lharje. Then, through cultivation of that method, a blissful warmth arose, and he could wear only a single cotton garment. Therefore, he was given the title Repa. Then, by receiving instructions on the transcendent perfections and gradual path of the teaching from precious Kadampa masters and the Great Seal from Lama Marpa, experiential realization was born within him.[164]

At Washo, in the presence of the learned teacher Ba Chenpo, he undertook combined study, reflection, and meditation, such that he perfected many oral instructions of the Kagyu lineage. By practicing the incantation of Vijayā, all appearances arose as stūpas.[165]

Then, traveling to U, he met glorious Taklung Tangpa and perfectly mastered the guidance of the Great Seal, such that the aforementioned realization was successfully matured. In particular, all phenomena of cyclic existence and nirvāṇa arose as auspicious circumstances. That is to say, all objective appearances, including the five external elements, arose as external auspicious circumstances, while the internal energy channels, winds, and generative essences and the secret enlightened mind—the immaculate awareness beyond objects of speech, thought, knowledge, and expression—were realized as relative appearances, a cycle of dependent origination of cause and result. He comprehended all outer and inner phenomena as auspicious circumstances, and an extraordinary devotion was born within him. Gradually, he completely received the guidance of the Six Doctrines and so forth, and he comprehended them. Inestimable enlightened attributes arose.[166]

Rechen Bom Gonpa attended upon Taklung Tangpa for three years, and then, when Rinpoche passed away, he attended upon Venerable Kuyalwa. He received the aural lineage of Cakrasaṃvara from Lama Sangye Rangjung and Cakrasaṃvara from Lhola Yakpa, and he beheld a vision of glorious Vajravārāhī.[167]

Traveling to Kham, {241} he then resided at Tamgon, and founded monastic seats at Washo and Drophu. Twice he brought great offerings to Taklung. Nurturing many congregations of the monastic community with the sacred doctrine and material resources, he expanded and developed the monastic estates of Taklung. He was never distracted from profound yoga. Simply by making a powerful declaration of truth, those who had been afflicted by ailments and spirits, wherever they resided within his domain, had good fortune and splendor. He extensively practiced the supreme teaching of the essential definitive meaning. On one occasion he said, "From the time when I was ordained as a mendicant, I have been untainted by defects and downfalls. I met Rinpoche Taklung Tangpa and his disciples and cultivated the sacred doctrine my whole life, so you too should be devoted and achieve that goal." In 1244 (wood dragon), in his sixty-fifth year, he passed away. There were innumerable wondrous signs, in consequence of which everyone was established in the ground of faith.[168]

The Four Heart Sons of Taklung Tangpa

The first of the four heart sons, known as Lama Mutowa, inhabited some sort of mountain hermitage, near the monastic seat of Taklung itself. He nurtured approximately two hundred monks. At the time when Rinpoche

Taklung Tangpa went to Tsogang, he arrived there to make obeisance, riding a blue horse. He said that in the lama's presence, at that time, he had received instruction on setting the mind on supreme enlightenment as a spiritual mentor of the Great Vehicle, and his perception then became extraordinary. Therefore, when he beheld the body of Taklungpa the Great, he saw Choje Rinpoche riding on a lion and traveling into the sky. Starting from then, the portals of pure vision opened, and he saw Rinpoche's physical body as the buddha bodies of perfect resource of the five enlightened families in union with their consorts, each with an entourage of six bodhisattvas. He saw him as Śākyamuni in the form Mahābodhi and as Avalokiteśvara, {242} each accompanied by two bodhisattvas and as the central deity alone; as Cakrasaṃvarasahaja surrounded by the four essential yoginīs; as Bhaṭṭārikā and sublime Lokeśvara in the form Jinasāgara, seated in a maṇḍala of rainbow light; and even as Rinpoche in his own form, seated within a tent of flowers; as Rinpoche in his eleven aspects, seated and aligned in a row; and so forth.

On one occasion, Lama Mutowa requested Taklungpa the Great to make a footprint on a piece of white silk, and he placed a piece of blue silk of the same size behind it. He laid out the latter in his own house and prayed to it, such that, through the power of devotion and blessing, an extremely clear footprint naturally appeared upon that blue silk, and upon it he drew whichever deities he wished, arranged in the manner of all his aforementioned pure visions. Nowadays that silk is kept among the blessed sacred artifacts of Taklung.

The second of the four heart sons was the accomplished master Tseringpo, also known as Dampa Gaton. He remained engaged in practice in the same place for fifty-seven years. The cotton painting of glorious Jñānanātha, nowadays kept in the lower chamber, which is known and proven to be endowed with blessings, was indeed his meditative commitment, and it had been consecrated by the blessed barley of Rinpoche Taklungpa the Great. The third of the four heart sons, named Dro Lotsun, remained one-pointedly engaged in practice in the same place for sixty years. The fourth, named Jowo Ngabulwa, remained seated in meditative stability, without distraction, for forty years, the door of his cave plastered with mud.[169] Lama Mutowa, Dampa Gaton, and Drubchen Lung Gawa were also called the three who were accepted as inseparable. {243}

As for the three disciples who did not have to be asked, in the land of Tsang Rongshang, Lama Oshawa nurtured two hundred monks; at Tselung, in On, Lama Tselungpa nurtured just a few monks; and at Namtso Semodo, Zaram mountain hermitage, and other places, with no fixed abode, Nyemo Dzegom Ngodrub Gyeltsen maintained the ascetic discipline of *Total Renunciation: The Natural Liberation of Attachment.*[170] These three were named Those Who Did Not Need to Be Asked because they were miraculously transported on alternate days from their abodes to Taklung in the service of Rinpoche.[171]

The last of these spontaneously brought forth a treasury of adamantine songs because the cakra of perfect resource within his throat had opened. Most of his anthology of sacred songs is extant—their words and meaning hard to surpass. It is known from the words of these songs that Rinpoche himself completed them at the behest of Venerable Sangye Gompa and the supreme incarnation Kuyalwa.

The Eighteen Close Heirs of Taklung Tangpa the Great

As for the eighteen close heirs, Mayo Gomnak, a preceptor of Vajrāsana in India, was the one who had a statue of Rinpoche made at Vajrāsana and is known to have traveled across the River Ganges and offered it to this monastic seat of Taklung. Nowadays it is displayed as the principal image of the Chapel of Bronzes within the Main Temple. At Rutok in Kongpo, Gomnak nurtured approximately one hundred monks. Here in Taklung, he distributed cups of saffron to a community of five thousand. In the island of Siṅghala, Lama Lhuk nurtured three hundred monks. At the sacred place of Jalandhara, Gompa Maṇiwa nurtured some seventy monks. {244} At Oḍḍiyāna, in the west Drakpa Gyeltsen lived as a hidden yogin. At the Asura Cave, there was Lama Mangkarwa, also known as Gazha. In Nepal, there was Rupo Drubtob; in Kyirong, Denma Lhachenpo; and in Rigang, Drubtob Rigangpa. At Drakar Taso, Tokden Naralwa nurtured seventy monks. At Tangchung, in Lato, one called Rinpoche Upa nurtured some seventy monks. At Tsangrong, there was Tokden Zhanakpa. In Nyemo, Cherton Zhikpo nurtured some twenty monks. At Tolung, there was Chone Karpo; in Yarlung, there was Margom Sonam Pel; and in Dam, there was Bapa Gyeltri. At Pel Chuwori, Sangye Gomre nurtured some seven hundred monks. In Chenga, Sherab Gyeltsen, a great exponent of Madhyamaka, served as an excellent government official. These were the eighteen. Those among them who did not nurture monastic communities lived as hidden yogins.[172]

Associates Representing Other Lineages

The three learned and accomplished masters who were particularly sublime were Jikten Sumgon Ratnaśrī, the great incumbent of glorious Drigung; Tsangpa Gyare Jñānavajra, the great master of Ralung who possessed the teaching of the lineage of attainment; and Trophu Lotsāwa Maitriśrī, the great learned and accomplished master of unrivaled isolation. The accounts of their realizations may be known from their respective biographies.[173]

Apart from them, there were also miscellaneous disciples, approximately thirty-four in number, who are clearly named in the early records, including the imperial tutor Drogon Repa Chenpo at the monastic seat of Jang Barom.[174] All of them either acted for the benefit of sentient beings or lived as hidden yogins; and in whatever ways, dependent on the nectar of Rinpoche's speech, they absolutely acquired supreme pristine cognition. {245} Only their names are listed in *The Great Biography*, but I will not write of them here for fear of being too verbose.

Lama Nakpa

Lama Nakpa, who witnessed the life of Taklungpa the Great, through the kindness of Rinpoche, excellently perfected the oral instructions, and he also received the cycle of Mahākāla from Selton Gomsho.[175] Through the enlightened attributes of such transmissions and realizations, he prospered and then traveled to Kham. By undertaking practice for a long period of time, his realization equaled space. He was also a recipient of many empowerments, transmissions, and guidance imparted by Kuyal Rinpoche and Venerable Sangye Yarjon. He was one who possessed extensive extrasensory powers and who undertook immeasurable enlightened activities for the benefit of others.[176]

Khepa Chenpo

Having completed this rough summary of the disciples of Taklungpa the Great according to the old recensions of his biography, we can see that there were many others who were not included therein. Among them, Lama Khepa Chenpo was born in Drigung Deu Rabdo as the son of Yaksum Gompa. In his sixteenth year, he was ordained as a mendicant by the monastic preceptor Magu Chochuk and the master of ceremonies Chenton Gewapel. The name Wangchuk Dorje was conferred upon him. Then he traveled to U, where he received the complete monastic ordination from Jadul. By attending upon Nyangdren, Yornyak, Chapa, Tsak, Tsang Nakpa, and so forth, he became a great upholder of the piṭakas. From certain great spiritual advisers, he received the Kadam cycle; from Mar Chokyi Gyeltsen, he received instruction on Cakrasaṃvara; and so forth. From Choje Rinpoche Taklung Tangpa, he received all the doctrinal cycles of the Kagyu lineage, and in particular, {246} the Six-Limbed Yoga[177] according to the tradition of Tsāmi and the entire cycle of Kākamukha Mahākāla, protector of the Buddhist teaching. He also composed texts on the Six-Limbed Yoga. Then, traveling to Kham, he established Washong Monastery. By making rainfall, he caused the nāga kings to actually bow before him, and he taught the sacred doctrine to them. He also took charge of many other monasteries including Namtok. Lama Khepa Chenpo lived a long life—Rinpoche Tashi Lama also studied the cycle of the doctrinal protectors under him. Finally, when he fell ill, the deities prepared a chariot adorned with ornaments and welcomed him. Riding an ash-white elephant bedecked with gems, he journeyed to a pure land, whereupon a stream of the water of pristine cognition flowed from the heart of the spiritual teachers of the Kagyu lineage and purified the obscurations of beings who were equal to the limits of space in number. He passed away, accompanied by many arrays of pure visionary appearance such as that. When the sacred corpse was cremated, two images of Vajrayoginī issued from the orifices of his mouth and nose and departed into space. Many such wondrous arrays were revealed.[178]

Other Disciples of Taklung Tangpa the Great

In the old chronicles, Trewo Tugon is counted among his disciples. He was preoccupied with hunting deer and fighting prowess when Onton Kyergangpa scolded him as a murderous killer of Trewo people.[179] But later, when he passed away, during the cremation, he began to experience dreams, and visions came to him. Accordingly, he arrived in the presence of the fifteen deity assemblage of Nairātmyā, above the funeral pyre, and was transformed inside her mouth, whereupon he confessed his thoughts in response to the previous scolding. In this way, he again had a vision of the visage of Nairātmyā, whereupon it is said that he delivered the verses that begin as follows:

> Since the liberating career of a yogin
> Who practices the way of Secret Mantra, is unfathomable . . .[180] {247}

The one known as Sangye Rongton from Jarnyal—the reincarnation of the great paṇḍita Prajñākara, the northern gatekeeper of Nālanda, was born in Loro. He attended upon Tengpa Lotsāwa and others, and excellently trained in all the piṭakas and the tantras. He perfectly received all the oral instructions of the precious Kagyu lineage from glorious Taklung Tangpa, without exception, and he acted extensively for the welfare of living beings. In four different locations, he simultaneously built four temples including Jolnang, with their four arrays of images. In his sixty-fourth year, light rays emerged from the heart of the Mahākāruṇika image in the Potala and were diffused into his own body, whereupon, guided by light that assumed the form of Mañjuśrī, they vanished again into the heart of Sublime Mahākāruṇika. It is said that through many pure visions, he journeyed through space and became invisible, letting his religious robe fall. Among his subsequent incarnations there was one known as Pawo Tulku, who nowadays has great enlightened activity.[181]

There was also one named Gyelwa Gangpa, who, on hearing extensively of the reputation of Rinpoche's physical presence, traveled to meet him. He just received a doctrinal connection, but after Taklungpa the Great had passed into nirvāṇa, when he again came to Taklung, the precious statue of Rinpoche within the grass hermitage taught him the Six Doctrines completely, on one occasion, such that he is said to have instantaneously brought forth all the successful signs associated with the meditational deity. Therefore, he should certainly be included among the disciples.

That much I have seen and heard. Later on, these narratives should be supplemented when reliable accounts, other than the mere mention of their names, have been discovered by historians. {248}

Concluding Verses

At this juncture, through this strenuous virtue,
May I and the realms of sentient beings,
Having perfected the paths through oceanic deeds, accumulated and refined,
Attain liberation in the presence of this Doctrinal Lord

Who has gone to bliss in an immaculate realm,
Satisfied by the nectar of his buddha speech!

Kuyalwa Rinchen Gonpo, Second in the Abbatial Succession

Verses of Homage

Reincarnation of glorious Dorje Gyelpo,
Immeasurable in miraculous abilities of buddha body, speech, and mind,
In order to hold dominion over the treasury of the space of existence and quiescence,
You were subsumed in the form of a supreme incarnation—
Rinchen Gonpo, lord-protector of living beings!

Rinchen Gonpo, the supreme incarnation of Phakmodrupa, who was a regent and emanation of the Conqueror, was born in 1190 at Rab Gang near Bongra Tengka, which is part of the Yangsho valley in Kuyung Gang. His father was the patron Benlon Goyak, and his mother was Joziza Tashitso.[182] At that time, the sugata Taklungpa the Great was in his forty-ninth year. While he was in the womb, his father traveled to Taklung, and one day, Taklung Rinpoche said, "Let Goyak come here!" When Goyak went to meet him, he said, "It seems that a son will be born on the estate as your inheritance. Offer him to me! Offer him, offer him!" Goyak indeed made that offering.[183]

When three years had passed [in 1193, water ox], Karmapa Dusum Khyenpa, the doctrinal lord of Tsurphu died, and all the attendants in the presence of Taklungpa the Great asked who would then occupy the monastic seat of Tsurphu. Rinpoche replied, "Who will occupy the seat of Tsurphuwa? I have already made preparations for one monastic seat!" The attendants asked him not to speak in that manner, but he said, "You need not be afraid. All that is now merely trifling!"[184] {249}

Right from birth, all of the child's modes of play were endowed with innumerable enlightened attributes, indicative of the greatness of buddha body, speech, and mind. Indeed, he exclusively acted with a demeanor of virtue, whether in teaching the sacred doctrine or cultivating meditative stability, and so forth. Taklung Rinpoche sent him many useful gifts, including a child's cloak and a letter that said, "Let this boy become a novice! Give him the name Rinchen Gonpo and bring him to us!" The child's mother was somewhat unwilling, but the child himself said, "I will become a novice and go to Taklung. Once I have become a spiritual mentor, I will master the sacred doctrine, and send a message to you, my parents, concerning the oral instructions."[185]

Accordingly, in 1202, when in his thirteenth year, he was ordained as a mendicant at Gothar Lhakhang in Tangkya in the presence of thirteen monks, including Onton Sonam Lama, who acted as monastic preceptor; Go Lhakhang Takpa, who acted as master of ceremonies; and the faithful and virtuous Lama Nakpa and Lama Dawopa. He studied *The Stanzas on the Novitiate, The Compendium of Learning,*[186] and so forth, under those two—the preceptor and master—and also under Naklungpa.[187]

That same year, he set out for U. The local people escorted him a short distance, and his mother said, "If my son practices the sacred doctrine, it will not matter if he were not to meet me again! Go practice the sacred doctrine!" So saying, she returned home. He met the men from Taklung who had come to welcome him at Langling Lakha Pass.[188]

On the day of his arrival at Taklung, Rinpoche said, "Make a silken path with a piece of white silk, and fix a banner behind him. At Rithel, raise a small banner in front of him and one behind him. A procession of monks should welcome him." {250} They did as commanded. On meeting Taklungpa the Great, Rinchen Gonpo presented a roll of silk and inquired politely about his health. Rinpoche said, "Are you not tired, sir?" in response to which Kuyalwa replied, "By the grace of Rinpoche, I am attentive." They made many such carefree preliminary inquiries.[189]

On one occasion when he galloped a horse, his father said to Rinpoche, "You should control the young monk!" Taklungpa the Great replied, "Be silent! You cannot restrict this young monk. He will be beneficial." And, "I did not summon this nephew of mine out of attachment to humanitarian righteousness but for the sake of meditation, the recitation of MAṆI, and so forth. I summoned him, thinking you will need him."[190]

Some days after his arrival, he made a communal tea offering, and immediately after that, in accord with Taklung Rinpoche's instruction, he stayed in a grass hermitage in the upper part of the monastery to practice meditation. He passed six years there in retreat, with the entrance walled up, seated in a single position and without meeting anyone, except when he saw Taklung Rinpoche during the teachings, he gave the great setting of the mind on enlightenment, and except for the times each month when he imparted the *Three Objectives of Guidance*.[191]

Rinchen Gonpo completely received all the oral instructions, in the manner of a vase being filled to the brim. The signs of experiential cultivation and all enlightened attributes that he naturally perfected were simply put to the test. He raised the supporting pillar of his house and placed someone else's robe underneath it. He ground beans to powder between his thumb and index finger, taking about seven beans at a time. He could play with bricks of tea, juggling them like eggs. While sitting cross-legged, he could throw a large load onto the roof of his house. Such were the miracles he exhibited.[192] {251} Once, he said to two boys who were woodcutters, "I'll go up into the forest. You two shouldn't go." Those two went to a brick kiln, and while they sat there drinking some hot beverages, he arrived in an instant and said, "Have you two eaten?" "We've not eaten," they replied. "I'll take your pulse," he said, whereupon he examined their pulse and said, "It seems you have not had anything except some hot drinks." While they were puzzling how he knew that, he brought two large bundles of wood and said, "How much wood is this?" "It's a large quantity," they replied, and it swayed when they placed a finger on the rope. "I can throw it onto the roof with a single finger," he said. At that time, his precious predecessor Taklungpa the Great said, "In this monastery, there is a single young monk who is acting for the welfare of innumerable sentient beings."[193]

In 1208, (earth male dragon), in his nineteenth year, he received full monastic ordination in the lower hall with Geshe Tsangpa acting as monastic preceptor, Sangye Gompa acting as master of ceremonies, and Gyelwa acting as confessor, in the midst of a large gathering of learned and venerable monks, headed by the devout monk Geshe Tangchungwa.[194]

Rinchen Gonpo attended upon his precious predecessor Taklungpa the Great for seven years. During that time, Taklungpa Lama Mutowa, on seeing the body of Taklung Tangpa, also made a life-size cotton painting of him.

When Khenpowa asked him to inspect the books in the library of Taklung concerning the setting of the mind on enlightenment, he replied, "Khenpowa, in this tradition of ours, a suitable teacher should know how to teach any doctrine in accordance with the determinations of the lineage as soon as a disciple appears before him. Apart from that, {252} will anything come of a geshe inspecting books?"[195]

In his twentieth year, when his precious predecessor Taklungpa the Great fell ill, he went into his presence and asked if he should dust the bookshelves [that is, recite prayers] or summon a patron[196] or skilled physician. Taklungpa replied, "There will be no difference if the scriptures are recited and the monks pray. I have not appropriated wealth and materials; they have been dispersed. If a doctor were to help, the benefit could come about even through luck itself."

Also, one day, Taklungpa the Great, his precious predecessor, summoned him into his presence and had him wear his mantle and hat. He hung glorious Phakmodrupa's rosary around his neck and entrusted the staff of Phakmodrupa into his hands. He made him sit on his cushion and said, "Stand up! Move around! Compose yourself!" When he had done so, Taklungpa the Great said, "That will do! You will have a merit greater than mine." Entrusting him with the key to the library, he said, "There is a single section of doctrinal texts that is unknown here in this monastery. I have not acted miserly with respect to the sacred doctrine, but I have concealed it owing to an essential point of auspicious circumstance and owing to the advice of the Sugata Phakmodrupa. Since you are able to reveal it, you should inspect those who request this text, and you should consider all of them in advance. Those persons are staying in the place where these texts are kept right now!" Thereupon, Rinchen Gonpo requested Rinpoche to entrust the library key to him by his own hand. He also requested an aspirational prayer that would benefit sentient beings, whereupon Taklungpa the Great responded, rejoicing fervently.[197] {253} Rinchen Gonpo requested him to give an audience to the monks and patrons, and bestow his advice upon them, and he said he would do so. Then, on the seventeenth day of the lunar month, Taklungpa the Great went into the assembly, and after teaching the sacred doctrine, he said, "You should treat my precious nephew just as you have devotion and respect for me. Since it is the advice of the Sugata Phakmodrupa, he will perform great miracles and the like."

After Taklungpa the Great had passed into nirvāṇa, Rinchen Gonpo attended to the sacred corpse and completely performed the offering clouds of the funeral rite and so forth. He also held an excellent funeral ceremony for master Sangye Gompa following his death. On the thirteenth day of the waxing half of the month of Puṣyā, 1210 (iron male horse), he assumed the monastic seat and was enthroned as a master of the Buddhist teaching. Commencing with the three non-separations,[198] he turned the wheel of the profound and vast doctrine, satisfying all beings. There were a great many who saw him as his precious predecessor, Taklungpa the Great, or who saw him as a meditational deity, and so forth. The master Khu Rinpoche, who had seen his precious predecessor on many occasions determined that these two were indivisible and said, "If this Rinpoche were not here, the lineage of our precious predecessor would be interrupted."

One day, when Rakshi Gyelpo displayed the image of Taklungpa the Great in the Layel Courtyard, on the occasion when Rinpoche Rinchen Gonpo took his seat on the teaching throne, he saw the image as the body of Lama Rinpoche and Lama Rinpoche's body as the image. On the day when the offerings were being made, on the occasion when he turned around, and on the occasion when he was seated behind a screen within the grass hermitage, Rakshi Kyikar saw him as the spitting image of his precious predecessor, extremely large in size.

When he performed the consecration of the Tashi Pelbar reliquary,[199] one body was seen on the teaching throne, {254} and another body was seen moving back and forth in order to scatter the flowers. When he gave teachings on the sacred doctrine on the summit of Nyingri, another body was seen on the teaching throne of Taklung teaching the sacred doctrine. Jangrin saw him cover his face with his tongue, extract pearl relics from his eyes, and conceal them in his robe. Moreover, he was seen with three eyes, and he was also seen as Śākyamuni in the form Mahābodhi, and as Saṃvarasahaja, Bhaṭṭārikā, Eleven-Faced Avalokita, Khasarpaṇi, Four-Armed Mahākāla, and a very large image of Mahākāruṇika.

The marks of the eight auspicious symbols were complete on his body. Wherever he was seated, in sunlight, moonlight, or in the glow of butter lamps, and so forth, his body cast no shadow. He dressed modestly and was seen to be unobscured in spiritual songs, and so forth. When Gelong Tsonseng asked him whether these monks of the present were reincarnations of their former lives as monks, he said, "The faithful ones are; the unfaithful ones are not. However, leaving that aside, through the connection of having accumulated and refined acts of merit such a prostration and circumambulation, they will eventually become disciples."

There are also innumerable accounts of his extrasensory powers. When he commissioned a large silver image of his precious predecessor Taklungpa the Great, there was an important female patron who thought that the icon was small, there was too much silver, and they should use some of it to prepare a manuscript version of *The Transcendent Perfection of Wisdom in Twenty-Five Thousand Lines* on cotton. At that time, he summoned her into his presence and said, "Ponmo, should we prepare a manuscript of one text of the sacred doctrine?" At that, she was ashamed and offered her confession. She did not ask for the cotton and instead asked for a grass hermitage, saying she would stay there in his presence.

Once, when he had summoned two monks, they had a somewhat unsuitable conversation on the way there, {255} and when they arrived in his presence, he said, "Wouldn't you two old monks be ashamed if someone were to hear such conversation?"

When a gatherer of household dung departed for Lower Plain in Kham, in his place he found a spear and a sickle, and he stored up some dung. He said to those who approached him, "You might catch fever!"

When the grid lines for the foundation of the Offering Chapel were being marked out, Rinpoche Rinchen Gonpo sent an attendant from Yang Gonteng, saying, "The grid lines should not be mistaken!" Just by looking from that distance, he could detect that mistakes had been made.

When two monks who had eaten some meat at Latsepak near Chak Pass went into his presence, he said, "It's embarrassing to be seen by people from Latsepak who eat meat!"

When he was preparing to set out for Chom to bring the cheesecake, which was to be transported from Uma for a great offering ceremony, he said that he felt numb and unable to walk. Those who went in his place found him there, already having loaded the cheesecake on to the pack animals.

When Zhangtra the Blind went upstairs in the Great Offering Chapel, he stumbled and injured himself. Rinchen Gonpo said, "It will not matter at all if you dispense with the doctor!" Immediately, he recovered.

When an official named Atsara suffered from paralysis, Rinchen Gonpo said he should receive treatment, but he was negligent and one day in the latter part of the month, after handing over his walking stick to those he had just received, he became gravely ill. Rituals were undertaken, and when it was determined that he would immediately die, Rinpoche came there to stay just for the day and said again that nothing at all would help. Consequently, on the tenth day of the lunar month, he passed away.

Rinchen Gonpo insisted to Shewu Oro that he should give back the cattle that he had belonging to Beri, but Shewu Oro did not pay attention, whereupon Rinchen Gonpo said, "No good will come of this!"[200] Consequently, he was slain by Beri.

Through his insistent commands, Rinchen Gonpo tried to avert Trewo Jetsun from traveling to Kham, when he was carried away by great desire for merchandise, {256} but he did not pay attention and was consequently defeated by Beri.

Knowing that his attendants had secretly discussed swindling him, Rinpoche said, "This plan to swindle me will likely become clear later on!"

When Tangpa Shak Seng asked if he should go into retreat, Rinpoche said, "If you remain under the yoke of human laws, you will have a son who will sustain the monastery." Consequently, that is exactly what came about. There are countless stories of his extrasensory powers, such as these.

Many times, he would say, "I myself aspire to dedicate offerings to the icons commissioned in the day that followed the passing into nirvāṇa of my precious predecessor—the image inside the grass hermitage that blazes with the glory of blessings and is no different from the precious Taklungpa the Great himself, and the image in the middle of the assembly hall, on the teaching throne in the Layel Courtyard." These two were the foundation upon which all the auspicious circumstances of spiritual and worldly affairs would be arranged for posterity in that community of Taklung.

At first, he made a silver reliquary measuring one handspan and another measuring one cubit, which would contain the former. In both of these, he inserted the hair, pearl relics, heart, tongue, and eyes of Rinpoche Dewar Shekpa, Taklungpa the Great. He also inserted a mole, which had been above the right eyebrow and within which the shape of a wheel had emerged, along with the fourth finger of the left hand, which had been left intact.[201] Later, even when the Main Temple was threatened by fire, the outer offering reliquary, up to its *harmikā*, and the smaller stūpa within it remained undamaged. Consequently, even nowadays, a small fraction of the erstwhile spiritual and temporal teachings of Taklungpa the Great imbue the meritorious terrain of this sacred place. {257}

Afterward, in 1216 (fire male mouse), Rinchen Gonpo commissioned the great reliquary named Tashi Pelbar of pure silver that had been refined seven times through smelting and that had then been poured into a casting mold. This precious stūpa, which bore the motif of a lotus heap or auspicious symbol, measured twenty-five handspans. On a cushion in the form of a solar disk, there was inserted an image of glorious Phakmodrupa, fashioned of seventeen ounces (*sang*) of gold, the marks of which were unrivaled anywhere in Tibet. He also commissioned the silver reliquary of Sangye Gompa, with a parasol, the contents of which included a small lotus-heap motif, made of silver, and the heart, tongue, eyes, and other relics of Gompa himself. These were the work of the emanational artisan Pon Zhange and others.[202]

Then, Rinpoche Rinchen Gonpo himself undertook a divination with the oracular mirror concerning the silver image of his precious predecessor, named Ornament of the World. It was carefully sculpted by Ponlha Chungwa, a master skilled in classical learning. The flesh of the body was fashioned of pure silver and the monastic shirt of pure red copper. The religious robe and staff were fashioned of brass and embellished with many thread patterns and motifs in gold and silver. The image was insatiable to behold, and fashioned from a single molding. For such reasons, all intelligent persons of the past and present concur that it is inseparable in its craftsmanship from Jowo Rinpoche in the Rasa Trulnang temple, which had been sculpted by the emanational craftsmanship of Viśvakarman, an emanation of Mañjughoṣa. But the fact that the actual body—the robes, and staff, and so forth—of this image were created from different materials and that it was fashioned completely without mixing of the different materials renders this workmanship particularly sublime. So they all concurred. Later, when it was damaged by fire and a monk just ushered it to the rear, {258} out of compassion it naturally moved to the great Layel Courtyard. On its rear curtain, the array of the seven lineage holders was fashioned, and on its throne was the array of an immeasurable host of meditational deities, doctrinal protectors, and mundane protectors such as Vasudeva.[203]

On the friezes carved upon the surfaces of the lion throne of the Tashi Pelbar Stūpa and on its tiers and multiple niches, there were also about ten thousand larger and smaller images depicting the hosts of the deities of the maṇḍalas of the infinite classes of tantra, along with the oceanic oath-bound protectors of the transmitted teachings and the group of yakṣas including Kubera. In addition, about two-thirds of those that were well made and executed in painstaking detail were successfully completed by Venerable Sangye Yarjon and his nephew.

Rinchen Gonpo gathered the monastic preceptors, masters, and others who had a right to participate in discussions, and he said to them, "There are too many representative images and scriptures. They cannot fit inside, so you should discuss the construction of a large Offering Chapel and give me your answer." The master Khu said, "Any kind of Offering Chapel will suffice. Since one proficient meditator is preferable to a hundred copies of *The Transcendent Perfection of Wisdom in One Hundred Thousand Lines*, inscribed in gold, let us foster guidance on meditation." Others said, "Let us do both." Consequently, in 1224 (wood male monkey), in his thirty-fourth year, on the first lunar day that was flourishing and bountiful, on which the constellation Puṣyā and the planet Jupiter converged, he began the construction of the Main Temple. They sought out wood from all parts of Tibet. Timber was brought from Do in large quantities. At first, the Drigungpa somewhat objected, but later the estate of Podo came into his possession. Consequently, the nephew of Drigungpa also asked him to bring timber from Naksho, and they transported an inconceivable amount of wood. {259}[204] To those who brought the wood, he said, "The auspicious circumstances of the masters and disciples in this teaching tradition of ours should converge here! The biographical accounts of the former Kagyu lineage holders who undertook innumerable austerities for the sake of the sacred doctrine are also complete in this tradition of ours. As far as the conditioned roots of virtuous actions are concerned, there is no greater merit than that generated by the construction of a temple. In India, when powerful kings and so forth constructed stūpas, the materials offered by others were unavoidably mixed together, such that when earth stuck to cotton it seems to have been held that one could probably dislodge it slightly by shaking it out. Though some may well think that the refinement of many wealthy persons accrues through the merit generated by constructing an Offering Chapel, actually the hybrid cattle transporting the timber from this moment on will not acquire rebirth in an animal form. Just as when the great grass hermitage of Phakmodrupa was made, Drogon Rinpoche established the auspicious circumstance and said that the living creatures within it would be reborn in the next life in the immaculate pure land of the east and attain the maturational empowerments and liberating guidance, so in this Offering Chapel of mine the merits of mixing even a single ball of adobe will be innumerable. O you workers, this is a great wonder!"

Drenka examined the geomantic location for the construction and said, "It will be good if we construct it as an annex." So it was built in its present location, and they then eliminated the defects associated with hostile earth spirits. Rinpoche himself performed the geomantic rite, based on the yoga of the Glorious Saṃvarodaya. The foundation stone was first laid by Dong Karpo Dzomjawa. The four cornerstones were laid by three sons of the mercantile class, along with the official Tashi Gon. Vases and treasures were inserted in nine places—the eight cardinal and intermediate directions and the center. In brief, {260} the construction was indeed sealed securely and rendered auspicious through the perception of pristine cognition that definitively knows and sees the abiding and apparent circumstances of all knowable phenomena of the three times, as found in the sūtras and tantras, and in the texts on temple construction. The Offering Chapel had eighty pillars, composed of thirty-two pillars in four rows in the upper courtyard, twenty-four pillars in three rows in the lower courtyard, twelve pillars (six in each of the two side wings), four pillars (two in each of the two projecting bays), four in the entrance hall, and four in the veranda. So it was that the chapel was supported by eighty pillars. The elegant building was well constructed, with thirteen stacked beams—large, high, triumphant, and captivating. The workers, headed by Pon Gyagar, were pleased with offerings of material wealth, amounting to twenty thousand *sang* of gold. Then the representational images, books, and stūpas were ushered in and installed. The concluding ceremonies were carried out with a consecration and an auspicious feast. In general, there were immeasurable virtuous signs, and in particular, the precious predecessor Taklungpa the Great was seen scattering flowers while seated in the midst of rainbow light in the sky.[205]

Then, when he thought of building this Kumbum Chenmo stūpa that sits in the lower part of the valley at Taklung, Gompa Sherab Gyeltsen said that his precious predecessor Taklungpa the Great had actually predicted, "Next year my teaching throne will be established here." And so it was constructed near the cliff. When the dome was being built, the workers had to excavate the cliff, such that their health was weakened. Thereupon, Rinchen Gonpo arranged many auspicious circumstances. The task was implemented by Geshe Chomtangpa, and an offering reliquary symbolizing the great enlightenment was constructed, replete with the defining characteristic marks. {261} The foremost of the relics contained within it was the aforementioned tooth of the Tathāgata, and apart from that, it was filled with representative artifacts of buddha body, speech, and mind and innumerable blessings. When the consecration ceremony was held, the virtuous signs that occurred were immeasurable. This structure is nowadays known as the Northern Stūpa. So it was that in consequence of the excellent approach heralded by the extensive construction of the Main Temple and its representations of buddha body, speech, and mind, disease, strife, famine, and other such disasters were interrupted throughout the whole country. For thirteen continuous good years, and so forth, the perfect glory of existence and quiescence was produced, such that all sentient beings also freely experienced the ocean of joyfulness. All the excellences of the twofold tradition of the glorious Taklungpa were indeed enhanced in the manner of the rivers of summertime.

During the lifetime of Venerable Rinchen Gonpo, the anniversary ceremonies of former spiritual teachers, the regular offering ceremonies associated with the precious jewels, the respectful offerings made to the monastic community, the donations of ordinary persons, and so forth were undertaken unstintingly. After appointing a monastic preceptor and master of ceremonies, he had them ordain neophytes as novices and full-fledged monks. They conferred the bodhisattva vow, through which the mind is set on enlightenment, and opened the portals of the sacred doctrine. They differentiated the objectives of the actions to be renounced and adopted, including their respective precepts, commitments, and so forth, and after these had been implemented, Rinpoche Rinchen Gonpo conferred guidance upon them.

As far as his daily life is concerned, Rinchen Gonpo never wavered from the actions and deeds of his precious predecessor. He never confused or adulterated the oral teachings, let alone change even one word of the liturgical prayers and aspirations. He imparted the teachings, intimating them through all his activities, great and small, and he did not act casually except in the aftermath of those teachings. {262} He always sat upright and never rested his head against a cushion. Even after not sleeping for many days, his health was not adversely affected. He did not allow meat or wine to be brought to his tongue, let alone permit them to be brought across the threshold of the monastery while he was in residence. And when he was out traveling, there was no place for meat or wine within his encampment. Any weapons that were offered were broken in his presence. He accepted the representative artifacts that were offered with his own hands. Other offerings were collected by his attendants. He did not engage in meaningless talk. He filled the monastery with advice concerning minor rules and other regulations, commencing from and including the minor ones. He engaged in exclusively virtuous conduct, without squandering in the meantime the material offerings that manifested there, like a wild blizzard.[206]

Tashi Gon, while acting as steward of the monastery, fought with Drigung, in consequence of which he was reprimanded and the role of steward then entrusted to his venerable uncle. There are countless instances of Rinchen Gonpo liberating people from ailments, demonic possession, and so forth simply through prayer, conferral of blessing, or auspicious connection. Whatever rites were required for dispelling obstacles and achieving success, he knew them just when someone arrived in his presence, and he disclosed whichever were appropriate. All feelings of malice he assuaged by vast material offerings and by the teachings that he imparted in pursuit of the truth.[207]

One day, while Rinchen Gonpo was praying in the Kumbum reliquary, amid an assembly of all the monks, a heatwave occurred, whereupon the pearl relics in the Kumbum reliquary were scattered. Then they multiplied, more and more, and the ground became covered with auspicious white markings. An image of his precious predecessor Taklungpa the Great appeared within the Kumbum reliquary. The pearl relics were gathered and distributed, such that each of the four groups obtained them.[208]

When Rinchen Gonpo first assumed the monastic seat, his patrons were in decline, {263} yet his prosperity increased, although there were no other patrons apart from them. Despite the need for provisions within his community, there were a great many people to whom a half measure of grain was distributed each month, and he offered guaranty on behalf of others. For one group, he supplied all that they needed, and he sustained eighty-two households, each of which were composed of approximately one hundred people from his own residence. When those on the outside saw this influx of resources, they would wonder where all this could be stored. And when those on the inside saw his outgoings, they would wonder if these would be replenished.[209] At the time when he had to present gifts to those who constructed the Tashi Pelbar Stūpa, eyewitnesses said, "He has shown off his wealth, but how can he possibly present all this to the artisans?"

The number of grass hermitages and monks also increased threefold from before. About five hundred of them were engaged in plastering alone. The entire residence was completely filled with wealth and resources, including gold, silver, and silk. There were nineteen corrals holding about one thousand cattle and horses at the most and about five hundred at the least. These were supplemented by the ten thousand people within the domain of the Taklungpa.

In general this supreme incarnation, Kuyalwa Rinchen Gonpo, had seven physical attributes: noble form, virtue and luster, clarity of the senses, smiling countenance and majesty, purity of conduct, fragrance of moral discipline, and beauty and insatiability on the part of those who beheld him. His speech also had seven attributes: it was easy to understand, grammatically correct, without falsehood, honest, stern in disciplinary matters, skilled in answering questions, and agreeable on account of its slow enunciation. His mind had the following seven attributes: radiance; directness, without deception; discipline and calmness; nobility; affection and compassion; engagement and earnestness in all respects; and immeasurable grace with respect to the three virtuous, unvirtuous, and indeterminate aspects of mind. He also possessed the following seven attributes: a sense of conscience, a sense of shame, forthrightness, long-term friendship, appreciation, {263} gratitude, and endurance. He was endowed with the following seven qualities: faith, perseverance, discriminative awareness, inspiration, generosity, dynamism, and the great armor of the bodhisattvas. He also had the following seven qualities: inscrutability, adaptability, inexhaustibility, reliability, agility and wisdom, judgment, and natural freedom from conceptual elaboration. So it was that his character effortlessly possessed these six groups of seven attributes.

Having been installed on the lion throne of the sacred doctrine, when he nurtured the community, he was skilled in giving explanations because he understood without error the enlightened intention of the transmitted teachings and treatises. He was skilled in the causal attributes to be attained because, having internally demonstrated the salient points, he could speak, mingling them with his own thoughts and integrating them with the pith instructions on meditation. He was skilled in establishing realization in the minds of others because he could guide them on the path that coalesces view, meditation, conduct, and fruit. He was skilled in nurturing others through guidance on meditation because he willfully understood the dispositions of his disciples and was therefore unimpeded in teaching the means by which they could be trained, in dispelling their obstacles, and in bringing forth their successful achievements.

He was skilled in nurturing the monks because he possessed the following seven qualities: he was beneficial to the monks; whatever they did, he did not forsake them but made them secure; he was controlled because he knew the essentials of the scope of the monastic vows; he made discussions meaningful; he was tolerant; he was of benefit in both matters of doctrine and secular affairs; and he assumed great responsibilities and the great armor of the bodhisattvas. He was skilled in council because the circumstances and perceptions of all were clear in his mind, he was adroit in means, he was reliable with respect to anything he undertook, he could not tolerate those who were overreliant and dependent, and he was skilled in council because he would teach all the monastic precepts and oral instructions without reservation. {265} He was skilled in making offerings and nurturing beings because he cared dearly for the following seven: the representations of the spiritual teachers and the precious jewels, the teaching of the Buddha, the virtuous activities of experiential cultivation, the disciples who practice the sacred doctrine, the primary patrons, the sentient beings who were donors, and the residence of the spiritual teacher. So it was that he possessed those seven kinds of skill.

He was endowed with the seven following kinds of resources: the resources associated with the locations of the doctrinal wheel, the resources of the retinue who form the congregation, the resources of material wealth, the resources of the sacred doctrine that is taught and studied, the resources of the views of philosophical systems, the resources of the mantras of attainment, and the resources of realization that is experienced.

He was endowed with the seven following kinds of power: the power of guiding beings from the level of an ordinary person to the buddha level, the power of disclosing the defining characteristics of the path and those that are not of the path, the power of accepting beings until they reach the point of enlightenment, the power of teaching the skillful means that purify faults and obscurations, the power of perfecting the provisions and enlightened attributes, the power of bringing forth all harmonious circumstances and of revealing the skillful means that bring them forth, and the power of not bringing forth all disharmonious aspects and of revealing the skillful means by which they are not brought forth.

The year before he passed away, the senior monks requested permission to build a wall around the monastery, but he refused them. At their further insistence, he said, "Very well then, but build a good one." They said that all that would not be necessary, whereupon he resigned.

On that day, in 1236, when he was in his forty-seventh year, rainbow lights, sounds, earth tremors, and so forth occurred. When asked if this was a sign that the Mongols were approaching, he replied, "I do not have long to live." His horse, named Druk Kyung Senge, fell ill with mange. To the monks who were moving about to the left and right, he said, "Stay here! Don't go anywhere!" {266} To the attendants, he said, "You will have to gather tea, brown sugar, and firewood." To those he was instructing, he said, "Make an effort and meditate because the dawn is almost breaking and the night watch is almost ending!"[210]

On the nineteenth day of the first summer month, they assembled, and he extensively gave a public teaching and advice on setting the mind on enlightenment, along with the aspiration prayer for the dedication of merit. From the middle summer month, they arranged sacraments within the Offering Chapel. When asked if the Tashi Pelbar Stūpa and the new reliquary with the silver parasol should be placed together, he said, "Leave a gap there! Another representational structure will be forthcoming. I am contented by the excellent performance of service with respect to these representations that presently exist."[211]

From the fourteenth day of that month, he felt slightly unwell. Rites were extensively performed to sustain his health, by all general and particular means. Many kinds of wealth, one hundred and ten horses, and so forth were offered to the Tashi Pelbar Stūpa. He said, "Henceforth, all that is dedicated to me should be offered to the stewards. There should be an extension, buttressed by the ravine on this northern side of the Offering Chapel, furnished with a cloud of offerings and alms, similar to those made to the Mahābodhi of Vajrāsana, to the three sibling images of Sublime Avalokiteśvara, to all the buddha fields, to the Five Peaks of Wutai Shan, to the three sibling Jo Shāk images of Lhasa, and to Gampopa, Phakmodrupa, and Taklungpa.[212] The wood for the rain canopy[213] is indeed sufficient, apart from one set of planks. I think it should face toward the roof of the Kumbum, but I did not make it." To the attendants, he also imparted oral advice, and he entrusted the library keys to Rinpoche Sangye Yarjon, saying, "I am the enlightened activity of Choje Rinpoche Taklungpa the Great. You too are the enlightened activity of Choje Rinpoche. {267} Nurture this place in accordance with his former exemplary life! You are the most responsible of all." And then he said, "Once my gross body has disintegrated, secure it to a pillar in the temple. That is a sign that you should firmly uphold the vows of ethical discipline. I am going to meet Lama Rinpoche, and there will be no tonight for me. Once my gross body has disintegrated, I will no longer lie down."[214]

In the evening of the twenty-fifth day, his emanational maṇḍala was absorbed into the expanse of reality. The sacred corpse was displayed, and on the morning of the first day of the next lunar month, the remains were cremated. Shang Khyer saw Rinpoche appear in a trail of smoke, seated within the crematorium. Wherever the smoke wafted, a shower of pearl relics fell. The skull became a mass of rainbow colors. Innumerable pearl relics were retrieved, along with the heart, tongue, and eyes, as well as a finger in the form of an icon and seed syllables.[215]

Immediately after Rinpoche Rinchen Gonpo passed away, Atri Zhonu was welcomed by ḍākinīs holding various offering sacraments. He saw the sacred corpse in the form of Phakmodrupa. The elder Kaṃtsikpa saw Rinpoche looking in all directions. Gompa Rongpa saw the sacred corpse in the form of Bhaṭṭārikā. He then saw rays of light being diffused from it in the four directions, and many ḍākinīs that were also presenting offerings. Jamchungwa saw Rinpoche's body in an extremely large form, surrounded by the eight closest heirs.[216] Denma Lharje saw the body seated in an aureole of light. Khoyo Gomrin saw innumerable ḍākinīs seated within all of its pores.[217]

On the day when the sacred corpse was cremated, Shakgyu Tsunchung {268} saw Rinchen Gonpo seated in good health. Rinchen Gyeltsen from Dome saw him seated above the fire with a red complexion and robe. Khoyo Gewapel saw his heart with an extremely large icon of glorious Phakmodrupa, with both father and son Choje [that is, Taklungpa the Great and Kuyalwa Rinchen Gonpo] seated at the right and left shoulders. Through reliance on the teaching and the auspicious circumstances that blessed his mind, Rinpoche Sangye Yarjon saw the sacred corpse in the form of Mahākāruṇika. The foregoing is but a fraction of the miracles that occurred. These are elucidated in detail in *The Great Biography*, composed by Duntso Gawa Loden Sherab.[218]

The Disciples of Kuyalwa Rinchen Gonpo

Venerable Rinchen Gonpo had an inconceivable number of disciples, but among them the most renowned was clearly Dezhin Shekpa Konchok Yenlak, who was also known as Tashi Drak or Yakru Repa, an emanation of Mahāvajradhara, Lord of the Dance. He was born in Dokham in 1200 (iron male monkey). His father was Wangchuk Lekpa, a yogin of Phakpa Tachok,[219] and his mother was Dolmatso. In his previous life, as a monk named Namkha-o, he had resorted to maturational empowerments and liberating guidance through the oral instructions of Dewar Shekpa Taklung Tangpa and had applied himself to the essence of spiritual attainment. Reborn with faith on that account, he traveled to U, where he touched his head at the feet of the supreme incarnation Kuyalwa Tulku Rinchen Gonpo at Taklung and was extremely delighted. He received all the oral instructions of the Kagyu lineage, in the manner of a vase being filled to the brim, and he stayed his whole life in this monastery of Taklung, engaged entirely in spiritual practice. {269} The grass hermitage where he lived at that time is even now recognizable. Later, he was also favored by Venerable Sangye Yarjon, and he became known as Yakru Repa on account of his signs of spiritual accomplishment. When Karma Pakshi traveled to Taklung and met him in his retreat hermitage, he requested a connection with the sacred doctrine, and so the latter said, "In his next life, he will become my disciple." He passed away in 1282 (water male horse), in his eighty-third year, in this very hermitage. His subsequent incarnations were known as The Crown-Bearers of Zhamar, and in the past, five of them appeared in succession.[220] The sixth incumbent is alive at the present time, and it is said that in the future, too, many others will appear.[221]

Concluding Verses

Here, through this virtuous endeavor, pure as the roots of a lotus,
May the deluded darkness of these beings who are equal to space be dispelled.
May they swiftly attain the level of Mañjuvajra,
Omniscient in the abiding and apparent realities of infinite fields of knowledge!

Choku Sangye Yarjon, Third in the Abbatial Succession

Homage to the undisputed Buddha, Venerable Yarjon,
Perfect in the pure ascetic discipline of the glorious three trainings,
Whose life was engaged in the essence of spiritual practice,
Unrivaled in the three planes of existence.

With regard to the biography of Choku Sangye Yarjon, this supreme venerable master who filled the three planes of existence with his reputation for resolute spiritual practice, he was born in the village called Bongra Tengkei Dongna in Yangsho.[222] His father was the great patron Gongyel, and his mother was Lhamo Seldron, who had been preordained by the ḍākinīs. She gave birth to four sons, of whom the eldest was the patron Yeshe Gon, the one below him was the patron Dorje Rinchen, {270} the one below him was Choje Rinpoche (Sangye Yarjon), and there was another who was the youngest.[223]

Among them, Venerable Sangye Yarjon was born in 1203 (water pig), accompanied by innumerable auspicious signs. His physical presence was handsome and pleasant, his acumen sharp and his mind intelligent. He was endowed with the excellence of faith, perseverance, and discriminative awareness. He possessed all the defining characteristics of the enlightened heritage of the Great Vehicle. Even in the modes of childhood play that he demonstrated, he enabled his companions to avoid negative acts and engage in virtuous acts. He naturally acquired the state of absorption in the meditative stabilities of spiritual attainment. In 1218 (earth male tiger), in his sixteenth year, he was ordained as a mendicant at the temple of Tangkya Gothar in the presence of many learned and venerable monks, headed by the monastic preceptor Gaton Lama, the master of ceremonies Lhakhang Takpa, and the faithful monk Lama Nakpa. He was given the name Sherab Lama.[224]

He extensively studied the texts and pith instructions under the guidance of that same monastic preceptor and that master of ceremonies, as well as under Lama Nakpa and others. While staying for three years engaged in one-pointed spiritual practice, in the sacred retreat hermitage called Saphu Gon,[225] flocks of ravens would sweep away the snow from the roof of his hut, and he could clearly see from afar the four modes of conduct in which the monks of Taklung engaged.[226] Lama Nakpa also predicted that this nephew of Choje Rinchen Gonpo would become an upholder of the Kagyu teaching.

In 1221 (iron female snake), in his nineteenth year, he set out for U along with Gontsen Chenpo—all the provisions of his journey being provided by the patron Tsangtsa Phurpa. At that time, the travelers were stopped by the people of Rakshi who prepared to steal their possessions, but when they heard that Rinpoche was present in the party, they could not attack and instead offered their service and respects. {271} Immeasurable acts of kindness such as these and auspicious signs occurred, such that everyone felt astonished and praised him as One Progressing This Year to Buddhahood. This name was proclaimed by the deities who delight in virtuous acts, such that it permeated the three world realms.[227]

Sangye Yarjon had first met his precious predecessor when the latter traveled to Chomtang. He was reminded of this at Podo, and he then reached the great seminary of Dorjeden Taklung. After some days, he made donations and distributed communal tea and alms. Gompa Jangseng offered him a grass hermitage in the monastery that he had built, whereupon he stayed in secluded retreat. He excellently received all the sacred doctrines that his precious predecessor possessed and experientially cultivated them, demonstrating completely the meditative experiences and signs of accomplishment. In 1222 (water male horse), in his twentieth year, he excellently received the precepts of a fully ordained monk according to the final ordination in the midst of an assembly including the faithful monk Gar Jose, with Tsangpa acting as the monastic preceptor, Khuton as the master of ceremonies, and Donmo Ripa acting as confessor. He became one who possessed the aggregate of peerless ethical discipline, a crown ornament of the hundred thousand upholders of the vinaya.[228]

Sangye Yarjon also attended upon certain other spiritual mentors who possessed the authentic defining characteristics. He integrated the study, reflection, and meditation of the impartial ocean of texts and pith instructions that extensively reveal the objects to be accepted and renounced in terms of the three kinds of vow—namely, the vows of individual liberation, the bodhisattva vows, and the mantras of the awareness holders. He remained one-pointedly in spiritual practice for sixteen years, during which time he donated the resources for sustenance that he had received from the lama's household as provisions for the practitioners of the monastery {272} while he himself subsisted on extracted elixirs.

On one occasion, someone named Apel Konchok Senge offered him tea, butter, cheesecake, and tsampa, and he immediately said to his attendant, "Make a torma offering seven cubits in height!" The attendant did as he commanded, such that when that patron saw it, through the fruit of the sacred doctrine, he became a wealthy man in Taklung Monastery.

On one occasion, in a dream, two conch shells hung from his ears as he rode his horse, and the sound emitted by them when blown permeated the entire world.[229]

In 1236 (fire male monkey), in his thirty-fourth year, when his precious predecessor Kuyalwa Rinchen Gonpo passed away, he performed the cremation rites and undertook virtuous acts of skillful means in connection with the funeral ceremonies, beyond expectation. Then, on the eighth day of the waxing half of the first autumn month, he was appointed as master of the Buddhist teaching upon the lion throne of the sacred doctrine, and an uncountable number of auspicious feasts were held.[230]

According to Rinpoche's own biography, just as his two late predecessors had done, like their reflection transposed on a clear mirror, each year, around the morning of the Great Offering Ceremony, he would proceed to the teaching throne, and deliver a teaching on the great setting of the mind on enlightenment. On any day in the waxing half of the summer months, he would convene an extensive congregation in the afternoon. Other than that, until he himself later passed into nirvāṇa, having reached his seventieth year, he spent the time exclusively in retreat, seated upon a single seat.[231]

During that time, when his precious predecessor Kuyalwa Rinchen Gonpo was passing into nirvāṇa, he went there and pledged that he would prepare a strict monastic charter[232] based on the council and auspicious intimations of the sacred doctrine that he had received. For a while, he entered into retreat at Sengling Dorje Drakdzong. {273} Then, he gathered together the authorized councillors of Taklung and went there in response to their invitation, whereupon he said, "If this monastic charter is implemented, it will be in accordance with our wishes." They accepted it, and he immediately departed.

Sangye Yarjon made the monastic regulations even purer and stricter than they had been according to the rules and charter of his two predecessors. They included thirteen regulations based on the exemplary life of Choje Kuyalwa, thirteen rules concerning monastic discipline, and thirteen regulations concerning the charter of the monastic assembly—thirty-nine altogether.

Among them, the first set, the thirteen based on the exemplary life of Choje Kuyalwa were as follows: (1) Having assumed the teaching throne, the responsibilities should be assumed in accordance with the four great religious activities, and so forth,[233] and apart from that, Rinpoche should not give advice on matters of government, lawsuits, war, punishment, and so forth. (2) Monks should attend the teachings from the first to the fifteenth day of any lunar month, and stay in retreat from the sixteenth to the thirtieth day. (3) Meat and alcohol should not be exhibited within sight. (4) Weapons offered to the monastery should be broken in a visible place. (5) It would not be permitted to offer a hand empowerment to women. (6) When there are disturbances in the community, prayers and offerings should be made to the precious jewels. (7) One should not incite the wrath of the doctrinal protectors. (8) Monks should always ask for leave of absence when visiting or staying with outsiders, be they powerful or weak. (9) They should never waver from teaching, debate, and composition. (10) They should always be seated in the four-session yoga. (11) Each day the offerings should be changed three times in the presence of the three representations (images, books, and stūpas) indicative of body, speech, and mind. (12) They should not turn away powerful or weak individuals including the sons of the nobility from the region who have escaped to take refuge in the sacred doctrine. (13) From the time when they are newly ordained as mendicants, the door of the sacred doctrine should be opened for all monks, and they should apply themselves to guidance. {274} These are the thirteen regulations based on the exemplary life of Choje Kuyalwa, which integrate and implement all the experiential cultivations, engagements and abstentions associated with all the turnings of the doctrinal wheel of the tathāgatas, without exception, in the essential nature of the three vows and the two stages of meditation.

As for the second set of rules concerning monastic discipline, these generally consist of the pure experiential cultivation of all the three vows, including the outer vows of individual liberation, the inner vows of the bodhisattvas, and the secret vows of the awareness holders. Then, in particular, the following regulations applied: (1) Meat and alcohol should not be exhibited within the monastery. (2) Even the mother of the venerable Rinpoche himself should be excluded from the monastery, and attending upon the doctrinal protectors, there should never be a place for women to come. (3) The monastic preceptor and the master of ceremonies should confer the vows of the novitiate and full ordination and teach their respective precepts. (4) Those who need to request vows and empowerments should be assembled in one place by eight elders of Taklung, and they should then make their request to Rinpoche and to the monastic preceptor and master of ceremonies on the occasion of an auspicious planet, constellation, and conjunction.[234] (5) They should not wear robes that are crushed or torn or unclean.[235] (6) They should not accept water from a layperson. (7) They should not let people go on to the roof.[236] (8) They should not keep a dog on the roof. (9) They should not participate in the buying and selling of fish, pork, eggs, garlic, or onions. (10) They should hold two confession ceremonies each month. (11) They should observe the summer rain retreat and maintain it for three months. (12) They should observe the restrictions and the lifting of restrictions associated with the summer rain retreat in the correct manner. (13) In order to protect the temple from damage caused by water, they should repair the dams in the uplands, transport earth for blocking leakages on the roofs, construct high barriers where streams flood together, repair bridges, whitewash earthen stūpas and chapels containing clay images, and take care of the roads during the autumn season.

These rules are also imbued with three cycles—namely, the cycle of recitation, study, and reflection; the cycle of renunciation and meditative concentration; {275} and the cycle of duties and actions—and they entail the implementation of the three vows, profound view, extensive conduct, and the Great Seal of experiential cultivation, blessing, and respect. That is to say, these thirteen regulations concerning monastic discipline integrate the two streams of the Kadam instructions and the Great Seal.

As for the third set of regulations concerning the charter of the monastic assembly, they are as follows: (1) The monks should undertake the outer prostration circuit in order that they might be amenable to study and receive the teachings. (2) They should undertake the inner prostration circuit so that they might swiftly be invited to form orderly rows. (3) The monks should chant the sūtras. (4) They should ask after the health of Choje Rinpoche. (5) They should request teaching in the assembly and make the maṇḍala offering. (6) Rinpoche should give the teaching. (7) The lower ranks should request advice, and the higher ranks should impart advice. (8) They should dedicate torma offerings. (9) They should recite the twelve volumes of *The Transcendent Perfection of Wisdom in One Hundred Thousand Lines* once. (10) They should recite prayers and the hundred-syllable mantra of Vajrasattva. (11) They should accomplish the recitation of the sūtras. (12) They should encourage deceased persons by means of mnemonic incantations. (13) Finally, those who respect the patrons, those who execute the pure aspiration prayers of dedication for the living and the dead, and those monks who partake of the three sublime levels or the status of an ordinary person, equal in number to the particles of the earth maṇḍala, should undertake rites that purify the donations of their patrons, practice experiential cultivation, and demonstrate the sacred doctrine, commencing with the exemplary lives of former buddhas and their disciples who consolidated the merit of their disciples. These are the thirteen regulations concerning the monastic assembly.

Furthermore, meat could not be displayed within the monastery. Patrons had no authority to stay more than three days within the monastery. Monks were not allowed to increase their wealth. Even wealthy persons who came from afar bringing offerings were not allowed to stay more than three days in the monastery. {276} After being ordained as a novice monk, up until the harvest time, they were not permitted to engage in activities that were harmful to living creatures, including construction work and the gathering of firewood and aromatic herbs. Monks were not allowed to thresh hay and so forth, to indulge in the gossip of the marketplace, or to profit from business and so forth. Even if there were one or two laymen who initially stayed in the monastery, they too would become mendicants, such that all those present would be exclusively novices or fully ordained monks. In brief, they did not only pay lip service to all the rules concerning renunciation, acceptance, engagement, and abstention, which are explained in the monastic discipline of the sacred doctrine, but they certainly undertook to implement them in practice.[237]

On one occasion, when the large army of Hor Dumur arrived in Tibet,[238] he sent his venerable uncle bearing gifts to the place where the Hor were encamped. By resorting exclusively to prayer, Dumur's inimical thoughts were calmed, and he became a disciple. At the time when he reached the place where the Hor were encamped, a band of travelers saw Mahākāruṇika seated above the head of the man bearing those gifts within a tent, and they prostrated. Those who engaged in occasional negative pursuits, such as fishing, butchering, and hunting, changed their outlook just upon seeing him, and thereafter they continued to abandon those negative pursuits.[239]

Although in terms of the sacred doctrine, there were no teachings that he did not receive and none that he did not know, Sangye Yarjon exclusively granted guidance in both the Great Seal and the Six Doctrines of Nāropā. He built the extension bay of the Main Temple and the middle story that was supported by eighty pillars and adorned with a gilded roof. He also built the reliquary chapel containing the blessed relics of the supreme Kuyalwa Tulku Rinchen Gonpa, along with its Chinese-style roof, which is known as the Central Reliquary Chapel. In addition, he built the Silver Reliquary Chapel called Tashi Obar, which resembled a snow mountain, and its life-size silver image of Rinpoche Taklung Tangpa. {277} Behind the thrones of both these silver reliquary and image, more than three thousand five hundred peerless statues were installed, depicting the spiritual teachers of the lineage, buddhas, bodhisattvas, the assemblages of deities according to the tantras, the doctrinal protectors, and the wealth deities. He also commissioned forty-eight large paintings on a cotton base, using a twelve-cubit roll and an eight-cubit roll, which reached the height of the roof of the Great Lower Hall of the Main Temple. As for the murals of the upper and lower walls of the Main Temple, he commissioned depictions of eighty-six large buddha fields, and it is said that not even a palm-size part of the wall surface was left empty.[240]

Each year, on the fourteenth and fifteenth days of the fifth lunar month, he made no less than twenty-three hundred thousand small terracotta icons with their mantra cores, which had the objective of warding off the Hor, and so forth. And each day, he newly made many terracotta icons and small statues and innumerable volumes of the sūtras, tantras, and treatises, inscribed on both white and blue paper. It is said that each year, while he was requested to remain at Taklung, one set of scriptures was printed on white paper and double that quantity on blue paper.

In all respects, the teachings were maintained without interruption. In the great hall for daily assembly, there were ten sessions; in the middle story, there were six sessions; and in the hall for minor rites, many different sorts of rites were undertaken, including those of Uṣṇīṣa, the hundred thousand names,[241] and the vase consecration. There were also three sessions of mantra recitation pertaining to rites of protection and the warding off of obstacles and of the doctrinal protectors. The offerings made to the representations of buddha body, speech, and mind, and the veneration of the monastic community were absolutely awesome. These were embellished in particular with incense powders of precious metals and gemstones and ornaments including many hundreds of brocade hangings, made from thousands of rolls of silk. Once each year the awnings covering the two reliquary stūpas were gilded, a hundred incenses compounded of excellent mountain medicines, valued at innumerable gold *sang* coins, were offered forty times, {278} and many sticks of incense, thirty-seven fingerspans in length, were offered on a daily basis. In each temple, each evening, butter lamps containing ten loads of melted butter were offered. On the fifth offering ceremony of each month, held on the nineteenth day, sixty loads of butter were offered, and twenty on each of the other four monthly offering ceremonies. Each month, no less than four hundred and forty loads of butter—and each year, five thousand and eighty loads of butter—were offered without interruption. During the Great Offering Ceremony, one thousand seven hundred large clay and copper lamps and lamps of pure copper, which had to be lifted by more than ten men, were filled with clarified butter and into each ten wicks, approximately the length of the human arm, were inserted, such that they burned for up to forty days. Each day, one hundred and eight butter torma were continuously offered, and during the Great Offering Ceremony, butter sculptures fashioned from fifty loads of butter were offered. The details of such auspicious anniversaries and regular offerings are indescribable.

In the great assembly, held during all months of the year, alms were distributed five times all day long, and the sustenance of many hundreds of monks was provided by the lama's household. The entire assembly was continuously nourished with tea, and on certain occasions many distributions of alms were made. In particular, during the Great Offering Ceremony, when the Layel Courtyard was filled with the entire congregation, like a mass of sesame seeds, one hundred thousand tormas were prepared, teachings were given, prayers recited, and countless ritual procedures of doctrinal conduct were undertaken. It is estimated that each load of butter in the morning and each load of brown sugar for the tea in the evening weighed eighty *sang*. A roll of silk was distributed for every five monks, and regular distributions of tea were made. The magnificence of the offerings made to the precious jewels {279} and the respect shown to the monastic community on that occasion appear to have been found nowhere else.

Furthermore, there was a prediction that had been made by the late Taklungpa the Great:

> The spacious, the strong, and the brown-headed—
> These three will be no different from me.[242]

"Spacious" denotes the supreme incarnation Kuyalwa the Great Rinchen Gonpo, the omniscient one who was also broad-minded and profound with regard to provisional matters. "Strong" denotes Rinpoche Sangye Yarjon, who was steadfast as a vajra in the three higher trainings and who maintained a meditative resolve that could not be moved by any circumstance whatsoever. "Brown-headed" denotes Tashi Lama, the emanation of Lord Ajita—the regent of the Conqueror, who like Vajrapāṇi, maintained the secret treasury of all the buddhas and for a while had the appearance of a brown-haired person. Only the physical projections of these three lineage holders, uncle and nephews, were revealed to have been different. Since their minds had a single continuum, they cannot be quantified, as if the deeds undertaken by the previous one were preparatory to the deeds undertaken by the next.

Kuyalwa Rinpoche had said to one Nyemowa Tsul Lek—who had formerly been born as the riding horse of glorious Taklung Tangpa the Great at the time when in a previous life he had incarnated as Geshe Jayulwa—"I am building a temple that will be called great throughout the country of Tibet. You should construct the golden spire!" He agreed to do so. At that time, even the foundations of the temple had not been laid, but later, when Venerable Sangye Yarjon was completing the white parapet of the temple roof, the golden spire indeed arrived there.

Again, Kuyalwa Rinpoche had said, "These painted scrolls of Caṇḍa should each have a metal peg and a ring attached to the wall. {280} Later on, the deities will have to be displayed!" This was done. Later, Venerable Sangye Yarjon fastened three straps to each of the large painted scrolls and said, "Now they should be displayed!" "Should we prepare the place for displaying them up there?" they asked, whereupon he said, "That will do."

When the scrolls were displayed, they fit onto the rings that had formerly been fixed on the wall.

Once the venerable patron Śākrin dreamed that Kuyalwa Rinpoche appeared to him, saying, "Śākrin, you are strong. Do not disrespect me! Change this mat and parasol!" The very next day, at Yang Gonteng, Rinpoche Yarjon said, "Śākrin, change this mat and parasol of mine!" Thus, there were a great many anecdotes determining that the father and son were indivisible and so forth.

When Tsangdar was in retreat, Sangye Yarjon said, "Can you not see the grass hermitage from your outer courtyard?" He replied, "It is obscured because the middle door is blocked off." "Can you not see it from the rim of your ladder?" He replied, "I cannot see it because it is obscured by Garing's upper story." Then, one day, he heard many monks making a noise. That evening, when he looked around, the upper story had been transformed, and he clearly saw the grass hermitage. Immediately thereafter, his mind distinctly realized inner radiance in the buddha body of reality, and he offered a spiritual song of realization.[243]

Most of the congregation, exemplified by them, pleased Sangye Yarjon exclusively through the service of spiritual attainment. Some were sculptors of sacred representations. And those who painstakingly arranged external activities and so forth, and who completed the communion offerings and engaged in virtuous activities, were innumerable. At the very least, the saintly persons who were present at that time unimaginably perceived the letters inscribed on the reverse side of each large painted scroll and even the drawn *tsakali* icons that had been inserted within each of the small images. {281}

Representations of buddha body, speech, and mind and offering sacraments were also newly brought to Taklung. These included representations of buddha body, such as a turquoise Amitābha, an ivory set of the eight stūpas, an image of Kuyalwa Rinpoche containing his own eyes, and the great female deity of Shara Pondrak. There were countless volumes of sūtras, tantras, and treatises, representative of buddha speech, and representations of buddha mind, such as the silver vajra that had been the hand emblem of the master Padmasambhava, the gilded metal vajra that had been the hand emblem of Neuzurpa, and the great reliquary of Geshe Megewa.[244] Innumerable offering sacraments also came into his possession, including the gong of Lato Khenpo; the large patterned brocade of Lhadok Tonpa; the large brocade hangings of Zhorang; the sling of Dzakolpa, called Ocean Quaking

Resonance; the brass conch of Karmapa, called Thunderous Sound; and his cymbals, called Strong and Mighty Lion.[245]

Sangye Yarjon displayed many arrays of buddha body. Khenpo Tangkarwa saw him as eleven-faced Mahākāruṇika. While Rinpoche was residing there in Taklung, he was seen to be traveling, visible in the common perception of many people in Lhasa and by the caretaker at Jayul. Gompa Dargon saw him as Vajradhara. Drongbu Tonpa saw him transform into Hevajra and then actually grant him scriptural transmissions. Gyawa Hralmo saw him as Rinpoche Kuyalwa. When he conferred oral instruction on Jodrub of Tsongdu Gurmo, one night the latter had a dream in which an image of the Great Compassionate One in the form of Khasarpaṇi appeared and imparted that same oral instruction. After he had meditated accordingly, other people later saw him as the Great Compassionate One.

Gomdar saw Sangye Yarjon as the maṇḍala of skeleton-clad Heruka. {282} The patron Yungdrung Tsunpa, on whom he had conferred oral instruction, engaged in experiential cultivation, such that at the time of his death, he perceived that Rinpoche directly arrived there. Nyawo Gomchung saw his body as a white syllable A. When he conferred oral instruction on Lama Dzakolwa, at the time when the transmission passed to him, the earth shook, and he had a vision of Rinpoche. When Sangye Yarjon conferred oral instruction on Darpa Lotsāwa, the latter engaged in experiential cultivation, whereupon he saw Rinpoche traveling in the sky on three occasions. Gompa Taklo saw Rinpoche's physical form on the roof of the Great Offering Chapel. Many monks saw Rinpoche riding a blue horse and traveling to Drakchuka, whereupon that region was cured of smallpox.

The venerable patron Śākrin dreamed that a white, peaceful Vajrapāṇi, dressed in silk robes, touched the cast images with a bamboo staff and that they then formed an array. The next day, he went to inspect the casting room, and he saw Rinpoche touching them with bamboo and giving advice to the sculptors, such that he knew him to be an emanation of Vajrapāṇi. Once, Sangye Yarjon said to Gompa Sherab Gyeltsen, "Gompa! Today did you not see the elder Aṅgita come here?"[246] He replied, "A while ago I saw a form of Rinpoche seated in the sky. Was that him?" "Yes!" said Rinpoche. When Sangye Yarjon extracted books, mold engravings, and precious jewels from the summit of a hill in Trekyi Dramotang, he was accepted as an emanation of Putowa.[247]

The stories indicative of his extrasensory powers were innumerable. On one occasion, he said, "Sell all the horses and cattle of our nomad camp, without exception! Make butter lamps!" They kept some back and sold the majority. Then, they offered butter lamps, the light of which filled the adjoining valley and was seen from Reteng in the north. {283} The remaining horses and cattle had been rustled by the people of Beri, and Rinpoche knew this through his extrasensory power. He knew that a hundred villagers[248] of Beri had drunk a cup of tea that morning and had a cup of gruel in the evening, and then he said, "You have been drinking. That's out of order! Later, don't do that!"

When he was residing at Sengling, the carpenter Ponśāk Tumbu came bringing a load of birchwood, and Rinpoche knew that he had almost fallen into the Ojo ravine. As soon as he arrived in Rinpoche's presence, Rinpoche said, "But for me you almost fell!"

Again, when he was residing at Sengling, Tsondru Chok brought a novice monk, and they went to request guidance on the hundred-syllable mantra of Vajrasattva. Rinpoche gave them this instruction. Tsondru Chok then asked, "Wouldn't he not know how to meditate?" Rinpoche replied, "He will have no option but to learn how to meditate." When they had climbed uphill and reached the Ojo Plateau, meditation surged within that novice monk. He knew that the latter had a small cloth that Gompa Umawa had used as bedding, and in his presence, he sent an attendant to collect it, saying, "I make the rules for everyone. If the meditator is feeling cold, he may have the fleece cloak that I am wearing." Consequently, the novice felt ashamed.

There was an itinerant monk named Gying Nawa Rindor, who was in retreat and who, when the roof leaked in summertime, would sometimes change his seat and sometimes sit covering his head with a bamboo pannier. When Rinpoche went to give guidance to him, he said, "You will make the leak bigger! During your time here, you may listen to the teachings, but for those in the future, the grass hermitage will be ruined! Apart from covering your head with a damaged bamboo pannier, what will you achieve that is not uncomfortable?"

When the monks who were bringing birchwood to him could not singe the wood because there had been no rain and it was too dry, he prayed, and immediately afterward the rain fell. When they arrived in his presence, he said, "I feared there would be some need since there has been no rain."

A blind servant named Neltsul {284} went to him for guidance, having inserted a *sang* of gold inside his waist belt, whereupon Sangye Yarjon said, "Instead of acting as a blind servant, why do you not like to buy a grass hermitage and do retreat?" When he said, "I have no means of paying for a hermitage," Sangye Yarjon replied, "All that is inside your waist belt will indeed be sufficient!"

Then there was one Dampa Gyachung, who had requested him to consecrate an icon. One day, Sangye Yarjon suddenly said to Gompa Lodro Pel, "You do the consecration!" He replied, "There is no water." Sangye Yarjon said, "Do not fear that water will not come!" Gompa then conveyed that injunction to Gyachungwa, such that it was impressed upon his mind. There being no water, he was planning to assign ten young monks to help in the morning and have them fetch water from the Drakchu so that there would be a sufficient amount for the consecration ceremony, but in the morning, a large spring of water burst forth from the side of the calf pen.[249] Gompa reported this to Sangye Yarjon, who remarked, "Well, you said there was no water!"

Seeing that the hybrid cattle of the monastery were grazing at Lata, he repeatedly said that they should be moved slightly, but they were not moved, and so civil strife ensued. He said, "From the time when I was in retreat in the forested valleys of Kham, I knew how the monks of Taklung were engaging in the four modes of conduct.[250] It is insulting for some of you to call me Yatawa and ask whether I am informed or not regarding your conduct."

When Nyawo Gomtsul was transporting two loads of rancid butter of different sizes, and had many disturbing thoughts arising in his mind, he came into Sangye Yarjon's presence, whereupon the latter said, "Is it all right for this butter of yours to give rise to many thoughts?"

When Lama Gyel Otsen had received guidance and was practicing in solitude, without meeting anyone, two attendants suddenly appeared, carrying him on a litter since it seemed that he was on the point of death, having fallen ill, and they brought him into Sangye Yarjon's presence. Rinpoche gave him a blessing, {285} whereupon he immediately recovered and walked into the house.

Once, when he was making small terracotta icons in the Layel Courtyard, with the intention of inserting them into the Kumbum, there was a heavy downpour of rain on all sides. An attendant therefore asked him if the monks should go to fetch the terracotta icons. He replied, "Prepare a torma offering. They will not be soaked with water." By granting his blessing, the rain fell all around, but from the start, it did not fall in the Layel Courtyard, and so the terracotta icons were not disturbed.

The great saintly being Sakya Paṇḍita traveled to Taklung, and they met. Later Venerable Sakya Paṇḍita informed Khache Paṇchen Śākyaśrī, "If I had not held discussions about the sacred doctrine with Taklung Sangye Yarjon, I would not have held any discussions again in this world.[251] There is no spiritual adviser like him elsewhere. Isn't that very astonishing?" Paṇchen replied, "Ordinary talk is incompatible with the sacred doctrine. If one can merely talk, making a single connection with a few words, one will not become a spiritual mentor."[252]

Then, at the place where they escorted Venerable Sakya Paṇḍita at the time of his departure from Taklung, Rakye Drakpa asked him, "Will it be all right if my old mother engages in any sort of whatever virtuous action?" He replied, "My son! This lama of yours is the buddha himself. Those assembled in his presence will entirely become bodhisattvas, so she should respect the monastic community in all ways!"

Later, when Lama Sakyapa the Great (Sakya Paṇḍita) was traveling to Mongolia, he and his nephew Chogyel Phakpa both visited Taklung.[253] At that time, Rinpoche Sangye Yarjon entreated Choje Sakya Paṇḍita as follows: "It seems that there will be a need for this nephew of yours in China, Tibet, and Mongolia—all three. So, at that time, please offer council that will also be beneficial to us Taklungpas." {286} Later, that is what transpired.[254] When Phakpa Rinpoche's enlightened activities were equal to space, at the time when he was returning to Tibet from the imperial palace in Beijing, Tashi Lama was sent to Podo to invite him, whereupon Phakpa said, "If your teacher, Sangye Yarjon, will attend the assembly, I will come. If he does not come, I shall proceed directly to Lungsho." When Rinpoche Sangye Yarjon was asked to attend the assembly, he said, "It has been my intention not to cross the threshold of Yang Gon before my death, but now I cannot disobey the words of this great teacher." Then, he went down to the Layel Courtyard where they met each other by prostrating simultaneously. Phakpa said to the congregation, "No one has seen Sangye Yarjon and his nephew, but today you have seen them. This is my present to you!" And he presented Sangye Yarjon with fine offerings. One day, when Sangye Yarjon was left in his presence without an attendant, they engaged in a limitless question and answer session, commencing with the essential definitive meaning, whereupon the great lama Phakpa became most respectful.[255]

When the great accomplished master Karma Pakshi was about to be immolated due to the punishment of the Chinese emperor, he felt Sangye Yarjon riding on a lion, traveling through the sky, and imparting oral instruction, such that he did not succumb to the harmful impact of the fire. As repayment for this kindness, he offered a jade cup, which exists even nowadays and is bestowed upon those appointed to the teaching throne at Taklung.[256]

Previously, when Sangye Yarjon was engaged in practice within the monastery, he went to do retreat at Lake Namtso Chukmo, and while he was staying in a cave at the larger of the two stone pillars of Tashi Dowoche, through the power of the blissful heat of caṇḍālī, all the stones above and below him, in all directions melted and merged together. They formed a plaster and he left many impressions of his handprints and footprints in the wet clay. {287} Even nowadays, when one goes up there, these are said to be in the cave.[257] Commencing from then, until he eventually passed into final nirvāṇa, all the miraculous powers and abilities of body, speech, and mind that he manifested, surpassing the imagination, cannot be documented in writing.

On the day of the anniversary offering ceremony of the late Taklung Tangpa the Great in 1271, when Sangye Yarjon was in his sixty-ninth year, he attended an assembly and extensively imparted teachings and advice. From the midwinter month, he seemed to fall ill due to the pollution caused by an attendant who had eaten meat and approached him. At that time, he had visions of innumerable buddha fields and meditational deities. For seven months, innumerable rituals to restore his health were undertaken here at Taklung and all around. He bestowed representative images, manuscripts, and so forth on his two nephews for their respective protection and extensively gave them advice. He appointed them as authentic masters of the Buddhist teaching in Kham and U.[258]

Then, on the third day of the waxing half of the last summer month in 1272 (water male monkey), he passed away and departed for the taintless eastern buddha field. Solzhowa saw his body seated in the form of rainbow light. Dronkhangwa Zhonu saw the master and his two disciples traveling and seated in the sky, within the old Kumbum stūpa. On the fifth day, the sacred corpse was displayed, whereupon Sonam Dorje saw four-armed Avalokiteśvara seated upon a lotus stem, then vanishing into the sky in the form of threefold rays of light. {288} Those who were chanting heard Rinpoche's voice resonate from the sky, saying, "I am present everywhere. Pray so that the chanting may continue without interruption."

Even the body was cremated, his heart, tongue, and eyes were retrieved, along with an indescribable number of relics, including clockwise-spiraling conch shells, icons, seed syllables, stūpas, and hand emblems. Wherever the smoke from the cremation wafted, there was a downpour of flowers and pearl relics.[259] Also at that time, when the sacred corpse was seated within the vault of the crematorium, Drombu Tonpa saw him as Hevajra. One person from Tre saw him as the Buddha Krakucchanda. Drom Dorje Pel saw him as Avalokiteśvara with a thousand arms and a thousand eyes. A Newar saw him as Mahāmuni. The artist Ongom saw him as Phakmodrupa. Gendun Shenyen Tok saw him as the Sage Śākyamuni. Geshe Darzhon saw him as Venerable Taklung Tangpa the Great.[260] Moreover, there were some who saw him seated at Yang Gon and seated in the place where the crematorium vault had been. There were a great many who had visions such as these, and the wondrous indications were infinite.

Here at Taklung, in the sacred places of India, China, Nepal, and all the regions of Tibet, a cloud of offerings was presented to the representations of buddha body, speech, and mind, and magnificent offerings were made to the entire assembly of monks and laymen. In this way, his enlightened intention was excellently fulfilled.

This account has been written, integrating to some extent both *The Great Biography* of Sangye Yarjon based on the tradition of Taklung Lower Plain—which was composed by the lord of yoga, Dampa Rakye Drakpa Rinchen Dorje—and the verses contained in *The Golden Rosary of Taklung Upper Plain*,[261] which was composed by Tokden Chenpo Tsangdar Dombuwa. {289}

The Disciples of Choku Sangye Yarjon

During the lifetime of Venerable Sangye Yarjon, it is said that his disciples included two nephews who were his equal in renunciation and realization and who were recipients of the teachings, endowed with enlightened activity for the sake of living beings. He also had four spiritual sons; five hundred meditators, in whom the realization of the common savor arose; one thousand five hundred who were proficient in the control of vital energy and mind; two thousand eight hundred who were introduced to the blissful warmth of caṇḍālī; and three thousand six hundred who belonged to the precious monastic congregation. Among them, a somewhat detailed account of the two venerable nephews is presented below.

Drington Barlewa Chenpo Śākya Rinchen

Drington Barlewa Chenpo Śākya Rinchen was one of the four spiritual sons. He was born at Drilung in 1201 (bird) in the family line of Dringpel Luse. His father was the great mantrin Yeshe Dorje, his mother was Nyentokza Dolma Bum, and he was the oldest of their three sons. He was given the name Chemchok Lhundrub. In his thirteenth year, he studied writing and reading. He received many doctrines of the new and ancient traditions from his father and his paternal uncle. At Kokhyim, he was ordained as a mendicant by the preceptor Chokyi Tsenchen and given the name Śākya Rinchen. Traveling to Sangphu, he trained excellently in the transcendent perfections and logic. In his twenty-fifth year, at Ojo, he received the full monastic ordination in the presence of the monastic preceptor Narawa and the master of ceremonies Lhundrubpa. His younger brother Lama Dar was also ordained as a mendicant and received the name Tsultrim Sherab.

Drinton Śākrin received teachings on monastic discipline and *The Treasury of Phenomenology* from his monastic preceptor and from Tsulchen Rinchen Zangpo, on *The Adamantine Garland*[262] and other works from Chak Lotsāwa, {290} and on the cycle of *The Litany of the Names of Mañjuśrī* from Nyelde. When he first met Venerable Sangye Yarjon, he saw him in the form of the sublime Khasarpaṇi. All the maturational empowerments and liberating oral instructions were bestowed upon him profoundly and extensively. He stayed at Gotsangchen in the uplands of Taklung, practicing one-pointedly for six years, dependent on austerities. He acquired realization by relying on the blissful warmth of caṇḍālī, and he was also proficient in the control of the energy channels and winds. During the dawn session of meditation practice, he would circumambulate the monastery three times, without interrupting his adamantine posture, and on the circumambulatory path, he would hover above the snow that had fallen in the manner of a bird while others would hold on by the hem of his robe. When this was reported to Rinpoche Sangye Yarjon, he said, "It appears that Drington Śākrin is circumambulating the monastery while maintaining his adamantine posture. This is simply an auspicious circumstance associated with the experiential cultivation of vital energy."

Kongpo Darshe, his younger brother Tsulshe, and Minyak Gyelshe went to meet him. He saw them from afar and came out of his doorway. They paid homage to him and asked after his health, whereupon Tonśāk said, "I will go ahead into my cave hermitage. You should come on in, my friends!"

But even the heads of those three would not fit. Darshe then said, "Lama Rinpoche did not give these oral instructions to us, whether they are profound or not. There is no difference between us in terms of discriminative awareness and perseverance, but we three have been deceived by this poor reputation of ours. He has not succumbed to substantial phenomena. Now, I too will go to Semodo at Lake Namtso and so forth and not come out until I have obtained fearless confidence in my mind. Dringon Śākrin, you too should see your practice through to the end!" Dringon Śākrin then set out, and in that sacred place of Semodo, he had visions of Jñānanātha accompanied by eight ḍākinīs. {291}

When Venerable Sakya Paṇḍita and his nephew visited Taklung, Dringon Śākrin went to meet them, and he received many empowerments and transmissions. Rinpoche Sangye Yarjon also bestowed on him detailed oral instructions, including the aural lineage and the cycles of six meditational deities. But when Rinpoche said he should set out for Kham, he expressed his wish to travel to the highland direction, Kailash and so forth, whereupon, Rinpoche consented, saying, "Come back here after three years!" He moistened eight lumps of sugar with his tears and gave them to Dringon Śākrin, who then set out.

At Namgyi Sildzong, he received the doctrinal cycle of the Karma Kamtsang tradition from Tokden Yeshe Wangchuk, and at Lato Dechen, he received the cycle of the Drukpa tradition from Choje Gotsangpa.[263] After visiting Kailash and Lake Manasarovar, he meditated in a large cave for six months, whereupon Śākyamuni, foremost of the thousand buddhas of the Auspicious Eon, appeared on the surface of the snow mountain and said, "After carrying out your deeds, then, through the truth of the path, you will bring the rebirth process to its conclusion and obtain nectar in the taintless buddha field." Elated by this vision, he danced on the surface of a boulder and left an impression of his footprint.

Returning to U, he then traveled to Barle Drakmar, at the "neck" of Nyenchen Tanglha, where his own younger brother Tsulshe had founded a monastery. The brothers joyfully met, and Tsulshe requested him to stay there, but he refused. The next day, he gave teaching to the meditators from the surface of the rocky teaching throne, and immediately thereafter—from who knows where—a man wearing the dress of Minyak appeared, riding a gray horse and requesting him to stay there, saying, "I will achieve all your enlightened activities!" and then he vanished. It is said his younger brother Tsulshe was summoned toward the great snow face of Nyenchen Tanglha. {292}

Drington Śākrin then journeyed to Taklung, where he offered as a gift to Rinpoche Sangye Yarjon his realization of the common savor of meditation. Rinpoche also granted him some profound oral instructions and then said, "Now you should practice at the neck of Nyachen Tanglha on that sacred mountain in order to enable living beings and so forth to leave behind their conceptual elaborations." Accordingly, he traveled to Barle Drakmar and stayed there. He diligently composed the biography of Rinpoche. He nurtured disciples through his oral instructions, the foremost of which concerned the Great Seal and the Six Doctrines of Nāropā. Consequently, he gathered about five hundred persons there, who were exclusively meditators.

When, after the Mongolian army had encamped at Nyingdrung, the monastery was about to be destroyed, he invoked the doctrinal protectors, whereupon a black cloud suddenly gathered, hailstones lethally fell, many lightning bolts struck, and many soldiers died, so they fled in fear.[264]

He also traveled to Taklung to repel the sorcery of the Tselpa. On that occasion, the master and his disciples, nine altogether, interrupted their retreat and turned the wheel of the thirty proud spirits, whereupon the potions boiled, fire blazed, the effigy bounced, and during the application of the rite, everyone saw a bloody human head within the cavity marked with the syllable HAṂ. Onpo Rinpoche recovered his health. The Tselpa were inflicted with a fatal disease and many people died.[265]

Masang Dawu Ngongen himself knew the time when he was about to die and he came to Taklung. He requested Rinpoche Sangye Yarjon to accept him as a disciple out of compassion, whereupon Rinpoche said, "When, in a former life, you were a householder in India, your household priest was the monk Dharmaguṇa. His reincarnation is Drington Śākrin, so you should go to his place!" Then Masang set out. Drinton Śākrin also knew this and went to welcome him at Drongchung Rabkhawa. As soon as he arrived there, Masang alighted from his horse, {293} placed his head in the lama's lap, and said, "Accept me as a disciple out of compassion!" He replied, "When you have passed away, your obscurations will be purified. Departing from here, you will be reborn as the son of a mantrin in the western direction, and then you will be guided to liberation."

Then Drinton Śākrin resorted to the patrons of the Nampa myriarch—of Gongde, Minyak, and so forth—and his resources extensively increased. When an attendant asked the reason for this, the lama said, "It is simply a change in circumstances. Even after some minor propitiation of Śrīdevī, whatever I wanted immediately came to pass. Without making even a leather pouch for tsampa, I am indeed like Aparājitā!"

In 1273, after Venerable Sangye Yarjon had passed away, Drinton Śākrin came to Taklung and made great offerings. For his share of the sacred relics, he constructed the extraordinary stūpa called Naturally Arising Pure Vision, which exists even today.[266] Some of the five sacraments that Nyenchen Tanglha had actually offered him are also extant today, including the crystal stone called Blazing Light, the three-eyed gemstone, the white cane flute, the offering scarf with the lion head, and the flint striker. There were others, such as the one fashioned by demonic spirits that were kept on his cushion, but just that will suffice. There were offerings of spiritual accomplishment made by many nonhuman beings, and there were countless other offerings, visible even to the attendants, who requested a doctrinal connection with him. In the upper story at Barle Drakmar, he constructed an image of Munīndra, surrounded by the buddhas of the ten directions, and the images of the authentic lineage of blessings. He installed about five hundred volumes inscribed on white and blue paper. Many times, he brought great offerings to the two Taklung residences in Kham and U. Each month he held an extensive anniversary offering ceremony on behalf of Choku Sangye Yarjon. He also established a great many essential writings that condensed the nucleus of the oral instructions. {294}

Drington Śākrin passed away in his eighty-eighth year, on the eighth day of the seventh month of 1288 (mouse). Rainbow lights formed in the smoke of his funeral pyre, and there was a shower of flowers. A ray of white light, the size of a clay pot, along with sounds, emerged above the crematorium and shot way up into the sky. Finally, it set off in the eastern direction, accompanied by a rainbow resembling an extended rope. This was visible to everyone. His heart, tongue, and eyes, along with many pearl relics, were retrieved from the crematorium. His next reincarnation is said to have been the peerless Choku Orgyen Gonpo of the monastic seat of glorious Riwoche.

The following is the manner in which masters of learning and accomplishment, maintaining celibate conduct, emerged in the family line of this saintly being Drinton Śākrin. His nephew was Lama Rinchen Gyeltsen. The latter had four nephews who were mendicants—namely, Zhonu Senge, Zhonu Gyeltsen, Namkha Lekpa, and Zangpo Pel, a master of Severance who had the status of a great lama at Taklung. They in turn had four celibate nephews—namely, the supreme incarnation Ngawang Zangpo, Pema

Peltsek, Chokyi Tsemo, and Namkha Ozang. They in turn had three celibate nephews—namely, Tashi Pel, who was a meditator from Tsang, Sengewa, and Tsulwang. These three in turn had four mendicant nephews—namely, the master Tashi Gyatso, Sonam Wangchukpa, Tashi Wangpa, and Lodro. Their nephews were Drakpa Wangchuk and his brother.

Drinton Śākrin's abbatial succession descended through the nephew Rinchen Gyeltsen, Lama Zhonu Senge, Choje Namkha Ozang, and Garewa Zhonu Gyeltsen. Then, Lama Ngawang Zangpo formed a separate monastic seat, and he was followed in succession by Cho Tsewa, Tashi Senge, and Tashi Wangchuk. Meanwhile, at the seat of Namkha Ozang, the succession fell to Pema Peltsek, Tashi Pelzang, Sonam Wangchuk, Tashi Gyatso, Lodro Wangpo, the master Tsulwang, Drakpa Wangchuk, and Tashi Drakpa. The last mentioned was the father of my great tutor, His Presence Vijaya Ratnaśrībhadra (Gyelwa Rinchen Pelzangpo).[267]

The second spiritual son of Venerable Sangye Yarjon was Tsulshe, the younger brother of Tonśāk. A brief account of his life has already been indirectly presented.[268]

Kongpo Darshe

The third spiritual son was Kongpo Darshe, an emanation of glorious Vajrapāṇi and mighty lord of occult power.[269] He was born at Gode Dora in 1228 (earth male mouse). His father was Konchok Senge, and his mother was Goza Nyene. He received the mendicant ordination at Ojo from the great preceptor Narawa and was given the name Darma Sherab. He studied logic at Sangphu, Madhyamaka at Tang Gon, monastic discipline at Kyormolung and Traphu, transcendent perfection at Tsome, and phenomenology under Tsulchen Rinzang. And he received teachings on Mahākāruṇika from Kyergangpa, on Uṣṇīṣa from a mantrin of the lower Kyichu region, on Cakrasaṃvara and Vārāhī from Chak Lotsāwa, on *The Litany of the Names of Mañjuśrī* from Nyelde, {296} and on the yoga tantras from Gangtonpa Ledrak. He also received the empowerments and three tantras of the Hevajra cycle from Sakya Paṇḍita and his nephew, the symbolic empowerment of Vārāhī and other teachings from the accomplished master Tseringpo, the cycles of Cakrasaṃvara and Hevajra from Zhangton Gomchen, and many cycles of the doctrinal protectors (and in particular the entire cycle of Mahākāla in the form Trakṣad "on foot" from the master Trewo Gyelyonchi.

It is said that this lama would converse with the doctrinal protectors as if he were talking to human beings. He presented gifts, saying, "Trakṣad, you should go this month!" and "You have no reason to dislike me!"

In the words of his spiritual song, he also said,

> Formerly, we met during the time of Indrabhūti.
> For many lifetimes, you have favored me.
> Now, may I completely acquire your kindness.[270]

It was in this way that he met the peerless Sangye Yarjon who completely bestowed upon him all the doctrines of many cycles, including the maturational empowerments of the path, the liberating generation and perfection stages of the path, the Six Doctrines of the Profound Path, the direct guidance of the aural lineage, the method of practicing austerity by subsisting on elixirs, the introduction to experiential cultivation, the ritual dispelling impediments, the ritual ensuring success, the pith instructions of the profound essentials, and minor oral instructions.

To the detriment of his food and clothing, he persistently engaged in practice at Taklung Monastery. One day, when Rinpoche Sangye Yarjon said he should come, he went into his presence, whereupon Rinpoche said, "Do you not have any barley?" "I have none" he replied. "Do you definitely not have any?" "I definitely do not have any" "Is there none at all?" Thereupon, he fiercely replied in the midst of his anger, "I doubt that there is a single grain! I do not have anything to eat!" Laughing, Rinpoche then said, "Starting from now, you should be the one to blow the conch to summon three hundred odd monks. Now you should eat all this and continue with your practice!" He gave him a barley cake. {297} In his thoughts, he pondered, "Since you only gave me a single barley cake despite all that I said about not having anything to eat, how will I, starting from now, blow the conch to summon three hundred odd monks?" Thereupon, Rinpoche said, "This cake has an auspicious circumstance. Come quickly to fetch it! Starting from now, since you are receiving it, a hired assistant[271] will come!" When he fetched it, a sentient being with large eyes, like a cat, arrived at his grass hermitage, looked back, and then went off somewhere else. It is said that later, when he asked Rinpoche about him, Sangye Yarjon said, "That was Aparājitā, the deity of wealth. If you had touched him, or covered the flaps of his robe, or scattered earth and so forth, great resources would have swiftly come. Although that did not happen, because he looked back, in a future life you and your family line will have great wealth."

Also, at the time when, for the sake of the long life of Rinpoche Sangye Yarjon, Kongpo Darshe was circumambulating a volume containing *The Thousand Offerings of Vijayā*,[272] he did three circuits without his feet touching the ground. Since his persistence was unrivaled, at the time when he subsisted on elixir extracted from water, his limbs were crippled, and yet he made three shuffling circumambulations of the Kumbum. On that occasion, a wolf cried out, and he was frightened, in consequence of which he was able to stand upright. He understood that this was the blessing of the lama.

It is reputed that Kongpo Darshe had great ascetic discipline because in order to avert the sorcery of the Tselpa, his thread crosses and tormas were carried to Gola Lakha. Just by reciting the *Tantra of Uṣṇīṣa*,[273] he had a vision of that sublime female deity.

When he was engaged in practice at Sewalung, {298} a form of the Tathāgata appeared in the sky in front and prophesied that he would attain the ninth level, saying, "You will be the bodhisattva named Sumati."

When he thought of going to Tashido at Lake Namtso, he asked Rinpoche Sangye Yarjon, who said, "Starting from now, it's a good time to go. If you would go now, then set out!" One night when he traveled via Drilam and stayed at the head of the lake, he dreamed that there was a beautiful woman who said, "If you stay in this Tashido region, we will serve you." This was the mermaid of the lake. With the protectors Nyenchen Tanglha and Namtso Chukmo acting as patrons, his sustenance was provided. At Drongke Dzalung, he was robbed by brigands, whereupon at Ngotra he engaged in the ritual practice of *Three Sibling Razors*,[274] such that his foes were vanquished. In this way, the fame of his sorcery first surfaced.

Kongpo Darshe stayed at Ngotra for ten years. When he considered making a painting of Uṣṇīṣa, just as he had seen her in his vision, one night he dreamed that a large-eyed woman taught him how to draw. The next day, he did not have the artist do the drawing. Instead, he himself spread out colored pebbles on a piece of white felt, in the excellent form of the required icon. Relying on that, the artist then made a copy, and so a perfect painting was produced. At that time, many such paintings were commissioned, including one depicting Mahākāla in the form Trakṣad "eating dry tsampa."[275]

As his contribution to the representations of Taklung, when Venerable Sangye Yarjon passed away, he built a stūpa that is still extant among the artifacts of the Main Temple in the present day.[276]

With Bari Zingkhyung acting as patron, his resources cascaded like rain. He went to Semodo at Lake Namtso and remained there for four years upon a single seat. In that place, he brought forth the water of accomplishment. One day, he thumped the rock with his hand and told his female patron to take some alms. {299} The next day, the carcass of a calf and two carcasses of female yaks were washed up by the waves of the lake. Thinking that this was a present offered by the local deity, he again engaged in practice at Jadur and brought forth the water of accomplishment. The cakra of perfect resource situated within his throat then opened, such that the treasury of adamantine song burst forth.

In the mouse year,[277] the patrons Belpa and Belmur offered him land for a monastery in Kongpo. About three hundred monks gathered, and they built grass hermitages. He said, "This monastery of mine is built on a precious geomantic site. The four deities of Juyakare are completely present. Starting from now, a golden-roofed temple will spring up. At Uridong, a meditation hermitage with a splendid turret will appear."

He said that Atsara Pakshi should send bellows for the kitchen and a kitchen assistant, but he had nothing to give that would keep the kitchen fire going. Then he said, "It will suffice if you can send a kitchen assistant," whereupon a monkey blew the fire, another ground the flour, and another brought the water, such that he was consumed with doubt and wrote a letter stating that he, Atsara, was responsible for the lives of eighty people and horses. A messenger was sent, and a great commotion ensued when he said he was building a monastery. When they all asked what they should do, the lama himself said, "Like a vase filled to the brim, I possess all the instructions of Choku Sangye Yarjon. Now, in this abode of the malign gods and demons of the red springs of Kong, in order to build a monastery, I have not made a third request for things that should be provided. If I have a finger-size wound, your cattle will have an arm-span-size one! Actually, I am one of the thousand and eight emanations endowed with the inheritance of the past actions of aspiration, made in the presence of the master Padmākara!" He then sent an official letter, in which he wrote, {300} "This carries the authorization of the lord-protector Mahākāla. It carries the words of Dopa Darshe, and it is addressed to Atsara Pakshi. You are responsible for the lives of eighty disciples and horses. You will be banished for three years. Surrender within three days!" The letter was sealed with his thumbprint impressed in incense and shellac wax and dispatched. The lama then said, "He is a leader appointed by men. I am a leader appointed by gods and demons. Look out for as many battles as possible!" He then summoned the doctrinal protectors. That night, a great light was emitted from the summit of Konglha Yangkar of the Bonpos. Indeed, he had even made preparations to bring about the victory of the Bonpos. So the lama inscribed a dark spell[278] and cast it, along with an imprecation. Wherever it manifested, a fatal disease struck and Bonpos died, such that the chieftain also became terrified and adopted the correct laws of the sacred doctrine.

At the time when Kongpo Darshe was engaged in practice, an attendant dreamed that a wolf of the Kongpo plain was being pursued by seven dogs from the lama's residence. When he asked about it, Kongpo Darshe replied, "If they did not encounter someone like me, the Bon protectors would not be weakened." One night, in the hermitage, the attendant saw through the window someone with a naked form carrying a torma over the shoulders and summoning the doctrinal protector, and he asked, "Is it better for us to don the protective rhino-hide apron now?" Kongpo Darshe replied, "They are trying to weaken my doctrinal protector. Check this out! Come and see who is victorious!" When he went to see, the foremost of the Bonpo was dead. The attendant asked, "Are the Bonpo continuing to use sorcery against us?" He replied, {301} "Their use of sorcery against us is like using sorcery against the sky. My propitiation of Acala created a landslide, such that I was unharmed by the sorcery of the Bonpo. People of exhausted merit have encountered me!" So saying, he subdued the sacred places of the Bon.[279]

When the horses that he sent in order to offer a large brocade hanging to Taklung were stolen by an imperial envoy, Kongpo Darshe made a torma and said, "Now, sheldrake, flow from the middle plain!"[280] He struck the ground with his hand whereupon hailstones traveled from the middle plain and fell, as the arc of a rainbow formed. He sent an army of monks, and they beat the imperial envoys who said, "If he does that, we will take this lama to our superior." The lama replied, "If you take me to your superior, I will rejoice. Even if you place me in the charge of the Great Imperial Preceptor, that will be all right. I am going even if Beng Trakṣad with his retinue of seven dog-faced deities takes me to the depths of the ocean at midnight! My gods and demons will protect me from any obstacles within the imperial domain. They do not have to take me to their superior. They themselves will have to go to their superior!" So it was that they died in Mongolia.[281]

His hair was reddish brown and he was accepted as an emanation of Vajrapāṇi. When he had to make rain fall just by lying down at the source of a spring, the nāga spirits could not resist him, and they would immediately cause rain to fall. If rain fell when he was teaching the sacred doctrine, it would fall everywhere, but not a drop would fall on the seminary where he was teaching. He bound a brown yak demon, which he found outside the range of the brass horns of the monastery, and appointed it as a lord of wealth in the monastery. All the horses that he had were offered to Taklung and all the woolen fabric that he had was offered to Riwoche.

Kongpo Darshe acted extensively for the benefit of the Buddhist teaching and sentient beings until his eighty-third year. Then, in 1310 (iron female dog), {302} on the eighteenth day of the first spring month, he passed away. When his sacred corpse was cremated, the sky was clear, rainbows gathered, and many pearl relics, the size of *sang* coins were retrieved. His heart, tongue, and eyes were also retrieved, along with an image of Vajravārāhī, a clockwise-spiraling conch, a white syllable A, and so forth.

To the present day, the lineage of his nephews is uninterrupted, starting with his own nephew Maṅgalaratna, and thereafter continuing through Nyame Drakpa Gyelpo, the supreme incarnation Namkha Nyingpo, Namkha Peltsek Gyelpo, Peltsek Gyatso, Peltsek Zangpo, Drakpa Peltsek, and Chenga Draka Pelzang.

The fourth spiritual son of Venerable Sangye Yarjon is said to have been Minyak Gyelshe.

Concluding Verses

By virtue of all the many excellent tales
Forming the narrative of Choku Sangye Yarjon,
Like fresh lilies threaded on the string of excellent instruction,
May all living beings, free from fear,
Attain the nature of the Lord of Secrets!

Tashi Lama, Fourth in the Abbatial Succession

Verses of Homage

Containing all knowledge in the vase of his mind,
Permeating all sentient beings and world systems with the light of
compassion,
Ever endowed with a mind of meditative equipoise,
Homage to the body, speech, and mind of Tashi Lama!

Tashi Lama, the incarnation of the lord-protector Acala (Maitreya), regent of the Conqueror, was born in 1231 (iron female hare) at Yangsho Bong-rateng, accompanied by infinite virtuous signs.[282] His father was the patron Choyak, a brother of Kuyal Rinpoche, and his mother was Joziza Zungdron. He was the second of their five sons, who were Lopon Lingpa, Venerable Tashi Lama himself, Zhelkyab, Tubpa, and Lopo.

From childhood, Tashi Lama wished to be emancipated from cyclic existence. {303} Through the mighty wave of the threefold approach to the setting of the mind on enlightenment,[283] he was exclusively intent on accomplishing the well-being of others. In 1246 (fire male horse), his sixteenth year, he was ordained as a mendicant at the great seminary of Tangkya by the incumbent monastic preceptor of that seminary and the master of ceremonies Drakpa Pelzangpo. The name Tashi Lama was conferred upon him. He studied *The Stanzas on the Novitiate* and many doctrinal cycles of Kadam, including *The Lamp of the Path*, under that preceptor and that master of ceremonies.

From Lama Khepawa, he then received the *Kālacakra*, *The Four Seats*,[284] *Cakrasaṃvara*, *Hevajra*, *Mahāmāyā*, *Vārāhī* according to the Chel tradition,[285] the trio of *Vajrapañjara*, *Hevajra*, and *Saṃpuṭa*,[286] *Clarifying Lamp: The Great Commentary on the Secret Assembly*,[287] the profound doctrines of glorious Taklung Tangpa the Great, the combined threefold approach to the setting of the mind on enlightenment, *The Precious Staircase*,[288] the practical implementation of empowerments, the profound blessing of the spiritual teacher, the exegeses and pith instructions of *The Five Paths*,[289] the symbolic empowerment of Vārāhī,[290] the four primary doctrines of Nāropā and their commentary, the aural lineage of Cakrasaṃvara, and the cycles of six meditational deities.[291]

In his twenty-fifth year, when he traveled to U, he was escorted for a short distance by his teacher, Khepawa the Great, who sang him the spiritual song titled "Fortress of the Eightfold Happiness,"[292] which begins,

> Grassy knoll of inner radiance, abundantly beautiful,
> Dense with trees of diverse experience and realization,
> Bright with flowers blossoming with pristine cognition,
> From the neck of that mountain, the following words arose:
> Master of enlightened heritage! Lord of the sacred doctrine!
> Precious One in whom the three buddha bodies are indivisible,
> Homage to glorious Taklung Tangpa!

> Think upon us with compassion and grant your blessing.
> The lineage of the four transmitted teachings is uninterrupted,
> And the rivers of the aural lineage have not vanished,
> The lineage of the auspicious mother has been maintained, {304}
> And the blessings of the lineage of attainment are extant.
> Therefore we are happy.[293]

In this way, the journey was rendered auspicious, and he set out.

Here in Taklung, Tashi Lama touched the lotus feet of Rinpoche Sangye Yarjon. On the day they met, there were also some students from Dokham—the nephews of spiritual teachers and the sons of lay officials—who had come to pay their respects. The lama knew them but pretended to ask, saying, "Who are all these?" He was offered an explanation of their circumstances, and Sangye Yarjon replied, "In the time of all our predecessors, lords of the sacred doctrine, people feared the sufferings of cyclic existence, birth, and death. There were many who, after abandoning this life, said they would engage in one-pointed practice, relying on just a single gold coin. Now it seems that many of you have come here, boasting that you are of a certain birthplace. If you want to study, there is a monastery to the south called Sangphu. You should all go there and master a few books. You should pursue the antidote for afflicted mental states, which is the sacred doctrine, combining both exegesis and experiential cultivation. But you, my nephew, should take barley to the value of five *zho* from my household, and starting from tomorrow, you should stay in retreat. The study that you have already undertaken in Kham is sufficient. This lineage of ours is a lineage of spiritual attainment. So spiritual attainment is very important. It was dependent on their perfection of spiritual attainment that the teachers who were our predecessors acted for the benefit of themselves and others. You should be diligent in your spiritual attainment!"[294]

The next morning, he met his older brother Lama Lingpa and requested permission to stay in retreat. All those accompanying him also said they should meet Lama Lingpa, so Tashi Lama had no choice but to meet his older brother on one occasion. {305} Lingpa was engaged in practice, contented above all with a single oral instruction, and it was difficult to meet him because he was staying in strict retreat. However, Sangye Yarjon said, "Since you are disciples from a distant land, you should have an opportunity to meet on one occasion!" They met the next morning.

In *The Biographical History of Taklung Lower Plain*,[295] it is written that the one called Lopon Lingpa was Venerable Sangye On. In *The Doctrinal History of Lhorong*, it is written that he was the elder brother of Venerable Tashi Lama, with the same father and mother, that he was known as Lopon Lingpa because he solely engaged in practice at Taklung Monastery, and that he died during the lifetime of Venerable Sangye Yarjon. Although I do not know which of these is correct, it seems that the latter is more likely.[296]

Thereafter, Tashi Lama received all the maturational empowerments, liberating paths, supporting textual traditions, and the props of the minute pith instructions that Venerable Sangye Yarjon possessed, as if the contents of one vase were poured into another. For sixteen years, he stayed one-pointedly, sealed in strict seclusion, endowed with the three isolations of body, speech, and mind, without meeting anyone at all. From the start, he was manifestly a sacred being, endowed with the level of unsurpassed pristine cognition, but in the perspective of others, he appeared to stay in retreat out of great respect, resolutely intent on the nature of his spiritual teacher and all the buddhas, and he seemed to actualize in succession the twenty-four yogas of experiential realization.[297] In the presence of his precious predecessor, Sangye Yarjon, he then offered his clear realization of the great state of nonmeditation, embellished with an aspiration prayer in the form of a eulogy to the arising of meditative experience, along with thirteen profound painted scrolls depicting the meditational deities, and eleven gold *sang* coins. {306} Thereupon, Sangye Yarjon granted him extensive purposeful teachings.[298]

Tashi Lama met the king of the sacred doctrine, Phakpa Rinpoche, and offered him a eulogy in lines of excellent metrical verse. Venerable Sangye Yarjon then said to Lama Phakpa, "Once my nephew Tashi Lama has taken charge, may you be cognizant of the administration of the patrons and monks of Taklung." The great Lama Phakpa replied, "Henceforth, I will be cognizant of the administration of Taklung and its short-term and long-term prospects." In brief, this denoted just the start of the Mongolian hegemony that seemed to cover with a white parasol the entirety of the thirteen myriarchies of Tibet. Since Phakpa Rinpoche was extremely noble-hearted with regard to the exceptional domains, saying he would not take them under his control, throughout his life he protected friend and foe without partiality. However, his lifespan was not very long. Afterward, a Chinese army arrived in Tibet, owing to the conflict that ensued between the ministers, and so many estates were laid waste. With regard to the many fluctuations that occurred, such as these, Sangye Yarjon, knower of the three times, had correctly understood that this would come to pass, and he skillfully established that this estate of Taklung would accrue auspicious circumstances that would render it perpetually secure like a golden mountain.[299]

Then Tashi Lama's precious predecessor Sangye Yarjon fell ill. In the evening of the third day of the first summer month, he summoned his nephew to the grass hermitage and they met. He placed his foot upon Tashi Lama's head, saying, "You should nurture all the patrons and monks of the Taklungpa tradition, just as I have previously nurtured them. {307} You should maintain the charter of the monastic assembly and the regulations of Choje Kuyalwa, as in my time!"[300]

On this occasion, Choku Sangye Yarjon actually saw without obscuration the situations and appearances of all things pertaining to the three times, without exception, and so he saw that if the teaching of Taklung were to flourish in both Kham and U, then the three planes of existence would be uninterruptedly covered by the immaculate tradition of the lineage of practice. Consequently, he bestowed upon Venerable Sangye On the separate representative artifacts that he should protect and that were portable, actually entrusting him to teach with the words, "You should take these and firmly plant the sacred and noble wish-granting tree, the teaching of this Kagyu lineage, at glorious Riwoche, in the valley of Yisho, and protect the sentient beings who live there from all the feverish torments of physical and mental affliction, by dispelling the obscurations that cover the instructions of the aural lineage!"

To Tashi Lama, the emanation of Maitreya, he assigned the representational objects of buddha body, speech, and mind that were not portable, but fixed like Mount Sumeru, along with the monastic complex of Taklung and its Main Temple, and entrusted him with the teaching, saying, "Hold these and, residing at the point of enlightenment, the Adamantine Seat, you should constantly and increasingly illuminate the teaching of the essential meaning for all posterity, uniformly permeating the three worlds with the light of virtuous buddha activity, which is like that of ten million suns!"[301]

However, this inconceivable objective, which was to be achieved exclusively through the fruitional realization of the supreme enlightened activity of the perfect buddhas, profound and vast, is within the perceptual range of the tathāgatas alone, and apart from them, it is the reality that cannot be fathomed even by the bodhisattva heirs of the conquerors. {308} On that occasion [the approaching death of the third abbot, Sangye Yarjon], there were ordinary persons with eyes only for this world who misunderstood the inexhaustible wheel of adornment that is buddha activity and who clamored that the two nephews took their respective inheritances and that their precious predecessor, Sangye Yarjon, had said, "I entrust the teaching to this one! I entrust the teaching to that one!" In order to resolve their doubts, when Rinpoche Sangye Yarjon had no visitors, Rinpoche Tashi Lama (Maṅgalaguru) said to him, "Now that you are alive here, if you did not say that I should be entrusted with the teaching, may this waist of mine become even more decrepit! If what you said is true, may this body of mine become straighter than a plantain tree!" It is said that because Tashi Lama spoke with the power of truth, he insisted on reminding Sangye Yarjon of this pledge a few times even before he returned from the Yang Gon hermitage to Kadruk. Consequently, his body, decrepit with such chronic ailments, later recovered and became straighter even than the shaft of an arrow.

It is certainly good for bodhisattva heirs of the Conqueror themselves to reach the enlightened intention of the Conqueror, but since the distinction between perfect buddhas and bodhisattvas resembles that between the amount of water contained in an ocean and the footprint of an ox, Tashi Lama then made a momentary investigation and, understanding only a fraction of the real situation, Kong Dopa Darshe first had the negative thought that the Buddhist teaching of Taklung was being divided between Kham and U, and he blazed with anger. Later, when he understood the auspicious circumstances of the lama's extensive enlightened activity, and the Buddhist teaching of Taklung had been divided between Kham and U, {309} he then made a confession, saying, "In the presence of the banner of the Buddhist teaching, I apologize for having contemplated dissension." However, there was no difference at all between the two nephews themselves in terms of both the abiding nature of reality and its appearances. Among them, Venerable Tashi Lama has a mind that was profound and vast, like an ocean, even to those of mundane perspective.

So, when Venerable Sangye On was requested to assume the lion throne at Taklung, for a while Maṅgalaguru attended to his ascetic discipline, which was pure and blissful in terms of the three isolations of body, speech, and mind. After one year, Venerable Sangye On saw that the time had come for him to train disciples in the east, and he set out for Kham. On that occasion, Tashi Lama seems to have sent a messenger with the request that the separate representative artifacts that were to be protected by Sangye

On should be kept here in Taklung. Even later on, he sent another message, which said, "My supreme guide! Lord of our enlightened heritage! You should bring from Taklung Lower Plain the representative objects of buddha body, speech, and mind, along with the library of the profound and vast sacred doctrine, which has many blessings, and come here to this great residence! That will establish an auspicious circumstance for this shared wealth of ours." This also alludes to the report, known in the narrative of the lineage, that Venerable Sangye On himself on one occasion received a prophecy declaring, "The sleeve will be connected to the main part of the costume!"

In brief, Gyelwa Taklungpa the Great himself had made a prophetic declaration concerning Sangye On in the following words:

> After me, there will be a young monk with reddish ears.
> After him, there will be a disciplined yak,
> Then a yogin will arrive.
> I will be all these![302]

He had also made a prophetic declaration concerning Tashi Lama, emanation of Maitreya, in these words:

> The spacious, the strong, and the brown-headed—
> These three {310} will be no different from me.[303]

So, these two nephews were definitely of a single mind. Residing separately in Kham and U, their activities had the exclusive purpose of ensuring that the Buddhist teaching of Taklung would equal space in its reach and range. Whether provisionally or conclusively, they were without defect even to the extent of the hundredth part of a hair-tip. Since the benefits that they brought diminished the three worlds, it is right that we should respect them with utmost faith.

On the occasion of Sangye On's departure, he laid down the flaps of his robe near the Kumbum Jangma and prayed. Consequently, a second tooth relic emanated in the manner of a multiplying bone relic, without impediment, from the tooth relic of the Buddha within the Kumbum and the reliquary chapel. When it alighted on his robe, he brought it to Riwoche. Such was the array of miraculous powers that he mustered. However, in order to dispel the thoughts of those small-minded persons that the tooth relic was not contained in the original reliquary, Rinpoche Tashi Lama approached the Kumbum and made the following declaration of truth: "If the tooth relic of the Buddha is definitely present, right now, within this reliquary, may some naturally arising artifact appear on this side of the lion throne!" Immediately, there appeared as a substitute the naturally arisen impression of the six-syllable mantra, which is nowadays visible in the common perception of all, and so the doubts of everyone were assuaged.[304]

Then, in his forty-third year, in 1273 (water female bird), Tashi Lama fearlessly assumed the lion throne of Taklung. He nurtured the entire congregation and resided there, turning the precious wheel of the sacred doctrine in all its aspects. On the north wing of the Main Temple, he built as his residence a small room with a gilded pillar.[305] {311}

Tashi Lama maintained the regulations of Choje Kuyalwa, the charter of the monastic assembly, and all the disciplinary rules of the monastery, just as his precious predecessor had done. He was endowed with extensive extrasensory powers. Later, when he was constructing a large image of Śākyamuni in the form Sangye Tongsum Zilnon,[306] he said, "I have no gold, but the emperor does." So when the time came to ask for the gold, the emperor Qubilai Qaγan sent him an offering of six measures of gold.[307]

When he went to Nyingdrung to receive the master Dharmapāla, who was traveling from Sakya to China, the servants did not know that the master would be arriving in a few days. In the valley of Siwu, there was a conspicuously small but excellent meadow, so he said, "Let's stay here. It's better to wait." They made a small settlement there and encamped. Rinpoche then said, "You should go over there. We have come to receive the great master Dharmapāla, so go!" He went over to a wall near the Lhachu spring. When the servants also caught up with him, at Chusergang, they met the great master who was traveling with some four hundred laypeople.[308] It is said that while staying at Siwu, the servants were unaware that Tashi Lama had moved on, and in order for them to catch up, he had to wait at Dam.

Tashi Lama once said, "Build a teahouse at the top of the steps of the Great Reliquary Chapel!" When they were constructing the hearth and arranging the planks and the cushions, he leaned his staff against the surfaces of the walls. "Dig here and here!" he said, whereupon the carpenter Rinchen Sonam had the thought, "This wall resembles rock. How can we break it by digging!" Understanding his thoughts, Tashi Lama then said, "Dig, without thinking such thoughts! If I say dig, you will break through, even though it is rock!" {312} When he had finished digging, the newly created windows were sealed from below, plastered from the outside, and evenly aligned.

When he was cutting the wood for the large eastern gate, he drew the outline of Avalokiteśvara and said, "Do you know how to engrave it like this?" Since there was no one else who knew, Pon Namkha that night prayed to Rinpoche and then clearly had the thought, "It is intended to be like this." By praying outwardly and inwardly in his presence, he pleased Tashi Lama, who said, "You and your name [Namkha meaning "space"] are in conformity. This has been achieved through my merit."

He then drew the measurements of the three small doors for the carpenter and had him make them, saying "Doors such as these have not been made anywhere!" When the work was finished, he drew the outline of his staff on the back side of the eastern door from top to bottom vertically and said, "Cut into it at these three places!" When the carpenter had cut in that manner, three apertures appeared that were properly aligned with the four panels on the front side of the gate. When the time came to ward off the army of the governor of Dokham,[309] everyone said they would come from Lungsho and head toward Yangra, whereupon Rinpoche said, "There is not a part of the army that will not come this way. They are going through Gangkar. Let's drink tea, and then you should set out! You should go this very day! Tomorrow evening, you should reach Zhomda. If you do not do this, they cannot be quelled." It is said that Pon Ozer Zhonu was sent, as he had commanded, whereupon the army was quelled to some extent.[310]

When the master Yaktakpa came to meet him, he said, "You have a desirable possession," and he pretended to play cymbals[311] with his hands. {313} "I have an excellent set of cymbals. Should I offer them and place them in the reliquary of Sangye Yarjon?" Tashi Lama then replied, "There is no difference between the father and his sons. Since we meditators esteem above all the root teacher, you may do just that! Offer tea and curd to this master!" Since there was nothing but ordinary tea upstairs, there was a slight delay as they went to buy some fine tea. As the master was about to leave, Tashi Lama said to him, "Stay a little! The tea is coming." At that very moment, a wealthy Khampa arrived and offered three bowls of tea, which he had strained. Tashi Lama said, "Offer the first to the representations of buddha body, speech, and mind, hand the second to the master, and send the last to the nomad tents. Although he had previously been someone without reason to be faithful, the master Yaktakpa from then on became extremely faithful.

When Riwo Goklungwa, who had arrived to request a doctrinal connection, was thinking that Tashi Lama had a decrepit body, the latter said, "You should sit there!" Right in front of him, Tashi Lama then flexed his body back and forth. Also, when he was wondering whether the lama's chronic waist ailment might be alleviated if he were to eat meat, Tashi Lama said, "From the time when I arrived at this monastic seat, I have not eaten meat," whereupon Riwo Goklungwa became afraid. "You should perform some virtuous acts!" said Tashi Lama. "I did have such a thought" he replied. Tashi Lama continued, "What are you doing, holding thoughts! You should let them go!" Thereupon, he became extremely faithful and departed after requesting the blessing of his foot empowerment

Moreover, when Sherab Ga of Dome went to meet him, along with his brother, he had the younger one stay by the door, and he gave an instruction on consciousness transference to the older one, without being requested to do so. After seven days, the older one passed away. The nephew of the official Shercho went off to pursue his studies, without heeding Tashi Lama's insistent admonition that he should delay, and he died of smallpox. When Taknawa Pelwang had a severely choked throat, Tashi Lama placed his tongue over Pelwang's mouth, {314} such that it seemed to block his gullet. Immediately thereafter, he recovered. He did not let out any mouthful of food from his throat, but whatever he ate did him no harm. He was able to live into his eightieth year. Zhangsun Maru had a severe case of brown phlegm disorder from the time when he had gone into the Tanglha valley to smelt copper for a large icon, but Tashi Lama conferred a foot empowerment, such that the disease was alleviated, enabling him to live into his seventy-ninth year.

When the time came to fasten the garuḍa motif to a large icon, Tashi Lama said, "You are preparing to fix it up there but that will not be necessary. Fix the garuḍa motif above the throne!" There was a spike with a ring at the end, which had previously been thrust into a beam, and that was suitable for the garuḍa motif. That winter when Tashi Lama was about to die, many hidden bamboo containers were found at Kachu. Leaning his staff against them, he said, "If these were bricks of tea they would be useful to you all!" Lachi Gyawo, a master from Kongpo, saw Tashi Lama as Rinpoche Kuyalwa, whereupon everyone understood that their minds were identical. His body and his robe were untainted by dirt. His naked body was untouched by others. Even the edge of his seat and his robe were untouched by those who were not meditators. During the time when he was being served, he drank tea but avoided meat. His body and robe had the fragrance of ethical discipline, resembling the scent of the primula flower, and simply by smelling them, one would feel healthy. Rinchen Sonam acted as his attendant for forty-one years, never saw him sleep with his waistband loose or with his head down on a pillow. Even when he looked at him by night in the light of a butter lamp, his body remained in meditation, and apart from that, he did not know whether he was sleeping or not. {315} He did not take dividends from the wealth of the household and did not engage in commerce. During the three anniversary offering ceremonies for his three precious predecessors, there was no opportunity for others to do anything outside the household.[312]

At the time when he assumed the monastic seat, the construction of the Southern Kumbum was not quite finished, so he completed the task in a timely manner, including the gilding and the repairs to the damaged parasol and dharma wheel spire. The lotus motifs on the lion-throne podium of the Tashi Pelbar Stūpa had been finished, and so, on the lower tier above the back-to-back lotuses, he added the buddhas of the ten directions, and in each corner an image of Venerable Sangye Yarjon himself. Below the lotuses, he added Tārā, who protects from the eight fears, and Avalokiteśvara, who protects from the eight fears, and along the edges two sets of the ten wrathful deities. On the vajra barrier motif of the podium base below it, he added a cubit-size set of the ten wrathful deities. After completing such acts of service, he consecrated the stūpa.

Then, intending to construct a large image of Śākyamuni in the form Tongsum Zilnon,[313] he built the wooden frame, but he did not entertain the thought that anyone other than the emanational sculptor Pon Bawa could make the image. Even the elders of the monastery suggested that there was no way that such an image could be made, and the official emissary of the emperor also made a similar point, but he replied, "When I have finished making the image, you will come to the feast of Mahākāla."[314] He sent people everywhere to prepare the copper, such that they acquired the brightest of materials. They collected chalcopyrite ore and requested permission to make brass, but he refused. Since the scale of the image was so great, Rinpoche himself filled them with advice. It was a little difficult even for mold-casting sculptors to understand the measurements and the design. They mixed various precious metals and gems with the copper material and poured it into the mold. The gold that had been chiefly offered by the emperor Qubilai

Qaγan was definitely sufficient, {316} so the work was effortlessly accomplished. They made an extremely thick layer of gilding, and escorted the image of Munīndra, which was insatiable to behold, into the lower story of the Main Temple, where it could just be accommodated, along with its throne and back screen. Then, he had a second thought. Above the protuberance of Munīndra, he constructed a one-and-a-half-cubit-size image of Buddha Dīpaṃkara, fashioned of cast gold. Exemplified by that, he then constructed the throne with its six supports,[315] and the four ornaments of the back rest,[316] along with the motifs of a youthful nāga, garuḍa bird, and town. This is the first of the thirteen large images within the Main Temple, renowned like the wind by the name of Tubchen Tongsum Zilnon. Within it are contained blessed artifacts, such as the bone relics and innumerable pearl relics of the tathāgata, and a tooth of the sovereign Lord Marpa Lotsāwa,[317] as well as an infinite number of icons, volumes of scripture, stūpas, and so forth. It was consecrated by many learned and realized monks, headed by Rinpoche himself. The entire congregation also recited the verses of good auspices and offered flowers. There were indescribable auspicious signs that occurred. The official emissary of the emperor also came to the festival, in compliance with an imperial decree, carried by a servant because he was very old. He bestowed gifts to the value of ten thousand large *sang* of gold on the sculptors. Inside the eastern gate, there were constructed on the right side an image of Mahākāla in the form Lekden and on the left side an image of Śrīdevī, while the murals depicted the oceanic assemblage of the oath-bound male and female protectors of mundane existence. The two images of Śrīdevī and Mahākāla were the actual handiwork of Viśvakarman, first and foremost of artisans. Their magnificence and beauty were hard to bear.[318] {317}

Later, even when the Main Temple was threatened by fire, this image of Munīndra could not be damaged even slightly, and moreover, it was at the very least not even tainted by particles of smoke. The planks and beams above its head were burned, and just as they were about to fall down, they were held by the crown of Mahākāla's dreadlocks and the tip of Śrīdevī's sword, so they did not fall down. It is reported that even the donkey mount of Śrīdevī cried out.

Formerly, at the time when the consecration was being performed, it is said that a dark and strong wind arose from within the atrium of the Main Temple, and everything inside froze. After these two protector images had been constructed, it is reported that henceforth when there was even the slightest misapprehension, without having to be summoned or incited, they would swiftly manifest endless signs, so this indeed formed an auspicious circumstance, suggesting that Tashi Lama and the emperor would both to some extent discipline their followers.

After nurturing the community in that manner for twenty-five years, in the midsummer month of 1297 (fire female bird), he said, "This year, you should postpone the ceremony that falls on the fifteenth day. During the ceremony, you will be busy. Hold it instead on the last day of this month!"

In the evening of the sixth day[319] of the midsummer month, he summoned the venerable lord of the sacred doctrine Sangye Pelzangpo, along with the senior preceptors and masters of ceremony and extensively advised them, saying, "Henceforth, joined to me by your fourth finger, you will have no fear of the lower realms." Khenpo Tsangpa lamented and offered a prayer that he should remain, but he replied with an adamantine song that began with these words:

> This conceptual thought that grasps signs
> Vanishes in the expanse of nonconceptual space.[320] {318}

And then he passed away without ill-health.

The sacred corpse was displayed and cremated in the upper story of the Old Offering Chapel. His heart, tongue, and eyes were found fused together. His skull had become an offering receptacle for pearl relics. A clockwise-spiraling conch fell into the hands of one faithful person. Also, a mass of four sorts of pearl relics fell into the hands of another faithful person and multiplied. One relic fell into the hands of one of his nephews and multiplied a hundredfold, the last of which was offered to Rinpoche Pelzangpo and inserted within the protuberance of the Jangchen image. Another relic fell into the hands of Tortungma and multiplied into eighty-four. When two people were in front of the funerary stūpa, they found three pearl relics that issued from the crematorium at the tail end of what resembled smoke. The human and divine practitioners who attended and the wondrous signs that occurred were indescribable. The funerary rites that fulfilled his enlightened intention were accomplished on a great scale.

The Disciples of Choje Tashi Lama

This venerable lord of the sacred doctrine had innumerable disciples, among whom Chung Jadrelwa the Great was particularly sublime. He was born at Yangsho Bongrateng in 1267 (fire female hare)[321]—the youngest of four sons born to the patron Zhangkyab and Chocham. He was ordained as a mendicant by the great preceptor of Tangkya and the master of ceremonies Duldzin and given the name Yeshe Lama. Thereupon, he embarked on a rather intermittent study of the sūtras and mantras. In his sixteenth year, he traveled to U, where he studied all the oral instructions of the precious Kagyu lineage in their entirety under the venerable lord of the sacred doctrine Tashi Lama. In particular, he undertook the experiential cultivation of the Great Seal, the Six Doctrines {319} and the Six Yogas, and he usually stayed exclusively in retreat. In his twentieth year, he received full monastic ordination at Taklung from the preceptor Yangopa[322] and others. His precious predecessor Tashi Lama said to him, "Your virtuous activities will have a successful outcome at Taklung. You have no reason to depart. Thereafter, you will accomplish the benefit of yourself and others in other places and your reputation will permeate the world." He requested a blessed support for his meditation practice, and Tashi Lama gave him a cushion. But he thought, "Since this is the Lama's mat, how could it be right to lay it down?" So he made a patched cushion, whereupon Rinpoche said, "Let this mat for sitting become a shawl[323] for going about in!"

After Rinpoche Tashi Lama had passed away, he was appointed in charge of Kadruk, but he was slandered by someone called Geserwa, in consequence of which, when Rinpoche Pelzangpo assumed the monastic seat, he appeared to reprimand him slightly, even though he was blameless.[324] So he stayed at Sengling. At Taklung, he established the medical tradition.

In his thirty-fourth year, he adopted the ascetic discipline through which renunciation naturally liberates attachment, and then he, the master with his four disciples, set out for the first time for Lhasa, where they saw Jowo Śākyamuni in the Jokhang, and continued via Densatil, Lhodrak, Sakya, Tsibri, Dingri Langkor, and so forth, to reach the Jarung Khashor Stūpa in Nepal. From the summit of the stūpa, five rays of light emanated and were seen vanishing into the crown of Choje Jadrelwa, so everyone paid him respect. The four monks accompanying him had many misapprehensions and said, "If you depart for India, we will not go." Then, they returned home, and he traveled on alone.

In one small place, he nursed three venerable monks who were ill with fever, {320} so the two younger ones befriended him and accompanied him to a meditation cave. Over a period of five months, his meditation thrived. When he was out begging for alms, he was summoned to a place where the mayor of a town had fallen ill. He cast a torma and conferred his blessing, whereupon that evening, a ray of light was exorcised from the channels of the invalid and exited the door, where everyone saw a monkey. By freeing the mayor from disease, Jadrelwa acquired a great reputation.

On the road between India and Nepal, he unknowingly partook of some poisonous alms, without having tested the food, such that he had a severe pain. At that time, he had a vision of Rinpoche Tashi Pel walking in front of him, wearing a patched robe,[325] a saffron meditation hat, holding a bamboo staff, and imparting oral instructions, whereupon he recovered.

In the midst of a jungle, he cured a sick monkey and protected it from being injured by wild beasts and hunters, so it brought fruits, on which he subsisted. He stayed there for approximately one month, and then set out for India.

Somewhere in a small country in the south, he alleviated a plague of locusts, and the people offered him a stone image of Mahākāla, which had been the meditative commitment of Indrabhūti. Two people from Taklung then arrived in his presence, along with the attendant Tsulzhon, to invite him back, bringing a communiqué from Rinpoche Pelzangpo, but he replied that he was not willing to go. They returned to Nepal, with Tsulzhon following them.

Then, thinking that he should travel on to Oḍḍiyāna in the west, he undertook a divination at a temple. Tashi Tsering, the caretaker, did not find his work appealing, so he agreed to act as his servant during the journey to Oḍḍiyāna. {321} They gradually set out. In the middle of a charnel ground in Oḍḍiyāna, there is a temple containing a naturally arisen engraving of the six-syllable mantra where the caretaker seemed to have reached the old age of one hundred and fifty. He said, "During my time, there were two people who arrived from Tibet." One was Drubchen Orgyenpa.[326]

One day, while looking at the sky in the eastern direction, he said, "The Taklungpas are indeed busy!" It is said that he prepared offerings and recited *The Seven Branches.*[327] At that time, Rinpoche Pelzangpo had passed away and Venerable Ratnaguru had assumed the monastic seat. The latter then made a petition to Jadrelwa. Two physicians and the master Kyab came to invite him back to Tibet. With persistence and through the compassion of the lama, they traversed a mountain pass that could not be crossed by anyone at all, without incurring any mishap. Then, they arrived in the presence of the venerable lord of the sacred doctrine, who had reached Zangkar following his pilgrimage to Oḍḍiyāna. But he did not agree to journey back to Tibet.

They petitioned a petty king who merely said, "You may visit the most sacred place on pilgrimage to Jalandhara." The master and his twelve disciples then set out for Jalandhara. On the way, the venerable lord of the sacred doctrine said, "We will have some trouble!" Then, in a short while, they were stopped by a group of some forty tax collectors. The venerable lord of the sacred doctrine said to a servant, "You should sing a song." He intoned a lament in verse, in Tibetan, and performed a dance, whereupon the tax collectors praised him and joyfully let them go.

They traveled easily, passing a place where a river flowed between two very large mountains and the mountain sides were joined by a rattan bridge, and so forth. They held a communion feast offering under the place where the master Lūipa had stopped the shower of stones hurled by heretical ḍākinīs in the sky {322} and where, when they subsequently fell lower, they had halted on merely being touched by his hand.

He practiced for seven days, inattentive to the need for food and drink, near the naturally arisen image of Tārā in Kashmir, whereupon he had a vision of Tārā. He was guided by a yogin who had attained the spiritual accomplishment of the Great Seal, who had passed the age of two hundred without dying and who happened to be drinking vegetable broth. At his invitation, Jadrelwa consumed the broth without preconceptions.

He made a hundred feast offerings at places such as the one where vermilion had dripped from the vagina of an image of Vajravārāhī, the place where there were impressions of the head, body, hands, and feet of glorious Nāropā on a boulder, the place where there is a square-shaped hole in the earth, inside of which there are eight sacred abodes of the ḍākinīs[328] and so forth.

A large town was filled merely with the news of his arrival there. It was a place that was terrified by the noise of nonhuman spirits and the cries of jackals during the night. A Drukpa monk who was acting as his servant cast an imprecation but to no avail. When he went out to the bathroom, he was slain by an obstacle.

The master and his disciples then passed without mishap over the seven steps that formed the end of a fearsome bridge spanning two cliffs. Traveling into a valley, they encountered seven brigands, but the venerable lord of the sacred doctrine was not harmed at all, although his attendants were beaten.

On reaching the far side of that valley, they arrived at a place where they saw what was said to be an extraordinary stūpa in the middle of a lake. That country was one filled with forests where many tigers roamed. In the middle of that land, there was a lake, about the same size as Taklung Monastery, and at its center on a platform of sweetflag wood[329] that could accommodate about one hundred people, {323} there was a naturally arisen stūpa made of black onyx,[330] which had been brought there from Trāyastriṃśa by the gods, headed by Śakra, and there was what seemed to be an eight-year-old boy praying that it should remain there.

When the master and his disciples had traveled almost the distance of an arrow, the stūpa and its plinth gently moved aside, and then they reached the shore of the lake. When they arrived on top of the platform, they slowly reached the center. They prostrated and circumambulated it and recited *The Seven Branch Prayer*. The venerable lord of the sacred doctrine had in his hand a lotus garland, which he offered to the stūpa. He fastened a square of red silk to a piece of hardwood and attached it to the pinnacle of the stūpa. The attendants were utterly exhausted, thinking that if this stūpa did not allow them to go back, they would simply die. Among his servants, there was a non-Buddhist teacher who had been acting as a guide. Seeing that there were also rain clouds in the sky, he said, "We'd better go back now!" The venerable lord of the sacred doctrine Jadrelwa stood up and made a recitation of *The Seven Branch Prayer*, and as soon as he had completed it, the stūpa and its plinth moved aside, and they slowly reached the lake shore. At that time, when the master and disciples requested a blessing and were about to return back, the stūpa set out toward the center of the lake. The venerable lord of the sacred doctrine Jadrelwa recalled what had transpired and sat there while he watched the stūpa. When they, master and disciples, had arrived at the mountain pass, it had reached the very middle of the lake.

It is held that that platform of sweetflag wood, which acted as the seat of the stūpa, had materialized in antiquity when a non-Buddhist accomplished master was subduing nāga spirts and had cast an antelope hide mat into the lake. Consequently, non-Buddhists make offerings directed toward the small plinth. {324} Buddhists make offerings directed toward the stūpa.

On auspicious days, countless people from different lands would gather there, and they would all offer necklaces. Having seen what transpired on this occasion and after asking why, those people acquired faith, and the fame of Jadrelwa permeated all directions. Although there are many accomplished masters in India, there was no one at all who had been welcomed by the stūpa in that manner. Saying, "There is such an accomplished master in Tibet," they came for oral advice, to hear the sacred doctrine, to pay their respects, and to make offerings, which cascaded like rain. About a hundred monks who were all meditators gathered there in his presence.

When he resided in one petty kingdom, another petty kingdom sent an army. They surrounded the palace and fired arrows. As soon as they struck the seat of the venerable lord of the sacred doctrine, a white light burst forth and surrounded the entire army, such that they retreated homeward. Asking how he did that, they acquired faith and offered him the role of councillor. The protector deity Traktsen[331] then arrived in his presence wearing Mongolian dress and many times requested him to return to Taklung.

When he left his retainers behind in order to make sacred medicine in Kashmir, although he set out alone, his fame was so great that he was venerated by everyone. There were ten people who transported him by palanquin and about one hundred who went in front, carrying incense burners. There were innumerable paṇḍitas, *kusulu* mendicants, and yogins, and also many non-Buddhist teachers who served him out of faith. All the hills and valleys were filled with people who came for advice, and they offered him innumerable quantities of medicine, which he accepted. He departed, after dispensing with all the remaining offerings and services that he had received.

On the way, Jadrelwa cured the illness of a petty king, such that he acquired faith. {325} The inhabitants of a land where the custom was to burn three nuns alongside the corpse of a religious king who had died completely offered to desist from that practice and pledged to do so henceforth.

There was in one land a stūpa reported to have been built after an emanational king had summoned three ogres from Cāmaradvīpa. Each of its sides was about the distance of an arrow shot, and its height was approximately double that, so its dimensions could not be grasped by the intellect. In front of it there was a stone sculpture depicting the great and glorious Virūpa, which is said to have been no different to the master Virūpa himself. In that place, which seemed to be imbued with such blessings, he also made offerings.

He was obliged to perform, unwillingly, a consecration ceremony at the place of a patron, and through the pollution of having recited mantras near one whose commitments had been broken, he fell ill. He went to the land known as Margun, which is identified as Maru, one of the twenty-four sacred lands of Buddhist India,[332] and there he stayed at the residence of a petty king.

One day, he imparted extensive advice to the meditators who attended upon him. Then he said, "You should cremate this corpse of mine and throw the ashes in the Zangkar River. Take these medicines to Taklung! Hereafter,

I will be born as the son of a brahmin in eastern India and perform acts of benefit for the sake of inestimable sentient beings."

Jadrelwa passed away on the fifteenth day of the tiger month in 1312 (water male bird) in his forty-sixth year. The king of that land constructed a golden image, the size of an arrow and half the size of the sacred corpse. Faithful patrons and attendants then cremated the sacred corpse and made the funerary offerings, which fulfilled his enlightened intention. For two months, the sky remained clear. The auspicious signs that occurred, such as this, were inconceivable. {326} A clockwise-spiraling conch was retrieved from the ashes and brought to Taklung, where it is contained inside a golden statue of Amitāyus that he had made. In a dream, he manifested his visage and accepted as a disciple a devout person from the India-Nepal borderlands. With the medicines, they established at Taklung an excellent medical tradition, the transmission of which is said to have been maintained to the present day by the older generations who remember it.

Concluding Verses

By any virtue that is acquired through this clear narrative,
May the sentient beings of the three world systems,
Without abiding in the confines of existence and quiescence,
Attain the thirteenth level, the adamantine holder,
And undertake maturational empowerments and liberating guidance!

Sangye Pelzang, Fifth in the Abbatial Succession

Verses of Homage

Wide-eyed with knowledge of all the classical sciences,
Adorned with the three pure trainings
And the glory of the two stages of meditation,
His responsibility for meditative practice and his altruism are hard to estimate.
Homage to the feet of Venerable Sangye Pelzang!

The peerless Sangye Pelzangpo was born at Yangsho in Dokham in 1257 (fire female snake).[333] His father was the patron Zhangkyab, his mother was Gyagar Cham,[334] and he was the oldest of their four sons who were respectively called Se Rinpoche,[335] Tuje Kyab, Yungdrung Kyab, and Chung Jadrel. From his youth, he exuded compassion, resolve, perseverance, and virtue. As such, he was one who had excellently perfected the signs of the enlightened heritage of the Great Vehicle.

In 1272 (water male monkey), his sixteenth year, Sangye Pelzangpo traveled to U and bowed at the lotus feet of Tashi Lama—the incarnation of the lord-protector Maitreya; mighty lord of knowledge, understanding, and compassion; the omnipresent lord of enlightened heritage—at the great seminary of glorious Taklung, home of the universal emperors of meditative attainment. {327} After a short time, Chogyel Phakpa Rinpoche, the glorious Sakyapa, after serving as the crown ornament of Emperor Qubilai Qaγan and establishing him in maturational empowerment and liberating guidance, returned to the region of U. At that time, Sangye Pelzangpo traveled to the great seminary of glorious Sakya as an attendant and was ordained as a mendicant. There, he excellently studied and comprehended all the outer and inner classical sciences, without exception, including the mantra tradition that this great lama Phakpa Rinpoche possessed, as well as dialectics, Sanskrit grammar, logic, arts, and medicine. He acquired a brilliance that was not dependent on others with respect to the three activities of a scholar.[336]

In that same place, Sakya, he excellently received the full monastic ordination according to the later rite, accepting the precepts of a monk in the midst of a monastic assembly who resembled sublime arhats, supreme elders pure in the three trainings, praised for the number of their concluding aspiration prayers and supplementary rites. In this way, he became a crown ornament among the hundred thousand strong upholders of monastic discipline.

Then, he returned to the great seminary of glorious Taklung, where he paid respects to his precious predecessor Tashi Lama, the venerable lord of the sacred doctrine who was the essential nature of the great pristine cognition of all the buddhas. The latter conferred upon him the genuine empowerment through which this precious Kagyu lineage is acquired, he explained the tantras, of which the fruit cannot be stolen, and granted him the pith instructions of the great seal of coalescence.

Sangye Pelzangpo obtained a successful outcome by means of the intermingling of the generation- and perfection-stage practices during the day and night, the transference of consciousness at death, and vital reincarnation, whereupon all the attributes that he formerly had resembled bark and chaff. The sun that shone from within was radiant and unobscured. All the glacial ice of conceptual thought melted in the river of pristine cognition. The natural fullness of unreal appearances was revealed. He excellently awoke to the four yogas of the ground, {328} he perfected the four yogas of the path, and he attained the kingdom of the four yogas of the result. He rejoiced in the joy and bliss that is unchanging and coemergent.[337] The entirety of existence and quiescence became pure in the maṇḍala of pristine cognition. During the night, he journeyed to infinite buddha fields and became transcendent in supreme inner radiance. He was free from the distinction between the object of consciousness transference and the subject of consciousness transference. Without depending on the oral instructions of the intermediate states, he actualized the body of coalescence, which is the fruit of the path of No More Learning. However, in order that his demonstration of the lineage of practice might be visible, he remained one-pointedly in strict meditation practice.

Then, at the time when he was enjoying the infinite meditation of the horizon, his precious predecessor, Tashi Lama, turned his mind toward the training of disciples in other fields, and on the sixth day of the waxing half of the midsummer month in 1297, he passed away after entrusting the treasury of the Buddhist teaching in its entirety to Sangye Pelzangpo. At that time, Tashi Lama said, "Just as Satśvetaketu empowered Venerable Maitreya as his regent, in accordance with the injunction of Lama Sangye Yarjon, I too have nurtured this great monastic seat for twenty-five years. Just as I have nurtured it, the master Onpo has also excellently nurtured the monastic seat, the monks, and patrons. Others headed by my youngest brother Jadrelwa have also practiced in accordance with his injunction and enlightened intention, but you should excellently nurture the teaching tradition of the practice lineage!"

Rinpoche Sangye Pelzangpo then took control of the great domain of the sacred doctrine that is the Taklung lineage. Through his great strength, which possessed attributes such as the eighteen distinct qualities of the buddhas and had mastery over the seven precious things,[338] he surpassed the celestial abodes of all mundane beings, including the gods. {329} He established all spheres of the three planes of existence on the auspicious level where the glory of the Perfect Age[339] of the Buddhist teachings concerning the essential definitive meaning can be appreciated.

Dedicated on behalf of his precious predecessor Tashi Lama, as an inner representation, he built a replica of the Śrīdhanyakaṭaka Stūpa, resembling a golden mountain, and as an outer representation, he constructed the image that is universally known nowadays as Chulonma, Brought Forth from the Water, blazing with the glory of the major and minor marks, its dimensions, the height of the throne and its back rest corresponding to the dimensions of the lower story of the Main Temple. This image was equal in size to the Mahābodhi image of Śākyamuni at Vajrāsana in India, which depicts for all disciples in common Śākyamuni in the form Great Enlightenment at the age of thirty-five, when the Blessed One attained manifestly perfect buddhahood, and which had been fashioned by Viśvakarman, modeled on the reflection of the buddha body that had arisen in water when the Buddha disciplined Udrāyaṇa, king of Roruka, by means of a drawn image.[340] When he consecrated these, an infinite number of auspicious signs filled the world. He secured sustenance for the spiritual and temporal well-being of the Buddhist teaching and sentient beings.

This saintly being absorbed the essentials contained in the myriad words and meanings that encompass the ocean of the scriptures and pith instructions, like the great Anavatapta Lake from which a hundred thousand rivers of eloquence flow and like the lion that completely overpowers the strength of ten million hostile elephants. Stringing the rosary of learning on the thread of excellent metrical verse, he was capable of granting in this very lifetime the banquet of the fruits of liberation. Endowed with the trunk of correct view, the branches of meditation, the leaves of conduct, and the fully ripened fruits of the result, his blessings were unrivaled in their power of aspiration with respect to the Great Seal. {330}

In brief, for thirteen years, Sangye Pelzangpo nurtured the entire congregation, without deviating even slightly from the regulations, the monastic charter, the established form of spiritual practice, and so forth, in the sequence that his predecessors had implemented. In addition, he also embellished the lineage of the Adamantine Vehicle with his eloquent custom of elucidating its enlightened intention.

Eventually, in 1308 (earth monkey), Sangye Pelzangpo fell ill. At that time, the monks of Taklung displayed, practiced, and made offerings to many maṇḍalas of the four classes of tantra. They excellently read aloud all the Buddhist scriptures that they had. But despite such extensive acts of service on his behalf, his health did not recover. At an auspicious time in 1309 (earth female bird), in his fifty-third year, he went to the assembly hall and empowered his nephew Ratnaguru as master of the teaching, bestowing the profound and extensive doctrines and oral advice upon him. He renounced whatever property he had and conferred its ownership upon

Ratnaguru. Then, in the morning of the fifteenth day of the third month in 1310 (iron male dog), while he was in his fifty-fourth year, he passed away in peace, accompanied by many wondrous signs. On the twenty-first day, his sacred corpse was displayed in public and offerings were extensively made with an ocean-like array of offering clouds. When the sacred corpse was cremated, his heart, tongue, and eyes were retrieved, along with innumerable five-colored pearl relics, and they became objects of offering for the three worlds. On the twenty-third day, they concluded the funeral ceremony, and on the sixth day of the next month, the auspicious circumstances that had excellently transpired were made visible to the entire congregation. {331} On all these occasions, they were enveloped by a canopy of rainbow light, a shower of flowers fell, a symphony of music resounded, and the fragrance of perfume wafted. Such were the innumerable wondrous signs that occurred.

The foregoing account is but the seed of his biography composed by Zhonu Senge of Dome, in which these events are assiduously explained.

Concluding Verses

By virtue of this sliver of his oceanic biography,
May the substratum of ocean-like sentient beings, the continuum of the ground,
Be refined through the continuum of the path of ocean-like maturation and liberation,
And thus may the continuum of the result, the ocean-like pristine cognition, be accomplished!

Ratnaguru, Sixth in the Abbatial Succession

Verses of Homage

Possessing the trunk of supremely pure ethical discipline,
Profusely extending the foliage of a hundred thousand meditative stabilities,
Radiantly adorning the anthers of training in discriminative awareness,
Homage to the *udumbara* lotus of learning and accomplishment!

His Presence Ratnaguru, the omniscient lord of the sacred doctrine, the glorious accomplished master of the seal of coalescent pristine cognition, took birth in the manner of the disk of the sun emerging on the horizon of a great ocean in 1288 (earth male mouse), at Bongra Tengka, a town in Yangsho, replete with the ten virtuous actions.[341] His father was the patron Tuje Kyab, who was great in merit, and his mother, the supreme consort who gave birth to this conqueror, was named Zungcham. Being disposed toward the sacred doctrine from childhood, the boy turned away from ordinary childish pursuits. His play was a wondrous ocean of the inconceivable three mysteries of buddha body, speech, and mind, communicating by means of the magical display of pristine cognition.

Once he had come of age, at the great seminary of glorious Tangkya, genuine source of the hundred thousand upholders of monastic discipline, {332} he received the precepts of the novitiate according to the ancient rite, with its three complete phases—preparation, actual conferral, and subsequent advice[342]—from the most sublime elder Sonam Yeshe, the upholder of the collection of monastic discipline Sangye Zangpo, and other faithful monks who participated in the quorum. The name Ratnaguru was conferred upon him.

In his seventeenth year, he met Jamyang Rinchen Gyeltsen, who was en route to the imperial palace in China.[343] He paid his respects, made excellent offerings, and received many teachings of maturational empowerment and liberating guidance. He also received some transmissions and pith instructions from Pelden Larupa. In 1306 (fire male horse), he traveled to U and proceeded to the great seminary of glorious Taklung, supreme power place and source of the buddha body of emanation, which is similar to Vajrāsana. In the presence of Sangye Pelzangpo, the glorious lord and teacher who was like an emperor among accomplished masters of the ocean of the sacred doctrine, he was empowered into many great maṇḍalas, including the tantras of skillful means, such as the *Guhyasamāja* and *Yamāntaka*;[344] the tantras of discriminative awareness, such as *Cakrasaṃvara*, *Hevajra*, *Mahāmāyā*, and *Catuḥvajrapīṭha*,[345] and the oceanic nondual unsurpassed yoga tantras, such as *Paramādibuddhakālacakra*;[346] along with those of the three classes of lower tantra—namely, yoga tantra, caryā tantra, and kriyā tantra. He was excellently established by means of extensive exegeses in their adamantine verses[347] that emphasize the six parameters of expression, the four modes of expression, and the seven ornaments of expression,[348] reaching the far shore in their profundity, most secret and beyond the perceptual range of the outer and inner pious attendants. {333}

With regard to the perfection stage of the father tantras, including *The Five Stages*,[349] which are without conceptual elaboration; the perfection stage of the mother tantras, including the Path and Its Fruit, which embodies the nine cycles of the path;[350] and all the nectar of the nondual tantras, without exception, including the Six Branches of Yoga, he did not merely receive guidance on their words, but he also received guidance on their meaning, with a certainty that was transplanted in his mind, such that he perfectly manifested all the enlightened attributes of clear realization, without exception.

In particular, Ratnaguru excellently received three modes of guidance concerning the oral instructions that are imbued with blessings and intended for experiential cultivation, extracting them from the essential and unique definitive nature. These were as follows. First was Coemergent Union of the Great Seal of the Profound Path,[351] which illustrates the real nature of fundamental reality and is the crest of all the rows of the victory banners of profound guidance concerning the definitive and unsurpassed secret essence of all the Buddha's turnings of the doctrinal wheel. Second was the four great primary methods of guidance, which are the nectar of the ocean of tantras, the heart essence of ten million learned and accomplished masters, and the heart blood of a hundred thousand ḍākinīs—namely, the pure inner heat of the activating and supreme phases; the utterly pure illusory body, in which the illusions that appear during the day are intermingled with the inner radiance of the path; Dream Yoga; and the yoga of inner radiance, in which the illusions that appear during the night are intermingled with the inner radiance experienced during sleep. Third was the two great secondary methods of guidance—namely, the oral instructions concerning the intermediate states and consciousness transference, in which the illusions that occur during the intermediate states are intermingled with the inner radiance of the moment of death. Collectively, the last two categories are named the Six Doctrines of Glorious Nāropā and they are renowned like the sun and the moon. This is the peerless Kagyu lineage of Lord Marpa, in which the nature of reality is communicated by being pointed out and buddhahood is then delivered in the palm of the hand. {334}

Within this tradition, too, he excellently examined and experientially cultivated in the correct manner the essentials through which the entire physical constitution composed of the psychophysical aggregates, the sensory elements, the sense fields, and the sense organs and sense objects that derive from them is likened to the alchemical base metal of iron and then actually transformed into the four indestructible realities of buddha body, speech, mind and pristine cognition, which resemble the alchemical transformation into gold. This is achieved through the accomplishment of the four delights of uncontaminated pristine cognition that resemble alchemical mercury, in which the flow of generative fluids of supreme bliss is melted by the yoga of Inner Heat when the mantra syllables within the channels of the subtle body of the visualized commitment seal are ignited. The implementation of this practice—according to the perfect Kagyu lineage, the tradition of Gyelwa Taklungpa the Great—is made by maintaining strict celibacy of body, free from desires. As such, it is dissimilar to the path of supreme bliss pertaining to the lower gate that is taught with an intention directed toward the stabilizing of individuals imbued with desire and exemplified by the image of a snake placed inside a bamboo tube and that therefore resembles a precipitous shortcut.[352] Consequently, in the perception of others, he gradually perfected the infinite glory of the renunciation and realization that constitute the path and its fruit. However, in the definitive sense, he had already been excellently accomplished in the nature of Lord Mahāvajradhara, and from that point onward, it was merely in a provisional sense that he performed the dance that actualizes the fruit through having meditated on the path. In brief, he perfectly received all the sacred doctrines pertaining to the two modes of the Great Vehicle, which his precious predecessor Sangye Pelzangpo, the venerable lord of the sacred doctrine, possessed.

Afterward, in 1309 (earth female bird), in his twenty-second year, during the auspicious festival when the excellently sculpted image of Mahāmuni, the meditative commitment of his precious predecessor, was consecrated, he was appointed as the authentic regent of the Conqueror upon the lion throne to which the crown ornaments of all mundane beings, including the gods, pay homage. {335} After being openly empowered as such, he was rendered peerless.[353]

All the rivers of the infinite and countless gateways to liberation, one hundred billion trillion in number, flowed into the Anavatapta Lake of the thirteen regulations of Choje Kuyalwa. All the infinite precepts and commitments contained in the corpus of monastic discipline according to the Lesser Vehicle, and in the oceanic sūtras of the most extensive class, and the tantras of the Adamantine Vehicle, which constitute the discipline of the tathāgatas, were handed down, embodied in the charter of the monastic assembly and the twenty-six disciplinary rules of Taklung Monastery.[354] Their practical application was implemented by means of *The Summation of the Scale Balance*,[355] the great textual pathway that had been entrusted by his saintly predecessors. That is to say, to those persons who take delight in elaborations, he first offered guidance in accordance with the textual traditions of the sūtras and tantras in a public exegesis, and finally sealed that with direct guidance on the definitive, essential meaning. To those who took delight in the nectar of the ultimate truth, discontented with the lower, long, and artificial paths, he granted the yoga of the intermingling of the generation and perfection stages by day and night, consciousness transference, and essential rebirth, as well as the blessings and nectar of the commitment of the Great Seal, sealing it with the nectar of pristine cognition, and thereby enabling them to encounter exclusively in this very lifetime the taste of this coalescence, which is supreme bliss. In such ways, he exemplified the deeds of the buddha body of emanation that acts on behalf of living beings, training each according to need.

However, just as a great ocean is not satisfied by a river, even though he was accomplished in the volumes that contain all the symbols and meanings of the scriptures, without exception, through which great sublime beings provisionally benefit those who require training, still, in search of eloquence and with a joyful demeanor, {336} he journeyed to the great monastic seat of glorious Sakya. In the presence of Lama Daknyi Chenpo, Drakpa Gyeltsen, Kunga Senge, Pelye Jungwa, the accomplished master Konchok Pelwa, and others, he infinitely studied the texts and oral instructions.[356] In the glorious hermitage of Jomonang, he received the precepts of full ordination according to the later transmission from Kunpang Chenpo Zhang Tuje Tsondru acting as monastic preceptor, Jangsem Gyelwa Yeshe acting as master of ceremonies, and Geshe Yonten Gyatso acting as confessor. Thus, in the manner of Upāli, he became a great upholder of monastic discipline, supreme among those who bear the victory banner of the saṃghāṭī. From that same monastic preceptor, he extensively received the complete empowerments of the glorious *Kālacakra*, an exegetical teaching pertaining to *The Great Commentary on the Kālacakra Tantra*,[357] guidance on the Six-Limbed Yoga, and so forth. On account of the attributes of clear realization that his mind possessed, Kunpang Choje also established him as a "glorious upholder of virtue whose resolve could not be captivated."[358] At that time, a messenger arrived from U to invite him back. With Ponchen Ozer Senge in attendance, he traveled swiftly and, with his retinue, reached the great monastic seat of glorious Taklung on the fifteenth day of the fifth month in 1310 (dog). On that very day, his precious predecessor, Sangye Pelzangpo, passed away, so he performed the essential service on behalf of the sacred corpse and undertook magnificent funerary rites that fulfilled his enlightened intention.

In dedication, as an outer representation, he excellently constructed the image of Śākyamuni in the form Tupa Jangchub Chenpo, which was the height of the first story of the Main Temple. It was in the form of the supreme buddha body of emanation, depicting the array of a hundredfold offerings and harem that were respectfully presented to the Conqueror in Trāyastriṃśa, {337} distinguished by its crown that sprouted diamonds and with two bodhisattva figures[359] who were known as the "head ornaments of the Sage." The blazing magnificence of its major and minor marks was insatiable to behold, as if the Buddha was actually present.[360]

As an inner representation, he excellently constructed the Great Golden Reliquary Stūpa, which resembled a second Mount Sumeru and shone as if with the light of ten thousand suns.[361] Consecrating these, he sustained the glory of the merit of all worlds and the genuine, supreme happiness of limitless realms of sentient beings. In such ways, he authentically cherished the precious Buddhist teaching, consisting of scriptural transmission and realization.

Moreover, on the day when he completed a careful inspection of the Great Offering Chapel in the area above the eastern gate, he began to construct an unrivaled ten-pillar Offering Chapel, along with its sacred artifacts, including countless large and small representations of buddha body, speech, and mind.[362]

The building here at Taklung that is known as the hermitage had formerly been founded in the time of glorious Taklungpa the Great himself. It had a pillar of potentilla and a pillar base of sand and contained representational images. Taklungpa the Great had ordered the monastic assembly to perform rites of enlightened activity there because it was always frequented by the protectors Wangchuk Tashi Tseringma and her four siblings. Later, during the time of Choku Sangye Yarjon, it had functioned as an assembly hall for retreatant monks who were known as the "four and a half thousand supplicants." It had also housed many common artifacts, including a copper cooking pot that had been used by the ancient Tibetan kings. This venerable lord of the sacred doctrine, Ratnaguru, now renovated it and made it more sublime by designing a courtyard for the monastic community.

Ratnaguru adopted without error the adamantine spiritual songs of all the mighty lords of accomplishment from the great monastic seats of the Kagyu lineage, {338} along with their chanting intonations. He widely propagated the profound adamantine spiritual songs of those who had formerly appeared in the authentic lineage of this great residence of Taklung itself, forming a lineal garland of buddhas, and then adopted them completely at all the auspicious anniversaries. In particular, he established the tradition of the ceremony called The Great Spiritual Songs of Taklung, which continues unbroken day and night on the fourteenth and fifteenth days of the twelfth month, coinciding with the anniversary of Venerable Mila Repa Zhepa Dorje. At that time, he was praised by many faithful, industrious, and intelligent monks, including those from Lachi, so the "transmission of the spiritual songs" was adopted. On that occasion, while they were practicing the great spiritual songs that form the cycles of answers to the questions of Tashi Tseringma, he went there. There was some hesitation concerning the intonation of the great spiritual song titled "Land of the Red-Faced Tibetan Ogre," which is contained within the first of those cycles, whereupon Tashi Tseringma actually appeared in the atrium of the assembly hall, riding a lion. Then, arising from the necklaces adorning the legs and head of the lion mount, there was a shrill voice, saying, "The intonation of that spiritual song goes like this!" So they adopted this advice and the defects in the intonation were eliminated.[363]

Internally, at this monastic estate of Taklung, Ratnaguru imposed stricter rules, ensuring that there was no place for meat to be brought inside. For groups of travelers who arrived at this great monastic seat with an interest in the sacred doctrine and mundane concerns, Ratnaguru granted the gift of fearless protection so that the community would not have to engage in corvee labor. This would apply not only to imperial officials and the like but even if the emperor himself were to come.[364]

In the upper eastern side of the Main Temple, he established a Protector Chapel, and he commissioned an image of Four-Armed Mahākāla in the raven-headed form, the adamantine leader of the oceanic protectors of the Buddhist teaching, {339} along with Gache Wangchuk, Marmo Tsajib, raven-faced Karmamahākāla, Shaza Siṃhavaktrā, and eight ḍākinīs, the central deity and entourage forming a group of thirteen altogether, along with the great king Vaiśravaṇa with his queen and treasure store, and the eight forming the entourage of the yakṣa Kubera, lord of horses.[365] The representative sacraments of these protectors also included eighty-three pieces of armor, such as the great leather armor of the Tibetan emperor Relpachen,[366] the armor of Rakram with the motif of an open-jawed lion, the garuḍa armor of Gomde, and an inconceivable number of weapons, including the crystal sword that had been a hand emblem of the emperor Relpachen, and the poisonous sword from the wooden stockade of Taklung.

Thus, the Protector Chapel was filled to the brim with innumerable outer, inner, and secret representations and sacraments of commitment. Owing to the vicissitudes of time, formerly, within this same east-facing Protector Chapel, the images of Jñānanātha and entourage and of Vaiśravaṇa and entourage had their respective tsakali icons fixed behind the corresponding images—tsakali that had indisputably been the meditative commitments of Gyelwa Taklungpa the Great himself. So it was that Ratnaguru built this chapel, which is nowadays generally known as the Old Protector Chapel.

Faith uncontrollably arose in those who simply saw the maṇḍala of Ratnaguru's body. His authentic speech severed the net of hesitation and established beings in unconfused view, meditation, conduct, and fruition. In the mirror of his mind, untarnished by obscuration, all the reflected images of the knowable phenomena of past, present, and future unimpededly arose, such that he could dispel the defects of living beings who were to be trained, and he established them in the glory of provisional benefits and conclusive happiness. {340} In whichever places he resided, living beings were free from thoughts of strife and disputation, and maintained a loving attitude toward one another. Even the smallest particles of dust from his footprints could offer protection from contagious life-threatening diseases. In such ways, this supremely great incarnation, endowed with immeasurable attributes indicative of the greatness of buddha body, excellently nurtured a large community for thirty years by the combined means of exegesis and attainment as if it were the assembly of Lord Ajita (Maitreya).

Finally, in his fifty-second year, in 1339 (earth female hare), one day, when Gompa Drakpa Gyeltsen and he—master and disciple—were present in the middle story, while staring fixedly into space, he said, "It seems that the two of us will have to depart this year by whatever means." Gompa immediately prostrated and said, "Please remain for the sake of living beings! I will depart!" to which he replied, "How would I have the power to do so?" Not long afterward, during the seventh month, he fell ill. At that time, there was an earthquake, a comet passed, and other inauspicious signs appeared. Although innumerable rites were undertaken to secure his health, he did not recover, and in the morning of the twenty-second day of the ninth month, the senior monks assembled, headed by the master Chungpowa, and he imparted many words of advice, saying, "Since I am certainly about to go, Ratnākara should excellently maintain this blessed residence, the source of glory, for a while. Just as in the lives of our predecessors, father and sons,

{341} he should nurture the disciples and the patrons in the correct manner. The disciples should also act in accordance with the teachings he imparts."[367]

In the morning of the twenty-third day, while seated in the assembly, he requested the venerable lord of the sacred doctrine, Ratnākara (Rinchen Jungne), to be seated upon the teaching throne and offered the necessary insignia to him, including his hat and robe. Entrusting him with the keys to the library, he empowered him as master of the entire Buddhist teaching, and he presented excellent alms and offerings to the monks. That evening, he passed into nirvāṇa in his chamber within the Great Offering Chapel. On the fifth day, his face was screened, and the sacred corpse was displayed. Then, on the morning of the sixth day, accompanied by many wondrous signs, the sacred corpse was cremated. Consequently, his heart, tongue, and eyes were retrieved, along with a clockwise-spiraling conch and innumerable five-colored pearl relics, and these were brought to the grass hermitage. Offerings were made until the evening of the forty-ninth day. As a representation of devotion, a single pearl relic was distributed to each of the resident monks and to all those monks who traveled there from all directions. In the morning of the seventh day, the great funeral ceremony was completed, the oceanic array of unsurpassed offering clouds was hard to measure, and so the sky was filled with pure intentions.[368]

This has been written based on a mere kernel of the biography contained in *The Golden Rosary* that Gelong Drakzhon extrapolated in some detail from the works of His Presence, the great scholar Jamyang Drakpa. {342}

The Disciples of Ratnaguru

The one who touched the dust of this supreme incarnation's feet out of service was the bilingual Taklung Lotsāwa Śākya Zangpo, who is said to have been an emanation of the elder Vajrīputra.[369] He was born around 1321 into the family line of the spiritual adviser Dromtonpa at Namgyi Jelung. His father was Drom Yonten Bumdar, and his mother was named Takmo Jiwa. From about his ninth year, he had a strong urge to enter into the portals of the sacred doctrine. He met Choje Rinpoche Ratnaguru on the road while traveling from Tsang to Taklung and followed in his service. At the great monastic seat of Taklung, he was ordained as a mendicant in the presence of the preceptor Tsultrim Wangchuk, who had mastered the four subjects,[370] and the master of ceremonies Gyelwa Ritsawa. The name Śākya Zangpo was conferred upon him. He excellently trained in the piṭakas and the classes of tantra, along with the four subsequent fields of classical learning, relying upon those two (the preceptor and the master of ceremonies), as well as Lopon Zopa Pel, Lodro Tsungme, Pang Lotsāwa Lodro Tenpa, Chenga Sonam Gyeltsen, Lochen Jangtse, Jamyang Donyo Gyeltsen, and others.

In his twenty-fourth year, he met the lord among scholars Buton Rinchendrub, and he received the full monastic ordination, with the latter acting as preceptor, Sakya Lama Dampa acting as master of ceremonies, Lochen Jangtse acting as confessor, and Nedrukapa Lodro Tsungme acting as the timekeeper.[371]

Taklung Lotsāwa undertook infinite studies in the presence of the omniscient great scholar Buton Rinchendrub and became a paṇḍita with knowledge of all the five fields of classical learning. Again, he traveled to Taklung, where he touched the feet of Choje Rinpoche Ratnaguru, who was peerless like a second Buddha, and of Ratnākara, the supreme incarnation of Gyeltsab Tulku. {343} By excellently studying all the profound doctrines of the precious Kagyu lineage, he acquired spiritual accomplishment.

Taklung Lotsāwa's compositions were extensive, headed by the thirteen great illuminations, which include *The Great Illumination of the Two Truths*,[372] *The Treatise That Attains the Single Enlightened Intention of the Six Ornaments*,[373] *The Great Commentary on Glorious Hevajra*,[374] and *The Great Illumination of the Methods of Reasoning: A Commentary on "The Exposition of Valid Cognition."*[375] He established a residence at thirteen major monasteries including Reteng, Langtang, and Nyenpo. There were many excellent disciples, spiritual mentors who were raised by him, including his own nephew, Khenchen Zangpo Ozer, and Lachen Mañjuśrī. He took Vajrapāṇi in the form Mahācakra as his meditational deity and Vaiśravaṇa as his doctrinal protector.

Taklung Lotsāwa commissioned many representations of buddha body, speech, and mind, including the image of Munīndra Śākyamuni at Reteng, and in the form Jotse at Yangpachen, along with the three-dimensional maṇḍalas of Vajradhātu and the speech empowerment of Dharmadhātu, as well as the Collected Works of Buton Rinpoche.[376] He passed away in his eighty-third year, on the twenty-eighth day of Māgha[377] in 1404 (wood monkey).

Following the cremation, images, including one of Vajrasattva, and many pearl relics emerged. It is said that immediately after he passed away, Venerable Tashi Peltsek heard a voice whispering that he had departed in the form of Mañjughoṣa to Śambhala with a large entourage.

The lineage of his nephew descended through Zangpo Ozer, Dechen Gyatso, Pelden Jangchub, Jangchub Zangpo, Phuntsok Gyatso, Ngodrub Pelzang, Drakpa Wangchuk, Namgyel Lhundrub, and so forth, down to the preceptors of the present day, Ngawang Sonam Chokdrub and his brother. {344}

Tsamla

Tsamla appeared in the family line of Odren Pelgyi Zhonu, who had been an actual disciple of master Padmasambhava.[378] He was appointed as Lama Olawa Gendun Rinchen, in accordance with a decree of Venerable Ratnagurupada. Thereafter, the titles Tsamla and Lachen were gradually conferred on the successors in his lineage, during their respective epochs—namely, Lachen Rinchen Zangpo, Tsamla Namgyel, Tsamla Śāksengwa, his brother Lachen Namkha Tashi, Tsamla Namkha Wangchuk, Lachen Namkha Peltsek, Lachen Gelek Gyatso, Chodzongwa Ngawang Gyatso, Jadrel Yeshe Wangpo, Densawa Lodro Wangpo, Lachen Kunga Nyingpo, Tsamla Sangye Tashi, and Tsamla Namgyel Rinchen. From the later, the lineage passed to Tsamla Ngawang Gendun Peldrub of the present day.[379]

Jamyang Drakpa

Venerable Ratnaguru also had a learned disciple named Jamyang Drakpa, who had studied much and attained the profound path. Although an excellent anthology of the lives of his disciples could be expanded into a more extensive garland of composition, I have not yet seen their definitive life stories.

Concluding Verses

May this mighty sal tree of virtuous narrative,
With the beautiful hanging snowflake flower[380] garlands
  of spiritual and temporal well-being,
Offer excellent shelter from the feverish torments
That are the afflictions of sentient beings
And beautify the domain of the Buddhist teaching!

Ratnākara, Seventh in the Abbatial Succession

Verses of Homage

His body mature with the major and minor marks and meaningful to behold,
The mystery of his speech combining all manner of eloquence
And offering liberation by hearing, {345}
His mind always in equipoise and never forgetful,
Homage with a hundred expressions of faith
To the lord-protector Ratnākara!

The supreme emanation Ratnākara, after teaching in the forms of the great paṇḍita Vidyākokila, the great translator Kawa Peltsek, the mighty lord of occult power Ra Lotsāwa Dorje Drak and so forth, took birth, accompanied by many wondrous omens, in 1300 (iron male mouse) at Bongrateng in Yangsho.[381] His father was the patron Tuje Kyab, and his mother was Zungcham. From childhood, he was manifestly adorned with the excellence of the four immeasurable aspirations and so forth, which are of benefit to others, and the four gateways to liberation, and so forth, which are of benefit to oneself. When he had come of age, he received the lay vows and the intermediate vows of a mendicant—the ordination of the novitiate, which embodies the ten preliminary precepts[382]—at the great seminary of glorious Tangkya, with Śrīpuṇyajñāna Pel Sonam Yeshe, an upholder of the Vinayapiṭaka acting as preceptor, and Buddhabhadra Sangye Zangpo, an elder and teacher of the sacred doctrine who resembled a lion acting as the master of ceremonies. The name Ratnākara was conferred upon him. Not long afterward, he traveled to U and reached the seminary of glorious Taklung, which the Conqueror had foreordained as a place where experiential cultivation and realization would increase, in the manner of Mount Potālaka. He touched the lotus feet of Choje Ratnaguru, who became his crown ornament, the lord of his enlightened heritage. Ratnākara then constructed the six-pillar Kadruk residence. In the presence of his precious predecessor, Ratnaguru, supreme sovereign of the Buddhist teaching composed of scriptural transmission and realization, he received the actual teaching of *The Sūtra Titled King of Meditative Stability*,[383] the conclusive definitive meaning of the ocean-like piṭaka composed of both aspects of the Great Vehicle,[384] as well as the content of *The Seven Sections of Spiritual Attainment*,[385] {346} *The Six Essential Cycles*,[386] *The Twenty-Four Doctrinal Cycles of Nonmentation*,[387] and so forth.[388] He also excellently received Coemergent Union of the Great Seal, where the essential nature of the innate mind is established as the view, and the Six Doctrines of Nāropā, which are pith instructions on meditation, integrating the three aspects of illusion and the three aspects of inner radiance, and which conform to the perfection stage of the six tantra approaches—namely, the *Secret Assembly*, which is a father tantra; *Mahāmāyā*, which is a mother tantra; the essential *Hevajra*, the quintessential *Cakrasaṃvara*; *Catuḥpītha*, which is conjoined with the protectors of the transmitted teachings; and the blessed Kālacakra. These are renowned in the precious Kagyu lineage as the "instructions in which the tiger and lion come face-to-face."[389]

In order to induce confidence in those to be trained and to exemplify spiritual attainment, Ratnākara remained in one-pointed practice, with an ascetic discipline that embodied the three unwavering modalities of body, speech, and mind.[390] He engaged his mind in experiential cultivation with uninterrupted perseverance that resembled the flow of a river or the point of a flame. Consequently, he cut off the movement of subtle and gross conceptual thoughts, and purified the signs of the subject-object dichotomy in the expanse of reality. His mind transformed into the buddha body of reality, and he mastered the object to be equipoised in meditative stability, the subject that enters into equipoise, and the pristine cognition that realizes meditative stability, without objectifying its essential nature. So it was that for him there was no difference between meditative equipoise and post-meditation, no difference between day and night, and no difference between the symbolic and the nonsymbolic. Like a merchant on a treasure island, all that appeared was of the nature of inner radiance. All that arose was the emanational play of the buddha body of reality. His recollections and perceptions engaged with the immensity of the buddha body of reality, the uncontrived and innate essential nature, and he acquired the inestimable approaches of meditative stability. Skilled in the practice based on the melting of the inner heat of *caṇḍālī*, {347} he practiced so as to secure the generative essence (or chyle) without leakage (ejaculation), and in this way, the pristine cognition integrating bliss and emptiness arose in the course of daytime appearances. All that appeared was of the nature of deities, the pure illusory body that is radiant, clear, unsullied, and consummate from the beginning. All phenomena of cyclic existence that manifest as bewilderment arose as insubstantial fictions, like the proverbial multicolored rope that appears as a snake, and so he determined this to be the nature of all objective appearances since such modes of perception were manifest to him even during periods of dreaming, when he acquired stability in the impure illusory body.[391] He attested to such experiences many times.[392]

As mentioned above, Ratnākara actualized the profound abiding nature of the yoga of the great seal, the inner radiance that permeates space, without requiring elucidation or establishment. By the power of integrating all movements of the channels, winds and vital essences associated with past actions in pure union with the channels, winds, and vital essences associated with pristine cognition, he actualized the level on which the path of No More Learning is integrated, disregarding the need for refinement of the buddha fields during the intermediate state after death and the consciousness transference with an object, which are suitable, respectively, for those of average and inferior acumen.

Then, he excellently received the full monastic ordination according to the later rite and in accordance with the ten aforementioned precepts, with Sherab Chogon, the supreme elder and abbot of the Jonang community of Cholung,[393] who held the immaculate transmission of the great paṇḍita Śākyaśrī of Kashmir, acting as preceptor, and with Geshe Sonam Wangchuk who was learned in the meaning of the words of the hundred thousand verses of the vinaya and worthy of supreme veneration for his observance of the monastic precepts, acting as the master of ceremonies, in the midst of quorum, which included the master who acted as confessor, and was supplemented by many noble monks.[394] {348}

Ratnākara was distinguished in that from the start he had mastered the two trainings of higher discriminative awareness and higher meditative stability, and now these were embellished with the ornament of training in higher ethical discipline. Replete with ten million light rays of noble activities, like a golden reliquary of the three trainings, he became an authentic object of refined offerings for all worlds including the gods.

Afterward, he traveled to the great seminary of glorious Sakya, where he received innumerable teachings of empowerment teachings of exegesis and teachings of pith instruction headed by the three main tantras and their pith instructions from Lama Daknyi Chenpo, Lachen Kunlowa, Kunga Gyeltsen, Khetsun Namlekpa, Jamyang Donyo Gyeltsen, Pang Lotsāwa Lodro Tenpa, Lama Dampa Sonam Gyeltsen, and others.[395] Then, in the retreat hermitage of Jomonang, from Jangsem Gyelwa Yeshe, he received in detail the empowerment of glorious Kālacakra, the three cycles of commentaries by bodhisattvas and in particular, the six-branch yoga—including the yoga of adamantine buddha body, in which composure and meditative concentration are virtuous in the beginning; the yoga of adamantine buddha speech, in which breath control and apprehension of the compete deity are virtuous in the middle; and the yoga of adamantine buddha mind, in which recollection of this and meditative stability are virtuous in the end.[396]

Then again, he traveled here to this great seminary of Taklung, where he received, in the manner of a vase that was filled to the brim, all the doctrinal cycles of the Kagyu lineage that his precious predecessor had possessed, exemplified by extraordinary teachings such as the Cycle of the Six Meditational Deities of Glorious Taklung Tangpa the Great[397] and the Three Hundred and Eight Compilations of Supreme Oral Instruction,[398] {349} and he manifested his expertise in them.

Since his precious predecessor succumbed to ill-health, on the twenty-second and twenty-third days of the ninth month in 1339 (earth male hare), Choje Rinchen Jungden Ratnākara, in his fortieth year, was requested to take his seat on the lion throne in the midst of an assembly of monks. To symbolize that he would turn the wheel of the sacred doctrine, he was offered the keys to the library. To symbolize that he would serve as the crown ornament of living beings, he was offered a hat. To symbolize that he would protect sentient beings from the torments of afflicted mental states, he was offered a robe. To symbolize that he would liberate living beings from the wasteland of rebirth, he was offered boots. In order to establish the auspicious circumstances for his continued long life, he was offered the teaching throne and seat. To symbolize that he would provide stability to unprotected living creatures, he was offered a staff. In order that he might demonstrate the genuine lineage that all the series of buddhas partake of a single continuum of buddha mind, he was offered a rosary. To symbolize that he would exclusively enjoy the nectar of the essential definitive meaning, he was offered a bowl. To symbolize that he would nurture his flock by means of the nectar of the oral instruction of the precious Kagyu lineage, he was offered a silver bird. To symbolize that he would bear responsibility for the Buddhist teaching, he was offered a riding horse and saddle. To symbolize that he would protect his spiritual and temporal dominions through peaceful acts of great compassion, he made a wide distribution of alms. His precious predecessor and the preceptors, teachers, and officials of the monastic community scattered garlands of precious flowers and chanted auspicious prayers. {350} He was then empowered as a universal monarch of the sacred doctrine, lord of the Buddhist teaching in its entirety.[399]

From that day on, he occupied the residence. That is to say, he spoke at the time of his precious predecessor's nirvāṇa and prepared a magnificent funeral ceremony on behalf of the sacred corpse. As a representation of buddha body, he erected an image of the Conqueror Śākyamuni, twenty-one handspans in height, surmounted by a crown protuberance, with two standing images of Maitreya and Avalokiteśvara, one on either side, their crown jewels reaching the tip of the earlobe of the central figure. These three central and peripheral statues were made of copper and brass, weighing approximately one and a half thousand loads and three thousand steelyard measures. Their threads were fashioned of gold weighing one hundred and thirty *sang*, which was multiplied eightfold with the addition of mercury. Even the throne and back screen were fashioned of copper and gold.[400]

As a representation of buddha speech, he commissioned a recension of all the treatises that had been translated in Tibet, commenting on the enlightened intention of the sūtras and mantras, and elucidating the four further subjects of classical learning, grammar, logic, art, and medicine, containing as many as two thousand three hundred and forty doctrinal discourses.

As representations of buddha mind, he erected this great golden reliquary, which nowadays is situated in the Old Offering Chapel. It is twenty handspans in height, in the design known as the "stūpa that displays great miracles" or "the stūpa that defeats extremists"—the original of which was built at the time when the genuinely perfect Buddha demonstrated the great miracles that subdued the six extremist teachers. Moreover, he gathered together innumerable other representations of buddha body, speech, and mind, such as the extraordinarily sublime image of Cakrasaṃvara in the Northern Chamber.

In order that the Buddhist teaching—composed of recitation, study, and reflection—might flourish in this great residence of Taklung, {351} he established many exegetical traditions, including commentaries of the enlightened intention of the three piṭakas,[401] such as *The Root Sūtra of the Vinaya*,[402] *The Ornament of Clear Realization*,[403] *The Supreme Continuum of the Great Vehicle*,[404] *The Introduction to the Conduct of a Bodhisattva*,[405] *Discriminative Awareness: The Root Stanzas of the Middle Way*,[406] *The Treasury of Phenomenology*,[407] and *The Compendium of Phenomenology*,[408] as well as the tantras of glorious *Kālacakra*, *Cakrasaṃvara*, and *Hevajra* and their pith instructions.

In order that the teaching composed of practice and meditative concentration might flourish, he established many traditions of guidance, such as the Great Seal, the Six Doctrines of Nāropā, and the Six-Limbed Yoga. He established those who required training in maturation and liberation in accordance with their dispositions, faculties, and inclinations, guiding them in a way that was commensurate with their capacity. He maintained the regulations of Choje Kuyalwa, the charter of the monastic assembly, and the thirty-nine disciplinary rules of the monastery, and so forth, without deviating from the ways in which they had been kept during the time of his predecessor, the venerable lord of the sacred doctrine. Due to the glory and excellence of the sacred doctrine and the desirable attributes of the senses, this manifestly ornate community of Taklung indeed flourished and expanded like a lake in summer.

Envoys also arrived in his presence, dispatched by the great emperor of China to present sacraments of offering, empowering him as a doctrinal king of the three world systems, indivisible from the transcendent lord Ratnasambhava.[409] These gifts, with an elaborate official certificate, were exemplified by the jade seal with a dragon-motif handle, its design bearing the name Ratnākara inscribed in the Rañjanā script, and by the "edict of permanent office,"[410] proclaiming him as a spiritual teacher of the emperor himself and as an object of offering throughout the entire empire, and by the many utensils that were made of precious gems of inestimable value.[411] {352}

These he accepted in a ceremonial manner that accorded with the great emperor's own judicial protocol handbook. The envoys in turn were allowed to accept the gifts of the sacred doctrine and of material things, which could fill the treasury of the emperor's intellect. So it was that the great drumbeat filled all worlds, including those of the gods, with the proclamation of the glorious and holy Taklungpa the Great, who is an object of homage, an object of offering, and a convergence of merit for all worlds associated with the wheel of inexhaustible adornment—the enlightened activity of the virtuous Buddhist teaching, and with the red seal of the Newly Ascendant and Youthful Emperor.[412] But he was not someone who would speak fine words face-to-face with deceitful persons engaged in devious machinations or in the presence of officials and fools. Nor was he one who would deviously pursue gifts of food and property. Rather, the fragrance of his talents, maintaining the glory of a lord-protector who was as noble as a learned scholar and a venerable monk, was wafted by the fresh breeze of intelligent beings.

Excellently appointed by the mighty power of heaven, endowed with long life as an earthly embodiment of Śakra, who virtuously protects the great empire under the sun in accordance with the sacred doctrine, he responded to the confident questions posed by the emperor, great king of the sacred doctrine, not once but repeatedly. For this reason, a spiritual mentor such as this is hard to find, like an udumbara lotus, worthy of veneration on account of all the necessities it provides. {353} Though he maintained this role over a long period of time, he gazed with the eyes of nonreferential great compassion, which neither lapsed nor were indifferent. It is certain that there was none superior to this fertile field of provisions that gave rise to a foundation of meritorious action,[413] and the emperor regarded him with faith, as if actually meeting him face-to-face. The venerable lama accepted the flowers that were excellently offered and accepted gifts and proclamations of unchanging authority over the nephews who maintained his enlightened heritage and all those who would become regents of the sacred doctrine in the future, starting from then until the end of future time. In this manner, he was capable of maintaining the standard of all systems of the ancient spiritual and temporal sciences, such that they did not decline, even provisionally. What is the point of those who nowadays implement whatever comes into their minds, having been appointed as authorities, thinking all sorts of utterly shameless thoughts, and who, because they have merely acquired dye of a red color for Buddhist robes, proclaim for the sake of a few gifts, "I am great! I am good!" but are in fact dependent on the fever that causes all their activities to perish! So it was that he examined things with an intellect that maintained his integrity and did not act with an intellect that lapsed into partiality, agitated by attachment or aversion.

It was in this way that he excellently nurtured the entire congregation by means of the combined exegesis and attainment for twenty-two years. Having widely increased acts of service and enlightened activity on behalf of the residence at Taklung, he passed into nirvāṇa, accompanied by many wondrous signs, on the twenty-fourth day of the fourth month in 1361 (iron female ox), when he was in his sixty-second year. Innumerable funerary offerings were presented {354}. When the sacred corpse was cremated, an inestimable number of seed syllables, pearl relics, and so forth were retrieved from the body. These were displayed to the assembly of monks and patrons, and part of them were distributed as representations of faith. The entire sky was also dense with rainbows. A shower of flowers, mingled with pearl relics, descended in waves. The fragrance of divine incense wafted, and the sound of cymbals played by the offering deities resounded loudly. The wondrous signs such as these that appeared were countless.[414]

The Disciples of Tulku Ratnākara

Kadrukpa Rinchen Gyeltsen Pelzangpo was excellently nurtured by nectar from the vase of this venerable lord's oral instruction. He was a sibling and the monastic official of Choje Kunpangpa Rinpoche, sharing the same father and mother.[415] Ordained as a mendicant in his youth, he perfected his studies, reflections, and meditations. In particular, owing to the kindness of Choje Ratnākara, he drank from the pure river of the Kagyu teachings, ever free from the polluted river of sophistry, such that his body, speech, and mind matured into the nature of the three purest adamantine realities of buddha body, speech, and mind. Experiencing the common savor in the disposition of the Great Seal, the abiding nature of all phenomena, all meanings and words of all the sūtras, tantras, and treatises, without exception, burst forth from the expanse of his buddha mind. He was also able to question other great teachers such as Daknyi Chenpo Sakya Lama Dampa Sonam Gyeltsen about many crucial points concerning the sacred doctrine. However, the emphasis of the experiential cultivation in which his own mind engaged and of the teachings that he widely imparted to others was exclusively the profound sacred doctrine of the Taklung Kagyu tradition. Dependent on that, {355} the disciples born of his buddha speech were also many, including the great learned and accomplished master Tamdrin Ozer and Ba Rinchen Senge. Those who followed these master and disciples manifested their expertise in the oceanic oral teachings of Lord Taklungpa the Great and his cycle of the six meditational deities, such that they were most beneficial for the teaching of the textual tradition. Although he was indisputably the monastic disciplinarian, he did not accede to the monastic seat, for which reason he is not actually counted among the holders of the authentic lineage and the successive hierarchs of the abbatial succession of Taklung. Since he passed away while living in Kadruk, he acquired the title On Kadrukpa.

Here in the udumbara grove of effort and virtuous action,
May the fragrant glow that delights all intelligent beings

Assuredly exude the milk of spiritual and temporal well-being in the form of gold,
And entice the minds of all beings, without exception, toward the sacred doctrine!

Namkha Pelyang Zangpo, Eighth in the Abbatial Succession

Verses of Homage

Endowed with the six-limbed yoga of adamantine reality,
Extracting the nectar of the oceanic lotus groves of scripture,
Manifestly humming the great commentaries of the nondual tantras,
Homage to Pelyang Zangpo, king of bumble bees!

The great learned and accomplished master Kunpang Namkha Pelyang was born with inconceivable virtuous signs in 1333 (water female bird year) at a place called Daryul, in Penyul, the "source of knowledge."[416] His father was the patron Yeshe Rinchen, the son of Yungdrung Kyab, and his mother was Chukmo Pele. He was the first of all the venerable incumbents of Taklung to be born in U. He was the oldest of three brothers, the younger ones being On Kadrukpa and the patron Kunye. In childhood, he felt that he was the small child of an enfeebled being, and so he was given the nickname Beggar. {356} On reaching his fifth year, as soon as he saw *The Verse Summation of the Transcendent Perfection of Wisdom*, the indications of the enlightened heritage of the Great Vehicle were excellently aroused, and his faith surged. His body hairs stood on end, and he shed tears. Loving-kindness and compassion for the worlds of sentient beings, the inconceivable mind that is set on enlightenment, burst forth of their own accord. His physical conduct grew diverse due to the influence of the propensities he had developed over the series of his past lives, and consequently he was also known by the names Yonten Gyatso, Kungawo, and Namkha Rinchen.[417]

In 1339 (earth female hare), in his seventh year, he received ordination not as a layman but as a novice monk from the preceptor Lama Namlekpa, the master of ceremonies Dinyopa, Drokdenpa Lopon Wangseng, and others, and the name Namkha Gyeltsen Pelzangpo was conferred on him. During his tenth year, he perfectly mastered the commentaries on *The Glorious Tantra of Hevajra*.[418] Since he had earnestly applied himself to adamantine yoga over many lives, in this lifetime the ten signs of realization and so forth naturally arose, without him studying the pith instructions or engaging in experiential cultivation.[419] In his eleventh year, his mind set on enlightenment was most profound, such that he had the ability to actually exchange his happiness with the sufferings of others. When he saw the volumes of the extensive, medium, and abridged *Transcendent Perfection of Wisdom*, the definitive secret of the profound abiding nature arose from within. For a while he had boundless experiences. He felt a strong sadness aroused by the impermanent appearances of the worldly environment and its sentient inhabitants, just as described in the biography of Kharak Gomchung, {357} his dreams were self-controlled, without depending on the need for a subjective focus, and so forth. Experiencing the common savor of the eight worldly concerns in the expanse that is without acceptance or rejection, he said,

> Nauseated at this cyclic existence,
> Tormented by suffering exclusively,
> Genuine awareness is arising from within,
> Uncontrived and easily.
> This mind of mine that resembles milk—
> Sometimes good and sometimes bad,
> Embarks on or conceives of the blissful path
> Through the blessings of Avalokiteśvara.[420]

Namkha Pelyang could remember an innumerable series of past events, including the array of the physical environment and its inhabitants in India, in the Tsang region, and so forth, during his former lives, and the respective modes of conduct in which he had engaged there.[421] When he was afflicted by fever, he practiced the union of the upper and lower winds, and by the power of inducting the winds into the central channel, he had visions of many such former lands. When he was equipoised in meditative stability, he said that all the maṇḍalas of knowable phenomena pertaining to past, present, and future clearly arose in his mind, without exception, but he did not speak of them. In his dreams, he perfectly experienced signs of the absorption of appearances, of the absorption of conceptual thoughts, of the absorption of subtle phenomena, and of the absorption of gross phenomena, and when he awoke therefrom, his consciousness would depart from his body and move unimpededly like the body of a *gandharva* in space, whereupon he knew that he had previously been born in the Tsang region. Then, after he had said some prayers, as soon as he exited from his cave hermitage,[422] his memory of that past life was immediately prompted by a specific circumstance.[423] When his consciousness went elsewhere, apart from his body, he said that he had no hardship and was incapable of physical action. On one of those occasions, in a vision of pure pristine cognition, he received a great many approaches of the profound and extensive doctrine over two nights from sublime Avalokiteśvara.[424] {358} Then, not long afterward, he actualized the real nature integrating bliss and emptiness, entirely as an object of comprehension, within the perceptual range of the pristine cognition that is particularizing intrinsic awareness, as if meeting a former acquaintance. Expressing this realization, he said,

> O when intrinsic awareness is blissful,
> I, the second Chowang, have found
> The precious emptiness endowed with all its finest aspects,
> Naturally radiant and undeluded![425]

That is to say, he clearly remembered having been Dharmeśvara, the son of the accomplished master Yumo.[426] Although he certainly knew where he had settled with that physical form of Dharmeśvara, he did not mention it for a while because it could be disconcerting. He said, "Avalokita is very kind to me. I just prayed that I might stay in this place for eighteen years. In general, my lifespan was to have been thirty-four years, but by the blessing of the profound oral teachings, that period became uncertain. It did not come to pass because I am consistently happy wherever I go."[427]

In the presence of Choje Ratnākara, the supreme head of the authentic lineage and unique lord of enlightened heritage, he received all the profound scriptures of the profound teaching of the glorious Taklung Kagyu lineage in their entirety, like the essence of butter originating from the churning of an ocean of milk. And so he became a master of the Buddhist teaching, integrating the two streams of Kadam instructions and the Great Seal.

When the great translator known as Jangchub Tsemo—the nephew of Pang Lotsāwa, whose intellect was unimpeded in all the subjects of classical learning, including the three piṭakas, the four classes of tantra, and Sanskrit grammar, and who had mastered the Six-Limbed Yoga— {359} arrived at Taklung to join the advance welcoming party for Sakya Lama Dampa, the precious Ratnākara made the following request to this Lotsāwa Tsemo: "Please act as teacher to my nephew!" And the latter replied, "I will do so!"[428]

Jangchub Tsemo then imparted the teachings and in his presence Kunpang Namkha Pelyang perfectly received the oceanic textual traditions of the mantras and dialectics, and in particular the empowerments of *The Glorious Wheel of Time*, along with *The Great Commentary on the Tantra*[429] and its pith instructions. At that time, also, he comprehended all the words and meanings of all that he received in their entirety, without error, just by hearing them only once. Not only did the meaning of all the great textual traditions penetrate the expanse of his enlightened intention, he also had an ability to retain in mind all the arrangements of their words, without omitting one iota, and to recite them aloud without looking at the books. It is said that he could enunciate texts such as the twelve thousand verses of *The Taintless Light*—the great commentary on the extensive version of *The Abridged Tantra of the Glorious Kālacakra* from memory, without adding or omitting a single syllable. So it was that he dwelled in the genuine meaning. He said, "I have studied this *Kālacakra* over many lives. Nowadays, indeed, there is no one with a greater interest in this tantra than I. Even though I did not painstakingly exert myself with regard to this definitive meaning, it spontaneously arose from within. A ray of light was diffused from the gemstone in the shoulder ornament of the tathāgata Amoghasiddhi, who held in his hand an alms bowl made of beryl and filled with nectar, and it illuminated my body. Seeing this, I became steadfast in meditative stability. In a past life, I meditated for a long period of time in Tsang, {360} and my swift development of meditative stability nowadays is also due to that. I am grateful for the kindness of Choje Ratnākara, who bestowed the profundities of the short path in the form of experiential guidance, entrusting the oral teachings of the precious Kagyu lineage, as if holding a buddha in the hand. I also nurtured the profound pith instructions on *The Commentary on the Kālacakra Tantra*, imparted by Lotsāwa Tsemo, such that nowadays I have acquired fearless confidence. Otherwise, even positive propensities have to be sustained."[430]

When he received the Six-Limbed Yoga, he dreamed that he was drinking a bowl full of milk, such that he instantaneously perfected all the realizations associated with meditative experience. He actualized the authentic level of manifestly perfect enlightenment in the essential nature of the *Kālacakra*, where on the lion throne of emptiness endowed with all its finest aspects the letter E—symbolizing the outer, inner, extraneous, and real natures—rejoices in the supremely unchanging and permanent supreme bliss symbolized by the letter VAṂ, and the binding seal of all the buddhas is attained, blissful, permanent, and authentic.[431]

He also said, "Nowadays, there are some who count the mantras HŪṂ and PHAṬ, emphasizing the meditational deities and the doctrinal protectors, and they are imbued with many supreme aspirations. I have many times imparted spiritual accomplishment to all by means of the meditational deities and doctrinal protectors, and I am without arrogance in that regard. The activity of the deities is said to be the unique inner radiance of one's own mind."

He was one who was never satiated when seeking out the eloquence of others. That is to say, he received teaching many times from Jamyang Donyo Gyeltsen, Khenton Namkha Gyeltsen, Lama Dampa Sonam Gyeltsen, Gyelse Tokme, and others.[432]

In his twenty-seventh year, in 1359 (earth female pig), at the Great Emanational Temple of Lhasa, in the presence of Jowo Rinpoche Śākyamuni, {361} he excellently received the precepts of the full monastic ordination, with Tashi Tsultrim, the supreme and sublime elder, abbot of the Jonang assembly, acting as monastic preceptor, Tsul Lawa acting as master of ceremonies, and the master Ton Gyelwa acting as confessor and timekeeper.[433] The ordination took place in the presence of a devout monastic community, including the master Jo Tenpa, and embodied the "fourfold rite including the request"[434] and the requisite ten presences,[435] reaching the culmination of entry into the Buddhist teaching on account of its purity, with the three phases—preparation, actual conferral, and subsequent advice taking place without error and in the correct order.[436]

Kunpang Namkha Pelyang never transgressed the proscribed limits of the precepts, observing the ten advantages as found in the oceanic piṭaka concerning the vows of individual liberation, where the Teacher (the Buddha) and the teaching are of a single modality.[437] He was a vase of white beryl, consisting of mindfulness, alertness, and carefulness, filled with the pure water of precious ethical discipline, endowed with eight qualities, and never sullied by the slightest blemish. He was worthy of veneration as a crown ornament by those disciples of extraordinary inspiration and virtue who seek liberation and follow the great sage Śākyamuni. He excellently prepared the marvelous sacraments of good auspices that sustain the precious Buddhist teaching, the source of spiritual and temporal well-being, enabling it to flourish and expand over a long period of time in all places, times, and circumstances.

In his twenty-ninth year, in 1361 (iron female ox), when his precious predecessor Ratnākara passed away into the taintless pure land, he performed the funeral rites in service of the sacred corpse, in the course of which he made most extensive offerings and so forth.[438] Afterward, {362} he was manifestly empowered on the precious adamantine throne, which is an object of homage for all the mighty lords of the three world systems, by the great transference of blessing of the series of buddhas, perfect in the genuine lineage. In this way, he was empowered as a universal monarch of the sacred doctrine, with dominion over the precious Buddhist teaching, consisting of the entire corpus of the Conqueror's supreme skillful means, integrating exegesis and attainment. All the buddhas of the ten directions uttered noble words of good auspices, bestrewing him with garlands of precious flowers, and uttering their aphorisms. At that time, all classes of living beings—not only the human beings who live upon the earth but also the gods who frequent celestial abodes and the nāgas who frequent subterranean abodes—were delighted, saying, "Emaho!" A perfect buddha has appeared in the world. Behold him turning the wheel of the sacred doctrine!" So they exerted themselves to the utmost in the rites of offering, and through their power, infinite signs of good auspices manifested even within the common perception of human beings.

Commencing from then, the regulations of Choje Kuyalwa, the charter of the monastic assembly, the disciplinary rules of the monastery, and so forth, were applied, just as they had been in the time of Venerable Sangye Yarjon, in the manner of a reflection transposed on a clear mirror. Above all, he focused exclusively on the inner yoga of absorption in unlimited and diffusive meditative stability, without moving from the state of ascetic discipline, in which the three isolations of body, speech, and mind are pure and at ease. In uninterrupted sessions of summer teaching and winter teaching, he caused the supreme lotus of intelligence to blossom in innumerable fortunate disciples, by means of the *Kālacakra Tantra* and its *Extensive Commentary*, the explanation of the glorious *Hevajra*, {363} the *Past Lives*[439] of the Tathāgata, the Six Doctrines of Maitreya, the exegesis of *The Introduction to the Conduct of a Bodhisattva*, and so forth.[440]

For some time, he constantly turned the wheel of the sacred doctrine of definitive meaning alone, including the Six-Limbed Yoga, the Six Doctrines of Glorious Nāropā, the cycle of *The Great Seal of the Profound Path*,[441] the extremely unelaborate instructions, *The Five Stages of the Secret Assembly*,[442] and *The Direct Guidance of Avalokiteśvara*.[443] Based on those teachings, there evolved an assembly of disciples with auspicious marks on their bodies, proficient masters of yoga in whose minds realization arose, all of whom, like the stars in the sky, held the three vows—namely, the outer vows of monastic discipline, the inner vows of the bodhisattvas, and the secret vows of the awareness holders, in accordance with the oral tradition of this precious lineage of attainment, and they relied exclusively upon the essential meaning. So it was as if they filled this precious monastery of Taklung itself and all regions of the three provinces of U, Tsang, and Kham.

As an outer representation of his precious predecessor, he constructed an image of Buddha Amitābha encircled by two bodhisattvas and the thousand buddhas, with the array of the buddha field of Sukhāvatī on its lion throne, and with a rear curtain that was particularly sublime, on account of which it resembled a golden mountain, the size of the lower story of the temple. As an inner representation, he built an extraordinary sublime Victory Stūpa, fashioned of diverse precious gems.[444]

He composed a great many works, including prayers, oral instructions, official prayer ceremonies, particular sorts of means for attainment, summations of many great textual traditions, essential writings on many profound pith instructions, and manuals on the essentials of astrology, poetics, {364} and medicine. Usually he remained in solitude, and he wished to stay exclusively in that state, instructing his many disciples in the form of whispered teachings.[445] However, in the face of the repeated entreaties of the monks, disciples, and patrons, he did travel six or seven times as far as Sok in the northern region.[446] He made all the sentient beings of those regions see that cyclic existence does have an end. He also mediated successfully between vengeful factions, granting them indiscriminate gifts. The assembly of the monastic community here, in this great monastery of Taklung, also greatly expanded, such that not even a grass hermitage could be purchased with gold. Since spiritual and temporal wealth were in abundance, it is said that this community was unrivaled in the whole world.[447]

Then, he thought that he should refine the buddha fields through the diffusion of his meditative stability in an isolated hermitage and saw that On Rinpoche Gyelse Jikten Wangchuk should become the fountainhead of the many excellent assemblies forming the array at this monastic seat of Taklung. Then, in his forty-third year, on an auspicious day in the first month of 1376 (fire male dragon), Venerable Tashi Peltsek Nyima Wangpo Sungwei

Gocha was empowered with dominion over the sacred doctrine. He himself stayed thereafter in one-pointed meditative commitment at Sengling Drakya Dorje Dzong, the sacred hermitage of glorious Taklung Tangpa the Great. Furthermore, he said that through the auspicious coincidence of staying in retreat, without being absorbed by emanational maṇḍalas in the world, spiritual attainment drew near, and his visualization became radiant. Then, he adopted Cakrasaṃvara as his foremost meditational deity during the generation stage of meditation, {365} and as the foremost practices of the perfection stage of meditation, he adopted the Six-Limbed Yoga and the Six Doctrines of Nāropā, integrating them in the definitive secret of a single essential point. That is to say, he remained moderately absorbed in meditative stability that combines the generation and perfection stages for four full years, in the manner of the flow of a river, after which he appeared to fall ill. After bestowing the verses of his oral instruction, which were profound and vast, he passed away on the fifth day of the sixth month in 1379 (earth female sheep). His mortal remains were properly cremated, and countless deity images, seed syllables, and pearl relics, and so forth were retrieved. A silver reliquary called Jangchub Chenmo was constructed as an inner representation, and a large image of Śākyamuni in the form Great Sage Meaningful to Behold was constructed as an outer representation, and so forth. The blessings of the funerary offerings greatly multiplied.[448]

By the rain of inexhaustible doctrine, cascading
From the cloud of virtuous provisions,
Acquired through the array of this biography
And created in the mental disposition that is the ocean of the disciples,
May the harvest of maturation come to ripen!

Tashi Peltsek, Ninth in the Abbatial Succession

Noble white beryl vase of ethical discipline,
Well filled with the musk[449] of perfect meditative stability
and discernment,
Peerless dispeller of afflictions of the rebirth process,
Homage to the feet of Venerable Tashi Peltsek!

This lord-protector, whose full flowering name was Gyelwang Tashi Peltsek Nyimei Sungwei Gocha, was born at Daryul Tengkhang in 1359 (earth female pig).[450] His father was the great patron Kunga Yeshe, and his mother was Jampel Kyi. He was the older of two brothers. While he was in his mother's womb, she dreamed {366} that there was a mountain of precious gems supported by surrounding grassland, that there was a bridge spanning a river, and that various musical instruments were playing. When his mother brought him to meet Choje Ratnākara, who was on his way to the north, the latter conferred the hand empowerment upon him and blessed his body, speech, and mind, predicting that he would become an object of worship for many beings.[451]

Even while in his fourth and fifth years, and so forth, all his childhood play exclusively had a pure mode of expression, as if explaining and practicing the sacred doctrine and the like. He learned how to write and read without difficulty. Then, relying on Geshe Rinchen Pelwa who possessed the glorious attributes of learning, dignity, and nobility, he received and mastered the three tantras of *Hevajra*, along with their pith instructions, the textual commentary on *The Introduction to the Conduct of a Bodhisattva*, the treatises on human behavior, the cycle of Vaiśravaṇa, and so forth.

In his seventeenth year, in 1375 (wood female hare), he was ordained as a mendicant with Choje Namkha Pelzang acting as preceptor and the elder Rinchen-o acting as master of ceremonies. He was given the name Tashi Peltsek Nyimei Sungwei Gocha, in conformity with a prophecy that Choje Rikden Chenpo (Namkha Pelzang) had received in a dream, and he became one who maintained the three trainings.[452]

In the presence of his precious predecessor, Tashi Peltsek received many steps of maturational empowerment, headed by the seven empowerments required for the entry of beginners in the maṇḍala of glorious Kālacakra, along with the three higher supreme empowerments and the fourth in its mundane and supramundane aspects, as well as the conclusive empowerment of great embodiment as an adamantine master.[453] {367} Along with these, he excellently received all the cycles of guidance of profound meaning, including The Profound Innermost Path of the Oceanic Tantras,[454] which integrates the Six Doctrines of Nāropā and the Great Seal, *The Mind Training according to the Great Vehicle*,[455] *The Direct Guidance of Mahākāruṇika*,[456] *The Five Stages of the Secret Assembly*,[457] the Six-Limbed Yoga, *The Extremely Unelaborate Phase*,[458] and the Path and Its Fruit.[459] In the perspective of others, he experientially cultivated these cycles in the correct manner, and by doing so, he perfected renunciation and realization and manifested the attainment of receptiveness with respect to the level of integration.[460] In addition, he completed an infinite number of studies, the titles of which cannot even be mentioned, concerning the sūtras, tantras, and commentaries, along with their liberating and maturational pith instructions.

Choje Rikden Chenpo Kunpang then informed Tashi Peltsek that he would enter into the absorption in the expanse and unlimited meditative stability, relying on the ascetic discipline of the three isolations of body, speech, and mind.[461]

Consequently, in his eighteenth year, on the eighth day of the first month in 1376 (fire male dragon), auspicious flowers were offered, enthroning Tashi Peltsek as master of the Buddhist teaching. Then, in his twentieth year, in 1378 (earth male horse), Tashi Peltsek journeyed to Lhasa in the lower Kyichu region. When one and two-quarter mansions had passed on the sundial in the afternoon of the fifteenth day of the waxing half of the month of Kārtikka, he excellently received the precepts of a fully ordained monk in the presence of Jowo Rinpoche, the representative image of the Teacher in the Great Emanational Temple of Lhasa, with Jangchub Tsemo, the peerless great translator and learned and accomplished emanation of Virūpa, acting as preceptor; Lochen Drakpa Gyeltsen acting as master of ceremonies; and Lotsāwa Namkha Zangpo acting as confessor and timekeeper, in the midst of a devout monastic community including master Jomo Tongyel.[462] {368} So it was that with regard to all activities associated with the Buddhist teaching, he became a promoter of enlightened activities who was no different from the Teacher himself. He received inconceivable empowerments, transmissions, and pith instructions from those preceptors and masters.

While he was receiving the Kālacakra empowerment from Lochen Jangtse, Tashi Peltsek had a long-lasting vision of the lama as Kālacakra, in the form of the buddha body of perfect resource. At that time, the secret name conferred on him by the mediational deity was Pelchok Dangpoi Dorje Rinpoche.

At the time when Kunpang Rinpoche fell ill, Tashi Pelstek performed extensive acts of service, attending on his behalf, and afterward, when the lama had passed into nirvāṇa, he cremated the mortal remains. In the course of the funerary ceremonies, he made an unimaginable number of offerings. The bone relics were at first inserted within a cubit-high silver reliquary, and that too was inserted within the Great Enlightenment Stūpa, fashioned of forty measures of silver. Nowadays, it is housed at the center of the Old Offering Chapel.[463]

As a representation of buddha body, Tashi Peltsek commissioned a relief image known as Meaningful to Behold, which was created according to the understanding of cotton-drawn images presented in *The Root Tantra of Mañjuśrī*.[464] The central image depicting the transcendent lord Buddha was twenty-four hands in height, and those depicting Maitreya and Mañjuśrī on either side were two-thirds of that in height. On the back screen of the throne, there were two nāga kings, sixteen bodhisattvas, eight hermit buddhas, eight pious attendants, two divine princes, and a host of sages, along with the arrays of the buddha fields of wrathful Yamāntaka, Tārā, and so forth. When the rear curtain was attached, Rinpoche himself touched it with his staff and said, "Cut it here!" There was a stone handle for each of the incisions, and these were fastened to the garuḍa at the top, so they had no difficulty hanging it.[465] {369} He performed the consecration on the thirteenth day of the first autumn month. In the Old Offering Chapel, he commissioned images and many volumes of texts inscribed in gold and silver, and an acacia reliquary for sacred bone relics. Then, when the large army of Desi Phakmodrupa poured into Penyul, they reprimanded the people of Gyama. They in turn were subdued by the Drigungpa who backed the people of Gyama. So Tashi Peltsek went there, unable to tolerate the outbreak of a period of chaos.[466] With fine gifts and advice, he first negotiated a military disengagement and later convened an excellent meeting. At that time, when Dzongji Gyeltsen Zangpo of Drigung was preparing to throw five hundred loads of poisonous aconite into the lake at the old dzong, he averted that catastrophe through his injunctions, and the aconite was buried underground. He also brought about a reconciliation between both the Drigungpa and General Rapa of Phakmodru. Journeying on to the highlands of upper Jang, he established innumerable sentient beings in maturation and liberation. He spared many thousands of animals destined for slaughter by paying their price.

On returning to Taklung, he established the boundaries of a retreat, such that no one would cross the outer and inner thresholds of the Offering Chapel for seven years. During that time, he gave teachings exclusively in terms of experiential guidance on many profound systems of guidance, including the Five Stages, the Great Seal and the Six Doctrines, and *The Introduction to the Conduct of a Bodhisattva*. All the regulations of Choje

Kuyalwa and the charter of the monastic assembly were observed strictly and even more precisely than before.[467] The entire congregation also maintained the three vows; relied on the threefold isolation of body, speech, and mind; and focused exclusively on inner yoga.

In no way did he transgress the series of symbolic and nonsymbolic meditative commitments over the course of a single day or the ways in which positive rites should be conducted during sessions of practice. {370} Even during the night, he changed seats without untying his waist belt. From time to time, he would simply change his lower robe completely. Formerly, it was not allowed to bring meat just inside the precincts of the monastery, but later in this period, he proscribed the carrying of meat specifically into each of the temples and into the monastic estate. In the assembly hall and so forth, a single recitation of *The Transcendent Perfection of Wisdom in Twenty-Five Thousand Lines* was permitted, but a single recitation of the longer and more time-consuming version in *One Hundred Thousand Lines* was not permitted. He repaired the old murals[468] of all the temples.

Tashi Peltsek was then invited by the people of Magsar and Jamo. He traveled to the north and conferred maturational empowerments on countless disciples. At that time, Taklung Lotsāwa had a vision of Rinpoche, his body in the form of Śākyamuni, which lasted for five days. He composed a eulogy in three stanzas and included it among the observances of his own meditative commitments. To others, also, he said, "It is our good fortune to meet in person such a perfect buddha!"

On returning to Taklung, Rinpoche Tashi Peltsek inaugurated one hundred recitations of *The Transcendent Perfections of Wisdom in One Hundred Thousand Lines* and one billion recitations of *The Fourfold Rite of Tārā*.[469]

On the day when the great preceptor Śākseng, incumbent of the monastic seat of Draknak in Ngari, first met him, he momentarily saw Rinpoche in the form of Four-Armed Avalokita.[470]

Rinpoche sent offerings to Puṣpahari Monastery in Kashmir, to Svayambhu in Nepal, to the Jowo image of Kyirong, and to the incumbent of the monastic seat of Chi Lhepa, Jangchub-o. As an indication that these had been received, he dreamed of himself wearing a precious headdress, from which rays of light were diffused.[471] Then, he made offerings to the lamas, masters, and monasteries of Tibet, which contained the three representations of buddha body, speech, and mind and had monastic communities, headed by the temples that had been constructed by the three ancestral religious kings, {371} and by the great residences of the Kagyu lineage.[472]

He also extensively donated sacraments of offering to Wutai Shan, to the sandalwood Jowo image, and to Minyak Ghei Lhakhang in China,[473] and he inaugurated pure aspirational prayer ceremonies. He bestowed fine gifts on all the patrons of the Buddhist teaching, including the emperor of China.[474] To each patron and priest, he sent a communiqué concerning precepts that would bring about immediate and long-term spiritual and temporal well-being. So it was that all those who saw or heard him determined that he was an emanation of the supreme buddhas.

For four years, he remained undistracted, exclusively in genuine meditative equipoise. When he had a severe illness, he carried it on the path by means of the common savor. On meeting the glorious Sakyapa Tekchen Choje Kuntrepa, he received countless doctrines of the Sakya tradition and of the Shang tradition.[475]

Consequent on the civil unrest caused by Desi Phakmodrupa, the whole of U and Tsang had been greatly disrupted, apart from the Taklungpas.[476] In particular, when the army of Drigung, Gyama, and Draknel arrived, Tashi Peltsek went in person to remonstrate and secured the peace. Traveling to Lhasa, he was met by Kongting Gushri Drakpa Gyeltsen of Phakmodru, who took a liking to him.[477] When Rinpoche made offerings and aspirational prayers to Jowo Śākyamuni, the gilded roof of the Great Emanational Temple was covered with a network of rainbow light. He also went to Ramoche, Drakla Lupuk at Potala, Tsel Gungtang, and elsewhere, and made offerings. When he gave teachings at Yerpa, there was a shower of flowers.[478]

When he returned to Taklung, he first placed a silver lamp fashioned of four measures of silver, along with provisions for the upkeep of the lamp, in the temple. {372} Observing the crucial mound of auspicious circumstances, he commissioned a human-size image of Glorious Taklung Tangpa and had it carried into the new Offering Chapel at Daklha Gampo. He presented sacraments of offering including a golden lamp to the Yizhin Norbu image. He also made offerings to Chenga Chokyi Senge, who was staying at that residence, and received instruction from him.[479]

When an envoy of the Chinese emperor, with the support of Khyungpo, informed him that a Chinese army would come to Tibet, Tashi Peltsek's heart could not bear the impending terror, and so he set out for Khyungpo.[480] First, at Reteng, he offered a pearl necklace and so forth to the image of Jowo Mañjuvajra, and inspected the Sanskrit manuscripts that were housed there. He also delivered a public teaching.[481] On the way, he was then invited by the Barompa and visited their monastery.[482] Inconceivable donations and service was offering by the people of Shopo and Jamo, as well as by the three districts of Bel, Ser, and Tsen. At Kangzhung in Shak, when he gave teachings, the sky was filled with rainbows, and there was a shower of flowers.[483]

He then offered most awesome gifts in Khyungpo, and liberated that faction through his advice, whereupon he was given all of their surplus merchandise, weighing one hundred and twenty thousand *sang*, headed by eleven official certificates of provenance. He also bestowed fine gifts on the imperial envoy, on his companion who had come to U and Tsang to collect donations, and on all the merchants who were there. So it was that he established a secure and lasting platform for discussion. All the hostilities between Drigung and Khyungpo, Gare and Khyungpo, Bel and Sok, and so forth were pacified. The material offerings that were then presented by the people of Khyungpo, Gare, Drosho, Naksho, Bo Sok, and elsewhere filled the entire valley. He bestowed on them the magnificent gift of the sacred doctrine. {373} Countless persons undertook to make one hundred million recitations of the six-syllable mantra, and pledged that they would renounce the killing of living creatures, in general and in particular. There were a great many who also offered to release living creatures from certain death. To thieves who had come to steal riding horses and had been apprehended by the horse herders, he gave whatever food and property they wanted and let them go.[484]

When he was invited by Duensha Konchok Zangpo, he reached the central parts of Magsar and Jamo and gave all the offerings he had to the destitute. He presented great gifts to fishermen, cutting off the course of their negative actions.[485]

After remaining there for approximately nine months, Tashi Peltsek returned to Taklung. There, he commissioned cotton paintings of the sixteen sublime elders as a meditative commitment, and when he performed the consecration, that night the master Yonrin (Yonten Rinpoche) dreamed that most of the elders were traveling through the sky, riding on dragons, and vanishing into their respective painted scroll.[486] He commissioned innumerable cotton paintings such as these.

When the Kagyu College was under construction, he said to the artist Tashi Gyeltsen, "If you meet Situ Genpo of Gyama, I think you should withdraw from your weekly tax obligation with him. There's to be no meeting with him starting this morning! Even Gyamawa himself does not know what will come to pass." The following year, there was civil unrest among the people of Gyama, and Situ died.[487]

Tashi Peltsek commissioned countless stūpas and images of cast metal, of beaten metal, of medicinal clay, and of carved wood. Through many extraordinary artifacts depicting the three representations of buddha body, speech, and mind, which were distinguished by his blessing, including the ivory image of the bodhisattva Maniratna, who had been the meditative commitment of the great brahmin Saraha,[488] {374} he performed acts of service and made offerings that delighted those into whose hands they fell, time and time again. His compositions were also voluminous, including biographies, prayers, oral instructions, official letters, aspiration prayers, maṇḍala rites of attainment, and guidance manuals. All of these works exclusively reveal the profound and vast meanings, with brevity of expression. They are of use to those seeking liberation and most beneficial for the continuity of the Buddhist teaching. In order to take into his following many disciples of good fortune, his acts as a preceptor of the full monastic ordination and as vajra master of empowerment were indescribable.

On one occasion, he traveled to Mongolia at the invitation of Jampon Senge of Mongolia. On the way, at Kong Monastery, he acted as preceptor during the full monastic ordination of Lama Namkha Peltsek Gyelpo. At Ong Yetak, he delivered teachings on the generation of the mind that is set on enlightenment, and a shower of flowers fell. There were a great many people who pledged not to kill living creatures, and he established reconciliation between Mongolia and Xixia. Then, after teaching in the northeast, in order to deter Drigung Dzongji's military preparations in Rongpo, he went there. In ways such as these, he was indeed untiring.[489]

On his return to Taklung, Khen Lotsāwa asked him to bless a three-dimensional maṇḍala of the Adamantine Expanse (Vajradhātu).[490]

Then, he set out again to visit Samye, Densatil, and so forth. On the way, the Nyenpowa and the Minyak were opposed to one another, but he gave gifts and oral advice, whereupon the senior elders said they could not contradict his injunctions. However, the majority did not listen and made preparations for war. As the conflict drew near, he arrived at the frontline of the battle, without wavering from the meditative stability of great loving-kindness, and simply on seeing his body, the malice of all the combatants was assuaged. {375} Without having to impart oral advice, the warring factions themselves dissipated. Although a ringleader of the Nyenpowa faction had to be handed over to Minyak, he arranged a peaceful settlement, cajoling them with gifts and injunctions. The Nyenpowa presented him with offerings and acts of service out of gratitude and requested a public teaching.[491]

He then struck camp and gradually headed across Gokar Pass.[492] At the Utse Temple in Samye, he saw the three representations of buddha body, speech, and mind, and he made offerings and aspirational prayers. While going to visit the sacred place of Chimphu, many people saw him moving without his feet touching the ground.[493] The next morning, after they reached lower Do, the attendants first went to collect his sleeping tent. There was a crowd of people from Nedong, larger than expected,[494] so Tashi Peltsek said, "We will not reach the ferry crossing for a while." And they remained there at the campsite for a long time. Then, when they did reach the river bank, there was a line of pack horses with loads of sacred artifacts moving through a gulley. Rinpoche himself went uphill to inspect them, and the attendants followed. The first arrivals had pitched their sleeping tents in the middle of the sand and said that they would have to pass midday there because the ferry boat was stuck hard[495] and could not be dislodged. Rinpoche ate some bread and, immediately after that, drank some tea and poured the remainder on the ground. Then he said, "All the attendants should buckle and roll up the tents." While they were rolling the sleeping tents, an official named Yungdrung Pel swiftly appeared with two servants, saying, "The boat has been dislodged from its hard mooring. There is a danger that the boat will sway. A long time has passed since his excellency the king arrived at Changling Drubzhi to receive you on the south bank of the river. {376} There is also a line of monks from the four communities[496] who are waiting, so please go as quickly as possible!" A group composed of the teacher and students paid the boatman's fee, and the boatman said, "Although it is late in the afternoon, there is no swaying today." An attendant said, "That is due to the kindness of the lama himself!" "This late in the day, we have never gone to Ngamsho without swaying." When they were preparing for the last ferry crossing, the boat did sway, but they reached the south bank on time.

Tashi Peltsek was welcomed by the ruler Drakpa Gyeltsen and his entourage, along with a line of monks from the four communities, and they proceeded to the palace of Neudongtse. The acts of service and offerings that were respectfully presented were inconceivable. He went to visit Tradruk and distributed an extensive cloud of offerings. Wherever he taught the sacred doctrine, there was a shower of flowers. Wherever he went, the place was connected with a net of rainbow light. On the way, he was invited to Tsetang and then proceeded to Densatil, where he presented offerings to the representations of buddha body, speech, and mind and made most awesome donations of tea and alms to the monks. The residents of Til, for their part, also undertook measureless offerings and acts of service on his behalf. He went to the Taklung Cave at Densatil and taught the sacred doctrine, saying "This trap of rebirth is most terrifying. I think that this cave is even more so than that!"[497]

They continued on to Lhasa via Drak.[498] When he was invited to Ratsak Jomo, and undertook self-empowerment in the maṇḍala of Jetsunma, his sleeping tent was shrouded in red light.[499]

Then, on the return journey to Taklung, he went to see the sacred place of Langtang. When he was invited to Gyabdrak and taught the sacred doctrine, there was a shower of five-colored flowers that resembled dust falling. On reaching Taklung, he brought about a reconciliation between the Drigungpas and Rongpo. He was presented with offerings by the Chinese official Hu Dacheng and others.[500] {377} When another official offered him an excellent ball of tea, he knew that Tokden Shonak Gyawo was envious and said, "Gyawo! Take this tea of yours!" Gyawo ran away in shame, but an attendant pursued him outside, bringing the tea, and placed it inside the fold of his robe.On another occasion, he knew that Gomo Choje Zangpo Pelwa and Lama Gyeltsen Zangpo both had bowls full of tea and curd but no butter and were discussing which was better. Then he summoned them into his presence, and after giving a lump of molasses[501] to other guests, as he continued laughing, he brought those two each some butter and vegetables. On one occasion, he said, "We should make this tradition that rests upon a tanned deerskin hide excellent and long-lasting!" and he went downstairs. Attached to a ceiling beam, there was a blue ceramic vase from the time of Venerable Kuyalwa, filled with many sacraments that would ward off the harmful effects of fire in the temple. So he said, "Secure a long ladder that leads directly to it!" Knowing in his mind that the handle of this vase had broken and was about to fall off, he said, "I'll change it!" Accordingly, the cook climbed the ladder, and simply by holding the vase with his hand, it broke off by itself and the new replacement handle was directly attached.

When he fell severely ill due to pollution, he distributed tea and alms to all the monasteries of Utsang. Two hundred and fifty monks worked hard for three years to dust the volumes of the scriptures that were there, such that the task was excellently completed, and he bestowed fine patronage.[502]

Formerly, in the land of Menzhang Mustang, there was a custom of cremating six or seven people alive along with the corpse of each person who had died. Chung Jadrelwa had manifested many signs of spiritual accomplishment and persuaded those people to discontinue that ritual, and so they interrupted it for thirty years. {378} Afterward, Tashi Peltsek's precious predecessor had sent a hillman there, and they offered a pledge to abstain from that practice for a further twelve years. The present lord of Taklung, Tashi Peltsek, then sent Lama Jampel Senge, who taught the sacred doctrine, to the Ṭhakur of Menzhang. He bestowed blessings, representations of buddha body, speech, and mind, and empowerments, and he also gave presents to the two ministers Vimala and Thirumala, and he made a proclamation. Accordingly, the king Ṭhakur replied, "In general, from the time of Maṅgalaguru, the protectors of Menzhang have been the Taklungpa. This Taklung Rinpoche of the present day in particular is one who possesses extrasensory powers and the great enlightened attributes of meditative stability. In the treasure doctrines of Maṅgalaguru, it is also said that the ninth lineage holder will bring forth a great wave of compassionate spirituality. Therefore, I am abandoning our custom of the "fire circle of life." Thereupon, Lama Jamseng attached the protective amulet of Cintāmaṇicakra to the body of the king's son, who had succumbed to a severe illness. By praying to Taklung Rinpoche, he recovered within three days. Rejoicing, the king said he would abandon the custom of the circle of fire in its entirety. In proximity to the golden reliquary and statue of Chung Jadrelwa, he swore this oath, with four great brahmins, including Chandhohari Brahmin, acting as witnesses. He also gave much gold to one named Menlungpa, turning him away from the practice of the circle of fire. The king Nyungti Ratna also abandoned this ancient, pre-Buddhist practice.[503] Carrying an abundance of offerings from Mustang, when that lama Jampel Senge came into the presence of Taklung Tashi Peltsek, there was a tea-maker holding a white square cloth in his hand. "Will he give such a cloth as this and such tea as this to me?" he wondered. Knowing this, Rinpoche presented him with a porcelain cup full of tea and a cloth such as that one. {379}

At that time, Da Ming Cheng Zu, emperor of China, sent his Indian envoy, the imperial minister Xiguang and others to bring offerings to Taklung,[504] and Tashi Peltsek accepted the offerings that were presented, along with the following imperial decree: "We think that all of your enlightened attributes, Taklung Rinpoche, are unlike those of others. Relying on the power of the truth of the sacred doctrine, among those who practice the sacred doctrine, you are handsome and supreme, inducting all persons into the path of virtuous actions. You are the protector of the empire. You are assuredly worthy of praise!"

When he was on the way to the hot springs in Nangong, he had visions of divine princes. When he taught guru yoga in the cave of Karleb Dzom Puk, there were immeasurable blessings endowed with splendor. Having been invited to the grass hermitage of Tsamla Tsonlekpa at Taklung, when he blessed the Neten Lhakhang with consecrated barley, in the space directly above the images of the deities, there were about fifty grains of barley that stuck together, as if bound by a rope, and remained like that for one year.[505] He said that he knew Lama Nangompa had passed away in China. They waited a long time for the word of travelers arriving quickly from China to receive them, doubting that they would come, but when they did swiftly come, the news was clearly correct. Then Rinpoche said, "About one year from now, we will flee away." Just as he said, even more than that would transpire.[506]

Lama Dewa Zangpo invited him to Tsibar Jamokyil. At Tokar Zhung, he taught the sacred doctrine, and all the bones of his dead riding horse, named Trichok, turned into pearl relics. Tashi Peltsek remained in retreat for a long period of time on the roof of the Main Temple at Taklung. On one occasion, he said, "There is a great disaster that will befall this kingdom of Tibet." He then undertook major ritual ceremonies {380} and encouraged all the lamas, officials, laity, and monastics of the region to perform rites of service. He said, "In this Offering Chapel, everything will disintegrate into ruins." Then, during the eleventh day of the ninth month of the hare year (1411), he went downstairs. He inspected all the representations of buddha body, speech, and mind, straightened them, and placed all the unstable shelves for the offering utensils on the floor. Then he said, "It seems that there will be a disturbance in the bookshelves at the doorway of the Old Protector Chapel." And, "If this mural depicting the array of the buddha fields of yoga tantra on the north wall below the gilded roof falls off, I would like to replace it." And, "Won't that torma of Uṣṇīṣa collapse?" That night, around midnight, there was a great earthquake, and at daybreak, it became even more intense. Many houses were destroyed. The east wall of the Offering Chapel, about five or six armspans in length, and the parapet above the door collapsed. From the doorway of the Old Protector Chapel there was a crashing sound of approximately fifty volumes of scripture. The plaster also fell off the area below the gilded roof, covered by the mural depicting the array of buddha fields, and it is said that the torma of Uṣṇīṣa also collapsed.[507]

He set up a camp to the rear of the Kumbum Stūpa and stayed there. Even now, he strove to engage the community in ritual service. "None of the monks should sleep indoors!" he said. On the evening of the fifteenth day, there was another large earthquake. Since the place was permeated by his compassionate spirituality, no further damage could be inflicted. Elsewhere, the mountains crumbled, lakes burst open, valleys were sealed, the earth itself was greatly fissured, and innumerable animals died. Such losses were unimaginable. While staying behind the Kumbum Stūpa for one and a half months, in the evenings, lay officials would visit the monastery, and once they had left, a large herd of mountain sheep would come down into the midst of the camp. {381} Rinpoche would go back and forth among them and move them onward, swinging his rosary, and then some of the mountain sheep would play with his robe and follow him. He would drink cool water on the high grasslands and sit there, eating tsampa from his pouch[508] and so forth. The repairs to the monastery were carried out during the following summer.

When Tekchen Choje Kunga Tashi was on his way to have an audience with the emperor Ming Chengzu, they met and exchanged gifts.[509] Then, Tashi Peltsek said, "A large group of travelers will arrive from this eastern direction. A reception party will also have to go this year to Rong." Just so, a large group of envoys and travelers headed by Hutāzhidrak[510] arrived via the "easy route" and the reception party had to travel as far as Rong.[511] He accepted a letter and representations of buddha body, speech, and mind from the emperor Ming Chengzu and Tekchen Choje, patron and priest.

Then he said, "Within the next year, there will be an auspicious event securing the good health of Choje Kunga Tashi." After about two months, a messenger arrived saying that Chojepa had reached Sok. He dispatched someone to serve tea, and they had a meeting. Then, as Tashi Peltsek traveled toward the south, when three days had passed, he remarked, "It seems that Chojepa's pet parrot has been lost." When Chojepa received that report, the parrot was indeed lost.

In front of the White Temple at Taklung, Tashi Peltsek then renovated the Neten Lhakhang. The murals were principally in accord with the chapter on the ten levels from *The Sūtra of the Great Bounteousness of the Buddhas*,[512] including the depiction of the transcendent lord Buddha seated in the celestial palace of Norbu Dampa, the abode of the powerful king of the gods; and the depictions of the alms bowl offered by the four great kings, the milk gruel offered by Sujāṭā, and the honey offered by Trapuṣa, {382} as well as the sublime elders. Other murals depicted *The Prophetic Declaration of Maitreya*,[513] *The Narrative of Nindimitra*,[514] *The Sūtra of the Prophetic Declaration of the Elders*,[515] and *The Tracts on Spiritual Attainment by Chim*.[516]

The folds of the robes, the background, the attendant figures, and so forth were extraordinary, in accordance with the Chinese tradition. Along with them, he commissioned murals depicting the great layman Dharmatāla, the Chinese Hoshang, and the four great kings. The consecration was held in conjunction with extensive gifts and patronage, and he established the auspicious circumstances that would enable the monastic community of this great monastic seat to expand like a lake in summer.

Even when he was severely ill, Tashi Peltsek did not mistake the correct order of his symbolic and nonsymbolic meditative commitments. Even when he sat in sunlight, moonlight, or the glow of a butter lamp, his body cast no shadow. Without opening the door of a room, he could go in or out without impediment. Even in the middle of winter, the water in a vase placed alongside him did not freeze. His body exuded the fine fragrance of ethical discipline, such that articles that had been placed alongside him for a day retained it, without it fading for a month. There are a great many stories exemplifying his noble robes.[517] When the Mongolian Jampel Sonam Gyeltsen was captured by the Rongpo, they took off his armor, and although they struck him many times with their swords, he was unharmed because he was wearing a vest that had belonged to Rinpoche.

The nobility of that region and even stern Mongolian and Chinese envoys became humble, without bravado, when they arrived in his presence.[518] If there was someone who strove to practice the sacred doctrine, free from activities, he would bestow the profound and vast teaching completely, despite the lack of material offerings.

From his eleventh year until he passed into nirvāṇa, {383} he did not permit meat or wine to touch his tongue. He even partook of foods such as the three dairy products[519] in the correct manner. While he was alive, his body maintained a lustrous complexion. Simply by seeing all things once, he comprehended them without forgetfulness. He focused exclusively on commissioning representations of buddha body, speech, and mind, on making offerings, teaching, making respectful donations to the monastic community, and so forth. Generally, he remained in retreat and, for the most part, gave teachings and guidance from the White Temple. In order that he might serve as an example to others, he acted virtuously at all times and, apart from that, did not even for an instant adopt an ordinary perspective. He undertook many acts of generosity on behalf of the local community and the monastery. Wherever sentient beings were afflicted by suffering, when he heard that, his heart could not bear it, and he undoubtedly would try to dispel that suffering. He had visions of innumerable buddha fields and meditational deities. He accomplished all enlightened activities directly through the agency of many doctrinal protectors, including the great king Vaiśravaṇa. Infinite were the acts he performed on behalf of many arrays of physical beings and also nonhuman beings, and so forth. At those times, in order that the monastic assembly might thrive like rivers of summertime, all his disciples exclusively adopted as their essential practice the attainment of the three isolations of body, speech, and mind. For example, for three years and three months, they engaged progressively in the visualization cycle of the Six Doctrines. For six years, they adopted the approach of meditative equipoise, and for three years, they engaged in the conduct associated with post-meditation. So it is said that the course of his experiential guidance was designated as completed after twelve years.

Again, on a certain occasion, he went to meet a powerful official of Drigung, after which he said that a minor miracle would occur. Some days later a meteor struck the summit of Tanglhazo, {384} but due to his exorcism, it scattered into pieces, and nothing came to pass except that small blue-gray fragments of iron were found everywhere.

Bon travelers also made great offerings to him and requested a doctrinal connection, whereupon he said, "Henceforth you should take care!" They encountered an earth spirit[520] in Penyul, in consequence of which the Bonpo were defeated by the people of Dome.[521]

That autumn, he said, "It seems that there is a malign nonhuman spirit in the vanguard of a large party of travelers coming from the east." He organized ritual ceremonies, and some days later, a large party of Chinese travelers arrived, headed by two imperial ministers.Then, the ruler Drakpa Gyeltsen sent Tashi Tsekpa an insistent letter, requesting him to preside over the rows of monks conducting the funeral of the late Chenga Rinpoche Sonam Zangpo.[522] Since the monks of Densatil also insisted that he should go, he did set out for Densatil. The entire reception party was arranged by Drakar Ringyelwa. The ruler Drakpa Gyeltsen received him at half a day's march, and the next day, they reached Densatil. The sky was filled with three complete rainbows in the form of a gateway with an arched pediment, and about four or five half rainbows of that sort, as well as various others that were round, semicircular, square, and so forth. Some saw Rinpoche riding up to the edge of the rainbows, as if on an extended white blanket. He presided over the rows of the great assembly. The offerings and alms that were distributed surpassed the imagination. At this time, he stayed in Til for four days. When the second day had passed, as he was about to depart for Yang Gon Nangso[523] to have a midday meal, he set out saying, "All the days are auspicious! All the stars are excellent! {385} We will be very busy today!" After the midday meal, he sat in meditation for a while and later said, "Prepare some tea in an isolated hermitage. You should invite all the preceptors, masters, and meditators of Densatil, young and old, and I will make a show of offering them tea here. Arrange a high seat for Choje Sonam Gyeltsen and spread out my red carpet on it. My attendants should invite him to be seated upon it." When Choje had taken his seat, Rinpoche made large offerings to him and said, "Lord Phakmodrupa, the emanation of Buddha Krakucchanda, acted for the benefit of infinite living creatures in this location. After him, Kyura Rinpoche and so forth nurtured the residence in succession. Now, you should be the regent and guide an infinite number of disciples. Your compassionate spirituality and enlightened activity will not be inferior to those of your predecessors!" Choje replied, "I shall do as you have commanded!" Flowers of benediction were scattered. So it was that this supremely perfect buddha, Choje Sonam Gyeltsen, who had been enthroned as master of the Buddhist teaching, nurtured the residence of Densatil from 1417 (fire female bird) to 1434 (wood male tiger), with a mind that did not discriminate between positive and negative or agreeable and disagreeable discussions with regard to all matters, whether minor or major.[524] In accordance with that prophetic declaration, he sustained in a peerless manner the spiritual and temporal well-being of the Buddhist teaching and all sentient beings without exception, and his marvelous deeds and enlightened activities were indeed greater than those of his predecessors.

The newly appointed Chenga Rinpoche then said to Tashi Peltsek, {386} "Now, owing to your busy schedule and the like, we are unable to request you to stay here for a long time. But in the future, we shall invite you to confer your experiential guidance, so please come back by whatever means!" Tashi Peltsek declined.

The ruler Drakpa Gyeltsen escorted him a short distance to Jasa Dongwa. Then on the way back to Taklung via Ngamsho, the Neudong Dzongpa made offerings to him out of respect. And in Penyul he had a meeting with Minyak.[525] When he reached the hot springs of Nang Gong, the practitioners of Severance in that place perceived that for about one month all the spirit lords of that locality were gathered together and the place was cleansed by sweeping and so forth. A usable hot spring that had not previously been there newly burst forth to one side. They bestowed unimaginable gifts upon him, and he established a reconciliation between Rong and Khyung. He also turned back a large army that the ruler Drakpa Gyeltsen had sent to reprimand Nangso Nelpa. On that occasion, the Chinese Da Ming emperor Cheng Zu, who held authority over the great empire under the sun and was the embodiment of Indra on earth, owing to his power over longevity and heaven, dispatched envoys headed by the four great Nulgon, proclaiming as follows: "Nowadays, among all the lamas and spiritual mentors in the region of U, the one called Taklung Rinpoche Tashi Peltsek resembles the crown ornament." Therefore, we offer him the title of National Preceptor, a silver seal, and an official certificate, along with these representations of buddha body, speech, and mind. The messengers arrived in his presence, and the certificate and the silver seal were inserted within a sandalwood chest, embellished on the outside with inlays of various precious gemstones and the auspicious symbols. {387} Along with these, they offered an ocean-like array of offerings and gifts, resembling those emanated by Samantabhadra, including a gold seal that was restricted because it was hard to classify articles proclaiming the noble imperial edicts; an image of the founder of the Buddhist teaching fashioned of cast gold; offering sacraments; insignia of authority; personal utensils; a silk robe patterned with the design of the wish-fulfilling palanquin, and so forth; many artifacts of crystal, stone, and metal, which were either self-originated or fashioned from precious gems and metals; and exquisite tea that had not previously been known. In order to bring forth the greatness of the imperial edict, he accepted in his lotus hands the image of the Buddha, the certificate, and the silver seal. In general, this lord of the earth, Yongle, developed measureless faith in Taklung Rinpoche because he had heard of his reputation. By virtue of that, he intentionally dispatched those offerings, but there was nothing at all that Rinpoche accepted with an ulterior motive. So it was very special.[526]

Tashi Peltsek's own nature is reflected in the rank of Anointed National Preceptor.[527] The label of the silver seal also reads National Preceptor of Chengzu,[528] indicating that he was "a great meditator, omniscient imperial teacher, and national preceptor." It is a manifest wonder that the silver seal offered on this occasion and the crystal seal that had previously been offered to Je Ratnākara by the Yuan emperor were both never destroyed in later times, even when fire broke out inside the temple. As far as the destruction inflicted by fire is concerned, even the silk wrapping tied around the crystal seal was not at all damaged by the slightest trace of fire. In exchange for these gifts, he bestowed the perfect gifts of the sacred doctrine and material presents, which the envoys carried back to China.

Tashi Peltsek was invited by nomadic and village communities, of Bel, Ser, and Tsen, of Partang Jamo, of Sok, and so forth and they presented him with offerings. There was an extremely inhospitable place called Nakyi Ruru Namoche where Karmapa Dezhin Shekpa had erected a stone teaching throne.[529] But when he taught the sacred doctrine, a lightning bolt had struck, killing two people. The mountain to the rear was a wild and extremely hostile environment called Shen Jangur, foremost of the thirteen Ngotulchen demons,[530] such that no one could erect a teaching throne there. Tashi Peltsek did, however, erect a teaching throne there, and he taught the sacred doctrine, such that the area became very auspicious and a shower of flowers cascaded. An inconceivable number of offerings were presented to him by the host of living creatures who filled that entire mountain region. Thieves offered up their booty and held him in esteem to the extent that they would henceforth not steal again. There are many such tales of his extrasensory powers.

On returning to Taklung, he immediately fell ill, but through the performance of extensive rites he recovered well. He completed the restoration of the reliquary chambers in each of the three Kumbum stūpas at Taklung.[531] At the invitation of Horkhangpa, he performed the consecration of the Neten Lhakhang at Drangzhi Dzong.[532] Then, Tashi Peltsek enthroned Choje Jangchub Gyatso Pelzangpo at the monastic seat and scattered flowers of good auspices. He said, "When I was taken ill and my mind had been disturbed, due to a strong sense of emancipation from cyclic existence, I gathered the vital energy and mind at the heart and induced them into the central channel of the subtle body. Consequently, in the sky in front, the Kagyu lineage holders appeared, from Vajradhara down to my own root guru. Below them were the divine hosts of the maṇḍala of meditational deities, {389} and alongside them were the buddhas, bodhisattvas, pious attendants, and hermit buddhas. Below them were the ḍāka heroes and ḍākinī heroines, along with the doctrinal protectors. After that I remained pervasive for a long period of time in the great seal."[533]

There was a considerable amount of definitive evidence suggesting that Gyelwa Taklungpa the Great had himself reincarnated as Tashi Peltsek, knowing that it would be for the benefit of the Buddhist teaching and sentient beings. On one occasion, while giving a public teaching, he digressed, saying, "It is said that Taklung Tangpa resembled the earth, Kuyalwa resembled the sky, and Yarjonpa resembled the eyes—that is, they respectively exemplified great responsibility, great tolerance, and precise conduct. Sometimes, I'm sure that I am Taklung Tangpa."[534]

He would speak coherently of many events that were unknown to others, saying, for example, that Drogon Rinpoche Phakmodrupa had predicted that glorious Taklung Tangpa would found the monastery at Taklung and that while he, Taklungpa, was serving as an attendant of Drogon, Kyura Rinpoche Drigungpa had first traveled to Taklung and at that time contributed to the injunction of Drogon and its auspicious circumstance.[535]

He also extensively said that glorious Phakmodrupa had given the monastery called On Tangkar Gonpa to Venerable Taklungpa the Great, that he had owned it until the present, and now offered it to Densatil as an endowment, and that all the excellent auspicious connections between Drigung and Taklung and so forth should be correctly maintained at the great seat of Densatil.

Finally, he succumbed to a cold, and in his sixty-sixth year, in 1424 (wood male dragon), on the nineteenth day of the mid-spring month of Caitra, he passed away. At the time of his death, he was asked, "To whom should we pray?" and he replied, "On the day of the funeral, {390} I will arrive in the sky above the grass hermitage and receive your prayers. The other lamas who have preceded me as incumbents of Taklung will also be present there and receive your prayers in the immaculate eastern direction." He had a vision of countless buddha fields of the ten directions.[536]

Immediately after he passed away, a basin-full of chyle (white generative fluid) emerged from his nostrils. A symphony of divine music resounded. Above his room, everyone saw a white light resembling an erect pillar. Some clearly saw an infinite array of great maṇḍalas, consisting of their containing palaces and the deities contained within them. Following the cremation, four clockwise-spiraling conch shells, his heart, and countless five-colored pearl relics were retrieved. Wherever the smoke from the pyre wafted, a shower of flowers cascaded, their four-petal anthers formed from the pearl relics, and some of them even fell into the teacups of the monks within the assembly. After about a day, the flowers faded, but in their place were pearl relics that remained, and these are nowadays designated as "raining pearl relics."[537] At that time, there was also a cascade of five sorts of precious gems and metals; its flow was filtered by the monks, and later on, some had among their collection of blessed representations five-colored pearl relics of gold, silver, copper, iron, and so forth. When I was a boy, I myself saw a small pouch containing such items.[538] A perfume arose from the smoke of the funeral pyre that was absolutely fragrant, resembling the incense that is a sacrament of the gods. During the cremation and its funeral rites, and at other times, there were many of pure vision who saw Rinpoche's body actually present.

Here, I have fully abridged the actual description of these funeral events, which derives from the work titled *Great Wave of Offerings Acquired Through the Funeral Ceremony That Arose in This Place and in All Directions*,[539] {391} composed by the omniscient Ngagi Wangpo and the awareness holder Tsultrim Pel.[540]

The Disciples of Jetsun Tashi Peltsek

Although the disciples who had gratitude for the teachings of Venerable Tashi Peltsek were countless, roughly speaking, they included (1) his brother Gyeltsab Dampe (Jangchub Gyatso), whose biography is explained in somewhat greater detail below in the context of this continuing narrative of Taklung; (2) Khenchen Zangpo Ozer, the nephew of Taklung Lotsāwa, who possessed the moisture of the nectar of supreme accomplishment, unimpeded in the pulverizing rites of King Pehar and so forth, which can store the oceanic treasures of the texts of the Adamantine Vehicle and its pith instructions; (3) Lachen Jampel Gocha, who was spiritually and materially nurtured by Ongyu Khenchen Lotsāwa of Barlewa and who was a repository of the treasures of the texts and pith instructions, accomplished in holding the three vows, which he received through the kindness of Rinpoche Tashi Peltsek; (4) Jadrel Chenpo Chokyi Gyeltsen, who had attained certainty with respect to the subjects of classical learning and was satiated with the nectar of spiritual accomplishment; and (5) Monlam Peljor, the supreme incarnation who integrated together the guidance and oral instructions of the precious Kagyu lineage and who, in particular, attained all enlightened activities through the agency of adamantine Kākamukha Mahākāla, without transgressing his injunctions and pledges.

The majority of his disciples were saintly beings who upheld the Buddhist teaching throughout the ten directions and who sustained the domain of learning and spiritual accomplishment. Although they were innumerable, they gathered like bees in a flower garden and endeavored to partake of the nectar of Tashi Peltsek's buddha speech.

Jangchub Tsemo

Among all the great promulgators of the Buddhist teaching in this Land of Snows, Jangchub Tsemo, the nephew of Pang Lotsāwa Lodro Tenpa, {392} was peerless in the composition of grammatical treatises that elucidate the enlightened intention.[541] In particular, Lord Vajrasattva and his consort Vajrayoṣit manifestly bestowed the secrets of all the vehicles of the awareness holders upon him, such that he was fearless in commenting on the adamantine verses through his own initiative. These writings were not only drawn from definitive sources among the scriptures and profound pith instructions that inspire confidence, but above all they could be established as acceptable in their own terms through the power of reasoning.

Bodong Chokle Namgyel

The great leader of living creatures—who had many names, including Amarasena, Buddhapālita, and Mañjuśrīkīrti, but who was generally known as the Omniscient Bodong—was indeed a geshe with mastery of the entire Buddhist teaching.[542] In order to satiate the treasury of his inexhaustible intellect in all the philosophical traditions upon the earth, he became a student in all the seminaries of Utsang. In the course of his travels, he reached Taklung. Since Rinpoche Tashi Peltsek's body, speech, and mind were perfect in the enlightened attributes of greatness, Bodong's mind was captivated, and he actually touched Rinpoche's lotus feet. He excellently received *The Coemergent Union with the Great Seal: The Essential Definitive Mystery*,[543] the Six Doctrines of Nāropā, which are the essence of the oceanic classes of unsurpassed yoga tantra, and *The Guidance Manual Titled Garland of White Light*,[544] which was bestowed by embellishing that wish-fulfilling jewel of the Six Doctrines with many precious gems of pith instruction. So it was that, in the manner that grain mash is fermented by yeast, {393} all the rivers of his infinite studies and reflections flowed in a common savor into the ocean of the definitive meaning.

Tsongkhapa Lobzang Drakpa

Similarly, the glorious Tsongkhapa Lobzang Drakpa from the east also touched Rinpoche Tashi Tsekpa's lotus feet and savored the nutritious taste of the nectar of his teaching.[545] Among all the supremely perfect saintly beings in Tibet, the Land of Snows, Tsongkhapa was peerless in the three deeds of the learned—namely, enlightened activities, profuse explanations, and compositions that pertained to the pure Buddhist teaching. In particular, with reference to the sacred doctrine, he applied discrimination with regard to the minor rules of the precepts that concern the refutation, proof, and maintaining of monastic discipline, along with the minor points to be accepted or rejected. He engaged in the definitive experiential cultivation of the gradual path on behalf of persons of lesser, mediocre, and higher acumen, as explicitly indicated in Atiśa's *Lamp for the Path of Enlightenment*.[546] He excellently disclosed the tantra class of the glorious *Secret Assembly*[547] by means of the key of exegesis endowed with the adamantine seal of the six limits and four styles of the scriptures. Even in this degenerate age, the monks who made up his monastic community have exemplified the exegetical tradition of the old and new classes of tantra, the traditions of teaching and study that preceded him. In general, his actions with regard to the entire Buddhist teaching were those of a second buddha. According to reports that have been passed down aurally, the supreme scholar Rendawa[548] and Tsongkhapa, master and student, traveled here to Taklung by chance. At Chak La pass, they had lunch. Then they packed the alms bowl into its pouch, while a sliver of meat remained stuck inside it, and went on their way, carrying it. While they were approaching the temple without hesitation, Rinpoche Tashi Tsekpa sent an attendant, {394} saying, "In your alms bowl there is a small item that is impermissible to bring inside our temple. You should eat it and then come in!" Tsongkhapa thought, "This is a great lie, just like *The Sūtra of the Hundredfold Homage of Renunciation and Fulfillment*! There is nothing at all in my alms bowl that is impermissible to bring into the temple. However, I should inspect it." On examining the bowl, there was a piece of meat. Then he thought, "He does have extrasensory powers. We should just meet him, but I will not request a doctrinal connection, since he will have nothing satisfactory to teach." When they came into his presence, they conversed with him in turn in a tea line. Rinpoche Tashi Tsekpa raised many important questions, starting from the Tathāgata's gateways to liberation, but the master and the student Rendawa and Tsongkhapa were both stifled in their response and, apart from that, had no opportunity to offer any complete answer. Then, he delivered a perfectly profound and vast teaching on all the questions that they asked, commencing with the higher definitive meaning. Also, to the side, he easily and freely elucidated many difficult essential points, such that an uncommon faith and devotion were uncontrollably born in Tsongkhapa's mind. He stayed there for about half a month and received the Six Doctrines of Nāropā. Then, at the time of his departure, Rinpoche said to Venerable Tsongkhapa, "Your enlightened activity will equal the sky! You should benefit the combined teaching of the generation and perfection stages that has descended from Lord Marpa!" It is hard to measure individually these approaches to liberation of the lamas of the precious Kagyu lineage who know the three times.

Changlungpa Zhonu Lodro of Choding

Furthermore, the glorious authentic awareness holder Changlungpa Zhonu Lodro also touched the lotus feet of Rinpoche Tashi Peltsek here at Taklung.[549] He had taught many learned and accomplished masters who appeared within this Buddhist tradition of Dang,[550] the countless sugatas of the three times, {395} and he exemplified those who maintain the glory of learning, dignity, and nobility. Until his hundred and fourth year, he undertook a great wave of activity for the benefit of the Buddhist teaching and sentient beings. From Taklung Tashi Peltsek, he received in the form of experiential guidance the profound oral instructions of the Fivefold Great Seal,[551] the Four Syllables,[552] the Great Seal of Bliss and Emptiness,[553] and the Six Doctrines of Nāropā. Finally, Rinpoche covered Changlungpa's head with a meditation hat that he wore on his own head and that had been imbued with the fragrance of pure ethical discipline.[554] It is said that he bestowed on Changlungpa the empowerments of the oral teachings, saying, "Formerly you performed great deeds on behalf of our teaching tradition. Now again you should do so!" He made a definitive prophetic declaration that this saintly being had previously been Venerable Sangye Yarjon and that in the future he would become the wondrous supreme Tulku Namgyel Tashi.[555]

By the thunderous rain cloud of endeavor and virtuous action in this
place,
Arising from the ocean of untrammeled admiration,
May the harvest of liberation of the Marpa translations[556] ripen
Instantly through the downpour of spiritual and temporal well-being!

Jangchub Gyatso, Tenth in the Abbatial Succession

Verses of Homage

Homage from the heart to this glorious and excellent protector,
Who, bound by the constraints of the three trainings,
Prepared the ship of precious **enlightened** (*byang chub*)[557] mind
And liberated all beings from the **ocean** (*rgya mtsho*) of suffering!

Choje Jangchub Gyatso Tsemo Pelzangpo was born in the district of Penyul in 1403 (water female sheep).[558] His father was the king of the sacred doctrine Rinchen Gyeltsen, who was the younger brother of Gyelwang Tashi Peltsek, and his mother was Minyakza Budren. Without moving from the buddha body of indestructible reality, the expanse of all-pervasive space, he had manifested buddhahood as Garwang Dorjechang, the buddha body of perfect resource, and as the Sugata Konchok Yenlak, the buddha body of emanation.[559] {396} In the abode of Tuṣita, he had manifested as Venerable Lord Maitreya, mighty master of the ten bodhisattva levels. However, from an ordinary perspective, he had been Kholpo Gawa, the disciple of Tilopā; the brahmin Sarvavid, the disciple of Nāropā; Zhonu Sangtsol, the disciple of Venerable Mila Repa; Tsultrim Pel, the disciple of Nyame Dakpo Gampopa; Gelong Namkha-o, the disciple of glorious Taklung Tangpa; and Tashi Drak, the disciple of the supreme emanation Kuyalwa. Then, he had been Drakpa Senge, the first upholder of the banner of the Zhamar tradition, and Pelden Khacho Wangpo, the second in that line.[560] Thus, he had manifested at one and the same time in two distinct emanational forms.[561]

From a young age he excellently perfected all the signs of the enlightened heritage of the Great Vehicle. Even all the details of his childhood play were engaged with the dance of a great wave of bodhisattva conduct. In his tenth year, in 1412 (water male dragon), he arrived at the great seminary of glorious Taklung Dorjeden, where Gyelwa Taklungpa the Great had manifestly attained buddhahood. He was ordained in the Main Temple of Taklung in the midst of an assembly of faithful and virtuous monks, with Tashi Peltsek Nyimei Wangpo Sungwei Gocha, king of the three world systems, acting as preceptor and others, including a master of ceremonies and timekeeper, who all resembled sublime arhats and were summoned to perform the supplementary rites. {397} As a preparation, his personal affirmation concerned the precepts of a layperson and those of an intermediate mendicant. Then, in the actual conferral, he received the vows of the novitiate, having abandoned the four contradictory circumstances[562] and fully acquired the five compatible circumstances.[563] When the subsequent advice was imparted, he affirmed the points that are to be understood and the precepts. Thus he was ordained according to the ancient rite, in which the ritual aspects of the ceremony are endowed with their proper defining characteristics. When he adopted the third transformation of a mendicant, which is the transformation of name, he was given the name Jangchub Gyatso Pelzangpo.[564]

Jangchub Gyatso then attended upon learned masters, and commencing with writing and reading, his mind engaged with all fields of classical learning without exception. Thus, the extraordinary virtue of intellectual brilliance that gathered all these fields of knowledge was instantly born within him. He set his mind on supreme enlightenment, the wondrous higher aspiration that derives from the two great chariots—the lineages of profound view and vast conduct—which he received through the kindness of his precious predecessor Tashi Peltsek, the lord of his enlightened heritage. In addition, he received from the latter all the myriad texts and pith instructions that clearly demonstrate the topics of renunciation, acceptance, engagement, and reversal in accordance with the ways in which bodhisattvas of excellent endowment magnanimously act, as well as the techniques that are purely applied in the symbolic maṇḍala and the empowerments of general meaning that communicate the words of mantra. Then, in particular, he excellently perfected the four empowerments of hidden meaning—namely, (1) the vase empowerment, through which all phenomenal existence arises as the spiritual teacher through the perception of pure admiration; (2) the secret empowerment, through which the generation stage of supreme skillful method integrating radiance and emptiness and the originally pure perfection stage are coalesced; (3) the empowerment of discerning pristine cognition, through which perceptions and sounds arise as the great seal of bliss and emptiness and emanate within the disposition of magical display, disregarding the symbolic methods whereby generative fluids forcefully descend through the central channel from above and are sustained forcefully within the central channel from below; and (4) the fourth empowerment, through which all attributes included within the ground, path, and result are liberated in the expanse of reality that is intrinsic awareness {398} and all attributes such as the three buddha bodies and the five buddha bodies are recognized to be natural arising, originally purified of apprehensions that engage in dualistic rejection, and acceptance.[565]

He also received the infinite details of the guidance of profound meaning, including (1) those definitive methods of guidance such as the gradual path, the sequence of the Buddhist teaching and mind training that actually demonstrates the precious sūtras; (2) those methods of guidance such as the Five Stages, the Four Stages, the Path and Its Fruit, and the Six-Limbed Yoga, which derive from the short path of the supreme way of mantra; and (3) those methods that constitute the Direct Guidance of Cakrasaṃvara, Hevajra, and Avalokiteśvara by means of instructions vomited by accomplished masters.[566]

In particular, among the cycles of pith instruction, the doctrines of the founding fathers of our own Taklung Kagyu lineage, he received in the form of experiential guidance (1) the sap of the ocean of the tantras that radiate like the moon, (2) the essence of the buddha mind of ten million learned and accomplished masters, (3) the heart blood of a hundred thousand ḍākinīs, (4) the authentic instruction that lays bare the intermediate states, (5) the pith instructions that intermingle the three modes of magical display and the three modes of inner radiance titled *Mingling, Transference, and Reincarnation*,[567] *Wish-Fulfilling Gem of the Aural Lineage*,[568] and the Six Doctrines of Glorious Nāropā; (6) the direct demonstration titled *King of Meditative Stability*,[569] which elaborates on the natural sameness[570] of all phenomena, based on *The Sūtra of the King of Meditative Stability*; (7) distinct from that, the indirect demonstration that derives from the entire oceanic piṭakas of the two approaches of the Great Vehicle; and (8) *Coemergent Union of the Great Seal of Definitive Meaning*,[571] which is the sole path traversed by all the buddhas.

As for the way in which he acquired the attributes of clear realization at those times, how could that lie within the perceptual range of ordinary beings such as ourselves? It cannot be fathomed from any quarter of space even by great bodhisattvas who are the offspring of the Conqueror, {399} and it cannot be written down because it lies within the perceptual range of the perfect buddhas. Saintly beings are not satiated by hearing of his attributes. So it was that under the authentic and mighty lord of discriminative awareness named Lachen Mañjuśrīvarman (Jampel Gocha), he received a great many methods of profound meaning, including all the transmissions of the infinite canonical scriptures and treatises, and all the empowerments that confer maturation. Moreover, he also attended on many other spiritual mentors who upheld the glory of learning and accomplishment, and he received from them the inestimable approaches of the profound and vast doctrines.

When he came of age, Jangchub Gyatso then received full ordination in a timely manner. That is to say, he traveled to the peerless great seat of glorious Phakmodru, where Chenga Rinpoche Sonam Gyeltsen Pelzangpo was a great elder, endowed with the five aggregates—namely, the aggregate of ethical discipline, the aggregate of meditative stability, the aggregate of discriminative awareness, the aggregate of liberation, and the aggregate of the uncontaminated vision of liberating pristine cognition. With him acting as the senior preceptor, and with the assistance of two other masters and in the midst of the monastic community in attendance, Jangchub Gyatso excellently received the vows of a fully ordained monk, which is the pinnacle for those who enter into the Buddhist teaching. Instantly, he became a master of the entire teaching, a preceptor of many tens of thousands of monks.

Then, when he was in his twenty-second year, in 1424 (wood female dragon), on an auspicious day at the start of the new year, he was invited to be seated upon the lion throne of Taklung.[572] He donned many particular robes and the meditation hat that is the crown insignia indicative of authority over the precious Kagyu lineage. He was then handed the ruby rosary that had been the meditative commitment of Nāropā; {400} the vajra, bell, and inner offering skull cup of Venerable Marpa; the staff of Venerable Mila Repa; the meditation belt of peerless Gampopa; the representations that guard against disconnection from all the series of buddhas of the authentic lineage; the keys to the library; the sacraments of empowerment; articles of offering; personal items;[573] and so forth. The parasol, the victory banner, the ensign of the lineage, and so forth were raised. He sat alongside Venerable Choje Tashi Peltsek. That is to say, in the forefront of the general assembly—including the preceptors, masters, and monastic officials—his precious predecessor held an extensive enthronement ceremony, with oral injunctions and auspicious predictions, and empowered him as master of the Buddhist teaching.

After a short time, when his precious predecessor passed away into the immaculate expanse, the mortal remains, like a wish-fulfilling gem, were properly cremated through the pure rites that accord with the tantras, and he arrived at the buddha body of reality. Jangchub Gyatso donated offerings for use in the funeral ceremonies. He also made meritorious offerings to communities belonging to the highland region of Ngari, including the bordering valleys of Nepal and Kashmir, and of Tsang; as well as to the communities of U, including the Emanational Temple of Lhasa, Chokhor Samye, Lhodrak, and the monastic seats of Gampo, Densatil, Tsurphu, Drigung, Tsalpa, and Druk; and to all the temples and representations of buddha body, speech, and mind in upper and lower Dokham, China, and so forth, from Riwoche to Wutai Shan. In all the assemblies, he distributed communal tea offerings and alms, and he undertook a great wave of generosity for the sake of living creatures.

Over one day and night, he opened many maṇḍalas pertaining to the classes of tantra, with the assistance of many hundreds of monks, and then, during the ritual offerings and the great funeral rite, he distributed butter and curd to each person in the assembly, consisting of many hundreds of thousands of laypersons and monks. {401}

As for the external representations of buddha body, speech, and mind, he constructed a cast-metal image of Munīndra depicting the turning of the doctrinal wheel of the transcendent perfection of wisdom, with a throne back twenty-five handspans in height, perfect in its fruition and covered with gold extracted from one hundred and fifty gold coins. On the rear curtain, there were depictions of the buddhas of the ten directions, the thousand buddhas of the Auspicious Eon, the sixteen elders, the four pairs of realized persons, the eight types of realized individuals, and the offerings of the wheel and conch that were made respectively by Brahmā and Indra in the presence of the Buddha. The thrones was supported by strong lions, bulls and other figurines, and between them were depictions of gods, antigods, gandharvas, garuḍas, kiṃnaras and so forth, as well as a great many offering deities, the four great kings, the six great cities of India, and so forth. As for its decoration, it was gilded with the gold extracted from sixteen gold coins. The casting of this image was made by Ponmoche Kyabpa whose assistants were about forty in number. The area behind the throne was the work of some eighteen persons, including Gelong Pelden and Pelden Ozer. These artisans excellently performed their tasks, along with a great many miscellaneous craftsmen who inscribed incantations, drew tsakali icons, and so forth. As for their fees, alms, and so forth, from start to finish, Dzongkar Obar and others contributed more than one hundred pieces of armor and three hundred horses, and in addition they sent innumerable varieties of precious things. Gathered together, these were unmistakenly valued at approximately three thousand *sang*. The full-size medicinal images in the row of images depicting the authentic lineage within the Old Offering Chapel were constructed by a sculptor named Gejong Phuntsok.

It is indisputably held that during great ceremonies, he would make the requisite number of lamp offerings. On auspicious occasions, pearl relics were retrieved. {402} A particularly superior manuscript of the Kangyur, inscribed in gold and silver ink on parchment, was commissioned and installed in the grass hermitage. The sacred artifacts that he inserted within those outer representations, inner representations, and statues are correctly said to have been flawless, without addition, omission, or error.

Many maṇḍalas pertaining to the classes of tantra were opened up. When the entire congregation headed by Rinpoche himself performed the preliminary consecration in the correct manner, the entire sky was filled with rainbows. A rain of flowers and pearl relics fell to the ground, and other such inconceivable auspicious signs occurred. While this aforementioned image of Munīndra was being cast, scrupulous cleanliness was maintained and rays of light burst forth. Later, also, when the consecration took place, there was a great luminance of light rays. Consequently, the image was named the Sage Diffusing Rays of Light.

Regarding Jangchub Gyatso, when people saw that even the maṇḍala of his body was endowed with the blazing splendor of the major and minor marks, they would have great faith in him. The color of his hair was azure blue, and the soles of his feet were adorned, in the common perception of all, with letters inscribed in the new Mongolian script of Chogyel Phakpa. As for the regulations of Choje Kuyalwa, the charter of the monastic assembly, the disciplinary rules of the monastery, and so forth, as in the past, he was strict in observing the proscribed boundaries and implemented them in detail. He was uninterrupted in all respects in his turning of the wheel of the profound and vast sacred doctrine, and the community at Taklung also flourished and expanded to its utmost, conspicuously on account of its glorious endowments that were both spiritual and temporal.

Who could describe the infinite emanations of this great saintly being throughout the three times? {403} Even in the perception of this world, apart from simply the display of different physical forms, there was not the slightest difference between him and the upholders of the Zhamar lineage. The future incarnations of glorious Khacho Wangpo would, according to a prophecy, "frequent the abode of the lama in the region around Jang and nurture his enlightened activity."[574] The reference to "frequenting the abode of the lama and so forth" means that through auspicious circumstances whereby Gelong Namkha-o had in the past approached Gyelwang Taklung Tangpa the Great and Drubchen Tashi Drak had approached the supreme incarnation Kuyalwa, the upholders of the Zhamar lineage would continue traveling to this supreme monastic seat of Taklung and nurture enlightened activity there. When his former entourage was about to offer him the crown of Zhamar and invite him there, he made a prophetic declaration, saying, "It seems that the people of Taklung will not let me go. So look for an incarnation in the Nyangpo region!" Continuing on from that, glorious Khacho himself said, "I will practice meditation in a place near the great eastern river, near a mountain that resembles an elephant with its trunk stretched out by a noose." Accordingly, Venerable Chophel Yeshe was born in Nyangpo.[575]

In general, Jangchub Gyatso nurtured the community at Taklung for eight years. In his thirtieth year, in 1432 (water mouse),[576] he enthroned Choje Pel-o Zangpo at the monastic seat, and then he became a renunciate, residing in a grass hermitage. Gradually he moved residence. That is to say, he traversed many districts of Utsang, and in particular, he visited sacred places such as Daklha Gampo and Densatil and paid respects to their representations of buddha body, speech, and mind. He went to Cāritra, the wheel of pristine cognition, which is classed as a subsidiary place free from obstruction,[577] and the infinite pure visions that he had were beyond number. {404} from Gungmo La pass, he went via Kurab and Dungkar Drak to reach this sacred place of Bayo Tashijong that had been blessed by the great master Padmākara.[578] There, he met Venerable Zhamar Chophel Yeshe, and their minds merged together. Day and night, they passed the time in free and frank discussion concerning the sacred doctrine. Both of them had the soles of their feet similarly embellished with letters in the new Mongolian script. Through such miraculous arrays, they established all living creatures on the level of faith. He acted for the benefit of innumerable disciples from Kongpo, Lung, and Ral.[579] Via Lhorong Dzong, he continued on to glorious Riwoche, the residence of Taklung Lower Plain, where the entire congregation welcomed him in procession.[580]

At Yang Gon, near Riwoche, he delightedly met Choje Miyo Gonpo,[581] and he saw the three reliquary stūpas, including the outer and inner representations contained in the Tashi Gomang and the Six-Pillar Chapel, as well as the Kangyur housed at the center of the upper story of the Great Temple of Riwoche. Then, camping at Lhalung near Riwoche, he stayed there for a long period of time. All of the better class of monks invited him into the grass hermitage and paid their respects to him. The material offerings were like a turbulent blizzard. His kindness to those who requested the novitiate and full monastic vows and in granting empowerments, transmissions, and pith instructions was incalculable. Again, on the occasion of the summer-rain-retreat offering, which coincided with the anniversary of Orgyen Gonpo,[582] he oversaw the drumming and dancing and was given detailed access to the outer and inner representations. There was a mutual meeting of minds. Many meritorious and auspicious circumstances converged, after which he struck camp.

Wherever he went in the southern region, the sky in all these places was filled with rainbow light, {405} there were downpours of divine flowers, green grass would grow, and flowers blossom even in winter. As he went, he was accompanied by innumerable auspicious signs such as these. He established a residence in the estate of Gyeltang, he taught the sacred doctrine at Lang Ngakhol, and newly founded the monastery of Ngakpel Tashi Namding. Up to the present, this monastery purely maintains the doctrinal lineage of Taklung itself.[583] He bound under an oath of allegiance the two powerful local deities who were known as Lhari Pelchuk and Pema Gotri. Then, again, he traveled via Dartsedo on the northern road.[584]

At the sacred place called Dentik, in the district of Tsongkha,[585] in his forty-sixth year, in 1448 (earth male dragon), he seemed to fall ill. On this occasion, an imperial envoy from the palace of the Chinese emperor arrived to invite him to Beijing, but knowing that the circumstances were not auspicious, he offered spiritual and material presents in return and sent him back. On the seventeenth day of the seventh month, he passed away. At that time, the omniscient Ngawang Drakpa,[586] who was seated in the toilet on the roof of Sengling near Taklung, is said to have had a vision of a tall and beautiful blue rocky mountain in the eastern sky, with nine caves occupying its center, the four cardinal, and the four intermediate directions. Among them, Vajradhara was seated in the central cave, but then that buddha body of form became invisible. In the eight surrounding caves, eight great accomplished masters headed by Nāgārjuna were actually seated, each of them reciting a *śloka* of eulogy, but while that was going on, he awoke from that visionary experience. This coincided with the actual date that Rinpoche Jangchub Gyatso passed away in Dome. {406}

Furthermore, although the great omniscient Ngawang Drakpa had previously received the initiation of Vaiśravaṇa, he said that he now had a vision that endured for a long time of the great king Vaiśravaṇa in the midst of his celestial palace with the eight lords of horses, corresponding to the description that Jangchub Gyatso had given him, and so an extraordinary certainty was born within him. He also said that he perceived Choje Jangchub Gyatso in the form of Vajradhara and that he had not previously had such a perception of his elder brother. At the time when he heard the news that Rinpoche Jangchub Gyatso had passed away, he immediately composed the prayer titled *Setting the Mind on Enlightenment*,[587] which concludes with the words, "In all my lives, may I view the victory banner of your buddha body, may I be sustained by the nectar of your buddha speech, and follow after your buddha mind with love!"[588] With these words, he made extensive aspiration prayers that, although enlightenment is identical in the buddha body of reality, Rinpoche Jangchub Gyatso might always manifest as his lord of enlightened heritage, commencing from his past appearance in the entourage of the Teacher Śākyamuni until reaching the point of enlightenment in the future. The great omniscient one Venerable Ngawang Drakpa further said that although there were many teachers such as the erudite Bodong Rinpoche, this venerable lord Jangchub Gyatso alone was the root teacher who had mastered meditative commitments by means of the definitive meaning.

The mortal remains were cremated in Dentik—the very place where he passed into nirvāṇa. In general, innumerable representations and pearl relics were recovered. In particular, among the relics that were retrieved depicting Eleven-Faced Avalokiteśvara was this perfect bone image of sublime Khasarpaṇi that is nowadays kept among the blessed inner representations at Zhuntik. In that very place, an excellent reliquary stūpa was constructed, and even nowadays it is seen by all pilgrims, and offerings are made to it.[589] The funeral rites {407} were carried out elaborately in this place, and an outer representation and an inner representation were constructed. Such virtuous acts of service cannot be measured.

As for the foregoing account, I arranged all the histories that I have seen and heard in the form of a commentary on the aforementioned prayer and then abridged and presented the gist of it as a biographical narrative.[590]

The Disciples of Choje Jangchub Gyatso

As for the disciples who obtained the kindness of profound meaning from this venerable lord, the seniormost was the great omniscient Ngagi Wangpo, whose narrative is given below.[591] In addition, they included Chokyi Gyatso, a profound and vast emanation of the ascetic Kṛṣṇācārin; Go Lotsāwa Zhonu Pel, a saintly being who was distinguished on account of his learning and accomplishment; the great tulku known as Changlungpa Zhonu Lodro, an entirely authentic spiritual mentor whose enlightened attributes of greatness in learning, dignity, and nobility blazed with splendid light that is immeasurable; Pa Tashi Gyatso, the master of Barle; Khenchen Dechen Gyatso, the nephew of Taklung Lotsāwa; Lachen Gelek Gyatso; Kongpo Peltsek Gyatso; and so forth.[592]

As for the subsequent incarnation of Choje Jangchub Gyatso Pelzangpo, *The Biography of Glorious Khacho Wangpo* mentions "a wandering practitioner who would emanate near that sacred place, delighting to attain the enlightened intention of Venerable Vajrarāja." This points toward his reincarnation as the fourth holder of the Zhamar crown, Chokyi Drakpa.[593] The description of "a young boy engaged in acts conducive to liberation,[594] protected by Vasudhara,[595] and seeking the inexhaustible mystery of power over material resources" points toward the fifth, Konchok Yenlak.[596] {408} And it continues to describe "one traveling to that sacred place and its subsidiary sacred place, delighting in drinking the nectar, thereby reaching the summit of realization exclusively four times in succession, and moving in all directions," which points toward the sixth Dorje Garwang Chokyi Wangchuk, who is alive at the present time.[597] Subsequently, too, it is said that not only will the dance of his emanations arise inconceivably but that there will be approximately fifteen incumbents to hold the crown of Zhamar.[598]

May the wish-granting tree of virtuous provisions, born of this
biography,
Heavy with the branches and fruit of spiritual accomplishment,
Offer all living beings, without exception, protection from suffering,
And grant the desired maturation and liberation!

Tashi Pel-o Zangpo, Eleventh in the Abbatial Succession

Verses of Homage

Going beyond the ocean of the magnificent two provisions,
Renouncing from afar the stains of the three obscurations[599] and their
propensities,
Venerable lord of the sacred doctrine,

In whom the twofold benefit of self and others is spontaneously
present,
Homage to the feet of Pel-o Zangpo!

Choje Tashi Pel-o Zangpo is counted among the lineage holders of the monastic seat of Taklung.[600] Without moving from the buddha body of reality, free from conceptual elaboration, coalescence of inner radiance and emptiness, this lord of the entire world and its inhabitants manifested to bodhisattvas abiding on the pure tenth level in the buddha body of perfect resource, endowed with the seven aspects of mystic union,[601] and then after manifesting to disciples of three classes in the supreme buddha body of emanation, he demonstrated the dance of the twelve deeds.[602]

Although the array of his bodies that permeate space have given rise at each instant to infinite acts of benefit for sentient beings, he provisionally took birth in 1408 (earth male mouse) according to the terrestrial system, also known as Sarvadhāri in India, in a holy and virtuous town in the upper reaches of Penyul, where the ten virtuous actions are fully present, the source of knowledge, a location in Uru to the north of Lhasa, blessed by Lokeśvara, the valley endowed with glorious snow mountains. {409} His father was the governor Ratnadhvaja (Rinchen Gyeltsen)—a product of many hundreds of merits, peerless in profound and vast intelligence that engages with every detailed and cursory action associated with the twofold spiritual and temporal tradition, a prominent artist[603] renowned like the child of dawn.[604] The mother who gave birth to this conqueror was the sublime Minyakza Budren, accomplished in aspiration prayers.[605] At that time, Venerable Jangchub Gyatso was in his sixth year.

For ten months in his mother's supremely holy womb, Tashi Pel-o Zangpo resided in an adamantine stacked mansion of precious gems. Then, since his elder brother, prince of the ten directions, was manifesting countless million trillion doctrinal approaches, as many as the sands of the River Ganges, he thought it would be timely to act for the benefit of his actual disciples, inspiring them toward unsurpassed enlightenment. Without harm to his mother, showing to the world the mature major and minor marks of his physical body, he took birth untainted by the blemishes of the womb, like a fine vase of treasure extracted from the great ocean. Even when he was breast feeding, his body lacked the lumpiness associated with the ordinary body, speech, and mind that resembles an ordinary vase. Of his own volition, he engaged in the four modes of appropriate physical conduct and so forth, without depending on others.[606] Then, when he had grown slightly, all the activities of childhood play that he undertook exclusively manifested the dramatic dance of teaching the sacred doctrine, granting empowerments, {410} nurturing disciples, and being equipoised in meditative stability. He grew finer, just as glory is enhanced on calendar dates in the waxing half of the month.

At the start of his eleventh year, in 1418 (earth male dog, or Vilaṃbhi), he occupied the estate of the Layel Courtyard, a pure buddha field where a succession of buddhas of the authentic lineage had rejoiced to the utmost, and the meditation hat, crown of the Kagyu lineage, was fastened to his head. He released the living creatures of this place, even as far as straw-eyed worms, from the fetters of negative rebirth.

Then, he traveled here to Taklung, the great glorious seminary that can bless ordinary individuals, who will assuredly be subject to rebirth, into the presence of the incarnation of Akṣobhya, Mikyo Tukyi Dorje, mighty lord of the taintless wheel in the east. He absorbed the blessings of the lamas of the root lineage. All of his sense organs and sense objects, arising from the psychophysical aggregates, sensory elements, and sense fields, were purified, as in the complete empowerment of the three seats.[607] From the six cakras within his subtle body, the maṇḍalas of the six enlightened families were diffused and absorbed. All the maṇḍalas of animate beings and their environment, all the gnostic mantras, and the entirety of the oceanic pure lands were perfectly present without intermingling, even in each individual hair pore of his body, and his emanations continued to endure as long as the expanse of reality. His body was that of a mendicant—a member of the sublime monastic community, his speech intoned the melody of the wheel of the sacred doctrine, and his mind was the buddha—immaculate and pure. In brief, his body had internally absorbed all the objects of refuge.

He then properly touched the topknot of his azure blue hair at the wheel-marked lotus feet of Venerable Tashi Peltsek Nyimei Wangpo Sungwei Gocha, whose fame resounded like the sound of the great drum of the gods, upholding the power of the sacred doctrine in the three worlds. {411} Although he had from the beginning been accomplished as a great sublime being in whom the uncontaminated vows were perfect, in order to demonstrate this to his disciples, he requested the ordination of a layperson and the preparatory ordination of a mendicant. Formally requesting his monastic preceptor, he adopted the three changes of appearance. That is to say, in the transformation of lifestyle,[608] he abandoned the dress of a layperson and of a non-Buddhist extremist and adopted the personal items of a mendicant. In the transformation of thought,[609] he eliminated mundane refuges and the turbid obscuration of excellent aspirations and set his mind on the wish to attain the nonabiding nirvāṇa for the benefit of sentient beings. In the transformation of name,[610] he tamed the pursuit of grandiose titles associated with the time when he had formerly acted inappropriately as a layperson, and instead enhanced the names of his school and monastic preceptor, such that he was given the name Tashi Pel-o Zangpo. After accomplishing such preparatory steps, he excellently received the precepts of the novitiate according to the ancient rite, with its phases of actual conferral and subsequent advice.[611]

Later, when Tashi Pel-o Zangpo came of age and the time arrived, he controlled the flow of nonsensical talk, and like a dike that dams a river, he excellently received the precepts of a fully ordained monk—the pure ethical discipline that entails seven renunciations with respect to physical forms, both apperceived and nonapperceived, along with their peripheral renunciations.[612] He became an elder, upholding the Buddhist teaching. His own nature identified with the Taklungpa Tradition of Perfect Ethical Discipline, which is renowned for entering into the definitive meaning. Similarly, he experientially cultivated both aspects of enlightened mind—the relative aspect that arises from coarse symbols and the ultimate aspect that is obtained through subtle reality—which are the source of all spiritual and temporal well-being and the main cause of perfect buddhahood. {412} Engaging in a great wave of bodhisattva conduct, he became a most saintly being, infinite in the power of his higher aspiration and training, and indistinguishable from the Samantabhadra-like career of his older brother, the prince Jangchub Gyatso.

Although he had already achieved mastery over the wheel of the fruitional vehicles, from the very start—including the maturational empowerments, the exegesis of the tantras that generates certainty, and the conferring of essential pith instructions that are profoundly secret—even so, he later showed himself listening to, pondering, and meditating on these, such that he became a supreme adamantine master, adorned with pristine cognition, a conferrer of the supreme empowerments that transfer the blessing of mastery over the ten aspects of tantra (outer, inner, and secret), an expositor of the classes of tantra of expressed meaning, a giver of pith instructions that offer buddhahood in the palm of the hand, and an elder and sovereign of mantra.

In particular, dependent on the traditional descent of the teachings in this precious Kagyu lineage, he received and experientially cultivated in the correct manner the oral instructions of the Great Seal—the sole path that all the buddhas have traversed, the essence of the entire definitive meaning, profounder than the profound, condensing the essentials of all the scriptures subsumed in the sūtras and tantras of the Great Vehicle, and establishing ultimate truth by manifestly pointing it out through the blessings of understanding and testing without simply resorting to inference.

So it was that he excellently examined the four yogas of the ground, {413} and by mastering the twenty-four yogas of experiential realization on the path, he perfected the renunciations and realizations associated with the ten levels and the five paths. Then, by means of his inconceivable buddha body of emanation that manifests the four conclusive fruitional yogas, he one-pointedly acted for the benefit of sentient beings.[613] Through the buddha body of essentiality, he was isolated from the conceptual elaboration of formative predispositions. Through the buddha body of perfect resource, which is endowed with the five certainties, all entities, animate and inanimate, became of a single savor.[614] Through the buddha body of reality, which is the essential nature of all things, he manifested the truth that is without meditation.

Similarly, he eradicated the objects of purification—namely, the obscurations of body, speech, and mind, along with the propensities for transference of consciousness at death. He did so, refining them by means of the four primary doctrines that (1) generate the four provisional objects of purification within the four cakras of the subtle body that constitute the ground of purification, and (2) apply the perfection stage that constitutes the act of purification in the imperishable vital essence of the cakras and the channels. Thereafter, the rank of the four buddha bodies that constitute the result of this purification was manifestly conferred in this very life.[615]

So it was that he received profound oral instructions concerning intermingling, transference of consciousness, and reincarnation, embodied in the six practices that consist of four primary doctrines and the two subsidiary doctrines.[616] It was this natural momentum of the essential, self-originated path that brought forth his success in the Great Seal, integrating bliss and emptiness. That is to say, he actualized the authentic rank of the imperishable Mahāvajradhara, who is the identity of the four buddha bodies of coalescence. Not only did he perfect the vital energy of pristine cognition internally but externally, too, his appearance was one endowed with excellent exegesis and attainment, the defining characteristics of a spiritual mentor of the Great Vehicle. As it is said in *The Gathering of Precious Enlightened Attributes*,[617] {414}

> Rely on the buddhas, the bodhisattvas who have set out for the supreme enlightenment,
> And those who have the transcendent perfections as spiritual mentors.

And in *The Ornament of the Sūtras of the Great Vehicle*,[618]

> One should serve a spiritual mentor who is disciplined, calm, serene,
> Outstanding in enlightened attributes, energetic, rich in scriptural transmission,
> Realized in the nature of reality, skilled in speech, kind, and indefatigable.

And in *The Ornament of Clear Realization*,[619]

> Those whose minds are not cowed and such,
> Who teach the nonexistence of the nature of entities and so forth,
> And who cast aside the discordant factors of those entities
> Are in all respects spiritual tutors.

And in *The Precious Garland*,[620]

> The defining characteristics of spiritual mentors,
> Briefly, are that they are a repository of knowledge,
> And they have knowledge of the sacred doctrine, compassion, discipline,
> And discriminative awareness that dispels afflicted mental states.
> If you serve them . . .

And in *The Introduction to the Conduct of a Bodhisattva*,[621]

> One should never abandon, even for the sake of one's life,
> A spiritual mentor who is skilled in the meanings of the Great Vehicle,
> And who keeps the supreme ascetic discipline of the bodhisattvas.

And in *Twenty Verses on the Bodhisattva Vows*,[622]

> One should accept a teacher who keeps the vows
> And who is learned and capable.

And in *The Commentary on "The Four Hundred Verses of the Middle Way,"*[623]

> Teachers who know the minds of their disciples
> And who can take them into their following
> Should gather their disciples,
> But those who are deluded are unworthy of gathering disciples.

And in Śākyaprabha's *Illuminating Commentary on the Monastic Discipline of the Novitiate*,[624]

> Ethical and knowledgeable in monastic discipline,
> With compassion and love for the sick
> And with a retinue that is pure,
> Striving to benefit beings both spiritually and materially, {415}
> And teaching in a timely manner—
> A teacher such as this is praised.

It is explained that the defining characteristics of spiritual mentors are that, among the oceanic piṭakas of the scriptures and the commentaries on their enlightened intention, they enhance virtuous actions by relying on the meaning of the sūtras that were extensively taught. Indeed, these attributes were excellently and fully present in this saintly being Tashi Pel-o Zangpo. It says in the Adamantine Vehicle,[625]

> Kind, disciplined, and learned in the treatises,
> The teachers who are particularly revered
> Are those who know completely the ten aspects of tantra.

He was endowed with compassion that seeks to liberate all sentient beings from suffering and its causes. He continuously maintained the three vows of the pious attendants, bodhisattvas, and the awareness holders. He comprehended all the treatises of sūtra and mantra without error. He was preeminent and certainly revered for conferring empowerments and pith instructions. It is explained in the yoga tantras that the ten outer aspects are maṇḍala construction, mantra, gestures of sealing, protective circles, invitation to the deity of pristine cognition, recitation, meditation, burnt offerings, embrace,[626] and the request to remain present. In the unsurpassed tantras, the ten inner aspects of mantra are maṇḍala construction, meditative stability, gestures of sealing, demeanor, posture, recitation, burnt offering, offerings, ritual applications, and reabsorption. And the ten secret aspects include rites of the two kinds of averting, the secret empowerment, the empowerment of discriminating pristine cognition, rituals of mystic union, torma offerings, recitation of adamantine verses, rites of wrathful attainment, consecrations, and attainment of the maṇḍala.[627] As for his knowledge of those ten secret aspects, {416} all the defining characteristics that are explained as those of an adamantine master were excellently perfected in him. So it was that this preceptor among the hundred thousand upholders of the vinaya, this leader among ten million princely bodhisattvas, this master among the ocean of awareness holders perfected the activities of study, reflection, and meditation.

Tashi Pel-o Zangpo pledged to live as an exemplary leader, roaring the lion's roar among his entourage, and in order to permeate the three planes of existence with the enlightened activity of the pure Buddhist teaching, he manifestly accrued a hundred billion trillion auspicious circumstances that would pave the way for future lives in the splendid emanational line of Sixth Zhamar, Choje Gongma Gargyi Wangchuk Jangchub Gyatso Pelzangpo.

In order to propagate his efficacious medicine for the sake of the Buddhist teaching and sentient beings in the districts of Utsang, Kham, Kongpo, and so forth, it is said that he relied on the discipline of total renunciation. However, in his twenty-third year, in 1430 (iron male dog), he was installed on the lion throne of the sacred doctrine that had been occupied by the ten successive hierarchs of Taklung and appointed as a master of the great domain of the sacred doctrine that is filled, in the manner of Anavatapta Lake, with the complete excellent endowments of the two sciences, spiritual and temporal, and to whom all worlds including the god realms bowed their crown ornaments in homage. This was accompanied by a million trillion arrays of wondrous auspicious circumstance. Garlands of auspicious coral[628] flowers were strewn. On account of his activities with respect to the three wheels that combine both knowledge and liberation, he lived in the midst of his timeless monastic assembly, radiant and resplendent like Lord Ajita (Maitreya), teaching the sacred doctrine at the center of the maṇḍala of his entourage. {417} Starting from then, Taklung became even more distinguished than in the past, uncontrollably captivating the minds of those who strive toward the rank of liberation and omniscience due to its resplendent array, consisting of (1) the celestial thirteen regulations of Choje Kuyalwa that are radiant and pure like the parasol above a teaching throne, (2) the subterranean thirteen disciplinary rules of the monastery that are firm and enduring like the earth, and (3) the thirteen points of the charter of the monastic assembly that are pristine and beautiful like a range of mountains fashioned of precious gems and metals.[629]

As his older brother, the supreme tulku Pema Gargyi Wangchuk had wished, Tashi Pel-o Zangpo perfected through his actual physical body all the approaches of enlightened activity that benefit living beings who are to be trained. Even though he sojourned for a while in his own abode, the field of the blissful array,[630] he was unstinting in his generation of bountiful deeds, including offerings that stifled the minds of those smitten by desire and that transcended exemplification.

On behalf of his deceased teacher, as an internal representation, he erected the precious gilded reliquary stūpa that illustrates all phenomena of the ground, path, and result and that seems to overpower Mount Sumeru, fashioned of four kinds of precious gems and metals, both in its essence and in its form. It blazed with the splendor of no less that ten thousand suns, as a glorious field of genuine merit for all mundane beings, including the gods.

As an external representation, he constructed a buddha image called Munīndra in the form Mound of Good Auspices, of which, however long it was examined by one skilled in critical analysis, {418}one would think, "This is an image blazing with the glory of the major and minor marks, born from many hundreds of merits and created through the workmanship of an artisan who induces conviction in the field where he actually resides, engaging in meditative equipoise in the myriad approaches of meditative stability." Incapable of arising as a mere mental object, it filled the central space of the Main Temple.

He also prepared the volumes that gave physical form to the entire Buddhist teachings contained in the complete Kangyur, the canonical teachings of the buddhas, with great translators epitomizing the epithet Eyes of the World, correcting them in accordance with the Indian manuscripts. Their inscribed pages resembled finely arranged rows of adamantine sunlight and taintless moonlight against the wide pathway of the gods, shining with the natural light of sapphire.[631] The stacks of these incomparable volumes are ornaments adorning the Northern Chapel.

Tashi Pel-o Zangpo then commissioned a three-dimensional mind maṇḍala of Kālacakra, insatiable to behold, depicting the glorious transcendent lord Kālacakra with four faces and twenty-four arms, standing within a celestial palace fashioned of various precious gems and metals, in mystic union with the innate female consort Viśvamātā, who has four faces and eight arms,[632] along with the eight powerful female deities,[633] the four symbols, the male and female buddhas of the six enlightened families,[634] the ten vases, the ten wrathful male and female gatekeepers,[635] the twenty-four male and female bodhisattvas,[636] and the twelve offering goddesses.[637]

At the insistence of the scholar Lewuchung, he also commissioned a perfect image of glorious Cakrasaṃvara, according to the tradition of Gaṇṭhapāda, {419} with four faces and two arms, in union with his female consort, and accompanied by the four essential yoginī, and so forth.[638] He placed these images within the Southern Chapel, at the heart of a depiction of the emanational land Śambhala.

Tashi Pel-o Zangpo occupied the lion throne for thirty-one years, during which time he increased the excellence of the spiritual and temporal domains of the Taklungpa, just as glory is enhanced during the waxing half of the month.

When he taught the wheel of the profound and vast sacred doctrine, the inexhaustible modalities of the words and meanings of the ocean of sūtra and tantra arose, and when he entered into their practice, he bestowed the Great Seal, such that with regard to all names, words and letters in their entirety, his mind, and the sacred doctrine were intermingled, and he could clearly point out and behold the innate and uncontrived pristine cognition, spontaneously present within his own mindstream. He secured the appearances of the energy channels, winds, and vital essences that constitute the abiding nature of the physical body and the certainty of unimpeded emptiness and radiance that constitutes the abiding nature of the mind, with the four branches of ritual service and attainment according to the generation stage of the path and the essentials of the adamantine Six Doctrines of Nāropā according to the perfection stage. Thereby, he bestowed the certainty that the four fruitional buddha bodies, free from obscuration, are present in the state of original buddhahood, where cause and result are simultaneous. The gatherings of his disciples, who were exclusively strict monks maintaining the inner yoga, formed a series as numerous as the sands of the earth, and while he was domiciled at the monastic seat of Taklung, he traveled to many regions—south, north, highland, and lowland—establishing many monastic and lay communities and bringing an end to cyclic existence through noble enlightened activities whereby innumerable corporeal beings saw him and heard his voice.

He also traveled to glorious Riwoche, to the monastic seat of Taklung Lower Plain, the residence of the supreme tulku Pel Ozer Zangpo,[639] whereupon he had a vision of Lord Acala, and immediately {420} many meritorious and auspicious circumstances manifested. Out of reverence for the impartial Buddhist teaching and its upholders, he founded the monastery of Rinchen Drak—with its temple and the representations of buddha body, speech, and mind contained within it—and a Protector Chapel. The place was filled with many gatherings of monks listening to the teachings of the piṭakas and nurturing the practical application of the tantras. And at the very least, the planted trees of the debating courtyard and so forth also contributed to the great temple of this great monastic seat. Through practical implementation of dialectics, he overpowered all opposing factions with his charisma. He constructed countless paintings—images of the Buddha and his heirs that were made of medicinal paste, cast in a mold, miraculously beaten into shape, and so forth—as well as volumes of scripture and reliquary stūpas representing the buddha body of reality.

So it was that for a saintly person such as him, whose creations were indicative of enlightened attributes, whose speech was indicative of the oral instructions, and whose undertakings were indicative of enlightened activity, even the approaches to liberation that contributed a single day could not be measured. This being the case, one should understand how the positive enlightened activities in which he engaged throughout his entire life could not be documented, let alone contemplated.

After establishing all his actual disciples, without exception, in purification and liberation by means of the pure liberating career of his buddha body, speech, and mind, and through the excellent path of positive deeds, finally, in his fifty-third year, in 1460 (iron male dragon), he appeared to fall ill. During that time, he had to pitch camp in the northern direction, and while he was seated there at that campsite, renowned for its rainbows, like a garden of the gods being transferred to earth, the appearance of his physical body succumbed, and he passed away into the expanse of reality. {421} The precious remains, like a wish-fulfilling gem, were brought here to Taklung. Kunkhyen Rinpoche Ngawang Drakpa offered words of advice that were widely spread. He then inserted the remains completely in a gilded-copper reliquary stūpa with the proper defining characteristics inside the South Chapel, and he donated inconceivable sacraments of offering. He commissioned two images of his precious predecessor that were fashioned from medicinal paste, in which medicines and precious gems were mixed together. Some five hundred spiritual mentors presented offerings to the remains. On the day of the great funeral ceremony, some thirty thousand laypeople and monks gathered, and copper coins were distributed, one for each of them. Innumerable offerings were made to those who were seated at the head of the row. In all the affiliated monasteries and sacred places of the surrounding region, offerings were presented to the three representations of buddha body, speech, and mind, and it is said that the respect, alms, and so forth shown to the monks were unimaginable.

The virtue of this biographical composition, which resembles a *ketaka* stone,[640]
Has clarified the three obscurations and turbid propensities of sentient beings
Who are on a downward course, wandering in the ocean of rebirth.
May it grant the noble fruit of eternal bliss that is desired!

Ngawang Drakpa Pelzangpo, Twelfth in the Abbatial Succession

Homage from the heart to the **glorious** (*dpal*),[641] and **noble** (*bzang po*) lord,
Treasure of the **speech** (*ngag*) contained in oceanic volumes of scripture,
Synonymous with Vajrasattva, **mighty** (*dbang*) lord of attainment,
Famed (*grags pa*) as a master of the Buddhist teaching!

The omniscient Ngawang Drakpa Pelzangpo was an embodiment combining the knowledge, love, and enlightened activities of all the conquerors of the authentic lineage, none excepted.[642] He was born in 1418 (earth male dog) in the estate of Daryul Jema. His father was Miwang Rinchen Gyeltsen {422} and his mother was a hidden yoginī, youngest of the six offspring of Minyakza Budren. Immediately, he was sent for protection to Venerable Tashi Peltsek, who gave him a protection cord made from a square of white silk and then named him Tashi Pel, saying that he would be of benefit to the Taklungpa tradition. Although childhood is a time for developing strength, all his childhood play showed him engaging in exegesis and attainment. When a hybrid dzo was lost, he sat briefly in meditative equipoise and then said, "Here it is!" When he had a wound on his head and was being treated by a physician, he said, "The physician of Riwoche did not act in that manner!" That is to say, he asserted himself to be the reincarnation of Choje Ratnākara of Riwoche.

After Venerable Tashi Peltsek had passed away, while he was residing at Dzongnyak, Ngawang Drakpa Pelzangpo actually met the deceased Choje Rinpoche, prostrated before him and requested his blessing, whereupon he heard a symphony of divine music and found on the ground an eight-petaled lotus, its anthers marked with pearl relics. After one day had passed, the flower vanished but the pearl relics remained.

Controlling his dreams, Ngawang Drakpa Pelzangpo set off in flight and had a precise vision of the grass hermitage of a local lama named Ngaripa, as well as the offerings he had made there to the representations of buddha body, speech, and mind. On another occasion, the arrow that he fired in sport pierced a stone. When he fell ill with smallpox, he thought nothing of it and remained without moving from his meditative stability. At that time, he had repeated visions of the spirit lord of the locality moving through the sky, riding a blue horse, and encircled by many attendants. Such miraculous occurrences were infinite. {423}

Traveling to Taklung, he served Lachen Mañjuśrī and received instruction in writing and reading. He then studied and refined his understanding of texts such as *The Lamp for the Path*,[643] *The Tantra That Clearly Realizes the Pith Instructions of All Conduct Pertaining to the Sacred Doctrine*,[644] and *The Root Tantra of Hevajra* and its commentaries.

In his fourteenth year, in the midst of a large gathering of monks—headed by the preceptor Choje Jangchub Gyatso Pelzangpo, the master of ceremonies Khenchen Zangpo Ozer, the timekeeper Lachen Jampel Gocha, and the devout monk Jadrel Chenpo Chokyi Gyeltsen—he received the vows of a layperson, the intermediate mendicant vows, and the vows of the novitiate. The name Namkha Tashi Jangchub Gyeltsen was conferred upon him. That night, in his grass hermitage, he had a dream in which he saw a boy of about eight years of age playfully sitting upon a white flat beam, and both he and the boy were adorned with dark Jambu gold, precious gems, and flowers. He offered a roll of white silk to the boy, whereupon he was given in exchange a silk rope embellished with a blue knot.

At Kadruk, while he was practicing the ritual service and attainment of Jñānanātha, in a dream, he saw a leper woman chopping with the sword that Mahākāla carries. Along with her was the head of a large flock of ravens who came to take the offering cakes, larger than the others, holding a skull cup and a ritual spike. Finally, that main raven appeared on the window sill of his room, wearing a gold ring around its throat. Entering within the room, it sat for a long time on the table and then vanished into the heart of a drawn image.[645]

Knowing that many clay sculptures in the Southern Storeroom had been disturbed and moved due to the miracle of a demon, {424} he emanated in the form of the transcendent lord Vajrabhairava and eradicated it. Such were the miraculous events that occurred.

On another occasion, when he was drinking tea, a miraculous apparition that resembled a calf appeared, whereupon his ceramic cup slipped out of his hand and spun around, without breaking when it struck the surface of the stone floor. At the time when he received the initiation of Vaiśravaṇa from Choje Jangchub Gyatso, he had a vision of this great king who is a doctrinal protector within his celestial palace, accompanied by eight yakṣa horsemen. On returning to his room, the vision was even clearer than before. That night in a dream, he saw many people with dreadlocks from Minyak who were unloading an inconceivable quantity of merchandise and placing it into a storeroom. They offered the key into his hands and he said, "Put some boxes outside. These should be opened after this year has passed!" Later, when he was invited there by Tsibarwa,[646] the calculation tallied with his dream.

In general, he excellently received innumerable doctrinal discourses from Jangchub Gyatso Pelzangpo, who was the embodiment of the lord Mahāvajradhara. In particular, he received the entire secret treasury of the sacred doctrines of the taintless aural lineage of the glorious Taklung Kagyu, including experiential guidance on the Great Seal and the Six Doctrines of Nāropā, as if pouring the entire contents from one vase into another. From the perspective of this world, he appeared to engage in experiential cultivation with great insistence and to gradually perfect all the experiential realizations that accorded with his individual fortune, but actually he had over innumerable past eons been an embodiment in whom the emptiness endowed with all finest aspects and supremely unchanging great bliss were coalesced. Moved by nonreferential great compassion, {425} he had completed his actualization of the level of the glorious holder of adamantine reality, and his enlightened activities were spontaneously present, uninterrupted as long as rebirth endures. This being the case, it was merely from the standpoint of provisional meaning that he experientially cultivated the pith instructions here in Taklung and exhibited the clear realization of the path on that basis, and so forth. From Lachenpa he received the transmitted doctrines of the Sakya tradition and the Buton tradition, including the three tantras and their pith instructions. He studied the teachings of Taklungpa, the Kagyu lineage in general, the Shangpa doctrines, and so forth under Jadrel Cho Gyeltsenpa.[647]

When he considered visiting the omniscient Bodongpa, in a dream he saw the form of that master's body with precise clarity alongside an array of many ornate torma offerings, from the midst of which two threads of light diverged, their ends being spun by two blue-colored women. The evening when he set out for Bodong from Taklung, there was a path of white light. A flock of ravens showed the way, and some black dogs followed behind. The following day when he did not know which path to take, a man wearing red clothes pointed it out. Such miraculous events occurred.[648]

Ngawang Drakpa Pelzangpo worked for the benefit of the monastery and so forth. When he taught the sacred doctrine at Ngomar and Tokar, there was a shower of flowers.[649] From Takdruka, he was welcomed by the household of Rinpungpa. On reaching the jetty, he saw the reflection of the sun in the water, whereupon the meditative stability coalescing appearances and emptiness was born within him.[650] When he reached the Jamkhang in Tak, someone arrived there with interesting news, saying that at that very moment Venerable Bodongpa had gone to Gyantse. In the evening, when he reached Lhundrubtse in the lower part of Nyangto, in a dream he saw a sun rising from the mountain peak in the east, ten times larger than this sun of the present. It illuminated Nyangto, {426} and a ray of light penetrated his heart, such that infinite meditative stability was born within him. He was welcomed from afar by the monks of Venerable Bodongpa and by the lay officials of Gyantse.[651] Later, Bodongpa received him at the entrance of the new temple.[652] They offered prostrations to one another, and seats were prepared for them without distinction of higher and lower. In the presence of the venerable and omniscient Bodongpa, he studied the four subsequent fields of classical learning and an inconceivable number of sūtras, tantras, and pith instructions, even the names of which are hard to describe. When he caught a contagious fever during his sojourn at Gyantse, he saw a raven freely alight on his pillow and sit there, whereupon he instantly recovered.

As an act of service, he performed a torma empowerment when the king of Gyantse was afflicted by a breathing disorder whereupon the latter was released from illness.[653] When the essential medicinal water and thermal waters were being prepared, a raven directly entered the room from who knows where, and thereupon the disease with its subsidiary causes were alleviated.

In order to avert obstacles caused by the king spirit Tsang Drang Gyelpo, at Jamchen he performed torma ceremonies of Mahākāla for twenty-one days, whereupon something resembling an intestine was seen emerging from the mouth of a raven and entering Tsang Drang Gyelpo's gullet, such that he was naturally tamed.

At Pelmo Choding,[654] he received full monastic ordination with Venerable Bodongpa acting as preceptor, and the vinaya master Ngawang Gyeltsen acting as master of ceremonies, in the midst of a monastic body that made up the quorum. By dint of this auspicious circumstance, he was given the name Ngagi Wangchuk Drakpa Pelzangpo. He acquired an inspiration within the great monastic assembly that did not rely on others—this was the actual mystery of the buddha speech of Venerable Bodongpa, and he became a peerless promulgator. {428}

He received many cycles of the doctrinal protectors from Draklo, the lord of the glorious Sakyapa,[655] and he also visited Gotsang, Samling, Namding, Lhadong, and so forth.[656] At Tsibri, he received the texts of the Drukpa cycle, *The Mountain Retreat Doctrine*,[657] *The Service and Attainment of Urgyenpa*,[658] and so forth from Choje Jangchub Zangpo.[659]

He then traveled to Dingri Langkor, Nyenam, and Chubar.[660] In Labchi, he received the doctrinal cycles of Drigungpa and Karmapa from Choje Dulwadzinpa.[661] In Kyirong, he saw the image of Phakpa Wati, and he also visited Drakar Taso, Rakma Jangchub Dzong, Kyangpa Namkha Dzong, Minkhyuk Dribma Dzong, and so forth.[662] The monk Sangrin, who requested a doctrinal connection with him, donated as a maṇḍala offering a ginseng plant along with the relevant instructions. Although he had a strong intention to focus on spiritual attainment in those great power places, he was pulled back by Choje Jangchub Gyatso and Nangso Tashi Gyatso, who repeatedly and persistently sent messages from Taklung, such that he resolved to go back. He departed after Venerable Bodongpa had offered him as a parting gift eloquent instructions combining the experiential cultivation of all doctrines in four parts—namely, the emancipation that is common to pious attendants, the higher aspiration that is common to bodhisattvas, the extraordinary pure vision of the mantras, and the view of Madhyamaka, which is common to all.[663]

When he gave teachings on the Great Seal at Mengab,[664] the spirit lord-protector of Taklung appeared in a youthful form, wearing white clothes, with bow, arrow, and quiver attached, and riding a wild horse. Offering him shoes made of elk skin, he encouraged him to go swiftly on his way. {429} He next visited the sacred places of glorious Sakya and its threefold representation of buddha body, speech, and mind.[665] At Rinpung, he was venerated by Drungchen Norzang, who requested teaching.[666] At Yamdrok, he was invited by the Tripon and his brother, who were descendants of the great chieftain Alen, and he turned the wheel of the sacred doctrine on their behalf, such that they obtained faith. At Zhung Trewuzhing, in the presence of Ngoton Rinpoche Jangchub Pelwa, he received the transmitted teachings of empowerment, the transmitted teachings of exegesis, and all the transmitted precepts of the pith instructions without exception that had descended from Ngadak Marpa and Ngok, and he comprehended them.[667] Rinchen Zangpowa, the great chieftain of Yargyab, then invited him to Dol, and when he gave teachings on the sacred doctrine, a shower of flowers fell.[668] He also visited the Great Emanational Temple of Lhasa and made offerings to Jowo Śākyamuni.

In 1444 (mouse), in his twenty-seventh year, Ngawang Drakpa Pelzangpo arrived back at Taklung and took up residence at Kadruk (the Six-Pillar Temple). The following year, he established the offering ceremonies of *The Array of the Three Commitments*,[669] *The Awakening of Vairocana*,[670] *Vajradhātu*,[671] *Sarvavid Vairocana*,[672] *Nine-Aspect Uṣṇīṣavijaya*,[673] *Guhyasamāja in the Form Akṣobhyavajra*,[674] *Guhyasamāja in the Form Mañjuvajra*,[675] *Vajrabhairava*,[676] *Cakrasaṃvara according to the tradition of Kṛṣṇācārin*,[677] *The Ocean of Ḍākas*,[678] *The Combined Enlightened Heritage of Pañjara*,[679] *Hevajra*, and *Kālacakra*.

That same year, he commissioned a complete manuscript copy of the treatise titled *Summation of the Real*,[680] numbering a hundred volumes.[681] During that period, he remained entirely in retreat, and he orally taught the profound and vast transmitted teachings of guidance, including the Great Seal, the Six Doctrines of Nāropā, *The Service and Attainment of Urgyenpa*,[682] and the Path and Its Fruit.

At the invitation of Yamdrokpa, he went there and extensively propagated the enlightened activity associated with the sacred doctrine.[683] Encouraged by the doctrinal protectors, {429} he then returned to Taklung, after which he fell ill but carried this illness on the path by means of the pith instructions on common savor.

Once, when he was going to the toilet, he was welcomed and escorted by the gods and demons of phenomenal existence in the forms of people riding horses and pack animals, moving from Ojo to Drelung. And, on another occasion, directly above Sengling, he saw an extremely high and beautiful cliff of sapphire in the eastern direction that had nine caves. In the central one, it is said there was seated Vajradhara, the color of a cloudless clear sky, translucent and otherwise "invisible in physical form," while in the eight caves of the cardinal and intermediate directions there were seated Nāgārjuna, Indrabhūti, Saraha, Kukkurāja, Ḍombhi Heruka, Lūipa, and Vajragaṇṭha. He offered a *śloka* of praise to each of them, and at that time the central Vajradhara image "who was invisible in physical form" cringed due to the death that very day of Venerable Jangchub Gyatso at Dentik.[684] He clearly held Jangchub Gyatso as his root teacher, the lord of his enlightened heritage, secured with the seal of that primordial lord Vajradhara.

Furthermore, once Ngawang Drakpa Pelzangpo had finished his daily meditative commitments, in his mind, he experienced a large gathering of ordained persons and laypeople, carrying various gifts and requesting the empowerment of Vajrayoginī. At that time, their leader, a most charismatic woman dressed in dark brown robes, was possessed by the being of pristine cognition, and she danced while there appeared many in the entourage of Venerable Tseringma, chanting melodic verses.[685]

At Ojo, he had a vision of an extremely clear image of the solitary central deity Jñānanātha, and when he performed the ritual attainment of the torma offering of Jñānanātha, {430} he recalled a former life in which he had been a mantrin with matted hair, taking Vajrabhairava as his meditational deity.

Under Lama Monlam Penjorwa, who resided in that very monastery of Taklung, he also studied completely the Collected Works of Phakmodrupa and the cycle of the rite of attainment pertaining to Jñānanātha. He established the minute offerings for the rites of attainment of Hevajra and Sarvavid Vairocana, and he commissioned volumes—including *The Collection of Tantras* and a manuscript of *The Transcendent Perfection of Wisdom in Eight Thousand Lines*, with many folios inscribed in pure gold—as well as many hundreds of painted scrolls. He made extensive offerings to all the temples and their three representations of buddha body, speech, and mind in Utsang.

Constantly, each morning he engaged in the meditations and recitations pertaining to Hevajra, Cakrasaṃvara, Bhairava, Amitāyus, Sarvavid Vairocana, and so forth, and he performed the torma offering rites, the rites of fulfillment, eulogies, recitations, and so forth pertaining to the renowned tenfold group of doctrinal protectors including Mahākāla in the forms Six-Armed Glorious Jñānanātha, Pañjaranātha, Thūmāṅgārī, Four-Faced Caturmukha, Vaiśravaṇa, Trakṣad, the ritual acolytes of Yama,[686] Lekden and his two siblings,[687] and the spirit lords of the locality, and so on.[688] In brief, from the disposition of the great seal, he undertook symbolic virtuous actions that could not be maintained by ten people, and, as his memoranda and writings on those combined meditative commitments actually reveal, he exclusively exhibited the magical display of pristine cognition, transcending the bounds of the intellect. He performed the funerary rites with respect to the two Rinpoches of Taklung who passed away (Jangchub Gyatso and Tashi Pel-o Zangpo) and prepared a vast cloud of offerings and so forth that fulfilled their enlightened intentions.

In 1451 (iron female sheep), in his thirty-fourth year, he formulated a clear plan, and in 1461 (iron female snake), in his forty-fourth year, coinciding with an auspicious conjunction of planets and stars in the waxing half of the first lunar month, he came to preside over the monastic seat. {431} In the summer of that year, he made wondrous restorations of the temples, large and small, and their three representations of buddha body, speech, and mind, and he donated inconceivable sacraments of offering. At that time, in a dream, he saw the spirit lord of the locality in a joyous form, the whole of Taklung filled with horsemen, armed with plume-topped hats, the ground covered with riding horses, and the air filled with paeans.

In 1463 (water female sheep), he invited Go Lotsāwa Zhonu Pel from Yarlung and studied under him without interruption *The Exposition of Sūtra and Tantra*[689] and a countless number of empowerments, transmissions, and pith instructions over a year.

During that same year, he acquired the service of a group of artisans from Kathmandu, including the skilled artist Jīvatija, and over the following three years this Newar artist who had reached the pinnacle of excellent craftsmanship in the sculpting of cire perdue beaten images in the Land of Snows, excellently fashioned the image of Munīndra called Tubchen Yulgyal Pelbar. Behind it were upright standing images of Maitreya and Avalokiteśvara, twenty-seven handspans in height. The throne and back screen were also fashioned of gilded copper and studded with jewels. The pearl relics that were inserted within the image had defining characteristics, exemplified by blessed objects such as the cotton painting of Hevajra that had been the meditative commitment of the supreme incarnation Marpa and the tooth of the peerless Dakpo Lharje Gampopa. During the consecration, the being of pristine cognition descended five times, on the last of which the lama saw it actually vanish into the image of Munīndra, and there were an infinite number of other auspicious signs—rainbows, showers of flowers, and so forth.

He also intended to commission a multiarmed image of his preferred deity, glorious Vajrabhairava, but because it could not be comprehended by the craftsmen, he instead commissioned an image of Venerable Mañjuvajra {432} that was insatiable to behold. Within it, he placed particularly sublime relics, including six different Sanskrit manuscripts of *The Litany of the Names of Mañjuśrī*.

When a Drigungpa army arrived at Tsatang Gangwa in Podo, he prayed to the three precious jewels, and after examining the auspicious circumstances, he rendered the local villagers fearless through the lion's roar of his exhalation. The large force of the opposing army was defeated by the protector deity Masang Tsewang Drakpa and a few acolytes.

In 1466 (dog), he fell ill owing to an infectious disease but carried that on to the path and composed *The Adamantine Spiritual Song of Common Savor*.[690] In 1469 (ox), when elaborate rites were undertaken to support his life, he had a dream in which he scaled a long white ladder within a mansion. On reaching the top, each rung of the ladder symbolized one of the five paths or the ten levels, and on arriving at the summit, an inconceivable feeling of joy and bliss was born within his mind. During the summer of 1472 (dragon), he made a great recovery. On that occasion, he said, "It seems that I probably won't partake of even a fraction of the deeds of Choje Ratnākara," and he promised that he would incarnate again.

In a dream, Bodong Rinpoche empowered him in the maṇḍala of *The Awakening of Vairocana*,[691] and said to him, "Meditate on the ḍāmaru and vajra within the ears of the being of pristine cognition as it descends!" He then rang his bell, whereupon the meditative stability of radiance and emptiness arose.

Owing to his service on behalf of the monastic seat, Ngawang Drakpa Pelzangpo was invited joyfully to the palatial abode of the spirit lord of the locality. He assumed the form of a person with matted hair, and the spirit lord of the earth assumed the form of White Pañjara. Along with his retinue, the spirit lord of the locality then requested instruction on setting the mind on enlightenment, and he offered to disclose for inspection his manifold subterranean treasure stores.[692] {433}

On one occasion, when he caused rain to fall through his meditative concentrations because there had been no rainfall, in his perception, the gods and nāgas said, "We have no spare time to assist because we are restoring the damage to an offering shrine," but they nonetheless stopped work, and immediately there was a great downpour of rain.

On the day of the autumn festival in 1472 (dragon), he presided over the investiture of his nephew On Rinpoche Tashi Pelwa.[693] He then traveled many times to the northern direction, where he manifoldly imparted advice to the communities of Rong, Khyung, and so forth. His compositions were extensive, including works on Sanskrit grammar, astrology, medicine, exegeses of canonical scripture and treatises, cycles of practical application, many writings on spiritual guidance, prayers, spiritual songs, oral instructions, official letters, and answers to questions.

When he went on pilgrimage to Reteng, the moment he saw the blessed painted scroll depicting Black Yamāri, he firmly maintained meditative stability that entire day, visualizing the whole environment as the celestial palace of Black Yamāri and all its inhabitants as the divine assembly of Vajrabhairava, unobscured by anything at all including endless processions, stops, and busy events. Things manifested in that manner since he had previously received the empowerment of Bhairava at Yamdrok from Bodong Rinpoche.

Ngawang Drakpa Pelzangpo revised the translation of *The Glorious Tantra of Hevajra* based on six Sanskrit manuscripts containing commentaries on that tantra. He also revised the translation of *The Litany of the Names of Mañjuśrī*, integrating six Sanskrit manuscripts, and he revised the translation of *The Attainment of Mañjuśrī: The Solitary Hero*[694] based on a single Sanskrit manuscript. He revised the translation of *The Great Paradise of Uṣṇīṣasītatapatra*,[695] integrating four Sanskrit manuscripts. He made a great redaction of *The Introduction to the Conduct of a Bodhisattva*, integrating three Sanskrit manuscripts; {434} a great redaction also of *The Supreme Continuum of the Great Vehicle*, integrating three Sanskrit manuscripts; and a great redaction of *The Transcendent Perfection of Wisdom in Eight Thousand Lines*, relying on three Sanskrit manuscripts, taking as their basis the translation of Ngok and integrating with it five other translations including that of Vairotsana. Furthermore, he also made important redactions of the *Heart of Wisdom*,[696] *Tārā*, *The Chapter of Vijayā*,[697] *The Eulogy of Tārā Titled Holding a Flower Garland*,[698] *The Eulogy of Cakrasaṃvara Titled Daṇḍaka*,[699] and *The Eulogy to Wisdom*.[700] He made an accurate revision of the *Mahāvyutpatti*.[701]

He excellently studied all the profound pith instructions of the perfection stage that were known and practiced here in Tibet, and experientially cultivated them in his own mind. Although he had no obstacles in teaching extensively to others, when he imparted guidance in the correct manner to students who were desirous of liberation, he exclusively praised the oral instructions of Coemergent Union of the Great Seal and the Six Doctrines of Nāropā, and he would teach with emphasis on these and nothing else.

When he taught the conclusive standpoint of the view, he emphasized the analytic meditations of the learned paṇḍitas that had been systematized through the natural power of the great masters who were erudite in the orthodox, unadulterated, and uncontaminated precious Kagyu teaching tradition. And after imparting that teaching, he would, without approval, also reveal those profound empowerments concerning the uncontrived, unorthodox path, known as the focused meditation of the *kusuli* yogins. Thus, it says in his own adamantine song,

> I pray that this coemergent pristine cognition of the luminous
> mind
> May not be perceived as a stain to be renounced, {435}
> And that those persons who hope the conquerors' pristine
> cognition will emerge
> From the accumulated propensities of analytic emptiness
> May not come to resemble the beaten chaff of those desiring rice
> Or the mirage pursued by those desiring water.[702]

Furthermore, leaving aside the other physical attributes of this mighty one among learned and accomplished masters, he ransomed many thousands of animals bound for certain death and extracted them from the jaws of the Lord of Death. He bestowed the bountiful gifts of medicine, including the compound known as "thirteen harsh ingredients,"[703] the compound of "six white ingredients,"[704] and the making of medicinal balls. He tamed by means of compassion and ritual activities gods and demons who were otherwise certain to steal physical vitality. He used the material resources that fell into his hands and that resembled the treasury of Vaiśravaṇa for offerings and donations, without squandering even a single piece of gold on unsuitable purposes. Subduing even the ferocious wild beasts in the vicinity of his residence, the wild ungulates and so forth in that place lived carefree. All that he told others would come to pass in the short and long term directly happened, and from Ngari in the highlands to Jang in the lowlands, all actions that were permeated by his enlightened activity were achieved by the imposing force of his presence. All holders of the piṭakas, when they arrived in his presence, were cowed, unable to fathom the depths of his learning. All his guidance and oral teaching directly introduced exclusively the ancient writings and were otherwise unadulterated. In addition to constructing new temples and their threefold representations of buddha body, speech, and mind, he also exerted his energy in the restoration of old buildings and artifacts. {436} His robes, seat, books, and physical necessities all exuded the fragrance of some sort of medicinal incense and indeed of unerring ethical discipline. He gave complete answers without hesitation to all those who requested him to cut off their doubts concerning subtle and minute points regarding the words, meanings, and experiential cultivation of the texts and pith instructions by accomplished masters who were renowned for their learning in scripture and realization. Each casual remark made in his speech could also completely sever hesitation. Although he possessed the treasury of inexhaustible space, he lacked the slightest trace of avarice in constructing temples and representations of buddha body, speech, and mind, or in acting on behalf of the community and the poor, and so forth. In all directions from south to north, and from first to last, he acted honestly, distinguishing between truth and falsehood, siding with the truth and keeping the shortcomings of miscreants in mind, such that in all respects he did not transgress the actual facts. Even when he appeared in the perception of this world to train those who had entered on a mistaken course, it was impossible for him in any way to be without the genuine truth. He made no distinction between the community leaders who requested teaching and action-free mendicants who requested teaching but perfectly granted them the profound and vast doctrine. Those who were afflicted by severe ailments, demonic possession, and so forth, he not only brought under the shelter of his compassion but cleansed them through healing, oral instructions, and the like. He did not overpraise or flatter his great-disciples, who resembled the sky covering the earth, or even his aristocratic patrons, who were proud like Brahmā, apart from training them by means of the sacred doctrine. Other than emphasizing truth and falsehood in approaching the definitive meaning, his mind could not be deeply swayed in any respect by deceit or obsequious flattery. {437} In brief, not to mention his activities with respect to the sacred doctrine, at the very least in all worldly dealings pertaining to governance, he did not rely on any consultations of those who were appointed in his service or of his subjects, whether in the short or long term, detailed or cursory. He was not persuaded by orders nor did he leave any aspect of a matter alone without examining it. So it was that he could never make mistakes and he did not in the slightest dismiss buddha activities as the trivial affairs of sentient beings. In these respects, his actions were consistent with and superior to even the liberating careers of other saintly persons who upheld the Buddhist teachings.

On one occasion, when he established the regular practice of Sitātapatrā, he had a wonderful dream in which that deity said, "Even without practicing the ritual service and rites of attainment, you are taken into my following." He then established the dance of the geomantic rite according to the lineage of yoga tantra and the torma offering rite of the doctrinal protectors, along with the drum dance.[705]

In 1476 (monkey), he founded Gepel Chodzong at Tangdrok.[706] The monastic seat was offered to him by the spirit lord of the locality. When Tsetang Kachupa Drakpa Tujewa came into his presence, he revised the translation of the root text and commentary of *The Treasury of Amarasiṃha*.[707] Minyak Drakdorwa composed the biography covering the first part of his life.[708]

Returning to Taklung, Ngawang Drakpa Pelzangpo knew that there would be a disaster due to the decline in support for the master in charge of offerings and the monastic estates of lower Kham, and his words turned out exactly to be true. The people were required to raise an army in the northern direction, but then, in the vanguard, many saw the spirit lord of the locality magically transformed into an envoy. The lama, on the other hand, saw him accurately as a smallpox-causing demon and persuaded them to abandon that military venture. {438} He constructed a large torma below his chamber. Many times, he performed the rite of summoning the demon of disease into an effigy and made offerings to it. Although the entire marketplace of the neighboring village was virulently infected, the disease was controlled from that place onward in the direction of Taklung, and subsequently, for a long period of time, reports of smallpox were unknown there.

In the fourth month of 1477 (fire female bird), when he was over the age of sixty, he planned to become a total renunciate, staying in retreat, and to that end, he went to Tangdrok. He issued an official letter of spiritual and temporal advice, and one-pointedly entered into firm retreat, without permitting outsiders within an earshot. He fell ill due to an insect bite in the side of his liver, but without immersing himself in the Dzaki River, it vanished when someone offered him an oral instruction concerning enchanted water.

Ngawang Drakpa Pelzangpo cherished the Collected Works of Buton,[709] which Nyenpo Nangso had offered him in exchange for some merchandise. He commissioned twelve copies of the Trengwachen version of *The Transcendent Perfection of Wisdom in Eight Thousand Lines*, inscribed in refined gold on Chinese paper.[710] He also built an iron bridge over the Lhachu.[711]

In the early summer at Tangdrok, he gave many empowerments, transmissions, and pith instructions, including *The Exegesis of Hevajra according to the Ngok Tradition*,[712] the Collected Works of Drogon Phakmodrupa, the Great Seal, and Mahākāla in the Form Kurukma to his sibling Rinpoche and approximately five hundred monks intent on the sacred doctrine.

Around that time, Zhika Nelpa[713] was deceived by the Phakmodrupas and, although Taklung was troubled, when the large army of Nangso Donyo Dorje and Yungpa Tsewang, chieftain and minister, poured into U, Onsa Ngawang Drakpa invited them up to Taklung.[714] From the time of Drungchen Norzang, Taklung and Rinpung had embraced a patron-priest relationship, and through this act of service, the situation calmed of its own accord. {439} In the spring of 1481 (ox year), Nangso Donyo Dorje Gyelpo, with some hundred officials and servants, arrived at Taklung, where they received many times the kindness of the lama's empowerments, transmissions, and pith instructions. Perceiving him as an actual buddha, Donyo Dorje accepted him as his root teacher. In addition to spending the autumn at Gepel Chodzong, Donyo Dorje went to the encampment of Venerable Karmapa Chodrak Gyatso. They had tea and established an official relationship.

In 1483 (hare), Ngawang Drakpa Pelzangpo went into the presence of Chokyi Drakpa Yeshe Pelzangpo, the fourth holder of the Zhamar crown, and bestowed upon him many empowerments, transmissions, and pith instructions of Drigung, Densatil, and Taklung—all three. Zhamarpa was extremely devoted and accepted him as his root teacher. He also composed works including the earlier and later hagiographies of that master.

When obstacles were instigated by demonic forces, Ngawang Drakpa Pelzangpo subdued them through the meditative stability of Vajrabhairava. One evening, in the early summer, he went up onto the roof, wearing his felt cloak and hat, and he performed the rites of wrathful mantras, assuming many diverse demeanors. About five thunderbolts fell around there that evening, but he said, "Now there will be no harm!" Immediately, there was thunder, hailstones fell, and although a thunderbolt struck, the residence and the people were unharmed.

He traveled in the northern region several times, and he founded many monastic communities. He brought Gungpa Tongkor under his authority. While he was residing at Kyil in Sokpo, in a dream he gathered all the many great gods and demons of U, Tsang, and Kham. The forest deities and hybrid tsen spirits also were present. They donated offerings to him and requested the setting of the mind on enlightenment. Also, one night in a dream, many noblemen arrayed offering sacraments, including the seven precious things on a golden wheel and offered them to him. They undertook a confession rite, affirmed their vows, and requested the sacred doctrine. {440} He said that these were the local deities of the Drigungpa.

Again, he returned to Taklung. In 1485 (monkey) Venerable Tashi Pelwa retired, and Choje Namgyel Drakpa was enthroned, while Rinpoche Sonam Pelzang was appointed at Kadruk. Although the Zhika Nelpa had not previously respected him, from that time on, they had a profound patron-priest relationship. In 1487 (sheep), alms and festival foods were dispatched throughout Utsang as a meritorious act of service to sustain his life. In 1488 (monkey), he fell ill and said that he would soon pass into nirvāṇa. In 1491 (pig), he began a construction project. In the summer of 1492 (mouse), he contributed a wonderful golden roof to the grass hermitage and varnished the Great Offering Chapel. Simultaneously, he presented twenty-one excellent artifacts to the Old Protector Chapel, including armor, helmets, and swords.

On one occasion, when he fell ill, he was asked to receive bloodletting treatment, but he said, "There's no need for bloodletting! Freedom from disease ensues from the cure of the spirit lord of the locality, as well as from bloodletting. The spirit lord of the locality also has a disciple!"

From the start of 1493 (ox), he received an insistent invitation from Neudongtse, from Onsa Dungyu Rinpoche, Chenga Rinpoche, Nangso Tsokye Dorje, Drung Donyo Dorje, Zhika Nelpa, and Yargyab Ponchen.

In the third month of that year, he set out. On the near and far sides of the gate of Taklung, there were people offering an image of Mañjughoṣa and of Bhairava, so he said that this was an excellent auspicious coincidence indicative of the gathering of the peaceful and wrathful meditational deities. In Lhasa, he visited Nelpa, who requested the initiations of Cakrasaṃvara, Mahākāla, and Vaiśravaṇa, as well as the Six Doctrines of Nāropā, and became a devout patron. At Lhunpotse in Chushul, he was presented with offerings by the encamped Donyo Dorje, {441} who requested many empowerments and pith instructions. He visited the power place of Drangsong Sinpori.[715]

In the estates of Dra, Dol, and Zhung, he was venerated by Yargyab Ponchen, who offered him an image of Munīndra in the form Serlingma, and so forth. He delivered teachings there on the profound and vast sacred doctrine, and then proceeded to Yarlung, where he was welcomed by Nangso Tsokye Dorje, the secretary of Neudongpa and a retinue of some five hundred horsemen. He went up to Norgye in Neudongtse, and was perfectly venerated there. In Tsetang, he gave excellent alms, and the entire river valley was filled with people who had come to see him and hear his teachings. Nangso Tsokye Dorje invited him to Khartok Gonsar and presented immeasurable offerings and acts of service. He requested many empowerments and guidance, including the empowerment of Mañjuvajra. At Tse, when a somewhat miraculous disturbance manifested due to demonic forces, he carried that on the path by means of the practice of common savor.

From Nyenpodru,[716] he traveled via Tarma to Densatil. The sacred seat of Phakmodrupa had been afflicted by drought, but that night there was a great downpour of rain, and everyone was astonished. Some days before, on the rock behind the image of Kundra Rinpoche Tongwa Tongden, the robe of the deity had been snagged in a crack. It could not be extracted, and so a whole cubit of the robe was squashed in front. In this way, they arrived at the certainty that they should welcome the omniscient one. He distributed a cloud of offerings to all the three representations of buddha body, speech, and mind that were hard to measure, and he offered communal tea to the assembly, along with gold and alms. He then delivered public teachings on the Great Seal and the Six Doctrines of Nāropā.

Ngawang Drakpa Pelzangpo then journeyed on to Tsongdu Drak Kha, where Onsa Dungyu Rinpoche requested the lay vows.[717] He also requested the blessing of Cakrasaṃvara, the initiation of Jñānanātha, guidance on the

Six Doctrines of Nāropā, and so forth and adopted him as his root teacher. {442}

Traveling on to Chokhor Samye, he refused to wear a red or black ceremonial hat and went there wearing an ordinary hat.[718] Since he was untainted by such flaws, he was definitely an indisputable great accomplished master. On teaching the sacred doctrine there, a shower of flowers fell, coloring the ground. He visited the Main Temple with all its representations of buddha body, speech, and mind, and he made great offerings.

Saying that it would not matter at all that there was no time to visit the Tsang region on an extended gradual itinerary, he went by coracle across the Kyichu and, at that time, avoided recriminations. In Lhasa, he was presented with offerings by Nelpa, and after donating offerings and making aspiration prayers in the presence of Jowo Śākyamuni in the Jokhang, he returned to Taklung.

Once again, the holder of the Zhamar crown and his disciples came to receive his teachings. They requested innumerable empowerments, transmissions, and pith instructions. With the venerable lama himself acting as preceptor and Tulku Zhamarwa acting as master of ceremonies, they conferred the complete monastic ordination on Choje Namgyel Drakpa and his brother. On that occasion, a lightning bolt fell upon the eastern gate, and although it struck the painted scrolls inside, there was no damage at all apart from a mere bluish glimmer around the protective wire mesh, and so everyone, residents and visitors, was astonished.

When the incumbent of Taklung, Choje Tashi Pelwa, fell severely ill due to lymphatic disorder, Ngawang Drakpa Pelzangpo went to perform a torma empowerment, whereupon just as he mounted his riding horse, an unceasing, strong windstorm arose. Afterward, his complexion turned red like vermilion, and he blazed with majesty. He said that although the course of the disease might continue somewhat, in the long term there would be no harm. Accordingly, that is exactly what happened.

In early and later life, about a hundred Sanskrit books came into his hands, and he published most of the textual commentaries they contained in volumes that were free from modification, addition, omission, or error, inscribed on parchment, {443} the Sanskrit in gold and the Tibetan in silver. These were said to have been finer in quality than an ordinary Kangyur.

He unquestionably engaged in ritual activities and so forth. Although his mind was without even a trace of spitefulness, he cast ominous and miraculous spells against those who held wrong views concerning the Buddhist teaching, such that only their names were left behind. Just by the thoughts in his mind, any material thing whatsoever would effortlessly fall into his hands.

In 1494 (tiger), he was invited by the governor Donyo Dorje, a mighty lord of faith and power. He set out during the eighth month. In upper Dam, he was invited by Bongsung, and on the way up, he visited the temple of Tseding.[719] From Zhupu, he was welcomed by the great governor with about one hundred horsemen and a golden line of monks.[720] He went to the settlement of Zhu Kungarawa.[721] The service and veneration he received were inconceivable.

In Rinpung, to that great patron Donyo Dorje, he granted many approaches of maturational empowerment, including the empowerments into the maṇḍala of Guhyasamāja in the form Mañjuvajra, many details of the generation and perfection stages pertaining to Cakrasaṃvara, Bhaṭṭārikā and so forth, the introductions to Coemergent Union of the Great Seal, the Four Syllables, and the Fivefold Great Seal. In particular, he granted maturational empowerment and liberating guidance in accordance with the detailed steps of visualization of the Six Doctrines of Nāropā, which constitute the profound path. Many great geshes of Utsang also assembled there. They requested the teachings they desired, and he resolved all their doubts concerning the essential points of the transmitted teachings. At that time, he conferred all the teachings that he gave, without relying on texts and exclusively from memory, including most of the well-known tantras, {444} *The Three Commentaries by Bodhisattvas*,[722] the cycles of oral transmissions,[723] the Sublime Cycle[724] of the Guhyasamāja including the Five Stages and *The Lamp That Subsumes Conduct*,[725] the Five Doctrines of Maitreya,[726] and the Six Collections of Madhyamaka Reasoning,[727] such that all were astonished.

In particular, the great governor Donyo Dorje was captivated by the enlightened attributes of the greatness of his buddha body, speech, and mind, and felt an intense wave of devotion, determining that he was actually a perfect buddha. Even in his own morning and evening meditations, he stopped his other outer and inner practices, without engaging at all in ordinary meritorious acts, symbolic or nonsymbolic. Immediately, there arose within the reach and range of his thought the very physical form that he had first seen at Taklung, and he had a feeling of contentment. In his meditation, he could successively name the relay stations on the way and arrive at the temple of Taklung, where he made a connection, saying, "I see the body maṇḍala of the precious father!" and then he recited the lama's name as a mantra, saying, "Ngawang Drakpa knows!" He would prolong this meditation even beyond the periods that had been provisionally set and, in the estimation of most ordinary people, he said, "I remember! I have found certainty! A great deed will come to pass!" It is said that, immediately after that, the lay officials who had been waiting would approach him to offer assistance once his meditation had dissolved.

Ngawang Drakpa Pelzangpo was then invited via the Rongchung valley to Lhunpotse in Chushul. There too he turned the extensive wheel of the sacred doctrine. He consecrated a torma for the ingress of the doctrinal protectors and offered prayers, such that after the ritual triumph in the battle of exorcism, the reputation and strategy of the Rinpungpa became vast as the sky. The veneration {445} and the offerings he received resembled those amassed in the offering clouds of Vaiśravaṇa's treasure store. In particular, he was offered from the estate itself many rare distinctive artifacts, including an image of Munīndra in the form Serlingma and a woven tapestry of Bhairava.[728] The governor Wangpo, with many attendants, requested permission to escort him as far as Gyere Lhakhang.[729] While in Lhasa he made offerings and aspiration prayers in the presence of Jowo Śākyamuni in the Jokhang. Zhika Nelpa paid his respects and received the kindness of his instruction on the profound path.

As soon as Ngawang Drakpa Pelzangpo reached this great seminary of Taklung, a group of Newar artisans, including the sculptor Lakṣmipāla arrived, and he intended to commission an image of glorious Jñānanātha, utilizing more than ten thousand *sang* of silver. Knowing that he would soon pass into nirvāṇa, he gave his instructions instantaneously. He also undertook the preliminary rites with respect to the relics to be inserted within that image, and he delivered many teachings pertaining to the profound and vast sacred doctrine to interested persons who gathered from all directions and to those who permanently resided there. In a dream, he had a vision in which all the doctrinal protectors were setting out, saying they were going to the place of Choje Densapa. Rainbow lights and a shower of flowers encircled him.

In the sixth month, he camped at the plain below the monastery and stayed there for some days. He then offered a fine feast to a party from Dranang, headed by his brother, Choje Kumche, and he went there to impart extensive oral instructions. When he reached the Drokha chamber, he immediately seemed to fall ill. His demeanor was one of utmost contentment, and he sang many spiritual songs. He accepted some responsibility for the ritual service undertaken to prolong his health. Then, in his seventy-ninth year, he passed away on the twelfth day of the seventh month of 1496 (fire male dragon). {446} Offerings were presented to the sacred corpse by some five hundred geshes. On the twenty-first day after the sacred corpse had been displayed, it was inserted within a precious basket and placed within the Northern Chamber. On the eighteenth day of the eighth month, Chenga Rinpoche was invited from Densatil to be seated at the head of the row, and a great funeral ceremony was held. Alms and feast offerings were lavishly distributed to some five thousand monks and more than eighty thousand laypeople. A gold image and an image fashioned of medicinal herbs, which was a representation of him, were constructed. A silver reliquary representing the great enlightenment was fashioned to contain the precious corpse, which had not decayed, in the manner of a wish-fulfilling gem, and it was placed at the center of the chamber known as Zimsak Jangma.[730] An extensive consecration rite was performed, such that the splendor of his blessings was incomparable. All avenues of auspicious coincidence naturally fell into place, and the occasion was rendered most positive.

The foregoing account presents merely the gist of the narrative up to his fifty-eighth year, which was composed by Minyak Drak Dor, and the biography of the later years, which was compiled by Tsamla Sonam Zangpo.

The Renowned Disciples of Ngawang Drakpa Pelzangpo

It is known that among all the great upholders of the Buddhist teaching who were illustrious for their learning and their venerable and noble conduct at that time—and who were exalted in lineage, birth, and rank—there was no one who did not bow down at the lotus feet of this lord-protector. Among them, those whom I definitely saw or heard authenticated in the records were the following: the glorious Chenga Rinpoche, who was the doctrinal regent and nephew in the family line of Choje Gampopa, lord of all the Kagyu lineages; {447} and the omniscient Chokyi Drakpa Yeshe Pelzangpo, the fourth holder of the Zhamar crown, the emanation of Gyelwa Konchok Yenlak and district governor of Phakmodru.

Zhamar Chokyi Drakpa Yeshe Pelzangpo

When the latter first met Ngawang Drakpa Pelzangpo, he received the symbolic empowerment of Vārāhī, the profound doctrines of Drigung, *The Drigungpa Circle of Devotion and Vitality*,[731] the blessing of Cakrasaṃvara, the complete initiation and four empowerments pertaining to Jñānanātha, and the entire outer, inner, and secret pith instructions concerning Mahākāla in the form Kurakma, which are known to be given in the Taklung tradition.

On their second meeting, he received the complete Collected Works of Drogon Rinpoche;[732] *The Narrative Titled Wish-Fulfilling Creeper*;[733] the empowerment of Vajrapāṇi, Subduer of the Lord of Death; and the blessing of *The Six Texts of Vārāhī*,[734] together with the oral instructions on the texts.

They met yet again at Lhunpotse while on the way to Densatil, and so forth. On such occasions, Zhamarpa received manifold empowerments, transmissions, and pith instructions. It was at the encouragement of the most venerable Sonam Yeshe Pelzangpo from Yargyab that he composed the two earlier and later hagiographies of Ngawang Drakpa Pelzangpo that are renowned in the present day.[735]

Drukpa Rinpoche Gampopa Chenga

The glorious Drukpa Rinpoche, Gyelwang Choje Kunga Peljor, who was perfect and peerless in learning, realization, and compassion, acted as the Chenga of Gampo Monastery for approximately six years.[736] He met Ngawang Drakpa Pelzangpo in the Drokha chamber at Taklung and received from him a profound and concise doctrinal connection.

Other Drukpa Connections

On some three occasions in early and later life, Drukpa Rinpoche Ngawang Chokyi Gyelpo, who had previously manifested in India as Ḍombhi Heruka and in Tibet as Marpa Lotsāwa,[737] also met Ngawang Drakpa Pelzangpo and largely received the empowerments of the seven maṇḍalas that are implemented according to the tradition of Ngok,[738] {448} as well as all the pith instructions of the generation and perfection stages pertaining to the exegesis of the tantras that the venerable master had himself conferred on Ngok Jangchub Pel,[739] and a great many essentials concerning the profound doctrines of Drigung, Taklung, and Druk. Later, Drukpa Rinpoche offered all those teachings to the wondrous supreme tulku Namgyel Tashi of Taklung,[740] such that the transmission of the teaching of the lineage of attainment became more beneficial.

Drigungpa Connections

When Rinchen Chogyel, the glorious potentate of the Drigungpa,[741] did not find a worthy person from whom to receive the unadulterated instruction of the Kagyu lineage, in his twenty-second year, he studied under Rinpoche's direct disciple, Chiwa Namkha Gyeltsen, and the latter's direct disciple, Duldzin Ngawang Gyeltsen. Then, on hearing that the entire unadulterated oral instruction of the Kagyu lineage in general and the Drigungpa lineage in particular rested in Taklung Ngawang Drakpa Pelzangpo, he went to meet him five times in early and later life. He excellently studied the cursory doctrinal cycles of the Kagyu lineage in general and all the profound doctrines of Jikten Gonpo without exception, and he said that the title Master of the Sacred Doctrine was then conferred upon him. At that time, in Drigung, leaving aside the transmission of the profound sacred doctrines of their own pure tradition, even the books were extremely rare. Thus, Rinpoche therefore restored the transmissions from their foundation and maintained the ancestral heritage of the Kagyu lineage at Drigung.

Furthermore, Mangto Rabjampa Konchok Rinchen also requested teachings completely from the venerable omniscient Ngagi Wangpo Pelzangpo here in Taklung, and he applied them in practice. He in turn offered them to Choje Kunga Rinchen, such that they were indeed more clearly elucidated.[742] In brief, during that period, the doctrinal lineage of the Drigungpa was unbroken due to the kindness of this lord-protector of Taklung. {449}

Sakya Connections

The great paṇḍita, masterful in the entire five subjects of classical learning, named Śākya Chokden Drime Lekpei Lodro Jampel Gawei Shenyen, was a renowned and unrivaled scholar.[743] He first met Ngawang Drakpa Pelzangpo at Daryul Rinchen Gang.[744] He received the permission rite of white Sarasvati, and on that occasion the attendant Paṇchen Pelden Tsultrim and the secretary Cho Gyeltsenpa were both also present. Later, they met at

Taklung, where he received the profound exegesis of the Trilogy of Spiritual Songs based on the commentary of Phub Lodro Senge, the Fivefold Great Seal, the Four Syllables, and so forth, and, as a supporting teaching, the Seven Sections of Attainment, the Six Essential Cycles, *The Twenty-Four Doctrinal Cycles of Nonmentation*, the complete extensive and concise empowerment, precepts, and pith instructions pertaining to Jñānanātha, and *The Golden Rosary of the Kagyu Lineage*.[745] On that occasion, his attendant Venerable Kunga Gyeltsen and Drakmarwa Kunga Tsepel were both also present. Paṇchen Śākya Chokden made a petition that he offered to the lama in Sanskrit, along with a most excellent hagiography.

The Close Disciples of Ngawang Drakpa Pelzangpo

Chime Pelzangpo

Foremost among the spiritual sons of Venerable Ngawang Drakpa Pelzangpo was the learned and accomplished master Chime Pelzangpo.[746] At the time when glorious Chime Drubpa, the emanation of the body of lord Phakmodrupa, was about to pass away, he had said to Pa Rinpoche Ngawang Drakpa, "Since I hope to be associated with you in my next reincarnation, you should accept me with compassion!" Accordingly, he would later be reborn as a hoopoe bird in the line.[747]

In recognition for his service, Chime Pelzangpo was given incomparable rewards. The transmission of Bodongpa's extensive *Summation of the Real*[748] descended to him, and he was favored with the mysteries of the pith instructions of the precious Kagyu lineage. Later, in other places too, he undertook extensive study and reflection and became a magnificent upholder of the Buddhist teaching, unsurpassed by anyone in all fields of classical learning, including sūtra, mantra, Sanskrit grammar, logic, art, and medicine. {450} Later, when he went to meet Venerable Karmapa Mikyo Dorje,[749] the latter's personal assistant said, "Which lama do you have faith in?" He replied, "I have faith in Lama Taklung Ngawang Drakpa himself!" "To what extent do you have faith in him?" "If Taklung Ngawang Drakpa were seated on one side in front and the thousand buddhas of the Auspicious Eon were seated on the other side, I would pay homage to Taklung Ngawang Drakpa, and my eyes would not have regard even for the buddhas of the Auspicious Eon!" "That is most wonderful!" he said. The personal assistant then praised him, saying, "I have traveled throughout Tsang and U, but nowhere have I seen anyone more magnificent that Chime Pelzangpo!"

Later, when Pawo Tulku Tsuklak Trengwa met him and received teachings, his mind could not embrace the magnificent exegesis of even a single session of Chime Pelzangpo's doctrinal connection. It was through this that the gateway of his expertise in teaching and composition opened like the break of dawn. So it is written in his biography.

He passed the time in the activities of teaching, debate, and composition, and he established the philosophical system of his own view. When he had excellently established this view based on scriptural authenticity and logical reasoning and had refined his skill in debate, he roared a lion's roar, asserting, "How can this possibly be contradicted without examining the writings of us three—me, Amarasena, and the son of Śuddhodana!" He repeatedly said that all the major and subtle points of debate concerning the perspective of the mantras were exclusively adopted through the enlightened intention of Pa Rinpoche. Inspired to the utmost through prayer, he continued to perform acts that were solely of benefit. He lived a long life, and finally, after appearing to fall ill, {451} he lit a long stick of incense. Holding it in his hands, in a most splendid and sweet melody, he intoned *The Prayer of the Six Doctrines*[750] that had been composed by Pa Rinpoche, saying, "I pray to omniscient Ngawang Drakpa from the monastic seat of Taklung Tang. Grant your blessing that I too might become like you in knowing all things!" It is reported that he passed away alone, as the incense fell from his hands.

Zhalu Lotsāwa Rinchen Chokyong Zangpo

Zhalu Lotsāwa Rinchen Chokyong Zangpo, a spiritual adviser who had refined the three trainings and was adorned with learning and spiritual accomplishment like a golden reliquary stūpa, also paid homage to Ngawang Drakpa and received a doctrinal connection with him.[751] At the insistence of Pa Rinpoche, he made a marvelous revised translation of *The Eulogy to Mahākāla in Eight Stanzas*,[752] which was in conformity with the Sanskrit manuscript. I, Ngawang Namgyel, think this translation of that text alone is excellent.

Sharawa Rabjampa Sangye Senge

Sharawa Rabjampa Sangye Senge, who first had been a geshe of the Riwo Gedenpa tradition, refined in sūtra and mantra, also paid homage at the feet of the omniscient and venerable Ngawang Drakpa here in Taklung.[753] He received maturational empowerment and liberating guidance according to the oral instructions of the precious Kagyu lineage, headed by the aural lineage of Cakrasaṃvara.[754] He became a mighty lord of yoga, resembling a snow lion, in whose mind realization arose because the auspicious indications were arrayed within his physical body. Later, his enlightened activity was even greater because he became the root teacher of Tsangpa Heruka.[755]

He also requested profound instruction on the curing of poison and propagated that based on the exegeses of Lato Zurkharwa and others.[756] {452} He alone requested a specific part of the guidance and oral instruction of the venerable and omniscient Ngawang Drakpa, and he benefited its transmission.

Drukpa Kunga Lekpa

The divine madman of Bhutan, Kunga Lekpa, had perfected the power of pristine cognition internally, and yet he acted externally as a child, free from astrological determinism.[757] He met Ngawang Drakpa while in the service of Drukchen and received a doctrinal connection with him. Later, he remarked to others, "I went to Taklung and offered a puppy to Choje Rinpoche. I requested a doctrinal connection and the lama appeared to be one who has both spiritual and material attributes."

Pawo Tulku Chowang Lhundrub

Pawo Tulku Chowang Lhundrub, a master of the ascetic practice that liberates phenomenal existence in the buddha body of reality, also touched his feet and requested many times the profound sacred doctrine of the Kagyu lineage.[758]

Lhunde Rabjampa Peljor Gyatso

Lhunde Rabjampa Peljor Gyatso of Densatil requested experiential guidance on the Great Seal and the Six Doctrines, attending upon his lotus feet for a long period of time. He requested the lama to cut off doubts regarding each distinctive point in *Distinctive Threefold Eloquence: Guidance on the Six Doctrines*,[759] and in his presence the lama presented a perfect guidebook (*khrid yig*) that established the abiding nature of reality.

Minyak Rabjam Drakpa Dorje

Minyak Rabjam Drakpa Dorje also served him for a long period of time and, as mentioned above, composed *The Great Biography*.[760] Later, considering that the Sakya and Geluk views were not of a common savor, it is said that he was able to secure the enlightened activity of the five venerable founders of Sakya, formulating the core texts of his own Sakya tradition.

Sangye Nyenpa Tashi Peljor

Sangye Nyenpa Tashi Peljor, the sole lord of the enlightened heritage of Venerable Karmapa Mikyo Dorje, an accomplished master who was an emanation of paṇḍita Smṛti, stayed in both the hermitage and monastery of Ngawang Drakpa and attended upon him for a long period of time, determining him to be a perfect buddha.[761] {453} He requested many cycles of instruction pertaining to the three lineages of Drigung, Taklung, and Druk, and in particular *The Experiential Guidance on the Six Doctrines according to Taklung*.[762] Accordingly, his realization increased and became steadfast. He held Ngawang Drakpa as a root teacher, equal to Venerable Chodrak Gyatso. In his spiritual songs, the following words are repeatedly found:

> Taklungpa, the great paṇḍita of the six subjects of classical learning;
> Karmapa, the knower of all things . . .

When he was present at a rain-stopping ritual,[763] there was a white cloud billowing in the direction of Taklung, and a fervent thought of immeasurable strength arose, thinking, "Underneath yonder cloud dwells my lama, the omniscient Ngawang Drakpa!" and he composed a spiritual song in the form of a prayer. This is known from many similar anecdotes, but in the official biography of Sangye Nyenpa, compiled by his disciples, there is no mention of this incident. It appears to have been intentionally discarded, owing to the prevailing circumstances.

Zhango Lungpa Choku Yeshe Tashi

Zhango Lungpa Choku Yeshe Tashi, the emanation of Lord Maitripā, was a most wonderful realized meditator from Tsang who maintained the ascetic practices of Kunpang Zhenpa Rangdrol.[764] His realization of the great seal of the abiding nature was like the sky, and his body and mind were liberated in the uncontaminated state through the nectar of the great seal of bliss and emptiness. He was a devotee of Pa Rinpoche Ngawang Drakpa.

Drilungpa Tokden Sonam Wangchuk

Drilungpa Tokden Sonam Wangchuk obtained the kindness of instruction on the three vows from Venerable Lama Ngawang Drakpa himself. Dissolving all bewilderment of the subject-object dichotomy in the disposition of reality, he conversed with meditational deities as with human beings, and the doctrinal protectors including Six-Armed Jñānanātha were assigned to his service, such that, at the very least, they were included among his playful companions. Although the enlightened attributes of his clear realization were internally radiant, like the sunrise at the break of day, {454} outwardly he was a lord-protector secretly engaged in the practices that control the central channel. His reincarnation was my crown ornament, Vajradharapāda.

Tsamla Sonam Zangpo

Tsamla Sonam Zangpo, who had perfected the enlightened attributes of scriptural transmission and realization, was dispatched to lower Jang,[765] where he greatly benefited the Buddhist teaching. As mentioned above, he composed the biography covering the latter part of Ngawang Drakpa's life. He presented an exquisite screen of gilded copper to be placed behind the precious reliquary. By engaging in the ritual service and rites of attainment of Jñānanātha and Legon Takṣad, he could eradicate the enemies of the Buddhist teaching just by cursing them. It is in his lineage that the monastic officials of Taklung have descended in succession.

Uma Onpo Peljor Gyatso

Uma Onpo Peljor Gyatso was most venerable and broad-minded.[766] He composed a particularly sublime and definitive memorandum on the transmission of Pa Rinpoche's teaching on *The Six Doctrines according to the Taklung Tradition*,[767] which later became an ornament of the Buddhist teaching.

Kyase Tokden

The great exponent of Severance known as Kyase Tokden,[768] who was endowed with the attributes of refinement, also many times requested guidance and oral instruction from Ngawang Drakpa. The one who was foremost in his meditative commitments was the previously mentioned Drilungpa Sonam Wangchuk.

Dungtsuk Namkha Wangchukpa

Dungtsuk Namkha Wangchukpa was a disciple and devotee of Pa Rinpoche himself. Most advanced in meditation, he was one who asked preeminently about the essentials of the oral instruction. He guided many hundreds of renunciate practitioners at the great hermitage of Tangdrok.

Papom Zhamarwa

There was also one called Papom Zhamarwa, who became an exemplary upholder of the teaching of the lineage of attainment.[769] Here at Taklung, he excellently requested the immaculate oral instructions of the Kagyu lineage in the presence of Ngawang Drakpa. {455} Through his explanations, he brought up countless disciples in the upper and lower regions of Dokham, including the area around Riwoche, guiding them with certainty through the path of experience. Nowadays, also, there is an extant introduction to the Great Seal, known as *The Established Method of Papom Zhamarwa*,[770] which is said to be esteemed in the region of Kham as an oral instruction conferring buddhahood in the palm of the hand.

Others

In addition, Śākya Gyeltsen, the master of Serdokchenpa; Nyuklha Paṇchen, Ngawang Drakpa; Drepung Choje Onpo Śākyadhaja; Ngotro Rabjampa Wangchuk Pelwa; Khedrub Gyamawa; Langtang Chenga Lodro Gyeltsen; Gyel Lhakhangpa Yonten Gyatso; Lowo Choje Kunga Chokdrub; Nyenpa Rinpochepa; Rabjampa Monlam Pel; and Rabjampa Tashi Rinchen, or Neljorpa Zabsal Dorje, were all summoned by the prince of Rinpung Gangpa Donyo Dorje to Lhunpotse in Chushul, where in a great row within the assembly hall, they powerfully chanted the renowned prayer to Pa Rinpoche Ngawang Drakpa titled *Embodiment of All the Conquerors*. However, the strength of his resolve was not captivated by patrons or priests, in consequence of which his reputation spread like the wind throughout Utsang. In my childhood, I had to accept this occasionally, while seated in the row occupied by all the noble officials.

The "Brown" and "Striped" Communities of Taklung

At this great monastic seat of Taklung, the great preceptor Gendun Senge, Dechen Gyatsowa and his nephew, and Lachen Pelgon Rinchen, who was in the line descended from the nephew of Dampa Lotsāwa, were appointed by Pa Rinpoche Ngawang Drakpa as leaders of the "brown" monastic community. {456}

This succession was subsequently maintained by Jangyampa Lodro Chowang who was descended from his own nephew, Ngawang Gyeltsen, Chokyi Wangchuk, and Phuntsok Gyatso, and from them down to Ngawang Samten Gyatso and his brother of the present day.[771] They have acted as the dharma gatekeeper and confessor, and so forth, during monastic ordinations, and they have the title Kyilsangwa.[772]

In general, the "striped" monastic community would recite the explanations of the emanational maṇḍalas pertaining to the meditational deity Vajrapāṇi in the form Mahācakra, the protector deity Vaiśravaṇa, and Sarvavid Vairocana, in accordance with the tradition of Buton. And the "brown" monastic community would engage in reciting those of the meditational deities Vajrakīla and Sarvavid Vairocana in accordance with the tradition of Pelden Lama.[773] Apart from just these, no other rites were established because they would be superfluous.[774] There was no difference between these two communities because they all exclusively focused on the actual foundation of experiential cultivation according to the monastic regulations of the Taklung Kagyu lineage, the generation and perfection stages, and the doctrinal protectors.[775]

Lokottaratama

While the paṇḍita Lokottaratama from eastern India was residing at Neudongtse, he received a letter from Taklung written in the Vartula script, which reads in Tibetan as follows: "Paṇḍita, what is your country? What is your social class? To which of the four monastic orders do you belong? What vows do you maintain—the novitiate or full monastic ordination? What are the names of your preceptor and master of ceremonies? What path and practice do you follow—sūtra or mantra? How many years have you been in Tibet? Are you now in good health?" In response to these questions, he sent the following clear reply: "My country is Saṅgharatna in the east. My parents are of the brahmin class. I belong to the Sammitīya order. My preceptor is Sarvajñāmitra, and my master of ceremonies is Vādisiṃha. My confessor was Abhayānanda. My own name is Lokottataratama. I have trained in the fields of Madhyamaka and logic. I have memorized the commentaries on Dharmakīrti's *Exposition of Valid Cognition* by Devendramati[776] and Śākyamati.[777] I also know *The Ornament of the Exposition of*

Valid Cognition,[778] and the commentaries of Dharmottara[779] and Yamāri.[780] {457} I have also brought many Sanskrit manuscripts concerning logic. I even have Śāntideva's own *Commentary on the Introduction to the Conduct of a Bodhisattva*.[781] With regard to the way of mantra, I know the cycles of Cakrasaṃvara and Vajrayoginī. I practice Dvimukhavajravārāhī as my meditational deity. I have come on the road down from Kashmir via the lands of Guge and Lowo Mentang. Having received a letter from Lama Karmapa, I am now going to Kongpo. My age is one hundred and twenty. Since the land of Tibet is cold and the food is harsh, I am weary."[782]

Later, when he came into the presence of Lama Ngawang Drakpa, he also offered him some Sanskrit manuscripts and satisfied him with the nectar of his buddha speech. In the course of conversation, he also seemed to cut off superimpositions and doubts concerning Sanskrit and so forth, and there were also many minor pith instructions that he offered.

Dharmadinakara

The great paṇḍita known as Dharmadinakara, who had been born on the island of Siṅghala, was a reincarnation of master Kṛṣṇācārin.[783] He was a great scholar who wrote practices concerning the guru in the form Manuṣyasūrya, the meditational deity Tārā with a Single Hair Knot, and the protector of the transmitted teachings Harisiṃha. He also touched the feet of Ngawang Drakpa and was favored with both spiritual and material gifts. In turn, he offered many Sanskrit manuscripts including *The Transcendent Perfection of Wisdom in Eight Thousand Lines*, and set his mind at rest.

Tsultrim Chodrub

As for the master and great geshe Tsultrim Chodrub, who arrived in his presence while reflecting upon the teaching of the glorious Taklungpa, he was born in a nomadic tent in the grassland pastures belonging to Taklung Monastery.[784] Having been ordained as a mendicant and then as a full-fledged monk, he touched the feet of the omniscient Ngawang Drakpa. Knowing the future accurately, the lama bestowed on him the pith instructions of this precious lineage completely and in their entirety. {458} In general, he was learned in all the outer and inner fields of classical learning, and in particular, he trained in Sanskrit grammar. His service in commissioning and editing manuscripts and so forth was also inestimable. All the essential points of the outer, inner, and secret pith instructions pertaining to glorious Jñānanātha in their entirety were bestowed upon him in the form of guidance that lays bare the practical application. Resorting to solitary retreat, he applied himself in the continuous stream of experiential cultivation, such that in actuality, meditative experience, and dreams, he obtained infinite signs of spiritual attainment. This saintly individual undertook unsurpassed acts of spiritual service on behalf of Pa Rinpoche and his three nephews. Later, he acted as the teacher who first imparted advice on study and reflection to the wonderful supreme tulku Namgyel Tashi, and after that he served as the lama with whom the latter studied on a regular basis. He offered Namgyel Tashi all the secret resources of the immaculate buddha mind that constitute the aural lineage of this glorious Taklung Kagyu tradition in their entirety, just as he had received them from the omniscient Pa Rinpoche. So his legacy on behalf of the Buddhist teaching was uniquely great. Later, after he had passed into nirvāṇa, his sacred corpse was brought to Tangkar, where it was transformed into sacred pills that liberate by taste, such that even if it were given to a bird, a fragment of the skull would burst into rainbow colors, and an image of glorious Cakrasaṃvara would most clearly emerge. For such reasons, the people who saw and heard of him were united in the way of devotion.

May the clouds of the provision of merit and the Perfect Age of the
sacred doctrine,
Imbued with hundreds of physical and mental endeavors in this sacred
place,
Yielding all exalted and definitive results that are desired,
Instantaneously alleviate the decline of existence and quiescence!

{459}

Tashi Pelwa

Master of the magical display of pristine cognition,
Simultaneously revealing tens of millions of wondrous miraculous
appearances
Through mantras arising from emptiness
And supreme sacraments arising from compassion—
Respectful homage to Venerable Tashi Pel!

The former incumbent Tashi Pelwa was an emperor of spiritual attainment who presided over the abbatial succession.[785] He was born in 1461 (iron female snake), the same year in which the omniscient Ngawang Drakpa was enthroned at the age of forty-four. His father was the governor Tsewang Drakpa, and his mother was Jayulza. He was sent to request instruction on meditation in the presence of Venerable Ngawang Drakpa, who bestowed on him a knotted mantra protection cord and a blessed item, and said, "Last night in my dream a solar disk fell into my lap, and inexplicably my hands were clearly warmed by its touch. Though he is an indisputable emanation of the supreme buddhas, it seems that his enlightened activity will not be great."

In actuality, the Conqueror Taklungpa the Great himself once again definitively knew the circumstances under which the dominion of Taklung would be firmly maintained with the sustenance of spiritual and temporal well-being on behalf of the Buddhist teaching and sentient beings. So when the time arrived, he summoned Tashi Pelwa, inviting him to this great seminary of Taklung, which had been foreordained by the Conqueror. Here, he excellently served as an attendant of the omniscient Ngawang Drakpa, doctrinal king of the three world systems. At first, preceded by the vows of a layperson and the intermediate mendicant ordination, he obtained the precepts of the novitiate, and the name Tashi Pel was conferred upon him. When he had then come of age, the vows of the full monastic ordination were conferred upon him according to the later ritual procedure. {460} His senses were controlled, and he became supreme among those who were respected for their monastic training, a crown ornament among the oceanic upholders of monastic discipline endowed with scriptural transmission and realization, resembling a second Teacher. Under the supremely omniscient Ngawang Drakpa, who was an ocean of the sacred doctrine, he studied the exegeses of the three piṭakas and the four classes of tantra, which that master possessed, along with the maturational empowerments, the liberating sequence of the path, and other instructions of which even the names cannot be described. In particular, he reached perfection in devotion and the regulations of Choje Kuyalwa, and he kept in mind the glorious Taklung Kagyu lineage, with respect to which he received (1) the outer instructions, including the profound history of the lineage that generates confidence, like the wish-fulfilling gem, grasping the essentials of experiential cultivation through which spiritual teachers are accomplished; (2) the inner instructions, including aspiration prayers that generate meditative experience like the wish-fulfilling gem, and that, after empowerment has been conferred with symbols in the fourfold symbolic maṇḍala,[786] apply the profound generation stage, along with authentic mantra recitations and atemporal commitments,[787] whereby the entire environment and its inhabitants are revealed as an infinitely pure, uncontrived, and originally consummate maṇḍala; and (3) the secret instructions, including the path of liberation that introduces the coalescent, coemergent pristine cognition, like the wish-fulfilling gem, and including the great seal of the view that secures all things of cyclic existence and nirvāṇa with the seal of coalescent pristine cognition. He also received the essential nectar of the oceanic classes of unsurpassed tantra and the complete heart essence of the mother Vajraḍākinī, whose warmth does not fade, unadulterated by negative sophistry and philosophical systems and uncovered by the stains of those who have misunderstanding, wrong understanding, and doubt. Not merely paying lip service to these, an immediate certainty arose within him by homing in on the narrow pathway of their practical application. {461}

Dependent on masters who were adroit in the instructions of the lineages of the four directions and numerous basic pith instructions, he received uncommon experiential guidance on meditation—the two profound paths[788] decisively established in the Six Doctrines of Nāropā. He also received the accessories that facilitate the path in their entirety, like the wish-fulfilling gem, including the ritual service of the pith instructions of the oceanic oath-bound protectors of the Buddhist teaching and of the Lord of Wealth, along with the host of yakṣas.

In 1473 (water female snake), in his thirteenth year, in conjunction with the festival of Lhachen Yulgyel Pelbar,[789] he was enthroned upon the lion throne from which all the conquerors who were his predecessors had revealed the sacred doctrine. The Main Temple, with its sacred representations, was manifestly filled with the entire congregation of Taklung Monastery. The nobility of the southern and northern estates resembling the frozen surface of a lake multiplied the offering sacraments that filled the temple with the wealth of the two sciences,[790] resembling Lake Anavatapta. The monastic community, endowed with both knowledge and liberation, resembled the fearless and omniscient Munīndra coming into the world. And the government officials resembled the moon surrounded by a cluster of stars. They all recited many auspicious verses, and there was a cascade of the individual flowers of good auspices that they tossed. They reenacted the protocol, exactly as Prince Śvetaketu had placed the crown on the head of Venerable Ajita (Maitreya) and empowered him as regent.

Afterward, while Tashi Pelwa implemented the peerless monastic rules and regulations of the successive hierarchs of Taklung {462} and widely increased the positive enlightened activities that definitively protect and guard the Buddhist teaching, he precisely knew the circumstances of all the maṇḍalas that consist of the phenomena of the three times, transparent as a moist gooseberry placed in the palm of the hand. Endowed with the body of pristine cognition that quantitatively knows all things that are seen, he then deliberately abandoned the activities of maintaining and protecting the domains of Taklung. Instead, he conducted himself with supreme virtue while maintaining the ascetic discipline of carefree and relaxed mind, in which subjective grasping is naturally liberated, and he was equanimous in his approach to activities that concern this material and mundane world.

On one occasion during that period, glorious Śākya Chokden Drime Lekpei Lodro Jampel Gawei Shenyen, who was alike in name and meaning and whose pure white banner of reputation extended beyond the three world systems, went to attend upon the venerable and omniscient Ngawang Drakpa, who had become a total renunciate and had settled down in retreat with extremely strict boundaries in a sacred white hut in the hermitage of Tangdrok. He entered through a secret pathway via an isolated ravine because of the restrictions imposed by those responsible for maintaining the retreat boundaries, who blocked the movement of people from the lower part of the valley within an earshot of the hermitage. He approached the door of the grass hermitage without anyone knowing and apprised Ngawang Drakpa of his situation. Thereupon, since Paṇchenpa Śākya Chokden was alone, and he previously had immeasurable spiritual and material kindness, Ngawang Drakpa broke with the conventions he was keeping and delightedly granted him a swift audience. Paṇchen Rinpoche said, "There was a master who maintained extremely great kindness to me and who has passed away. {463} Although I thought of commissioning a large reliquary for the funeral ceremony, there was a doubt that a logician such as I, of feeble means, could achieve that aspiration. So for the sake of spiritual accomplishment, I request you to grant the initiation of Vaiśravaṇa." Pa Rinpoche Ngawang Drakpa replied, "Formerly, when you were young, you made an extensive study of Vaiśravaṇa in the form Vaiśravaṇa of the Eight Great Families at the seat of Kyormolung.[791] I only have this transmission of Vaiśravaṇa in the form Great Yellow One with the Eight Masters of the Horses.[792] Previously, at the south-facing cliff on the side of Rinchen Gang, on the banks of the Nyenpo River,[793] I propitiated Vaiśravaṇa, such that one early morning, I held an ear of corn and said, "May a pile of *tsampa*[794] gather inside a *dre* measuring box!" Thereupon, tsampa did gather, and later on, simply through thought, various sorts of select items would appear. Nowadays, even though all sorts of southerners selling donkeys may not make a profit, they cross Chak La pass, saying "This is for spiritual accomplishment! You should become successful by engaging in business on the backs of others!" Nowadays, although I have no authority here in Taklung, I continue to write. On the way here, I offered an initiation to a monk from Taklung Chokhang. In general, there is a worldly saying to the effect that "You should request a means for attainment of longevity from an aged lama. You should request a means for attainment of wealth from a wealthy lama!" So he advised Śākya Chokden that auspicious circumstances would come about by sleeping amid tea and silk.

Accordingly, they returned to this great monastic seat of Taklung. Upstairs in the Offering Chapel, the senior monks who were expositors of the three piṭakas, along with their disciples, paid respects to Choje Tashi Pelwa—embodiment of Lord Vajrasattva and dancer of the pristine cognition that extensively increases the tradition of blissful accomplishment of the Kagyu lineage—since he maintained the pure ascetic discipline of celibacy. They touched their heads at his feet, which were adorned with the noble insignia of the wheel of excellent virtue. {464} In the presence of the omniscient Pa Rinpoche Ngawang Drakpa, this glorious mighty lord of accomplishment Tashi Pelwa himself conferred the initiation of the great king, peaceful Vaiśravaṇa, in the form Great Bliss Great Yellow One with the Eight Masters of the Horses,[795] according to the teaching transmission and practical technique of Buton Rinpoche, mighty lord of discriminative awareness, which had been transmitted through Taklung Lotsāwa Śākya Zangpo and the omniscient Lachen Jampel Gocha.[796] Just as he had received it, with unadulterated and uncontaminated authenticity, he imparted the skillful preliminaries, and immediately afterward, the disciples perceived him as the deity Guhyapati Nilambaradhara, arising from the emanational display of the five aspects of manifest awakening.[797] He secured this visualization with the majestic seal of Māyājāla, the being of pristine cognition, and then excellently empowered them, wearing the crown that is the insignia of empowerment. He then had the pride to induce the oceanic oath-bound protectors of the Buddhist teaching, mundane and supramundane, to accomplish involuntarily the injunctions with which they are charged. In the presence of this graceful emanational display of the protectors, he purified the material substance of the tormas, which were the support for their visualization, with mantras and sealing gestures that were naturally pure. He then undertook to materialize mentally the supporting environment as Alakāvatī, the palace of the mighty yakṣa Guhyapati, a particularly abundant array fashioned of diverse blazing gemstones, and to bring forth the great protector deities with their retinues and further retinues who were the beings supported within that environment, perfectly and distinctly present. This he did based on the unerring rite of the generation stage that gives rise to definitive certainty—within reach and range of the mind—that the divine assembly of symbolic protectors manifests through the modulations of the liturgical verses. {465}

Thereupon, there was a learned and saintly individual adorned with spiritual accomplishments named Ngotro Rabjampa Wangchuk Pelwa, who acted as an attendant to Paṇchen Mawei Senge Śākya Chokden. He had a vision in which he saw, in accordance with the descriptive basis of the deities, that His Presence Tashi Pelwa had outlined a square celestial palace with four gates, ornaments, and pediments, with three successive encircling walls, at the center of which was a nine-story mansion, in the middle of which was a three-story palace. In the midst of this environment, endowed with such completely perfect characteristics, he saw the great king Vaiśravaṇa and, within the first encircling wall, the eight lords of horses. Within the second encircling wall, these were encircled by the twenty-eight generals, the thirty-two powerful acolytes, the sixteen sacred places,[798] the five hundred Rāṣṭrapālas, Hārītī and her son, the seven great ogresses,[799] the eight mātaraḥ,[800] the eight nāgas,[801] and yakṣas holding diverse forms. Within the third encircling wall, these in turn were encircled by the eight classes of semidivine ogres[802] and so forth. This vision had a clear and stable radiance, extending the light rays of a hundred thousand suns. Afterward, they elaborately received the initiations of buddha body, speech, and mind, along with the services pertaining to the injunctions of the wrathful rites.

After the initiations had ended, he said to Paṇchen, "Now there will be a representation of Vaiśravaṇa that will fulfill the aforementioned auspicious circumstances from your time at Kyormolung!"[803] On his way back to Tsang, the incumbent of Gakhang College at Kyormolung offered Śākya

Chokden an excellent yellow parasol for the new image of Vaiśravaṇa, so he was most pleased, thinking that the auspicious connection would be excellently fulfilled. So I have heard. {466}

Later, when building the great seminary of Tubten Serdokchen—with its representations of buddha body, speech, and mind, as well as incomparable brocade appliqué scrolls of Śākyamuni in the form Beauteous Ornament of the World, the Ten Power Places of the Teacher, and so forth—all the facilitating conditions fell into place without effort. Indeed it says in the biography of Paṇchen Chokyi Gyelpo himself that this was indicative of the compassion of that initiation of Vaiśravaṇa.[804]

In general, with regard to the biographies of the emperors who attained accomplishment in the precious Kagyu lineage, since to them the mighty lord of the three world systems and a nest of ants are alike, they destroy the knot of the eight worldly concerns. Although they know the five fields of classical learning, they do not lose a single word of the oral instruction in poetry. Although they can pulverize Mount Sumeru, they do not undertake rites of mystic union and liberation for the sake of this life. Although they are endowed with the five eyes and the six extrasensory powers, they do not act as household fortune tellers. Although they have mastery over the eighty-four thousand aggregates of the sacred doctrine, they do not release them in the incontinence of this life by the acquisition of transmissions, public empowerments, and exegeses. After making a careful examination, they disclose the oral instructions to disciples of good fortune who are known to be worthy recipients in an experiential manner such that—apart from resorting to the sacred doctrine as the sacred doctrine and resorting to the oral instructions as the oral instructions—they do not at all consider their reputation for study, reflection, or meditation but remain focused in reality. Although the exemplary, glorious Nāropā is the crown ornament for all paṇḍitas, they do not discard the activities of the great elders like spittle, but they seek out spiritual teachers through their ascetic discipline of the central energy channel. Venerable Mila Repa said, "An old parasol and a gold vase are identical."[805] {467}

The king of the Newars and the descendants of King Tsede of Ngari did not bother to invite him, saying, "Although glorious Phakmodrupa, Gyelwa Taklungpa the Great, and so forth have enlightened attributes that are equal to space and are the spiritual teachers of the three world systems, they pass the time in retreat in their grass hermitages and so forth without speaking and with the door walled up with clay and so forth. Apart from that, they do not hold administrative office and the like but teach according to their custom, focusing on a career that is free from activities."[806]

They display certain modes of behavior that are strong and unimpeded, free from the norms of artificial airs and graces. Among them, Kunkhyen Rinpoche Tashi Pelwa also, rather than staying in the monastic seat, turned to the welfare of the Buddhist teaching and sentient beings by relying on the ascetic discipline of total renunciation. Looking widely through the portals of enlightened deeds and activities, he would reprimand slightly those clinging to the perspective of this life and invite them to stay strictly in the monastic hermitage.

At that time, Rongpo Tsonzang[807] sent a sealed request encouraging him to set out quickly from the retreat, but the lama recited a solemn declaration of truth, such that Rongpo's family line immediately came to an end.

Tashi Pelwa then stayed about half a month in monastic retreats such as Kyilsang Gong and after that continued on to the large nomadic enclave of Sokpo. A great commotion occurred when the Hor arrived, and so the nomadic herds had to be secured. Straightaway, the Nakchu River overflowed, and there was no hope of crossing. When they did not know what to do, Choje Rinpoche scattered sanctified grain, and just when they saw it, the mighty flow of that fearsome torrent instantly receded, and the river banks became distinct. Fish, frogs, tadpoles,[808] and other aquatic creatures started to flounder while the master and disciples crossed to the other shore. {468} Following in their wake, most of the herds and the people were able to get out. One small camper group were there to the very end. They retorted, "How could it be that they (the Horpa) do not understand the reality of the buddhas!" They stayed in that valley for a long time and were seized by the Hor. As soon as the other camper groups had gotten out, the river resumed its previous course. Owing to this wondrous display, all the people who saw and heard of it invited him because they had true certainty, actually determining him to be a perfect buddha. They saw him whenever he gave an audience. They heard whatever he said. They received whatever empowerments his hands imparted. They reached the limit of whatever material offerings they made, even though he did not accept them. They requested the meditation and recitation of Mahākāruṇika, the setting of the mind on enlightenment, prayers of dedication and aspiration, and so on, such that a commotion ensued, and the horses, alone numbering more than a thousand, could not be offered.

On one occasion, Pa Rinpoche Ngawang Drakpa requested him to come back by sending a sealed letter to Jampon Senge that read, "One of our people has arrived in your direction. Take care of him, without letting him roam elsewhere!"

Taking whatever arose onto the path, Tashi Pelwa proceeded gradually without formalities. He went to attend upon the venerable and omniscient Ngawang Drakpa, who was living at Gepel Chodzong in Tangdrok, his enlightened activity combining meditation and the turning of the doctrinal wheel of definitive meaning. Having cast away thoughts of the subject-object dichotomy, since he epitomized to some extent the river of the real nature, which is the expanse of reality, Tashi Pelwa, just by being in Ngawang Drakpa's presence, rejoiced in the manner of a monk of the third meditative concentration and did not think at all of the pointless rebuke he had previously received. {469} Instead, he renounced all the material things in his possession, including more than a thousand horses and offered them in Rinpoche's presence. In return, Pa Rinpoche granted him, as his share, Pena and a guesthouse.

Tashi Pelwa devoted himself to genuine meditative equipoise on the foremost of meditational deities, including Vajrakīla, according to the generation stage. Even while he was in the presence of the omniscient one Ngawang Drakpa, he would sit secretly among the crowd of common attendants, and he performed acts of service without having even the slightest trace of arrogance. Assuming a playful guise in all circumstances, upstairs and downstairs, he would go into the lama's presence repeatedly but immediately look out of the window, such that ordinary foolish people who did not understand the perceptual range of a buddha permanently closed off the window of the room. Since he had loving-kindness toward lowly beings who were afflicted by hunger, thirst, and poverty, wherever he stayed in Pena and the guesthouse, he took turns cooking. When he went with three relatives to receive the empowerment of Kālacakra from the fourth holder of the crown of Zhamar in the Ten-Pillar Chapel, a thunderbolt actually fell on his lap, but not only was he unharmed, even his clothes had no trace of fire. Turning in the flaps of his robe, he dismissed the incident, such that all the locals and visitors were astonished and determined that he was an indisputable accomplished master.

Tashi Pelwa commissioned many images of the meditational deities in the form of paintings and relief sculptures, as well as accurate manuscripts. While he was residing at Pena, all the astrologers of the area unanimously determined that an eclipse of the moon would be clearly visible from the monastery itself, whereupon he made a solemn declaration of truth and {470} uttered the following injunction: "Rāhu, you should not obscure the moon!" Consequently, there was no eclipse.

When an iron bridge was being built across the Lhachu River, it was reported that the iron was short by about half an armspan. So, while it was being dragged by the efforts of a hundred men, he took hold of the end of the iron chain and single-handedly pulled it, squeezing it as if it were wool. It then easily stretched across the width of the river, and not only that but it could also be anchored down on the river banks by approximately one armspan. Nowadays it is still there, in the common perception of all.[809]

At Taklung, on the anniversary of Venerable Mila Repa, which falls on the fourteenth day of the horse month,[810] the monks and retreatants perform an elaborate recitation of his spiritual songs all night long. All the local people come and go without sleeping in order to hear the chanting, do circumambulations, and so forth, and there were occasional fights that would break out, probably due to intoxication. For this reason, the ceremony was deficient. On one occasion, someone officiating on the anniversary day of the fourteenth said, "The five sisters, including Tashi Tseringma, have actually appeared in the presence of this Venerable Tashi Pelwa at Pena. Now, they no longer even appear at Taklung during the anniversary of Mila Repa!" According to my research here, and according to the historical accounts, henceforth, Pena was permitted to undertake the nighttime ceremony of the fourteenth-day anniversary. When Venerable Namgyel Drakpa Pelzang fell ill, Tashi Pelwa went there to perform an initiation. On that occasion, he recovered as soon as a steward carried a censor of Tashi Pelwa's incense into the room.

The subsequent precious incumbent of the monastic seat also had great difficulties in his construction projects and management of the monastery, and so forth, due to some other persons,[811] such that he fell ill. Someone then said to Tashi Pelwa, "Since you appear to be well, you should transfer his illness to yourself!" That very night, he made the transfer, and the precious incumbent immediately recovered his health.

When the venerable and omniscient Ngawang Drakpa passed away into the taintless expanse, {471} the incumbent asked the monks to bring the wealth that they found appealing, as if the treasury of Vaiśravaṇa had been opened. Apart from being smitten with fervent devotion, Tashi Pelwa was purely without craving for material things, for which reason he did not accept anything except a hand drum with a yak-hair handle and an old riding horse called Drochung. The incumbent said that some riding horses had escaped from Pena and that he could not find them. Tashi Pelwa replied, "The horses are in Drosak Langma valley." The incumbent searched for them there and found them.

He once said that they should go out for recreation and boil some tea but was informed that they had no stove or utensils. "Dismiss the attendants, and be seated in meditation for a while!" he said. "Now come up!" When they went into his presence, the stove and all the necessary containers were there, so they could boil the tea. When it was time for him to go back, no one knew where the attendants had gone.

Thinking that he should depart for another realm, Tashi Pelwa manifested illness at Pena, whereupon the precious incumbent of the monastic seat arrived and inquired after his health and well-being many times, but he did not recover. He traveled to Sengling directly, and indirectly he made excellent offerings, but Tashi Pelwa refused them. Since, however, the incumbent of the monastic seat had a mind that was profound and broad with skillful intent, he offered Tashi Pelwa a pleasant environment at Sengling, where there were nightingales. Delighting in these, Tashi Pelwa did not depart immediately. Then in 1508 (earth male dragon year), in his forty-eighth year, he passed away into the pure and taintless expanse. That is to say, he continued working for the well-being of infinite sentient beings through the reflection of the kingly transcendent lord Akṣobhya. His sacred corpse was cremated and the ashes then fashioned into a representation of the buddha body of reality. Representative images were made, {472} and the offerings presented in conjunction with the funeral ceremony were most magnificent. Although these events occurred in the middle of winter, rhododendrons glistened, and there were other such wondrous signs that were indescribable.

Though these words are advantageous, in that they are wondrous,
By incidentally hearing this brief description of the lineage,
May old ladies who are equal in number to space
Reach the level of that supremely accomplished master.

Namgyel Drakpa Pelzangpo, Thirteenth in the Abbatial Succession

Vastly omniscient in the fields of classical learning,
Supreme lord of accomplishment in the path of the Adamantine
 Vehicle,
Unsurpassed lord-protector of all who desire liberation,
Homage to the hermit Wangchuk Namgyel Drakpa!

Choje Rinpoche Namgyel Drakpa Pelzangpo, who dwelled in the authentic lineage of realization, was born in 1469 (earth female ox) at Tregang in the upper reaches of Rikpei Jungne in Penyul. His father was the brave and courageous governor Tsewang Drakpa, who was exalted on account of the glory of his great merits, and his mother was Gyamaza Pelmo Budren.[812] He was the eldest of three brothers. He was sent into the presence of the venerable and omniscient Ngawang Drakpa to request instruction on meditation, and the name Tsewang Tashi was conferred upon him. He was indisputably known to have been the reincarnation of Drigung Choje Rinchen Pelzangpo, whom Drubchen Guṇawa of Zholungtso had foreordained to be an emanation of the great accomplished master Śavaripā.[813] When he was in his third year, in the summer of 1471 (iron hare), the venerable and omniscient Ngawang Drakpa went to Tre and, on meeting him, bestowed his blessing, saying, "He will be of benefit to the Taklungpa." {473} The child learned writing and reading without difficulty. In his seventh year, in 1475 (wood female sheep), he was invited to glorious Taklung Upper Plain. In the presence of the venerable and omniscient Ngawang Drakpa Pelzangpo, he received the vows of the novitiate completely, including the phases of preparation, actual conferral, and subsequent advice, and he was given the name Namgyel Drakpa Pelzangpo.

In his ninth year, in 1477 (fire female bird), he went to the monastic seat of Kadruk, where he built a grass hermitage with an enclosing wall from the foundations to the rooftop. In the presence of the glorious and omniscient Ngawang Drakpa, he received in the form of experiential guidance Coemergent Union of the Great Seal and Six Doctrines Like the Wish-Fulfilling Gem,[814] and he perfected the experiential realization that was his individual destiny. In particular, this supreme leader of men, endowed with the vast eye of the sacred doctrine, compiled an anthology of all the unadulterated volumes containing the outer, inner, and secret pith instructions preceded by the extensive and brief empowerments pertaining to the protector deity mighty Kākamukha Mahākāla. These books are nowadays known as the Father and Mother Yellow Manuscripts of Taklung. He then studied in detail all the Doctrinal Cycles of Kurakma,[815] and he also completed the experiential cultivation of meditation pertaining to the latter's four perfect cycles of pith instruction concerning the perfection stage, which are (1) the fivefold cycle concerning the essential core, which is the basis of separation, resembling a tree trunk; (2) the fourfold cycle that concerns separation, resembling branches; (3) the twofold cycle resembling beautiful flowers; and (4) the single cycle that concerns the main points, resembling fruits.

Then, while staying in an absolutely strict and restricted retreat, he entered into meditation uninterruptedly, like the flow of a river, {474} such that in actuality, in meditative experiences, and in dreams, how could it be doubted that he acquired countless stable signs of having accomplished infinite rites? Above all, through the experiential cultivation of the channels, winds, and vital essences, refining the essentials within the subtle adamantine body, he cut off all impurities of the psychophysical aggregates, sensory elements, and sense fields, and his chyle became strong, with the result that his material body was transformed into the rainbow body and his mind was liberated in the supreme bliss of the uncontaminated coemergent delight. Furthermore, the vitality of his chyle was sealed with the view of the Great Seal, such that he became a lord-protector of the natural abiding nature, liberated from the hollow of adventitious stains. This lord-protector of the path that is to be attained understood the natural expressive power of awareness. He was a lord-protector of the spontaneously present fruit, arising from within in a self-originated manner, and he became a mighty lord of peerless yoga, the crown ornament of all those who uphold the lineage of spiritual accomplishment.

However, he also achieved the rank of a great scholar who brought an end to the stains of ignorance with respect to all the conventional sciences. That is to say, he knew the practical astrology of the *Kālacakra*,[816] the systematic textbook astrology, the charts of the *Svarodaya Tantra*,[817] the positive and negative prognostications according to the great astrological and divinatory systems, the calculations pertaining to the duration of the Buddhist teaching, the four-phase appearance and decline of great temporal eons,[818] and so forth. He also composed many new texts on astrology and divination.[819]

He excellently mastered *The Kalāpa Grammar*;[820] the complete *Grammar of Candragomin*;[821] the supplementary *Treatise on Uṇādi*;[822] *The Paradigms of Verbal Roots*;[823] and *The Treatise on the Termination Si and Others*,[824] composed by Mañjuśrīkīrti; as well as *The Precious Source of Prosody*,[825] *The Mirror of Poetics*,[826] and *The Treasury of Amarasiṃha* and its commentary on the subject of synonymics.[827] In terms of calligraphy alone, he knew how to write and read Rañjanā, Vartula, {475} Nāgarī, Gauḍa, Ghahura, Sindhu, Tāmaralipti "ocean end" script, and Kashmiri, as well as the script of the *cīvaṃcīvakas*, the script of the rākṣasas, the two Mongol scripts, and the Chinese scripts.[828] He was especially familiar with the treatises of medical science and their esoteric instructions, and above all, he acquired an inspirational confidence, independent of others, in all the sūtras, tantras, and their treatises. In brief, he was like a vase containing all the teachings that he had received from the omniscient Ngawang Drakpa and all knowledge based on scriptural authority and logical reasoning.

From Pa Rinpoche Ngawang Drakpa, he received the uncommon instructions on meditation according to the Taklung Kagyu lineage, as well as the profound doctrines of Marpa and Ngok, the exegesis of the tantras, and all the sequences of maturational empowerments and liberating guidance. He received in their entirety the doctrinal cycles of the Drigungpa, the doctrinal cycles of the Drukpa, the exegeses of the Sakya tradition in general, and in particular Bodongpa's cycle titled *Summation of the Real*,[829] which is an extensive treatise imbued with mystic blessings,[830] along with their complete empowerments, transmissions, and pith instructions. After receiving the empowerment of Venerable Ngawang Drakpa's own preferred meditational deity, Vajrabhairava, he received *The Commentary on the Tantra of Glorious Vajrabhairava*, and all the empowerments, transmissions, and pith instructions according to the tradition of Ra Lotsāwa; the pith instructions of *Dhūmāṅgārīśrīdevī*[831] according to the tradition of Ngok; instruction on the great king Vaiśravaṇa according to the tradition of Buton; and so forth.

From Rinpoche Tashi Pelwa, he received completely the Collected Works of the religious king Songtsen Gampo. From Chenga Rinpoche Chokyi Drakpa Pelzangpo, he received the seven maṇḍalas of Ngok; *The Adamantine Garland of Empowerment*;[832] *The Ocean of Means for Attainment*;[833] *The Hundred Means for Attainment*;[834] the four scrolls containing the aural instructions of Marpa; the fifteen scrolls of pith instruction; {476} the empowerments, exegetical teachings, and pith instructions of the *Kālacakra*; the cycles of the Karma Kamtsang; and many streams of transmission pertaining to sūtra and tantra.

From the scholar Choje Rinchen Chowang, who was a master of the single volume containing all the sūtras and tantras, he received the entire streams of transmission of the complete Kangyur, the Collected Works of Lama Zhang, and many cycles of Kadam and Pacification. He did not simply hear all these but perfectly comprehended all their words and meanings, and he was unimpeded in teaching, debate, and composition.

Rinpoche Tashi Pelwa was permitted to retire, disinclined as he was toward the distractions of administration. Consequently, in the waxing half of the first month of 1485 (wood female snake), when he was in his seventeenth year, Namgyel Drakpa Pelzangpo came to preside over the monastic seat, and with the best of all beings, including the gods, paying homage, he was invited to take his place on the fearless lion throne as an object of their prostrations. The omniscient Choje Ngawang Drakpa and his nephew Tashi Pelwa, along with the entire congregation, chanted auspicious verses and scattered flowers of offering. The wealth and excellent resources of the twofold tradition of the great seminary of glorious Taklung, along with the subjects of the southern and northern estates and the mother and subsidiary monasteries, were offered as the vessels of his command. Thus, he was enthroned as a king of the sacred doctrine presiding over the three world systems.

In terms of the regulations of Choje Kuyalwa and the charter of the monastic assembly established by his Kagyu predecessors, the arrangement of the retreats and meditation, the establishing of maturational empowerment and liberating guidance by means of the four attractive qualities for all those to be trained,[835] and so forth, he definitively applied the regulations of the omniscient Choje Ngawang Drakpa. {477} Through the authentic blessings of Mahākāruṇika, all the subjects of the estates also thrived and flourished like the rivers of summer, and he brought the four directions under his sway. He would manifestly praise and practice exclusively the teachings that Pa Rinpoche Ngawang Drakpa had given. Consequently, all his enlightened activities were spontaneously accomplished. Pa Rinpoche too was especially pleased and compassionately favored him, such that, as uncle and nephew, they developed an extremely positive methodology.

On one occasion, when Tsekhawa Peldrak and his servants[836] brought considerable disgrace upon the Taklungwa tradition, through the power of the protectors of the transmitted teachings, Peldrak himself died of leprosy not long afterward, his family line was cut off, and almost half of his subjects fell into the hands of Namgyel Drakpa.

On occasions when the time came for him to train the disciples of the northern region, taking virtuous action as his basis and conjoined with pure aspiration prayers, he would encamp there. He visited that region many times. The material offerings that were made were inconceivable, and he turned the wheel of the profound and vast sacred doctrine. On these occasions, too, the entire sky was filled with rainbow light, divine sacraments fell as a shower of flowers, and so forth. The meritorious signs such as these that appeared were inestimable.

At Chak Khorwedong,[837] also, the people offered gifts to Pa Rinpoche, and they distributed offerings and alms to Choje Namgyel Drakpa and his brother, along with the entire congregation of monks. The people of Puborgang in the east {478} and the people of Dzakhol Gyeltang also prepared most distinguished new sacraments of offering, including the gilded spire of the great temple, the gold offering bowls and silver offering bowls that were placed before the representative image of Śākyamuni in the form Tashi Obar, as well as decorative hangings and canopies.[838]

During the sixth month of 1493 (water female ox), in his twenty-fifth year, Namgyel Drakpa excellently received the vows of a full-fledged monk in the midst of many learned and venerable monks headed by the omniscient Choje Ngawang Drakpa Pelzangpo, who acted as preceptor; Chokyi Drakpa Yeshe Pelzangpo, holder of the crown of Zhamar, who acted as the master of ceremonies; the retired Rinpoche Tashi Pelwa, who acted as confessor; and Khenchen Ngawang Zangpo. He became a second buddha, a monk holding the vajra, in whom the defining characteristics of the following verses are fully perfected:

> Maintaining the ethical discipline of a monk,
> Endowed with study and reflection,
> And proficient in meditation . . .[839]

When the time drew near for Pa Rinpoche to pass into nirvāṇa, in a dream Namgyel Drakpa saw the ḍākinīs and doctrinal protectors moving camp and saying "We are going into the presence of Choje Densawa!" They resembled dark people, dark horses, armed and raising their many banners, in dice-spot formations, and circumambulating groups whose movement caused the heavens and the earth to reverberate. He said, "This is a bad sign for us! The doctrinal protectors are circumambulating Choje Densawa."

After Ngawang Drakpa had passed into nirvāṇa, Choje Chokyi Drakpa, the holder of the crown of Zhamar, was invited to be seated at the head of the row presiding over the great funeral ceremony. Hundreds of offerings were made, more than four of which were particularly awesome. {479} Tea was distributed to some five thousand monks, equivalent to the value of a gold *zho* coin. Approximately eighty thousand laypersons distributed butter and curd to the assembly. He commissioned a gold image one cubit high in Choje Densawa's bedroom and a representative image that was an actual likeness of him, fashioned of medicinal herbs and paste, with a covering of fine brocade, in the Drokha chamber. That central silver image of Jñānanātha in the Drokha was also made then and there. Communal tea was distributed to all the monastic institutions of Utsang, including Densatil, Tsetang, Sangphu, Tsurphu, Drigung, Langtang, Nalendra, the three monasteries of Drepung, Sera and Ganden, Sakya, glorious Choding, and Bodong.[840]

In the winter of 1496 (dragon), Namgyel Drakpa himself began the construction of the silver reliquary, and it was excellently completed in the third month of 1497 (fire snake). The sacred corpse, like a wish-fulfilling gem, was inserted at its core, along with its casket. Moreover, all the other artifacts that were inserted within it were, according to estimation, replete with the appropriate defining characteristics. At the center of the solar disk was an image of Venerable Jangchub Gyatso fashioned of six *sang* of silver, and within the door of the vase was an image of Pa Rinpoche himself, fashioned of twenty-six *sang* of silver. The lion throne supporting the reliquary, which was made of gilded copper was embellished with more than five hundred gemstones, while the screen to the rear was exquisite and well designed. It depicted the successive Kagyu lineage holders, starting from Vajradhara, and it was half the height of the Northern Chapel. An elaborate consecration ceremony was held.

Later, in accordance with an injunction that Pa Rinpoche had previously given, behind the gilded-copper throne of the silver image of Jñānanātha, he made cubit-size silver images depicting the three primary retainers, a hand-span-size gold image depicting each of the eight retainers with different faces, and a depiction of a terrifying charnel ground on the throne itself, and so forth.[841] {480} Alongside these, he installed peerless sacraments of offering and approximately thirty continuously burning lamps. On the door of the Northern Chapel, within a protective grill of wire netting, he commissioned a mural depicting the life of Pa Rinpoche in Sukhāvatī Buddha Field, and so forth. He then performed the consecration and offered unsurpassed gifts and provisions.

On the occasion of a festival, in the seventh lunar month of that same snake year (1497), he instated an eight-day offering ceremony of spiritual attainment, which included, in addition to the ritualist monks who had previously attended, singers of spiritual songs; the sacred dance of suppression by means of the maṇḍala of multicolored Vajrakīla according to the Sakya tradition, the sacred dance of Pañjaranātha, and the sacred dance of Vajrakīla, which vanquish unsurpassed obstacles during the geomantic rite; and the sacred drum dance of Vajrakīla, which is enacted on the last day; and so forth.

In the twelfth month, he introduced a sacred offering dance and—at the new year ceremony, which followed a communion feast-offering ceremony that could continue all day—a lavish distribution of alms on the twelfth day of each month.

In the eighth month of 1498 (earth male horse), a group of skilled Newar artisans arrived, so he established a workshop for the construction of large images. They made a perfect start, constructing an image of Munīndra in the form Victorious Over Demons, the back of which was thirty-eight handspans in height, along with standing images of Maitreya and Avalokiteśvara, which were six cubits in height, and on the screen to the rear, images of the thousand buddhas and of the six ornaments, and so forth. The task was excellently completed on the anniversary of Ngawang Drakpa's passing in the seventh lunar month of 1500 (iron monkey). Namgyel Drakpa then inserted the relics within the statue and carried out the consecration ceremony perfectly. There were authentic auspicious signs that occurred. The new sacred images were said to have been auspicious because the country remained peaceful, the year was excellent, and not even the words *disease*, *conflict*, or *famine* were heard. Many particularly sublime sacraments of offering were presented. {481} At the feast, Choje Kumche, the brother of Namgyel Drakpa, Nangso Yabse, and others gathered, and people paid their respects with a bountiful distribution of alms in the Great Assembly Hall that lasted all day. The artisans were delighted with the donations and provisions that were offered. Many were contributed by seven communities from Khyungpo, Gyeltsang, Hor, Sokpo, Lhato, Gyepa,[842] and so forth.

In 1499 (sheep), Donyo Dorje of Rinpung had attacked Zhika Nelpa with a large army. At that time, Namgyel Drakpa was invited in order to protect the lives of Zhika Nelpa's subjects. On the way, he made offerings and prayers of aspiration in the presence of Jowo Śākyamuni in the sacred pilgrimage place of Lhasa. Then, he actually saved the lives of Neudzongpa and his relatives.[843] Without disparaging their wealth and their subjects, he calmed the noblemen. Previously, when Governor Donyo Dorje had visited

Taklung, he had received the initiation of Jñānanātha at the time when Venerable Namgyel Drakpa was just in his eleventh year. But now, he acquired faith and requested the gist of the admonitions of glorious Phakmodrupa, and the transmissions of the great prayers of the Taklung Kagyu lineage, and so forth. Neudzongpa also requested some initiations and guidance and made excellent material offerings in exchange for this act of kindness.

Then, Namgyel Drakpa established a community to take responsibility for spiritual practice at Sengling Drakya Dorje Dzong, which had been one of the six citadel-like hermitages of glorious Taklungpa the Great. As an act of service to the image of Choku Sangye Yarjon kept there, and as a rite of offering, he undertook a great construction project there, which included restoration and new building. He had the precious representative image of Choku Sangye Yarjon that had previously been kept within the monastery brought into the center of a viewing room that had been newly constructed for its circumambulation and presented it with many sacraments of offering. He then determined the multiple circumambulations that should be undertaken there. {481}

After nurturing the community in this manner for sixteen years, in the first lunar month of 1501 (iron female bird), when he was in his thirty-third year, he appointed Choje Rinpoche Sonam Pelzangpo to the monastic seat. Venerable Namgyel Drakpa, having renounced responsibility for administration, then became a total renunciate at Yangdzong, a remote outpost that belonged to Sengling hermitage, and while staying exclusively in retreat, he became one-pointedly equipoised in the profound meditative stability of the two stages. During retreat sessions, he would extensively turn the doctrinal wheel of profound guidance on the definitive meaning.

Starting from 1498 (horse), Namgyel Drakpa commissioned an accurate manuscript edition of the Kangyur of high quality, which was his commitment, inscribed on parchment in gold and silver, with outer and inner covers, wooden boards and straps. This project was excellently completed over three years, and then he conducted a most awesome consecration ceremony with fine offerings and provisions.

Privately, he inaugurated at Sengling, on the anniversary of Pa Rinpoche's passing, a five-day offering of spiritual attainment, combining Cakrasaṃvara, Hevajra, Vajrabhairava, Vajradhātu, and Sarvavid Vairocana, with approximately a hundred participating monks. And at all the other monthly ceremonies, the offering of spiritual attainment was conducted for a day by some fifty monks.

Namgyel Drakpa repeatedly conferred the empowerments associated with the great maṇḍalas that he applied in practice. Above all, to many interested persons, he exclusively delivered continuous teaching on experiential guidance according to the Great Seal, the Six Doctrines, and Mahākāla in the form Gonpo Kurak. To those persons, he also visibly demonstrated practical guidance on the training of vital energy with regard to the essential points of the subtle body and so forth. Without being perfunctory or pompous, he subtly and finely differentiated the meditative experiences and realizations offered by his disciples, the dispelling of obstacles, successful outcomes, and so forth. Assisted by such antidotal techniques, he could easily be consulted, {483} such that the meditators and disciples of that era were largely brought forth by this venerable master alone. It is said that he filled with practitioners the uplands of Taklung and Drilung, the heights and lower reaches of Sengling and Tangdrok, and the entire shaded and sunny sides of Urulung.[844]

Formerly, when the precious representative image of Sengling was being reinstalled in the monastery, it was struck at the heart by the end of a falling beam within the temple and slightly damaged. He then wrote a eulogy proclaiming that this precious image should be placed at the highest point of Taklung. He presented it with the sacraments of offering, a hat, robes, silk offering scarves, and so forth, and established the custom of arranging offerings before it and making prayers. Consequently, the image was naturally restored to its former state.

Later, while Namgyel Drakpa was residing at Sengling, the subterranean protectresses revealed their own forms to him in a vision and offered him their vital heart mantras. He conferred on them the setting of the mind on enlightenment and commissioned cotton paintings that corresponded to this vision, entrusting them to posterity with his injunctions, so that even nowadays, they continue to manifestly reveal miracles and assist in positive endeavors. Relying on the inspiration of those paintings, I myself have also arranged a book of liturgical prayers.

Then, in the ninth month of 1508 (dragon), he undertook extensive virtuous acts, including bountiful offerings that he presented during the funeral ceremony for the late Choje Sonam Pelzangpo, and he commissioned the appropriate representative images, along with outer and inner representations of buddha body, speech, and mind, and so forth. With no option but to resume responsibility for the monastic seat and its branches, he once again sat upon the lion throne of the sacred doctrine and continued to support the great seminary and the governance of the Rinpungpas unswervingly.

On one occasion, due to the times, a large Mongol army arrived in Tibet.[845] {484} While they were oppressing and afflicting great hardships on the entire northern region, Rinpoche himself subdued the malign forces in accordance with the sacred doctrine by the blessings of his genuine meditative stability, endowed with the pristine cognition of supreme bliss in which cyclic existence and nirvāṇa are of a common savor, and by means of his skillful enlightened activity, endowed with the four attractive qualities. Consequently, the Mongols became the enactors of his enlightened activity, unable to transgress whatever was his command, and he planted the seed of enlightenment within them. But with respect to those among them who had not become fields of taming through peaceful rites and who continued to attack in order to inflict harm upon the communities of the Taklungpa, the severe punishment of the protector deities fell of its own accord, without being invoked. They were reduced to suffering, afflicted by diverse disagreeable circumstances.

Namgyel Drakpa renovated the Main Temple and all the Kumbum stūpas with their reliquary chapels and made extensive offerings. He changed the top and bottom brocade borders of the large story-high painted scrolls. His compositions are also extant, including a guidance manual on the Six Doctrines that is adorned with profound advice based on scriptural authority, reasoning, and pith instructions, as well as many essential memos on the pith instructions, many exegeses on the stages of empowerment and the maṇḍalas of attainment, prayers, spiritual songs, details of oral instruction, *An Abridgment of the Lives of the Abbatial Succession*,[846] *The Foundation of the Fivefold Astrological Calculation*,[847] and *An Inventory to the Temples of Taklung*.[848]

Finally, in his sixty-second year, on the twenty-second day of the second month of 1530 (iron male tiger), his enlightened intention displayed the dissolution into the expanse of reality. At that time, there were also wondrous and marvelous occurrences that appeared visible to all. The entire expanse of the sky was filled with floating white flowers, divine sacraments {485} that entirely covered the ground in the vicinity of the precious corpse and the valley around the glorious monastic seat. All creatures who saw and heard of this were moved with faith and devotion, such that their body hairs stood erect, and they shed tears.

Although that venerable and wondrous supreme Tulku Namgyel Drakpa was of a tender young age at that time, he was served by a group of ministers who were profound and vast in knowledge. They undertook bountiful acts of offering during the funeral ceremonies, and extensively commissioned representations of buddha body, speech, and mind, and so forth. So it was that his enlightened intention vastly filled the divine pathway of reality's expanse with a hundred million trillion clouds of the path of excellence through which he had formerly accrued merit.

The foregoing account of his life is actually abridged from the biography composed by the master Rinchen Tsultrim Chokdrub, who was powerful in learning, venerable conduct, and spiritual attainment.[849]

The Disciples of Namgyel Drakpa Pelzangpo

The foremost of the disciples of Venerable Namgyel Drakpa Pelzangpo was the wondrous and supreme tulku Sonam Yeshe Pelzangpo, who was entrusted with the succession of genuine blessing and empowered as his genuine regent. The account of his life is presented below.[850] Moreover, his other learned and accomplished disciples, who were beyond number, included the glorious Drukpa Ngawang Chokyi Gyelpo, uncle and nephew;[851] the two nephews of Venerable Bodongpa; Monlam Drakpa, the nephew of Choje Yezang Tsepa;[852] Khedrub Āryaśrī;[853] master Tsokye Dorje, who composed *The Ascertainment Clarifying the Meaning of the Tantra of Sarvavid*;[854] Lampei Chenga of Tolung; Geden Choje Chokyi Shenyen;[855] the master of the lower ramparts of Nalendra; Choje Jamyangpa; Nartang Khenchenpa; {486} Jangpa Rabjampa Rinchen Zangpo;[856] Drakchokpa, the preceptor of Densatil, who was the teacher of Unyonpa;[857] Tsultrim Wangchuk, the nephew of Burampa, who received the scriptural transmission of the Kangyur from Pawo Tsuklak Trengwa;[858] Rabjampa Zopa Pel of Pelkhor Dechenpa;[859] Japukpa Kunga Samten; Langtang Chenga Jeon Śākya Gyeltsen,[860] who offered into his hands the image of Tārā that had been the meditational deity of master Candragomin and that had an attached certificate of indisputable provenance; Mengom Śākya Wangchuk, the preceptor of Yabpa; Drulgang Trulzhikpa; Drulgang Gyapa, uncle and nephew; Kongpo Chenga, uncle and nephew; Zurmang Choje Lodro Gyatso;[861] Jangsem Tarpa Gyeltsen, uncle and nephew;[862] Gekhawa Gendun Gyatso;[863] Drigung Rechenpa; Barompa; Targonpa; Trabkhapa; Langtang Chenga Khenpo Ngawang Zangpo, uncle and nephew; Nangchen Sangye Drakpa; and Jadrelwa Śākya Gyeltsen, who revealed his experiential guidance in Drilung and nurtured the community there.[864]

Namgyel Drakpa was exalted by the faithful patron Sonam Chenpo Pel, who revered him, since he actually conceived of the venerable one as the Buddha. However, there were an inestimable number of other patrons, including the governor Donyo Dorje Gyelpo Pelzangpo, Yungpa Tsewang,[865] Neudzongpa and his relatives, Governor Rinchen Gyelchok of Chongye Taktsewa,[866] and Lingpon Chen.[867]

May this virtuous biography, excellently presented in this manner, {487}
Like the moon in winter, momentarily dispel the darkness
Of the minds of living beings of the three levels.
And may the lily flowers of liberation blossom
Through the hundredfold illumination of its excellent virtue!

Sonam Yeshe Pelzangpo, Fourteenth in the Abbatial Succession

Homage to the feet of Sonam Pelzang, lord-protector of living beings,
Fruition of excellent conduct with regard to the ocean-like two provisions,
Who mastered the dominion of the buddha body of reality for his own sake
And possessed the seven precious things that benefit others!

Choje Sonam Yeshe Pelzangpo, who is included in the lineage of the abbatial succession, was born in 1472 (water male dragon). His father was the peerless and heroic Masang Tsewang Drakpa, who nurtured his own community while overwhelming those of others, and his mother was Gyamaza Pelmo Budren, endowed with the signs of a saintly woman.[868] He was the second of their three sons. Even in childhood, when his demeanor lacked vigor, he was never tainted with the stains of ordinary propensities. His conduct that delighted in positive actions resembled the glory of the waxing moon, and he even made his childhood playmates reject negative actions and adopt virtuous actions. Perceptive persons who observed his astonishing glory would pass on wonderful reports from one to another, and when these reached the ears of the omniscient Ngawang Drakpa, he had the thought that this child was a most saintly individual who could definitively act as regent of Taklung. Then he said to the parents, "Bring him to Taklung!" There he excellently received the vows of ordination, from those of a layperson to those of the novitiate, and the name Sonam Pelzangpo was also conferred upon him. {488}

Then, he resided in the palace of the sacred doctrine, which was the grass hermitage. Attending upon learned masters, he began by learning to write and read, and he trained in many texts great and small, and in many means for attainment, extensive and concise, such that he comprehended them without difficulty. In the presence of the venerable and omniscient Ngawang Drakpa, he undertook the rite that sets the mind on the supreme enlightenment of the Great Vehicle, just as it had definitively originated from the individual implementation of the two traditions of the promulgators of profound view and vast conduct, Nāgārjuna and Asaṅga, to whom the descent of these teachings had fallen, respectively, from Prince Mañjughoṣa and Prince Maitreyanātha. Commencing with the setting of the mind on supreme enlightenment, he studied the oceanic textual traditions that reveal topics appropriate and inappropriate for the most bountiful conduct of a bodhisattva. In particular, his mindstream was brought to maturation through inconceivable streams of empowerment, originating from the respective ascertainment of the higher and lower tantras of the Adamantine Vehicle and dependent on the ascertainment associated with the implementation of each of the former lineages that were authentic in India, Land of the Sublime Ones, and in Tibet, exactly and as many as they were, unadulterated by mutual contradictions. He excellently trained in Ngok Zhedang Dorje's *Commentary on the Glorious Hevajra Tantra*, which is known as *The Resemblance to a Precious Ornament*,[869] and he studied and trained in many other tantra commentaries along with their branches until the essentials of the adamantine verses were clarified. These included the profound exegesis established on the basis of the precise and detailed memorandum of Ngok Chokyi Gyeltsen, titled *Spiritual Attainment through Reading Aloud*.[870] He studied all the different precious unsurpassed tantras that are definitively secret, without duality of skillful means and discriminative awareness, {489} integrating the generation stage and its branches and the many particular aspects of the symbolic and nonsymbolic perfection stage, and his mind was liberated through the unbewildered signs experienced on the path.

Among them all, the glorious and omniscient Ngawang Drakpa advised that the most essential of all his essential, oceanic studies should focus on Cakrasaṃvara and Vajravārāhī in the generation stage and the Six Doctrines and the Great Seal in the perfection stage, and that for him the protectors of the transmitted teachings should be Jñānanātha and Dhūmāṅgārīśrīdevī.

Guided by this certainty, he refined the experiential cultivation of *The Glorious Tantra That Equals Space*,[871] which is the essence of the ocean-like instructions of the generation stage, and its pith instructions on the stages of self-consecration, differentiating the content of Indian treatises according to superior, mediocre, and inferior acumen, along with the three stages of the divine body, inner radiance, and integration and their branches.

He also received the four profound, symbolic empowerments that favor the most powerful among those of sharp acumen with the maturational path of the heart essence that is associated with the twofold descent of the short and long lineages, derived respectively from the great and glorious brahmin Saraha and lord Maitripāda. He also received teachings on the integration of the generation and perfection stages of Satyadvayamukha Bhaṭṭārikā, which accords with the path of liberation, and the four empowerments of all the general yoginī tantras, along with their sharp bullets of blessing that confer maturation according to the elixir of the oceanic oral instructions introduced by Lord Marpa Lotsāwa in *The Oral Transmission of the Twofold Supreme Vision*.[872]

He then received *The Coemergent Generation Stage That Confers Liberation*,[873] *The Wish-Fulfilling Gem of the Aural Lineage of the Perfection Stage*,[874] and its related hidden and concealed extracts from the six tantra approaches[875] that are contained in twenty-five doctrinal sections. {490} He absorbed the essential core of this profound aural lineage.[876]

With regard to the Six Doctrines, although there is no difference between the definitive secrets of the instructions contained in their different recensions within the precious Kagyu lineage, there are ostensibly many dissimilar stages of visualization. So here in Taklung, he received the basic guidance manual known as *The Six Doctrines: Darkhukma*[877] or *The Wish-Fulfilling Gem*,[878] which is the adamantine teaching of Gyelwa Taklungpa the Great, adorned with the gems that extract the profound essentials of other profound instructions on the perfection stage of the unsurpassed yoga tantras by Jikten Wangchuk Tashi Peltsek and slightly embellished by the elaborate visualizations titled *Garland of White Light*.[879] The latter is Tashi Peltsek's guidance manual on the path of skillful means that focuses on the vitality channels[880] and contains unbewildered essential points pertaining to Taklungpa's own aforementioned adamantine teachings concerning the intrinsic nature.

Sonam Pelzangpo could easily write down the venerable and omniscient Ngawang Drakpa's introductions to the concealed and hidden essential points of experiential cultivation, without disordering them, as they pertained to the aforementioned *Six Doctrines: The Wish-Fulfilling Gem*, such that the later recensions of *The Wish-fulfilling Gem* are easier to understand and more profound in their essentials than all the earlier recensions of this guidance manual because he did not in the slightest alter the words or their meanings.

Furthermore, the profound pith instructions of the Six Doctrines of Nāropā (which contain the concealed meaning of the infinite tantras, the heart essence of as many spiritual heroes and ḍākinīs as there are particles of Mount Sumeru and the quintessence of their unsurpassed secrets intermingling the three aspects of illusion and the three aspects of inner radiance) and the great seal of the abiding nature (which yet again carries that same path of the Six Doctrines onto the path within the nonsymbolic expanse of reality in order to bring forth a successful outcome) {491} are both embraced by many dissimilar titles. Although they are all essentially identical in their directly pointed introductions, they are somewhat dissimilar in their presentation of the stages of symbolic visualization. Among them, here in this Land of Snows, Da-o Zhonu Dakpo Lharje Gampopa[881] was the great promulgator of the Buddhist teaching, foreordained by the Conqueror as the one who would open up the tradition of the path of the great seal of definitive meaning, unrivaled in his acquisition of inspiration that did not rely on others. The oral instructions revealed by him are explained to be a coemergent union because the mind, conceptual thought, and the buddha body of reality are coemergent at the outset and united as one through the instructions.

So it was that Sonam Pelzangpo perfectly received the experiential guidance of the great seal of the abiding nature, which is endowed with this symbolic meaning. By manifesting its experiential cultivation with devotion and constant fervent perseverance, he seemed to acquire in succession all the attributes of the path and fruit without exception that are described for the sake of those to be trained in accordance with the provisional meaning. But as far as the definitive meaning was concerned, over countless past eons of time, it is certain that he had attained manifestly perfect enlightenment as a mighty lord possessing the diverse glorious wheels of existence and quiescence, and the wheel indicative of dominion that is secure in the real nature, the expanse of reality. This being the case, his gradual introduction to the teaching from this point onward, his receiving of the oral instructions that confer maturation and liberation, and his acquisition of the attributes of experiential realization are indeed only with reference to the provisional meaning.

Then, in his twenty-second year, in 1491, he turned his mind toward receiving the vows of full monastic ordination, which are the foundation of all the teachings of sūtra and mantra. With the omniscient Choje Ngawang Drakpa Pelzangpo (Vāgīśvarakīrtibhadra), the steadfast and learned one who had reached the summit of the branches of learning and altruism, acting as preceptor; {492} with Chodrak Yeshe Pelzangpo (Dharmakīrtijñānaśrībhadra), the crown holder of Zhamar, acting as the master of ceremonies; and with Venerable Tashi Pelwa (Maṅgalaśrī), distinguished for his venerable conduct and mastery of spiritual attainment, acting as confessor, in the midst of a number of fully ordained monks replete with all the appropriate indications who made up the quorum, he excellently received the vows of the complete ordination.

This saintly individual who perfected the three vows deeply cherished the precious training of ethical discipline, such that he assumed strict responsibility to ensure that even the most minute of the rules might not be infringed. Throughout his life, he did not allow meat to touch his tongue, even if it were one of the three sorts of pure meat,[882] and he lived as one who was untainted in the slightest by minor downfalls.

Under the supreme emanation who had acted as the master of ceremonies during his full monastic ordination (that is, Fourth Zhamar), he studied an infinite, inconceivable number of empowerments, transmissions, and pith instructions, the foremost of which were the profound doctrines of Lord Marpa and Ngok, so he received them insatiably. In general, he understood that all his spiritual mentors—and especially the glorious omniscient Ngawang Drakpa, embodiment of Mahāvajradhara, endowed with three kindnesses[883]—were themselves the foundation of spiritual accomplishment, such that he pleased them with many things that were pleasing. Their minds merged together, and he acquired the extraordinary transference of authentic blessing.

In 1500 (iron female bird), in his thirtieth year, Choje Namgyel Drakpa renounced his responsibility for the monastic administration, wishing to stay in isolated retreat. So, this saintly individual Sonam Pelzangpo was inaugurated upon the lion throne of the great monastic seat. Flowers of offering were scattered, {493} and he assumed authority over the infinite spiritual and temporal powers, headed by the Main Temple of Taklung, which outshone even the most glorious of victorious divine realms.

Even at that time, his adamantine body, a basket filled with the glorious gems of the three trainings, remained calm and disciplined, and so he excelled through his habitual conduct, which was supremely steadfast. There was no one at all in the world, including the god realms, who was perceived as surpassing him in demonstrating the path of truth and observing onerous and strict boundaries with respect to the transmitted teachings and transmissions, free from falsehood, like a golden yoke. Fastidious, painstaking, upright, and steadfast, however much he was examined, he was devoid of defects, and his mind, profound and vast like a great ocean, was endowed with the three mysteries of buddha body, speech, and mind, blazing with the radiance of countless million trillion attributes of transmission and realization. It suffices to say that human beings would serve this saintly wish-fulfilling gem, even if arrayed on the crown of a hundred proud deities, including Brahmā, Viṣṇu, and Maheśvara. Through the enlightened activity of the loving-kindness of Mahākāruṇika, endowed with the four attractive qualities—making generous donations of necessities, speaking respectfully, acting purposefully, and acting harmoniously—he spontaneously accomplished the welfare of both himself and others, disregarding laborious effort. This being the case, how could the instances of his engagement in the lesser four rites possibly be differentiated?

In brief, since he held authority over his domain through the power of loving-kindness like the great kings of yore, it was reiterated that none of his subjects could be harmed by nonhuman spirits and that even the words *fear* and *sorrow* were unheard. {494} Even in this great monastery, which had formerly been home to one hundred and thirty-six bodhisattva princes, he established the custom of ever stricter observance of the rules and regulations, which were not violated, just like the injunctions of his saintly predecessors. In order to set an excellent example for others in taking care of the Main Temple—which was filled to the brim with extraordinary representations of buddha body, speech, and mind—at the very least, he offered advice on removing vegetation and plugging leakages in the upper story of the temple, and he also showed how it should be swept clean and maintained. He restored all the rooftop victory banners in the cardinal and intermediate directions, into which the incantation of sublime Sitātapatrā had been inserted as a core, their copper tops in the shape of a gemstone, excellently covered with thick gilding. With the inconceivable artifacts that others had offered, he rejoiced above all in making offerings. Even though he did not differentiate between equipoise and post-meditation, in his meditation, which was unelaborate like space, he did not dwell in one extreme alone but passed the time, day and night, in the infinite, uninterrupted, and elaborate meditations. At the very least, the prostrations and circumambulations that he alone made were unimaginable. Since he was without the stains of sleep, sluggishness, and indolence, without even untying his waistband at night, he passed the nighttime hours in meditation. Since he was powerful in the expression of the intense love that he had for beings with specific expectations and for those who were powerless, destitute, and afflicted by ill-health or suffering, even ordinary worldly people developed the faculty of intense faith, saying that his mind was profound and upright, an unfailing {495} refuge with the broad vision of extreme generosity.

On one occasion, at the meritorious invitation of many faithful persons, he went camping in many enclaves of the upper and lower northern region. Through the meditation and recitation of Mahākāruṇika, setting the mind on supreme enlightenment and so forth, he secured a countless number of living creatures in the definitive enlightened heritage of the two modalities of the Great Vehicle. Through material and spiritual gifts, he also encouraged butchers, hunters, fishermen, and others who earned a living exclusively through negative actions and made them turn away from their negative behavior. Just by scattering consecrated barley upon a terrifying and awesome flood, the waters subsided, and the master and all his disciples could proceed safely.

Again, through his vast miracles, as in the case of the just mentioned flooding river, he planted the seeds of faith in an immediate manner in those who saw and heard him. To those nomadic encampments that were not on friendly terms, he bestowed a mass of material things like a mountain, filling the terrain with horses and cattle, and so forth, without regret. He made excellent verdicts without falling into bias by pursuing the truth through boundary treaties[884] that did not transgress the limits of the three judgments of innocence and guilt, which had constituted the legal code of the religious king Songtsen Gampo. He brought those who were extremely pernicious under his sway by the great torma offerings that are the antidote of the doctrinal protectors. Imposing commitments upon them, he meditated excellently and established the country in peace.

All the fine and bountiful possessions that were offered by his faithful patrons were not squandered. Although he did not forsake the roots of virtuous action, {496} he set aside the best artifacts for lowly persons, and so forth. Without the stains of defect, he would devise ways of donating them exclusively for causes such as the commissioning of representations of buddha body, speech, and mind; the offering sacraments of the temple and its amenities; the offerings for anniversary ceremonies; and offerings for rites of attainment, appropriate for the entire congregation of monks. He secured the monastic assembly with his extensive dedications and prayers of aspiration, such that it increased more and more.

In 1508 (earth male dragon),[885] he offered alms and communal tea to the great monasteries of Tibet in order to fulfill the enlightened intention of his elder brother, Venerable Tashi Pelwa, dancer of the magical display of pristine cognition, whose physical reflection had dissolved into the taintless buddha field that was his natural abode. It is difficult to estimate the alms and so forth, consisting of innumerable material things that he dispensed to many thousands of upholders of the sūtra and mantra traditions who assembled here in Taklung and to the many hundreds of thousands of laypeople. After the funeral, as an outer representation, he commissioned perfectly designed artifacts including an image of Śākyamuni with his two retainers, as if Munīndra were actually present, and with a throne and back screen that filled one story of the Great Offering Chapel. He perfectly performed the consecration, along with the entire congregation of preceptors, masters, and monks headed by his venerable brother Namgyel Drakpa.

On one occasion during that period, Choje Drigungpa Kunga Rinchen, the regent and scion of Kyopa Jikten Sumgon, master and disciples, arrived in this direction of Taklung. In order to extol the upholders of the teaching of the lineage of attainment, {497} he was invited with a great welcoming reception by the preceptors, masters, and monastic community of Taklung, their hands adorned with an array of marvelous offering sacraments. From the eastern gate of the Main Temple, the two venerable brothers Namgyel Drakpa and Sonam Pelzangpo also honored him with a reception. Simply on sight, those most saintly individuals seemed to rival one another in their expressions of devotion. They greeted each other face-to-face, touched their heads together, and first they meritoriously secured excellent, auspicious circumstances, their hands adorning each other with silk scarves of good auspices. In the great upper chamber of the Offering Chapel, they took their seats correctly on fearless lion thrones that were high, resplendent, and individually bedecked with an unsurpassed array of ornaments. The resident and visiting monastic officials, preceptors, masters, and spiritual mentors—a multitude whose vases of intelligence were filled with the ocean of the piṭakas and whose minds were disciplined by the immaculate three trainings—and many senior and minor lay officials, learned in the noble ways of the world, in an orderly manner took the splendid seats that had been allocated to them. They were honored with bountiful food and drink that was admissible in terms of the vinaya and that could rival the supreme attributes of the food of the gods, endowed with a hundred flavors. The holy ones passed the time engaged in mutual, profound, and extensive discussions concerning the sacred doctrine. On that occasion, since it was the time of month when the moon was very large during the summer, for recreation, the rows of resident and visiting monks assembled together in sleeping tents and held an inconceivable feast. Even later on, wondrous conversations would be held concerning the ensuing elaborate discussions in which those saintly beings engaged on that occasion, {498} and their demeanors infused with the pure visions of buddha body, speech, and mind, the attributes of scriptural transmission and realization that the spiritual mentors headed by the preceptors and masters possessed, the hierarchy and pageantry of their entourages headed by the major and minor officials, the places where they sat, and the gifts that were presented, and so forth.

Moreover, Sonam Pelzangpo established unsurpassed spiritual and material connections with Choje Bum Rabjampa, who in word and meaning was described as "a learned master who had gone to the other shore of the ocean of the piṭakas;"[886] with Choje Chime Pelzangpo, lord of the infinite sūtras and tantras, who maintained the treasure store of Venerable Ngawang Drakpa's teachings;[887] with the white-robed mantrin Kunga Drakpa, who was a great upholder of the teaching of the ancient way of Secret Mantra;[888] and with Drukpa Rinpoche, the axis of the teaching of the lineage of spiritual attainment, who visited early and later in the course of his life. Consequently, his mind and theirs merged identically into one another. From many sides, he was greatly praised and complemented.

To all, including monks who locally resided in this precious monastery of Taklung, those who gathered from all directions, and those who maintained the vows concerning the three isolations of body, speech, and mind in the four retreat hermitages associated with Taklung,[889] he freely conferred maturational empowerments, many sequences of initiation, and the essential maturation of the cycles of profound guidance without interruption. In brief, for nineteen years, Sonam Pelzangpo had the kindness to meaningfully restore and expand without decline the two traditions of the precious teaching of the glorious Taklungpa. {499} Then, for a while, he inspected all the disciples of this field. Intending to pass away into another field, in the perception of the disciples, he appeared to fall ill for a long period of time. Many learned physicians recognized the symptoms of lymphatic disorder and offered medical treatment. Since his body was weak, they offered him a little meat, but he refused this, saying he was pledged not to eat meat. Although infinite rites were performed here in Taklung and in all other directions in order to secure his long life, he sometimes directly and indirectly went to the places where his attendants were staying, informing them that he would not live long.

In the morning of the twenty-eighth day of the ninth lunar month in 1520 (iron male dragon), he passed into nirvāṇa in the Northern Chamber. Through the upward motion of white vital essence, phlegm dripped in a swirl from his nostrils. Starting from then, the sky was filled with a net of rainbow light, a shower of flowers fell, and the entire ground became warm, as in summertime. Although it was the height of winter, flowers bloomed, and there were many to be offered. Since the land was permeated with such a wondrous array of auspicious signs, the great upholders of the Buddhist teaching who resided elsewhere also praised him.

At that time, his older brother Choje Avadhūtipa the Great (Namgyel Drakpa) conducted the funeral rites. The large gathering of monks who assembled in the monastery opened the maṇḍala of the secret mantras and undertook offerings of attainment, day and night. In the presence of the precious corpse, offerings were made with an infinite number of butter lamps and offering sacraments. In all the monastic communities of U, Tsang, and Kham, including the large and small monasteries of the new and ancient traditions, {500} and of the Sakyapa and the Gedenpa, there was an inconceivably large distribution of boiling tea and alms. On the day of the great funeral ceremony, the fourth holder of the crown of Zhamar was invited. Innumerable offerings were made and there was a day-long extensive distribution of alms in the Great Assembly Hall. The throngs of laypeople were also satisfied with infinite gifts. The precious sacred corpse itself was offered for cremation on the annual anniversary. Relics were distributed as a token of devotion to all the faithful monks and disciples. In the Old Offering Chapel, a precious representative image of the deceased was fashioned and an anthology of the canonical scriptures of the Buddha was commissioned in vermilion, gold, and silver, and so forth. In ways such as these, his enlightened intention was fulfilled.

Establishing all hermitages and monasteries that follow
The virtuous path beyond cyclic existence and nirvāṇa,
In the ground with dominion over the provision of merit
That originates from this biography,
By the merit of this lord-protector who was imbued with such offering sacraments,
May the twofold benefit of self and others be perfected!

Namgyel Tashi, Fifteenth in the Abbatial Succession

Emanating as the ten million buddhas of the three times,
Assuming forms that are mighty in hundredfold learning and accomplishment,
Inconceivable in the mysteries of knowledge, love, and power,
Homage to Gyelwang Namgyel Tashi!

The wondrous supreme tulku, Ngawang Namgyel Tashi Drakpa Gyeltsen Pelzangpo in past time had emanated as ten million conquerors, as is elucidated in the venerable master's own *Sealed Narrative*.[890] At the present time, he continues to teach in the form of the countless buddhas of the ten directions, including the sage Lokaśubhakṛtsna. {501} In the future, he will attain buddhahood in the form Sugata Ratnakūṭa in the field of Diffusing Light[891] in the zenith, and teach the sacred doctrine for eighty thousand years to an entourage numbering four billion. Having displayed ten million attributes—the rolling of thunder, infinite rays of light, mounds of glory, and so forth—he will discipline those to be trained, and his emanational display that acts for the welfare of the Buddhist teaching and living beings in ways that are superior, inferior, and mediocre is inconceivable. Above all, in the past, he had assumed the forms of eight great householders, including Anāthapiṇḍada, who were the patrons of eight tathāgatas of the three times; of Satyadarśana, who was ordained as a mendicant from the householder class in the presence of the Buddha Kāśyapa; of Śikṣādara, who was ordained as a mendicant from the lower class in the land of Saṅprana; of the great king Indrabhūti; the great preceptor Śāntarakṣita; Nanam Yeshe De; the mighty lord of yoga Tilopā; the great hermit sage Śūrasena; Daṃkipa; Nakasoripa in Ekākāra; Jinipaṭu in Nepal; Jñānadvaja in Kashmir; Sañcanātha in Vaiśālī; Tingbidhura in China; and as Putowa Rinchen Sel, during the later phase of Buddhist propagation in Tibet; as well as Taklung

Sangye Yarjon,[892] Martonpa Rinchen Śākya,[893] and Changlungpa Zhonu Lodro.[894] Of an identical mindstream, and simultaneously, he had also assumed the forms of Taklung Jangchub Gyatso[895] and the twenty-second Drigung Chenga,[896] and just prior to this present reincarnation, he had been Choje Tsokye Dorje of Zangzang Neuringpa.[897] In general, all these successive incarnations had shared an identical mindstream, and in particular, it is accepted that Venerable Karmapa Mikyo Dorje and this lord-protector were of an inseparable mindstream, merely manifesting in different physical forms. {502} This is clearly elucidated in the successive lives of the glorious Karmapa and elsewhere.

Having worked for the welfare of as many worthy living beings as there were, through Padmavajra's undiminished and unenhanced pristine cognition of intrinsic awareness, supreme among authentic holders of gnostic mantras, here at Taklung, as had been foreordained by Jikten Wangchuk Tashi Peltsek, he reincarnated, continuing the primordial, consummately present maṇḍala of the transcendent lord Cakrasaṃvara, with its supporting palace and the deities within it. His father was the governor Sonam Drakpa, who resided in the governor's palace known as Lhundrub Dzong, which was adorned with the complete excellences of existence and quiescence, and his mother was Dekyi Budren Gyelmo, princess of Olkha, an emanation of Vajravārāhī, embodiment of supremely unchanging great bliss, endowed with the glory of the auspicious oceanic assembly of Śrīheruka, and the essential nature of emptiness in all its finest aspects. After entering the womb, in the situation of the ground, he manifested the rank of the five pristine cognitions, or ten levels, within the womb and then was born at the sacred monastery called Rinchen Drak[898] on the thirtieth day of the midwinter month, also known as Pauṣya in 1524 (wood male monkey). The venerable hierarch Namgyel Drakpa, with great delight, named him Chokyong Tashi, saying that because he was a gift bequeathed by the doctrinal protectors, guardians of the transmitted teachings, his name should conform to that.

Then, as soon as a date associated with noble enlightened heritage arrived, this divine prince with a topknot—bearing the youthful glory of the major and minor marks, which are fully perfected through aspects of renunciation and realization— {503} just after reaching the age of five, traveled to this great seminary of Taklung, the Adamantine Seat foreordained by the Conqueror. He served as an attendant at the feet of Venerable Avadhūtipa the Great, Namgyel Drakpa Pelzangpo, emanation of the compassion of the great mighty lord of yoga Śavaripā, who was foremost in the lineage of authentic blessing and the sole lord of his enlightened heritage. He received the vows of a layperson, maintaining the threefold refuge, and the name Namgyel Tashi was conferred upon him. That is to say, after first completing the virtuous ordination[899] associated with the excellent path through which the gate of the precious Buddhist teaching is entered, he then received the threefold vows of definitive meaning. He was empowered as a genuine regent of the sacred doctrine and attained manifest enlightenment in the unique buddha body of reality by securing the expanse of reality with the seal of pristine cognition.

At first, Namgyel Tashi stayed in a grass hermitage, where he began learning to write and read under the learned Kunga Lodro. Then, he undertook extensive study and reflection on the minor fields of classical learning, including Sanskrit grammar, poetics, astrology, and prosody, as well as the oceanic sūtras and tantras of Buddhist learning. During that period, he comprehended them just by seeing the texts since he had been accomplished in the power of refinement over his successive past lives. However, his intelligence did not merely possess the volumes of all the scriptures—this mighty lord of speech also instantaneously became learned in all fields of knowledge.

Then, in his seventh year, in 1530 (iron male tiger), after elaborate funeral rites had been undertaken to fulfill the enlightened intention of his late precious predecessor Sonam Pelzangpo, in the midst of the entire congregation of monks who were endowed with both knowledge and liberation, he was immediately appointed as a master of the Buddhist teaching upon the lion throne of the sacred doctrine, which the line of the buddhas of the authentic lineage had occupied as a focal point for the offerings and remembrance of all worlds, including the gods. {504} He was invested with authority over the treasury, replete with spiritual and secular excellence. With an oceanic display of empowerment as a child of the conquerors, the conquerors of the ten directions without exception bestrewed him with flower garlands of awareness and filled all their fields with the unending melody of their benedictions. They acquired certainty that he was a learned master and requested him to satisfy beings with the nectar of spiritual accomplishment.

He received the profound and concise empowerments, transmissions, and pith instructions associated with the two approaches of the lineage, derived from the attainment of occult power and the attainment of ethical discipline, through which he excellently refined all the subtle and coarse topics of his own textual tradition.

In his eighth year, coinciding with an auspicious stellar conjunction[900] on the thirtieth day of the autumn month of Uttarabhadrapāda, in 1531 (iron female hare), in the presence of Venerable Ngagi Wangchuk, a great paṇḍita of Sakya,[901] he excellently received the vows of the novitiate in accordance with the ancient ordination rite, and the name Ngawang Namgyel Tashi Drakpa Gyeltsen Pelzangpo was conferred upon him.

In the presence of the glorious Drukpa Rinpoche Ngawang Chokyi Gyelpo, common ancestor of the lineage of spiritual attainment, he mastered the ocean-like oral instructions of the glorious Phakdru Kagyu lineage, exemplified by Coemergent Union of the Great Seal of the Abiding Nature,[902] the Great Seal of Bliss And Emptiness,[903] and the Six Doctrines of Nāropā. Here, at Taklung, he also received scriptural transmissions, commencing with the complete Kangyur, which consists of the wealth of the entire Buddhist teaching in general.

In his sixteenth year, at the hermitage of Sengling Drakya Dorje Yangdzong, {505} for almost a year, he propitiated Mahākāla, the lord of enlightened heritage of all. That is to say, he propitiated Mahākāla externally in the form of the adamantine universal monarch, Kākamukha, in the manner of a protector deity that is visualized in front, then propitiated him internally in the manner of a meditational deity that is visualized as oneself, and then, secretly, he propitiated him as the pure essence of the vital heart mantra.[904] By refining the experiential cultivation that integrates these three steps with the meditative stability of the great seal, the vitality of the pure essence, he perfectly obtained the signs of supreme and common spiritual accomplishment, just as they are explained in the manuals of pith instruction. Starting from that time onward, this great adamantine holder of the attainment of supreme awareness easily accomplished all enlightened activities that he intended through the power of the protector deities and their entourage.

Afterward, in 1542 (water male tiger), the year in which his calculated period of "nine womb months plus three intercalary months" was complete,[905] he received the precepts of full monastic ordination, with Jamyang Ngagi Wangchuk, the great saintly being of glorious Sakya,[906] acting as monastic preceptor and master of ceremonies and Jetsun Dampa Drolchok[907] acting as confessor. With the patronage of the world, including the gods, he was calm and disciplined in the manner of the sublime Aśvajit;[908]

devout in monastic training like Rāhulabhadra, son of the Conqueror;[909] and like the second elder Upāli, maintained the vinaya of word and meaning.[910] Simply by entering his room, stains of body and mind were dispelled by the fragrance of ethical discipline that exuded from his body. He became supreme among those who wear the victory banner of the monastic robe, a preceptor of many thousand recipients of ordination, holy sovereign of the vows of individual liberation according to the Great Vehicle, which are distinguished from the vows of the pious attendants by the setting of the mind on supreme enlightenment. {506}

At that time, Venerable Eighth Karmapa, Mikyo Dorje, and his disciples traveled here to Taklung. Although there were no appropriate auspicious circumstances for them to actually meet one another as tulkus, Venerable Karmapa is said to have composed the following verses of meditative inspiration inscribed as a letter in Rañjanā handwriting, and he sent it for Yung Gelong Rinchen Gonpo[911] to offer:

Supreme mighty power, familiar with the accumulation of the two provisions,
Inspired by the enlightened intention of the glorious emanational body,
In order that your past experiences might be reborn,
May the causal basis of supreme enlightenment,
The bountiful uplifting of the mind, be radiant in your mind!
May your conduct that is powerful and perfect through the commitments,
That cannot be accommodated in the minds of ordinary people,
Guard the gates of nectar that cures infinite living beings
With awareness, wherever past propensities are present!
May the unsurpassed secret discourse of past lives,
Profound in words sealed with adamantine reality,
And manifested by this Venerable One (Namgyel Tashi) alone,
Please take place here in my presence!
With words that form a continuum,
Rejecting the basis of doubt,
And clearly foreordained, without obscuration,
May you learn the marvelous approaches to the magical display of pristine cognition,
The discourse that is presented throughout the three times

In the supreme emanational land of the ḍākinīs of pristine cognition!
May the three stages (of generation, perfection, and great perfection),
Enunciated by the great master (Padmākara),
Be practiced in the mountainous ravines of the northern direction!
May enlightened activity that is not untimely or overdue
Not be forgotten with regard to the conferral of scriptural transmissions
And the positive practice of the Buddhist teaching,
Just as they are both taught by this great Venerable One,
Inasmuch as they are profound topics!
Let this be auspicious!

On that occasion, {507} Namgyel Tashi delighted this teacher (Karmapa Mikyo Dorje) with the three things that are pleasing[912] on account of the enduring signs of his supreme spiritual accomplishment. He was also endowed with the eye of omniscient pristine cognition, aware that he had been reincarnated in succession as eleven mighty lords of learning and accomplishment in India and Tibet, starting with the mighty lord of yoga Kanhapā, whom the Conqueror had clearly foreordained in many tantras would obtain the supreme accomplishment during the intermediate state of rebirth, and finally as one named Jamgon Drupei Pawo Pelden Kunga Drolchok Losel Gyatsode, a holy spiritual adviser who appeared in the world like Munīndra.

There was unimaginable astonishment when he completed the empowerments of the forty-five maṇḍalas of the Adamantine Garland in a single day. In general, from different teachers, he painstakingly received classes of transmission that were very rare, including one hundred and eight ancillary scriptures of the four tantras that were not included in general transmitted teachings of the canon and one hundred and eight tracts of profound guidance that were subsumed in three collections—the tradition of the sūtras, the tradition of the tantras, and the meditative experiences vomited forth by accomplished masters—as well as one hundred and eight details concerning the doctrinal protectors, guardians of the Buddhist teaching.[913] Exemplified by these compilations, his studies of the exegeses of the sūtras and tantras, maturational empowerments, and liberating guidance that had come down to him through the lineages of the Sakyapa, Jonangpa, Zhalupa, Ngorpa, Bodongpa, Nyingma, Kadam, Pacification, Severance, and the two approaches of the Kagyu lineage (those of Dakpo and the Shangpa), and so forth, were infinite. He received teachings, even the names of which were hard to enumerate, and all of the teachings that he received were instantaneously absorbed through pristine cognition, along with all their essential points without exception, as objects of his mind, such that the expanse in which all these were gathered {508} surpassed the reach and range of thought. This may be inferred from the certainty of those saintly beings endowed with the broad vision of the sacred doctrine who praised him.

Again, in 1543 (hare), Namgyel Tashi entered into strict retreat at Sengling Dorje Dzong. Without accepting anything inadmissible, as was appropriate, he received his food, consisting of the three dairy products, through a hand-span-size aperture and at teatime. He communicated by symbols since he would go there having written things that were permissible for him to say on a wooden board. He became absorbed in a continuous flow of profound adamantine yoga, without distinguishing between meditative equipoise and post-meditation, integrating the king of meditative stability that diffuses the natural sameness of all things with the three magical displays and the three aspects of inner radiance.

Prior to and after those events, he commissioned a countless number of artifacts, including the silver reliquary of his venerable predecessor Vajra Avadhūtipa the Great (Ngawang Drakpa) in the form of an enlightenment stūpa, which was resplendent like a massive mountain, and gilded-copper images of Munīndra and his retainers, with a throne and back screen that were the height of the Lower Hall of the Main Temple, as if the Conqueror had actually arrived there. He also commissioned the complete Kangyur inscribed in gold and silver on parchment; a gold image of glorious Jñānanātha with entourage, which was an extraordinarily sublime creation, blazing with the light of splendor; the complete lineage of the Six Doctrines fashioned of red sandalwood; an awesome silk tangka depicting Munīndra with the sixteen elders, for which the brocade had been purposefully sent from many hundreds of sources; the lineage of the Shangpa Kagyu; and a set of the ten doctrinal protectors.

In the presence of Jetsun Dampa, among the ocean of oath-bound protectors of the transmitted teachings, on whom countless adamantine holders of India and Tibet had relied, {509} he completely received the extraordinary pith instructions concerning Kṣetrapāla; Glorious Four-Faced Mahākāla with his sister, who cannot be rivaled by others in mighty battles; and also the extraordinary outer, inner, and secret pith instructions concerning the propitiation of Yakṣa in the form of male and female consorts in mystic union; the propitiation of the Mother Protector (Śrīdevī) in the form of male and female consorts in union; and the propitiation of Yama in male and female forms. He said that he saw the signs of the might of the protector deities following him, as a shadow follows the body, and that they would accomplish all his enlightened activities.

Later, when he was commissioning a painted icon according to his meditative commitment, while consecrating the canvas base, he visualized the individual faces and torso of the lord-protector on the blank canvas, and he perfectly turned the canvas base into a bulging relief form with folds, upon which the artist then applied the gold lines. Just to see the unbearable wrath and splendor of this self-originating lord-protector that is free from artificiality was enough to know how different it was from any others in all its hair-raising magnificence. He said that there were many certain indications that the aspiration of the glorious lord-protector was actually embodied in this image.

In general, the perfect paintings that he alone commissioned of different forms of the deity, according to the ritual service and means for attainment and the ritual applications, were approximately five in number. It is said that these paintings were displayed in his chamber with their faces exposed and that some of his retainers blacked out and fainted merely at their sight, collapsing on the ground, and were then revived by being smeared with his saliva.

In his grass hermitage, the outer, inner, and secret representative images of the glorious Four-Faced Lord-Protector Mahākāla, in the guise of a brahmin and their sacraments of commitment, in painted and relief forms, {510} were installed,[914] along with a cotton painted icon of the great divine Genyen in wrathful guise, and so forth.[915] These were created in conjunction with a continuous display of terrifying miracles by the deities of the Protector Chapel.

In the Protector Chapel of the Main Temple, he commissioned a story-high brocade scroll depicting raven-faced Karmamahākāla, a wondrous array that accorded with an ancient rite of attainment.[916] At dawn, following the night after he had performed the consecration, he had a vision of a large emanational raven flying from the southern direction with flapping wings and then vanishing into that icon. When it was brought into the Protector Chapel, there were also innumerable miraculous signs that occurred.

As a precursor,[917] he also excellently commissioned and installed in that Protector Chapel a brocade scroll depicting the glorious Four-Armed Jñānanātha in the form Coemergence of Secret Attainment, which derives from the pith instructions of the second promulgation of the doctrinal wheel.[918]

In early and later life, the artist who was asked to make those paintings of his meditative commitments was Bernak Sangye Gyatso alone. Once, when he was making a small cotton drawing of the lord-protector Jarok Dong, based on the lama's meditative commitment, he made the sketch replacing the little finger of the left hand of the central deity, which holds the ritual skull with a thumb. Thereupon, Namgyel Tashi said, "From past time until the present,[919] when the time comes to cast out the torma of Legon, it seems they do so while concealing the fingers of the left hand, so your drawing is not mistaken!" On examining the drawing, it has been exactly adjusted by an inch. It is said that Namgyel Tashi previously drew it during the night upon a surface of molten butter while performing the ritual service of Four-Faced Kākamukha Mahākāla in the presence of an inch-perfect full-story-size apparition of Mahākāla {511} and that, consequently, the artist could clearly see the perfect form that accorded with the drawing to be made on the surface of the canvas base.

In brief, this holy individual had inestimable visions of the deities that were his meditative commitments. All the doctrinal protectors and guardians exactly performed the injunctions that he assigned them. The circumstances pertaining to all knowable phenomena of the three times were clear in his mind like reflections on the surface of a clear mirror, such that his life was an infinite, profoundly secret narrative of visions, prophetic declarations, and so forth. When he disclosed this to the master Kunlo, who was preparing a rough biographical account of his life, although the latter was erudite, he informed Namgyel Tashi that it would not be auspicious because his life would be endangered were he to disseminate such narratives, as if oppressed by darkness of Māra. Consequently, it is said that Namgyel Tashi did not permit him to continue with the composition, owing to such adverse circumstances, and even gathered in the parts of the biography that had previously been formulated. Actually, although he explained that his life would be endangered by the proclamation of those secrets and so forth, that was simply for the sake of a few individuals on the path of conventional human behavior. He knew the immediate and long-term advantages that accrue for perfect and omniscient buddhas who proclaim and conceal profound secrets in that manner. Disciplined with self-control over life and death, he was repelled by the arrogance[920] of those who seek profit and fame with a liking for wishful and material long-life rituals that resemble the iterations of parrots. His mind was measured, and he was one who had to strive to abandon violations of commitments and so forth. Even at that time, in his enlightened intention, there arose the thought that the actions of such acquisitive sentient beings would mostly be undone of their own accord.

Then, on the twenty-ninth day of the tenth lunar month of 1547 (fire female sheep), {512} when he went to replenish the tormas in the protector chapels, he foresaw that fire would break out in the Main Temple, outside and adjacent to the image of glorious Four-Armed Mahākāla in the Old Protector Chapel, and he foresaw clear signs that every auspicious circumstance would be arranged for the effortless rebuilding of the temple and its representations.

During the night of the twenty-seventh of the twelfth lunar month of that year (1547), in order to bring forth the greatness of the enlightened activity of the conquerors, the representations of buddha body, speech, and mind, the sacraments of offering, and so forth in the Main Temple, which were filled with all the excellences of existence and quiescence, were engulfed in the midst of a blazing fire, like the unimaginable demeanor of someone absorbed in the perfection stage of meditation. At that time, the objects that were damaged by fire included the silver image of glorious Taklungpa the Great, known as Ornament of the World; the image known as Gyagarma; the reliquary called Tashi Pelbar, which was damaged from the harmikā upward, along with the cubit-high silver stūpa within it that contained the heart, tongue, and eyes of Gyelwa Taklung Tangpa the Great; the reliquary of Kuyal Rinpoche, which was filled with tens of thousands of pearl relics, along with his complete skull and heart; the heart of Venerable Tashi Peltsek; the complete relics and rainbow-like body of glorious Ngawang Drakpa; the complete relics and skull of Venerable Namgyel Drakpa; more than a thousand relics of Munīndra; the two thousand images positioned behind the back screen of the Tashi Pelbar reliquary; and the new and old protector chapels.

Then, {513} he began the restoration in conjunction with his great pledge to restore the layout of the temple and its contents exactly to their former appearance, transcending the boundaries of the ordinary intellect, on the third day of the month of Caitra in 1548, a year that is called Kīlaka in India and earth male monkey in Tibet and China, on a day of auspicious planetary and stellar conjunction. Through the power of Mahākāruṇika, the building materials, including the timber, and all the skilled craftsmen spontaneously appeared without difficulty. They newly built the projecting bay extending along the north wall upon the exact area that it had previously occupied. Within three years, they excellently rebuilt the temple that rivaled the mansion of Vijaya, and simultaneously they also set up a workshop for the construction of representative images. Namgyel Tashi then commissioned an image of glorious Taklung Tangpa the Great, fashioned from a *sang* of gold, along with its silver throne and back screen; a likeness of Phakmodrupa, the lord of living beings, called Ornament of the World, which was fashioned from seven hundred and fifty *sang* of silver; the section of the precious Tashi Pelbar silver reliquary from the harmikā upward, which was newly cast; a peerless image of the Sugata Taklungpa the Great in a form representing the buddha body of reality, which was fashioned from one thousand two hundred *sang* of silver; an image of Cakrasaṃvara according to the tradition of Kṛṣṇapāda, known as Knower of the Three Times, the actual body of which was fashioned from four and a half thousand pure *sang* of silver that had been smelted and refined seven times, with a seat and ornaments fashioned from four hundred *zho* of gold and the female consort fashioned of copper; an image of Munīndra, the back of which was thirty-five handspans in height, along with its throne and back screen, the body of which was fashioned from two hundred and seventy loads of copper and gilded with a thousand *zho* of gold; {514} and other images, including Dakpo Lharje Gampopa, Phakmodrupa, and Venerable Taklung Tangpa the Great, each fashioned of thirty *sang* of silver. The construction of the temple and its contents was more greatly esteemed than before, and so, as far as Tibet is concerned, it is completely unrivaled in the present day.[921] This splendid achievement, which was unanimously praised by knowledgeable and honest persons, was excellently completed within five years, so his manifestation of miraculous ability was a marvelous supreme gateway to liberation.

Such magnificent acts of rebuilding the temple and its representations of buddha body, speech, and mind that surpass the boundaries of the intellect were in all circumstances—beginning, middle, and end—under the protection of marvelous Mahākāruṇika. So, leaving aside those workers who eventually injured their limbs during the construction and so forth, it is clear that, apart from that, the project was completed without anyone even falling ill. To that end, the entire congregation applied themselves one-pointedly to their tasks with body, speech, and mind, scorning difficulties, and all worldly persons who saw and heard them were astonished. To that end, even the resources that were contributed, including tea, clothing, silk, horses, armor, salt, and barley, donated by each of their respective owners, are said to have been continuous. During those years, with regard to the congregation of the workers and the coming and going of resources, it seemed that there was no shortage at all, and this was due to the blessings of Mahākāla himself.

Afterward, at the southern gate of the new temple, he constructed an image of the protector deity Genyen Chenpo, wearing wrathful garb, {515} and he was appointed as the doctrinal protector of the temple. Taking as a basis *The Verses of Torma Offering*[922] bequeathed by Gyelwa Taklungpa the Great and the liturgical texts composed by Choje Sangye Onpo and Rinpoche Maṅgalaguru, he gathered together the best of the texts composed by the learned Jampel Drakpa and so forth and created this new composition titled *Delightful Supplement of Liturgical Offering*,[923] which is nowadays renowned like the wind.

The venerable and holy Namgyel Tashi presented many representations of buddha body, speech, and mind endowed with the blazing light of blessed splendor, exemplified by a high-quality bronze-alloy image of the Buddha, which had been the meditative handiwork of the glorious Indian master Candrakīrti, with an attached certificate of indisputable provenance written on the surface of its border band in the capital letter Sindhu script, which read *sāramahācārya candrakīrti deya dharme yaṃ*. This translates into Tibetan as "This is a sacred doctrine to be granted by the supremely great master Candrakīrti." Along with that, he presented innumerable awesome material objects, the value of which was inestimable. He also made icons that were the meditative commitments of three traditions—Drigung, Taklung, and Druk—having indeed received their many profound doctrines. So it was that this holy individual was most wonderful, making use of two qualities, in that he was the best of tutors based on his infinite studies and the best of disciples based on his devout acts of service, which in all respects surpassed the bounds of the intellect.

Afterward, owing to his bountiful and positive enlightened activities, Venerable Kunga Tashi—who had lotuses upon his hands and was the ideal image of a vajra-holding monk and my holy lord of refuge, {516} sustaining the spiritual and temporal well-being of the Buddhist teaching and living beings—was crowned on the lion throne of the sacred doctrine in 1555 (wood female hare) and flowers of offering were scattered.

For a while, Namgyel Tashi then stayed in retreat at Sengling. He traveled several times for the sake of his disciples in the northern region, and through the four attractive qualities, he brought innumerable disciples of good fortune to maturation and liberation. Though he intended to visit Taklung Lower Plain, he was asked publicly and privately to stay in Utsang, and so he consented and postponed his journey.

The incumbent Choje Kunga Tashi then permitted him to construct the gilded spire of the Main Temple and so forth. He consecrated the incantations inserted within the newly commissioned representative images, and he extensively restored the old shrines—the Kumbum and so forth. Upon the host of the entire resident congregation of monks, exceeding one thousand in number, who gathered from different directions, he conferred forty-five empowerments, which included the actual forty-two maṇḍalas presented in the glorious *Adamantine Garland*, with the addition of three auspicious maṇḍalas described in *The Compendium of Rituals*.[924] He bestowed these over a whole month, relying on cotton painted maṇḍalas. On these occasions, also, he spoke unimpededly and absolutely from the heart concerning all the sequential procedures of maṇḍala construction and empowerment ceremony—generating the maṇḍala in front of oneself, consecrating the ritual vase, and the entry of oneself into the maṇḍala—and besides that, he never relied upon books and so forth. In order to demonstrate that he looked after the lineage holders, who saw him accept prostrations in a manner that was not perfunctory, he ensured that all the root and subsidiary empowerment sacraments were passed down to the great monastic assembly by his own hand. {517} The physically strong adult attendants, who carried the offering sacraments, would be utterly tired and exhausted and left behind, and yet Venerable Namgyel Tashi himself would immediately maintain his dignity. Despite the heaviest swaying of the crowd at those times, he would proceed without ever perspiring or being short-tempered. Also, during his introduction to the deities in the main part of the empowerment, he would accurately communicate each attribute of the supporting celestial palace and the deities contained within it, based on the pure words found in the text of Buton's *Perfect Garland of Yoga*.[925] With regard to the deities also, he would enunciate their body colors, hand emblems, ornaments, costumes, and all the authentic features of their postures. Other than that, he would not permit the symbols to be compared or contracted even slightly. He perfectly bestowed the individual empowerments of the higher and lower classes of tantra and the tantras of skillful means, discriminative awareness, and nonduality in their entirety, without confusing the distinctive procedures of each and certainly without omitting any item that was essential or adding any item that was not essential. At those times, whenever there was a discussion between the vajra officiants of the empowerment ceremonies and the many knowledgeable persons in the rows of those receiving the empowerments, he would examine them in detail. Such an approach to the implementation of empowerments is astonishing to those of later generations.

Nowadays, most of those who perform the recitations and rites employ rites that are deficient in many aspects due to the defects of addition, omission, or error, and those who would explain the empowerment rites solely on the basis of their intellects find that the essentials to be appraised are covert because there are slight difficulties with regard to the rites of the generation stage—self-generation, generation in front, the attainment of the vase, and so forth. For this reason, those who are lax and those who are slightly hesitant merely recite the texts. With regard to the activities of the main part of the empowerments, {518} they have little difficulty because they go on to repeat the words of a single rite, but when they abridge the introduction to the deity and so forth, they may even say, "Through the resolve to see directly the preferred deity in such and such a maṇḍala with its supporting celestial palace and supported deities, may that come to pass just by means of this rite!" How could such persons, who find only names attractive, reach even a hundredth part of the empowerment![926]

Again, in the case of those masters endowed with profound discriminative awareness—who are steadfast, broad-minded, and illustrious and who do not act in a perfunctory manner, even though the words of the empowerment rite may not be retained in their minds—the entire meaning does arise unbewildered in their minds. Over and above the text-based rites of such realized persons, it is not clear that the aforementioned mind-based rites of that sort have a particular purpose that can communicatively or meaningfully take effect. In general, even when a verbal transmission is interrupted, if the rite is not brought forth from the mind, the empowerment would not take effect, but if it can indeed be retained by the mind, all its words could then be recited carelessly and indifferently. It is clear that both of these techniques are incorrect. At the present time, approaching the eon's end, I think it will be better if one does not fall into either of those positions.[927]

Accordingly, this lord-protector Namgyel Tashi, mighty lord of knowledge and love, bestowed in a public gathering the empowerments of the Adamantine Expanse,[928] relying on a maṇḍala of colored sand, along with the infinite transmissions and guidance of the glorious Six Doctrines of Nāropā, and so forth. He also bestowed without interruption and in an abridged manner innumerable other empowerment teachings, including the great empowerment of *Kālacakra* according to the Buton tradition, relying on a cotton painting, and infinite profound guidance, including the detailed exegeses of many essential sūtras, tantras, and treatises, the Luminosity of All Hidden Meanings,[929] the Four Doctrines,[930] the Mind Training,[931] the Direct Guidance on Avalokiteśvara,[932] the Great Seal, the Two Approaches,[933] {519} and Mahākāla in the form Gonpo Kurak. All knowledgeable persons unanimously praised him, saying that nowhere among a million trillion teachers of the sacred doctrine was anyone like him seen or heard, owing to his teaching method.

Even at times when all the actual, knowledgeable disciples of Venerable Namgyel Tashi would meet in person and converse, these were most pure, owing to the magnificence of his exegeses, the essentiality of his experiential cultivation, and his conversations concerning the basic steps of visualization, which were direct and timely, imbued with scriptural authority and reasoning, and unadulterated with other teachings. Having comprehended without bewilderment the words and meanings of these sacred doctrines that were to be explained, by pointing out the definitive secrets, those of high and low intelligence would easily understand and easily retain them. Since his teaching sessions were very long, they would last all day, but in his speech, he was without the slightest trace of unnecessary repetition of words and meanings, contradiction, disconnection, and adulteration of words. He never discriminated between petitioners of great and little influence, those who greeted him politely and those who did not, or those who asked him about the sacred doctrine and those who did not, and so forth. People could be heard saying unanimously that he resembled the steadfast flow of a wide meandering river.

On one occasion, he covered the pillars of the inner sanctum in the Great Temple of Rasa Trulnang—abode of Jowo Rinpoche, representative image of the Teacher—with a gilded canopy of beaten metal, studded with a cluster of precious gems, the value of which was inestimable. He donated a beautiful silver parasol to the image of Self-Originated Eleven-Faced Mahākāruṇika, a brocade canopy to the image of Jowo Mikyo Dorje in Ramoche, and so forth. When he made his aspiration prayers in Lhasa, {520} the entire sky was permeated with rainbow colors, and a shower of flowers fell.

All of his compositions on the infinite classes of the sacred doctrine that are extant also arrived at the enlightened intention of the sūtras, tantras, and treatises. They concisely reveal the profound and extensive meanings, they delight the learned, and they are easy for the foolish to understand. They exclusively resemble a concentrated mine of gemstones that have been purified by means of the three sorts of scrutiny.[934]

The list of Namgyel Tashi's extant writings is separately documented in a catalog that I prepared.[935] Among them, if one were to mention just the most important, they include his two outer autobiographies, his *Secret Narrative with Its Sealed Injunction*;[936] *The Ascertainment of the Essence of the Precepts, Restrictions, and Attainments of the Vinaya*;[937] *Ornament of the Enlightened Intention of Fearless Eloquence: Implementation of the Adamantine Garland of Maṇḍala Rites*;[938] *General Framework of the Tantras*;[939] *Ascertainment of the Vinaya of the Tathāgata*;[940] *Chariot That Attains the Definitive Meaning, Combining the Meaning of "The Sūtra of the King of Meditative Stability" with the Pith Instructions*;[941] *Wishing Tree of Eloquence: The Explanatory Method concerning the Wish-Fulfilling Gem of the Great Seal according to the Taklungpa Tradition*;[942] *Feast of Pure Blissful Attainment: An Explanatory Method of the Coemergent Union of the Great Seal*;[943] *Extracting the Essence of the Adamantine Reality of Pristine Cognition: The Great Guidebook on the Wish-Fulfilling Gem of the Six Doctrines*;[944] *The Threefold Explanatory Method of the Six Doctrines of Niguma*;[945] *The Oral Transmission of the Section on the Setting of the Mind on Enlightenment according to the Preliminary Practices from the Luminosity of All Hidden Meanings*;[946] *The Oral Transmission of Jamgon Lama: An Explanatory Method concerning the Luminosity of All Hidden Meanings Titled Captivating the Minds of the Learned*;[947] *The Concise Visualization Steps of the Coemergent Union, Gauma, and Fivefold Traditions of the Great Seal, along with the Twofold Six Doctrines, the Common Savor, the Guidance on the View of the Middle Way, the Four Stages, the Three Pure Recensions of Hevajra,* {521} *the Guidance on Bhairava according to Ra Lotsāwa, and the Two Methods of Propitiating the Vitality of Mahākāla*;[948] *The Lamp of the Crucial Points Elucidating the Tenfold and Threefold Doctrinal Supports of Mahākāla in the Form Kurakma*;[949] and *Granting Desire for the Two Accomplishments: The Great Guidance Integrating All the Outer, Inner, and Secret Cycles of Attainment pertaining to Glorious Jñānanātha*.[950] In addition, they included innumerable biographical prayers, oral instructions, eulogies, garlands of song, official letters, aspiration prayers, supplements on guidance, and so forth.

In all respects, Namgyel Tashi uninterruptedly turned the profound and extensive doctrinal wheels of empowerment, transmission, and pith instruction, in consequence of which the disciples born from his speech were innumerable; perfected in all sorts of auspicious fortune, refinement, and enthusiasm; excellently endowed with the virtue of resolve; delighting solely in conversations concerning the irreversible wheel that emulates the perceptual range of all the tathāgatas; without depending on others, their minds undeceived in terms of the provisional, definitive, and conclusively definitive meanings of all the essential teachings; and relying above all on the sacred doctrine, its meaning, definitive ascertainment, and pristine cognition. Among those saintly individuals there were an inconceivable number who are counted as the greatest—a brief account of some is given below.

Finally, Namgyel Tashi went to Nyemo in Tsang and eventually met Jetsun Dampa Drolchok. Then, he intended to return to the great monastic seat of Taklung, but he put off that plan because there was a blight afflicting the crops, and he took up residence in a tented camp in the northern regions. {522} He criticized as a false report a later prediction that he would pass into nirvāṇa in the mountain hermitage of Zanglung. That is to say, although it was said to be clear, he was uncertain. He went to the mountain hermitage of Sengling, where he succumbed severely to a combined humoral disorder. Though he was requested to take some medication and to undertake rites of long life, he did not recover. In general, it says in his *Secret Narrative*,[951] "Although I hope that my lifespan will be short, owing to the misconduct of the uneducated people of the degenerate age, in one circumstance that may not be certain. Since I have control over the circumstances of birth and death, if the merits of the disciples are extensive, I could continue living for a decade with the name Nāga.[952] But even if that were the case, there is no certainty with regard to time."[953]

Accordingly, in his fortieth year, on the twenty-sixth day of the eleventh lunar month in 1563 (water female pig), his physical form dissolved into the taintless eastern field, the terrain enjoyed by the transcendent lord Akṣobhya, Bhaiṣajyarāja, and glorious Maṅgalaśrī (Taklung Tashi Pel). At that time, the array of his body that filled the sky assumed the appearance of the buddha body of perfect resource, and it would be depicted in a cotton painting just as it arose in the vision of pure pristine cognition of glorious Dorje Drolchok. At the heart of this pure field, upon a lion throne and with a back screen adorned and resplendent with diverse motifs and lotus and moon cushions, there seated in the posture of royal ease is the transcendent lord Paramādya, his vajra the color of exquisite saffron. He wears the three religious robes, blazing forth a maṇḍala of reddish yellow light, the vajra in his first right hand held toward his heart and the bell in the corresponding left hand supported at the hip. {523} His head is adorned with a swaying silken crown of diamonds, and he is surrounded in front by innumerable sublime mendicant monks of the Great Vehicle, endowed with both knowledge and liberation, holding infinite offering sacraments that resemble the emanational offerings of Samantabhadra. It is this very painting that nowadays guides the mental faculty of all scholars, without exception, who are endowed with the vast perception of intrinsic awareness.

Then his disciples, headed by the regent Jikten Wangchuk,[954] brought forth an inconceivable oceanic array of offering clouds that filled the heavens of his enlightened intention. The reliquary depicting the great enlightenment of the buddha body of reality was constructed, the entire sacred corpse placed within it, and it was established as a field of merit for all beings. The whole country of Tibet, without exception, was then filled with magnificent offerings that were the means of fulfilling his enlightened intention.

It is clearly indicated in *The Secret Narrative with Its Sealed Injunction*[955] that Namgyel Tashi's future line of reincarnations will also include an emanational bodhisattva in the field of Sukhāvatī, a portion of the emanations in this field, one with the guise of a hidden yogin in Lato, seven beggars sojourning in a ravine in the region of U, an emanational king in the region of Kham, and as countless emanations training each according to need in many enclaves of India, China, Tibet, and so forth. Afterward, he will attain buddhahood in the presence of the Sugata Ratnakūṭa and ensure that the Buddhist teaching will indeed endure for a hundred thousand years.

Although its sealed injunction was extremely strict, after Venerable Namgyel Tashi had passed into nirvāṇa, {524} glorious Kunga Drolchok Losal Gyatsoide—whose body, speech, and mind were indivisible from those of this supreme lord-protector and who had attained the accomplishment of lord Mañjuśrī—released the sealed injunction at the retreat hermitage of glorious Changlung, and it was disseminated in all directions, consequently enabling me to write this account of his life that combines the essential points of six distinct biographies. These are (1–3) the three outer and inner biographies that this supremely wondrous tulku permitted, which are said to have been written merely listing events in the earlier and later periods of his life; (4) *The Narrative Titled Cornucopia of Excellent Virtue*,[956] which was composed by Jetsun Dampa Kunga Drolchok; (5) *The Brief Catalog and Inventory of the Silver Reliquary*,[957] which was compiled by Gelong Sherab Zangpo; and (6) *The Great Divine Drum of Renown*,[958] which I wrote as a subdivision of *The Narrative of Past Lives Titled Wondrous Gong of Brahmā*.[959]

The Disciples of Namgyel Tashi

Repachenpo Namgyel Phuntsok

An inconceivable number of disciples of Venerable Namgyel Tashi have appeared, among whom were his two younger brothers, who had both the same father and mother. The first of these was the lord-protector of living beings and king of the sacred doctrine Repachenpo Namgyel Phuntsok. He was born in 1532 (water male dragon). In his eighth year, he was invited to Taklung, where the mendicant ordination was conferred upon him. In 1550 (iron dog), he came to the monastic seat of Taklung, and after two years, he adopted the lifestyle of a total renunciate. He constructed within the Main Temple the image of Mahendra in the form Subduer of the Host of Demons,[960] and in addition, he constructed many other representations, large and small. He obtained steadfastness in the generation stage of glorious Vajrabhairava and reached the requisite number of recitations, such that he acquired mastery in his attainment of myriad rites. He journeyed to the extremities of Riwoche, Dartsedo, and so forth, and he continued to nurture living beings. Finally, in 1603 (water female hare), in his seventieth year, he passed away. {525} The biography of the second younger brother, who had the name Gyeltsab Jikten Wangchuk Tuje Terchen Kunga is recounted below.[961]

Furthermore, although those who savored the nectar of the speech of this sacred and venerable master, Namgyel Tashi, permeated the ten directions, among them the ancestor of all lineages of spiritual attainment, the son of Drukpa Rinpoche, Ngagi Wangchuk Gyeltsen Pelzangpo, who subsequently became known as Gyelwang Pema Karpo, also received his entire transmission of the teachings and their authorization.[962]

Also included among them were Paṇchen Dorje Gyelpo, an authority among translators and charioteer of the teachings of exegesis and attainment according to the *Glorious Kālacakra Tantra*;[963] Kunga Pelzangpo, the nephew of Jamgon Lama, a spiritual mentor resembling a golden offering lamp, who was exemplary in attainment and venerable conduct;[964] the saintly lord of the sacred doctrine Konchok Jungne, an erudite and discriminating incumbent of the pure seat of Drom, the noble vase of whose mind was filled with the nectar of perfect and supreme attainment;[965] Choze[966] Rinchen Pel, pure in the three trainings, a model of the pure view and conduct of the Dakpo lineage, who at that time raised the axle of the actual teaching of the Drigung Kagyu lineage;[967] Jangchub Nyingpo, the younger nephew of Uma and guide of many reclusive practitioners, who continued to act for the sake of living beings through the excellence of his enlightened attributes of scriptural transmission and realization, and through his profound guidance;[968] Samten Wangchuk, a yogin of the Great Seal embodying bliss and emptiness, who at all times was intent on isolation, an exemplary model in whom the harmonious conditions for the sacred doctrine converged;[969] and Geshe Sherab Zangpo, who was imbued with the blessings of Venerable Namgyel Tashi since he engaged exclusively in service of body and speech, taking care of and measuring the materials for the construction of sacred representations, managing projects, domestic matters, and so forth.[970] {526}

Namgyel Rinchen Pelzangpo

In particular, his disciples also included my own tutor, His Presence Namgyel Rinchen Pelzangpo, a peerless master to whom the teachings of the authentic lineage descended and who was realized in the supreme body of genuine coalescent pristine cognition.[971] His father was Tashi Drakpa, a lord among yogins, a yogin of Pacification and the Great Seal, in the line descended from the stainless family of Barle Tonśāk, who as previously mentioned was one of the spiritual sons of Venerable Sangye Yarjon. His mother was named Konchok Tso. He was born at Namkhok in 1532 (water male dragon). He spoke much earlier than other children, and he clearly brought to mind many former lives. In his fifth year, he was ordained as a layperson, holding the three vows of refuge by Venerable Karmapa Mikyo Dorje. The name Sangye Pelzang was conferred upon him. In his thirteenth year, in 1544 (wood dragon), at Tringda Gartok, he received ordination as a layperson, mendicant, and novice in the presence of Gyelwang Namgyel Tashi, and the name Namgyel Rinchen Pelzangpo was conferred upon him. His wisdom eye opened wide in the study of sūtra, mantra, and classical learning. He attended upon many tutors, including Pawo Tsuklak Trengwa, the venerable master of the sacred doctrine; Konchok Yenlak, who worn the crown of Zhamar; and Rikdzin Dudjom Dorje.[972] He endlessly received infinite teachings of empowerment, scriptural transmission, and esoteric instruction. In his twentieth year, in 1551 (iron female pig), in the Main Temple of Taklung, he received full ordination as a monk in the midst of a quorum of five, including Gyelwang Namgyel Tashi, who acted as preceptor, with the assistance of four others acting as the master of ceremonies, {527} the confessor, the timekeeper, and assistant. In this way, he perfected ethical discipline.

One night, when he fell severely ill while staying at the large encampment of Karmapa in Tsāri, a black man with the head of a lion presented him with a letter sealed with red wax, saying, "This is the seal of Taklung Rinpoche!" Thereupon, he immediately recovered.

On many occasions, he journeyed to Taklung, where, in the presence of Venerable Sangye Kundu,[973] he received all the particular instructions of this Taklung Kagyu lineage. Not satisfied with merely acquiring all these, he ascertained the maturation of the continuum of empowerment. Through the generation stage of meditation and the control of the channels, vital essences, and winds, he determined the pure maturational body, and through the Inner Radiance and the Great Seal, he determined phenomenal appearances to be the three buddha bodies. He trained in emancipation, resolute devotion, and the mind of enlightenment, and he actually reached the conclusion that his spiritual teacher was a perfect buddha. Appearances arose as the bodies of deities, his mind was satiated with supremely unchanging bliss, and he became a supremely great accomplished master who arrived at the perception of luminosity in the supreme union of the body of coalescence.

In the short and long term, Namgyel Rinchen Pelzangpo was also granted many prophetic declarations. Having obtained the power of mnemonic retention that did not forget anything, with the aid of a lamp during the night, he could present in the form of a memorandum all the exegetical teachings of sūtra and mantra that his authentic teachers had imparted in the course of the entire previous day, without confusing word and meaning. By making consecrated medicine of *The Peaceful Guru*[974] at Sebuka Hermitage,[975] he permeated the valley with a fragrant perfume. He had a vision of Śrīdevī in the form Rematī, and on the day when that vision ended, the entire sky turned to rainbow light. {528} In a dream he had a vision of a woman who offered him a bale of wool, saying, "You will bring maturation and liberation to sentient beings, equal in number to the strands of hair forming this bale." At Langdong, when he practiced *The Attainment of the Mind of the Guru*,[976] the offerings remained warm in the middle of winter, and he had a vision of the Eight Manifestations of the Guru. At the time when he cured the Mongolian pox, in the experience of a meditator from Jomo Gang, this master was seen entrusting a small child to Gangkar Shamema.[977] At Ngangtsang Cave, in the sky in front, he had a vision in which Vajradhara appeared at the center, with Tilopā in the east, Nāropā in the south, Marpa in the west, and Mila in the north. And then, in place of Vajradhara in the center, Venerable Gampopa appeared and moved about, almost harshly pointing in front to the great seal of bliss and emptiness, saying the words, "This is the path of the Karmapa Kamtsang lineage!" and then purely, gently, and slowly pointing to the great seal of the abiding nature with the words, "This is the path of Taklungpa!"

This venerable master Namgyel Rinchen Pelzangpo predicted my own birth in 1571 (iron sheep), in his fortieth year. He established monastic seats at Nenang and Uma Drakar.[978] On the occasion when he performed rites of attainment, combined with the casting of tormas directed toward the enemies of the Buddhist teaching, fire burst off from the tips of the charms and tormas, shot into the sky, and eventually fell resoundingly upon the targeted area.

In the context of a service to support the life of Choje Rinpoche, when he performed the aversion rite of the tormas of the Eight Pronouncements, a dark tornado connecting the earth with the sky moved directly through Urulung and encircled the dwelling of the enemies of the Buddhist teaching for two days. There were an infinite number of such omens and miracles that occurred. {529}

On the third day of the seventh lunar month in 1577 (fire female ox), he made an inspection and founded a monastery and college at Nyelung.[979] From the waxing half of the fifth lunar month in 1579 (earth female hare), I requested the first of his teachings. Commencing from then, I requested the complete Kangyur except for the Domang section, the seven maṇḍalas of Ngok, the Adamantine Garland,[980] *The Hundred Teachings of Mitrayogin*,[981] the twelve maṇḍalas of *The Purification of the Lower Realms*,[982] *The Five Pentads*,[983] and *The Ocean of Means for Attainment*,[984] and so forth, as well as general teachings, particular teachings, and countless other teachings of empowerment, scriptural transmission, and guidance according to the lineages of the Taklung Kagyu, Karma Kamtsang, Drigung, Druk, Kadam, Sakyapa, Jonang, Zhalu, Bodong, Nyingma, and so forth.

In general, this saintly individual nurtured me with the kindness of the sacred doctrine, such that in all respects I did not resort to cyclic existence. Speaking of his extrasensory powers, there were countless instances that indeed occurred within our range of vision and hearing. It was thanks to the kindness of this venerable master that the long tradition of the glorious Taklung Kagyu and the teaching of its taintless scriptures and realization were illuminated again in this degenerate age, without decline.

As for myself, insofar as outer and inner talents can be investigated, I do not at all think that I have even the slightest ostensible amount of talent, and that is absolutely due to the kindness of this lord-protector.

Namgyel Rinchen Pelzangpo also composed a large number of works, including tracts on guidance adorned with the exegesis of the supporting teachings, and *The Ease of Entry into the Maṇḍala of Attainment.*[985] When he performed the auspicious ceremony for averting the Mongols at Lingkar,[986] the entire terrain was filled with a flock of birds, and in a dream, he had a vision of the goddess Rematī, who offered a copper basin containing a moist human heart.

One day, when he bestowed the empowerments of the Adamantine Garland upon me, {530} the water inside the empowerment vase of Vijaya[987] boiled strongly. In the hot springs of Nyingdrung, he had a vision of the eight manifestations headed by Padmasambhava. He served as monastic preceptor of the great seminary at Dechen Yangpachen.[988] When he went to see the power place of Zabulung,[989] he had a vision of the peaceful and wrathful deities according to *The Net of Magical Emanation*[990] at Nakding Lake. When he went into the valley of the seven treasures, three wonderful lotus flowers appeared on the visage of the image of Master Padmākara that sits within the temple on the side of the Zangdok Pelri hill.[991] Tobgyelwa, a descendant of Meton Chenpo[992] and Nyemowa, a descendant of the maternal uncle of Rutsam Tripon Che, bowed at his feet.

Namgyel Rinchen Pelzangpo spoke repeatedly of his impending nirvāṇa, both directly and indirectly. Finally, he passed away on the eighth day of the third lunar month in 1599 (earth female pig), in his sixty-eighth year. On the fifteenth day of that very month, his remains were cremated. An infinite number of pearl relics were retrieved. The sky was permeated with rainbows. The sacred bone relics were inserted within enlightenment reliquary stūpas fashioned of silver, gold, and copper.

In general, it is held that this saintly individual had in former lives been the brahmin child Maitreyamitra in the presence of Buddha Kāśyapa; the great master Buddhajñāna;[993] the child Pemasel;[994] Kongpo Gomnak, the disciple of glorious Taklungpa; Barle Tonśāk, the direct disciple of Choku Sangye Yarjon; Orgyen Gonpo of Riwoche;[995] Dharmeśvara, son of

Drubtob Yumo;[996] Kunpang Rinpoche Namkha Pelyang;[997] the great preceptor Tamdrin Ozer; Zangpo Pel, the master of Severance; the attendant Jangchub Pel; Pel Zhiwa Zangpo, the disciple of Chogyel Rinchen Lingpa; Taktsang Lotsāwa Sherab Rinchen; {531} and Serdingpa Donyo Drakpa. Even to mundane perception, the attributes of greatness that his body had in terms of learning, dignity, and nobility surpassed the bounds of the intellect. In this age of degeneration, he was a great tulku who took charge of worldly affairs while thinking of the teaching of the Taklung Kagyu lineage.

Through the illumination of the three planes of existence,
By the blazing rosary formed of supreme magnifying crystal of innately present virtues,
And assisted by the daylight rays of accumulated virtues,
May the dark vale of twofold obscuration shrouding the minds of living beings be ended!

Kunga Tashi, Sixteenth in the Abbatial Succession

May this embodiment of the great pristine cognition of **all** (*kun*)[998] the conquerors—
Capable of conferring the **joyous** (*dga'*) feast of liberation,
The supreme root and branches of the entire **auspicious** (*bkra shis*) Buddhist teaching—
Be present as an ornament of the heart until enlightenment!

Gyelwa Kunga Tashi, whose name is hard to mention,[999] is our own crown ornament and master of inconceivable compassion and enlightened activity who manifested in the body of form that is identical in nature to all the perfect buddhas. With regard to his appearance, since, in general, it is difficult to estimate the emanational display of the teachers, the inconceivable sons of the conquerors who have passed away, how could one even slightly conceive of the continuum of the ten levels? And yet, this much I have personally heard: This embodiment of the knowledge, love, and deeds of all the buddhas, enactor of the discipline of awareness that eradicates heretical views by dint of miraculous abilities, imbued with blessings by sublime Avalokiteśvara and Mañjughoṣa, {532} and that illuminates the Buddhist teachings through the deeds of explanation, debate, and composition had in former lives manifested as glorious Śāntideva, who attained the rainbow body of coalescence; Puchungwa Zhonu Gyeltsen, authorized inheritor of the emanational volume containing the secret teachings of Jowo Atiśa and his son Dromtonpa, who acquired pure pristine cognition with respect to all things in the essential nature of the sixteen vital essences;[1000] Kunga Tashi, venerable master of the doctrine of the Great Vehicle and supreme throne holder of glorious Sakya, crown ornament of all the mighty lords of inviolable discriminative awareness and compassion in the authentic Khon family; Gyelse Ngulchu Chodzongpa Zangpo Pel, lion of speech endowed with scriptural authority and reasoning, sovereign of the twofold enlightened mind, possessing the ornaments of the three trainings;[1001] and Tokden Sonam Wangchuk,[1002] the spiritual son of omniscient Ngawang Drakpa and destroyer of all bewilderment in the space of reality.

Thereafter, in time, he was born in this present life at Lhundrub Dzong in 1536 (fire male monkey) as the youngest sibling of five brothers and two sisters.[1003] His father was the bodhisattva Tashi Gyatsoi Pel, a nephew in the family line of glorious Taklungpa the Great, mighty lord of the world, respected and perfectly accomplished in his career, who took charge of worldly affairs, while known as an authentic regent of the Buddhist teaching. His mother was called Olkaza Dekyi Budren Gyelmo. At the time of his birth, a torma offering was sent with a petition to the venerable and wonderful supreme tulku Ngawang Namgyel Tashi and joyfully presented, whereupon he was given a protection cord and the name Tashi Dondrub was conferred upon him. {533}

In childhood, he absolutely had the propensities of one whose body, speech, and mind were withdrawn from worldly affairs. During that time, he received ritual ablutions and initiations from Sakyapa Dakchen Ngagi Wangchuk, Drukpa Ngawang Chogyel and Drigung Rinchen Phuntsok.[1004] When he received the initiation of Hayagrīva from Tokden Cho Gyeltsen, he beheld the face of Aśvottama Heruka. Immediately thereafter, his mother passed away. In his seventh year, in 1542 (water male tiger), he traveled to Taklung. There, in the presence of Jamgon Drupei Pawochok,[1005] the twelfth reincarnation of the ascetic master Kṛṣṇācārin, he received the precepts of the novitiate according to the ceremony that embodies the complete rite of three phases—preparation, actual conferral, and subsequent advice. The name Ngawang Namgyel Kunga Lekdrub Tashi Gyeltsen Pelzangpo was also conferred upon him. This auspiciously coincided with the time when, as a religious king of the Great Vehicle, his enlightened activity became extensive in the lands of China and Mongolia,[1006] and in consequence of that, his principal name became Kunga Tashi. I heard Yongdzin Rinpoche say that this indirectly presaged the gateway from his former state to his present enlightened activities.

Afterward, Kunga Tashi bowed at the lotus feet of his elder brother, the wondrous supreme tulku Ngawang Namgyel Tashi Drakpa Gyeltsen Pelzang, whom he recognized alone as his glorious root teacher, the lord of enlightened heritage, whose nature was that of the countless buddhas of the three times. At first, he learned to read under one named Lhodre Sherab Zangpo. In addition, he understood immediately and without difficulty all the cycles of the meditational deities and protector deities, which he practiced. {534} He also trained in the correct manner in the textual traditions and the conventional subjects of classical learning that he received. Consequently, when he performed an offering rite of Hevajra, green shoots, one thumb deep, grew from within the vase of Vijaya, even though it was the middle of winter. When he performed the recitations of Mañjuvajra according to the *Guhyasamāja*, the door of his discriminative awareness opened, and his tongue could easily make the recitations. Such were the events that occurred.

From the holy Jetsun Kunga Drolchok, he impartially received an infinite number of empowerments, scriptural transmissions, and esoteric instructions of the two approaches of the Kagyu lineage, Dakpo and Shangpa, along with the Sakyapa, Ngor, and Dzongpa traditions, the Jonang and Zhalu traditions,[1007] the Kadam tradition, and so forth. From Gyelwang Namgyel Tashi, among the empowerments that nurture the immediate needs of practical implementation, he received many details of maturational empowerment and liberating guidance of the four classes of tantra according to the tradition of Jikdrel Sangwa Jin.[1008]

In particular, he received all the profound and extensive doctrinal cycles of the glorious Taklung Kagyu tradition in their entirety. Through profound oral instructions on propitiating the spiritual teacher, he perfected the resolve whereby the spiritual teacher appears as the buddha body of reality, and he was imbued with an extraordinary transference of authentic blessings. When he received the oral instructions of maturational empowerment and liberating guidance pertaining to Cakrasaṃvara and Jetsunma Vajravārāhī, which essentialize the ocean of the generation stage, his body was transformed into the great seal of the deities' body, liberated from attachment to ordinary, imaginary appearances; his speech resembled the pleasant resonance of a thousand peels of thunder, the natural sound of profound mantra that is different from the expression of ordinary speech; and his mind turned toward the horizon of the meditative stability of the great seal, the union of awareness and emptiness, the abiding nature that is the opposite of the bewildering thoughts of the subject-object dichotomy characteristic of ordinary mind. Also, in particular, he received in the form of experiential guidance an oral instruction on the coemergent union, which concerns the great seal of the abiding nature; and the Six Doctrines of Nāropā, which concern the great seal of bliss and emptiness. {535} Through experiential cultivation, his mind was liberated internally from the bonds of the eight worldly concerns. The knots of all the channels that ripen into relative appearances were destroyed. The movement of all the winds that come and go within them was severed. The white and red vital essences were freed from the elaboration of blazing and melting. The wind of pristine cognition gathered in the central channel, endowed with two purities.[1009] Sleep entered into the stream of inner radiance. Free from the flux of the obscurations of meditative equipoise, appearances then arose as the bodies of the deities, and he was satisfied with unsurpassable bliss. Through his infinite activities, Kunga Tashi favored fortunate beings and conferred blessings upon their minds. He became a peerless mighty lord of yoga, actualizing the body of coalescent pristine cognition.

Moreover, in the course of an entire year, without interruption, he received without exception the empowerments, transmissions, and pith instructions of adamantine Kākamukha Mahākāla, mighty among protectors, retaining the words and their meanings. In particular, following a prayerful entreaty, this venerable master composed *The Great Guidebook: Granting Desire for Accomplishment*,[1010] which integrated all the stages of experiential cultivation—the outer, inner, and secret esoteric instructions pertaining to Jñānanātha. During such times, there were many auspicious indications that occurred—seeds sprouted from the offering cake of raven-faced Karmamahākāla within the torma receptacle and so forth. In particular, he had an actual vision of a body manifesting as the supreme planetary divinity Rāhula, the lord-protector of rites and great hermit sage. Starting from then, there were inestimable proofs that all the enlightened activities of this venerable master were undoubtedly attained through the agency of Jñānanātha.

In his twentieth year, immediately after the new year in 1555 (wood female hare), {536} in the Main Temple of glorious Taklung, Kunga Tashi excellently received the precepts of a fully ordained monk in accordance with the ten requisite presences, just as they are explained in the vinaya texts. In the midst of a quorum of five, including the supreme tulku Vijayamaṅgala (Namgyel Tashi), who resembled a second Teacher,[1011] acting as monastic preceptor, and others with the appropriate characteristics acting as the master of ceremonies, confessor, timekeeper, and so forth. He became a master of the Buddhist teaching, no different from the Tathāgata in terms of all the deeds that he undertook with respect to the Buddhist teachings.

Kunga Tashi was then enthroned upon the monastic seat at dawn on a day of auspicious planetary and stellar conjunction in the waxing half of the first month of that same year. Officials representing the venerable supreme tulku—Second Dalai Lama, Gendun Gyatso—scattered flowers of benediction and appointed him as a doctrinal king of the three world systems.[1012] On that occasion, the sun, moon, and constellations converged in the heavens. Although it was the high point of extreme cold in the last winter month, the weather on that day was excellent and warm. A stream of water formed of melting ice on the Phachu[1013] flowed down into the river in the lower valley. Starting from then, he unswervingly maintained the peerless regulations of Choje Kuyalwa and the charter of the monastic assembly, even more than before, for although his saintly predecessors had been equal to space in their deeds and enlightened activities, his period turned into a progressive eon. Even his disciples formed a circle that was exclusively pure in terms of the accumulation of the two provisions and the application of occult power, such that they were easy to train. During that era, which was even more degenerate than the proverbial final five hundred year period of strife and degeneration, this lord-protector was particularly sublime in many respects because he trained, in accordance with the sacred doctrine, an entourage that was more difficult to train and impure owing to a preponderance of coarse deeds and afflicted mental states. {537} He did so through his inconceivable loving-kindness, compassion, enthusiasm, and perseverance. Although his legacy in maintaining, nurturing, and increasing the Buddhist teaching at this great monastic seat by means of the two traditions of sūtra and mantra was extremely great, he was without pride and did not make a big deal of it. His sacred outlook increased impartially with respect to all things and all persons, without falling into bias, and apart from that, he neither praised himself nor disparaged others. In order to bring forth the greatness of the Buddhist teaching, he esteemed those who upheld even the mere indication of being readers, meditators, and mantrins. Besides that, with regard to those who had pride in their clans, their talent for study, reflection, and meditation, and their prowess in the two traditions of sūtra and mantra, and so forth—even though it was his duty, he did not engage in disputes concerning prostrations or disputes concerning seating arrangements except when it suited him. In his mind, too, he was without the apathy and faults that ensue by not investigating things with engagement and judgment. Although there were laypersons and monks within his own community who acted ignorantly and without respect, he secured them with the same influence and individual rights that they had previously enjoyed, and he did not implement any new changes. Even when they started to misinterpret him somewhat through body, speech, and mind, he continued to benefit them through his responses, and apart from that, he did not resort to revenge through verdicts and punishments. When he heard of or saw the mutual antipathy between the upper and lower Mongols[1014] and so forth, he was not partisan in requiring material resources to be given but brought about a reconciliation, thinking of the security of the entire country. He instantly maintained his composure in all circumstances, whether pleasant or unpleasant, and so forth, but he did not make light of profound mistakes on the part of those who were destructive and those who strove for rewards. {538} Although in the short term it was as if he granted greater rewards to those who cared for his legacy, in the longer term, his own mind was without attachment whenever they engaged in positive actions or shamelessly squandered resources. Even when those relatives, patrons, and so forth who had formerly been close and had performed acts of service became ineffectual, he secured them in modesty and long-term friendship. Even though he did not now have to grant rewards, gifts, and so forth that had been absolutely necessary in the past, since he could not be harmful, he definitely continued to bestow them. Even though it seemed that his own immediate wishes were subservient to those who petitioned him, Kunga Tashi's approach to enlightened activity with respect to the sacred doctrine was not dependent on others. He observed whether the taxes of his subjects and so forth were presently in conformity with those that had formerly been levied or not, and then he set an appropriate rate. Apart from that, he did not impose excessive levels of taxation or impose new taxes. He did not even investigate the income of the monastic estates, and so forth, that was offered according to the determination made by the steward.

In brief, during the early part of this venerable master's life, there was much turmoil within the Taklungpa.[1015] External enemies were in the majority, much land belonging to the administrative estates was lost, and the noble landowners looked out for their own interests. Though there was no one at all who even thought of external loyalties, this lord-protector Kunga Tashi, in consideration of this period alone, was an actual, cognizant reincarnation of Gyelwa Taklungpa the Great himself. Therefore, in the manner of the proverbial tongs extracting something hot from an oven, this venerable master alone assumed entire responsibility for administrative affairs—both religious and secular. From the religious perspective, he was served by my tutor Yongdzin Rinpoche, {539} and on the secular side he was served by my dear father, the governor. One should know that it was mostly due to the kindness of those three, master and disciples, that the vitality of this Taklungpa tradition was maintained during that period.

Later, Kunga Tashi traveled to glorious Riwoche, and he received the entire doctrinal cycles of Taklung Lower Plain in the presence of Venerable Tsokye Dorje.[1016] In return, he offered him the doctrinal cycles of Taklung Upper Plain. He brought with him extraordinary representations of buddha body, speech, and mind and sacred artifacts imbued with perfect blessings. He acted with kindness to the people who were his disciples, including myself, such that Taklung Upper Plain again became a unique stream of the Buddhist teaching. He illuminated the stainless tradition of the practice lineage like sunrise, such that, even from the religious perspective, I greatly understood the legacy of this venerable master with respect to the long term.[1017]

On one occasion, Choje Pawo Tsuklak Trengwa journeyed here to Taklung, and they had a meeting. Acquiring the service of a group of Newar craftsmen, he excellently commissioned the gilded roof of the Main Temple, seventy-five handspans in height, fashioned of gold applied with nine hundred and eighty-five *zho* of gold. The insertion of relics and consecration were performed by Kunpang Rinpoche (Namgyel Tashi). A great feast was held, and bountiful donations were made.

Similarly, on the surface of the white parapet of the Main Temple and on the walls of its lower story, he commissioned murals depicting the buddha field of Amoghadarśa (Beautiful to Behold), and the five conquerors of the three times encircled by the thousand buddhas of the Auspicious Eon. He further commissioned twenty-three cotton paintings depicting Munīndra with the sixteen elders, Hashang, Dharmatāla, and the four great kings; {540} as well as two-story-high appliqué scrolls depicting Jñānanātha and Vaiśravaṇa, a series depicting the three meditational deities (Cakrasaṃvara, Hevajra, and Bhairava) and ten protector deities, and a series of corner appliqué scrolls depicting Karmamahākāla and consort, which are all housed in the Old Protector Chapel.

When the mighty Conqueror and supreme tulku Kunpang Rinpoche (Namgyel Tashi) passed away on the twenty-sixth day of the eleventh lunar month in 1563 (water pig), Kunga Tashi presented an extensively elaborate cloud of offerings in connection with the funeral ceremonies. As material for the silver reliquary, he offered eleven large and small pieces of silver and more than two hundred *zho* of gold. He also prepared all the lavish earthly ornaments, heavenly ornaments, offering sacraments, and so forth that are contained in the silver reliquary chapel known as the Northern Chapel.

On that occasion, Kunga Tashi also commissioned the extant image of glorious Jñānanātha, fashioned of a thousand *sang* of silver, along with its ornaments and throne fashioned of gold amounting to forty *zho* of gold. When he inserted within that image the relics, including a stone image of Mahākāla called Mebarma that had been the meditational deity of glorious Ga Lotsāwa, and had completed all the rites of consecration without exception, at the very moment as the being of pristine cognition was invited into the image, an emanational raven cawed its various sounds and purposefully made a small aperture with its beak on the back side of the image. Such were the wondrous indications that manifested. It is indisputable that dust does not settle on the face of this image.

When in 1564 (wood mouse) Kunga Tashi fell ill, extremely potent rites to sustain his life were undertaken here in Taklung and in all directions, whereupon he immediately recovered. In 1566 (tiger), when Jamgon Drupei Pawo (Tsuklak Trengwa) passed away, here in Taklung, he also undertook vast offerings and donations during the funeral ceremonies. In particular, {541} in order to see the precious silver reliquary of Pawa Tsuklak Trengwa, in 1567 (hare), he traveled to the hermitage of Cholung Jangtse.[1018] When he first arrived there, the entire sky was permeated with rainbows, and a shower of flowers fell. He extensively made offerings and recited aspiration prayers in the presence of the precious silver reliquary.

The official secretary Tsewang Pendar performed acts of service on his behalf and presented him with offerings.[1019] Kunga Rinchenpa, the lord of North Lato, also respectfully paid homage to him and presented an abundance of offerings.[1020] In 1568 (dragon), when the large encampment of Zhamarpa and Karmapa reached the Taklung area, with the thought of responding to the request of the resident and visiting monks, he met them and presented extensive offerings. They invited him to the seminary of Dechen Yangpachen, and he went there. He was welcomed with great pageantry by the lay officials of the venerable father and son[1021] and by the monks of each community. On that occasion, he received all the crucial doctrinal cycles of the Karma Kamtsang tradition from Venerable Zhamarpa Konchok Yenlak. He offered for inspection an elaborate display of offerings in the gandhola shrine and held an inconceivable prayer festival to mark the new year. All the lamas and custodians of that community—along with the heads of the college,[1022] Namkha Rinchen,[1023] and so forth—paid homage to him and requested a doctrinal connection. On his return to Taklung, he received many doctrinal cycles of the Sakya tradition including Śrīheruka and Vajrakīla combined from Tsedong Dakchen Kunga Samdrubpa, a mighty lord of the saintly and powerful Khon family.[1024] Choje Kunga Tashi offered him in turn the extraordinary red handbell of Drogon Chogyel Phakpa, which had been preserved at Taklung. {542}

Around this time, Kunga Tashi commissioned forty-one painted scrolls depicting the complete hundred deeds of the Buddha's past lives. In 1570 (iron male horse), a Newar artist named Jatipāla constructed an image of Mahāmuni in the form Amoghadarśa, the back of which was forty-five spans high, utilizing one thousand nine hundred *zho* of gold. It had both the size and grace of all the former and recent great images of the temple. Along with its lion throne and back screen, it is manifestly extant in the present time.[1025] Such is its blazing splendor, endowed with blessings. The relics were inserted within it, and the consecration undertaken in the appropriate manner. Although this was a period of extreme difficulty, owing to the conflict between Drigung and Taklung, and so forth, through the power of his great compassion, he achieved this without obstacles.[1026]

He invited to Taklung Lopa Chenga Ngawang Chokyi Drakpa, revered as a completely great spiritual mentor who was the reincarnation of Chenga Tsultrim Bar,[1027] and he undertook extensive study of the texts and oral instructions of Kadam. At that time, he also cleaned and adorned the extraordinary image of Mañjuvajra according to the Guhyasamāja that had been the meditational deity of Pa Rinpoche and that had later been damaged by the fire. He completed this act by inserting the pearl relics and performing a consecration. He then repaired the damage of the Nechu Lhakhang and had new murals painted. He also repaired the damage of the Kumbum reliquary and the Old Offering Chapel and had new murals painted.

Kunga Tashi journeyed many times to the north on horseback, and on one such occasion, the people were shocked at the mere sight of a wide river, but he caused it to recede just by splattering it with his hand. Even those who were present in his camp could not be harmed by contagious diseases, obstacles due to spirits, and the like. Even when they did not take the slightest precautions to avoid such contagions, the herds of yak in the camp never succumbed to diseases that impact livestock. {543} He reconciled all the mutual antipathy of the upper and lower Mongols by spiritual and material means. Bringing them under the sway of the large remedial torma of the doctrinal protectors, henceforth they would act with kindness toward one another in the manner of a younger and older brother. There is no doubt at all that it was through the kindness of this master that these communities of the north were established, for a while, in peaceful coexistence.

In 1573 (bird), he received many times the empowerments, scriptural transmissions, and pith instructions of the extensive cycle of Bodongpa's *Summation of the Real*[1028] from Choje Bogongwa Tendzin Ngawang Drakpa,[1029] a great lineage holder of the Bodongpa tradition.

In order to benefit this great monastic seat of Taklung in the short term and in the long term, he rebuilt the Chodzong Namgyel Rabten.[1030] Choje Chime Ozer, the reincarnation of the lord of speech Chime Pelzangpo, bowed at the feet of Kunga Tashi, who then imparted the entire empowerments, scriptural transmissions, and pith instructions pertaining to the Collected Works of omniscient Ngawang Drakpa.

In 1574 (wood male dog), Kunga Tashi acquired the services of a group of Newar artisans, including one named Buddhapāla, who made beaten copper arrow-size images of Munīndra, with the sixteen elders, Hashang, Dharmatāla, and the four great kings, gilded utilizing four hundred *zho* of gold. The images had hand emblems that were fashioned of diverse precious gems and metals. The craftsmanship was most excellent, blazing with golden light, as if the Conqueror and his disciples had actually appeared there.[1031] During that period, he was invited by the chieftain of the upper Mongols. They encamped in a region of quartz and clay. Focusing his enlightened intention, he scattered soil with his hand, which the Newar official Metsowa here in Taklung unquestionably scattered upon the sculpted image of the transcendent lord Munīndra. {544} This wondrous event, surpassing the intellect, was clearly demonstrated to all.

Alongside the door[1032] of the temple, he also commissioned a most exquisite image depicting Vaiśravaṇa in the form Great Yellow One with the Eight Masters of the Horses, the fruit of craftsmanship that brings forth all necessities and desires, utilizing fifty *zho* of gold. He inserted the relics in the correct manner and performed a consecration ceremony that delighted the skilled artisans with donations and gifts.

In 1576 (fire male mouse), he commissioned the extant perfect manuscript edition of all the canonical scriptures of the Buddha that had been translated into Tibetan, on parchment, embellished with gold and silver, amounting to eighty-six volumes, with their wooden boards, ties, and cloth covers. During the consecration, the official Drak Opa[1033] arrived with men representing Altan Qaγan, bearing donations and gifts and offering an inaugural ceremonial arrow.[1034] Thus, Taklung acquired an inconceivable number of offerings, including gold, silver, garments, silk, tea, cotton, horses, mules, and camels. At that time, the venerable official Kunga Pelzangpo also journeyed in that direction and met him. They received and exchanged many profound doctrines.

During the twelfth lunar month of that year (1576), I also went into his presence. In 1577 (fire female ox), he fell severely ill due to poorly prepared food, so for almost three months his body appeared to be exhausted. Yet, through the performance of extensive life-sustaining rites and prayers, he excellently recovered his health. Even though he clearly knew those miscreants who had held such bad intentions toward him, he did not speak of them.

Appointing the monastic preceptors, masters, monk officials, the eight seniors of Taklung, stewards, and so forth, {545} he made the observance of the charter of the monastic assembly secure, exactly as it had been in the past.

From the start of 1578 (earth male tiger), Kunga Tashi intended to travel to Mongolia. At first, he went to see the image of Śākyamuni in Lhasa, where he made aspiration prayers and so forth. In the waxing half of the fourth lunar month, he struck camp, departing from there. They took the northern road and traveled from Dang La as far as the Yangtze[1035] through his display of miraculous power. From Tsaka, on the far side of the Yangtze,[1036] he was welcomed by an inviting party from Mongolia. In the place called Qagan Usu,[1037] he was met by the official Abel, and at Dawu Tsatsokha,[1038] he was received by an emissary of the chieftain Altan Qaγan. Proceeding to the encampment of Abel, at a place called Tselmar, he was offered bountiful gifts and donations.[1039] He then reached the encampments of the religious king Altan Qaγan on the shore of Lake Trisho Gyelmo.[1040] Owing to innumerable wondrous signs, he turned the mind of Altan Qaγan toward the sacred doctrine. Through Kunga Tashi's profound and vast teachings, the seed of enlightenment was born within him. The offering of articles made to Taklung was inconceivable. Washul Bum Kyabdar[1041] then invited him and presented offerings. Kunga Tashi brought about a reconciliation between those factions and satisfied the monastic communities with the sacred doctrine.

From the start of 1579 (hare), he was invited by Bingtu Qaγan of Ordos[1042] and Karma Lama, who had formed a patron-priest relationship.[1043] Taking an unprecedented route across the neck of Machen Pomra, he reached the northern direction.[1044] At Chumik Ringmo, he was presented with offerings by the religious king Altan Qaγan, who conferred upon him the title Tathāgata, a seal fashioned of eighty-five *sang* of silver, a royal edict,[1045] with an official certificate,[1046] hat ceremony, silk robes, many thousand *sang* of silver, and so forth.

Then, from the environs of Lake Trisho Gyelmo as far as the place called Taklung Lasar, which belongs to Tsongkha, he was presented with offerings by Jina Nangso, Brati Nangso, {546} the Chinese governor of Ziling Fort, and so forth.[1047] In Pari,[1048] monks maintaining the earlier Sakya and Kagyu transmissions paid homage to him.[1049] He easily crossed the river known as Julak Chongrong through his display of miraculous power.[1050] The Chinese chiliarch commander[1051] made offerings to him. Ordos, priest and patron, performed unfathomable acts of offering and service.

Again, in the autumn of 1579 (hare), the religious king Altan Qaγan offered Kunga Tashi a large metal pot, fashioned of one thousand five hundred *sang* of silver and other artifacts. His mind was brought to maturation through the doctrinal promulgation of empowerments, initiations, the setting of the mind on enlightenment, meditation, recitation, and so forth. The encampment of Altan Qaγan then moved to lower ground, where the governor of the Ordos encampments, the imperial crown prince Sečen,[1052] presented offerings to him. The Chinese commander with the rank of *ganzhou dutong*[1053] also presented him with gifts.

Then, Kunga Tashi was invited to the palace of Göden, king of the Mongols in Liangzhou.[1054] Exhorted in this way, he went there. Offerings were present by the two Chinese commanders, and he inspected the four temples—namely, the emanational temple of the east, the powerful temple of the south, the lotus temple of the west, and the ocean temple of the north.[1055] He was presented with donations by the Karma Lhakhang, and the governor of Ordos offered him a maṇḍala fashioned of five hundred *sang* of silver and so forth. He imparted profound and vast teachings.

Kunga Tashi then prepared to leave for the Ziling area. On the gentle route from the Chinese fortress of Trongnang,[1056] he was presented with donations by the Taklung officiant of offerings at the aforementioned Lasar pass. On that occasion, knowing that my dear father would pass away, he informed me accordingly. From the third month of 1580 (dragon), he traveled up to Tibet, and on the way, he was presented with offerings by the official Abel. Crossing the same northern route as before, he reached this great monastic seat of Taklung during the eighth lunar month. Here, he donated bountiful presents and offerings to all the lamas, masters, and monasteries of Utsang. {547} At the end of that year, he invited Konchok Yenlak, the fifth holder of the crown of Zhamar, and made innumerable offerings and acts of service on his behalf. Zhamarpa received a hundred long-life empowerments and in return offered artifacts including the extant peerless statue of the Buddha that had been the meditative commitment of master Dharmottara.

During 1581 (iron female snake), Kunga Tashi repaired the golden roof and wooden frame of the central inner sanctum of the Great Temple of Lhasa, which was mostly old, utilizing gold amounting to a continuous string of five thousand *zho* and six rounds of mercury. The wooden frame was mostly replaced. He refurbished the gutters and the four dragon gargoyles. This peerless restoration was accompanied by feast and donations. Starting from then, the glorious spiritual and secular excellence of the Taklungpa flourished like the rivers of summer.

Thereafter, Kunga Tashi had a skilled artisan work carefully for one year making a carving from which he would not part. It was fashioned exclusively from white sandalwood kept in the chapels housing the astonishing charred remnants of the gandhola spire that had been carved from stone by the hand of the master Nāgārjuna. In 1582 (water male horse), he built the massive precious perimeter wall of the great monastic seat of glorious Taklung and offered that statue to be inserted within the wall. He then sealed the foundations of the wall with his foot and, after blessing it, also scattered consecrated barley.

In the summer of that year, he was invited to act as monastic preceptor conferring the mendicant vows on Tāranātha Gyelwei Tenpa, a supreme emanation of Mañjuśrī. He set out in the direction of Tsang, and at the hermitage of Cholung Jangtse, {548} he conferred the vows of the novitiate preceded by the vows of a layperson and the intermediate mendicant vows on the precious tulku and conferred upon him the name Jamyang Kunga

Nyingpo Tashi Gyeltsen Pelzangpo.[1057] Doring Onpo Kunga Gyeltsen,[1058] a direct disciple of his predecessor, Jetsun Kunga Drolchok; Draktopa Lhawang Drakpa;[1059] Tendzin Tulku; and others also paid homage at his feet and savored the nectar of his speech.

Traveling on to Jonang, he bestowed a doctrinal connection on the female practitioners there. Then, he again returned to Taklung, and in 1584 (wood male monkey), he commissioned the large appliqué depicting Mahendra and his retinue, ten double armspans in width and the height of the temple, which was drawn and created by Mentangpa Lobzang Gyatso from excellent pieces of fine fabric that were in his possession.[1060] Elaborate donations and gifts were presented during the consecration. An appliqué depicting the meditational deity Jñānanātha was also made at this time.

In 1585,[1061] he commanded me to assume responsibility for the monastic seat of Taklung, and although, in all respects, I was incapable of possessing the necessary inner and outer qualifications, thinking that it would be wrong to disobey, I complied.

In the fifth lunar month of 1586 (fire male dog), he struck camp for Riwoche. Traveling gradually through the encampments of the upper and lower Mongols, including Adrakpa So Namgyel, he meritoriously met Choje Tsokye Dorje. He completely received all the empowerments, scriptural transmissions, and guidance contained in the seven large volumes that constitute the Collected Works of Venerable Sangye On. In return, Kunga Tashi offered him the uncommon distinctive doctrines of Taklung Upper Plain. {549}

With an uncommon enlightened intention directed toward the unique vitality of the Buddhist teaching of Taklung Upper Plain, Jedrung Rinpoche of Riwoche[1062] presented him with an inconceivable number of particularly precious objects, including a silver statue depicting glorious Phakmodrupa; a silver reliquary called Tashi Obar; silver statues depicting Vajradhara and the three hierarchs,[1063] with their thrones and backs; the eight deeds of the Buddha fashioned of the adamantine clay of the nāgas by the hand of sublime Nāgārjuna; innumerable wonderful old paintings depicting the self-manifested footprint of glorious Taklungpa the Great, and so forth; artifacts, such as the meditation belt of glorious Taklungpa the Great, that were replete with the blessings of the precious upper Kagyu lineage; two sets of the Collected Works of Venerable Sangye On; an incense censor fashioned of clear crystal; and the armor of the great patron Gazi.[1064]

Kunga Zangpo then turned the wheel of the sacred doctrine at places in

Nangchen and so forth, including Zurmang and Karma Gomde.[1065] Returning to Riwoche, he held wide-ranging discussions concerning the teachings that were meritorious in the short term and in the long term. Then he returned home.

Not long after, he set about further reconstruction. Utilizing gold amounting to six *zho*, he excellently decorated the eaves of the gilded roof of the Main Temple of Taklung[1066] and the east and west lattices of the roof canopy above the two-pillar temple in the palatial assembly hall of Reteng, which had previously been left uncovered with gold.[1067]

On the nineteenth day of the fourth month of 1589, he had the kindness to act as monastic preceptor when I received the precepts of a fully ordained monk. Then, in consequence of the insistent invitation of his faithful Mongol patron Abel Qaγan, {550} he set out again for Mongolia during the sixth month. Unbearably wide rivers such as the Yangtze and Chumar,[1068] which are on the way, naturally reduced their flow simply when he scattered consecrated barley, and so he journeyed with ease. Taking the road between the lakes Kyaring and Ngoring,[1069] at a place named Chalchi, he met the king and his retinue. He, the qaγan, had previously been smote by a strong wind disorder to his life-breath. Medical procedures and rituals had not helped, but Kunga Tashi restored his health simply by means of ablutions and some initiations.

In 1590 (tiger), he was presented with bountiful gifts and offerings by Sečen Qaγan, the ruler of Tümed, and at Taklung Lasar pass he was presented with offerings by the Taklung offering officiant. The Chinese commander Guyeng Jongči Daiqing paid homage at his feet and requested teachings.[1070]

In 1592 (dragon), Kunga Tashi was invited by the ruler of Ordos, Qoloči Bādur.[1071] When he consecrated the temple and its Kangyur there, the sky was filled with rainbow light, a shower of flowers fell, and that great patron was established in the ground of faith. He mollified the ruler's mind with the nectar of the sacred doctrine, profound and vast.

Then, while riding back, he encamped at the place called Yige Bakhowo on the way. One night, wondering if the lama might not be giving many teachings to some gentleman, the offering attendant went to look, and he saw an inconceivable commotion[1072] alongside Kunga Tashi's tent. The next morning, when he asked what that was, Kunga Tashi said that he had been explaining the sacred doctrine to Machen Pomra.[1073]

Nyenchen Tanglha also welcomed him with a great display. He then took the highest of the northern routes. Even though it was in the twelfth month of the year, the land and the rivers all remained warm, as in summertime. With such wondrous displays, he arrived at the monastic seat. {551}

Immediately, he commissioned a gold image of Coemergent Cakrasaṃvara, the size of an eight-year-old child, and an arrow-size image of Dvimukhavajravārāhī, along with three large statues fashioned of medicinal herbs that depicted Jowo Atiśa, Dromtonpa, and Orgyen Rinpoche. In accordance with his command, I performed the consecration.

During the summer of 1594 (horse), Kunga Tashi excellently commissioned Mentangpa Lobzang Gyatso, assisted by an entourage of many silk weavers, to make two appliqués that would be positioned alongside the great appliqué of meditative commitment that had previously been made. These new appliqués depicting the sixteen elders, Hashang, and Dharmatāla, with the four great kings and some peripheral invited deities, were fashioned mostly of gold-threaded satin with the *tā jus* motif and the *nya jus* motif;[1074] their height equaled that of the temple, and in width each of them was three double armspans. Jetsun Tulku (Tāranātha) performed the consecration ceremony and presented a bountiful feast of gifts. Afterward, Kunga Tashi received from the great tulku a great many doctrinal cycles that he himself had newly translated.

On the surface of the hill to the rear of Chodzong, many relief images clearly appeared that had not previously been conspicuous, including a self-arising image of master Padmasambhava, Vajravārāhī, a swirling gemstone motif, and a white doctrinal conch.

In 1595 (sheep), Kunga Tashi commissioned the medicinal clay statues depicting the main form of Jñānanātha with three retainers, which are on the four pillars of the Chodzong.[1075] He restored the Protector Chapel—which was densely packed with outer, inner, and secret representations and infinite cloud-like sacraments—and performed the consecration ceremony in the correct manner. At the beginning, middle, and end of all these activities there was an inconceivable number of miraculous signs and countless indications of his splendor and virtue that occurred. {552} In that place, he repeatedly had visions of the visage of sublime White Tārā in the form Cintāmaṇicakra. He completed two hundred million recitations of the secondary heart mantra of Cakrasaṃvara, along with its supplement. Thereafter, he stayed mostly in seclusion and remained in meditation.

In 1600 (mouse), Jetsun Tulku was invited. He bestowed the doctrinal cycles of glorious Riwoche, undertook longevity rituals, and performed many intricate rites of service. He inquired about the great restoration of the monastery and offered appropriate gifts. The Mongol prince known as Qadan Bagatur,[1076] who was a powerful strongman throughout the northern regions of Tibet by virtue of his past actions and merit, also paid homage at his feet.[1077] He spoke of his many extrasensory powers, dismissing them as dreams.

The glorious Drukpa Rinpoche Mipham Chokyi Gyelpo[1078] and his son Mipham Tenpei Nyima[1079] both met him, and he imparted many traditional doctrines including the Profound Collected Works[1080] of Venerable Sangye On, and *The Hundred and Eight Teaching Manuals of Jonang*. The Mongol prince Qadan Bagatur invited him to his encampment and presented offerings to him.

From the Drokha chamber, he returned to preside over the funeral ceremony and cremation of his older brother, the lord-protector of living beings who had passed away. He encased the relics in a reliquary symbolizing the great enlightenment, which was displayed in the temple at Sengling.

When he was taken severely ill with pulmonary fever, I performed the rite of exorcism known as Shinje Charkai Dongzor[1081] and offered a ritual that sustained his life, in conjunction with the ritual aversion of irritants, such that he immediately recovered.

In Drigung, he was seated at the head of the row during the funeral ceremony when Venerable Chogyel Phuntsok Tashi Pelzangpo passed away.[1082] {553} In the late winter, when my dear mother passed away at Lhundrub Dzong, he was also invited to that place, and he embraced us with his compassionate refuge. Then, when Jedrung Karmapa Wangchuk Dorje passed away, he also dispatched extensive offerings there, and even from his encampment, he performed a perfect funerary offering ceremony.

Based on Hevajra, I performed an extensive consecration of the aforementioned great appliqués depicting Mahendra and the sixteen elders, the set of corner appliqués depicting the protectors of the Kagyu lineage, and the complete Kangyur that he had newly commissioned. The supreme sixth incarnation of Zhamar, Dorje Garwang Chokyi Wangchuk, and Yonten Gyatso, the tulku of Drepung,[1083] both met him, and they immediately embraced as before.[1084] He commissioned four cast-metal stūpas, fashioned of pure silver.

From the late winter of 1604 (wood male dragon), he succumbed to ill-health due to contaminated water. Immediately after the new year in 1605 (wood female snake), while on pilgrimage in the south, I returned to his presence and obtained many carefree injunctions that were extremely easy to ponder. Although in person I undertook intricate longevity rites and rituals to induce auspicious circumstances—offering a prayer that he should prolong his life and offering a large torma dedicated to Mahākāla and Khabarma[1085]—I observed that his enlightened intention was focused on another realm, such that his mind turned toward space. On the thirtieth day of that same month, the array of his physical body dissolved into the expanse of pristine cognition, indivisible from the mind of the transcendent lord Akṣobhya, the Conqueror Mahāvajradhara, in the taintless eastern buddha field. For forty-nine days and nights, great ceremonial offerings were maintained in conjunction with eulogies. {554} At each juncture, conspicuous offerings and bountiful donations of alms were made. At the head of the row during the funeral ceremonies were the glorious Drukpa Choktrul Paksam Yongdu Wangpo[1086] and his entourage. Vast donations and alms were presented all day long on the fifteenth of the month of Citra, which was the first of a duplicated [that is, intercalary] third month, and vast offerings were presented to all the holders of the Buddhist teaching and the monasteries of Utsang. The sacred corpse was inserted within a stūpa endowed with the defining characteristics of the great enlightenment, the buddha body of reality, the undiminished wish-fulfilling gem, that had been fashioned of silver, gold, and copper. It was installed in the Palace of Blissful Attainment of the Kagyu Lineage, the Southern Chapel, embellished with a great array of sacred representations and offerings amid inexhaustible and auspicious sacraments that formed an exquisite mass indicative of the two traditions of this monastery, sūtra and tantra.

The Disciples of Kunga Tashi

Among the inconceivable number of disciples who partook of this venerable master's kindness, roughly speaking, were Khamsum Chokyi Gyelpo Tsokye Dorje, uncle and nephew, who occupied the lion throne of Taklung Lower Plain; Drukpa Rinpoche, father and son, who were ancestors of the teaching of the lineage of attainment;[1087] Kunga Nyingpo, the supreme emanation of Mañjuśrī;[1088] Tulku Chime Ozer, charioteer of the teachings imbued with fearless mystery; Venerable Onpo Kunga Pelzang, incumbent of the monastic seat of Jonang; Yongdzin Rinpoche Namgyel Pelzangpo, whose mind had merged together with his as one; the reincarnation of Pema Gyelpo of Riwoche; Doring Onpo Kunga Gyeltsen, the incumbent of the monastic seat of Cholung; {555} Chakzampa Tendzin Tulku Drubchen

Draktopa Lhawang Drakpa; Kabzhi Chodze Tsultrim Gyurme;[1089] Yung Chadrel Rinchen Gonpo; Bokhar Choje Maitri Kelzang Wangpo;[1090] the incumbent of the monastic seat of Changlung;[1091] Tongom Chodrub Pelzang;[1092] Gelongwa, incumbent of the monastic seat of Lo;[1093] Rin Gonpa of Barom; Drongu Tingdzin Drakpa;[1094] the lamas of the different seminaries of Drigung, Taklung, and Druk; and Kabchupa Tashi Chophel.[1095] As such, they were infinite in number.

Whatever virtue I obtain through such narratives
I dedicate to the ocean of sentient beings that equals space.
May they attain the rank of this glorious lama,
The great sage who is faultless and perfect in all enlightened attributes.

Ngawang Namgyel Kunga Rinchen Pelzangpo, Seventeenth in the Abbatial Succession

I pray that he who trains all sentient beings hard to train,
Through superior compassion and all sorts of virtuous actions
That derive from all the conquerors,
Might always be present as a heart ornament of the Supreme Pair!

With this prayer, there now follows my own life, the monk of the Śākyas, narrator of this great history, who has become a servant of the teachings of all garlands of buddhas holding the authentic lineage. My name is Ngawang Namgyel Kunga Rinchen Pelzangpo, or alternatively Pelden Chokyi Nyima Jikme Zangpo Chok Tamchele Nampar Gyelweide. My father, the governor of Lhundrub Dzong called Kunga Gyatso, was profound, vast, and radiant like the aureole of Mahābrahmā, progenitor of the world. He was supremely devoted to those upholding the impartial Buddhist teaching, {556} and he was well versed in the logical topics pursued by all beings and in the yoga that entails the generation stage of meditation, recitation, and torma offerings. My mother, Monlam Phuntsok Butri, was a natural yoginī who had been definitively foreordained, the daughter of the great adamantine master Chogyel Rinchen Phuntsok of glorious Drigung, holder of gnostic mantra. Her conduct was unbewildered in terms of acceptance and rejection, and she had a disposition that was utterly respectful to the practice lineage.

I entered her womb at the monastery called Rinchen Drak and was born at Lhundrub Dzong on the eighth day of the fifth month in 1571 (iron female sheep). At that moment, the house was penetrated by rainbow light, and that year the harvest was reckoned to have been most excellent. I was given the name Tashi Tobgyel, and a bountiful festival was held to commemorate my birth. All my childhood play exclusively had a modality that maintained, nurtured, and enhanced the Buddhist teachings as a spiritual mentor. I recognized, without being taught, a painted scroll depicting Trakṣad Mahākāla with the demonic force of invited deities.[1096] I fell over the precipice of Toknga while pursuing a lamb in play, but I did not die. Even the things that I said haphazardly and in excess, whether good or bad, came to pass. Above all, based on the indications of his dreams, Yongdzin Rinpoche said that I had been born through the compassion of Gyelwang Namgyel Tashi. Through such events, the whole district proclaimed that I was a tulku.

In general, I instinctively rejoiced greatly in the location, teaching, and upholders of the Buddhist teaching in the region of Taklung. In my sixth year, in the eleventh month of 1576 (fire male mouse), I was summoned by Venerable Mahāvajradhara (Kunga Tashi), and my father, the most gracious governor, was well disposed. {557} So it was that I arrived at the great seminary of glorious Taklung, Adamantine Seat of the manifest awakening of Tashi Pel (Maṅgalaśrī), the embodiment of the transcendent lord, the Conqueror Akṣobhya. At the hermitage of Chodzong Namgyel Rabten, the palace where the most sublime Lokeśvara always rejoices, it seemed that Padmapāṇi—heir of the Conqueror; sovereign of knowledge, love, and power; essential nature of the great pristine cognition of all the conquerors—was to become my master, endowed with the threefold adamantine reality of buddha body, speech, and mind. Actually, I was introduced to the maṇḍala of the visage of Ngawang Namgyel Kunga Lekdrub Tashi Gyeltsen Pelzangpo. Simply through that, I obtained a modicum of the three aspects of faith—conviction, longing, and clarity—and virtuous propensities awoke within me. At that time, Venerable On Kunga Pelzangpo arrived there. I met him and was also ordered to attend upon him.

In my seventh year, in the waxing half of the second month in 1577 (fire female ox), on the occasion of an auspicious conjunction of Puṣyā and Jupiter, in the Northern Chapel of the Main Temple of glorious Taklung, I completely received the precepts of the novitiate, preceded by the vows of a layperson and the intermediate vows of a mendicant, in the presence of Kunga Tashi (Ānandamaṅgala) himself, sovereign of the entire Buddhist teaching, doctrinal king of the three world systems, who acted as monastic preceptor, along with a master of ceremonies, timekeeper, assistant, and a quorum of devout monks. The name Ngawang Namgyel Kunga Rinchen Pelzangpo was conferred upon me.

I learned to read under the guidance of the master Namgyel Chophel. I also received initiations and meaningful advice from Choje Tendzin Ngawang Drakpa. {558} On the third day, in the waxing half of the seventh month of that year, I first met Yongdzin Dampa Namgyel Rinchen Pelzangpo. When we, master and disciples, went to meet him at Tsene, I asked him many nonsensical childish questions without careful consideration, but Yongdzin Rinpoche, guided above all by the certainty of his buddha mind, determined that I was the emanation of my venerable predecessor. Among those who upheld his instructions on the Drigungpa *Clear Doctrinal Practice of Kudzi*,[1097] Sakya Paṇḍita's *Treasury of Precious Eloquence*,[1098] and so forth, I alone retained what I heard. I also received the complete instructions of Hevajra and the cycle of the doctrinal protectors, which that former master had applied in practice.

Through prayers of dedication, doctrinal connections, and so forth, I then started to subsist on donations. After obtaining the necessary empowerments and scriptural transmissions in the presence of Venerable Mahāvajradhara Kunga Tashi, the large caravan of the master and his students set out on horseback for Mongolia in 1578 (earth male tiger). At first, I stayed in the grass hermitage and afterward in the upper story of the Offering Chapel. Since I was without responsibilities, I mostly cherished my studies, which were pure. All the responsibilities were assumed by Benponpa and Uma Solpon. Affairs were managed by those two companions, and I was sustained by the great dance of the adamantine expanse. I performed the springtime offering ceremonies and the summertime offering ceremonies in the correct order. I reintroduced all the maṇḍala draftsmanship, colored lines, and recitations of the ritualists that had formerly been in vogue, and I too dwelled as an adamantine master of the maṇḍala of Hevajra. Since all my recitations were clear, I myself fearlessly acted as the chant master in accordance with the age-old custom. {559}

In 1579 (earth female hare), Yongdzin Rinpoche was invited, and I requested the extraordinary empowerments and scriptural transmissions of the profound doctrines of the Taklung Kagyu lineage. When my father, the governor, passed away at Lhundrub Dzong, he (Yongdzin Rinpoche) took us entirely under the refuge of his compassion. During the summer of that same year, in the Great Lower Hall in the midst of the entire congregation, everyone rejoiced at his transmission of *The Biography of Omniscient Ngawang Drakpa*,[1099] and at his extensive exegesis of *The Guru Yoga of the Profound Path*.[1100] At Lhundrub Dzong, I also met my maternal uncle from Drigung, Chogyel Phuntsok Tashi Pelzangpo, and requested some minor teachings of the new and ancient traditions from him.

That year, we restored the teaching throne known as Satri Marpo, which is renowned like the sun and the moon, the lion throne of the sacred doctrine belonging to all the rows of the buddhas of the authentic lineage, without exception, to which the crown ornaments of the entire world, with its god realms, pay respects. We carefully redrew the murals of that room. When we, master and disciples, though few in number, roughly undertook the consecration dependent on Hevajra, the sky cleared, the air was warm and gentle, and a shower of flowers fell. When we scattered the flowers that conferred good auspices, many barley grains stuck to the murals, and so forth. Such were the virtuous signs that manifoldly manifested.

Starting from then, Venerable Zhamar Konchok Yenlak, foremost of those upholding *The Jewel Ornament of Liberation*,[1101] which expounds the graduated path according to the Great Vehicle, kindly offered me the following verses, which begin,

> May the new moon of buddha body
> Enhance the lordship of the three realms of existence,
> Permeating them with the white light of excellent virtue,
> And may this gem of the Kagyu lineage be victorious! {560}

When I was called to the place where Choje Rin Gonpa of Barom passed away, I traveled through Damzhung where bountiful gifts and offerings were presented to me. Horpon Karma Pel and others also made offerings and undertook outstanding acts of service.

I then heard the news that the great caravan of lord Mahāvajradhara (Kunga Tashi), who had been training the borderlands of Mongolia in the sacred doctrine would soon arrive back in the region of Utsang.

When a meditation hermitage had adopted some erroneous notions and practices, I was called to assist on behalf of the precious jewels, and so those malpractices were completely eradicated. Not long afterward, I was satisfied by the feast of beholding yet again the actual face of the Conqueror, Kunga Tashi.

When the fifth crown holder of Zhamar, Konchok Yenlak, arrived in this region, I met him and attended upon him, whereupon he conferred upon me hundreds of long-life empowerments. I have widely conferred those teachings of empowerment and scriptural transmission on those who were interested.

Without effort, I learned scripts such as Rañjanā and Vartula, as well as the painting of sacred icons. I also had a penchant for Sanskrit grammar, poetics, astrology, and so forth. Then, I obtained experiential guidance on the profound instructions of the Six Doctrines of Nāropā concerning the perfection stage of meditation from the lips of lord Mahāvajradhara (Kunga Tashi), who rejoiced in supreme authority and was radiant like the moon amid a cluster of stars. In addition, I extensively received the empowerments, scriptural transmissions, and pith instructions that derive from the glorious Taklung Kagyu lineage and from the tradition of fearless Amarasena.

Around that time, my maternal uncle was appointed to the lion throne of Choje Jikten Gonpo due to a division within the house of Drigung, and he also reinstated the territory of the Taklungpa that had been lost. Yongdzin Rinpoche came, and I requested the essential empowerments and scriptural transmissions of *The Ocean of Means for Attainment*[1102] and so forth. {561}

In my twelfth year, in the summer of 1582 (water male horse), in the Great Lower Hall of the Main Temple, to more than a thousand assembled monks, including residents and others who spontaneously arrived, over extremely long daytime teaching sessions, I delivered from memory an exegesis of *The Jewel Ornament of Liberation: The Graduated Path of the Great Vehicle*,[1103] which is the nectar of the speech of the peerless king of the sacred doctrine Gampopa, without adding or omitting a single word. Everyone present was astonished.

In 1584 (monkey), I performed the consecration ceremony for the large appliqué of meditative commitment that had been commissioned at Taklung. On the occasion of the summer teaching, we—the masters and disciples of Taklung, approximately fifty in number—performed the great sacred dance of Vajrakīla, according to the upper rite and the lower rite.[1104] I then acted as vajra master during the offering of attainment with respect to the maṇḍala of Cakrasaṃvara according to the tradition of Kṛṣṇācārin.

In my fifteenth year, in 1585 (wood female bird), Venerable Mahāvajradhara Kunga Tashi commanded me to act as his regent. Although I was poorly educated in the two traditions of sūtra and mantra and, above all, although I was never happy to assume responsibility for monastic discipline, I complied with the words that my teacher had spoken. Then, whether I was able or unable to carry them out, at the risk of my body and vitality, I indeed assumed that responsibility, perceiving whatever had to be done for the sake of the teaching tradition of this lineage. In a great ceremony on the nineteenth day of the first month, or Māgha, which is the last winter month according to the system of the *Kālacakra*, I was installed upon the doctrinal throne known as Satri Marpo, on which nineteen successive incarnations of the completely perfect buddhas had sat, {562} to which the crown ornament of all mighty lords of the world pay homage, and in which all phenomenal existence is consecrated as the pristine cognition of adamantine supreme bliss. The throne was bedecked with the color indicative of the enlightened activity[1105] that overpowers in accordance with the sacred doctrine. In the midst of the monastic body endowed with awareness and liberation, as many as the stars in the sky, who filled the great Layel Courtyard completely, the crown of the precious Kagyu lineage was fastened upon my head. The lord of all enlightened heritage, the venerable, glorious, and holy lama Mahāvajradhara (Kunga Tashi) and his disciples scattered garlands of precious flowers with their hands and made a supreme benediction with all their auspicious verses. I offered my *Guru Yoga of the Profound Path*[1106] to the assembled host as my first doctrinal feast.

Starting from then I focused on major cultural studies, I was supported by Benbon Kunga Gyelzang, whose excellent intelligence was refined in all activities associated with the two traditions of sūtra and mantra; officials of major and lesser status headed by Kudzi Kunga Namgyel, who was appointed by the power of aspiration and past actions to assume responsibility for all the wheels of activity in which I engaged during my lifetime; lay officials of varying capability; and the subjects of the monastic body. I dwelled simply with the higher aspiration to maintain, nurture, and enhance the Buddhist teachings.

At first, Yongdzin Rinpoche held a reception at which he conferred the title Pelden Ngawang Chokyi Nyima Jikme Zangpo Chokle Namgyelde upon me, along with bountiful gifts. Starting from then, {563} my estates were separate. The monastic preceptors, masters, and senior monks, along with the subjects of the monastery, made great voluntary contributions to commemorate the enthronement. Gyelwang Karmapa, the lord-protector Drigungpa, the glorious Drukpa, venerable tulkus, the great monastic preceptor of Tsok Cholungpa, and people in all regions of the upper and lower Mongols and in Kyisho[1107] and so forth presented innumerable bowls of tea.

In the Great Lower Hall, a maṇḍala of colored sand was displayed, and for the sake of the entire congregation, I conferred the elaborate empowerments embodying the sixty-two aspects of the glorious transcendent lord Cakrasaṃvara, according to the tradition of Kṛṣṇācārin. At the anniversary ceremony of Ngawang Drakpa, in the seventh month of that year, I established a great offering of attainment in accordance with past custom. From then until the present day, this custom has not been broken even for a single year. That year, I also acted as vajra master for the attainment offering ceremony in the maṇḍalas of *The Great Encampment of the Adamantine Expanse*[1108] and *Forty-Nine-Deity Bhairava.*[1109] In the presence of Yongdzin Rinpoche, I received the empowerments and initiations for the seven maṇḍalas of Ngok and so forth; the transmission for the complete cycle of unsurpassed yoga tantras from *The Collection of Tantras*[1110] section of the Kangyur; and many instructions of guidance, including the experiential guidance of Coemergent Union of the Great Seal.

During the eleventh month, I went to inspect the religious estates of Dar and Tre. Commencing with a ceremony on the nineteenth day of that month, for one whole month, until the nineteenth day of the following month, I completed an uninterrupted ritual pertaining to Coemergent Perfection Stage of the Aural Lineage.[1111]

In 1586 (fire male dog), in the presence of Yongdzin Rinpoche, I many times received the empowerments, scriptural transmissions, and minute pith instructions of the complete *Collection of Tantras* and *The Hundred Teachings of Mitrayogin.*[1112] I revered Trakṣad Mahākāla, lord of demonic forces, as the lord-protector of enlightened activity. {564} I cleaned the hundred and eight assorted thumb-size images behind the charred image of glorious Taklungpa the Great and tidily arranged their sacred relics by hand.

There were approximately five hundred threshold planks from Reteng Monastery, the seat of Dromton Jikten Wangchuk, a supremely powerful place foreordained by the Conqueror, which came into the possession of us Taklungpas. Using them, I excellently restored the chapel of the protector deity Genyen Chenpo. I commissioned the murals, including depictions of this deity and his entourage in three demeanors: completely peaceful, semi-peaceful and wrathful, and extremely wrathful. I also commissioned a well-composed large silk appliqué depicting the series of ten meditational deities and consecrated it according to the Cakrasaṃvara tradition of Kṛṣṇācārin.

During the summer teaching, I established the attainment offering ceremony associated with the colored sand maṇḍala of the five deities of Coemergent Union of the Aural Lineage,[1113] which concludes the generation stage of meditation, according to the Taklung Kagyu tradition. I also encouraged the distinctions between our own philosophical system and those of others and ensured that there was no confusion between the objects of prayer and the sacred doctrine that is to be experientially cultivated.

That autumn I went on pilgrimage to Reteng and made offerings, along with aspiration prayers. In the dry summer season of 1587 (fire female pig), I built a high and spacious gallery above the Main Temple, eleven pillars in area, with its adobe walls and borderlines. His Presence Kunga Nyingpo, emanation of the supreme lord Mañjuśrī, then arrived with his entourage. He offered many empowerments, scriptural transmissions, and pith instructions. Duzhapa Jampa Lhundrub was also present as an attendant.[1114] I, too, requested certain teaching connections pertaining to the permission initiations. {565}

I made prayers and offerings in the protector chapels of Genyen in the upper and lower valleys of Draklung.[1115] I gave the initiation of Tashi Tseringma to a large gathering. During the eighth month, the large caravan of Venerable Mahāvajradhara Kunga Tashi returned from glorious Riwoche. Not long afterward, at my request, I completely received from him all the empowerments, scriptural transmissions, and esoteric instructions contained in the fourteen volumes that constitute the Collected Works of Venerable Sangye On.

In 1588 (earth male bird), from Yongdzin Rinpoche, I received empowerments, scriptural transmissions, and guidance many times, commencing with the Experiential Guidance of the Six Doctrines[1116] and the complete transmission of the vinaya. That year, I sent Kunga Yarpel, the reincarnation of Denma, to Mongolia to collect offerings on behalf of Taklung.

In order to promote reconciliation between the upper and lower Mongols, I went to the encampments of lower Hor during the middle of winter. On the way, I inspected Barom Lhakhang. During the dry summer season of 1589 (ox), I returned to Taklung. The reconciliation of the Mongols had been rendered secure. From Yongdzin Rinpoche, I then received many empowerments and scriptural transmissions, including the great empowerment of the *Kālacakra*, the twelve maṇḍalas of *The Purification of the Lower Realms*,[1117] the Six Empowerments and Six Guidances of Mitrayogin,[1118] *The Five Pentads*,[1119] and so forth.

On the morning of the seventeenth day of the fifth month, an auspicious conjunction of planets and stars, when the sundial had passed one lunar mansion and one quadrant, in the Lower Hall of the Main Temple of glorious Taklung Dorjeden, in the presence of the actual silver image of Maṅgalaśrī, the lord-protector and perfect buddha of the three worlds, peerless in his liberating life, which is called Supreme Auspicious Ornament of the World, in accordance the "fourfold rite including the request,"[1120] I obtained the seven sacraments pertaining to physical forms, both perceptible and imperceptible,[1121] which are indicative of the precepts of a fully ordained monk and resemble a dam controlling and blocking off the flow of confusion. This ordination was excellently conferred with kindness in the presence of Ngawang Namgyel Kunga Lekdrub Tashi Gyeltsen Pelzangpo, religious king of the three world systems, and sovereign of the precious Buddhist teaching, who acted as monastic preceptor, {566} and by Yongdzin Rinpoche Namgyel Rinchen Pelzangpo, a sublime and great elder endowed with the primary and ancillary commitments, who acted as master of ceremonies, confessor, and timekeeper. So it was that I was granted the wealth of the three trainings that elucidate the victory banner of the saffron tradition.

The caravan of Venerable Mahāvajradhara (Kunga Tashi) then set out again for Mongolia. I went to escort them as far as the hot springs of Nyingdrung. Since an encampment of the upper Mongols was in the vicinity of Galta Latok,[1122] they summoned me there and presented me with gifts. I recognized the steep hill of Yuki Pari as a bastion of the divine protector Genyen Chenpo.

At Taklung, when the fully ordained resident monks had observed the fourteenth of the confession ceremonies, which are held at half-monthly intervals, when the time came to observe the fifteenth, they would recite the discourses recounting the liberation of each of the sixteen elders without interruption, and I myself would also undertake that recitation. Then, during the winters, I would stay in closed retreat, focusing on the ritual service and attainment of the meditational deities and the protectors.

In the summer of 1590 (iron male tiger), in the presence of Yongdzin Rinpoche, I received the transmission of *The Transcendent Perfection of Wisdom in One Hundred Thousand Lines* and some important empowerments. I sent the vajra disciple {567} Ngawang Sherab to serve as the teacher of the king of Jang and to maintain, nurture, and enhance the Buddhist teaching of the Taklung tradition. One named Lama Ngawang Tsultrim arrived to deliver offerings.

In the eleventh month, I undertook to offer a new throne and back screen to the silver image of glorious Taklungpa the Great. Five Newar craftsmen, including one named Lāgashing, were employed. The wide and high lion throne was then embellished with the motifs of the doctrinal wheel and the two deer. On its tiers, the throne back had ornaments and many extraordinary features that were arrayed, and it was replete with the six distinct ornaments. On either side of the image, it had the stacked motifs of elephant, lion, śarabha deer,[1123] and dwarf, supporting a beam of gemstones, above which were sea monsters with young nāgas issuing from the spiral motif[1124] of their tails, and at the top, in the middle, was the majestic king of garuḍas. On a decorative frieze that extended from this throne back screen, there were rows of letters in Rañjanā script, depicting the name of Venerable Taklungpa the Great, the seed syllables of the three adamantine realities, and a verse of homage, along with a geometric poetry chart with more than one hundred and eight squares, divided according to auspicious lines of verse. Surrounding it was the perimeter rim of a maṇḍala, completely imbued with garlands of blazing light rays.

While this was going on, to avoid smallpox, I went into solitary retreat at Sengling Dorje Dzong. From Yongdzin Rinpoche, I received the extensive empowerments and scriptural transmissions of the ancient tradition of Secret Mantra. His Presence Mipham Pema Karpo, the great omniscient incumbent of the glorious Drukpa journeyed here to Taklung. I met him, since we had word that he should be accommodated, and an excellent meritorious outcome was achieved. {568} We had an extensive discussion concerning the scriptures, and he was pleased with the wondrous array of the representations of body, speech, and mind in the Main Temple, along with the monastery. Wherever he subsequently went, in all places and at all times, he expressed only praise for us. He also obtained in great abundance acts of service, gifts, and offerings from this Taklung area. In brief, it suffices to say that we mutually acted as master and disciple, imparting doctrinal connections. Apart from that, any opportunity that might have arisen for a return visit ended simply in this perfect encounter.

At the end of the eighth month of 1591 (iron female hare), I went down into the lower Kyichu valley to see Jowo Śākyamuni in Lhasa. On the third day of the waxing half of the ninth month, coinciding with an auspicious planetary and stellar conjunction, I had an excellent visit to the Great Temple of Rasa Trulnang, with its sacred representations and their chapels. I extensively presented sacraments of offering, including face gilding, butter lamps, and offering scarves. At each glimpse of the sacred image, I immediately called to mind the excellent words and meanings of each aspiration prayer, such that intelligent and impartial bystanders in our own and other groups were astonished. I was paid respectful homage by the glorious governor Yulgyel Norbu.[1125] At his thoughtful request, I undertook some empowerments and initiations. Since this governor was of the highest intelligence, his heart had deep devotion and aspiration.

I then went on pilgrimage to Yerpa and imparted to Ena Drungpa the sundry teachings he desired. On the way, I was summoned to Changlung Choding. I went there and distributed fine tea and alms. They reckoned that I was the reincarnation of the great learned and accomplished master Zhonu Lodro, so with fervent devotion they offered presents and donations that surpass the imagination. {569} I expounded many teachings continuously, night and day, to everyone there, in general and in particular, commensurate with those that would satisfy their minds. The local official also sent presents from Khartse, and I undertook certain initiations.[1126]

Also, in the eleventh month, I received a summons from the upper Mongols regarding the funeral rites of the late Taklung niece Guru Butri. Since my sister was ill, I went via Lingkar. The offerings and acts of service that I received were immeasurable. On the way back down, I extensively expounded the setting of the mind on enlightenment according to the lineage of profound view to the monastic assembly of Dechen Yangpachen, embellished with infinite empowerments, scriptural transmissions, and pith instructions, such that everyone rejoiced.

In succession, I then conferred the mendicant ordination and the full monastic ordination, as appropriate, on four nephews of the preceptor, master of ceremonies, and retreat supervisor of this place,[1127] the reincarnation of Barom, and so forth. That year I gave many empowerments according to both the ancient and new traditions, including The Seven Maṇḍalas of Ngok,[1128] Cakrasaṃvara, Guhyasamāja, Vajradhātu, and *The Hundred Teachings of Mitrayogin*.[1129] I composed *The Great Commentary on Two-Part Hevajra*,[1130] and performed the profound and extensive torma aversion rites of Jñānanātha, based on the ritual arrangement of our own uncommon tradition. I also administered without mishap the funeral rites of the late Ponsa Namgyel Pelmo and the property and estates of Je Lama, considering this an act of service, and accomplished it well.

After that, since the copper work of the throne and back screen of the central image of Taklungpa the Great had mostly worn away, I gilded it with no less than eight hundred gold *zho* and adorned it with diverse precious gems. I tended to the throne, complying with the auspicious guidelines that concern all its sacred relics and defining characteristics. On the reverse side, it has charts depicting one hundred and eight icons of the Conqueror Taklungpa the Great, {570} along with fifteen peripheral icons depicting the deities of The Four Stages of the Generation Stage,[1131] and the six meditational deities, along with other meditational deities, doctrinal protectors, Vasudeva, and so forth.

With Yongdzin Rinpoche acting as the sacred vajra master, we then reconsecrated the actual library of Drogon Rinpoche (Phakmodrupa) and Gyelwa Taklungpa the Great and his heirs, according to the rite of Venerable Vajrayoginī, without mingling or adulterating it with other ritual applications. The preliminaries were undertaken on the first day of the waxing half of the second month of 1592 (water dragon), and the main practice on the second day. This rite was embellished by an infinite array of auspicious feasting. The artisans were delighted with awesome gifts. My hopes were fulfilled when this straightaway coincided with the return of the great caravan of the venerable lama Mahāvajradhara (Kunga Tashi).

In 1593 (water female snake), I moved residence, basing my calculation on the exact sidereal year according to the five astrological components of the *Kālacakra*, and it was easily done. Choje On Rinpoche then traveled here from Drigung, and we had a meeting that was most meritorious. The rows of monks were satisfied with the desired teachings.

I then went to Uma Drakar,[1132] where I was offered bountiful presents and donations with respect to the funeral rites I undertook on behalf of the late Lama Jangchub Nyingpo. That summer, I received from Yongdzin Rinpoche the Adamantine Garland and the complete cycles of the Kadam lineage, which he himself had received from Lozim Okpa Jampa Chojor.[1133]

In 1594 (wood male horse), I prepared the cross thread of fulfillment for the local protector and positioned it well, such that it was fixed in his path of vision. Venerable Tulku Ponlob[1134] arrived, and I offered him *The Hundred Teachings of Mitrayogin*,[1135] six ancillary teachings, {571} ten initiations, *The Root Sūtra of Monastic Discipline*,[1136] and some twenty-eight sundry and concise transmissions of tantra. In return, I received *The Hundred Means for Attainment*,[1137] *The Twenty-One Tārās*,[1138] *The Eighty Accomplished Masters*,[1139] three large ancillary teachings, three distinct initiations, the complete maturational empowerments and liberating guidance of the Six Doctrines of Niguma, and many transmissions of major and minor Sanskrit texts. Kabzhi Chodze Tsultrim Gyurme Ponlob[1140] then arrived, and I conferred the initiations and transmissions in accordance with his considered request. He was extremely devoted.

With Gelong Tashi Namgyel acting as a scribe, I then composed *An Extensive Exegesis of the Precepts according to the Three Vows,*[1141] along with its *Summary.*[1142] That winter, Dakchen Rinpoche arrived from Sakya and Tsedong, and I met him. I satisfied Onpo of Tsib Nesar,[1143] Gyabdrak Choje Gelong, and others with the desired teachings.[1144]

Since the new year of 1595 (wood female sheep) coincided with an obstacle year, with the intention of averting misfortune, I prepared the thread cross that secures Trakṣad Mahākāla and performed many times the offering rites of the sixteen elders, along with the burnt offerings and recitations associated with the rite of pacification. At that same time, I extensively expounded the transmissions and guidance to resident monks and those who had assembled from all directions.

Ben Onpa made two images of medicinal clay depicting my two supreme guides (Yongdzin Rinpoche and Kunga Tashi), from which I would never be separated. Then, from the tenth month of that year, I commissioned paintings on twenty-eight distinct large painted scrolls, which were exquisitely drawn, fashioned of excellent materials, and distinguished in particular by narratives depicting the Kagyu monasteries. The work was completed during the ninth month of 1596 (fire monkey), and the consecration ceremony was performed by the glorious lord, my teacher Mahāvajradhara (Kunga Tashi). The artisans were satisfied to the utmost by excellent donations and gifts. {572}

In the interval between 1595 and 1596 (sheep and monkey years), I was invited up to the household of Karma Yulgyel, the Mongol chieftain, when my maternal aunt Onsa passed away, and in the winter of 1596 (monkey), I was invited up to the encampment of the upper Mongols when On Tseten Gyelpo passed away.

I also went to Lhasa when summoned by Onsa Ane Drungpa Ngotsar Konchok Tsewang Pelmowa from the lower Kyichu region to reconsecrate the temple of Ramoche, which had been built by the Chinese princess Wencheng. They had carried out an extraordinary restoration of the murals on the wooden beam-ends and commissioned thirty-six gold painted scrolls depicting the tathāgatas of confession, the materials and design of which were both perfect. Based on the colored sand maṇḍalas of the five deities associated with Coemergent Perfection Stage of the Aural Lineage, I performed the preliminary rite on the fourteenth, the main part on the fifteenth, and the concluding festival of benediction and so forth on the sixteenth. Intelligent persons were captivated. I also conferred empowerments, initiations, and so forth, complying with the wishes of the glorious governor of the lower Kyichu region.

I then went to Phakmodru when summoned by Phakmotse. There, I met On Choje Rinpoche, a descendant of Jikten Sumgon. I offered him many empowerments and initiations to sustain his health, as many as he wished, including The Hundred Long-Life Empowerments,[1145] The Multiple Deities of Sitātapatrā,[1146] Siṃhavaktrā, and Loktripāla. I performed many detailed rites to sustain his health and protect his life, including the great torma of Mahākāla and the averting thread cross of Śrīdevī. At Namseling, I also performed long-life empowerments for Dungyu Rinpoche and his wife.[1147]

That summer, I began working on the extensive biography of Taklungpa the Great. {573} Plaster and an adobe coating were added to the outer walls of the Main Temple, which were seen to be unsatisfactory. I then met Drukpa Dungyu Rinpoche Mipham Tenpei Nyima and his disciples when they visited Taklung. Then, when Choje Dorje Lingpa Mangto Pekarwa[1148] arrived as an act of service, at that time I delivered an exegesis of the outer and inner Collected Works of glorious Taklungpa the Great, along with the six meditational deities and so forth. Later I conferred an infinite number of teachings. To return this favor, he assisted with the preparation of the woodblocks of *The Great Biography of Venerable Taklungpa the Great*. I also brought maturation to Chodze Lama Zangpo from the Rinpung Estate through empowerments, scriptural transmissions, and pith instructions.

From the new year of 1598 (earth male dog), I began to prepare a manuscript version of the complete Kangyur with ink of gold and silver on parchment paper, without external and internal grid lines.[1149] In succession, we prepared and consecrated fifty volumes, including *The Collection of Tantras*,[1150] *The Collection of Discourses and Incantations*,[1151] and *The Transcendent Perfection of Wisdom in Twenty-Five Thousand Lines*.[1152]

In the presence of Yongdzin Rinpoche, I then received many times all the intermediate and concise texts belonging to the cycle of *The Transcendent Perfection of Wisdom*, along with *The Great Bounteousness of the Buddhas*, *The Six Books of Kadam*,[1153] *The Pagoda of Precious Gems*, the cycle of the Drukpa school, and the empowerments, scriptural transmissions, and pith instructions of the Nyingma. Then, when Kabzhi Chodze returned here, I satisfied him with the teachings he desired.

On the eighth day of the third month in 1599 (earth female pig), Yongdzin Rinpoche, who was peerless in his kindness, passed away. On the sixteenth day, I myself performed the cremation, based on the ritual of five-deity Bhaṭṭārikā. I commissioned a reliquary stūpa depicting the great enlightenment—fashioned of silver, gold, and copper and replete with the defining characteristics—and inserted excellent relics including the sacred bones and blessed representations. {574} I consecrated it and installed it in the Northern Chapel. The funeral offerings were performed in all sorts of ways.

I also composed *The Biography Titled Illumination of the Sublime Path.*[1154] Woodblock carvers from Jayul cut one hundred and thirty-eight woodblocks, including *The Fourfold Preliminaries,*[1155] *The Basic List of Visualizations according to the Great Seal and the Six Doctrines,*[1156] *The Offering to the Spiritual Teachers,*[1157] *The Attainment of the Spiritual Teacher*[1158] with its torma rite *The Doctrinal Practices: An Illumination,*[1159] and the complete *Rites of Fulfillment.*[1160] They were delighted with our dispensing of the customary provisions and donations, which was excellent. I also satisfied Chodze Ngawang Tubten Yangdak of Trerapa College[1161] with empowerments, scriptural transmissions, and pith instructions.

Around that time, the Mongol king known as Göden Bādur,[1162] a descendant of Qubilai Qaγan, who surpassed everyone in the northern regions, like a powerful universal monarch, suddenly arrived in Taklung. He was one who generally obliged those of the south and the north to function as his servants. However, owing to an inheritance of past actions, he became intensely devoted immediately upon meeting me. Earlier and later in life, I went many times to his encampments. The offerings and acts of service that he made were incalculable. Since I was widely responsible for monastic discipline, I also undertook the protector rites and the many associated teachings of empowerment.

On one occasion, Jetsun Tulku arrived, and he requested the profound doctrines of Marpa and Ngok, the aural lineage of Rechung, *The Six Books of Vārāhī,*[1163] ten major empowerments, ten initiations, and many scriptural transmissions. I also offered him seven or eight empowerments and initiations of the ancient and new traditions and the swift guidance of the Six Doctrines.

That summer, after consulting all the officials of the upper Mongols,[1164] {575} we restored the monastery and newly built one hundred and eight grass hermitages within the restored monastery. With me acting as monastic preceptor, one hundred and eight assembled monks were given the mendicant ordination in a single day. I also extensively performed consecrations and auspicious enthronement ceremonies. When Kudzi constructed perfect images of Munīndra and the sixteen elders, I correctly performed the consecration based on Satyadvayamukha Bhaṭṭārikā. Tendzin Choje Chak Nangpa of Bodong and all his monastic body traveled here just for that purpose. There were many mendicant and full-ordination ceremonies to be conferred, and I carried them out correctly. I extensively dispensed the empowerments, scriptural transmissions, and pith instructions. I commissioned a cotton painting of glorious Taklungpa the Great in full color and of Genyen brandishing a mighty banner in his hand.

In 1601 (female iron ox),[1165] I commissioned nineteen volumes from the Kangyur including *The Vinaya Scriptures*, *The Great Bounteousness of the Buddhas*, and *The Transcendent Perfection of Wisdom in Ten Thousand Lines*. The consecration was undertaken by Venerable Mahāvarjadhara (Kunga Tashi). The glorious Drukpa Chenpo Choje Mipham Chogyel also came and I met him. I contributed bountiful doctrinal gifts for their seminaries. Then I venerated the reincarnation of Denma as the crown ornament of all the seniormost Mongol princes; and he brought forth, as it were, the sunrise of the Buddhist teaching. He passed away in the Chakhar heartlands.[1166] Offerings on his behalf arrived unimpededly in Taklung. There were extraordinary riches of immeasurable value heaped up like a mountain.

In 1602 (water male tiger), Choje Drogon passed into nirvāṇa at Drokha.[1167] Jetsun Tulku was invited to sit at the head of the row during the funeral ceremony. I received from him the complete empowerments of Vajrakīla according to the Sakya tradition and Unsurpassed Acala.[1168] {576} In return I offered him a torma empowerment of The Peaceful and Wrathful Guru.[1169]

In 1603 (water female hare), my dear mother departed Lhundrub Dzong for another world. It was estimated that she had been ill with measles. Though we had no opportunity to meet just before that occurred, I undertook many purposeful offerings at Kudzi. I wrote a note and sent it with an offering to the officials of Venerable Karmapa Wangchuk Dorje at Namling in Shang.[1170] This also ensured that things turned out all right after her death, and so Gyeltsab Rinpoche performed acts of service.[1171] In a petition to Gyeltsab Rinpoche that I made from here, there was a verse requesting him to assume responsibility in the manner of the enlightened activity of sublime Mahākāśyapa. Though there were no suspicions at that time, later it seemed that my request was aligned with the circumstances of that period.[1172] Perceptive individuals, for the most part, held that I was a holder of extrasensory powers. At that time, Zhamar Choktrul (Chokyi

Wangchuk)[1173] came here to Taklung on pilgrimage, and although his visit was timely, I had no opportunity to meet him in person because I was staying in extremely strict retreat, avoiding the infection of measles.

That year, I excellently commissioned the large brocade appliqué, each side of which was symmetrical, eleven double armspans in width. These depicted the meditational deities surrounded by Munīndra and the sixteen elders, forty-one icons in all. The skilled artisan Mentangpa Lobzang Gyatso drew it and cut the sections of silk, and it was sewn by some twelve silk craftsmen. Its materials included sixty-five rolls of brocade, which was excellently colored, mostly with the motifs of *dā jus* and *nya jus*, and unadulterated with common silk, {577} as well as some twenty-five rolls of manufactured silk of superior, mediocre, and inferior quality. The consecration was held on the waxing half of the seventh month. I invited the glorious lama, lord Mahāvajradhara (Kunga Tashi), and we sat for three days in a tented camp behind the Kumbum. The distinctive items that we had acquired from Mongolia were put on display. The face of the appliqué was then revealed and blessed with consecrated barley. This was to bring about an auspicious circumstance of excellent merit. It transpired that those who were devoted could even engage with the doctrinal terminology that the lama had mastered.

When Drepung Tulku Yonten Gyatso arrived from Mongolia, I served him tea and met him in person. On Eighteenth Choje,[1174] I bestowed *The Hundred Teachings of Mitrayogin*,[1175] the blessings of the Eighty-Four Accomplished Masters, and approximately twenty ancillary teachings, and so forth. Then, when a Mongol army launched an attack from Dzongnyak against the traders of Dakpo, by determining the truth of the matter, the signs of future foreboding immediately appeared to me.

During 1604 (wood male dragon), I commissioned twenty-one volumes, including *The Transcendent Perfection of Wisdom in One Hundred Thousand Lines*, *The Transcendent Perfection of Wisdom in Eighteen Thousand Lines*, and *The Pagoda of Precious Gems*. In conjunction with the excellent completion of the Kangyur and the appliqué, the glorious lama lord Mahāvajradhara (Kunga Tashi) and his disciples graciously performed the consecration based on Hevajra. Denma Abo Gonpo sculpted pure images of the sixteen elders, and I performed the consecration.

Since it seemed there was a need to travel to the encampments of the Tongso Mongols,[1176] I traveled around them to some extent. Then, I directly went to Lhasa in the lower Kyichu region along with our patron. At the maṇḍala of Lhasa, I met Drepung Tulku Yonten Gyatso and was presented with gifts and offerings by the Mongols. {578} As for the peripheral deities in each chapel of the Great Temple of Lhasa, if there was one that I did not know, I was able to identify it according to ancient archives. I then went to the great seminary of Sera,[1177] at the behest of the tulkus, masters, and disciples there. They held an elaborate reception. I saw the precious artifacts that they had, including the tapestry depicting Munīndra, the printed edition of the Kangyur from China,[1178] and a manuscript of *The Transcendent Perfection of Wisdom in Eight Thousand Lines* inscribed in gold in Rañjanā script on Chinese paper. In the Potala, I conferred on Lama Dungkar Drukdra, at his personal summoning, the transmission of the maṇḍala of attainment of Mahākāruṇika.[1179] Since the governor Yulgyelwa had a great wish to receive an esoteric instruction of definitive meaning, I stayed about one month at the Drakar Estate and the best part of ten days at Dewugong, giving a detailed explanation of the visualization sequence of Coemergent Union of the Great Seal, and a great many empowerments, initiations, and scriptural transmissions. Through the foundation of life-sustaining rites, a protective circle, and auspicious coincidence, I fulfilled his wishes. At Changlung Choding, I explained many teachings that they wanted.[1180]

On the second day of the first month of 1605 (wood female snake), I returned to Taklung. Venerable Mahāvajradhara (Kunga Tashi) had been unwell, but when I went into his presence, he was pleased and conversed quite freely. Knowing that his enlightened intention was about to focus on another pure land, I became introspective. His health did not manifestly improve at all despite the life-sustaining rites and medical treatments that were requested. On the last day of that lunar month, he displayed the yoga of dissolving into the expanse of great immaculate peace. {579} A most bountiful funeral ceremony was held here in Taklung and in the surrounding area. In his bedroom, a single gold image of Munīndra, one cubit in size, was commissioned, and at Chodzong, a life-size representation of him was fashioned of medicinal clay. The glorious Drukpa Choktrul Paksam Wangpo was invited to preside over the funerary assembly, and we had a meritorious meeting. I offered him a long-life empowerment, the complete scriptural transmission of each volume of *The Transcendent Perfection of Wisdom in One Hundred Thousand Lines*, beginning, middle, and end, along with the complete transmissions of *The Sūtra Demonstrating the Three Vows* and *The Sūtra Demonstrating the Purification of Infinite Approaches*,[1181] completely but in abridged form. Choje Lhatsewa Ngawang Zangpo, Choje Drapukpawa Pelgyi Senge, the great preceptor Jam Drakpa, Choje Dor Dzinpa, the lama of Chokdra Nyingpa, and Lotsāwa Sangye Pelzang were also present in attendance among those who received the transmissions. Aside, I imparted to them the complete Collected Works of glorious Taklung Tangpa the Great, and instruction on the channels and winds according to the Six Doctrines. Under Choje Dra Pukpawa, I ascertained and studied the charts of elemental divination. I satisfied them by both spiritual and temporal means. Having formed a mutual friendship, they all (masters and disciples) returned home.

During the second of the duplicated (intercalary) third month of that year, a group of Newar artisans including one Ponmoche Amipāla arrived, so I set up a factory for making a silver reliquary. {580} I blessed their materials and tools, and starting from then, I gave particular instruction on the intricacies, intricate details, and implementation regarding the geometric proportions of the reliquary and its entire design.

Jetsun Tulku (Tāranātha) then arrived, and I requested the initiation of the Twenty-One Tārās, according to the tradition of Sūryagupta, three cycles of Khecarī, five great empowerments, approximately fifteen miscellaneous initiations, *The Four Paper Scrolls of Marpa*,[1182] certain Sanskrit texts, and the Collected Works of Lama Zhang. I in turn offered him many empowerments, initiations, and scriptural transmissions, including the Peaceful Guru,[1183] the Dark-Red Wrathful Guru,[1184] the Razor Vajrakīla,[1185] Most Secret Amitāyus,[1186] and Fierce Vajrapāṇi.[1187]

At the entrance to the dome of the silver reliquary, I placed a miniature icon[1188] of Venerable Kunga Tashi himself, and at the center of the solar disk at the top of the reliquary, an image of Gyelwa Taklungpa. At the top of the ornate entrance was an image of the lord of our enlightened heritage, Venerable Namgyel Tashi, and on the pedestal surfaces supporting the fourth tier of the reliquary base were inscribed the long incantations of Immaculate Uṣṇīṣa and Vijaya. On the thirteen stacked rings symbolizing the sacred doctrine were metrical verses praising the names of the Kagyu lineage holders and eulogizing the body of Venerable Kunga Tashi. At the middle of the lowest tier of the base, coordinated letters in Sanskrit and Tibetan were carved by the Newar artisans as if they had been written. The smelted and refined silver that was used weighed seven hundred steelyard measures, and the gold amounted to a continuous string of six hundred *zho*. The reliquary was embellished with an incalculable cluster of gemstones. The undeteriorated remains and their receptacle were inserted within it, along with other relics, complete with the appropriate defining characteristics. The reliquary was installed in the center of the Southern Chapel, The Blissful Palace of Attainment of the Kagyu Lineage. {581} To its right was placed the silver image of glorious Phakmodrupa, Ornament of the World and common representation of the Kagyu lineage in general, along with its offering platform, and on the left was placed the silver image of Gyelwa Taklungpa the Great, Meaningful to Behold, the uncommon representation of the Kagyu lineage, along with its offering platform. In addition, there were newly arranged and amassed wondrous representations of buddha body, speech, and mind, including inconceivable and inexpressible icons filled to the brim with offering sacraments, as well as ornaments of heaven, ornaments of earth, and their receptacles, captivating the minds of perceptive persons.

In the eleventh month of 1605 (wood snake), I revealed the colored sand maṇḍalas of the five deities of Satyadvayamukha Bhaṭṭārikā and infinitely propagated all the rituals of consecration, without exception, performing the preliminaries on the twenty-sixth day and the main part on the twenty-seventh. The Newar artisans were pleased with their gifts.

In the new year of 1606 (fire male horse), I edited the Collected Works of the wondrous and supreme tulku Ngawang Namgyel Tashi Drakpa Gyeltsen Pelzangpo that were extant only in the form of handwritten paper scrolls—supplementing them and correcting errata. I adorned them with introductory verses of homage and colophons and ensured that they would become a resource for all fortunate beings endowed with faith and the clear eye of discriminative awareness.

That dry summer season, I restored the three Kumbum. Most of the wood had to be replaced. About two-thirds of the tiled roofs were refurbished. The corners of the actual stūpas were repaired, and they were newly painted with the application of gold, silver, copper, and so forth. In such ways, I was contented. {582} During this restoration, each day, from start to finish, I looked upon it with delight because there was indeed a wondrous array of miracles that occurred, including a shower of flowers. I also prepared an extensive catalog of the Kumbum contents, a tract concerning the calculation of multiple circumambulations, and so forth.

In the Tanglha Chapel of the Main Temple, I introduced some changes, prepared wire mesh screens, and so forth. Then, I constructed the Chapel of Bronzes, in which were installed one hundred and eight authentic Indian representations, headed by the central image of Gyelwa Taklungpa the Great, which had been made by Mayo Gomnak at Vajrāsana in India, and the image of Munīndra Chokorma of natural copper, which had been made at Vārāṇasī in Madhyadeśa and had once been one of the foremost sacred icons in the Lhasa Potala. Along with these were twenty-two Chinese bronzes including the image of Jowo Jangkye and Avalokiteśvara in the form Chenrezik Chudzin, as well as twenty-three consecrated icons from Tibet and their sacraments of offering and up to a thousand volumes containing canonical texts and treatises.[1189] I then elucidated the writings of *The Throne Array*[1190]—the adamantine speech of Venerable Sangye On concerning the rite of sixty-two-deity Cakrasaṃvara according to the tradition of Lūipa, which was the uncommon meditational deity of the Taklung Kagyu lineage. I restored the custom of making offerings in connection with it on the last day of the lunar month, and I revived its sacred offering dance.

I satisfied with desired teachings Lama Shorokpa Kunga Zangpo of Yangri,[1191] who belonged to the large encampment of glorious Karmapa, along with his disciples. Then, within the space of a single month, I excellently made the appliqué of Gyelwa Taklungpa the Great, doing myself the work that was worthy of being undertaken by an artist. This is one of the best appliqués in Tibet—if its material and provenance were examined, it would not be considered inferior. I undertook the consecration ceremony based on Cakrasaṃvara, {583} and the event was naturally rendered auspicious.

During the new year of 1607 (fire female sheep), I founded the great monastic institution of Kagyu Domsumling where one hundred and eight assembled monks were given the mendicant ordination simultaneously and committed themselves to study and reflection. The beauty of this institution captivates perceptive persons on account of its bountiful endowments, both spiritual and temporal, its code of monastic regulation, and its erudition. I then started to write my autobiography titled *Wagon of the Mind*.[1192] This is written in detail based on my own experiences, from my birth until the present, including the fictions of my bewildered thoughts. If one were to wish for a more detailed account, that would be clear!

I then trained some forty well-qualified monks of our monastery in the sacred dance of Vajrakīla and in the sacred drum dance. In the context of the offering of attainment their perfect performance was pleasing.

It seems that the Mongol king Göden Bagatur could not adapt to the physical conditions in Tibet, the terrain and the water, so he became unwell and returned to Mongolia. On the way back, he died. I went there at their behest out of charity on his behalf. En route, I visited the sacred place of Tashi Dowoche at Namtso.[1193] I then directly reached their encampment at Drong Shelkha Lake. The material offerings that they made were incalculable. For the most part, they included public property for the monastic assembly of Domsumling. On the return journey, I rested for some days at Tangdrok. Back at Taklung, on behalf of the monastic assembly of Domsumling, I then conferred the elaborate empowerments according to the cotton-drawn maṇḍala of Cakrasaṃvara, along with the four empowerments, common and uncommon, pertaining to Satyadvayamukha Bhaṭṭārikā and Sahajā combined, and the initiations of Sahajasaṃvara, Parṇaśavarī, Citriṇī, Vaiśravaṇa, {584} Aparājitā, the Great Genyen, and so forth, along with useful scriptural transmissions, major and minor.

Then, I returned to my residence at the great monastic seat. The monks of Domsumling went begging for alms in places under the control of Tibetan villages. I took up residence at Chodzong and appointed suitable and educated individuals as the preceptor of that monastery, and as the Lachen, the Chogo, the Tsamla, the eight seniors of Taklung, and the steward. The charter of the monastic assembly and the disciplinary rules of the monastery did not deviate from the custom that had formerly been established.

Then, Mongols headed by the three Taiji[1194] and newcomers arrived in large numbers in the area of lower Hor. Consequently, there were also some disturbances and upheavals that occurred in the lower Kyichu (Lhasa) region.

In the new year of 1608 (earth male monkey), I received offerings in connection with the funeral ceremony of Yulgyel Norbu, the glorious governor of the lower Kyichu region who passed away at Banam. I was asked to write an obituary notice and so forth. Then, in order to avoid contacting smallpox, I stayed in strict retreat at Khartok, Setsa, Sengling, Nyentok, and so forth.

During the early summer, I also finished work on the restoration of the monastery. I composed *The Gong of Wondrous Brahmā: A Biography of Past Lives*,[1195] and four printers from Jayul carved about thirty woodblocks, containing my own autobiography and my writings on orthography, consecration, and the torma rite of Vaiśravaṇa. In the context of an offering rite of attainment, the monks of Domsumling displayed the colored sand maṇḍala of Cakrasaṃvara and performed a peerless offering rite of attainment. I had a set of the eight stūpas made from white and red sandalwood at Kudzi and also consecrated the woodblocks in a suitable manner {585} based on the yoga of Cakrasaṃvara at Tsomka Gye Tashi Sarma[1196] in Yang Gon.[1197]

In the new year of 1609 (earth female bird), in my twenty-ninth year, on the anniversary of the miracle of Śrāvastī, I performed the empowerment of attainment based on the colored sand maṇḍala of Mahākāruṇika, Tamer of Living Beings. Onsa Ane Drungpa, from lower Kyichu, commissioned a most exquisite set of paintings depicting the nine successive incarnations of the wondrous supreme tulku Ngawang Namgyel Tashi, and I performed an elaborate consecration based on Cakrasaṃvara.

Starting from the twenty-third day of the first lunar month, I sat down to write this *Great Doctrinal History*[1198] of Taklung. At that time, I received the particularly sublime image of Zangtangma, lord of the Buddhist teaching, which was offered by Desi Tsangpa.[1199] I therefore considered that this would widely establish an auspicious circumstance of excellent merits for the short term and the long term.

Concluding Verses

Entering into the essential teaching at birth
Through excellent deeds of pure auspicious circumstance
That threaded the confines of my own natural fetters
Onto the string of this precious garland, the narrative of the Kagyu lineage,
May I achieve the fruit of having engaged in correct study, reflection, and meditation,
Ending forever all obscurations that are to be renounced,
And attain the glory of the auspicious, undisturbed lord-protector,
The antidotal pristine cognition, youthful and mature!

The Abbatial Succession of Taklung Lower Plain

Sangye On Drakpa Pel, the Founder

Glory (*dpal*)[1200] of body, speech, and mind, **renowned** (*grags pa*) in the three planes of existence,
Illuminated with sacred **light rays** (*'od zer*) of inconceivable attributes and activities, {586}
Manifesting among living beings without concealment the **noble** (*bzang po*) life of a perfect **buddha** (*sangs rgyas*),
Homage to that supreme lord-protector and his abbatial succession—
The second Taklung Kagyu lineage!

No perceptive persons can recount even one of the many hundreds of wondrous narratives associated with the supreme buddha body of emanation, which are uninterrupted from one continuum to another. Even so, in this case, I will summarize the main points, since these may be suitable for the minds of present-day disciples, and I shall recount this narrative, which is easy to grasp. It should be heard respectfully.

The supreme tulku Sangye Onpo, Drakpa Pel Ozer Zangpo, holder of the secret treasury of the immaculate sacred doctrine that is the aural lineage of Taklungpa the Great and compiler of the teachings, appeared in the world in the following manner. The patron Dorje Rinchen, who was the older brother of Choku Sangye Yarjon, with the same father and mother, married Tseza Jodar, the daughter of Jowo Amchok. Among their offspring, first of all, the lady Rinchen Tsomo was born. She was the reincarnation of Lotsāwa Drubpa Pelzangpo.[1201] Owing to her naturally accomplished inspiration, she was unimpeded in poetics and prosody. Undoubtedly, she was an accomplished yoginī. In the perception of disciples, superior and inferior, she went off to get married and passed away, but at the moment of her death, when she engaged in spiritual practice, she departed in the manner of a sky farer. Such were the diverse displays of miraculous ability that she manifested. The second child was Venerable Sangye On, and the third sibling was Tashi Gyeltsen, who had a different mother.[1202]

When Dorje Rinchen was in his sixteenth year, he had traveled to Taklung, {587} where he had requested guidance on the Six Doctrines from Rinpoche Sangye Yarjon. Having engaged in spiritual practice from his fifteenth year, his realization was equal to space, and he was most inquisitive about the oral instructions.[1203] By practicing consciousness transference, he manifested uncommon signs of realization. His acts of blessing had innumerable results: liberating beings from diseases and demonic possession and so forth.

Once, when he was traveling from Tre to Taklung, at the head of Chak La pass there was an unattractive woman carrying a loaded basket while holding on to her horse's bridle. "Take this gift from me!" she said. "Send someone to request a child from Jowo in Lhasa!" So saying, she vanished. Consequently, the mother (Tseza Jodar) went to Lhasa. On seeing the sacred image of Jowo Śākyamuni, she prayed for her desired objective. That night, in a dream inside the temple, she dreamed that she requested a son in the presence of Jowo Śākyamuni, who replied, "Go to the chapel of Avalokiteśvara (Rangjung Ngaden) and tell him I say to give you a son!" So, she went into the presence of the Great Compassionate One, offered her prostrations and asked accordingly. Avalokiteśvara replied, "If Jowo Rinpoche says to give you a son, I will make your son!" When she seemed to be dancing with intense joy, she awoke. The woman who had previously delivered the prophecy at Chak La was a ḍākinī.

Then, the father and mother journeyed to Kham. In a dream, she beheld an Indian paṇḍita named Vijayamati,[1204] an accomplished master of Hevajra, who arrived there and said, "Take these medicines that will purify your womb, without engaging in sexual intercourse for one month. Through the threefold perception[1205] of Nairātmyā, you should visualize the womb as a celestial palace, and meditate on the syllable HŪṂ, red and lustrous. You should perform ablutions in accordance with the oral instructions that do not forget the sacred doctrine, in the presence of a miniature image of Mañjuśrī, and through the hundred-syllable mantra of Vajrasattva. {588} You should draw a lotus motif on an exposed plain, and then undertake the rituals and so forth!"[1206] She did so in accordance with certain secret commitments that hit their mark, and consequently she saw the father vanish into the fontanelle of the mother in the form of a bone-clad yogin. The father and mother swooned, owing to their bliss, for a long time.

Once the child had entered her womb, deities and ḍākinīs also congregated, the mother was without afflictive mental states, and satisfied with uncontaminated bliss. She spoke in Sanskrit and had extrasensory powers. In a dream, she stood in the midst of volumes of books, and there were many women offering wine from a skull cup. When a black man did not permit her to drink, an aspect of Acala cut him to pieces with his sword. Then, many people from afar said, "An aspect of Padmākara has appeared in yonder woman's womb!" On examining her womb, she saw an image of Mahākāruṇika telling the beads of a rosary and revealed it to them. Many pearl relics spilled out of the image, and though she tried to stop them, she could not, such that the whole valley was filled with them. Her body became as clear as crystal, and in its midst a child appeared reciting mantras. He said, "Look here! Each day I recite seven syllables. Today, I am in good spirits, so I did twenty-one!" When he said this, she awoke. In her womb, a sound distinctly echoed.

The child was born in 1251 (iron male pig) at Zalung in Yangsho Bongrateng.[1207] When his umbilical cord was cut, eight verses of the sacred doctrine resounded. One day, while he lay in his bed, he levitated about two cubits into the air, and steam wafted up. Not long after his birth, he began to speak. To his mother, he said, "When I had been practicing the discipline of awareness in India, I went to Sosadvīpa, and even though the heretical ḍākinī Kauṇapeśvarī {589} made obstacles, it seemed that I lacked the perception of death. Instead, I manifested in Akaniṣṭha and requested the sacred doctrine in the presence of Vairocana, assuming the guise of a bodhisattva." Vairocana foreordained, "During a powerful and auspicious phase of the teaching, you will become the foremost in the retinue of the lord of refuge, Śākyasiṃha. Since this portends the Land of Snows, you should ride the horse of pure aspiration!" The bodhisattvas who were present concurred. In a celestial mansion of crystal, on the left side, an eight-petal lotus appeared, surrounded by the eight female deities headed by Gaurī, and at its center it seemed that I was seated in the anthers of a sixteen-petal white udumbara flower. At that moment, I swooned in the union of bliss and emptiness. Many women were making offerings, lamas were teaching the sacred doctrine, I myself was teaching, and that flower appeared at the center of a great lake. I took birth, thinking that was awesome.

The father went to one Rakton to request a name for the child, but on the way a sound was heard from the sky, proclaiming "His name is Konchok Se!"[1208] So he was given that name. In 1254 (wood male tiger), actually in his fourth year, his parents brought him to U. On the way, the child, knowing all languages, taught the sacred doctrine to horses in the language of horses. He had a vision of Hevajra with garuḍa wings. One night, seven ḍākinīs asked him about many terms, and by way of reply,[1209] he composed in the form of a spiritual song *The Ancient Path of Purification*.[1210] When he reached his fifth year, his maternal uncle Sonam Pel met him as a five-year-old and immediately said, "Is he Prajñāgomin?"

In childhood play, he poured a cupped handful of hot ashes, {590} and by squeezing them with his hands, they became cold like water. When many horsemen were racing, by giving them a gift, there were none that could be harmed, and they entered into his service. He conferred blessings in the place called Utse Ganglha Rolsa in Setsa,[1211] and he could retain in his mind verses of the sacred doctrine that had been spoken only once. Starting from then, he acquired the power of unforgettable retention and held sacred songs in mind. He imparted five oral instructions concerning Mahākāruṇika in the form Ocean of Attributes and on Hayagrīva, and so forth, which he had actually been granted by the meditational deities in his former lives.

When the lama turned his intention toward liberation, wondrous signs manifested, indicating that he had been protected from obstacles. Henceforth, in order to simplify his elaborate modes of emanational play, Sangye On summarized them in verse, the salient points of which I shall repeat:[1212]

The lord-protector and perfect buddha Taklungpa
Manifestly revealed his visage and I was pierced by his oral teachings.

On Mount Potālaka in the south,
The deity Mahākāruṇika then gave instruction.
He playfully turned a gorge into an abyss.
My body hovered in space and descended slowly.[1213]

On the surface of the cliff of Gyawodong,[1214]
The natural image of glorious Aśvottama was indistinct.
Through subsequent prayer it appeared as if drawn.
For three days, there was a profusion of rainbows and light rays,
And these were arrayed with lotuses
As an antidote for spirits of anger and attachment.
There was a treasure consisting of eighteen ogre skulls
And this six-syllable mantra, carved by a skilled minister.

And it was said of him,

Knowing covert matters, he spoke of them.
Though he could naturally and effortlessly
Write and recite many scripts,
He trained his playmates
And, unknown to others,
Secretly bestowed instruction upon them.[1215] {591}

His body, swollen and vacuous, vanished in water
And emerged from solid grassland to the rear.[1216]

He threw a sheep's stomach, bloated with air, into the river,
And upon it, he sat in the adamantine posture and stood in the posture of equipoise.

Consequently, he cut and scattered riverside boulders like dough.
With a finger snap, he could reverse the river's flow
And walk wherever he wished.[1217]

When the villagers of Khongdrong were making an irrigation ditch,
He churned the waters and offered a handful to the female king spirit.
When someone sought to accuse him of being a fraudster,
He seized that person by the hand, threw him afar,
And paralyzed him when he started to get up again.[1218]

With his cupped handful of sacraments and nectar,
He delighted the deities and filled the sky.
He had visions of glorious Pañjaranātha and his retinue.
In the middle story of the local temple,
There was a skillfully executed mural depicting the twelve deeds,
From which he emanated the maṇḍala of the deity Hevajra.
He filled the sky with an inch-size Hevajra.
Nearby the supreme reliquary called Tashi Pelbar,
He had visions of the maṇḍalas of glorious Kālacakra and Black Yamāri.
He said that they came from the skylight aperture via the staircase.

There was a grove of *caragona* bushes,[1219]
In which dwelled a hybrid nāga and *menmo* spirit,[1220]
Which no one could even touch.
Later, he cut them to pieces and uprooted them,
And then the spirit's body emerged from its former lair
In the terrifying form of a weasel
And paid him respectful homage.
It went repeatedly wherever Jetsun was seated.
So when a great fire blazed from that grove of bushes,
And he was nowhere to be seen,
Aso Se[1221] called out to him by name,
And he instantly emerged from within the fiery mass,
But when they touched his body there, it was cool as stone.
He sat in meditative posture in the middle of a spring of water,

And the hood of a snake covered his head,
And he was surrounded by many aquatic creatures. {592}
Aso Se saw him seated with hands in the gesture of teaching the sacred doctrine,
But when others went to look, they saw nothing at all.[1222]

There could be no ill effect when the dust and soil of his footprints
Was placed on curd or wine.[1223]
While six playmates carried him across a flooding stream,
He jumped through the sky by the height of a spear length.[1224]

At the waterfall of Nene Sertang,
He moved like a flash of lightning
And strode across the waterfall.
While all the venerable one's attendants crossed,
The cascading water clearly became motionless,
And with Jochung holding on to his robes,
He went flying across the Tselchu.[1225]

When a crow's nest in the sacred place of Gyawodong
Was disturbed by the children of Khongdrong,
The venerable one carried the nest and the chicks in the sleeves of his robe,
And he climbed a cliff, smooth like the palm of the hand
And steep, as if scaling a ladder.
He carried them up to a lofty cave, a place of safety.
On the way back, extending with his hands the sleeves of his robe,
He flew down, gliding like a bird.
In front of that cliff, at the distance of about an arrow shot,
He alighted slowly, seated in a meditative posture.[1226]

He said that in general, this place will be blessed and respected.
It has, as a representation of buddha body, a self-arising Hayagrīva.
It has, as a representation of buddha speech,
The syllable A in the form of a sacred spring.
It has, as a representation of buddha mind,
The stūpa called Caragona Grass Courtyard.
Because it is set in at the center of these three representations,

The entire environment of glorious Taklung
Was thereby transformed into a sacred place.

An incarnation of Yamartsen offered him
His vital heart mantra, out of fear and faith,
And promised henceforth to do whatever he said.
He was also invited by the deity Genyen Chenpo,
Who offered him fermented curd and natural butter in a beryl bowl. {593}
In return, he gave food and imparted meditative stability,
Such that, it is said, his body and mind were satisfied.

A disciple formerly associated with him,
Whom he said, with clear recall of past and future lives,
Had once been a king bee, came to harm him,[1227]
But by simply raising his ten fingers in that direction,
He impeded that person due to his elaborate power over water.

He said to Jochung, "Do not go outside!"
But he went on a wayward path, fractured his skull,
And suffered pain that was hard to bear.
At that time, the venerable one went there, scattering diverse flowers.
In the sky, he arrayed the eight auspicious symbols,
And not a single one of them fell to the plain.
Due to this wonder, he caused Josung to forget his pain,
And henceforth he had no sharp ache.[1228]
On one occasion, he suddenly approached Josung
And, taking a pill from his mouth with his left hand,
Rubbed it on the wound and pressed it with his palm,
Such that he recovered, without a trace of the wound, and tapped his feet in dance.

Again, on a certain occasion, he sat upon a stone teaching throne
And gathered all the children of Khongdrong.
He wanted to make great offerings and a feast.
He spoke of the liberating deeds of his teacher,
And then he instantly entered meditative equipoise,

Whereupon the sky above was filled with rainbows and with light.
Diverse birds gathered, chirping sweetly,
And he then taught the sacred doctrine,
Speaking many words of prose
And a hundred words of verse.
The earth slightly shook, and there was a tumultuous thunder.
A shower of flowers, divine sacraments, then fell,
Resplendent like the color of pearl.
Unskilled ordinary children beat the drum of service,
Proclaiming him the village mantrin.
And the folk of Gamtangpa made a hundred thousand circumambulations.
"Now go see this spectacle," they said. {594}
"It seems that snow like this is falling!"
Jochung's unbearable faith was enhanced.
Finally he said, "Now, I will offer a feast of molasses!"
He smeared a stone slate with saliva from his tongue.
The taste of it, when licked, was actually of molasses.[1229]

He cast a spell on the point between the eyebrows of his playmate
And left the mark of his fingers behind the ears.
He tested mantra-enchanted saliva on his own body,
And though he was on a main road, no one saw him.
Some people approached where he was invisible and called out to him.

When Jochung's hair ornament was lost in the river,
He thrust a ritual spike of barberry wood this way and that.
He cast a spell upon a cogon grass straw and placed it across the river.
After eddying, it came decisively to a halt.
In the sand below it, they found a small turquoise.[1230]

"You should stay here," he said to Jochung,
"I will look for some playmates!"
In a moment, he arrived with eleven boys and girls
Who resembled local boys and girls.

Assuming the dramatic role of universal monarch and spiritual
mentor,
He taught them innumerable doctrines, profound and vast.
He and his disciple Jochung then went ahead,[1231]
And later, though Jochung watched out for them many times,
Their other playmates did not arrive.
As for all the local boys and girls,
Some were actually staying in their own homes,
And some were just arriving from cattle herding in the hills.
Now the certainty grew within him
That all those playmates were emanations of the venerable lama.[1232]

In the hermitage of glorious Tashi Sapuk,
He received a secret repository of prophecies from the ḍākinīs.
When he brought Lhatsenchok Donden Sonam Pel to maturation
Through the empowerment of the lord-protector Hevajra,
After the lines of the maṇḍala had been completely laid
And they were about to spread the colored sand,
They could not find the sand that had been left behind in the cave.
At that time, Venerable Sangye On said the supporting gnostic
mantra, {595}
And immediately all the distinct lines of the maṇḍala completed
elevated into space
And then descended onto their platform
After the colored sand had been obtained from the cave.
He set up four wooden posts,[1233] accurately measuring one
handspan,
Which filled the valley with fine fragrance,
Such that it was naturally present all through the night.
And when he finally performed the communion feast offering,
The sour wine that entirely filled the small vase
Was actually transformed into nectar, consecrated by Venerable
Sangye On,
And though the offerings continued through the night, it was
endless.
Later, when the residual torma offering was presented,
As before, he inserted into a skull container

Many fruits, each with a hundred savors,
And however much they were enjoyed, they could not be exhausted.[1234]

When the region was smitten by drought[1235] and there was no rainfall,
And all the monks, mantrins, and yogins were afflicted,
He said, "Last night the nāgas arrived and scattered flowers.
This morning four species of nāgas said that
We should now make this offering out of gratitude
In order that Drogon Lama[1236] might protect you
From the fear of the garuḍa bird.
They will offer a queenly rain cloud to me.
Now henceforth rain will come!"
They asked him to describe the form of those nāgas.
Thereupon, the venerable one crushed a handful of river pebbles
And kneaded them into shape, as if they were moist dough.
He also arrayed a cluster of white and black divinatory pebbles.
Jochung brought a skin, resembling an actual snake,
That had been wrinkled on the back with finger nails,
And his father made the gesture of menace.[1237]
Not daring to look, he offered much wine as a bribe,
And that evening there was an unimaginable downpour of rain.[1238]

When Jochung killed a small rabbit,[1239]
He delivered an oral instruction:
Confession of the Six Doors to Rebirth.[1240]
Going into the presence of his mother and her servants,
In order to secretly perform the cremation rite,
The venerable one sat in a meditative posture upon the fire,[1241] {596}
Such that the strength of three persons could not move him,
Even though they tugged the venerable one's hands.
When they had gone, the venerable one arose from meditation.
The force of the fire was still unabated, no different from before.
Even the venerable one's robe was undamaged.
Rainbow lights pierced the place where the ashes of that rabbit were strewn.
He said that this was the last life in which it would have an animal's body.[1242]

Seeing Domjoden making votive images,
While reciting *The Heart Mantra of Dependent Origination*,[1243]
The venerable one placed the mold into clear water
And instantly made many votive images of water,
Which possessed the five rainbow colors,
Most radiant and exquisitely formed.
But when they sought to stretch out toward them,
They could not grasp them with their hands.
When the ripples of the water cleared, they were as before.
They could not be examined anywhere, above or below.
The following day, they were placed in a pool and vanished.[1244]

On one occasion, when there was an epidemic
In the evening of the eighth day of the horse month,
He placed a mold in water, causing it to freeze.
The next day the votive image was brought out and placed in the sun.
Though placed all day in the sun, it could not melt.
When he prayed with his hands together at sunset,
It instantly melted, as if placed on a butter lamp.
Mixing that sort of potion, he sprinkled it at the perimeter of the
village,
And on the day when he threw it at the cattle, the epidemic ceased.[1245]

Again, on one occasion he said,
"The turnips[1246] have been taken by evil spirits!"
That year, all that had been planted were eaten by worms.

Getting up from his bed one night,
He went to look, and the entire valley of Setsa
Appeared as a blazing expanse, forming a single flame.
And within it appeared Venerable Hayagrīva with three faces and
six arms,
His body permeating heaven and earth.
He saw how to draw this deity and other deities,
And immediately thereafter the venerable one instantly drew
Four icons depicting Lord Śākyamuni, Avalokiteśvara, Tārā, and
glorious Atiśa. {597}
The execution was most exquisite.[1247]

He knew all habitations of the three times and their inhabitants
And all the aspirations of individuals, without exception.
Also, once, when he stayed at Podo,
He brought Jochung inside the temple
And revealed to him countless assemblages of deities,
According to the way of Secret Mantra.
He assumed the form of Venerable Hevajra
And transformed himself into many bodhisattvas and buddhas,
Such as the four meditational deities, Cakrasaṃvara, and Guhyasamāja.
Their sizes were the same size as his body.
Then, again, the lama turned back into his own form,
And within the five cakras of his subtle body,
He revealed five celestial palaces, with innumerable deity clusters.

How could we speak of his visions of the deities' visage?
Some have been documented as follows:
In the lake of Gyawodong,
He saw the dancing white form of glorious Hevajra.
At the summit of the hill called Zom,
He saw the red form, with a yellow bowl of wine,
And a green fire pit for burnt offerings.
At the end of a mass of clouds, he saw Nairātmyā
And Avalokiteśvara within a pea-size amulet.
At Kharkokchen, he saw the Newar,[1248]
At Gyawodong he saw Dharmata,
At Godzong, he saw the six-syllable mantra,
And at the meadow of Podo, he saw Vaiśravaṇa.

Also, it was after Guru Padmākara manifested in a blazing, resplendent form,
That his exploits in the profound treasure doctrines ensued.
From the cliff face of Gyawodong, he brought forth seventeen doctrines, like the heart.
In particular, he brought forth *Yamāntaka: Black Slayer of Death*.[1249]
From Godzong Drak, he brought forth thirteen treasures.
From Lumodza, he brought forth a vase.

From Utse Gang Lhayi Rolsa,
Gonpo Rawa Ngalokjong, and so forth,
He brought forth many treasure doctrines.
He said that there were also prophecies that he would extract treasures
From Tsangdrang Lhakhang in Lhasa
And from the cliff of Zhoto Tidro. {598}

For the sake of disciples of the future, this venerable one
Concealed at the great power place of Gyawodong
The doctrinal cycle of The Gathering of the Black Slayer of Death.[1250]
At the summit of Zhungkhen Cliff, he concealed elixir alongside the self-originated stūpa.

As far as the doctrinal cycles of Hevajra and the Black Slayer of Death are concerned,
This became known as the tradition of Jñāna.
As far as his esoteric instructions are concerned,
There is a lineage derived from the region of Lato,
And it may also possibly be widespread in Nepal.
As far as the tantric commentaries are concerned,
In Kham, China, and in U,
His instructions on the female deity Nairātmyā were widespread.
He said that the treasures that he brought forth at Damcho Nubkha
Would be of benefit to the Buddhist teachings and living beings.

He said it was predicted that in the future, in the supreme abode of Akaniṣṭha,
In the presence of Hevajra,
He would become the bodhisattva Lodro Nyingpo,
Taintless, resplendent, and glorious.
He would perfect the conduct of a bodhisattva,
And then in the eastern world system called Indestructible Mirror,
He would attain manifestly perfect buddhahood.
Instantaneously, he would bring to maturation and liberation
An innumerable host of pure retainers.

The lama also said to his father,
"Last night a pleasant fragrance arose at my pillow.
Three young girls appeared
And said, 'The sky farers invite your elder brother!'"
His father said in reply,
"That is a sign that I will depart.
However, as an auspicious circumstance for averting that,
You should send me a cubit-size image in human form made of clay
And adorned with earth of five colors."
So, that year, his health improved.
The following year, he said to his son,
"The body of this old man, this charioteer,
You will have to cremate.
The outlook of the local people will be transformed.
Within this skull of mine, a precious image depicting Hevajra and the syllable A will appear." {599}
Later, on the twenty-ninth day, he passed away.
They did not permit the sacred corpse to be brought from Zhuwateng,
And when it was brought to Menchukha,
The sky was covered with rainbows and lights.
Inconceivable phenomena were seen,
Including the forms of deities and masses of fire.[1251]

After his father passed away, he stayed
For half a month at Setsa.
He covered the entire valley of Sari on foot,
Many adamantine songs of profound importance arose,
And he brought his mother to maturation through the sacred doctrine.

When he placed his vajra and bell in the sky,
In the middle of winter, the supreme wish-granting tree
And the stems of lotus flowers manifested.

He displayed many imprints of his hands and feet
On surfaces of solid stone.

Whenever he needed utensils for communion feasts, offerings,
and so forth,
They became spontaneously present.

When he stayed at Nesertang,
At that time the venerable one could not be found,
Wherever they looked for him.
Of that he said, "I was staying cool to protect myself from the heat!"

He saw a celestial palace in the hollow of a lotus flower
And saw that it was endowed with the defining characteristics.

In the midst of a tent of five lights in the sky,
There was a white syllable A that vanished into the lama.
When they were afraid, he was seated on his bed.
And his single body diffused and absorbed multiple forms.
He even made a mustard seed appear the size of Mount Sumeru.
Such were the countless miraculous powers that he manifested.

In general, among his teachers,
He had gratitude first to these four:
Rinpoche, Jñānatapa, Kuṇḍalī, and Drojorwa.[1252]

In a previous life, in India,
He had been the great paṇḍita Vijayamati.
He had attended upon eighty-five teachers,
The foremost being Nirtikaru.
He had known three hundred and five tantric commentaries,
Including those on Hevajra and the Slayer of Death.
All of these were clear in his present mind.
So he said to his maternal uncle, Sonam Pelwa,
Having had his preferred deities actually manifest their visages to him
In the course of his previous life. {600}
And here, in this present life, he brought them forth
For the most part as spiritual revelations.[1253]

His teacher, the supreme exemplary incarnation
Named glorious Jñānatapa,

Was a peerless great accomplished master of India
Who appeared in order to deliver the approaches of the sacred doctrine.[1254]
His father was Candramati, of the royal class,
In the city of Thaga, in Bengal,
A land in the east of India,
And his mother was named Bimanā.
In her womb he appeared as a child, holding a sword,
And reciting *The Litany of the Names of Mañjuśrī*,
Which could be clearly heard outside.
The father knew him to be an incarnation.
He trained in the eighteen fields of classical learning
And assumed the self-originating adamantine reality of pristine cognition.
Having attended upon many learned and accomplished masters of India and Nepal,
He knew all the sūtras, tantras, and treatises, without exception.
The supreme lineage holder of Tilopā and Nāropā,
Who was named Avagarbha,
Extensively revealed to him the empowerments and esoteric instructions
Of the ocean of the unsurpassed tantras.
He attained all the supreme and common accomplishments,
And was given the secret name Lilāvajra.
He traveled to the Land of Snows
And went via Lhasa to Lungsho.
At Setsa he met Venerable Sangye On,
Who gave him some food and drink to share
And medicine to ward off hunger.
When they met again at Taklung,
He conferred upon the venerable one seven ordinary oral instructions,
Reciting them, without a text.[1255]
After mastering excellently the ocean of Secret Mantra,
The venerable one made an occasional study of minor oral instructions.[1256]

Having been offered three different sorts of auspicious sacrament,
Jñānatapa then set out temporarily for Nepal.[1257]

One night, while sleeping in Kathmandu,
He received a clear authentic prophetic declaration
That he would propagate the teachings on
Hevajra, the Black Slayer of Death, and so forth
Here in this land of Tibet.
Returning directly to Tibet,
He found the venerable one asleep at Setsa.
At daybreak, he was aroused by a disembodied voice {601}
Saying, "Get up immediately and go to the roof!"
In a vision, he saw a yogin in the grassland below,
Beckoning him with a cloth.
Going there, they had a joyous meeting.
Also, by comparing the former prophecies,
They found that the circumstances were appropriate.
In the hermitage of Tashi Sapuk,
The venerable one then received, in the manner of a vase filled to the brim,
The complete empowerments, transmissions, and esoteric instructions
Pertaining to four primary meditational deities:
Hevajra, Black Slayer of Death, Pañjaranātha,
And Vaiśravaṇa in the form Norbu Sampel,
And also all the inconceivable and wondrous teachings that he possessed.[1258]

From the ḍākinī of pristine cognition, Kuṇḍalī,
He also received instruction on the generation and perfection stages of Nairātmyā.[1259]

After staying there for two full years,
Jñānatapa then again departed for the Sublime Land of India.

Then, when Venerable Sangye On was in his twelfth year, in 1262 (water male dog), on the eighth day of the waxing half of the month of flower offerings,[1260] he received the mendicant ordination from Tangkarwa acting as monastic preceptor, Khen Onpa acting as master of ceremonies, and a quorum of seven faithful monks.[1261] Choku Sangye Yarjon himself inscribed his ordination name on the board, and the name Drakpa Pel Ozer Zangpo was conferred upon him. Also during these events, the monastic preceptor had a vision of glorious Phakmodrupa. The attendant Gomtsul and Gompa Taklo saw him as Sangye Yarjon. A lay visitor saw him as Hayagrīva. A visitor from Tsang saw him as Four-Armed Avalokiteśvara. A grandson of Hor Khangpa Gyelwa saw him as the transcendent lord Buddha. Onpo Jungseng saw him as the elder Aṅgita. {602} In addition, there were many who saw the sixteen elders. Denchungwa Chudo saw him as Red Avalokiteśvara, holding a vase. Again the monastic preceptor saw him as Hevajra, and there were a great many who saw him as Avalokiteśvara. Moreover, there were those to whom he appeared with a crown protuberance on his head, with his body in the form of a golden stūpa, and with the third eye. Diverse rays of light were perceived being diffused from his body, and there were some who could never see him even though he was actually present. Such events were innumerable.

The night before Drakpa Pel Ozer Zangpo (a.k.a. Sangye On) went to receive the mendicant ordination, the monks and meditators in common dreamed that tomorrow a paṇḍita who would bless the northern regions would appear, that two transcendent lord buddhas would manifest in the White Temple of the Layel Courtyard, teaching the sacred doctrine, and vanishing into one another (such that their luminosity would fill the region), that a banner would proclaim that Choje Taklungpa had arrived, and that Sangye On was seated in the lap of Rinpoche Kuyalwa.

In the perception of other disciples, Sangye On studied the entire secret repository of buddha mind, which was the immaculate aural lineage descended from his precious predecessor, and he seemed to undertake the essentials of practice. Great meditators offered him their signs of experiential cultivation, requested him to dispel obstacles, and so forth. Great upholders of the piṭakas, such as Geshe Monlam Senge and the nephew of Se Chilpuwa also questioned him about the essential points of the scriptures.[1262]

When he consecrated representations of buddha body, speech, and mind, there were a great many flowers that manifested of their own accord. Simply on account of him preparing an obstacle-removing torma, there was a cast image that exclaimed "Ouch!" And then, when he scattered mustard seeds of exorcism, ten million of them indeed appeared owing to his words of censure. {603} When he stayed in a flower meadow in the vicinity of the Phuchu at Taklung, he recited verses for offering flowers, and then as soon as he said the words "*varja puṣpe*," the flowers vanished. When he composed *The Prayer Titled Storehouse of Precious Treasure*,[1263] there was a meditator who thought, "Will such dexterity in speaking not result in mistakes in the composition?" But he said, "You need not fear! There will be no mistakes!"

Knowing that Khenpo Ba was ill and that the time of his death was approaching, while some were writing petitions, questioning this, Sangye On drafted a response and distributed it. The outcomes of all his prognoses came to pass, just as he had predicted. Occurrences such as these were innumerable.

On those occasions, too, he acquired representations of buddha body, speech, and mind and a multitude of assorted artifacts that were perfectly consecrated. By his own hand, he prepared the best canvas[1264] and drew an icon depicting glorious Phakmodrupa,[1265] which he consecrated a hundred times. On seeing this icon, which became the meditative commitment of Geshe Mok Chokyi Lodro,[1266] it appeared as if the attributes present in the mind of glorious Taklungpa the Great were born within him.[1267]

When Rajak Rinla commissioned an image of Rinpoche, Sangye On himself performed the consecration. Its sacred artifacts included a stūpa containing hair from the head of Venerable Mila Repa, a tooth relic of Venerable Mila Repa, two vase icons of Hevajra, which had been the meditative commitments of Nāropā and Serlingpa, an upright icon of Dīpaṃkara, which had been consecrated by Nāgārjuna, and a vajra that had been the hand emblem of master Padma.[1268]

On the eighth day of the month of Pauṣya in 1270 (iron male horse), in his twentieth year, he received the full monastic ordination in the midst of a quorum of five: Galungpa as monastic preceptor, Khen Onpa as master of ceremonies, Bagompa Yeshe Gonpo as confessor, and the faithful monks Gelong Gendun Kyab and Gompa Lodro Pel.[1269] {604}

He then received the transmitted teachings of empowerment, the transmitted teachings of exegesis, and the transmitted teachings of esoteric instruction from both Dzington Neljor Gawei Dorje and one known as Lopon Gompa, who was a disciple of Ngok residing at Merge Monastery, the seat of Lama Chokro (Chokyi Gyeltsen). Moreover, he also received many empowerments, transmissions, and esoteric instructions from Hrulchungwa, Ling Gongwa, Ukarwa, and others.[1270]

In 1272 (water male monkey), at the time when Choku Sangye Yarjon was about to pass away into the taintless expanse, he bestowed upon Sangye On the representative artifacts, with which he had a connection and which he was to keep safe. In order that the precious teaching of the lineage of practice might spread, triumph, and long endure in all directions, times, and circumstances, he gave Sangye On oral advice, made predictions concerning him, and appointed him as regent. He did likewise to his other nephew Maṅgalaguru. Afterward, he performed an elaborate cremation ceremony. During that same monkey year (1272), when he was in his twenty-second year, he assumed the monastic seat. He taught the profound and vast sacred doctrine. An inconceivable auspicious enthronement ceremony was held. He rendered the regulations of Choje Kuyalwa, the charter of the monastic assembly, and all the disciplinary rules of the monastery exactly as they had been in the time of his predecessors, father and sons.[1271]

On those occasions, it was as if he had held the neck of a brass vase filled with water and, turning it upside down, poured out the water so that it, as it were, reached the stomachs of the disciples who observed his commitments. When he dispelled the obscurations of others concerning the oral teachings, a ritual doughball belonging to the attendant fell to the ground, and in its place, at the side of the throne, there appeared a pebble, which split in two. Rubbing them, he made fermented balls,[1272] {605} one of which he placed on the torma plate, and the other he gave to a meditator.

To those who requested to make an image of him, he said, "Make images of Śākyamuni, Avalokiteśvara, and the peerless Dakpo Lharje," the point being that he was indivisible from them.

Sangye On was a great scholar who had exhausted the stains of ignorance with respect to all things. To Khenpo Tangsakpa and others, he excellently taught *The Great Commentary on Madhyamaka.*[1273] For the benefit of others, as well, he gave many teachings, including *Clarifying Lamp: A Commentary on the Guhyasamāja.*[1274] On one occasion, a yogin[1275] offered him a set of the eight offering receptacles fashioned of stone, which were said to have been consecrated by the great brahmin Saraha and sublime Nāgārjuna, along with a footprint from the Mahābodhi and volumes of Sanskrit manuscripts. Since he had authority over the consecration of the three reliquaries of Choje Rinpoche (Taklungpa the Great), father and sons, by means of the auspicious circumstances of his excellent consecrations, he performed in the correct manner the consecration of all the sacred representations here in Taklung, headed by the Tashi Pelbar Stūpa. Also, although he was an emanation resembling Lama Zhang,[1276] he refused three times to undertake the casting[1277] of the head of Mahākāla in the form Lhachen Pelbar.[1278] He said that afterward he did undertake the consecration by bringing a vase that was said to have been the personal vase of Choje Rinpoche Taklung Tangpa and then throwing it into the mold.

During the nights, he went on a walkabout, and in a place where the hot ashes of the communal kitchen were spread out, he would say to his attendant, "Pass that way over the ashes! Pass this way over the ashes!" His shoes were not burned, let alone his feet.

When someone visited Rinpoche (Sangye On), he said that he saw him in the form of a golden stūpa, whereupon Rinpoche replied, "I have mastered the wind of the earth element." When it seemed to Gomye that his lungs and heart were bursting from his fontanelle, he asked him, "Since I am ill, should I not cultivate the control of energy channels and winds?" {606} "There will be no fault," he replied. "You should cultivate the Inner Heat by applying these yogic exercises to the vital points of your body in the morning and at daybreak. Then, in the evening and at twilight, you should cultivate the Great Seal and the Illusory Body! For a period of one month, you should focus on the element water!" By doing as advised, realization arose within him. When one Tsangnyak said that he wanted to cry out freely, Sangye One replied, "It is so because your meditation belt is short!" By slightly lengthening it, he recovered. Apart from such examples, there are countless instances of him measurably dispelling obstacles and bringing forth spiritual success.

In the summer of that year, when he assumed the monastic seat, he constructed the Reliquary Chapel of the Kumbum Lhoma in the form of a stūpa symbolizing the great enlightenment, along with its roof.[1279] The measurements and design were prepared by Geshe Zhangton. It was filled with relics, above all with the sacred bones and pearl relics of Choku Sangye Yarjon, which had the appropriate defining characteristics. The base of the Tashi Pelbar Reliquary was also leaking, but he undertook all sorts of repairs. Through this peerless consecration, perfect in its attributes, he gathered together the blessings of all the buddhas and established the Buddhist teaching and all beings in spiritual and temporal well-being, mitigating disasters.

In his twenty-third year, on the eighth day of the sheep month in 1273 (water female bird), alongside the Kumbum Jangma, he spread out the sleeves of his robe and prayed. Thereupon, a second tooth relic unimpededly issued from the Buddha's tooth relic, within the stūpa,[1280] the reliquary, and so forth, taking the form of a multiplying bone relic. Bringing all the wondrous relics such as these that alighted and carrying a continuous supply of consecrated grain from the storerooms and a continuous flame from the Naktsang Chenmo, he set out in the direction of Kham. {607} He stayed for about six months in the vicinity of Podo. There, too, his body was uncontaminated. He could seize with his bare hand the blade of a fine knife, and even though it broke, his hand was unharmed. Whatever teachings he was asked to give—whether on Kadam, Pacification, Severance, or dialectics—he could impart them without impediment.

He then struck camp on the eleventh day of the mouse month. At Ser in Shak, an envoy of the Sakyapa arrived, but owing to Sangye On's conduct of yogic discipline, the envoy was unable to cross the river. Instead, he asked Sangye On to send across some counterfeit representations to placate the people of Taklung, but he did not do so. He denied that request, saying, "From that point on, there would be no confidence in either the relics of Upper or Lower Taklung!" When the envoy repeated that request, he then said, "Lama Rinpoche (Sangye Yarjon) entrusted this seat of the Kagyu tradition to me. Wherever I stay, that will be my seat. As long as my life faculties endure, I will not entrust these sacred representations, with which I have a connection and which I am to keep safe, to anyone at all!"[1281]

Then Sangye On fell ill, such that everyone outside and inside his entourage was afraid. The official returned to Sakya via Taklung, and the master and his disciples then prepared the road ahead to Aryo. When they arrived at Ngitang on the way from Labzhi to Jakto, there were a hundred precious children mounted upon a hundred fine horses from Rakshi. The first of these to make offerings was Pongom Tashi Ozer.[1282]

Sangye On conferred maturational empowerments and liberating guidance by means of the sacred doctrine on all beings wherever he encountered them. He held discussions with the people of Yelpa, and they offered the monastery of Yelpa Cave to him, with the request that he stay there. He went there, saying he could not stay forever, but remained for about one summer and winter. The people of Chambu also invited him to their monastery. {608} They offered him a handbell of Jowo Atiśa and so forth. Then, he returned to the Yelpa Cave.[1283]

He acquired the staff of glorious Phakmodrupa, the bone ornaments of Kaṇakaśrī, a self-originating footprint of glorious Taklungpa the Great, a painted scroll that Venerable Phakmodrupa had consecrated a hundred times with his own hand, a monastic robe of the Sugata, and a Lotus-Mound Stūpa into which he inserted the sacred tooth relic and so forth.[1284] He made a thumb imprint on a stone, and at Drugu in Tsawagang, he impressed his footprint in stone.[1285]

the *kapāla* of the master Śāntarakṣita and other relics that glorious Taklungpa the Great had offered to Jetsun Drakpa Gyeltsen, and these were dispatched. Consequently, he said that there were astonishing teachings that appeared to him in his dreams and that he gave him pills of nectar and so forth. During the great offering ceremonies of Sonam Tsemo and Chakna Dorje, and so forth, Chogyel Phakpa had Sangye On take his seat at the head of the row.[1287] He traveled on to Markham, covering most of the area around lower Le, including Muru Gonpa and Lingji. At Usik, he acquired a speaking image of glorious Taklungpa the Great.[1288]

While staying at the white spring in the Yelpa Cave, while he was walking about, a large impression of his naked footprint appeared on the Pedraktek boulder. {610} He stayed here and there, but even those who were received at his camp did not see him. On the other hand, while he was traveling in the mountains, some people would indeed see him seated in a sleeping tent.

Then, in 1276 (fire male mouse), Sangye On reached Chamlakha. In his twenty-seventh year, during the first month of 1277 (fire female ox), he arrived in the region of Yisho.[1289] There, he recited the auspicious verses of *The Auspicious Flower Garland*[1290] at Riwoche, king of mountains, the auspicious verses of Vajrasattva at Lhajatang plain to the east, the auspicious verses of Vajrasūrya at Gyelmo Richuk to the south, the auspicious verses of Padmendra at Jamtang plain to the west, and the auspicious verses of Kubera, king of the seven horses, at Tatak Khorbu to the north.[1291]

On the eighth day of that month, he pitched his tent at Nedomtang, which is nowadays the site of a corral for hybrid cattle. He tamed the geomantic site, protected it from obstacles, consecrated it, and so forth. Then, on the third day of the dragon month, he began the construction of the Yang Gon monastery. Under his direction, the foundation stones of the residence were laid.[1292] Two four-pillar temples, one six-pillar temple, the throne room, and the Protector Chapel were excellently built. His attendants from Taklung and large numbers of monks who assembled from all regions of Dokham established many separate monastic residences, and the monastery flourished greatly.

From 1283 (water female sheep), Sangye On set about constructing the sacred representations that were his meditative commitments. These peerless artifacts included a silver image of Vajradhara, surrounded by the eighty-four great accomplished masters; silver images of the supreme incarnation Kuyalwa Rinchen Gonpo and Choku Sangye Yarjon, surrounded by twenty thousand lineage holders of the Kagyu and Great Seal traditions and countless meditational deities; the silver reliquary containing the sacred relics of Choku Sangye Yarjon; the Great Golden Stūpa called Tashi Pelgyi Lhunpo Obar; {611} Hevajra holding weapons,[1293] Cakrasaṃvara with four faces and twelve arms, according to the tradition of Lūipa; and the complete Kangyur inscribed in gold on parchment, with syllables that were elegantly arranged and correctly spelled,[1294] along with the wooden boards, book ties, and cloth covers.[1295]

In 1285 (wood female bird), he constructed the image of Śākyamuni in the form Great Enlightenment, and the large silver image of Choku Sangye Yarjon called Auspicious Ornament of the World. Within them, he inserted as sacred relics a complete manuscript of the Kangyur inscribed on paper scrolls in gold and silver. This project was excellently completed and the consecration performed in 1288 (earth male mouse). The artisans, headed by Pon Sopo, were delighted with the donations that were made.[1296]

On many occasions, Sangye On traveled at the invitation of the disciples who were in his entourage to engender a glorious field of merit on their behalf. The female chieftain Yaga Tahu erected the tented awning on the roof of the palace. Champhu Ponchen offered various artifacts including the headdress of King Indrabhūti. All the monastic bodies of Dokham respectfully venerated him and held him to be supreme among the fields of offering.[1297]

As far as the teaching of the practice lineage is concerned, he rendered it like the sunrise at dawn. During that period, he also assumed the teaching throne at Zheda. When some three thousand monastic and laypeople gathered en masse to hear the sacred doctrine, they rushed into the market accompanied by the horses and cattle of those who followed to present offerings, but Rinpoche (Sangye On) performed a hand gesture, ensuring that even their skin was not grazed. Khenpo Darzhon offered him a stone image depicting Tārā that had been the meditative commitment of the spiritual teacher Vajrāsana.

There were also countless occasions when he spoke with prescience. Prior to building the monastery, he said to Tashi Senge, "Something will happen to you before you reach yonder fields!" {612} Consequently, while that person was loading the outer and inner sacks [onto the pack animals], a falling package struck his leg. And once, he said to Gompa Zhondar, "You should take care on the ice!" Consequently, that person's horse slipped on the ice, and he injured his head.

On yet another occasion he said, "All the stacked possessions of the retreatants should be moved together!" When they had moved them some distance, a large falling rock was found in the place where they had previously been.

One day, he said to Rinchen Sherab, "Come here!" In the place where he had been, a falling rock then struck his felt tent. And when he did not like the rear of the cattle corral being so close to the cliff, he said, "Move it right now!" On the evening after they had moved it, the cliff collapsed. A falling rock directly hit his grass hermitage, but he recited a mantra and made certain hand gestures so that it could be carried away.

When he said to someone else, "You are probably not going on this date!" the concerned person passed away at that very time. When certain people had their time of death determined by astrologers, diviners, physicians, and the like, and the indications of impending death had arisen, he would confer oral instructions for prolonging the lifespan, so that through experiential cultivation, they would recover.

Sangye On could make a dry hot spring reemerge by making tormas, and when earthquakes repeatedly occurred, he could stop them by making tormas. When a monkey was staying behind the hermitage of a certain geshe and throwing rocks down, he caused the monkey to flee away by making tormas. Moreover, simply by making a torma, he could avert misfortune, benefit the populace, cut off hailstones,[1298] and bring rain to places afflicted by drought. Even when it was estimated that negative omens were appearing in the world, he ensured that no harm came. When he heard that beings were afflicted by severe ailments, simply by directing his enlightened intention toward them, he could alleviate them immeasurably. When he simply gave guidance to those afflicted by demonic possession who requested his blessing, they would instantly recover upon seeing his wrathful body or seeing his fiery conflagration, and so forth. {613}

When Saṅgaśrī, a paṇḍita from Vajrāsana and a yogin of Tāmradvīpa named Varamati, and so forth, met him, he could speak the sacred doctrine in the languages of India and Tāmradvīpa. One named the yogin Suprahipa, whose body could not sink in water, came to meet him and said, "I will practice the extracting of elixir for twelve days!" So he stayed in retreat, but when five days had passed, Sangye On sent an attendant to spy on him, and he had almost died. Rinpoche Sangye On then performed certain yogic exercises and auspicious remedies, whereupon he recovered. Buddhasena, king of Vajrāsana, then sent Paṇḍita Gotaṃśrī with two servants, carrying offerings that included a shimmering bone relic of the Tathāgata's index finger, a handprint of Mahābodhi, and a petition written in Sanskrit.

To those who spoke dissimilar languages, he could teach the sacred doctrine in their own distinct languages. There was no one of any country whose language he did not know how to speak. When he had visions of the visage of Mahākāruṇika and Venerable Tārā, he composed innumerable teachings of pure vision, including *The Oral Instruction of Thirty-Three Aspects: Carrying Appearances on the Path*[1299] and *The Attainment of the Sacred Syllable HŪṂ*,[1300] a few of which he propagated among his fortunate disciples. For the most part, he instructed Kuzhang Rinpoche Lhei Tsunpa in the aural lineage.

In general, Sangye On turned the wheel of the profound and extensive sacred doctrine without interruption, so that two-thirds of Jambudvīpa was filled with his realized students. His commonly known compositions, the transmission of which is extant until the present,[1301] sufficed to fill fourteen volumes. As for the teachings imparted to him face-to-face by his preferred deities in the course of his former lives and during this very lifetime, as well as {614} the profound doctrines that he brought forth as spiritual revelations, most of these were untimely in terms of their auspicious inauguration and propagation, but some were inserted within stūpas and the like. It is said that some of them even now are preserved in the libraries of Taklung Lower Plain, sewn in leather casing and undamaged.

On one occasion, Sangye On said to Gomtsul, "Last night I had a dream." Pongom Tashi Ozer then asked him the circumstances, and on being asked insistently, he replied, "I wondered where this doctrinal lineage of mine would find its suitable repository, and on inspecting the whole of the world, it did not appear to be anyone other than an unkempt nephew in this locality who has the name of Tashi Gyeltsen. He is one blessed by the spiritual heroes and ḍākinīs. Last night, I entrusted the doctrinal lineage to him." "Is there not a difference between speaking to him in a dream and speaking to him in actuality?" he was asked. "When consecrating sacred representations," he replied, "It's necessary to secure great power with respect to the being of pristine cognition. In this context too, since I prayed to the spiritual teachers and ḍākinīs, there was no difference whether he was actually present or not."[1302]

In addition, he appointed a well-known preceptor of Tangkya and sealed a document stating, "It will be pointless if my monastic seat should fall to Onpo Drakpa!"[1303] Then, after some years had passed, Rinpoche Sangye

On said, "If I send these sacred representations and the monks to Taklung Upper Plain, I will guide some two hundred yogins, and then if I go to Khawa Karpo or Mount Kailash, I will live a long life and also be of benefit to the Buddhist teaching. My reputation will equal space, and I will have an entourage of five hundred cotton-clad yogins. {615} On the other hand, if I stay here, I will not live long." Thereupon, Gomtsul asked him not to talk in that manner, saying, "Since Lama Rinpoche possesses those sacred representations with which he has a connection, please establish that as the auspicious circumstance for your long life!" Sangye On replied, "If I sustain the pledge concerning those sacred representations with which I have a connection, they will be maintained here, but the merit of sentient beings will be small. It will be greater as a result of not sustaining that pledge!" "We will do as you say by all means!" said Gomtsul. "Please fulfill that pledge!" Thereupon Sangye On replied, "Do not buy a wooden box for storing grain, and do not buy a black horse! Do not bring petitions inviting me to other places! Do not send Indian yogins to meet me! I am staying in strict retreat for three years! If you maintain these four pledges for the duration of the retreat, your purpose will be fulfilled!"[1304]

Sangye On then entered into retreat. After one year had passed, however, Gompa Jong secretly bought a box for storing grain, and since he had no suitable horse to ride, he bought a fine black horse from Khyungpo. Insistent invitations were directed toward the meditation community requesting permission to come to meet him, and these were repeated three times, after which he finally relented. Eleven ācāryas, each offering a golden *sang* as a gift, came to meet him and asked many questions in the Indian language, saying, "We have come from India in fear of the Turuṣka army. In order to avert that, we have come to invite Lama Rinpoche. Please consent to travel there now!"[1305]

Thereafter, no one knew where he went from the Layel Courtyard. He summoned the meditators and steward into his presence and then said, "Last year when I was about to depart for Khawa Karpo or Mount Kailash, I stayed on, and you said you could maintain four pledges concerning the sacred representations with which I have a connection. {616} Now, I must depart for another pure land. You should paint that grain box with red ocher and place this body of mine inside it!" Thereupon, they all gathered in the Protector Chapel and cried. Rinpoche came to the White Temple and gave them teachings on the setting of the mind on enlightenment and union with the guru. They asked, "From this day on, what sacred doctrine should we request?"[1306] "Send a message to the disciples in other places!" he replied. "You yourselves are not to blame!"[1307]

Sangye On then turned the doctrinal wheel extensively on behalf of the resident and visiting monks, and there were a great many who indeed offered signs of realization without having meditated. On the third day of the fourth month, there was a rain of flowers. On the third day of the sixth month, he said, "Onpo of the Taklungpa tradition is going to be renowned." Although that statement was intentional, they did not understand. He gave detailed advice to Gomtsul concerning the size of the pyre, of how the offerings should be made, and so forth.[1308]

Then, on the first day of the ninth month, the conch was blown and the congregation arrived. He gave teachings on the profound and extensive doctrine, and he imparted inconceivable words of advice. On the morning of the second day, a group including his attendants, the evening tea-maker Gandhewa, and the cattle herder were sent into his presence, and he said to them, "I look toward the teaching of the sacred doctrine and the oral instructions. You who experientially cultivate it are most industrious. Surely this is my final piece of advice." On the morning of the third day, he met the retreatants and gave them extensive advice concerning the sacred doctrine. After eating, he sat in his room. To the three attendants who were present, he said, "At the time when I came here into the world, I arrived assuming the appearance of a heruka. {617} Now, as I am about to depart this world, I will depart, assuming the appearance of a heruka. Bring the six ornaments here!" He sent those three out the door and locked it, but they looked through the gap in the door. He donned the six ornaments on his body, and seated on his throne, he assumed the adamantine posture. Holding the vajra and bell in his two hands, he crossed them at his heart, and with his eyes fixed, he sat in meditation. After a while, both of his eyes dissolved inwardly, the vajra and bell fell into his lap, and his body rested against the back screen as a support. At teatime on the third day of the ninth month of 1296 (fire male monkey), in his forty-sixth year, he passed away into the immaculate field of the eastern direction. Immediately, the earth quaked and emitted a mighty rumbling. All the retreatants came out, and all the monks assembled. They made inconceivable offerings and prayers. From the sixth day after his passing, the sacred corpse was displayed in public. Then, on the tenth day of that month, it was placed on the funeral pyre. All the cardinal and intermediate directions were densely filled with clouds of offering. The preceptor Galungpa acted as the chant master. The preceptors, masters, and spiritual mentors presented their funerary offerings. When they kindled the pyre, at first it was somewhat difficult for the fire to burn. Then, Kuzhang Rinpoche arrived and prayed, whereupon a self-originating flame instantly and directly emerged from the heart of the sacred corpse and engulfed the pyre, producing *śarīraṃ* relics[1309] marked in the center with the syllable HAṂ. It is said that the heart, tongue, and eyes were fused together, that pearl relics permeating the tent of the funerary smoke poured down in a rain of five colors, that the miscellaneous pearl relics formed from the white and red generative fluids that appeared were distributed among the thousand monks, {618} and that, on that basis, three thousand six hundred icons were later fashioned of gold, silver, copper, brass, sandalwood, soft stone, and so forth. The wondrous indications that manifested were indescribable. At Vajrāsana in India, Wutai Shan in China, and at all the monastic seats of the Kagyu lineage, headed by Taklung, and in all the monasteries of Ngari, Utsang, and Dokham headed by glorious Sakya, offerings were presented, and communal alms bountifully distributed. It was hard to estimate the offerings that were presented to the congregation of monks and laymen who gathered in that very place (Riwoche). Under the direction of Kuzhang Rinpoche Sonam Pel, the Eastern Stūpa was constructed, and sealed manuscripts inserted within it, surrounding the sacred bone relics, ashes, and other items. A gilded "lotus-mound" reliquary was also commissioned.[1310]

At that time, the bodhisattva Rangjung Dorje[1311] sent an edict in the form of a prophetic declaration to the monks and patrons of Riwoche, which read, "This Rinpoche of yours has been installed in a golden palanquin by four ḍākinīs of pristine cognition with golden earrings. Borne through the sky, he arrived at Vajrāsana as an ally against the Turuṣka army. After taming the hosts of that army, in the place called Padmavat, a city of eastern India, he is now teaching the sacred doctrine called the Great Seal to a retinue of seven hundred thousand. In his wake, projecting the array of his own incarnations, there will appear a great many descendants, articulate and erudite, endowed with loyalty, purity, high hairline, distinct eyebrows, and noble complexion. You should obtain sustenance without partiality or bias, {619} and this monastic seat will flourish with good auspices and glory as an ornament of Jambudvīpa!"

Although Onpo Drakpa was appointed to the monastic seat, due to the fault of having infringed the lama's previous injunction, he greatly incurred the enmity of the protector deities, in consequence of which it is said that a party headed by Pon Gom Tashi Ozer was sent to U to invite Choku Orgyen Gonpo.[1312]

The Disciples of Sangye On Drakpa Pel

Foremost among all the disciples of Venerable Sangye On was Kuzhang Rinpoche (Sonam Pel), who acquired the power of unforgettable retention, and whom Ma Khandro said was an "upholder of the spiritual songs of prophetic declaration." He was the youngest of the four sons of Tsepo Shomarasa and Jowo Amchok. From his fifth year, he met Venerable Sangye On and served him inseparably, like a shadow that follows the body. He even traveled to Kham to attend upon him. He built the residence at Riwoche and was appointed as senior lama. Venerable Sangye On even said to him, "You perform the maturational empowerments, and I will undertake the liberating guidance." It seems that as a lay practitioner, he had the name Sonam Pel, and that later on, after receiving the mendicant ordination, he was called Kunga Pel.

In the manner of a vase filled to the brim, Sonam Pel was given all the profound doctrines associated with the many dissimilar lineages and traditions that Venerable Sangye On possessed. All of these, without exception, he in turn offered to Choku Orgyen Gonpo, so that the latter was appointed Lord of the Sacred Doctrine. Thereafter, Kuzhang (Rinpoche Sonam Pel) resided in the mountain retreat nearby the great monastery of Riwoche, and he passed away there.

Onpo Lha Wangchuk Pel was a disciple of both the uncle and nephew. {620} He constructed the reliquary of Khuwolha,[1313] the size of the Jowo image of U, along with its throne and back screen, and placed it within the Central Hall. His disciples were Onpo Lha Lodro Pel, Drakpa Pel, and Lhapel Zangwa, the last of whom built the monastery of Ganden in Bubordob. From him, it is said that some transmissions of the On lineage also originated.

Gangchung Repa Tsultrim Gyeltsen was mentioned in *The Spiritual Song of the Dzong*[1314] as The Second of the Three Cotton-Clad Yogins. He traveled to Markham and had a large number of disciples. His disciple Dzeng Re was also nurtured mainly by the oral instructions of Venerable Sangye On himself. From him, there were many sublineages that successively emerged, so that his service to the monastic seat of Riwoche was exceedingly great.

There was one Gompa Lodro Pel with hair wrapped in a turban who requested him to provide relics for insertion in a representative image. Sangye On replied, "That will not do!" and threw them out of the window. Searching for them, they could not be found. Then, when the time came to install the icon, after the consecration of the incantations, those relics appeared in the lap of the dreadlocked Gompa himself, such that he became astonished.

When he went to Kanado, he crossed the river without impediment and placed his foot upon a boulder. In the place where he had sat for a while, there appeared a perfect impression of his naked foot, with its hairlines.

When he went to Trara, there was a fierce local deity named Jowo Drakmar, in whose presence even the great Sakyapa and so forth wore inconspicuous clothing. When he went there and was informed that that was the case, he went on his way saying, "It does not matter!"

When he was returning to the market place of Ba by the back road, a completely pale dust storm arose from the southwest. By pulling the reins slightly, he swiftly made three circuits of the storm, and it subsided as before. Someone went to welcome him there and attend upon him, offering him a sack of honey, but that person could not see his body from the start. Though Sangye On was delivering many teachings, he did not hear them. {609} Again, even though Sangye On granted him the blessing of seeing his visage and hearing his teachings in the place from which the sound was coming, he did not see the lama's body, apart from a pale white light.

Previously, too, when he was residing at Trangtak, someone went to make offerings in the daytime, and although Sangye On was teaching the sacred doctrine, his body could not be seen at all apart from the uppermost third, including the throne back and parasol. When he went to Daryul, a husband and wife couple could hear his teachings, but apart from just that they could not see his body. Such events indeed transpired.

At Kyerka, he met the great lama Chogyel Phakpa. On that occasion, meeting face-to-face, Sangye On offered *The Memorandum on the Path and Its Fruit* that Drogon Phakmodrupa had composed and presented to Venerable Sachen (Kunga Nyingpo) for inspection. Consequently, Chogyel Phakpa said, "Your vajra is placed inside Jose's mouth!" He asked him to conceal the text for a while and placed it in the library, such that it became known as the "library text." And he said, "This should not be revealed while the master Jose is alive!"[1286] and so on. He also made a petition requesting

Repa Tisewa practiced at Mount Kailash. He traveled to Markham, where he founded the monasteries of Rurulu, Sokdong, and so forth. His enlightened activity was extensive. His monasteries and the lineage of his disciples continued into later times.

Repa Lhei Gyeltsen practiced at Lake Namtso. After founding monasteries at Khawa Karpo, Gyadang, and Tromyul, the lineage of his disciples was later interrupted. Repa Khoyo Gyeltsen nurtured his enlightened activity in the lower reaches of Rab Gang. Chakmo Repa built Trer Monastery. These last two also had disciple lineages that were long-lasting. Moreover Tokden Zhenpen Nupa was inconceivable.

May this marvelous narrative, resembling the blubber of a great whale,
Insulate from harm all living creatures inhabiting the ocean of
obscurations
Due to afflicted mental states, past actions, and knowable phenomena,
The actual fruition experienced by all sentient beings, equal to space! {621}

Orgyen Gonpo

Homage to the supremely named Donden Orgyen Gonpo,
Who amassed marvelous great temples
Through the authentic magical display of his regency,
Although his essential nature was inseparable from that of the Conqueror!

As for Choku Orgyen Gonpo, it was at the invitation of his parents that Venerable Sangye On had originally traveled to U. At that time, the consort of the patron Dorje Rinchen became pregnant and gave birth to a son. On growing up, Tashi Gyeltsen became accomplished in consciousness transference, "attaching a blade of grass to his head."[1315] He served as an attendant when His Holiness Sakyapa Lachen Chogyel Phakpa was on his return journey from China and traveled to U in his service. He also stayed in Tsang for almost one continuous year. Then, following his marriage to Jetsun Onmo Sangye Bum, he stayed at Shara and other places in Penyul. Sooner or later, he had three sons, of whom the eldest was born at upper Sharatang in 1293 (water female snake).[1316] Many wondrous signs occurred—a symphony of music, the fragrance of incense, a parasol circling directly over his body, and so forth.

The child was placed in the protection of Rakye Drakpa Rinchen Dorje, an actual disciple of Sangye Yarjon who had acquired proficiency in the control of energy channels and winds. The latter had a dream in which a voice said, "This is an emanation of Orgyen Pema. You will have no difficulty protecting him. He should be called Orgyen Gonpo." So he was named accordingly.[1317]

In 1296 (fire male monkey), about the time when Venerable Sangye On passed away, around midnight he arose from his bed and said, "I will survive on horse flesh. I must travel to Kham!" Not long afterward, people arrived to invite him. In his fourth year, {622} he was placed inside a small wooden box. Wearing a sacred text on his head,[1318] he was transported on horseback. He departed from the estate of Sharatang during the twelfth month. His mother escorted him as far as Chak La, where he said to her, "Practice the refuge in this manner!" and bestowed upon her the practice of union with the spiritual teacher and an oral instruction of Nairātmyā. Then she returned home.[1319]

One day, in Lhoto as he arrived following after some people who had gone ahead, he made a gesture with his hand and said, "Don't go that way! We should go on this side!" "They have gone ahead in that direction," his attendant said. "They too will come back here," he replied. They did not find the way and hurried back, arriving late at night.[1320]

Again, one day, he said to his attendants, "Don't dress as travelers or wear ordinary clothes. People will ridicule us!" As they asked, "Who will ridicule us in this empty place?" many people forming a reception party arrived in front, and the monks had no time to don their robes. Rakshi Tujekyab[1321] was the first to come up, responding that he would escort them to the monastery. The reception party then met them at Jak. Lama Lha Wangchuk Pel offered him a hat, which he put on, and it pleased him. From Puto they gradually reached Yangragang on the fourteenth day of the second month of 1297 (fire female bird). The residents turned out to meet him. He delivered teachings that were suitable for the minds of each, so that everyone had confidence in him. He stayed there for two full months. Then, while he was playing, the tips of a flag fluttered in the direction of Riwoche Monastery, although there was no wind, so he said, "Let's go now!"[1322] {625}

On the first day of the fourth month, they reached Yangdon Kadruk. Access to all the other temples including Kabzhi and Kanyi was cut off by a curtain. Moving straight toward the ladder of the Kabzhi temple, he said,

"Let's go up here." "There are no stairs," they replied. "There are if you remove this curtain!" On reaching the top of the ladder, he said, "Open the door of the Kabzhi!" The resident caretakers had about ten keys in their hands, and he inspected them all one by one. "Open it with this one!" he said. They went inside. "Open that library padlock!" he said. "There is no key" they replied. "Bring that small brown leather box here!" he said. He went directly toward Sangye On's former teaching throne and marked it with his hand, saying, "My lama sat here!" Seeing that all the library keys were inside that leather box, he said, "Open it with this one!" Before entering the room, he said, "Pull out the catalog using this meditation staff!" In the catalog, he saw that there was a decree of advice, which he took out. Examining it once, he placed it on his head and reinserted it in its former place. "Now you should cultivate this advice!" he said.[1323] In this way, he caused all the resident and visiting monks in the Kadruk Temple to remember Sangye On.[1324]

Orgyen Gonpo stayed from 1297 (bird) until the sixth month of 1304 in that chamber that is nowadays known as the treasury. During that period, at the great offering ceremonies of the autumn and spring, he would grant his blessings in public, and afterward he would appear to be reading a book. There are countless episodes of him passing unimpededly through walls, opening the door of the treasure storeroom without a key, moving everywhere without obstruction, mastering the power of each of the four elements, {624} and arriving at certainty with respect to past and future circumstances.[1325]

On one occasion, he took his seat during roll call in the Protector Chapel. When his attendant brought a ladder and said, "Go ahead!" he replied, "I don't need a ladder. You go!" At that moment, he arrived at his proper place, without anyone knowing how he got there. He could subsequently explain with precision the remaining visualization steps pertaining to the guidance that older monks had previously received. The wondrous episodes that occurred such as these were unimaginable.

In the morning of the eighth day of the month of flower offerings in 1304 (wood male dragon), in his twelfth year, in the presence of the sacred representations with which Sangye On had a connection and that he was to keep safe, he received the mendicant ordination in the midst of a quorum of devout, virtuous, and accomplished monks, with Sonam Yeshe of Gaji Tangkya acting as monastic preceptor and Lhatsun Sonam Tashi acting as master of ceremonies. The name Rinchen Sherab Zangpo was conferred upon him, in accordance with an injunction of Venerable Sangye On. A great feast was then held. Henceforth, he would reside in the four-pillar residence. He took possession of the sacred representations that had been his predecessor's meditative commitment and of the library. He established all the regulations prescribed by Kuyalwa Rinchen Gonpo, as in the past. On the third day of the autumnal offering ceremony, he assumed the teaching throne. Extensive offerings were presented by the entire community. He delivered profound and extensive teachings, commencing with *The Tale of Gyelwa Dropei Kyemche,*[1326] and citations from *The White Lotus of the Sacred Doctrine.*[1327] All gods and humans were contented.[1328]

From Fourth Sakya Dakchen, Jamyang Rinchen Gyeltsen, Orgyen Gonpo then received the setting of the mind on enlightenment, the empowerment of the body maṇḍala of Cakrasaṃvara according to the Gaṇṭhapāda tradition, and so forth.[1329] {625}

From 1305 (wood female snake), in his thirteenth year, Orgyen Gonpo began to impart spiritual guidance. Previously Venerable Sangye On had given instructions to a servant of Sangye Yarjon and to Kuzhang Lha Kunga Pel, who was his own likeness, assuming the appearance of a heruka, saying, "These will later be required due to the importance of their auspicious circumstances. You should practice them at that time!" Having acquired them, along with that prophecy, Kuzhang Lha Kunga Pel consequently offered Orgyen Gonpo all the empowerments, transmissions, and esoteric instructions of the precious Eastern Kagyu tradition contained in the eleventh chapter of the treatise titled *Ornament of the Genuine Appearance of Pristine Cognition,*[1330] along with all teachings contained in the associated spiritual songs of *The Treasury of Esoteric Instruction and Prophecy.*[1331]

On the monkey day of the monkey month in 1320 (iron male monkey), in his twenty-eighth year, Orgyen Gonpo held an elaborate sacred drum dance in association with Venerable Sangye On's *Discussion with the Sixteen Wrathful Deities*[1332] and his *Discussion with the Four Great Kings,*[1333] and so forth,[1334] in order to tame the site for the construction of the Great Temple. He placed great treasures in the eight cardinal and intermediate directions, nine including the center, marked out the lines, and employed artisans, including the Newar Jaya, Wangchuk Bum of Gungtang, and Pon Sonam of Dokham. The single-layered outer wall was fashioned of adobe, and the double-layered inner walls were fashioned of stone, while the upper story was fashioned of latticed wood. Eclipsing the pride of the celestial mansion of Vijaya, it was insatiable to behold. The construction was excellently completed in seven years. On the twenty-fifth day of the eighth month in 1326 (tiger), they erected the gilded spire.[1335]

During 1328 (earth male dragon), they brought into the temple sacred representations including the image of Śākyamuni in the form Tubwang Lhunpo, which depicted the Teacher at the age of twenty-five and had been the meditative commitment of Venerable Sangye On,[1336] {626} along with the silver reliquary called Tashi Pelbargyi Lhunpo Obar and the precious likeness of Lama Sangye Yarjon called Ornament of the World,[1337] along with their offerings. To these, he offered lion thrones and back screens, fashioned with an array of superior precious gemstones. He newly constructed a great reliquary of pure cast silver, which resembled the supreme Mount Sumeru, and an image of Venerable Sangye On that blazed with the splendor of his blessings. On its seat there was a saddle blanket called Galel Tajakma, which had been donated by a ḍākinī of Tasho, a girl named Pematso, which until the present day has not incurred any damage due to insects and the like.[1338] The temple had three celestial ornaments, skylight canopies extending from south to north, and it was filled without intervening spaces with excellent sacraments of offering including the incense pouch with a motif depicting the ripples of an ocean,[1339] as well as terrestrial ornaments, the butter lamp donated by the Mongol Queen Yakha Tahu, and so forth.

Orgyen Gonpo Rinpoche himself performed the consecration, and at the time when obstacles were expelled, Karmapa Rangjung Dorje, who was staying at Sokzam knew of this in his mind and said repeatedly, "The son of Gazi has expelled the obstacles from the temple!" The Great Temple was then given the name Tashi Lhunpo Dzamling Gyen, and he said, "I am not one who nominally has the title Monk. I am a genuine monk." Scattering consecrated barley from the outer circumambulatory pathway, he arrived eventually at the gilded spire. He bestowed offerings and donations on the artisans who were masters of the classical sciences. To the monks and the crowd who assembled there, he delivered teachings, offering liturgies, dedications of merit, and prayers of good auspices, conjoined with a feast of alms. {627}

Orgyen Gonpo then installed sacred representations in the chapel at the Rachung Cave in Yang Gon. He gave guidance during the night to all the meditators and retreatants. The walking stick that the venerable one himself used when moving around the hermitage during the night is still preserved. He then struck camp and, from Drakgi, Genyen Dorje Tsendrak traveled here and there throughout upper and lower Markham. He created an unimaginable stack of sacred texts for installation in the lower story of the Great Temple of Riwoche with the innumerable volumes of scripture that were offered.

When Yaka Tatu, the queen of the Mongol emperor Qubilai Qaγan, was on her way to see the image of Jowo Śākyamuni in U, she made great offerings of extraordinary wealth at Riwoche, and Orgyen Gonpo delivered a sermon. When she requested permission to go upstairs in the temple, he replied that it would not be appropriate because they had made a pledge that women could not go there. However, she went anyway on the basis of her authority. A lavish reception was held. Then, on the road back to Mongolia, she passed away. In her will she bequeathed all her body ornaments to Orgyen Gonpo Rinpoche, along with more than a hundred Mongolian trunks of varying sizes and their contents, as well as Mongolian saddles, Mongolian copper pots, and silk clothes, which are preserved there in Riwoche.[1340] Her attendants did likewise, while butter lamps were prepared. Therefore, the Chinese and Mongolian artifacts arrayed among the offering sacraments of the temple of glorious Riwoche mostly date from this period. A Mongolian dragon-motif silver coin was distributed to each of the assembled monks.

The duties of the temple were hard for him to relinquish. The monastic charter of the monks who focused solely on meditative concentration was relaxed, a mere mental observation. So, in order to properly reinstate it, he constructed a grass hermitage at Yelpuk and stayed there for a great many years. {628}

The monks thereafter managed not to transgress his command concerning the code of monastic regulation and petitioned him to return. But he stayed in a stone building that housed spring water of spiritual accomplishment of which he partook. Gathering such resources himself, he remained for six years in strict retreat, without seeing anyone.

During that time, Jangchub Gyeltsen, the chieftain of Ling, banged on the small eastern door of his hermitage with a golden hammer and asked to see him. He responded back and forth to the entreaties of the resident monks, officials, and disciples; issued direct reminders; held discussions; and acted skillfully and meticulously with regard to the monastic charter and so forth. In these ways, he rendered the situation meritorious.

Starting from 1332 (water male monkey), Orgyen Gonpo extensively taught the doctrinal cycles of the profound aural lineage. By establishing a rotating three-year retreat that accommodated approximately fifty persons, he produced innumerable wonderfully realized yogins. In the monastery itself, the resident monks who assembled were never fewer than two thousand three hundred in number. They were adorned with the excellent endowments of higher rebirth and definitive excellence.

This saintly being definitively comprehended all the subjects of classical learning, and the tales of how he applied them in practice are indeed countless. When Laka Lama met him, he perceived Orgyen Gonpo Rinpoche in the form of the sublime Eleven-Faced Avalokita, and later also saw him in the form of Mañjughoṣa. This Laka Lama was a senior disciple of Zhang Tselpa. When he went to met Drigung Jikten Gonpo, the latter said to him, "Your power is that of Vajrapāṇi, and your ascetic discipline is equal to that of Virūpa." {629} He accepted Drigungpa's prostrations, and they exchanged offering scarves. Gonsa Lungtenpa belonged to the lineage of his nephew. On this present occasion, when he met Orgyen Gonpo Rinpoche, he had the name Laka Wangtsonpa. He offered his main monastery and its branches to Riwoche.

In the presence of master Bashingpa Tashi Gyeltsen, Orgyen Gonpo said, "I constructed this great temple to fulfill the enlightened intention of Venerable Sangye On. Its design is commensurate with the buddha field of Amitābha. At Tāmradvīpa in India, there is a temple with this design.[1341] Above all, it is said to depict the maṇḍala of glorious Kālacakra. Its consecration, moreover, was undertaken by Jowo Je Atiśa and Lord Marpa. Deshek Phakmodrupa composed *The Hundred Oral Instructions*[1342] there, and thereafter, they were applied in practice by Choje Rinpoche Taklung Tangpa and his sons."

When he had grown old, he made a square temple resembling a parasol upon a wooden palanquin, and then it is said that the attendants brought him to a low-lying place adjoining the plains and the hills, near a hot spring. On the eighth day of the fifth month of 1366 (fire male horse), he passed away into the taintless expanse. The sacred corpse was displayed on the thirteenth day. On the seventeenth day, the sacred corpse was cremated and the funeral ceremony performed. On the twenty-fourth day, the crematorium was opened. The heart, tongue, and eyes were retrieved, along with images including sublime Eleven-Faced Avalokita, the six-syllable mantra, and countless pearl relics. It was indisputably seen by all that a shower of flowers continued to fall upon the monastic seat of Riwoche, and its environs on the eighth day of every month, starting from that month of his passing and continuing for four or five years. {630} A small relic was distributed to each of the monks in the great assembly, so that many icons depicting the venerable one himself were subsequently made. These they placed within their respective temples, monasteries, and hermitages.[1343]

With regard to Chenga Yonten Gyeltsenpa, who was most beneficial to this lineage of the sacred doctrine, the patron Gongyel, who was the younger brother of Venerable Sangye Yarjon had two sons, the older one named Yeshe Gonpo and the younger one named Sangye Kyab. Chenga Yonten Gyeltsenpa was the son of the latter. He received the vows of a mendicant and the vows of complete monastic ordination from Sonam Rinchen, the monastic preceptor of Tangkya, and he then completely received the oral instructions of the Kagyu lineage from Orgyen Gonpo Rinpoche. He resided at Muru and in the monasteries of upper and lower Markham, and he brought forth many monks and disciples, headed by Mangpel Yonten Ozer. After elucidating the teaching of the lineage of practice, he passed away.

Strung on the thread of words forming a beauteous garland
Of lotus flowers that captivate the minds of the fortunate
With the collection of tales concerning the deeds of this venerable one,
May all beings become similar to him!

Khedrub Gyelwei Tsenchen

Definitively prophesied by the ocean of Conquerors
To hold sway over the dominion of the Conquerors' sacred doctrine,
Imbued with the incomparable lives of the Conquerors,
Homage to the lord of doctrine, Gyelwei Tsenchen!

Khedrub Gyelwei Tsenchen was born in the east, in the environs of the monastic seat of glorious Riwoche in 1344 (wood monkey).[1344] His father was the patron Chokyi Gonpo, the younger brother of Orgyen Rinpoche, and his mother was Seryikpa Gomza Pema Dron. He was the fourth of six siblings born to them. The name Rinchen Gon was conferred upon him. In his sixth year, he took the vows of a lay practitioner in the presence of his elder brother Lopon Drakpa Rinchen, {631} and he received teachings including Hevajra and the Six Doctrines of Nāropā. He met Choku Orgyen Gonpo, the lord of the enlightened heritage of the supreme Conqueror, in his tenth year, in the waxing half of the sixth month in 1353 (water female snake). Then, he was ordained as a mendicant, with Sangye Rinchen, the incumbent of the monastic seat of Yelpuk acting as monastic preceptor, Chichopa Sonam Gyeltsen acting as master of ceremonies, and Repa Gyeltsen acting as timekeeper. The name Lodro Gyeltsen Pelzangpo was conferred upon him by the monastic preceptor, as advised by Orgyen Gonpo Rinpoche himself.

In the presence of his precious predecessor, Gyelwei Tsenchen then made a complete study of all teachings of the ancient and new traditions, including the cycle of the essential profound doctrines of the Taklung Kagyu lineage, the general Kagyu tradition, the Kadam tradition, the tradition of Ngok, the tradition of Jñāna, the cycle of Mahākāruṇika, and the Doctrines of the Shangpa. He also studied all sorts of texts under the monastic preceptor Sonam Gyeltsen, Gelong Senge, and so forth. Without leaving the profound esoteric instructions as merely names to be heard, he focused on the essential points and experientially cultivated them, such that he perfected the experiences and realizations associated with each.

In his twenty-second year, on the full moon of Pauṣya in 1365 (wood female snake), in the presence of the particularly sublime representations with which Sangye On had a connection and that he had to keep safe, Gyelwei Tsenchen received the vows of full-fledged monastic ordination in the midst of a quorum consisting of his former preceptor and master of ceremonies (Sonam Gyeltsen), as well as Gelong Senge, who acted as confessor, and the devout monks Lingre Chogyel, Robpa Gyeltsen Bum, and so forth. He became a crown jewel among the hundred thousand upholders of the vinaya, pure with respect to the three trainings.

In 1366 (fire male horse), he performed bountiful offerings that fulfilled the enlightened intention of the late Choku Orgyen Gonpo {632} and undertook the funerary rites in the correct manner. That same year, a divination was made in the presence of the precious jewels, and it alighted on this venerable master, who was duly enthroned under an auspicious planet, constellation, hour, and date. The image of Venerable Lord Maitreya that had been the meditational deity of glorious Ga Lotsāwa was bedecked with grand silken drapes depicting the thousand buddhas, and the entire congregation of monks scattered flowers commemorating the auspicious enthronement. Great offerings and an immeasurable feast were held. Chengawa Gyelwei Tsenchen then taught the profound and extensive doctrines.

Those who came to hear the sacred doctrine and who could not cross the river heard from the hillside on the far bank, such that the teachings that were given made no distinction between them and those who were seated in close proximity. To contain the inner relics of his deceased precious predecessor, he commissioned a gold image of Munīndra called Meaningful to Behold,[1345] a representative icon depicting Orgyen Gonpo as he was when actually alive, and a silver reliquary.[1346] All three had particularly sublime throne and back screens. As an outer representation, he then commissioned the Kumbum Barma Rinpoche and a well-proportioned icon named Lhunpo Tashi Chokden, which was fashioned of medicinal paste mixed with fine silk, medicines, funerary ash, sacred bones, and so forth, and covered thickly[1347] with refined gold. The dome, with its wooden tiers and its tiled and gilded roof, was constructed in the Chinese style. The insertion of the relics, the consecration, donations, and so forth were particularly great. Karmapa Rolpei Dorje came and inspected the temple with its artifacts. He presented a large silk hanging that had been offered by the Mongol emperor as a sacrament of offering. {635}

During the lifetime of this venerable master Gyelwei Tsenchen, the chieftains of different regions offered monastic estates and the devout populace, who were their subjects and under their authority, made most bountiful offerings, such that the reach and influence of Riwoche expanded. He also displayed many manifest signs of spiritual accomplishment. He expertly promoted the profound oceanic doctrines of the Taklung Kagyu tradition, and incidentally he taught without interruption many hundreds of doctrinal traditions to anyone who desired them. The regulations of Choje Kuyalwa Rinchen Gonpo, the charter of the monastic assembly, the disciplinary rules of the monastery, and so forth were maintained without wavering from their former observances.

Gyelwei Tsenchen presided over the monastic seat for nineteen years. Then, after appointing Choje Ratnākara as his regent, he became a total renunciate,[1348] dwelling principally at grass hermitages in Kharnak and Lhalung, but also passing some time at Ritangshong, Chiyi Yelpuk Kak, and so forth. He made an enormous skylight canopy of silk that was totally exquisite and sent it to be hung between the southern and northern pillars of the great temple at Riwoche, and it fit well, such that everyone was astonished.

He became the primary patron of the monks at Tsang Sarwa, Ripakha Chogye, Retsang Gomde, and so forth, and he took under his sway all the gods and humans of Lhaten Pesum at Lhodang Dzong in Yelpa, as well as those of Seri, Yuri, Tapu Dartso, Drelpang, Dangado, and so forth. He provided the bedding for Ta, Yak, and Gyang at Laka Gon, and he took charge of the support for the monastery, lamas, and monks. He went to the summit of Lhoyi Dugri Nakbal and bound the local deity under an oath of allegiance, establishing it as a lay practitioner, and renaming it Ugyel Tongtub. Thereafter, that local deity harmed no one at all, {634} and a meditation hermitage was even built on the side of that hill. He tamed many arrogant spirits including Genyen Kana of Tsawagang, Mukmori, and Dretso Chukmo, and he established many beings of Atsetsa, Rongpo Mide, and the Dachu and Sechu region, in maturational empowerment and liberating guidance.

Gyelwei Tsenchen's compositions were also most extensive, including prayers, offering liturgies, epistles, descriptive maṇḍalas, guidebooks, introductions to the nature of mind, and prophetic declarations. He secured all those afflicted by ill-health in spiritual and temporal well-being through the bountiful gifts of medicines, which included yellow powders.

His disciples included retreat masters of the ancient and new traditions, adhering to the Nyingma tradition of the preceptor Śāntarakṣita, the master Padmākara, and the religious king Tri Songdetsen, such as Kabzhipa Sonam Lodro and his brother, Donyopa, Upa Jamyang, Yonten Ozer, and Sonam Gyeltsenpa. And they also included the realized yogins of Lingchawu Topa and Richenpa Ozer Gyeltsen, who had become accomplished in the peaceful and wrathful rites of Severance. Headed by them, there were a countless number who benefited the Buddhist teaching and sentient beings throughout China, U, and Kham.

As a protector deity, he revered Mahākāla in the form Trakshe Kangtang, according to the lineage derived from master Dhanasaṃskṛta. This protector carried out all his injunctions in the manner of a servant assigned to a task, such that he triumphed over all disharmonious factions.

In his fifty-eighth year, in 1401 (iron female snake), Gyelwei Tsenchen fell ill, and on the fifteenth day of the first month, he passed away. On the twenty-first day, the cremation was held at Kharnak. The whole skull was bedecked with large *śarīraṃ* relics, the eyes and heart were fused together, and innumerable pearl relics of five colors were retrieved. The area was shrouded in a tent of rainbow light, a rain of flowers fell, and each of the pearl relics multiplied countlessly. {635} Such were the unimaginable wonders that occurred.

To contain his inner relics, Onpo Kumche of Kharwa commissioned a perfect image of Munīndra in the form Great Enlightenment, along with its throne and back screen.

Dzorawa, the Elder and the Younger

The two known as Dzorawa the Elder and the Younger were immaculate individuals born into the same familial line, but they did not reach the heights of enthronement. Their father was also Chokyi Gonpo, and their mother was Seryikza Pemo Dron.

The elder brother was born in 1330 (iron male horse). In his eighth year, the mendicant name Drakpa Rinchen Pelzangpo was conferred upon him. He received full monastic ordination from Sonam Rinchen, the monastic preceptor of Tangkya, and all the oral instructions from Orgyen Gonpo Rinpoche and others. He was endowed with the inestimable enlightened attributes of scriptural transmission and realization. After practicing in the border area between Nepal and Tibet, he intentionally journeyed to U and passed away at Sok.

The younger one was born in 1339 (earth female hare). He had the same parents as the elder one. The mendicant name Rinchen Senge was conferred upon him, and he attended upon Choku Orgyen Gonpo and others, successfully integrating study, reflection, and meditation.[1349]

He commissioned many images, relief carvings, and manuscripts, including the silver image of Vajradhara in the Utse Temple at Riwoche.[1350] He was commended for his chanting of *The Oceanic Spiritual Songs of the Precious Kagyu Tradition*[1351] and the practical liturgies of the way of Secret Mantra. He satisfied Choje Ratnākara, master Telkhangpa, his brother, and others with the nectar of the profound aural lineage of Venerable Sangye On. Venerable Drakpei Tsenchen offered him sacred representations headed by the mottled stone image of Venerable Sangye On, {636} as well as all sorts of artifacts that he owned as his rightful share. In 1416 (fire male monkey), in his seventy-eighth year, Dzorawa the Younger passed away. Following the cremation, innumerable pearl relics were retrieved.

May the mercury that forms these narratives
Consume the iron element that constitutes the past actions
And afflicted mental states of living beings,
And generate the precious gold of omniscience!

Ratnākara

Homage at the feet of Choje Rinchen Jungne,
The drizzle of whose instructions of the **precious** (*rin chen*)[1352] aural lineage
Moistened all the fields of **precious** (*rin chen*) disciples,
And ripened well the harvest of **precious** (*rin chen*) attainment and bliss!

Ratnākara, the peerless incumbent of the monastic seat of glorious Riwoche, was the subsequent reincarnation of Choje Ratnākara of Taklung Upper Plain.[1353] His father, the patron Rinchen Dorje, who was the second son of the great patron Chokyi Gonpo, had married two consorts, one of whom was his mother, Dongza Konchok Gyen. He was the youngest of the six siblings to whom she gave birth. He was born in 1362 (water male tiger). During his fourth and fifth years, he met Orgyen Gonpo and was blessed as a lineage holder of his buddha mind.

In his thirteenth year, on the eleventh day of the second month of 1374 (wood male tiger), on the occasion of an auspicious planetary and stellar conjunction, Ratnākara received the vows of a lay practitioner and the intermediate mendicant vows of the novitiate amid a quorum of eight, which included Nangso Sangye Rinchen of Yelpuk acting as monastic preceptor, Drungpa Wangchuk Gyeltsen acting as master of ceremonies, Ling Repa acting as confessor, and the devout and virtuous lama Lha Drakpa Pel. The name Rinchen Sherab Wangchuk Pelzangpo was conferred upon him. {637}

Until his tenth year, Ratnākara resided at Dzora and Telkhang,[1354] where he refined his studies. For the most part, he stayed in retreat. In the presence of master Rinchen Senge, he received all the profound doctrines of Venerable Sangye On in their entirety. He also studied under his aforementioned preceptor and master of ceremonies and under Gaji Dorzang, Tazhi Kunzang, Pongom Dolma, and others. He then received the full monastic ordination in the midst of a quorum of devout monks from Joten Namkha Sonam, the incumbent of the monastic seat of Yelpuk, acting as monastic preceptor, and two masters of ceremonies.

After Choje Gyelwei Tsenchen had confined himself to isolated retreat and had become a total renunciant, focusing on meditative commitments, Venerable Ratnākara was enthroned at the precious monastic seat of

Riwoche in his twenty-third year, in 1396 (wood male mouse). By means of the four attractive qualities of a bodhisattva, he acted for the benefit of innumerable sentient beings. At all times, he remained absorbed in the meditative stability of loving-kindness, and as far as all the current regulations were concerned, he applied the basic monastic discipline of the sacred doctrine, adorned with the thirteen regulations of Kuyalwa Rinchen Gonpo, as his predecessors had done. All the monks present in his entourage and all those who resided at the precious monastery of Riwoche also applied the threefold vows, consisting of the outer vows of individual liberation, the inner vows of the bodhisattvas, and the secret vows of the awareness holders. With respect to the three trainings as well, at all times, he unwaveringly maintained the state of equanimity.

By imparting instruction exclusively on the experiential guidance of The Attainment of the Guru, the Great Seal, the Six Doctrines, and Severance, Ratnākara educated countless disciples who were realized yogins, possessing the discipline of the ascetic virtues, and who essentialized their spiritual practice by means of mountain retreat, silence, and walling up their hermitages. {638}

He also composed many new works, including prayers to the Kagyu lineage, adamantine spiritual songs implying meditative experience, major and minor treatises that essentialize the enlightened intention of the sūtras and mantras in terms of experiential cultivation, and guidebooks on spiritual practice. At the request of Chenpo Lama Gyeltsen, he also delivered many elaborate public teachings.

The lord of Gonjo at first had a profound patron-priest connection with him, but later Ozer Pel instigated many misdeeds. When Ratnākara went directly to his camp, since their mutual merit had been exhausted, as an example of the malign thoughts that he had acquired, he said that he required Ratnākara to prostrate before him. When such requests are made, saintly beings have a disposition that can withstand criticism, and so Ratnākara consented and said, "I will do so!" The next day, as Gonjo held consecrated artifacts in the fold of his robe and sat upon the throne, Rinpoche Ratnākara directly made a series of nine prostrations toward him. Then, when the master and his disciples had almost returned to their campsite, a great tornado appeared and carried away the tents of Gonjo. That night, Gonjo dreamed that a woman had extracted his heart and carried it away. The next morning, he saw that there was a blood stain on the posts of his outer and inner tent. His life came to an end that same year. Afterward, Gonjo Ozer Namkha also made many harsh comments, but not long afterward, his family line was interrupted, leaving only the residue of his name.

When a great quarrel broke out between two branches of a meditation hermitage and the villagers of Khyungpo, and so forth, he tamed all the mutually hostile parties with gifts of the sacred doctrine and material things. Bringing about a reconciliation, he secured the country pervasively in peace. {639} He entrusted legal duties and affairs to his senior attendants, who were endowed with profound and magnanimous intelligence. They indeed acted meritoriously by carrying out the enlightened intention of Venerable Ratnākara with devotion and commitment, unadulterated by self-interested negativity.

On one occasion, when a large herd of frontier horses was lost to the brigands of the Adro people, Ratnākara was asked if they should raise a large army from Ramda, but he said, "Even if you are victorious, the monks will lose. Even if you are defeated, the monks will lose." They then postponed the attack.

The saintly Drakpa Tsultrim Ozer also bowed at his feet, and Ratnākara granted him the nectar of his profound and extensive teachings. In return, he completely offered the monastic estates of Drak to Ratnākara.

Starting from then, Ratnākara gradually appointed lama officials, including Drungpa Lodro Rinchen, who excellently maintained the tradition of Riwoche. Chengawa Sonam Gyeltsen, the incumbent of the monastic seat of Choje Marpa at Marsho Gon, also made great offerings and many times requested his profound doctrines.

Choje Zhonu Sangyepa, the incumbent of the monastic seat of Yerpa Lhari Nyingpo, commissioned manuscripts of *The Transcendent Perfection of Wisdom in One Hundred Thousand Lines*,[1355] *The Sublime Sūtra of the Transcendent Perfection of Wisdom in Eight Thousand Lines*,[1356] *The Hundred Thousand Names of the Buddhas*,[1357] and so forth, on parchment, inscribed in gold, and accompanied by a petition offered them in the presence of Choje Rinpoche Ratnākara during a public teaching at glorious Riwoche.

To the south side of the great monastery of Riwoche, Ratnākara constructed a hundred and eight hermitages, and he prayed that the meditator monks of the monastery and those who gathered there from the respective mountain retreat centers of the region would stay there by whatever means.

He introduced the custom of inspecting the teaching of the practice lineage of experiential cultivation during sessions of meditation and their intervals.

In the autumn of 1413 (water female snake), in his fifty-second year, {640} he struck camp and went to meet Kunga Tashi, the venerable lord of the Great Vehicle of the glorious Sakyapa tradition.[1358] The venerable lord Kunga Tashi said to him, "There is a great purpose in our traveling now in this direction. It is so that we may meet you, Choje Ratnākara of Taklung." So it was that they held many delightful conversations. As a memorandum, in the midst of the assembly of all the resident and visiting monks, Choje Ratnākara astonished everyone by reciting *The Setting of the Mind on Enlightenment: The Great Pearl Necklace*.[1359] On returning to the monastery, he commissioned two large painted scrolls depicting Mañjughoṣa and Uṣṇīṣavijaya. In 1416 (fire male monkey), he commissioned three hundred volumes of the Kangyur and Tengyur, along with *The Hundred Thousand Teachings of the Kagyu Tradition*,[1360] and the maṇḍala of buddha mind according to Kālacakra fashioned of precious gems, and so forth.

Along with the monastic preceptors, masters, and monks, Venerable Ratnākara correctly consecrated the actual library collection of Riwoche, according to the integrated sūtra and mantra tradition. When master Dzorawa Rinchen Senge passed away, he undertook the preparation of the sacred corpse, the funeral rites, and so forth. Later, he entrusted the monastic seat to Onpo Drakpei Tsenchen. Then, in his fifty-seventh year, at dawn on the twelfth day of the waxing half of the twelfth month in 1418 (earth male dog), he departed for Akaniṣṭha. The cremation was held on the third day of the following month. The heart, tongue, and eyes were retrieved, along with countless pearl relics. Most bountiful offerings were undertaken as a means of fulfilling his enlightened intention. {641}

Ritsewa

The one named master Ritsewa was a mendicant in the familial line of that time who did not accede to the monastic seat. He had the same father as Venerable Ratnākara, and his mother was Sangye Bum. When he entered the womb, his mother dreamed that her body was adorned with lotus flowers, and she heard the sound of ARAPACANA.[1361] He was born in 1372 (water male mouse). In his ninth year, he was ordained as a mendicant by Joten Namkha Sonam, with the incumbent of the monastic seat of Yelpuk acting as monastic preceptor and Chogowa Yonten acting as master of ceremonies. The name Drakpa Tashi Pelzangpo was conferred upon him.

The child received the transmission of the scriptural authorization of the precious Collected Works of Venerable Sangye On from Lama Ozerwa, and in the presence of master Rinchen Senge he received the related cycles of empowerment, guidance, and oral instruction. From Choje Gyelwei Tsenchen, he received experiential guidance on the Great Seal and the Six Doctrines. He then resorted to isolated retreat and focused on the profound inner yoga.

In his twenty-second year, Ritsewa received the full monastic ordination from the preceptor Yonten Ozer and others. In his thirtieth year, in 1401 (iron snake), when Chengawa Gyelwei Tsenchen passed away, the brothers in common commissioned an image of Munīndra in the form Great Enlightenment, with its throne and back screen, to contain the inner relics. He then exclusively cultivated the empowerments and the generation and perfection stages based on the Collected Works of Venerable Sangye On, above all focusing on his own experiential cultivation and all the approaches of further instruction for the sake of others.

Ritsewa compiled and established in fourteen volumes the extant doctrinal discourses of all the successive hierarchs of the Kagyu lineage in general and the compositions of Venerable Sangye On in particular, without adulterating them. And he made great efforts to propagate the transmission of their empowerments, transmissions, and esoteric instructions. {642} Consequently, although he did not accede to the monastic seat, his kindness to the doctrinal lineage of Riwoche was exceedingly great. There are also many works that he himself composed. He had visions of the meditational deities, and there are innumerable anecdotes concerning his extrasensory powers and so forth. Finally, in his thirty-eighth year, in 1409 (earth ox), he passed away.[1362]

May the magnifying crystal of these narratives,
Exuding the nectar of spiritual and temporal well-being,
Cleanse the stains of the threefold obscuration of all beings,
Without exception, and emerge victorious!

Drakpei Tsenchen

Homage to the lord of sacred doctrine, Drakpei Tsenchen,
The divine drumbeat of whose **fame** (*grags snyan*)[1363] marvelously resounded

As the reincarnation of the earlier Drakpei Pel himself,
His compassion commensurate with the meaning of that **fame** (*grags pa*)!

Choje Drakpei Tsenchen, who was alternatively known as Rinpoche Drak Khawa after the name of his residence, had the same parents as master Ritsewa and was the youngest of their three sons.[1364] He was born in 1376 (fire male dragon). In his ninth year, he arrived in the presence of Choje Gyelwei Tsenchen and then attended upon him continuously for eighteen years. In his twelfth year, on an auspicious day in 1387 (fire female hare), he received the mendicant ordination from Joten Namkha Sonam, the incumbent of the monastic seat of Yelpuk, and others. The name Drakpa Tashi Gyeltsen Pelzangpo was conferred upon him. In the presence of Lama Chogowa Yonten Ozer, he received the complete empowerments and transmissions of the precious Collected Works of Venerable Sangye On and also many general and particular doctrines of the Kagyu tradition.

On the eleventh day of the first autumn month, in 1398 (earth male tiger), {643} in the temple of glorious Riwoche, he received the full monastic ordination in the midst of a quorum of devout monks, including Geshe Yonten Ozer, who acted as monastic preceptor, as well as a master of ceremonies and a timekeeper. From the great renunciant Gyelwei Tsenchen, he received in the form of experiential guidance all the profound aural lineages, including the Great Seal and the Six Doctrines of Nāropā, and by experientially cultivating them, he became a peerless universal monarch of spiritual accomplishment, not dissimilar to Saraha, the mighty lord of yoga.

The two brothers, acting as monastic preceptor and master of ceremonies, ordained innumerable novices and full-fledged monks. Since Drakpei Tsenchen was adroit in anything to which he turned his mind, he designed the renovations at Kharnak, and for this reason his actions were particularly sublime. He liberally supplied materials and land for the use of major and minor offering ceremonies, including the fifteenth-day ceremony.

Drakpei Tsenchen was on good terms with all persons—high, low, and middling. On one occasion he traveled to Chamlakha in Dokham and clearly impressed his large footprint on a flat stone at Letsasho, which is a revered sacred object for all the monastic and lay communities of the region. Through his bountiful gifts of the sacred doctrine and material offerings and the power of his pervasive and constant enlightened mind, imbued with loving-kindness and compassion, he pacified all conflicts in Minyak Godong and elsewhere, and peace spread throughout the land.

At Riwoche, for the outer relics of Chengawa Gyelwei Tsenchen, he commissioned a reliquary stūpa of gilded copper with a throne and rear curtain. Nangso provided him with an excellent continuous source of materials for commissioning a manuscript of the Kangyur and Tengyur.

In his forty-second year, in 1418, Drakpei Tsenchen himself acceded to the monastic seat of Riwoche. When Choje Ratnākara passed away during the twelfth month, {644} Drakpei Tsenchen undertook a magnificent and auspicious funerary rite that fulfilled his enlightened intention. He took care of and made offerings to the sacred representations kept at the residences of his predecessors, and in Rachung, Kadruk, the two Kabzhi temples and his own dwelling. His wheel of the ornament of inexhaustible enlightened activity resembled space, nurturing and increasing the Buddhist teaching without permitting any deviation from the regulations of Choje Kuyalwa and the charter of the monastic assembly, as they were previously observed.

For the outer relics of the late Choje Ratnākara, he commissioned the Upper Kumbum. The entire design and its implementation, including the geomantic rites and the drawing of the lines, were undertaken by the master Pema Gyeltsen. It was constructed of medicinal paste, in which fine medicines, supreme fragrances, various grains, essences, diverse jewels, funerary ash, and bones, and so forth, were mixed together. In the vault within it,[1365] he inserted an inestimable number of the hundred thousand incantations; representations of buddha body, speech, and mind; the staff of Zhuye Neljorpa;[1366] and the heart of Drogon Sangye Yelpa in a silver reliquary that was brought from Lhodong Dzong; as well as a particularly sublime likeness of the master Ratnākara himself, fashioned of cast silver, with its own throne and back screen; and so forth. The stūpa, with its Chinese-style roof, was insatiable to behold. The rite of consecration that accorded with the teaching transmission of glorious Taklungpa the Great and the Great Seal—a tradition in which sūtra and mantra are definitively without duality, was immensely enhanced with auspicious feast offerings.

During the lifetime of this master, Drakpei Tsenchen, the entire congregation of monks at Riwoche increased like the swelling rivers of summertime. By turning the wheel of the profound and extensive sacred doctrine without interruption, headed by all the profound esoteric instructions of the precious Kagyu lineage, {645} he ensured that the three pure vows were experientially cultivated, and he succeeded in bringing forth an inconceivable number of disciples endowed with the inspiration and extraordinary virtues that engage for the sake of the Buddhist teaching and sentient beings.

With regard to this lord-protector Drakpei Tsenchen, Venerable Sangye On had himself prophesied, "Starting from now, when forests grow on this bare hill in front, I will come here again." Since the prophecy coincided with that time, it is indisputable that this wondrously supreme buddha body of emanation Sangye On had himself reincarnated for the sake of the Buddhist teaching and sentient beings.[1367]

Once, when the war with the inhabitants of Khyungpo reached Khangnye,[1368] the commanders, including Machen Rokdzi, said they would muster an army of monks and fight, but he refused them permission. Instead he sent an offering scarf and gifts to Teng Gom Sonam Gyeltsen and dispatched them to the battlefield, and in this way averted conflict. Later, the chieftain of Khyungpo and his servants arrived in the monastery and met him in person. They were then pacified.

When he went to the hot springs at Chukordo in Nedu, he incidentally taught the sacred doctrine to countless persons who gathered there, eager to see him and hear his teaching, commensurate with their capacities.

In general, Drakpei Tsenchen nurtured the community at Riwoche for four complete years. Then, in his forty-sixth year, in 1421 (iron female ox), he fell ill, and in the morning of the third day of the seventh month, he passed into nirvāṇa. When the cremation was held, a replica of the syllable HAṂ[1369] and the images of the deities Hevajra, Avalokita, Mañjughoṣa, and so forth were retrieved, along with the heart, tongue, and eyes and countless relics, large and small. For one day and night, the offerings of attainment associated with many outer and inner maṇḍalas of the way of Secret Mantra were prepared, {646} and offerings of melodious spiritual songs and so forth were made. Finally, presents and great alms were distributed to the monks all day long, and a mass of food resembling a hill heaped with gemstones was distributed to the large crowd of people who assembled, surpassing the imagination. An innumerable foundation of meritorious action was offered to all those with whom Riwoche had a patron-priest relationship in all lands—India, China, Nepal, and Tibet.

May the magnifying crystal of limitless beings
Encounter the sunlight of these narratives,
And therefrom may unbearable devotion blaze forth,
Illuminating the path of liberation in its entirety!

Miyowa Gonpo

Homage to the one renowned as Miyo Gonpo,
Abiding in the supreme calmness
Of **unwavering** (*mi g.yo*)[1370] adamantine meditative stability,
Imbued with the three **unwavering** (*mi g.yo*) states,[1371]
Indivisible from the **unwavering** (*mi g.yo*) wrathful king Acala!

Choje Miyowa Gonpo was the son of On Senge, the younger brother of Choje Ratnākara's father. His mother was Zhonuza Alo. The oldest of the four siblings was Pontsang Sonam Rinchen, and this venerable master was the one below him. He was born in Zholsar in Dzong Namlhadrak Karpo, in 1409 (earth female ox).[1372] A white letter A at his heart diffused light, which was seen by Tsenpa Budzi and did not fade for some days. Venerable Ratnākara gave him a protection cord of white silk and blessed him. In his ninth year, in 1417 (fire female bird), he was ordained as a mendicant at the Khar Residence in Riwoche, with Choje Drakpei Tsenchen acting as monastic preceptor and Tsampo Gompukpa Konchok Gyeltsen acting as master of ceremonies. The name Rinchen Sherab Pelzangpo was conferred upon him. {647}

From his venerable predecessor Drakpei Tsenchen, he received completely the maturational empowerments for the Collected Works of Lama Rinpoche Sangye On, the supremely accomplished saint, along with the liberating guidance and the supporting transmissions of scriptural authority. He also received many general teachings based on the turning of the doctrinal wheel of the Kagyu lineage from Tsamponpa. By integrating study, reflection, and meditation, unimaginable attributes of clear realization were born within him. When Choje Drakpei Tsenchen passed away into the taintless field that was his natural abode, Miyowa Gonpo presided over the cremation of the sacred corpse and his precious enlightened intention at all times extended a cloud mass of auspicious offerings that extensively filled the expanse of reality, the pathway of the gods. So it was that his devotion to the late lama billowed forth from the ocean, endowed with water of eight qualities.[1373]

In his fourteenth year, in 1422 (water male tiger), he returned to the monastery, and in his sixteenth year, in 1424 (wood male dragon), he acceded to the lion throne in the midst of the entire congregation. He taught the profound and extensive doctrine. Then, when he met Atang Tsasolwa, an emanation of Mahākāruṇika, the latter saw his body in the form of dark-blue Acala, holding a sword and an adamantine lasso, his index finger in the gesture of menace, and bedecked in the garb of a wrathful deity. Consequently, he became renowned as Choje Miyowa throughout the three world systems.

He commissioned a set of volumes of the Kangyur of the Conqueror and the Tengyur in their entirety, inscribed with a gemstone solution on parchment, with master Pema Gyeltsen making the arrangements, managing the project, undertaking corrections, and so forth. In the middle story of the Great Temple, which represents the wheel of buddha speech, artists, headed by Drak Gyel, drew murals depicting the lamas of the Kagyu lineage, the deeds of the Teacher, the divine assemblages of the tantras, the buddhas of the ten directions, {648} the ocean of oath-bound protectors, and the assemblage of the yakṣas, headed by Vasudeva. Ponmoche Pegyelwa made an image of Munīndra in the form Great Enlightenment, along with its throne and back screen. Khepa Goyu commissioned medicinal clay icons of Munīndra and the sixteen elders, along with Hashang, Dharmatāla, and the four great kings, forming a playful array, with a rocky mountain backdrop. Venerable Miyowa Gonpo himself acted as the vajra master, and they performed a peerless consecration, replete with auspicious feasts and the dispensing of gifts.[1374]

In a dream, he met Deshek Phakmodrupa, who revealed to him the profound doctrine. The next day, he commissioned an image of glorious Phakmodrupa fashioned of medicinal paste, composed of fine silk and various precious medicines. After he had finished partaking of the fruits of that communion feast offering, two marks spontaneously appeared of their own accord at the heart and cheeks of that image.[1375]

When he met the late Drakpa Gyeltsen in a dream, the latter delivered an introduction to the view, meditation, conduct, and result. Consequently, the realization of the meditation known as the single savor was born within him, free from the constraints of meditative equipoise and post-meditation. In 1431 (pig), he commissioned a specially produced Tashi Gomang stūpa.

Forming a great caravan, Miyowa Gonpo then set out for the hot springs at Chukhordo. On the way, he visited the meditation cave, maṇḍala platform, and naturally originated stone hand drum and so forth of Venerable Jñānatapa. There, he had a vision of the divine assemblage of Hevajra, along with the lineage of spiritual teachers, in consequence of which he also composed *The Prayer to the Lineage Succession of Hevajra according to the Jñāna Tradition*.[1376] An infinite number of auspicious signs arose, including a tent of rainbow light and a shower of flowers. He also taught the Fivefold Great Seal.[1377] {649}

On reaching that hermitage,[1378] he turned the wheel of the sacred doctrine on behalf of many realized yogins who were learned and venerable, including Kabchupa Pema Senge. On reaching the banks of the river in Jamda, he recited an aspiration prayer to allay fear of the water and left the impression of his foot in stone. In the presence of Gyara Sangye Yeshe, he received many doctrines of the ancient and new traditions and in return granted the profound doctrines of Venerable Sangye On. He also received teachings from Drung Lodro Rinchen.

Without interruption, he bestowed infinite profound and extensive empowerments, transmissions, and esoteric instructions, including guidance on the aural lineage of Cakrasaṃvara, the Great Seal, and the Six Doctrines. He commissioned an exemplary manuscript of *The Collected Works of the Kagyu Tradition*.[1379]

In 1436 (dragon), he met Choje Kunpang Rinpoche Jangchub Gyatso, who arrived from Taklung Upper Plain.[1380] They received teachings from one another, and then, without even taking turns, their minds merged together. As long as the visitors, master and disciples, stayed at Riwoche, Miyowa Gonpo undertook immeasurable acts of service and respectful offerings on their behalf. They inspected in detail the large and small temples, the representations of buddha body, speech, and mind, and the collection of blessed inner relics. The resident monks in return received the precepts of the novitiate and full-fledged ordination in the presence of Venerable Jangchub Gyatso and extensively requested the kindness of his empowerments, transmissions, and esoteric instructions. When the visitors, master and disciples, departed, they then undertook extensive acts of benefit for the sake of living beings in upper and lower Pubor, before heading back toward Taklung.

On a later occasion, Venerable Jangchub Gyatso again returned to Riwoche via upper and lower Lho, and he again met Choje Miyowa Gonpo. At that time, Rinpoche Jangchub Gyatso appeared to have fallen ill. Thus it is documented in *The Golden Rosary of Riwoche*[1381] {650} that Venerable Jangchub Gyatso seems to have visited Riwoche on two occasions.

In the autumn of 1437 (snake), on behalf of the entire congregation of Riwoche, the great monastic seat, Venerable Miyo Gonpo bestowed in the context of a public teaching the empowerments of *The Guru Yoga: Meditative Stability Endowed with Blessings*,[1382] which had been the meditative commitment of glorious Taklung Tangpa the Great, along with two guidebooks—the guidance that lays bare its practical application and the guidance of Mahākāruṇika.

In 1440 (monkey), the great caravan of Karmapa Tongwa Donden arrived at Ngartok. Although there is an account stating that Miyowa Gonpo offered him tea and had a meeting, actually the circumstances for them to meet were incomplete. With just as few disciples, the Karmapa Tulku is said to have secretly made an inspection of the layout of the monastery.

Choje Miyowa Gonpo excellently commissioned images depicting the fifteen holders of the authentic lineage of Riwoche, from Vajradhara to Choje Drakpei Tsenchen, along with the great accomplished master Jñānatapa, which were fashioned of medicinal paste that was made from combining various gemstones, fine medicines, silk, earth, and stone from extraordinary places of attainment, and water that had been used for cleaning sacred artifacts.[1383] These blazed with a light of blessed splendor, as if the lineage holders were actually present. They were installed with the proper procedures, in accordance with the enlightened intention of the aforementioned consecration rite of glorious Phakmodrupa titled Library, and the feast offerings that were made were hard to imagine.

In his thirty-fifth year, in the fifth month of 1443 (water female pig),[1384] his caravan set out, and keeping to the narrow horse trail, he passed through Chubzang, the sports ground of Riwoche. At Mayoksumdo, he observed the anniversary of the Sugata and delivered a teaching on the great setting of the mind on enlightenment. Then, he received an invitation from Kyorak Choje Sonam Zangpo. {651} He traveled directly to Chudu in the Dachu valley,[1385] where he taught the profound and extensive doctrine. Simply through engaging in discussion, he enabled Kyorak Choje to achieve the great success of meditative commitment.

Then, he set out promptly on a day-long journey to Parkha. The great caravan of the enthroned Rinpoche Tashi Pel-o Zangpo, master and disciples, arrived from Taklung Upper Plain. A meritorious meeting took place. They invited one another to each other's encampment, and their minds merged together. They made awesome offerings and acts of service to one another. Then, Miyowa Gonpo continued on to Yelpuk Monastery, where he donated offerings of material things that resembled a downpour of rain.

In his thirty-eighth year, in the eighth month of 1446 (tiger), he traveled to Kumbum and then brought about a reconciliation between the local meditators and the people of Minyak. He went to Drekhuteng in Chi, where he was presented with fine offerings and acts of service by Namkha

Gyeltsen of Nangchen and his brother. On returning to the monastery at Riwoche, Tulku Zhamarwa, Karma Situpa, and others arrived, and he held a reception with offerings and acts of service.[1386]

In 1449 (snake), Miyowa Gonpo commissioned a life-size precious gold image of Venerable Sangye On, along with its extraordinarily sublime throne and back screen. He consecrated it according to the tradition of Phakmodrupa's Library, based on the maṇḍala of Guhyasamāja Mañjuvajra. At that time, many of the dancers saw him as Aṅgita, one of the set of paintings depicting the sixteen elders.

Moreover, he commissioned about eight or nine other images fashioned of gold and silver, hundreds of painted scrolls, and hundreds of immaculate manuscript volumes. Dong Gampopa Chokyi Gyeltsen presented him with great offerings consisting of distinctive artifacts of Chinese and Mongolian origin, and he requested the sacred doctrine. {652} When the lama delivered teachings in public during the summer of 1450 (horse), both those who were nearby and those who were far away could hear him without distinction.

In his forty-fourth year, in 1452 (monkey), his caravan set out for Pozhung in Chamlakha in Dokham. He granted many desired teachings to Zurmang Rinpoche, Puri Dejung, master and disciples, and so forth, and he brought about a reconciliation between Minyak and Kora. On being invited by Adro, he established all the beings of the Mekong valley to maturational empowerment and liberating guidance. The female chieftain offered many riches and prayers to him, such that she recovered from her skin disease that the nāgas had provoked.

Many of his compositions—including prayers, epistles, maṇḍala descriptions, fulfillment rites, and guidebooks—are still extant.[1387] He perfected the meditative commitments associated with the two stages, and his acts on behalf of others were like the sky. He also filled the great community of Riwoche with the excellences of the twofold tradition of sūtra and mantra in the manner of Anavatapta Lake, such that he became a focal point for the aspirations of all.

In his forty-fifth year, in 1453 (bird), he fell ill, and he passed away at dawn on the tenth day of the tiger month of 1454 (dog). Following the cremation, images of Mañjughoṣa, Vajravārāhī, and so forth, were retrieved, along with his heart, which was embellished with countless minor relics. When they started to make clay figurines representing him, they were naturally indistinguishable from him in person. Marvelous funerary rituals were performed, including the most auspicious and bountiful of the means that fulfilled his enlightened intention and the commissioning of outer and inner representations.

Through these wondrous waves,
Arousing ancient clouds of narrative,
May the superior communities of the Auspicious Eon
Playfully perform the dance of faith and enthusiasm! {653}

Gonpo Yeshe

Homage to the one named **Gonpo Yeshe,**
Lord-protector (*dgon po*)[1388] who summited the three trainings and two stages
And who, as regent of the **lord-protector** (*dgon po*) Drakpei Pel,
Was offered authority as **lord-protector** (*dgon po*) by gods and other living beings!

Choje Gonpo Yeshe, also known as a total renunciant, was the second of six siblings born to Pontsang Sonam Rinchen and his consort Rongza Alhama. He was born in 1430 (iron male dog). The name Trowo was conferred upon him. In his eighth year, after his father passed away, the mother and her son made donations, commissioned a gold image of the Teacher with its throne and back screen that was installed in the lower hall of the Great Temple, arranged butter lamps, and so forth.[1389]

In his sixteenth year, in the waxing half of the snake month, in 1445 (wood female ox), he was ordained as a mendicant by Sonam Rinchen acting as monastic preceptor, Chogowa Sangzang acting as master of ceremonies, and Geshe Lodro Zangpo acting as sundial timekeeper. The name Drakpa Tashi Pelzangpo was conferred upon him.

He then received completely the profound doctrinal cycles of the Kagyu tradition and all the empowerments and transmissions of the ancient and new mantra traditions from Drung Lodro Rinchen, and the Shangpa doctrines from Tsampon Tsultrim Ozer. From Choje Miyo Gonpo, he requested all the empowerments, transmissions, and esoteric instructions of the precious Collected Works of Venerable Sangye On in their entirety. With the disposition of an exclusive retreatant, he applied himself to study, reflection, and meditation, and thus became a mighty lord of accomplishment, a master of the doctrines of transmission and realization.

Gonpo Yeshe commissioned many representations of the meditative commitments, {654} and undertook the maintenance, nurturing, and enhancement of the great monastic seat of Yelpuk, in accordance with the two traditions of sūtra and mantra. He acted for the well-being of all the monks and laity of Ta, Yel, and Cham, and of Dachi. Appointing the reincarnation Sangye Rinchen as the frontier official of Yelpuk, he secured the monastic precepts in the short term and in the long term.

In 1454 (dog), when Venerable Miyowa Gonpo passed away, he performed the cremation and made bountiful funerary offerings. He commissioned a perfect image of Munīndra in the form Great Enlightenment, with its throne and back screen.[1390]

In his twenty-fifth year (1454), Gonpo Yeshe received the full monastic ordination from Sherab Yeshe, the great monastic preceptor, with Sherab Zangpo acting as master of ceremonies, Sonam Zangpo as confessor, and the devout monk Tashi Zangpo and others completing the quorum, and he brought to perfection the aggregate of ethical discipline. He also received the precepts of the vinaya and some minor doctrines from that monastic preceptor. During the summer, the season when fruit trees and flowers blossom, on an auspicious day, he was enthroned, and he resided at the palace of the sacred doctrine in Riwoche Monastery, where he ensured that there was no wavering in the regulations of Kuyalwa Rinchen Gonpo, the charter of the monastic assembly and all the disciplinary rules of the monastery, just as they had been observed in the past. He turned without interruption the wheel of the profound and extensive sacred doctrine, and he did not deviate from the profound meditative commitments, symbolic and nonsymbolic.

Gonpo Yeshe appointed the monastic preceptor, the master of ceremonies, the stewards, the eight seniors of Taklung, and so forth and cut off negativity by rewarding good behavior and reprimanding bad behavior. Without laxity, the charter of the monastic assembly and the regulations of Kuyalwa Rinchen Gonpo, endured like a steady stream of water. Throughout the region, he enhanced the Buddhist teachings and strove for the extensive well-being of the disciples.

In 1462 (water male horse), {655} he appointed Choje Jikten Wangchuk as the dharma regent. He traveled to Retsang Gomde and Lhochi Tsawagang. Then, while he was staying at Yelpuk, during the autumn of 1463 (sheep), he was invited by Zurmang Rinpoche and traveled there.[1391] In order to secure the country in peace, he brought about a great reconciliation.

Sooner or later, Gonpo Yeshe traveled to Lhochen four or five times. Miwang Tsegyel and Nangso Kunga Gyeltsen both offered him Tatsak Lhakhang, with its sacred representations of buddha body, speech, and mind, as well as the land and villages of Dzongkhar Ngisho and the temple and monastic estates of Ngodu. He established all the monks and laity of upper, lower, and middle Lho in maturational empowerment and liberating guidance by means of the four attractive qualities of a bodhisattva.

In 1468 (mouse), on the horse trail to the north, he tamed many pernicious nonhuman spirits. When he cleaned the natural image of Tārā at Paratang, it became brighter, and a rain of flowers fell. From the Dungbumchen reliquary of Jowo Smṛti, he traveled through Litang, Pubor, Upper and Lower Dza, Dob, Gyeltang, Phowa, Yangdang, and so forth, acting for the well-being of innumerable sentient beings.[1392] The material offerings that he received were hard to measure, and the monasteries that were offered were also very many.

During the tenth month of 1469 (ox), Gonpo Yeshe returned to Riwoche. He set up a factory for the maintenance of the gilded roof. Then, in 1471 (hare), his caravan departed again, and he journeyed through many lands. During 1472 (dragon), the work on the gilded roof was completed. In general, sooner or later, he commissioned some sixty gold images of varying sizes, along with about one hundred and fifty paintings and some eighty manuscript volumes.

In his forty-fourth year, during the first month of 1473 (snake), {656} Gonpo Yeshe fell ill. Extensive rituals were performed to maintain his health. Then, on the twenty-first day of the seventh month, he passed away at Rachung in Khar. The cremation was held at Naktsangteng on the eighth day of the eighth month. The sky was filled with rainbows and a shower of flowers fell. When the cremation chamber was opened, images of Hevajra, Vajravārāhī, and so forth were retrieved, along with his tongue, which remained undamaged, and countless minor relics. One night, around that time, there was a pillar of rainbow light that penetrated both Rachung in Khar and the crematorium. At the residence of Tasho Bako, a rain of flowers fell. Representative images of the late teacher were immediately made from medicinal paste that combined medicines, silk, and gemstones. As an outer relic, an image of the lord-protector Maitreya was commissioned.[1393] Between 1473 (snake) and 1474 (horse), there were outbreaks of smallpox and measles in all the lay communities, but eyewitnesses said, "The local deities and spirit lords of the ground cured our illness through the funerary smoke of the late Choje Kunpangpa of Riwoche. Pacifying the harm done to others, they have released everyone from ill-health." So it is said.

Through the resonance of the mighty divine drum of this narrative,
May all who have been our mother, equal to space,
Awaken from the sleep of fundamental ignorance
And acquire omniscience with respect to knowable things!

The Four Successors of Gonpo Yeshe

I pay homage, touching the crown of my devotion at the feet of these three—
Jikten Wangchuk, resplendent with the glory of immortal life and pristine cognition;
Pema Gyelpo, supreme leader among awareness holders, maintaining strict vows,
And Tsokye Dorje, master of vows integrating E and VAṂ in supreme bliss! {657}

Now, at this juncture, I will establish somewhat
The tales that I have simply heard from reliable sources,
As the kernel for an extensive future narrative,
And on that basis, I will quantify them to some extent
With my words of approximation.

Jikten Wangchuk

All the common biographies that partially reveal for the sake of the disciples of this world the inexhaustible wheels of adornment of buddha body, speech, mind, attributes, and activities, through the seven universal monarchs of the sacred doctrine, who successively occupied the lion throne of the monastic seat of Taklung Lower Plain, commencing with Venerable Sangye Onpo Drakpa Pel Ozer Zangpo, were written by Choje Jikten Wangchuk in a work titled *Pearl Necklace: Biographies of the Lineage Holders of Taklung Lower Plain.*[1394] Condensing this text, I have also incidentally included a brief account of the saintly beings who did not accede to the monastic seat but who were beneficial to the doctrine and indisputably holders of the familial line. Now, without having seen any book outlining the lives of the subsequent successors to the monastic seat, and even though I have not found a reliable informant, I will have to write the remainder based on all that I have heard, abandoning exaggeration and deprecation.

Choje Jikten Wangchuk, who is briefly mentioned at the end of the foregoing account of the Kagyu lineage of Taklung Lower Plain, was born at Tramo Rachung in 1454 (wood male dog). He was given the name Jikten Wangchuk based on a prophecy that his babysitter had received in a dream. For eight years, he lived at Lhatsang Khangmoche, where he studied writing and reading under Lama Rinchen Zangpo and Chophel.

In his ninth year, in 1462 (water male horse), {658} during the waxing half of the month of miracles, in Tashi Gomang, alongside the sacred representations with which Sangye On had a connection and that were to be kept safe, including the naturally originated sandalwood image of Jowo that had been the meditative commitment of Shawarawa and the image of Munīndra that had been the inner relic of Sangye Gompa, and in the presence of Choje Gonpo Yeshe, he was ordained as a mendicant with Neten Sonam Zangpo acting as monastic preceptor, Geshe Gyelwa Zangpo acting as master of ceremonies, and Gelong Gendun Pel acting as the timekeeper. The name Sonam Rinchen Gyeltsen Pelzangpo was conferred upon him. He was enthroned ten days later.

From Khenchen Sonam Zangpo and Lopon Gyelzangpa, he received many doctrinal cycles pertaining to the Buddhist teaching in general and the Kagyu lineage in particular. From Choje Gonpo Yeshe, he received in the manner of a vase being filled to the brim all the profound doctrines of the Taklung Kagyu lineage, headed by all the empowerments, transmissions, and esoteric instructions pertaining to the precious Collected Works of Venerable Sangye On. Comprehending these, he became a sovereign of all the doctrines of transmission and realization, a saintly leader capable of deeds like those of a second Teacher with respect to the Buddhist teaching, and a progenitor of all sorts of practitioners—monks, vajra holders, and accomplished masters.

In 1467 (pig), at the entreaty of Drubchen Chuphurwa Śākya Rinchen, he undertook a strenuous reconstruction of the monastery and gave the mendicant ordination to many venerable elders.[1395] By making and implementing these arrangements, the precious monastery was maintained and secured, such that the number of assembled palanquins[1396] also greatly increased. Above the residence, he newly constructed a temple replete with the three representations and perfect sacraments of offering. {659} He then commissioned a complete manuscript of the Kangyur and Tengyur inscribed in gold and silver on parchment and the complete *Collected Works of the Kagyu Tradition*, which were most immaculate, with eaglewood book covers, as well as countless images, paintings, and relief statues, headed by a silver image of Hevajra with a gilded-copper back screen.[1397] He maintained without error the noble custom of observing the charter of the monastic assembly and all the former regulations instated by Kuyalwa Rinchen Gonpo but slightly widened access to meetings and teachings.

Leaving aside his other magnanimous religious acts, at the very least, Jikten Wangchuk cheated death by paying the price for many thousands of creatures that were bound for slaughter, and brought them forth from the jaws of the Lord of Death. He permitted birds, herds of deer, and all aquatic creatures to move freely and safely without being endangered by hunters or fishermen, and he constructed a great many iron bridges and wooden bridges spanning wide rivers that could not otherwise be crossed, thereby granting the refuge of fearlessness to all persons who came and went. Such activities indeed surpassed the confines of the imagination.

In 1523 (water female sheep), sixty-two years after his enthronement at the age of nine[1398] in 1462, Jikten Wangchuk composed the aforementioned *Doctrinal History of the Kagyu Tradition of Taklung Lower Plain*.[1399]

In the fifty-fourth year of this venerable master, in 1507 (fire female hare), Karmapa Mikyo Dorje was born. In the latter's autobiography it says, "I have outer, inner, and secret parents. In the field of the buddha body of perfect resource, in the form of the syllable HRĪḤ, the essential nature of the pristine cognition of all the buddhas, {660} I arose from the mouth of my secret father Choje Jikten Wangchuk (Lokeśvara), who assumed the form of Cakrasaṃvara. I then entered the womb of my secret mother, Adron—an emanation of Vajrayoginī. These two are bodhisattvas of the tenth level, and it is owing merely to the perception of deceitful senses that my origins ostensibly appear to be inferior. Thereafter, I was born with the form of a heruka, the causal basis of the buddha body of perfect resource. I arose from the mouth of my inner father, the mendicant of Ser Jampa Shenyen, and entered the womb of my inner mother, the nāginī Darseldron. In consequence of that, my speech is slightly stilted, and my relatives are ostensibly dim-witted. These two had both attained the path of connection, according to the way of mantra. Having completely received the inner empowerments of the Adamantine Vehicle in those secret and inner wombs, I now took birth from the womb of my inner mother in the form of the buddha body of emanation. My outer father is Jampa, and I entered the womb of my outer mother, Domza Lala Madron. These two had both attained the path of provisions according to the way of mantra."[1400]

Later, when Amdo Tulku Kyase Tokden and all the nomadic populace determined that Mikyo Dorje was the Karmapa, this was decisively confirmed by Choje Jikten Wangchuk, who indisputably recognized him, saying, "This is the genuine Tulku!" Thus, his service to the lineage of the Karmapas was unrivaled. Later, when Jedrung Karmapa visited Riwoche, he was enthroned there with great respect and offerings. The tulku in return also said, "This is the auspicious coincidence, on the basis of which the teachings of Choje Jikten Wangchuk will flourish like the rivers in summertime."

In brief, Jikten Wangchuk lived a longer life than all his predecessors, and his enlightened activity with respect to the twofold tradition of sūtra and mantra was great. {661} In establishing the regulations of Kuyalwa Rinchen Gonpo and in the meditative commitments associated with practice, he was without rival. Since his learning was extremely vast, he comprehended all doctrines and was unimpeded in teaching and composition. Indeed, by instructing others in the immaculate profound doctrines of Venerable Sangye On and by experientially cultivating them himself, he ensured that the philosophical framework of the Riwoche tradition was intact and that it became a unique sustainer of the precious teaching of the practice lineage in later times. Finally, in his seventy-eighth year (1532), the array of his physical body dissolved.

Pema Gyelpo

Choje Pema Gyelpo, the familial nephew of Jikten Wangchuk, was the one who became his doctrinal regent. As a mendicant, the name Pema Gyeltsen Pelzangpo was conferred upon him. He acquired the extraordinary practice of authentic consciousness transference endowed with blessings from Choje Jikten Wangchuk.

Pema Gyelpo excellently received all the oral instructions of profound maturational empowerment and liberating guidance of the glorious Taklung Kagyu tradition from his father Choje Kharwa, who was a master of gnostic mantras and others. Moreover, he attended upon many spiritual mentors and infinitely studied the vehicle of dialectics as well as the way of mantra according to the ancient and new traditions. Through excellent yogic discipline imbued with the three isolations of body, speech, and mind, he experientially cultivated the profound esoteric instructions, such that he perfected all the meditative experiences and realizations that were his lot.

Following his accession to the lion throne of the great monastic seat of Riwoche, Pema Gyelpo excellently maintained the entire congregation through his enlightened activities endowed with the authentic twofold tradition of sūtra and mantra. He commissioned sacred representations of buddha body, speech, and mind, and through the positivity of his great offerings and liberality, he ensured that the precious Buddhist teaching would emerge triumphant in battle with the demonic Lord of Desire who bears the crocodile ensign.[1401] {662} He ensured that the charter of the monastic assembly and all the regulations of Kuyalwa Rinchen Gonpo without exception did not degenerate but were enhanced even higher, just as they had been implemented by his teachers and predecessors. Through his skillful means and the power of his great compassion, the lay community and the monastery flourished with the excellent resources of the twofold tradition of sūtra and mantra. Finally, he instantaneously departed for the taintless buddha field where Venerable Sangye On resides.

Drung Sonam Tashi

During the period after Choje Jikten Wangchuk had passed into nirvāṇa and when his heir Pema Gyelpo was in his infancy, the great monastic seat of Riwoche was exclusively maintained by local kinsmen and celibates, and apart from that, it lacked the continuity whereby monastics integrating the regulations of Kuyalwa Rinchen Gonpo with respect to the twofold tradition of sūtra and mantra could accede to the teaching throne. Since the nominated monastic head was also young, Choje Khardrung Sonam Tashi assumed responsibility for all the affairs of glorious Riwoche, spiritual and secular, without ostensibly acceding to the monastic seat.

In general, this precious master had in a previous life been the omniscient Choje Ngagi Wangpo at Taklung Upper Plain. Like the sun rising at daybreak, he pervaded the three world systems with the precious teaching of the practice lineage through his liberating career of buddha body, speech, and mind and through his magnanimous enlightened activities. Thereafter, he had been reborn in the familial line of Riwoche.

From childhood, Sonam Tashi was intent on emancipation from cyclic existence, and he had unique devotion to genuine liberation. He took flight, into the presence of one known as Zhamarwa of Papom, {663} a saintly being in whom perfect meditative commitment had been born through the definitive oral instructions of Venerable Ngagi Wangpo. Reaching his residence during the night, Sonam Tashi waited until daybreak at the door of the grass hermitage. Zhamarwa then saw in his mind Venerable Ngagi Wangpo seated at the door, and although he was engaged in a period of very strict retreat, at dawn he immediately broke open the door, and they had a joyful meeting. There was a felt garment dyed with saffron that Pa Rinpoche (Ngagi Wangpo) had given him placed next to a pile of a hundred gold coins.[1402] He recognized it, saying, "This is mine!" So it was that the lama Zhamarwa comprehended with certainty that he was the reincarnation of Venerable Ngagi Wangpo and completely offered him all the doctrinal cycles of the Kagyu tradition that he possessed, without exception.

Sonam Tashi received all the father doctrines of the glorious Taklung Kagyu lineage from Choje Jikten Wangchuk and all the profound doctrines of the great accomplished master Sangye On from one named Chophel Zangpo. He integrated study, reflection, and meditation and became a mighty lord of yoga, equal to space, who had internally perfected the expressive energy of pristine cognition. Although he sought to adopt the precepts of a monk that would have fulfilled his own inclination, because the line of monastic heads was extremely tenuous, Venerable Jikten Wangchuk advised that he should get married, and all the monks and patrons unanimously insisted that he do so. He agreed, his intention turning toward the continuity of the teaching.

During the lifetime of this venerable master, many lay communities of the upper and lower valleys, here and there, held many misconceptions about the practitioners of Riwoche. {664} Accordingly, from the perspective of the doctrine, Sonam Tashi performed numerous rites of wrathful sorcery based on the manifold meditational deities and doctrinal protectors of the ancient and new traditions. From the mundane perspective, also, although there was some need to engage in disputation, warfare, and so forth, his enlightened activity was indivisible from that of the unborn Lama Zhang, in acting for the well-being of the Buddhist teaching and sentient beings. Finally, through this venerable master's myriad rites of pacification, enrichment, subjugation, and wrath, all the inimical thoughts of the opposing factions were calmed. The precious monastic seat of Riwoche flourished even more, based on the two traditions of sūtra and mantra. Even those who had formerly been condescending later became his disciples, subdued in accordance with the sacred doctrine. Even those who were most pernicious were unable to bear the ailments and mishaps that, not once but repeatedly, afflicted their bodies, vitality, resources, and family lines as the punishment of the protectors of the transmitted teachings, and they came to bow at his feet.

With regard to the sacred representations of buddha body, Sonam Tashi disapproved of people entering the monastic seat and visiting or staying in the room in Yang Gonteng, where the representations with which Sangye On had a connection and that were to be kept safe were housed, and he did not actually permit that. Even so, with regard to the nectar of the empowerments, transmissions, and esoteric instructions of the oceanic profound doctrines of Venerable Sangye On and so forth, he conferred the maturational empowerments and liberating guidance upon innumerable fortunate persons.

On one occasion, on the basis of a mutual dispute, one named Sangye Drakpa of Nangchen, who had been an actual disciple of Pa Rinpoche Ngagi Wangpo, began to perform a wrathful rite against Choje Khardrung, master and disciples, but at that time, he experienced a vision in which Pa Rinpoche arrived in the sky in front, just as day was breaking {665} and regretfully said, "Is it right that you do such things against me?" Sangye Drakpa then offered his confession.

Sonam Tashi advised that the monastic charter and the rituals and charms for long life, protection, and aversion, and so forth should be unwaveringly maintained, as they had been observed in the past. He gave birth to three sons in his familial line, including Choje Pema Gyelpo; His Presence Tsokye Dorje, who was endowed with the great enlightened activity of the supreme incarnation Drakpa Pel; and the glorious governor Wangdrak Dorje. After establishing innumerable sentient beings in maturational empowerment and liberating guidance, finally, the array of his physical body vanished into Akaniṣṭha.

First Jedrung, Tsokye Dorje

After Choje Pema Gyelpo, the next person empowered with the blessing of the supreme pristine cognition of all the lines of the buddhas of the authentic lineage as a universal monarch of the sacred doctrine, upon the lion throne of the monastic seat of Riwoche, was the peerless supreme incarnation, His Presence Choje Tsokye Dorje. He was born in 1530 (iron male tiger). Since he received monastic ordination from a preceptor, master of ceremonies, and quorum of monks who were perfect with all the defining characteristics, according to the threefold affirmation,[1403] he was no different from the Tathāgata in all acts associated with the Buddhist teachings.

Under many extraordinary spiritual mentors of the Great Vehicle, Tsokye Dorje excellently cultivated both the relative and absolute mind of enlightenment, and he became a unique ford for all the transcendent perfections, identical to all the great heirs of the Conqueror. He attended upon the great adamantine holder Choje Pema Gyelpo; his own father, the supreme awareness holder Drung Sonam Tashi; {666}, Rinchen Nyingpo of Yelpuk; the meditation supervisor Tashi Zangpo; and so forth, in the correct manner and with manifold acts of service and the three means of pleasing the spiritual teacher. Above all, he became a perfect successor to the transmitted teachings of supreme coalescent pristine cognition, since the genuine transference of the blessing of the Kagyu tradition of peerless Phakmodrupa was transferred to his mind, in the manner in which one butter lamp expires in a second one. To his disciples, it was as if he received all the teachings of the different lineage traditions that were known in Tibet, headed by the maturational empowerments, liberating guidance, and supporting transmissions for the precious Collected Works of Venerable Sangye On.

After Choje Pema Gyelpo had passed into the expanse of reality, Tsokye Dorje alone acceded to the fearless lion throne and enhanced his enlightened activity, teaching the sacred doctrine. He implemented all the regulations of Choje Kuyalwa Rinchen Gonpo, the charter of the monastic assembly, and the disciplinary rules of the monastery, without deviating even slightly from the regimes of his successive predecessors. In a skillful manner, he experientially cultivated all doctrinal cycles including the texts and oral instructions of the Kagyu tradition in general and the Taklung Riwoche tradition in particular. Without interruption, he constantly turned the doctrinal wheel of excellent instructions for the sake of others.

The glorious life of this Taklungpa, king of the sacred doctrine, excellently endowed with the essential precious ethical discipline, knowledge, and conduct, was manifestly akin to that of Rāhulabhadra, son of the supreme Conqueror, who respected the precepts.[1404] His mind was not confined solely to the cultivation of the elaborate meditational deities, headed by his three billion combined recitations of the mantras of glorious Sahajasaṃvara[1405] and of Four-Armed Adamantine Kākamukha Mahākāla, which culminate the generation stage of meditation, and the ocean of the protectors of the transmitted teachings. {667} Nor did his supreme quiescence of nonconceptual meditative stability partake of the distinction between meditation and post-meditation. Without neglecting even those who slightly transgressed the prohibited boundaries to be negated or established, he immediately seized upon their faults and uprooted them, such that there was no one who transgressed his onerous command, as if it were a golden yoke. The mightiest of mundane and supramundane protectors were assigned their tasks in the manner of a servant, such that he achieved all enlightened activities without impediment. The injunctions that he made, saying, "Later this will come to pass," certainly came about in a timely manner—other than that, there could be no mistake. Not only did human beings fear the transgression of his injunctions, even the birds in the sky would pass over that land, without resisting to chirp, "Here we are again!" Even when the Chagar Mongol army actually arrived, they turned back, unable to harm the great monastic seat of Riwoche. And afterward, he made many ritual devices for suppression, incineration, and bondage, saying, "The Mongols will not come within the range visible from the monastery from my rooftop!" That is exactly what transpired.

Later, in his fifty-sixth year, in 1585 (wood female bird), Tsokye Dorje thought that he should engage in the approach to liberation whereby the two rivers of the lineage descending from Upper and Outer Taklung might always converge in common savor in the oceanic expanse of excellent merit. To that end, he invited from Taklung Upper Plain my supreme guide, the lord of our enlightened heritage, Kunga Tashi, such that the heads of Taklung Upper and Lower Plain had an auspicious meeting. They exchanged profound teachings, {668} and their minds merged together. Their philosophical perspectives were indivisibly one, and the teaching of Taklungpa came to resemble the sun rising at the break of day. They joyfully offered one another representations of buddha body, speech, and mind and innumerable consecrated inner relics. They stamped their seals on an official document pledging that, without contaminating the pristine waters of the familial lineage and doctrinal lineage of glorious Taklungpa with the muddy waters of other traditions, even to the extent of a hair, starting from then until the end of time, all the great saintly incarnations, who were holders of the Buddhist teachings, would focus on the innermost spirituality of buddha mind and otherwise not permit needless acceptance and rejection.

In brief, the kindness of this approach to liberation, commencing from the encounter of these two saintly individuals of Upper and Outer Taklung, ensured that cyclic existence would be rendered nonexistent due to whatever acts of service we, the disciples and subjects of the future, might perform.

On that occasion, as soon as I met the uncle and nephew, I too abandoned idleness and requested all the doctrinal cycles of Taklung Lower Plain that had been excellently offered to Zhabdrung Kunga Tashi. I was encouraged by a sealed document that stated, "It will depend upon you that these profound doctrines of Venerable Sangye On, with their empowerments, transmissions, and esoteric instructions that resemble molten gold, do not fade but are widely propagated." I am proud to achieve even a fraction of that injunction by cherishing effort.

In general, Venerable Tsokye Dorje restored all the sacred representations and the chapels housing them at the monastic seat of Taklung Lower Plain. He also commissioned new ones as well and extensively propagated this tradition. It is impossible to write adequately of his enlightened activities in maintaining, nurturing, and protecting the teaching in ways such as these. {669}

Finally, in his sixty-first year, in 1590 (iron male tiger), the reflection of Tsokye Dorje's physical body was absorbed into the great adamantine maṇḍala, the taintless eastern buddha field bedecked with flowers, where all the conquerors and his predecessors without exception supremely rejoice. The cremation was excellently conducted, and an offering reliquary commissioned, representing the great enlightenment of the buddha body of reality.

Namgyel Drakpa Pelzangpo

Gonpo Dorje, a mighty lord of the two sciences who cultivated virtue in accordance with the sacred doctrine, was the son of the chieftain Wangchuk Dorje. He in turn had three sons, of whom the middle one, on being ordained as a mendicant, received the name Namgyel Drakpa Pelzangpo. He in recent times acceded to the monastic seat. In old age, he became a lay practitioner and lived in a large mansion. It is said that there is some suggestion that the reincarnation of the late Jedrung Tsokye Dorje is his young nephew.[1406]

So it is that I have recounted merely the kernel of the lives of these four generations, along with other incidental anecdotes. In the future, this should be supplemented if an authentic historical document is seen or a reliable and rational report is heard.

May the vessels of all intelligent beings be well filled
With continuous drops of wondrous nectar
That give birth to the wish-fulfilling tree of history,
And, with tongues of faith and enthusiasm, may they relish the taste of liberation!

Concluding Verses

Emaho!
Embodying the compassion of the ocean of auspicious conquerors,
Glorious field of the ocean of new merits,
Immersed in the ocean of wondrous biographies,
Essence of the ocean of the unsurpassed precious jewels, {670}
At this adamantine monastic seat of manifest enlightenment.
The heirs of the Conqueror of the ten directions, none excepted,
Have conferred empowerment through the ritual arrangements of auspicious song,
Combined with musicality and a great downpour of *mandārava* flowers,
In the vital essence of the expansive means of the supreme doctrinal kings.

The great regents rejoicing on the golden throne of positive enlightened activity,
Elevated by their gemstone mansion of the three trainings,
The great drum of their reputation reaching out with complete clarity,
Form until the very end, on behalf of living beings,
An uninterrupted beauteous garland of emanational lineage holders.

In the white sandalwood forest of history,
Imbued with the anthers of good tidings,
May the best of my faithful intentions,
Playing with the dance of new delights,
Eschew inappropriate words at this time,
Concerning the chronicles composed by past masters,
And render this book that gathers together
The requisite and definitive essentials worthy of being retained!

The power of the blessings of the glorious authentic lineage,
The attractive **power of speech** (*ngag dbang*)
Is nameworthy as the sun of the sacred doctrine.
As for its noble and fearless enlightened activity,
By virtue of laboriously compiling
The garlands of wondrous tales
Of those who have appeared in the lineage of supreme incarnations,
Upholding the three piṭakas of definitive meaning,
Nucleus of the teaching **triumphant** (*rnam rgyal*)
Over all demonic directions,
And maintaining the adamantine vows that are most secret,
May the expansive foliage of this enlightened activity
Encompass all directions.
And may the glory of its branches of liberation
Surpass even the summit of exalted existence! {671}

May this place where inexhaustible feasts emerge,
Ripe with exquisite fruits of pristine cognition
That captivate the minds of intelligent bees
With their fine fragrance of merit,
Be adorned with flower garlands of esoteric instruction—
The great seal of definitive meaning,
Conferring bliss on the hearts of many scholars
Through the shining emerald hue of scriptural transmission!

May the wish-granting tree that gathers the entire teaching,
Filling the spacious confines of the three world systems,
Shelter the minds of all living beings
From the tormenting heat of existence and quiescence
And cast the cooling shade of supreme bliss!

This completes chapter eight of the extensive exegesis of the biographies of the Taklung Kagyu lineage holders from *Wondrous Ocean of Eloquence: A Narrative of the Wish-Fulfilling Gem of the Lineage* compiled by Gelong Ngawang Namgyel.

9. The Biographies of the Diverse Kagyu Traditions

Herein is contained a rough biographical account of the Kagyu lineage holders in general, chapter nine of *The Doctrinal History Titled Wondrous Ocean.* {675}

Verses of Homage

OṂ SVĀSTI

I offer the crown of my head to the precious Kagyu lineage,
Essence of the doctrinal wheel of the conquerors,
Its word, meanings, and concepts without exception
Actually born in the minds of disciples![1]

Preamble

The ninth part of this book is a rough biographical account of the Kagyu lineage holders in general. Overall, the emancipation that is not captivated by existence or quiescence, the enlightened mind through which the self cherishes others, the devotion to the spiritual teacher, the buddha body of reality, the pure vision that perceives all things as sameness, the dislike for pointless attachments in all respects, the realization that the genuine mode of being arises internally, the fruition that buddhas acquire from the mind, and the understanding of "total liberation through singular knowledge"[2] are said to characterize the Great Vehicle of quintessential definitive meaning that has been revealed in the wake of all great accomplished masters.[3]

The mighty lords of accomplishment of India and Tibet who have maintained this tradition, endowed with the bountiful promulgation of the two methods of the Great Seal, constitute the precious Kagyu lineage that is renowned throughout the three world systems. Within it, the biographies associated with the four descents of the transmitted teachings,[4] the two masters of supreme vision,[5] Śavaripā and his disciple Maitripā,[6] and the four predecessors of Taklungpa the Great[7] have already been extensively presented, along with the names of just the most senior of their disciples. Now I shall briefly mention the most important of the other lineage holders, continuing on from that discussion.

Among the disciples of Lord Marpa, who were known as the "four pillars," {676} the three comprising Ngok, Tsur, and Me held the exegetical transmission, and Mila Repa held the practical transmission.

Ngok Khacho Wangpo Choku Dorje

The vajra holders who successively appeared in the familial line of glorious Ngok were mighty lords of Hevajra, Catuḥvajrapīṭha, and Mahāmāyā. Included among them were some who rendered as bright as sunrise the teaching of the Adamantine Vehicle, endowed with the exegesis of the tantras and the enlightened activity that imparts the esoteric instructions.

The first in line was Ngok Khacho Wangpo Choku Dorje (1036–1097), who held the descent of the oral teachings of the great Marton Lotsāwa's *Exegesis of the Tantra of Hevajra*. His disciples included Ram Tsenchen, Pa Wabachen, Ngok Depachen, Gya Amachen, Sumpa Pokachen, Lhopa Chungmachen, and Nyelpa Ngok Chungmachen.[8]

Thereafter, in his succession came Ngok Dodei Zhedang Dorje (1090–1166), who had visions of fifteen female deities including Nairātmā and who had mastered the path of skillful means. He in turn had many disciples, including Tsak Dharmarāja, Gar Tashi Rinchen, and Gyeltsa Rinchen Gonpo.[9]

Ngok Kunga Dorje (1157–1234) was the founder of the sacred hermitage of Trewu Zhing (1243–1319). Until him, the lineage holders had the status of a mantrin. The latter's son was Ngok Ziji Drakpa, and he was followed by Lama Rinchen Zangpo, renowned as an emanation of Venerable Marpa. These last two had the status of a monk. Ngok Chokyi Gyeltsen dictated *A Great Memorandum on Hevajra*.[10] Then there were Ngok Dondrub Pelwa and Ngok Jangchub Pelwa, these being foremost among their many contemporary upholders of the Buddhist teaching. They also widely propagated the empowerments, transmissions, and esoteric instructions of the Ngok tradition.

Ngok Tashi Peldrub, Ngok Jangchub Peldrub, Ngok Jangchub Drakpa, and Lodro Pelzang, who was in the family lineage of Ngok, and so forth, also appeared. They are merely mentioned in the dynastic succession of this monastic seat that derived from the clan of Tsangtsa at Trewu Zhing,[11] {677} and there were many who issued from the same familial line. They had innumerable disciples who could act for the well-being of others through teaching and composition. In particular, Gyeltsa Tokme Drak (1120–1156), the son of Dode, composed many excellent commentaries on the tantras, and the lineage of his sons was also long-lasting.[12] This concludes the section on Ngok.[13]

Mechenpo Sonam Gyeltsen

Mechenpo Sonam Gyeltsen many times expounded the *Hevajra Tantra* at both Nyangrong and Tsangrong, and he composed an excellent commentary. He then took over the seat of Nezhi Bado. His familial line extended from Mekunpo and Joto through to Lodrak, and the exegetical line of his doctrinal transmission continued through Zhang Sonam Bar, Deshek Yeshe Nyingpo, Zhangton Kunga Drak, Lama Rinchen, and Śākya Gyelpo, down to Zhangton Drakjor. There were also many disciples in this lineage, including Gyatso Drak, who composed commentaries. This concludes the section on Me.[14]

Tsurton Wangi Dorje

Lord Marpa completely conferred the exegesis of the esoteric instructions of *The Five Stages according to the Guhyasamāja*[15] and of the *Guhyasamāja Tantra* itself upon Tsurton Wangi Dorje. His disciple was Khampa Tonyam Dorje, who composed an excellent commentary on this tantra. Khon Gepa Kīrti, Cheton Sonam Gyeltsen, and others were also among his disciples.

Khon Gepa Kīrti's disciple was his brother, Jakhangpa Sonam Rinchen. Thereafter, in succession, there appeared Turlawa Tsultrim Kyab, Tangpewa Phakpa Kyab, Serdingpa Zhonu-o,[16] Kunkhyen Choku Ozer (1214–1292),

Kunkhyen Pak-o, {678} and Buton Rinchendrub (1290–1364), the mighty lord of discriminative awareness, by whom the transmission was extensively propagated.

Moreover, Chogyel Rinchen Lingpa requested the exposition of the *Tantra of the Guhyasamāja* from the three disciples of Khon and from Gyalungpuwa the Younger, who was in the disciple lineage of Khampa Ronyam Dorje. There were also exegetical transmissions of the tantra itself and of the empowerments and transmissions of *The Great Exegetical Tantra Titled Nondual Victor*,[17] which Gyapowa Lungpa and Nyemdo the Omniscient[18] propagated in succession. This concludes the section on Tsur.[19]

Aural Lineages of Rechung Dorje Drak and Namdzong Tonpa Bodhirāja

As for the oral instructions of maturational empowerment and liberating guidance, including the aural lineage of Cakrasaṃvara and the Ḍākinī,[20] which descended to Rechung Dorje Drak, the saintly emanation of glorious Vajrapāṇi, who was the "moonlike" spiritual son of Venerable Zhepa Dorje (Mila Repa), there were twelve actual disciples who completely received his empowerments and were genuinely introduced to pristine cognition, as well as one who received the complete empowerments and thirteen spiritual sons, and so forth, who extensively appeared. Among them were Loji Gowa (fl. twelfth century), Tsangpa Sumpa, Burgom Nakpo, Zangri Repa, and Khyung Tsangpa (1115–1176), whose enlightened activities were great. From Khyung Tsangpa, the lineage descended through Machik Ongjo (fl. twelfth to thirteenth centuries), and from her to Zhanglo Drubpa Pel (b. 1237), and so forth. In this way, the doctrines of the aural lineage of Rechung flourished.[21]

One named Namdzong Tonpa Bodhirāja also completely received the oral instructions of the great venerable one (Mila Repa), and became their compiler. From him the lineage descended through Gungtang Repa, Gyapowa Lungpa, and so forth. There was also a disciple of Ngamdzongpa named Nyelpa Sungche, from whom the lineage in succession passed through Marbu Drakpa Zhonu Sherab, Dromton Rinchen Sherab, and so forth. In this way, the aural lineage of Ngamdzong[22] flourished.[23] {679} This concludes the section on the two aural lineages.

The Abbatial Succession of Gampopa

Gampo Tsultrim Nyingpo (1116–1169) was an actual disciple of Venerable Gampopa and the son of his elder brother. Venerable Gampopa had indeed said of him, "He is the only bodhisattva of all the ten levels that I brought to awakening." At Gampo, he constructed a Tashi Gomang reliquary to house the relics of Gampopa,[24] and he also undertook construction of the Old Offering Chapel and the meditation hermitage. After him, there appeared master Gomchung Sherab Jangchub (1130–1173), and thereafter in succession Dakpo Duldzin (1134–1218), On Sherab Jungne, Damcho Lingpa, Chenga Chotsulwa, Rinpoche Lhalungpa, Rinpoche Bornepa, Rinpoche Chowangpa, and so forth. At a later time, there was a learned and accomplished master named Choje Tashi Namgyel (1513–1588), who founded a new assembly hall and repaired the old one. He composed many treatises, gave teachings on profound guidance, and so forth. Widening the influence of Daklha Gampo, he passed away after living a long life. Nowadays, a clear incarnation of his has appeared and a familial line also continues at the monastic seat. This concludes the section on the monastic succession of Gampopa.[25]

Barompa Chenpo Darma Wangchuk

The actual disciples of Venerable Gampopa were uniquely wonderful, including the great accomplished master Choyung (1100–1177); Olkha Choyung (1103–1199), who had perfected the enlightened attributes of the Six Doctrines; and Lho Layakpa Jangchub Ngodrub, who composed a commentary on the Four Doctrines.

Glorious Barompa Chenpo Darma Wangchuk (1127–1199) was the reincarnation of Kṛṣṇapāda, a practitioner of yogic discipline. He founded Barom Monastery in the North, {680} and he had a reputation for intermingling and transforming his meditative experiences in the great seal of bliss and emptiness and for following awareness alone, the path toward the great seal of the abiding nature. In this way, he brought innumerable fortunate beings to maturational empowerment and liberating guidance.[26]

His seniormost disciple was Drogon Tishrī Repa,[27] and the monastic seat was maintained in succession by the following familial line: Jotsun Namkha Gyeltsen, Drakpa Sherab Jangchub, Wangchuk Gyeltsen, Wangchuk Gyelpo, Wangchuk Rinchen, Khedrub Zhonu Sherab, Lama Chowangpa,

Tsezhiwa Senge Pelwa, Tsechuwa Rinchen Gyeltsen, Nyerchikpa Drakpa Gyeltsen, Namkha Gyeltsen, Kunpang Cholo, Tsultrim Gyatso, and so forth. This concludes the section on Barompa.

Karma Kamtsang

The accomplished master Use[28] had been a celibate practitioner during the teaching period of Buddha Siṃhaśākya in the Auspicious Eon.[29] He was also known as Gomsen Chewa, among the eight hundred great meditators who were disciples of Venerable Gampopa, and he perfected the oral instructions of seven actual disciples of Venerable Mila Repa. In particular, he was a master of the indivisible practices of the innate generation stage and vital energy and mind according to the perfection stage. All the ḍākinīs of pristine cognition offered him an azure crown and conferred upon him the name Karmapa. Consequently, he is universally known as the glorious First Karmapa Dusum Khyenpa (1110–1193).

Although Dusum Khyenpa had innumerable disciples, he was blessed with an unbroken line of his own emanations, and he entrusted the lineage to Sangye Rechen (1148–1218).[30] The latter's disciple was Choje Pomdrakpa Sonam Dorje (1170–1249).[31] Thereafter, the accomplished master Karma Pakshi (1204–1283) ensured that the Mongol Emperor Quiblai could not destroy the Buddhist teaching.[32] {681} His disciple was the accomplished master Urgyenpa Rinchen Pel (1229–1309).[33] Then, Venerable Third Karmapa, Rangjung Dorje (1284–1339) brought forth an infinite number of accomplished masters.[34] His main disciple was Yungton Dorje Pel (1284–1376).[35] Thereafter, Fourth Karmapa, Rolpei Dorje (1340–1383) overwhelmed China, Tibet, and Mongolia.[36] The latter's disciple was the second crown holder of Zhamar, Khacho Wangpo (1350–1405).[37] Then, Venerable Fifth Karmapa, Dezhin Shekpa (1384–1415), protected Tibet from the fear of an invading Chinese army.[38] The latter's disciple was Sokon Rikpei Reldri Rinchen Zangpo. Then, Venerable Sixth Karmapa, Tongwa Donden (1416–1453), tamed his disciples through the way of mantra.[39] The latter's main disciple was Gushri Peljor Dondrub. Then, Venerable Seventh Karmapa, Chodrak Gyatso (1454–1506), propagated the teaching of both scriptural transmission and realization.[40] The latter's main disciple was the accomplished master Sangye Nyenpa. Then, Venerable Eighth Karmapa, Mikyo Dorje (1507–1554), permeated U, Tsang, and Kham with his exegetical colleges and meditation hermitages.[41] His disciple was the fifth crown holder of Zhamar, Konchok Yenlak (1525–1583). Then, Venerable Ninth Karmapa, Wangchuk Dorje (1556–1603), established all the sentient beings who saw, heard, recalled, and came into contact with him in provisional temporal well-being and conclusive spiritual bliss.[42] His main disciple was the sixth crown holder of Zhamar, Dorje Garwang Chokyi Wangchuk (1584–1630), who nowadays serves as the regent of the lineage, teacher of the sacred doctrine.[43] The supreme emanation Tenth Karmapa, Choying Dorje (1604–1674), not long afterward appeared in the world, in accordance with the correct procedure.[44]

The first of the six successive crown holders of Zhamar was Tokden Drak Seng, who stayed in solitude and focused on meditation practice.[45] The second was Venerable Khacho Wangpo (1350–1405), who nurtured living beings through perfect knowledge, love, and power.[46] The third was Choje Chophel Yeshe (1406–1452), who {682} crossed the ocean of secret mantra.[47] The fourth was Chenga Chokyi Drakpa Yeshe Pelzangpo (1453–1524), who permeated Tibet with his positive enlightened activities.[48] The fifth was Venerable Konchok Yenlak (1525–1583), who rendered indivisible the enlightened activities of the red-hat and black-hat hierarchs (Zhamarpa and Karmapa). The sixth was glorious Dorje Garwang Chokyi Wangchuk (1584–1630), who became a unique repository of all the scriptures. Although in general it is said that there will be eleven successive crown holders of the black-hat Karmapas and twenty-one successive crown holders of the red-hat Zhamarpas, these emanations cannot be appraised.[49]

Each of these emanational lineages also produced a countless number of disciples, the foremost of whom could act on behalf of the Buddhist teachings and living beings. Among them, there are two renowned lines in the present day that have supported the teaching of the Kamtsang tradition.

The first of these is that of Gushri Peljor Dondrub (1427–1489), an emanation of Odren Pelgyi Wangchuk and Repa Zhiwa-o, who held the scriptural transmission of both the Kangyur and the Tengyur.[50] His successive emanations included Second Gyeltsab Tulku, Tashi Namgyel (1450–1518), and Third Gyeltsab, Drakpa Peljor (1519–1549), up to Fourth Gyeltsab Tulku, Drakpa Dondrub (1550–1617), who presently has the complete defining characteristics of a virtuous spiritual mentor with respect to both the traditions of Kadam and Great Seal.[51]

The second is that of the genuine saintly being Second Pawo, Tsuklak Trengwa (1504–1566), adorned with learning and accomplishment, the reincarnation of First Pawo, Chowang Lhundrub (1440–1503), who had brought together the twofold benefit of self and others through his great accumulated provisions, triumphant over all directions, previously revealed in the succession of his past lives as many mighty learned and accomplished masters, starting with the great Indian paṇḍita Prajñākara. His reincarnation, Third Pawo Tulku, Tsuklak Gyatso (1567–1633), is alive at present, teaching the sacred doctrine.[52] This concludes the section on Karma Kamtsang.

Dungtso Repa's *Guidance concerning the Nature of Mind*

Dungtso Repa, an incarnation of Venerable Gampopa's disciple Kyepo Yedor, brought forth *Wish-Fulfilling Gem: Guidance on the Nature of Mind*[53] from Lake Maṇḍala Nakpo behind Gampo, along with the rite of the doctrinal protector that had been concealed there by Venerable Gampopa.[54] He taught it to Trukzhik Nawupa Dorje Dze, and thereafter it was propagated through the lineage of Tsungme Rinchen Zhonu (b. 1333), Chenga Sonam Gyeltsen, and so forth. This concludes the section on Dungtso Repa's *Guidance concerning the Nature of Mind*.[55]

Zhang Tselpa Tsondru Drakpa

Drogon Zhang Rinpoche Tsondru Drakpa (1123–1193) was an actual disciple of Venerable Gompa Tsultrim. Through his former emanations in a billion places within Jambudvīpa, he had transformed his pure physical body, the deeds of which he had ripened for the sake of living beings, into a body endowed with the net of magical emanation. His body has attained buddhahood in the buddha body of form and his mind in the buddha body of reality.[56] His monastic seat was successively maintained by the incomparable Śākya Yeshe (1147–1207), the master Jang Ye, Lhachukpa Nyiza-o, Sangye Bum, Sangye Nyingpo (d. 1238), Sangye Repa (d. 1260), Serkhang Tengpa Kunga Gyeltsen (1223–1292), and so forth. The actual disciples of Drogon Zhang Rinpoche were inestimable, including the four with the name O, (namely, Lhariwa Namkha-o, Lhachukpa Nyima-o, Kharak Drapa Dulwa-o, and Drirawa Śākya-o).

From Ponchen Darma Zhonu, the attendant of Zhang Rinpoche (d. 1220), the great attendants of Tsel Gungtang, who were appointed as masters of the twofold tradition of sūtra and tantra, and as representatives of

Zhang Rinpoche himself, are successively identified. Among them, from the time of Tselpon Sangye Ngodrub (b. 1261) onward, the great governors of Tselpa, who were descended from the clan of Lonpo Gar, appeared in succession. For many years, they took care of political affairs in Tibet, and as long as they did so, the Buddhist teaching continued undiminished. Later, the great temple at Tsel Gungtang was destroyed by fire. Nowadays, at this monastic seat, merely the representations of Zhang Rinpoche's body, speech, and mind have been preserved, along with the Protector Chapel and so forth. {684} The transmission of his profound doctrines does exist elsewhere, taught and studied by great upholders of the Buddhist teachings. This concludes the section on Tselpa.[57]

The Abbatial Succession of Densatil

After the glorious lord-protector of living beings Phakmodrupa had passed away at the most sacred place of Densatil, Kyura Rinpoche of Drigung protected the monastic seat to some extent. Afterward, the omniscient Chenga Rinpoche Drakpa Jungne (1175–1255), who had been born into the family of Langlha Zik and who was a supreme saintly being, totally unrivaled in all realms including that of the gods, stayed there. Then, in succession, there appeared at Densatil Chenga Tok Dukpa Drakpa Tsondru (1203–1267), Chunyipa Rinchen Dorje (1218–1280), Rinpoche Drakpa Yeshe (1240–1288), Nyichopa Drakpa Rinchen (1250–1310), Tsezhi Nyingma Drakpa Gyeltsen (1293–1360), Chunyi Sarmawa Drakpa Sherab (1310–1370), Tsezhi Sarmawa Drakpa Jangchub (1356–1386), Choje Sonam Drakpa (1359–1408), Chenga Pelden Zangpo (1383–1407), Nyernyi Rinpoche Sonam Gyeltsen (1386–1434), Choje Pel Ngagi Wangchuk (1439–1495), and so forth. Later, the monastic seat was occupied by three successive crown holders of Zhamar.[58]

By the power of glorious Phakmodrupa having established auspicious circumstances for the recovery of the aged Geshe Lang, the rulers of Tibet subsequently appeared in the family line of Lhazik Lang.[59] The Tripon Dorje Pel founded some large estates including Neudong. Later, Tai Situ Jangchub Gyeltsen (r. 1350–1371), the elder brother of Chunyi Sarmawa, served as the governor of Utsang for some forty years. He founded the monastery of Tsetang and many large forts. Onpo Jamyang Gushri Śākya Gyeltsen (r. 1372–1384) then obtained a prophetic declaration that he would "know the three provinces of Tibet." {685} In his lineage, the dynasty known as the Rulers

Who Secured the Wooden Gates of Tibet has long endured, and even now there are many descendants.[60] This concludes the section on Densatil.

The Abbatial Succession of Drigung

It was through the kindness of the great saintly being, glorious Phakmodrupa, an emanation of Nāgārjunagarbha, that glorious Drigungpa the Great, Jikten Gonpo Rinchen Pel (1143–1217) perfected his realization, and his enlightened intention became comparable to that of all the buddhas.[61] He obtained auspicious circumstances, enabling birds and wild deer to meditate. This venerable master acted like the rising sun on behalf of the Buddhist teachings, through the doctrinal wheel that reveals causes and results to be indivisible in emptiness. His community is said to have numbered fifty-five thousand five hundred. On one occasion, for example, the tally stick counted one hundred thousand monks.

The seniormost of his disciples were innumerable, including the Four Chenga; the Trio of Nye Gyelwa Lhanangpa, (1164–1224), Gar Dampa Chodingpa (b. 1180), and Cho Pelden Choye; and the Twelve Great Glorious Ones.[62]

As far as the dynastic abbatial succession of Drigung is concerned, this line consisted of Khenchen Rinchen Tsultrim Dorje (1154–1221), On Rinpoche Sonam Drakpa (1187–1234), Venerable Chenga Drakpa Jungne (1175–1255), Chung Dorje Drak (1211–1279), Tokhawa Rinchen Senge (1227–1285), Samchepa Drakpa Sonam (1238–1286), Chogowa Dorje Yeshe (1223–1293), Chunyi Dorje Rinchen (1278–1314), Nyergyepa Dorje Gyelpo (1283–1350), Nyernyipa Chenga Chokyi Gyelpo (1335–1407), and Choje Dondrub Gyelpo (1369–1427). Then came Chogyel Rinchen Pelzang (1421–1469) and Choje Rinchen Chokyi Gyeltsen Pelzangpo (1449–1484), the sons of Wang Rinchen the Elder (1395–1467), who both had to maintain the familial line and did not accede to the monastic seat but who nonetheless protected the Buddhist teachings. Furthermore, Wang Rinpoche studied under Taklung Ngawang Drakpa and revitalized that lineage of the sacred doctrine. {686}

Thereafter, Kunga Rinchen (1475–1527) greatly elucidated the teaching of the practice lineage, and Rinpoche Chokyi Gyelpo Gompei Tsul of Drigung[63] resided at the palace of Phakmodru. Later, the monastic seat was successively occupied by Wang Rinchen Phuntsok Chokyi Gyelpo (1509–1557), Choje Rinchen Namgyel (1519–1576), Choje Paṇchen Sonam

Gyatso (1527–1570), Dungyupa Chokle Namgyel (1557–1579), and Chogyel Phuntsok Tashi Pelzangpo (1547–1602). Nowadays, Choje Tashi Phuntsok (1574–1628) is the incumbent.[64] This concludes the section on the Drigungpa.[65]

Yamzang Choje

Zarawa Kalden Yeshe Senge (c. 1168–1207) was a disciple of Drogon Phakmodrupa. His disciple in turn was Yamzang Choje (1169–1233). The latter's disciples included four with the name Gom.[66] The monastic seat was held in succession by the attendant of Yamzang Choje named Rinchen Jose (d. 1242), Tokden Gyelpo Gedze-o (tenure 1243–1280), Kharchungwa Chosam-o, Zarawa Delek-o, Dungyupa Tashi-o (tenure 1281–1298), and so forth. This concludes the section on the Yamzangpa.[67]

Trophuwa Gyeltsa Rinpoche Rinchen Gon

Furthermore, there was a disciple of Drogon Rinpoche Phakmodrupa named Gyer Gomchen, who founded Nyepu Shukseb and whose enlightened activity was great. In Kham, also, there were Marpa and Zolpukpa, who both engaged directly and indirectly in great enlightened activities.

Gyeltsa Rinpoche Rinchen Gon (1118–1195) was the disciple of glorious Phakmodrupa, who founded Trophu.[68] His nephew was Kunden (1148–1217). Tro Lotsāwa Jampa Pel (1173–1236) was the son of Jopen, the latter's younger brother. It was he who invited Mitrayogin;[69] Śākyaśrī, the great paṇḍita of Kashmir; and the great paṇḍita Buddhaśrī to Trophu, and he commissioned a large image of Maitreya. After him there appeared Lachen Sonam Wangchuk (b. thirteenth century), Sempa Chenpo Sonam Senge (b. thirteenth century), and the latter's disciple, Yangtsewa Rinchen Senge (b. thirteenth century). {687} His disciple in turn was Buton Rinchendrub (1290–1364). This concludes the section on the Trophuwa.[70]

The Middle Drukpa: The Abbatial Succession of Ralung

The disciple of Drogon Rinpoche named Drubchen Lingre Pema Dorje (1128–1188) was renowned for his high realization on this side of the River Ganges. He dreamed that Vajraḍākinī entrusted a book to him and that he swallowed it. Consequently, the stain of unknowing with respect to all things came to an end. He lived as an actual embodiment of glorious Heruka and acted for the well-being of living beings.

His disciple who had determined all things through his singular understanding was Tsangpa Gyare Yeshe Dorje (1161–1211). He was one in whom a sky-like realization of the great seal arose. All auspicious circumstances clearly appeared to him like the image on a mirror. He was endowed with twelve approaches to liberation that were uncommon.[71] The teaching that he imparted to a series of disciples permeated all directions for a distance of eighteen vulture flying days.

The foremost of his disciples were Pariwa and Kyangmo Khapa, Gya Yakpa, and Dre Mopa, along with Lorepa and Gotsangpa Gonpo Dorje. Onre Darma Senge (b. 1177) resided at the monastic seat. Thereafter, the lineage of this nephew appeared in succession as follows: Zhonu Senge (1200–1266); Nyima Senge (1251–1287); Pokyawa Senge Rinchen (1258–1313); Senge Gyelpo (1289–1325); Jamyang Kunga Senge (1314–1347); Lodro Senge (1345–1390); Sherab Senge (1371–1392); Yeshe Rinchen (1364–1413);[72] and Second Gyelwang Drukchen, Choje Kunga Peljor (1428–1476), the last of whom had most extensive enlightened activities and even occupied the monastic seat of Gampo. Then, there appeared in succession the peerless Ngawang Chokyi Gyelpo (1465–1540), his son Ngawang Drakpa Tenpei Gyeltsen (1506–1538), his younger brother Ngagi Wangchuk (1517–1554), and glorious Mipham Chogyel (1543–1604). At present, Dungyu Rinpoche Mipham Tenpei Nyima (1567–1619) resides there.[73]

Later, one named Fourth Drukchen Mipham Pema Karpo (1527–1592), a great paṇḍita learned in all the five fields of classical learning, appeared like the rising sun, in accordance with the former aspirations of Lord Nārotapa and Tsangpa Gyare that the essence of the enlightened activity of Ngawang Chokyi Gyelpo might again work on behalf of the teaching of the glorious Drukpa tradition. {688} He filled the entire country of Tibet with communities engaged in exegesis and practice and realized disciples. The writings that he composed elucidated, clarified, and authenticated with sources concern all the texts and esoteric instructions that are known within the glorious Drukpa Kagyu tradition.

Pema Karpo established individuals who definitively belonged to the precious Kagyu lineage in the liberation of Lord Mila through the path of direct guidance of esoteric instruction. He also made degenerate individuals who were unable to enter instantaneously into the teaching of definitive meaning study and reflect upon the five fields of classical learning: sūtra and mantra, Sanskrit grammar, logic, arts, and so forth. He passed away having rendered clear as day the teaching of both scriptural transmission and realization.

He then revealed his supreme reincarnation, Fifth Drukchen, Paksam Wangpo (1593–1641), who is alive at present, acting as a genuine source of infinite spiritual and temporal well-being for the sake of the Buddhist teaching and living beings. He continues to reveal the excellent path that engages the approaches of reading, study, and reflection according to the perspective of others.

This concludes the section on the Kagyu lineage holders of the monastic seat of Ralung, who are known as the Middle Drukpa.[74]

The Upper Drukpa, the Lineage of Gotsangpa Gonpo Dorje

Gotsangpa Gonpo Dorje (1189–1258), the disciple of Drogon Tsangpa Gyare, was a mighty lord of yoga, unrivaled under the sun, endowed with twelve meditative commitments—thirteen, including the protective armor—and approaches to liberation that includes the three pledges of buddha body, speech, and mind; the seven immediate pledges; and the five extraordinary pledges.[75]

Although his disciples were like the constellations in the sky, among them, the one who was his equal in yogic discipline was the great accomplished master Urgyenpa Rinchen Pel (1230–1309).[76] He manifestly received the profound instructions of ritual service and attainment from Vajrayoginī, and he acted as a master of the Buddhist teaching in India, Tibet, and Nepal.

Gyelwa Yang Gonpa (1213–1258), his equal in terms of realization, attended upon many fine teachers, including Venerable Gotsangpa. It was as if there was no doctrine that he would not receive, and all those that he did receive he condensed into the quintessential special doctrines titled *The Three Doctrinal Cycles of Mountain Retreat*[77] and *The Six Mothers of Most Essential Content*.[78] Teaching these, his reputation pervaded Jambudvīpa.[79] In addition, Bari Chil Karwa was equal to Gotsangpa in his mode of practice, and Puriwa Konchok Gyeltsen was his equal in austerities. Madunpa was his equal in compassion. Delek Gyeltsen was his equal in auspicious circumstances, and so forth.[80] Urgyenpa's disciples included Venerable Third Karmapa, Rangjung Dorje, Rinpoche Kharchuwa, Khetsun Sonam Ozer, and Tokden Dawa Senge, along with Nyemdowa's brother Kunga Dondrub (b. 1268).[81] The foremost of Yang Gonpa's disciples was Chenga Rinden (b. 1202). And in the lineage of the latter's disciples there appeared Zurpukpa Rinchen Pel and Barawa Gyeltsen Pelzang (1310–1391), along with his students, and so forth.[82] This concludes the section on the Upper Drukpa.

The Lower Drukpa, the Lineage of Lorepa

The disciple of Tsangpa Gyare named Gyelwa Lorepa (1187–1250) was endowed with a career consisting of thirteen pledges—that is, six major pledges, six incidental pledges, and one extraordinary pledge.[83] He adroitly composed the oral instructions of *The Fivefold Capacity*.[84] There were many who appeared in the lineage descended from his nephew and in the lineage of his disciples,[85] and {690} they elucidated the teaching of the definitive meaning. This concludes the section on the Lower Drukpa.[86]

Conclusion

In brief, based upon the emancipation of the pious attendants, the setting of the mind on enlightenment according to the Great Vehicle, and the pure commitments of Secret Mantra, the distinctive features of the precious Kagyu lineage are the exegesis of the tantras by Marpa and Ngok; the fortitude and oral instructions of Mila Repa; *The Flagging of the Essential Nature of the Great Seal* by Gampopa;[87] the indivisible vital energy and mind of Karmapa; the conclusive supreme path of Zhang; the path of Barompa, which integrates the mingling of meditative experience and transference of consciousness; the secret mantras of Phakmodrupa; the thirty-nine regulations of the Taklungpa; the unique essential of the three vows according to the Drigungpa; the auspicious circumstances and common savor of Tsangpa Gyare; and the devotion and detachment of Lorepa and Gotsangpa.[88]

These distinctive features are said to have an extraordinary compatibility. Although all practices are complete in each of these approaches, they are adroitly differentiated in order to guide and nurture disciples. These techniques are worthy of being established as the sacred doctrine, and in their totality they are renowned throughout the three world systems as the teaching of the precious Kagyu tradition.

The rain of the oceanic teaching of the conquerors—
The precious Kagyu tradition, king of power,
Causes a downpour of authentic accomplishment
To dispel all deterioration of existence and quiescence.
May its hanging ornate garland of lineage holders,
Their fame flapping and fluttering with respectful veneration,
Ever endure as long as beings are reborn
In the beautiful, glorious maṇḍala of the three planes!

This completes the rough biographical account of the Kagyu lineage in general, chapter nine of the extensive exegesis of the biographies of the Taklung Kagyu lineage holders, from *Wondrous Ocean of Eloquence: A Narrative of the Wish-Fulfilling Gem of the Lineage* compiled by Gelong Ngawang Namgyel.

10. The Origins of Diverse Doctrinal Traditions

Herein is contained a partial account of the diverse doctrinal lineages, chapter ten of *The Doctrinal History Titled Wondrous Ocean*.

Verses of Homage

OṂ SVĀSTI
Having understood the genuine source
Of the wish-fulfilling gem of great enlightenment
Through which all attain definitive excellence
In this abode of compassionate Avalokita,
An expanse of golden sand girded by snow mountain ranges,
Swirling in the ocean vastness of scripture and realization, of the
Buddhist teachings,
I bow toward it with pure vision, impartial in all respects,
And propagate this wondrous history.

The Earlier Promulgation of Buddhism in Tibet

With regard to the partial account of the diverse doctrinal lineages that constitutes chapter ten of this book, in general, the teaching of Secret Mantra according to the Great Vehicle has never faded here in Tibet, and it has survived until the present. All the texts that were translated prior to the arrival of paṇḍita Smṛtijñānakīrti are known as the Ancient School of Secret Mantra.[1] At first, the religious king Songtsen Gampo extensively taught the generation and perfection stages of Mahākāruṇika, and there were an inestimable number who experientially cultivated this practice. The supplication of Sublime Mahākāruṇika and the recitation of the six-syllable mantra flourished throughout the country of Tibet.[2] The sovereign lord Tri Songdetsen invited the precious master Padmasambhava, and by means of the instructions of Secret Mantra, he conferred on the twenty-five disciples including the king and his subjects maturational empowerments and liberating guidance. In addition, many vajra holders of India—including Śāntigarbha, Hūṃkara, and Vimalamitra—arrived, and {694} innumerable fortunate individuals followed them, such that the Buddhist teaching extensively flourished.[3]

Foremost among the teachings of the generation stage in this tradition are the five supramundane cycles known as Mañjuśrī, the Buddha Body;[4] Padma, the Buddha Speech;[5] Viśuddha, the Buddha Mind;[6] Amṛta, the Buddha Attributes;[7] and Kīla, the Buddha Activities;[8] with the addition of the three mundane cycles, Imprecatory Mātaraḥ,[9] Malign Mantra,[10] and Mundane Praise.[11] There are eight cycles in all.[12]

There are also the esoteric instructions renowned as the Great Perfection, which are composed of three classes: the class of mind, the class of space, and the class of esoteric instructions. Five of the texts belonging to the class of mind originated from Vairotsana, and thirteen from Vimalamitra. The class of space also originated from the former. The class of esoteric instructions, known as Innermost Spirituality, originated from Vimalamitra.[13]

Transmission of *The Net of Magical Emanation* and So Forth

The exegesis of the tantras according to the Ancient Translation School is also extant until the present. This mainly concerns the cycles of the *Guhyagarbha from the Magical Net of Emanation*.[14] Vimalamitra (fl. late eighth to early ninth centuries) taught this tantra to Ma Rinchen Chok (fl. late eighth to early ninth centuries), and they translated it. The latter explained it to both Tsukru Rinchen Zhonu and Gyere Chokyong, who both instructed Darje Pelgyi Drakpa and Zhang Gyelwei Yonten. The lineages descended from Zhang are known as the lineage of esoteric instructions. Darje propagated it many times in U, Tsang, and Kham, such that his lineage is known to include both the U tradition and the Kham tradition.[15]

Moreover, Nyak Jñānakumāra (fl. late eighth to early ninth centuries) was a disciple of Vimalamitra. His disciple was Sokpo Pelgyi Yeshe, and his disciple in turn was the master Nub Sangye Yeshe (late eighth to late ninth centuries). It seems that there are also lineages that stem from them. Nub Sangye Yeshe had four spiritual sons, including So Yeshe Wangchuk, or five with the addition of his most authentic spiritual son, Yonten Gyatso.[16] {695}

Nyang Sherab Chok (fl. late ninth century) was a disciple of Yonten Gyatso (fl. ninth century) and his sons, as well as of So Yeshe Wangchuk (fl. ninth century).[17] His disciple was Zurpoche Śākya Jungne (1002–1062), and the latter's disciples included the Four Summits—five including the Summit Ridge—and one hundred and eight great meditators.[18] Foremost among the Four Summits was Zurchung Sherab Drak (1014–1074). The disciples of the latter included the Four Pillars, Eight Rafters, Sixteen Beams, Thirty-Two Planks, Two Great Meditators, One Great Boaster, Two Simple Ones, Two Venerable Ones, and The Three Useless Men.[19] Zurchungpa's son was Venerable Dropukpa Chenpo Śākya Senge (1074–1135). His disciples in turn included The Four Grandfathers,[20] The Four Black Ones, and The Four Teachers—twelve in all.[21] Supreme among the Four Black Ones was Lharje Cheton Gyanak (1094–1148). He in turn had many excellent disciples, but the foremost was his nephew, the great lama Yontenzung (1126–1195). He in turn had a great many disciples, but his authentic spiritual son was Tulku Zhikpo Dutsi (1149–1199). The latter had six foremost disciples, of whom the best was Taton Joye (1163–1230).[22]

Two other disciples of Dropukpa Chenpo Śākya Senge were Tsangpa Jiton and Nyeton Chokyi Senge. From them the lineages also descended in succession through Tsangnak Obar, Meton Gonpo, and Lama Song, from whom Pakshi Śākya-o and Tanak Dudul received the transmission.[23]

From Tanak Dudul, it then descended to Zur Jampa Senge (fl. thirteenth century), under whom Yungtonpa (1284–1365) and Jamyang Samdrub Dorje (1295–1376) both studied.[24] From the latter, the lineage descended through Venerable Sangye Rinchen, and from him to Go Lo Zhonu Pel (1392–1481).[25] Also, the lineage of Dropukpa's disciples included Sangye Gonglawa of Dakpo, who extensively propagated this transmission of the tantras in Kham.[26] In addition, there are the familial line and disciple line of Rok Sherab-o (fl. twelfth century), many of whom received empowerments and the exegesis of the tantras.[27]

The transmission of the tantras exemplified by the *Guhyagarbha* also greatly flourished in Denpak, Tsangton Mangkar, and the northern and southern reaches of Lato,[28] {696} as well as at Kaḥtok Monastery in the environs of Pobor, on the far bank of the Yangtze, and so forth.[29] This concludes the section concerning the transmission of the tantras, above all *The Magical Net of Emanation*.

Transmission of *The Sūtra That Gathers All Enlightened Intentions*

The Sūtra of the Gathering[30] includes *The Root Tantra Titled "The Sūtra of All-Gathering Awareness"*[31] and *The Exegetical Tantra Titled "The Sūtra That Gathers All Intentions."*[32] Dhanarakṣita expounded these in Nepal to Dharmabodhi and Vasudhara. They expounded them at Trom in Gilgit to Chetsenkye and translated the texts into Burushaski. These three together expounded the texts to Jowo Nub Sangye Yeshe (fl. late eighth to late ninth centuries), and the lineage gradually descended from Jowo Yonten Gyatso and so forth. Lharje Shangpa and Togar Namkha bestowed this transmission on Zurpoche Ukpalungpa (1002–1062), and from then on, it descended in tandem with the lineage of *The Magical Net of Emanation*. Under Jetsun Drolmawa Samdrub Dorje (1295–1376), it was studied by Venerable Go Lotsāwa Yizang Tsepa (1392–1481). This concludes the section on *The Sūtra That Gathers All Enlightened Intentions*.[33]

Transmission of the Perspectives of the Class of Mind

There was a reincarnation of master Kṛṣṇācārin named Rongzom Lotsāwa Chokyi Zangpo (1042–1136), who became a great peerless scholar. He also received the trio of *The Sūtra That Gathers All Intentions*, *The Net of Magical Emanation* and *The Class of Mind*,[34] which together constitute the distant lineage of the transmitted teachings. Then his enlightened activity was enhanced through experiential cultivation and imparting instruction to others.[35]

As far as the perspectives of mind according to the Great Perfection are concerned, Nyak Jñānakumāra (late eighth to early ninth centuries) requested them from Vairotsana (late eighth to early ninth centuries) and Yudra Nyingpo (late eighth to early ninth centuries). The four great rivers of the transmitted teachings then converged in him.[36] His disciples included ten authentic ones, among whom Sokpo Pelgyi Yeshe in succession transmitted the lineage to Nub Sangye Yeshe (late eighth to late ninth centuries).[37]

Also, there was a disciple of Vairotsana named Pang Sangye Gonpo (fl. ninth century) who expounded it to Ba Rakṣita, and he transmitted it to

Yazi Darma Sherab and so forth. Gradually, the lineage then descended in succession through Marpa Sherab-o and Langpa Tonpa Darma Sonam, {697} from whom Dropukpa received it. He in turn passed it on to Śākya Dorje.[38]

Moreover, there is also a lineage that descended in succession from Vairotsana, through Jomo Dremo, Marpa Sherab-o, and from Sangdak Datsa Horpo to Drogon Dampa Śākya Gyeltsen, and so forth. Go Lotsāwa received it to some extent in the presence of Sangye Rinchen. This concludes the section on the transmission of the perspectives of mind.

Transmission of *The Vajra Bridge: The Class of Space*

Within the cycles of *The Class of Space*, according to the Great Perfection, the esoteric instructions of *The Vajra Bridge* are based on the "nine spaces" revealed in *The Lesser Tantra Equal to Space*[39] and on other texts, such as the *Secret Pristine Cognition*.[40] Vairotsana (late eighth to early ninth centuries) imparted these to Pang Mipham Gonpo (fl. ninth century), and then gradually the lineage passed in succession through Ngenlam Jangchub Gyeltsen (fl. ninth century), Zadam Rinchen Yik (fl. tenth century), Khugyur Selwei Chok (fl. tenth century), Nyang Jangchub Drak, Nyang Sherab Jungne (fl. late tenth century), master Bagom Yeshe Jangchub (fl. eleventh century), and Dzeng Dharmabodhi (1052–1136). Then indeed there were five including Nyang Dharmasiṃha, along with Venerable Ngor and Dzeng Jose and so forth who requested these instructions from Dzeng, after which they were manifoldly propagated.[41]

The lineage then descended in succession through Kyetsa Yeshe Wangchuk, Zik Yeshe Wangpo, Ngurpa Sonam-o, Ngurton Vajreśvara, Khenchen Sonam Gyeltsen, Sherab Gyeltsen, Zhonu Sherab, Zhonu Drakpa, Sangye Zangpo, Lama Tsondru Wangchuk (b. fourteenth century), Tazhi Drakpa Rinchen (b. fourteenth century), and master Śākya Gyelpo (1384–1474), from whom Venerable Go Lotsāwa (1392–1481) received it. He in turn offered this instruction to the fourth crown holder of Zhamar, Chokyi Drakpa (1453–1525).[42] This concludes the section on *The Vajra Bridge*.

Transmission of *The Innermost Spirituality: The Class of Esoteric Instruction* {698}

As far as the most profound Innermost Spirituality of the Great Perfection is concerned, the earlier master Vimalamitra (fl. eighth to ninth centuries) taught this to the sovereign king Tri Songdetsen (742–796) and to Nyang Tingdzin Zangpo (fl. ninth to tenth centuries).[43] Nyang Tingdzin Zangpo constructed the temple of Uruzha and concealed the instructions there in the form of treasure.[44] He explained the verbal transmissions to Drom Rinchen Bar (fl. tenth century), who in turn explained them to Be Lodro Wangchuk (fl. tenth to eleventh centuries).[45] One named Neten Dangma Lhundrub Gyeltsen (fl. eleventh century) then brought forth the treasures. He explained *The Innermost Spirituality* to Chetsun Senge Wangchuk (fl. eleventh century) and Kharak Gomchung Wangchuk Lodro (b. eleventh century). Chetsun taught Nyang Kadampa, and then he reconcealed the instructions in three separate treasures. These were later unearthed by Chegom Nakpo of Rongnangda, by Shangpa Repa from Langdro Chepa Takdra, and by Zhangton Tashi Dorje (1097–1167), who was born at Lado on the nine-isle Yamdrok Lake, and also by Melong Dorje. Later, Zhangton also met Chetsun in person.[46]

Zhangton's son was Nyima Bum (1158–1213), and from him the lineage gradually descended through Guru Jober (1172–1231), Trulzhik Senge Gyabpa (fl. thirteenth century), Melong Dorje (1243–1303), Rikdzin Kumārādza (1266–1343), and Longchen Rabjam (1308–1364).[47] From Melong Dorje, the transmission also descended through Jangsem Sonam Lodro, Jamyang Samdrub Dorje (1295–1376), and Drolmawa Sangye Rinchen (1350–1431), from whom Go Lotsāwa (1392–1481) received it.[48]

The lineage of *The Innermost Spirituality of the Ḍākinī*[49] is as follows: male-female Samantabhadra in the form of the buddha body of reality, the five classes of peaceful and wrathful deities in the form of the buddha body of perfect resource, Mahāvajradhara in the form of the buddha body of emanation, Prahevajra in the form of a further emanation, the awareness holder Śrī Siṃha, the master Padmākara (fl. eighth to ninth centuries), the great consort Yeshe Tsogyel (f. eighth to ninth centuries), Pema Ledreltsel (1292–1316), Gyelse Lekpei Gyeltsen (fl. thirteenth to fourteenth centuries), omniscient Karmapa Rangjung Dorje (1284–1339), Gyelwa Yungtonpa (1284–1365), Khedrub Tsultrim Gonpo (fl. fourteenth century), {699} Drubchen Gonpo Gyeltsen (fl. fourteenth century), Gyelse Tukchoktsel (a.k.a. Longchen Rabjam, 1308–1364), Nyangton Sonam Zangpo, Nubchen Ratnaśrī (b. fifteenth century), Jetsun Namkha Sherab (b. fifteenth century), Tulku Nyida Ozer (fl. fifteenth century), and Yongdzin Rinpoche Namgyel Pelzangpo (b. sixteenth century), from whom I, Ngawang Namgyel (1571–1626), requested it.[50]

As far as the perspective of the spiritual revelations is concerned, there are many discoverers who have been prophesized in *The Injunctions of Pema,*[51] commencing from Sangye Lama (c. 990–1070) and continuing through to Dechen Lingpa (1562–1592).[52] The most renowned are Ngadak Nyang (c. 1124–1192), Guru Chowang (1212–1270), Rikdzin Godempa (1337–1408), and so forth.[53] So there are many treasure doctrines, most of which were concealed by master Padma but also by many other saintly persons of the past, for the sake of fortunate beings of the future, that have already been discovered. Even nowadays these revelations and the saintly persons who are the masters of their doctrines continue to come forth in succession.

This concludes the section on *The Innermost Spirituality and Revelations* according to the Ancient Translation school of Secret Mantra, which approximately condenses the main points explained in *The Blue Annals,*[54] supplemented by some corroborating comments.[55]

New Translation Schools: The Sakyapa

The fountainhead of the new translation schools of Secret Mantra was Lochen Rinchen Zangpo (958–1055).[56] Also, the Buddhist teaching was propagated by Loton Dorje Wangchuk (b. tenth century), who appeared at the start of the later phase of dissemination.[57] During that period, Tri Tashi Tsekpa Pel (ca. 911–950), the son of the king Pelkhortsen (c. 881–911), protected the kingdom in the region of Rulak. His sons were the three siblings named Pelde (ca. 980–1000), Ode (995–1037), and Kyide Nyima Gon (fl. early tenth century).[58] They requested from Loton Dorje Wangchuk a pair of monks, a monastic preceptor and master of ceremonies, who could propagate the teaching, so he sent the monastic preceptor Śākya Zhonu and the master of ceremonies Yeshe Tsondru, and they established the monastic community in far-west Tibet. {700} Following consultations with those two, the monastic preceptor and master of ceremonies, Drokmi Śākya Yeshe (993–1050) and Tak Lo were sent to India with the command, "Listen to the vinaya because it is the foundation of the Buddhist teaching, to *The Transcendent Perfection of Wisdom* because it is the nucleus, and to the Secret Mantra because it is the essence." They acted accordingly, and Drokmi became a great monastic preceptor. He propagated the Buddhist teachings through exegesis and practice, principally of the mother tantras.[59]

Lochen Rinchen Zangpo elucidated *The Transcendent Perfection of Wisdom*, the exegetical precepts of both the father tantras and the mother tantras, and in particular the yoga tantras. Venerable Go Khukpa Lhetse (fl. eleventh century) propagated the exegetical precepts of, principally, the *Guhyasamāja* according to the tradition of sublime Nāgārjuna.[60] Lord Marpa filled the land of Tibet with the empowerments and exegeses of the *Guhyasamāja*, which is a father tantra; the *Mahāmāya*, which is a mother tantra; the *Hevajra*, which is the essence of tantra; and the *Cakrasaṃvara*, which is the quintessence of tantra, as well as *The Four Seats*, which embodies the protectors of the transmitted teachings, and so forth.[61] By propagating extensively the transmitted teachings of the esoteric instructions, he filled the land of Tibet with learned and accomplished masters, and he became a master of the teaching of the way of Secret Mantra. The teaching of the new translations of Secret Mantra is held to have originated from these three great translators.

With regard to the oral instructions of the Path and Its Fruit, which are renowned like the sun and moon, the lineage of succession begins with Vajradhara, Nairātmā, Virūpa the mighty lord of yoga, Kṛṣṇapāda, Ḍāmarupa, Avadhūtipa, and Gayadhara (fl. tenth to eleventh centuries), the last of whom traveled to Tibet and instructed Drokmi Śākya Yeshe. The latter possessed the Path and Its Fruit, along with the associated nine cycles of the path, and although he had many disciples who mastered the texts, it was Seton Kunrik (1029–1116) who mastered the esoteric instructions. He (Seton Kunrik) instructed Zhangton Chobar (1053–1135).[62]

The latter's disciple was Venerable Sakya Chenpo Kunga Nyingpo (1092–1158), {701} whose learning was like the sky and who had attained the supreme spiritual accomplishment. His son, Venerable Sonam Tsemo (1142–1182), comprehended all the piṭakas and perfected the ethical discipline of celibacy. His most venerable younger brother, Drakpa Gyeltsen (1147–1216), perceived the reality of all things and crossed the ocean of Secret Mantra. His spiritual power was equal to that of Virūpa. The son of his younger brother was Choje Sakya Paṇḍita Chenpo Kunga Gyeltsen Pelzangpo (1182–1251). He perfected the five fields of classical learning in their entirety, and he subdued the extremist Haranandin in debate. He possessed the major and minor marks and was endowed with extrasensory powers. He established the emperor of China, Göden Qaγan (1206–1251), in the Great Vehicle. His disciples who held the lineage of scriptural transmission and realization were inestimable in number. His nephew, Phakpa Rinpoche (1235–1280), was one who perfected learning, realization, and compassion. The Mongol emperor Qubilai Qaγan (1215–1294) subjugated Tibet, and conferred authority and patronage upon him. Although he would issue decrees, he had a good heart that did not seek to modify any of the preexisting schools, and he was unrivaled owing to the twofold tradition of the Sakyapa.[63]

The nephew of Drogon Chogyel Phakpa, the glorious Lama Dampa Sonam Gyeltsen (1312–1375), was equal to Sakya Paṇḍita in his discriminative awareness.[64] Tekchen Choje Kunga Tashi (1349–1425) served as a spiritual teacher to the Da Ming emperor. Later, those who appeared in the familial line, like an unbroken bridge, until the present, including Dakchen Rinpoche Ngagi Wangchuk (1517–1584), had an incalculable number of disciples and great-disciples. Consequently, all the exegeses, practical transmissions, and experiential cultivations of the glorious Sakyapa school {702} are pure in terms of the three modes of investigation.[65]

The division into the subschools of Ngor and Dzong derives from Kunga Namgyel of Gongkar Dorjeden (1432–1496), a mighty lord of spiritual power,[66] and Ngorpa Dorje Chang Kunga Zangpo (1382–1456), who were both adherents of the tradition of Secret Mantra.[67] Most of those who adhere to the mantra perspective of the Sakyapa became the Ngorpa. In general, the instructions of the Path and Its Fruit divided into eighteen branches, including the tradition of Zhama, which Seton imparted to Machik Zhama.[68] Exemplified thereby, this school became exceedingly pervasive, and there are multiple sources of the lineage.

This concludes the section on the origin of the new translation schools of Secret Mantra and in particular the glorious Sakyapa.[69]

The Exegetical Traditions of the Tantras

In general, the exegetical traditions of both the kriyā and caryā tantras were not conspicuously widespread during the later promulgation of the Buddhist teaching. The yoga tantras were at first adroitly manifested by Lochen Rinchen Zangpo (958–1055), and also they were eloquently explained by Zangkar Lotsāwa Phakpa Sherab (fl. eleventh century). They were greatly propagated by the disciples and great-disciples of those two, and they are extant, without decline, supremely elucidated by Buton Rinchendrub (1290–1364).[70]

As far as sublime Nāgārjuna's tradition of the father tantra titled *Guhyasamāja*[71] is concerned, this was excellently translated and expounded by Go Lotsāwa Chenpo Khukpa Lhetse (fl. eleventh century) and Lord

Marpa Lotsāwa (1002–1097). Foremost among the disciples of Go were the group of six: Mangra Senge Gyeltsen, Ngok Upa Geser, Ngabmi Jangchub Gyeltsen, Lhopa Dorje Nyingpo, Nyelpa Gar Chokyi Dorje, and Upa Gabum. Rongpa Gyele and Shongton Dorje Gyeltsen (fl. thirteenth century) both requested it from these six, and it was propagated extensively by them.[72] Tsurton Wange directly received the teachings from Venerable Marpa, but he also paid homage to four actual disciples of Go, {703} receiving and propagating the traditions of Go.[73]

Later the exegetical streams of both Marpa and Go mostly descended through Kunkhyen Choku Ozer (fl. thirteenth century) and Kunkhyen Pak-o Yonten Gyatso (1260–1327). Then they were absorbed into the ocean of Buton Rinchendrub's buddha mind and greatly elucidated. In addition, Patsab Lotsāwa Nyima Drak (b. 1055) and Chak Choje Pel (1197–1263/64) and others also propagated this sublime tradition to some extent through their exegeses.[74] Both Marpa and Go also expounded the tradition of Jñānapāda, and it was adroitly propagated by Nyo Jungpo (fl. eleventh century).[75]

As far as the cycles of Yamāntaka are concerned, Naktso Lotsāwa Tsultrim Gyelwa, (1011–1064) requested them from Jowo Atiśa (982–1054), and so forth. He expounded them to Rongpa Chaksorwa, by whom they were also propagated. Go also expounded them.[76]

Above all, Ra Lotsāwa Dorje Drak (1016–1128) traveled to Nepal, where he received the cycle of the three related meditational deities—Yamāri, Ṣaḍānana, and Vajrabhairava—from the Newar Mahākāruṇika and then translated and expounded them. Among his some two thousand disciples, the nine main ones were renowned. The exegetical transmission descended in succession through his nephew Ra Chorab (b. eleventh century), Ra Yeshe Senge (b. twelfth century), Ra Bumseng (b. twelfth century), Venerable Ga Lo Namgyel Dorje (1203–1282), and his sons, and so forth.[77]

The empowerments of the tantra of Cakrasaṃvara, which is a mother tantra, along with the exegeses of this tantra and the related practical writings that have manifoldly appeared at first, also originated in the lineage of the disciples of Lochen Rinchen Zangpo. Then, Jowo Atiśa imparted these teachings to Rongpa Gar Ge, while Phamtingwa (Vagīśvara) of Nepal also instructed Lokya Sherab Tsek, his lineage descending to Mel Lotsāwa Lodro Drakpa (fl. eleventh century).[78]

Then, there is the exegetical tradition of Mardo: Marpa Dopa Chokyi

Wangchuk (1042–1136), who had perfected all the texts and esoteric instructions held by four disciples of Nāropā, expounded them to Zepa Loden (b. eleventh century) and Chogro Chogyel (1108–1176), and so forth, {704} and they then propagated them.[79] Trewo Gonpo also requested them from the learned Gya Namkha and propagated them. Lochung Drakjor Sherab, who passed away as a sky farer without relinquishing his physical body, received these instructions from the teachers of Mardo and from Bhīmadeva,[80] and expounded them.[81]

Chel Lo Kunga Dorje requested the cycles of Cakrasaṃvara and Vajravārāhī from the Newar Hamu Karpo and propagated them.[82] Then, there are a great many transmissions, including the cycle of *The Ocean of Ḍākas*, which were translated and expounded by paṇḍita Jayasena and Sumbha Lotsāwa Dharma Yonten (fl. eleventh century).[83]

All the extant unadulterated empowerment precepts, exegetical precepts, and precepts of esoteric instruction pertaining to the three traditions of Lūipa, Kṛṣṇapāda, and Ghaṇṭapāda were then excellently received by Buton Rinchendrub himself, who comprehended and elucidated them.[84]

As for the empowerments, tantra commentary, and esoteric instructions pertaining to the *Kālacakra*,[85] Somanātha of Kashmir (fl. eleventh century) journeyed to Tibet, and the tantra commentary was translated by Dro Lotsāwa Sherab Drakpa (fl. eleventh century). The tradition of Dro then descended in succession from that paṇḍita through Gompa Konchok Sung (fl. eleventh century), Droton Namla Tsek (fl. eleventh century), Yumo Mikyo Dorje (fl. eleventh century), the latter's son Dharmeśvara (fl. eleventh to twelfth centuries), Khangsarwa Namkha Ozer (fl. twelfth century), Semochewa Namkha Gyeltsen (fl. twelfth century), Choje Jamyang Sarma Sherab Ozer (fl. twelfth century), Kunkhyen Choku Ozer (fl. thirteenth century), Kunpang Tuje Tsondru (1243–1313), Jangchub Gyelwa Yeshe (1247–1320), Phak-o Yonten Gyatso (1260–1327), and the great, omniscient Dolpopa Sherab Gyeltsen (1292–1361).[86]

As far as the Ra tradition of the *Kālacakra* is concerned, Ra Chorab traveled to Nepal, where he received the empowerments, transmissions, and esoteric instructions completely from paṇḍita Samantaśrī. The Ra tradition then passed in succession through Ra Yeshe Senge, Ra Bumseng, Ga Lo Namgyel Dorje (1203–1282), {705} Lama Sherab Senge (1251–1315), Lama Pelden Senge, Lama Dorje Gyeltsen (1283–1325), and Buton Rinchendrub.[87] Buton also received the transmission from Pak-o Yonten Gyatso and propagated it greatly, combining the transmissions of both Ra and Dro in a single lineage. The great, omniscient Dolpopa Sherab Gyeltsen also received the Ra tradition.

The Ra tradition was extensively propagated by Buton's disciples Dratsepa Rinchen Namgyel (1318–1388), Gongsum Dechenpa Chokyi Pel (fl. fourteenth century), the glorious Lama Dampa Sonam Gyeltsen (1312–1375), and so forth. The last of these also composed *A Great Commentary on the Kālacakra*.[88] The disciples of the great omniscient Dolpopa Sherab Gyeltsen included Kunpang Chodrak Pelzang (1283–1363), Choje Bodong Chokle Namgyel (1306–1386), and Nya On Kunga Pel (1285–1379). The disciples of the last two included Rinpoche Sonam Zangpo (fl. fourteenth century).[89]

The disciple of Semochewa Namkha Gyeltsen was Bodong Rinchen Tsemo (b. twelfth century). Then, gradually the lineage descended through Takdewa Senge Gyeltsen (1212–1294) and Shongton Dorje Gyeltsen (fl. thirteenth century). It was from Takdewa that the mighty scholar named Pang Lotsāwa Lodro Tenpa (1276–1342) received it. Then gradually, the lineage descended through Lochen Jangchub Tsemo (1303–1380), who had acquired supreme accomplishment and unsullied inspiration with regard to the words and meanings of the ocean of sūtra and tantra; Lochen Drakpa Gyeltsen (fl. fourteenth century), who had acquired learning and accomplishment, and the omniscient Jikme Drakpa (1315–1391), who had actually been granted the mysteries of the supreme vehicle by Lord Vajrasattva and Queen Dorje Tsunmo.[90]

Trukhang Lotsāwa Sonam Gyatso (1424–1482) received the definitive secrets of the *Kālacakra* from Namgyel Drakpa Zangpo (1395–1475) and Yaron Sonam Namgyel (1401–1475), who were disciples of Bodong Rinpoche Chokle Namgyel (1376–1451), and later he received it from the great Indian paṇḍita Vanaratna (fl. fifteenth century).[91] {706}

Furthermore, Venerable Sangye Rinchen received these instructions from Choje Chokle Namgyel, and Go Lotsāwa Zhonu Pel in turn received them from him.[92] These all refer to the instructions of the *Kālacakra* that were propagated through both the Ra and Dro traditions.

Then, with regard to the distinct tradition of Lotsāwa Tsāmi, the lineage descended in succession through Kālacakrapāda the Elder (Caurayaśa), Kālacakrapāda the Younger (Nālendrapa, fl. eleventh century), Bodhibhadra, Tsāmi Sangye Drakpa (fl. eleventh century), Se Lotsāwa

Zhonu Tsultrim, Nyo Darma-o, Lama Tashi Rinchen, Dukhorwa Sangye Dorje, and Khedrub Orgyenpa (Rinchen Pel, 1229–1309).[93]

There are also precepts pertaining to *The Means for Attainment of Coemergent Kālacakra*[94] and the esoteric instructions of the Six-Limbed Yoga, the lineage of which descended from Tsāmi through glorious Phakmodrupa and Gyelwa Taklungpa the Great.

This concludes the section on the origin of the exegetical traditions of the tantras.

The Texts and Oral Instructions of Kadam

With regard to the manner in which glorious Dīpaṃkarajnāna (982–1054) enabled the ethos of the Great Vehicle to flourish in Tibet, although he had been born as the son of the king of Zahor and had practiced the conduct of Secret Mantra, in the perception of others he was ordained as a mendicant through the Mahāsāṃghika order. He was without the stain of unknowing with respect to all the fields of classical learning, the sūtras and tantras, and he overwhelmed all beings with his enlightened mind. This saintly upholder of the Buddhist teaching, named Dīpaṃkaraśrījñā**na, lord-protector of all yogins, unrival**ed in Jambudvīpa, was invited by the bodhisattva princes Podrang Jangchub-o (984–1078) and Zhiwa-o (1016–1111),[95] and having also been exhorted by his preferred deities, he journeyed to Tibet [in 1042]. {707} There, he established the people in the roots of the sacred doctrine, the acceptance of positive acts and rejection of negative acts in accordance with karma and its fruits, and in the taking of refuge. He secured ordained mendicants in immaculate ethical discipline, and he rectified the view of those who were erudite. He also united meditators in pure calm abiding and higher insight, and he enabled those who entered into the way of mantra to adopt pure commitments. All of them he guided through the central pathway of enlightened mind. All fabrications that resembled the sacred doctrine but were not the sacred doctrine naturally vanished. The upholders of the tradition of this saintly being, known as the Kadampa, are renowned like the sun and moon.[96]

Atiśa's seniormost disciple, to whom he entrusted the treasure store of his oral instructions in their entirety, pertaining to the three lineages of profound view, extensive conduct, and blessed experiential cultivation, was Dromtonpa Gyelwei Jungne (1004–1064) an emanation of sublime

Lokeśvara who was appointed lord of the Buddhist teaching while maintaining the status of a celibate layperson.[97]

Moreover, Atiśa had five extraordinary Indian disciples;[98] noblemen such as the princes Jangchub-o and Zhiwa-o; as well as translators including Lochen Rinchen Zangpo (958–1055), Naktso Tsultrim Gyelwa (1011–1064), Go Lotsāwa (Khukpa Lhetse, fl. eleventh century), and Gya Tsonseng (b. tenth century); upholders of Secret Mantra, including Chaktri Chok of Lhodrak, Rongpa Gar Ge, and Yol Chowang (b. eleventh century) and his three siblings; spiritual mentors, including Khuton Tsondru Yungdrung (1011–1075) and Ngok Lekpei Sherab (fl. eleventh century); and innumerable great meditators including the great yogin Ame Jangchub Jungne (1015–1077),[99] Gonpawa Dzeng Wangchuk Gyeltsen (1016–1082), the yogin Sherab Dorje (b. eleventh century), Chakdar Tonpa (b. eleventh century), and Jampei Lodro (b. eleventh century).[100] {708}

Although Geshe Dromtonpa had many fine disciples, headed by Kyura Zhonu Ozer (fl. eleventh century), the most exalted among them were known as the Three Siblings—namely, Jamyang Putowa Rinchen Sel (1027–1105), Chakdor Chengawa Tsultrim Bar (1038–1103), and the emanation of Avalokita, Puchungpa Zhonu Gyeltsen (1031–1106). With the addition of Khampalungpa Gang Śākya Yonten (1023–1115), they are also called the Four Faces.[101]

After the death of Dromtonpa, the great yogin Ame Jangchub Jungne resided at the monastic seat of Reteng. His disciples included Tolungpa Rinchen Nyingpo (1032–1116), and after the latter, the abbatial succession of the monastic seat passed through Gonpawa Dzeng Wangchuk Gyeltsen (1016–1082), and the latter's disciples Neuzurpa Yeshe Bar (1042–1118), Zhangkamapa Sherab-o (1057–1131), and so forth, who are known as the Four Sons of Gonpawa.[102]

The monastic seat of Reteng was then maintained in succession by Shawo Gangpa Pema Jangchub (1067–1131), Kharak Gomchung Wangchuk Lodro (fl. eleventh century), and so forth, and then, after being protected to some extent in the interim by Putowa, it was maintained by Ojowa (fl. twelfth century). Then Khenpo Gurton (fl. twelfth century) was appointed, and then Neten Maton (fl. twelfth century) was appointed, the auspicious circumstance being arranged by Lhadrowei Gonpo. His successors included Khon Shedorwa,[103] Dulwadzinpa (fl. thirteenth century), and Khenpo Jamyangpa (fl. thirteenth century).[104]

Putowa had innumerable disciples, but in general the most sublime among them were the Ten Great Pillars, including Ramdingmawa Jungne Dorje (fl. eleventh to twelfth centuries); Rok Sherab Gyatso (1059–1131); Sharawa Yonten Drak (1070–1141), who resembled the sun; and Langtangpa Dorje Senge (1054–1123), who resembled the moon.[105]

Sharawa's disciples included Tabkhawa (Darma Drak, fl. twelfth century), Ja Chekhawa Yeshe Dorje (1101–1175), and Nartangpa Tumton Lodro Drak (1106–1166).[106] The disciples of Langtangpa included Shawo Gangpa (Pema Jangchub, 1067–1131) and so forth. {709} The monastic seat (of Langtang) was successively maintained by Langtang Zhang, Geshe Nyen, the master Gompa, and so forth.[107]

The lineage of Ja Chekhawa Yeshe Dorje's disciples began with Se Chilbupa (1121–1189). His monastic seat was maintained in succession by Lhalungi Wangchuk (1158–1232), Lha Drowei Gonpo (1186–1259), Lha Drakhawa Lodro Yeshe (1250–1286), Lha Zurkhangpa (1277–1337), Lha Lodro-o (1285–1350), Lha Rinchen Senge (fl. fourteenth century), Lha Śākya Sonam, and so forth.[108]

Tumton Lodro Drak founded the monastic seat of Nartang. In succession, there then appeared Doton Sherab Drak (b. eleventh century), Zhang Zhung Dorje-o (1122–1194), Droton Dutsi Drak (1153–1232), Zhangton Chokyi Lama (1184–1241), Sangye Gompa (Senge Kyab, 1179–1250), Chim Namkha Drak (1210–1285), Kyoton Monlam Tsultrim (1219–1299), Nyima Gyeltsen (c. 1225–1305), Zeu Drakpa Tsondru (1253–1314), Drakpa Sherab (1259–1325), Chim Lobzang Drakpa (1299–1375), and so forth.[109]

Foremost among the disciples of Venerable Chakdor Chengawa Tsultrim Bar (1038–1103) were Tulku Jayulwa Zhonu-o (1075–1138), Tolungpa Rinchen Nyingpo (1031–1116), and so forth. The disciples of Jayulwa included five hundred in whom meditative stability arose, one hundred and ten great spiritual advisers, nine outsiders who were great, eight moderately close ones who were great, and three who were the inner sons of buddha mind. Among them was Shawa Lingpa the Great.[110] The monastic seat of Jayulwa was maintained by Tsangpa Mikyo Dorje (1077–1161),[111] and then in succession by Rinpoche Langlungpa Tsondru Zhonu (1123–1193), Sangye Gompa Dorje Zhonu (1160–1229), Zom Rinpoche Drakpa Senge (1191–1256), Khampalungpa (1232–1282), Sangye Jowo Wangchuk Zhonu (1232–1312), Sangye Tonpa (d. 1325), Sangye Gompa the Younger (Tsultrim Sherab) (1284–1338), Gyeltengpa Sangye Onpo, and so forth.[112]

The disciple of Jadul (Jayulwa) {710} named Tromzher Chenpo (1100–1170) founded Kaṃkaṃ. There were many who acceded to his monastic seat, starting with Kyoton Jangchub Rinchen (1126–1200).[113]

Sangye Onton Zhonu Sangye (1138–1210), who was the younger brother of Gyer Gom the Great (1090–1171),[114] built Gyama Lhakhang, and the abbatial succession was maintained by Sangye Yonten, Deshek Chenpo, and so forth.[115]

Jangchub Gedze (1084–1167) was the disciple of Neuzurpa Yeshe Bar (1042–1118), and his disciple in turn was Korchenpo (fl. twelfth century). He resided as the monastic seat of Takchen, and subsequently there were many who appeared to maintain the monastic seat, including Marpa Phukpawa (d. 1228).[116]

Rongpa Chaksorwa (fl. eleventh to twelfth centuries) met Dromton in person. He composed *The Biography of Jowo Atiśa.*[117] His disciples were known as the Four Sons of Rongpa.[118] The disciple of the great yogin Ame Jangchub Jungne was Mangra Gyeltsen. The latter's disciple was Nyukrumpa Tsondru Gyeltsen (1042–1109).[119]

Puchungwa Zhonu Gyeltsen resorted to solitude and focused on spiritual practice, so he did not have very many disciples. But his own mind concisely conserved the instructions of the sixteen vital essences, the seven divine doctrines, the five recollections, the four immeasurable aspirations, and the two inspections. All these doctrines gathered together composed Dromtonpa's *Book of Kadam*, and their transmitted teachings of maturational empowerment and liberating guidance descended to Puchungwa. It appeared that his physical body was different to that of Geshe Dromtonpa himself, but apart from that, their minds were indivisible.[120]

One actual lineage of *The Book of Kadam*, including its empowerments, guidance, and transmissions is as follows: Glorious Jowo Je Atiśa (982–1054), who brought the streams of the three lineages together; Drom Gyelwei Jungne (1004–1064); Ngok Lekpei Sherab (fl. eleventh century); Ngariwa Jangchub Sempa Sherab Gyeltsen (fl. eleventh century); Puchungwa Zhonu Gyeltsen (1031–1106); Kamawa Dromton Rinchen Gyeltsen (fl. eleventh to twelfth centuries); {711}Zhangton Darma Gyeltsen (fl. twelfth century); Tabkawa Drom Jangchub Zangpo (fl. twelfth century); Tonpa Namkha Rinchen; Nartang Khenpo Nyima Gyeltsen; Rinlingpa Rinchen Jangchub; Galungpa Riki Dakpo Pel; Galung Jangchub Pel; Nyukpei Lopon Sonam Ozer; Gongon Chuserwa Sangye Zangpo; Jadrelwa Sonam Zangpo; Lama Peldenpa (1333–1399); Taktsang Chokhorwa Khenchen Namkha Ozer; Patsab Gawa Dongpa Neten Yeshe Tsultrim; Nub Cholungpa Khenchen Ratnākaraśāntipa (fl. fifteenth century); Nyuklha Paṇchen Ngawang Drakpa (1458–1515); Lopa Chenga Ngawang Chokyi Drakpa (fl. sixteenth century); Lozim Okpa Lopon Rinpoche Jampa Pelden Chojor; and Yasedzin Dampa Namgyel Rinchen Pelzangpo (1532–1599); the last of whom excellently bestowed the transmission upon me, Ngawang Namgyel.

This concludes the section on the texts and oral instructions of Kadam.

The Transmission of Ngok Lotsāwa

Ngok Lotsāwa Loden Sherab (1059–1109) was the son of Chokyab, the younger brother of Ngok Lekpei Sherab. He comprehended all doctrines simply by receiving them. As a Tibetan translator there are many doctrinal texts that he translated, and he taught the entire Kangyur and Tengyur from memory. When he expounded it at Lhasa and elsewhere, twenty-three thousand monks would gather, and even for his assistant teachers some two thousand one hundred and thirty would gather. He lived as a great bodhisattva who had perfected all modes of conduct associated with the six transcendent perfections, a great upholder of the supreme awareness of the definitive meaning who illuminated Tibet with the light of his exegeses of the three piṭakas.[121] {712}

Senior among his disciples were the group of four: Zhangtsepong Chokyi Lodro (fl. eleventh century), Drolungpa Lodro Jungne (fl. eleventh century), Dre Sherab Bar (fl. eleventh century), and Khyung Rinchen Drak (fl. eleventh century), but many others including Gangpa Shewu also appeared.[122]

At the monastic seat of Sangphu, the abbatial succession following Lochen Ngok Loden Sherab himself was as follows: Zhangtsepongwa Chokyi Lodro (fl. eleventh century), Nyelpa Rilu, Neparwa, Chapa Chokyi Senge (1109–1169), Tsak Wangchuk Senge (fl. twelfth century), and so forth. The monastic seat was split into two by Tsangpa Jamseng and Khepa Jonam owing to the distinct exegeses that they gave in the upper and lower colleges. At each of these, a great many incumbents have appeared.[123]

Chapa Chokyi Senge was the disciple of Drolungpa (Lodro Jungne, b. eleventh century) and Tolung Gyamar (Jangchub Drak, b. eleventh century).[124] He had innumerable disciples including The Eight Great Lions, The Eight Minor Lions, The Four with the Name Jose, and The Three Accomplished Masters.[125]

Ar Jangchub Yeshe (fl. eleventh century) was the disciple of Dre Sherab Bar (fl. eleventh century), and his disciples in turn were Khu Sherab Tsondru (1075–1143) and Karchung Ringmo. Their disciple was Zhang Yepa Monlam Tsultrim (b. twelfth century); the latter's was Nyel Zhik Jampei Dorje;[126] and his disciples in turn, including Zering, were known as The Nine Sons, who founded exegetical colleges at Trophu, Tolung, Yarlung, Zhalu, Sakya, Drakri, Kyangdur, Nartang, Nyetang, and so forth.[127]

Later, Yaktruk Sangye Pelwa (1350–1414) propagated the teaching of the transcendent perfections to the utmost. His senior disciples were Mawei Senge Rongton Śākya Gyeltsen (1367–1449) and Rendawa Zhonu Lodro (1349–1412), who had become a supreme scholar, having attended upon Nya On Kunga Pel (1285–1379), a student of both Buton and Dolpopa. Rendawa's disciple was Shar Tsongkhapa Lobzang Drakpei Pel (1357–1419), who had unrivaled knowledge of both the causal and fruitional vehicles and was renowned for maintaining regulations that never transgressed the proscriptions of the vinaya of the sacred doctrine, permeating the earth with his enlightened activities.[128] {713}

Supreme among the latter's disciples were Gyeltsab Darma Rinchen (1364–1432), foremost in debate; Khedrub Gelek Pelzangpo (1385–1438), who attained power through refinement of both sūtra and mantra; First Dalai Lama, Choje Gendun Drubpa (1391–1474), who was an emanation of Dromton; the disciplinarian Drakpa Gyeltsen (1374–1434); Jamyang Tashi Pelden (1379–1449); Sera Jamchen Choje Śākya Yeshe (1354–1435); Jangsem Radrengwa Śākya Sonam (b. 1357); and Nartangpa Sherab Senge (1384–1445), who later propagated the exegetical precepts of the *Guhyasamāja*.[129]

The next incarnation of Venerable Gendun Drubpa was Second Dalai Lama, Khedrub Gendun Gyatso (1475–1542), and the next again was Third Dalai Lama, Choje Sonam Gyatso (1543–1588).

The disciple of Rongton Sheja Kunrik was the great paṇḍita Śākya Chokden (1428–1507), learned in the five complete fields of classical learning, who maintained an exegetical college at Serdokchen. Jamchen Sangye Pelwa (1412–1485) founded the Dreyul Kyetsel monastic college. His disciple, the omniscient Gorampa Sonam Senge (1429–1489), founded Tanak Tubten Namgyel, Dedunpa Drakar Rabjam Tenpa Rabsel founded Tubten Rawame, Bumtruk Sumpa Jampa Chodrub (1432–1504) founded Nyenyo Jarshong, and Zhung Gyapa Ngodrub Pelbar (1456–1527) founded Chokhor Lhunpo. In such ways, the lineage was well propagated.

Furthermore, there is also an exegetical transmission of Madhyamaka that stems from Patsab Nyima Drak (b. 1055),[130] an exegesis of *The Compendium of Phenomenology* based on the teachings of Drangti Darma Nyingpo (fl. eleventh to twelfth centuries),[131] an exegetical transmission of *The Treasury of Phenomenology* originating from paṇḍita Smṛtijñānakīrti,[132] an exegetical transmission of *The Exposition of Valid Cognition* that descended from Paṇchen Śākyaśrī of Kashmir (1127–1225) to Sakya Paṇḍita (1182–1251),[133] {714} and also *The Doctrines of Maitreya* that were propagated by Tsen Khawoche (b. 1021), who had received them from Sajjana.[134]

Although there are many enumerations of the transmissions that appeared, the master of the teaching of the vehicle of defining characteristics in these snow ranges of Tibet is recognized to be Ngok Lo Chenpo himself, along with his disciples and great-disciples.[135]

This concludes the section on Ngok Lotsāwa and his lineage.

The Transmission of Pacification

Padampa Sangye (fl. eleventh to twelfth centuries) was one who had unique kindness for the later promulgation of the Buddhist teaching in Tibet.[136] He perfected the oral instructions of fifty-four accomplished masters, male and female, and he was favored by thirty-six teachers who were sky farers. He had visions of meditational deities to the extent of the heavenly constellations, including the twelve deities that were his meditative commitments.[137] Having acquired the eight common accomplishments and the supreme spiritual accomplishment in the correct manner, he is said to have lived in Jambudvīpa for five hundred and seventeen years. He journeyed many times to Tibet.[138] Residing at Dingri, he acted for the benefit of countless fortunate beings. He elucidated the defining characteristics of the Pacification of suffering in accordance with the sequential cultivation of *The Transcendent Perfection of Discriminative Awareness*.[139]

The transmission of *The Trilogy of Tārā of Pacification*[140] that Padampa Sangye imparted to Jñānaguhya of Kashmir constitutes his first lineage.[141] Padampa Sangye then gave instruction on the Great Seal to Ma Chokyi Sherab (b. 1055), on seeing naked awareness to Sochung Gedunbar (d. 1128), and on carrying conceptual thoughts on the path to Kaṃ Tsultrim Gyeltsen. Consequently, the transmission of the trio of Ma, So, and Kam is known as his intermediate lineage.[142]

In the transmission descended from Ma, the following appeared in succession: Sokpo Dode[143] and Gyelwa Teni (1127–1217).[144] The successors of So were Shami Monlam Bar (1085–1171), Chupa Dartson (1117–1192), Mel Kawachen (1126–1211), and so forth.[145] The many who appeared in the succession of Kaṃ are known as the upper lineage and the lower lineage,[146] {715} and the instructions of this lineage also fell from Kam to Chupa Dartson.[147]

Finally, Padampa Sangye conferred maturational empowerment and liberating guidance on Chokro Nyonpa, Lokya Relpachen, and so forth.[148] He also gave instruction that he brought forth from within the austerities of the five paths and the three paths to Dampa Kunga (1062–1124).[149] He further conferred maturational empowerment on the Four Yogins of the Gates: namely, Gyagom, Vajrakrodha, Charchen, and Charchung,[150] as well as on the twenty-four nuns, and so forth.[151] All this constitutes his later lineage of the sacred doctrine.

Dampa Kunga later entrusted all the *Instructions of Kunga*[152] to Patsab Gompa (1077–1158),[153] and he in turn taught Gyelwa Tine,[154] and the Rok Brothers met him. Separately, in Tsurpa, Dartson taught Tsurpa Tson Seng, and then all the lineages converged in Rok Sherab-o (1166–1244).[155] The latter's younger brother Zhikpo Nyima Senge (1171–1245)[156] and Khepa Mawei Senge (1186–1247)[157] both also became highly learned masters of Pacification. Thereafter, the oral instructions of Pacification were extensively propagated.

In general, the entirety of Tibet was permeated with his threefold lineage of Pacification, along with his many random transmissions. Commencing with Gyadrakpa Yeshe Zhonu (1257–1327) and Tokden Samten Pel (1291–1366), at the hermitages of Gomo Choding and Yab Choding and elsewhere, there were those who were exclusively practitioners of Pacification,[158] but nowadays [that is, in the time of Ngawang Namgyel], it seems that the transmission has become somewhat rare.

However, in the addendum to the father doctrines of the Taklung Kagyu lineage, many profound instructions are still extant, including the Oral Instruction of Pacification that Dampa bestowed on glorious Phakmodrupa in a dream, and the Cycle of the Attainment of HŪṂ.[159] This concludes the section on Pacification.

The Transmission of Severance

The esoteric instructions of Severance are so called because they gather all the demonic actions described in the chapter on demons in *The Transcendent Perfection of Wisdom* into four classes—those that are impeded, those that are unimpeded, those that delight, and those that are arrogant—and {716} then directly sever their rope of arrogance.[160]

In this regard, the one called Machik Labkyi Dronme (1055–1149), a female embodiment of the Transcendent Lady of Wisdom, Mother of the Conquerors, from the perspective of others, excellently realized the genuine truth by reciting *The Sūtra of the Transcendent Perfection of Wisdom*. Having decisively determined the nature of mind, this instruction of Severance then arose in her mind. On meeting Padampa Sangye, the blessing of that practice was transferred, and pristine cognition manifestly arose within her through the empowerment that she received from Kyo Sonam Lama (fl. twelfth century).[161]

She conferred maturational empowerment and liberating guidance on innumerable disciples, and her esoteric instructions of Severance covered the whole of Tibet. The lineage of her disciples included Khu Gom Chokyi Senge (fl. twelfth century) and Ngagi Wangchuk of Dakpo Tsongde, after whom the instructions were greatly propagated through the lineage.[162]

With regard to the lineage of her sons, her son Nyingpo Drubpa had three sons by his earlier marriage—namely, Tsewang, Khuyuk, and Neljor Drak. Khambu Yale was the son of his later marriage.[163] Tsewang had three sons: Gyelwa Tonzung, Tonyon Samdrub, and Kyeme Osel. Among them, Tonyon Samdrub was known as Gangpa because he resided in the snows of Mount Yarlha Shampo, and in the lineage of his own son, the following appeared in succession: Gangpa Muyen, Gangpa Lhundrub, Sangye Tensung, and so forth.[164]

There were also other lineages of her sons that descended from Machik's son Drubpo, whom his mother called Gyelwa Dondrub, and from her grandson Khambu Yale.[165] This concludes the section on Severance.

The Transmission of the Shangpa Kagyu

The Shangpa Kagyu tradition is known to derive from Khyungpo Neljor Tsultrim Gonpo (990–1127).[166] This saintly being had attended upon one hundred and fifty learned and accomplished teachers, and had perfectly acquired all the oral instructions. In particular, he received two approaches of the instructions concerning the Six Doctrines from the mouths of Niguma and Sukhasiddhi.[167] {717} He then acquired perfection in the supreme and common accomplishments. He could instantaneously manifest one hundred and eight arrays of his physical body, and he actually conversed with the meditational deities. In five different places, he could manifest as the deities of five classes of tantra,[168] and his body could appear as the infinite peaceful and wrathful deities. He gathered eighty thousand disciples and was capable of living for one hundred and fifty years.

Foremost among the disciples of Khyungpo Neljor were the Five Earlier Sons and his One Later Son.[169] Among them, the master of the sealed precepts that were passed down through a single lineage holder was Mokchokpa Rinchen Tsondru (1110–1170).[170] From him, in succession, the lineage descended through Drubchen Kyergangpa Chokyi Senge (1154–1217),[171] Nyenton Rigongpa Chokyi Sherab (1175–1255),[172] and Choje Sangye Tonpa Tsondru Senge (1207–1278), who was the reincarnation of Drubchen Khyungpo himself.[173]

The last mentioned, Sangye Tonpa, was the one who released the sealed precepts and propagated them pervasively throughout Tibet. His main disciple was Khedrub Tsangma Shangton (1234–1309), and his disciples in turn were Jakchen Gyeltsen Bum (1261–1334) and Samdingpa Zhonu Drub (d. 1319).[174] From them, there originated the conventional divisions into the upper tradition and lower tradition of Niguma, the tradition of Jak, and the tradition of Sam, and the approaches of the lineage infinitely diverged.

Nowadays, it is said that although there are still one or two lineage holders of the doctrine that are exclusively Shangpa, these oral instructions permeate all the other doctrinal lineages. This concludes the section on the Shangpa Kagyu.

The Spread of Buddhism in Adjacent Countries

If one were to offer incidentally a partial account of how the sacred doctrine made its appearance in other adjacent lands, it would be as follows:[175] In Khotan, it arrived in accordance with a prophetic declaration of the Conqueror. One hundred and seventeen years after the Teacher's nirvāṇa, the queen consort of the religious king Aśoka gave birth to a son conceived by the guardian king Vaiśravaṇa. The boy was named Salenumanu (Suckled from the Earth).[176] Vaiśravaṇa gave him to the emperor of China. Then, on growing up, he was given the means of a king and an army of ten thousand men. He took possession of these and was then sent to search for the place where he had been born. {718} At that time, the minister of King Dharmāśoka named Yaśa was exiled by the king, along with his entourage of seven thousand. Arriving there, in Khotan, they met together with Prince Salenumanu, who occupied that land and built a fortress.[177] The prince's son was Yewu. One hundred and sixty-five years after the founding of the country of Khotan, the latter's son, Prince Vijayasambhava, an emanation of Maitreya, appeared.[178] At that time, Mañjughoṣa emanated as the monk Vairocana and he taught the Khotanese language and the Khotanese script. The king then built the Great Temple of Tsārma. Since he had a great wish to build temples and stūpas, he ordered all those who possessed the relics of the Buddha to build a great temple. Encouraged by the king, the monk Vairocana invited an emanation of the Teacher, along with the entourage of the sixteen elders, and venerated them.

Then, during the time of Vijayavīrya, the ruler of Khotan who was seventh in the royal dynastic succession, four arhats arrived from India, and they informed the king about the Stūpa of Kāśyapa that had been foreordained by the Teacher. In that locale, he then built the Great Temple of Gauto Shan upon the summit of Gośīrṣa Hill. A young prince was ordained as a mendicant, and he attained arhatship. It was starting in this way that the Buddhist teaching became widespread in that land. Many exclusively religious kings subsequently appeared, and they constructed countless temples and stūpas.[179]

With regard to the land of China, Mañjuśrī actually resides at Mount Wutai Shan. A natural image of Bodhisattva Samantabhadra of precious agate resides at Mount Emei Shan in the body of perfect resource, resembling the palace of Vaiśravaṇa. The kings who first held sway over that country were the thirty-seven[180] kings of the Zhou dynasty. Among them, it was in the time of the fourth ruler of that dynasty, Zhou Zhao Wang[181] (d. 977 B.C.E.), that **Śākyamuni** Buddha appeared in the world.[182] {719} After the Zhou dynasty had ended, there were two emperors of the Qin dynasty, Qin Shi Huangdi (r. 221–210 B.C.E.) and his son Qin Er Shi (r. 210–207 B.C.E.). Then the imperial throne was seized by one named Han Gaozu (r. 202–195 B.C.E.).[183] During the reign of the fourteenth emperor of this dynasty, Han Mingdi[184] (r. 57–75), a paṇḍita endowed with truth and insight named

Dharmaratna[185] arrived in that land, introducing the doctrines of the Lesser Vehicle. In 68, he built the White Horse Monastery[186] in Hunan. Starting from then until the present day, the Buddhist teaching has been widespread in China. After some time, the dynastic succession of Wei and Jin divided into two branches: the Eastern Jin (Dong Jin, 317–420) and the Western Jin (Xi Jin, 265–316). During the period of the Western Jin, an envoy was sent to bring a sandalwood image of Jowo Śākyamuni. They returned at the time when a provincial governor[187] became emperor.

After some time, Tang Gaozu[188] (r. 618–626) seized power, and he became the first emperor of the Tang dynasty. During the reign of Tang Taizong[189] (r. 626–649), there was a translator named Xuan Zang[190] (602–664) who translated many doctrinal texts. Prior to him there had been two hundred Chinese translators. Generally speaking, there were twenty Tang emperors or empresses.[191] During the reign of the last Tang emperor Ai Di[192] (a.k.a. Zhaoxuan, r. 904–907) the vinaya master Drum Yeshe Gyeltsen became a protector of the Buddhist teaching in Kham.[193]

After the Tang dynasty had come to an end, the capital was transferred to the Liang city of Kaifeng. Through five successive dynasties including that one, the Liang, there were fifteen emperors from different families who ruled in Kaifeng (907–960). Thereafter, during the reign of Song Taizu[194] (r. 960–976), the original capital (Chang'an) was lost to Xixia. There were eight imperial successors of the Northern Song who all belonged to the clan of their predecessor, Song Taizu.[195]

Afterward, in 1127, the Kitan Da Liao forces under the Jurchen[196] seized the northern half of the empire including Kaifeng.[197] Song Gaozong, a princely descendant of Qinzong, the erstwhile ruler of that northern half, then occupied the country of Southern China.[198]

In the north, there were nine emperors who appeared in the Jin dynastic succession following Wanyan Aguda Qaγan. In the time of Wanyan Chenglin,[199] the ninth of his successors, they were taken over by Qinggiz Qaγan in 1234.[200] {720}

The country of Xixia is delimited by China in the east, Naxi in the south, Tibet in the west, and Mongolia in the north.[201] At first, the entire land of Xixia was under China. Later, a child was born to a woman in the northern fortress, conceived by a local deity residing at the mountain range called Alasha, which is situated between Liangzhou and Xiazhou.[202] Whenever he went missing, as he was inclined to do, he was nurtured by vultures, cows, and so forth. He, on reaching adulthood, seized the kingdom from China by means of strategy, and he became the lord of a populace that was mainly Chinese and Mongolian. He was called Jingzong (r. 1038–1048)[203] or Guang Sheng Huangdi.[204] Renzong (r. 1139–1193) was the fifth in his dynastic succession. During his time, a disciple of Karmapa Dusum Khyenpa (1110–1193) named Geshe Tsangpo arrived, and the emperor revered him as his teacher, such that his empire was established in the sacred doctrine. His son, Huanzong (r. 1193–1206), was slain by a minister,[205] so the imperial line was interrupted, and the capital later came under the power of an emperor named Mozhu (r. 1226–1227).[206] It was during his reign that Qinggiz Qaγan seized the kingdom.

In general, it is said that Jingzong appeared after the Chinese emperor Song Zhao Zheng (r. 1022–1063)[207] and his brother had occupied the kingdom and that there were twelve emperors of Xixia who held dominion for two hundred and sixty years.[208]

The imperial succession of the Mongols is as follows:[209] First there was Borte Chino, The Son of Heaven. Then there was his son, Badači Qaγan, who was succeeded for eighteen generations until Bartan Bagatur (fl. eleventh to twelfth centuries).[210] The latter's son was Yesügei Bagatur (1134–1171) who, with Queen Hoelun (1142–1221), had a son named Qinggiz Qaγan (1162–1227). It was he who subjugated the Chinese empire.

Then, in succession there followed Ogodei (r. 1229–1241) and Guyuk Qaγan (r. 1246–1248). The latter's younger brother was Göden (1206–1251), who invited Venerable Sakya Paṇḍita (1182–1251) to Mongolia. Guyuk Qaγan was succeeded by Mongke Qaγan (r. 1251–1259), who acted as a patron of the great accomplished master Karma Pakshi (1204–1283). {721} Then there was Gopela, also known as Qubilai Qaγan (r. 1260–1294), who served as the patron of Lachen Phakpa Lodro Gyeltsen (1235–1280). After him, there were ten further emperors, from Oljeitu (a.k.a. Temur, 1294–1307) to Rinchinbal Qaγan (r. 1333). After that, Toγon Temur (r. 1333–1368) was appointed, but in his thirty-sixth regnal year (1368), he fled to Mongolia.

In that same year (1368), the Da Ming dynasty acquired imperial power. Commencing from then, without fluctuation, they have maintained their rule in China proper. The Da Ming emperor Hongwu (r. 1368–1398) invited Karmapa Dezhin Shekpa (1384–1415), Sakya Tekchen Choje Kunga Tashi (1349–1425), and Sera Jamchen Choje Śākya Yeshe (1354–1435). After him, there have been eight successive emperors from Jian Wen (r. 1398–1402), Yongle (r. 1402–1425), and so forth, to Zheng De (r. 1505–1521). Approximately eight have been chronicled. Later, when my sacred lord of refuge journeyed to the great kingdom of Mongolia, he mentioned that one named Wan Li (r. 1572–1620) had acceded to the imperial throne.[211]

This concludes the section on the partial account of how the sacred doctrine made its appearance in Khotan, Early China, Xixia, Mongolia, and Later China.

Conclusion

By virtue of this labor, may the supreme Buddhist teaching,
Embodiment of scriptural transmission and realization,
Ever flourish within the minds of limitless beings who resemble space.
And traversing the ocean of suffering that is cyclic existence,
May they all easily arrive at the precious isle of liberation!

This completes chapter ten of this book, a digression offering a partial and incidental account of the origins of the various lineages of the sacred doctrine from *Wondrous Ocean of Eloquence: A Narrative of the Wish-Fulfilling Gem of the Lineage* compiled by Gelong Ngawang Namgyel. {723}

11. The Origins of the Outer Fields of Classical Learning

Herein is contained an account of the origin of the four outer fields of classical learning, the eleventh part of *The Doctrinal History Titled Wondrous Ocean*. {915}

Verses of Homage

I pay homage so that the precious, peerless Kagyu lineage,
Lucidly expressed as omniscient and renowned as unerring,
Observing, out of love for infinite beings,
The clear reflections of qualitative and quantitative knowledge
In the clear crystal mirror of supreme pristine cognition of buddha mind,
Free from the tarnish of the three obscurations,
May ever be arrayed as an ornament of my heart
And so that authentic devotion might increase!

Having abundantly discussed the foregoing chronicles,
Now I should supplement them with a separate chapter
That recounts the origin of the four fields of classical learning,
Which eradicate the mistaken views of others
And bring them into the fold.

An Introduction

The eleventh chapter of this book will conclude with the origins of the four outer fields of classical learning. In general, the lord-protector Maitreya said in *The Ornament of the Sūtras of the Great Vehicle*,

Even the most sublime beings will not attain omniscience
Without having been skilled in the five fields of classical learning.
Since they eradicate the mistaken views of others,
Bringing them into the fold,
And consist of all sorts of knowledge for ones own benefit,
We should persevere in them.

Definitively understanding these verses, the fields in which those who wish to better themselves should train consist of the five fields of classical learning, which are the apex of knowledge.

Among them, the essential inner field of Buddhist learning consists of the authoritative treatises that excellently interpret the meaning of the three scriptural baskets and the four classes of tantra, {916} commenting on their enlightened intention, along with the three trainings and two stages of meditation that are the nucleus of the expressed meaning they establish. In brief, in the beginning, there were so many countless paṇḍitas in India, Land of the Sublime Ones, who, knowing the complete five fields of classical learning, having been foreordained by the conquerors and having acquired the glory that is triumphant over all directions, widely propagated the precious sacred doctrine of the Buddhist teaching, embodying transmission and realization by means of teaching, debate, and composition. And there were innumerable lords of yoga, holders of adamantine reality, who had actually attained the level of Glorious Heruka, who conferred maturational empowerment and liberating guidance on innumerable fortunate beings by opening the portals of the swift path, the mysteries of the Adamantine Vehicle.

These lines of transmission later flourished in Tibet, this glorious Land of Snow Mountains, blessed by sublime Lokeśvara, due to the kindness of knowledgeable paṇḍitas, yogins who had actually mastered spiritual accomplishment, and the emanational religious kings and bodhisattvas who nurtured this great land in virtuous actions in accordance with the sacred doctrine. Such events have been well presented in the foregoing ten chapters.

Here, I will briefly present the origins of the four outer fields of classical learning, along with their peripheral subjects. These are the fields of Sanskrit grammar and Buddhist logic that eradicate the mistaken views of others and the fields of the arts and medicine that bring others into the fold.[1]

The Origins of Sanskrit Grammar

With regard to the field of Sanskrit grammar, formerly, in the realm of Trāyastriṃśa, one named Sarvajñādeva, the master of the gods, composed a treatise on Sanskrit grammar titled *The Grammar of Sarvajñā*.[2] {917} His disciple Śakra composed *The Grammar of Indra*.[3] His disciple Bṛhaspati was filled with the arrogance of pride, which Śakra dispelled with these words:

> The field of Sanskrit grammar is infinite,
> As much as the oceans in their entirety.
> Indra knows merely the water in a jar.
> Bṛhaspati knows merely a drop![4]

Then he urged Bṛhaspati to become a teacher to others. Except for the four restricted days when he observed the vow of silence,[5] Bṛhaspati engaged in exegesis, such that the study of Sanskrit grammar flourished in the god realms, and he became renowned as a master of Sanskrit grammar and the teacher of the gods.

As for its propagation in the human world, the brahmin child Pāṇini, who had been foreordained in *The Sūtra of the Descent to Laṅkā* and *The Root Tantra of Mañjuśrī*,[6] was taken into the fold by sublime Avalokita, such that he became extremely learned in Sanskrit grammar. He composed the text titled *The Grammar of Pāṇini*,[7] and the nāga king Vāsuki composed a great commentary upon it, titled *The Great Exposition*.[8] It is said that these two textual commentaries had to be studied and explained, one each year.

As for *The Kalāpa Grammar*, King Śaṅkarabhadra, patron of sublime Nāgārjuna, was ignorant of Sanskrit grammar, and teased by the queen, he had his own maternal uncle Śvaravarman[9] engage in the propitiation of Kārtika. After seven days, he saw Kārtika mounted on a peacock and made the request, "Please may I know Sanskrit grammar!" Kārtika revealed to him the paradigms of verbs up to the fourth stanza, beginning with *siddhovarṇasanamnāyaḥ*, and as he said the word "please," the peacock mount soared upward, and he saw its multicolored tail feathers, whereupon Kārtika said, "Apologize to Kalāpa!" Śvaravarman committed these paradigms to writing and then composed the four later stanzas of the paradigm of verbs and the six stanzas concerning the primary nominal suffixes. {918} He taught these to the king, such that he became learned, and the queen was delighted.

Also translated into Tibetan were Durgasiṃha's commentary *Paradigm of Verbal Roots*, *The Useful Study Commentary*[10] composed by the brahmin Yaśobhūti for the sake of Buddhist students, *The Commentary of Ratnacchatra*[11] composed in Kashmir by Ratnacchatra, two works titled *The Treatise on the Termination Si and Others*[12] composed by the brahmin Sarvadhara and Mañjuśrīkīrti, Trilocanadāsa's *Explanation of the Durgasiṃha Commentary*,[13] and so forth.[14]

With regard to the *Candrapa*, this was composed by the master Candragomin for the sake of a disciple. On it there is *The Commentary in Six Thousand Lines*,[15] composed by his own maternal uncle Dharmadāśa; *The Subandhu Commentary*[16] by Haribhadra; *The Accomplished Commentary* of Sūryagarbha;[17] and so forth. In addition, Ratnamati composed *The Commentary on the Six Thousand Lines*,[18] and Purṇacandra composed a further commentary on that,[19] and so forth.[20]

Furthermore, Rājaśrī composed an abridgment of both the *Kalāpa* and the *Candrapa* grammars titled *The Grammar of Rājaśrī*.[21] Both the *Kalāpa* and the *Candrapa* became, as it were, the lamp of the field of Sanskrit grammar here in Tibet. Formerly, they were widely propagated, and even nowadays, their line of transmission is uninterrupted, and there are those who expound and study them.

Sanskrit is the foremost of all languages. Because it is astonishing in relation to other languages, and because those who do not know Sanskrit grammar are known to resemble oxen, it is the sole objective of the wise. In general, Sanskrit is so called because it "excellently combines" primary stems[22] with affixation[23] and morphological derivations.[24] The teaching of it is called the field of Sanskrit grammar.

As for the ancillary aspects of Sanskrit grammar, these are the four lesser fields of classical learning, on which is it said,

> If one knows synonymics, one will be undeluded with regard to names.
> If one knows prosody, one will be undeluded with regard to verse. {919}
> If one knows verbal ornaments, one will be undeluded with regard to poetry.
> If one knows dramaturgy, one will be undeluded with regard to languages.[25]

Among these, the first is synonymics, which concerns the expression of things through multiple synonyms. It is exemplified by the treatises titled *The Treasury of Amarasiṃha* and *The Wish-Granting Commentary.*[26]

The second is prosody, which includes works such as *The Primary Sūtra*[27] by the hermit sage Piṅgala, and *The Examples*[28] by Jinadeva. Among them all, in particular, *The Precious Source of Prosody*[29] and its commentary exemplify eloquence because, as it is said,

> It has eight qualities—namely, brevity, clear versification,
> Model examples, which are themselves sūtras,
> Distinctiveness, progression, ease of recitation,
> Pauses, and combinations.[30]

The third is poetics, which establishes the body of poetry in terms of prose, verse, and mixed verse and prose. *The Mirror of Poetics*, composed by the master Daṇḍin, perfectly reveals these three aspects through its analysis of the traditions of Gauḍa and Vaidarbha, the thirty-five ornaments of sense, the ornaments of sound, the sixteen ornaments of enigmatic innuendo, and the rejection of the ten flaws in composition.[31] This treatise itself is extremely widespread, even in Tibet, and those interested in poetics will not succeed without first relying on this introductory treatise. As for the model exemplars, *The Wish-Granting Tree* [of Kṣemendra exemplifies the tradition of the easterners (Gauḍa), and the thirty-four *Tales of Past Lives*, narrated by Śūra, exemplifies the tradition of the southerners (Vaidarbha).

The fourth is dramaturgy, which gives form to ancient tales, employing dialogue in different languages, as well as song and dance. It is exemplified by Harṣadeva's *Drama Titled Utter Delight of the Nāgas*,[32] which portrays the past lives of Meghavāhana and Candragomin's drama titled *Utter Delight of the World*,[33] which portrays the past lives of Maṇicūḍa.[34] {920}

The Origins of Logic

Logic includes both non-Buddhist and Buddhist approaches.[35] Among them, non-Buddhist logic[36] accepts the existence of the self as a descriptive base and makes imputations concerning it through notions about objects, subjects, and their diverse relationships. These are the antitheses of Buddhist logic. Buddhist logic, by contrast, shares only the name "valid cognition" in common with non-Buddhists, and there are significant differences.

Though generally based on the enlightened intention of the scriptures, in particular the field of logic conventionally originated as follows: Mañjuśrī taught the arhat Dharmatrāta, and the latter composed the treatise on logic titled *Chest of Speech*.[37] He instructed the learned Narendradeva, and he in turn taught Vasubandhu. The latter instructed Dignāga who was skilled in the methodology of logic itself. He composed *The Sūtra of Valid Cognition*,[38] and his grand-disciple Dharmakīrti composed the seven sections of valid cognition. These include the three primary treatises that resemble the body (the extensive *Exposition of Valid Cognition*,[39] the mid-length *Ascertainment of Valid Cognition*,[40] and the concise *Point of Reason*),[41] as well as the four ancillary treatises (*The Point of the Axioms*,[42] which demonstrates detailed modes of reasoning; *The Inquiry into Relations*,[43] which refutes the relations imputed by heretical extremists; *The Proof of Other Minds*,[44] which concurs that there are other minds even though appearances are mind; and *The Reasoning of Polemics*,[45] which demonstrates the modes of disputation).

The sequence of disputation in *The Exposition of Valid Cognition* accords with the order of the expressed meaning—that is, the chapter on proof is followed by the chapter on direct perception, followed by the chapter on inference for one's own sake, and followed by the chapter on syllogisms for the sake of others. However, when one trains in logic, Dharmakīrti initially reflected upon the important framework of reasoning. Observing that it was hard to understand, he composed *A Commentary on the Chapter concerning Inference for One's Own Sake*,[46] so that later students would begin with the chapter on inference for one's own sake.

Paṇḍita Devendramati {921} was exhorted to write a commentary on the remaining three chapters, and he started to do so on three occasions, the last of which[47] was pleasing to Dharmakīrti.[48] Moreover, Śākyamati,[49] Prajñāgupta,[50] Jinapāda,[51] Jamāri,[52] Sūryagupta,[53] and the brahmin Śaṅkarānanda[54] also authored all sorts of commentaries on *The Exposition of Valid Cognition*, either on the entire treatise or on one or two chapters.

Dharmottara,[55] Jñānaśrībhadra,[56] and Vinītadeva composed commentaries on *The Ascertainment of Valid Cognition*. Dharmottara and Jayadatta composed commentaries on *The Point of Reason*. Vinītadeva authored an extensive commentary on each of the four ancillary treatises.

In Tibet, the concise treatise *The Point of Reason* was propagated initially, then the mid-length treatise *The Ascertainment of Valid Cognition*, and finally the extensive treatise *The Exposition of Valid Cognition*. Among all these treatises, the last became the sole focus for subsequent generations.

The Origins of the Arts

Within the arts, in general, the unmodified arts of the mind denote all things pertaining to the attainment of cyclic existence and nirvāṇa, and so forth, including within them also the field of Buddhist studies. The functional arts of speech denote the transformations of voice, subsuming within them poetic words, intonations, lyrical songs, and all verbal expressions. The modified arts of form include both the formation of the world and so forth that is not associated with a creator and the arts described in this context that are associated with a creator.[57]

Foremost among the latter are the representations of buddha body, buddha speech, and buddha mind, and among these the first to emerge was drawing. In antiquity, when human beings had a lifespan of less than a hundred thousand years, there was a king of men named Bhayajita. He protected the land in accordance with righteousness, {922} so that the lifespan increased to one hundred thousand years and all were extremely happy. By practicing great austerities, the king attained the eight attributes of Iśvara,[58] and Brahmā granted him three supreme boons. Among his subjects, there was a brahmin whose young and beloved son suddenly died. The brahmin therefore approached the king and said, "If you do not grant me my son again, I will commit suicide here!" The king led the brahmin, and they approached the Lord of the Yama realm. He begged for the son, but the Lord of Death said, "I did not take him. This came about due to the exhaustion of his individual karma." Though the king repeated his request, he received the same reply, so the two sides prepared for battle, and they fought. The king hurled down a cascade of divine weapons, and the entourage of Yama was defeated. They then both took up staffs and the king prevailed in the fight, such that the entire world was in awe. Thereupon, Brahmā arrived and said, "Since his individual karma has been exhausted, Yama is not at fault. However, you may make a drawing of the son of that brahmin!" Accordingly, the king drew the boy, Brahmā restored him to life on that basis, entrusted him to the brahmin, and said to the king, "Since the anguished spirits are bereft, you should tame them!" The king consented, and accordingly was named Tamer of the Bereft. Since he was the first to draw, he was also named First Artist. In accordance with the exhortation of Brahmā, the king also paid homage and made offerings to Yama, so he was placated.[59]

Again, the king journeyed to the world of Brahmā, and when he requested permission to continue drawing, the latter praised him, saying,

The best of mountains is Sumeru.
The foremost of the egg-born is Garuḍa.
The foremost of humankind is that king himself.[60]
Similarly, drawing is the foremost of the crafts . . .

And,

This king similarly, among all the crafts,
Relies on the activity of drawing. {923}

Viśvakarman then foreordained that he would become the Teacher, and he acted as the foremost of universal emperors, demonstrating the need for aesthetics and so forth, with these words:

I demonstrate the defect of lacking proportion,
The advantage of having proportion, and so forth.
If there is no aesthetic proportion with respect to the body,
To what would proportion be applied?

So it was that these defining characteristics of drawing, titled *Tract on the Proportions of Brahmā*,[61] originate from their application by the hermit sage Atreya.[62]

In particular, the Conqueror elucidated and extensively demonstrated the proportions of his physical body in the *Kālacakra*, *The Emergence of Cakrasaṃvara*, and so forth.[63] Moreover, all the tantras of the Adamantine Vehicle mention the infinite activities associated with maṇḍalas,[64] along with the advantages of making drawings and relief images of icons. And in the sūtras of the Great and Lesser Vehicles, the defining characteristics of temples, icons, books, stūpas, and so forth are revealed, along with the advantages of constructing them. Such references are infinite, and these creative endeavors are themselves to be accomplished through the activity of the arts. Therefore, this field of classical learning constitutes an unrivaled approach to the provision of merit.

The initial appearance of the representations of buddha body, speech, and mind, in accordance with the Buddhist teaching, has already been mentioned, somewhat extensively in this book,[65] and the manner in which the learned and accomplished masters of India and Tibet and the religious kings documented them incidentally emerges, as it were, from their respective biographies. At first, when the Buddhist teaching was propagated, in each corner of Tibet, through the compassion and merit of the spiritual mentors and the great patrons of the Buddhist teaching, there were innumerable persons skilled in making metal cast icons, metal beaten icons, and icons of medicinal clay. {924}

As for the stylistic embrace of the arts, all the styles of India, China, Nepal, and Tibet are integrated, and among them, for the most part, artists may emphasize any one specific style through the engagement of their own minds, rendering the others subsidiary.[66]

In the case of iconography, initially because drawing accorded with the styles of India and Nepal, these were well established. In the intermediate period, the Indian and Chinese styles were integrated, so that paintings juxtaposed both of these styles. Later, Mentangpa (Menla Dondrub) of Lhodrak (fl. late fifteenth century) and Khyentse the Great (fl. fifteenth century) integrated these painting styles. It is said that they had emanated through the compassion of the buddhas and bodhisattvas in order to establish from their own perspectives the enlightened activity of the great upholders of the Buddhist teaching in the land of Tibet and of the devoted and wealthy patrons of the Buddhist teaching. Indeed, there were two unmistaken stylistic traditions that evolved. Nowadays, there are many who exclusively follow these two stylistic traditions.[67] Those who require metal beaten and metal cast icons mostly engage with the Newar sculptors themselves.

Then again, the basis of all erudition, even for those who do not engage with all the fields of classical learning and philosophical systems, is exclusively writing, and, in all activities, both writing and reading are indispensable.

The Origins of Medicine

With regard to the field of medicine, in general, medical science is indispensable for maintaining the well-being of the precious human body, free from disease, since it is foremost of the supports for achieving the sacred doctrine, wealth, and all that is desired, and also for facilitating the recovery from ill-health, whether one wishes for liberation or does not wish for it.[68] In this regard, non-Buddhists hold that the four Vedas—*Ṛg*, *Sāma*, *Yajur*, and *Atharva*—all originated from the four faces of Brahmā, along with the six branches of elocution, grammar, prosody, astrology, divine revelations that are "heard," and ritual sacrifice, as well as two subsidiary branches consisting of commentaries of human authorship that are "remembered" and righteousness.[69] {925}

Brahmā revealed medical science to the divine physician Prajāpatidakṣa, and he taught the Aśvin twins, Nāsatya (Nose-Born Being)[70] and Dasra (Universal Boon). The former was named Nāsatya because they were born from the nose of Saraṇyu, the wife of Sūrya, and Aśvinīja because they were born under the constellation Aśvinī.[71] They in turn revealed medical science to Śakra. Brahmā also differentiated the texts of[72] Ayurvedic works, including *The Hundred Thousand Verses of Medical Science*.[73] Śakra is known to have had seven outstanding disciples, including the divine hermit sage Atri.[74] These seven fathers cohabited with females who were human mothers, and therefrom there emerged their respective sons: Atreya, Agniveśa, Dhanvantari, Dvitapaścaraṇa,[75] Nemindhara, Kāśyapa,[76] and Punarvasu.[77] They all studied under Śakra and their fathers, and they each composed a commentary on the primary text. There were also nine others including the hermit sage Bheḍa who authored many texts,[78] and there were extensive compositions by Śālihotra, Suśruta, Jajaya, and so forth, their lineage continuing up to and including Atreya, the physician of Takṣaśīla.[79]

Regarding the propagation of medical science in the human world, in antiquity, not long after the appearance of sentient life, there was one Manu who could not digest the primordial nutrients of the soil. He cried out in lamentation, whereupon Brahmā arrived and prepared boiled water. That is said to have been the earliest incidence of invalids, diseases, doctors, and medications known to them [that is, human beings].[80]

In general, all the fields of classical learning at first originated through the power of the buddhas and bodhisattvas, and since Brahmā, too, is a being of the Auspicious Eon, he himself originated from the power of the buddhas. Although there are no sūtras or tantras that specifically teach medical science, it is incidentally and abundantly demonstrated in the ground rules concerning medicine from the transmissions of the vinaya, the chapter on the merchant's son Jalavāhana (Water Bringer) from *The Supreme Golden Light*,[81] and also from other references in *The Tantra of the Adamantine Sky Farers*, the *Kālacakra*, and so forth.[82]

Among the treatises, *The Hundred Compounds*,[83] The versified *Discourse on Sustenance*,[84] {926} *The Preparation of Ava Grass*,[85] *The Precious Garland of Mercury*,[86] and *The Alchemical Transformation of Gold*[87] were composed by sublime Nāgārjuna. *The Great Treatise of the Eight Branches*,[88] *The Intro-*

duction to the Eight Branches,[89] *The Concise Essence,*[90] and *The Summation of the Eight Branches*[91] were composed by master Vāgbhaṭa. Brangti Pelden Tsoje and others hold that Candranandana of Kashmir actually met master Vāgbhaṭa. He composed *Moonbeams of Word and Meaning: A Commentary on the Concise Essence,*[92] *Precise Terminology: A Supplement to Materia Medica,*[93] and so forth.[94]

In Tibet, at first the Chinese princess Wencheng brought the text titled *Supreme Medical Science,*[95] and it was translated. Three physicians were invited from India, China, and Persia, and they translated many texts pertaining to their respective traditions. In common, they composed a text titled *Weapon of Fearlessness.*[96]

During the time of Jinsheng Konjo, *The Somarāja* was translated. From Byzantium, one named Bitsi Tsanpa Shilaha was invited,[97] and he was granted seven awards.[98] He adhered to fifteen commitments[99] and established seven admonitions.[100]

Tongsum Gangwa, the foremost among the celebrated nine physicians, was given the hermitage of Yorto Chuwori, and his fame reached as far as the four extremities of the Tibetan empire.[101]

During the time of Lord Tsede (c. 1057–1090), one Melhajung, who had been exiled from Oḍḍiyāna, composed *The Outer, Inner, and Secret Rites of Fulfillment concerning Divinatory Pebble Calculations,*[102] and he translated many texts. The paṇḍita Janardana and the great translator Rinchen Zangpo translated Vāgbhaṭa's aforementioned *Concise Essence*, and Candranandana's *Summation of the Eight Branches: Its Root and Commentary*, and so forth. Cheje Tipam encountered a disciple of that great translator named Mangmo Mentsun, and in his lineage there were many learned physicians including Cheje Zhangton Zhikpo.[103] Also from the great translator, there is a lineage through Zhangzhungpa Sherab-o, Gyaton Drakpa Sherab, and Yutok Gyagar Dorje. Also, there was a further lineage from the great translator through Zhangzhungpa, Ngok Jongmen Yungdrung, Yutok Drakpa, and Yutok Yonten Gonpo (1126–1202).[104]

In Tibet, Zhang Zijibar, who was greatly learned in *The Summation of the Eight Branches,*[105] encountered nine learned Tibetan physicians, as well as the Indian hermit sage named Candrabi. He composed works including *The Immaculate Splendor: Root and Commentary*[106] and *The Thirty Instructions: Root and Commentary.*[107] His disciples included the three named Chung, who numbered four with the addition of Rok and five with the addition of Nekyok.[108]

Toton Konchok Kyab (b. eleventh century) traveled to India and trained under the later Śāntipā (b. eleventh century). He authored many writings.[109]

All these rivers of the lineage flowed into the lake that was the mind of Yutok Yonten Gonpo (1126–1202). This great emanational being generally acquired skill and accomplishment in all the fields of classical learning, and, in particular, he became a master of all the texts and pith instructions of medical science. He revealed innumerable wondrous signs of his attainment, and he was an actual buddha body of emanation. He expounded *The Four Tantras*, making the citadel of medicine, Sudraśana, his own residence; the expanse of reality, Bhaiṣajyaguru, his mind; the four assembles of the retinue, the diversity of his investigations; the hermit sage Manoja, his desire for composition; and the hermit sage Vidyājñāna, the essential nature of his awareness.[110] This author, Yutok Yonten Gonpo, is ascertained to have been an emanation in accordance with the fruitional signs. Since this work of his in many respects excelled all the other texts of medicinal science without exception, and it was appropriate for the land of Tibet and its time, his kindness was beyond any possible estimation. *The Four Tantras* are therefore regarded as the actual word of the Conqueror.[111] In addition, Yutok Yonten Gonpo also authored many minor tracts including *The Eleven Collected Cycles*,[112] and *The Cycle of the Attainment of the Secret Guru*, which is the supreme means for attainment associated with medical science. {928} The land of Tibet was filled with the lineage holders of his disciples and grand-disciples, and their compositions are also incalculable.[113]

Later, there was one Zurkharwa Nyamnyi Dorje (1439–1475), who, from birth, as it were, was naturally learned in all fields in general, and in particular in the texts and pith instructions of medical science. His many compositions included *The Pearl Relics of Ten Million Pith Instructions*.[114] He greatly elucidated the teaching of medical science, and although later there were many skilled physicians who appeared, that was due to his kindness.[115]

In general, there are said to have been one hundred and four physicians who were universally renowned and fifty-eight who were renowned for all their propagation. The ones who appeared first were Lochen Rinchen Zangpo and Kyebu Melha. The one who appeared in the intermediate period was Yutok Yonten Gonpo. The one who appeared later was Zurkhar Abo Choje (1439–1475). All of these are absolutely regarded as most wonderful.[116]

Nowadays, I have heard that there are many in each corner of the land who not only maintain the practical techniques of medical science, but also can expound, study, and pay attention to it. Therefore, this field of classical learning is exceedingly great in its activity, and it is the source of spiritual and temporal well-being for all corporeal beings.

Conclusion

By virtue of this, may the dawn of Sanskrit grammar, logic, arts, and medicine
Connect with the sunlight of inner Buddhist studies,
Eclipsing the dense obscuration and darkness of the three planes of existence,
And may they be diligently applied with the supreme light of omniscience!

This completes chapter eleven of this book, a digression presenting the origins of the four outer fields of classical learning, from *Wondrous Ocean of Eloquence: A Narrative of the Wish-Fulfilling Gem of the Lineage* compiled by Taklungpa Ngawang Namgyel. {929}

Colophon

OṂ SVĀSTI

With a hundred thousand light rays of transmission and realization, clearly renowned and unmistakenly described as "the glorious maṇḍala of knowledge that is spacious, precious, and second to none," the Buddhist teaching thoroughly eclipses the darkness of the minds of living beings and is resplendently beautiful as the crown of the entire world with its god realms, yielding all wishes—the inexhaustible banquet of higher rebirth and definitive excellence.

Lifting this teaching in their hands, rippling great waves with their long tails that are the supreme conduct of the bodhisattvas amid the ocean of kindness, and magnificently adorned with many distinctions including diverse ornaments of immeasurable knowledge, love, and enlightened activity, the two nāga lords of learning and accomplishment raise the thousand cobra hoods of the profound two stages of meditation.

Accurate narratives that recount the origin of this Buddhist teaching and the two stages are insatiable to behold, their noble meanings forming an adamantine mansion, expansive and elevated like the expanse of reality. Their words, too, form portals of four precious substances,[1] embellished with the body of mixed verse and prose. Their ornaments of sense form pedimental arches of bright crystal, exclusively opening avenues accessible and appropriate for place and time.

This book holds no fear for those who would inspect it. Though lacking even a drop of pristine cognition, when polished with the genuine nectar of faith, the unsullied water of this wondrous and credible narrative lucidly manifested. The lines of this book are wondrously arrayed like an ear ornament of gems dangling at the neck. Washing away blemishes of doubt with the water of reflection that excellently examines them firsthand and within range of the sense faculties, {930} it shone forth and was composed with great diligence!

The power to generate infinite realms of diverse sentient beings
As buddhas of inexhaustible purity
Will not be produced by any means
Apart from virtuous activities of heaven and earth.

Dedicated in the manner of the exemplary life of Samantabhadra,
The vital silken crown of the Sage's empowerment
Over the dominions of the sacred doctrine
Has reached this land of ours.

I pray that we may easily become accomplished here,
In accordance with his intent and aspiration to emanate
Through the guides, their heirs, and disciples
Who acquire the treasure of unsurpassed pristine cognition!

May devout corporeal beings always worship atop their victory banner
The supreme wish-fulfilling gem of transmission and realization—
Source of all good auspices of existence and quiescence,
And eliminator of constant poverty!

In particular, may the great chariot of the attainment lineage
Impartially introduce across the earth
The innate pristine cognition
Originally present within our own hearts,
Manifestly establishing it like a treasure in the hand!

A vital essence within that heart, may the teaching
Of exegesis and attainment of the Taklung Kagyu lineage
Spread forth and distend the branches and leaves
Of enlightened activity of the coral jasmin tree
So that it permeates all spatial spheres!

Embellished with noble body, the three trainings;
Steadfast limbs, the four attractive qualities;

And a golden web of enlightened activities—
May the supreme vehicle supporting the entire Buddhist teaching
Live long within the forest of existence!

May the prowess of accomplishing gnostic mantras
Embodying the compassion of the precious jewels, {931}
Accessing the clear crystal mirror of the three world systems,
Be enjoyed by living beings as a feast,
Transfiguring them in the new forms of a present Perfect Age!

May monasteries endowed with the blissful essence
That attains the definitive meaning of the Kagyu lineage,
Nurturing through appropriate study, reflection, and meditation
The treasure of sacred nectar, unique essence of the three vows,
Constantly flourish in their authentic priest and patron relationships!

With this unfading adamantine pen,[2]
May I elucidate the history of the activities
Of the Buddhist teaching on this earth,
Like the supreme appearances of whiteness in meditative
  consummation,
As if clad in a translucent robe of finest silk!

May the auspicious aspirations finely arranged in verse form
At the end of each of chapter,
Delineating the origin of the sacred doctrine in a hundred wondrous
  approaches,
Become a springtime of joy for beings of the three planes of existence!

May the array of the inanimate world and its life forms,
A magical emanation of appearances and emptiness,
Created from materials arising from the deeds of sentient beings
And through the power of secret mantra that refines the buddha fields,
Be actualized as a great maṇḍala, consummately perfect!

May we strive to be born into the following of that lord-protector,[3]
Who can fill the expanse of reality with a rain of particles,

The camphor of the two provisions accumulated over many eons,
And whose half-moon toenails are the crown ornament of a hundred deities!

When raised on the solid platform of the cycles of renunciation, recitation, and activity,
May we mount the courageous and peerless śarabha,
The eight-footed one endowed with faith, diligence, and wisdom,
And eyes that look up toward the conduct of Samantabhadra!

Through the gems of word and meaning
Contained in the vinaya, abhidharma, and sūtras,
May we acquire unlimited intelligence like a celestial treasury,
And may the forces that slay and quell the fever of signs and concepts
Resemble a forest of white sandalwood,
Exuding words of adamantine reality! {932}

May the flock of mighty garuḍa that constitutes the four seals
Swallow the three serpents that constitute the aggregates,
Sensory elements, and sense fields, along with the sense organs and sense objects,
And then, having digested the poison of the three obscurations,
May they fashion of beryl the innate pristine cognition!

Penetrating with the light rays of the Buddhist teaching
Those who are ill due to the dense blackness of negativity
That has shrouded them for eons,
May the pure daylight of the sacred doctrine be able to refresh them
Just as the celestial mirror of the sun befriends the lotus flower!

Manifestly establishing all endowments of the vajra-holding tradition
In the body, speech, and mind of fortunate disciples with a hundred merits,
Inexpressible even by the tongue of the teacher of nāgas,
May these wondrous deeds shine forth as ornaments!

May the supreme and adamantine gemstone mansion of exegesis and attainment,
With its high golden tower of liberating lives,

Excellently introduced by the hundred thousand garuḍas of
enlightened activity,
Manifest in the three worlds without impediment!

Unfurling supreme and calm meditative stability as a great canopy,
Thinking to fill the vacuum of space,
May this cause all the lotus groves of corporeal beings
To swell with genuine and auspicious liberation!

May voyagers who unimpededly reflect
The diverse modes of the sacred doctrine
In the pools of pure vision, endowed with the eight qualities,
Purged of the turbid stains of bias,
Come look upon this work with eyes of clarity!

Having scaled the staircase of grammar, logic, art, and medicine
And opened the portals of the three scriptural baskets,
May all realms of infinite sentient beings
Enter within the celestial palace of the Adamantine Vehicle!

Though there are all sorts of oceanic upholders of the pure Buddhist
teaching,
Depicted on the surface of Benares cotton that is the mind with
mastery of speech, {933}
The essential incantations are drawn by calligraphers
Endowed with the compassion of the precious Kagyu lineage
Who delight in the distinguishing features of iconography.
Since this work has been well composed, simply as a gateway
For impartial beginners, disciples of faith, diligence, wisdom, and noble
wealth,
May the transformation of great pristine cognition,
The blessing of Maṅgalaśrī (Tashi Pel), emanation of the Conqueror
Akṣobhya,
Enter into this heart of mine and of others!

Although I, slightly earlier, had an intention to write this *Wondrous Ocean of Eloquence: A Narrative of the Wish-Fulfilling Gem of the Lineage*, due to indolence, I procrastinated somewhat. Then, encouraged by the entire congregation of Kagyu Domsumling with one-pointed devout faith, it was with joy that I, Pelden Ngawang Chokyi Nyima Jikme Zangpo Chokyi Tamchele Nampar Gyelweide, a monk and vajra holder from the northern region, when four hundred and sixty-seven years had passed since the birth of Taklungpa the Great Maṅgalaśrī and four hundred and twenty-eight years had passed since that same lord-protector set foot in this great monastic seat of Taklung, during the four hundred and twenty-ninth year, when I, the author, was in my thirty-ninth year, I set myself to the task of writing on the twenty-third day of the first lunar month of 1609, known in India as Śānti and in Tibet as the earth female bird year. Then, on the fifth day of the waxing half of Vaiśākha, the fourth lunar month that is also known as the last spring month—the day on which Munīndra had clearly foreordained his setting out upon the spiritual path, I completed the task at the great seminary of Taklung Dorjeden, the place where Tashi Pel, emanation of the Transcendent Lord Akṣobhya, had attained manifestly perfect buddhahood. {934} The scribe who first set down the memorandum in book form was named the Śākya novice Gala Namgyel. May it become like the sun and moon upon the earth!

MAṄGALAṂ ŚUBHAṂ

PART TWO

Great Divine Drum of Wondrous Renown

Ngawang Tenpei Nyima

Herein is contained the supplementary biographies of the later incumbents of the abbatial succession of Taklung Upper Plain Dorjeden, titled *Great Divine Drum of Wondrous Renown*, continuing on from the extensive exegesis of the biographies of the Taklung Kagyu lineage holders, which constitutes chapter eight of *Wondrous Ocean of Eloquence: A Narrative of the Wish-Fulfilling Gem of the Lineage*. This supplement was compiled by Ngawang Tenpei Nyima.{725}

Verses of Homage

Perpetual homage to the supreme mighty lords of spiritual accomplishment and logical reasoning within the Kagyu lineage, whose essential nature is inseparable from the entire ocean of spiritual teachers and the precious jewels!

I pray that you may swiftly grant your blessing so that this act of composition might reach its perfect conclusion!

I have sincere faith in the all-illuminating expanse of the buddha body of reality,
The supreme teacher of vast kindness, transcending worldly affairs,
Whose nature is the emptiness of sound,
Devoid of arising, cessation, and present continuity,
That mighty circle of the sun, lord of all, consummate from the beginning,
In whom the two truths are indivisible,
Whose thousand light rays of enlightened activity, supreme bliss, dispel the darkness of the hundredfold defects of these sentient beings, including myself!

I worship the crown ornament of the entire golden rosary of the authentic lineage of the Taklungpa,
Which emerged from the beauteous ornament of the world and its inhabitants throughout the three times,
With its inconceivable emanations, names, and methods for the sake of those to be trained,
Diversely arising from the unique, authentic pristine cognition in which they are inseparable.

Until enlightenment, I worship and attend inseparably upon the teacher
Whose multiple arrays permeate all sacred places and fields,
Cakrasaṃvara in male-female union, and the infinite deities of the tantra class,
Whose mighty wish-granting power fulfills the hopes of all supreme desires.

I bow and pay hundredfold homage with resolute devotion
To Munīndra, who planted his toenails upon the crowns
Of all the greatest gods, nāgas, and yakṣas,
Whose body like a mountain of gold refined a hundred thousand times crushes pride,
Supreme in the blazing glory of its major and minor marks that dispel mental afflictions,
Whose speech is the gateway of the sacred doctrine composed of the two truths, provisional and definitive, {726}
Teachings satisfying the minds of countless living beings,
Along with his heirs, pious attendants and hermit buddhas who train in this approach.

May the protectors Magon Chamdrel[1] come to my assistance!
Having mastered the great path of the supramundane noble ones
In order to dispel the causes, fruits, and afflictions of miserliness in the minds of living beings,
I request the accomplishment of the glorious lord-protector Vasudeva,
Arisen in the physical form of a yakṣa bestowing a stream of wealth and desired necessities.

May the lord of the soil Yirabdel and his retinue,
Guardian of all that is indestructible,
Mighty *genyen* protector whose fame conforms with actuality,
Such that his wrathful prowess in this mundane existence is unrivaled and marvelous.
Render everything excellent in this community!

Writer's Pledge

If the extent of these lives of our Kagyu predecessors,
Each fraction of their deeds embellished with a hundred wonders,
Cannot be expressed by those who have mastered the path of the noble ones,
How could I, a stupid and dull person, possibly do so!

These writings compiled by my blind intelligence
Are mute expressions—a source of embarrassment for the wise.
This is why my inclination to write treatises has been discouraged.
And yet through my resolve and various means,
Since even the slightest mention of the biographies
Of lineage holders who act on behalf of beings in this existence,
Exudes a positive maturation,
I especially hold upon the anthers at the center of my heart
The face of my lord of enlightened heritage in whom all refuges are gathered,
And the supremely secret teachings of my teacher, Mahāvajradhara. {727}
As I then donate, in the form of an offering cloud, a somewhat labored supplement
To the foregoing doctrinal history,
May this lotus offering fall within reach of his joyous eyes,
And in all my rebirths, may I be accepted inseparably by my lord and spiritual teacher,
My mind and his buddha mind merging together,
And may he bestow spontaneously present good auspices,
The excellent endowments of existence and quiescence!

Synopsis of the Text

Having arranged these verses of the offering prayer and the writer's pledge in lines, like neatly aligned garlands of coral flowers, I now turn to the venerable master and perfect buddha Ngagi Wangpo, universally known as the late Ngawang Namgyel Kunga Rinchen Pelzangpo. Wearing the saffron robe, he emanated the dance of the Sugata Ratnakūṭa in the world in general and particularly in this northern region of Uru, in order to elucidate more intensely like cloudless sunlight the precious teachings of Taklungpa the Great, embodiment of the Conqueror Akṣobhya. These teachings concerning the sacred doctrine and worldly affairs constitute the wheel of the profound and vast sacred doctrine that emerged from the glorious voice of this sacred teacher who comprehended all things quantifiably and definitively and that he turned without interruption. They have been well analyzed by means of the three analytical methods—analysis conducted in the manner in which gold is smelted, cut, and polished—indicating that they are indeed without any deviations, errors, or flaws. Their verbal expression is pleasant and magnificent in form, consistent with the rules of the textual tradition of poetics. Through each casual expression, profound and vast with respect to expressed meaning, the particular realizations experienced in the minds of intelligent persons and all the incontrovertible meanings of the scriptures, general and particular, are easily understood. {728} Even topics that may be accepted or rejected in accordance with the twofold tradition of sacred and secular affairs are incidentally understood.

Among the quantifiable volumes of his great treatises, the compositions forming his Collected Works, *The Doctrinal History Titled Wondrous Ocean* contains a complete but cursory account of the origins of the Buddhist teaching in general and particular, and, above all, it contains a somewhat extensive account of the Kagyu lineage in general and the biographies of the spiritual teachers and lineage holders of its subschool, the upper and lower monastic seats of Taklungpa the Great. This commences with a description of the three mysteries and five wheels of adornment[1] of the one renowned as Taklung Tangpa Tashi Pel, the peerless Sugata, the buddha body of reality, progenitor of the monastic succession of Taklung Upper Plain, and it continues down to Vajradhara Kunga Tashi, who was Venerable Ngawang Namgyel's own lord of enlightened heritage. The narrative resembles a rust-free mirror of ideation and scrutiny on which the wondrous deeds and great profound mysteries of each lineage holder are clearly reflected, arising within range of the recollection of all persons, wise and foolish.

Recently, from the monastic seat of Riwoche in Yisho Pel, the great buddha field of Dorje Melong Drubpa, our crown ornament, an embodiment of peerless and unrivaled kindness in the three planes of existence, reminiscent of the discerning Mañjunātha Pañcaśikha who manifestly sees all abiding and apparent objects of knowledge that there are without obscuration, as clear as a gooseberry in the palm of the hand, emanated as a saffron-robed monk, in accordance with the wishes of sublime Lokeśvara. {729} Disregarding hardship over many eons for the sake of even a single sentient being of the three world systems, through steadfast courage, with great love that cherishes others rather than oneself and never becomes obsolete, he overwhelmed the four classes of demonic forces and effortlessly guided all those associated with him through sight, hearing, recollection, and contact toward the positive path of liberation and omniscience, reminiscent of the manner of vajra-holding Guhyapati. In brief, it was in the presence of this embodiment of all the maṇḍala circles, essential nature of all the tathāgatas of the ten directions and three times, source of the eighty-four thousand sections of the sacred doctrine, sovereign of all monastic communities, unrivaled lord-protector of refuge, my root teacher, the most sublime wish-fulfilling master, omniscient Mahāvajradhara, whose actual name is difficult to say—Drakpa Choying Lhundrub Rinchen Tendzin Namgyel Trinle Gyelweide Chenpo—that I, of coarse realization, at the lowest level of those who nowadays preach the sacred doctrine, merely having the external form of a teacher but lacking the doctrine, acting arrogantly by exaggerating my grand title, and responsible for maintaining an ascetic discipline that is titanic and powerful, was offered, along with material gifts, the noble inspiration of his injunction, as if he were looking upon a clod of earth as gold. He insisted that I should compile and contribute cursory biographies of the complete succession of the monastic seat of Taklung, which would appropriately serve as a supplement to *The Doctrinal History Titled Won-*

drous Ocean, commencing from the later part of the life of the venerable sugata Ngawang Namgyel and continuing down to the two tulkus of the present day. {730}

As a preceptor of eight counterfeit attributes, I have not greatly examined the teachings of the scriptures in general, or even the integration of sūtra and mantra, and I am without erudition. Though there are some minor parts of the scriptures that I have obtained through the kindness of my gracious, peerless, and venerable teachers, my analytical skill in appraising perfect words and meanings is inferior, and although I have obtained as my share a mere fraction of refined guidance on the outer and inner fields of classical learning, poetics and so forth, from the teachings of those scholars, mighty lords of discriminative awareness, masters, and tutors, I am submerged in the swamp of forgetfulness and indolence, such that these have vanished like the tracks of a bird. This being the case, how could I joyously fulfill the wishes of Mahāvajradhara, mighty lord of the four buddha bodies, let alone pass the inspection of intelligent persons? Mediocre in terms of wisdom and foolishness, I am even uninspired to preach a minute fraction of the profound words and meanings that can withstand scrutiny. As the master Daṇḍin has said, "When speech is inappropriately used, this indeed declares the stupidity of its writer."[2] Since I lack expressive words that would cause the learned to rejoice, in general I am discouraged. That would certainly be a source of embarrassment for others. So how could I possibly be worthy of composing a supplement to a work written by that great omniscient one of the past! And yet, if I do not take the injunctions of the teacher's word as my standard, and if I do not do as he bids, even if I were to slay all the sentient beings in the three world systems, there would be no more onerous crime than that of once infringing the command of the teacher. This is said in the commentaries on the enlightened intention of the Conqueror in general, {731} and in particular, I had doubts, thinking I might be contaminated by the extremely unbearable downfalls described in *Fifty Stanzas on the Spiritual Teacher*.[3] The venerable one then bestowed on me the teachings on *The Spiritual Teacher: Gathering of All That Is Rare and Precious*,[4] and I requested the outer attainment.

In these circumstances, I detailed the most important activities distilled from the extant individual biographies recounting the later part of the life of Venerable Ngawang Namgyel, and those of Choktrul Tashi Peldrub, Venerable Chokyi Gyelpo, omniscient Tendzin Namgyel, and Tashi Drakpa Yeshe, and then I supplemented these, arranging them according to my understanding. With regard to Dzong Zhabdrung Namgyel Lekdrub, Tashi Jampel Gyatso, and so forth, since I did not find even an inkling of their biographies, I had no way but to present the definitive points that fell within the range of my understanding, in collaboration with the two senior and junior tulkus. After arranging all this in the form of a memorandum to be presented in an orderly manner before the eyes of my supreme teacher, the venerable buddha, lord of enlightened heritage, I embarked on the task of offering this supplementary historical narrative.

1. The Later Life of Zhabdrung Ngawang Namgyel, the Seventeenth Hierarch

Respectful homage to you, lord-protector, Ngawang Namgyel,
Gathering all excellent endowments in the entirety of existence and quiescence
As ornaments of the apparitional wheels of adornment,[1]
Emanating as many conquerors including Ratnakūṭa!

Among all the incumbents of the monastic seat of Taklung, forming a garland of buddhas, Ngawang Namgyel reveals himself in many emanational forms, including the peerless buddha of the future, Ratnakūṭa, a universal emperor of the sacred doctrine, and the buddha of the present Lokaśubhakṛtsna. {732} In this field of ours, he appeared in the past as Anāthapiṇḍada who was consolidated on the divine path by offering lodgings to our teacher, the King of the Śākyas, and arraying a revered cloud of offerings. In the Kalāpa Palace of Śambhala in the north, he appeared as the great sage Vīrasena, a mighty accomplished master endowed with the body of pristine cognition on whom the Kulika king Mañjughoṣakīrti excellently conferred the doctrinal wheel of the outer, inner, and extraneous Kālacakra maṇḍalas. He appeared as Nanam Yeshe De, a spiritual son of the mighty accomplished master Padmākara, who could summon the mental faculties of beings of the three planes of existence through many displays of miraculous power in the sky. He appeared as the supreme elder Aṅgita, and, later, emanating as a spiritual mentor, pure with respect to the three trainings, he manifested as Potowa Rinchen Sel. He then appeared as Taklung Sangye Yarjon, establishing the codes of monastic discipline and the rules of the assembly, acting in the manner of a second teacher with respect to the Buddhist teaching, and manifestly perceiving internally the pristine cognition of the real nature. Subsequently, he appeared as Marton Rinchen Śākya, an emanation of the mighty accomplished master Śavaripā, who actualized the signs of having attained supreme spiritual accomplishment. He appeared as Janglungpa Zhonu Lodro, who after becoming an awareness holder with power over the lifespan, disciplined the realms of living beings for up to a hundred years and displayed a liberating career that was profound and extensive. He appeared as Gyelwang Tsokye Dorje, who beheld the faces of many assemblies of preferred meditational deities, and attained spiritual accomplishments. He appeared as the wondrous and supreme tulku Namgyel Tashi, who raised aloft the banner of spiritual and temporal activities, exemplifying the teaching of the Conqueror Akṣobhya through many magnificent deeds. Then, after revealing all these forms, he once again took birth in the familial line of Taklung, tall like a great sal tree. {733} His father was Taklung Gaji and his mother Drigung Kyurama. In his thirty-ninth year, starting from the thirteenth day of the first month of 1609 (earth female bird), he composed *The Great Doctrinal History Titled Wondrous Ocean*. Up to that point, the full account of his enlightened activity, his detailed biography and the events surrounding his composition of the *Doctrinal History* have already been presented in the context of the actual narrative of this monastic succession. Distinct from that, here I shall recount his later life, presenting it in the form of a supplement, starting from the events that immediately followed his composition of *The Doctrinal History*.

On the fourth day of the sixth month of 1609 (earth female bird), also known as Saumya during the tenth sexagenary cycle, the Newar Maṇipāla, with a group of fifteen artisans, arrived in his presence. He began by blessing the tools of the artisans and the materials for the sculptures, and this continued until the insertion of the inner relics had been completed, thereby ensuring that the excellent custom of handcrafting representations of the perfect buddha himself reached perfection. So it was that, with the exception of the two exalted images of Jowo Śākyamuni in the Lhasa Trulnang and Ramoche and the image of Jangchub Chenpo at Samye, among all the lesser representations of Śākyamuni that were constructed here in Tibet by the religious kings, great paṇḍitas, learned and accomplished masters, and kingly hierarchs, they constructed this extraordinarily perfect creation known as Lhachen Pelgyi Lhunpo Dzamling Gyen (Ornament of the World: Glorious Mound of Great Gods),[2] the meaning of which is in conformity with its name. As for the relics that were inserted within it, foremost among the authentic consecrated objects were the multiplying bone relics of many authoritative, reliable, and authentic beings, including tathāgatas, pious attendants, and hermit buddhas, as well as pearl relics of the buddha body of reality. There were also many representations of buddha speech, including more than ten thousand incantation scrolls, a complete manuscript of the Kangyur, and ten complete manuscripts of *The Transcendent Perfection of Wisdom in Eight Thousand Lines*. {734} He effortlessly gathered all the excellent provisions of existence and quiescence, none excepted, including images, incantations, wish-granting prayers, and charts of the meditational deities, buddhas, bodhisattvas, and the doctrinal protector Vasudeva, which saintly beings had handwritten, and exuberantly ensured that this seminary of Taklung would until the end of worldly existence effortlessly acquire excellent provisions and limitless opportunities for auspicious coincidence that were well presented, like the waxing moon. He then performed the consecration ceremony based on the sixty-two-deity Cakrasaṃvara sand maṇḍala, and he satisfied the artisans with gifts of material wealth, as if they had arrived at the mythical treasury of Paulastya.[3]

At that time, Ngawang Namgyel was invited by five itinerant groups of Ponmo Apa, the wife of Pon Yulgyel from lower Hor, to dedicate virtuous actions to perfect enlightenment on behalf of the deceased. Detouring via Dzutse, Bipu Lungring, and Sangto Tsachuk, at Pontsang Rutok the Yangri Garpa of Drigung[4] incidentally arrived en route from Kham, and they stayed together, along with Gelong Karma Demchok and others from the encampment of Karmapa,[5] approximately fifty from Zuri, and all the monks and lamas of Meldro Gungkar Hermitage.[6] He and Drigungpa went back and forth meeting each another, and profound and elaborate receptions were held. Owing to profound and extensive discussions concerning the sacred doctrine, including a prayer dedicated to the life of Chogyel Rinchen Phuntsok that he had written,[7] his mind was utterly pure, rivaling the snows of Mount Kailash. He imparted the view of meditative cultivation to the communities of Yangri and Zuri, and the initiations with respect to the desired teachings to the lamas of Katsel. {735} Fulfilling their hopes in ways such as these, his good fortune was absolutely authentic. Seated at the head of the row of the recipients of the great offerings of the roots of virtue, he performed the rite of purification of the dead along with the empowerment, pointing out the path and so forth through his supreme individual guidance. Finally, he made an extensive solemn declaration of truth, along with an oral exegesis, dedicating virtuous actions to perfect enlightenment on behalf of the deceased. All those who had assembled there acquired pure vision and steadfast resolve.

In addition, he was invited by each of the nomadic communities from lower Hor and held most extensive feasts at which bountiful doctrinal and material gifts were bestowed, along with teachings on the higher realms of rebirth and the definitive excellence of liberation. Afterward, with the resident monks of the monastery who held the three vows in the vanguard, the great encampment also traveled to the great seminary of Taklung Tangpa, illustrious among those of subdued mind.

That autumn, Ngawang Namgyel excellently executed a painted image of Taklung Tangpa Chenpo, the supreme Conqueror, in the form Jakchil Kutsab Rinpoche—the maṇḍala of its visage was as if Taklung Tangpa were actually present. The drawing was made by the lord-protector himself, and the colors were added by Drukgyampa. He then commissioned the masks of the protector deity Genyen Chenpo,[8] including those of the protector of the Buddhist teaching himself and his retainers, which are preserved even now in the Great Offering Chapel.[9] He inserted *dhāraṇī* within the statues of the thousand buddhas to be placed in the background of the aforementioned large Śākyamuni image.[10] After he had completed exemplary eye-opening and face-gilding rites, and so forth, the artisans who made the throne back did so exclusively through the strength of their compassion and discriminative awareness, which were of the highest order.

In 1610 (iron dog), also known as sādhana, when Ngawang Namgyel was in his fortieth year, Tsering Gyelpo, a venerable junior chieftain of Hor, passed away. In order to secure him on the genuine path of refinement, he went to Galta Latok and acted as a pilot, leading the deceased to blissful realms. {736} On returning to the monastic seat, he offered the silk robes that are contained within the Munīndra image. In such ways, he reached the pinnacle of perfection. As if Munīndra had actually returned, this image was consummately created as a supreme field of merit for persons who excel to reach a level of pure virtuous symbols.

When the elderly Kunga Namgyel, who had previously been the venerable master's official at Kudzi, succumbed to fever due to a phlegm disorder, he went to Seling, a place deemed conducive to pilgrimage,[11] after which Kudzi was then sent out on pilgrimage.

The stūpa known as Tashi Pelbar, which had in ancient times held the reliquary of Venerable Taklung Tangpa the Great and had gradually been constructed since the time of Kuyalwa, was four or five stories in height.

It had been consummately accomplished, but at the time when the temple was previously damaged by fire, the flames had reached up to the harmikā, which supports the relics. The cubit-size silver reliquary containing the heart, tongue, and eyes of Choku Taklung Tangpa the Great, which forms the core within it, had been undamaged by the fire. More recently, Ngawang Namgyel's venerable predecessor Namgyel Tashi, knowing that it would be an auspicious circumstance causing the Buddhist teaching and its enlightened activity to expand, had restored the dome and the dome plinth and so forth from the harmikā downward of pure white silver, as in the past. Although its aperture of beaten gold and the silver icon of Venerable Taklung Tangpa inside it with its exquisite and splendid throne back had been commissioned, at that time no lion throne and plinth had been constructed for the icon. By the power of the unrivaled aspiration of his late teacher, Ngawang Namgyel was not content to imagine it in the form of a lotus stūpa or a stūpa symbolizing the birth of the buddha with four tiers, a foundation slab symbolizing the ten virtuous actions, a lion throne, and so forth, {737} but he actually commissioned the throne and plinth without difficulty. He inserted its inner relics and so forth, a cubic meter of the four sorts of pearl relics, and in addition, he also filled it to the brim with excellent auspicious artifacts, including many particular diagrams for gathering the monastic community, overpowering, increasing resources, and so forth, as well as treasure vases, medicinal seeds, exquisite fragrances, and essences.

At Seling, he then constructed representations of the subterranean protectors and perfectly accomplished the service of the main image depicting Tashi Pelbar. After that, he had hoped to carry out an inspection and bestow extensive acts of kindness on all the monastic communities and sacred places of U, Tsang, and Kham. However, the occasion did not arise for him to go in person because he had to nurture the excellent spiritual and secular provisions of the monastery at Taklung through the many great methods that enhanced them, and so forth. And yet, at least among the noble and ordinary monks of his field, who knew how to recite a single verse of the scriptures, the pure vision of his enlightened intention was directed toward the sacred field of merit consisting of prostration and offering, motivated without partiality or bias. He made offerings to the monasteries, artifacts and sacred places representing the impartial philosophical systems up to and including the four divisions of the monastic community, and he presented communal tea offerings and contributed excellent facilities to them. He exclusively paid attention to the authentic connections that engendered unsurpassed meritorious deeds in all monasteries representative of the different doctrinal traditions and philosophical systems, from Tsang, Yarlung, Lungsho, the Drigung region, and Lharigo, as far as Dartsedo. Indeed, the fame of his achievements, pleasing to the ear, caused all living beings, including the gods, to rejoice. {738}

Kudzi Kunga Namgyel set out from Taklung with health-giving water and went to fulfill the hopes of living beings at Sitsa, Khartok, Nyonruk, and so forth. On that occasion, at Nyon Dzong, before the day was out, Kudzi passed away in the supreme field of liberation. Ngawang Namgyel performed the immediately beneficial ceremonies. Immediately, at Taklung, all the official and private monks then extensively performed an auspicious funeral ceremony, following an official directive. In particular, Ngawang Namgyel commissioned a pure gold manuscript of *The Transcendent Perfection of Wisdom in Eight Thousand Lines*, and a pure silver manuscript of *The Transcendent Perfection of Wisdom in One Hundred Thousand Lines*, and so forth, and he consecrated them. He appointed the treasurer Ngawang Rabten in charge of all responsibilities concerning religious and secular affairs, external and internal.

Then, after establishing a residence in the taintless field of Yang Gon hermitage, Ngawang Namgyel met Drungpo Tsewang Dondrub, the chieftain of Lowo who was a descendant of Jamgon Kunga Drolchok on pilgrimage at Lhasa, and with a letter of permission, they went together to visit Radeng. Ngawang Namgyel joyfully bestowed upon him the empowerments and initiations of *The Long-Life Empowerment Titled Innate Supreme Bliss*[12] according to the maṇḍala of the buddha mind of Vajrapāṇi and of White Tārā, and so forth, along with the guidance, experiential cultivation, and synopsis of the Great Seal. His mind was satisfied with these teachings, the sight of the representative images at Radeng and so forth, and he obtained joyfulness.

Ngawang Namgyel made line drawings, tracing by hand the ancient drawing of Gyelwa Taklungpa and the drawing of Drogon Phakmodrupa that had been prepared face-to-face, and he had artists color them.

Similarly, he had a meeting with the reincarnation of Geshe Gyelwa Dadzin Chogon, the lord of Desi Gyangkar Tsewa, and also with Langtang Chenga Choje; {739} and he brought them to maturation through many initiations, including that of Amitābha.

At that time, the army of Desi Tsangpa conquered the hinterland of Yamdrok and took possession of the dzong estates and their governance.

On that occasion the Desi Tsangpa Karma Phuntsok Namgyel[13] had utmost devotion to the three precious jewels that held sway through the wheel of powerful merit throughout the land of Utsang with its four horns and to the upholders of the enlightened heritage of attainment in the Kagyu tradition. Along with some eight hundred attendants, he traveled to Lhasa to see Jowo Śākyamuni. Then, by virtue of a connection in former lives that resembled that between sandalwood and the fragrance of sandalwood, he sent a messenger to Taklung, to invite Choje Deshek Rinpoche Ngawang Namgyel. A grand procession of all the senior masters of Taklung, accompanied by the assembled community of monks upholding the three vows, set out from the monastic seat. They reached the region of Lhasa where they were escorted by some two hundred lay officials on horseback.

On behalf of the ruler Desi Chenpo, along with most of his ministers and generals, and about three hundred attendants, in the presence of the image of Jowo Śākyamuni, the most essential representation of the Buddha in the world, he bestowed the elaborate practice of the one-day fast and the eightfold precepts of lay ordination, according to the lineage descended from Mañjuśrī and Nāgārjuna, and the most extensive rite of setting the mind on supreme enlightenment, in accordance with the lineage of profound view, which descends from Śāntideva. He also kindly favored the Desi in private with the initiations of *White Amitāyus according to the Tradition of Taklung*,[14] *Blue-Clad Vajrapāṇi according to the Tradition of Buton*, and the *Attainment of Hayagrīva according to the Tradition of the King*.[15] {740} Then, in the upper gallery of the Great Temple of Lhasa, in front of the Maitreya Chapel, on behalf of the Desi and his official entourage, the assembly of resident monks, and a countless host of monks and laypeople, he gave extensive oral guidance on the profound path, adorned with the pith instructions of his spiritual teachers. At that time, in sight of everyone, there were wondrous signs, including a shower of flowers. Each day, he met with the Desi and bestowed upon him hundreds of empowerments pertaining to Amitābha, White Tārā, and Amitāyus, along with the verses of their aspiration prayers. He turned the wheel of the sacred doctrine unceasingly, in accordance with the faculties of those to be trained, including initiations and the specific guidance of the mantras, ancient and new, on behalf of the Desi and his official attendants, and also the communities of Namling, Chakpa Gyatso, Yamdrok, Pelde, and, in U, of Yangpachen, Shakpa, Trebupa, and Lhagyari. Drungpa Śākya Lhundrub donated the offering lamp of Jowo and a large silk offering scarf. The government of the Desi produced a prayer festival catalog, including *The Daily Burnings during the Great Prayer Festival*.[16]

In the Kyilkhorteng,[17] Ngawang Namgyel bestowed on the Desi subsidiary estates[18] and a hundredfold pure material offerings; and in return he extensively paid his respects to Deshek Rinpoche Ngawang Namgyel, along with his senior monks and monastic body in the Ganden Khangsar Palace at Drepung.

In addition, Ngawang Namgyel donated to the Jokhang a hundred gold *zho* coins, and five hundred consecutive leases, and so forth. By methodically securing this patron-priest relationship, like that of sun and moon, the stable prayer festival offerings were arrayed in detail in all the upper and lower stories of the Great Temple. {741}

Then, seen off by the governor of Kyisho and his brother, along with an escort of some five hundred attendants, who mostly belonged to the nobility, and attended upon by Onsa Anedrung, he returned to the monastic seat of Taklung, after visiting the sacred place of Yerpa, earliest of the sacred places in the Land of Snows, where he presented an excellent cloud mass of offerings.

In the late summer of that year and part of autumn, he brought to maturation in the minds of the monastic assembly headed by the four preceptor masters and each master of the ritualist monks, the supreme fruit of maturational empowerment and liberating guidance by imparting without interruption the gift of the sacred doctrine. During the eleventh month he composed *The Rain of Adamantine Fire: Inspecting the Wrathful Rites of Genyen Chenpo, Protector of the Transmitted Teachings, the Sharp Dart of Wrathful Activity*,[19] and on that basis he also extensively composed a torma offering rite and the temporal sequence of the rite.

In his forty-second year, in 1612 (water mouse), also known as *paradhari*, Dungyu Rinchen,[20] the nephew of Drigung Phakmo, then in his seventeenth year, arrived at Taklung with some eighty attendants. The lama performed the ritual tonsure and bestowed upon him the lay vows that uphold the three precious jewels, conferring upon him the name Ngawang Rinchen Peldrub Kagyu Nampar Gyelweide.

Soon after, the venerable master's own nephew Zhabdrung Ma Rinpoche Tashi Peldrub,[21] sacred sovereign of knowledge, love, and power, then in his thirteenth year, arrived. Indeed, when he set foot in this supreme seminary of Taklung, the great monastic seat exalted through the glory of existence and quiescence, they, father and son, met together. The entire congregation of monks welcomed him with a cloud of offerings similar to those mentioned in the biography of Samantabhadra. {742} Ngawang Namgyel then opened the door of auspicious coincidence, commencing with the biography of Gyelwa Taklungpa. Straightaway, in the manner of Śākyamuni, Tashi Peldrub discarded his stands of bluish black hair there in the god realms, and the precepts of the novitiate were bestowed upon him, preceded by the lay vows and the intermediate mendicant vows. He was given the name Ngawang Tashi Peldrub Ngedon Chokyi Nyima Namdrol Chokide.

Then, the two supreme tulkus of Taklung and Driging in tandem extensively bestowed the sequences of the sacred doctrine. In opening the portal of the sacred doctrine, they bestowed the precepts that set the mind on enlightenment, and the initiation of White Amitāyus, the meditational deity of glorious Taklungpa. Thereafter, they conferred the empowerments and initiations of Cakrasaṃvara according to the tradition of Lūipa, the eighth succession,[22] as well as Dvimukhavajravārāhī, the seven maṇḍalas of Ngok, Akṣobhya in the form Guhyasamāja, Buddhakapāla, Vajrapāṇi, Sarvavid Vairocana, The Peaceful and Wrathful Guru, the five empowerments of The Compassion of Dark-Blue Guru Drakpo, Vajravidāraṇa, Siṃhavaktrā, Lokṭipa, Long-Living Hayagrīva according to the tradition of Drubgyel, and Coemergent Cakrasaṃvara. And in a monastic congregation holding the three vows, they conferred *The Ocean of Means for Attainment*,[23] the initiation of Mahākāla, the fourteenth vase empowerment, *Dhūmāṅgārīśrīdevī*,[24] Vaiśravaṇa, Tseringma, and so forth. They granted the immeasurable kindness of the nectar of the sacred doctrine, including many oral transmissions and crucial points of specific guidance concerning the Collected Works of Venerable Mila Repa, Dakpo Lharje, and Phakmodrupa; *The Golden Books of Drigung*,[25] the Great Seal, the Six Doctrines, the purificatory rites of The Peaceful and Wrathful Guru, the purificatory rites of Four-Armed Mahākāla, and so forth. To Drigung Rinpoche he offered bountiful acts of service, respect, and donations. {743} They formed an unsurpassed resolution that profoundly secured the extremely close mutual friendship between Drigung and Taklung. For about two and a half months, they sat together, acquiring authentic gems from one another and satisfying one another. Then, as if turning away,[26] Drigung Rinpoche returned to his own abode at Drigung.

Tashi Peldrub, the nephew of Venerable Ngawang Namgyel, focused on a profound resolve to completely receive, in the manner of the contents of one vase being poured into another, whatever empowerments, transmissions, and guidance of the profound doctrine Deshek Rinpoche possessed, without residue or remainder. Starting from then, he vowed to undertake without interruption at best three, on average two, and at least one daily session of teaching that mostly entailed empowerments and initiations during the summer and transmissions and guidance during the winter. Throughout all the four seasons, his time was passed in accordance with the wheel of the sacred doctrine. Here, I have not listed the names of the various teachings that were given, lest that be too verbose.

Starting from the fourth day of the fourth month of that year, Ngawang Namgyel restored the precious grass hermitage containing the celestial palace of the Conqueror Akṣobhya, as well as the cave hermitages, and he newly built the small Layel Courtyard. On that occasion, he correctly provided the fees and lavish feasts on behalf of the foreman and the artisans. He brought that precious image of Gyelwa Tangpa, which had formerly been placed within the lower Kagye Chapel, into the center of the grass hermitage and consecrated it, such that it was established as an object of offering for the living beings of the three planes of existence.

During the fifth month, eleven Newars, headed by one named Amirāja, set up a workshop for embellishing with gold and silver the lion throne of the Tashi Pelbar reliquary of the supreme Conqueror Tangpa in the Offering Chapel, which had previously been carved. {744} They enhanced the base and the sides of the lion throne with silver and gilded copper. They excellently enhanced with *salung* flowers the four round tiers in the shape of lotuses, adorned with railings, as well as the eight relief-carved lions, and the pillar ornaments supported intertwined silver dragons. Such an array was insatiable to behold. On the hub of the perimeter wheel, which was of dark crystal, with insets of many kinds of crystal stone headed by a hundred *sang* of silver, in clear crystal they excellently inscribed information concerning the patrons of the saintly Taklung Tangpa himself, along with a bilingual inventory of its contents and a gold vase.

Afterward, On Rinpoche went to Lhundrub Dzong. Deshek Rinpoche went to upper Nyingdrung at the invitation of the governor of upper Hor, where he exceeded all their expectations through the ritual casting of tormas and the granting of empowerments, initiations, and ritual prayers. He introduced all the teachings and received excellent donations. On the way back, in the sacred places of the protector Genyen Chenpo in the slate and snow peaks of Phodo, he incidentally entrusted that deity with his activities. Then, when uncle and nephew were reunited at Taklung, he bestowed

The Collection of Tantras along with the empowerments of the Adamantine Garland and so forth, and incidentally, as an act of service, he also conferred the ten difficulties and eight signs of Shang Karpowa on Karma Wangchuk and others.[27]

During the tenth month, he held a consecration and feast in connection with the completion of the reliquary, the lion throne, and so forth. He presented the Newars with a large quantity of gifts, including seven large rolls of fine brocade, ten mules, and fifteen cattle. {745}

In his forty-third year, from the twentieth day of the second month in the new year of 1613 (water ox), through to the twenty-fourth day of the third month, Ngawang Namgyel then bestowed the extensive *Experiential Guidance on the Wish-Fulfilling Gem of the Six Doctrines*[28] and supporting doctrines including the transmission of the *Guhyasamāja Tantra*, the initial and conclusive Coemergent Venerable Tseringma,[29] and the empowerment of Cakrasaṃvara according to the tradition of Gaṇṭhapāda.

At the start of that year, the Tsangpa army reached southern and northern Lato, and those regions were brought under the authority of Tsang. Though Yarto, including the foremost sacred place of U, Yar Lhacho,[30] was damaged by the war, once the Tsangpa forces had proceeded beyond Yarto, restoration was undertaken. In Yarlung, one named Jadren Kuncho of Taklung was sent to convene all the warring parties of Utsang. On that occasion, the great Desi of Tsang said that ownership of Langtang Degon should be taken by Taklung. He ordered that each year a precise lease fee amounting to six hundred loads of grain should be handed over to the persons who would make the transfer, the monks who were in charge, along with the store that the trustees of the upper villages[31] had donated from Yarto here at Langtang through the power of faith.

For a whole month, Ngawang Namgyel then bestowed on his nephew, On Rinpoche, and the entire congregation of monks who held the three vows the guidance of *The Seven-Point Mind Training*[32] and the empowerment of *The Hundred Means for Attainment of Mitrayogin*. Since virulent smallpox was greatly spreading, he himself went to stay in retreat, along with those who took care to avoid it. In that circumstance, he granted On Rinpoche a great many teachings in succession, including the empowerment, guidance, and transmission of Four-Armed Mahākāla in the form Kurakma.

When the titular king of the whole of Tibet, Dungyu Rinpoche of Nedongtse, who was a descendant of Lhazik Lang Phakmodrupa, passed away,[33] {746} Ngawang Namgyel received the dedicatory articles of the deceased, and had the kindness to perform the purificatory rite that guides the consciousness of the deceased to a pure land, and the aspiration prayers of dedication, but he did so while staying in retreat. Although he was invited to be seated at the head of the row during the funeral ceremonies, there was no occasion for him to go, so he procrastinated for a while. But when the request that he go was repeated with great insistence, consequently, on the twentieth day of the ninth month, he set out. Traveling via Daryul and Langtang, in front of the estate of Orgyen, and through parts of Penyul, lower Phudo, the upper Kyichu, and so forth, he went to take his seat at the head of the row of the congregation of three thousand monks of the impartial philosophical traditions. As offerings, he was three times presented with a hundred pure material things—representations, paintings, and relief sculptures of India and China; items that were of Chinese and Mongolian appearance, including a jade bowl of Muslim provenance, and a crystal vase; as well as garments, various precious metals and stones, including gold, silver, coral, and pearl, and cloth; weapons, horses, and mules, and so forth. Ceremonies of communal tea offering, lodging,[34] alms distribution, and so forth were endlessly undertaken.

In this gathering, Venerable Ngawang Namgyel exclusively brought to maturation the authentic fruit of virtuous actions through his extensive detailed exegeses of the origin of the inhabited world and its sentient inhabitants, the systematic presentation of the Buddhist teaching, its purposes, circumstances, and so forth, and also through his pure dedications and aspirations. To the queen of Neudong, he respectfully offered the empowerment of Vajravārāhī and so forth. Although there was an extremely virulent plague at that time, Deshek Rinpoche held the invalids with his hands in public gatherings, such that their contagion decisively ceased. In this way, the power of faith in all who were present was intensely enhanced. Nor did the contagion spread among the senior masters of Taklungpa or around their monastic camps. Although this was a perfect object of wonder, it arose through the immeasurable compassion of the venerable one himself. {747}

Ngawang Namgyel then stayed for almost a month at Langtang. To the three thousand monks and laypeople who gathered there, he bestowed guidance on mind training, along with the transmission of the biography of Paṇchen Śākya Chokden. To De Khartsepa and other officials who magnanimously offered him the respects of Penyul, he granted doctrinal connections that satisfied each of them, so that all gods and humans experienced the feast of liberation. He returned to Taklung via Daryul.

That winter, when a large group of travelers, including one named Lhatsun arrived from Mongolia, Darqan Čogtu presented him with bountiful material offerings. Starting from then, earlier and later, the entire region of the northern Chahar in Mongolia became his disciples through the endeavors of Denma Kukye and a lama named Chopa, whom he sent there. He offered a large maṇḍala fashioned of one thousand two hundred silver *sang* to Jowo Rinpoche of Lhasa. Many Mongolian monks who were disciples of Denma Kukye arrived. Khondule Sechen Dalching, the chieftain of Shopo in Mongolia, donated a maṇḍala to the temple of Taklung that was fashioned of six hundred *sang* of Chinese silver. A large group of travelers headed by Governor Asing and his brother donated large offerings. Thereupon, he satisfied all the Mongolian monks with a banquet of the outer and inner fields of classical learning, the empowerments, transmissions, and esoteric instructions. He delighted them with an abundance of material presents, and they then returned to their own land.

That summer he bestowed the oral transmissions of *The Pagoda of Precious Gems*, *The Great Bounteousness of the Buddhas*, and *The Transcendent Perfection of Wisdom in One Hundred Thousand Lines*. The treasurer of the monastery Rabten passed away due to a pale-phlegm disorder, and he appointed the latter's brother Lhundrub.

During the twelfth month, {748} when Deshek Rinpoche himself fell ill due to fever, communal alms distributions were made in all the monasteries. His nephew undertook the longevity prayers and the torma offering of Mahākāla, and then the doctor Rikdzin offered him profound medication so that he recovered without trace of the disease.

That autumn, a large group of travelers from Mongolia presented an inconceivable number of material offerings to the official in charge of donations here at Taklung from Dalching Nangso, who was the lama of the Yong Gil Ching Tümed, and the Qaγan of the Dolon Tümed, and others.

During the second month of 1615 (wood hare), Jewo Dongpa Tendzin Choje and his disciples arrived from Yamdrok, and they immediately began to hear his teachings. Ngawang Namgyel bestowed upon them an infinite number of empowerments, transmissions, guidance, and esoteric instructions pertaining to many doctrinal cycles of the Sakya, Kagyu, and Nyingma traditions, including *The Elucidation of All Hidden Meanings*,[35]

The Systematic Presentation of All the Tantra Classes,[36] and on Cakrasaṃvara, Hevajra, and Guhyasamāja.

That summer, within one month, he restored the grass hermitages of the monastery, not a small task, including the construction and the imposition of a new monk supply tax, and he completed approximately a hundred new grass hermitages. He performed the consecration along with his nephew. The new monks were given the vows of a mendicant and applied themselves to study and reflection. He gave them all sorts of materials, and he appointed the eight seniors of Taklung. In ways such as these, he repaired the violations of the monastic vows and commitments.

Ngawang Namgyel also acquired the services of all the woodblock carvers from Jaryul, as many as there were, and offered them excellent patronage. Then, when Gyelwa Zhanak Karmapa Choying Dorje went to Damzhung, he greeted him there with a cloud of offerings. He restored the Old Temple of Taklung and changed the wooden timbers. He conclusively restored the images of the authentic lineage holders, who resembled a chain of golden mountains, {749} coloring them with gold lines, gold leaf, and so forth, and then he installed them in the Northern Sanctum of the Upper Offering Chapel, embellishing them with face gilding, hats, robes, and other sacraments of offering. He led a consecration ceremony in which the being of commitment and the being of pristine cognition merged together.

Then, the uncle and nephew stayed together for about one month at Setsa. They held a communion offering and tenth-day ceremonies at the treasure place of Gyawodong, and they stopped over for two days and nights at Podo. After they returned to Taklung, Venerable Dewar Shekpa Rinpoche, Ngawang Namgyel, had by that time himself maintained the administration and held responsibility at Taklung for thirty-one years, filling this monastic seat with the wealth of the twofold tradition of sūtra and mantra, like the Anavatapta Lake. He had perfected without impediment and according to his wishes extensive acts on behalf of the Buddhist teaching, headed by his exegeses and compositions.

Consequently, he then resolved to appoint his nephew, On Rinpoche Tashi Peldrub, with the responsibility of maintaining the monastic seat. Although his relatives, the monks, and so forth requested him to stay for a while, the ocean of his enlightened intention, the profundity of which was hard to fathom, could not be swayed by the winds of trifling external circumstances. On the conjunction of Puṣyā and Jupiter, on the twenty-fourth day of the ninth month, he had the peerless On Rinpoche, Choje

Ngawang Tashi Peldrub, take his seat upon the heavenly lion throne of the Ten-Pillar Chapel. Venerable Ngawang Namgyel himself took a seat in the side row to the left, and the enthronement ceremony was carried out in the midst of the highest of those holding the twofold tradition, including the official disciplinarian, the monastic preceptors and masters of ceremony, the treasurer, and the eight senior monks, along with a monastic gathering of high, middle, and low ranking officials, numbering approximately one thousand two hundred, as well as Nangso Barlewa, {750} the Tsang Desi, representatives of lower Hor, Kyisho, and so forth. He was widely acclaimed and appointed as master of the Buddhist teaching in general and of the teaching of Gyelwa Taklungpa the Great in particular. During the concluding ceremony, the cotton paintings of the protector deity Genyen Chenpo, hoisting the banner of enlightened activity in the sky above the monastery, were handed over to him, along with images indicative of auspicious circumstances, representing buddha body, speech, mind, attributes, and activities, including a handmade image of Venerable Maṅgalaśrī, a silver image called Blazing Glory of Blessing, and a representative image of the Teacher of sūtra and tantra, as well as robes, resources, riches, daily implements, and all the sacred artifacts and their shrines throughout the temple that were undamaged and extant from the past, in addition to many that were newly made, progressively filled by the monastic assembly, and those that derived from the monastic estates and lay communities in the Tibetan nomadic areas. This connection was established through the profound kindness of Ngawang Namgyel.

Tashi Peldrub then assumed the monastic seat as the supreme tulku, sitting upon the Satri Marpo throne, where all his venerable predecessors had sat in succession in the midst of the entire congregation that filled the Layel Courtyard like sesame pods. As he, along with the monastic assembly, scattered assorted flowers of good auspices, rainbow colors arose in the sky, a shower of flowers fell and other such most wonderful auspicious coincidences manifested.

Thereafter, Deshek Rinpoche himself stayed at Chodzong Namgyel Rabten, where he remained one-pointedly in meditative stability—a continuously uninterrupted equipoise combined with the ascetic discipline of total renunciation. {751}

During that time, to facilitate the nurturing of the monks of Drokha and Kagyu Domsumling in the short term, he yet again tended to the Buddhist teaching by assuming the great responsibilities of Langtang Chenga and of all the Tibetan nomadic communities of Jemata Khadongpa, the village communities of Nyon, Ruk, and Khar, and the camper groups of the south and north who had formerly provided a share of alms to the late Kunga Tashi and his brother, including the income for the rows of monks receiving communal tea. Monastic estates including upper and lower Namar,[37] the upper monastery, upper and lower Tsongdu, Gonbuk, Khang Lhonubpa, Nyena, Gardrong, and Penyul were gradually offered him as endowments from the top. Such activities his enlightened intention accomplished without effort.

During that period Ngawang Namgyel invited his nephew, Choje On Tri Rinpoche, and his disciples to Chodzong, where he conferred in detail the meaning of the precepts to be undertaken according to the twofold tradition of sūtra and mantra. He received at Chodzong all those who requested an audience, including persons who made offerings to the teaching throne and groups who came from all directions. That summer, the workers whom he had restore a reliquary of Geshe Langtangpa were supplied from the monks of Rikter Dratsang.[38] He provided the gold, silver, mercury, and so forth, and they embellished the reliquary with a golden spire. He provided the artisans needed to restore the assembly hall, the cells, and so forth, along with the patrons who provided their salary, and succeeded in this endeavor without impediment. During the winter, on the days that he passed in Yasang, Uma, and Trang Takrama, however short the day, he tended for the local communities by making torma offerings and so forth. Then, when he went to Langtang, immediately he offered a doctrinal connection to all sorts of ordained and laypeople of upper and lower Penyul. {752} In ways such as these, he acted extensively for the welfare of others.

When Ani Drungpa from Yerpa arrived directly at his hilltop retreat in her eighty-seventh year, he nurtured her with maturational empowerments and liberating guidance according to the sacred doctrine and with material things.

Invited by the governor of Kyisho,[39] Ngawang Namgyel performed ritual aversion by tormas and long-life empowerments, and he granted many empowerments and initiations pertaining to The Peaceful and Wrathful Guru, and so forth.

He then returned to Langtang on the twentieth day of the twelfth month and undertook an extensive great torma ritual in connection with the seasonal fulfillment and reparation of vows.

At the new year, in 1616 (fire dragon), those who requested his teaching accompanied him for a while to each of the sacred mountains, after which he stayed in strict retreat mainly practicing *The Attainment of the Mind of the Guru*.[40] Then, immediately after coming out of retreat, he consecrated the aforementioned reliquary and conferred on the assembly the instructions that they desired in the form of public teachings. To people from Riwoche, Chamdo, Beri, and so forth, he gave advice on the means of securing happiness and pacifying obstacles as well as binding contracts, oaths, empowerments, and so forth. Shortly thereafter, he returned to Chodzong via Lhundrub Dzong. To some who were interested, he gave guidance on mind training, and when Dungyu Rinpoche of Druk Ralung[41] visited Chok Trawa, Bentsang, and so forth, he gave him oral guidance on *The Four Doctrines of Dakpo*.[42]

During the third month, in the place where the monks of Domsumling gathered in the morning on the north side of his grass hermitage, he newly built twenty-five cells and ten retreat hermitages, with a garden enclosure and so forth. The entire monastic community and the Tibetan villagers who were their subjects undertook the construction with effort. Ngawang Namgyel actually went there in person and prepared the plans, the laying of the foundations, and so forth. {753} Immediately after its completion, along with his nephew, he performed the consecration.

Although at the Chodzong Palace, the murals and so forth depicting the earlier Kagyu lineage had formerly been executed with utmost purity, at that point in time they had faded to some extent. The image of Vajradhara that had been the meditative commitment of Venerable Sangye On, and the silver images of Kuyalwa and Sangye Yarjon with their individual throne backs had survived, but he had a metal-casting sculptor from Langtang construct a miniature thumb-size cast silver image of Taklung Tangpa the Great, as well as an image of Four-Armed Mahākāla that was approximately one foot in height. Excellent pearl relics were inserted within it and Choje Tri Rinpoche Tashi Peldrub performed the consecration.

Then, Ngawang Namgyel set out for the hot springs of Lhei Gatsel in Nyingdrung. Immediately after completing that pilgrimage, he arrived in the environs of Kyisho Rukpa, the monastic seat of Geshe Kamawa. Even there, an assembly of monks gathered. He bestowed the transmission of *The Hundred Former Lives of the Teacher*,[43] guidance on the Great Seal, and so forth, and made a detailed examination, testing his meditative experiences.

Consequently, the blessings of the authentic lineage were transferred to that venerable master Kamawa, so that an exclusively excellent meditative realization arose within him.

To a large gathering of Tibetan nomads from south and north banks of the Kyichu river[44] he kindly bestowed the guidance of the preliminary practices and the main practices. As the teaching was near completion, someone from the mountain hermitage of Ngarnang offered him a gold manuscript of *The Sūtra of the King of Meditative Stability*. Thinking this to be a great auspicious coincidence that would enhance the exegesis and attainment of the profound definitive meaning, he granted its transmission to those who were gathered there, and as a blessing on the last day, he conferred in the context of a communion feast offering the profound and extensive empowerments of *The Attainment of the Guru of the Profound Path*,[45] which is the king of all empowerments. Finally, he empowered them on their heads with all the drawings that he had of the natural stone footprint of Taklung Tangpa the Great. {754} A shower of flowers fell from the sky, and these were connected with a net of rainbow light. So the auspicious signs that occurred were beautiful. Then, the monks returned to undertake an offering ceremony of attainment at Taklung.

Venerable Ngawang Namgyel himself stayed on for about one further month, and he continuously granted doctrinal connections to Nyen spirits and people as far as Drigung Dzongsar. On the way back to Taklung, he traveled to Chodzong via Khartok and Tsangto.

When Ton Maryon Samdrub Dar passed away, he received an invitation and went there to guide the deceased on the path of great liberation. During the eleventh month, Ngawang Namgyel fell ill, and offering ceremonies were held at Taklung. Torma offerings were restored in the Protector Chapel, a public distribution of alms was made, and so forth. Those who were encamped there held a hundredfold communion feast offering pertaining to Satyadvayamukha Vajravārāhī, after which he made an excellent recovery.

Ngawang Namgyel brought to fruition the hopes of the devout inhabitants of Upper and Lower Hor. He participated in the offering ceremonies at the time when the venerable and omniscient Fourth Dalai Lama, Yontan Gyatso passed away at Drigung, and he performed extensive aspiration prayers in connection with the funeral ceremonies.

Thereafter, he traveled to Sertsa via Ulung. While he was there, he invited Tri Rinpoche Tashi Peldrub with the entire monastic assembly from Taklung, and they performed profound and extensive *gutor* ceremonies, casting out the torma of exorcism on the twenty-ninth day and making the divine incense offering and so forth on the thirtieth day. On the following day, the new year of 1617 (fire snake), they held a feast. Immediately afterward Tri Rinpoche and his people departed for their own homes.

Ngawang Namgyel Rinpoche himself stayed on in retreat, during which time he received an invitation from Kartsenpa, the chieftain of upper Hor, at whose devout insistence he set out the next day. {755} Arriving at the residence of the chieftain[46] in Pelchen Nawa, he conferred the empowerment of Hayagrīva, along with a burnt offering, the great torma offering of Jvalamukha, and so forth, such that the chieftain recovered.

Then, he traveled at the insistence of Yulgyel, the chieftain of lower Hor, to his residence at Muchu. He granted him a water purification rite, a long-life empowerment, and longevity prayers, and so forth, concurrently with Drigung Rinpoche, such that he to some extent recovered from his ailment.

While he was staying there, he received an invitation from Choje Rinpoche Tashi Peldrub at the Taklung Palace, who had seemingly fallen ill due to a blood and wind disorder. Traveling day and night, he arrived there promptly, reaching Taklung after a brief stop in upper Hor. There, he performed many empowerments and initiations on behalf of Tri Rinpoche Tashi Peldrub, as well as granting him long-life prayers in conjunction with the burnt offering and the rites of reception and aversion of Jvalamukha, and so forth. Consequently, he recovered completely, like a cloudless moon.

When the aforementioned chieftain Yulgyel passed away, Ngawang Namgyel established the deceased in the glory of exalted rebirth and definitive excellence over ten successive days in upper Dam by perform the funeral rite, along with prayers of dedication and aspiration. Then he took up residence for some time at Drokha in Taklung. During that time, he also imparted guidance on Severance to Bale Drungpa and others.

While staying in the palace of lotus light at the treasure-trove of Gyawodong, and in Tsangdong near Setsa, a medicinal valley for spiritual attainment, he again traveled to the monastic seat of Choje at Taklung and gave transmissions of *The Root Sūtra of Monastic Discipline*, and so forth. At that time, the crown holder of Zhamar[47] and his disciples were in lower Hor on their journey up to Kham. When sent by Zhamarpa to offer him tea, Zuri Lama Karma Demchok and his disciples and a resident of Riwoche named Drupa and others presented the offerings and incidentally received his doctrinal connection.

The painting of glorious Phakmodrupa and the offering scarf that Venerable Taklungpa the Great {756} had acquired on his return visit to Phakmodru were unimaginably precious relics in his possession, among the things from which he was never separated.

A band of a thousand Mongols, including the chieftain of Qalqa Khondu Litsokhu,[48] Qaraqud, Talji, and Tuphu arrived in Utsang,[49] and when they approached this area, he offered tea and received them. He met them on the way when they were encamped at lower Namrab. They offered him a hundredfold pure artifacts, along with Chinese merchandise. He undertook the rite of the fulfillment and reparation of vows, pertaining to the year end, along with a large torma offering.

At New Year, in 1618 (earth male horse), Ngawang Namgyel poured many burnt offerings pertaining to the rites of pacification, enrichment, subjugation, and wrath for many preferred deities. Then, while sojourning for a while at Lhundrub Dzong, he composed *The Root Verses of the Three Vows*.[50] He carefully protected the supplies of that castle in the appropriate manner when the old steward passed away. Then, he went to Taklung.

About three hundred soldiers of that Mongol army who had arrived in the central part of Tibet reached Penyul via Dar La pass. They destroyed the harvest and turned it into fodder. So a mediator from Taklung and an envoy who was similarly urged by the Tsangpa Desi to bring about reconciliation were appointed. However, the army did not inflict disaster upon the Buddhist teaching, and the Qalqas returned home from Dam. The Tümed army, however, did reach Lhasa via Chak La and Go La, afflicting their customary damage wherever they stayed. In order to protect Lhasa, which was rightfully to be guarded by all means, since Sera, Drepung, and so forth were situated above the encampment of the Mongol army, many were killed at one time. Consequently, the Tsangpa Desi marched out at the head of an army. His armed forces that were mustered from the highland region of Ngari in the west as far as the lowland region of Kongpo Gya La in the east were far more numerous. {757} An envoy was sent from Taklung to Desi Tsangpa, insisting that the monasteries should not be damaged and that even those that had been embroiled in the conflict should be reconciled. Although the Tsangpa agreed, the Mongol army, greatly enraged, inflicted immense harm on them all. Consequently, the foremost of the masters and disciples, teachers and students, of Sera and Drepung, along with five hundred monks, encamped at Chodzong Namgyel Rabten near Taklung. Ngawang Namgyel personally offered them sustenance for seven days and daily communal tea offerings. Sometimes, they requested him to take his seat at their head. Then again, using his connections with the Tsangpa and Mongol nobility, the monks of Sera and Drepung monasteries were permitted to return home. This was certainly a marvelous act of benefit that he undertook out of loyalty to the Buddhist teaching. After appointing the bursar, Ngawang Norzang, to carry out spiritual and secular activities, with both external and internal responsibilities, on the sixteenth day of the eighth month, he set out from Chodzong and arrived at Langtang via Lhundrub Dzong. Thereupon, he allayed the fears of the monks of Sera and Drepung, who had fled to the precincts of Taklung Monastery out of fear. With the permission of the Desi, the monks of Drepung and Sera then converged at Langtang. On the eighth day of the first ninth month, Choje Rinpoche Tashi Peldrub and his disciples also set out from the palace at Taklung for Langtang. Then, the following day, the uncle and nephew set out together, and via Go La, they escorted the monks of Drepung and Sera to their respective residences.

When Tsangpa Desi invited Taklung Choje, the seniormost figures of Sera and Drepung, including the masters and bursars, gathered together. They prostrated before the Desi, {758} and served Taklung Choje by providing a boat fee.[51] Via Dewu Gong Norgyeling, he reached the hill on the near side of Kharok Shan. Yangri Lama and his disciples also arrived there from the camp of Karmapa, and at Chakra on the far bank, the glorious great Tsangpa Desi[52] arrived within his entourage. On meeting the uncle and nephew from Taklung, the ruler immediately prostrated at their feet in great devotion. The Desi and his four hundred attendants welcomed them with white scarves and diverse musical instruments—conch shells, trumpets, long horns, and so forth. When the priests and patrons together reached Dechen Palace in Zhigatse, they stayed there for some days and were offered incomparable veneration and excellent offerings. Thereupon, Ngawang Namgyel and Taklung Choje bestowed empowerments and initiations with respect to the mind maṇḍala of Vajrapāṇi, White Tārā, Cakrasaṃvara, and Dark-Blue Guru Drakpo according to the Jangter tradition. Afterward, they were presented with great donations. In recognition of their neutrality, Tashi Dzong and Khangsar Gong also made offerings to Taklung, estimated as one thousand five hundred loads of grain, and so forth.

When Tri Rinpoche Tashi Peldrub had been served with a large mass of offerings, they, priests and patrons, then set out, all in harmony, for Lhasa.[53] In the presence of Jowo Śākyamuni, image of the Teacher in the Jokhang, they conferred the eightfold precepts of lay ordination upon the ruler, Tsangpa Desi. In the Kyilkhorteng Hall, they held an innumerable feast that enhanced good auspices, with an extensive array of sacraments, an offering cloud of veneration. With their respective excellent offerings, the ruler and his attendants then proceeded in the direction of Yerpa. The uncle and nephew completed an elaborate pilgrimage in Lhasa, and then {759} via Kyisho and Langtang, and so forth, in succession, Tri Rinpoche set out for Taklung and Venerable Ngawang Namgyel himself set out for Chodzong.,

To some interested monks of the college and the monastery he granted guidance on the Great Seal, the Six Doctrines, and on the lord-protector Mahākāla, and so forth. Traveling in the direction of Rong, he then stayed at Khartok Dzong, where he also constructed a maṇḍala of Akṣobhya. At Tashitse, he offered a Ṣaḍānana ritual missile along with the combined rites of protection and aversion in association with Mañjuśrī-Yamāntaka, and a large torma offering that conferred the enlightened activity of the protector deity

At the start of the new year of 1619 (earth sheep), Ngawang Namgyel fell ill, whereupon communal alms distribution and long-life prayers were extensively undertaken, in public and in private, so that he gradually recovered.

He excellently completed the restoration of the three reliquary stūpas at Taklung, along with their domes and murals. Although the exquisite great spires of gilded copper surmounting each of them were extant, he properly repaired and stabilized them. He made the murals and so forth as they had been in the past.

At Horkhang, he then stayed for a month, during which time he conferred upon the monks of the monastery the guidance of the Great Seal, and in the monastic assembly he conferred the empowerments of nine-deity Akṣobhya. After restoring the perimeter wall of the monastery, he passed some time for health reasons at the hot springs of Dromalung. He received copious and extensive offerings from upper Hor and from Matrogyel.

To mark the auspicious coincidence of him averting the army of Tsangpa Desi, a stone image of the great guardian king Dhṛtarāṣṭra was constructed at the perimeter of Radeng Monastery. Monks were especially sent there to perform the consecration. Here at Taklung, the reliquary stūpas were also consecrated.

When the king of Beri passed away, offerings were presented to him, and when Agon of Namru passed away, he was offered auspicious donations that he might go to guide the deceased and so forth. {760}

Once the leaders of the Mongol forces had also departed for Mongolia, he traveled to Zhika Tashitse, Taktse, and Tashi Dzong. On Gyelpo Dondrub he conferred a great many teachings, including the initiation and guidance on the seven maṇḍalas of Ngok and so forth. For Choje Phakmowa of Ganden Shar, the meditation hermitage of Ganden, and a multitude of monks from Sera and Drepung who came to see him, he established doctrinal connections, fulfilling their hopes.

Then he went to Logon where he met Drigung Choje, father and son, who had arrived there with some two hundred attendants. Seated on the teaching throne of Chenga Tsultrim Bar, he gave an extremely extensive doctrinal guidance in public on *The Seven Points of Mind Training*.[54] In the presence of Drigung, he privately conferred experiential guidance on the Great Seal, the empowerments of Glorious Lord Vajrapāṇi, and so forth. Gradually, he arrived at the forest of Kama.

At the new year of 1620 (iron make monkey), in conjunction with an auspicious planet and constellation, he reached Khartok Phushing. Choje Tri Rinpoche Tashi Peldrub also arrived there. They performed a hundred long-life empowerments and so forth, combining Sitātapatrā, Vajrapāṇi, and Amitāyus, Lord of Death, and then they returned to Taklung. Reaching the hillside of Pushing Hermitage, he composed this additional biographical account of his life, up to the age of fifty.

From Riwoche, the mighty lord of knowledge, realization, and compassion, Jedrung Drakpa Gyeltsen[55] and his disciples then arrived at Taklung and stayed at Gepel Chodzong. Ngawang Namgyel conferred the great rite of aversion through Mañjuśrī-Yamāntaka, and the uncle and nephew together undertook the most extensive rite of protection and aversion associated with the Inception of Yama.

Although Ngawang Namgyel himself had previously intended to travel to restore Taklung Lower Plain, {761} on this occasion in a dream a portent arose, indicating that he could not travel to the east. At that time, Tsangpa Desi was stationed at Chumdo Chakor with a large army, and two Mongol armies from Tsokha arrived in the vicinity of Tsomo Rawa, after striking the camper groups of lower Hor. Then, as in the past, he offered them tea and advice on the need for a peaceful solution, along with material gifts. While he was establishing the country in peace, discussions were held about inviting Paṇchen Rinpoche from Tsang to protect the monks of Sera, Drepung, and Ganden from fear.

At the new year of 1622 (iron bird), a large Mongol force, under Lhatsun Chungwa Lobzang Tendzin and Kyishopa arrived in Penyul. They inflicted great devastation on the religious estates of the Karmapa and the Drigungpa and so forth but did not at all harm the southern and northern Tibetan nomadic pastures of Taklung. In addition, Ngawang Namgyel extensively bestowed the gift of protection, such that living beings did not fear falling on bad times. Paṇchen Rinpoche also arrived from Tsang and held discussions with our representatives from Taklung. A treaty was established to some extent between Tsang and the Mongols, and the saintly monks of Sera withdrew back to Jang for a while.

Ngawang Namgyel had some twenty monks from Domsumling train in the melodic spiritual songs of the earlier Kagyu lineage holders, and he established the custom of chanting them in all months of the year. He and Paṇchen Rinpoche had a meeting at which they prostrated simultaneously to one another.

He correctly dedicated and sealed with aspiration prayers the merit of all the bountiful offerings he received when the Tsangpa Desi, Karma Phuntsok, passed away. {762} To that end, he composed an aspiration prayer for offering golden maṇḍalas in the presence of Jowo Śākyamuni in Lhasa, and he presented it along with the woodblocks.

When Desi Karma Tenkyong Wangpo took over, in order to drive out the invading forces, he arrived in Penang,[56] intending that his large army should march directly against them. The holy lord of refuge, Ngawang Namgyel, himself went to Luding in Lhundrub Dzong. By means of copious gifts and advice, he persuaded the generals not to proceed to the north and counseled them of the need to withdraw by securing a peaceful solution. The Desi agreed and turned back via Chak La.

When Ani Drungpa of Kyisho passed away, Ngawang Namgyel undertook aspiration prayers of dedication and guided the deceased to supreme bliss, the path of liberation. When he then reached Gepel Chodzong, the peoples of the south and the north were on the move again, but he could not immediately succeed in establishing peace. On account of the situation in Chongye,[57] the Tsangpa forces reached the plateau of Lhundrub Dzong and then arrived in Lhasa in order to confront the Mongols directly. Many northern banners of the Mongolian forces made haste. From Taklung, an envoy was specially sent so that the battle could be delayed to some extent. Then, following discussions with Paṇchen Rinpoche, a major treaty was secured between the Tsangpa and the Mongols. The Gelukpas retained the monastic estates that they formerly held, while Kyishopa, Taktse, Drakar, and so forth were also given to them as their share. Our people also returned here to Taklung, and the armies dispersed to their own domains. Although Ngawang Namgyel had made preparations to travel to Riwoche, he could not find the means to travel there since he was delayed by Tsangpa Desi. {763}

While undertaking extensive long-life prayers and rites of reparation and fulfillment in connection with the end of the year, he wished to study under Zhamar Chokyi Wangchuk the doctrinal cycles of the Shangpa Kagyu, headed by the Six Doctrines of Niguma, which had been given to Drungpa Karma Kunga and transmitted from him to Sixth Zhamar, Chokyi Wangchuk, and from him to Karmapa Choying Dorje. So this transmission would be most beneficial for the continuity of the Buddhist teaching. On that occasion, however, the teaching was disturbed by a cold, and he fell ill due to unhealthy water. Through the health that comes to maturity in consequence of essential long-life prayers, he gradually recovered, just as when water is sprinkled on flowers. In addition, he went to the hot springs at Drowalung in the uplands of Nyingdrung. While camping one week at the springs and at Nyingri Gungtang, he performed an elaborate offering to Tanglha. Then, gradually he returned to Chodzong. He commissioned black painted scrolls depicting Coemergent Cakrasaṃvara and all the ten doctrinal protectors and then had the two artists earnestly undertake the means for attainment.

During the seventh month, he completely granted the remainder of his guidance, empowerments, and transmissions to Tri Rinpoche Tashi Peldrub. In the twelfth month, he undertook elaborate rites of reparation and fulfillment at Domsumling, and cast out the torma offering of Mahākāla in the form Gonpo Trakshe toward the northern direction. Although the Tsangpa and the Mongols around there were at peace, the nomads of upper Hor had fled, and Mongols had inflicted damage by striking at many camper groups in the north. The army of Zhungzhik Lhatsun[58] and Kyishopa descended upon the estates of Drigung and Phakmodru. Both the Zhabdrung Rinpoches of Drigung and Phakdru had to go away on account of the Mongol armed incursion, and as such it was difficult for the Drigungpa to handle. At that time, a bursar was sent from Taklung to offer them security. {764} This was of utmost benefit to all the officials and subjects of Drigung, and so Taklung granted them the unsurpassed gift of protection from fear. Afterward, the Mongol forces invited the Zhabdrung of both Drigung and Phakmodru back, and they withdrew to the north.

On account of his utterly exhausting activities in securing the well-being of Drigung and Phakmodru, this saintly lama Ngawang Namgyel had frail health. Although he indeed had a great wish to meet with the two Zhabdrung, he could not travel, but an elaborate reception was held below the Dzong, at which Tri Rinpoche Tashi Peldrub requested simply to meet the two Zhabdrung.

The Tsangpa forces mobilized his militias of the south, the north, Dakpo, Kongpo, Ngari, and so forth, and he adopted a strategy to take over all the lands under the control of the Mongols in Penyul and lower Hor. At that time, Tri Rinpoche and Paṇchen Rinpoche many times sought to reconcile them, and for a while peace was restored. That autumn, Ngawang Namgyel went to the hot springs at Nyingdrung.

At the new year of 1624 (wood mouse), to the entire assembly of monks of the college and the monastery who gathered with great concern for the sacred doctrine, he gave the initiation of *The Hundred Means for Attainment*[59] and elaborate guidance on the twenty-one responses of Kadam. They exclusively practiced the essential points, their minds in harmony with the sacred doctrine.

Then, Choje Mokchokpa, the disciple of Jamgon Kunga Nyingpo, arrived with his attendants, and he gave a great many tracts of guidance and transmissions.

From the eighth day of the third month, Ngawang Namgyel gradually set out via Podo. He set up camp at Sewalung. On the nineteenth day, during an anniversary offering, on behalf of some residents of the cave hermitage of Taklungpa the Great, he started to confer the profound and extensive *Guidance on the View of Vajrayoginī: A Wish-Fulfilling Gem of the Aural Lineage.*[60] {765} He stayed a little more than one month there, and during that time he successfully restored the residence at Chodzong and so forth.

Setting out on pilgrimage from the hot springs of Drowalung, he went via Rakchen and stayed a few days in the sacred place of Tarlukhok, where Orgyen the Great had actually trod. Then, he remained for two months at Tsang Dong Forest. Earlier and later on these occasions, he twice granted important guidance to many interested disciples. Each day, also, the minor empowerments and transmissions that he conferred were countless and inconceivable. Since the bursar Ngawang Norzang had assumed office, he instated the nineteenth day offering ceremony, and he also prepared an inventory of the scheduled anniversary offering ceremonies.

When the young Zhabdrung from Drigung passed away, they persistently requested him to go there to preside over the rows of monks performing the funeral ceremonies. Accordingly, with a monastic congregation from the college, he rode there and was welcomed by a thousand monks who escorted him to Drigungtil in procession. He met Drigung Choje and his brother in the midst of an excellent assembly. Seated upon the high teaching throne, he performed extremely elaborate funeral offerings. The communal alms, the exhibition of sacred representations, the offering donations, and so forth were perfect, beyond the limitations of the intellect. He revisited Drigung Dzongsar, and then proceeded swiftly via Tsewa, Gang La, and Hor, to reach Chenga Bumpa. After offering victory banners, silken ropes, butter lamps, and so forth to the great stūpa, he returned to Chodzong.

In his fifty-fifth year, as the year 1625 (wood ox) dawned, {766} Ngawang Namgyel was extremely dispirited because he had not managed to travel to Kham. Consequently, he asked Tri Rinpoche whether it would be of some benefit to the Buddhist teaching and living beings if he himself were to travel in the direction of Yisho [that is, Riwoche]. No answer was immediately forthcoming,

On the tenth day of the first month of that year, in the Hall of the Blazing Glory of Existence and Quiescence in the Main Temple of Taklung, in the presence of the three extraordinary images of Taklung Tangpa the Great and the Tathāgata Munīndra, with Dewar Shekpa Ngawang Namgyel himself acting as the monastic preceptor and master of ceremonies, and in the midst of an assembly of monks, Jeon Tri Rinpoche Tashi Peldrub received the precepts of a fully ordained monk, and he became accomplished as a veritable second Upāli, upholder of monastic discipline.

The next day, he arrayed an infinite number of particular offerings, and on behalf of an assembly of resident monks who at that time exceeded a thousand, for an entire day, he delivered an extensive and detailed exegesis of the transmitted teachings and treatises associated with Jowo Serlingpa's tradition concerning the setting of the mind on supreme enlightenment, and so he clearly planted the seeds of enlightenment within them.

When the Gazi governor Tseten Dorje appeared to fall ill due to a phlegm disorder, Deshek Rinpoche Ngawang Namgyel was invited. He undertook torma offerings, ritual ablutions, initiations, and so forth, but there was no way to benefit him except through the transference of consciousness to a pure land, and the ruler expired. Ngawang Namgyel performed all sorts of rites for the purification of obscuration. At that time a bursar suggested that it would be proper for him to change his drinking water and move to another place, but he was disinclined to move elsewhere, delighted with the new residence at Chodzong.

On Rinpoche gradually requested permission to go to Kham, {767} but he said, "You should do not go now. I suspect that if you are subjected to pollution in this Taklung region, your extensive activities will become threadbare in the middle, and even though you set out eventually, I would say the same as before to your request for leave of absence because it would be shameless to go without having a prophecy concerning future circumstances. And yet, you should consider going because it will be of benefit for the Buddhist teaching and sentient beings in the Kham area."

Thereupon, he set about making preparations to go abroad to Riwoche with half of the monks of the monastic college. He prepared a foreign travel permit sent notification for Taklung Lower Plain in Riwoche, and he performed incense offerings and prayers of good auspices. On the twenty-seventh day, he constructed a large torma. The saintly lama Ngawang Namgyel himself arrived from Chodzong and performed elaborate rites, mantra recitations, and rites for aversion of negativity through torma offerings. He set out just as a large whirlwind of dust and other omens arose.

Around this time, extensive donations were made because the son of king Julang from Mongolia[61] and our master of offerings, among others, also arrived. Intending to establish a Kagyu contemplative college, Ngawang Namgyel first of all commissioned eleven paintings depicting the lineage holders, from Vajradhara to Venerable Yarjon, which were carefully executed by talented artists, and these were enhanced in the context of an excellent consecration ceremony.

Beyond that, the most wonderful biographical account of Ngawang Namgyel's buddha body, speech, mind, attributes, and activities is extremely hard to fathom. Since he had mastered calm abiding with respect to the precepts of the transcendent perfections of ethical discipline, meditative stability, and wisdom, there was never any occasion when he could be without renunciation.

During his long tenure as the Zhabdrung of Taklung, it was as if the perfect buddhas had actually manifested. Indeed he was without the slightest stain of bewilderment. Since he abided on the bodhisattva levels, {768} he was beyond objects of appraisal. He had effortlessly accomplished all the distinct qualities of the conquerors. His inconceivable symbolic and nonsymbolic meditations could never be interrupted, and at these times he would confer empowerments, explain the tantras, grant the esoteric instructions, compose treatises, commission particular manuscripts and newly created representations of buddha body, speech, and mind. He would insert mantra cores within these representations, undertake the scheduled anniversary offering ceremonies of his predecessors, and rites of reparation and fulfillment, dispel the obstacles of meditators, cut off the doubts of geshes, issue sublime decrees, and so forth. In brief, having perfected bountiful acts of benefit to the Buddhist teaching and living beings, passing days and nights exclusively in the ten modes of doctrinal conduct and in deeds that maintained, protected, and enhanced the Buddhist teachings, in this field he brought to maturational empowerment and liberating guidance the disciples whom he was destined to train through his actual body in this field.

Then, for the while, he considered displaying the means of passing into final nirvāṇa. During the ninth month of 1625 (wood ox), his physical strength became increasingly frail due to pale-phlegm disorder, and his complexion lost its luster. Apart from that, he was not at all ill. However, the bursar Ngawang Norzang was concerned. Here at Taklung and in all the monasteries of Utsang, large and small, they distributed communal alms, performed elaborate long-life prayers, made offerings to secure his long life, and all such ritual means, but these did not greatly help. In the evening of the twenty-fifth day of the eleventh month, a mighty earthquake reverberated throughout Utsang. Then, on the night of the fifteenth day of the twelfth month, there was a most intense light that could illuminate the Taklung area, coinciding with a loud sound, rumbling, as it were, from the northeast to the southwest. {769} In addition, many particular inauspicious omens occurred pertaining to living creatures and pertaining to the heavens and the earth.

Although his health did not deteriorate further, he advised those who had been appointed as Zhabdrung in detail concerning all that should be done in the future, commencing with the important actions that maintain and protect the Buddhist teachings, and concerning how all minor rites should be carried out here at Taklung in order for his enlightened intention to be absorbed into the expanse of reality. Thereupon, their minds became spacious. Now, they did not dare to do more than merely request that he should have long life.

Ngawang Namgyel settled into meditation day and night on the fifth day of the fourth month of 1626 (fire tiger). In addition, he dedicated a torma offering to the doctrinal protectors and undertook extraordinary acts of entrustment. The next day, on the sixth, when even the constellation Gemini moved gently, he had On Rinpoche and others recite *The Aspiration Prayers of the Taintless Field: A Eulogy of Venerable Taklung Tangpa.*[62] When they reached the verse of the taintless aspiration prayer that says, "At the time when the deeds of peerless Choje are perfected," he clearly recalled the image of Taklung Tangpa and looked at it for just a moment. After that, he looked at On Rinpoche, and at noon on the sixth day his emanational form was instantly absorbed into the expanse of great quiescence.

The divine course of his enlightened intention was fulfilled by great offerings of attainment and multiple arrays of most extensive offering clouds for forty-nine days. The precious corpse was dressed in the costume of a universal emperor and offered on the funeral pyre in conjunction with the burnt offering of Sarvavid Vairocana. Choje Konchok Rinchen was invited from Drigung to be seated at the head of the row of monks performing the great funeral ceremony. Then, {770} the vast assembly of monks representing the impartial philosophical systems—including those of Drigung, Taklung, and Karmapa[63]—were satisfied with a great distribution of alms.

Commencing from the day when Ngawang Namgyel passed into final nirvāṇa, Chodzong was entirely enveloped, outside and inside, by an inverted tent of rainbow light, and pearl relics poured out of the images that he had commissioned when he was alive. Many such auspicious signs were within the perceptual range of all. The parts of the sacred corpse that were brought to Taklung, including his heart, tongue, and eyes, were inserted within a most exquisitely crafted reliquary in the form of an enlightenment stūpa, fashioned of gold, silver, and diverse precious stones, which was positioned in the left corner of the Southern Chapel.

The Disciples and Patrons of Zhabdrung Ngawang Namgyel

The disciples who acquired the kindness of Venerable Ngawang Namgyel were uncountable. Among them, the foremost were On Rinpoche Tashi Peldrub, the lord of the Buddhist teaching who combined the spiritual and secular affairs of this monastic seat; as well as Drigung Choje Rinchen Peldrub, Choje Langtang Chengawa, who promulgated *The Gathering of the Real;*[64] Chime Ngagi Wangchuk, Karma Kunga, the reincarnation of Drubwang Tsemlung; Kyabdak Drubchok Wangpo, the emanation of Gotsang

Rechen; Drubwang Kabzhipa Tsultrim Gyurme; Tenpa Namgyel, who offered profound guidance on the profound truth of definitive meaning to Gyelwang Karmapa Choying Dorje; the incumbent of the monastic seat of Shang Neutok; the head lama of omniscient Drepung; Lingme Choje, the throne holder of Ganden; Lopa Chenga, the senior lama in charge of discipline among the Sakyapa; Lama Nangselwa, tutor to Drigung Choje Rinpoche; {771} Druk Cho Lhatsewa;[65] Karma Tendrel of Riwoche; Sharok Lama Kunga Nyingpo, the elder and younger eighteenth Choje of Nalendra; and so forth. In brief, the lamas, masters, and most of the monks associated with each of the monastic institutions of the Sakya, Kagyu, and Nyingma traditions savored the nectar from the mouth of this venerable master, so the number of his disciples emanating from each of these traditions cannot be mentioned.

Foremost among his patrons were Tsangpa Desi and his son, mighty lords of heaven and earth; Rinpung Chogyel Dawa Zangpo; and Mongol kings including Qadan Bagatur, who held whatever he said as their standard because they believed this venerable master to actually be the perfect buddha, and who pleased him with body, speech, mind, and resources.

It is said that in the future, Ngawang Namgyel will appear successively as a disciplined hidden yogin in the region of Lato in Tsang, and then he will appear in many hundreds of emanational forms in diverse lands, including India, Tibet, and China. Also, he will, for a while, assume the guise of a great king in the region of Kham and cause the Buddhist teaching to spread and flourish. He will manifest in diverse emanational forms such as these, training each according to need. Finally, he will attain buddhahood as the Tathāgata Ratnakūṭa in the buddha field named Diffusion of Celestial Light and then turn the wheel of the sacred doctrine for a retinue of four billion. The teaching of that buddha will also endure for six hundred thousand years.

Through the realization and scrutiny of those with enhanced power of faith,
In all realms of existence and quiescence where this drum of the conquerors resounds,
May all beings to whom his excellent reputation and splendor are all-pervasive
Bring to maturity the noble fruit of excellent bliss! {772}

2. Choktrul Tashi Peldrub, the Twentieth Hierarch

Devout homage to this extensive light of supreme liberation,
Spontaneously **accomplishing** (*grub*)[1] all that is **glorious** (*dpal*)
Through a billion **auspices** (*bkra shis*) throughout the three planes of existence,
Observing the entirety of the sacred doctrine of provisional and definitive meaning,
Spiritual mentor to all, with the luminosity of a hundred thousand suns of compassion!

With regard to the appearance of Choltrul Tashi Peldrub, the mighty lord of wisdom and compassion who acted above all on behalf of the precious Buddhist teaching of essential meaning, sun of the sacred doctrine of definitive meaning, since the enlightened activities of the conquerors are of the nature of space and hard to estimate—how could this life of his possibly be appraised within the perceptual range of the disciples of this world? And yet, as indicated in the succession of the former lives of Yongdzin Rinpoche Namgyel Pelzangpo, he had indeed manifested in the successive forms of Paṇdita Maitrimitra, who had been blessed by sublime Mañjughoṣa; as the great awareness holder Sangye Yeshe, heart son of Orgyen the Great Padmākara; as Khyeu Pema Chodrub, who had the courage to sacrifice his own life for the sake of Vairotsana; as Khyuchok Drington Śākya Rinchen, who maintained the teaching of the aural lineage; as Orgyen Gonpo, regent of Gyelchok Drakpa; as Chokyi Wangchuk, who possessed the supreme and common accomplishments of the original buddha; as Drubwang Pema Karpo, who possessed the attributes of renunciation and realization; as Tamdrin Ozer, sage vast in the supreme scrutiny of teaching, debate, and composition; as one named Lachen Zangpo, who actualized nonconceptual meditative stability; as Sempa Jangchub Pelwa, who supported the enlightened activities of Garwang Chok; {773} as Zhiwa Zangpo, who possessed the supreme and common accomplishments through the compassion of Pema Gyelpo; as Taktsang Lotsāwa, who reached the summit of learning by inspecting all doctrines; as Rikdzin Donyo Drakpa, heart son of the original lord Samantabhadra; and as Namgyel Rinchen Pelzangpo, elucidator of all the general and particular doctrines associated with the Buddhist teaching.

Subsequently, he was born in 1600 (iron male mouse) during the tenth sexagenary cycle at Pelto Lhundrub Dzong. His father, Gazi Tseten Dorje, belonged to the Gazi family, one of the six clans of Dong, and he was endowed with the seven attributes of the higher realms, including the seven attributes of scrutiny that pertain to rulers of men. His mother was Drigung Kyura Butri Gyelmo, and at birth he resembled a new lotus, untainted by the stains of the womb. He was recognized as the reincarnation of Yongdzin Sangye Peldzin. This was reported to Konchok Tsekpa, the secretary of Ngawang Namgyel, along with a request for a torma offering, and so the child was named Donyo Namgyel and given a protection cord. He had the utmost delight when seeing those wearing the garb of a mendicant. In his fourth year, on the day when his mother was about to pass away, he pointed toward the sky and said, "Nanam Dorje Dudjom is up there!" to which his mother replied, "He is not up there today. He will come tomorrow!" Since he was somewhat erudite, he was offered the cloak and undershirt of Yongdzin Rinpoche, a special white conch that had been offered to Ton Śāk by Nyenchen Tanglha, and an income of sixty loads of grain. In this way, his former propensities were strengthened.

In childhood, Donyo Namgyel's faculties were clearer than those of other children. The attributes of disillusionment, compassion, {774} enlightened mind, the meditative stability in which appearances and emptiness are coalesced, and so forth, were naturally and spontaneously present.

When the lord of refuge Ngawang Namgyel returned to Taklung from Lhasa, he incidentally pleased him with empowerment precepts and blessings that dispelled unfortunate circumstances.

In his seventh year, in 1606 (fire horse), the child was brought to stay at Kudzi, where he learned to read under the monk Śākya Zangpo from Taklung. Gradually, he adopted and comprehended simply through being shown the gestures the essential practical applications, communion feast offerings, rites of reparation and fulfillment, *The Ornament of the Precious*

Vows of Individual Liberation,[2] and so forth. He dreamed of auspicious signs, such as a raven smiling, and although he had a severe illness resembling fever due to one or two breaches of the commitments, he recovered when particular long-life rituals were undertaken many times.

From his eighth or ninth year, he was naturally learned in the composing of texts on Buddhist doctrine. Through the power that he had refined in former lives, his propensities awoke, and with utmost faith and steadfast confidence, he even had a strong desire to approach his former teacher Pawo Tsuklak Trengwa. After inspecting the latter's *Sacred Songs*,[3] *Biography*, and so forth, he instinctively knew that cyclic existence with its coarse processes of deeds and fruition was pointless, that all things were impermanent and of the nature of emptiness, and he experientially cultivated the foundation of the sacred doctrine, nurturing it in his mind.

In his twelfth year, he met the foremost hierarch of Sakya, the great throne holder, on his visit to Lhundrub Dzong.[4] When he requested a doctrinal connection, the latter asked to inspect the extent of the scriptures held at Taklung and decreed that there was no need to fear that Taklung might lose its independence and come under the sway of others.

Until then, the child had mastered the root verses of *The Two-Chapter Tantra of Hevajra*, *The Ornament of Clear Realization*, *The Definitive Presentation of All the Classes of Tantra*,[5] {775} the three vows according to the aural lineage, and so forth.

In his thirteenth year, on the fifteenth day of the first month of 1612 (mouse), he was received by a procession of the monks of the entire congregation, and he beheld the image of the Conqueror Akṣobhya in the form of the buddha body of reality. The uncle and nephew met together in the Six-Pillar Chamber, and they made manifest the meritorious and auspicious circumstances of existence and quiescence. Immediately, the saintly lama Ngawang Namgyel conferred upon him the precepts of the novitiate, preceded by the lay vows and the intermediate mendicant vows, with himself, the perfect buddha, acting as the preceptor and master of ceremonies, Drung Kadrukpa acting as the timekeeper, and others including Drung Kyilsangpa and Gelong Rinlingpa making up the quorum. The name Ngawang Tashi Peldrub Ngedon Chokyi Nyima Namdrol Chokide was conferred upon him. The vows associated with the setting of the mind on enlightenment were also conferred upon him in accordance with the lineage of profound view.

The next day, they performed the rite of Vajrayoginī, and on completion of the rite, Tashi Peldrub asked if the physical presences of Phakmodrupa and Taklung Tangpa were actually extant in the old paintings depicting Drogon Phakmodrupa and his disciple. "They are," replied Ngawang Namgyel. "They are the physical presences of Drogon Rinpoche and glorious Taklungpa the Great." After introducing these paintings in detail, he bestowed them upon Tashi Peldrub, as icons from which he should never be separated.

Henceforth, by inspecting each aspect of the attributes of learning, dignity, and nobility that the saintly Ngawang Namgyel possessed, his resolve in harmony with the sacred doctrine increased beyond his years and months. Perfecting this resolve and devotion, he made manifest the liberating career of Taklungpa the Great.

Then, Ngawang Namgyel bestowed inaugural teachings upon him, starting with the initiation of White Amitāyus, the meditational deity of Gyelwang Taklungpa. {776} And then, he bestowed upon him, together with the assembled monks of Domsumling, Cakrasaṃvara according to the Lūipa tradition, Satyadvayamukha Bhaṭṭārikā, the seven maṇḍalas of Ngok, Sarvavid Vairocana, the Peaceful Guru along with the Red Wrathful Guru and the Dark-Blue Wrathful Guru (all according to the tradition of Chowang), Vajravidāraṇa, Siṃhavaktrā, Loktri, Coemergent Saṃvara, Vajrapāṇi, and *The Ocean of Means for Attainment*.[6]

Commencing therefrom, as Tashi Peldrub would perfect each day all the modes of the sacred doctrine that his venerable predecessor Ngawang Namgyel himself possessed, the latter bestowed the sacred doctrine upon him continuously, over three, two, or a single session, such that the teacher and the retinue became inseparable in the manner of a vase being filled to the brim. These sessions cannot be described individually.

Moreover, Tashi Peldrub perfectly studied and reflected upon the many textual traditions of the Buddhist teaching, general and particular; the ritual applications of the ancient and new traditions of the Secret Mantra; and the outer and inner fields of classical learning, including scripts, poetics, and divination. Consequently, after a short time, he became perfectly skilled in the deeds of teaching, debate, and composition.

Then, when the venerable lama Ngawang Namgyel had excellently completed the construction of the lion throne for the supreme Tashi Pelbar reliquary along with its tiers, over three days they undertook an elaborate consecration based on the colored sand maṇḍala of Cakrasaṃvara.

Thereafter, Ngawang Namgyel bestowed detailed and extensive teachings on the Six Doctrines, Mahākāla in the form Kurakma, and guidance on Amitāyus. He also privately composed a memorandum on the sequences of visualization, and when the masters, officials, and so forth saw it, they brought it to the attention of Venerable Ngawang Namgyel, who made corrections to it. This was a work composed with inspiration, {777} but there were also many other writings of his that he could not present for inspection. Gradually, he came to enjoy presenting them for inspection, and he was repeatedly praised for his usage of the ornaments of sense, including poetic similes, when offering oral exegeses and many essays that employed simile.

While fulfilling according to their wishes the results for which the people in Mongolia hoped in connection with the sacred doctrine, empowerment, and so forth, the uncle and nephew traveled incidentally together to the terma sites of Setsa and Gyawodong. On Rinpoche Tashi Peldrub bestowed empowerments, transmitted teachings, and so forth on the monk officials at Podo. Immediately on their return to Chodzong, Ngawang Namgyel expressed his gratitude with guidance and transmissions, including *The Transcendent Perfection of Wisdom* and the six branches [of the *Kālacakra*].

Until then, Tashi Peldrub had received without interruption all modes of the sacred doctrine associated with the impartial philosophical systems, along with the authentic lineage of their blessings. Consequently, through the vase empowerment, he held as his constant horizon the great seal of the deities' body that is free from attachment to ordinary appearances, consisting of the inhabited world and its sentient inhabitants; the great seal of profound mantra in which sound is naturally empty, liberated right where it is from the pleasant and harsh expressions of ordinary speech; and the meditative stability of the great seal, the abiding nature of which transcends the imaginations of the ordinary mind.

In particular, he received, in the form of experiential guidance, oral instruction on Coemergent Union of the Great Seal of the Abiding Nature, as well as Profound Path of the Great Seal of Bliss and Emptiness, and the Six Doctrines. By experientially cultivating them, all mistaken understandings that perceive the eight worldly concerns as happiness and suffering were liberated right where they were, as if awakening from a dream. The knotted energy channels that enable relative appearances to ripen were unraveled. The winds of inhalation and exhalation were interrupted, and the extraordinary blazing and melting bliss of the white and red generative essences grew. {778} The wind of pristine cognition entered into the central channel, endowed with two purities, and he was satisfied with the great bliss that is supremely unchanging, in which the rays of light neither come nor go.

Then, on the tenth day of the ninth month, it was decreed through his father, the governor Tseten Dorje, and Benbonpa Kunga Gyelzang that he should be enthroned at the monastic seat of Taklung. With the exception of those monastic officials who were disinclined, it was agreed that they should do as ordered. Tashi Peldrub offered a letter of acceptance in verse, with profound meaning and elegant words, and he held in his heart the meanings conveyed in the verses of the eulogistic reply that he received.

On the twenty-fourth day of the ninth month of 1615 (wood hare), coinciding with a conjunction of Puṣyā and Jupiter, they set out from Chodzong for Taklung. In the Ten-Pillar Hall, On Rinpoche Tashi Peldrub took his seat upon the heavenly lion throne. Deshek Konchok Tsekpa Ngawang Namgyel was seated in the corner row to the left. Then, in the midst of a gathering of one thousand two hundred, headed by the governor Gazi Tseten Dorje and his son, the preceptors and masters and dignitaries from all directions, including Tsangpa Desi, all the auspicious offerings that were appropriate, including the three kinds of representation and useful implements, embellished with many auspicious symbols, were presented to him for inspection. Then, he sat upon the red throne, which eclipsed the color of rubies, in the great Layel Courtyard, and along with the saintly lama Ngawang Namgyel and the assembly of preceptors and masters, they scattered assorted flowers and chanted their felicitations with a sweet and auspicious melody.

Thereupon, {779} Tashi Peldrub gave a somewhat detailed doctrinal exegesis of *Union with the Guru*,[7] and there were many perfect indications of auspicious signs that occurred: there was no wind, his parasol was extremely warm, a shower of flowers actually fell, and so forth. Then, seated in the golden hall of the temple, alongside the sacred representations, he was offered the first fruits of all those offerings.

Starting from then, many monastic communities including those of the Karmapa, both Zhamar and Zhanak, and of Jonang, Drigung, Phakmodru, Ralung, Ganden Podrang, Sakya, both official and private, Yangzur, Yangpachen, and Nyinje Lingpa, and dignitaries including Tsangpa Desi, Kyisho Taktse, and the chieftains of Upper and Lower Hor presented an abundance of excellent offerings to commemorate the enthronement, as if the monsoon rain clouds of summer had gathered, and he satisfied them with the sacred doctrine and material artifacts.

On the twenty-ninth day, in the Old Protector Chapel, he was presented with torma offerings, swords, armor, and so forth. On his return to Chodzong, the saintly lama Ngawang Namgyel decreed that inaugural rites of auspicious coincidence should be extensively undertaken. Over one and a half months, in accordance with the command of the holy lama, he bestowed the guidance of the Six Doctrines and the supporting background teachings of *The Sūtra of the King of Meditative Stability* on the hill-dwelling yogins of the Taklung uplands, the Nangso of Langdo, and so forth. Consequently, he acquired a resolve imbued with immeasurable pure vision.

On behalf of those who had built the monastic cells of Domsumling, the uncle and nephew together performed a consecration rite. In the sacred abodes of the great protectors of the transmitted teachings, such as Pogyi Yagangchen, he composed many offering prayers for restoring the divine cairns, which he presented for inspection. Coincidentally, there arose the most astonishing phenomena including swirling[8] hailstones and thunder.

During the tenth month, {780} when he was enthroned in the Tibetan villages and monastic estates, in accordance with the ancient custom, he accepted offerings and gave initiations, public empowerments, public teachings, and so forth, which fulfilled their immediate and long-term aspirations. Then, on returning to Taklung, he also placed a thread cross of reparation representing Genyen Chenpo, the great protector of the transmitted teachings, at the southern entrance of the temple.

At the time when Lama Rinpoche Ngawang Namgyel was away visiting Sertsa, Tri Rinpoche Tashi Peldrub undertook as scheduled elaborate rituals including rites of reparation and fulfillment, torma offerings, ritual bombardments, incense offerings to the local deities, and so forth, in conjunction with the monastic college.

In 1617 (fire snake), while engaged in retreat in the ritual service of Amitābha, he became unwell but gradually recovered after the saintly lama Ngawang Namgyel had conferred empowerments, initiations, ritual ransom, and great torma offerings, as well as rites of welcoming and aversion, and so forth.

That summer he restored the Ten-Pillar Hall of the temple. In Tsangdong forest, he perfectly received the transmission of the texts of monastic discipline from Deshek Rinpoche Ngawang Namgyel.

When the monks of Sera and Drepung took up residence at Taklung, consequent on conflict between Tsang and the Mongols, his achievements in the service of the Buddhist teaching—sustaining their lives, protecting them from fear, escorting them back home, and so forth—were henceforth unsurpassed.

When Tsangpa Desi invited the uncle and nephew together, he gradually visited Dechen Tse and places around Lhasa. When they met together, he immediately established a doctrinal connection with the Desi, received his material offerings, and so forth. He returned to Taklung via Yerpa and Langtang.

When the precious Kumbum reliquary was restored, they excellently performed the consecration, and the feast of good auspices limitlessly increased. He received fine respect and service at Nyingdrung, and at Pontsang Jarik, and so forth. Then he repaired the golden spire of the temple at Taklung, {781} and in stages, he successfully completed without impediment the construction of the White Temple.

Tashi Peldrub studied the offerings, sacred dances, root verses, and so forth of *The Maṇḍala of Indestructible Expanse* and the *Kālacakra*. He trained anew in the drum dances and the Vajrakīla dances and also improved the dance costumes by sewing them anew. He had the Collected Works of Venerable Ngawang Namgyel inscribed and correctly arranged in volumes of gold and silver.

Although the uncle and nephew appropriately considered going to Riwoche, at each crucial point, the circumstances for them to go were unsuitable. With regard to the conflicts between Hor, Mongolia, and Tsang, they brought about a peaceful resolution by excellently forging reconciliation through spiritual and material gifts. The offerings—including horses, cattle, and possessions of the Hor and Mongols that he personally received—were abundant.

In all, he received the infinite stream of empowerments, transmissions, and esoteric instructions, and the treatises that he composed, pure in terms of the three modes of scrutiny, from the earliest to the latest, amounted to some twenty volumes. So, he merited the flowers of praise that were scattered upon him a hundred times by impartial observers. He excellently completed the restoration of the Old Offering Chapel of Genyen, the old and new murals depicting Munīndra and the sixteen elders in the White Temple, and the Great Lower Hall of the Main Temple. Everyone was satisfied with his excellent patronage. On that occasion, awesome and astonishing events occurred. For example, someone fell from the roof of the Main Temple but did not die. All this was attributed to the magical means of the compassion of the saintly Tashi Peldrub himself.

He paid homage to others headed by the venerable lord of refuge Ngawang Namgyel, {782} and when the latter fell ill due to a phlegm disorder on the occasion of a feast, which was pleasing to him above all, Tashi Peldrub completed thirty thousand circumambulations of the grass hermitage, such that he gradually recovered.

During the first month of 1625 (wood ox), in the presence of the three images in the Main Temple that were no different to the actual Buddha, and, with Deshek Rinpoche Ngawang Namgyel acting jointly as the preceptor and master of ceremonies, with two monk officials acting as confessor and timekeeper, and others making up the quorum, the precepts of a fully ordained monk were correctly conferred upon him, and he perfected the aggregate of ethical discipline, untainted by even the slightest trace of misdemeanor or downfall.

The next day, to a congregation of one thousand, he gave an extremely detailed and extensive exegesis concerning the vow of setting the mind on enlightenment, such that he had manifestly trained in accordance with the liberating career of Upāli, holder of monastic discipline, and of the bodhisattva Padmapāṇi.

Then indeed, when the uncle and nephew in association had nurtured most bountiful acts of benefit for the Buddhist teaching and living beings, Deshek Rinpoche Ngawang Namgyel fell ill. At that time, Tashi Peldrub made the great torma offering of the protector-lord Mahākāla in the form of a torma of bombardment. However, a mighty dust storm of red wind and so forth appeared. Other inauspicious signs also occurred, including lights and an earthquake. Everyone, in public and private, was encouraged to perform extensive rites, but since the time had come, they were unable to avert the strong river of their negativity. On the sixth day of the fourth month of 1626 (fire tiger), Venerable Dewar Shekpa Ngawang Namgyel passed away into the immaculate field of the eastern direction.

Tashi Peldrub performed the rituals on behalf of the sacred corpse and a limitless funeral ceremony, at which a reliquary was excellently constructed in the form of an enlightenment stūpa, fashioned of three thousand five hundred *sang* of silver, and plated with one hundred *sang* and five *zho* of beaten gold, insatiable to behold. {783}. He performed the consecration.

He then brought to maturation and liberation a congregation from the impartial monasteries of Utsang—headed by the Drigungpa, Taklungpa, Karmapa, and Drukpa—and the entire assembly of fortunate disciples belonging to the local community by means of empowerments, guidance, transmissions, and pith instructions that opened the repository of the sacred doctrine, consisting of the Buddhist teaching in general and the essential definitive meaning in particular. The inconceivable manner in which he did so, at many times, is elucidated in his detailed biography, but here I can only offer an approximate description. Nor can I describe all the major and minor details of his early and later travels when he encamped in order to bring into his following all the inhabitants of the Tibetan nomadic areas, south and north.

Tashi Peldrub gradually traveled to Samdrubtse Palace at the invitation of Tsangpa Desi, where the offerings indicative of their bountiful mutual respect manifestly engendered an attractive, heart-trembling display, like the wealth of Vaiśravaṇa. He set foot in all the monasteries of Utsang, including Tashi Lhunpo and Nartang Takten Damcholing, and visited the sacred pilgrimage places.

In all, the communal alms offerings and doctrinal connections that he made with those who were interested were hard to estimate. He installed the particularly astonishing representations originating from India and China within an iron grill in the Main Temple, and he excellently embellished them so that they would not deteriorate until the end of future time, furnishing them with an offering cloud of sacred doctrine as if it were the second liberating career of Samantabhadra.

He removed the image of Munīndra, Meaningful to Behold, which had served as the meditative commitment of Venerable Kunga Tashi, the contents of which, including the hide of a lesser panda, had been damaged, along with the dilapidated artifacts of the northern wing of the Main Temple, {784} and moved them, with due construction rites, to the southern side. He repaired the wood in the northern wing of the Lower Main Hall and newly commissioned a two-cubit-size silver image of the venerable lama Ngawang Namgyel himself and perfectly concluded the rites of inserting the contents and consecration, along with the offerings.

From this time on, Tashi Peldrub also began the custom of offering communal tea in a joint assembly of the congregated monks of the college and monastery. He newly commissioned large communal kitchen pots and communal ladles, which were of immeasurable value. Also from this time on, he newly built and completed the restoration of the Precious Array Chamber and the Blissful Attainment Chamber of the upper monastery.

When Miwang Rinchen Gyeltsen arrived from Riwoche, their minds merged together as one. During that year, he constructed the inner sanctum of the college assembly hall, completing it in accordance with a marvelous design, commencing with the measurement of the subterranean geomantic spirit lord and continuing through to the painting of the woodwork.

Around that time, he focused his mind on the peaceful resolution of the harmful conflict between the Tsangpa and the Mongols, which erupted to some extent in this northern region near Taklung. Once the situation had been resolved, the country was rendered very secure. In the sanctum of the college, he correctly reinserted the contents and undertook the reconsecration of the images of Munīndra and his eight supreme pious attendants, along with those of Hayagrīva and Vajrapāṇi, and he ended with the concluding rites, directing his intention toward the purposeful auspicious circumstances appropriate for each of them.

Then, Tashi Peldrub restored the Buddhist teaching by pacifying the conflict between Yisho Riwoche and Beri. He concurrently made preparations to travel to Riwoche in order to fulfill the enlightened intention of Venerable Dewar Shekpa Ngawang Namgyel, but distracted by the Tsangpa and the Mongols, he postponed that journey for a while. He stayed in retreat at Seling and elsewhere {785} and at the end of the year also undertook the extensive rite of torma aversion in connection with the display of the eight wrathful meditational deities. In that regard, when certain harsh omens arose in his dreams, earlier and later, these were portents that concerned the monastic seats of Tibet and Kham in general. The bursar Norzang also passed away. After performing consciousness transference on his behalf and establishing the roots of virtuous action and so forth, he appointed Ngawang Zangjin to that role.

Thereafter, Jedrung Drakpa Gyeltsen and his attendants reached Taklung from Riwoche. Since they were persons inclined toward the sacred doctrine, they passed the time here, and then Tashi Peldrub fixed an astrologically auspicious day to set out in order to benefit the Buddhist teaching of Taklung Lower Plain.

Tashi Peldrub gave an initiation to the Mongolian Ding Jue Wei and to their leader Karma Chungwa. As for the leaders of this community at Taklung, Miwang Gelek Gyatso was staying in retreat,[9] but both Wang Mengyel and Nangso Welne were active. The supreme tulku Jedrung also stayed here in Yang Gon Monastery, along with them.

Tri Rinpoche Tashi Peldrub, along with sixty monks from Domsumling, then traveled via Tardo, Bilung, and Lungrik, and gradually via Tashi Pargam, Ka Zhung Shak (also known as the abode of the protector Ngamchen Gonchen), Sok Zam, Musarwa, Tanang Gon, and so forth, and after making a divinatory inspection of which sites in Nangchen and Riwoche were pure, they descended to Riwoche. While there, he stayed for some days in Yangra, offering protection to the people of Beri and its Bonpo monasteries. The monks of Riwoche, on seeing him, immediately offered their respects and gifts. He conferred on them empowerments, initiations, and doctrinal connections, at which time he also gave the king of Beri all sorts of counsel concerning mutual reconciliation. At Jama Gon, he also made a similar doctrinal connection.[10] {786} At Chamzhi, he bestowed empowerments and bountiful alms.

Then, traveling via Nabun Dzong, the place of attainment of master Padmasambhava, and via Sorak Mikye and Karyol Sumdo, he arrived at Karma Gon, where he saw the sacred representations and offered butter lamps and so forth. He established a mantra transmission of Jñānanātha there and experienced wondrously clear signs including dream indications, in consequence of which he also made certain predictions concerning future events that later came to pass. So, he could certainly see all knowable phenomena, definitively and quantitatively, as clear as a gooseberry in the palm of the hand. Then, via Tamka, he arrived at Zenda.

The congregation then considered traveling on to Chamdo and Lijiang, but Tashi Peldrub gave detailed advice, empowerments, and so forth to the lamas and monks of Domsumling along with the populace. Like an auspicious ewe and her offspring, they did not go beyond the domains of Taklung. Inconspicuously, an innumerable number of sacred relics were forthcoming, and apart from that, they did not even slightly hold on to other material artifacts of gold, silver, musical instruments, and so forth. They did leave some portion of these including ceremonial scarves and butter lamps for aspiration prayers to be offered to the sacred representations, reliquary stūpas, and so forth at Riwoche. At Yeruchok, he fulfilled the hopes of some devout persons from Riwoche, and he had Depa Rinchen Gyeltsen stay nearby him at Riwoche, donating to him even his smallest possessions.

For a while, the king of Beri carried out Tasho Peldrub's orders and lived securely, replete with his tents and artifacts. When it seemed that the times were changing for the better, Tashi Peldrub inspected the border and advised the Depa at Riwoche to make his home there, and then he gradually set out on the return journey back to Taklung. Traveling via Putokzhung and Khyungpo Ling Dzong, he met the chieftain of lower Hor from Malazhi. Then, continuing gradually via Pangtsik Gon, Sokrong, {787} Atrakpa, Nakso, and so forth, he exclusively bestowed on the communities en route in both directions the feast of maturational empowerment and liberating guidance concerning the precious leisure and endowments of human birth through savoring the nectar of his doctrinal connections.

Tashi Peldrub was then welcomed by the spiritual and secular dignitaries of Taklung at Chom. He resumed his seat at the monastery, accompanied by a procession of monks who gathered there. On the many occasions when he prepared to journey to Kham, early and later, he also bestowed worthy gifts in return on those who offered him parting gifts.

At Lhundrub Dzong, he extensively conferred empowerment through Akṣobhya and the tantras of conduct on Ama Drung and so forth, but not long afterward, she passed away. At that time, he performed the consciousness transference, along with elaborate auspicious prayers of aspiration. Then, he gradually conferred doctrinal connections and infinite streams of empowerment, transmission, and esoteric instruction on On Zhabdrung Ngagi Wangchuk, who had the title Hundredfold Blazing Light, and on On Rinpoche Namgyel Lekdrub.

A paṇḍita named Balabhadra then arrived at Taklung from Vārāṇasī in India. Despite fulfilling his wishes with respect to the study of Sanskrit grammar, Tashi Peldrub was greatly distracted by the need to maintain and protect the monastic community, so he was not interested. But he had the chamberlain Lama Tashi Pelzang and others study an unbroken session of Sanskrit grammar each day.

After the summer-rain-retreat offering ceremonies had been completed, in the autumn he bestowed diverse teachings as an act of service on Jedrung Rinpoche. In response to the king of Beri, who asked him to send someone acting in accordance with the sacred doctrine, he dispatched Drongchok, Lhunpo, and Tubten.

Then, he composed an offering prayer on behalf of the monks of Drak Temple. He went for the sake of his health to the hot springs at Kharak and Tolung Tsatok and then gradually returned to the monastic seat. {788} Simultaneously he bestowed on Jedrung Drakpa Gyeltsen and his nephew the experiential guidance on the sixteen spheres according to Kadam, and in addition he incalculably conferred empowerments, initiations, guidance, and so forth, opening the treasury of the sacred doctrine.

As a precaution, Tashi Peldrub then took up residence for a while at the mountain retreat of Taklung Upper Plain because there was an outbreak of smallpox, and in this location, he also took into his following Namgyel Peljor, the reincarnation of Barom; the reincarnation of Taktsang; and so forth. Then, he moved his residence from these uplands to Setsa. He also made preparations to travel, intending to study *The Sarasvata Grammar* with the omniscient Jayulwa, but he delayed. Instead, he completed this extant exemplary manuscript of *The Collected Works of the Kagyu Predecessors*, inscribed appropriately in gold and silver on red parchment and dark-blue paper. He repaired the interior of the reliquary stūpas and, after removing[11] their old roofs, rebuilt them with golden spires.

After a while, Ojoltrone[12] built a fairly large new residence for him. On receiving an invitation from the governor of Rata while he was on tour,[13] Tashi Peldrub went there, received his respects, and infinitely nurtured the welfare of living beings.

At that time, Beri inflicted great damage on Riwoche. Consequently, the merit of the king of Beri declined like the waning moon. The monks and inhabitants of Riwoche Monastery were protected by Depa Rinpoche himself, as best he could. Afterward, Gushri, king of the Oirats, conquered the forces of Čogtu at Tsokha. When he arrived here in Taklung, a reception was held, tea was offered, and they met in person. In such excellent ways, their friendship was secured.

In 1626 (fire tiger), Jedrung and his nephew and so forth moved their residence to Chodzong. {789} That summer, Tashi Peldrub consecrated the reliquary stūpas and the Red Throne, and individually drew the deities that avert war, misfortune, and infectious diseases. Since some negative indications occurred together in his dreams, he focused on pilgrimage, charitable donations that have a remedial effect, and so forth. He reported through Miwang Gelek Gyatso and Ngawang Samdrub that his nephew, On Zhabdrung Ngagi Wangchuk, should take responsibility for the monastic seat.[14] On the morning of the auspicious twelfth day of the fourth month, he presented On Rinpoche Ngagi Wangchuk with the gifts and other articles appropriate for enthronement on the monastic seat, which had been handed down from the past and survived undamaged, and he abundantly expressed the wish that he would continuously perform noble deeds that maintain and enhance the Buddhist teachings.

Afterward, he completed all his worthy acts, requesting gold and silver for the precious Kumbum reliquaries and so forth. The three of them—uncle, nephew, and Jedrung—performed a public consecration ceremony.

When he fell ill due to a serious leg inflammation and received medication, he gradually recovered like the sun released from the trap of clouds. Starting from then, Venerable Tashi Peldrub was perfect in knowledge and realization among the great individuals who maintained the Buddhist teaching of Taklung Upper Plain. On account of his seniority, he was venerated by all, so that the Zhabdrung of Taklung had the name of Tashi Peldrub. At Ojo, he stayed in retreat along with Jedrung for a long time. He commissioned innumerable representations, murals, and relief sculptures. He also brought the Tselpa edition of the Kangyur from Jang, and as an inauguration, he had it recited aloud once and then installed it in the Southern Chamber. In addition, many important artifacts came into his hands, including the religious conch of Marpa and the headdress of Indrabhūti. {790}

At Seling, Nyima Lhechen, and so forth, he stayed in retreat for some three years altogether in order to remain absorbed in the expansive and limitless approaches of meditative stability.

Jedrung Rinpoche sent notification that he was about to depart for Kham and requested permission to go ahead, along with his itinerant monks, but he then postponed his departure, thinking that he should go with Zhabdrung Machen.[15] In the Monastic Assembly Hall, he extensively commissioned murals including *The Pagoda of Precious Gems*,[16] *The Array of the Vinaya*, and so forth, which were insatiable to behold.

The army of the Oirat king then encircled Samdrubtse in Tsang, and soon Gushi Tendzin Chokyi Gyelpo brought the whole of Utsang under the sway of his patron-priest relationship. Starting from then, all parts of the country under the sun and upon the earth have been covered by the white parasol of the most exalted spiritual and temporal administration of the Ganden Palace, Victorious Over All Directions, and continue to enjoy the purging of obscurations to temporal well-being and spiritual bliss.

When Zhabdrung Rinpoche Tashi Peldrub fell ill, Jedrung Drakpa Gyeltsen performed empowerments, initiations, rites of reparation, thread-cross rites, burnt offerings, rites of welcoming and aversion, subjugation of the inimical *si* demons, and so forth, such that his condition did not deteriorate. When Gushi Tendzin Chogyel, priest and patron, arrived in Lhasa, they sent excellent material gifts to Taklung. Jedrung Rinpoche requested permission to set out for Riwoche, and they went their separate ways. He set out from Taklung Monastery, heading east via Ojo, but on the way he did not survive, and so he did not succeed in reaching the monastic seat of Riwoche.

Zhabdrung Rinpoche Tashi Peldrub then traveled gradually to the doctrinal palace of Drepung, where he attended upon the lotus feet of the supreme all-seeing Fifth Dalai Lama. {791} He offered to mediate between the priest and patron and some other factions, and the response he received was encouraging and excellent. He set out via Kyisho and then arrived at Marser. On reaching the snow mountainsides of outer and inner Lhokha, there he found, among the possessions of the Karmapa camp that had been lost in the snow, two jade bowls and so forth. Some bronze representational images also came into his hands. He passed about one month visiting the sacred place of Pemaling, Dowo Dzong, Tro Monastery, Mawochok Ode Gung Gyel, and so forth. Then, via Yabzang, Ombu Lakhar, Tradruk, Tsetang, and so forth, he went by boat and reached Phakmodru. There he made a detailed inspection of the sacred representations, presented communal alms, and stayed in retreat for almost three weeks, along with the sublime saffron-robed community, a multitude of monks who had obtained the mendicant and full-fledged ordinations. After passing some days at Drakha Tang, he then made a detailed pilgrimage of the sacred places at Chokhor Samye. Then, traveling via Gungtang, he fulfilled his profound aspirations by making offerings in the presence of Jowo Śākyamuni in Lhasa. In all those travels, he bestowed an infinite number of empowerments and doctrinal transmissions on those who were interested. Then, traveling via Yerpa, Langtang, and Daryul hot springs, he arrived back at Taklung Monastery.

Zhabdrung Ngagi Wangchuk remained on the teaching throne of this monastic seat for about two years, and after that, he appointed Miwang Gelek Gyatso with the outer and inner responsibilities of Taklung and their handover. He then went off to Riwoche. Although previously this Ngagi Wangchuk had lapsed in his practice of celibacy while traveling in Hor, it is said that Zhabdrung Ma Rinpoche and others in Riwoche did not know this, and so he was appointed to assume responsibility for the sacred doctrine at the lower monastic seat in Riwoche. The governor Tashi also had a son {792} named Zhabdrung Tashi Chokyi Gyelpo.[17] When a gilded Chinese-style roof was erected above the image of Munīndra in the monastic college, the uncle and nephew performed the consecration together.

When Tashi Peldrub was invited to Riwoche on account of the external hostilities and the extensive internal damage, he requested permission to go from the Supreme Conqueror, Fifth Dala Lama, and bountiful parting gifts were bestowed upon him. Here at Taklung and in all directions en route, a great many parting gifts were successively presented. He rode out from Taklung on the sixth day of the eighth month, and initially met Gushi Tendzin Chokyi Gyelpo and his son at the Nyingdrung hot springs.

Then, gradually traveling via Naksho, Kong Gon, and inner Hor, he was welcomed at Taktang near Riwoche by Depa Rinpoche and continued on the Great Temple of Riwoche. He was seated in the Ground Floor Assembly Hall, where he performed the torma rite of Uṣṇīṣa and so forth at the head of the row of monks in the congregation during the scheduled communal alms ceremony. At Yang Gon, he combined as his residence the Two-Pillar Chamber, the Rachung, and so forth, and while staying in retreat, his meditative stability did not transgress the seals of appearance and radiance, bliss and emptiness, such that the aforementioned hostilities abated. From the third day of the fourth month, he appointed monks to restore Yang Gon and the area around the temple, and his great drumbeat exhorted some seventy new monks to undertake the precepts. He extensively propagated the rites of Sarvavid, Hevajra, and so forth, together with their new compilations. In succession, he also excellently arranged the necessities required for the scheduled anniversary ceremonies. He fashioned life-size clay images of his late teacher Ngawang Namgyel and the supreme guide Taklung Tangpa the Great and also commissioned magnificent lifelike images of Sangye On, Pañjaranātha, and so forth. He excellently completed the restoration of the three reliquary stūpas, the gilded roof, {793} and also various mural and relief icons depicting the meditational deities and doctrinal protectors, and also restored the Hevajra Chapel and the five grass hermitages of the monastery, and he commissioned various new artifacts. His kindness in restoring the Buddhist teaching at Riwoche was inconceivable.

As a replacement for the areas around Riwoche, which were lost to Chamdo, the ownership of Karma Gon was settled in favor of Riwoche. On that occasion, the gilded roof of the White Temple at Karma Gon was attached, and the building reconsecrated by Taklung Upper Plain. The two icons of the lamas at Yang Gon Ngonga in Riwoche were prepared and consecrated in a single day, such that many auspicious signs were manifestly visible, including a shower of flowers. Tashi Peldrub then undertook extensive positive actions, inspecting the shrines and their sacred artifacts at Shar Yerpuk, installing butter lamps there, and so forth.

During the fourth month of 1627 (hare), a messenger arrived reporting that Miwang Gelek Gyatso had passed away at Lhundrub Dzong. Therefore, in the Hevajra Chapel, he conferred to some extent the funeral rites according to Cakrasaṃvara and so forth, and he restored the temples, including the shrine of the local deity Yigyel and his entourage. Although there were some signs of rejoicing that arose, there were no celebrations in Kham as a whole.[18] He went to Tsawagang to act for the benefit of living beings, and then again he bestowed on a congregation of laypeople and monks from Riwoche *The Four Doctrines of Dakpo*,[19] *The Seven Points of Mind Training*,[20] *The Direct Guidance of Mahākāruṇika*,[21] *The Union with the Guru*,[22] and so forth. Also, to groups of varying size from upper and lower Ma,[23] the colleges and the monastery and so forth, he gave more than twenty times guidance on the Great Seal, and apart from that he also gave a great many times guidance on Severance, the Attainment of the Guru, and the Six Doctrines. Consequently, he had countless disciples with perfect meditative experience and realization. {794}

Tashi Peldrub then focused his attention on rites of confession and purification of the hardship caused during those prior restoration works and so forth when human beings, livestock, and many hundred millions of living creatures had perished. He commissioned a manuscript of the hundred and thirteen volumes of the Kangyur, inscribed entirely in gold and silver, using materials amounting to more than four hundred *zho* of gold and approximately four hundred and fifty-four *sang* of silver.

During that period, Zhabdrung Rinpoche Tashi Peldrubwas engaged in experiential cultivation of the attainment of the guru on a year-long retreat, and he experienced innumerable signs of warmth associated with the path and its fruition. He also consecrated relief sculptures depicting Orgyen Guru Rinpoche, Mahākāla, the goddess Mārīcī and so forth, as well as the entire Kangyur manuscript. He established the custom of the scheduled anniversary offering ceremonies and the ritual service of Amitābha, lord-protector of Sukhāvatī. During the month of Puṣyā, he instated The Attainment Rite of Vajrakīla according to the Nyingmapa, the torma aversion rite from Ratna Lingpa's *Attainment of Buddha Mind*,[24] and the torma aversion rite of Jñānanātha according to the Sarmapa, and so forth. He appointed

Lama Mitruk Trinle Rabgye to the rank of monastic preceptor. Moreover, he also had each of the teachers of the three colleges representing Nyingma and Sarma traditions perfectly revive the Nyingma and Sarma recensions of doctrinal practice, the rites of reparation and fulfillment according to Hevajra, and so forth, as well as the sacred chanting, the sacred dances of Vajrakīla, the drum dances, and so forth. He supplied the three stories of the Main Temple—upper, lower, and middle—as well as the Kumbum reliquaries and the Yang Gon temple with sacraments of offering, butter-lamp wicks, and so forth.

When the great all-seeing Fifth Dalai Lama departed on invitation to China, he offered parting gifts that were sent to Drichukha on the Yangtze. He completed refurbishment of the outer and inner murals and the sacred artifacts in the Protector Chapel of Yang Gon and ensured that the incense offerings to the lord-protector Mahākāla would not be interrupted.

Then to Tse Zhabdrung Ngagi Wangchuk, Depa Rinpoche, {795} and the monks and laity of the college and monastery who were present, he unreservedly imparted advice concerning the duties of the two traditions, spiritual and secular.

Then, with parting gifts of all sorts, private and public, Tashi Peldrub set out from Yisho on the nineteenth day of the fourth month of 1630 (horse), escorted by a riding party as far as Gyelmo Richuk. Proceeding in the direction of Putokpa Tsomgo, which belonged to the communities of Drongpa and Sok Tsanden Gon, he bestowed guidance, empowerments, and initiations on Pungri Nangso and so forth. Lama Lotsāwa, his interpreter, gathered all the things, domestic and imported, that he acquired on the way, and he again sent them to Riwoche in order to commission a manuscript of the Kangyur.

Gradually, via Shakchu and so forth, he reached Drakkar at Uma in Dam. Taklung On Namgyel Lekdrub went there to welcome him, and on the third day of the month, he arrived at the Main Temple and the college in Taklung Monastery, along with a procession of monks. The following day, he gave presents by degree to all the high and low persons who were sent to greet him from Setsa in the service of Gyeltsab Rinpoche.

For a while, Tashi Peldrub remained in retreat. Then via the pass of Setsa, he traveled east to Lhundrub Dzong, and via Langtang to Lhasa, where he met Fifth Dalai Lama, the lord of heaven and earth, and made offerings and aspiration prayers in the presence of Jowo Rinpoche, the precious representative image of the Teacher. He stayed in Lhasa for almost one month and received the particular doctrinal cycles, transmissions, and many initiations of Tsongkhapa, along with the transmission of *The Great Graduated Path*.[25]

When Konchok Rinpoche of Drigung passed away, he was invited to be seated at the head of the row during the funeral ceremonies. He arrived at Trelung and Changling with a reception party. The next day, he met Choje Rinpoche, and in the midst of a congregation from Drigung Til, {796} he presided over the great offerings of the funeral ceremony and dedicated the merit of that practice. Inspecting the sacred artifacts of Drigung, he made an extensive offering of butter lamps and bestowed communal alms and doctrinal connections. He and Lama Dampa Ratna Zhab from the Drigung Palace took turns at receiving the sacred doctrines from one another.

Then, via Jukpei Chenga Bumpa, Tashitse, Gonpa Sewa, Khartok, and Chodzong, he arrived back at Taklung. There, he gradually gave the entire transmission of the Kangyur to On Rinpoche Namgyel Lekdrub.

While staying a year in retreat at Ojo, Tashi Peldrub then completed a hundred thousand times the attainment of the guru, along with prostrations. On the nineteenth day of the seventh month of 1632 (water monkey),[26] he came out of retreat and offered long-life sustaining prayers to On Rinpoche. He restored an important icon given by Drung Kadrukpa and consecrated it as the essential nature of the being of pristine cognition.

On the nineteenth day of the ninth month of 1633 (mouse), he appointed On Rinpoche Jetsun Ngawang Namgyel Lekdrub as the master of spiritual and secular affairs in this community of Taklung. In accordance with the writing of an ancient edict, the successive clouds of offerings were gradually handed over to him by Miwang Tensung. In the midst of a congregation endowed with reason and liberation in the great Layel Courtyard, Onjo Rinpoche recited prayers of good auspices and turned the wheel of the sacred doctrine, such that he became the nectar of the minds and ears of all those who were assembled there. He assumed the teaching throne, and excellent offerings from all directions were amassed like clouds.

Zhabdrung Ma Rinpoche, Tashi Peldrub, traveled from Ojo to the hot springs at Nyingdrung. On the way back, in Sewalung, he stayed in strict retreat for a year. Then, when Gyeltsab Rinpoche of Tsurphu passed away into the expanse of reality and On Rinpoche was invited to be seated at the head of the row during the funeral ceremonies, he went briefly to Sewalung. {797}

In 1634 (wood dog),[27] he excellently completed the second reliquary of his late teacher Ngawang Namgyel—the lotus-mound stūpa fashioned of red sandalwood that is nowadays within the Tsanden Lhakhang. He also received from Riwoche a supplement to the second Kangyur, which was near completion, and he sent it back after making a catalog.

Some years had passed since the official Trangtakpa Wangyel considered that all neighboring arable land should be acquired as an endowment for offerings. He said, "This year, it is appropriate for arable land to be offered to the monastery," and so the fields of Trangtak, Nyena, Gardrong, Drongbuk, and so forth were donated as endowments for offering, and then Trangtakpa Wangyel himself received the mendicant ordination. His mind focused on the sacred doctrine in mountain retreat, such that he arrived at the essential point concerning the eight freedoms, the ten endowments, and material wealth.

In the Lama Lhakhang of the monastery, Tashi Peldrub arrayed and arranged as the foremost representations those icons that were extant from the past and those that had been newly acquired, mostly brought from Riwoche, as well as the blessed artifacts gathered from the statue of Lama Dampa Phakmodrupa in the form Rinpoche Jonlek,[28] and he transformed the monastic assembly into a field of merit.

He had his attendant[29] Ngawang Ledrub travel to Drigung to request the transmission of the Domang section of the Kangyur, while he stayed in a somewhat isolated retreat at Seling. Then, again, he dispatched Ngawang Monlam in order to commission a third manuscript of the precious Kangyur.

When Drigung Rinpoche fell ill and passed away, he composed an elaborate biographical prayer in the context of the funeral ceremony. Although the people invited him to be seated at the head of the row, he insisted that Choje Tri Rinpoche be invited in his place.

Then, when Zhabdrung Rinpoche Tashi Peldrub ended his retreat, he went to Lhasa where he offered prostrations to the All-Seeing Conqueror, Fifth Dalai Lama, and received some doctrinal connections from him. {798} He also met Yamdrok Chime Tulku, who arrived there in Lhasa, and at Langtang, he commissioned texts including the seventeen volumes of *The Collected Works of the Kagyu Lineage*[30] and also the thirteen volumes of his own Collected Works.

Lest these activities might simply lead him astray,[31] he set out on the third day of the seventh month for the abode of the Five-Tufted Nyenchen, which had been blessed by the great master Padmasambhava and many lamas belonging to the lineage of attainment, the crystal cave that had served as the place of attainment for Lhangang Choje, Tsangpa Gyare, and so forth, and he arrived there on the sixth day. A group of six or seven masters and disciples including Gelong Dode Pelyang then entered into strict retreat for three years. During that period, it was decreed that they should not partake of offerings including things dedicated on behalf of the dead. Each year, they undertook once the means for attainment of the guru, but the contemplation of regular observances was uninterrupted. Consequently, his mind itself secured cyclic existence and nirvāṇa in a common savor, the meditative stabilities free from the elaborations of bliss, radiance, and nonconceptuality, intermingling equipoise, and post-meditation. Finally, he nurtured that experience without wavering even for an instant from the real abiding nature, free from the objects and acts of meditation. He was satisfied with whatever food he obtained, and as in the biography of Venerable Mila Repa, he focused on one-pointed attainment. He conferred the whispered teachings of *The Aural Lineage of the Five Stages*[32] on the monastic preceptor Śākya Zangpo and Taktsang Ngawang Tashi.

Depa Rinchen Gyeltsen from Riwoche and his attendants invited Zhabdrung Rinchen to Kham, and after being reproached in due course by Chamdo, they came to ask for advice at his hermitage and met with him. Then, when Tri Rinpoche Namgyel Lekdrub from Taklung also arrived with a reception party, he conferred upon them the liberating guidance of the Five Stages, the Aural Lineage, and so forth. {799}

When Drung Lung Rikpa was en route for Kham, he arrived on the way at Lhanang, where he received the transmission of the Domang anthology and the transmissions of four medical lineages. He restored the representations that were extant from before in the crystal cave, and newly commissioned two images of the master Padmasambhava. Depa Rinpoche and the official Trangtakpa, priest and patron, then said that Taklung Zhabdrung (Tashi Peldrub) should not delay in Kham for more than three years but return to Taklung. Accordingly, he stayed in that strict retreat from the nineteenth day of the seventh month of 1636 (mouse) until the sixteenth day of the third month of 1639 (hare), and then after coming out, he stayed for one week at Phodang Kaleb. Then, via Nyingdrung hot springs and Tangdrok, he traveled in succession through Ojo, Seling, and Chodzong.

On the second day of the fifth month, in the Main Temple, he ordained the peerless Tri Rinpoche as a full-fledged monk and also granted him instruction on the setting of the mind on enlightenment. After conferring the transmission of the Domang anthology and so forth, he arrived in Lhasa via Uma, Lhundrub Dzong, Langtang, and Ngode. Then, he went to see the two images of Jowo Śākyamuni, and at the Potala Place, he joyfully met the supreme Conqueror Lokeśvara and six hundred dignified attendants. He bestowed upon him the guidance and transmission of *The Graduated Path of Guhyasamāja*[33] and so forth, and a long-life empowerment with the actual vase that Tangtong Gyelpo had used. Then, after receiving fine parting gifts from the Dalai Lama and his regent, and after making a connection through pure aspiration prayers, blessed in the presence of the two sibling sublime images, he arrived at Langtang. After many parting gifts, both public and private, {800} that had been profoundly and extensively offered from Taklung and so forth, along with blessings and advice, he headed toward the east on the twenty-seventh day.

While acting for the benefit of the inhabitants of Tarlugok, Sewalung, Kongkong, Drelgyido, Maryonang, Barde, Amdo, and so forth, people arrived from Riwoche via Memo La, and inner Hor on numerous occasions to serve him tea.

At Khangsar Shangkhyim, he went briefly into the presence of Zhabdrung Tsenang. Then at Taktang near Riwoche, a welcoming meal was offered, and he alighted at the glorious great temple, accompanied by a procession of monks. From the sixth day of the eleventh month of that year, he established a workshop at Riwoche, dedicated to the replacement of the gilded roof of the Main Temple and so forth. He continuously granted guidance and transmissions, without interruption. He also stayed in retreat in the great chamber, and he held a detailed discussion with Phakpa Lha of Chamdo who was then en route for U. On the sixth day of the seventh month, he scattered the flowers of good auspices, reconsecrating the manuscripts of the Kangyur that had been commissioned, the painted scrolls depicting the doctrinal protectors, and so forth. Below the gilded roof of the temple, he commissioned perfectly executed varnished murals depicting an array of buddha fields and so forth.

Gradually, he completed the upper and lower stories of the temple at the second Domsumling Monastery in Yisho, along with the monastic cells. The iconography, relief sculptures, inner relics, consecration rites, and so forth manifested an array of miraculous ability that transcended the bounds of the intellect. In the old chapel, he elaborately commissioned murals in conformity with the perspective of the ancient translations. He secured and consecrated the exquisitely fashioned gilded roof ornament, along with its excellent inner relics as a pure infinite display, consisting of all the shrines and sacred artifacts in their entirety. {801}

On many interested residents of the college and the monastery, Tashi Peldrub then bestowed the guidance of *The Seven Points of Mind Training*.[34] On On Jedrung Drakpa Lekdrub[35] he bestowed instruction on the calligraphy of Rañjanā, in addition to empowerments and initiations. At Domsumling, the monastic college of Taklung, he spread out the flowers of benediction, naming the upper and lower assembly halls, as well as the residential monastic cells as embellishments of the pleasure garden of Anāthapindada, and labeling each of their individual internal plaques with the appropriate relief inscription.

In accordance with an injunction of Jedrung Rinpoche, he also arranged the representative images in the Protector Chapel above the east gate of the monastery, and he roughly completed the painting of the small rooms and so forth. Then, in the presence of the images in the Abhirati Room, he conferred the full monastic ordination on Jedrung Dampa. Immediately ascending the lion throne of the Tashi Gomang, along with the monastic officials and the monastic assembly, he bestowed upon him enjoyable offering clouds and rejoiced, appointing him as the highest master of spiritual and secular affairs in Riwoche.

In the maṇḍala circle of buddha mind in the Main Temple, together with the monks of Domsumling, he performed an extensive consecration ceremony by means of the three-day Hevajra empowerment. For all, in public and private, he had perfect kindness in granting advice concerning direct guidance, oral instruction, legal charters, regulations, and so forth.

Then, once he had also excellently undertaken service and restoration work at Shar Yerpuk, he focused on the sacred image of Munīndra in the form Tupa Otsen Wangpo and went there. In addition, he newly composed an elaborate smoke-offering rite dedicated to the local deities of Riwoche, which was based on the ancient rituals of thanksgiving. {802} At an overnight stop in the uplands of Gang, he gave extensive initiations and oral advice to his mounted escort, which included the brother of the Zhabdrung.

Then, traveling in succession via Putoktang, Sharu La, Gam La, Khyungpo, Drongu, Shakchu, and so forth, on the thirteenth day of the eighth month, Taklung Tri Rinpoche and Depa Tashi went out to welcome him. Rinpoche Tashi Peldrub then turned back, after sending presents to the preceptors, disciples, and monks of Taklung. Aristocratic officials and so forth then accompanied him via Nyingdrung hot springs and Trelgyi La, to reach Zadam Chalking, where the omniscient Gyelwang Dalai Lama was encamped. They offered a hundred horses, six hundred bricks of tea, and half that amount to the regent, and they bestowed upon him in turn excellent gifts as a reward for services rendered, which engendered mutual rejoicing. The inhabitants of upper and lower Penyul paid their respects.

Then, on the twenty-third day of the ninth month, Tashi Peldrub did reach the great monastic seat of Taklung, and he moved into the Great Temple. Since the walls had been replastered in an excellent, exemplary manner, he rejoiced to the utmost. He gave return gifts to the people who came from all directions to offer him donations. Then, he went to Chodzong and stayed there, following the regulations of Choje Kuyalwa concerning retreat that maintained the lineage of practice.

He commissioned an excellent collection of paintings depicting the successive former lineage holders of Taklung, which were to be displayed in the inner sanctum of Riwoche Monastery. When some monks from Zuri received the mendicant and full monastic ordinations, Tri Rinpoche was also present in the line of ritual officiants.

Tashi Peldrub himself had previously composed the first part of the biography of Drigung Lama Konchok, and there was a need to preserve the remainder. Without receiving encouragement from Drigung to do so, he finished the composition, which they then brought back to Drigung. {803} In addition, during that period, there were a great many other works that he composed, including his *Commentary on the Three Vows*.[36]

Zhabdrung Ngagi Wangchuk and his family arrived from Riwoche and met him, and it was then that he mostly completed the woodblock[37] of *The Pagoda of Precious Gems* (*Ratnakūṭa*) scriptures that had been newly commissioned. A phlegm disorder that he had previously had flared up. Two lama physicians offered purgatives, and Tri Rinpoche performed the rites of fulfillment and confession that cheat death, and so forth.

On the basis of *The Spiritual Songs of the Precious Kagyu Lineage* that were extant and unadulterated, he arranged in the correct sequence *The Adamantine Songs*[38] of Venerable Drakpa that had been preserved in ancient writings. Every month, he held a recital of these spiritual songs so that their melodies would not be lost. Woodblocks for some of them had previously been prepared in Lhodrak, and these gradually came into his possession. He commissioned new woodblocks for *The Sūtra of the King of Meditative Stability*.

The Dalai Lama and the Great Regent Sonam Chophel inquired after his health. Long-life prayers were also undertaken on his behalf at Drigung. He composed an extensive *Word Commentary on the Mantra Vows of the Awareness Holders,*[39] which was a teaching of his late teacher Ngawang Namgyel. While he was focusing one-pointedly on the ascetic discipline of *Total Renunciation: Natural Liberation of Attachment*[40] at Khuyuk Rolpei Dzong in Sewalung, Choje Tri Rinpoche implemented extensive long-life rituals and composed the verses of a prayer dedicated to him, along with an auspicious chart. Accordingly, the enlightened body of this peerless and precious lord of refuge Tashi Peldrub became lustrous and bright. His physical stature acquired the strength of a most powerful supreme bull. His enlightened speech {804} became pleasant like the voice of Brahmā, and he became a lion of speech, exuding without impediment all the words and meanings of the eighty-four thousand approaches of the sacred doctrine.

As far as his enlightened mind, which distinguished the vision of the real abiding nature of the ultimate truth of emptiness, is concerned, how could one estimate the number of ordinary persons whom he trained? In all common affairs as well, he was simply steadfast, profound, and unswayed by any circumstances. However much he was investigated by others, the profound depths of his enlightened mind could not be fathomed. Even when scorned and strongly censured by all, he was utterly without anger, calm, and disciplined. He was vast in his approach to learning with respect to all the ten outer and inner fields of classical learning. Even a small fraction of each of his enlightened attributes diffused without impediment and without interruption all the approaches to liberation that cannot be appraised over many eons, and he captivated the mental faculties of all.

The unique white parasol of his enlightened activities became a sustaining shade for all living beings of the three world systems, without exception. Although there were many bountiful acts that he undertook on behalf of self and others, the array of his miraculous abilities that would be accomplished at each instant was inexhaustible. It is hard to estimate such profound and vast modalities that clearly manifested, such that even in the perceptual range of negative beings, a powerful faith uncontrollably arose.

In this disposition, from 1667 (fire sheep), in his sixty-eighth year, he renovated the residence at Khuyuk Rolpei Dzong in Sewalung and enthusiastically engaged in practice. There, he simply gave audience through an aperture, when attending to the most essential matters, and gave hand empowerments, and besides that, apart from just his bursar, his attendant, his brother, his two lama physicians, and the cook, no one at all met him. He focused exclusively on retreat in a hermitage with a sealed aperture. {805}

He would speak alone to Zhingtse, Ngagi Wangchuk, Pema Tulku Jedrung Drakpa Tekdrub, and others who at all times would come to see him, granting audience through an aperture during the day, and extensively bestow upon them countless guidance, transmissions, and empowerments on the Great Seal and so forth. He nurtured each of them through his particularly gracious kindness in dispensing hospitality, parting gifts, and advice.

He propagated his innumerable compositions during the intervals between his meditation sessions and edited his own early and later works, as well as many newly published texts on medical science, above all. He consecrated representational images, paintings, and relief sculptures, and guided beings on the path of liberation by inscribing the names of the dead and the living. In such ways, his achievements were infinite. He also commissioned representative artifacts, including a set of the eight stūpas, fashioned of black myrobalan and gold painted scrolls.

As far as the disagreement with the retired incumbent Zhabdrung is concerned, the government decreed that the commander Kyangpo On should arrange a settlement of the rift at Taklung through Ma Rinpoche Tashi Peldrub, and he went there, but the advice was not accepted.

When Tashi Peldrub's body showed signs of ill-health, in all the monastic estates of Taklung, Riwoche, and so forth, the official bursars again assumed responsibility for performing communal alms offerings and extensive long-life ceremonies on his behalf. The physicians in succession offered him medical treatment, such that he slightly recovered on a number of occasions. The retired incumbent, uncle and nephew, the monks of the college and monastery, and people from Dakpo, Drigung, and so forth also offered prayers for his longevity.

In brief, over a period of four years from 1667 (fire sheep) until 1671 (iron pig), he effortlessly accomplished a great wave of benefit for the Buddhist teachings and living beings, directly and indirectly, without wavering from meditative stability because, in the manner of bubbles vanishing of their own accord in water, he dissolved all grasping based on the insistence of refutation and proof with regard to substantialism in the unchanging disposition in the expanse of the luminous great seal. {806} Then finally, in order to rouse the eternalist disciples of this field (world) for a while toward the sacred doctrine, in his seventy-second year on the twenty-first day of the third month in 1671 (iron pig), he was welcomed in front by many miraculous offering clouds, and the array of his physical body vanished into the mind of the Conqueror, mighty Akṣobhya, in the taintless buddha field of the eastern direction. Then, the expanse of his enlightened intention was extensively fulfilled with honors and a great cloud of virtuous offerings, as manifold as the material offerings that were donated in the presence of the sacred corpse. The mass of pearl relics from the funeral pyre was inserted within an enlightenment stūpa, fashioned of many precious metals and gems, and it was positioned to the left of center in the Southern Chamber.

The Disciples of Choktrul Ngawang Tashi Peldrub

Zhabdrung Ngagi Wangchuk

Those who were the disciples of this venerable master cannot be counted, like the constellations of the sky. Among the two nephews who were the foremost of his spiritual sons, the senior nephew was named Riwoche Tse Zhabdrung Ngagi Wangchuk Ogya Barwa. The main part of his biography accords with the description repeated in the section on the abbatial succession of Riwoche, since he nurtured the community at Riwoche in Kham. This can be known from the account elucidated in *The Supplement to the Doctrinal History of the Lower Plain*,[41] which represents the actual words of Venerable Lama Choku Dorje Chang, who was his own crown ornament.

Zhabdrung Namgyel Lekdrub

As far as the younger nephew named Zhabdrung Namgyel Lekdrub, or Sungrab Kungyi Nyima Tashi Pelyang Choktu Drakpeide, is concerned, since I have not seen even a kernel of his biography documented, {807} we do not know it in detail. However, the inspiration of his learning in all the crucial points of the outer and inner sūtras and mantras was supremely wide-ranging. He possessed the noble signs of one who had attained the supreme and common accomplishments with respect to many preferred deities. He received from his predecessor Tashi Peldrub the ocean of pith instructions of the profound doctrine, without remainder, and he was appointed to the rank of throne holder of the sacred doctrine at the monastic seat of Taklung. He brought the entire congregation to maturation in the feast of the sacred doctrine. He opened the door of enlightened activity that sustained living beings of the south and north, without partiality. In the temples, he carried out extraordinarily perfect restoration and maintenance, laying aggregate plaster in the upper and lower floors of the hall called Blazing Glory of Existence and Quiescence, displaying gold painted scrolls, and so forth. In the grass hermitage, he fixed a golden spire and so forth. Such was the wheel of enlightened activity that he extensively performed on behalf of the Buddhist teaching and living beings.

The compositions of this venerable master included *Ocean of Buddha Fields: A Prayer to the Life of Tashi Peldrub,*[42] official letters, *An Offering Prayer to the Tsen Spirits of Khartok Dzong,*[43] and *The Smoke Offering of the Great King Vaiśravaṇa,*[44] some of which were endowed with excellence of word and meaning, attractive to the minds of intelligent persons.

After engaging in such acts of exegesis, composition, and teaching, finally it transpired that the public and private obstacles to the Buddhist teaching could not be averted. At that time, when the monastic officials were not close, the mass of monks indulged in various acts of exaggeration and deprecation, and although he was without the stains of bewilderment in his mind, he knew that the time to train the disciples by various peaceful and wrathful methods had arrived, and then he immediately retired. {808}

He appointed his nephew Tashi Chokyi Gyelpo to both monastic seats when the latter had reached the age of ten. He himself then went on pilgrimage to Dakpa Shelri. Then, he traveled about on account of various deceitful machinations of untamed *damsi* demons that concerned his entourage,[45] an allusion to which is slightly made in the biography of Tashi Chokyi Gyelpo. He stayed a long time at Chodzong Namgyel Rabten, such that he became known also as Dzong Zhabdrung Namgyel Lekdrub.

Later, on the day when Venerable Tendzin Namgyel arrived at that monastic seat, it is clear that Chodzong Zhabdrung Namgyel Lekdrub passed away into the expanse of reality. After his nirvāṇa, the silver reliquary that was constructed, resplendent like a snow mountain and embellished with many precious gems, was positioned on the left side of the Southern Chamber. Apart from that, I have not seen a kernel of an account of that intervening period of his life, so I do not dare to speak of it here.

Depa Tensung

Among the brothers of Tashi Peldrub, the governor Depa Tensung had an approach to wisdom equal to that of Brahmā Hiraṇyagarbha, while his bravery and courage were equal to those of Nārāyaṇa. He performed perfect acts of service on behalf of the spiritual and secular affairs of the Ganden Palace administration. In particular, during the Southern Wagon War with Bhutan, he was sent as a general to eastern Mon. Since his reputation as a military strategist was particularly great, he emerged victorious in battle over the attacking Drukpa forces and so forth and was decorated for his bravery.

Apart from them, the other actual disciples of Venerable Tashi Peldrub himself included Jedrung Drakpa Gyeltsen of Taklung Lower Plain, Khyabdak Drakpa Lekdrub, Drigung Konchok Phuntsok, and Yamdrok Chime Tulku. {809} These are clearly implied from the biography, but I tremble at the uncountable number of disciples in whose minds he planted the seeds of liberation simply through sight, hearing, memory, and contact.

3. Zhabdrung Ngawang Tashi Chogyel, the Twenty-Third Hierarch

By taking just a drop of water from the ocean
That is the liberating career of the supremely accomplished one,
Embodying all the glory of the enlightened activity of the Conqueror
And the source of all good auspices,
May you encourage us and others to act on behalf of the Buddhist teaching!

Sincere homage to Zhabdrung Tashi Chogyel—
The top-knotted **official** (*drung*),[1] the dust of his **feet** (*zhabs*) pure as sunrise,
Who possesses the glory of ten million exquisite **good auspices** (*bkra shis*),
And is the **king** (*rgyal po*) leading beings to the springtime
That is the joyous banquet of the **sacred doctrine** (*chos*) of definitive meaning!

Zhabdrung Ngawang Tashi Chokyi Gyelpo was the twenty-fourth of the incumbents of the lion throne of Taklung, who appeared in the succession of the blessed authentic lineage, an heir born to the *oncho*,[2] who belonged to the same family as peerless Tashi Pel, Taklung Tangpa the Great, the mighty lord of the world, illuminating the essential meaning of the precious Buddhist teachings.

Emanating from the Conqueror Mahāvajradhara, embodiment of the body, speech, and mind of all the conquerors, and of the five wheels of inexhaustible adornment, the buddha body of reality in whom the enlightened intention of all the buddhas is of a single savor, he appeared as the five enlightened families and the three enlightened families of the buddha body of perfect resource, and also in diverse emanational forms, among which, here in this world, he emanated from the light rays of Mañjughoṣa himself, the mighty lord of discriminative awareness, who actually represents the adamantine reality of buddha body.

In the presence of Śākyamuni Buddha, he had been the pious attendant Śāriputra, and during the early dissemination of the Buddhist teaching in Tibet, the Land of Snows, he had been the religious minister Pemei Gungtsen and the great translator Kawa Peltsek, {810} and, as mentioned in the sealed precepts of prophetic declaration from *The Gathering of Enlightened Intention* of the great master Padmasambhava himself, he later manifested as many scholars and accomplished masters of India and Tibet.

As far as the perspective of this Taklung Kagyu tradition is concerned, he appeared in succession as the supreme incarnation Choje Kuyalwa, as Choktrul Drakpei Pel, as both the earlier and later peerless Ratnākara, as the omniscient Ngawang Drakpa, and as Rikdzin Sonam Tashi.

Finally, in the area of Penyul, Source of the Quick-Witted, at Lhundrub Dzong, he was born in 1660 (iron mouse), as the oldest of three sons born to the father Gaji Miwang Tashi and the mother Kyishoza. They requested the lord of refuge, Rinpoche Tashi Peldrub, to protect him, and he bestowed upon the child the name Tashi Chokyi Gyelpo. From childhood, his physique was resplendent, his speech was pleasant, and his mind was clear and circumspect. In all his childhood play, too, he had a disposition that transcended the ordinary range of perception.

When his uncle Zhabdrung Namgyel Lekdrub, the incumbent hierarch, suddenly expressed the wish to become a total renunciate, he invited the child to Taklung without delay and bestowed upon him the lay and intermediate mendicant vows, as well as the vows of the novitiate. The name Ngawang Tashi Chokyi Gyelpo was conferred upon him, and then, in his tenth year, he was appointed as the hierarch. He stayed separately at Dzong Zhabdrung Namgyel Rabten and went to visit the power places of Cāritra and so forth. On his return, certain demonic forces caused discord, and consequently his mind was agitated from its depths. {811} The Dzongzhab official led a random group of servants and monks from Domsumling and occupied the entrance to the Labrang Yangon Tse during the night. With their many lay domestics, they lapsed into a state of mutual great hostility. However, they did pay attention to the request of the lay official Agon, and then On Tashi Chogyel retired that night to Horkhang. All this transpired in accordance with a prophetic declaration in the treasures of Ratna Lingpa, which says, "During the civil war at Taklung, monks will die at the sword."

Then with his uncle Ngawang Lekdrub, Tashi Chokyi Gyelpo traveled via Lhundrub Dzong to Drepung and reported this to the government. The government ordered that the commander Kyangpo should grant them sanctuary at the residence of Tashi Peldrub in Sewalung and protect the lives of the governor and the incumbent Zhabdrung here. He accordingly went there and said, "You should settle this internal dispute between the incumbent throne holder and the retired throne holder, which entailed violent struggle during the night. When you settle it, if nothing but armed insurrection comes about, it will be inappropriate that you should protect the interests of Taklung in that manner." But in response, his relative did not listen to that request, and so in the manner of food that sustains the mind,[3] he said, "Please desist! Maintain kindness! Do not abandon your long-term objective of protecting the interests of Taklung!" He communicated this advice, with parting gifts.

The Great Fifth Dalai Lama then negotiated a mutually agreeable settlement and granted the monastic body authority to select who should preside over the monastic seat. In accordance with a petition made to On Rinpoche, Tashi Chokyi Gyelpo again took up residence at the monastic seat of Taklung. {812}

The physician Lekchok offered him instruction on calligraphy and poetics. From Gelong Demchok, he received and perfectly mastered all the outer and inner subjects of classical learning, commencing with *The Kalāpa Grammar*. Under Dzong Zhabdrung himself, he made an extensive study of the sacred doctrine, including the cycle of the aural lineage of the profound doctrines of glorious Taklung Tangpa Rinpoche and the transmission of the Kangyur.

Since, until a Conqueror attains buddhahood, both the actions of the substratum and the pristine cognition of buddha mind are integrated, the defects of suffering may be scrutinized, their indications generated through the past actions of fundamental ignorance, and since the inconceivable attributes of the excellent path of liberation originate in the apparitional aspect of the pristine cognition that is awareness, here the natural radiance of this age of degeneration is mostly subject to untamed demonic forces. Consequently, exemplified by the wounds and sores of a slanderous verbal communication between father and son, they were pierced by the weapons of the five-arrowed one, the demonic lord of obstacles. So when this reached

His Holiness the Dalai Lama, the lord of discipline, in order to settle the difference between the truth and falsehood of positive and negative speech—since they were lost in the perspective of their negative arrogance, and the merit of all their dependents had simultaneously declined and obstacles had arisen that were stifling to the Buddhist teaching—the government took over the monastery and its domains, with the exception of just a small number of officials who were of good fortune.

Tashi Chokyi Gyelpo, in his twentieth year, then moved his residence to Ojo, and he traveled on pilgrimage to Cāritra and so forth. He received the maturational empowerments and liberating guidance of many old and new treasure revelations in the presence of Mindroling Chogyel Terdak Lingpa, and the cycle of the Northern Treasures from Dordrak Rikdzin Chenpo. {813} Then, in the presence of the Great Fifth Dalai Lama, Ngawang Lobzang Gyatso, he received the mendicant and full monastic ordinations, and the name Kunga Sonam Chokdrub was conferred upon him. He also received certain empowerments and transmissions from Gelong Jamyang Drakpa and undertook many rites of service and attainment, including The Great Ritual Service of Cakrasaṃvara, The Peaceful and Wrathful Guru, and Mañjuśrī Yamāntaka. Inestimable pure visions were born within him, whereby appearances, sounds, and awareness arose as a display of deities, mantra, and meditational stability, and he acquired the supreme and common accomplishments without effort.

In these ways, he unimpededly accomplished the infinite rites of pacification and so forth. He commissioned representative images, paintings, and relief sculptures, along with many volumes of profound scripture. Earlier and later in life, he traveled to Upper and Lower Hor in the northern region for the benefit of living beings. Since he possessed the mind of enlightenment, he abided in the natural state and accepted everyone with love.

Since the spaciousness of his awareness was vast and the propensities of his former experiences had awoken, in his seventeenth year he engaged in composition. His new works included *Rejoicing in the Protectors: An Offering Prayer to the Divine Genyen Chenpo*[4] and *An Extensive Offering Prayer to the Demons of Malaise*,[5] which is widely practiced nowadays. And he edited the original ancient manuscript pertaining to the Kyagu Drenchu protectors. Furthermore, when one examines the arrangements of his oral instructions, spiritual songs, and rites of service and attainment, it is certain that his discernment and erudition were unrivaled. He conferred empowerments and guidance on Hor Lotsāwa Lama Loden, some officials of Taklung, and others, and among his subjects, he bestowed the mendicant ordination and so forth on eighty new monks. He had a great many disciples who had the good fortune to obtain the sacred doctrine. {814} Since he mostly established his residence at Ojo Okmin Chodzo, he was universally known as Ojo Zhabdrung.

Though the schism between uncle and nephew had occurred in the past, his perception later on grew morbid. He did, however, meet up with Zhabdrung Ngawang Tsangpa, Khuwo Tsetrul Ngagi Wangchuk, and others, and their minds merged together.

Finally, when an outbreak of smallpox occurred all over the country, he undertook a strict retreat, but the physician who was attached to him prescribed a purgative for bile disorders that was incompatible, and on account of that, his enlightened intention dissolved into the expanse of reality. He passed away in his thirtieth year on the twenty-first day of the first month of 1689 (earth snake). For seven days, rainbow clouds arose in a clear sky, water suddenly burst through the east side of his meditation cave, rhododendrons bloomed, and other such wondrous signs occurred—seeds inducing the faithful assembly to pray and those without faith to hesitate. The sacred corpse was placed inside a funerary reliquary constructed at the confluence of Ojo. Since whatever wealth he had was used for the funeral ceremonies, a small silver reliquary was commissioned. Nowadays, it is the one placed inside the Dromton Chapel in the Utse. It is said that some small articles were left as an endowment for recognizing his tulku and so forth.

At Taklung, after the retirement of Zhabdrung Ojo, there were about seven who held the title of monastic preceptor, including Kadrukpa, who was appointed by the other preceptors, and those who were appointed by the government—namely, Sera Umdze, Nang Jungne, Kyormolungpa, Jangtse Lodro Dondrub and Kyilsangpa Deno Gyatso. {815} Some of them were virtually alike in their maintenance and preservation of the monastery and so forth, whereas others subjected their monastic and lay subjects to suffering. I have indeed heard a great many such depressing stories.

Among those who obtained the kindness of the profound doctrine from Venerable Tashi Chokyi Gyelpo, the foremost was Tashi Jamyang Gyatso, who himself was renowned as the incarnation of Venerable Tashi Peldrub. However, he never took his seat upon the throne of this monastic seat. He was of great benefit to the continuity of the sacred doctrine through his empowerments and transmissions, and some of his official letters and writings are extant. Only a part of his biography is clearly known from the time of Chotrul Trinle Chokdrub—apart from that I have not seen any other books, so I could not present it here.

May those with supreme knowledge and power that sees all things,
After inspecting this fragmentary biographical account,
Understand their own affairs to be illusory, without truth,
And accomplish the signs indicative of essential meaning!

4. Kyabgon Ngawang Trinle Tendzin

Heartfelt homage to Ngawang Trinle Tendzin Namgyel—
Divine **lord of speech** (*ngag dbang*)[1] who maintained subsequent rebirths without forgetting,
Sun whose thousand lights of marvelous **enlightened activity** (*phrin las*) at the time of near attainment,
Who emanated as a lotus, **holder** (*'dzin*) of the **Buddhist teaching** (*bstan*),
And recalled the three mysteries of the Supreme Conqueror!

In this northern region of Uru, the sphere that maintains the Land of Snows, the detailed account of the precious Buddhist teaching of the Sugata Akṣobhya at Taklung combining both religious and political affairs is well known to have had three phases—the early dissemination, the intermediate dissemination, and the later dissemination.

Among them, at the start of the later dissemination at Taklung, it was Ngawang Trinle Tendzin Namgyel Pelzangpo, the peerless lord of refuge, who perceived all knowable things and elucidated the Buddhist teaching. {816} Concerning him, it says the following in a sealed prophetic declaration of the great master Padmasambhava:

> When you, Lotsāwa Kawa Peltsek, have passed away
> And journeyed to the divine land of Tuṣita,
> Here in Tibet many emanational translators will quarrel,
> But in this ordinary time, one named Gyadrong will emanate
> And perform acts of great benefit to living beings.

And,

Having established the old tradition of the teaching of the sacred doctrine,
From this point until cyclic existence has been emptied,
He will maintain the Buddhist teaching and establish sentient beings in happiness.

In accordance with such extensive prophetic declarations, and in accordance with the wishes of the emanations of the ocean of conquerors of infinite pure lands, one named Gyadrong manifested in human form in Penyul, Land of the Quick-Witted. He was descended from the Khyung family of mantrins and adept in the occult power of mantrins who espouse the following teachings: The Peaceful and Wrathful Guru as the spiritual teacher, The Eight Pronouncements of Spiritual Attainment as the meditational deities, Four-Armed Mahākāla as the doctrinal protector, and Dorje Lekpa as the guardian. His father was On Tashi, and his mother was Tashi Lha, and he was the youngest of four siblings. He was born along with wondrous signs on the thirteenth day of the twelfth month of 1691 (iron female sheep). After seven days, his mother passed away, and he was nursed by his stepmother Tsering Dzompa. There was a prediction pertaining to him that said "In the valley of the local deities of Namtel and Choding, the sun will become a man of the northern region."

Venerable Tashi Jampel Gyatso from Taklung clearly revealed that the child recognized the possessions of his predecessor, {817} and when the Lamo Chokyong oracle also indicated that he was the reincarnation of Taklung Zhabdrung, who had to undergo a change of name and physical appearance, the authorities of Taklung gave him the name Losal Peljor. He traveled via Chak La to Lhundrub Dzong, where in front of the Tsepak Lhakhang, he had a vision of Padmasambhava, almost human size, that was most clear. Below the finest grass-covered hill near the confluence of Shara, he also perceived a blue-complexioned dwarf, his head covered with a white turban, but the accompanying government officials did not see this.

On reaching Ojo, in his fourth year, the child met Tashi Jampel Gyatso and, upon offering his ceremonial tonsure to become a mendicant, the name Ngawang Tashi Kunga Dondrub was conferred upon him. He attended on Gelong Peltso, Pema Chokchen, and others, and extensively studied without difficulty the writing and reading of the Tibetan alphabet and memorizing of the practical cycles of Secret Mantra according to the ancient and new traditions, and so forth. In Lhasa he paid homage to and witnessed the enthronement of Gyelwang Tsangyang Gyatso and saw in detail the supreme representative images of Lhasa headed by Jowo Śākyamuni, the representation of the Teacher. At the residence of the potentate [that is, Desi Sangye Gyatso, the regent of that time], he met Minling Terton Rinpoche and offered a ceremonial tonsure in his presence, indicative of ordination, whereupon the name Orgyen Tendzin Dondrub was bestowed upon him. He was given the empowerment of Guru Drakpo according to the new treasures, and the rites of renunciation and empowerment associated with that doctrinal cycle. Then, he traveled to Seling via Gyadrong. Henceforth, certain visions would arise to him that were beneficial for nurturing the doctrinal tradition of the monastic seat at Taklung. So it was that on this occasion when Tashi Jampel Gyatso had gone to Riwoche and was on his return journey to U, {818} the child rode out to welcome him at Dolema.

Commencing on the new year of 1699 (earth hare), Tashi Jampel Gyatso gradually conferred on him the empowerments and guidance of Vajrapāṇi and Sarvavid Vairocana. It was during the fifth month of that year that he first arrived at Taklung. At the time when Matang was in the government,[2] they arranged for his arrival there to be signaled with the blowing of a conch from the roof of the temple, and so an auspicious connection was spontaneously and properly established. He was ordained as a mendicant at Chodzong in the midst of a divine assembly, headed by the preceptor Jedrung Drakpa Lekdrub, Tere Namgyel, and Nyingla Dargye, and he was given the name Drakpa Tashi Ngedon Phuntsok. Along with Jam Gyama, he received many initiations and empowerments including *The Hundred Empowerments of the Peaceful Guru.* When he offered his ceremonial tonsure in the presence of Gyelwa Tsangyang Gyatso in Lhasa, he also became known under the name Rinchen Gonpo.

When Venerable Tashi Jampel Gyatso fell ill due to pollution, he could not receive more than the minor essentials of empowerment and transmission, but he did acquire a steadfast resolve and sacred outlook. Then the venerable one went to stay at Horkhang, taking with him very few possessions. The wealthy monks of that place provided good facilities for him in succession and arranged all necessities. During 1703 (water sheep), in a vision he clearly saw the three protectors—Ya, Du, and Tsen—and Genyen Chenpo revealed to him a document with a red seal from underneath an overhanging rock. This was an edict of Taklung Tangpa, which included the following prophetic declaration: "In the future, you should act as the master of the Buddhist teaching and also experientially cultivate the meaning contained in this document." Later, he understood that this was an auspicious coincidence, indicating that the teaching of the Taklung tradition would come into his hands.

During 1704 (wood monkey), for the benefit of living beings, he traveled to Sok via the nomadic encampments of Namtso and Tsomgo, {819} so thirty-seven horses and three hundred yaks came into his possession. Then, with the intention of immediately setting out for Mindroling, traveling via Uma Gyadrong, Kyechi Rabdon, Sel La, and Yangadruk, he was welcomed on horseback at Dramada and reached Mindroling. His mind merged together with the buddha mind of Terdak Lingpa, the great treasure-revealer and king of the sacred doctrine, who bestowed upon him the empowerments, guidance, and transmission for *The Heart Essence of the Awareness Holder: Subduer of Arrogant Spirits*,[3] *The Gathering of Arrogant Spirits by Norgyamama*,[4] and all of his new treasures in their entirety. At that time, he also experienced many visions due to his sacred outlook.

By studying and contemplating the major and minor fields of classical learning—including Sanskrit grammar, poetics, astrology, and divination, prosody—and the scripts of Rañjanā and Vartula, he comprehended them unimpededly, as if he had acquired the wisdom of Five-Tufted Mañjunātha, and he totally reached the summit of learning. He naturally learned how to make torma offerings, draw deity icons, and so forth, without having studied. He formed a close bond with his spiritual brethren, including the monastic official Rinchen Namgyel, Gyeltsab Tulku, Mawochok Dungyu, Kaḥtok Gyelse, Tsokchen Tulku, Pelri Tulku, the son of Dokharwa who was a student of classical learning,[5] Lolha Teji, and Tara Dopa. He made a detailed inspection of representative images of Mindroling, including the sacred relics within them.

At that time, the regent Sangye Gyatso was killed, and other such events occurred, so that the whole region was engulfed by unhappiness and chaos. Consequently, without delay, he returned home via Drak La. His former possessions were lost, all the herds of horses and yaks that he had were devastated, and so on. Just as in the biography of Venerable Mila Repa when he returned to his native land, this directly became a device for him to understand impermanence and the illusory nature. {820}

He met the venerable teacher Jampel Gyatso, received the sacred doctrine and requested a great many study methods, but it is said that he was slightly displeased. Not long after that, Venerable Jampel Gyatso passed away. He went to pay his respects to the sacred corpse and composed a prayer, and so forth. The minutiae of the funeral rites were carried out and a small silver reliquary, which is kept in Dakgyu Podrang, was commissioned by the ordinary monks.

Starting from then, Venerable Ngawang Trinle Tendzin, on many occasions, early and later in life, undertook infinite rites of service and attainment with respect to Vajrasattva, The Peaceful and Wrathful Guru, Cakrasaṃvara, Vajrapāṇi, and so forth. He possessed the three wheels of the generation stage of meditation, perfecting the appearances of the world and its inhabitants as deities, sounds as mantra, and recollections and thoughts as the wheel of buddha mind, and he was liberated in the inner radiance arising from the apprehension of the complete deity and subsequent recollection according to the perfection stage of meditation. Consequently, there were excellent indications that he had acquired spiritual accomplishments. In actuality, meditative experiences, and in dreams, he would meet his preferred deities and hear their teachings. All the infinite pure visions such as these that he had are clearly mentioned in his inner and secret biographies, so I will not present them here.

Ngawang Trinle Tendzin requested the Dolha of Gyadrong for Changling, Choding, and Taktsawa and took possession of them. Without delay, he then went to Choding and occupied the teaching throne of Marton Rinchen Śākya and Khedrub Zhonu Lodro. There, he conferred maturational empowerments and liberating guidance on many fortunate disciples.

At that time, the whole region was afflicted by an outbreak of smallpox, and so for that reason, he stayed in retreat. When his attendant arrived there one evening, there was a raven flying that had not been previously noticed. It alighted above his dwelling, cawed, vomited, flapped its wings in various ways, and then flew off. The next day, {821} his voice was stuffed with cold, and consequently he caught nothing but a wheeze and a mild, nonvirulent form of the pox. He intentionally mingled with those in his entourage, and then from Yungwada this mild contagion gradually spread through the region. More than a thousand people were saved. Accordingly, it was known that the local deity had offered this protection to him, and everyone had faith and paid homage to him.

After that, he went to Taklung, where Jangtse Khenpo instructed him in the use of the poetic ornament of denial according to the second chapter of Daṇḍin's *Mirror of Poetics*. He also focused his intention on repairing the gilded roof above the Great Offering Chapel at Taklung. Thereafter, he again had to assume responsibility for Janglung Choding and appointed

Tsultrim as his representative teacher here. He made offerings in the hilltop protector chapels of Draklung Ya Gangchen and then traveled on horseback as far as Tsowok and Namru, where he took possession of some two hundred horses and three hundred and fifty yaks. He then met Minling Terton when the latter traveled to Lhasa, receiving some doctrinal connections and presenting fine offerings.

On the waxing half of the third month, in his twenty-first year, he received in succession from the retired Ganden Tripa Dondrub Gyatso the lay, novitiate, and full-fledged ordinations. The name Lobzang Tenpei Nyima Pelden Lodor was conferred upon him. He also requested the extensive empowerment of Vajrabhairava according to the tradition of Ra Lotsāwa. Then traveling via Gyeldrong, Penkar La, Ruk La, Kama, Nyonruk, Khartok, Nyingpo, Setsa, and so forth, he returned home.

Zhabdrung Tashi Tobgyel from Riwoche passed away, and he went there for the funeral ceremony, and perfectly conferred the maturational empowerment rites. He commissioned the thirty-eight painted scrolls of the Kagyu Dratsang, {822} and then he went to Drigung because he was interested in the doctrinal cycles of the Kagyu tradition as a whole and met in person with Lord of the Buddhist Teaching Wheel, Konchok Trinle Zangpo, emanation of the Sugata Phakmodrupa. An extraordinary power of faith was born within him, and he received infinite teachings, including the great empowerment of Cakrasaṃvara and guidance on the Great Seal and Great Perfection. Incidentally, he also resolved his doubts concerning astrology and the Rañjanā and Vartula scripts.

Under Bondrong Chodze he received instruction on *The Grammar of Sarasvata*, and then, when Dharmaśrī, the great monastic preceptor of Mindroling, was en route for Chamdo, he met him on the way and held a doctrinal discussion, such that their minds mutually rejoiced. He received many doctrines pertaining to the cycle of monastic discipline.

Then, wishing to see the sacred places of the south, Ngawang Trinle Tendzin traveled directly to Gya La and made all sorts of pilgrimages, passing days at Onbu Taktsang, Densatil, Tsetang, Nedongtse, Tradruk, Tsechu Bumpa, Sheldrak, Samye, and Chimphu. The five images of Pehar at Samye actually bowed before him and received commitments from him. Also, the acolyte Gopo Tare at first assaulted him with miracles, but later he subdued that spirit by means of meditative stability and bound him under an oath of allegiance. Gradually, he made his way to the Drigung Tsewa estate, where he met the lord lama and encountered the inestimable kindness of his combined spiritual and material activities.

On returning to Taklung via Lungsho, Ngawang Trinle Tendzin cremated the body of Zhabdrung Gongma Ojowa. After restoring a reliquary stūpa, he inserted within it most of the sacred bone relics and funerary ash and performed a consecration ceremony. {823} He made icons of the former hierarchs, including those of thirty-seven Kagyu monasteries and the lineage of teachers of the Great Perfection, and he inserted their mantra cores. Along with the assembled monks of Domsumling, he imbued these with the essential nature of the being of pristine cognition and installed them separately in Utse, in the Northern Chapel, and at Choding. He performed the ritual service of two colored sand maṇḍalas, those of Vajrasattva and Amitāyus, and bestowed the extensive empowerments at the elaborate offering of attainment in Choding upon a large public gathering of monks and laity.

Ngawang Trinle Tendzin composed a fervent prayer for the benefit of others when Terdak Lingpa of Mindroling passed away. In early and later years, in times of severe drought, he induced downpours of varying intensity, weak and strong, and he consecrated the springs of Namar and Dara. Consequently, there were many early and later occasions on which he protected many beings from the torments of heat by means of rainfall and most excellent water. Then, he traveled to his disciples in the north.

Yizhin Trinle Chokdrub, the supreme tulku of Venerable Jampel Gyatso, sent gifts along with an invitation from Riwoche. He set out on the fourth day of the third month of 1715 (wood sheep) and traveled via Tsomo Rawa, Jangkhu La, Drong Ngur, Shakhul, Druya, and so forth. He met together with Zhabdrung Phakchok Tashi Wangyel, Tse Zhabdrung Orgyen Tashi Namgyel, and others at the glorious monastic seat of Yisho. They convened an extensive and most excellent banquet of the sacred doctrine, combined with material hospitality, and at that time the monasteries and all the monks and laity offered him their sincere respect. He commissioned a manuscript of the twelve volumes of *The Transcendent Perfection of Wisdom in One Hundred Thousand Lines*, and at that time six hundred and thirty-two loads of offering tea were used. The precious teacher performed the consecration. Blessed objects and artifacts including a footprint of Taklung Tangpa and about a hundred multiplying bone relics sequentially came into his possession. {824}

After received parting gifts that were publicly and privately offered, Ngawang Trinle Tendzin returned gradually to U. He stopped to undertake practice successively at Semodo and Jangur by Lake Namtso and then reached the great monastic seat of Taklung during the seventh month. There, he met up with Tsetrul Kunga Tendzin Nyima from Powo and Ngawang Tashi Trinle Chokdrub, the reincarnation of Jampel Gyatso, and bestowed excellent reciprocating gifts upon the two groups of ritual officiants and three groups of ordinary monastic officials.

To Kunpang Zhab, he imparted guidance on the first and second chapters of *The Mirror of Poetics*, and he bestowed this along with the most profound doctrinal connection of Drigung. After that, the venerable tulkus set out for Mount Kailash and to see the power places of Nepal. In that somewhat insecure period, they performed extensive long-life rituals, including a hundred smoke offerings, a hundred rites of fulfillment, the recitation of *The Transcendent Perfection of Wisdom in One Hundred Thousand Lines*, and so forth. When he dreamed that he was in the presence of the image of Taklung Tangpa in the Lower Hall of the Offering Chapel, he had signs and meditative experiences suggesting that the monastic seat would revert to its former auspicious state.

When Drigung Kuzhab extended an invitation, he went there to Drigung. Although he himself was unwell, he accepted and conferred empowerments, guidance, long-life empowerments, and so forth. He also offered a longevity prayer, but because the times were adverse, Drigung Zhabdrung passed away into nirvāṇa. The lamas of Drigung and Taklung assembled together and performed the cremation. On the way back to Taklung, he performed many acts of benefit to living beings in Lungsho, and then at Choding he entered into retreat, practicing the great ritual service of Cakrasaṃvara.

Kunpang Tenpei Nyima Rinpoche returned after completing his pilgrimage. They met together at Taklung, and Kunpang excellently fulfilled his wishes with empowerments, transmissions, and so forth. {825} In turn, he offered Kunpang parting gifts and useful necessities. For the monastic community of Choding, he extensively prepared elaborate day-long communion ceremonies, communal alms offerings, and offering sacraments.

On the third day of the first month of 1719 (earth pig), with just a couple of attendants, he conveniently departed from Choding and went down to the ford on the Kyichu. Traveling via Mangra, Drigung, Gyelra, and Gang La, he reached Jeri Taktse. He visited Buchu Lhakhang in Kongpo, and traveling together with Kunpang Rinpoche, the people of Kanam in Powo respectfully paid homage to him. He received assistance and excellent support on the way. Fulfilling the hopes of all according to their wishes, he acted for the benefit of many living beings through his manifold doctrinal connections and so forth.

Then he traveled through Menchu Gon, Demo Chamnak, Chongrong, Trelo, and so forth. Reaching the valley of Makung, the great power place where ḍākinīs gathered, he experienced an inconceivable array of pure visions, as is clearly stated in his spiritual songs and in his secret biography.

He undertook the great ritual service of Amitābha, lord of Sukhāvatī, and he refined experiential cultivation of the yogic exercises of vital energy, such that the pristine cognition of bliss and emptiness was effortlessly born within him. He secured all phenomenal existence in the great seal of inner radiance, the wheel of pure deities and mantras.

He offered service to Drigung Zhabdrung Chodrak and his attendants, and they formed a close bond. When an anthrax contagion was extremely virulent in Sikkim, he was invited there to implement remedial means. By propitiating the Wrathful Krodha, there were harsh signs of success that abundantly manifested, including earth tremors and lightning bolts. Although the village was destroyed and many people and cattle died, {826} and the house where Venerable Ngawang Trinle Tendzin himself was staying was destroyed from its foundations, a ceramic cup on the table in front of him fell but did not break and the shrine and the torma offerings were also undamaged. This most astonishing event was ascertained to indicate the miraculous ability through which he had acquired self-control over the vital winds and mind. Although the earth shook without interruption over two days and nights, on the night of the fifteenth day, he performed the burnt offering of the Wrathful Krodha, and starting from then, the disturbances were calmed, pacified, and assuaged. On behalf of the entire population of that land, he performed the empowerment of the Wrathful Krodha, the burnt offering of *The Gathering of All Rare and Precious Things*,[6] and so forth, and then he went to Latsoka.

After that, Ngawang Trinle Tendzin intended to travel in stages directly to Riwoche. That year, the supreme leader of gods and men, Seventh Dalai Lama, Kalzang Gyatso, was enthroned in the Potala Place, and the army of the Manchu emperor returned home. Around that time, he traversed the southern route without harm, though the trail was extremely narrow. He went via Drongra Gon, Olhung Gon, Lho Dzong, Delamok Gon, Gyangshok, Netrab, Ngangpo Gon, and Bu La,[7] and in each location he was respectfully received. He accepted their offerings and excellently planted the seeds of omniscience and liberation in all those who saw, heard, recollected, and came in contact with him. At the glorious monastic seat of Yisho, he met together with Kyabgon Phakchok Rinpoche and Tse Zhabdrung Orgyen Tashi. Bountiful material offerings were made, and he satisfied the great assembly with the resources for a hundred million recitations of the six-syllable mantra, communal tea offerings, public alms distribution, and so forth. Thinking to stay there for some years, he cut off contact with the outside world at the Achok Mountain Hermitage. While he was staying there, one night, in a dream, {827} the protector of the transmitted teachings Genyen Chenpo appeared with a large entourage and was hospitably received by a proud local horseman raising a banner. The next day, when he was making a smoke offering to the gods, people carrying an invitation from Taklung Lower Plain arrived.

In U, the times were all peaceful due to the enthronement of Gyelwang Seventh Dalai Lama. In particular, all the monastic officials and subjects of Taklung were in retreat, and so Zhabdrung Ngawang Tsangpa had assumed responsibility, and the monastic seat had naturally been bestowed on him. Though the descendants of Gaji, who had maintained the monastic seat in the past were to be appointed in the service of the Ganden Podrang government, the son and heir of that line had fallen ill, and for a while, the family was incapable of serving. In his place, the young tulku Trinle Chokdrub was found, but he had not studied much, so Zhabdrung Tashi Chokyi Tulku [that is, Ngawang Trinle Tendzin], who was older and erudite, was ordered to maintain that seat. He was presented with a decree issued by Lord Rakshak and letters issued by three monastic officials belonging to the *labrang*, the public administration, and the private residents, insisting that he should go to Taklung by all means. The holy lama thought that it would be excellent if he were to perform any sort of service on behalf of the Buddhist teachings, but if the external and internal circumstances were to change, he would not be of benefit to the Buddhist teaching and in addition the meditative commitments between teacher and disciples would be interrupted. After making a detailed consideration of these reasons in their entirety, he resolved that he should decline that request, but the venerable masters of the sacred doctrine from Riwoche, headed by Jetsun Phakpei Chok, said that that would not be appropriate and that he should go. As soon as the thought arose in his mind that he should return to U, he made his decision during the last month of the year[8] and {828} swiftly set out for the monastery. At Yangri, he propitiated Cakrasaṃvara and offered the empowerments of the Adamantine Garland and the twelve maṇḍalas of *The Purification of the Lower Realms*[9] to Lama Rinpoche.

Yet again, he passed the time in propagating the teachings by means of empowerment, transmission, pith instructions, and exegeses. All the monks of the palace, the public administration, and private residents, then presented him with parting gifts, and he gradually set out via Drigung Til, Yangri Gar Tsewa, and so forth, and on the twelfth day of the eighth month, he reached Setsa, where he was welcomed on horseback by Choktrul Yizhin Trinle Chokdrub Rinpoche. After offering scarves had been presented, this was an event resembling the meeting described in the account of Orgyen Rinpoche and Tri Songdetsen. Indeed Choktrul Rinpoche went to study under him, saying, "By all means please make this your monastic seat!"

To repay the kindness of his predecessor, the supreme tulku Tashi Jampel Gyatso, and so as not to neglect the injunction of the Lord Tsangpa Rakshak and not to disappoint the monastic community of Taklung—for these three reasons and since from birth he had had the title Taklung Tulku and until now had been contented with food given through faith and vegetarian or dairy food—his service on behalf of the Buddhist teaching also fell into three phases—early, intermediate, and later. Among these, at the start of the later phase, he considered that it would not be permissible for him to avoid assuming great hardships, like those required to raise Taklung from its foundations. So, he pledged to fulfill the hopes and aspirations of all. Welcomed in front by a procession of the assembled monks, and by dances performed by the lay subjects of Taklung, and so forth, he then presented an offering maṇḍala in front of the image of Gyelchok Taklung Tangpa the Great, in the grass hermitage of Taklung, and at a thanksgiving banquet in the hall known as Zimdrub Deko, {829} he gave an oral exegesis that was endowed with the five excellences at the beginning, middle, and end. He satisfied the assembled groups of lamas with excellent gifts, and on the nineteenth day of the ninth month, a day coinciding with an auspicious planet and constellation, he assumed his seat upon the lion throne of the sacred doctrine belonging to the succession of supreme conquerors of Taklung, the soles of his feet marked with auspicious wheels. Together, the tulkus, monastic preceptors, and teachers scattered flowers, and at the same time the peaceful and wrathful deities and their heirs who reside in the expanse caused a downpour of coral flower garlands, saying, "Let virtue prevail! May this be auspicious!"

Thereupon, on behalf of the assembled monks, he gave an extensive exegesis on the doctrine of guru yoga, such that the entire monastic assembly experienced the hairs of their faith standing on end, horripilating strongly. This was the first joyous feast at which the indications of virtuous action were newly expressed, as they clasped their palms together on the crowns of their heads. The second occurred when he took his seat on the throne of the sacred doctrine in the Ten-Pillar Chapel of the Main Temple. The third was when he took his seat on the dark throne in the midst of the assembly in the Lower Hall. He was granted the official government status, and he accepted the enthronement offering scarves presented to him by all the high, low, and middle ranking lamas of the monastery, headed by the Choktrul, the Dokhar Zhabdrung, and the Ling Zhabdrung. He made a dedication of merit, accompanied by an exegesis on patronage.

On the twentieth day, he then went to Domsumling, and he established this residence once more at the labrang of the monastery. He met the officer in charge of the imperial Chinese army, as well as the senior and junior Sino-Mongol officials including General Yan Xin[10] and General Dorje Amban,[11] who respectfully paid homage, knowing that he had accepted to gather all the important responsibilities naturally under his control. {830}

Then, on the twenty-ninth day, when he placed the representative torma offering in the Protector Chapel of Oselko and performed the rites of reparation and fulfillment, there were some large drops of dew that actually gathered on the image of glorious Four-Faced Mahākāla. In addition, he ensured that the scheduled anniversary offerings, the smoke offerings, and so forth were undertaken more profoundly and more extensively than in the past. In the winter, he went to Penyul, where he acted greatly for the benefit of living beings, and in Lhasa he had a joyous audience with the omniscient and all-seeing Gyelwang, Seventh Dalai Lama, with whom he had a patron-priest relationship. He met the *zhabdrungs* of Gaji and their minds formed a close bond. He went to see the two images of Munīndra, the natural image of Mahākāruṇika, and other images in Lhasa and the Potala, and altogether he made a hundred offerings along with aspiration prayers.

At the new year of 1722 (water tiger), in the Tromzikhang in Lhasa, he met Tendzin Wang, Pelrab Khangsar, the secretary of the Senior General Yabje, and so forth, and they presented him with offering scarves. Each of them obtained joyous teachings and transmissions. Then, heading back via the same road as before, he reached the monastic seat of Taklung.

Starting in the third month of that year, he began the first of his restoration projects, removing and replacing the Flower Garden Wall and the area around the Layel Courtyard and the grass hermitage. When there was some risk of a contagious disease spreading in the Dratsang, he performed a burnt offering of the four rites, which was most beneficial. He established a workshop for restoring the Great Offering Chapel. Over two and a half months, he stripped and redecorated the vestibule, the middle hall, the entire northern wing, the ten-pillar Lama Lhakhang, the Lima Lhakhang, the Ngulku Lhakhang, and so forth. At the same time, he rebuilt from their foundations the Old Offering Chapel and the chapel of the local deity Dobuk. Without obstacle, he successfully repaired the White Temple, {831} the Red Throne, the reliquary stūpas, and the small chapel for propitiating the Kagyu lineage, which were certainly very dilapidated and in need of reconstruction. He was efficacious in matters that were charged and entrusted to the protector deities, such that there were clear signs and indications that the protectors had been accepted into his service.

Starting from then, Ngawang Trinle Tendzin opened wide the treasury of guidance, empowerment, transmission, and pith instruction with respect to the Great Seal and the Six Doctrines on behalf of certain interested persons, such that, by giving them whatever they needed, they attained liberation. Those who experienced this feast of the doctrine were inconceivable.

Tsetrul Tendzin Nyima from Riwoche suddenly passed away, and he effectively performed the funeral ceremony. That autumn, in the area of Penyul, he granted maturational empowerments, liberating guidance, and oral instructions to those who wished for them, and he received abundant offerings of grain. Then, Tse Zhabdrung Tashi Namgyel arrived from Riwoche and met him. During the excellent reception held on his behalf, news arrived that Mine Rinpoche Phakchok Tashi Wangyel had passed away into the taintless Akaniṣṭha, so immediately he had the local and visiting monks prepare an extensive cloud of offerings for the funeral ceremony.

Tse Zhabdrung then returned to Riwoche, and he accompanied him on horseback as far as Nak Gu. On the way, at Drigung Tsewa, he met Choktrul Tendzin Drodul and went to request a doctrinal connection. On the way back, at Taphur, Childa, Dre Nak Gu, Chor, Kama Gon, Lege, Kharto, Kharchung, Namde, and so forth, he fulfilled the wishes of all that were publicly and privately expressed. Then, after passing the new year at Nyon, he stayed for a short while at Khartok, {832} Chage, Gyawodong, and

Seling, before immediately returning to the monastic seat. He excellently completed the drapery of the upper and lower offering chapels, the murals of the entire Main Temple, and so forth. From that year on, he also extensively reinstated those offerings of attainment that had been discontinued in the intervening period.

Ngawang Trinle Tendzin then focused his intention on newly constructing a gilded roof above the Main Temple. The master, together with an entourage of thirteen, went via Drakpu and Drilam to the five lakes of Namru, around Drong Tso, and via Bardha and so forth, and they stayed a while at Namtso. They obtained a large quantity of offerings including horses, yaks, butter, and silver, and he assigned these to be placed in trust in a storeroom to be used for the restoring of the gilded roof. He set up a workshop, commencing on the nineteenth day of the fourth month. The unadulterated smelted gold amounted to one hundred and forty-six *sang*, and the mercury was three times that. The wages, food, expenses, and gifts on behalf of the artisans and corvee laborers altogether amounted to six thousand four hundred and forty-seven silver *sang*. The materials were not squandered. Everything connected with the project was exclusively auspicious and spontaneously accomplished. In addition to the inner relics that were extant from before, the building was filled to the brim with an abundance of new offerings, including pearl relics, representations of buddha body, speech, and mind, the doctrinal conch of Marpa, and so forth. Commencing with the initial construction rites, until the concluding profound and extensive consecration ceremony, the work was perfectly carried out in an authentic manner and without impediment, such that its wonders exceeded those of the Brahmā realms. He replastered the walls of the Central Offering Chapel, and reconstructed the cliff grottoes of the sixteen elders, the murals, the stūpa symbolizing enlightenment, and the receptacle of long-life attainment. {833} When he brought the Hair of Dromton relics to be placed here, within the Ten-Pillar Temple, he knew the ways in which benefit would come to hundreds of spiritual and temporal traditions. He asked that it should be installed at the center of Utse.

That summer, behind the reliquary stūpas, he conferred empowerments and undertook burnt offerings on behalf of Pontsang Drasar, his wife, and children. He climbed the hill to the rear and had a vision in which the pebbles laid out below the palace[12] on this side, representing the clusters of the deities upon their seats in the supreme maṇḍala, appeared as the buddha bodies and pristine cognitions.

Ngawang Trinle Tendzin many times received encouragement from the protector deities, and so forth, in dreams, and accordingly he set out via Drak Phu, Dechen, Yangpachen, and Shogu La, and reached Zabulung in Tsang. He extensively bestowed a hundred communal feast offerings in connection with this sacred place, and so forth. Although he saw that according to *The Seven Treasure Prophecies*[13] there were many treasure troves there, he was not particularly interested. He visited sacred places of the ancient and new traditions including Tana, Mishang, and Sobuk, and then he went to Shogu Marnang via Ribgong, where he met Drigung Tulku Rinpoche. After obtaining offerings of attainment, he raced back via Yer La to reach the monastic seat of Taklung, where he remained in retreat for seven days in the Utse and also experienced certain visions and prophetic declarations.

During the waxing half of the fourth month, he extensively performed over three days the preparatory rite and main part of the consecration ceremony in the Upper Offering Chapel,[14] according to the Luipāda tradition of Cakrasaṃvara. The sky was filled with rainbows, and in the perceptual range of all, the rainbow clouds entirely assumed the form of the eight auspicious symbols. {834} When the Tulku Rinpoche of Gampo arrived, he offered hospitality and a profound doctrinal connection.

Then, on the twenty-ninth day of the third month, Venerable Ngawang Trinle Tendzin with entourage, about twenty in all, rode off from Taklung. He considered whether he should go via Ulung and upper Bidam to the borders of lower Hor to collect offerings, but when he reached the northern region of Nakchu, the protector deity of Riwoche insistently exhorted him. Accordingly, he traveled gradually instead via Jangkhu La, Omchang, Drong Ngur, Shakchu, upper and lower Atrak, Memo La, Bonzhung, Serzhun, Drongpa, and so forth, and reached the glorious monastic seat of Yisho on the waxing half of the tenth month. There, he was welcomed and met by Tse Zhabdrung Tashi Namgyel and was received with fine hospitality. He bestowed gifts on all, in public and in private. In an auspicious gathering coinciding with the enthronement of Jedrung Tulku of Yangon, he offered the vows of the novitiate to him and conferred the name Drakpa Rinchen Sherab Lhundrub upon him.[15]

Then, carrying bountiful material gifts, he journeyed via Dra La, Shetang, and so forth. He offered many treasure vases at Tamekor and was sincerely respected also by many red-hat and yellow-hat monasteries. He pitched camp at Seyi Zampa, and traveling gradually via Memo La, he was welcomed by Choktrul Rinpoche at Gode and, with him, reached the plain of Taklung. He replenished the storerooms with altogether six hundred and forty loads of tea, two hundred horses, and hybrid cattle. And to the common monks, he bequeathed wealth to the value of a hundred silver *sang*.

Then, setting out for Lhasa at the end of the fourth month, he made offerings in the presence of the supreme guide, Seventh Dalai Lama, Kelzang Gyatso, {835} presenting him with three hundred and one horses and yaks. The latter bestowed upon him more extensively than before woven carpets, rear curtains, dairy products, tables, and so forth, and he decreed, "Since you Taklungpa are great in your service to the Ganden government, you are the sort that should be rewarded. Accordingly, you are formally instated as the proprietor or executor of the monastic seat of Taklung. Since you have indeed shown excellent respect for this institution, from now on you may come and stay, as you did in the past. The government will receive you hospitably when going and coming, and so forth. You may assume your former station and your former place." Thereupon the regent displayed his great pleasure, saying, "This decree, which cannot be rescinded, includes that very expression of gratitude. We sanction this, your humble manner of traveling and staying!"

Moreover, he had detailed discussions and meetings with the minister Zhabdrung Tsering Wangyel, just as in the past he had been received with hospitality by the kingly father of the Dalai Lama and the administrative offices of the spiritual and secular authorities and so forth, and they expedited the offerings of attainment for Taklung.

Although in the past the public property of the monastery had been maintained by the monastery itself, in the intervening period, there had been diverse fluctuations in the harvest and water supply, and he had therefore assumed responsibility for the donations prepared by everyone. So, in 1728 (earth monkey), intelligent persons considered that these provisions should be of great benefit for any of the three institutions at Taklung—the palace, the college, or the monastery. He stayed in retreat during the eighth month of that year and undertook the great ritual service of Cakrasaṃvara and Guru Drakmar, along with the supplementary burnt offerings, and he experienced diverse visions.

In 1729 (earth bird), Drupa Chojung purposefully arrived from Riwoche. Taklung insisted to him that either only two lamas or one alone should come to visit. {836} Although Tashi Gelek, the supreme reincarnation of Jampel Gyatso, who was also known as Trinle Chokdrub, wished to come,

Venerable Ngawang Trinle Tendzin considered that that would be disastrous. Though firmly postponed, the matter was not settled, whereupon Choktrul himself made the decision to come.

Early and later during that year, Ngawang Trinle Tendzin performed the vase consecration ritual about fourteen times, including two vase consecration rites on behalf of Pon Banak and two vase consecration rites of Maṇivajra[16] on behalf of Lama Chogyel's household at Drong. The monastic communities there satisfied him with their respect.

Then, on the first day of the fifth lunar month, at Yang Gon Samdrub Dechen, in the presence of the representative icon of the Teacher named Zangtangma, and the lifelike image of Venerable Taklung Tangpa, the Choktrul received the full monastic ordination, with Venerable Ngawang Trinle Tendzin Namgyel acting as the monastic preceptor, Deno Gyatso acting as an officiant, and others acting as the timekeeper and confessor, in the midst of forty monks who made up the assembly. The name Ngawang Tashi Pelden Chokyi Nyima was conferred upon him.

Then, in accordance with the venerable lama's injunction, they excellently prepared camping equipment, tents, cooking utensils, saddles, an entourage, and so forth—in short, the necessities for a journey away from home—and he appointed superior servants and a resolute muleteer, and a feast was held on behalf of the master Choktrul and his entourage of twenty-five, at which a stipend and provisions were offered. Everyone, great and small, offered appropriate parting gifts, and then although they announced that they would prepare together for a year-long journey, it transpired that, owing to the prearranged riding escort and cooking escort, Venerable Ngawang Trinle Tendzin went with them only as far as Dam Uma. {837} On the way back, he traveled via Yangra and Setsa and reached the monastic seat.

When various signs appeared to him concerning the Seng Cham Karmo Lhakhang, he moved the representative artifacts from that temple.

During the eighth month, certain dignitaries arrived in connection with the funeral ceremonies for Jetsun Dampa of the Qalqa Mongols, who had passed away, and they met him, thereby achieving excellent merit. To each of the monks, they sent about fifteen different sorts of alms, including a silver *sang*, silk brocade, offering scarves, herbal medications, an assortment of Mongolian silk, five-colored silk threads, and needles.

When he visited Lhasa, he met with and paid homage to the Governor Sonam Tobgyel and pleased him, such that excellent merits were secured. As commanded, he also bestowed the desired sacred doctrine upon Rakshak

Zhabdrung Kalon and Tashi Pel Rinpoche. Then, after visiting, paying homage, and presenting offerings to the representation of Jowo Śākyamuni in the Jokhang, he returned home to Taklung.

When Tā Lama, the representative of the emperor, was on his way back to Lhasa, and stayed overnight at the monastery, he met him, and their minds were compatible.

When he received the invitation of Namar Pontsang Basar to undertake activity on behalf of the sacred doctrine, without sustenance being provided, although he was sure that there was a lot of snow there, he set out, disregarding hardship, for the sake of others. By rites of purification and so forth, he brought them on to the path of liberation. Having fulfilled the hopes of the Banak tribes and so forth, he returned to Taklung. Before that, in conformity with a dream of Seling Gomchen Zhiwo, he performed rites of reception and aversion in order to dispel obstacles to the continuity of his lifespan and obtained excellent signs that the obstacles had been calmed for fifteen years.

He decided that Gaji Zhabdrung Tashi Pelden should, for a while, not travel to Kham. Ngawang Trinle Tendzin himself went as far as Nak Gu and escorted him on the way back {838} from Lhakhang Chenga Bumpa, through the mountains, and back to Taklung.

He then performed the ceremonies marking the period at the end of 1729 (earth bird) and the new year festival of 1730 (iron dog). He repaired the hermitage and the college for the study and practice of spiritual songs.[17] He constructed a Tashi Gomang–style stūpa in lower Seling as a means to secure the well-being of Tibet and Kham. He also completed the assembly hall of Janglung Choding Monastery.

He greatly worried that in a dream the Choktrul was displeased, and although all his entourage had arrived, he himself was not actually present. He therefore went to pray at Ya Gangchen, and on the way back down at Drewulung, positive indications and excellent signs arose.

He stayed for some days in retreat there and established the recognizable features of that sacred place. Within it, there was a hermitage of Lhungyi Sherab, the emanation of Drogon Pema Karpo and a rock in the shape of Vajravārāhī's body, with representations of the three primary channels and the five cakras. The latter included a cave where nāgas are tamed at the bliss-sustaining secret cakra, the abode of Rāhula at the navel cakra of emanation. And among the three caves—upper, middle, and lower—at the heart cakra of the doctrinal wheel, there were the naturally arising deities and mantras in the lower cave, the maṇḍala of Guru Drakpo in the middle cave, and the naturally formed throne and offering platform of Guru Rinpoche in the upper cave, and many unclear footprints in all three caves, as well as natural formations representing Cakrasaṃvara, the deities of *The Eight Pronouncements of Spiritual Attainment*,[18] and the divine assemblage of Mahākāla. In addition, there was the inconceivable naturally arising cave of the peaceful and wrathful deities at the throat cakra, and the energy cakra of supreme bliss at the crown. He had visions of many wondrous arrays, including the palace of the pure buddha field of the buddha body of reality.

Zhabdrung Tashi Pelden was then sent back to take care of Riwoche with a facilitating band of monks and laypeople. {839}

On the fourteenth day of the eighth month in 1731 (iron pig), whether on account of his travels or simply due to a change in physical appearance, Riwoche Choktrul's mind and speech became extremely frail. Before his twenty-fifth year had passed, it was said that he should stay in strict retreat, but he was prone to obstacles since his studies had not been great. When he was brought to Rongnakgu, he suddenly passed away due to a severe illness. For the sake of others, Ngawang Trinle Tendzin perfectly carried out the funeral ceremonies and the outer, inner, and secret activities that are appropriate, replete with advice.

Then, in a vision, he encountered one named Kyabgon Phakpa, who said, "It is appropriate to change your name and physical appearances since obstacles have arisen." So, he assumed the name Rikdzin Tsewang Tashi, and in dress he adopted the ways of an awareness holder. He said that henceforth Guru Padmākara would actually manifest to him and sometimes appear in the form of his root guru and that he also obtained certain prophetic declarations.

At the end of 1731 (iron pig) and the start of 1734, as commanded by the king of Tibet, he undertook rites of service and attainment and rites of aversion through the continuous mantra recitation of Mahākāla and so forth, to secure the well-being of the whole of Tibet and Kham. At the request of Menwa in Jang, he prepared elaborate torma offerings representing the sense fields, and prayed one-pointedly to Mahāguru (Padmākara). Consequently, he experienced ecstatic pure visions on the basis of which he recorded in writing *The Mother and Child Doctrinal Cycles of the Three Roots*.

From the seventh day of the fourth month, for the benefit of the Buddhist teaching and living beings, he established a workshop for the construction of an image of Mahāmaitreya. This task was completed without impediment, and an excellent accumulation of auspicious circumstances that had not been prearranged unfolded of their own accord. {840}

He made the reliquary for Choktrul out of medicinal clay, in the form of a Tashi Gomang stūpa, and installed it in the story-high Lower Hall of the Main Temple, and in the aperture of the Gomang, he positioned the cluster of the deities of confession, along with the bodhisattvas and protector deities. This reliquary is indeed extant at the present time.

When he fell quite seriously ill due to food poisoning, the government and private individuals offered rites to secure his long life and so forth. According to the advice of Gyelwang Karmapa, he traveled to undertake the circumambulation of the lake at Namtso, and he stayed in retreat for a week at Jangur. Then, after recognizing the reincarnation of the lama Norbu Gyatso Dzong Namgyel Lekdrub, he was invited to Riwoche. He went there in the guise of a mendicant and was received with fine hospitality.

While staying at Yang Gon Tse, he became the focus of the wishes and aspirations of all. But eventually, he stayed at Horkhang without any fixed abode and became like a proverbial rolling stone. On the basis of the manuscript of *The Heart Essence of the Three Roots*,[19] he granted empowerment to five supplicants headed by Drigung Zhabdrung Konchok Tendzin Drodul, and extraordinary signs of meditative experience arose.

When he was invited by the Governor Dargye to Lhundrub Dzong, he repaired the chapel of the local deity and its shrine. When he placed a treasure vase in the direction of Dar and Tre, the soil became nutritious and the rainfall moderate. Jedrung Tulku and his disciples then arrived from Tonkham. He fulfilled their aspirations with the transmitted teachings of the sacred doctrine in general, full-ordination ceremonies, and so forth. And when Kalon Tsering Wangyel and his entourage came to Taklung for the offering of attainment, he joyfully fulfilled their wishes with spiritual and material gifts, such that the minds of the incumbents of the familial line and incarnation line of Taklung merged together like water and water. {841}

The reincarnation of that Tsetrul Tendzin Nyima, born in the Khyungpo area, was Tashi Gewei Wangpo. When he was invited to Riwoche, Ngawang Trinle Tendzin again considered going through Powo. Traveling in that direction, they were hospitably received with food and the like, as in the past.

During the seventh month, when the omniscient Gyelwang (Seventh Dalai Lama) was returning from Kham, he was incidentally invited here, to this sacred place of Taklung. He was offered an inspection tour of all the representative artifacts and sacred places, and they also requested the blessings of his entrustment, seated in the original temple at the center of the monastery. Since excellent arrangements were made to the measure of their ability, including servants, the supreme Conqueror, Seventh Dalai Lama, favored Taklung with his inspiration and great love.

In 1736 (fire dragon), Ngawang Trinle Tendzin experienced visions concerning the circumstances at Taklung, extending from the past to the future. Accordingly, the perception arose that the teaching of the Taklungpa would spread, expand, and thrive, at best for three hundred human years if they were to build a temple on the hillside behind the reliquary stūpas, on average for two hundred years if they were to build a temple at the footprint of Marpa, and at least for one hundred years if they were to build a temple in the center of the monastery. However, the first and second opportunities were both successively lost due to the actions of his attendants. They were lost because the auspicious season for undertaking such projects was not correct. Thinking that the last or third option should be carried out by all means whatsoever, he laid the lines at the geomantic center of the monastery. He then excellently performed the preliminary rite that consecrates the site and so forth in accordance with procedures outlined in the texts of the tantras and divination science, and he constructed the three-story temple that is known as Tashi Khangsar. Inside, he commissioned the three-dimensional palace of Cakrasaṃvara, perfect in all defining characteristics that are the unmistaken enlightened intention of the tantras—its array, ornaments, encircling rings, and so forth appearing as if the maṇḍala of naturally manifesting pristine cognition had actually been invited into it. Moreover, the task of making representational artifacts, exemplified by the image of Taklung Tangpa, the bas-relief sculptures, the murals and their varnishing, was well-organized and without obstacle. Finally, he performed the consecration by means of the ritual service and attainment of his preferred deities, headed by Cakrasaṃvara, and the excellent auspicious circumstances of fertile ground were actualized in the essential nature of that maṇḍala, where the being of commitment and the being of pristine cognition were indivisible. Zhabdrung Tashi Pelden then arrived from Riwoche and together, the resident and visiting monks offered an extensive long-life prayer on behalf of the emperor and the Dalai Lama, patron and priest, who resembled the pairing of sun and moon. To the visitors, he offered parting gifts, along with profound instructions that pertained to both traditions of sūtra and mantra.

In 1739 (earth sheep), after completing the excellent central temple, in order to renovate the sacred artifacts of the impartial traditions throughout the eight cardinal and intermediate directions, he understood that there were many meritorious signs concerning the flourishing of the Buddhist teaching and the blazing merits of the citizens of Tibet, and so, in the east, he constructed a Tashi Gomang stūpa. In the south, he repaired from its foundations the golden reliquary of Changlung Monastery. In the southeast, he repaired the Lama Lhakhang of Domsumling and newly commissioned the artifacts and fixtures of the Zhalgyi Gonkhang and so forth. In the west, he repaired the Great Offering Chapel and offered the deities white and red robes. In the southwest, sooner or later, he completed the upper and lower chambers of the Palace along with the chamber called Immortal Garden. In the northwest, he focused his attention on Drewulung. In the north, he restored Tashi Dowoche at Lake Namtso. By effortlessly accomplishing these gateways to subtle auspicious circumstances and the like, without error, {843} he was great on account of his unrivaled kindness that secured the well-being of the Buddhist teaching and living beings, in general and particular.

In 1740 (iron monkey), on the tenth day of the sixth month, he conferred maturational empowerments on some twenty monks at Driwulung and on more than a hundred attending the tenth-day ceremony from Dar, Tre, and Rong. And he established the places for attainment and the circumambulatory path, and so forth.

During 1741 (iron bird), when the reincarnation of the aforementioned Choktrul was born at Ojo, he undertook a detailed examination of the one who had been recognized. In a dream, there arose from the eastern direction a moon obscured by clouds that was sometimes clear and sometimes unclear. Thinking that the recognition would not be very beneficial for the Buddhist teaching, he merely accepted the ceremonial tonsure, and apart from simply naming the child Tangpa Tashi, he did not pay much attention to him.

When Ton Zhabdrung Phakchok Tulku Drakpa Gyeltsen arrived at Taklung, he was welcomed by a procession of monks in the former traditional manner. Ngawang Trinle Tendzin accepted his ceremonial tonsure and opened the gates of the sacred doctrine on his behalf. Without delay, he then set out for the seat of the nation in Lhasa, along with an entourage of the entire monastic body, and he offered extensive service on behalf of the emperor and the Dalai Lama, patron and priest. In return, he was rewarded with both spiritual and material wealth and also with fine words of praise. On returning to Taklung, he attended to his remaining activities, which included the conferral of the novitiate ordination.

Although some years had passed since Tsetrul Tashi Gewei Wangpo came here to Taklung, while he was staying in the Chotse, the grass hermitage of Gyelto, and so forth, the flower blooms were delayed and the grain was scarce. At that time, he was invited to Zurenang by Lama Gardampa. Ngawang Trinle Tendzin encouraged him to go and bestowed upon Tsetrul the empowerments, transmissions, doctrines, and so forth on which his intention had focused.

At the dawn of 1742 (water male dog), he received a prophetic declaration to the effect that if he were to produce a hundred copies of the Kangyur within three years, {844} the teaching of Taklung wound not undergo change for thirteen years. The monks of the college, monastery, and palace combined to produce a hundred copies of the Kangyur within three years.

He also received a prophetic declaration from the region of Cāritra to the effect that if he were to build a temple at the estate of Driwulung, it would revitalize the Buddhist teaching and political affairs, in general and in particular. Accordingly, after laying out the ground plan, he established a workshop and excellently completed the Single-Story Temple. He commissioned an image of Mahāmaitreya in the Lower Hall of the Offering Chapel, and he dismantled the poorly constructed old representative icon of Maitreya that had not been properly proportioned, and remodeled the lower legs. He completed these two bodhisattva figures, along with Śākyamuni in the form Tubwang Drongkhyer and Lokeśvara, and then held a grand consecration festival.

A group then arrived from Riwoche to invite him back, but he delayed and procrastinated lest the continuity of his lifespan come to an end. Tsetrul therefore went to stay in solitary retreat in Sewalung and Ojo.

When Venerable Ngawang Trinle Tendzin was staying at Nyingdrung hot springs, his former ailment recurred. Long-life rites were performed, and then through medical treatment, he slightly improved. In order to alleviate the course of his lifespan, he knew that he should go on pilgrimage—at best to Mount Kailash, on average to Tsāri, and at worst to Namtso—but he did not manage to go in person and sent one Ngakpel Gelong in his place. The venerable one himself went to Tashi Dowoche at Namtso via Ulung and Dri Lagen. He had a vision in which, in the sky directly above the pinnacle of the stone, in the midst of five masses of cloud, five groups of ḍākinīs clearly appeared, along with the eight manifestations of Padmākara. He asked his attendants what they could see, and they replied that they could see only clouds. {845} He stayed there in retreat, and on breaking the retreat, he went on a circumambulation of the lake, during which he also saw an inestimable number of the guru's clear handprints.

At that time, his extensive outer life was at its end. The patron Golon Migen Tsering invited him to Tsokzhing. He traveled south on the third day of that month, and when he passed the night there, the great protectress of the Buddhist teaching Dorje Kundrakma actually bowed with respect at his feet and said, "In this place the rites of service and attainment pertaining to the transcendent lord Cakrasaṃvara have not been observed for a hundred years, but you yourself have performed them—so thanks be to you!"

At Sharka Chujangma, he performed the rite of *The Attainment of Mind: Gathering of the Sugatas* and then gradually traveled home via Lagen. He went first to Sewalung and then reached the monastic seat of Taklung in the company of a welcoming party that received him at Drak La. He presented a cloud of offerings to the representative images and gifts to the monastic assembly.

He then performed the vase consecration rite from *The Profound Path: Gathering of the Sugatas*[20] at Mindroling, seat of Terchen Lama. At Driwulung, he bestowed the great empowerments of *The Heart Essence of the Ḍākinī*,[21] along with the profound guidance of the Great Perfection and so forth, on about thirty persons headed by Nagon Samling Lama.

Then, he went to Lhasa. At Pabongkha, he bestowed blessings and doctrinal connections on Sumtreng Zhabdrung, Neten Jampa Kelzang, and so forth, and they acquired authentic good fortune, as if they had reached the level of the Joyful. Then, via Kam La, he traveled to Lhunding, Ringang, Rongpo, and Garpa. On that occasion, he placed a long-life vase and a porcelain cup directly on Garpa's teaching throne. {846} Then, he placed one foot outside the threshold of the outer door and the other inside and stood there for a long time. "The patron will come to have a fine warhorse," he said.

Then, he dismounted in a valley called Charlok and said, "This valley, with its many white cliffs, is the buddha field of Mahākāruṇika." From there, he reached his monastic seat via Lhundrub Dzong and presented to the assembly in general bountiful offerings and gifts including a wheel containing one hundred million seven-syllable mantras. For a while, he stayed at the Labrang Palace and then moved to Tashi Khangsar at the center of the monastery. He took his seat at the head of the row of those undertaking the communion feast offerings of Bhaiṣajyaguru and Malikkā, and he sealed that with the oral instructions and aspiration prayers of dedication that he made on behalf of the entire congregation, satisfying the minds of all.

Then, he became somewhat unwell, and as he grew weaker, he stayed, as it were, in closed retreat. A great many sorts of long-life ritual were performed on his behalf, including loud recitations of the teachings, attainment rites of the incantations, rites of fulfillment and reparation, and ritual aversion through tormas, and so forth. Certain physicians of external ailments requested that he regain health by taking medications that would alleviate the symptoms, but since the course of his lifespan had been determined in a prophetic declaration of the meditational deity and since the merit of living beings was weak owing to the imprecations of untamed *damsi* demons, and so forth, his mind was intent on traveling to another field. He placed on his tongue sacraments of commitment consisting of sacred multiplying bone relics and gave a little also to his retinue.

Then, in the evening of the twenty-seventh day of the fourth month, his physical body passed away into the taintless state, in the profound expanse of quiescent reality. His mind itself remained clear in the coalescence of radiance and emptiness, without wavering from natural supreme bliss. His right eye assumed the gaze of the bodhisattvas. This {847} appeared to be an auspicious circumstance, indicating that he would always nurture beings through the vision of compassion and pristine cognition and that he would swiftly reincarnate.

Immediately thereafter, the circumstances of his passing were reported to Rakshak Kalon Chenpo. A bountiful cloud of offerings was prepared for the funeral ceremony in the presence of the great saints of the impartial tradition and the three sorts of representations (images, books, and stūpas) within the monastery. Nearby the sacred corpse, all the monks and laity, loudly chanting the sacred songs of the Kagyu hierarchs as an offering, had a glimpse of the sacred corpse. On the auspicious day of the sixth of the fifth month, some twenty monks, headed by the tutor Dakpo Geshe, dressed the sacred corpse in the garb of a Cintāmaṇicakravartin. They placed it within an enlightenment stūpa and performed an authentic cremation in conjunction with the maṇḍala rite of Cakrasaṃvara according to the Luipāda tradition. The sky was filled with rainbow clouds that were seen by all. In the perception of the devout senior official Yarjon Tashi, a trio of Orgyen and his entourage was clearly visible within a rainbow tent in the southwest, the trio of Mahākāruṇika and his entourage were present within another rainbow tent, and a trio of Munīndra and his entourage were present within yet another rainbow tent. The end of one rainbow was seen penetrating the sacred corpse and encircling the roof of Tashi Khangsar. In the perception of the master Lodro Tendzin, a loud sound was heard distinctly coming from the body of the lama while he was seated within the smoke of the fire. The smoke also, for the most part, billowed in the direction of Taklung Upper Plain, and consequently, most people discussed whether that was a causal basis for his reincarnation to take birth at Rongpo Garpa. {848}

After three days had passed, when the crematorium was opened, the skull with a round hole, the heart, tongue, and eyes, and the hands and feet remained intact, with many undamaged naturally arising forms, including the six-syllable mantra and many deities. These were inserted within a casket. A silver reliquary stūpa representing the Descent from Tuṣita with twenty-five rungs was fashioned of one thousand one hundred and eighty silver *sang* and forty-three gold *sang*. Embellished with gems and ornaments and filled to the brim with the four sorts of pearl relic, this beauteous ornament of the teaching of the lineage of attainment was placed as a field of merit for the sake of infinite beings in the northeast of the Great Lower Hall of the Main Temple, blazing with the glory of existence and quiescence, while the monastic assembly scattered the flowers of auspicious consecration. This was an unsurpassed auspicious circumstance indicating that all excellent provisions of merit of existence and quiescence were gathered, effortlessly present like clouds, in the spiritual and temporal facilities of this community.

The Collected Works, including oral instructions, advice, aspiration prayers, ritual arrangements, biographies, catalogs, official letters, and offering prayers to mundane and transcendent protectors, and so forth, which Venerable Ngawang Trinle Tendzin composed through the expressive power of his unimpeded learning in exegesis and composition were excellently arranged in three volumes. His oral instructions and so forth have exceedingly great blessings, which can rouse the mind toward the sacred doctrine through the nourishment of heartfelt faith and mindfulness of death, and they contain many capacities to transform mental attitudes, simply by seeing and hearing them. They are apparent to the eyes of all and within the actual perceptual range of the substratum.

So it was that this venerable lama's attributes of greatness {849} unraveled the knots of the eight ostensible and worldly concerns right where they were, knowing that both modes of conduct, imperial affairs of state and the actions of a beggar, are false and like an illusion. Although he was adroit in the five fields of classical learning, in order to show his affinity with the minds of foolish disciples, he did not pursue poetic ornaments of speech but for the most part undertook doctrinal teachings that were easy to understand, employing colloquial language. Although he was endowed with extrasensory powers, including clairvoyance, he did not make prophetic declarations concerning future events, thinking that they would become a causal basis for exaggeration and deprecation. After making careful examination, he would reveal to fortunate persons of intelligence his oral instructions as doctrines to be savored, such that manifold meditative experiences would arise without difficulty. In brief, he satisfied the minds of beings, training them in accord with their needs by means of the four sorts of gift—namely, gifts of the sacred doctrine, material gifts, the gift of fearlessness, and the gift of sanctuary.[22] He carefully guarded the renunciation of crimes and downfalls that contravened even the most minute practices to be adopted and rejected in terms of the three vows. However well or badly government officials and those who became his followers behaved, he did not have anger but remained calm and disciplined. He repeatedly donned the steadfast armor of perseverance, without indifference or indolence, with respect to his magnificent acts of benefit for the Buddhist teaching and living beings. He was equipoised in genuine meditational focus, without wavering for an instant from the profound meditative stability of the generation and perfection stages. And since he possessed discriminative awareness that was innately present, acquired, and refined, he could perceive without impediment the origin of all things, definitive and quantitative. Effortlessly accomplishing the twofold objective (the benefit of self and others), which was his inexhaustible enlightened activity, by means of the six transcendent perfections and the four attractive qualities of a bodhisattva, he was glorious on behalf of the Buddhist teaching and living beings. Such were his perfect attributes of greatness. {850}

The Disciples of Ngawang Trinle Tendzin

The foremost of all the disciples who were favored with the oral transmissions of Venerable Ngawang Trinle Tendzin were Jedrung Rinchen Sherab of Taklung Lower Plain, mighty lord of knowledge, power and compassion; Tashi Wangdrub, emanation of Rikdzin Sangye Yeshe; Choktrul Yizhin Trinle Chokdrub, reincarnation of Jampel Gyatso; Phakpa Jikten Wangchuk;

Phakchok Drakpa Gyeltsen, who was a holder of the Adamantine Vehicle, maintaining the secret repository of the teachings while playing the part of a saffron-robed monk; and Tsetrul Kunpang Tendzin Nyima, who had attained supreme spiritual accomplishment and unimpeded ascetic discipline and who, the lama had asserted, was indivisible with his buddha body of reality and of the same essential nature, although their physical bodies were different.

His disciples also included Tsetrul Tashi Gewei Wangpo, mighty lord of learning, veneration, and attainment, who was the manifestation of that lord-protector, his predecessor, through the unborn magical display of rebirth; and also the sublime minister Tsering Wangyel, who raised aloft the pure parasol of political affairs, integrating a hundred traditions through the powerful force of his merit; and the latter's brother Zhabdrung Tashi Pel, whose conduct resembled that of the yogin Avadhūti.

They also included the Mongol Genghiz Drubgyu Tendzin, who was skilled internally in authentic ascetic discipline and adept in all the details of classical learning; Drubwang Phulden, who maintained the treasure store of the lineage of empowerment, transmission, and esoteric instruction; Gelong Tsokchen, who acquired the accomplishment of deity visualization and mantra recitation with respect to Cakrasaṃvara; and others who were associated with our upper and lower seats of Taklung.

Moreover, there were those such as Tendzin Drodul, the supreme incarnation of Drigung, and so many saintly beings upholding the impartial philosophical systems, Sakya, Geluk, and Nyingma, great and small, who simply obtained a doctrinal connection with him. {851} And there were many tens of thousands of monastics and laypeople of Kham and U altogether who acquired a connection with him, enabling the shoots of liberation and well-being to grow in their minds. So it was that the limits of his acts on behalf of sentient beings were hard to enumerate.

Among them, the wondrous deeds of Jedrung, Phakchok, and so forth may be understood from *The Doctrinal History of the Abbatial Succession of Taklung Lower Plain*, which was composed by my teacher, Yizhin Norbu, Mahāvajradhara, in whom the three buddha bodies are subsumed. There is also extant a biography of Gazi Zhabdrung Tsering Wangyel, who, despite living as a householder, should also be placed provisionally among these masters. As for Choktrul Yizhin Trinle Chokdrub, the enlightened activities in which he engaged through his life were not extensive, but a somewhat short account of his life can be found below.

Tsetrul Kunpang Tendzin Nyima had the appearance of a yogin free from mundane activities, who practiced in the great sacred places and who exclusively, through his association with those sacred places, nurtured living beings impartially throughout the entire land. And yet, since there is nothing but an inkling of his deeds mentioned within the biographical documents of Taklung Lower Plain, it would also not be reliable to include that here. A few short spiritual songs of his are extant, and apart from that, the reincarnation of this venerable master is listed among the lamas who nowadays act for the welfare of Taklung.

As for Tsetrul Tashi Gewei Wangpo, I have heard that he was born at Taksho in Kham, but according to *The Biography of Venerable Ratnanātha*,[23] it is clear that he was born at Karu Gyaleb in Khyungpo. Later, there was also a householder purporting that Tsetrul was incarnated at Sertsa in Khyungpo. {852} However, in actuality, I have not seen an account of his deeds and do not know. As I have heard through the oral communication of the aged monks of the past, after he was recognized at Riwoche, he was invited to the Tse Palace, where his studies of sūtra, mantra, and classical learning were not inconsiderable. Subsequently, although he did not act as a throne holder of this monastic seat of Taklung, in accordance with the tradition of retired doctrinal lords, he stayed for some years indefinitely at the palace, the monastery, and so forth. Later on, at the time when the monastic seat of Riwoche was being oppressed, he endured many hardships due to the unseemly attitude of the harsh inhabitants of the Yisho area, who were hard to discipline. So, he traveled again to U and stayed for quite a long time at Ojo mountain retreat and so forth, and there were also some disciples who obtained empowerments, transmissions, and esoteric instructions from him, including Kyilsang Sechen Lama Konchok Yeshe. If one were to appraise the infinite maṇḍalas of his successive past lives and the offering ceremonies that he randomly performed with respect to Gesar, Gurkarma, and so forth, it seems that his learning and conduct in precise fields, such as poetics, was particularly exalted. I also think I have heard reports that at many early and later times, he supported the welfare of living beings in Penyul, Lungsho, and elsewhere. Afterward, he passed away at Tsedrung in Riwoche in 1763 (water sheep year of the thirteenth sexagenary cycle). As his testament, he had wanted to construct a story-high image of Vajradhara of medicinal clay in the Lower Hall of the Great Temple of Taklung. His followers, including his sister, clearly carried this out in accordance with his injunction. {853}

I should also speak a little of the foremost disciples of Tsetrul Gewei Wangpo Tendzin Namgyel. In that regard, the writings of my precious teacher also were enunciated to some extent to supplement the monastic succession of Taklung Lower Plain.

By diffusing a mass of the virtuous provisions of cyclic existence and nirvāṇa
In the four continents of Sumeru, upon the mighty earth of excellent attainment,
An offering cloud that pleases all the conquerors and their heirs,
May the provisions of merit and pristine cognition be perfected!

5. Choktrul Tashi Jampel Gyatso and Yangsi Tulku Yizhin Trinle Chokdrub

Homage to Tashi Jampel Gyatso—
He who attained all glorious, **auspicious** (*bkra shis*)[1] endowments of existence and quiescence,
Embodiment of the deity **Mañjuśrī** (*'jam dpal*), **oceanic** (*rgya mtsho*) treasure of scripture,
Wellspring of marvelous emanational activities for the Buddhist teaching and living beings,
Best among those of supreme accomplishment!

This master had in the past taken birth as many saintly beings, including the bodhisattva Maitreyamitra who was a magical display of the compassion of Mañjughoṣa, the all-seeing natural form of the infinite omniscient conquerors, as well as Rikdzin Sangye Yeshe, Drington Śākya Rinchen, Choku Orgyen Gonpo, Yongdzin Namgyel Pelzang, and so forth. In particular, as Venerable Ngawang Tashi Peldrub, the precious refuge and great sunlight of the Taklungpa teaching, he had perfected knowledge, love, and power and kindly expanded the activities of the Buddhist teaching at both our upper and lower monastic seats. As such, he became a focal point for the flowers of praise that were scattered by all his contemporaries, superior and inferior.

His reincarnation, Choktrul Tashi Jampel Gyatso, was born at a place called Chodrak in the three districts of Lhomon, {854} in 1672 (water mouse year of the eleventh sexagenary cycle). In his childhood, he was brought to Taklung, and he became equal to his predecessor, the lord of refuge, in his wide-ranging and insightful engagement with all aspects of knowledge including the five outer and inner fields, the ten aspects of classical learning. It is clear that he also received certain connections to the sacred doctrine from Tashi Chokyi Gyelpo, who had the title Gaji Zhabdrung Ananta, while the latter was residing at Ojo.

Then, from the uncommon lord of his enlightened heritage, Jedrung Drakpa Lekdrub of Taklung Lower Plain, he received in the manner of a vase being filled to the brim the general doctrinal traditions of the three vows and in particular all the empowerments, transmissions, and esoteric instructions of *The Four Gems: The Profound Doctrines of Taklungpa*,[2] and then he became a supreme saintly being who maintained the teaching of essential meaning and acquired mastery over the exegesis and attainment of this lineage of attainment. There is extant a rather slim volume containing his essential letters and so forth, which were of eloquent composition.

Although he did not hold and maintain the throne of the monastic seat of Taklung, Tashi Jampel Gyatso did extensively bestow all the sacred doctrines that he possessed with respect to the Buddhist teaching, general and particular, including the empowerments, transmissions, and esoteric instructions of *The Four Gems: The Profound Doctrines of Taklungpa* upon the peerless holder of the teaching of Taklung Lower Plain at Riwoche, Phakchok Yizhin Wangyel Ngawang Drakpa Damcho Trinle Phuntsok, who was also known under the alternative name of Phakpa Tashi Wangyel. He also had great kindness to the continuity of the sacred doctrine at both the upper and lower monastic seats of Taklung by propagating the empowerments and transmissions of the cycle of requisite practical applications on behalf of the venerable teacher Tendzin Namgyel. {855}

Tashi Jampel Gyatso mostly stayed in different places such as Chodzong, Drokha, and Horkhang, and on one occasion he went to Riwoche. After undertaking such great acts of benefit for the Buddhist teaching and living beings, both directly and indirectly, his mind on certain occasions became unsettled, and he succumbed to ill-health for many years, falling ill, as it were, due to material distraction and pollution. Finally, after displaying physical hardships, and although he was not actually transformed into the buddha body of adamantine reality, the thought arose in his mind that he should pass away into quiescence through his conditioned physical body, in order to encourage indolent beings to swiftly approach the sacred doctrine, and in order to undertake great acts of benefit for the sake of living beings in other realms. On the twelfth day of the fifth month of 1706 (fire male dog), in his thirty-fifth year, his physical body became equipoised in the disposition of reality, the expanse of great quiescence, free from conceptual elaboration.

Intricate funeral rites were carried out, and the small silver reliquary containing the core of pearl relics from the cremation of his sacred corpse is nowadays kept in the Dakgyu Podrang of Domsumling. The responsibility for these ceremonies was assumed by the followers who were disciples and attendants of that venerable master. It is reported that a silver coin was collected from each of the ordinary monks of the congregation in the monastic college, and the reliquary was constructed on the basis of these offerings.

Yangsi Tulku Yizhin Trinle Chokdrub

The reincarnation who was the emanation of that lord-protector was born in conjunction with many virtuous signs in 1709 (earth female ox). His father was Sonam Norbu, the younger brother of his predecessor, and his mother was Tashi Tsomo. Facilitated by the venerable teacher Tendzin Namgyel Rinpoche and the devout patrons of the college and the monastery, Tokarwa, an old attendant of his predecessor, and other devout persons went to recognize him, {856} and after finding a clear and certain proof, without error, they invited him to Taklung in 1715 (wood sheep) during his seventh year. He took up residence at Horkhang and received the lay and novitiate vows from Yongdzin Rinpoche of Dechen Chokhor; Gyelwa Drigungpa Konchok Trinle Zangpo; Kunpang Tendzin Nyima, the reincarnation of Riwoche Tsetrul Ngagi Wangchuk; and Kyilsang Gongkhen Deno Gyatso. He also received minor sorts of empowerments for dispelling immediate obstacles and a great many stages of empowerment and transmission pertaining to the general and particular doctrinal modes of the Buddhist teaching. The name Yizhin Trinle Chokdrub was conferred upon him.

From the day when he met face-to-face with the lord of refuge, Tendzin Namgyel, on the nineteenth day of the seventh month of 1717 (fire bird), the latter's enlightened intention was drawn toward the marvelous kindness that his predecessor Jampel Gyatso had displayed by means of the two traditions of sūtra and mantra, and he pledged by whatever means to repay his kindness and assist this reincarnation. Immediately, he performed empowerments, ritual ablutions, entrustments, and so forth in order to dispel obstacles, and in addition he gradually bestowed all the ocean-like blessings of the empowerments, guidance, and esoteric instructions in accordance with the wishes of the Tulku himself. {857}

Since, until that point, the monastic preceptors of Taklung had been appointed by the government, it was not easy even for tulkus to act independently or to travel and stay as they wished. From the seventh day of the seventh month of 1718 (earth dog), however, the monastic preceptor Kyilsangpa was appointed, and the whole of Taklung was taken under the ownership of Gazi Yakdrong Zhabdrung Tsangpa and his son. This ensured that even the tulkus were secure and could freely nurture living beings.

After the troubles of 1721 (iron ox), the Chinese imperial patron and his Tibetan priest (the Dalai Lama) reverted to the previous arrangement, bestowing the responsibility for the monastic seat of Taklung on the family of Lord Gazi. At that time, there were few aristocratic members of that family line, and they had to act in the service of the central government, and so on. Consequently, they could not assume the role of hierarch at the monastic seat, and for a while Gazi Yakdrong Zhabdrung decreed that either of the two tulkus should act as the hierarch. Since, at that time, the senior tulku Tendzin Namgyel was staying at Riwoche in Kham, for the sake of harmony between Mije Zhabdrung and all the subjects of the college and the monastery, he was invited here to Taklung. Gradually, he set out from Yisho. On the twelfth day of the eighth month, Choktrul Yizhin Trinle Chokdrub arrived at Labrang Yangon Tse from Horkhang. After that, on the sixth day of the ninth month, the peerless lord of refuge and elucidator of the teaching Ngawang Trinle Tendzin Namgyel reached this monastic seat, {858} and after a short time, on the nineteenth day of that same month, the lord of refuge was enthroned.

Starting from then, the aspirations of the two tulkus, senior and junior, merged together, and by, as it were, eating from a single bowl and sitting on a single seat, they assumed greater and lesser responsibilities for the sake of the Buddhist teaching, in accordance with their seniority. Apart from that, without selfish concerns, they passed the time complying with the excellent and auspicious tradition of Taklung. For nine years, they resided at this Yang Gon Labrang, as father and son, sun and moon, integrating, as it were, skillful means and discriminative awareness, such that the entire community experienced positive feelings of happiness. By repairing the Main Temple, erecting a new gilded roof and so forth, they meritoriously fulfilled the aspirations of the great teacher, the lord of refuge Rinchen Gon.

Choktrul Yizhin Trinle Chokdrub himself again authentically received the precepts of a fully ordained monk along with those of a mendicant and the novitiate, and the name Mipham Ngawang Tashi Pelden Lekdrub Chokyi Nyima was conferred upon him. Although he engaged in discriminative awareness born of study and reflection with respect to the outer and inner fields of classical learning, he was an exemplary scholar due to the awakening of the propensities of his past experiences. From the venerable teacher Rinchen Gon, he received for the most part the infinite profound and vast maturational empowerments and liberating guidance of the ancient and new traditions of Secret Mantra, along with the instructions of the generation and perfection stages that had been preserved. Altogether, he also spent more than one year in retreat, focusing on the ritual service and attainment of his preferred deity, and he acquired genuine supreme and common spiritual accomplishments. His mind and that of Gazi Zhabdrung, father and son, merged together, such that they became a field of admiration and respect on which the higher and lower members of this community depended for all their provisions. {859}

During that time, the lord of refuge, the teacher Rinchen Gon (Ratnanātha), stayed strictly in retreat for one week in the Upper Hall of the Offering Chapel, and the thought arose that he should now confer on Choktrul Yizhin Trinle Chokdrub the responsibilities for maintaining and nurturing the monastic seat of Taklung and that he himself should become a total renunciant, maintaining the threefold isolation (of body, speech, and mind). Thereupon, in a vision at dawn, the protector of the transmitted teachings Genyen Chenpo clearly manifested his own form and offered the following prophetic declaration: "I rejoice in the manner in which you have undertaken to nurture this monastic seat of Venerable Tangpa in the past. Now, again, it falls to you to maintain, nurture, and enhance it. It will be difficult for this Choktrul to live beyond the age of twenty-five or thereabouts, and it is perfectly evident that this present body of his is enacting the remainder of the lifespan of his predecessor. Since there is no way of prolonging his life, he will not be of great benefit to living beings." At this, Rinchen Gon was saddened.

At the end of 1728 (earth monkey), the authorities of Riwoche insisted that when Zhabdrung Tashi Namgyel passed away in order to make offerings when the sacred corpse was cremated, both the tulkus should travel there together from Taklung, or at least one of them should do so. The Choktrul himself was undertaking retreat since the obstacles associated with his twenty-fifth year had not yet passed, and he remained here. Venerable Ngawang Trinle Tendzin Namgyel therefore made preparations to travel to Kham, but he postponed the journey at the insistence of the entire community, in general and particular.

Since there was no alternative, he properly prepared equipment, tents, and so forth on behalf of Choktrul Yizhin Trinle Chokdrub and his attendants and, after extensively offering them eloquent advice on how they should proceed, insisted that even if they were delayed, they should return within one year.

Choktrul and party then set out on the twenty-second day of the fifth month of 1729 (earth bird) {860} and arrived at Riwoche on the nineteenth day of the seventh month. In accordance with that schedule, the sacred corpse of the late Zhabdrung was cremated. Choktrul offered the incantation scrolls for the reliquary and perfectly undertook the consecration ceremony. He fulfilled the hopes of both Jedrung and Phakchok of Yang Gon, the widow and heir of the palace, and so forth, and of all the superior and inferior persons belonging to the three colleges of the ancient and new traditions[3] according to their wishes. He distributed communal alms to the assembled congregation and established a patron-priest relationship for sponsoring a hundred million recitations of the six-syllable mantra. In such ways, he greatly enhanced the continuity of virtuous actions. He also received many empowerments and transmissions of the supreme vehicle from Mikyel, Lhotrul Rinpoche, Pangleb Terton, Drubchok Tenpel, and others. He was attended upon by the king of Nangchen and his servants. Since he extensively increased his enlightened activities for the sake of living beings, the duration of his stay there approximated two and a half years.

Then, he gradually set out. On the fifteenth day of the eighth month of 1731 (iron pig), he was welcomed by the venerable teacher Rinchen Gon and the assembled community and escorted back to this monastic seat of glorious Taklung. When father and son met together face-to-face, everyone was transported to the glory of happiness. He presented fine material offerings as gifts to the supreme teacher, the lord of refuge, along with prayers for his long life, and he satisfied all the assembled congregation with a bountiful offering cloud of communal alms. He then rested for some days and undertook retreat. He also made a brief excursion to Nyingdrung hot springs.

From the start of that year, the physician Sonam reported that the Choktrul's pulse was slightly unhealthy. The venerable teacher also saw him in person and determined that his demeanor was not the same as before, and he wondered whether he might not come to have a similar illness to that of his predecessor, whose mind had been unsettled, seemingly by the arising of obstructing *si* demons. {861} Although, on account of that, he did not doubt that there were obstacles to Choktrul's life, even before Choktrul had returned to Taklung, he also had some doubts owing to inauspicious signs, such as an owl that hooted behind Yang Gon. Immediately, therefore, he requested many divinations, on account of which he undertook strong remedial rites.[4]

After a short time, Choktrul meritoriously presented offerings to Jowo Śākyamuni Yizhin Norbu at the Jokhang in Lhasa, and he met with the illustrious governor. He also established a close rapport with the heir of the Gazi clan, who hailed from his own family, the venerable minister and governor of Tibet, Zhabdrung Tsering Wangyel. When, as the essential point of his advice, he offered extensive prayers that Tibet should become a beauteous ornament of the Buddhist teaching in the short and long term, expounding virtuous actions and releasing beings from negative actions, all the attendants also were inspired.

On the way back to Taklung, he nurtured living beings at Langtang, Sumtreng, upper and lower Daryul, and so forth. He was invited to Lhundrub Dzong by Depa Dargye. Then, on the morning when he met that lama, he was immediately invited into the temple at his hermitage, where they undertook the rites of Pehar and the means that purify enmity. He requested Depa Dargye that he should emphasize retreat practice, including the ritual service and attainment of the meditational deities.

On the tenth day of the eleventh month, he reached Taklung and stayed there for four days. He caught a mild cold that became persistent but recovered by relying on meditation. Then, when he was invited to a memorial service on behalf of Depa Tseten from Rong Nak Gu, he fell ill on the way up and said, "You should request the remaining empowerments and guidance. I will see whether I should return to Kham in the warm season." {862} Following his return, he did not stay long here in Taklung and turned his thoughts toward traveling to Riwoche and staying there.

In any case, he rode toward Rong on the thirteenth day of the month, and from the night following his departure,[5] he suddenly fell ill due to pollution. His condition deteriorated as he reached Nak Gu, and as this news was passed on to Taklung, a physician was dispatched, and profound methods for securing long life were undertaken, and so forth. When these did not take effect, and he was about to pass away in his twenty-third year on the morning of the twenty-first day of the eleventh month, in response to the entreaties of his attendants and servants, he revived and said, "I have come!" They once again arranged auspicious circumstances in accordance with his injunctions, but their wish that he remain could not be accommodated within the confines of the merit of all his followers. In order to display the magical appearance of impermanence to those who adhered to permanence, the array of his physical body was then absorbed into the expanse of reality. His actual mind came to rest in a disposition of luminosity, without coming and going.

The steward Peldzin and the monastic preceptor Takchak and others were sent from Taklung to bring back the sacred corpse, and on the evening of the twenty-third day, the precious corpse was received by the congregation with many sacraments of offering. It was placed in the Zimdrub Deko chapel of the Yang Gon Tse Palace. Although that night, when it was brought there, was the high point of the cold winter season, the warmth of the sacred corpse did not fade, and it was sealed off in retreat for four days. The venerable lama Ratnanātha undertook the prayers with respect to his post-death meditation and so forth. {863} On the morning of the twenty-fourth day, blood and serum emerged from his nose, and his head was upturned.[6] From the twenty-fifth day, people were gradually admitted to see the sacred corpse, and at the time when offerings were made at the funeral ceremony, colored sand maṇḍalas were erected for *The Offering to the Spiritual Teachers*,[7] Cakrasaṃvara according to Lūipa, the five deities of Vārāhī, Sarvavid, and Nivāranaviṣkambhin.[8] Above the assembly of the monastery, the tents of the colleges and Tibetan villagers were also clustered.

When the attendants, including those groups of varying size that performed the means for attainment and all the congregations of monks of our own enlightened heritage had assembled, a monastic congregation of some four hundred and fifty participated in the offering of the attainment of the maṇḍalas. They recited the adamantine spiritual songs of their Kagyu predecessors and the timely scriptures. Excellent gifts were respectfully offered to them, and until the forty-ninth day, here at Taklung and in all directions, the Choktrul's enlightened intention was fulfilled by an extensive cloud mass of communal alms. The heavens were densely filled with a cloud mass of bountiful and uncontaminated offerings that were worthy of praise by all gods and humans.

On the twenty-fifth day of the lunar month, in conjunction with the rite of Cakrasaṃvara, the venerable lama Ratnanātha conferred an empowerment, whereupon a rainbow of five colors and various transformations of rainbow clouds arose in the sky. Then, as the sun rose on the hilltop on the third day of the twelfth month, the sacred corpse was cremated. The multitude of monks headed by the lord of refuge, the teacher Rinchen Gonpo, placed the sacred corpse on the pyre in conjunction with the rites of Sarvavid and Nivāranaviṣkambhin. As an external sign of success, rainbow light swirled in the sky and a white rainbow cloud, resembling an outstretched blanket, extended directly from the west to the east. There were also three internal signs: smoke from the pyre wafted to the east; within the pyre, there was little disturbance and no smell of burning; and as a secret sign, {864} a fragment of the legs of the sacred corpse from the eastern aperture of the pyre alighted directly in front of the venerable lama. After that, a palm-size fragment emerged from an opening in the skull, and Jambhala arose in the common perception of all the astonished persons who were in his presence. The venerable lama Tendzin Namgyel then made the following adamantine statement: "When I examined these signs, from my perspective, I think that he was one who genuinely and sincerely kept his commitments, disregarding any sort of adversities that would arise and in consideration of the commitments of his predecessor and the immediate reputation of the teaching. That being the case, my mind is somewhat at ease." These words of his became a basis that induced pure confidence in those who heard them. When the pyre was opened, he said that the heart remained undamaged, but apart from that there were very few bones, traces of charcoal, and so forth, indicating that the remains had been taken as an object of offering by the ḍākinīs. Such were the wondrous matters that were conjectured.

Two golden reliquaries, large and small, were commissioned. The larger one was placed in the upper hall of the Offering Chapel and the smaller one in the Tashi Khangsar. As funerary representations, an image of Mahāmaitreya was excellently commissioned, the size of a story of the Main Temple, and as a reliquary stūpa, a Tashi Gomang Chorten, the size of a story of the Lower Hall. In its aperture an image of Munīndra, the size of the Jowo, was inserted, and in its lattices were icons depicting the thirty-five confession buddhas, all of them covered in gold gilt. On its throne base there were colorful representations of glorious Mahākāla, Vasudhara, and Tseringma. Inside, it was filled to the top with four kinds of pearl relics. {865}

Yangsi

After Choktrul Yizhin Trinle Chokdrub had passed away in that manner, just before a full year had passed, the venerable lama Ratnanātha had a vision of inner radiance, in which a crescent moon clearly arose from the eastern direction, obscured by clouds. The next day, in accordance with his dream of the previous night, it seemed to him that a tulku had appeared, and so he ordered his servant Loten to offer incense smoke and erect a flag. The servant said, "When no tulku appeared we were quite joyful. Now trouble will come!" Thereupon, the venerable master had a slight change of heart, but later on he said that the tulku was almost exemplary because eloquent and prescient expressions emerged from the child's mouth.

On the fifteenth day of the tenth lunar month of 1733 (water ox), in conjunction with a lunar eclipse, a baby boy was born into the Ojo clan of Radeng, and it was widely proclaimed that he was the reincarnation of that Choktrul. In the autumn of 1734 (tiger), an outstanding monk inspected the child but could not recognize him as the reincarnation because, although there were auspicious circumstances, the child was too young, and he permitted him to come later to Taklung. Kunzang Rangdrol and others were gradually sent to Radeng, and they just named him Tangpa Tashi and gave him robes to wear. In 1739 (earth sheep), the venerable lama himself went there and made a detailed inspection of the child. Although earlier and later on, he had many hopes, because no permission was forthcoming from the Dalai Lama, he could not take possession of the child or bring him to the monastic seat of Taklung. It was under these circumstances that in 1743 (water pig), the venerable lama Tendzin Namgyel also passed away, his enlightened intention dissolving into the expanse of reality. And it was no longer said of this child that he was the reincarnation of Choktrul. Indeed, that proposition vanished without a trace like the tracks of a bird in the sky. {866}

Since this magical play of successive incarnations
Exemplifies the magical display of all things of phenomenal existence,
I have described the compassionate magical display of Jamgon.
May all beings attain buddhahood, endowed with magical display
And devoid of true existence!

6. Tulku Tashi Drakpa Yeshe, a.k.a. Chokyi Nyima

I pay homage at the feet of Tashi Drakpa Yeshe Chokyi Nyima—
Treasure among all **good auspices** (*bkra shis*)[1] of existence and quiescence,
Healing the afflictions of all beings with the medicine of compassion,
Renowned (*grags pa*) authentic and peerless master **of the sacred doctrine** (*chos kyi*),
Supreme **sun** (*nyi ma*) of **pristine cognition** (*ye shes*)!

The conquerors assume diverse emanational forms that discipline those to be trained without moving from the buddha body of reality. Great bodhisattva beings, who are the heirs of the conquerors, reveal the modalities of death, transference, and rebirth by the power of compassion, and according to the wishes of sentient beings, they instantly, just in the time it takes to stretch out and withdraw a hand, send forth billions of emanations. Among them chiefly in the field of Akaniṣṭha is the emanational play of Mahāvajradhara, endowed with the five certainties, indivisible from Mañjughoṣa, embodiment of the discriminative awareness of the conquerors. His emanations have included sublime Śāriputra; the monastic preceptor Lhungyi Sherab; the paṇḍita Rikpei Khuyuk; Lotsāwa Kawa Peltsek; the religious minister Pema Gungtsen; the learned and accomplished Nāropā the Great; the mighty lord of yoga Mila Repa; the mighty lord of occult power Ra Lotsāwa; the supreme incarnation Kuyalwa Rinchen Gon, who was a relative of Taklung Tangpa; Sangye Onpo, the emanation of Hevajra; Ratnākara, the doctrinal lord of Taklung Upper Plain; Jedrung Ratnākara of Taklung Lower Plain; the madman of Bhutan Kunga Lekpa; the omniscient Ngagi Wangpo; Janglungpa Zhonu Lodro; the great accomplished master Neljor Shukchangtsel; {867} Rikdzin Sonam Tashi; Zhabdrung

Ojowa Tashi Chogyel; and Tendzin Namgyel, the all-seeing elucidator of the Buddhist teaching—who all manifested in different forms but were of an identical essential nature.

Finally, he took birth as Chokyi Nyima, the reincarnation of the venerable lama Tendzin Namgyel, conjoined with many virtuous signs including thunder that reverberated and rainbows that arced in the sky all around Taklung, in the upper region of Penyul, Land of the Quick Witted on the sixth day of second month of 1744 (wood male mouse year of the twelfth sexagenary cycle). He was the son of Rongpo Garpa, who hailed from a powerful clan and was head of the militia in the uplands of that district.[2]

At the time when his venerable predecessor had been invited to Rong Gar and declined to stay,[3] he had placed a long-life vase, a porcelain cup, and so forth on Garpa's seat and returned from that long journey on horseback. A household priest of Garpa had a dream in which an exquisitely perfect stūpa of crystal appeared from the northeastern direction and the merchant Tashi Sonam had a dream in which a stone stūpa manifested of its own accord to the southwest of his house. In the seventh month of 1743 (water pig), the child's mother had seen a rainbow body in the sky when she was approaching Serkok Chora, and it actually penetrated her. Also, on the evening when he was born, his mother had accepted the token gift of a steward while the lama was staying in the chapel of Garpa, and the household priest Rabjampa experienced many auspicious signs in dreams, a moon of the third day and a cloudless sun arose and so forth. On the day after the child was born at sunrise, when he was bathed and then carried upstairs, {868} everyone saw the sky filled with rainbow light.

Gomchen Pulden, a disciple of his venerable predecessor, obtained many authoritative and definitive signs. During the ninth month of the year when the venerable predecessor passed away, three women wearing ornaments appeared, saying, "The emanation of your lama is over there to the south from here." And he found himself in the area of Daryul, looking at the house of Garpa, as if seeing it in a looking glass. Also, in the perception of his vision and the perception of his hearing combined, someone with the appearance of a heruka pointedly said, "He should be named Pema Tsewang Tendzin." Furthermore, in the sky, the body of his venerable predecessor clearly appeared, and from below his right armpit, a small boy with loose brownish hair alighted on the right side of Pulden and so on.

The Dalai Lama also undertook clear divinations and conferred upon the child a prayer for long life. One day, he said that the tulku should travel to

Taklung, and when he was not permitted to stay there, he insisted that he be brought as far as the river bank. At that time when the child was small, as a propensity associated with his former monastic seat, it was determined that he had a rosary held at his heart. At the time of his actual recognition, the child accepted a painting of the six meditational deities of Taklung Tangpa, along with the rosary of his venerable predecessor, such that a strong recognition took place, and it became clear in the manner of a bee finding a flower or a swan entering water that the child was the incarnation of that saintly being.

Kaḥtok Rikdzin the Great[4] named him Tashi Chokyi Nyima, offered him a hat, a mat, and the tokens of the treasury, and then he was enthroned as master of the teaching of the lineage of attainment. {869} The auspicious connections for his long life were arranged in succession by three communities of Taklung—the palace, the monastery, and the mountain hermitage, and so forth.

The nineteenth day of the third month of 1749 (earth snake) was held to be astrologically auspicious for his journey to Taklung. He set out on horseback accompanied with dancing and singing, and at the time of that auspicious circumstance, the protector deity Yamar Tsengo prophesied that he would preside over the monastic seat of Taklung from that very day. The household priest Rabjampa dreamed that an extraordinarily wonderful golden spire had been erected above the image of Cakrasaṃvara in Yang Gon. The news was reported to the Dalai Lama and to Gazi Kalon Tsering Wangyel and others. As decreed, he was brought to Taklung, and his arrival at the crossroad of Tak was arranged to coincide with the sun rising at the monastery—an auspicious indication that clearly manifested, emerging of its own power, like the light of the sun. The congregation and community of monks presented offering scarves to him in the Hall of the Blazing Glory of Existence and Quiescence in the Main Temple at the monastic seat, and an auspicious feast was excellently observed, as if the Perfect Age had come again. Then, when Siddhu Rinpoche was en route for Kham, he also offered him the tonsure ceremony.

That summer, in Sok, he received from Gomchen Pulden the essential empowerments and transmissions of the Taklung Kagyu lineage. Then, during the eighth month of 1750 (iron horse), in the midst of a quorum headed by the monastic preceptor Gelong Pulden and Gelong Rabdrub, supplemented by others, in the grass hermitage of Samdrub Dechen, he received the lay vows and the intermediate mendicant ordination. His name, Tashi Chokyi Nyima, was left unchanged.

At first, he went to stay at Tashi Khangsar, where he also had visions of Genyen {870} and his retinue, and of Nyenchen Tanglha. That is to say, the protector deities clearly manifested their own characteristics, enacting his activities, like the body and its shadow. Then, when he received the invitation of Setsa Kadrukpa, the latter saw the master and his two disciples approaching from the upstairs east balcony, and there arose in Setsa's mind the perception that he had been favored by the lama in his past life. The patrons of his predecessor including Ruknamter, Nak Gu, and so forth also extended him their invitations and paid him abundant respect.

When long-life prayers were offered by the assembled monks of the college, he also had a vison of the face of Four-Armed Mahākāla. Outwardly, his own physical form assumed the appearance of a proud protector, inwardly the protector dwelled within the energy channels and cakras of his body, and secretly, with regard to the nature of mind, the natural energy of the buddha body of reality arose as Jñānanātha. In this way, the indications clearly manifested that he was certainly indivisible from the glorious lord-protector Mahākāla.

From Drubchok Phulden, he received many sorts of empowerments and initiations of the old and new traditions, including *Cakrasaṃvara: Means for Attainment of the Teacher*;[5] *Vārāhī*; *Akṣobhya*; the maṇḍala of *The Purification of the Lower Realms*; *The Ocean of Means for Attainment*, with its forty-three initiations; *The Precious Source*;[6] and *The Gathering of the Sugatas of the Eight Pronouncements.*[7] And, undeterred, he also received the extensive transmissions and so forth that he was offered pertaining to the Collected Works of Taklung Tangpa, Sangye On, Ngawang Namgyel, and Tendzin Namgyel.

In 1756 (fire mouse), he met and paid homage to the all-seeing Dalai Lama Kelzang Gyatso and received the vows of the novitiate, at which time the name Kelzang Ngawang Namgyel Peldrub was conferred upon him. Rakshak Kalon Tsering Wangyel then decreed that he should take responsibility for the monastic seat of Taklung {871} and bestowed upon him an abundance of material gifts. He was then empowered as the throne holder and representative of the Gazi line. Limitless, profound, and extensive aspirations were made in the presence of the representative images of Lhasa, headed by Jowo Śākyamuni, to the effect that he would undertake bountiful acts of benefit for the sake of the Buddhist teaching and living beings. As soon as Tashi Chokyi Nyima arrived at the monastic seat, Gompa Pulden immediately passed away and the sky was filled with white clouds, indicative that his enlightened intention was unconditioned in the expanse of uncontaminated reality.

On a meritorious day of the month in 1757 (fire ox), he was appointed as the sacred spiritual and temporal lord of refuge. Enthroned on the great teaching throne of the lower hall of the Offering Chapel, a feast resembling a meeting place of the gods was offered, including the long-life prayers of the entire congregation and excellent offerings that were presented in order by the senior nobility, Tsetrul Gewang, Zhabdrung Tashi Pel of Riwoche, and Yang Gon, followed by his disciples and adherents, high and low.

The secretary Purpa Tsering was appointed in place of the bursar Sangye Jikten, who had gone to attend a spectacle outside of Taklung. The official Odze utilized the property of the retired bursar Horkhangpa, who had passed away, and commissioned a Chinese-style roof above the Lama Lhakhang within the monastic college, which was insatiable to behold. The venerable lama dissolved the being of pristine cognition into that temple and uttered a benediction to the sacred images contained within it.

He also had a meritorious meeting with the great all-seeing Paṇchen Lobzang Pelden Yeshe when the latter traveled to Taklung. Then, in 1760 (iron dragon), he was invited to attend an offering of attainment by the aristocrat Rabshi and his entourage and was pleased at the sight of that sacred place and the inspection of its retreat hermitage, and so forth. Their minds mutually blended together spiritual and temporal affairs. After Rabshi's father and mother passed away in succession, {872} he authentically conducted the funeral rites, the aspiration for the dedication of merit, and so forth.

In 1761 (iron snake), Tashi Chokyi Nyima traveled via Tala, Nyingdrung hot springs, and Lagen to the great stone pillar of Tashido at Lake Namtso in the north. That day, there was a rainbow canopy in the sky, and as he prostrated before and circumambulated the throne of master Padmākara in the Utse, the sky was filled with rainbow light, so there were many wondrous occurrences. On the surface of the lapis-colored lake, he saw, in an authentic pure vision, an extremely protruding white handprint of Orgyen the Great (Padmākara), and so forth. Innumerable pure visions such as this, for which he resembled his predecessor, arose in succession.

Undoubtedly, too, he assumed responsibility for pursuing the same exemplary career in relation to his hidden enlightened attributes. He did not speak much, even to say, for example, "This is wonderful," and so his words could not be objectified as this or that. The patrons of Tsomgo paid their respects, and he visited the sacred sites of Lhacham Khenpari, Dokya,

Jangur, and so forth. Then, he undertook extensive acts of benefit for the sake of the disciples of Sakya Ruwa, Namru, Hor Bardha, Yerchung Ruwa, Sangzhung, and so forth and established all who were connected with him on the level of authenticity. After staying at Uma Drakar, Dam Lungrik, Sewalung, and so forth, after not long, he set foot once again in the great monastic seat of Taklung.

That winter, Tashi Chokyi Nyima undertook the strict ritual service and attainment of Coemergent Cakrasaṃvara and experienced auspicious signs that he had acquired spiritual accomplishment. He recited prayers, exemplified by *The Encouragement in the Face of Severe Summer Drought*,[8] in the hilltop chapels of Ya Gangchen, the sacred place of the great protector of the Buddhist teaching. Accordingly, he obtained repeated signs that the deities and protectors were pleased, and there was an extremely abundant downpour of rain. {873}

In 1762 (water horse), he went to Riwoche at the behest of Tsetrul Gewei Wangpo and Lord Rakshak to stand in as a lama for Zhabdrung Tashi Pel, who could not be present there. On that occasion, Tsetrul was residing at Ojo.

Then, during the eighth month of that year, when the reincarnation of the all-seeing Dalai Lama, Jampel Gyatso, was enthroned in the Potala, he went to Lhasa and resided at Rakshak. Requesting an audience in the Potala Palace, he offered extensive long-life prayers, and in order of status, he presented gifts and met with the regent, the council ministers, the Chinese ambassadors, Rakshak Kalon, and so forth—such was his excellent way of making arrangements. In all respects, he pleased all those high officials with an ocean of joy. He established connections through the noble aspirations that he made and the ceremonial scarves that he presented to the representative images of Lhasa, headed by Jowo Śākyamuni.

On the way back, he visited the sacred sites of Drak Yerpa and made extensive offerings and aspiration prayers. Gradually, he arrived at the monastic seat of Taklung. At that time, there was a large gathering from Riwoche, including Zhabdrung Tashi Pel and Tseyang Kutsab.

He then focused his profound enlightened intention in order to receive the full monastic ordination from Zhabdrung Phakchok Rinpoche at Taklung Lower Plain, along with the instructions of the unique doctrinal lineage of Taklung, including its empowerments, transmissions, and guidance. He sought permission from Rakshak and others and then prepared to set out on receiving their positive approval. At the invitation of the college and the monastery, in public and in private, he was presented with a vast amount of perfect offerings. On the nineteenth day of the fifth month in 1763 (water sheep), he set out from Taklung. Journeying via Drakpu, Dam Nyingdrung, Sangzhung, Nakchu, {874} Sokchu, and Soklam, he was paid excellent respects by Ponpo Gutri Gyel and Seshur Lama, who offered him their horses, yaks, butter, and cheesecake. Fulfilling their spiritual and material hopes, he reached Yelchung and Drutsab.

At that time, news arrived that Tsetrul Gewang had passed away at Riwoche. He traveled via Phakmar and Phozhung to Tana Gon, where he opened the golden stūpa of Gesar, visited the sacred sites, distributed communal alms, and so forth. At Kartortang, he was welcomed by the senior groups of lamas headed by Kuzhab Jedrung Tulku.

Then, accompanied by a procession of monks gathering at the monastery, the circumstances for his opportune meeting with Rikdak Phakchok Rinpoche in the Abhirati Chapel of the monastery were well arranged. These saintly beings loved one another and were at ease and joyful, like old friends being reunited after a long time. He took up residence in the Tse Luding Tashi Khangsar. To each of the monks in the assembled congregation, he offered gifts, communal tea, and incense, and he presented a cloud of offerings, along with canopies and pillar hangings to the three representations of buddha body, speech, and mind, headed by those in the Tragyema Offering Chapel, to each as was appropriate.

Inside the Two-Pillar Chapel of Yang Gon, alongside the inner representation of Munīndra, from whom he was actually indivisible, he received the precepts of a fully ordained monk, preceded by the intermediate vows of a mendicant and novice, in the midst of a quorum of monks from Phakchok Drakpa Gyeltsen, a monastic preceptor and lord of the perfect teaching who was actually no different from the Teacher himself, and from the confessor Mitruk Kunga Pelzang and others who made up the quorum. {875} He became a beauteous crown ornament among the hundred thousand who maintained the monastic discipline, holding the victory banner of the saṃghāṭī robe. Alongside him, Jedrung Rinchen Lekdrub[9] and Khen Mitrukpa also received the full ordination. The name Tashi Drakpa Yeshe Gyurme Trinle Chokle Namgyel was conferred upon him. As an inaugural teaching, the initiation of *The Coemergent Union of Cakrasaṃvara*[10] was bestowed upon him. Starting from then, they alternately received from one another the extensive doctrinal wheel of the empowerments, transmissions, guidance, and esoteric instructions, exemplified by the Great Seal and the Six Doctrines.

Tashi Chokyi Nyima then stayed in retreat for a while at the Angchok Mountain Hermitage. By focusing on meditative stability, he manifestly had visions of the intrinsic face of the three buddha bodies, which are the essential nature of innate mind according to the Great Seal. By successfully completing the practices of the energy channels and winds according to the Six Doctrines of Nāropā, which concern the coalescence of bliss and emptiness, he forced the winds of past actions to enter into the central energy channel, such that his experience and realization of supreme inner radiance was unsurpassed. The transformation of the pristine cognition of authentic blessing was born—implanted, as it were, again in his mind. He consecrated the newly built silver reliquary of Kuzhab Tsetrul Gewang, and also sat at the head of the row when performing the twenty-ninth-day torma exorcism in the Taklung college and the Palace.

At the new year of 1764 (wood monkey), he performed a ritual ablution and made offerings in the Offering Chapel, simultaneously with the two *kuzhab* of Yang Gon. After gradually completing his studies of the sacred doctrine, he undertook an excellent hundredfold offering by means of *The Pure Vision of Long Life*,[11] which pertains to *The Offering to the Spiritual Teachers*,[12] and in return, too, he was served with an abundance of long-life prayers and gifts that were offered.

During that year, {876} news arrived that Rakshak Kalon Zhabdrung had passed away, so immediately he undertook, for seven days, offerings to the three representations of buddha body, speech, and mind along with the rite of Akṣobhya. Khenpo Drakchok arrived to assume responsibility for the palace at Riwoche, whereupon Venerable Tashi Chokyi Nyima himself witnessed this transfer of authority, as Rakshak had previously decreed. Residents of both the old and the new Hevajra Chapels, along with the monastic college of Taklung, requested an empowerment connection, and they honored him with their possessions.

The excellent vase of his buddha mind exquisitely filled them with the nectar of the profound doctrines of the aural lineage of maturational empowerment and liberating guidance, and then, without delay, he set out in the direction of Chulha. An equestrian escort of approximately a hundred monks and laypeople, including a group from the palace, went as far as Muktang. As their minds met one another, he imparted extensive words of advice and then set out gradually via Taktang, Putokha, Sertsa, Tselkar, Drutsab, Begupon, Sezhu Lama, Naksho, and so forth.

On the day when he arrived via Briti Tsara, he was welcomed by the assembled monastic body at the great seminary of Taklung, who lined up in front out of highest respect and placed him on the lion throne. He was invited by the college and the monastery separately and presented with many offerings, including exquisite gifts, long-life prayers, and so forth. He in turn bestowed in abundance communal alms, gifts, and so forth, in public and in private. Prior to his arrival at the monastic seat, he had excellently commissioned a silver reliquary for Rakshak Kalon, along with an image of Vajradhara and a silver reliquary to fulfill the enlightened intention of the late Tsepa Tulku, which are still extant.

Not long afterward, the Chinese emperor with the watchfulness of a great overlord sent an envoy to graciously confer on Sonam Wangyel, the heir of Lord Rashak, the status of Jue Wei, which is the first rank of public officialdom,[13] {877} and for all who were included among his subjects, he was of an exalted level.

With the permission of the bursar Purpa, Ngawang Sonam was appointed as the caretaker of the monastery. Tashi Chokyi Nyima then stayed in retreat for twenty-one days, focusing on the preliminaries of the Great Seal, along with ritual service and attainment, so that he actualized the signs of success on the path of the preliminaries and the main practice and the realization that beholds of its own accord the natural face of the buddha body of reality.

In 1765 (wood bird), according to the oral communication of the older monks, he exquisitely painted with vermilion and gold leaf a somewhat inauspicious black throne at the center of the assembly hall in the Great Offering Chapel. He opened the innermost door of the Tsenkhang of the Old Offering Chapel and made elaborate prayers and offerings for the security of horses, cattle, and so forth. He went on foot to the hilltop shrines of Drakpu, including Ya Gangchen, as well as to Driwulung, the summit of Seling, Ojo, and the uplands of Taklung, where he performed offering prayers, entrusting the local protectors with their rites and embellishing these locales with yak-hair banners. In the Great Offering Chapel, he presented a flat canopy made of finely woven silk, along with six pillar hangings fashioned of various sorts of brocade.

When a dispute arose between Rakshak Tseten and the monks concerning expenses for rituals, Rashak Kutsab introduced changes, so that, starting from then, the expenses would have to be weighed and measured. In this regard, at all times, Tashi Chokyi Nyima acted so as to reinforce the charter of the monastic assembly, the strict disciplinary rules of the monastery, and the regulations of Choje Kuyalwa that had been devised by the peerless Sangye Yarjon. {878} All infringements of body, speech, and mind were prohibited, and the scrupulous ethical discipline of celibacy was maintained such that no one at all could transgress the charter of the monastic assembly that is respected as the most sublime congregation of living beings. After consecrating a manuscript of the Kangyur, the pages of which had been out of order,[14] he went briefly to Nyunruk.

During the third month of 1767 (fire pig), he conferred the guidance of the Great Seal and the great empowerment of Cakrasaṃvara on about twenty monks. Those who requested the mendicant vows and the novitiate, as a precursor to full monastic ordination, over time altogether came to number approximately five hundred. In the Offering Chapel, he presented white and red food offerings, resembling conch and rubies, and over time he even changed the black and white curtains within it on a few occasions. He consecrated with barley a new stūpa that had been commissioned from Dam Gangrak and incidentally also performed acts of great benefit to other patrons outside the influence of Taklung, alleviating their misfortunes, aspiring that they be guided on the path of liberation, and so forth.

In 1768 (earth mouse), he undertook an extensive restoration of Tashi Khangsar, and during the sixth month of that year, he went out to welcome the regent Demo Rinpoche, who had traveled to inspect the sacred sites of Taklung. The reception included a procession of monks, a banquet, offerings, and service. While the noble regent made his inspection, different sorts of incense were offered, thereby facilitating the immeasurable inspiration of his joyous and excellent speech.

At the start of the eighth month, Kuzhab Jedrung Rinchen Lekdrub from Riwoche arrived along with Drakchok from the palace at Riwoche to visit the authorities. At Taklung, he was received elaborately with a procession of monks, a reception, and so forth. He offered many profound and extensive doctrinal connections, including *The Ocean of Means for Attainment*.[15] {879}

When Lama Gyelwang, who maintained the discipline of an accomplished master, arrived, Tashi Chokyi Nyima requested a divination and was told that he should practice the experiential cultivation of Guru Drakpo. Accordingly, starting from then, he adopted the continuous practice of contemplation and mantra recitation, which encompassed the new treasures of Mindroling, as well as Guru Drakmar, the three roots according to our own tradition, [the recitation of] VAJRA GURU that accords with the ritual service of the peaceful aspect, *The Attainment of Long Life: Seven Syllables of Cakrasaṃvara*,[16] and Vajrapāṇi in the form Slight Rage.

Moreover, every morning and evening continuously, he would not interrupt even for a single day his profound and innumerable liturgical arrangements, combining contemplation with prayers, prostrations, maṇḍala offerings, water tormas, and rites of fulfillment and reparation. Each year, he would pass the time focusing on the crucial points of excellent experiential cultivation, including the deity visualization, mantra recitation, and meditative stability, which essentialized the generation and perfection stages, commencing with his strict retreat on the preliminaries of the Great Seal.

The official Odze then offered the monastic college twenty dance costumes made of various dragon-patterned brocades and a pair of censers made of a hundred silver *sang*, and he donated to the monastery four ornate robes and twenty identical dance costumes. In addition, in the Offering Chapel along with a communal tea offering, he made an endowment with assurance[17] and offered a large number of presents, including vermilion-dyed woolen cloth, dress materials, horses, and so forth, and these were well appreciated.

Tashi Chokyi Nyima opened up the grass hermitage and Protector Chapel of the monastic college, and coercing the protectors with his contemplation, he entrusted them with their rites. He sent someone to recognize the reincarnation of Tsepa Tulku [that is, Tsetrul] who had taken birth at Banak in Pengye, and a clear recognition was made. He posted Gomchen Chaklungpa and later also Lama Sherab at Kudzi.

That winter, he consecrated the Kangyur that had been commissioned by Ulha and given to Rukpa Nam, and he restored the torma shrine of Depa Nakguwa. {880} In such ways, he fulfilled the hopes of his devout patrons and then returned to Taklung.

While staying in his retreat hermitage during the twelfth month, he went on the evening of the fourteenth day to attend a performance of sacred songs, and this laid the framework for an entirely auspicious circumstance. Gelong Tekchok then offered him dance costumes, short-length dance ponchos,[18] a pair of gold-plated censers made of a hundred silver *sang*, a bale of fine cloth, a pair of Chinese cymbals in a case, some golden drums, meditation hats, religious robes, a pair of long brass horns, skeleton costumes, and bird and lion dance costumes. He donated to the monastic college newly made articles including short-length dance ponchos, parasols, victory banners, and hangings, along with an abundance of other presents, including horses.

During the eighth month, Tsetrul sent him an invitation from the north, so he set out via Lho Śākya, Nyachu, Lagen, and Dam Ulung, and across Drak La, where he was received by an array of monks in procession. At Zimdrub Deko, they met face-to-face like father and son, or like sun and moon, and they observed a feast. On a number of occasions, the patrons, the assembled congregation of monks, and so forth together offered long-life prayers. To each in turn, he offered presents and gifts that were not small, and in this way everyone rejoiced. He left his personal attendant Lama Sherab in charge of the residence and his hermitage.

On the third day of the ninth month, he cut off the tonsure of Tsetrul's dark hair, and the latter received ordination as a layperson. The name Tashi Gelek Zangpo was conferred upon him. When Lama Sherab fell ill, Gelong Tendar was appointed in his place.

Smallpox then broke out in Lhasa, so Lord Rakshak and his heir retired to Dokhar. {881} In order to bring happiness and benefit to sentient beings, and in particular to avert the epidemic, Venerable Tashi Chokyi Nyima himself stayed in strict retreat, performing the ritual service of *The Fierce and Wrathful Meditational Deity*,[19] which is a profound doctrine revealed by the treasure-finder Rolpei Dorje.

During the fifth month of 1771 (iron hare), he went to offer rain-retreat prayers at the abode of the protector Genyen, and he avoided the threat of smallpox. At that time, he also performed an offering of attainment, and as a sign that he had overcome the epidemic, he also erected a large flag. In order to offer a wedding banquet for Lord Rashak Dzasak, his bursar set out for Dokhar.

Then, on an auspicious autumn day, Tsetrul Rinpoche received ordination as a mendicant novice in the midst of a quorum of the monastic preceptor Kyabgon Drakpa Yeshe, the timekeeper Gelong Tsedzin, and others who made up the number. The name Ngawang Jikme Chokyi Gocha Drubgyu Tenpei Nyima Tashi Gelek Pelzangpo was conferred upon him.

In 1772 (water dragon), Odze completed an outstanding restoration of the monastic college. Then, when Drigung Zhabdrung Chokyi Nyima traveled to the north, on the way he went to inspect the sacred sites of Taklung. He was welcomed, and a reception was held with due respect, excellent offerings, and acts of service. Consequently, the minds of Drigungpa and Taklungpa merged together.

From the first day of the second month of 1773 (water snake), they restored the tormas in the grass hermitage of the monastic college and held an extensive prayer ceremony. They plastered the rooftop floor above the Great Offering Chapel and revarnished the assembly hall of the monastic college, and so forth. Then, Odze provided the resources for carrying out the consecration and an auspicious feast. Furthermore, Odze, along with Chogyel, Chak Tseten, and Tekchok offered a hundred female yaks and silver as an endowment for the butter lamps that were to be offered to the image of the precious Conqueror Taklung Tangpa. {882} Two officiating monks were also appointed to make these offerings continuously. Thereafter, the offering cloud of continuously burning butter lamps was undiminished, and even in the present day, it has become even greater.

At the invitation of the Jang Pengyewa's family, the lord of refuge Tashi Chokyi Nyima and his heir, together with an entourage of some twenty attendants, undertook the pilgrimage circuit of Lake Namtso in the north and reached Drakdrong Tsokha. As he sat on a throne within a fenced enclosure, the Banak nomads of Pengye paid their respects. They stayed there for many days, fulfilling the hopes and wishes of the nomadic community with empowerments, transmitted teachings, and so forth. Similarly, they also briefly visited other patrons including the Tsebum family.

Then, Tsetrul and his entourage stayed at Batok while the supreme lord of refuge Tashi Chokyi Nyima went via Nakchu to confer empowerments, consecrations, burnt offerings, and so forth in the lands of many patrons, including Naktsang Tsengtre, Zhelngo Khangsar Nangso, Sodruk Ngakpa, and Zhung Sok Dharokha. At that time, some important travelers gathered there, including Nakchu Khen, Begu the chieftain of lower Hor, and Bekyang Mangwa, and there was a great deal of coming and going. On all those who made a connection with him, he conferred the bountiful splendor of exalted rebirth and definitive liberation, and they happily turned their possessions into a cloud of offerings to the precious jewels. Then, on the return journey, he fulfilled the hopes of the nomads of Bartawa, headed by the family group of the headman of Barta.

Tashi Chokyi Nyima and his heir Tsetrul reunited at Batok and gradually continued their journey through Chumar Gak, Dromdzo, Sangzhung, Choktse La, and Damtri Ulung, where they were received with bounteous respect. From Sewalung to the Podo Estate, {883} they were received with harmonious[20] respect, and then they reached Taklung.

Tashi Chokyi Nyima dispatched Dengsongwa Lamei Kocha to Kham, along with Singtei Nangkham Zangdrub Ponpo and Ngakpel Ponpo, with the aspiration that they might individually bring benefit and prosperity to the Buddhist teaching.

People then arrived from the chieftain of Tsakhor in Gyelmorong to distribute communal alms in the impartial monasteries of Tibet, and here at Taklung, they also donated as a gift a red-colored parasol that was of outstanding craftsmanship, along with three rolls of cloth and five *dotse* measures of silver.[21] They also donated communal tea to the entire congregation, along with a Chinese silver *sang* for each monk, and in this way, their aspirational provision of merits perfectly ripened.

Around the first day of the fourth month, it was decided that Zhabdrung Tendzin-la, the sibling of the late minister Lord Rakshak, should go to Riwoche to assume the teaching throne in the palace. After offering his tonsure to the supreme all-seeing Dalai Lama, Jampel Gyatso, he first traveled to Taklung to receive empowerments and doctrinal transmissions. On that occasion, as if filling a vase to the brim, Tashi Chokyi Nyima excellently bestowed upon him the empowerments, initiations, and all essential transmissions pertaining to *The Offering to the Spiritual Teachers*,[22] Cakrasaṃvara, Sarvavid, Vārāhī, Akṣobhya, and so forth, along with the vows of the novitiate ordination. The name Ngawang Chokyi Drakpa Tashi Gyeltsen Tenpa Rinchen Sherab Pelzangpo was conferred upon him. He in turn offered an abundance of possessions, including parting gifts,[23] and set out for Riwoche.

On the tenth day of the fifth month of 1776 (fire monkey), coinciding with the Dreulung Tsechu,[24] Tashi Chokyi Nyima conferred the great empowerment of the three roots, and a large crowd of monks and laypeople gathered. On that occasion, Doring Paṇḍita and his wife Cham Rinchen were traveling to the hot springs, and on the way, they arrived at Taklung. {884} Since Tashi Chokyi Nyima had previously considered constructing victory banners of gilded copper above the Great Offering Chapel, he went to Doring to request good quality gold and mercury and permission for the artisans to obtain leave of absence. The latter delightedly also offered a donation of one *dotse* of gold. The pair of victory banners that were constructed that year and the three that were constructed the following year altogether contained one hundred and three steelyard measures of pure gold, three hundred and thirteen steelyard measures of mercury, and one hundred and fifty-nine bushels of copper. Including these, and along with other materials, the wages of the artisans and the banquets, the total expenditure amounted to two thousand nine hundred and seventy-six *sang* of silver. To that end, Tashi Chokyi Nyima obtained all sorts of donations from individual patrons of regions that were sympathetic to Taklung. As for the relics contained within those victory banners, they were filled completely with many icons fashioned of gilded copper and bronze, the soiled robes, rosaries, and offering bowls of his venerable predecessors, as well as countless incantations representing buddha speech, including the canonical texts of the Conqueror and the commentaries upon their enlightened intention, and also earth, stones, and water from three main sacred places, and in addition the wealth of the precious treasury of the yakṣas, food, gems, and useful artifacts. These were inserted securely in such a way that the being of commitment and the being of pristine cognition merged indivisibly. The inauguration was well arranged in conjunction with an excellent feast of good auspices, and then the unfading victory banners of the teaching of the lineage of attainment were gloriously raised, exalted in the heavens.[25]

Dilapidated buildings of the monastery were also restored by Odze. {885} As an endowment, he planned to raise seven *dotse* of silver, or ten *dotse*, including tea, butter, and barley, and he acted in service of the restoration.

During the eleventh month, Namterwa invited Tashi Chokyi Nyima to consecrate a hundred icons of Orgyen Rinpoche that he had commissioned, and incidentally the funding for this was supplemented voluntarily by other patrons.

During the fourth month of 1777 (fire bird), Tashi Chokyi Nyima bestowed the guidance of the Six Doctrines of Nāropā on some ten monks. For the offering of attainment, Lord Rakshak and his entourage arrived at Taklung via Nyingdrung hot springs, and they had a meritorious meeting of minds.

Here at Taklung, there was a resident named Gazi Zhabdrung Awa Sonam Tobgyel, who could not understand the teachings and who passed away on the fifteenth day of the seventh month due to water pollution. In the sky at that time, wondrous signs appeared, including a rainbow cloud. The cremation and funeral rites were carried out without obstacle and with positive signs that were not insignificant.

When Lord Rakshak the Great decreed that the murals of the Great Offering Chapel should be varnished, Tashi Chokyi Nyima replied that they should begin with the timbers of the bow capitols, roof, and so forth in the Main Temple that was certainly very dilapidated. Thereupon, in accordance with the permission of Zhungsa Rinpoche, the regent, during the second month of 1778 (earth dog), they gradually cut down trees below Lhundrub Dzong, and from the start of the fifth month, the reconstruction project began. They finished work on the bow capitols, the roof, the wall plaster, the floor cement, and so forth of the north wing of the Main Temple, and then they also repaired the Old Offering Chapel, and it was decreed that stuffed images of Genyen and his entourage should be erected at the upper and lower monasteries. Some twenty artisans worked gradually on the murals and the relief sculptures. {886}

When the Dalai Lama was about to travel to Chokhorgyel, in accordance with his itinerary, the sibling of Lord Rakshak visited Taklung and inspected the restoration work that had been completed. He decreed that the restoration should be completed the next year. In 1779 (earth pig), the murals of the upper and lower halls of the Offering Chapel were restored or newly painted—the murals of the reliquary stūpas, the Satri, and the Old Offering Chapel, along with the lower hall of the Lhakhar Palace, and the main kitchen, and so forth, were all repaired, while the upper and lower spectators' galleries for sacred dances, along with the flagstones of the dance courtyard and the shrines of Nyenchen Tanglha, were newly built. These extensive plans were completed with many wondrous and effortless arrays.

While seeing off the all-seeing Paṇchen Lama Pelden Yeshe when he was invited to the Palace of the Chinese emperor, the omniscient, all-seeing Dalai Lama accompanied him, along with Trichen Nomon Qan, the Chinese ambassadors resident in Tibet, and other important aristocrats. They journeyed out via Yangpachen, escorting him as far as Uma Tashitang, and then suddenly they all changed direction to visit the sacred places in Radeng and Taklung. Elaborate preparations were made, including a riding escort and a procession of monks. The offerings that were elaborately made, including banquets, donations, silver, silk cloth, horses, hybrid cattle, and so forth surpass the imagination.

On this occasion, Zhabdrung Chodrak of Riwoche also arrived here in Taklung. When the ministers, the Zhabdrung Kumche, and the great lord of refuge Tashi Chokyi Nyima of Taklung visited the sacred places, they were escorted by incense carriers and so forth. Their happy demeanor, awards, and decorous attention were, as it were, matchless, and particularly great in terms of protocol. The reimbursements that the government provided were not insignificant, and they donated censers, pillar hangings, and so forth in the offering chapels. {887} The party sojourned for two days at the confluence of Tak. When they set out for Lhasa, Lord Rakshak escorted the Paṇchen Lama to Drichukha and then stayed at his own residence.

In 1780 (iron mouse), empowerments were held for fifty-three initiations on behalf of some fifty monks who were interested in the Great Seal. Then, the supporting rites of fulfillment were recited, along with the reading of *The Hundredfold Injunctions*[26] and so forth.

When the glorious hierarch of Sakya and his heir came to visit the sacred places, they were received with an elaborate reception. They requested *The Long-Life Empowerment Titled Queen of Accomplishment That Tallies Age*, and all the monks and laity who gathered there were satisfied with the empowerment and the meeting.

There was an auspicious coincidence that occurred when an award of *jiu wei* rank was made by an imperial edict of Nomon Qan to Tse Zhabdrung Chodrak Rinpoche of Riwoche. The latter gradually completed his studies, including empowerments, guidance, and esoteric instructions, headed by the Great Seal and the Six Doctrines, and on that occasion, here at Taklung, Rakshak awarded the supreme lord of refuge Tashi Chokyi Nyima a gold seal in Chinese and Tibetan that said, "This is the seal of the glorious doctrinal king, elucidating like daylight the teaching of the Kagyu lineage."

In 1781 (iron ox), when the bursar had to go to meet Lord Rakshak, he went there as in the past, and on reaching Lhunding, he suddenly contacted a serious illness. Returning to Taklung, he gradually recovered for a while, but later his condition deteriorated, and unable to hold on to life for much longer, he passed away.

Coinciding with the award of the aforementioned gold seal, in a communal tea offering ceremony, an auspicious scarf was offered to each of the monks, and Tashi Chokyi Nyima composed an edict reinforcing the monastic charter. {888} The gold seal was also handed over for safekeeping to the monastery.

A workshop was established for the construction of the silver reliquary of the late Lord Rakshak Senior, Wangchuk Tashi Lek. The entire monastic college and the monastery successfully raised the donations, mostly in a spirit of excellent cooperation.

When the lama's personal attendant Gelong Tsedzin suddenly fell ill and could no longer recognize anyone, rites that acquired positive and virtuous action were undertaken on his behalf. The minister Lord Rakshak arrived in Taklung during the consecration of the silver reliquary, and this coincided with the reception for the sacred corpse of Paṇchen Rinpoche when it was returned to Tibet from China. At meetings high and low, detailed discussions were held between the monasteries for the sake of the Buddhist teaching.

His bursar, the steward Trelgo, was then appointed as the ritual officiant. When he was invited by the retired steward of Seling and by the meditation hermitages in general, a most meritorious, auspicious connection was established.

Tashi Chokyi Nyima was invited by the patrons of Penyul, and he stayed there, carrying out public empowerments, private empowerments, incense offerings, rites of ablution, and so forth on behalf of Menlung, Daryul, Rong Gar, Yezhi, Chichen, the estate of the monastic college, and so forth. During that time, the reputation of Lord Rakshak resounded like thunder when it was announced that the Chinese emperor would confer on him a title, along with a plumed hat and so forth. On that occasion, as a gift to his dependents, they enjoyed as a concluding dance the spectacle of peacock plumage.[27]

Gradually, Tashi Chokyi Nyima effortlessly carried out the twofold benefit of self and others at all his domains including Drongma, Ringang, Nyenchuk, Sharbum, Yakdrong, Sumtreng, Khang Lhoga Lhun Dzong, and Unang, and then he traveled directly back to the monastic seat of Taklung.

In 1782 (water tiger), he commissioned the reliquary of Zhabdrung Awa in the form of a Victory Stūpa. {889} At the encouragement of the monks who requested the sacred doctrine on behalf of the entire congregation of the monastic college and the monastery, he conferred the fourteen-aspect maṇḍala of *The Purification of the Lower Realms*[28] and the great empowerment of Vārāhī. In the Great Offering Chapel, a large victory banner fashioned of diverse fine silks was offered.

In 1783 (water hare), although the previous year the salt caravans had been robbed and destroyed, and there was no way for the rebellious nomads of Gegye to provide compensation and so forth for the theft, here at Taklung they expressed their regret by replacing and substituting the lost salt and so forth, such that there were a few people who incurred losses. When the Zhabdrungpa of Riwoche Tseyang, while visiting the sacred places, was asked to provide assistance, his offerings caused their minds to rejoice.

Tashi Chokyi Nyima also sent presents from Taklung when Prince Doring was enthroned, and when the stūpa of Driwulung was rebuilt, he performed the consecration and rites of ablution.

On an occasion when a roaming king spirit entered this wilderness in the valley of Yamar Tsengo, Tashi Chokyi Nyima arranged all that was needed for ritually dispatching the requisite first fruits, including a tawny stallion, a black horse, a black dog, a royal costume, various silks, grains, medicines, and articles of offering. Then, four groups including the masters of the monastery carried out the torma rite of Four-Armed Mahākāla and cast the tormas separately into the cardinal directions. Drion Tashi Nyendrak then effectively reinforced this with the torma rite of the demon-taming Siṃhavaktrā and a thread cross, and the protector Tsengo Yamarwa proudly possessed his icon. As a further support, the assembly of monks recited *The Heart Sūtra of Wisdom* and *The Ritual Aversion of Siṃhavaktrā*.[29] In this way, the malevolent king spirits and bewitching spirits were banished by the distance of a yojana and an earshot, such that they no longer dwelled there. In addition, {890} long-life rituals, rites of fulfillment, offering prayers to the gods, and burnt offerings of pacification and enrichment were undertaken on behalf of the college, the monastery, and the palace. Tashi Chokyi Nyima then convalesced at Nyingdrung hot springs, and on the way back he incidentally also perfectly nurtured the well-being of his patrons.

In conjunction with an auspicious planet and constellation, on the fourth day of the ninth month, in front of the eastern gate of the Main Temple, he reconsecrated the sacred artifacts and the buildings containing them, headed by the central image of Taklung Tangpa the Great, and he spread forth the flowers of his benediction. The ritual officiant Pelgyur undertook on his behalf the aversion torma rite of Wrathful Guru Drakpo, along with the long-life prayers associated with the rite averting the reception of the ḍākinīs.

Thereafter, Tashi Chokyi Nyima restored the temple of Driwulung. He had the monks of the monastery recite aloud an arrangement of *The Sūtra of Supreme Golden Light*, and he had those of the monastic college study anew and perfectly restore the melodic chants associated with the rites of fulfillment and reparation. He also composed a liturgical arrangement supplementing the rite of the peaceful and wrathful deities in the context of his predecessor's pure vision of the three roots. The provisions for the performance of this supplementary rite were provided from the palace, but others also gradually contributed.

During the second month of 1785 (wood snake), when the official Odze suddenly succumbed to a severe illness and passed away, Tashi Chokyi Nyima presided over the extensive meritorious rites of the assembled offerings and imparted advice. He effectively supported the restoration of the grass hermitage and Protector Chapel of the monastic college, and the offering of new tormas to the representative images, and so forth.

The previous year, he had been invited to the north along with Choktrul Jola Abu Lama and Kyabne Kuzhab, but they did not go because Kuzhab Choku the latter had been unwell. Offerings were made in many dependent congregations in conjunction with daily symbolic rites, {891} and in many congregations an abundance of communal tea and alms distribution was offered. Four bass relief sculptors filled the victory stūpa, containing the skull of Gelong Tsedzin with the four kinds of pearl relics, and it was placed within the Lama Lhakhang of the Offering Chapel.

After sojourning annually at Nyingdrung hot springs, Rikdak Phakchok Rinpoche passed away for the benefit of others, whereupon in each of the communities of the monastic college, the monastery, and the mountain hermitage at Riwoche, communal alms and offerings were made to the sacred representations. Here, too, at Taklung, an extensive offering cloud of funerary rites was undertaken.

When it was decreed that the *si* demon of Yamar Kalung should be effectively suppressed, the ritual was elaborately undertaken for one week by Akhu Demchok of Lhunding, Namar Akhu, and so forth.

In 1786 (fire horse), they traveled together to Driwulung and repaired the shrine of the local deity, and so forth. In that regard, owing to the threat of smallpox in Lhasa, the two younger sons of Rakshak traveled to Taklung to avoid this virulent contagion, and Tashi Chokyi Nyima provided whatever extensive service he could from his hermitage residence.

The protector of Tibet, Trichen Nomon Qan the Great, then set out for the great capital city of Beijing, and at the confluence of Tak, Tashi Chokyi Nyima pleased him as best he could with meals, presentational offerings, receptions, escorts, and so forth. He in turn bestowed noble words, gifts, communal alms, and so forth. Jola Lakyab of Pengye initiated a Maṇi Bumdrub ceremony at all the congregations affiliated with Taklung.

During the high point, the beginning, and the end of the epidemic, Tashi Chokyi Nyima's service was most excellent. When he gave empowerments at the end, he bestowed the maturational empowerments of the five-deity assemblage of *The Great Compassionate One: Tamer of Living Beings*,[30] on approximately five hundred monks and laypeople. Opening the maṇḍala of *The Hundred Sacral Aspects of the Peaceful and Wrathful Deities*,[31] {892} he even brought his follower, the patron Abu, to maturation through the empowerment.

Once the threat of smallpox had diminished in the college and the monastery, the two Rakshak princes also returned to Lhasa. Everyone in the palace, the college, and the monastery, in public and in private, also carried out extensive ritual service to pacify the contagion.

That winter, while the supreme lord of refuge, Tashi Chokyi Nyima, was staying in strict retreat, during the twelfth month, small abscesses appeared on his feet when otherwise he had no illness or pain. The doctors did not speak of it as malignant. At the end of the year, on the occasion of the twenty-ninth day *gutor* ceremony, he attended as he had done in the past. Previously, he had been meticulous in the melodic chanting, but this year he appeared somewhat stricter, more fastidious and meticulous than before. Tsetrul Rinpoche had all sorts of inauspicious dream signs, but he could not mention them owing to Tashi Chokyi Nyima's majestic appearance. At the new year of 1787 (fire sheep), the abscesses on his feet slightly increased, so his attendants consulted individual lama physicians, including Nyenpo Drungtso, the senior and younger Namter Emchi, and Drigung Zhabdrung, but it did not appear to be very dangerous. Then, at the time when the divinations of lamas, including Gyelwang Karmapa, were gradually sought, along with the prophetic declarations of the doctrinal protectors, although he was without any pain, the pustules became more severe. Along with Lord Rakshak, they appealed to him, and then everyone, in public and in private, gradually undertook long-life prayers, the incantation of Amitāyus, all through the night, and so forth, but they could not avert the focus of his enlightened intention that was directed toward other pure lands. When midnight had passed on the twenty-seventh day of the first month of 1787 (fire sheep), at the end of the early part of the hour of the ox, the emanation of his physical body displayed the way of dissolving into the expanse of reality. {893}

When the attendants requested the venerable one to swiftly reincarnate for the benefit of the Buddhist teaching and living beings and to maintain his post-death contemplation without distraction, his eyes momentarily looked up toward the sky, without saying anything at all, his head suitably positioned and his legs equipoised in the posture of adamantine reality, his physical body became straight as an arrow, and he became equipoised in the disposition of the great seal, the luminosity devoid of all extremes of conceptual elaboration, the supreme quiescence of reality.

Thereupon, funeral offering ceremonies, extensive material offerings, the chanting of sacred songs, and prayers were sequentially requested. For three days and nights, he remained seated in post-death contemplation, and immediately after that, the sacred corpse was excellently bathed with fine perfume and medicine and then adorned with seed syllables in the sacred places of body, speech, mind, and so forth, and the costume of the buddha body of perfect resource. People were then gradually admitted to see the sacred corpse.

On the fourth day of the second month, in the small Layel Courtyard, Tsetrul Rinpoche and some forty attendants carried out the cremation in connection with the burnt offering of Sarvavid Vairocana. As soon as the sacred corpse was placed within the crematorium, the sky cleared and all the cardinal and intermediate directions were filled with rainbow light, a shower of flowers fell and other such signs occurred in the manifest perception of all. So it was that immeasurable devotion and pure vision arose within the assembled congregation of masters and disciples, along with the patrons. When the cremation stūpa was opened on the fifth day, the heart, tongue, and eyes emerged undamaged. These were inserted within this silver reliquary in the form of an enlightenment stūpa, which was fashioned of many precious elements, {894} and from nine hundred *sang* of silver, and then placed in the Lower Hall of the Main Temple. Its essential nature is one in which the being of commitment and the being of pristine cognition are inseparable.

The Collected Works of Tashi Chokyi Nyima, along with the catalog of his earlier and later restorations and the representations that he commissioned, fill eleven volumes. The first part was compiled by the lord-protector himself, and the second part is a supplement composed by Tsetrul Gelek Zangpo. Since the three mysteries and the five wheels of adornment of this teacher, the lord of refuge, were manifestly no different from all the conquerors of infinite buddha fields, these works of his cannot be measured, just like the sense field of space.

In the common perspective of his disciples in this world, too, his physical form was beautiful, majestic, and insatiable to behold. His speech was sweet, profound, and attractive, exclusively establishing the excellent path that is without defects, imbued with the wheel of the elaborate sacred doctrine, the pronouncements of which concern all positive and negative factors of existence and quiescence. His mind could accommodate all things, definitive and quantitative within the vast expanse of knowledge, and yet ostensibly he professed a disposition similar to that which Lord Atiśa refers to with the words, "The talents of others should be proclaimed. Your own talents should be concealed." Therefore, it seemed that he did not greatly study the outer and inner fields of classical learning and so forth, and he acted with modesty, saying to the attendants within his own inner circle, "I have the title Taklung Choje, but on investigation, I am feeble in attributes of study and refinement." However, in actual fact, he was effortlessly accomplished in omniscience. He absolutely maintained the skill in means that comprehends the most minute immediate and long-term circumstances and acts of acceptance and rejection in terms of the twofold tradition of sūtra and mantra. His noble enlightened intention was steadfast like the king of mountains Sumeru and hard to fathom like an ocean. {895} He made excellent appraisals in all his activities, and apart from that, he was extremely profound, unable to be swayed by the winds of external circumstances. Although he had the prescience in which many accurate but hidden prophecies concerning future events clearly arose, to those who indulged in exaggeration and deprecation, he had the demeanor of one who saw nothing at all. Other than that, he did not clearly speak of them. He was similar to Lord Songtsen Gampo, embodiment of the Great Compassionate One in immediately rewarding with awards and praise the positive actions of all his subjects, monastic and laity, and in critically repudiating those who would lead them astray into misconduct. In the meantime, he never squandered any of the material resources that were his by association. In order to acquire the essence of merit, he would respect acts of service on behalf of the three sorts of sacred representations within the Main Temple and sponsorship of the monastic community. He ensured that such authentic and positive contributions were used exclusively for their intended purpose, and so to all honest and knowledgeable persons, he was increasingly worthy of praise, and he had a career in which they rejoiced.

The Disciples of Tashi Chokyi Nyima

The foremost of the array of disciples on whom the fatherly descent of his oral transmissions were conferred was Zhabdrung Dampa Pelden Nomon Qan Chokyi Drakpa, sovereign of knowledge, power, and compassion, whose life story may be incidentally known from *The Supplementary Doctrinal History of the Abbatial Succession of the Palace: The Second Labrang of Taklung Lower Plain, Yisho*, which was authored by the root guru and all-pervading lord of enlightened heritage, Phakchok Yizhin Norbu Wangi Gyelpo. If one wishes to know his life story more extensively, I think it would not take long because it is extant in other documents. {896}

After him, there was our peerless and gracious lord of refuge Jikme Gocha. Although there are no documents pertaining to his life story, an approximation including the minor details of all that I have heard may be known from the account that follows below.

In addition, there was the physician and great hermit sage Drigung Zhabdrung Tashi Nyendrak, and all the many masters of the college and the monastery whose wondrous lives should be discussed but cannot be established because I have not seen their accounts.

May the enlightened activity of always pleasing the lama,
Extracted from this mere drop of this supreme lama's life story,
Composed of all excellent virtues of ground, path, and result,
Become a causal basis capable of liberating all three world systems!

7. Kunkhyen Jikme Gocha, a.k.a. Drakpa Choying Lhundrub

Devout homage to Jikme Gocha,
He who adopted the words of the eighty-four thousand doctrinal sections
Imparted by the divine Ngagi Wangchuk
As a melody of **fearless** (*'jigs med*)[1] resonance
And donned the robust **armor** (*go cha*) that upholds the Buddhist teaching
of the sacred doctrine of definitive meaning, of benefit to others!

Now, I will recount the appearance of our peerless and gracious guide, the omniscient Jikme Gocha, the twenty-fourth incumbent of the lion throne of the sacred doctrine at Taklung, who was an emanation of the second Conqueror Acala, in this fertile northern region. Without moving from the natural sameness, which is that of the buddha body of reality, the conquerors are endowed with profound methods that diversely reveal their liberating careers in accordance with the faculties of their disciples.

Not distinct from the perceptual range of the conquerors, it is clearly elucidated here from the succession of his former births that they included eight renowned great accomplished masters who were contemporaries in India, headed by Paṇchen Saraha and the yogin Śavaripā, and in Tibet the succession of his former births clearly included Mila Repa, Salton Gomshe, Druk Ling Repa, Gonpo Tashi Pel of Taklung, Kunkhyen Ngawang Drakpa, {897} Khardung Sonam Tashi, the three madmen (Druk Nyon, Tsang Nyon, and Gam Nyon), and so forth. Apart from his immediate predecessor, Ngagi Wangchuk, who composed the lineage prayers to the teachers who were the objects of his faith, they were, for the most part, exclusively of the same generation. For this reason, they did not form a lineage of incarnations from one to the next. Since all the conquerors exclusively emerge from the unique buddha body of reality, they can be counted as simply identical in the essential nature of the pristine cognition of buddha mind.

In this field, the first of his actual series of incarnations who appeared in common perception was Kunpang Tendzin Nyima, the incarnation of that Tsetrul Ngagi Wangchuk who had founded the Tse Palace at Riwoche, who lived as a carefree mendicant in all parts of the country, including the three sacred power places. His reincarnations took rebirth as the Tsetrul line, mighty in virtuous activities, who earlier and later occupied the teaching throne of the Tse Palace at Riwoche and who engaged the residents of Taklung and Ojo in spiritual attainment, study, and reflection.

Finally, he took birth at Pengye Banak in 1764 (wood male monkey). His father was Abu Tsoril, a devout patron in the region of Jang Namar, and his mother was Yangtsoma. Those from Taklung who undertook the rituals of recognition were exceedingly clear. In particular, there was a vase that had been the property of his predecessor, of which he said, "That's mine!" His father said, "That's not yours. It belongs to Tsetrul," and he replied, "If I am not Tsetrul, who is?"

Since events such as this were extremely well attested, they all acquired confidence in him and {898} escorted him to the monastic seat. He received the vows of the laity and the novitiate from Kyabje Tashi Drakpa Yeshe (a.k.a. Tashi Chokyi Nyima), and under him he received and studied as much as he could the empowerments and transmissions of the impartial ancient and new ways of Secret Mantra. From his personal attendant, Gelong Tendar, he received the practical applications of the Taklung tradition, and under Punkharcho Phuntsok Chowang, he perfected without distraction refinement and perseverance that reached the pinnacle of skill in the calligraphy of the Rañjanā and Vartula scripts and so forth.

Together with his lord of refuge, he once traveled to undertake the pilgrimage circuit of the lake at Lake Namtso in the north and to travel around his estates. Other than that, he resided at this seminary of Taklung.

In 1787 (fire sheep), in his twenty-fourth year, after Kyabgon Drakpa Yeshe had passed away into the expanse of reality, he excellently prepared the sacred corpse, performed the funeral rites and undertook the construction of the great silver reliquary. At the time of this consecration and festivity, Lord Rashak encouraged him, saying, "You yourself must take responsibility for the monastic seat as a provisional hierarch, since there is no one of the Gazi line now capable of assuming the role of hierarch, and even the reincarnation of your predecessor, the lord of refuge, cannot swiftly appear and assume that responsibility!" Accordingly, he took his seat on the great teaching throne in the midst of the assembly. The monks of the congregation and dignitaries lined up magnificently in rows, making offerings and reciting auspicious verses.

From Zhabdrung Pelden Nomon Qan of Riwoche, he acquired the full monastic ordination, and he perfectly received the lineage of authentic blessing pertaining to the Great Seal, the Six Doctrines, and so forth. From Gyelwang Chodze Peljor, he acquired the ocean-like empowerments, transmissions, and pith instructions, headed by the twenty-eight maṇḍalas of *The Maṇḍala Rites Titled Adamantine Garland*. {899}

In the crystal cave of Tanglha, a sacred place of attainment near Lhabu Gangi Rawa, that had been blessed by Padmasambhava, master of accomplishment, and the hierarchs of the Kagyu lineage, he stayed for some months, engaged in the experiential cultivation of the generation and perfection stages in general. In particular, with strong perseverance and one-pointed focus on the Six Doctrines of the profound path, including the four primary doctrines and the two ancillary doctrines, all appearances became fictitious, in the manner of a magical display or a dream, and he also attained control over the pure deities and mantras in the essential nature of pristine cognition. All the winds associated with past actions were inducted into the central energy channel of pristine cognition that is of pure appearance, and he acquired extraordinary experiences and realizations, manifesting all agitation of the ordinary subject-object dichotomy as the enlightened intention in the unchanging buddha body of reality.

Returning to Taklung, he then brought the minds of the masters of the college and some sixty disciples who maintained the vows of ethical discipline to maturation in the guidance of the Great Seal of the profound path and the maṇḍalas of the ocean of tantras.

In 1790 (iron dog), he graciously bestowed perfect acts of service upon Taklung, restoring the roof of the Upper Offering Chapel, replacing the internal wooden structures and so forth. At the end of 1790 (iron dog), there was danger due to the war with Nepal in the direction of Tashi Lhunpo in Upper Tsang. Consequently, a large Chinese and Mongol imperial army arrived, and great damage and destruction was inflicted upon all the southern and northern parts of Utsang. However, in this direction of Taklung, by the power of truth, combined with the aspirations of saintly beings and the receptacles of the three precious jewels, no damage at all was inflicted apart from some minor short-term commotion that was transitory. {900} At Podo, he met and paid homage to the senior lieutenant general Ho Si, and by pleasing him in these ways, he rendered the situation auspicious.

In 1792 (water mouse), I, the pretentious[2] Chokyi Gyeltsen, who timely assumes the appearance of a lama, also paid respects at his lotus feet, and starting from then, at all times, he looked after me with immeasurable great kindness.

In 1794 (wood tiger), he offered a flat canopy and so forth fashioned of various fine silks to the Offering Chapel, and he repaired the sacred dance masks, embellishing them with colored paint. In the Offering Chapel, he completed the restoration of the preexisting image of the Great Fifth Dalai Lama, and in earlier and later times, he newly commissioned many small images fashioned of medicinal clay, depicting Jowo Je Atiśa; the trio of Khuton, Ngok Lekpei Sherab, and Dromton; the Bodhisattva Śāntarakṣita; Khache Paṇchen Śākyaśrī; Sakya Paṇḍita; Buton Rinchendrub; Songtsen Gampo; Mila Repa; Vajrapāṇi; Hayagrīva; Acala; and so forth.

Every year at the uninterrupted major and minor anniversary ceremonies, the bountiful array of offerings that were made continuously, according to ancient customs, was astonishingly sublime. Many times, early and later, he obtained very clear signs of realization with respect to the supreme and common accomplishments, due to his skill in the profound yoga of the authentic generation and perfection stages—the recitation, ritual service, and rites of attainment pertaining to infinite preferred deities, of the ancient and new traditions, headed by the wrathful demon-subduing Siṃhavaktrā.

In particular, during 1795 (wood hare) and 1796 (fire dragon), there was extreme danger due to smallpox throughout the region, such that here at Taklung, there were also some thirty monks from the college and the monastery who died. Specially for that, he prepared strong, unrefined pills and so forth, in accordance with *The Wrathful Guru Drakpo*[3] of Rolpei Dorje. {901}

In 1797 (fire snake), when he felt ashamed at the state of the white and red robes[4] in the Main Temple, he clad them in white and red like the radiance of the sun and moon. He swept clean the parapet, repaired the slates, and so forth, so that they joined continuously just like two half moons. Incidentally, with extensive funds from the bursar Rin Gang, he constructed a window on the south side of the hermitage and so forth.

Afterward, he conferred upon me the vows of the laity and the novitiate and gave me the name Ngawang Tashi Chokyi Gyeltsen Drakpa Namgyel Pelzang. During the festivities, he rejoiced in inspecting an image of the protecting deity Apchi Lhamo, and even I, at that time, with the perspective of a small child, experienced this most amazing spectacle.

In 1798 (earth horse), Jikme Gocha granted forty-three instructions and initiations of the Great Seal of the profound path to some thirty who requested it, headed by Lama Kadrukpa. And in 1799 (earth sheep), on behalf of some twenty monks, he imparted the essentialized perfection stage of the profoundly secret unsurpassed tantras, along with guidance on the Six Doctrines, and the great empowerments of twenty-eight maṇḍalas according to the Adamantine Garland. I also had the kindness of receiving these early and later empowerments and initiations.

When Amban Song Yun (1794–1799) and Amban Ying Shan (1799–1804) came to inspect Taklung, Jikme Gocha met them and rendered the circumstance auspicious. And then, when the regent of Tsurphu, Chokyi Pelzang, came to visit Taklung, he offered service and an excellent reception. They passed the time in uninterrupted conversion concerning the profound and extensive sacred doctrine, and during his stay, he acknowledged the rows of monks, and in the Main Temple, he elaborately conferred over two days the great empowerment of Mahākāruṇika in the form Jinasāgara, {902} consisting of the preparation and the main rite. Then, after completing rites on behalf of the Palace and so forth, he set out for his own domain.

In 1798 (earth horse), Zhabdrung Nomon Qan of Riwoche visited Taklung, and over a stay of many days, he paid excellent respects, taking up residence in the hermitage. He bestowed upon Kyabje Jikme Gocha himself some empowerments and transmissions, including a long-life empowerment. Together with me, he received some essential transmissions including *The Mother and Child Rites of Reparation and Fulfillment for Jñānanātha*, based on volume twelve (*na pa*) of the Collected Works of Venerable Ngawang Namgyel. Kyabchok Jikme Gocha offered him bountiful material offerings and parting gifts, along with a long-life prayer, and in return he brought forth bountiful pristine presents, including monastic undershirts and other robes, as well as material necessities. Then, when he was about to depart via Drigung Lungsho, one day, at my request and that of some others who were interested, the supreme Zhabdrung bestowed in detail the blessing of the eighty-four great accomplished masters, based on the writings of

Venerable Tashi Peldrub. He had the kindness just to devote the whole day and the evening to that.

In early and later years, he presented to Taklung an offering cloud of gifts that would please the conquerors, along with exquisite newly made embroideries, six pairs of pillar decorations, and victory banners with many extraordinary embellishments, as if they had been mentally drawn. In early and later years, he also passed some time at the hot springs of the divine grove of Nyendrung. {903}

In 1799 (earth sheep), when Jikme Gocha went to make offering prayers at the sacred sites of the great protector deity at Pokyi Yagangchen, there was a great snowfall. Immediately after that pilgrimage, in order to see the circuit of the lake at Jang Namtso, to inspect his paternal estates and fulfill the hopes of faithful patrons, he set out for the north. He tarried there about three months and received the somewhat elaborate service of his disciples. He satisfied all those beings who inhabit the prosperous estates of the northern region with feasts of provisional benefit and conclusive great bliss. On his return, he presented me with gifts including a horse, and he also distributed all sorts of individual gifts to Lord Rakshak and to the congregation of the college and the monastery.

When he prayed for an offering cloud for the sake of the temples, I, too, accompanied him. That autumn when I succumbed to measles, and he sought out the responsible demon, thanks to his remedies, which included blessings and pills of nectar, I recovered without mishap. That winter, he stayed in strict retreat as before, and although he undertook the continuous mantra recitation of Jñānanātha for one week each year, on this particular year, he insisted on reciting for two weeks and an additional period the mantra GAVUVAVAPAŚAYA. Otherwise, the requisite auspicious circumstances would not turn out as intended. From then on, each year he would add the mantra VAPAŚAYA. It was later in 1815 (wood pig) that I reverted to reciting the thirteen-syllable mantra of Jñānanātha in accordance with the former custom.

Then, on the tenth day of the monkey month in 1800 (iron monkey), we set out together for Drilung. There, on behalf of a congregation of about one hundred monks and laypeople, he brought their minds to maturation in the empowerments of The Conqueror: Union of All Rare and Precious Things[5] and The Peaceful and Wrathful Guru. {904} When he was performing the offering of attainment, Lord Rakshak Tutob and his son arrived, and he satisfied them with a reception, acts of service, offerings, and other such bountiful and lavish gifts. For about ten days, they camped behind the reliquary stūpas and then departed in good spirits.

That winter, while in retreat, Gelong Tashi fell ill due to pollution, and although all sorts of remedies and rites were undertaken and Drubwang Dudul Puk was invited from Drigung, and so forth, he passed away in a timely manner, without holding on to life. At that time, the people providing the expenditure and the Palace performed extensive and auspicious funeral rites. The butler of his nephew acted as the ritual officiant and requested Jikme Gocha to remain in retreat. The bursar Rin Gang had permission for leave of absence and in his place, the official Pelpo was appointed.

In 1801 (iron bird), Kyabgon Phakchok Rinpoche, the lord of all enlightened heritage, and his entourage arrived from Riwoche. They stayed for about one and a half months, and Jikme Gocha perfectly undertook excellent service and reception on his behalf. Phakchok Rinpoche joyfully bestowed on his audience the transmission of the essential liturgical compilations from the Collected Works of Venerable Taklung Tangpa and of Sangye On, and a large number of empowerments including *The Precious Source of Means for Attainment*[6] and Four-Armed Mahākāla. Among his subjects, I, too, incidentally received these. Sundry matters were concluded, including the exchange of parting gifts, and then they set out gradually from the Lhasa area for Yisho.

As the master under whom I would study the fields of classical learning, {905} a teacher was requested from Mindroling, and he arrived in the autumn of 1800 (monkey), and in that regard I am now continuing with my training in the outer and inner fields of classical learning at all times.

Although Kyabgon Jikme Gocha himself had greatly intended to go to the Lhasa area in order to see Gyelwa Rinpoche, the Dalai Lama, to make offerings to Jowo Śākyamuni and so forth, he did not in fact go, not only because his eyesight, hearing, and so forth were very poor but because his attendants did not show much concern and so forth. Then, suddenly, in 1803 (water pig), he immediately purchased a large amount of gold and mercury from Lhasa. In the fourth month of that year, he established a workshop and commissioned the extant representation of Munīndra, fifteen spans in height, which is known as Conqueror in Battle of the Four Demonic Forces. However, the artisans, headed by the leader Rinchen Zangpo of Doring, were unhappy with the fees, provisions, and so forth. There were many reasons for disagreement and the deterioration of commitments, and the image itself was not completely attractive. The arrangement of the most auspicious circumstances did not naturally arise. The project was amicably completed at the end of the seventh month, and the supreme lord of refuge, Jikme Gocha, himself, with some twenty attendants, undertook the consecration ceremony in which the being of pristine cognition was absorbed into the image, and he also held a feast.

That autumn, Sakya Dakchen Pelden Chokyong arrived to visit the sacred sites at Taklung, and I asked to lead the way holding incense and so forth. They met together in the Lower Offering Chapel. In a public gathering, he kindly bestowed the extensive maturational empowerment of *The Long-Life Empowerment Titled Granting the Glory of Immortality*,[7] and an abundance of offerings was presented to him. Kyabje Jikme Gocha himself visited the rooftop corner tent of Horkhang, where he was staying, and received transmissions from him. {906} He also went to escort Dakchen at the time of his departure. In such ways, he paid him wonderful respect and praise.

Then, in the hiatus between the transition from old to new college bursars, there were a great many reasons for his frustration and lack of clarity. All sorts of outer and inner essential points relating to auspicious circumstances were mistaken, and consequently, during the first month of 1804 (wood mouse), he became somewhat ill-disposed, as if physically unwell. Minor rituals were undertaken, including the hoisting of prayer flags dedicated to the gods and vitality spirits, such that for a while he recovered, like a cloudless moon. The noble Lord Rakshak Sherpang arrived and made a long-life offering prayer. Many such prayers to secure his long life were offered by all sorts of people, in public and in private. However, at all times, inauspicious signs arose in our dreams, and an owl actually alighted on the Jema estate.

Such were the inauspicious signs that occurred. In such adverse circumstances, when the obstacles could not be warded off, his illness became more severe from the ninth day of the fourth month. Although we requested long-life rites and medical treatment on his behalf, that request could not be accommodated within the narrow meritorious enclosure of all his followers, and so at noon on the twenty-first day of the fourth month, the array of his physical body dissolved into the expanse of reality. His actual mind vividly remained in a state of great calmness, imbued with bliss, radiance, and nonconceptuality. In the morning of the twenty-second day, he let go of his post-death contemplation, and immediately, the master Tsultrim and I precisely undertook the procedures that were advised with respect to his post-death contemplation. Then, we presented the sacred corpse for viewing and so forth. {907}

Together with my teacher from Mindroling, I composed an aspiration prayer for his swift reincarnation, and it was introduced for recitation in the assembly hall. Assuming responsibility on behalf of the Palace Treasury, the two upper and lower retreat centers, the Rakshak Regent, the caretaker Tsewang, and so forth, I gradually prepared as many divine torma offerings as possible, estimating the materials for auspicious funeral procedures here at Taklung and in all the monasteries of the impartial traditions. After calculating the need to avoid fire and seared offerings in this, my seventeenth year, coinciding with the trigram Li, with agreement and unconcealed consensus, some thirty monks including maṇḍala draftsmen and the retired master and throne holder of Kadruk, we erected a crematorium in the riding enclosure and dressed the sacred corpse in the garb of a universal emperor, with a cloud-like array of offerings. The cremation was carried out in accordance with the burnt-offering rite of Sarvavid Vairocana, and the crematorium was then sealed for five days. Then, when it was opened, apart from a small fragment of his heart, the remainder of the sacred corpse had been consumed by the fire. Two relics and so forth that had been offered to it prior to his nirvāṇa emerged fire-resistant. Most of the funereal ashes were used to make terracotta imprints, and some were inserted within a casket and placed at the center of this, his extant reliquary, a supreme receptacle of the buddha body of reality in the form of an enlightenment stūpa, fashioned of many precious elements. Along with an image of this venerable master, it was actualized as a field for the material provision of merit. {908}

Although not even the slightest kernel of the biography of the supreme lord of refuge, Jikme Gocha, the great embodiment and lord-protector of the doctrinal wheel and lord of all enlightened heritage and maṇḍalas, had been written down, I have presented it as a memorandum, simply based on what I have heard from others and the precise activities that I undertook in common with him.

His compositions including adamantine songs of ultimate truth, prayers, oral instructions, and short incense offerings together amount to some fifty pages. These are all endowed with excellent words and meaning and are unsurpassed for those of intelligence and faith. He unimpededly knew by sight all the enlightened qualities that are included among the definitive and quantitative attributes of physical greatness. He had immeasurable compassion and kindness that was equal for all unbiased persons, like the light of the sun, regardless of whether they were near or far, or his official attendants, and so forth, and he could liberate sentient beings, taking them beyond the ocean of rebirth. In such ways, he could emulate the careers of the conquerors and their heirs, but he did not harbor even the most subtle aspect of the pride that is in my thoughts, and though his subjects indulged in so many rivalries that contradicted his intention, he never scolded them. Lacking such thoughts, he never wavered from calm and disciplined great compassion. Even a single facet of his activities caused fortunate beings to cringe speechlessly, for the astonishing hair-raising effect he had on the faithful is hard to appraise.

In the noble vase of expressive words arising from the clear lake,
The elixir that is the nectar of biography is worthy of savoring.
Thus do the gods move even now, deceiving the sun and moon. {909}
By this merit, may the enlightened intention of my guide be fulfilled!

The Disciples of Jikme Gocha

As for the so-called direct disciples who received the oral transmission of Venerable Jikme Gocha, they include me—one who merely assumes the appearance of a virtuous ascetic but is not dressed even in the slightest garb of the wondrous biographies of the sacred masters. My name is Ngawang Chokyi Peljor, otherwise called Tashi Chokyi Gyeltsen and Ngawang Tenpei Nyima.

Although there is a short separate memorandum documenting the apparent activities of this life of mine, in meaningless, nonsensical language to ordinary deluded persons, let alone genuine masters such as that lord of enlightened heritage, the actual embodiment of Vajradhara. To them it would be the cause of embarrassment and ridicule. Therefore, I myself dare not write of it here due to fear.

The other disciples of that venerable one included Drung Kadrukpa Śākya Tsultrim, who passed his life in calm, disciplined, and decorous activities in accord with the sacred doctrine, as well as some others who acquired realization. Their wondrous ascetic discipline that merits a most detailed description is not within the range of my sight or hearing.

Concluding Verses

Emaho!
I pay a hundredfold homage and respectful obeisance again and again
To the ring of golden mountains of the Taklung Kagyu lineage,
Those divine and human teachers who,
On hearing these wondrous and marvelous biographies,
Imbued with the inconceivable three mysteries of body, speech, and mind,
Swiftly strive for supreme bliss that eradicates all calamities of rebirth![1]

Manifoldly emanating all corporeal forms, resources, and continuous provisions of merit,
As a cloud of offerings that would eclipse the life, the disposition of Samantabhadra,
May we ever make offerings, permeating within the expanse of purity
The subject of offering, the object of offering, and the act of offering![2] {910}

Grant your blessing that the three vows might be pristine as a lake,
Having affirmed the vows and tearfully confessed with total regret
All negative actions generated by the five dissolute poisons
And under the sway of this human body, speech, and mind![3]

Rejoicing from the heart in the most sublime of all liberating careers
Of all the conquerors and spiritual teachers, pervasive as space,
Each of which has a billion wonders,
May I and all beings also have the power to engage in that manner!

Though the sound of sacred doctrine ever resonates in Akaniṣṭha field,
May the ways of the sacred doctrine endowed with the four gems of the aural lineage[4]

Not decline but remain clear for disciples of this field,
Adhering to the genuine path, as long as they are subject to rebirth!

As for all regents of the great, supreme Teacher who are present,
Most saintly beings repeatedly demonstrating birth and transmigration,
Although the adamantine body they possess is indestructible,
May they liberate living beings entirely from the vast ocean of rebirth![5]

I dedicate this short narrative of the astonishing history
And all provisions of merit that are valuable and positive
So that enlightenment endowed with astonishing glory might be obtained,
Inseparably coalescing skillful means and discriminative awareness![6]

May all schools that esteem the supreme Buddhist teaching,
Holding the monastic seats with their lineages of attainment, pith instructions, and tantras,
Gathering all the assemblies with the four excellent endowments,[7]
Be filled with beings of the three planes who possess the three trainings!

May the expanse of real nature, primordial natural expression,
Spontaneously present Vajradhara,
In whom the bodies of reality, perfect resource, and emanation are inseparable,
Unchanging in the essence of the seal of awareness and emptiness,
Be our crown ornament as long as space endures!

May all fathers and perfect mothers of the celestial paths of Lhasa,
And those frequenting the divine northern region, {911}
Always enjoy comforts and material wealth like that of Devendra,
And be blessed by the divine three precious jewels![8]

By the continuous downpour of the constant rain
Of spiritual and temporal well-being, auspicious and virtuous,
From the cloud mass of the conquerors' compassion,
Source of good auspices that fills the sky,
May fortunate beings enjoy the feast of wondrous bulging rice shoots
At this great monastic seat of Tashi Pel, endowed with auspicious glory,
And their fruits of liberation endowed with a hundred good auspices![9]

Colophon

The eighth chapter of *Wondrous Ocean of Eloquence: A Narrative of the Wish-Fulfilling Gem of the Lineage*, recounting in detail the biographies of the Taklung Kagyu lineage was composed by the perfect buddha Ngawang Namgyel, the seventeenth incumbent of the monastic seat of the great seminary of Taklung Upper Plain Dorjeden, supreme place of spiritual attainment. Distinct from that, this supplemental text titled *Great Divine Drum of Wondrous Renown* continues this narrative through to recent times, recounting a small portion of the long and concise biographies that I could find of all the successive incumbents who later appeared. The injunction to compose this supplement that resembles a wish-fulfilling crown was granted by my root teacher Vajradhara, whose name, hard to mention, is Phakchok Yizhin Wangpo Kunkhyen Drakpa Choying Lhundrub Rinchen Tendzin Namgyel Trinle Gyepei Dechenpo—the universal form of all the conquerors, none excepted, the lord of all enlightened heritage and maṇḍalas, the source of the eighty-four thousand sections of the sacred doctrine, the master of adamantine reality endowed with the three kindnesses,[1] and essential nature of all deities, mantras, and meditative stabilities. Taking this injunction as my crown ornament, {912} I, Ngawang Tenpei Nyima Chokyi Jungne, also called Tashi Chokyi Gyeltsen, who merely has the appearance of a contemporary lama, though lacking the sacred doctrine, like a trumpeting donkey or elephant[2] sitting on the lion throne of the sacred doctrine at Taklung Dorjeden, and assuming a counterfeit career, recorded these narratives in 1821 (iron snake), when I was in my thirty-fourth year. I subsequently delayed finalizing them for a long time, impeded by distraction and indolence. Then I once again received repeated encouragement through the injunction of my venerable lama Mahāvajradhara from Yisho, and so I awoke, and now, in the waxing half of the month of Uttarabhadrapāda, in 1824 (wood monkey), in my thirty-seventh year, I did finalize it. The scribe who first committed these notes to writing was my own maternal uncle Dondrub Tsering, and it was then arranged as a book by the secretary Dargye Tsering.

By virtue of this cloud mass of offering that is a spectacle for my venerable teacher, may the teaching of glorious Taklung, nucleus of the lineage of attainment, spread throughout the world, and consequently may all sentient beings who have been my mother acquire the causal basis to attain easily and unimpededly the rank of the omniscient teacher, Mahāvajradhara!

Let them be victorious! {913}

PART THREE

A Brief Chronicle of Riwoche, Including Jedrung Tulku Gongma and Gara Lama

Jedrung Jampel Gyeltsen

1. Riwoche Monastery

The monastery of Riwoche, which maintains the tradition of the Taklung Kagyu school, was founded in 1277 (fire ox) by Choje Sangye On, the fourth throne holder in the succession of Upper Taklung, who was born into the Gazi family. During the time of Choje Gyelwei Tsenchen, the third incumbent of Riwoche, sectarian border conflicts were reconciled, such that many monastic and lay communities became subservient to him. In consequence of that, he was granted the title Imperial Preceptor[1] by the Ming emperor Hongwu (r. 1368–1398), and a seal and other artifacts were conferred upon him. Around that time, the number of monks in the monastery was approximately six thousand, and the number of lay households under his authority exceeded ten thousand, and it was the earliest of the four monastic communities renowned for their combined spiritual and temporal authority in Doto. During that period, there were thirteen successive incumbent hierarchs of Taklung, venerable lords of the sacred doctrine who hailed from the Gazi family, who in succession maintained the sacred doctrine and the temporal affairs of the Gazi chieftain.

2. The Tulku Successions and Palaces of Riwoche

Later, around the time when the familial line of Gazi was interrupted, the tulku system was introduced. Since 1530, at Riwoche, there have been seven successive Jedrung Tulkus, commencing with First Jedrung Tulku, Tsokye Jungne (1530–1590), and continuing through to Seventh Jedrung Tulku, Trinle Jampei Jungne (1856–1922). {208} In addition, there have been six tulkus in the line extending from Phakchok Zhabdrung Ngawang Kyab (b. 1688) through to Phakchok Tubten Namgyel (d. 1979).

During the lifetime of Third Jedrung, Tulku Drakpa Lekdrub (1646–1708), there was an internal dispute, following which the Palace of Tse Zhabdrung broke away. Starting from then, there have been two palaces—with both Jedrung Tulku and the first Phakchok Tulku, who had been born in 1688 (earth dragon), presiding over the Yang Gon Palace and Zhabdrung Tulku presiding over the Zhabdrung Palace. In common, they established the methods of nurturing spiritual and temporal governance. There were nine successive incumbents, familial heirs and tulkus, who nurtured the Zhabdrung Palace, commencing with Tse Zhabdrung Ngagi Wangchuk, who was a son of the Gazi governor of Upper Taklung, and continuing down to Zhabdrung Lobzang Tsultrim.

Phakchok Ngawang Kyab was given the title Nomon Qan along with a seal in 1723 (water hare)—the first regnal year of the Qing emperor Yong Zheng. Previously, Third Jedrung Tulku, Drakpa Lekdrub, had been given the appropriate rank of supervisor of Drigung and Taklung by the Great Fifth Dalai Lama, and during the time of the regent Sangye Gyatso, he had been granted a clear measure of authority and autonomous tenure. Fifth Jedrung, Rinchen Lekdrub (1745–1829), received the title of Qutuktu and a seal from the emperor Jia Qing (r. 1796–1829).[1] Sixth Jedrung, Drakpa

Gyatso (a.k.a. Rinchen Obar, c. 1830–c.1855), received the title of Qutuktu along with a eulogy, jointly from Tenth Dalai Lama (d. 1837) and the Chinese ambassador Etuoshi who was resident in Tibet (from 1836 to 1837). {209} Seventh Jedrung Tulku, Trinle Jampei Jungne, was also confirmed and given his title in Lhasa by both Chinese and Tibetan masters and officials in connection with the formerly established protocol, as is the case with the casting of lots from the golden urn.

With regard to the number of monks, their expenditure, and income, at that time in the three monastic colleges of Riwoche, the total number of monks was not quite one thousand. The lead role was taken by two bursars, senior and junior, monastic or lay as appropriate, who were dispatched from the two palaces, and under them were the offices of the senior and junior stewards who had responsibility for major tasks, including the administration of Riwoche, its disciplinary code, wealth, the reception of Chinese and Tibetan visitors, and so forth. The sources of monastic expenditure included the grain tax known as *te*, the leasing of cattle, and the continuous butter tax, and these were dispatched annually by the subjects of Riwoche, farmers and nomads. When the estates, large and small, were estimated, they numbered approximately sixty. There were sixteen and a half herder groups in the inner circle, the private community of Riwoche, and thirteen and a half herder groups in the outer circle, along with Lho and Kar. As mentioned above, when these outer and inner communities or herder groups were tallied together, they numbered approximately two thousand households. There were more than two hundred households directly employed as dairymen and servants of the monastic estates by the palaces, the monastic colleges, and the main monastery with its branches. The expenditure extended as far as the stipends allocated to the three tulkus of the two palaces and their personal attendants, as well as their regular kitchens and two large kitchens. {210} Approximately one-third of the expenditure was allocated to the assemblies of the three monastic colleges, and there was also an allocation for the cost of the monastic and lay offerings presented to the teachers of the meditation hermitage, the stewards, and the teachers of the monastery, an expenditure of ten days supply that was sent each year for more than three hundred monks at the branch monastery known as Karma Gonchen, and the annual stipend and allowance for offerings presented to the seniormost thirteen teachers and monks. Such requirements reflected merely the basic modes of subsistence.

3. Jedrung Trinle Jampei Jungne

Seventh Jedrung Tulku, Trinle Jampei Jungne (1856–1922), the twentieth incumbent of Riwoche, was born in 1856 (fire dragon)[1] into the Dru family at Takgo Danang, which was named Pontsang Achak. In accordance with the casting of lots from the golden urn, he was invited by both Chinese and Tibetan officials to the monastic seat. After a short time, following the formerly established protocol, he traveled to Lhasa for his inaugural reception with the Thirteenth Dalai Lama. On that occasion, he was appointed with an official liaison aide by the government and welcomed with a reception and a meal on his arrival. While staying in Lhasa, he was ordained as a mendicant in the presence of Purbuchok Tulku Rinpoche, the tutor of the Dalai Lama, and the name Ngawang Drakpa Trinle Jampei Jungne was conferred upon him. He received the profound doctrines of the Taklung Kagyu tradition from Matrul Tekchok Jikme Pawo, the twenty-ninth incumbent of Upper Taklung. In addition, he studied many doctrines of the impartial philosophical systems and trained as a master in the five fields of classical learning. He promoted the teaching of exegesis, attainment, and enlightened activities, and his own compositions amounted to six volumes, including one volume that contained his spiritual revelations.[2] He is also known to have mastered Tibetan medical science. He had many direct disciples in all directions of Tibet.[3] His physical stature was short and corpulent, his temperament gentle, and he continuously wore the robes of a mendicant.

4. Gara Lama Sonam Rabten

Gara Lama Sonam Rabten was born in 1876 (fire mouse of the fifteenth cycle)[1] at Lungzangnang in present-day Basha township, Riwoche County, into a well-known family that, according to oral tradition, belonged to the clan of Garwa, a branch known as Gara Tsang or Hornya Gardrusum, into which the successive nobility of the Yang Gon Palace, monastic and lay, had formerly been born. He was the son of the niece of Seventh Jedrung, Trinle Jampei Jungne.[2] In his childhood, he had the title of a lama, living as a monk at the Nyingma College in Riwoche. Under Jedrung Jampei Jungne, he studied the fields of classical learning and doctrinal history, and as he grew, he acquired intelligence, dexterity, and great courage from a young age. There are also oral accounts of him revealing many miraculous powers including doctrinal activities and medicinal treatments, such that the public had great faith in him. His physical stature was powerful, his eyes bright and round, and his voice loud, wrathful, and fierce. Gara Lama habitually wore a maroon felt robe, and on his head he had a very large topknot of hair. When Jedrung Jampei Jungne took a wife, {211} she and Gara Lama had a liaison, after which Jedrung took responsibility for nurturing the sacred doctrine, and Gara Lama became head of the administration of the Yang Gon Palace at Riwoche.

5. The Opening of Pemako

During the period when Jedrung Trinle Jampei Jungne's activities on behalf of the sacred doctrine greatly expanded, in 1899 (earth pig), he, along with Gara Lama, petitioned the thirteenth Dalai Lama as follows: "In order to further and enhance the traditions of the sacred doctrine in the southwest border region, we request permission to open the hidden power place of Pemako!" Permission was granted. He, along with Gara Lama and their entourage, set out from Riwoche for Pemako in Powo. The governor of Kanam provided an escorting guard of about two hundred soldiers, headed by Nyerpa Namgyel, and along with them, they reached Adratang, a geomantic feature representing the right ear of supine Vajravārāhī. There, they turned the wheel of the sacred doctrine on behalf of the indigenous Dra nationality—a subdivision of the Lhopa ethnic group. Not only had there formerly been a patron-priest relationship with Abogye, the clan chieftain, which was known to have lasted more than two hundred years, they also established a patron-priest relationship with Orgyen Wangchuk, the regent of neighboring Bhutan.[1]

In Pemako, they established the sacred dances of the tenth day, and two communities, consisting of some forty monks of the monastic college and approximately fifty venerable mantrins of the mantra college. Up to fifty Tibetans settled there. The governor of Kanam in Powo offered Jedrung and Gara Lama the hermitage of Chendruk Gutang, along with dominion over the most secret power place as long as they stayed there. {213} Gara Lama and some of his entourage actually went to Yangsang Dopo Pema Sheri, foremost of the power places. While they were residing there, the wife of both Jedrung and Gara Lama gave birth to her middle daughter, Yang Ga, who would later become a doctor at the Mentsikhang in Lhasa. At that time, a small number of persons at the Zhabdrung Palace slandered them with false accusations at the seat of government in Lhasa, in consequence of which an urgent order was issued, decreeing that Jedrung and Gara Lama with their entourage should immediately return from there. Consequently, in 1907 (fire sheep), along with their entourage, they had to return to Riwoche. In place of the lama and master at Adratang, Datse Gelong Gyatso and Dzapu Kongtrul were both left behind, and they maintained that community until the end. Finally, in 1910 (iron dog), when one of the Tibetans went hunting at the sacred Markori, there was a quarrel with some of the ethnic Dra people, in consequence of which that midnight, an army of Dra tribesmen encircled the hermitage at Adratang and burned it to the ground, such that not a single building remained. The lama's regent, Dzapu Kongtrul, and Lama Rinchen Lhagyel, from the guesthouse, both jumped stark naked from the toilet cavity and finally escaped, but apart from just them, more than six hundred Tibetans, monks, and laity who had settled there were slaughtered all at once.

6. Chinese Invasions

In 1908 (earth monkey), during the first regnal year of Xuan Tong, the forces of the ambassador Zhao Erfeng reached Chamdo via Batang. {214} At that time, they were not favorably received by Chamdo monastery, the mother and branch monasteries of Drayab, Pasho Monastery, and so forth. On the contrary, those establishments overtly complied but covertly opposed them, so the forces of Zhao Erfeng burned them down. On the other hand, the Yang Gon Palace of Riwoche sent the chamberlain Tsega as a special envoy, along with thirteen attendants, to Chamdo and hospitably received the invading forces, offering them a thousand *dri* and yaks, a thousand goats and sheep, and a thousand Chinese silver coins in the denomination of three *zho*. Ambassador Zhao Erfeng considered Jedrung Jampei Jungne of Riwoche to be a noble person who was patriotic, with respect for the armed forces, but the underlying significance was that monasteries headed by Riwoche Temple that complied with his decrees obtained protection, and the property of those monasteries, including their sacred artifacts, was not destroyed even to the extent of a needle and thread.

In 1909 (earth bird), as the forces of Peng Daren approached Riwoche, Jedrung Trinle Jampei Jungne and Zhabdrung Lobzang Tsultrim had a meeting at the house of Drukpaka, a senior official of Riwoche, at which Jedrung said they should discuss the reception and they should provide for the armed forces of the Qing emperor as they approached Riwoche, above all—a position that would henceforth be acceptable with respect to the central authorities. On that occasion, the two palaces both pledged under oath to establish a united position, {215} but after Zhabdrung Lobzang Tsultrim and his senior officials went home, they conferred among themselves and then set out secretly for Lhasa with an entourage of some twenty persons, including his wife Pelmo, the retired bursar Tsedrak, and Madrong Togagyel. On reaching Lhasa, with the malign assistance of both Zholkhang Lonchen

Dondrub Phuntsok and Dokharwa, they presented their slanderous report to the authorities that the Yang Gon Palace of Riwoche, headed by Jedrung Rinpoche and Gara Lama, had sided with the Chinese, that they were traitorous, rebelling, and so forth. The Tibetan government then granted the estate of Nyarikhuk in Penpo to Tseten, the acting Zhabdrung Lama, and he also obtained a promise that awards would be granted them after Sino-Tibetan affairs had been peacefully settled.

At the end of 1909, the forces of Peng Daren reached Riwoche and stayed there for seven years. During that time the Yang Gon Palace, in accordance with the former pledge made by Jedrung and Zhabdrung, received the imperial forces favorably with handouts, including grain, meat, butter, firewood, and lamp oil.

At the end of 1912 (water bird),[1] the Kalon Lama Jampa Tendar, who was head of all the civil and military personnel sent by the Tibetan government to pacify lower Dokham, arrived at Lhodzong with his monastic and lay staff and an army. Not long afterward, {216} it was stated among the letters that reached Jedrung Rinpoche earlier and later in this sequence of events, "In order to pacify the Sino-Tibetan borderlands, Gara Lama should come to discuss this in person, a group from Riwoche should swiftly submit a petition to the government, and since it is an important general matter for the benefit of the Buddhist teaching and sentient beings, it should be investigated whether there is any truth in the petition previously made by the Zhabdrung. The Dalai Lama should not at all be displeased in this matter!"

7. The Detention and First Escape of Gara Lama

The attitude of Peng Daren was such that he disagreed that Gara Lama should go to Lhodzong and that the responsible monastic officials of Riwoche Yang Gon Palace should also deter him. Finally, however, in 1914 (wood tiger), Gara Lama, bringing a servant named Drodok Gelek, set out for Lhodrak Dzong without regard for the difficulties or his own life. There, the Kalon Lama Jampa Tendar, by gentle means in connection with a reception, detained Gara Lama alongside a group of other officials from the Kham region, including Chamdo Yabzang Lobzang Dechen, Derge Jago Tobden, and Jago Ama Tsewang Dolma.

On the other hand, the commander Dokharwa, who was stationed at Mari with his armed forces confiscated and stole all the property of Gara Lama, including the *dri*, yaks, horses, and mules of his private estate. Not only did they beat the local people by whatever means, they also beat the servants include Yangar who had accompanied him, confiscated their property, and treated them with various severe penalties. {217} Now, owing to the former deception of the faction of Zhabdrung Lama and the great enmity of the commander Dokharwa toward the Yang Gon Palace, suffering was piled upon suffering, and finally, it was secretly intimated to Gara Lama by Jago Ama that Gara Lama's own life was in danger. Consequently, by various means, Gara Lama repeatedly sought permission to inspect his estates but to no avail. In the end, he had no choice but to stay there.

One day, he ordered his servant Gelek to have two excellent riding horses prepared at a certain place nearby, and one evening, drinking a very strong cup of tea, he passed the whole night naked, practicing the yogic exercises of meditation that control subtle wind. As he had ordered his servant in advance, he had him mix the urine of a goat with his own urine and present a false sample for urinalysis. After completing this careful strategy, he had his servant Gelek call on the Kalon Lama Jampa Tendar, informing him that Gara Lama had been smitten by an extremely severe disease. The Kalon Lama Jampa Tendar then distributed alms to the entire assembly of Zhitram Monastery and had them undertake a day-long ritual for long life. At the same time, he sent his own lama physician, who examined the pulse and urine and reported immediately to Kalon Lama that there were symptoms resembling intoxication due to numbness and that this therefore indicated that a grave disease had befallen Gara Lama. {281} The Kalon Lama therefore sent Khenchung Lodon to inquire after his health, and along with him, he dispatched two of his own reliable servants jointly to act as nurses and to examine him. After that news broke, the regular guards who were monitoring Gara Lama became careless. The two servants who had been purposefully sent were hospitably received by Gara Lama's own servant Gelek, who plied them with food and drink, including tea and beer, so that they fell asleep out of intoxication. Taking that opportunity, around 2 o'clock in the morning, Gara Lama and his servant both set out on horseback from the prearranged place and crossed the Salween at Peto Druka. On reaching the border of Riwoche at Peto Drongtso lake, they had to go into hiding.

On learning that Gara Lama had escaped, a band of soldiers was immediately mustered and sent after him in pursuit. They reached Wago via Zhabye Bridge, whereupon after crossing the pass of Bokla, a local from Wago fired some bullets. Simultaneously, someone told them he had come from Ngomda to the Drongtso area, mentioning that a large platoon of Chinese soldiers had reached Bomdo, that a party of scouts had already reached Bom La pass, and that the Chinese forces at Riwoche had increased and almost reached that very place via Tre La pass. Consequently, the Tibetan forces fled out of doubt and panic like a pile of peas being scattered. On the way back, their possessions were robbed by locals from the regions of Mari and Zhabye, their quarters were set on fire, and so forth. {219} When Gara Lama came to know the news that the Tibetan forces had retreated, he joyfully accepted the escort of guards that the locals provided, and in 1915 (wood hare), he could safely reach Riwoche.

While Gara Lama had been detained at Lhodzong, Peng Daren had repeatedly sworn an oath directed toward Jedrung Rinpoche, saying, "Under various pretexts, above all, Gara Lama has surrendered to the Tibetan government and become a refugee!" And, around the same time, "If Gara Lama does not return to Riwoche, I will set fire to the temple!"

He had bundles of straw attached to the pillars and permanently stationed a platoon of ten Chinese soldiers there. In ways such as these, he incited forceful intimidation.

However, after Gara Lama reached Riwoche, Peng Daren esteemed him even more than before and appointed him as the commander of the northern district of Chamdo, which included both the upper and lower "white" herder groups of Khyungpo, upper and lower Drongpa Doshul, the upper and lower Ngomchu areas of Chamdo, upper and lower Dang La Gong, upper Rob, Meru, both the sunny and shady banks of the Dzachu, Lhato, and the two Bedru districts of Nangchen. Peng Daren also granted him a sealed decree accepting, in the context of a report made to the future Chinese government, that he should be appointed as the head of Chamdo district.

8. The Rebellion

After Gara Lama reached Riwoche, his own prowess was strengthened, and simultaneously, he drew to his side the might of Tashi Namgyel, the chieftain of the upper "white" herder group of Khyungpo Tengchen, who rebelled against the Tibetan government. {220} These two, together with the forces of Peng Daren, attacked the forces of the commander Jingpa, who were stationed at Khyungpo Tengchen, and a battle ensued. At the place called Khyung Nyelagyu, they slew the commander Jingpa and also slaughtered a group of solders apart from him.

Later, the Tibetan government distributed modern guns called English rifles that had been given to the Tibetan army by British imperialists, and then two camps—one thousand soldiers of the Zhigatse regiment commanded by the general Tashi Tongpa Gyurme Gyatso, and approximately five hundred soldiers of the Dingri regiment under the command of general Tangponpa Namgyel Wangdu—were dispatched to Chakzamka, and they guarded that frontier.

The army of General Pulung established a camp at Meru Kyilkhar Gon in Khyungpo, and then, along with people from the Zhabdrung Palace, they advanced toward Dzizamka in Riwoche and occupied the Main Temple of Riwoche Monastery. Two intense battles were fought, after which the Tibetan forces had to withdraw to Yangpon Shamkhyim at the Zhabdrung Palace. Immediately, the army of Peng Daren, along with reinforcements including more than a hundred volunteer soldiers mustered by Gara Lama, monks and laymen from the Yang Gon Palace, commanded on the battlefield by Gara Lama in person, attacked the forces of Pulungpa billeted at Shamkhyim, and on that occasion they slew and wounded a number of Pulungpa's officers and infantry. {221} General Pulung then withdrew to Dzizamka and fought guarding the ends of the bridge. Finally, he was isolated and hid under the bridge. Pursuing him while he was defending the bridge, the forces raised by Gara Lama launched a strong attack, after which General Pulung was actually killed. At sunset, the Tibetan soldiers at the end of the bridge threw the general's corpse into the river, and they had to retreat to Meru Kyilkhar.

Not long afterward, the army of General Tsogowa advanced against the forces of Peng Daren, which were permanently stationed at Drayab Kyiltang, and since they numbered more than one thousand, the Chinese army duly surrendered. An army of volunteer soldiers from Shopado, Pelbar, and Lhodzong, three hundred in number, under the command of Khenchung Dawa, blocked the road between Riwoche and Chamdo. Their objective was to capture Jedrung and Gara Lama alive if they were to flee toward Chamdo, and they prepared to advance against Riwoche in all ways.

Simultaneously, the Zhigatse and Dingri regiments commanded by the generals Tang and Tashi, who were both stationed at Chakzamka, reinforced by an army from Lhodzong, which was stationed at the encampment of Pulungpa in Meru, joined together, and they launched an intense assault against Riwoche. Consequently, the forces of Peng Daren who were based there were completely encircled and expelled, {222} and the Tibetan army occupied Riwoche.

Gara Lama, along with his relative Taklha, the latter's wife Tsewang Chodron, and also some twenty young braves and about ten advisers from Karu Kyangtsang, fled to Chamdo on a secret route, but apart from only these, everyone else was left behind at Riwoche. When General Tang, Commander Tashi, and Khenchung Dawa reached Riwoche, they placed a guard on both the Great Temple and the Taklung College, which included the Zhabdrung Palace. They did not harm Jedrung Rinpoche because he was chronically unwell, but apart from him, over three days and nights the Tibetan army ransacked the Yang Gon Palace, the New College, and the Nyingma College, as well as the monastic cells and houses, looting, damaging, and occupying them, and the air was filled with terror. The dwellings and property of all the inhabitants of the Yang Gon Palace, headed by Jedrung, were completely confiscated, down to their drinking cups, and their lines were extinguished.

9. The Detention of Jedrung Rinpoche

After three days had passed, Jampa Tendar, the Kalon Lama of the entire Do region, with his officials and armed forces, reached Gong Ngamda Tashigang in Riwoche district and began to investigate the crucial points concerning Riwoche. First, they summoned Jedrung and his wife Tsultrim to the court and proclaimed the crime of Jedrung and Gara Lama in rebelling against the government and siding with the Chinese. {223} In that regard, they reached a verdict that Jedrung Rinpoche should spend his whole life in exile in Lhodzong, on the basis of the following three provisos: (1) the three concerned persons including Jedrung should not be allowed to sit at the head of the row, (2) they should be deprived of their authority to speak in public, and (3) there should be no search for or recognition of subsequent Jedrung incarnations.[1] His wife Tsultrim was placed under house arrest at Ngamda village, and although she was handed over to the Tibetan army, after about three months of incarceration, by diverse means of patronage, though she was not permitted to go anywhere, with certain assurances, she went to stay with Jedrung Rinpoche at Lhodzong.

Since at that time, the doctrinal lineage of Taklung was frail, the great throne holder of Taklung Monastery, Tsetrul Ngawang Pelden, a relative of Thirteenth Dalai Lama, went to request the sacred doctrine from Jedrung of Riwoche, and he fortunately requested the governor general of eastern Tibet and the Tibetan government that Jedrung should not have to stay imprisoned. The appeal was successful in that he was permitted to stay at Sepu Mountain hermitage near Lhodzong. Later, after Tsetrul had returned to Lhasa, he again made a series of requests that Jedrung should be permitted to reside at Upper Taklung Monastery, but in reply he was informed that Jedrung's crimes were very great and that someone whose monastic discipline had lapsed should not be allowed to stay at Upper Taklung Monastery.

Moreover, it was certain that Tsetrul himself would have to be investigated and punished for supporting a guilty party.

Despite this, it was determined that the doctrinal lineage of the Taklung Kagyu tradition was indeed frail, and so, in connection with a petition submitted to the governor general of eastern Tibet, {224} he was handed over to the two monastic and lay officials of Nakchu and successfully permitted to stay at a place near the monastery of Jang Takring. About two years later, Tsetrul again presented a petition, saying, "Since I have great responsibilities and a karmic connection with the spiritual and temporal affairs of Taklung Monastery, but the distance from here to Takring Monastery is too great for me to go to request teaching, and it is difficult for me to travel at short notice, I request that Jedrung might be permitted to stay at a mountain hermitage within the area of Upper Taklung." The petition was successful, and he went to stay at Jang Taklung under the supervision of Podo Dzong, where, in 1923 (water pig), he passed away.

10. The Capture and Second Escape of Gara Lama

In 1917 (fire snake), Gara Lama and an entourage of about forty successfully reached Chamdo, and they resided there permanently, but when the army of the Qing emperor was defeated, Peng Daren was captured alive and ransomed. Coincidentally, Gara Lama and a small number of attendants stayed in hiding in the Yellow Cave on the banks of the Mekong on the outskirts of Chamdo city, and they built a wooden boat. They planned to escape by crossing the Mekong, but when they got into the boat, the wife of Gara Lama's relative named Tsewang Chodron shouted, "Please take me with you!" whereupon the Tibetan army understood his whereabouts, and they exchanged several shots there. After that, Gara Lama ran out of ammunition, and he, along with his servants, was captured alive.

In 1918 (earth horse), the council of ministers of Chamdo was first established, headed by the Kalon Lama Jampa Tendar, the head of the civil and military administration of eastern Tibet. {225} At Chamdo, Gara Lama and his faction were under arrest, his wife was exiled, and all the others were each given a hundred lashes, after which a criminal investigation was opened. Gara Lama's younger brother Taklha had his kneecaps broken, and three other men, his younger brother Samye, his nephew Kyuru Tsering Lhagyel, and his nephew Gonpo Namgyel, had their ears cut off, and they were handed over and detained at Shido and Pelbar Dzong. Twenty-eight men including Agya Pelden, the minister of Karu Kyangtsang, had their ears cut off and were handed over to the individual estates of Pelbar and so forth. Then, after about one month, Gara Lama was given a "departure whipping" and sent to Lhasa under the guard of a military platoon. On reaching Lhasa, at the Zhol Office, the verdict of life-imprisonment was imposed, combined with lashes. While Gara Lama stayed in prison, he taught the sacred doctrine among the crowd of prisoners, and in addition, he distributed among all the prisoners the things that were brought to him by sympathetic aristocrats and a group of merchants, and so forth. Consequently, the prisoners and most of the prison guards respected him.

After a few years had passed, in connection with a great amnesty for prisoners during an obstacle year of Thirteenth Dalai Lama, he was thrown into a cage and, with a notice proclaiming his crimes, he was brought out on the main road adjoining the Later Zhol Pillar for seven days, after which he was strapped to a bullock and exiled to Drongzhi, at Jayul in Lhuntse County, {226} where he was handed over to both the lay official Nyelungpa Namkha Tsewang and the monastic official Tredong Choze. Not long after that, Gara Lama established a patron-priest relationship with those two county governors, and coincidentally, since he was older than them, the two county officials concurred with his wish to pass the end of his life in retreat, so they arranged for him to stay ostensibly in prison but actually in a retreat hermitage.

Not long after that, Gara Lama sent a secret message to the formerly exiled minister of Karu Kyangtsang Karu Nawo—that being the name by which he was known after he had had his ears cut off, saying, "You should secretly flee ahead to Dartsedo and wait there!" On receiving this letter, he indeed fled, along with his younger brother Yungdrung, and they waited at Dartsedo.

Taking advantage of an opportunity when the Jayul estate manager was not in residence, one night Gara Lama arranged his own matted hair and the shavings of his fingernails and toenails, along with his own robe, upon the mat where he slept, and made his escape. Regarding the way in which Gara Lama escaped, there are many mythological stories, but later, Yungdrung, the brother of Karu Nawo, the minister of Karru Kyangtsang, told me that on that occasion, Gara Lama reached Dartsedo on the main road, accompanied by someone from Tawu who had come to Lhasa on pilgrimage.[1] {227} Some days after Gara Lama had fled, the deputy governor of that locality only then informed the government, but the local people who had great faith in Gara Lama said that he had attained the rainbow body! There were many such reports. Immediately, the Tibetan government summoned both the lay official Nyelungpa and the monastic official Tredong Choze to Lhasa, and requisitioning them, they were demoted, and a verdict was passed that they should be incarcerated at the Zhol Office.

11. Retribution against Riwoche

On early and later occasions, after Jedrung Rinpoche and Gara Lama had been imprisoned, the governor general of eastern Tibet had urged Kadrung Tashi Pelrawa to again investigate Gara Lama. The property and the livestock of the Yang Gon Palace and Gara Lama were completely confiscated. There were some important documents that had previously been concealed during the war, including the imperial decree with the gold seal that Emperor Yong Zheng had conferred upon Phakchok Ngawang Kyab[1] and the proclamation of the rank of Qutuktu that had been conferred jointly by the Chinese and Tibetans upon Jedrung Drakpa Gyatso. There was also the sword that Ling Gesar had tempered and used to slay Hor Gurkar, known as The Sword That Mollifies the World with Water. {228}[2] Some sacred relics apart from these were stolen and removed. As for the remnants, they sealed the door of the Great Temple and handed over the keys to the bursar of Taklung, Sangye Pelzang. Later, at the insistence of the Tibetan government, the finance minister and inspector Palhawa arrived in Riwoche, but, as is commonly said, it seems that he returned to Lhasa because his inspection was postponed and delayed due to Jedrung's wife Tsultrim and the relatives. Later still, there were many investigations opened into important establishments such as Riwoche, their controversial palaces and monasteries, and, above all, the so-called betrayal of the Tibetan government by Jedrung and Gara Lama, and consequently it was decided that henceforth, on the one hand, that the investigation should be carried through to its conclusion, and, on the other hand, that in the future the Tibetan government itself should send as a palace steward a monastic official to manage the spiritual and temporal affairs of Riwoche and the income and expenditure of the Yang Gon Palace.

In 1918 (earth horse), therefore, coinciding with an inspection of Riwoche, the first of these palace stewards, Khenchung Lobzang Gelek, reached Riwoche. The government officially confiscated all the upland nomadic grasslands and low-lying estates of the Yang Gon Palace, including their outer environment and inner inhabitants, and this became a source of income for the palace steward. Simultaneously, he reviewed the former private estates of Gara Lama and confiscated the remainder of the livestock along with the belongings of the Gara Lama faction. Yet again, Riwoche, headed by the Yang Gon Palace, was accused of having betrayed the government.

With a view to imposing further taxes, the livestock and the size of the fields belonging to the subjects of the monastery were examined, {229} and according to their quantity, taxes were levied on each household, "some in butter, some in barley, and some in money." Yet again, unlike in other places, approximately one hundred and thirty soldiers were stationed at Riwoche, and taxes had to be collected locally for the salaries of the soldiers. The ownership of the fields, livestock, and so forth that formerly had been the property of the Zhabdrung Palace and one group of officials within it was entrusted to the government, and afterward they were given a sealed authorization granting them life-long rights.

An exceptional succession of palace stewards granted Tsedrak, the bursar of the Zhabdrung Palace, eight taxpaying households as the servants of his estate. At the Yang Gon Palace, Phakchok Tulku was annually granted two hundred loads of grain, and sixty loads of butter, and the new Jedrung Tulku was granted one hundred and fifty loads of grain, fifty loads of butter, and four households to transport firewood. Annually, they were permitted, unchanged from the past, to gather taxes in kind—grain and butter for the rituals of the protectors who bring rain and prevent hail. Seven rooms were allocated for their use within the palace. Whereas in the past, the bursar's office of the Yang Gon Palace had certain responsibilities for the expenditure given to the subjects of the monastery, henceforth the unbroken custom was established whereby the palace steward himself would assess the quality and quantity by calculating the grain and butter.

As for political affairs, each year it was customary for the palace steward to get the tulkus and nobles of Riwoche to accept an agreement, proscribing Gara Lama, with his Chinese sympathies, and his outer and inner evil associates. The steward had a platoon of approximately five hundred Tibetan soldiers stationed at Riwoche, {230} and they continuously subjected the local subjects to various astonishing measures that were inappropriate and repressive. Once again, the palace steward Khenchung Lobzang Gelek imposed a new tax, called "hit them again," and although that for which he himself was responsible could not be implemented each year, when the second palace steward Rampa Tubten Kunkhyen considered putting it into practice, the people of Riwoche, headed by Dargen Samdrub Gyeltsen, all strongly rebelled. Around that same time, a petition was submitted concerning their welfare to the governor of eastern Tibet and the government, but some ten persons who were senior and elderly, headed by Dargen Sandrub Gyeltsen, were horsewhipped, and consequently, Dargen Samdrub Gyeltsen died. It transpired, however, that there was no need for the new tax called "hit them again" to be tested. At that time, among the monastic officials of the Tibetan government, there were many who willingly pushed to petition the authorities because the income of the palace steward of Riwoche was excessive, and, not least, among lowly subjects, there was even an oath that spread everywhere when playing dice, to the effect of, "Let's eat the foodstuff of the Riwoche palace steward!"

12. Gara Lama in China

Gara Lama, through certain Chinese officials, eventually reached Nanjing and changed his name to Nub Lama. There he first of all taught the sacred doctrine, disclosing the doctrinal traditions of Tibet, and he strongly propagated the practice of longevity rites, the casting of divinatory lots, the casting of mantra spells, the practice of medicine, and so forth. {231} A private employee of Jiang Jieshi entered into a patron-priest relationship with him, and with his help and council, he adopted various methods, including a petition to the Guomindang central authorities. Finally, not only did he meet Jiang Jieshi in person, he obtained extensive facilitating wealth, including a salary.

While Gara Lama was resided at Nanjing, he had a series of discussions with Pomda Tobgye, who was also staying there, and eventually they concurred in common that they should oppose the Tibetan government. In unison, they gradually informed the central authorities of the Guomindang of their discomfort and wish to have a Khampa army dispatched to Tibet, but many years passed while the project was delayed owing to the untimely circumstances that prevailed within the country during that period. Finally, in 1935 (wood pig), the Guomindang government conferred civilian and military titles on Gara Lama, and they placed approximately one thousand troops under arms with sufficient ammunition. He then explained in a communiqué to Liu Wun Hue, head of the nascent Sichuan Xikang committee (1934–1937), that his purpose was to return to Tibet and that Liu should later send the allied forces at his disposal, just as they were required. Not long afterward, Gara Lama reached Sichuan and presented in detail the aforementioned orders of the Guomindang central authority at the residence of Liu Wun Hu, whereupon Liu said that until then he had not received any document or radio communication and so forth directly from the central authority concerning that matter but that if he were to wait there in the meantime, it would be all right. {232} During that time, he was lavishly welcomed. Gara Lama yet again, in due course, sent a petition by telegram from Sichuan to the central authority of the Guomindang, and eventually it seemed that Liu Wun Hue did receive a telegram from the central government stating that he was required to provide whatever assistance was required for the military engagement.

On that occasion, Liu Wun Hue explained to Gara Lama, "Nowadays, the Red Army has almost reached Sichuan province, so it will be difficult to find a way of providing military assistance to you from here. To return to Tibet, you should proceed to Batang. I have decided that the troops belonging to an autonomous regiment stationed there should assist your army, so I have sent an order to the commander in Batang accordingly. When you have reached that area, you may discuss the details, but do not proceed immediately into Tibet. You should stay in Kandze and prepare to march on Tibet!"

Immediately after Gara Lama with his army reached Dartsedo, he sent Pomda Tobgye and his four servants to Batang to discuss sending an army into Tibet, as Liu had commanded. Though Pomda Tobgye did reach Batang, Liu had outwardly pretended to heed the orders of the central authority, demonstrating to Gara Lama that he would send the reinforcements, but in actuality he covertly dispatched a secret telegram to the permanent regimental commander in Batang, advising that he should not send reinforcements to Gara Lama, so how could the army have possibly been reinforced? {233} On the contrary, a high-level official of Ba Chode monastery and the Tibetan government had a convert relationship, on the basis of which Pomda Tobgye and his four servants were summoned to a banquet at the monastery, captured alive, and detained in custody. Afterward, Gara Lama just managed to get away. With his hopes of sending an army from Batang ended, while he was on the road to Kandze, Gara Lama encountered the forces of the Red Army who were on the Long March, and they fought a battle with his forces there. Consequently, the Guomindang forces belonging to Gara Lama were absolutely routed, and at the time when the forces under him fled, it is said that he was shot and so forth. In any event, Gara Lama's leg was wounded, and the Red Army brought him to Kandze, where they not only took care of his medical treatment fairly well but later also conferred a rank upon him. However, without fulfilling his aspirations, in 1935 (wood pig), he passed away at Kandze.

PART FOUR

Extracts from *A Guide to the Sacred Places of Utsang*

Third Kaḥtok Situ, Chokyi Gyatso

1. Taklung Upper Plain {58}

Traveling a short distance into the uplands of Tre in Pelyul, the upper reaches of that valley lead toward Chak La pass. On the mountain to the rear, which is a weathered rocky outcrop, there are many willows growing. Ahead there is a grass-covered mountain and some junipers. In its middle reaches, which offer access to Tolung through the uplands of that valley, there is the plain of glorious Taklung.

There, the temple to the right, which belongs to the tantric college, was founded by Venerable Ngawang Namgyel.[1] The hall has twenty-five pillars. In its inner sanctum, there is an exquisite clay image of Munīndra in the form Tokdu Toknyima, with the eight supreme pious attendants, standing and life-size, and also well-fashioned of clay. The murals depict the thousand buddhas, and there is a stacked wall of sacred scriptures, approximately four hundred in number. There is an excellent painted scroll depicting the *Avadānakalpalatā*. In the Two-Pillar Utse Chapel of the Lama Lhakhang, which is the residence of Taklung Ngawang Namgyel, there are images depicting himself and Tashi Peldrub, both approximately one cubit in height, as well as some two hundred statues in Mongolian bronze and East Indian bronze, forming five rows, headed by Vajrayoginī, Munīndra, and Tārā. {59} There are also bronzes depicting Taklung Tangpa, Phakmodrupa, and so forth, the former containing an artifact made by the hand of Peta, the sister of Venerable Marpa, and there are many painted scrolls and a glorious Protector Chapel on display. Above it are two gilded roofs, large and small, and two gold victory banners that are exquisitely polished.

In the five-pillar inner sanctum of the Dargye Khangsar,[2] there is a two-story-high image of Maitreya, a stacked wall of sacred scriptures approximating two hundred volumes, an image of Vajradhara containing a tooth relic of Dharmodgata, and more than two hundred other images including a gold and copper alloy statue of the previous Tsegyel, as well as the two-story silver reliquary of Tsetrul. The Twenty-Pillar Hall contains a platform and two thrones, and it is surmounted by a small gilded roof.

Separate from the Namgyel Reliquary, the adobe reliquary of Tangpa Rinpoche has five stories, the last containing a self-originating inscription of the six-syllable mantra in different colors, and the gold leaf applied in front of its relics blazes with light. It also has an Avalokiteśvara and several icons depicting former teachers, drawn in the Newar style. The adobe reliquary of the supreme incarnation Kuyalwa Rinchen Gonpo is white and in the center. Within it are half of the tooth relics that had been allocated as a sacred artifact to the king of Kaliṅga.[3] The adobe reliquary of Choku Sangye Yarjon is white and to the right. All three are similar in size, with gilded-copper spires and Rañjanā inscriptions in front. These have been restored by Ma Rinpoche, Tenpei Nyima.[4] In the circumambulatory pathway around them are murals depicting lineages of former teachers, including those of Geden and Sakya, Longchen Nyingtik, and Taklungpa. The complex is surmounted by a large gilded roof.

In the Zhelre Lhakhang containing Taklung Tangpa's cave of spiritual attainment, there are images of medicinal clay depicting the sixteen elders, and upstairs the face of the image of Taklung Tangpa is viewed from a distance through an aperture. It also contained approximately two hundred volumes of scripture that belonged to Matrul Tenpei Nyima.

In the Labrang Palace, there is a life-size image of medicinal clay depicting Maitreya, {60} three collections of scripture including the Kangyur and Tengyur, and *The Precious Store of Revelations*, as well as the residence of Matrul, with its miscellaneous sacred artifacts. This building is surmounted by a small gilded roof.[5] In the middle of the monastery, the Phuntsok Khangsar has a small gilded roof and a four-pillar inner sanctum containing a large wood-carved maṇḍala of Cakrasaṃvara in the center. It its interior, there are some statues depicting former teachers.[6] In short, Taklung has a twenty-pillar assembly hall, some thirty large buildings, and at the extremity of the monastery, there is a Protector Chapel dedicated to Tseringma.

The Red Offering Chapel

As summarized in *The Great Explanation of the Sacred Place: A History of the Red Offering Chapel*,[7] this sacred place of Taklung had been foreordained in *Compassion's White Lotus*, and it had been frequented by Guru Rinpoche. Three self-originating representations of buddha mind, buddha speech, and buddha body were emanated here. It was then frequented by Phakmodrupa, and Taklung Tangpa Tashi Pel himself stayed in the cave of spiritual attainment. His nephew, the supreme incarnation Kuyalwa Rinchen Gonpo, constructed the temple called Glorious Splendor of Existence and Quiescence, which has eighty large pillars, and thereafter the representations of buddha body, speech, and mind were multiplied and expanded by Choku Sangye Yarjon, Sangye On, Tashi Lama, and so forth. However, during the lifetime of Namgyel Tashi, the seventeenth incumbent of the abbatial succession, this building caught fire, and in its aftermath the sacred image of Taklung Tangpa the Great, the Tashi Pelbar reliquary, the two protector chapels, the books, and many statues that had survived the fire were restored.

The temple of the present-day measures twenty double armspans up and down and seventeen across. Within the ground floor, measuring seven double armspans, the Great Temple is filled exclusively with large murals in the Old Menri style, depicting the thousand buddhas, the golden lineage of the Kagyu tradition, and so forth.

Starting from the south side, in a clockwise direction are the following. (1) There is the image of Munīndra called Tubwang Sizhi Pelgon, fashioned of medicinal clay, twenty-one handspans in height {61} and covered with seven *sang* of gold leaf, with a rocky backdrop, which had been recently commissioned by Matrul Tenpei Nyima. (2) In its retinue are images depicting the two pious attendants Śāriputra and Maudgalyāyana, the seven previous buddhas of medicine, the master Guru Padmākara, the three deities of longevity, and the three-dimensional maṇḍala of Bhaiṣajyaguru. (3) Then there is the image of Mahāmuni, thirty-seven handspans in height, called Auspicious Ornament of the World, which had been commissioned by Ngawang Namgyel, fashioned of copper, gilded utilizing seven hundred *zho* of gold, with crown ornaments offered by Derge, and on the throne back are the thousand buddhas and additional protectors in red. (4) Then there is Kunga Tashi's Mahāmuni image called Meaningful to Behold, forty-five handspans in height, made of copper gilded with nine hundred *zho* of gold, and its core filled with one hundred copies of *The Transcendent Perfection of Wisdom in Eight Thousand Lines*. The catalog states that there are ten thousand volumes in the stacked wall of scriptures including those that survived the fire, and although there do not seem to be more than seven thousand according to my rough estimation, it is certain that there must be that many because they are also on the second and third stories of the building. (5) Alongside these is the arrow of the tsen spirit of the rocks, and (6) the image of Mahāmuni named Tubchen Tongsum Zilnon commissioned by Namgyel Tashi, which is of gilded copper, one story in height, and containing as its inner sacred artifact the painting known as Chulonma (Holding Back the Waters). Formerly, there were said to have been thirteen such images. It is slightly broader than the previous one of forty-five handspans. (7) Then there is the Tashi Obar reliquary, approximately one story in height and fashioned of one thousand *sang* of silver, containing the hair and pearl relics of Taklung Tangpa, his heart, tongue, and eyes, as well as the round mole of his forehead and the undamaged ring finger of his left hand. It also contains the tooth relics of Kuyalwa, and in the aperture of its dome, there is a buddha image of cast gold, fashioned of five hundred *sang* of gold. (8) Then there is the life-size statue of Fifth Dalai Lama, fashioned of medicinal clay, which was commissioned by Khenpo Janglingpa during the interim when the monastery was taken over by the government, (9) the statue of Atiśa that had been the sacred possession of fourth Tsetrul Tashi Gelek Zangpo, and so on. (10) Then there is the silver statue of Taklung Tangpa called Ornament of the World, which has a monastic jacket of copper and a brass cloak, and (11) the solid gilded-copper life-size statue of Kuyalwa, which had been brought out on to the flagstones of the courtyard during the fire. {62} Its throne-back screen depicts one hundred and eight gold icons of Taklung Tangpa, along with the meditational deities and doctrinal protectors. (12) Then there is the image of Cakrasaṃvara according to the tradition of Kṛṣṇācārin, slightly larger in size than a standing person, the male buddha in silver and the female in copper. It contains twenty-one pearl relics, a hundred pearl relics of Taklung Tangpa, the bone relics of Ngawang Drakpa, the heart of Tashi Peltsek, the chebulic myrobalan miraculously procured by Sangye On, and so forth. (13) Then there are five story-high appliqué banners depicting Munīndra with the sixteen elders, the eight manifestations of Guru Padmākara, and so forth. (14) Then there is the Buddha image called Subduer of the Host of Demons, which had been commissioned by Namgyel Phuntsok, twenty-five handspans in height, and fashioned of gilded copper with gold weighing fifty *sang*. (15) Then there is the Tashi Gomang reliquary stūpa and (16) the story-high clay statue of Vajradhara with throne back, which had been commissioned by Ngawang Tashi Chokyi Gyeltsen; (17) the life-size statue of Orgyen; (18) Coemergent Cakrasaṃvara according to the tradition of Ga Lotsāwa; (19) the likeness of Ngawang Trinle Tendzin Namgyel; (20) the adobe reliquary stūpa of Hor Pelden Gyurme; (21) the medicinal clay story-high statue depicting Maitreya, and (22) life-size statues of Mañjughoṣa, Vajrapāṇi, Śākyamuni in mendicant pose, and Lokeśvara. (23) Then there is the stūpa symbolizing the descent from the god realms, fashioned of one thousand *sang* of silver, which is the reliquary of Tendzin Namgyel, commissioned by Tsetrul Tashi Gewei Wangpo; (24) the reliquary of Gazi Tsering Wangyel, fashioned from four hundred *sang* of silver, and (25) the reliquary of Gazi Wangchuk Tashi Gepel, made of silver weighing three hundred *sang*. (26) Then there is a clockwise-spiraling conch; (27) the reliquary of Tashi Drakpa Yeshe, made of silver weighing nine hundred *sang*; (28) the image of the Buddha in the form Muni Victorious Over the Four Māras, twenty handspans in height, fashioned of gilded copper, including seven hundred *zho* of gold, and {63} (29) the silver reliquary of Gelek Zangpo, weighing nine hundred and sixty *sang* and gilded with twenty-five *sang* of gold.

(30) Then there is the recently made silver reliquary of Matrul Tenpei Nyima with gold ornaments, which does not appear in the inventory,[8] and (31) the new reliquary of Rakshak Kungo, the zhabdrung of Taklung, as well as (32) the reliquary of the Matrul who recently passed away. These are silver reliquaries, almost one story in height and particularly sublime. In the aperture of the dome, they have depictions of the twelve deeds of Śākyamuni, handmade by Nāgārjuna with clay from the nāga realm, which had belonged to Daklha Gampo, and so forth. On the latter two, there are exquisite ornaments including two clockwise-spiraling conches from Riwoche weighing seventy-five *sang* and rubies. They contain, respectively, a likeness of Matrul and the preserved sacred corpse of the Zhabdrung who died of smallpox. (33) Within this hall, there are also the thrones of both the Dalai Lama and the Taklung Lama.

In the Old Protector Chapel, which is accessed from within this hall, there is (1) a story-high image of glorious Four-Armed Mahākāla with an entourage of twelve figures; (2) Vaiśravaṇa and consort with the eight horsemen; and two hundred and forty sets of armor, headed by the leather armor of the king Relpachen, which had been arrayed there by Venerable Ratnaguru. (3) There is an image of Mahādeva commissioned by Mipham Tashi Lama (Maṅgalaguru), and inside the old door (4) there are story-high images of Mahākāla in the form Lekden and of Śrīdevī, which brayed like a donkey when the temple was threatened by fire. (5) The image of Mahākāla in the form Trakṣhad was commissioned by Ngawang Tenpei Nyima. (6)

Within a wooden lattice shrine there are stuffed effigies of spirits, including Draktsen, and by the southern door there is a statue of Draktsen, as well as thread crosses, and so forth.

The middle story, which exceeds two double armspans in height, is the Light-Diffusing Palace of Attainment. Within it, there is (1) the story-high silver reliquary of Ngawang Namgyel in the form of a lotus-heap stūpa, fashioned of gilded copper. In the aperture of its dome there is the stone footprint of Taklung Tangpa and so forth, and there are four Kadam-style stūpas in the four directions. It also has a clockwise-spiraling conch shell. (2) Then there is a sandalwood statue of Four-Armed Mahākāla, which had been carved by the hand of Choku Orgyen Gonpo, and {64} (3) forty-five life-size statues of medicinal clay with silken robes, depicting the golden lineage of the Kagyu masters, which had been commissioned by Namgyel Tashi. (4) There is the enlightenment stūpa in red sandalwood, one double armspan in height, and (5) the large silver reliquary of Tashi Gewei Wangpo, about one and a half double armspans in height. (6) Then there is a set of eight sandalwood stūpas commemorating the deeds of the Tathāgata, one double armspan in height, and among them, in the glass-paneled aperture of the dome of the sandalwood lotus-heap stūpa, there is a bronze figure of Tārā "triumphant in battle;" in the stūpa symbolizing enlightenment, there is a bronze figure of Śākyamuni; in the "multi-door" stūpa, there is a bronze figure of Hevajra that had been the sacred possession of Venerable Marpa; in the stūpa symbolizing miracles, there is the astonishing tooth relic of Venerable Mila Repa, which brings forth pearl relics; in the stūpa symbolizing the resolution of schism, there is an East Indian bronze statue of Vajrapāṇi with crystal ornaments; in the stūpa symbolizing the descent from the god realms, there is a bronze figure of Coemergent Cakrasaṃvara that had been the sacred possession of Sangye On; in the stūpa symbolizing victory over Māra, there is the tooth relic of Venerable Dakpo (Gampopa); and in the stūpa symbolizing nirvāṇa, there is a bronze Tārā. (7) Then there are two silver reliquaries, large and small, and (8) scroll paintings of Atiśa and Dromton that survived the fire, and so forth. (8) On the upper and lower floors, there are Newar-style maṇḍala scrolls and a large number of other old painted scrolls.

In the Southern Chamber, which is the Palace of the Class of Attainment of the Kagyu Tradition, there is (1) an exceptional statue of Drogon Phakmodrupa called Ornament of the World, which is fashioned of five hundred steelyard units of silver, containing one hundred and sixteen pearl relics, the tooth of Ga Lotsāwa, an image of Four-Armed Lokeśvara, and so forth, as well as (2) the silver statue of Taklungpa called Meaningful to Behold, weighing 750 steelyard units. These were both commissioned by Namgyel Tashi. It also contains (3) the life-size medicinal clay statue of Tashi Jampel Gyatso; (4) the reliquary stūpa of Kunga Namgyel, weighing two hundred *sang* of silver; (5) the silver reliquary stūpa of Gazi Sonam Wangyel made with three hundred *sang* of silver and gold, weighing fifteen *sang*, which had been commissioned by his lordship Gazi Sherwang Sonam Wangchuk; {65} (6) the reliquary stūpa of Ngawang Namgyel, fashioned of three thousand *sang* of silver, one thousand five hundred *zho* of gold, and five hundred steelyard units of copper, finely ornamented with gemstones; (7) the statue of Śākyamuni the size of the Jowo that had been the sacred possession of Drung Sangton; (8) the reliquary containing the preserved sacred corpse of Venerable Kunga Tashi, fashioned of two thousand five hundred *sang* of silver and five hundred *zho* of gold; (9) the reliquary of Tashi Peldrub fashioned of two thousand *sang* of silver; (10) the reliquary of Ngawang Namgyel Lekdrub fashioned of two hundred *sang* of silver and one hundred and fifty *zho* of gold; and (11) a woodblock print of the Kangyur in Chinese vermilion, with its own case, which was transported from Lijiang.

In the Northern Chamber there is (1) the reliquary of Gyelwang Namgyel Tashi, fashioned of four hundred *zho* of gold and five hundred and fifty *sang* of silver, containing his preserved sacred corpse, wearing the bone-ornament costume of Buton Rinchendrub, as well as twenty-one miniature inch-high figures depicting Taklung Tangpa, cast in gold. (2) There are also twenty-two life-size statues of former teachers, (3) an exquisite clay statue of Vajrapāṇi with a short skirt, and (4) approximately one hundred handwritten volumes of sacred scripture.

In the Central Chapel of the upper floor called Immaculate Palace, there is (1) the speaking image of Dromton with growing hair and (2) the image of Atiśa. Both of these are one arrow in height and had been brought here by Kunga Tashi from Kachu Lhakhang. There is also (2) the silver reliquary of Pelden Lekdrub, fashioned of two hundred *sang* of silver and three hundred *zho* of gold, containing the preserved sacred corpse of the recently deceased Taklung Matrul, wearing the lotus hat of Orgyen; (3) the sandalwood reliquary of Tashi Chogyel; (4) the statue of Phakmodrupa that had been the sacred possession of Taklung Tangpa; (5) two "tiger bronze" statues of Śākyamuni; (6) the small reliquary of Zhabdrung Dojo Tashi Chogyel; (7) the "tiger bronze" statue of Taklung Tangpa that had been the sacred possession of Sangye On; (8) approximately fifty hand-span-size medicinal clay statues of the golden lineage of Kagyu masters; {66} (9) the bronze image of Vajrakumāra that had been the sacred possession of Lang Pelgyi Senge; (10) a stūpa symbolizing triumph over Māra; and (11) a wonderful backdrop of stucco caves holding statues of the sixteen elders. Surmounting this chapel, there is (1) a middle-sized gilded roof and (2) five gilded victory banners that had been commissioned by Tendzin Namgyel.

In the Chapel of the Lotus-Heap Stūpa, there are (1) the arrow-high Kadam-style reliquary containing the heart of Geshe Potowa and (2) similar Kadam-style reliquaries of Dampa Gaton, Dor Yewa, Khuton, Rinchen Gyeltsen, and so forth, forming a heap of approximately three hundred.

In the Chain-Curtain Temple, there are (1) more than four hundred bronzes in the styles of East, Central, South, and West India, the Chinese Ming dynasty, as well as the styles of Kadam, of the royal dynastic period, of Newar bronzes, and of the Karma Kagyu, and so forth, depicting Munīndra in a precious gold alloy in the teaching gesture, in the prophesying gesture, and in the god realms, and so forth, as well as (2) the miniature *gandhola* spire made in marble by Nāgārjuna; (3) the two-story cubit-high model of the Vajrāsana Stūpa fashioned of a precious gold alloy; (4) the likeness of Taklung Tangpa commissioned at Vajrāsana by the Kashmiri Mayo Gomnak, a monastic preceptor of Vajrāsana, which had arrived here in Taklung from the River Ganges through his miraculous power. Taklung Tangpa had told him, "It doesn't look like me. It looks like you." (5) There is also a bronze image of Guhyasamāja in the form Mañjuvajra, which is more than one cubit in height.

In the Chamber of Tanglha's Divine Treasury there are (1) approximately two hundred images depicting Munīndra, the buddhas of the five enlightened families, the eight closest bodhisattva heirs, and so forth, most of which are bronzes from the royal dynastic period; (2) a life-size likeness of Tashi Peldrub; (3) the silver reliquary containing the heart of Sangye Yarjon, with a pillar of rainbow-reflecting crystal; (4) the exquisitely fashioned silver statue of Taklung Tangpa with throne and backrest, which had been the inseparable possession of thirteen successive lineage holders of the past; (5) the likeness of Phakmodrupa that he himself had consecrated with his own barley; and (6) the silver statue of Ngawang Namgyel that had been the sacred possession of Tashi Peldrub.

In the Chapel of Wooden Lattices, there are (1) two images of Śākyamuni, the same size as the two renowned Jowo Śākyamuni statues of Lhasa, each of them fashioned of Newari bronze; (2) a bronze Śākyamuni statue the size of an eight-year-old boy; {67} (3) three individual cubit-size figures; and (4) apart from them, fourteen slightly larger bronze Śākyamuni images.

In the Chamber of the Lama Temple, there is (1) the half of the black rock that was split open by Dromton, of which the other half is at Reteng, on which the torso of the form of Self-Originated Eleven-Faced Mahākāruṇika is extremely clear. (2) There are miscellaneous statues of teachers representing the impartial philosophical traditions, approximately seven hundred in number, including those of bronze, medicinal clay, stone, wood, and gold. (3) There is the Śākyamuni image that had been the sacred possession of Kunga Tashi, along with the images of the elders and their entourage—twenty-three individual cubit-size figures that had been commissioned by the noble and excellent Kunga Tashi and that had been consecrated miraculously when a grain of consecrated barley from the north landed here. (4) There is also a life-size bronze Śākyamuni and (5) approximately four hundred miscellaneous gilded copper and bronze statues, depicting Maitreya and so forth; (6) a statue of Ngawang Drakpa known for "bringing rain in summer and stopping snow in winter;" (7) a bronze Cakrasaṃvara that had miraculously flown here at the time when Drigung Monastery was sacked; (8) three footprints in stone, of Ga Lotsāwa, Sangye On, and Ngawang Namgyel; and (9) an Avalokiteśvara that had withstood the fire.

The inventory mentions a collection of more than three thousand miscellaneous volumes of scripture, but even among the five hundred or so random volumes on display, there are many old writings representing the new[9] and ancient translations.

In the Protector Chapel of the middle level, there are (1) Satyadvayamukha Vajravārāhī with a beautiful face of gilded copper, (2) a smaller than life-size image of Coemergent Cakrasaṃvara according to Abhayākara's tradition, and (3) a statue of Four-Armed Mahākāla fashioned of one thousand *sang* of silver and ornamented with four hundred *zho* of gold. (4) Also, there is a resplendent life-size statue of Four-Armed Mahākāla made of medicinal clay, which had been brought from the Protector Chapel of Chodzong Namgyel Rabten; (5) the Pañjaranātha statue that had been the sacred possession of Sangye On; (6) and the cast image of Kartṛkājñānanātha, as well as statues of his acolytes, Ziden Wangchuk, the raven-faced Karmamahākāla, the female consort Śrīdevī, and dark green Yama. (7) There are also more than one thousand volumes of scripture. This account has been summarized from the account of Ngawang Tenpei Nyima. {68}

In the Temple of the Eight Manifestations of Guru Padmākara, (1) there are images of Guru Padmākara in the form Dupung Zilnon and his entourage, three figures, along with the eight manifestations, life-size, probably made of clay, with decorative painting and elegant in demeanor. These were commissioned by the sublime Ngawang Tendzin. (2) There are also images of the preceptor Śāntarakṣita, the master Padmākara, and the religious king Tri Songdetsen and supplementary figures commissioned by the late Matrul.

There are four great walls in the four cardinal directions of the monastery, and above them is the divine cairn of Draktsen.

Formerly, the monastic body at Taklung numbered five hundred, but nowadays [in 1920], it exceeds three hundred. There are on display exquisitely made torma offerings associated with twenty sorts of ritual attainment, including those of *Cakrasaṃvara according to the Sixty-Chapter Tradition of Kṛṣṇācārin*,[10] Hevajra according to the tradition of Jñāna, Kālacakra according to the tradition of Buton and the Taklung writings, Guhyasamāja in the form Mañjuvajra, Vajrabhairava, Akṣobhya, Sarvavid, *The Rite according to the Discourse of Bhaiṣajyaguru*, Short-Skirted Vajrapāṇi, Amitāyus, Vijayā, Black Wrathful Vajravidāraṇa, Vajrakīla according to Ratna Lingpa, *The Attainment of the Heart of Taklungpa*,[11] *The Three Roots* according to Taklungpa, and Vaiśravaṇa. I did not observe any discussions indicative of textual knowledge and the fields of classical learning or of experiential realization and so forth. Indeed, since the teachers of the Taklung tradition have passed away, the present is a time of lean fragility at Taklung, Upper Plain and Lower Plain.

2. Taklung Lower Plain: Riwoche

Then, via the household of Nedodepa, which is the paternal estate of Chakme,[1] and crossing by boat from the birthplace of Karmapa Tongwa Donden,[2] which is called Selchen, from Malanyi, I reached glorious Riwoche in Yisho, the seat of Gyelwa Taklung Lower Plain, on the fifth day of the ninth month [in 1918]. An emanation of Avalokiteśvara known as Venerable Sangye On had traveled here from Taklung Upper Plain in his twenty-sixth year and founded the Doctrinal Palace of Yang Gon.

His nephew Orgyen Gonpo, in his twenty-eighth year, constructed the temple in the monkey year. Externally it is said to represent Tāmradvīpa in India; internally, Glorious Kālacakra; and secretly, the array of Sukhāvatī buddha field. The lowest story is the multicolored temple, resembling the three faces of Hevajra, the painting of which was offered by Drogon Phakpa. {19} It is seven times the height of a human being and represents the maṇḍala of buddha body. The middle story, red in color, is five times the height of a human being and represents the maṇḍala of buddha speech. The upper story is white in color, five times the height of a human being, and represents the maṇḍala of buddha mind. Known as the Awesome Multicolored Temple, each of its external walls measures one hundred and thirty-three double armspans.

The Ground Floor

The lower temple has sixty pillars, there are flagstones and a well in its hall, and it has a skylight gallery replete with many lion sculptures. The central pillars have a circumference exceeding two double armspans, and the spaces between them are extremely wide, like vallies.

The sacred representations contained within it are from right to left as follows: (1) There is a statue of medicinal clay depicting the fifth guide

(Maitreya) and commissioned by Phakchok Rinpoche Tashi Drakpa Gyeltsen, which overwhelms the forces of Māra and generates the glory of the Buddhist teaching and living beings. It has a carved wooden throne of excellent quality and an entourage of the seven closest bodhisattva heirs. (2) There is a clay image of Padmākara, painted with molten gold. (3) There is a gilded image of Mahāmuni, who overwhelms the forces of Māra, approximately two double armspans in height, which was commissioned by Khardrungwa Sonam Tashi, its back screen adorned with rows of approximately three hundred buddhas. (4) There is an image of Makākāruṇika with a thousand arms and a thousand eyes, fashioned of medicinal clay, which had been the sacred possession of Tse Zhabdrung Gewei Wangpo. (5) There is a medicinal clay image of Orgyen (Guru Padmākara). (6) There is a gilded image of Mahāmuni, two double armspans in height, which had been commissioned by Kunpang Gonpo Yeshe. It has an engraved wooden back screen engraved with the thousand buddhas, slightly incomplete, with the sixteen elders as throne adornments. (7) There is a set of ten doctrinal protectors. (8) There is a gilded image of Amitāyus, approximately the height of a human being, which had been the sacred possession of Depa Wangdrak Dorje. (9) There is a majestic gilded image of Guru Drakpo, almost human size, which was commissioned by Rikdzin Khardrung as an antidote for hostile border armies. (10) There is a silver cast image of Śākyamuni in the form Great Enlightenment, exquisitely inset with jewels, which had been the sacred possession of Tashi Drakpa Gyeltsen. (11) There is a medicinal clay image of Amitābha, along with a stūpa commemorating the descent from the god realms, which had been commissioned by Jedrung Drakpa Lekdrub. {20} (12) There is a life-size gilded image of Śākyamuni that contains the relics of Ritsa Drakpa Tashi, which had been commissioned by Venerable Drakpei Tsen, along with its throne back. (13) There is a gilded image of Mahāmuni, triumphant in battle, a double armspan in height and fashioned of tarnished bronze. It is known as the outer reliquary of Choje Gyelwei Tsen, and it was commissioned by Drakpei Tsen. (14) In the space in front of that, there is the gilded image depicting Śākyamuni, the size of a fifteen-year-old, which had been the sacred possession of Khenchen Chophel Zangpo and Drung Lorinpa. There are also some old artifacts. (15) Displayed in the offering case, there is the reliquary of Zhabdrung Ngagi Wangchuk, perfectly fashioned of cast silver and inset with exquisite jewels; (16) the likeness of Tashi Peldrub, its face fashioned of medicinal clay; (17) and the likeness of Jedrung Drakpa Lekdrub.

(18) On the inner wall, at the southern side, there is the gilded reliquary displaying the maṇḍala of the face of Choje Gyelwei Tsen, which had been commissioned by Ratnākara. (19) In front of these are the gilded reliquary commissioned by Jedrung Trinle Jampei Jungne as the outer representation of Venerable Kunga Tsen; (20) the image of Mahāmuni in the form Meaningful to Behold that had been commissioned by Chengawa as the outer representation of Choku Orgyan Gonpo; (21) the Kadam-style stūpa, one double armspan in height and fashioned of pure cast silver, which had been commissioned by Sangye On Rinpoche as the reliquary of Sangye Yarjon, (22) and the slightly-larger-than-life-size silver image of Sangye Yarjon called Ornament of the World that had been commissioned by Onpo Pel. (23) In front of these are "many old statues of various sizes," such that in this lower story of the temple, it is certain that there are more than a hundred cubit-size images, headed by those of Cakrasaṃvara, Hevajra, and Guhyasamāja, while the majority of the buddha images are bronzes of Indian, Chinese, Nepalese, and Tibetan origin.

(24) The central image depicting Munīndra, the size of a twenty-five-year-old, equivalent to the Mahābodhi image, {21} was a sacred possession of Sangye On, fashioned of white bronze that resembles cast silver. At the time when it was commissioned, an attendant named Ripa Gyagar was sent to Vajrāsana in India to take the measurements. His return coincided with the time when the construction of the image was completed, and it was astonishing that its proportional measurements were correct in and of themselves. Fashioned of pure *dzi kṣiṃ* gold,[3] it contains a miraculous manuscript of the Kangyur, inscribed in gold.

(25) In front of it to the right and left are pillars of nine conjoined sandalwood trunks that are said to have been offered by Pehar. (26) There is also a well-fashioned life-size gold image depicting Guru Rinpoche, which had been the sacred possession of Khardrung Rinpoche, and (27) an image of Venerable Ngawang Namgyel, fashioned of medicinal clay, that had been the sacred possession of Tashi Peldrub. (28) The foremost representative image to the left is the gilded speaking image that depicts Sangye Yarjon. (29) On the right side of the central buddha image, there is a life-size likeness of Sangye Yarjon, fashioned of pure cast silver, and (30) on its right there is a Kadam-style stūpa, one double armspan in height and fashioned of pure cast silver that is the reliquary of Sangye Yarjon. (31) Seated on the left side of the central buddha image, there is a medicinal clay image of the perfect buddha Drakpa Pel Sangye On that has spoken many times. On

its lotus plinth, (32) there is a gold image of Four-Armed Avalokiteśvara, made by the hand of Choku Orgyen Gonpo, (34) a cubit-size gold image of Mahākāla, which had been the sacred possession of Tsokye Dorje, and (35) a wonderful saddle that had been woven in a single day through the miraculous ability of Pematso, daughter of Lhotasho. (36) The Kadam-style silver reliquary to its left, one double armspan in height, was commissioned by Orgyen Gonpo as the outer representation of Sangye Yarjon. (37) Seated on its left is the life-size speaking image depicting Choku Orgyen Gonpo, which is fashioned of pure silver. {22}

(38) Below and in front, there are many extraordinarily sublime old artifacts, including a beautiful and exquisitely made image of Munīndra, the Blessed Lord Vajradhātu, a silver Hevajra, and a gold Cakrasaṃvara. (39) The silver offering reliquary commissioned by Orgyen Gonpo, containing the sacred corpse of Sangye On Rinpoche, (40) the silver image of Orgyen Gonpo and also his stūpa, fashioned of pure cast silver, both of which were commissioned by Gyelwei Tsenchen, and in front of which there is also his hand drum.

(41) There is also an old life-size Chinese statue of medicinal clay depicting an elder and an exquisite life-size clay image that had been made by Khyungpo Lhazo at the time when the Zhabdrung residency expanded and became dispersed. (42) There are also many life-size statues depicting many of the incumbent hierarchs of former teachers in the succession of Taklung.

(43) As for the sacraments of offering, there are ceiling ornaments, including the "canopy that covers the skylight," the "black umbrella amassed with gems," the "oceanic folds of the incense pouch," the "victory banner of precious flowers," and the "yak-tail whisk with the gemstone handle." On the ground, also, the altar is exquisitely arranged. (44) There is a brocade scroll depicting Bhaiṣajyaguru and also brocade scrolls depicting the sixteen sublime elders.

(45) Along the left side of the assembly hall and adjacent to the door curtain, there are the great stacks of sacred books. These include *The Turquoise Śatasāhasrikā of the Parrot*,[4] and also *The Secret Anthology of the Ḍākinīs*.[5] The volumes, representations of buddha speech collected through miraculous ability by the former teachers of Taklung, exceed ten thousand. That is to say, there are five square bookcases, each of which has twenty-seven long volumes that are vertically stacked. Also, in each of those bookcases, there

are thirty-eight vertical columns of major scriptures inscribed in gold and silver, and each of these has thirteen rows across. By my estimation, there are thirteen thousand volumes there, and it is certain that there are fifteen thousand when one adds those contained in the upper story.

(46) In the eastern hall, there is a story-high silver reliquary stūpa, {23} which is the reliquary of Jedrung Rinchen Sherab, commissioned by Phakchok Rinpoche. (47) There is the extremely elegant image of medicinal clay depicting the Conqueror Lord Maitreya, with its throne back in the form of a *gandhola* spire, replete with multiple buddha figures, which was commissioned by Choje Jikten Wangchuk as the outer representation of Venerable Kunpangpa. (48) There is the two-story-high silver offering reliquary, which is the reliquary of Ngawang Drakpa. (49) There is the exquisitely fashioned gold image of the Buddha in the form Mahādeva, two and a half double armspans in height, which had been the sacred possession of Lama Tashi Peldrub. (50) There is a copy of the precious Kangyur of the Conqueror, inscribed in ink of precious metals on dark-blue paper, which is of extremely high quality, and the two-story-high silver offering stūpa that is the reliquary of the latter. (51) There is the clay image of Mahākāruṇika with a thousand arms and a thousand eyes. (52) There is an image of Avalokiteśvara and (53) also a stūpa symbolizing the resolution of schisms.

(54) On the first great column in front, there is a painting of Four-Armed Mahākāla; on the second great column, there is a mask depicting the face of Genyen Dorje Kunkyong; on the third great column, there is a mask depicting the face of Makpon Yigyel, along with the knife of Jedrung that eradicates the enemies of the Buddhist teaching; and a large number of artifacts and sacraments on display. On the great column alongside the door, there is the hat of Ling Gesar, which resembles the felt hat of a nomadic herder, along with the sword of Trotung; the divine shield of Gaje On; and the arrows, bow, and armor of Donglha Gogyel.

(55) There are many labeled icons depicting Avalokiteśvara, and (56) there is the large gate of fitted acacia planks called Self-Resounding Acacia Gate. (57) To the right of the entrance portico and to the left of Four-Armed Mahākāla, there is an image of Pañjaranātha, both of which are three stories in height, and they have mansions of thread crosses, outer, inner, and secret representations, suspended in the air. (58) There are also murals depicting the thirty proud spirit generals in the retinue of glorious Mahākāla and Mahābala in the form Invincible Tamer of All.

The Middle Floor

On the east wall of the middle story, which represents the maṇḍala of buddha speech, (1) there is a golden manuscript of the Tengyur, the commentaries on the enlightened intention of the Conqueror, {24} and (2) within a frame, there are approximately twenty cubit-size images associated with the deities of the four classes of tantras, fashioned of white and red sandalwood, which had been the sacred possessions of Phakchok Tashi Drakpa Gyeltsen. (3) There is a mural depicting Pelden Dokham Lhamo, and (4) there are life-size statues of medicinal clay depicting Thūmāṅgārī, the eight manifestations of Guru Padmākara, and the five classes of Padma Totrengtsel, which had been commissioned by Phakchok Ngawang Drakpa. (5) Then there are the life-size gold image of the Buddha in the form Buddha as the Great Divine Being," which belonged to Jedrung Drakpa Gyeltsen; (6) the gold "arrow-size" icon depicting the Buddha, which had been commissioned by master Tunkhangpa; and (7) the clay image of Guru Dupung Zilnon, which had been commissioned by Rikdzin Sonam Tashi. (8) There is also a gold manuscript of the Kangyur, which was a sacred possession of the former hierarchs in the line of On, as well as (9) woodblocks of some two hundred volumes containing the Collected Works of the ancestors of the Kagyu lineage, which had been the sacred possessions of Venerable Ratnākara.

(10) In the middle, there is the foremost representation, the gold image, two double armspans in height, depicting the Buddha in the form Great Enlightenment, which had been the sacred possession of Venerable Miyo Gonpo.

(11) On the right wall, there are fifteen virtually life-size images depicting the succession of the teachers forming the golden lineage of the Kagyu school, starting from Vajradhara. (12) There are particularly sublime murals in Newar style, and in front of each of them is the corresponding clay image. If one touches one's cheeks against the face of Tunkhangpa Dzorawa, it helps alleviate the pains of tooth decay.

(13) In the middle, on the face of the column in front, there is a life-size gold image depicting Śākyamuni, which had been commissioned by Lha Jangchub Pel, and (14) to its right and left there are buddha images, both of gold. (15) Below it, there is an image of the Buddha in the form Tonpa Urgyenpa, the size of a seated human being, which had been the sacred possession of Lhatsun. (16) To its right, there is the story-high golden reliquary of Kuzhang Rinpoche, and on its left there is a lotus-heap stūpa with sun and

moon finial, one double armspan in height. (17) Then there is an image of Mahākāruṇika with a thousand arms and a thousand eyes that reaches the top of that story. (18) Around it are Secham, Chogyel, {25} Venerable Mila, and the six deities headed by Tseringma, which had been commissioned by Jedrung Rinpoche.

(19) To the left of the central representational image, there is a gold statue depicting On Heruka, a life-size Miyo Kudul, and a statue of medicinal clay depicting Drogon Phakmodrupa, its heart and cheeks with self-originating auspicious markings. (20) There is also the golden lineage of Kagyu teachers, starting from Venerable Nāropā, and the fifteen hierarchs in the abbatial succession of Taklung.

(21) On the north side, there are many volumes of sūtra and mantra, headed by the gold manuscript of the Kangyur that belonged to Kuzhang Rinpoche, as well as a complete Kangyur and two life-size gold buddha images that had been the sacred possessions of Jedrung Tsokye Dorje. (22) There are many other icons, more than a hundred bronzes labeled "worn bronzes," including a consecrated image of Vajradhara, and some fifty Kadam-style stūpas.

In brief, (23) on the face of each of the surrounding columns there is a miniature arrow-size image of the Buddha, fashioned of cast gold, each with its own throne back, and there are approximately forty-two columns. (24) There are also extraordinarily sublime icons depicting the Buddha, the entire array of the sixteen elders, and Śakra, as well as life-size images of medicinal clay that had been the sacred possessions of Ngawang Drakpa.

The Upper Floor

In the upper story, which represents the maṇḍala of buddha mind, (1) there is a room fashioned of timber containing the Kangyur of the Conqueror, which had been the sacred possession of Sangye On and an image with restricted access that had been drawn with the serum of Takshobu Pematso and into which Pañjaranātha had manifestly vanished. (2) There is a life-size silver image of Vajradhara, which had been the sacred possession of master Dzorawa, and (3) an image of medicinal clay depicting Choku Orgyen Gonpo, whose consecrated barley mothers use just to keep babies warm at their bosom. (4) Inside the perimeter wall of the timber room, there are images of Drogon Phakmodrupa and Drubchen Sangye Yerpa, which had been brought there from Yelpuk, (5) and there are also many extraordinary sublime icons, about fifty in number, including many different sorts of bronzes of Indian, Chinese, and Tibetan origin, {26} and (6) an image of Sangye On called Chuzikma.

On the north wall, (7) there is a gold manuscript of the Kangyur and (8) a gilded clay image of the deity of the means for attainment of long life (Amitāyus), which belonged to Rolpei Dorje.

(9) In the middle, the central representation is a medicinal clay speaking image depicting Sangye On called Tetakma, which had formerly been the inner representation of Dokham Usik Gon. And there is (10) an appliqué scroll depicting Sangye Yarjon, (11) a miniature "arrow-size" gold icon depicting Lopon Rinpoche, (12) a likeness of Tashi Drakpa Gyeltsen, and (13) an icon depicting Vaiśravaṇa painted by the hand of Drukchen Kadrukpa, along with (14) Pañjaranātha, and (15) an extraordinarily sublime bronze painted in gold line, (16) a Buddha image painted in Nepal that has an extraordinarily sublime radiance, (17) painted scrolls representing many classes of tantras, (19) scrolls depicting maṇḍalas and so forth and many pillar hangings drawn in Newar style that depict the golden lineage of the Kagyu school. (20) Then there is the offering shrine and torma chest associated with Chogyurlingpa's *Vajrakīla: Seven Profundities.*[6]

(21) Directly above the gilded roof, there is a large golden spire, about eight double armspans in height, with four golden hangings on its four corners.[7] (22) Interspersed between them, there are also four golden victory banners.

Other Buildings

Upstairs in the Zhabdrung Palace are the living quarters and the Protector Chapel. Downstairs, there is an assembly hall with sixteen pillars and a gold victory banner, but it was ransacked and left empty by the Chinese forces.

The Sarma College has a gilded roof, and there are ten retreat hermitages. Within the splendid guesthouse, there is an awesome and charismatic image of gilded bronze, more than one cubit in height, depicting Four-Armed Mahākāla, which had been the sacred possession of Ga Lotsāwa, as well as images depicting Cakrasaṃvara and Hevajra that had been the sacred possession of Jñāna, the hand drum of Choku Orgyen Gonpo, and a gilded bronze image of Jarok Dongma that had been found by a teacher from Riwoche who had taught *The Seven Conches of Cakrasaṃvara*[8] at Ga Lotsāwa's hermitage. There is also {27} a body ornament made of bone that belonged to the Indian accomplished master Jñānaśrī and more than a hundred bronzes and gold images, including representations that had been the sacred possessions of Orgyen Gonpo, along with a Kangyur. The remaining representations of buddha body, speech, and mind that were once visible in the twenty-pillar assembly hall were plundered by the Tibetan army.

The Yang Gon Palace, with its ceramic tiles and golden spire, houses the chapel of Gonpo Maning, many residential quarters, and a sixteen-pillar assembly hall containing three or four life-size gold images and some similar clay statues. Apart from these, all the remainder have been ransacked and emptied by the Tibetan army, so it presents an extremely sorrowful spectacle.

In the meantime, the three-story reliquaries of Ratnākara, Choku Orgyen Gonpo, and Sangye On Rinpoche are still covered with gold leaf, but they have been damaged by leakages. Thieves[9] have occupied the first two, and although there are many exquisite icons extant within the gilded-copper umbrella at the top, the roof tiles have collapsed. It is said that the third tooth relic of the Buddha, which was half of the allocation of the sacred artifacts that once belonged to the king of Kaliṅga, is contained within the reliquary of Sangye On.

The Nyingma college was also greatly plundered by the Tibetan army, and apart from that, there are about a hundred statues and a Kangyur. In the temple where the vase attainment of Ratnamaṇi is performed, there are four large maṇḍalas, the great chamber of xylographs called Bumlang, and a cubit-size sandalwood kīla with three faces and six arms that had been the sacred possession of Kaḥtok Dampa Deshek, which had been given to Riwoche by Kaḥtok Rikdzin Chenpo. It also houses a gold image of Vajrakīla with three faces and six arms that had belonged to Ratna Lingpa, along with its glorious secret kīla. Also there is the representative image of Guru Padmākara that had been brought forth as a treasure by Jedrung himself, a Mahākāruṇika statue that had been revealed within the treasures of Sangye Lingpa, and many others.

The Gonpo Maning chapel, the thirty-five-pillar temple with its gilded roof, and the Taklung College were undamaged, even by those armies. {28} Among them, the Thirty-Five-Pillar Temple with the gilded roof is of fine quality. It contains an image of Tashi Peldrub, a life-size gold image of the Buddha, a likeness and reliquary of Ngawang Namgyel, a gold manuscript of the Kangyur, a Tengyur, and more than two hundred gold images and bronzes. The Protector Chapel of Tsering Chenga is also extant.

In the past, the two palaces and the three colleges housed approximately three thousand gold images, numerous extremely exquisite painted scrolls, and many volumes of scripture that surpassed determination, but I am saddened because these have been destroyed by armies. The hermitage for the vase attainment of Mahākāruṇika, according to Jatson Nyingpo, and some nine hermitages are extant.

Reflecting upon the faith and present decline
In that sublime place frequented by holy beings of the past
Who stacked the threefold representations of Taklung Lower Plain like
  a mountain,
My sadnesses rival one another.

Abbreviations

BDRC	Buddhist Digital Resource Center. bdrc.org
Dg.K.	*sDe dge bka' 'gyur* [The Derge Kangyur]. Xylograph edition. 103 vols. Edited by Situ Chokyi Jungne. Freely accessible online at www.bdrc.org.
Dg.T.	*sDe dge bstan 'gyur* [The Derge Tengyur]. Xylograph edition. Edited by Zhuchen Tsultrim Rinchen. 213 vols. Freely accessible online at www.bdrc.org.
DNZ	Jamgon Kongtrul Lodro Taye ('Jam mgon kong sprul blo gros mtha' yas). *Gdams ngag rin po che'i mdzod* [The treasury of precious instructions]. 18 vols. Delhi: Shechen, 1999.
KPD	*Bka' 'gyur dpe bsdur ma* [The annotated Kangyur]. 1994–2008. Beijing: Krung go'i bod rig pa'i dpe skrun khang.
MVT	*Mahāvyutpatti*. Edited by R. Sakaki. Kyoto: 1916–1925.
THL	The Tibetan and Himalayan Library. https://thlib.org.
Toh.	H. Ui non. 1934. *A Complete Catalogue of the Tibetan Buddhist Canons*. Tohoku University catalog of the Derge edition of the canon. Sendai.
TPD	*Bstan 'gyur dpe bsdur ma* [The annotated Tengyur]. 1994–2008. 120 vols. Beijing: Krung go'i bod rig pa'i dpe skrun khang.
Treasury of Lives	Treasury of Lives: A Biographical Encyclopedia of Tibet, Inner Asia, and the Himalayas. https://treasuryoflives.org/

Notes

Taklung Painting by Jane Casey

1. Taklung Ngawang Namgyel 1992. Here and below, all page numbers of *The Doctrinal History of Taklung* refer to the Tibetan manuscript, and all cited passages are translated by Gyurme Dorje.
2. Funding from Robert Y. C. Ho, with additional funding from John Eskenazi, supported this multiyear effort.
3. Casey 2023.
4. For more on *tukdam*, see Casey 2023, 95–97.
5. See discussion in Casey 2023, 156–59.
6. See discussion in Casey 2023, 318–21.
7. In these inscriptions, the teacher's name is in Sanskrit, rendered phonetically in Tibetan script. Dan Martin notes that these name mantras (*mtshan sngags*) are usually rendered using the Sanskrit form of the person's name (personal correspondence, February, 2021). Kīrtiśrīraśmibhadra, which appears in many Taklung inscriptions, is the Sanskrit equivalent of the interim fourth Taklung abbot's ordination name, Drakpa Pel Ozer Zangpo (Grags pa dpal 'od zer bzang po). See Casey 2023, 67.
8. See Casey 2023, 1056–62.
9. Taklung Ngawang Namgyel 1992, 604. See below, p. 474.
10. Taklung Ngawang Namgyel 1992, 306. See below, p. 241.
11. Taklung Ngawang Namgyel 1992, 307. See below, p. 242.
12. Taklung Ngawang Namgyel 1992, 287. See below, p. 227. Gyurme Dorje notes that this information is also contained in *The Doctrinal History of Lhorong* (*Lho rong chos 'byung*) (see Tatsak Tse Wangyal 1994, 504–5) and in *The Doctrinal History Titled Scholars' Feast* (*Chos 'byung mkhas pa'i dga' ston*) (see Pawo Tsuklak Trengwa 1961, 426–27). Peter Schwieger (1996, 121) discusses the importance of such objects to attract pilgrims to a monastery.
13. Stag lung ya thang.
14. Stag lung ma thang.
15. Dan Martin notes, "Yang-dgon [Yang Gon] means an extra added monastery founded after its mother monastery perhaps to take in the monk overflow?

Sometimes it is a proper name, but it's still kind of ambiguously so" (personal correspondence, February, 2021).

16. Taklung Ngawang Namgyel 1992, 308. See p. 243.
17. Taklung Ngawang Namgyel 1992, 309. See p. 244.
18. Taklung Ngawang Namgyel 1992, 607. Gyurme Dorje refers the reader to *The Doctrinal History of Lhorong* (see Tatsak Tse Wangyal 1994, 527). See p. 476.
19. Taklung Ngawang Namgyel 1992, 614–15. See pp. 481–82.
20. Roerich 1976, 651–52.
21. Taklung Ngawang Namgyel 1992, 605.
22. See Appendix 2 in Casey 2023, 1056–63. In some cases, it is clear that these inscriptions were added to earlier paintings because the inscriptions are placed around preexisting inscriptions. Many of the inscriptions personalized by Sangye On are written in gold print script (*dbu can*), which also sets them apart from previous inscriptions.
23. Taklung Ngawang Namgyel 1992, 205. See p. 163.
24. Published in Casey 2023, 182–215.
25. Enthroned deities and revered teachers appear within mountain caves in other early Tibetan paintings. See Kossak and Singer 1997, 55, 95, 114, 131, 137, 175.
26. Matthew Akester (2016, 37n33) writes that the ancient willow hut was established on the northern side of the Old Offering Chapel (Mchod khang rnying ma). Dan Martin (2010, 203n22) describes these early huts (*spyil bu* or *spyil pu*) as "generally corresponding to Sanskrit *kuṭī* or *kuṭikā*." In the same source (203n23), he mentions *glang ma* to be the "usual spelling for the type of 'alpine willow' then in use for hut making."
27. Indian treatises on iconography, such as the *Mahāvastu*, describe thirty-two great marks (*mahāpuruṣalakṣaṇa*) of the enlightened being, as well as an additional eighty lesser marks (*anuvyañjanalakṣaṇa*). See Buswell and Lopez 2014, 463.
28. See, for example, Casey 2023, 252–59, 284–93.

Editor's Preface to the Tibetan Edition

1. *chos 'byung.*
2. *mda' tshad ma.*
3. The publication referenced here is *Chos 'byung ngo mtshar rgya mtsho*, published in 1992 in Lhasa by Bod ljongs bod yig dpe rnying dpe skrun khang. See BDRC MW17276. This is the Tibetan source on which Gyurme Dorje based his translation of parts one and two of this volume.—Ed.
4. *rig gnas lo rgyus rgyu cha rtsom 'bri tshogs chung.*
5. *lha sa chab gros.*
6. *bam po nya pa.*
7. *gdan rans rnam thar kyi kha skong.*

8. This supplement refers to the text that constitutes part two of this volume, *Great Divine Drum of Wondrous Renown*.—Ed.
9. *gtsang pa sde srid.*
10. *dga' ldan pho brang.*
11. *slob gzhi.*
12. The section corresponds to part one, chapter eight (see p. 153), there titled "The Biographies of the Taklung Kagyu Lineage."—Ed.
13. This system of annotation refers only to the Tibetan edition and not to the present translation.—Ed.
14. *dkar chags.*
15. *bam po'i sa bcad.*
16. *da pa.*
17. *nang gses.*
18. Following Gyurme Dorje's own arrangement, this order is not followed in this translated volume. Rather, here, Ngawang Tenpei Nyima Chokyi Jungne's supplement (part two) is placed after the eleven chapters of Ngawang Namgyel's main text (part one), which is why the pagination of the Tibetan source (in curly brackets) jumps from 723 at the end of chapter ten to 915 at the beginning of chapter eleven.—Ed.
19. *zur brten dpyad gzhi.*
20. This list of annotations refers only to the Tibetan edition and not to the present translation.—Ed.
21. *shig 'dzin gyi brtul zhugs.* This is a metaphor for emaciation. See Śrīdharasena, *"Clarifying All Varieties" or "The Garland of Pearls": A Treatise on Expressions, Abhidhānaśāstraviśvalocanamityaparābhidhānamuktāvalīnāma, Mngon brjod kyi bstan bcos sna tshogs gsal ba zhes pa ming gzhan mu tig phreng ba zhes bya ba* (TPD 120), 1281.
22. "The publishers of this work" here refers to Lhasa's Bod ljongs bod yig dpe rnying dpe skrun khang.—Ed.
23. *po ta la'i rig dngos do dam khru'u.*

A Brief Introduction to Zhabdrung Ngawang Namgyel and Ngawang Tenpei Nyima

1. *gdan sa pa.*
2. *dge bsnyen bar ma rab byung.*
3. *Sku rdzis chos spyod rab gsal.*
4. *Legs bshad rin po che'i gter.*
5. *'dus pa'i rgya mtsho.*
6. *Thams cad mkhyen pa ngag gi dbang po'i rnam thar.*
7. *Lam zab bla ma'i rnal 'byor.*
8. *mkhyen rab.*

9. *sde srid kyi skyong bdar.*
10. Bkra shis 'dzam gling rgyan mchog.
11. *Rgyal ba stag lung pa chen po'i rnam thar rgyas pa.*
12. *Rnam thar 'phags lam snang ba.*
13. *Skal bzang yid kyi shing rta.*
14. That is, part one, chapter eight. See p. 153.—Ed.

Part One: Wondrous Ocean of Eloquence

Verses of Homage

1. The five wheels of inexhaustible adornment (*mi zad rgyan gyi 'khor lo lnga*) are buddha body, speech, mind, attributes, and activities. See Dudjom Rinpoche 1991, 2:149.
2. The four buddha bodies (*catuḥkāya, sku bzhi*) are the buddha body of reality (*dharmakāya, chos sku*), the buddha body of perfect resource (*sambhogakāya, long spyod rdzogs pa'i sku*), the buddha body of emanation (*nirmāṇakāya, sprul pa'i sku*), and the buddha body of essentiality (*ngo bo nyid kyi sku, svabhāvikakāya*). The five pristine cognitions (*pañcajñāna, ye shes lnga*) are the pristine cognition of reality's expanse (*dharmadhātujñāna, chos dbyings kyi ye shes*), the mirrorlike pristine cognition (*ādarśajñāna, me long gi ye shes*), the pristine cognition of sameness (*samatājñāna, mnyam nyid kyi ye shes*), the pristine cognition of discernment (*pratyavekṣanajñāna, so sor rtog pa'i ye shes*), and the pristine cognition of accomplishment (*kṛtyānuṣṭhānajñāna, bya grub pa'i ye shes*). For a detailed presentation, see Dudjom Rinpoche 1991, 1:115–48.
3. These are to be identified with the four great principles (*sdom pa chen po bzhi*) of Taklungpa. See p. 9.
4. The three planes of existence (*srid pa gsum*) are the celestial, terrestrial, and subterranean abodes or, alternatively, the world systems of desire, form, and formlessness. See Nordrang Orgyen 2008, 457–58.
5. The threefold obscuration (*sgrib gsum*) pertains to knowable phenomena, afflicted mental states, and propensities. See Dudjom Rinpoche 1991, 2:118.
6. In Purāṇic mythology, the seven horses that pull the chariot of the sun are named after the seven meters of Vedic verse—namely, Gāyatrī, Bṛhatī, Uṣṇik, Jagatī, Triṣṭubh, Anuṣṭubh, and Paṅkti. See Mani 1964, 770–71.
7. The two stages (*dvikrama, rim gnyis*) are the generation and perfection stages of meditation, according to the tantras. See the references in Dudjom Rinpoche 1991, 2:108.

Writer's Pledge

1. The inexhaustible wheels of adornment (*mi zad pa'i rgyan gyi 'khor lo rnams*) are fivefold, including the buddha body, speech, mind, attributes, and activities.

2. Vasubandhu, *The Treasury of Phenomenology*, *Abhidharmakośakārikā*, *Chos mngon pa'i mdzod kyi tshig le'ur byas pa chos rjes kra shi* (Toh. 4089; Dg.T. mngon pa, *ku*, ff. 1b–25a; TPD 79, 3–59), chap. 8, vv. 39a–d. See the translation and commentary in Pruden 1988–90, 4:1308n217.
3. Ngag gi dbang po.
4. The citation is as yet unidentified.
5. *nyams skyugs kyi gdams pa*.
6. Phyag rgya chen po lhan cig skyes sbyor.
7. Dpal nā ro pa'i chos drug.
8. This citation is unidentified at present.
9. *thugs dam*.

1. The Presentation of World Systems

1. *Ḍākārṇava* (*Śrīḍākārṇavamahāyoginītantrarājanāma*), *Dpal mkha' 'gro rgya mtsho rnal 'byor ma'i rgyud kyi rgyal po chen po zhes bya ba* (Toh. 372; Dg.K. rgyud, *kha*, ff. 137a–264b).
2. *Buddhāvataṃsaka*, *Sangs rgyas phal po che zhes bya ba shin tu rgyas pa chen po'i mdo* (Toh. 44; Dg.K. phal chen, *ka*, ff. 1b–393a, *kha*, ff. 1b–396a, *ga*, ff. 1b–396a, *a*, ff. 1b–363a; KPD 37).
3. *Smṛtyupasthāna*, *'Phags pa dam pa'i chos dran pa nye bar gzhag pa* (Toh. 287; Dg.K. mdo sde, *ya*, ff. 82a–318a, *ra*, ff. 1b–307a, *la*, ff. 1b–312a, *sha*, ff. 1b–229b).
4. Maudgalyāyana, *Lokaprajñapti*, *'Jig rten gzhag pa* (Toh. 4086; Dg.T. mngon pa, *i*, ff. 1b–93a).
5. Asaṅga, *Abhidharmasamuccaya*, *Chos mngon pa kun las btus pa* (Toh. 4049; sems tsam, *ri*, ff. 44b–120a; TPD 76, 116–313).
6. That is, Vasubandhu's *Treasury of Phenomenology* (*Abhidharmakośakārikā*, *Chos mngon pa'i mdzod kyi tshig le'ur byas pa chos rjes kra shi*).
7. Kusumatalagarbhavyūhālaṃkāralokadhātu, Gzhi dang snying po me tog gis brgyan pa'i zhing.
8. This cosmology derives from *The Great Bounteousness of the Buddhas* (*Buddhāvataṃsaka*), on which see Cleary 1993, 202–53. See also Dudjom Rinpoche 1991, 1:409; and Jamgön Kongtrul Lodrö Tayé 1995, 101–4. More specifically, the narrative that follows in this entire first part of the book derives directly and verbatim from Pawo Tsuklak Trengwa's *Doctrinal History Titled Scholars' Feast* (*Chos 'byung mkhas pa'i dga' ston*). See Pawo Tsuklak Trengwa 1962, 6–9.
9. *sahalokadhātu*, *mi mjed 'jig rten gyi khams*. On the term *sahalokadhātu*, see Kloetzli 1983, 6n1. See also Jamgön Kongtrul Lodrö Tayé 1995, 104.
10. Vasubandhu, *The Treasury of Phenomenology* (TPD 79), 19. This is chap. 3, v. 45. See also the translation in Pruden 1988–90, 2:451. The latter renders the number six million one hundred thousand (*sa ya drug 'bum*) as "sixteen hundred thousand leagues." The term *yojana* (*dpag btshad*) denotes the yoking

distance of oxen, estimated in Abhidharma sources as the equivalent of 7,315 meters.

11. *īṣādhārāmātrā varṣyadhārā, sprin chen gser gyi gnya' ba.* Cf. Pruden 1988–90, 529n366. See also Jamgön Kongtrul Lodrö Tayé 1995, 108.
12. *kañcanamayībhūmi, gser gyi sa gzhi.*
13. Vasubandhu, *The Treasury of Phenomenology*, chap. 3, vv. 46–48. See Kloetzli 1983, 25.
14. The depth of the water is considered to be 1,120,000 yojana, of which the uppermost 320,000 yojana are transformed into the terrain of gold. See Vasubandhu, *The Treasury of Phenomenology*, vv. 47a–48a; and Kloetzli 1983, 26. Note that our text misreads 340,000 yojana (*dpag tshad sum 'bum bzhi khri*) for the thickness of the terrain of gold.
15. Vasubandhu, *The Treasury of Phenomenology*, chap. 3, vv. 50b–51b. See also Pruden 1988–90, 2:452–54; and Jamgön Kongtrul Lodrö Tayé 1995, 110.
16. These are, respectively, Yugaṃdhāra, Īṣādhāra, Khadirāka, Sudarśana, Aśvakarna, Vinatāka, and Nimamdhāra.
17. This brief description of the mountain ranges and seas derives from Vasubandhu, *The Treasury of Phenomenology*, chap. 3, vv. 48b–49c, 51c–52c. See Pruden 1988–90, 2:452–54.
18. On the dimensions of the four continents and their peripheral islands, see Pruden 1988–90, 2:455; and Kloetzli 1983, 26–28.
19. *cakravāla, lcags ri.* The *cakravāla* lends its name to the single world system thus formed. For a detailed description, see Kloetzli 1983, 23–50.
20. These are outlined in Vasubandhu, *The Treasury of Phenomenology*, chap. 3, vv. 58–59d. See also Pruden 1988–90, 2:456–60.
21. This accords with Vasubandhu's *Autocommentary on "The Treasury of Phenomenology," Abhidharmakośabhāṣya, Chos mngon pa'i mdzod kyi bshad pa* (Toh. 4090; Dg.T. mngon pa, *ku*, ff. 26b–258a; TPD 79, 65–630), on which see Pruden 1988–90, 2:455–56.
22. *asura.*
23. See Pruden 1988–90, 2:460–62.
24. Vasubandhu's account of Trāyastriṃśa, the paradise of Śakra, is translated in Pruden 1988–90, 2:463–64. See also Jamgön Kongtrul Lodrö Tayé 1995, 116–18.
25. Cf. Pruden 1988–90, 2:465–66. See also Jamgön Kongtrul Lodrö Tayé 1995, 118–19.
26. *kāmadhātu, 'dod khams.*
27. *rūpadhātu, gzugs khams.*
28. *arūpyadhātu, gzugs med bzhi.*
29. On the diverse god realms of desire, form, and formlessness that constitute these three world systems, see the charts in Kloetzli 1983, 33–39. See also Dudjom Rinpoche 1991, 1:14–15. Vasubandhu's account is found in Pruden 1988–90, 2:470ff. Cf. Jamgön Kongtrul Lodrö Tayé 1995, 119–21.

30. On the appearance of perfect buddhas, hermit buddhas, and universal emperors in the human world, see Pruden 1988–90, 2:480–87.
31. Sgra mi snyan.
32. See Jamgön Kongtrul Lodrö Tayé 1995, 132. See also Pruden 1988–90, 2:455.
33. Suvarṇadvīpa.
34. The sixteen traditional regions of ancient India (*yul 'khor chen po bcu drug*) are enumerated in Nordrang Orgyen 2008, 2962. The six major cities (*grong khyer chen po drug*) are listed in *Minor Transmissions of Monastic Discipline* (*Vinayakṣudrakavastu*) as Śrāvastī, Sāketa, Campaka, Vārāṇasī, Vaiśālī, and Rājagṛha. See Nordrang Orgyen 2008, 1329.
35. On the geomantic significance of the rigors of the Tibetan terrain being likened to a supine ogress (*srin mo gan rgyal du 'gyel ba*), see Aris 1979, 8–33; Mills 2007; Sørensen and Hazod 2005, 48–56; and Dorje 2009, 850.
36. *pṛthivīparpaṭaka, sa mo zhag.*
37. The myth of the divinely inspired origin of human beings on Jambudvīpa is recounted by Vasubandhu. See Pruden 1988–90, 2:487–88.
38. These are glancing, agitation, holding hands, and sexual intercourse. See Pawo Tsuklak Trengwa 1962, 8.
39. *tretāyuga*. See Jamgön Kongtrul Lodrö Tayé 1995, 133–34. On the four temporal ages (*caturyoga, dus bzhi*), including this Third Age, see Dudjom Rinpoche 1991, 2:138–39. The four ages are named after the four sides of a traditional Indian dice: "perfect" is the score of four; "second" place is a three; "third" place is a two; and "kali" is the name for the lowest score, a one.
40. Cf. the slightly dissimilar accounts in Pruden 1988–90, 2:488, and Jamgön Kongtrul Lodrö Tayé 1995, 133–34.
41. Thirteen years after the Buddha's enlightenment, the monastic community was confronted with the circumstances of the first defeating act for a fully ordained monk—sexual misconduct. The twelve preceding years are considered to have been the Perfect Age with the Third, Second, and First Ages subsequently unfolding, commensurate with the appearance of the other three defeating acts—stealing, killing, and lying. See Ngawang Zangpo 2014, 255–60; and Jamgön Kongtrul Lodrö Tayé 1995, 162–63.
42. Pawo Tsuklak Trengwa (1961, 9) reads *chu bur dang po byung ba'i tshe*. Arbuda is said to endure for as long as it would take to empty a container holding twenty dry measures of sesame seeds by removing a single grain every hundred years. See Patrul Rinpoche 1994, 68; Ngawang Zangpo 2014, 202; and Pruden 1988–90, 2:475.
43. See Pruden 1988–90, 2:481–82.
44. See Jamgön Kongtrul Lodrö Tayé 1995, 134.
45. See Pruden 1988–90, 2:488.
46. The appearances and circumstances of the thousand buddhas of the Auspicious Eon are recounted in *The Bhadrakalpika Sūtra*. See the translation in Yeshe De Project 1986a.

2. The Deeds of the Teacher

1. The appearance of these legendary universal emperors (*cakravartin, 'khor lo bsgyur ba*)—whose temporal authority is symbolized by wheels of gold, silver, copper, and iron and whose physical forms are said to be imbued with the thirty-two major marks and the eighty minor marks, just like the buddhas—is described in Jamgön Kongtrul Lodrö Tayé 1995, 134–38. See also Pruden 1988–90, 2:484–85; and the *Lalitavistarasūtra*, as translated in Dharmachakra Translation Committee 2013–16. Both Mahāsammata and Cārumant are considered to have been ancient ancestors of Nāropā. See Guenther 1963, 7. Ngawang Namgyel's immediate source is Pawo Tsuklak Trengwa 1962, 9–11, which details the lineages of the legendary kings.
2. Gnyen ldan.
3. The following version of the life of Śākyamuni Buddha derives directly and often verbatim from Pawo Tsuklak Trengwa 1991, 18–30.
4. The five degenerations (*pañcānantarīya, snyigs ma lnga*) are those of lifespan, wrong view, afflicted mental states, sentient beings, and time. See Dudjom Rinpoche 1991, 2:144.
5. The eighteen extremist teachers (*mu stegs kyi ston pa bco brgyad*) are listed in Nordrang Orgyen 2008, 3021. See also Dorje 2012, 841n1050.
6. See Dharmachakra Translation Committee 2013–16, 3.17–3.54.
7. *lokavit, 'jig rten rig byed.*
8. *dvipendra, gnyis 'thung dbang po.* See Dharmachakra Translation Committee 2013–16, 5.1–5.4.
9. *uragasāracandana, tsan dan sbrul snying.*
10. See Dharmachakra Translation Committee 2013–16, 6.41ff.
11. See Dharmachakra Translation Committee 2013–16, 7.72.
12. According to Pawo Tsuklak Trengwa (1961, 18–19), the entire city of Kapilavastu turned into precious metals and gems, and two young snow lions arrived there and played in the streets without harming anyone.
13. *butea frondosa, palāśa.*
14. See Dharmachakra Translation Committee 2013–16, 7.3–28.
15. See Dharmachakra Translation Committee 2013–16, 7.29–37. These eighteen signs are not enumerated in Pawo Tsuklak Trengwa 1962, 19.
16. See Dharmachakra Translation Committee 2013–16, 7.85, 7.89.
17. The four vassal kings (*rgyal phran bzhi*) were Prasenajit (Gsal rgyal) of Śrāvastī; Bimbisāra (Gzugs can snying po) of Rājagṛha; Śatānīka (Dmag rgya pa) of Kauśāmbhī; and Pradyota (Rab snang), the son of Anantanemi (Mu khyud mtha' yas) of Ujjayinī ('Phags rgyal). See Pawo Tsuklak Trengwa 1962, 19.
18. See Dharmachakra Translation Committee 2013–16, 7.65–72, 90–105. See also Taranatha 2003, 48–52. Araṇa (Nyon mongs med) is also listed among the eighteen exponents of extremist views. See Dorje 2012, 841–42n1050.

19. See Dharmachakra Translation Committee 2013–16, 10.
20. *mahāgrasārā*, *snying mchog chen po*. This number is also designated as the "application to the smallest particles" (*paramāṇurajaḥpraveśānugata*, *rdul phra rab la 'jug pa'i rjes su song ba*). See Dharmachakra Translation Committee 2013–16, 12.34–45.
21. See Dharmachakra Translation Committee 2013–16, 11.15–20.
22. See Dharmachakra Translation Committee 2013–16, 11.3–14.
23. See Dharmachakra Translation Committee 2013–16, 12.52–68.
24. See Dharmachakra Translation Committee 2013–16, 14.2–27.
25. Bsngags ldan.
26. 'Dun pa.
27. *rnam dag mchod rten*, "pure stūpa." See Dharmachakra Translation Committee 2013–16, 15.2–15.4.
28. See Dharmachakra Translation Committee 2013–16, 16.3–16.5, 17.1–17.5.
29. See Dharmachakra Translation Committee 2013–16, 17.6–77. These five were Ājñātakauṇḍinya (Kun shes kauṇḍinya), Aśvajit (Rta thul), Bāṣpa (Rlangs pa), Mahānāma (Ming chen), and Bhadrika (Bzang ldan).
30. For this account that accords with the tantras of union, see Lessing and Wayman 1968, 25–29.
31. The two village girls are more commonly known as Sujāṭā and Uttarā.
32. See Dharmachakra Translation Committee 2013–16, 18.24–49.
33. See Dharmachakra Translation Committee 2013–16, 19.1–80.
34. *jina*, *rgyal ba*. See Dharmachakra Translation Committee 2013–16, chap. 21.
35. See Dharmachakra Translation Committee 2013–16, chaps. 22–23.
36. See Dharmachakra Translation Committee 2013–16, chap. 24.
37. See Dudjom Rinpoche 1991, 2:139.
38. See Dharmachakra Translation Committee 2013–16, chaps. 25–26; and Dudjom Rinpoche 1991, 1:423.
39. See Dudjom Rinpoche 1991, 1:423–24.
40. See Dudjom Rinpoche 1991, 1:424, and on Mount Mālaya, 1:454–56.
41. On the five noble companions (*pañcavargika*, *lnga sde*), who were the original monks naturally ordained by the Buddha, see Buswell and Lopez 2014, 617–18.
42. On this incident, see Buswell and Lopez 2014, 944–45; and Lamotte 1988, 17.
43. See the brief account of these two in Dudjom Rinpoche 1991, 1:425–26. For a scholarly appraisal, see Buswell and Lopez 2014, 777–78, 498–99.
44. On the life of Mahākāśyapa, see Dudjom Rinpoche 1991, 1:432–34; and Buswell and Lopez 2014, 497.
45. *ārāma*, *kun dga' ra ba*. Located at Śrāvastī, which was then the capital of Kosala, ruled by King Prasenajit. This was where the Buddha spent much of his teaching career. See Buswell and Lopez 2014, 851–52. On the patron Anāthapiṇḍada, see Buswell and Lopez 2014, 42. On the Jetavana Grove, Buswell and Lopez 2014, 383.

46. *Daharopamasūtra* (a.k.a. *Kumāradṛṣṭāntasūtra*), *Gzhon nu dpe'i mdo* (Toh. 296; Dg.T. mdo sde, *sha*, ff. 295b–297a).
47. On Prasenjit, the king of Kosala, see Buswell and Lopez 2014, 664. On Bimbisāra (r. c. 465–413 B.C.E.), the king of Magadha, see Buswell and Lopez 2014, 119.
48. On the life of the model monk, Ānanda, see Buswell and Lopez 2014, 38–39; Dudjom Rinpoche 1991, 1:434–35; and Lamotte 1988, 19.
49. Ngawang Zangpo 2014, 86. Sāṃkāśya is identified with modern Sankissa Basantapura, located on the north bank of the Ikkhumati between Kampil and Kannauj in Uttar Pradesh.
50. This refers to the miracles displayed at Śrāvastī, on which see Lamotte 1988, 20. The six renowned extremist teachers (*mu stegs kyi ston pa drug*) who were contemporaries of the Buddha are Purānakāśyapa (Kun tu rgyu 'od srung rdzogs byed), Maskarī Gośālaputra (Gnag lhas kyi bu), Sañjayavairaḍīputra (Yang dag rgyal ba can), Ajitakeśakambalin (Mi pham skra'i la ba can), Kakudakatyāyana (Smra 'dod kyi bu), and Nirgranthajñātiputra (Gcer bu gnyan gyi bu). See Basham 1951, 10–26.
51. These syllables are indicative of the union of bliss and emptiness.
52. As enumerated in Nordrang Orgyen 2008, 1618, these seven aspects of union of Heruka and consort are perfect resource, union, supreme truth, lack of inherent existence, fullness of compassion, non-interruption, and non-cessation. Heruka is the generic name of the wrathful aspect of the buddha body of perfect resource (*sambhogakāya*). The diverse Heruka forms are prominent in the transmission and manifestation of the unsurpassed union tantras (*yoganuttaratantra, bla med rgyud*).
53. The prophecies regarding the spread of Buddhism in Kashmir are recounted in Dudjom Rinpoche 1991, 1:438. On those pertaining to Khotan, see Emmerick 1967, 3–77.
54. Vajrapāṇi—in his various forms, including Guhyapati and Vajradharma—is recognized as an important compiler of the tantras. On this, see Dudjom Rinpoche 1991, 1:451–60.
55. See Ngawang Zangpo 2014, 87; and Lamotte 1988, 22.
56. See Ngawang Zangpo 2014, 88; and Lamotte 1988, 23.

3. The Compilation of the Transmitted Teachings

1. The following narrative concerning the three councils derives from Pawo Tsuklak Trengwa, 1961, 31–41.
2. *praṇidhānasamādhi, smon gnas shes pa'i ting nge 'dzin.*
3. *gaṇḍi.*
4. The eight shortcomings (*nyes pa brgyad*) of Ānanda are recounted in Tāranātha's *Sun of Confidence*. See the translation in Taranatha 2003, 456–58.
5. Bri dzi.

6. *jñāptidvitīyakarmaṇa, gsol gnyis kyi las.* This denotes the first request concerning the compatibility of the recipient and the second request that constitutes the main part of the ordination rite. This is contrasted with the fourfold request, in which the main part of the rite is repeated three times. See Ngawang Zangpo 2014, 249.
7. For a summary of the first council, see Buswell and Lopez 2014, 198–99; and Dudjom Rinpoche 1991, 1:428–29.
8. *Minor Transmissions of Monastic Discipline, Vinayakṣudrākavastu, 'Dul ba phran tshegs kyi gzhi* (Toh. 6; Dg.K. 'dul ba, *tha*, ff. 1b–310a, *da*, ff. 1b–333a).
9. On the second council, see Buswell and Lopez 2014, 199; Dutt 1978, 11–33; Taranatha 2003, 472–76; and Dudjom Rinpoche 1991, 1:429.
10. These five hundred aspirations are contained in *The Sūtra of Compassion's White Lotus, Karuṇāpuṇḍarikasūtra, 'Phags pa snying rje chen po'i pad+ma dkar po zhes bya ba theg pa chen po'i mdo* (KPD 50), 444; see also Nordrang Orgyen 2008, 3848–67.
11. *Svapnanirdeśasūtra, Rgyal po kri kri'i rmi lam rgyal ba 'od srung gis lung bstan pa'i mdo* (Toh. 48; Dg.K. bkon brtsegs, *ka*, ff. 203b–237b). This is the eighth of the eighteen dreams of King Kṛkī of Kāśī, which are all enumerated in Nordrang Orgyen 2008, 3002–3. The original source cannot presently be traced to the extant Tibetan version of the sūtra, but there are references in other classical sources, such as Kṣemendra's *Wish-Fulfilling Vine: Narratives of Bodhisattvas, Bodhisattvāvadānakalpalatā, Byang chub sems dpa'i rtogs pa brjod pa dpag bsam gyi 'khri shing* (Toh. 4155; Dg.T. skyes rab, *ke*, ff. 1b–366a, *khe*, ff. 1b–329a). See the translation in Black 1997, 418.
12. These are listed in Buswell and Lopez 2014, 1091–92. It is clearly stated in Tāranātha's *History of Buddhism in India* (*Rgya gar chos 'byung*) that the division into eighteen orders occurred on the basis of the texts of monastic discipline rather than the sūtras. See the translation in Chattopadhyaya 1970, 339–42. For further detail on the eighteen monastic orders, see Dutt 1978.
13. These are listed in Nordrang Orgyen (2008, 339) as the ground of purification (*sbyang bya gzhi*), the path of purification (*sbyong byed lam*), and the fruition of purification (*sbyangs pa 'bras bu*). An alternative explanation is that they may denote the first three seals of the transmitted teachings—namely, impermanence, suffering, and no-self.
14. For traditional Tibetan accounts of the third council, see Dudjom Rinpoche 1991, 1:429–30, and Chattopadhyaya 1970, 91–95. Pāli sources, on the other hand, attribute the third council to the reign of Aśoka, and Chinese sources refer to Kaniṣka's council as the fourth. On the historicity of these, see Buswell and Lopez 2014, 199–200.
15. Cf. the description of the four main orders and their subdivisions given by Longchen Rabjam in Dorje 2016, 492–93.
16. *Questions of First Year Monks, Bhikṣuvarṣāgrapṛcchā, Dge slong gi dang po'i lo dri ba* (TPD 93), 913.

17. Vinitadeva, *A Summary of the Different Schools from the Wheel of Chronology of the Different Textual Traditions, Samayabhedoparacanacakrenikāyabhedopadeśanasaṃgrahanāma, Gzhung tha dad pa rim par bklag pa'i 'khor lo las sde pa tha dad pa bstan pa bsdus pa zhes bya ba* (TPD 93), 1166.
18. Dudjom Rinpoche 1991, 1:430–31; Chattopadhyaya 1970, 96ff.
19. For a traditional account of the compilation of the tantras, see Dudjom Rinpoche 1991, 1:441–57, and on the distinction between texts of provisional and definitive meaning, 217–18.
20. The principal source for this section on sacred representations is Pawo Tsuklak Trengwa 2016, 42–47. See also Konchog and Davis 2017, 41.
21. On the legacy of this painting for Tibetan iconography, see Konchog Lhadrepa and Davis 2017, 41–43.
22. These would presumably have included the sandalwood image commissioned by King Prasenajit, on which see Buswell and Lopez 2014, 664. Cf. other legends regarding the origin of Buddhist sculpture in Konchog and Davis 2017, 43–44.
23. *Dhvajāgrakeyūranāmadhāraṇī, Rgyal mtshan rtse mo'i dpung rgyan* (Toh. 612; Dg.K. rgyud, *ba*, ff. 45b–46b; KPD 91, 149–55).
24. Contemporary research (Falk 2011; Falk and Karashima 2012) has brought to our attention extant segments and fragments of a birch-bark scroll containing a portion of a generic manuscript of *The Sūtra of the Transcendent Perfection of Wisdom* in the Gāndhārī language, written in Kharoṣṭhī script, which was, by all accounts, retrieved from a stone case in the Bajaur region of the Afghan-Pakistan borderland. The manuscript has been carbon dated within the range of 25–74 C.E. Philological evidence suggests that this manuscript was the forerunner of a later Gāndhārī manuscript translated by Lokakṣema into Chinese, while certain peculiarities of transcription and the presence of conventional mnemonic abbreviations also presuppose an earlier manuscript, which may no longer be extant. These Kharoṣṭhī scrolls are among the oldest surviving exemplars of all Indic texts, with the exception of the Aśokan rock inscriptions and pillar edicts, and it has been speculated that their source manuscript may even predate the original redaction of the Pāli Canon at Aluvihāra during the fourth Buddhist council (29–17 B.C.E.). The oldest extant Pāli text, preserved on gold sheets in the Burmese Stūpa of Sri Ksetra, does not predate the seventh century.
25. The traditional eight stūpa models of the Tibetan tradition, commemorating the eight principal deeds of Śākyamuni Buddha, are illustrated and described in Dorje 2012, 272–82.
26. Spyan lnga. An epithet of the Buddha.
27. On these legendary artifacts and the origin of the two sacred images of Lhasa, see Dorje, Tsering, Stoddard, and Alexander 2010, 127.
28. These are, respectively, the Jowo images of the Lhasa Trulnang and Ramoche. On the former, see Dorje, Tsering, Stoddard, and Alexander 2010; and

Akester 2016, 65–81. On the latter, see Dorje 2009, 103–5; and Akester 2016, 81–86. Kṣemendra's *Bodhisattvāvadānakalpalatā* mentions a legendary stūpa constructed by King Kṛkī on behalf of the Buddha Kāśyapa. See the translation in Black 1997, 53.

29. This Mahābodhi image was the most revered statue in the Buddhist world—there are millennium-old records that mention it, and it served as the model for similar images in China, at Nālanda and Vikramaśīla in India, and at Gyantse in Tibet, where the measurements were taken in 1413. The image is not mentioned after the fifteenth century. The tenth-century gilded sandstone image now inside the temple was found in the ruins and placed there by Alexander Cunningham in 1880. See also Buswell and Lopez 2014, 493–94. According to UNESCO, the present temple with its fifty-five-meter central tower is one of the earliest and most imposing structures built entirely in brick from the Guptan period (c. 300–600 C.E.), although there are some older sandstone railings that have been dated approximately to 150 B.C.E. The structure was heavily renovated in the nineteenth century.

30. This is perhaps to be identified with the legendary sandalwood image commissioned by King Udāyana, on which see Buswell and Lopez 2014, 932–33.

31. The Mauryan emperor Aśoka (c. 300–232 B.C.E.) is renowned for having multiplied the eight original reliquaries holding the moral remains of Lord Buddha, by the construction of eighty-four thousand stūpas. This legend is recounted in the *Narrative of Aśoka* (*Aśokāvadāna*). See Buswell and Lopez 2014, 70–71.

32. Anon., *Nandimitrāvadāna*, *Dga' ba'i bshes gnyen gyi rtogs brjod* (Toh. 4146; Dg.T. 'dul ba, *su*, ff. 240a–44b).

33. Vasubandhu states in *The Treasury of Phenomenology* that human beings have an infinitely long lifespan at the end of an eon of creation, after which it will diminish in cycles of decrease, or waning (*apakarṣa*, *mar 'bri ba*), and increase, or waxing (*utkarṣa*, *yar 'phel ba*). See the translation in Pruden 1988–90, 2:478–79.

34. See Pruden 1988–90, 2:489–90; and Jamgön Kongtrul Lodrö Tayé 1995, 143–45. See also the definition in Thupten Phuntsok 2013, 448. Ngawang Namgyel's immediate source for this, and the following paragraphs through to the end of the chapter, is Pawo Tsuklak Trengwa 1962, 12–17.

35. On the sixteen elders, see p. 37.

36. The universal emperor Śaṅkha ('Khor lo brgyur rgyal dung) is mentioned alongside Maitreya in a prophetic declaration from the *Bodhisattvāvadānakalpalatā*. See the translation in Black 1997, 83.

37. Adhimukta (Mos pa mtha' nyas), also known as Ālokakara (Snang mdzad), is the last of the thousand and two buddhas foreordained to appear in succession in the course of the Auspicious Eon. For the full list, see Nordrang Orgyen 2008, 3869–4022.

38. See Pruden 1988–90, 2:475–80.

39. Vasubandhu, *Abhidharmakośakārikā, Chos mngon pa'i mdzod kyi tshig le'ur byas pa chos rjes kra shi*, chap. 3, v. 102. See the translation and commentary in Pruden 1988–90, 2:495.
40. The bright eon of Mahāmadhura (Snyan pa chen po) is mentioned, for example, in vinaya treatises such as Anon., *A Commentary on the "Bhikṣuṇī Pratimokṣa Sūtra" of the Noble Mūlasarvāstivāda, Āryasarvāstivādimūlabhikṣuṇīpratimokṣasūtravṛtti, 'Phags pa thams cad yod par smra ba'i rtsa ba'i dge slong ma'i so sor thar pa'i mdo'i 'grel pa* (TPD 87), 27.

4. The Appearance of Buddhism and Its Upholders in India

1. The threefold affirmation (*brjod pa gsum*) is made in the context of monastic ordination. These three steps are, respectively, the affirmation of the refuge (*skyabs brjod*), the personal affirmation of the candidate (*bdag brjod*), and the affirmation of others' acceptance (*gzhan brjod*). See Ngawang Zangpo 2014, 248–49.
2. See the traditional accounts in Dudjom Rinpoche 1991, 1:432–35, and in Chattopadhyaya 1970, 20–25. Also on Madhyāhnika, see Buswell and Lopez 2014, 490. Ngawang Namgyel's source for this entire section on the early development of Buddhism is Pawo Tsuklak Trengwa 1962, 31–41.
3. The double "armspan" (*gzhu 'dom*) is an ancient Indian measure, equivalent to four cubits, or about six feet. Other sources suggest that the cave was eighteen cubits in length and twelve in width. See Chattopadhyaya 1970, 38n19.
4. See Dudjom Rinpoche 1991, 1:434–37; and Chattopadhyaya 1970, 26–49, 68–75. On Śāṇavāsika, see Buswell and Lopez 2014, 766, on Upagupta, 939, and on Dhītika, 255.
5. *Lang kar gshegs pa'i 'grel pa*. See this chapter, note 7.
6. Bhi bhi ka la.
7. *The Sūtra of the Descent to Laṅkā, Āryalaṅkāvatāramahāyānasūtra, 'Phags pa lang kar gshegs pa rin po che'i mdo las sangs rgyas thams cad kyi gsung gi snying po'i shes bya ba'i le'u* (KPD 49), 403–4. This lineage does not appear to be attested in the two commentaries on *The Sūtra of the Descent to Laṅkā* that are extant in the Tibetan translation: those of Jñānaśrībhadra (Toh. 4018) and Jñānavajra (Toh. 4019). A succession of twenty-eight Indian hierarchs including the above is, however, prominently presented in Keizan Jokin Zenji, *Denkōroku* (*Record of the Transmission of the Light*), written circa 1300.
8. These figures are of seminal importance for the propagation of the nascent tradition of the Great Vehicle in Central Asia, China, Japan, and also in Tibet. They also figure prominently in painted and bas-relief imagery. See de Visser 1919; Tate 1989; and Thartang Tulku 1984.
9. *'Bum sde*.
10. For Tāranātha's traditional account of the lives of these six extraordinary exponents of the Great Vehicle, see Chattopadhaya 1970, 106–11 on Nāgārjuna

(fl. second century); 123–29 on Āryadeva (c. 170–270); 154–67 on Asaṅga (c. 320–390); 167–75 on Vasubandhu (fl. fourth and fifth centuries); 181–85 on Dignāga (c. 480–540); and 228–40 on Dharmakīrti (c. 600–670). Contemporary scholarship differentiates two Nāgārjunas and two Āryadevas on the basis of the earlier sūtra treatises and the later tantra commentaries. See also Buswell and Lopez 2014, 64–65 on Āryadeva; 69 on Asaṅga; 246–47 on Dharmakīrti; 259 on Dignāga; 561–62 on Nāgārjuna; and 961–62 on Vasubandhu.

11. Traditional accounts of the lives of all these illustrious writers of the Great Vehicle tradition are found in Chattopadhaya 1970, 186 on Buddhapālita (c. 470–540); 215–20 on Śāntideva (fl. eighth century); 130–36 on Śūra (fl. second century); 186–88 on Bhāviveka (c. 500–570); 198–99 on Candrakīrti (c. 600–650); 199–209 on Candragomin (fl. fifth century); 179–81 on Sthiramati (475–555); 188–90 on Vimuktisena (fl. sixth century); 179 on Guṇaprabha (fl. sixth century); and 259 on Śākyaprabha (fl. eighth century). Also see Buswell and Lopez 2014, 154–55 on Buddhapālita; 774 on Śāntideva; 381–82 on Śūra; 114 on Bhāviveka; 165 on Candrakīrti; 165 on Candragomin; 859 on Sthiramati; 974 on Vimuktisena; 337 on Guṇaprabha; and 742 on Śākyaprabha.

12. On Haribhadra (c. 800), see Chattopadhyaya 1970, 277; and Buswell and Lopez 2014, 345.

13. See Dudjom Rinpoche 1991, 1:441–42.

14. *Śrīcakrasaṃvarapañcakrama*, *'Khor lo sdom pa'i rim pa lnga pa* (Toh. 1433; Dg.T. rgyud, *wa*, ff. 224b–227a).

15. The extraordinary lives of these great accomplished masters are recounted in Abhayadatta's *Narrative of the Eighty-Four Accomplished Masters*, *Caturaśītisiddhapravṛtti*, *Grub thob brgyad cu rtsa bzhi'i lo rgyus* (TPD 48, 413–556). See the translation of this text in Robinson 1979. For the lives of these masters, see also Tāranātha's *Sevenfold Descent of the Transmitted Teachings*, on which see the translation in Templeman 1983. Specifically, the following biographies are to be found: For Indrabhūti, see Robinson 1979, 150–52; Templeman 1983, 24–29; and Dudjom Rinpoche 1991, 1:458–60. For Saraha, see Robinson 1979, 41–43; and Templeman 1983, 2–3. Nāgārjunagarbha in Robinson 1979, 75–80; and Templeman 1983, 3–8. For Lūipa, see Robinson 1979, 22–24; and Templeman 1983, 8–11. For Śavaripā, see Robinson 1979, 37–40; and Templeman 1983, 8. For Vajragaṇṭapāda, see Robinson 1979, 174–79; and Templeman 1983, 30–32. For Virūpa, see Robinson 1979, 27–32; and Templeman 1983, 15–17. For Kuddālapāda or Koṭali, see Robinson 1979, 155–57. For Guhyapati Bhadrapāda, see Robinson 1979, 103–5; and Templeman 1983, 44. For Ḍombhi Heruka, see Robinson 1979, 33–36, 110–11. For Kambalapāda, see Robinson 1979, 117–20; and Templeman 1983, 33–36; and Dudjom Rinpoche 1991, 1:485–87. For Kṛṣṇācārin, see Robinson 1979, 81–85; and Templeman 1983, 43–44. For Kukkurāja, see Robinson 1979, 128–30; Templeman 1983, 69–70; and Dudjom Rinpoche 1991, 1:460–62.

16. These six or seven "religious kings" (*chos kyi rgyal po*) are listed in Henning 2007, 365. Their dates are said to range from 977 B.C.E. to 377 B.C.E.
17. The Kulika, or Kalkī, kings (*rigs ldan gyi dbang po*) are enumerated in Henning 2007, 365–66. They are said to span the period from 277 B.C.E. to 2327 C.E.
18. On the activities of Prakāśacandra, see Chattopadhyaya 1970, 255, 285. The three learned in the tantras of union were Śākyamitra, Buddhaguhya, and Ānandagarbha. See Nordrang Orgyen 2008, 329.
19. On the teaching activities of Buddhaguhya, see Chattopadhayaya 1970, 280–83; and Dudjom Rinpoche 1991, 1:465–66.
20. This is the aforementioned *Narrative of the Eighty-Four Accomplished Masters* by Abhayadatta, translated in Robinson 1979.
21. The corresponding collection of spiritual songs and commentaries (*do ha 'grel bcas*) is contained in Vīraprabhāsvara, *The Essence of the Realizations of the Eighty-Four Mahāsiddhas, Caturaśītisiddhisambodhihṛdaya, Grub thob brgyad cu rtsa bzhi'i rtogs pa'i snying po* (Toh. 2292; Dg.T. rgyud, *zhi*, ff. 153a–158b; TPD 48, 562–667).
22. These works are contained in the supplement of TPD and are not found in the Derge Tengyur.
23. *gaṇacakra, tshogs kyi 'khor lo.*
24. That is, *The Essence of the Realizations of the Eighty-Four Mahāsiddhas*. See this chapter, note 21.—Ed.
25. On the primordial buddha Samantabhadra as progenitor of this transmission, see Dudjom Rinpoche 1991, 1:447–50.
26. See Dorje 2005; Dorje 2016; and Dudjom Rinpoche 1991, 1:458–84.
27. On the life of Prahevajra, in particular, see Dudjom Rinpoche 1991, 1:490–94.
28. Mchod rten, "mundane worship." These transmissions are detailed in Dudjom Rinpoche 1991, 1:447–84.
29. This chronological sequence of the kings of ancient India accords with the account of Tāranātha, on which see Chattophadyaya 1970. The temples of Samudragupta (*rgya mtsho sbas pa'i lha khang*) in Kashmir and Somapurī Monastery are mentioned in the same source, respectively on p. 267 and p. 266. Ngawang Namgyel had as a reference for this section the chapter on the royal dynasties of India in Pawo Tsuklak Trengwa 1962, 48–56.

5. The Four Lineages of Transmitted Teachings and the Two Masters of Supreme Vision

1. Nāropā's transmission to Marpa includes the instructions of the Six Branches of Yoga (*yan lag drug*) according to the perfection stage of meditation, which are encapsulated in three practices—namely, the mingling of the generation- and perfection-stage practices of daytime and nighttime (*bsre*), the transference of consciousness at death (*'pho ba*), and vital reincarnation (*gnad kyi mtshams sbyor*).

2. Mahāvajradhara, embodying the buddha body of perfect resource, is endowed with the five excellences of place, time, teacher, teaching, and retinue.
3. There are several traditional accounts of the life of Tilopā (988–1069) extant in Tibetan, including those compiled by Marpa Chokyi Lodro, Orgyenpa Rinchen Pel, Gyeltangpa Dechen Dorje, Dorje Dze-o, Montsepa Kunga Pelden, Tsangnyon Heruka, Drigung Choje Kunga Rinchen, Wangchuk Gyeltsen, and Lhatsun Rinchen Namgyel. On these, and for a translation of the first mentioned, see Torricelli and Naga 1995. See also Robinson 1979, 101–202. Ngawang Namgyel's sources include Pawo Tsuklak Trengwa 1962, 384–86. The four transmissions that Tilopā received from human teachers concerned Dream Yoga (*rmi lam*), Illusory Body (*sgyu lus*), Inner Radiance (*'od gsal*), and Inner Heat (*gtum mo*). Ngawang Namgyel's source for the lives of these predecessors of Tilopā is Pawo Tsuklak Trengwa 1962, 377–83. The first of these was imparted to him by Caryāpā, on whom see Templeman 1983, 44. On the ḍākinī Sumatī, also known as Lakṣmīnkarā, see p. 54, and Robinson 1979, 250–53.
4. See Templeman 1983, 25.
5. Bhina pa badzra. See Robinson 1979, 57–59.
6. See Templeman 1983, 26.
7. Padmavajra, otherwise known as Saroruhavajra or Padmasambhava. From the perspective of the new translation schools, see Templeman 1983, 26–29; and from the traditional Nyingma perspective, Dudjom Rinpoche 1991, 1:468–74, 1:481–83, 1:515–21. See also Douglas and Bays 1978; and Erik Pema Kunsang 1999. For contemporary historical assessments, see Hirshberg 2016.
8. See Templeman 1983, 29, 50–52.
9. To date, I have found no further references to this figure.
10. The four delights (*dga' ba bzhi*) experienced on the path of skillful means (*thabs lam*) are delight (*dga' ba*), supreme delight (*mchog gi dga' ba*), freedom from delight (*gda' ba dang bral ba*), and coemergent delight (*lhan cig skyes pa'i dga' ba*). See Dudjom Rinpoche 1991, 2:127–28.
11. On the four empowerments, see p. 310.
12. *Dohākośagīti*, *Do ha mdzod kyi glu*, also known as *Dmangs kyi do hā* (Toh. 2224; Dg.T. rgyud *wi*, ff. 70b–77a; TPD 26, 193–208; also in DNZ 7, 7–22). Translated in Guenther 1993.
13. *Dohākośopadeśagīti*, *Mi zad pa'i gter mdzod man ngag gi glu*, also known as *Rgyal mo'i do hā* and *Brtsun mo'i do hā* (Toh. 2264; Dg.T. rgyud, *zhi*, ff. 28b–33b; TPD 26, 1020–34.) Translated in Guenther 1993.
14. *Dohākośanāmacaryāgīti*, *Do ha mdzod ces bya ba spyod pa'i glu*, also known as *Rgyal po'i do hā* (Toh. 2263; Dg.T. rgyud, *zhi*, ff. 26b–28b; TPD 26, 1013–19). Translated in Guenther 1993.
15. On Saraha, also known as Rāhulabhadra, see part 1, chap. 4, note 15.
16. *Āryadvādaśasahasramahāmegha*, *'Phags pa sprin chen po stong phrag bcu gnyis pa* (Toh. 232; Dg.K. mdo sde, *wa*, ff. 113a–214b).

17. *Mūlamadhyamakavṛttiprasannapadā, Dbu ma rtsa ba'i 'grel pa tshig gsal ba* (Toh. 3860; Dg.T. dbu ma, *'a*, ff. 1b–200a; TPD 60, 4–483).
18. For references to the life of Nāgārjunagarbha, see part 1, chap. 4, note 15.
19. See Templeman 1983, 36–43; and Robinson 1979, 161–62.
20. This refers to the wrathful rites of liberation, on which see Boord 2002, Boord 2010, and Dorje 2016. These require the ability to both slay and resurrect the dead. See Dudjom Rinpoche 1991, 1:603–4.
21. *tarjanī mudrā*.
22. Lalitacandra was the last king of the Candra dynasty. See Chattopadhyaya 1970, 251.
23. See Templeman 1983, 30.
24. These are Sanskrit grammar, logic, arts, medicine, and Buddhist studies.
25. See Torricelli and Naga 1995, 28.
26. See Torricelli and Naga 1995, 29.
27. The words that he said are translated in Torricelli and Naga 1995, 29.
28. Cf. Torricelli and Naga 1995, 30.
29. *rtsva byi gzung, arctium lappa*.
30. Cf. Torricelli and Naga 1995, 35.
31. Cf. Torricelli and Naga 1995, 36–39.
32. Cf. Torricelli and Naga 1995, 39.
33. Cf. Torricelli and Naga 1995, 40–41.
34. Cf. Torricelli and Naga 1995, 41.
35. Cf. Torricelli and Naga 1995, 39–40.
36. Cf. Torricelli and Naga 1995, 40.
37. Cf. Torricelli and Naga 1995, 42.
38. See Torricelli and Naga 1995, 42–43.
39. See Torricelli and Naga 1995, 43.
40. Cf. Torricelli and Naga 1995, 44–45.
41. See Torricelli and Naga 1995, 45.
42. Torricelli and Naga (1995, 45) remark that this is Śiromaṇi.
43. See Torricelli and Naga 1995, 45–46.
44. The narrative of Tilopā's emanation Kālapa is found in Torricelli and Naga 1995, 56.
45. Bhairavahāsyaśmāśāna, 'Jigs byed bzhad pa'i dur khrod. This incident is mentioned in Torricelli and Naga 1995, 31. Mataṅgi is mentioned as a disciple of Nāgārjunagarbha in Chattopadhyaya 1970, 129, 273.
46. This prophecy is outlined in the verses cited in Torricelli and Naga 1995, 32.
47. See Torricelli and Naga 1995, 32–33.
48. See Torricelli and Naga 1995, 33–34.
49. See Torricelli and Naga 1995, 46–47.
50. See Torricelli and Naga 1995, 57.
51. See Torricelli and Naga 1995, 34.
52. See Torricelli and Naga 1995, 48–49.

53. See Torricelli and Naga 1995, 49–50.
54. See Torricelli and Naga 1995, 50–51.
55. See Torricelli and Naga 1995, 52–53.
56. See Torricelli and Naga 1995, 53–54.
57. See Torricelli and Naga 1995, 51–52.
58. See Torricelli and Naga 1995, 55–56.
59. Gsang ba mdzod.
60. Cf. Torricelli and Naga 1995, 59–60.
61. The hagiographies of Nāropā (956–1040) appear to be extant in three main texts, composed by Drakar Lhatsunpa Rinchen Namgyel (twelfth century?), Zhamarpa Khacho Wangpo (1350–1405), and Wangchuk Gyeltsen (fifteenth century). The first and third of these have been translated into English in Guenther 1963 and into German in Grünwedel 1933. See also Buswell and Lopez 2014, 576. Ngawang Namgyel's sources include Pawo Tsuklak Trengwa 1962, 386–93.
62. The title Nārotapa is cognate with the Sanskrit *narottama*, meaning "best of men." Guenther (1963, 7) suggests that he was descended from king Mahāsammata of the Śākya clan, on whom see p. 15. As for the hierarchy of the eight virtuous familial lines (*dkar nag brgyad*) within the brahmin class, this may perhaps be related to the original eight sages—Viśvamitra, Jamadagni, Bharadvāja, Gautama, Atri, Vasiṣṭha, Kāśyapa, and Agastya—from whom all brahmins are said to have descended.
63. Guenther (1963, 9–11) states that his birth name was Samantabhadra and his name as a lay disciple was Gaganagarbha.
64. Bhima ka la ba tta.
65. See Guenther 1963, 15.
66. See Guenther 1963, 16–17.
67. See Guenther 1963, 18.
68. Khri stan. Location unidentified.
69. See Guenther 1963, 18.
70. See Guenther 1963, 19–20.
71. See Guenther 1963, 20–21.
72. *The Ultimate Summary: An Explanatory Commentary on "The Summary of Empowerment," Paramārthasaṃgrahanāmasekoddeśaṭīkā, Dbang mdor bstan pa'i 'grel bshad don dam pa bsdus pa* (Toh. 1351; Dg.T. rgyud, *na*, ff. 220b–289a).
73. *'Dus pa rgyud phyi.*
74. See Guenther 1963, 19–20.
75. See Chattopadhyaya 1970, 295–303.
76. These characteristics are enumerated in Guenther 1963, 24.
77. See Guenther 1963, 24–25.
78. The thirty-seven factors conducive to enlightenment are the four applications of mindfulness, the four correct exertions, the four supports for miraculous ability, the five faculties, the five powers, the seven branches of enlightenment,

and the noble eightfold path. See Dayal 1932, 80–164. The thirty-seven deities are those of the Vairocanābhisambodhi maṇḍala.

79. See Guenther 1963, 27–28.
80. See Guenther 1963, 28.
81. OṂ HRĪḤ HĀ HĀ HŪṂ HŪṂ PHAṬ.
82. See Guenther 1963, 29.
83. See Guenther 1963, 29.
84. See Guenther 1963, 30.
85. See Guenther 1963, 30–31.
86. Cf. Guenther 1963, 32–33.
87. See Guenther 1963, 31.
88. See Guenther 1963, 31–32.
89. See Guenther 1963, 32.
90. See Guenther 1963, 33.
91. See Guenther 1963, 33–34.
92. See Guenther 1963, 34.
93. Cf. Guenther 1963, 35–36.
94. See Guenther 1963, 36.
95. See Guenther 1963, 36–37.
96. See Guenther 1963, 37.
97. See Guenther 1963, 37.
98. See Guenther 1963, 38–39.
99. Cf. Guenther 1963, 40–41, where these words are spoken by Nāropā.
100. See Guenther 1963, 41.
101. See Guenther 1963, 42.
102. See Guenther 1963, 42.
103. See Guenther 1963, 42.
104. That is to say, the first vase empowerment (*bum dbang*) was symbolized by the embers on a roll of cotton, the lump of crystal, and the wish-granting gem. The second secret empowerment (*gsang dbang*) was symbolized by the unmoving gaze, the vessel of pure water, and the untying of intricate knots. The third empowerment of discerning pristine cognition (*shes rab ye shes kyi dbang*) was symbolized by the mingling of water in a common savor, the sealing gesture of the source of phenomena, and the drawing of the vital essence. The fourth empowerment (*dbang bzhi pa*) was symbolized by the pointing of the finger, the smile, the silence, and the fruit.
105. See Guenther 1963, 43–46. This pertains to the instruction on the generation and perfection stages of meditation. The text here includes an annotation, suggesting that, in some manuscripts, it is also said that a sharp iron instrument was stabbed through his private parts, causing a pus-filled swelling that prevented his walking for a protracted period.
106. See Guenther 1963, 47–49.
107. See Guenther 1963, 53–61.

108. See Guenther 1963, 50–53.
109. See Guenther 1963, 67–69.
110. See Guenther 1963, 61–67.
111. See Guenther 1963, 69–71.
112. See Guenther 1963, 72–74.
113. See Guenther 1963, 76–80.
114. Cf. Guenther 1963, 75–76, despite dissimilarities.
115. See Guenther 1963, 82–86.
116. See Guenther 1963, 80–82.
117. The source of this verse is not yet identified.
118. This correlation between the twelve ascetic acts and the twelve instructions of the perfection stage, which Nāropā received from Tilopā, appears to diverge from the presentation found in Guenther 1963, 43–82.
119. *Phyag rgya chen po gangā ma*. This text is translated in Sangyes Nyenpa 2014, 1–17, along with extensive commentary.
120. On Kasoripā and Riripā, see Chattopadhyaya 1970, 306–7.
121. This prediction pertains to Marpa Lotsāwa (Chos kyi blo gros, 1002–1097, or 1097–1100).
122. See Guenther 1963, 95.
123. This episode is recounted in Templeman 1983, 48–49.
124. On the life of Atiśa (982–1054), see Buswell and Lopez 2014, 77–78; Chattopadhyaya 1967; Decleer 1995; Decleer 1997; and Sherburne 2000. On the life of Marpa Lotsāwa, see p. 108.
125. Among these, reference has already been made to Ḍombhipa and Śāntipā. On Maitripā, see p. 76. On Dharipā or Darikapa, see Templeman 1983, 8; and Robinson 1979, 236–39. On Jāyaka and the Kashmiri Jñānākara, also known as Ākārasiddhi, see Templeman 1983, 49; and Roerich 1949, 361. Kusulupā (a title indicating a practitioner of Severance and so forth) is equivalent to Kusalabhadra, or Kusali, on whom see Roerich 1949, 361; and Templeman 1983.
126. A pham badzra. Translator indicates that the Sanskrit rendering is uncertain.—Ed.
127. Among these, Śāntibhadra and Pitopa are also associated with Atiśa. See Roerich 1949, 261. Ratnaśrīmitra was a commentator on the *Samvarodaya Tantra*. See Roerich 1949, 389. Jowo Smṛtijñānakīrti (Jo bo smṛ ti) was an important commentator and was active in Tibet between the ancient and new translation phases. No further information appears to be available on either Śāntivarman or *Aparājitavajra.
128. On Prajñārakṣita, see Chattopadhyaya 1970, 306–7. Manakaśrījñāna is included in the lineage of the empowerment of Cakrasaṃvara that Marpa received. See Roerich 1949, 385. On the four Phamtingwa brothers from Nepal—Dharmamati, Abhayakīrti, Kālacakrapāda, and Tangchungwa—see Roerich 1949, 380–82.
129. This represents the first of Tāranātha's seven instructional lineages, on which see Templeman 1983, 1–14. On Śavaripā, see Pawo Tsuklak Trengwa 1962, 393.

130. See Templeman 1983, 8.
131. On Maitripā (c. 1007–1085), see the traditional account in Templeman 1983, 11–14; Buswell and Lopez 2014, 518–19; and Pawo Tsuklak Trengwa 1962, 393.
132. Cf. Templeman 1983, 11. The Sakara who is included among the eighty-four accomplished masters (Robinson 1979, 227–30) may be different, although both share an affinity with Śrīparvata.
133. *Phyag brgya bzhi pa'i bsam gtan.*
134. *Do ha theg chen nyi shu pa.*
135. See Templeman 1983, 11–12.
136. *A ma na si'i chos 'khor nyi shu rtsa bzhi.*
137. On these four senior disciples Maitripā and their work, see Roerich 1949, 842–43.
138. The seven medium and ten lesser disciples of Maitripā are enumerated in Roerich 1949, 843.
139. In the last three quatrains, the Tibetan verses are distinguished by the use of internal syllabic reduplication.

6. The Spread of the Sacred Doctrine in Tibet

1. In chapter 6, the author relies entirely on passages drawn verbatim from Pawo Tsuklak Trengwa's *Doctrinal History Titled Scholars' Feast*. The frequency of the references from that work in the following pages is testament to its importance.
2. Among the three ancestral kings (*mes dbon rnam gsum*), who were fountainheads of the Buddhist teaching in Tibet, Songtsen Gampo is revered as the embodiment of Avalokiteśvara's compassion, Tri Songdetsen as the embodiment of Mañjughoṣa's discernment, and Relpachen as the embodiment of Vajrapāṇi's power.
3. These are the four assemblies (*'khor bzhi*) of monks, nuns, laymen, and laywomen. The text reads *'khor zhi*.
4. See Thupten Phuntsok 2013, 48. This is an ancient name for the Yarlung Tsangpo (Brahmaputra), which appears to vanish when emerging from its mountainous gorge on to the Assamese plains.
5. The primary source for this paragraph is Pawo Tsuklak Trengwa 1962, 81. Marine fossils from the ancient Tethys Sea are frequently found in the high Himalayan regions. On the formation of the Tibetan plateau, see Yeshe De Project 1986a, 12–53. Tibet's legendary occupation by nonhuman spirits is examined in Namkhai Norbu 1996, 2–31.
6. The mythological simian origin of the Tibetan race is prominently mentioned in the *Mani Kabum* (*Maṇi bka' 'bum*), on which see Yeshe De Project 1986a, 102–13. The six original Tibetan clans are those of Se (Bse), Mu (Rmu), Dong (Ldong), Tong (Stong), Ba (Dbra), and Dru ('Dru). See the discussion in Namkhai Norbu 1996, 31–40; also Yeshe De Project 1986b, 126–33.

7. Dungkar Lobzang Trinle (2002, 1198) cites Pawo Tsuklak Threngwa, suggesting that this forest was located in Kongpo, while acknowledging an oral tradition that places it near Jasa Lhakhang (Bya sa lha khang) in Lhokha.
8. The twelve minor kingdoms (*rgyal phran bcu gnyis*) are listed as Chimyul Drushul, Zhang Zhung, Nyangdo Chongkar, Nubyul Lingu, Nyangro Shambo, Gyiri Jongdon, Ngamsho Tranar, Olphu Pangkhar, Sinrong Lamogong, Kongyul Drena, Nyangyul Namsum, and Dakyul Drubzhi. See Dudjom Rinpoche 1991, 2:176; and Pawo Tsuklak Trengwa 1962, 84. As for the forty principalities (*sil ma bzhi bcu*) into which these minor kingdoms divided, their names are mostly unknown. See Dudjom Rinpoche 991, vol. 2, 184.
9. Dungkar Lobzang Trinle (2002, 2166) indicates that this is nowadays known as Tsentang Lhari (Bstan thang lha ri), to the west of Tsetang, while acknowledging that other sources would place it in Kongpo. On Tsentang Lhari, also known as Lhababri, see Dorje 2009, 232; and Akester 2016, 428.
10. On Nyatri Tsenpo, see Namkhai Norbu 1996, 402–7; Yeshe De Project 1986a, 140–49; and Kapstein 2006, 35–38.
11. See Pawo Tsuklak Trengwa 1962, 85–87; Sonam Gyeltsen 2002, 55; and Dudjom Jikdrel Yeshe Dorje 1999, 16–17. This dynasty included Nyatri Tsenpo (1), Mutri Tsenpo (2), Dingtri Tsenpo (3), Sotri Tsenpo (4), Metri Tsenpo (5), Daktri Tsenpo (6), and Sibtri Tsenpo (7). The regnal numbers are in parenthesis. These seven kings are said to have been immortal beings who ascended to the heavens after fulfilling their reigns. The succession was matriarchal, the names of their respective mothers being indicated in the legendary accounts.
12. The second son, Chatri Tsenpo, was also known as Pude Gungyel. He hailed from Kanam and is revered as a culture hero who reputedly introduced base metals and agriculture and built the Chingwa Taktse castle in Chongye. See Pawo Tsuklak Trengwa 1962, 87–89; and Dudjom Rinpoche 1991, 2:99n1392.
13. These seven, literally known as the Seven Adroit Emanational Ministers of Tibet (Bod yul 'phrul blon mdzangs mi bdun) are listed in Nordrang Orgyen 2008, 1678–79. Among them, on Rulekye (Ru las skye), who was instrumental in restoring Chatri Tsenpo to dynastic power, see Yeshe De Project 1986a, 152–55.
14. On the appearance of early Bon in Tibet during this time, see Karmay 1972; Clemente 1995; and Namkhai Norbu and Rossi 2013. See also Yeshe De Project 1986a, 156–57; and Kapstein 2006, 44–50.
15. See Pawo Tsuklak Trengwa 1962, 89–90. This dynasty, known as the Six Kings of Earthly Succession, included Esho Lek (10), Desho Lek (11), Drongzhi Lek (14), Tisho Lek (12), Guru Lek (13), and Isho Lek (15). The regnal numbers are in parentheses. This listing accords with Orgyen Lingpa (1986, 114), except for the second, who is named as Lisho Lek rather than Desho Lek. Among the various alternative lists, Sonam Gyeltsen (2002, 58) enumerates the patrilinear succession of these six kings as Asho Lek, Desho Lek, Tisho Lek, Guru Lek,

Drongzher Lek, and Isho Lek. Dudjom Rinpoche (1991, 23–24) reads Esho Lek, Desho Lek, Tisho Lek, Gongru Lek, Drongzher Lek, and Isho Lek. It is said that during this period animals were domesticated, and that irrigation and taxation developed.

16. The six kings of the Lek dynasty built different palaces that were successively named (1) Taktse (Stag rtse), (2) Gotse (Rgod rtse), (3) Yangtse (Yang rtse), (4) Tritse (Khri rtse), (5) Tsemo Khyung Gyel (Rtse mo khyung rgyal), and (6) Tritsik Bumjuk (Khri brtsigs 'bum rgyugs). These were all in the environs of Chingwa Taktse Dzong in Chongye, although nonexistent at the present time. See Dungkar Lobzang Trinle 2002, 868; and Yeshe De Project 1986a, 158–59.

17. The dynasty of the eight kings of sundry succession called De include Zanam De (16), De Trulnam Zhungtsen (17), De Nolbe (a.k.a. Senol Namde) (18), De Nolya (a.k.a. Se Nolpo De) (19), Sor Nonam (a.k.a. De Nolnam) (20), De Nolpo (21), Sotelek (a.k.a. De Gyelpo) (22), and Trin Gyeltsen (23). The regnal numbers are in parentheses. See also Sonam Gyeltsen 2002, 59; and Yeshe De Project 1986a, 159. This succession is also known as the Eight Kings of Intervening Succession Called De (Bar la lde brgyad). It was during this period that Tibetan trade with the Chinese Shu Han dynasty prospered, with Tibetan horses being particularly valued.

18. The dynasty of the Five Connecting Kings Called Tsen (Tshigs la btsan lnga) includes Tongri Tongtsen (24), Tri Namtsen (25), Tri Dra Pungtsen (26), Tri Tokje Tsen (27) and Totori Nyentsen (28). See Sonam Gyeltsen. 2002, 59–60; and Yeshe De Project 1986a, 159–60. The Tibetan folkloric traditions were established through the activities of Bon priests during this period, and it is said that Buddhism made its initial appearance during the reign of the last of these kings.

19. *Dpang skong phyag brgya pa* (Toh. 267; Dg.K. mdo sde, *ya*, ff. 1b–5b).

20. *Āryakāraṇḍavyūhanāmamahāyānasūtra*, *'Phags pa za ma tog bkod pa zhes bya ba theg pa chen po'i mdo* (Toh. 116; Dg.T. mdo sde, *pa*, ff. 200a–247b).

21. See Pawo Tsuklak Trengwa 1962, 90–92; Dudjom Rinpoche 1991, 1:508–9; and Yeshe De Project 1986a, 166–69. The traditional dates given for Lhatotori are birth in 376 (fire mouse), accession in 433 (water bird), and death in 493. See Thupten Phuntsok 2013, 3820–22.

22. This dynastic succession therefore includes Trinyen Zungtsen (29), Drong Nyenderu (30), Takri Nyenzik (31), and Namri Songtsen (32). Among these, according to Thupten Phuntsok (2013), Trinyen Zungtsen is said to have passed away in 516 (fire monkey), Takri Nyenzik acceded to the royal throne in 555 (wood pig) and died in 608 (earth dragon), and Namri Songtsen was born in 592 (water mouse), acceded in 608 (earth dragon), and passed away in 629 (earth ox). This dating is tentative. According to Orgyen Lingpa (1986, 114–15), these monarchs are included among the thirteen kings of the Auspicious Imperial Succession. See also Yeshe De Project 1986a, 169–76; and

Kapstein 2006, 52–54. Drugu denotes the Turkic khanates established during the sixth century in present-day Xinjiang. On the origin of this nomadic tribe, also known as *thu kyu* or *thu gu*, see Dungkar Lobzang Trinle 2002, 561.

23. A contemporary appraisal of the life and reign of Songtsen Gampo is found in Dungkar Lobzang Trinle 2002, 2074–82. The main source of the present account is Pawo Tsuklak Trengwa 1962, 95–155. See also Dudjom Rinpoche 1991, 1:510–12; Yeshe De Project 1986a, 188–229; and Kapstein 2006, 54–62. The date of his death is established in Chinese and Tibetan chronicles as 650 (iron dog) but the date of his birth is disputed since Buton and others assert that he passed away in his eighty-second year. That would place his birth in 569 (earth ox) rather than 617 (fire ox). Some Tibetan sources including *The Blue Annals* concur with the earth-ox date. Cf. Gyalbo, Hazod, and Sørensen (2000, 174–76), who consider the later date (617) to be implausible. On this see Sørensen and Hazod 2005, 45. These issues are discussed in Richardson 1998, 3–6. Some contemporary historians, including Dungkar Lobzang Trinle, acknowledge the later date, which would imply that Songtsen Gampo passed away at the early age of thirty-three (unless the date of his death is to be adjusted).
24. See Pawo Tsuklak Trengwa 1962, 95.
25. This dating assumes that, as stated above (see this chap., note 23), Namri Songtsen lived from 592 to 629. The location of this coronation is considered to have been Mount Wangkur, near Ganden Monastery, on which see Dorje 2009, 170; and Akester 2016, 148–53.
26. The text here misreads *-gyi* for *-gyis*.
27. See Pawo Tsuklak Trengwa 1962, 95–96.
28. These are listed in Pawo Tsuklak Trengwa 1962, 99.
29. See Pawo Tsuklak Trengwa 1962, 98–99.
30. Our text reads *spo mthong mkhar*, but see Pawo Tsuklak Trengwa 1962, 100.
31. The six legal codes of Songtsen Gampo are elaborated in Pawo Tsuklak Trengwa 1962, 100–106. See Uray 1972; Yeshe De Project 1986a, 194–96; Dotson 2007; and Schaeffer, Kapstein, and Tuttle 2013, 92–94.
32. See Pawo Tsuklak Trengwa 1962, 100–101. See also Nyima and Dorje 2000, 359; and Yeshe De Project 1986a, 195.
33. These political divisions are discussed in Dungkar Lobzang Trinle 2002, 1455–56, 1860. The five regions included U, Tsang, Ngari, Doto, and Dome.
34. See Dungkar Lobzang Trinle 2002, 638–40.
35. See Dungkar Lobzang Trinle 2002, 1765.
36. As indicated in Dungkar Lobzang Trinle (2002, 1277), the highland army (*stod kyi dpa' sde*) guarded the border with Qarloq in the northwest; the middle army (*bar gyi dpa' sde*), with its twelve divisions, guarded the border with Jang in the southeast; and the lowland army (*smad kyi dpa' sde*) guarded the border with Azha in the northeast.
37. The six great ordinances (*bka' 'gros chen po drug*) were (1) to sustain the person

of the king and offer resources on his behalf, (2) to control the armed forces and support the servants' servants, (3) to not conscript servants and exempt the royal ladies from council deliberations, (4) to protect the borders and prohibit horses from riding through private agricultural land, (5) to subdue enemies and protect subjects, and (6) to practice the ten virtuous actions while renouncing the ten unvirtuous actions. See Nyima and Dorje 2000, 94; and Schaeffer, Kapstein, and Tuttle 2013, 94.

38. As indicated in Dungkar Lobzang Trinle (2002 1853) the six credentials (*yig tshangs drug*) were gold and turquoise credentials for ministers of the highest caliber, silver and gold-plated silver credentials for those who were average, and copper and iron credentials for those who were inferior. On their large and small subdivisions, see Schaeffer, Kapstein, and Tuttle 2013, 94.
39. The six official seals (*bka'i phyag rgya drug*) are (1) a chest symbolizing royal edicts, (2) a banner symbolizing the regional military governors, (3) a castle symbolizing the countryside, (4) a temple symbolizing religion, (5) a tiger skin symbolizing the heroic, and (6) a book symbolizing the wise. See Nyima and Dorje 2000, 106; and Schaeffer, Kapstein, and Tuttle 2013, 94.
40. The six titles of honor and dishonor (*rkyen drug*) are (1) the title "leopard" or "tiger" for warriors, (2) the title "fox" for cowards, (3) the title "divine doctrine" (*lha chos*) for noble persons, (4) the title "artisan" (literally "weaver") or "Bon" for servants, (5) the title "officer" for the wise, and (6) the title "thief" for the wicked. See Nyima and Dorje 2000, 132; and Schaeffer, Kapstein, and Tuttle 2013, 94.
41. The six insignia of heroism (*dpa' mtshan drug*) are (1–2) the tiger tunic and tiger kilt, (3–4) the larger and smaller girdles, and (5–6) the neckerchief (*gong ras*) and the tiger-skin dress (*stag slog*). See Dungkar Lobzang Trinle 2002, 1278; and Schaeffer, Kapstein, and Tuttle 2013, 94.
42. See Pawo Tsuklak Trengwa 1962, 103–4.
43. See Pawo Tsuklak Trengwa 1962, 104. Twenty dry measures (*bre*) are equivalent to one mule load (*khal*), and one-sixth of a dry measure is known as a *phul*. The *sang* is a measurement of weight and coinage, equivalent to the Chinese *liang/tael* (37.5 grams). The *zho* (3.75 grams) is one tenth of a *sang*, the *se* (0.0375 grams) is one hundredth of a *zho*, and the *sran* is the smallest unit.
44. See Pawo Tsuklak Trengwa 1962, 104.
45. See Pawo Tsuklak Trengwa 1962, 104.
46. See Pawo Tsuklak Trengwa 1962, 104. For a full enumeration of the sixteen pure humanitarian laws, see Dudjom Rinpoche 1991, 1:59–60.
47. See Pawo Tsuklak Trengwa 1962, 104.
48. Pawo Tsuklak Trengwa (1961, 104–6) presents these in detail. The first is a verdict in favor of the status quo, made simply to avoid the embarrassment of the dominant party in a dispute, who would otherwise be subjected to gossip, and at the same time to avoid punishing the weaker party, even though their case is unbelievable, in order not to disappoint those who are humble. It is

unclear whether Dolon is the name of a person. The second is exemplified by the tale of the brahmin Daṇḍin (Dbyug pa can), who borrowed an ox from another household and took it without asking, while the other householder was also negligent and culpable. The last mentioned is exemplified by the monk Dvikula, or Riknyipa (He of Two Families), who anecdotally is said to have belonged to two different families in consequence of a newly born child having been lost in a river, swallowed by a fish, and rescued by another family.

49. The Tibetan source text (Taklung Ngawang Namgyel 1992, 107, line 1) misreads *dge slong ma kā ra ma ti shī la*. The source of this passage is Pawo Tsuklak Trengwa 1962, 106–8. On Ākarmatiśīla, see also Dudjom Rinpoche 1991, 510.
50. The seven generations of past buddhas (*sangs rgyas rabs bdun*) are Vipaśyin, Śikhin, Viśvabhuk, Krakucchanda, Kakutsunda, Kanakamuni, and Kāśyapa. See Nordrang Orgyen 2000, 1729–30.
51. These are the eight most sacred places associated with Śākyamuni Buddha: Lumbinī, Vārāṇasī, Gṛddhrakūṭa, Śrāvastī, Vajrāsana, Nairañjanā, and Kuśinagara. See Nordrang Orgyen 2000, 1831–33.
52. See Pawo Tsuklak Trengwa 1962, 108. Of these, Sublime Wati ('Phags pa wa ti) was installed in Kyirong (Mang yul), Bhukaṃ (Bhu kaṃ, [*sic*] Byu kaṃ) was installed on the Tibet-Nepal border (exact whereabouts unknown), Ukhang (U khang) is said to be have been installed in Kathmandu (Yam bu ya 'gal), and White Jamali ('Jam' ma li dkar po) is installed in the Sveta Matsyendranāth Temple (Jana Bahāl) in Assan, Kathmandu, where it is known as Padmapāṇi. Sublime Lokeśvara was installed in the Phakpa Lhakhang of the Potala Palace in Lhasa. Cf. Dungkar Lobzang Trinle 2002, 1521, 1887–88, 2200.
53. See Pawo Tsuklak Trengwa 1962, 108.
54. See Pawo Tsuklak Trengwa 1962, 108–11. Princess Tritsun is said to have constructed the Great Temple of Lhasa in 639 (earth pig). On the Potala Palace, see Dorje 2009, 108–17; Akester 2016, 95–100; and Phuntsok Tseten (Ping Cuo Ci Dan) et al. 2000.
55. The chief minister Gar Tongtsen Yulzung (Mgar stong bstan yul zung) traveled to China in 636 (fire monkey) and passed away in 667 (fire hare). See Gozhul Drakpa Jungne and Gyelwa Lobzang Khedrub 1992, 333. On the significance of the Gar family during the royal period, see Richardson 1998, 114–23.
56. The source for the following narrative concerning Princess Wencheng is Pawo Tsuklak Trengwa 1962, 111–31; the items included within her dowry are listed in that text on p. 114. The princess is said to have reached Tibet in 641 (iron ox) and founded Ramoche in 651 (iron pig).
57. See Dungkar Lobzang Trinle 2002, 2099.
58. The eight methods of examination (*brtag thabs brgyad*) are (1) pulse palpation (*nad pa'i rtsa la brtag pa*), (2) uroscopy (*chu la brtag pa*), (3) examination of the tongue (*lce la brtag pa*), (4) examination of the eyes (*mig la brtag pa*), (5) examination of fevers (*tsha ba brtag pa*), (6) examination of breathing (*dbugs*

gtong lugs la brtag pa), (7) examination of the secondary causes of disease (*nad kyi slong rkyen la brtag pa*), and (8) inquiry (*na lugs dri ba'i sgo nas brtag pa*). See Parfionovitch, Dorje, and Meyer 1992, 123–50.

59. These five therapeutic techniques (*dpyad lnga*) are bloodletting (*gtar ga*), moxibustion (*me btsa'*), compress (*dugs*), fomentation (*lums*), and ointments (*byugs pa*). See Parfionovitch, Dorje, and Meyer 1992, 153–64.
60. These six purgative methods (*sbyongs drug*) are laxatives (*bshal sman*), emetics (*skyugs sman*), nasal medications (*sna sman*), mild enemata (*'jam rtsi*), strong enemata (*ni ru ha*), and cleansing of the channels (*rtsa sbyongs*). See Parfionovitch, Dorje, and Meyer 1992, 149–54.
61. The four sorts of medicinal compound (*sbyor sde bzhi*) are decoctions (*thang*), powders (*phye ba*), pills (*ril bu*), and pastes (*lde gu*). See Parfionovitch, Dorje, and Meyer 1992, 149–50.
62. See Pawo Tsuklak Trengwa 1962, 116–17.
63. According to the chronological tables in Thupten Phuntsok (2013, 3825), Songtsen Gampo married Tritsun in 630 (iron tiger), Ruyongza and Litikmen in 631 (iron hare), and Wencheng in 641 (iron ox).
64. See Dungkar Lobzang Trinle 2002, 2019–20.
65. The eight auspicious symbols (*bkra shis brda brgyad*) are (1) parasol, (2) golden fish, (3) lotus, (4) conch, (5) vase, (6) śrīvatsa, (7) victory banner, and (8) wheel. On their symbolism, see Dungkar Lobzang Trinle 2002, 192.
66. These are the four geomantic scrutinies in the environs of Lhasa—namely, (1) the scrutiny of the white tiger in the east (that is, Gamotrang, Dga' mo 'phrang), (2) the scrutiny of the blue turquoise dragon in the south (that is, Lhasa Kyichu), (3) the scrutiny of the red bird in the west (that is, Shungi Drakmar Diu Dong, Shun gyi brag dmar rdi'u gdong), and (4) the scrutiny of the black turtle in the north (that is, the cliff of Phabongka). See Dungkar Lobzang Trinle 2002, 1291.
67. See Pawo Tsuklak Trengwa 1962, 117.
68. This is a grove to the south of Chakpori, nowadays within the compound of the Tibetan Autonomous Region government. See Dungkar Lobzang Trinle 2002, 1816.
69. See Pawo Tsuklak Trengwa 1962, 119–21. On the miraculous origin of this celebrated image of Mahākāruṇika (*rang byung lnga ldan*), see Dorje, Tsering, Stoddard, and Alexander 2010, 68–69.
70. There are various traditions as to what exactly constitute these twelve geomantic temples and their specific locations within the grand design. The relevant sources are detailed in Sørensen and Hazod (2005, 48–56) and tabulated with illustrative material in the appendices on pp. 171–213. According to Pawo Tsuklak Trengwa (1961, 123), the four border-taming temples (*mtha' 'dul bzhi*) are Katsel, Tradruk, Tsangdram, and Drompagyang (on the shoulders and hips of the supine ogress); the four further-taming temples (*yang 'dul bzhi*) are Buchu, Khomting, Jamtrin Gegye in Mangyul, and Drongpa Tradun (on the

elbows and knees); and the four district-controlling temples (*ru gnon bzhi*) are Longtang Dolma, Kyerchu in Bumtang, Tselrik Dronma, and Tsangpa Lung Non (on the hands and feet).

71. As for this group of nine temples, there are three temples suppressing the earth element in the east that determine the sun, moon, and planets—namely, Kachu, Kamchu, and Lingchu. The pair of temples suppressing the fire element in the south are Nangdro and Longtang. The pair of temples suppressing the water element in the west are Gulang and Shinkun, and the pair of temples suppressing the wind element in the north are Geri and Pelri. See Pawo Tsuklak Trengwa 1962, 123; and Sørensen and Hazod 2005, 197.
72. On the construction and layout of Tradruk, see Sørensen and Hazod 2005, especially pp. 93–94 on this encounter with the beggar monk. Some sources suggest that the mendicant was appointed as the king's personal chaplain.
73. Other sources suggest twelve days, including four for the walls, six for the carpentry, and two for the ceiling. See Sørensen and Hazod 2005, 56.
74. See Thupten Phuntsok 2013, 2458.
75. See Pawo Tsuklak Trengwa 1962, 123–26. On the construction and layout of the temple, and the various traditions and anecdotes concerning Tibet's most sacred image, Jowo Śākyamuni, contained within its central inner sanctum, see Dorje, Tsering, Stoddard, and Alexander 2010. With regard to the names of this temple, the same source (p. 51) states, "The Great Temple was named 'Great Emanational Temple of Rasa, place of the goat' (*ra sa 'phrul snang gi gtsug lag khang*), firstly because the earth for its construction had been transported by an emanational goat and secondly because a particularly wonderful temple resembling an optical illusion had been constructed there once the lake had been filled. Others too described the building as 'an apparitional Great Temple giving rise to four delights' (*dga' bzhi 'phrul snang gi gtsug lag khang*). Firstly, it delighted Buddhists since its four gates were fashioned in the style of a celestial palace (*vimāna*), secondly it delighted Bonpos since its walls were fashioned in the design of a svastika, thirdly it delighted mantrins since its pillars were fashioned in the design of a ritual dagger, and fourthly it delighted the populace because its joists and beams were fashioned in the design of a lattice (*mig mang*)."
76. See Pawo Tsuklak Trengwa 1962, 124.
77. *be'u bum brgya rtsa*. This is the title of a booklet in the form of a memorandum or inventory to the murals of the Great Temple of Lhasa. See Thupten Phuntsok 2013, 2179.
78. For a brief description of Ramoche, see Akester 2016, 81–86; and Dorje 2009, 103–5.
79. This is identified with present-day Minyak Lhagang in Dardo County. See Thupten Phuntsok 2013, 3094; and Dorje 2009, 552–53.
80. See Pawo Tsuklak Trengwa 1962, 127–29.
81. *samayasattva, dam tshig sems dpa'*. This meditative process denotes the merging

of the actual deities (*ye shes sems dpa'*) with their visualized, or symbolic, simulations (*dam tshig sems dpa'*).

82. See Pawo Tsuklak Trengwa 1962, 129.
83. This is the name of the palace of Queen Tritsun, formerly located at Draklha Lupuk. See Dungkar Lobzang Trinle 2002, 1502; and Thupten Phuntsok 2013, 2291. According to the chronological charts in Thupten Phuntsok 2013, 3824–25, Gungri Gungtsen was born in 621 (iron snake), acceded to the throne in 633 (water snake), and passed away in 638 (earth dog)—but this is evidently implausible if Songtsen Gampo's birth date is accepted as 617 (fire ox). According to Dungkar Lobzang Trinle 2002, Gungri Gungtsen was born in 669 (earth snake) and died in 686 (fire dog). The more plausible chronology, stated and implied in *The Tang Annals*, would place his birth in 629 (earth ox), his accession in 641 (iron ox), and his death in 646 (fire horse). Cf. Kapstein 2006, 56.
84. See Pawo Tsuklak Trengwa 1962, 129–30.
85. Ratnadeva is the name of a gemstone brought to Tibet as part of the dowry of Princess Tritsun from Nepal. See Dungkar Lobzang Trinle 2002, 1891.
86. See Pawo Tsuklak Trengwa 1962, 131–32.
87. See Pawo Tsuklak Trengwa 1962, 132. For a description of the Chimphu hermitage above Samye, see Akester 2016, 329–41; and Dorje 2009, 216–19.
88. See Pawo Tsuklak Trengwa 1962, 132.
89. The text here reads "earth dog," which would be 698. See part 1, chap. 6, note 84.
90. Regarding the Red Mausoleum (Ban so dmar po) at Chongye, and the other tombs of the early kings located in that valley and in the adjacent Dungkar valley, see Akester 2016, 436–37; and Dorje 2009, 244–47.
91. Clay images traditionally had silk thread and fragments mixed with the clay. See Thupten Phuntsok 2013, 1487. Of the two bronze images that formed the dowry of the Nepalese princess, Jowo Mikyo Dorje was originally housed in the southern sanctum but moved to Ramoche, perhaps by the princess Jincheng, to replace the image of Jowo Rinpoche that had been relocated in the Jokhang within the Great Temple of Lhasa. On Maitreya in the form of Jampa Chokhor, see Dorje, Tsering, Stoddard, and Alexander 2010, 74.
92. See Pawo Tsuklak Trengwa 1962, 148–49.
93. See Pawo Tsuklak Trengwa 1962, 155. According to the chronological charts in Thupten Phuntsok 2013, 3825–26, Mangtsong Mangtsen was born in 638 (earth dog), became king on the death of his father in 650 (iron dog), and reigned until his death in 676 (fire mouse).
94. This incident is recounted in Dorje, Tsering, Stoddard, and Alexander 2010, 71. Richardson (1998, 251) adds that this image was known locally as Gungtang Meshor, meaning "Gungtang is on fire!" because a finger of its outstretched hand pointed in that direction. The invasion of Lhasa by Chinese forces following the death of Songtsen Gampo appears to have been a fabrication of later Tibetan historians. See Richardson 1998, 39–47.

95. 'Dus srong mang po rje lung nam 'phrul gyi rgyal po.
96. According to Deu Jose's *The Doctrinal History of Deu*, these were Ngok Ringla Nakpo (Rngog ring la nag po), Ngok Ling Gam (Rngok gling gam), Bego Dongtsen (Sbas rgod ldong btsan), Go Yak Chung ('Gos g.yag chung), Chokro Drongshor (Cog ro 'brong shor), Non Gyeltsen (Gnon rgyal mtshan), and Non Tride Yuljin (Gnon khri lde yul byin). All were renowned for their heroic superhuman exploits. See Nordrang Orgyen 2008, 1696. An alternative list appears in Peljor Zangpo 1985, 171–72.
97. See Pawo Tsuklak Trengwa 1962, 155–56. According to the chronological tables in Thupten Phuntsok (2013, 3826–27), Dusong Mangpoje Lungnam Trukgyi Gyelpo was born in 676 (fire mouse), became king in 679 (earth hare), and reigned until his death in Jang in 704 (wood dragon), following a military campaign in Jang against the kingdom of Nangzhao. Cf. the summary of his life in Dungkar Lobzang Trinle 2002, 1151–52. See also Kapstein 2006, 62–63.
98. Pho brang ldan dkar.
99. See Pawo Tsuklak Trengwa 1962, 156–57. According to the chronological tables in Thupten Phuntsok (2013, 3826–27), Tri Detsukten was born in 698 (earth dog), became king in 705 (wood snake), and reigned until his assassination in 755 (wood sheep). See also the summary of his life in Dungkar Lobzang Trinle 2002, 396–97. Our text here suggests he was born in 680 (iron dragon). The Denkar Palace, formerly located in the On Valley, north of Tsetang, was during the eighth and early ninth centuries a repository of texts, cataloged by Kawa Peltsek and others in *The Denkarma Catalog* (*Dkar chag ldan dkar ma).* See Dungkar Lobzang Trinle 2002, 1331.
100. The five temples constructed by this king were Lhasa Khardrak (Lha sa mkhar brag), Drakmar Drinzang (Brag dmar mgrin bzang), Chimphu Namrel (Mchims phu nam ral), Drakmar Keru (Brag dmar ke ru), and Masagong (Ma sa gong). Of these, on Drakmar Drinzang, see Akester 2016, 303–4. On Drakmar Keru, located in the On Valley, see Akester 2016, 367–69; and Dorje 2009, 226–27. The Pangtang Palace predates the construction of Samye but was destroyed by flooding—it was where King Tri Detsukten commissioned a catalog of the early translations of the Kangyur and Tengyur, known as *The Pangtangma Catalog* (*Dkar chag 'phang thang ma.* See Dungkar Lobzang Trinle 2002, 1338.
101. Mes ag tshom.
102. On the paternity of Jangtsa Lhaon, see Thupten Phuntsok 2013, 1095.
103. See this chap., note 94.
104. According to the chronological tables in Thupten Phuntsok (2013, 3828–3929), Jincheng Konjo reached Tibet in 712 (water mouse) and passed away there in 739 (earth hare). See also Kapstein 2006, 63–65.
105. The life of Tri Songdetsen is recounted in Pawo Tsuklak Trengwa 1962, 158–213. Regarding the controversial dating of his birth, see Dungkar Lobzang Trinle

2002, 404. The same source dismisses the fabrication that he was the son of Jincheng Konjo and abducted by Nanamza—who was his actual mother. This year of his birth, 742 (water horse), is attested in Dunhuang chronicles and in the astrological writings of Lochen Dharmaśrī and others. Our text, following Pawo Tsuklak Trengwa, reads "iron male horse," which would be either 730 or 790. Tri Songdetsen became king in 755 (wood sheep) and died in either 796 (fire mouse) or 797 (fire ox).

106. See Pawo Tsuklak Trengwa 1962, 158–59.
107. See Pawo Tsuklak Trengwa 1962, 161.
108. 'Gos padma gung bstan.
109. See Pawo Tsuklak Trengwa 1962, 166ff. On the activities of Śāntarakṣita (725–783) and Padmasambhava in Tibet, see also Dudjom Rinpoche 1991, 1:512–21.
110. Byang chub phyogs chos so bdun yongs su rdzogs pa chos 'khor chen po dpal bsam yas mi 'gyur lhun gyis grub pa'i gtsug lag khang.
111. See Pawo Tsuklak Trengwa 1962, 175. On Samye, see Shedragung Wangchuk Gyelpo 2000; Akester 2016, 305–28; and for a brief contemporary description, Dorje 2009, 208–15.
112. See Pawo Tsuklak Trengwa 1962, 175.
113. Brag dmar mtsho mo mgur.
114. Pawo Tsuklak Trengwa (1962, 185–86) adds that the foundations of Samye were laid in the iron hare when the king was in his twenty-second year—that would be 751. According to the chronological tables in Thupten Phuntsok 2013, 3829, Samye was founded in 761 (iron ox).
115. Rba khri gzigs.
116. According to Pawo Tsuklak Trengwa (1961, 185), these ordinations took place in the wood sheep year (755), when the king was in his twenty-sixth year. Thupten Phuntsok (2013, 3830) suggests 775 (fire dragon). If the king were in his twenty-sixth year at that time, 767 (fire sheep) would be more plausible. The seven were Ba Trizhi (Śrīghoṣa), Ba Selnang (Jnānendra), Pagor Vairocana (Vairocanarakṣita), Ngenlam Gyelwa Choyang, Ma Rinchen Chok, Khon Luiwangpo Sungwa (Nāgendrarakṣita), and Lasum Gyelwa Jangchub. See Dudjom Rinpoche 1991, 1:515; and Pawo Tsuklak Trengwa (1961, 190), who lists the variants and comments on their attributes.
117. See Pawo Tsuklak Trengwa 1962, 191–94; and Dudjom Rinpoche 1991, 1:537. Specifically on Yerpa, see Akester 2016, 133–39; and Dorje 2009, 169–71, and on Chuwori, 194.
118. Khri bzang yab lhag.
119. Stag bstan gdong gzigs.
120. The gradation and implementation of these laws regarding compensation are discussed in Nordrang Orgyen 2008, 1678–79. Pawo Tsuklak Trengwa (1961, 199) adds that Go Trizang Yablhak was included in the group of seven culture heroes because of his great kindness to later generations of ministers. Nyer

Taktsen Dongzik is also said to have allocated one horse and one dzo to each household.

121. See Pawo Tsuklak Trengwa 1962, 198–99.

122. See Pawo Tsuklak Trengwa 1962, 200. Śāntarakṣita died in a riding accident in 783. His skull is still preserved as a sacred relic at Samye Monastery.

123. See Pawo Tsuklak Trengwa 1962, 199.

124. See Pawo Tsuklak Trengwa 1962, 200–208.

125. See Pawo Tsuklak Trengwa 1962, 209–13. These four great ceremonies are the offering ceremony of the vinaya at Lhasa, the offering ceremony of the abhidharma at Tradruk, and the offering ceremonies of the sūtras and enlightenment at Samye. See Dungkar Lobzang Trinle 2002, 864. Mune Tsenpo was short-lived. According to the chronological tables in Thupten Phuntsok (2013, 829), he was born in 762 (water tiger), acceded to the throne in 796 (fire mouse), and was poisoned to death the following year 797 (fire ox) by his own mother Queen Tsepongza Metok Dron. Dungkar Lobzang Trinle (2002, 4615) points out that there are differing accounts as to how long he actually reigned—extending from one year and seven months to seven years and nine months, or even seventeen years. Some sources suggest he was followed by his exiled brother Mutik Tsenpo (a.k.a. Murub Tsenpo) from 797 (fire ox) to 804 (wood monkey), when the latter was intentionally killed by Queen Poyongza in a riding accident. Other sources suggest that he was assassinated en route from exile back to Central Tibet and was never actually crowned.

126. Sad na legs 'jing yon.

127. Rdo rje dbyings kyi lha khang.

128. See Pawo Tsuklak Trengwa 1962, 213–17. Tri Desongtsen was the youngest of Tri Songdetsen and Queen Tsepongza's four sons. The oldest, Mutri Songpo, died in infancy; the second, Mune Tsenpo, was poisoned to death in 797; and the third, Mutik Tsenpo, or Murub Tsenpo, was most probably killed while returning from exile to claim the throne (see this chapter, note 128). According to Thupten Phuntsok (2013, 3830), Tri Desongtsen was born in 776 (fire dragon), acceded to the throne in 804 (wood snake), and died in 815 (wood horse), which would mean that he was in his twenty-eighth year when the succession occurred. Cf. the account in Dungkar Lobzang Trinle 2002, 397–98.

129. See Pawo Tsuklak Trengwa 1962, 213–17. A somewhat detailed appraisal of his reign is found in Dungkar Lobzang Trinle 2002, 401–3. According to this account, he acceded to the throne in his tenth year. Our text, following Pawo Tsuklak Trengwa (1961, 217), suggests that this enthronement occurred when he was in his twelfth year. According to Thupten Phuntsok (2013, 3831–32), he was born in 806 (fire dog), acceded to the throne in 815 (wood sheep), and died at the hand of his older brother Langdarma in 836 (fire dragon). The last date is disputed—some sources (including Pawo Tsuklak Trengwa) suggest he was assassinated in 841 (iron bird), and others (including Go Lotsāwa) suggest

836 (fire dragon). Pawo Tsulkak Trengwa also mentions that he acceded to the throne in 817 (fire bird) rather than 815.

130. Bran ka dpal yon.

131. Cog bza' dpal gyi ngang tshul.

132. The three obelisks were erected in 823—one in front of the Great Temple of Lhasa (still standing), one in the Chinese capital of Chang'an, and one in the Sino-Tibetan borderland at Gung Gu Meru (Gung gu rme ru). On the inscription of the renowned Lhasa obelisk, see Sonam Kyi 1984, 21–58; also various articles in Khagang Tashi Tsering 2003, 8–40; and Richardson 1998, 300 (along with plates 10 and 24).

133. See Pawo Tsuklak Trengwa 1962, 219; and Dudjom Rinpoche 1991, 1:521–22.

134. Dpe med bkra shis dge 'phel.

135. U shang rdo.

136. This temple once stood at Ushangdo, on the banks of the Kyichu River, below Shugseb and Gangri Tokar. See Akester 2016, 230–31; Dorje 2009, 188; and Richardson 1998, plates 59–60.

137. On the exile of Prince Tsangma in Bhutan, see Aris 1978, 83–114; and Karma Phuntsho 2013, 110–15.

138. See Pawo Tsuklak Trengwa 1962, 220–23. Langdarma Udumtsen was the last, or forty-third, king of unified Tibet. See Dungkar Lobzang Trinle 2002, 578–79. The year of his birth is uncertain—possibly 802 (water horse) or even 815, according to Thupten Phuntsok (2013, 3831). *The Tang Annals* suggests that he was killed by Lhalung Pelgyi Dorje in 842 (water dog), having reigned for only one year and a few months after killing his brother, while others sources (Buton and others) suggest this occurred in 841 (iron bird). Pawo Tsuklak Trengwa (1961, 225) holds that this occurred in 846 (fire tiger), and our text concurs. Contemporary scholarship suggests that Langdarma may have had some Buddhist sympathies but aimed simply to reduce the extent of the official patronage. His actions may also have been influenced by a similar anti-Buddhist persecution that occurred in Tang China in 845. See Kapstein 2006, 80–82.

139. Smar g.yo gtsang gsum. See Dudjom Rinpoche 1991, 1:523–24. On Lhalung Pelgyi Dorje's hermitage in Amdo, see Dorje 2009, 722.

140. According to Pawo Tsuklak Trengwa (1961, 225), the brothers were both born after the death of their father in 847 (fire hare), and Namde Osung passed away in 885 (wood snake). During this period, the Tibetan empire disintegrated due to a series of three internal rebellions (*kheng log gsum*), extending from around 845 to 910, and particularly in 869 (earth ox). See Davidson 2004, 66–72. Various other dates have been suggested for Namde Osung (847–907, according to Buton; and 847–903, according to Richardson 1998, 112, 840–93). Sakya sources (including Drakpa Gyeltsen's *Royal History of Tibet, Bod kyi rgyal rabs*) suggest that he lived for sixty-three years. Regarding Yumten, Thupten Phuntsok (2013) suggests that he was born in 841 (iron bird), and Drakpa Gyeltsen suggests that he lived for thirty-six years. Some have even

questioned his existence—on the possible conflation of the two brothers, see Richardson 1998, 48–55; and Kapstein 2006, 90.

141. Pelkhortsen, according to the chronological tables in Thupten Phuntsok (2013, 3833), was born in 865 (wood bird) and reigned from 885 (wood snake) until his assassination in 895 (wood hare). He is said to have founded the original fortress of Gyelkhartse (modern Gyantse). Elsewhere his dates are given as ca. 881–910 or 911 and 892–923. See Richardson 1998, 112; Hazod, Gyalbo, and Sørensen 2000, 177–91; Davidson 2004, 68–69; and Dorje 2009, 308.

142. Nyima Gon fled to Ngari and founded Purang in 912. His son Tashi Gon established the Guge kingdom, and his son Yeshe-o (947–1024) invited Atiśa to Tibet. See Vitali 1996; Hazod, Gyalbo, and Sørensen 2000, 182; and Davidson 2004, 69. The family trees of both Namde Osung and Tride Yumten are outlined in Hazod, Gyalbo, and Sørensen 2000, 181–89; and Davidson 2004, 69, 91.

143. Ra sa 'phrul snang

144. This passage derives from Pawo Tsuklak Trengwa 1962, 236.

145. Be ri tshva mtsho.

146. Rma lung rdo rje brag.

147. Dan tig shel gyi yang dgon.

148. These are two distinct power places of Dome—both associated with Padmasambhava. Achung Namdzong is in Jentsa County, and Dentik is in Bayan Qar County. See Dorje 2009, 721–23 on Achung Namdzong, and 714–15 on Dentik.

149. Mu zu gsal 'bar. Otherwise known as Muzu Labar and Lachen Gongpa Rabsel. See Dudjom Rinpoche 1991, 1:524. According to the chronological tables in Thupten Phuntsok (2013, 3834) he was born in 895 (wood hare) and ordained in 906 (fire tiger), before passing on the ordination of the Lowland Vinaya to the ten men of Utsang in 910 (iron horse). The more plausible dates for Lachen Gongpa Rabsel are 892–975.

150. Mnga' ris pa 'od brgyad spun gnyis.

151. The source for these paragraphs on the Lowland Vinaya tradition is Pawo Tsuklak Trengwa 1962, 242–50. On the early development of this monastic tradition, see Davidson 2004, 86–107.

152. Mnga' bdag srong nges. The lord of Ngari who was the grandson of Tashi Gon. See Vitali 1996, 175–79.

153. These were Sadhupāla, Guṇapāla, and Prajñāpāla. See Dungkar Lobzang Trinle 2002, 1256.

154. See Pawo Tsuklak Trengwa 1962, 250–54.

155. This prophecy is mentioned in Pawo Tsuklak Trengwa 1962, 255.

156. These are Neudongtse Tsokpa (Sne'u gdong rtse tshogs pa), Drachi Tsongdu Tsokpa (Grva phyi tshong 'dus tshogs pa), Dranang Gyeling Tsokpa (Gra nang rgyal gling tshogs pa, founded by Jangchubpel), and Tsang Cholung Tsokpa (Gtsang chos lung tshogs pa).

157. This ordination line known as the transmission of Paṇchen (*paṇ chen sdom rgyun*) is detailed in Pawo Tsuklak Trengwa 1962, 255–62. The usual dates given are 1127–1225 for Śākyaśrī and 1173–1236 for Trophu Lotsāwa Jampa Pel.
158. This view of Dromtonpa is mentioned in Roerich 1949, 61. The determination of the earth tiger year in question is a matter of crucial importance for the subsequent history of Buddhism in Tibet. Go Lotsāwa (Roerich 1949, 60–61) adds that Sumpa Yeshe Lodro, one of the ten men from Utsang, was still alive in 1042, when Atiśa reached Tibet in the sixty-fifth year after the earth tiger. This would suggest that the later dissemination of the Buddhist teaching (*bstan pa phyi dar*) commenced in 978 (earth tiger). Following Buton, Go Lotsāwa also offers an alternative date, 973 (water bird), mentioning that this was seventy-three years after the assassination of Langdarma in the iron bird. Generations of Tibetan historians have sought to reconcile the long hiatus between Langdarma's assassination in c. 841 and the restoration of 978—a considerably longer period than seventy-three years. One view, reflected in the chronological tables in Thupten Phuntsok (2013, 3835), holds that the later dissemination commenced a full sixty years earlier, in 917 (fire ox), while others have brought forward the chronology of the Tibetan kings by as much as sixty years, suggesting that the assassination of Langdarma occurred in c. 901, rather than c. 841. The year 978 is credible for the start of the later dissemination. Gyengong Lhakhang near Zhalu was founded in 997 by Loton Dorje Wangchuk, one of the ten men from Utsang, and it is considered to have marked the reintroduction of temple building (see Dorje 2009, 327–8) following the hiatus. The reference to "seventy-three years" may perhaps refer to 901 (iron bird), as some point between the second and third rebellions when the Buddhist teaching all but disappeared, rather than the assassination of Langdarma in c. 841 (iron bird). See also the discussion in Roerich 1949, xiii–xviii.
159. *mi srid pa'i med pa'i srid snang*. Translation marked as uncertain.—Ed.

7. The Biographies of the Early Kagyu Lineage Holders in Tibet

1. The bolded terms, followed by Tibetan transliteration, represent the meaning of the names of the master who is being praised in the verse.—Ed.
2. The initial verses of homage in chapter seven are dedicated to the four progenitors of the Kagyu lineage in Tibet: Marpa Lotsāwa Chokyi Lodro (1012–1097), Mila Repa Dorje Gyeltsen (1040–1123), Gampopa Sonam Rinchen (1079–1153), and Phakmodrupa Dorje Gyelpo (1110–1170), whose hagiographies are detailed in the pages that follow. There are alternative dates given for Marpa (1002–1100) and for Mila Repa (1052–1135).
3. *rig byed grangs kyis 'khyud pa*.
4. Dkon mchog stod pa bkra shis ling nga.
5. The author's principal source for this brief hagiography of Marpa appears to

be Pawo Tsuklak Trengwa 2010. The birthplace of Marpa that is mentioned here accords with that work (see p. 32). Other sources (Go Lotsāwa and Tsangnyon Heruka) speak of this place as Lhodrak Chukhyer (Carried Off by Water)—an appropriate name for this gorge, which is prone to heavy landslides in the rainy season. See Akester 2016, 471n52; and Dorje 2009, 254–55.

6. Candrakīrti, *Pradīpoddyotananāmaṭīkā*, *Sgron ma gsal bar byed pa zhes bya ba'i rgya cher bshad pa* (Toh. 1785; rgyud, *ha*, ff. 1b–201b).
7. Pham ting ba rnam rgyal dbang po spyi ther ba. Otherwise known as Dharmamati, the eldest of the four Phamtingwa brothers.
8. *Dud gsol ma*.
9. Ri bo gser gyi dgon pa.
10. Me tog gis brgyan pa.
11. References to many incidents in the life of Marpa are found in the English translation of Tsangyang Heruka's elaborate work titled *The Life of Marpa the Translator*. On this specific stanza, see Nalanda Translation Committee 1999, 12.
12. *Do hā*.
13. *Gdan bzhi pa*.
14. Chu shing gi snye ma can.
15. See Nalanda Translation Committee 1999, 42.
16. *Yi ge bzhi'i chos*.
17. On Ngok Choku Dorje (1036–1097) and Tsurton Wangi Dorje, along with their disciples, see Go Lotsāwa's *Blue Annals*, translated in Roerich 1949, 403–26.
18. Nag po lwa ba pa.
19. Nag po zhabs.
20. The twenty-four sacred abodes associated with Cakrasaṃvara are understood in external geographic terms, as well as in terms of the spiritual progression of a bodhisattva and the network of energy channels within the subtle body of the meditator. See Nordrang Orgyen 2008, 3187–89; Gray 2007, 54–76; and Callahan 2014, 543–47.
21. *Ral gcig ma'i rtog pa*.
22. *Nges brjod bdud rtsi*. Translation marked as uncertain.—Ed.
23. Cf. Nalanda Translation Committee 1999, 202.
24. See p. 118.
25. These are the nine vehicles (*theg pa dgu*) expounded in Nyingma philosophical texts. See the recapitulation sections in Dudjom Rinpoche 1991, 1:223–37, 1:346–72. See also Cabazon 2013.
26. Cf. Nalanda Translation Committee 1999, 67–71.
27. Uru (*dbu ru*) is one of the four horns of Tibet. It corresponds to the Kyichu basin.
28. Cf. Nalanda Translation Committee 1999, 71–72.
29. Atiśa (982–1054), whose disciples established the Kadampa tradition in

Tibet. On his life and work, see Sherbourne 2000; Thupten Jinpa 2008; and Thupten Jinpa 2013, 23–36.

30. Cf. Nalanda Translation Committee 1999, 77–78.
31. Cf. Nalanda Translation Committee 1999, 78–79.
32. See Nalanda Translation Committee 1999, 80.
33. See Nalanda Translation Committee 1999, 80.
34. Rus pa'i rgyan can.
35. See Nalanda Translation Committee 1999, 80.
36. See Nalanda Translation Committee 1999, 79. Note missing verse.
37. See Nalanda Translation Committee 1999, 81, and the interpretation that follows.
38. See Nalanda Translation Committee 1999, 81.
39. See Pawo Tsuklak Trengwa 2010, 118. (*spu shad tshun gsal ba drod ma yal ba mthong nas . . .*)
40. All the foregoing signs of Nāropā's presence are said to have occurred over a seven-month period. See Nalanda Translation Committee 1999, 82–85.
41. See Nalanda Translation Committee 1999, 87–89.
42. Cf. Nalanda Translation Committee 1999, 87.
43. Cf. Nalanda Translation Committee 1999, 85.
44. *Snyan brgyud yid bzhin nor bu.*
45. *Thugs brgyud gdam bskor bco lnga.*
46. *Rgyud kyi snying po'i dmar khrid shog dril bzhi.*
47. *Man ngag gi shog dril bzhi.*
48. *Rlung sems gnyis med.*
49. *Sems khrid yid bzhin nor bu.*
50. *'Pho ba grong 'jug.*
51. *Thugs dam pad+ma dmar po'i phreng ba brgya rtsa brgyad pa.* An aspect of Vajravārāhī in the form Khecarī (Mkha' spyod ma).
52. These are the celestial, terrestrial, and subterranean.
53. The three yogas (*rnal 'byor gsum*) are those of buddha body, speech, and mind. See Dungkar Lobzang Trinle 2002, 1242. Alternatively, they could imply the generation stage, the perfection stage, and their integration.
54. Tāranātha's *According to the Intention of Marpa* (2008) remarks that the magical display of post-meditation (*rjes thob sgyu ma*) consists of the magical display of appearances (*snang ba sgyu ma*), the magical display of dreams (*rmi lam sgyu ma*), and the magical display of the intermediate state (*bar do sgyu ma*). According to Longchen Rabjam's *Excellent Wagon: A Commentary on "Finding Rest in Illusion," Sgyu ma'i ngal gso'i 'grel pa shing rta bzang po* (Chengdu: Si khron mi rigs dpe skrun khang, 2009), these constitute the magical displays of ground, path, and result.
55. The rite of resurrection (*grong 'jug*) is a method of entering into the corpse of a living creature to revive it for some temporary purpose. As such, it is dis-

tinguished from consciousness transference (*'pho ba*) into buddha fields or higher realms at the time of death.

56. Reading *phul* for *phur*.
57. Meton Sonam Gyeltsen and his lineage are mentioned in Roerich 1949, 405–6.
58. *Brtag pa dang po'i le'u drug pa yan gyi dka' 'grel bka' yang dag pa'i tshad ma.*
59. *'Bum chung nyi ma.*
60. *Gur gyi srog shing.*
61. *Chos drug bdud rtsi'i chu rgyun.*
62. *E vaṃ gyi man ngag.*
63. See Chan 1994, 932.
64. There are several extant sources for the life of Tibet's illustrious yogin Mila Repa, including traditional biographies, as well as the unrelated art forms of Tibetan opera and modern cinema. Among classical works, the author refers directly to Karmapa Rangjung Dorje's *The Black Anthology of the Sacred Songs of Mila Zhepei Dorje, Mighty Lord of Yoga* (*Rnal 'byor gyi dbang phyug mi la bzhad pa rdo rje'i gsung mgur mdzod nag ma*), as well as the accounts found in Go Lotsāwa's *Blue Annals* (Roerich 1949, 407–36); Pawo Tsuklak Trengwa 1962, 397–401; the well-known biography by Tsangnyon Heruka, translated by Dawa Samdrub in Evans-Wentz 1928; and Lhalungpa 1982. *The Hundred Thousand Songs of Mila Repa* (*Mgur 'bum*) are also referenced in the notes that follow, utilizing the Ziling edition of the Tibetan text (*Rnam mgur*) and the translation in Chang 1977. On this specific paragraph concerning the birth of Mila Repa, see Evans-Wentz 1928, 51–53.
65. Otherwise known as Lharje Hūṃchung, on whom see Dudjom Rinpoche 1991, 1:615.
66. *Māyājāla.*
67. *'Khrugs ser chen po.*
68. These would be the residents of Layak, later to be the abode of Guru Chowang. See Akester 2016, 477–78; and Dorje 2009, 257.
69. On the four rites of enlightened activity (*las bzhi*)—namely, pacification (*zhi ba*), enrichment (*rgyas pa*), subjugation (*dbang*), and wrathful destruction (*drag*)—see Dorje 2016, 349–51 in the context of the peaceful deities, and 731–43 in the context of the wrathful deities. See also Dorje 1987, 783–86 and 1258–64.
70. See Akester 2016, 464–69; Chan 1994, 698; and Dorje 2009, 254.
71. See Chan 1994, 697.
72. See p. 322.
73. This is the Taknya Lungten Cave, on which see Akester 2016, 471–72; and Chan 1994, 699.
74. *Gtsang la yar 'gro'i mgur.* Mila Repa 1999, 116–26.
75. Evans-Wentz 1928, 160.

76. Evans-Wentz 1928, 192.
77. See Chan 1994, 934.
78. The crouching posture for meditation is described as follows: "When the soles of the feet are touching together firmly, and the two legs assume a seated position, a full palm-width above the ground, this is the crouching posture (*tsog bu'i stabs*)." See Dorje 2012, 216.
79. Our text misreads *gzhis*, "fundamental nature," for *bzhig*, "loosening."
80. Evans-Wentz 1928, 192–208. The unraveling of the knots of the energy channels, including the serpentine *kuṇḍalinī*, are accompanied by the reversal and upward motion of generative essences through the central channel and the mastery of the bodhisattva levels. See Dudjom Rinpoche 1991, 1:340–41.
81. The external appearance of the ogress of the rocks here parallels Mila Repa's inner meditative experiences. The incident described in this paragraph is mentioned in Mila Repa 1999, 228–42. The annotations in square brackets correspond to that text.
82. *bshud pa*. Our text reads *bshugs pa*, but see Mila Repa 1999, 228.
83. *steng gi dkar cha'i nus pa 'og to song ba.*
84. Also known as Drakmar Khyunglung. See Chan 1994, 261–63.
85. On Rechungpa Dorje Drak (1085–1161), see Thrangu Rinpoche 2002; and Roberts 2007. Also Roerich 1949, 456–59.
86. *Lus med mkha' 'gro'i chos skor*. Marpa had already bestowed five of these nine cycles on Mila Repa. See Roerich 1949, 437.
87. Also known as Pārvātapada, he is considered to have been the Indian reincarnation of Marpa's son. See Roerich 1949, 437.
88. Pawo Tsuklak Trengwa (1961, 399) adds that Rechungpa hoped to receive reciprocal prostrations from Mila Repa, he had acquired misconceptions and arrogance. On this locale, see also Chan 1994, 262.
89. See Chan 1994, 261.
90. These are the three appearances associated with the dissolution of the elements at the approach of death: redness, whiteness, and blackness.
91. Chuwar in southern Rongshar, on the Tibet-Nepal border, is where Mila Repa passed away. See Chan 1994, 254–60; and Dorje 2009, 367.
92. These five primary winds (*pañcavāta, rlung lnga*) are life-sustaining breath (*prāṇa, srog 'dzin*), ascending wind associated with the vocal cords (*udāna, gyen rgyu*), pervasive wind associated with metabolism and muscular movement (*vyāna, khyab byed*), fire-accompanying wind associated with digestion (*samāna, me mnyam*), and descending purgative wind (*apāna, thur sel*). On their relationship to the five elements and their control within the subtle body, see the detailed explanation in Callahan 2014, 227–86.
93. In one major cycle of breath (*saṃkrānti*) consisting of 1,800 winds, there are said to be fifty-six and one-quarter winds of pristine cognition. The remainder are the winds of past actions. In one minor cycle of breath, consisting of three hundred and sixty winds, there are eleven and one-quarter winds of pristine

cognition, consisting of one thirty-second part of each breath. See Callahan 2014, 261–62.

94. On the downward and upward movement of the white and red vital essences (*bindu, thig le*) within the central energy channel, see Callahan 2014, 287–337.
95. See the illustration of the throat center and its subsidiary network of channels in Callahan 2014, 205.
96. On the separation of chyle and its residue or dregs, see Callahan 2014, 287–337.
97. See Karmapa Rangjung Dorje 2008.
98. *Gdengs tshod kyi mgur.*
99. The eighth level obtained by bodhisattvas is that point from which no regression is possible.
100. Cf. Roerch 1949, 435ff.
101. The primary biography of Gampopa is contained in the various recensions of his own Collected Works. The text is titled *The Biography of Glorious Choje Gampopa, Banner of the All-Pervasive Renown of the Precious Wish-Fulfilling Gem and Precious Ornament of Liberation* (*Chos kyi rje dpal ldan sgam po pa chen po'i rnam par thar pa yid bzhin gyi nor bu rin po che kun khyab snyan pa'i ba dan thar pa rin po che rgyan gya*). Abbreviated versions are also found in Roerich 1949, 451–62; and in Pawo Tsuklak Trengwa 1962, 401–12. See also Davidson 2004, 282–90. This particular quote attributed to Marpa is also found in Mila Repa 1999, 618.
102. Rin po che padma'i zla ba rnam par dag pa mngon par 'phags pa'i rgyal po.
103. See Roerich 1949, 451–52.
104. This is also cited in Mila Repa 1999, 618.
105. On the Nyel valley where Gampopa was born, see Dorje 2009, 238–39.
106. *Sman dpyad yan lag brgyad pa.*
107. *Lam rim.*
108. See Roerich 1949, 453.
109. This would be King Tsede (Rtse lde) of Ngari, a descendant of Namde Osung and son of Ode Jangchub-o, who lived from c. 1057–90. See the family tree illustrated in Davidson 2005, 69.
110. See Roerich 1949, 453.
111. See Pawo Tsuklak Trengwa 1962, 402.
112. See Chan 1994, 254.
113. See Pawo Tsuklak Trengwa 1962, 402–3.
114. See Mila Repa 1999, 626.
115. Cf. Roerich 1949, 455–56.
116. Our text misreads *stobs*, "power," for *thabs*, "means."
117. As stated in Pawo Tsuklak Trengwa 1962, 403, these are (1) the lapse into securing emptiness (*stong nyid rgyas 'debs su shor ba*) when one assertively meditates that all mental objects are emptiness, (2) the lapse into emptiness as the fundamental nature of knowable phenomena (*stong nyid shes bya'i gshis*

la shor ba) when one asserts that all things of cyclic existence and nirvāṇa are emptiness, (3) the lapse into emptiness as an antidote (*stong nyid gnyen por shor ba*) when one beholds the afflicted mental states and thoughts that arise and asserts that these are emptiness, and (4) the lapse into emptiness as nihilism (*stong nyiod chad ltar shor ba*) when one asserts that now one is without meditation.

118. See Pawo Tsuklak Trengwa 1962, 403.
119. The text reads *'khor stong*, whereas Pawo Tsuklak Trengwa (1961, 403) simply reads *'khor*.
120. Our text reads *bden bden gyi 'khor lo*, whereas Pawo Tsuklak Trengwa (1961, 403) reads *spyi bo'i 'khor lo*.
121. See Pawo Tsuklak Trengwa 1962, 404.
122. See Pawo Tsuklak Trengwa 1962, 404.
123. See Pawo Tsuklak Trengwa 1962, 404.
124. That is to say, it had not yet been transformed into the vital energy of pristine cognition (*ye shes kyi rlung*).
125. As described in *The Discourse on the Particularly Extensive Former Aspirations of the Seven Tathāgatas*, better known as *The Discourse of the Medicine Buddhas in Eight Hundred Lines*, these are Sunāmaparikīrtanaśrī (Mtshan legs yongs bsgrags dpal), Ratnacandrarāja (Rin chen zla ba), Suvarṇabhadravimalaprabhāsa (Gser bzang dri med snang), Aśokottoma (Mya ngan med mchog), Dharmakīrtisāgaraghoṣa (Chos bsgrags rgya mtsho'i dbyangs), Abhijñārāja (Mngon mkhyen rgyal po), and Bhaiṣajyaguru (Sman bla). See the description in Dorje 2014, 136.
126. See Pawo Tsuklak Trengwa 1962, 404; and Roerich 1949, 456–57.
127. See Pawo Tsuklak Trengwa 1962, 404.
128. See Pawo Tsuklak Trengwa 1962, 405.
129. The lacunae supplied by the editors of the Tibetan text and in this translation can be found in Mila Repa 1999, 645–48. The exact wording corresponds to the aforementioned *Biography of Glorious Choje Gampopa*. Our text suggests there were twenty-four rather than forty-two dream signs.
130. Our text here reads *mang dres* for *ma dres*.
131. This is missing in the Tibetan text.
132. Our text reads *sred pa*, "craving," for *srid pa*.
133. See Pawo Tsuklak Trengwa 1962, 405.
134. On Nyel (Gnyal) in Lhuntse County, see Dorje 2009, 239.
135. On Olka and Mount Ode Gungyel in Zangri County, see Akester 2016, 382–93; and Dorje 2009, 263–64.
136. This is Daklha Gampo, the site of his future monastery, in the environs of Gampodar, where Karma Lingpa is said to have revealed *The Tibetan Book of the Dead*. See Akester 2016, 394–401; and Dorje 2009, 267.
137. This is illustrated in Jikme Chokyi Dorje 2001, 290.
138. This form of Mahākala is alternately spelled *tra kṣad* and *trak shad*. Gyurme

renders the former Trakṣad and the latter Trakshe, and this difference has been preserved here.—Ed.

139. According to Dungkar Rinpoche (2002, 1586), these are attending to horses, cattle, birds, dogs, noncloven hoofed animals (*rmig zlum*), and wild beasts, as well as relationships with nuns, irreligious talk, meat, alcohol, and sex. Alternatively, they could denote the eight worldly concerns (*'jig rten gyi chos brgyad*).

140. The twelve ascetic virtues (*dvādaśadhūtaguṇa, sbyangs pa'i yon tan bcu gnyis*) are wearing clothing from a dust heap, owning only three robes, wearing felt or woolen clothes, begging for food, eating one's meal at a single sitting, restricting the quantity of food, staying in solitude, sitting under trees, sitting in exposed places, sitting in charnel grounds, sitting even during sleep, and staying wherever one happens to be. For the Sanskrit and Tibetan terms, see *MVT*, 127–39; and Dudjom Rinpoche 1991, 2:169.

141. Zangri County, on which see Akester 2016, 377–78; and Dorje 2009, 261–62.

142. The ten total consummations are (1) the total consummation of the earth element, (2) the total consummation of the water element, (3) the total consummation of the fire element, (4) the total consummation of the wind element, (5) the total consummation of the space element, (6) the total consummation of blueness, (7) the total consummation of yellowness, (8) the total consummation of redness, (9) the total consummation of whiteness, and (10) the total consummation of consciousness. For a detailed explanation in the context of meditative concentration, see Ñāṇamoli 1979, 122–84.

143. This narrative is derived from the aforementioned *Biography of Glorious Choje Gampopa*. Gampopa interprets the dream before Gyelwa Khyungtsang has an opportunity to make a full report, rebuking those Kadampa masters who disparaged his teachings.

144. These three men from Kham are the most famous disciples of Gampopa—First Karmapa, Dusum Khyenpa (1110–1193), who founded Karma Gon in Chamdo and Tsurphu in Tolung Dechen County; Phakmodrupa Dorje Gyelpo, who founded Densatil Monastery in Zangri County; and Selton Shogom, who founded Lho Miyel Monastery in Nangchen.

145. Dakpo Gomtsul Tsultrim Nyingpo (1116–1169) was the nephew of Gampopa, who took charge of Daklha Gampo monastery after the death of his uncle.

146. Barompa Darma Wangchuk (c. 1127–1194) was the founder of Barom Monastery in Nakchu.

147. Cf. Roerich 1949, 462ff.

148. There are extensive biographies of Phakmodrupa by Drigung Rinchen Pel and by Gyeltangpa Dechen Dorje. Abridged versions are found in Roerich 1949, 552–65; Pawo Tsuklak Trengwa 1962, 412–25; and Davidson 2004, 333–34.

149. *Snyan brgyud yid bzhin nor bu.*

150. Āryaśūra, *Jātakamālā, Skyes pa'i rabs kyi rgyud* (Toh. 4150; Dg.T. skyes rab, *hu*, ff. 1b–135a).

151. See Speyer 1895, 218–27, 244–53.
152. Cf. Pawo Tsuklak Trengwa 1962, 416. The Chinese emperor could perhaps be the third emperor of the Tang dynasty, Tang Gaozong (628–683), whose personal name was Li Zhi.
153. *Gsang ba'i de kho na nyid.*
154. Gayadhara (994–1043) introduced the Path and Its Fruit to Drokmi Lotsāwa, Kālacakrapāda the Younger was a key lineage holder of the *Kālacakra Tantra*, and Ame Jangchub (1015–1077) maintained the lineage of Atiśa.
155. On the Mesho valley in Kham, see Dorje 2009, 582–84.
156. See Roerich 1949, 553; and Pawo Tsuklak Trengwa 1962, 412–13.
157. See Roerich 1949, 554; and Pawo Tsuklak Trengwa 1962, 413.
158. A renowned Kadampa master (1091–1166).
159. The preeminent logician Chapa Chokyi Senge (1109–1069) of Sangphu. See Davidson 2004, 180–81.
160. Among these Kadampa masters, on Jayulwa (1075–1138), see Roerich 1949, 286–91.
161. Go Khukpa Lhatse (fl. eleventh century) was an important lineage holder of the *Guhyasamāja*. On his rivalry with Ra Lotsāwa and also with the Zur family exponents of Guhyagarbha, see Davidson 2004, 139–40, 152–53. Bari Lotsāwa (c. 1040–1112) was a custodian of Sakya and compiler-translator of *The Hundred Means for Attainment* (*Grub thabs rgya rtsa*). See Davidson 2004 297–99.
162. *Gdams ngag zab dgu.*
163. Sachen Kunga Nyingpo (1092–1158), the first of the five patriarchs of Sakya. See Jamgon Amezhab Ngawang Kunga Sonam 1986, 20–63; and on his life and legacy, Davidson 2004, 293–315. On the formulation of the Path and Its Fruit (Lam 'bras), see Davidson 2004, 178–94.
164. See Roerich 1949, 556; and Pawo Tsuklak Trengwa 1962, 413. The path of insight (*darśanamārga, mthong lam*)—the third of the five paths (accumulation, connection, insight, cultivation, and no-more-learning) is characterized by knowledge of phenomena (*dharmajñāna, chos shes pa*) and subsequent knowledge (*anvayajñāna, rjes su rtogs pa'i shes pa*) with respect to each of the four noble truths.
165. Cf. Roerich 1949, 557.
166. *A ro'i chos skor.*
167. *Thim pa rnam gsum.*
168. *Kha rag skor gsum.*
169. *Khyad chos rnam brgyad.*
170. On Kharak Gomchung and Aro Yeshe Jungne, see Roerich 1949, 999–1004. On the inspirational teachings of the latter concerning the mind class of the Great Perfection, see Patrul Rinpoche 2016.
171. See Roerich 1949, 557; and Pawo Tsuklak Trengwa 1962, 413. On Machik Zhama (1062–1149), see Davidson 2004, 291–93.

172. Tsāmi Lotsāwa Sangye Drak of Xixia and Ga Lotsāwa Zhonu Pel (1110–1198) are significant for the introduction of *Kālacakra* and for the cycles of *Mahākāla*. See Davidson 2004, 281, 333–34.
173. Sbyor ba yan lag drug pa.
174. See Roerich 1949, 555–56, and on Khampa Aseng, 386, 734, 736.
175. The quotation *'di las mi 'da'o* is cited in a few sources.
176. See Pawo Tsuklak Trengwa 1962, 413.
177. See Roerich 1949, 558–59; and Pawo Tsuklak Trengwa 1962, 413–14.
178. *khrigs kad de ba*. Translation marked as uncertain.—Ed.
179. See Roerich 1949, 559; and Pawo Tsuklak Trengwa 1962, 414.
180. Cf. Pawo Tsuklak Trengwa 1962, 414.
181. On the geomantic temple of Tsi Nesar in Gyantse County, see Akester 2016, 498–500; Aris 1979, 25; and Dorje 2009, 313.
182. *Zhi byed rmang lam ma* (in *Collected Works of Phakmodrupa*, vol. *nga*, ff. 146a–156b).
183. *Zab don gcod kyi skor*. On Machik Labdron (c. 1055–1149) and the Cycle of Severance, see Harding 2013 and 2016; and Davidson 2004, 290–93.
184. See Pawo Tsuklak Trengwa 1962, 416: *tshal bu'i rdor 'debs ma myong*. This suggests a fat- or meat-based seasoning.
185. Our text reads *reg pa*, "touch," for *rig pa*.
186. On Gampopa's integration of sūtra and mantra approaches to the Great Seal, see Davidson 2004, 286–90.
187. Za ma he.
188. Based on the date and the initial syllable *za* alone, this figure may be identifiable with Song Gaozong (1127–1187), the tenth emperor of the Song dynasty, and first of the southern Song, who reigned from 1162. His personal name was Zhao Gou.
189. Our text misreads *rnol zla* for *snron zla*.
190. See Pawo Tsuklak Trengwa 1962, 416, with slight variants.
191. See Roerich 1949, 563; and Pawo Tsuklak Trengwa 1962, 417.
192. Kun ldan gtsang pa ras chung.
193. Zwa ra'i skal ldan ye shes seng ge.
194. Mi nyag sgom rings.
195. Grub thob nyag re se bo.
196. Cf. Roerich 1949, 563–65; and Pawo Tsuklak Trengwa 1962, 416–17.
197. The first four lines allude respectively to Marpa, Mila Repa, Gampopa, and Phakmodrupa.
198. *rnam pa bzhi'i yon tan*. Yet to be identified.
199. *'phrul 'khor*.
200. The text reads *las kyi tsa ṇi ḍa* for *las kyi caṇḍālī*. The blissful female channel is known as *vasudharā* (*nor 'dzin ma*).

8. The Biographies of the Taklung Kagyu Lineage

1. Maṅgalaśrī, or Tashi Pel (Bkra shis dpal, "Auspicious Glory"), is the personal name of Taklungpa the Great (1142–1210), who founded the monastery of Taklung Upper Plain in 1180. As mentioned on p. 182, our author compiled the hagiography of Taklungpa the Great from three extant accounts to which he had access. These were composed respectively by Kuyalwa Rinpoche, Gompa Tsultrim Pel, and Tashi Peltsek. He also consulted Tatsak Tse Wangyel's *Doctrinal History of Lhorong* (*Lho rong chos 'byung*; 1994, 453–492), and his own more detailed composition titled *Springtime of the Excellently Flourishing Cornucopia of Devout Tales* (*Gtam mos gus kyi snye ma dge legs su mngon par dar ba'i dpyid*), which is based on *The Great Biography* (*Rnam thar chen mo*). Abridged biographies are also found in Roerich 1949, 610–27; and Pawo Tsuklak Trengwa 1962, 425–26. He is revered as the first hierarch of the abbatial succession (*gdan rabs*) of Taklung.
2. The bolded terms, followed by Tibetan transliteration, represent the meaning of the names of the master who is being praised in the verse.—Ed.
3. Here, the main building of Taklung Upper Plain is likened to a palatial tower (*ba gam 'bum*), its monastic community perfectly endowed with the three higher trainings (*lhag pa'i bslab gsum*) of ethical discipline, mental cultivation and discriminative awareness, the generation and perfection stages of meditation and activities imbued with the seven precious things (*rin chen bdun*)—that is, the symbols of royal authority in ancient India, which are the precious wheel, the precious queen, the precious minister, the precious elephant, the precious horse, and the precious general.
4. That is to say, the lineage of profound view stemming from Nāgārjuna, the lineage of vast conduct stemming from Asaṅga, and Tilopā's lineage of inner realization all converged in Gampopa Sonam Rinchen, on whom see p. 129.
5. This refers to the disciples of Gampopa, including Phakmodrupa Dorje Gyelpo, on whom see p. 140.
6. The eight pure qualities of water (*yan lag brgyad ldan dag pa'i chab*) are sweetness, coolness, gentleness, lightness, clarity, purity, the quality of not aggravating the throat, and the quality of benefiting the stomach.
7. It has been suggested that this is an oblique reference to 1273 (water bird), the year when Taklung Sangye On set out for Kham to found the monastery of Taklung Lower Plain at Riwoche.
8. *Karuṇāpuṇḍarikasūtra*, *'Phags pa snying rje chen po'i pad+ma dkar po zhes bya ba theg pa chen po'i mdo* (KPD 50), 217.
9. Shing kun skye ba.
10. See Akester 2016, 37; and Dorje 2009, 175.
11. Phodo Dudul Temple (Phod mdo bdud 'dul gyi gtsug lag khang) at Phodo Dzong, on which see Akester 2016, 35; and Dorje 2009, 176.

12. On the construction of the Main Temple (Gtsug lag khang chen mo) of Taklung by Kuyalwa Rinchen Gonpo, see p. 204.
13. Roruka may be identified with the capital of the Sauviras. See Edgerton 1953, 457.
14. The kingdom of Kaliṅga, corresponding to modern Oḍiviśa (Orissa) in East India, was conquered by the Mauryan emperor Aśoka in the eighth year of his reign—an act of total brutality and devastation that subsequently turned him toward the practice of dharma. See Buswell and Lopez 2014, 408–9. The association of the tooth relic with Dantapura, capital of Kaliṅga, is well documented. However, Sinhalese sources claim that this tooth relic was brought to Śrī Laṅkā during the reign of Sirimeghavana. On the life of Ga Lotsāwa Namgyel Dorje (1203–1282), see Roerich 1949, 789–90.
15. Concerning the establishment of the Great Offering Ceremony (Mchod pa chen po) for the sacred tooth relic by Choku Sangye Yarjon, see p. 220.
16. *Karuṇāpuṇḍarikasūtra, 'Phags pa snying rje chen po'i pad+ma dkar po zhes bya ba theg pa chen po'i mdo* (KPD 50), 217–18.
17. Cf. Dorje 2017, 520n542.
18. Phakmodrupa Dorje Gyelpo 2003, 199–214.
19. Citation not found.
20. See p. 39.
21. In this passage, the attributes of Taklungpa the Great are mentioned in ascending numeric order. Among them, the category of two includes the attributes of subjective understanding and objective knowledge, as well as the two attributes of skillful means and discriminative awareness. The three indestructible realities (*rdo rje gsum*) are those of buddha body, speech, and mind. The four buddha bodies (*sku bzhi*) are those of reality, perfect resource, emanation, and essentiality. The five pristine cognitions (*ye shes lnga*) are the pristine cognition of reality's expanse, the mirrorlike pristine cognition, the pristine cognition of sameness, the pristine cognition of discernment, and the pristine cognition of accomplishment. The seven worlds (*'jig rten bdun*) that he transcended are either the six realms along with the intermediate state or else the three lower realms along with the gods and humans of the realm of desire and the two sorts of gods associated with the higher realms of form and formlessness. The noble eightfold path (*aṣṭaṅgāryamārga, 'phags pa'i lam yan lag brgyad*; see *MVT*, 996–1004) is composed of correct view, correct thought, correct speech, correct activities, correct livelihood, correct effort, correct recollection, and correct meditative stability. The nine branches of the scriptures (*yan lag dgu dang ldan pa'i gsung rabs*) are discourses (*sūtra, mdo sde*), sayings in prose and verse (*geya, dbyangs bsnyad*), prophetic declarations (*vyākaraṇa, lung bstan*), verses (*gāthā, tshig bcad*), aphorisms (*udāna, ched brjod*), legends or frame stories (*nidāna, gleng gzhi*), extensive teachings (*mahāvaipulya, shin tu rgyas pa*), marvelous events (*adbhutadharma, rmad du byung*), and estab-

lished instructions (*upadeśa, gtab phab*), while excluding tales of past lives (*jātaka, skyes rabs*), narratives (*avadāna, rtogs brjod*), and fables (*itivṛttaka, de lta bu byung ba*). See the analysis offered in Buton 1988, 17–18. For a detailed discussion on the ten bodhisattva levels, see Dayal 1932, 270–91; and Williams 1989, 204–14. The twelve aspects of the four truths (*bden don rnam pa bcu gnyis*) are the four noble truths of suffering, its cause, its cessation, and the path leading to cessation, as they are respectively experienced in the contexts of the three realms of desire, form, and formlessness. See Nordrang Orgyen 2008, 2735. The sixteen aspects of the four truths (*de nyid rnam pa bcu drug*) are enumerated in Dudjom Rinpoche 1991, 2:173–74. Cf. Jamgon Kongtrul's explanation in Callahan 2007, 115–19. The twenty modalities of enlightenment (*rnam pa nyi shus mngon par byang chub pa*) are either the twenty aspects of emptiness; or the five pristine cognitions in terms of skillful means, discriminative awareness, physical analysis, and mental analysis; or the ten gross and ten subtle winds in terms of their movement and cessation; or the six cakras with the addition of the twelve cakras of the joints of the limbs and two located at the space between the eyebrows and below the navel. See Nordrang Orgyen 2008, 3085–86. The maṇḍala of the hundred enlightened families (*rigs brgya'i dkyil 'khor*) is that of the peaceful and wrathful deities of the *Guhyagarbha*, on which see Dorje 2005 and Dorje 2016.

22. The three upland regions of Dokham (Mdo khams sgang gsum) are identified as Tsawagang, Puborgang, and Markhamgang. To Kuyung Gang (Stod ku g.yung sgang) appears to be equivalent to Markhamgang. See Tatsak Tse Wangyel (1994, 454), where it is said that Upper Yangsho Bongra (G.yang shod bong ra stod) is located in a side valley of the Yangtze within Markhamgang. As the following narratives reveal, this is the ancestral place of several early hierarchs of Upper Taklung.
23. Bongra Tengka (Bong ra steng ka) in Yangsho (G.yang shod) is located on the Yangtze side of Markhamgang. I have not yet been able to place it in either present-day Markham or Gonjo counties.
24. The Gazi clan into which Taklungpa the Great was born has been influential at Taklung thorough the centuries.
25. This is Tangkya in the Markhamgang area, perhaps the site of the well-known Sakya Monastery of Tangkya (Thang skya) in Gonjo County, on which see Dorje 2009, 571; and Gruschke 2004, 117–18.
26. Roerich (1949, 610) mentions that he had to overcome his father's resistance to receive ordination and that the father later requested him not be placed at the end of the row.
27. Yaśomitra, *Abhidharmakośasphuṭārthā, Chos mngon pa'i mdzod kyi 'grel bshad* (Toh. 4092; Dg.T. mngon pa, *gu*, ff. 1b–330a, *ngu*, ff. 1b–333a).
28. The narrative that follows would suggest that Drakgon (Drag dgon) was located in Kham.
29. *Zhi byed sgron ma rnam gsum.*

30. Kolti (Kol ti) is a location in the east of Tibet, where conflict had to be pacified.
31. Mok Cholo (Rmog chos blo) is known to have corresponded with Phakmodrupa—the latter's advice and instructions to Mok are contained in the Collected Works of Phakmodrupa. The dates may suggest an identification with Mok Rinchen Tsondru (Rmog rin chen brtson 'grus, 1110–1170)—the disciple and lineage holder of the Shangpa tradition of Khyungpo Neljor, on whom see Roerich 1949, 733–37.
32. *Rnal 'byor ma'i gsang ba'i mtha' dpal sdom drug pa.*
33. *Gsang ba bdud rtsi'i phreng ba.*
34. This dream is recounted in Roerich 1949, 612; and Pawo Tsuklak Trengwa 1962, 425.
35. See Roerich 1949, 612; and Pawo Tsuklak Trengwa 1962, 425.
36. See Roerich 1949, 612–13; and Pawo Tsuklak Trengwa 1962, 425–26.
37. Jayulwa Zhonu-o (1075–1138), the disciple of Tsultrim Bar (1038–1103), as mentioned, is revered as a previous incarnation of Taklungpa the Great.
38. See Roerich 1949, 613; and Pawo Tsuklak Trengwa 1962, 426.
39. See Roerich 1949, 614; and Pawo Tsuklak Trengwa 1962, 426.
40. Snyan brgyud yid bzhin gyi nor bu'i bskor.
41. Gnas lugs phyag rgya chen po lhan cig skyes sbyor gyi bskor.
42. Bde stong phyag rgya chen po na ro chos drug gi bskor.
43. Gnyis su med pa'i rgyud dpal dus kyi 'khor lo'i bskor.
44. Rje bstun rdo rje rnal 'byor ma'i bskor.
45. Snying po dgyes pa rdo rje'i bskor.
46. Bka' srung can gyi gdan bzhi'i bskor.
47. Ma rgyud ma hā mā yā'i bskor.
48. Thabs rgyud 'dus pa dang gshin rje'i gshed kyi bskor.
49. 'Phags pa 'jig rten dbang phyug gi bskor.
50. Rgyal yum sgrol ma'i bskor.
51. 'Phags ma gdugs dkar.
52. Phyag na rdo rje.
53. Dpal rta mgrin.
54. Khro rgyal mi g.yo ba.
55. Rnam 'joms.
56. Sme brtsegs.
57. 'Jam dbyangs.
58. Tshe dpag.
59. Klu dbang rgyal po.
60. Ri khrod ma.
61. 'Od zer can.
62. Gtsug gtor rnam rgyal.
63. Khyung khra.
64. Ku ru kulli.

65. Mkha' 'gro sde lnga.
66. Bstan srung rgya mtsho'i ded dpon bya rog ma.
67. Dpal ldan dud sol lha mo.
68. Byin rlabs kyi mgon po phyag drug pa.
69. Yon tan gyi dgon po gri gug ma.
70. 'Phrin las gyi dgon po ta kṣa ra.
71. Rgyal chen rnam sras.
72. A pa ra tsitta.
73. Dzam bha la.
74. Tshogs bdag.
75. Mchod sbyin gtor ma'i bskor.
76. Mthun rkyen bcud len gyi bskor.
77. Phar phyin theg pa'i lam rim.
78. Sngags kyi bskyed rdzogs kha 'thor ba'i bye brag brgya rtsa gcig.
79. Yongs su ma grags pa mtshan brjod kyi bskor.
80. *Ye shes snang ba dam pa'i rgyan.*
81. Mngon pa sde bdun.
82. Tshad ma sde bdun.
83. Dbu ma rigs pa'i tshogs drug.
84. Byams pa'i chos lnga.
85. The three sublime levels are those of pious attendants, hermit buddhas, and bodhisattvas.
86. The eight great accomplishments (*grub chen brgyad*), otherwise known as the eight great common accomplishments (*thun mong gi grub chen brgyad*), are the enchanted sword, the enchanted eye salve, swiftfootedness, invisibility, extrasensory powers, elixir extraction, sky faring, and frequenting of the levels. See Nordrang Orgyen 2008, 1801. On Mangkar Gang in southern Lhartse County, see Akester 2016, 596–603; Dorje 2009, 351–52; and Chen 1994, 890–94.
87. See Roerich 1949, 616.
88. See Roerich 1949, 614; and Pawo Tsuklak Trengwa 1962, 426. Chekhawa (1101–1175) was a renowned Kadampa geshe. On the Meldro valley, see Dorje 2009, 178; and Akester 2016, 162.
89. See Roerich 1949, 614–15. On the Phodo region, see Akester 2016, 35; and Dorje 2009, 176. Tango (Thang mgo) appears to be located opposite Reteng Monastery (see www.tibetmap.com).
90. The site of Taklungpa's hermitage, also known as Sele Gotsang. See Akester 2016, 36.
91. See Akester 2016, 36n28.
92. This is the local protector deity of Taklung Monastery.
93. Not yet identified.
94. Not yet identified.
95. *Zhal gdams gyi zin bris.*

96. Not yet identified.
97. See Roerich 1949, 615. Sangye Gompa Tsultrim Sherab (1284–1338) appears to have been the tenth in the abbatial succession of Jayul, but the given dates for him are surely wrong.
98. The three ways of pleasing a teacher (*mnyes pa gsum*) are material offerings, offerings of service, and devotion to spiritual practice.
99. See Roerich 1949, 615; and Pawo Tsuklak Trengwa 1962, 426.
100. See Roerich 1949, 615.
101. See Roerich 1949, 615–16. Tatsak Tse Wangyel 1994, 465–66. On the renowned Kadampa master Potowa Rinchen Sel (1027–1105), see Roerich 1949, 268ff; and Davidson 2004, 250–55. On Kharak Gomchung Wangchuk Lodro (fl. eleventh century), see Roerich 1949, 1001–4.
102. See Tatsak Tse Wangyel 1994, 466–67. Lama Da-o (Zla 'od) would be the younger brother of Taklungpa the Great—Lenka Parko (Glan ka phar bsko).
103. The three unforgettable recollections (*mi brjed par dran pa gsum*) are those of the spiritual teacher, the monastic vows, and death. See Roerich 1949, 616.
104. Cf. Tatsak Tse Wangyel 1994, 467, which mentions only Kham.
105. Among these six, Ojo appears to be close to Sengling. Uma and Sewalung are in neighboring Damzhung County. Lang appears to be south of Taklung. I have not yet identified Parti.
106. Dar (Dar), Tre (Spras) and Rong (Rong) are the names of valleys in upper Penyul, lying to the west and north of Ganden Chungkor in present-day Lhundrub County. See Akester 2016, 37n31, and the map on pp. 47–48. This conflict and its resolution are mentioned in Roerich 1949, 617–18. Cf. Tatsak Tse Wangyel 1994, 467.
107. On the Main Temple (Gtsug lag khang chen mo), or Ancient Offering Chapel (Mchod rnying), see Akester 2016, 37n32, and the description on pp. 42–43. On the White Temple of Precious Spiritual and Temporal Well-Being and its annexes (*zhal dkar/skar rin po che phan bde rtsa lag*), also known as Zhelre Lhakhang (Zhal ras lha khang), see Akester 2016, 41. On the Red Teaching Throne (Sa khri dmar po), see Akester 2016, 37n33.
108. *Gsol 'debs rin chen byon legs ma.*
109. *Sa bon rin chen.*
110. See Tatsak Tse Wangyel 1994, 469.
111. See Roerich 1949, 620.
112. *Sdom pa gsum phyag rgya chen por gnad gcig pa'i grub mtha'.*
113. The first two categories, natural offenses (*prakṛtisāvadaya, rang bzhin gyi kha na ma tho ba*) and prohibitions (*pratikṣepaṇasāvadaya, bcas kyi kha na ma thob ba*), are specifically for monastics, the former including the five defeats and the latter including technical offenses concerning eating, deportment, and so on. The third category of mundane inadmissible transgressions (*laukikasāvadaya, 'jig rten gyi kha na ma tho ba*) includes the ten unvirtuous actions as generally understood.

114. Not yet identified.
115. Not yet identified.
116. Here "outer phenomena" denotes the external world, "inner phenomena" denotes the subtle adamantine body of the yogin, and "extraneous phenomena" denotes the maṇḍala circle. See Thupten Phuntsok 2013, 2062.
117. Cf. Roerich 1949, 619.
118. That is to say, the Collected Works of Taklung Tangpa the Great were collated by the author of our text, Taklungpa Ngawang Namgyel.
119. *Dri za'i rgyal po zur phud lnga pa.*
120. Not yet identified.
121. Not yet identified.
122. Roerich (1949, 620–21) suggests that relations with Drigungpa were not always ideal. For example, they appear to have disagreed over the roofing of the monastery at Densatil and the keeping of sacred texts there.
123. The life of Tsangpa Gyare Yeshe Dorje (1161–1211) is presented in Roerich 1949, 664–70.
124. Probably this is the renowned Asura Cave at Yanglesho in Nepal, although Tatsak Tse Wangyel (1994, 471) suggests it is in India.
125. See Roerich 1949, 620–21.
126. *Gtam mos gus kyi snye ma dge legs su mngon par dar ba'i dpyid.*
127. *Rnam thar chen mo.*
128. See Tatsak Tse Wangyel 1994, 470. Only four of these eight—Kuyalwa Rinchen Gonpo, Ago Zhikpo, Jamyang Dzase, and Jori Repa are mentioned in the narrative that follows.
129. On the life of Kuyalwa Rinpoche Rinchen Gonpo, see p. 197.
130. A more extensive biography of Ago Zhikpo is found in Tatsak Tse Wangyel 1994, 585–609.
131. Puborgang is the highland region of Kham that separates the lower Yangtze to the west from the lower Yalong to the east. As such, it includes the present-day counties of Pelyul, Batang, Litang, and Dabpa. See Dorje 2009, 458.
132. Lijiang (Ljang yul), the homeland of the Naxi, traditionally extends as far north as Tsakalho in Markham County. According to Tatsak Tse Wangyel (1994, 585), the rich man is said to hail from the southern borderlands (*lho phyogs kyi mtha'*), and there is an annotation suggesting that may be Dzayul, rather than Lijiang, as stated in our text.
133. This parable is recounted in detail in Tatsak Tse Wangyel 1994, 586–87.
134. This parable is explained in Tatsak Tse Wangyel 1994, 587–88.
135. See the detailed explanation in Tatsak Tse Wangyel 1994, 588–90.
136. See Tatsak Tse Wangyel 1994, 590–91.
137. See Tatsak Tse Wangyel 1994, 591.
138. Tatsak Tse Wangyel 1994, 596, reads *rdo ngar ba.*
139. This encounter with the five girls is detailed in Tatsak Tse Wangyel 1994, 591–96.

140. See Tatsak Tse Wangyel 1994, 596–97, recounts his travels in Gyelmorong, Lijiang, and Nyarong.
141. *Gsang bdud rtsi'i phreng ba.*
142. See Tatsak Tse Wangyel 1994, 596–97.
143. See Tatsak Tse Wangyel 1994, 599–600.
144. See Tatsak Tse Wangyel 1994, 605.
145. See Tatsak Tse Wangyel 1994, 606.
146. Our text reads *yul gyi bud med*. Tatsak Tse Wangyel 1994, 606, reads *grong pa'i bud med.*
147. See Tatsak Tse Wangyel 1994, 607–8.
148. See Tatsak Tse Wangyel 1994, 608.
149. Tatsak Tse Wangyel 1994, 609, also lists his principal disciples.
150. *Rin chen sku ma dbyangs kyi rta.*
151. The life of Dzam Dzase is summarized in Tatsak Tse Wangyel 1994, 609.
152. The biography of Jori Repa (b. 1163) is included in Tatsak Tse Wangyel 1994, 609–17.
153. Tatsak Tse Wangyel (1994, 610) adds that he received this cycle from his own father at Shuklung Gonpa.
154. See Tatsak Tse Wangyel 1994, 611.
155. See Tatsak Tse Wangyel 1994, 611.
156. Tatsak Tse Wangyel (1994, 612) suggests that this teacher was named Gomyal (Slob dpon Sgom yal).
157. Our text reads *rang bzhin gnyis kyi don*, "the meaning of the two natures," whereas Tatsak Tse Wangyel 1994, 612, correctly reads *rang bzhan gnyis gyi don.*
158. He passed four years at Sewalung and eleven years at Taklung. See Tatsak Tse Wangyel 1994, 612.
159. See Tatsak Tse Wangyel 1994, 613.
160. See Tatsak Tse Wangyel 1994, 614. Nenang, or Kampo Nenang, is the location of Lengu Gonpa, the seat of Karmapa Dusum Khyenpa, founded in 1165. It is located in Litang County; see Dorje 2009, 540.
161. See Tatsak Tse Wangyel 1994, 615.
162. See Tatsak Tse Wangyel 1994, 616–17. These places are in Markhamgang, but I have not yet been able to locate them.
163. Only the life of Rechen Bom Gonpa is described here. See also Tatsak Tse Wangyel 1994, 620–26. The biographies of the other two, Senge Gyeltsen and Sumbu Sertsang, have not been located.
164. See Tatsak Tse Wangyel 1994, 620–21.
165. Tatsak Tse Wangyel (1994, 622) says that in this way he averted the signs of death.
166. See Tatsak Tse Wangyel 1994, 622–23.
167. See Tatsak Tse Wangyel 1994, 623–24.
168. See Tatsak Tse Wangyel 1994, 625–26.

169. These four "heart sons" (*thugs sras*) are mentioned briefly in Tatsak Tse Wangyel 1994, 470–71.
170. *Kun spangs zhen pa rang grol.*
171. See Tatsak Tse Wangyel 1994, 471.
172. See Tatsak Tse Wangyel 1994, 471.
173. The lives of these three lineage holders are recounted in *The Blue Annals*. Among them, on Drigungpa Jikten Sumgon, also known as Rinchen Pel (1143–1217), see Roerich 1949, 596–601. On Tsangpa Gyare (1161–1211), see Roerich 1949, 664–70; and on Trophu Lotsāwa Jampa Pel (1173–1225), see Roerich 1949, 708–11.
174. The monastery of Jang Barom (Byang 'ba' rom) was founded by Barompa Drama Wangchuk (1127–1197).
175. Selton Gomsho (Gsal stong sgom sho), otherwise known as Selton Shogom, was one of the three men from Kham who were Gampopa's principal disciples.
176. See Tatsak Tse Wangyel 1994, 617.
177. Sbyor drug.
178. See Tatsak Tse Wangyel 1994, 617–20.
179. Kyergangpa (Skyer sgang pa) Chokyi Senge (1154–1217) was a disciple of Mokchokpa and an important lineage holder of the Shangpa Kagyu tradition. See Roerich 1949, 737–41.
180. Not yet identified.
181. On the line of the Pawo Tulkus of Nenang near Tsurphu, see the chart in Douglas and White 1976. The most renowned was Pawo Tsuklak Trengwa (1504–1566), whose *Doctrinal History Titled Scholars' Feast* (*Mkhas pa'i dga' ston*) is a key historical source utilized by Taklung Ngawang Namgyel, the author of our text.
182. Rinchen Gonpo is the personal name of the second hierarch of Taklung, Kuyalwa Rinpoche (1190–1236). As stated on p. 212, the author's principal source is *The Great Biography* (*Rnam thar chen mo*) composed by Duntso Gawa Loden Sherab. Cf. Tatsak Tse Wangyel 1994, 476–492; the abridged account in Roerich 1949, 621–27; and Pawo Tsuklak Trengwa 1962, 426. Like his predecessor and several hierarchs who would succeed him, Rinchen Gonpo was born at Bongra Tengka in Markhamgang.
183. See Tatsak Tse Wangyel 1994, 476–77.
184. See Roerich 1949, 621–22. The translation of "trifling" (*phrag phrug*) is marked as uncertain.—Ed.
185. See Roerich 1949, 622.
186. *Bslab btus.*
187. See Tatsak Tse Wangyel 1994, 477.
188. See Roerich 1949, 622.
189. See Roerich 1949, 622; and Tatsak Tse Wangyel 1994, 478.
190. See Roerich 1949, 622–23.
191. *Khrid kyi dmigs pa gsum.* See Tatsak Tse Wangyel 1994, 478.

192. See Roerich 1949, 623.
193. See Roerich 1949, 623.
194. See Roerich 1949, 623; and Tatsak Tse Wangyel 1994, 479.
195. See Roerich 1949, 623–24.
196. Our text misreads *yong dag* for *yon bdag*.
197. See Roerich 1949, 623.
198. The three non-separations (*mi 'bral ba gsum*) are the non-separation of the body from the deity, the non-separation of speech from mantra, and the non-separation of mind from meditative stability or reality (*chos nyid*).
199. According to Tatsak Tse Wangyel 1994, 481, this would have been in 1216 (fire male mouse).
200. The original manuscript is illegible at this point.
201. See Tatsak Tse Wangyel 1994, 481.
202. Roerich 1949, 624; and Tatsak Tse Wangyel 1994, 481–82.
203. See Tatsak Tse Wangyel 1994, 482.
204. See Roerich 1949, 624–625.
205. See Roerich 1949, 625.
206. See Roerich 1949, 625–626.
207. See Roerich 1949, 626.
208. The four groups are fully ordained monks and nuns, laymen and laywomen.
209. See Roerich 1949, 626.
210. See Roerich 1949, 626–27; Tatsak Tse Wangyel 1994, 487–88.
211. See Tatsak Tse Wangyel 1994, 488–89.
212. See Tatsak Tse Wangyel 1994, 489–90.
213. *thig khang*. Translation marked as uncertain.—Ed.
214. See Tatsak Tse Wangyel 1994, 490.
215. See Roerich 1949, 627; Tatsak Tse Wangyel 1994, 490–91.
216. The eight closest heirs (*nye sras brgyad*) are the foremost of the tenth-level bodhisattvas—namely, Kṣitigarbha, Vajrapāṇi, Ākāśagarbha, Avalokiteśvara, Maitreya, Nivāraṇaviṣkambhin, Samantabhadra, and Mañjuśrī. See their iconographic descriptions and symbolism in Dorje 2005 and Dorje 2017.
217. See Roerich 1949, 627; and Tatsak Tse Wangyel 1994, 491–92.
218. See Tatsak Tse Wangyel 1994, 492.
219. Phags pa rta mchog. This was marked in the text as uncertain, indicating either a place or Vārāhī and Hayagrīva.—Ed.
220. That is to say, his five subsequent reincarnations were First Zhamar, Drakpa Senge; Second Zhamar, Khacho Wangpo; Third Zhamar, Chophel Yeshe; Fourth Zhamar, Chenga Chodrak, the author of *The Blue Annals*; and Fifth Zhamar, Konchok Yenlak.
221. That would be Sixth Zhamar, Chokyi Wangchuk (1584–1630).
222. As stated on p. 228, the present hagiography of Sangye Yarjon (1203–1272) was compiled from his *Great Biography* (*Rnam thar chen mo*) based on the tradition of Taklung Lower Plain, composed by Dampa Rakye Drakpa Rinchen

Dorje, and the verses contained in *The Golden Rosary of Taklung Upper Plain* (*Tshigs bcad ma ya thang gi gser phreng du zhugs pa*), which was composed by Tokden Chenpo Tsangdar Dombuwa. See also Tatsak Tse Wangyel 1994, 492–507; Roerich 1949, 617–29; and Pawo Tsuklak Trengwa 1962, 426. His birthplace in Markhamgang is also the ancestral home of his two predecessors, and he was in fact a nephew of Kuyalwa Rinpoche.

223. See Tatsak Tse Wangyel 1994, 492–93.
224. See Roerich 1949, 627; Tatsak Tse Wangyel 1994, 493.
225. Saphu Gon (Sab phu dgon), according to Tatsak Tse Wangyel (1994, 493), is also called Bumbu Gon (Bum bu dgon), or Nag Gon (Nag dgon).
226. These four modes of conduct (*spyod lam rnam bzhi*) are walking, rising, sitting, and reclining. See Nordrang Orgyen 2008, 718–19.
227. See Tatsak Tse Wangyel 1994, 493–94, makes no mention of this potential conflict.
228. See Roerich 1949, 627; and Tatsak Tse Wangyel 1994, 494. Our text reads *'du 'dzin 'bum sde* for *'du 'dzin 'bum sde.*
229. See Tatsak Tse Wangyel 1994, 495.
230. See Tatsak Tse Wangyel 1994, 495.
231. See Tatsak Tse Wangyel 1994, 497.
232. The institutions of the monastic charter (*bca' khrims*) and its relationship to the vinaya rules of monastic discipline are discussed in Ter Ellingson 1990, 205–29.
233. These four great religious activities (*chen po ya bzhi*) are maṇḍala construction, mnemonic incantation, teaching, and ritual. See Nordrang Orgyen 2008, 583.
234. These astrological components entail calculations pertaining to the nine planets, the twenty-eight constellations, and twenty-seven conjunctions. On their names, permutations, and calculations, see Henning 2007 and the charts in the appendix to that work.
235. *yu can.* Translation marked as uncertain.—Ed.
236. *thog khar mi mi 'gro.* Translation marked as uncertain.—Ed.
237. See Tatsak Tse Wangyel 1994, 497.
238. This may be identified with the Mongol invasion of 1240 under the command of the generals Dorta Nakpo and Leje. See Shakabpa 1967, 61.
239. See Tatsak Tse Wangyel 1994, 498–499.
240. The translation of *sa gra stong par lus pa* is marked as uncertain.—Ed. See Tatsak Tse Wangyel 1994, 495–96.
241. *mtshan 'bum pa.*
242. Unidentified at present.
243. See Tatsak Tse Wangyel 1994, 500.
244. See Tatsak Tse Wangyel 1994, 500.
245. See Tatsak Tse Wangyel 1994, 500.
246. Aṅgita being one of the sixteen elders, on whom see p. 37.

247. The assumption here is that these artifacts had a past association with Putowa who formerly resided at Taklung prior to its foundation.
248. Our text misreads *rom pa* for *rong pa*.
249. *be'u ngos*. Translation marked as uncertain.—Ed.
250. See part 1, chap. 8, note 229.
251. See Tatsak Tse Wangyel 1994, 501–2.
252. This reference has not yet been found elsewhere. By forging an alliance with the Mongols and assuming the role of spiritual priest in the context of the newly established "patron-priest relationship," Sakya Paṇḍita (1182–1251), the fourth of the five founding hierarchs of Sakya, is credited by historians with warding off the destruction of Tibet that would otherwise have been inflicted upon it, as had occurred in neighboring Xixia (Minyak) in 1227. The illustrious Śākyaśrī, Great Scholar of Kashmir (Kha che paṇ chen, 1127–1225), is considered to have been the last abbot of Nālanda prior to its sacking by Islamic invaders in 1192. He visited Tibet from 1204 to 1214, traveling there extensively, and is revered as a seminal teacher of Sakya Paṇḍita and source of the Sakya tradition of Buddhist logic and epistemology.
253. Chogyel Phakpa Lodro Gyeltsen (1235–1280), the fifth of the five founding hierarchs of Sakya, was effectively ruler of Tibet due to the patronage of Qubilai Qaγan, who conferred upon him the title "national preceptor" (*guoshi*) in 1260 and "imperial preceptor" (*dishi*) in 1270.
254. Cf. Tatsak Tse Wangyel 1994, 502.
255. See Roerich 1949, 628; and Tatsak Tse Wangyel 1994, 502.
256. In 1260, Karma Pakshi (1204–1283), the second Karmapa, was burned at the stake by Qubilai Qaγan, who at that time saw him as a rival to Chogyel Phakpa. The flames reportedly burned for three days, but he remained unharmed and was subsequently exiled to Yunnan for ten years before returning to Central Tibet. The jade cup offered to Taklung by Karma Pakshi appears to be no longer extant.
257. On the stone columns at Tashido and the adjacent caves, see Dorje 2009, 16–167; and Chen 1994, 663–64.
258. See Tatsak Tse Wangyel 1994, 504–5; and Pawo Tsuklak Trengwa 1962, 426–27.
259. See Tatsak Tse Wangyel 1994, 506.
260. See Tatsak Tse Wangyel 1994, 506.
261. *Tshigs bcad ma ya thang gi gser phreng du zhugs pa*.
262. *Vajrāvali*, *Rdor phreng*.
263. Tokden Yeshe Wangchuk was a disciple of Karma Pakshi. See Roerich 1949, 517. Gotsangpa Gonpo Dorje (1189–1258) is revered as the founder of the Upper Drukpa school. See Roerich 1949, 680–88.
264. Nyingdrung (Snying drung) is located in Damzhung County on present-day Highway 109 between Damzhung County town and the Yangpachen intersection. See www.tibetmap.com.

265. The Tselpa (Mtshal pa) are the followers of Zhang Tselpa Tsondru Drak (1123–1193), who acted as sacristans of the Jokhang in Lhasa during the twelfth and thirteenth centuries. During the Sakya hegemony, Tselpa functioned as one of the thirteen myriarchs (*khri skor bcu gsum*) into which Utsang was then divided.
266. That is to say, in the time of Ngawang Namgyel. The location of this stūpa—called Naturally Arising Pure Vision (Mchod rten dag snang rang shar), presumably at Barle Drakmar near Mount Nyenchen Tangla—has not yet been identified.
267. On the life of Gyelwa Rinchen Pelzangpo, or Namgyel Rinchen Pelzangpo, the teacher of Ngawang Namgyel, see p. 410.
268. See p. 229.
269. See Roerich 1949, 652.
270. Cited in Roerich 1949, 651.
271. The text reads *mi gle ba* for *mi gla ba*.
272. *Rnam rgyal stong mchod*.
273. *Gtsug tor gyi rgyud*.
274. *Spu gri mched gsum*.
275. *trakṣad phye 'gam*.
276. Kongpo Darshe's stūpa at Taklung, extant in the time of Ngawang Namgyel, is no longer discernible at the present day.
277. This is probably either 1276 (fire mouse) or 1288 (earth mouse).
278. *'ud nag po*. Translation marked as uncertain.—Ed.
279. Kongpo is well known for its continuing affinity with the Bon religion. This is a richly forested region, composed of the valley of the Nyangchu (Gyamda county) and its wide confluence with the Yarlung Tsangpo (Menling and Nyangtri counties). On this region and its Bon sites including Mount Kongpo Bonri, see Dorje 2009, 274–92.
280. The middle plain (*thang 'bring*) is perhaps to be identified with the spacious confluence of the Nyangchu with the Yarlung Tsangpo.
281. Since this incident is not dated, the imperial envoys could have represented Qubilai Qaγan (r. 1260–1294) or one of his successors—either Temur Qaγan (r. 1294–1307) or Quluq Qaγan (r. 1308–1311).
282. Biographies of On Tashi Lama (1231–1297), the fourth hierarch of Taklung Upper Plain, are also found in Tatsak Tse Wangyel 1994, 546–54; and Roerich 1949, 629–32. See also Pawo Tsuklak Trengwa 1962, 426–27. He was born in the same location in Markhamgang as his uncle and predecessors.
283. The threefold approach to the setting of the mind on enlightenment (*sems bskyed gsum*) suggests that a bodhisattva may guide sentient beings as a ruler, as a friend, or as a shepherd.
284. *Gdan bzhi*.
285. *Phag mo dpyal lugs*.
286. *Gur brtag sam gsum*.

287. *Gsang 'dus kyi 'grel chen sgron gsal.*
288. *Rin chen them skas.*
289. *Pañcakrama, Lam lnga.*
290. *Phag mo'i brda dbang.*
291. See Roerich 1949, 629–30.
292. *Bde ba brgyad kyi rdzong mgur.*
293. Only an oblique reference to this spiritual song is found in Tatsak Tse Wangyel 1994, 546.
294. See Tatsak Tse Wangyel 1994, 546–47; Roerich 1949, 630.
295. *Ma thang gi rnam thar.*
296. On the life of Sangye On, see p. 454.
297. The twenty-four yogas of experiential realization (*nyams rtogs kyi rnal 'byor nyer bzhi*) are presently unidentified. They could be associated with the twenty-four yoginīs named in the *Buddhakapālatantra*, on which see Nordrang Orgyen 2008, 3189.
298. Roerich 1949, 631; and Tatsak Tse Wangyel 1994, 547–48. It is uncertain whether any of these thirteen profound painted scrolls depicting the meditational deities (*thugs dam thang ka zab bris bcu gsum*) are extant.
299. See Tatsak Tse Wangyel 1994, 548. Chogyel Phakpa died in 1280 at Sakya, allegedly poisoned by an unpopular local governor (*dpon chen*), which was the pretext for the Yuan invasion. It is said that Taklung was spared due to the commitment that Chogyel Phakpa had previously made to Sangye Yarjon.
300. See Tatsak Tse Wangyel 1994, 548; Roerich 1949, 631.
301. This heralded the divergence between the Taklung Upper Plain and Lower Plain traditions, at Taklung and Riwoche respectively.
302. Presently unidentified. These three would be respectively Kuyalwa, Sangye Yarjon, and Sangye On.
303. As stated on p. 221, these three are respectively Kuyalwa Rinchen Gonpo, Sangye Yarjon, and Tashi Lama.
304. This naturally arisen impression of the six-syllable mantra of Avalokiteśvara appears to be longer extant.
305. See Tatsak Tse Wangyel 1994, 549.
306. Sangs rgyas stong gsum zil gnon.
307. See Roerich 1949, 631–32.
308. Dharmapāla (r. 1280–1282, d. 1287) was the successor of Chogyel Phakpa. This incident is mentioned in Tatsak Tse Wangyel 1994, 549.
309. This would be the army sent by the governor (*dpon chen*) of Dokham to quell the power of Drigung. See Tatsak Tse Wangyel 1994, 549.
310. See Tatsak Tse Wangyel 1994, 549.
311. The text reads *cha la* for *cha lang*.
312. See Tatsak Tse Wangyel 1994, 551.
313. Stong gsum zil gnon.
314. Ber ka khrog ge. Translation marked as uncertain.—Ed.

315. The six supports of the throne (*khri drug 'degs*) are the motifs of lion, elephant, horse, peacock, cīvaṃcīvaka, and athlete. See Nyima and Dorje 2000, 357.
316. The four ornaments of the back rest (*rgyan snang bzhi*) are the motifs of water, rocks, clouds, and dragons. See Nyima and Dorje 2000, 721.
317. On this renowned image and its later replacement, see Akester 2016, 42. Tatsak Tse Wangyel 1994, 550, suggests that this was a tooth relic of Mila Repa.
318. See Tatsak Tse Wangyel 1994, 550–51.
319. According to Roerich 1949, 632, this occurred on the sixteenth day of the lunar month.
320. Not yet located.
321. The text reads 1279 (earth female hare), but this would be incompatible with him meeting Tashi Lama at the age of twenty and also with his death at the age of forty-six in 1312, as stated below.
322. Mkhen po g.ya' ngos pa.
323. A shawl or loose fitting garment, sometimes with tassels at the bottom (*gos tshar* or *gos dzar*).
324. It appears that Chung Jadrelwa was actually the youngest brother of Sangye Pelzangpo.
325. *bla gos stong hun*. Translation marked as uncertain.—Ed.
326. Orgyen Rinchen Pel (1229–1309) composed a guidebook to Oḍḍiyāna on his return to Tibet. See Tucci 1999.
327. *Yan lag bdun pa*.
328. The eight sacred abodes of the ḍākinīs (*mkha' 'gro ma'i gnas brgyad*) have not yet been identified.
329. *shu dag dkar po*, *Acorus gramineus/calamus*.
330. Black onyx (*ar mo ni ga*, Ch. *Wu ya tou zi*) is found abundantly in Lhodrak in its hexagonal, cube-like crystalline form.
331. Sprags btsan. Translation marked as uncertain.—Ed.
332. Maru, said to be "near Janandhara in the northern direction of Kashmir," is the twenty-third in the traditional listing of the twenty-four sacred places of India. For the complete enumeration, see Nordrang Orgyen 2008, 3187–89, 3194–95.
333. As stated on p. 260, this hagiography of Sangye Pelzangpo (1257–1310), the fifth hierarch of the abbatial succession of Upper Taklung, is derived from the biography written by Zhonu Senge of Dome (Mdo smad pa gzhon nu sang ge). See also Tse Wangyel 1994, 554–56; also Roerich 1949, 632–33; and Pawo Tsuklak Trengwa 1962 427. His birthplace is the same location in Markhamgang where his predecessors were born.
334. According to Roerich (1949, 632), her name was Chocham (Chos lcam).
335. Sras rin po che, that is, Sangye Pelzangpo.
336. The three activities of a scholar (*mkhas pa'i bya ba rnam pa gsum*) are teaching, debate, and composition. See Nyima and Dorje 2000, 392.
337. The text reads *lhun skyes* for *lhan skyes*.

338. The eighteen distinct qualities of the buddhas are as follows: (1) The tathāgatas are without clumsiness, (2) they are not noisy, (3) they are without false memories, (4) they are without differentiating perceptions, (5) they are without uncomposed minds, (6) they are without the indifference that lacks discernment, (7) they do not degenerate in their resolution, (8) they do not degenerate in their perseverance, (9) they do not degenerate in their recollection, (10) they do not degenerate in their meditative stability, (11) they do not degenerate in their wisdom, (12) they do not degenerate in their liberation nor in their perception of liberating pristine cognition, (13) all the activities of their bodies are preceded by pristine cognition and followed by pristine cognition, (14) all the activities of their speech are preceded by pristine cognition and followed by pristine cognition, (15) all the activities of their minds are preceded by pristine cognition and followed by pristine cognition, (16) they engage in the perception of pristine cognition that is unobstructed and unimpeded with respect to the past, (17) they engage in the perception of pristine cognition that is unobstructed and unimpeded with respect to the future, and (18) they engage in the perception of pristine cognition that is unobstructed and unimpeded with respect to the present. See the analysis in Konow (1941, 41–44), which discusses the etymology of *āveṇika* and compares alternative listings. See also Dayal 1932, 21–23; and Sparham 2012, 82. On the seven precious things (*rin po che sna bdun*), see part 1, chap. 8, note 3.
339. See p. 805n41.
340. On this see p. 29.
341. As stated on p. 268, this hagiography of Ratnaguru (1288–1339), the sixth hierarch of Taklung Upper Plain, is based on the account of Gelong Drakzhon, found in *The Golden Rosary* (*Gser phreng*), which itself was extrapolated from the works of Jamyang Drakpa. See also Tatsak Tse Wangyel 1994, 556–59; Roerich 1949, 633–34; and Pawo Tsuklak Trengwa 1962, 427. Ratnaguru's birthplace is the ancestral family residence of the Taklung hierarchs at Yangsho in Markhamgang.
342. The precepts of the novitiate (*dge tshul gyi dngos po*) are conferred according to the ancient rite (*tshigs snga ma*) in three phases—the preparation, the actual conferral, and the subsequent advice (*sbyor dngos rjes gsum*). See Nyima and Dorje 2000, 601.
343. Jamyang Rinchen Gyeltsen (r. 1286–1303) was the third imperial preceptor from Sakya during the Yuan dynasty, following Chogyel Phakpa and Dharmapāla.
344. *Gshin rje'i gshed.*
345. *Bde dgyes ma ya gdan bzhi.*
346. *Dam pa dang po'i sangs rgyas dus kyi 'khor lo.*
347. *Vajrapada, Rdo rje'i tshig.*
348. The six parameters (*mtha' drug*) of the tantras entail understanding (1) scriptures that employ the language of hidden intention (*dgongs pa'i skad*), (2)

those that do not (*de bzhin min*), (3) those that are literal (*sgra ji bzhin pa*), (4) those that are not (*de bzhin min*), (5) those of provisional meaning (*drang ba'i don*) and (6) those of definitive meaning (*nges pa'i don*). The four modes of expression (*tshul bzhi*) are (1) lexical (*yi ge*), (2) generic (*spyi*), (3) concealed (*sbas pa*), and (4) conclusive (*mthar thug*). For examples of all these, see Dudjom Rinpoche 1991, 1:290–93. There are various enumerations of the seven ornaments of expression (*rgyan bdun*). See Nordrang Orgyen 2008, 1626–27.

349. *Pañcakrama.*
350. On the Path and Its Fruit (Lam 'bras) and its subsidiary nine cycles of the path (*lam bskor dgu*), see Davidson 2005, 183–209.
351. *Zab lam phyag rgya chen po lhan cig skyes sbyor.*
352. That is to say, in the Taklung tradition, the transformational practice of Inner Heat is refined while maintaining celibacy as a monastic and without activating the lower gate of the sexual cakras that depend on a yogic partner.
353. See Tatsak Tse Wangyel 1994, 557; Roerich 1949, 633.
354. On all these regulations of the monastic charter, see p. 216.
355. *The Summation of the Scale Balance* (*Nya ga 'gag 'dril*) is the title of a text on the Great Seal by Gampopa.
356. See Tatsak Tse Wangyel 1994, 557; and Roerich 1949, 633. Among these Sakya masters, Lama Daknyi Chenpo Zangpo Pel (1262–1324, Bla ma bdag nyid chen po) was the eleventh throne holder of Sakya.
357. *Rgyud 'grel chen po'i bshad bka'.*
358. Ratnaguru's activities at Jonang are also mentioned in Tatsak Tse Wangyel 1994, 557; Roerich 1949, 633. Kunpang Chenpo Zhang Tuje Tsondru (1243–1313) was a renowned master of Kālacakra within the Jonang tradition.
359. The text reads *sems pa gnyis* for *sems dpa' gnyis.*
360. Tatsak Tse Wangyel 1994, 557, says that this was the inner representation (*nang rten*), that it rivaled the illustrious aforementioned image known as Tubchen Tongsum Zilnon (Thub pa stong gsum zil gnon), and that it was in the guise of the buddha body of perfect resource.
361. Tatsak Tse Wangyel 1994, 557, suggests that this was the outer representation (*phyi rten*).
362. See Tatsak Tse Wangyel 1994, 557.
363. The section of Mila Repa's spiritual songs titled "Answers to the Questions of Tashi Tseringma" (Bkra shis tshe ring ma'i zhus lan bskor gyi mgur chen) is contained in *The Hundred Thousand Songs of Mila Repa* (*Mi la mgur 'bum*). They include the song titled "Land of the Red-Faced Tibetan Ogre" (*Gdong dmar srin po bod kyi yul*), on which see p. 266.
364. The exemption from corvee labor at Taklung derives from the protection granted the monastery by Chogyel Phakpa, who persuaded Qubilai Qaγan to exempt Tibet from this tax.
365. These are enumerated in Nebesky-Wojkowitz 1975, 69.

366. See p. 100.
367. See Tatsak Tse Wangyel 1994, 558–59.
368. See Tatsak Tse Wangyel 1994, 559.
369. On Taklung Lotsāwa Śākya Zangpo (c. 1321–1404), see Roerich 1949, 310. Vajrīputra is one of the sixteen elders, on whom see p. 37.
370. The title *bka' bzhi pa*, "one who has mastered the four subjects," denotes a geshe who is accomplished in four fields of study—Madhyamaka, transcendent perfection, vinaya, and *The Treasury of Phenomenology*. See Nyima and Dorje 2001, 104–5.
371. Buton Rinchendrub (1290–1364) was a prolific author of twenty-eight volumes, trained in the Kadam, Sakya, and Trophu traditions. He is well known for working on the Tselpa and Zhalu manuscript compilations of the Kangyur and Tengyur. Lama Dampa Sonam Gyeltsen (1312–1375) was the fourteenth throne holder of Sakya.
372. *Bden gnyis snang chen.*
373. *Rgyan drug dgongs pa gcig tu sgrub pa'i bstan bcos.*
374. *Dpal brtags gnyis pa'i ṭīk chen.*
375. *Tshad ma rnam 'grel gyi tik rig tshul snang chen.*
376. For a description of Reteng, see Akester 2016, 27–34; Dorje 2009, 176–77, and on Yangpachen, 164–65.
377. *mchu zla ba*, the eighth lunar month.
378. On Odren Pelgyi Zhonu, see Dudjom Rinpoche 1991, 1:604–7.
379. That is to say, the time of the author, Ngawang Namgyel.
380. *kaliṅgaka.*
381. On the life of Ratnākara (1300–1361), the seventh hierarch of Taklung Upper Plain, who was also born in the Markhamgang enclave of Kham, where his predecessors had been born, see also Tatsak Tse Wangyel 1994, 559–62; Roerich 1949, 634–35; and Pawo Tsuklak Trengwa 1962, 427. As to the past lives of Ratnākara that are mentioned here, on Vidyākokila (Rikpei Khuyuk), who was a disciple of Candrakīrti (fl. seventh century), see BBRC P0RK297. On the great translator Kawa Peltsek (fl. eighth century), see Dudjom Rinpoche 1991, and Treasury of Lives; and on Ra Lotsāwa Dorje Drak (1016–1128), see Cuevas 2015.
382. The ten preliminary precepts (*sngon du sgro ba'i bslab gzhi bcu*) are the four primary precepts—not to kill, steal, lie, or commit sexual misconduct—and the further restrictions on (5) intoxicants; (6) song and dance; (7) garlands, incense, unguents, and ornaments; (8) high beds and mats; (9) afternoon meals; and (10) accepting gold and silver. See Ngawang Zangpo 2014, 727.
383. *Samādhirājasūtra*, *'Phags pa chos thams cad kyi rang bzhin mnyam pa nyid rnam par spros pa ting nge 'dzin gyi rgyal po zhes bya ba theg pa chen po'i mdo* (Toh. 127; Dg.K. mdo sde, *da*, ff. 1b–170b).
384. The two aspects of the Great Vehicle (*theg pa chen po rnam pa gnyis*) are the causal vehicle of the transcendent perfections (*rgyu pha rol tu phyin pa'i theg*

pa) and the fruitional adamantine vehicle of the Secret Mantra (*'bras bu sngags rdo rje theg pa*). See Nordrang Orgyen 2008, 58.

385. *Grub pa sde bdun.*
386. *Snying po bskor drug.*
387. *A ma na si'i chos bskor.*
388. *The Seven Sections of Spiritual Attainment* (*grub pa sde bdun*) are the seven treatises contained in the first part of volume *wi* of the Derge Tengyur (Toh. 2217–23; TPD 26, 3–191), which are respectively by Saroruhavajra, Anaṅgavajra, Indrabhūti, Lakṣmīnkarā, Darikapa, Cito, and Ḍombhi Heruka. The Six Essential Cycles (*Snying po bskor drug*) are (1) *The Treasury of Spiritual Songs* (*Do ha mdzod*) by Saraha (Toh. 2224); (2) *The Establishment of the Four Seals* (*Phyag rgya bzhi gtan la dbab pa*) by Nāgārjunagarbha (Toh. 2225); *The Pith Instructions of the Inconceivable Stage* (*Bsam gyis mi khyab pa'i rim pa'i man ngag*, Toh. 2228) by Kuddālīpāda; (4) *Purification of Mental Obscuration* (*Sems kyi sgrib sbyong*, Toh. 1804) by Āryadeva; (5) *The Luminosity of Pristine Cognition* (*Shes rab ye shes gsal ba*, Toh. 2226) by Devākaracandra; and (6) *The Synthesis of Abiding* (*Gnas pa bsdus pa*, Toh. 2227) by Sahajavajra. *The Twenty-Four Doctrinal Cycles of Nonmentation* (*A ma na si'i chos bskor nyi shu rtsa bzhi*) are the works of Maitripā (a.k.a. Advayavajra) contained in the *Advayavajrasaṃgraha* and in vol. *wi* of the Derge Tengyur. They are variously said to number twenty-four, twenty-five, or twenty-six (Toh. 2229–54, TPD 26, 288–523). On this corpus, see Higgins 2006.
389. The expression "instructions in which the tiger and lion come face-to-face" (*gdams pa stag seng kha sprod*) is reminiscent of a title in the Gesar series of epic poetry.
390. *mi g.yo ba gsum.*
391. On the distinction between the pure and impure illusory body, see Padmasambhava 1998, 141–50.
392. *la sogs pa'i bzhed dgur mdzad pa.* Translation marked as uncertain.—Ed.
393. This community appears to have been founded by one Chophel Zangpo.
394. See Tatsak Tse Wangyel 1994, 560; and Roerich 1949, 634.
395. See Tatsak Tse Wangyel 1994, 560; and Roerich 1949, 634. Among these, Lama Daknyi Chenpo Zangpo Pel (1262–1324), Jamyang Donyo Gyeltsen (1310–1344), and Dampa Sonam Gyeltsen (1312–1375) were respectively the twelfth, thirteenth, and fourteenth hierarchs of Sakya.
396. See Tatsak Tse Wangyel 1994, 560–61; and Roerich 1949, 634.
397. *Dpal stag lung thang pa chen po'i thugs dam lha drug gi bskor.*
398. *Zhal gdams chen mo chos tshan sum brgya rtsa brgyad pa.*
399. See Tatsak Tse Wangyel 1994, 561.
400. See Tatsak Tse Wangyel 1994, 561–62.
401. The text misreads *bde snod gsum* for *sde snod gsum*.
402. Guṇaprabha, *Vinayasūtra*, *'Dul ba'i mdo rtsa* (Toh. 4117; Dg.T. 'dul ba, *wu*, ff. 1b–100a).

403. Maitreya, *Abhisamayālaṃkāranāmaprajñāpāramitopadeśaśāstrakārikā, Shes rab kyi pha rol tu phyin pa'i man ngag gi bstan bcos mngon par rtogs pa'i rgyan* (Toh. 3786; Dg.T. shes phyin, *ka*, ff. 1b–13a; TPD 49, 3–48).
404. Maitreya, *Abhidhānottaratantranāma, Mngon par brjod pa'i rgyud bla ma zhes bya ba* (Toh. 369; Dg.T. rgyud, *ka*, ff. 247a–370a).
405. Śāntideva, *Bodhicaryāvatāra, Byang chub sems pa'i spyod pa la 'jug pa* (Toh. 3871; Dg.T. dbu ma, *la*, ff. 1b–40a; TPD 61, 951–1048).
406. Nāgārjuna, *Prajñānāmamūlamadhyamakakārikā, Dbu ma rtsa ba'i tshig le'ur byas pa shes rab ces bya ba* (Toh. 3824; Dg.T. dbu ma, *tsa*, ff. 1b–19a).
407. Vasubandhu, *Abhidharmakośakārikā, Chos mngon pa'i mdzod kyi tshig le'ur byas pa chos rjes kra shi* (Toh. 4089).
408. Asaṅga, *Abhidharmasamuccaya, Chos mngon pa kun las btus pa* (Toh. 4049).
409. This would be Torghon Timur (r. 1333–1368), the last emperor of the Yuan dynasty.
410. *yongjiu cefeng zhaoshu, gtan du ba'i las ka dang 'ja' sa.*
411. No longer extant, it seems.
412. *ham dmar 'char ka'i lang tshogs gsar pa rjes su 'brel ba.* Translation marked as uncertain.—Ed.
413. *puṇyakriyāvastu, bsod nams bya ba'i dngos po.*
414. See Tatsak Tse Wangyel 1994, 562.
415. Kunpang Namkha Pelyang, on whom see p. 279.
416. On the life of Kunpang Namkha Pelyang Zangpo, see also Tatsak Tse Wangyel 1994, 562–68; and Roerich 1949, 635–38. He was the first of the hierarchs of Upper Taklung to have been born outside Yangsho in Markhamgang. On the Penyul region, which lies between Taklung and Lhasa, see Akester 2016, 45–61; and Dorje 2009, 174–75.
417. Tatsak Tse Wangyel 1994, 652–53; and Roerich 1949, 635.
418. *Dpal brtag pa gnyis pa' rgyud.*
419. The ten signs of realization are smoke, mirage, clouds, fireflies, sunlight, moonlight, the blaze of gemstones, eclipse, starlight, and rays of light. See Dudjom Rinpoche 1991, 2:167.
420. See Tatsak Tse Wangyel 1994, 563.
421. See Roerich 1949, 635.
422. *phug gcig nas thon.* Translation marked as uncertain.—Ed.
423. See Tatsak Tse Wangyel 1994, 564; and Roerich 1949, 635.
424. See Tatsak Tse Wangyel 1994, 564.
425. The last two lines of this verse are cited in Tatsak Tse Wangyel 1994, 564.
426. Yumo, a.k.a. Yumowa Mikyo Dorje (fl. 1027), was the founder of the Jonang school and an exponent of *Kālacakra*. See Roerich 1949, 636.
427. Cf. Roerich 1949, 635–36.
428. On Lotsāwa Jangchub Tsemo (1303–1380), see Roerich 1949, 778–79, 787–88.
429. *Rgyud 'grel chen.*

430. Cf. Tatsak Tse Wangyel 1994, 564–65; Roerich 1949, 636.
431. The union of emptiness in all its finest aspects, symbolized by the Sanskrit letter E and supreme bliss, symbolized by the Sanskrit letter VAṂ in the context of the energies within the subtle body is discussed in Dorje 2016, 50–53.
432. See Roerich 1949, 636. Gyelse Tokme Zangpo (1295–1369) was an important Kadampa master and lineage holder of the seven branches of mind training. See BDRC P830; also Treasury of Lives.
433. See Tatsak Tse Wangyel 1994, 565.
434. *jñāpticaturtha, gsol bzhi'i las kyi cho ga.*
435. *daśapratyakṣa, mngon gyur bcu.*
436. The ordination of a full-fledged monk (*upasampadā, bsnyen rdzogs*) is conferred in the context of a ceremony known as the "fourfold rite including the request" (*jñāpticaturtha, gsol bzhi'i las kyi cho ga*). It is so named because the request for ordination (*jñāpti, gsol ba*) is immediately followed by the formal three iterations (*las dngos tshar gsum brjod pa*) of refuge, personal affirmation, and the acceptance of others. The ten presences (*daśapratyakṣa, mngon gyur bcu*) that are prerequisite for the conferral of the ordination include the presence of the buddhas, the sacred doctrine, the monastic community, the monastic preceptor, the master of ceremonies, the desire for ordination, the articles of ordination (*upakaraṇa, yo byad*), the proper quorum (*viśuddhi, yang dag*), the request for ordination (*jñāpti, gsol ba*), and the actual ceremony (*karma, las*). See Nyima and Dorje 2001, 918. These are sequenced according to the preparation, actual conferral, and subsequent advice (*sbyor dngos rjes gsum*). That is to say, the first nine are preparatory, the tenth is the actual conferral, and that is followed by the subsequent advice. See Ngawang Zangpo 2014, 716.
437. On the proscribed limits of the two hundred and fifty-three precepts (*bslab pa bcas pa'i 'tshams*) for a fully ordained monk, see Ngawang Zangpo 2014, 255–89, 717–24. The ten advantages (*phan yon bcu*) that accrue when the vows of individual liberation (*prātimokṣa, so sor thar pa*) are maintained are listed in Nordrang Orgyen 2008, 2263.
438. See Tatsak Tse Wangyel 1994, 565.
439. *Skyes rabs.*
440. See Roerich 1949, 637.
441. *Zab lam phyag rgya chen po'i bskor.*
442. *Gsang 'dus rim lnga.*
443. *Thugs rje chen po'i dmar khrid.*
444. According to Tatsak Tse Wangyel 1994, 565, the outer and inner representations are reversed.
445. *bug chos.* Translation marked as uncertain.—Ed.
446. On the Sokchu valley, see Dorje 2009, 465–67.
447. See Tatsak Tse Wangyel 1994, 566.
448. See Tatsak Tse Wangyel 1994, 566–67.

449. Or "camphor." The text reads *kapura*, but this would have to be either *ktura* or *karpūra*.
450. On the life of Jetsun Tashi Peltsek, see Tatsak Tse Wangyel 1994, 558–84; also Roerich 1949, 638–47.
451. See Tatsak Tse Wangyel 1994, 658; and Roerich 1949, 638.
452. See Tatsak Tse Wangyel 1994, 569; and Roerich 1949, 638. The three trainings (*bslab pa gsum*) are ethical discipline, meditative stability, and discriminative awareness.
453. The preparatory seven empowerments are those of water, crown, silk ribbon, vajra and bell, conduct, name, and permission. On their respective purifications, see Hopkins 1985, 73–74, 105–30. The three higher supreme empowerments (*mchog dbang gong ma gsum*) in this system are those of the vase, the secret, and the pristine cognition of discriminative awareness. The fourth empowerment has mundane, or provisional, and supramundane, or definitive, aspects (*'jig rten dang 'jig rten las 'das pa'i bzhi pa*), and these are followed by the conclusive empowerment of the adamantine master (*rdo rje slob dpon bdag po chen po'i dbang gi mthar thug pa*). See Hopkins 1985, 68–69.
454. Rgyud sde rgya mtsho'i khong snying zab lam.
455. *Theg chen blo sbyong*.
456. *Thugs rje chen po'i dmar khrid*.
457. *Gsang 'dus rim lnga*.
458. *Shin tu spros med*.
459. The Path and Its Fruit (Lam 'bras) is the definitive system of Buddhist practice followed within the Sakya tradition. See Davidson 2004, 183–204.
460. That is to say, he became receptive to the nondual coalescence of appearances and emptiness.
461. That is to say, he would retire from the abbatial succession to focus on meditation. See also Tatsak Tse Wangyel 1994, 569. The text misreads *dbon gsum* for *dben gsum*.
462. See Tatsak Tse Wangyel 1994, 570; and Roerich 1949, 639.
463. See Tatsak Tse Wangyel 1994, 571–72; and Roerich 1949, 640–41.
464. Regarding the cotton-drawn images (*ras bris*) presented in *The Root Tantra of Mañjuśrī*, see Kapstein 2001, 257–80.
465. See Tatsak Tse Wangyel 1994, 572.
466. See Tatsak Tse Wangyel 1994, 572–73; and Roerich 1949, 641–42. The desi in question would not have been Tai Situ Jangchub Gyeltsen (r. 1350–1371), the charismatic founder of the Phakmodru dynasty, since Tashi Peltsek was only twelve at the time of his passing, but one of his successors, but rather either the second desi Śākya Gyeltsen (r. 1372–1384), the third desi Drakpa Jangchub (r. 1385–1390), or the fourth desi Sonam Drakpa (r. 1391–1408).
467. See Tatsak Tse Wangyel 1994, 573.
468. *rgyud ris*. Translation marked as uncertain.—Ed.
469. *Sgrol ma maṇḍal bzhi ma'i cho ga*.

470. This Draknak in Nakchu prefecture is not to be confused with Draknak in Nakchu (Dorje 2009, 464).
471. The Puṣpahari Monastery (Me tog mdangs 'phrog gi dgon pa) in Kashmir is mentioned in the biographies of Nāropā and Marpa. See p. 108. On Svayambhu ('Phags pa shing kun) in Nepal, see Ehrhard 1989; and Dowman 1995, 24–29. Chi Lhepa Senge Pel (fl. twelfth century) appears to have been a disciple of Śākyaśrī.
472. See part 1, chapters 6–7.
473. On Wutai Shan, see Baumer 2011; and the classic work in Tibetan by Changkya Rolpei Dorje, titled *A Guide to the Sacred Places of the Pure Land Wutai Shan* (*Zhing mchog ri bo rtse lnga'i gnas bshad*, 1993).
474. *rgya nag stong kun gyi rgyal po*. On the origins of the term *stong kun*, which may render the Chinese Dongjing ("Eastern Capital") or Dongjun ("Eastern Ruler"), see van Schaik and Galambos 2011, 170–75. The emperor mentioned here is probably the founder of the Ming dynasty, Hongwu (r. 1368–1398).
475. See Roerich 1949, 641; and Tatsak Tse Wangyel 1994, 574–75. Sakyapa Tekchen Choje Kuntrepa (Kun bkras pa, 1349–1425) was invited to China by the Ming emperor, Yongle.
476. This was in consequence of the earlier campaign of Tai Situ Jangchub Gyeltsen and his successors against Sakya and the myriarchies of Utsang. See Shakabpa 1982, 73–82.
477. Kongting Gushri Drakpa Gyeltsen of Phakmodru (Phag mo gru pa'i kong ting gwa'i shri grags pa rgyal mtshan, r. 1385–1432) is the fifth of the rulers (*sde srid*) of this dynasty. He received his title and golden seal from the Ming emperor Hongwu in 1389. During his reign, the Great Prayer Festival was established at Lhasa, and the three main Gelukpa monasteries of the Lhasa region—Ganden, Drepung, and Sera—were founded by Tsongkhapa and his disciples. See Shakabpa 1982, 82–86.
478. See Tatsak Tse Wangyel 1994, 575; and Roerich 1949, 641–42.
479. See Tatsak Tse Wangyel 1994, 575–76.
480. Khyungpo is an important Bon enclave, lying to the east of Shel La pass, within the Gachu and Ruchu river valleys. See Dorje 2009, 467–69.
481. See Tatsak Tse Wangyel 1994, 576. On this sacred image at Reteng, see Akester 2016, 31–33; also Dorje 2009, 176–77.
482. This would be Barom Riwoche Gon in Nakchu, which was founded by Barompa Darma Wangchuk in 1160.
483. Shakchuka is the traditional name given to the barren upper reaches of the Shakchu-chu valley. See Dorje 2009, 464–65.
484. See Tatsak Tse Wangyel 1994, 576–77.
485. See Tatsak Tse Wangyel 1994, 577. It might possibly be that Duensha Konchok Zangpo is an epithet of Ngorchen Kunga Zangpo (1382–1446).
486. See Tatsak Tse Wangyel 1994, 577–78.

487. One might wonder if this could possibly be a bizarre, indirect reference to Tai Situ Jangchub Gyeltsen, who died in 1371.
488. See p. 46.
489. See Tatsak Tse Wangyel (1994, 578) states that this was Gompa Sonam Rinchen of Drigung. Roerich (1949, 642) adds that this Dzongji had imposed an exorbitant fine or tax on the people of Rongpo and that the lama's attempted meditation was unsuccessful. See also Dungkar Lobzang Trinle 2002, 1557. On Rongpo (Gyaruptang) in the Salween region, see Dorje 2009, 467.
490. This could be the elderly Taklung Lotsāwa who passed away in 1404. See p. 268.
491. These appear to be local villages or tribal groups within the upper Kyichu region.
492. An important watershed on the ancient "royal trail" between the Kyichu and the Yarlung Tsangpo. See Dorje 2009, 168–69.
493. Roerich (1949, 642) adds that his companions had difficulty climbing the steep pathway to Chimphu, while he traveled without his feet touching the ground.
494. *za bsam las che*. Translation marked as uncertain.—Ed.
495. The text reads *'khrags pa* for *mkhregs pa*.
496. These are the four communities (*tshogs pa sde bzhi*) established by Śākyaśrī during the early thirteenth century—namely, Tsongdu Tsokpa in Drachi, Tsetsokpa at Neudong, Gyaling Tsokpa in Dranang, and Jonang Tsokpa in Tsang. See Heimbel 2013. Go Lotsāwa includes Tsokpa Jadzong, Gendun Gang, and Cholung near Gyantse. See Roerich 1949, 1072–73.
497. See Tatsak Tse Wangyel 1994, 579.
498. This is the Drak valley to the north of Dorje Drak monastery, in Drangang County. See Akester 2016, 345–52; also Dorje 2009, 198–200.
499. On Ratsak, see Akester 2016, 200–203; and on the obelisk inscription at Ratsak Jomo (*ra tshag jo mo*), see Richardson 1998, 286–91.
500. Perhaps this official Hu Dacheng (*hu tā zhing*) is to be identified with Venerable Ozer Namkha Zangpo of Gonjo, on whom the title Hu Jiao Wang was conferred. See Sperling 1989, 77–78.
501. *bur khras*. Translation marked as uncertain.—Ed.
502. See Tatsak Tse Wangyel 1994, 579.
503. See Tatsak Tse Wangyel 1994, 579–81; Roerich 1949, 643–44. On the terrain and culture of Mustang (Glo bo sman thang) in northern Nepal, see Peissel 1967; Marullo 1995; and Matthiessen and Laird 1996.
504. The monk emissary Xiguang was sent by Ming Chengzu (r. 1402–1424) to Nepal, and to places en route including Drigung and Taktsang (Taklung). See Slobodnik 2004, 163.
505. See Tatsak Tse Wangyel 1994, 581.
506. This portends the earthquake of 1411, on which see p. 298.

507. See Tatsak Tse Wangyel 1994, 581–82; and Roerich 1949, 644.
508. *bag phag nas sdod pa.* Translation marked as uncertain.—Ed.
509. Kunga Tashi (1349–1425) was a member of the illustrious Khon family of Sakya and lineage holder of the Dzongpa, or Lhakhangpa, branch. He was one of the five "dharma princes" (*fa wan*) invited from Tibet to China by Ming Chengzu. See Slobodnik 2004, 164; and Sperling 1989, 79.
510. This might possibly be the same Hu Dacheng mentioned in part 1, chap. 8, note 500.
511. The "easy route" (*'jam lam*) is probably the old China trail (*rgya lam*), which crosses the Mekong–Salween divide to reach Rongpo Gyaruptang and then continues across the Nyenchen Tangla range to Drigung.
512. *Buddhāvataṃsaka.*
513. *Byams pa lung bstan pa.*
514. *Nindimitrāvadāna.*
515. *Gnas brtan lung bstan pa'i mdo.*
516. *Chims kyi sgrub yig.*
517. See Roerich 1949, 644.
518. See Roerich 1949, 644.
519. Curd, milk, and butter.
520. *sa ba.* Translation marked as uncertain.—Ed.
521. Nonetheless, Bon communities did survive in Dome (Amdo).
522. This was Chenga Sonam Zangpo (1380–1417), the twenty-eighth monastic preceptor of Densatil.
523. This is the name of a hermitage at Densatil.
524. See also Roerich 1949, 644–45.
525. See Roerich 1949, 645.
526. See Roerich 1949, 645–46.
527. *guanding guoshi, kon ting gwa'u shri.* On this title, which Ming Chengzu offered to the Dharma princes (*fa wang*) of Tibet, see Slobodnik 2004, 163–64.
528. *chengzu tungyu guoshi, cing ze'u thung ū gva'i shri.*
529. On the life of Fifth Karmapa, Dezhin Shekpa (1384–1415), see Douglas and White 1976, 61–65; Sperling 1980; Thinley 1980; and Lama Kunsang et. al 2012.
530. This location is unidentified.
531. These stūpas contain the relics of the first three hierarchs of the abbatial succession, Taklung Tangpa, Kuyalwa, and Sangye Yarjon.
532. Unidentified.
533. See Roerich 1949, 646.
534. Unidentified.
535. Kyura Rinpoche is Jikten Gonpo, the first hierarch and founder of Drigung (1143–1217). See Treasury of Lives; also Roerich 1949, 596–601, and Khenpo Könchog Gyaltsen 1984 and 1990.
536. See Roerich 1949, 646.

537. See Roerich 1949, 646–47.
538. This is a direct observation of the author, Ngawang Namgyel.
539. *Dgongs pa rdzogs thabs kyi mchod sbyin rlabs po che 'di dang phyogs thams cad du bskrun no.*
540. The biography of Ngawang Drakpa Pelzangpo is found p. 329.
541. Jangchub Tsemo (1303–1380) was the nephew and disciple of Pang Lodro Tenpa.
542. Bodong Panchen Chokle Namgyel, the Omniscient Bodong (Bo dong thams cad mkhyen pa, 1375–1451) was the grand-nephew of Pang Lodro Tenpa, and author of 137 volumes of scriptural commentary.
543. *Gnad kyi nges gsang phyag rgya chen po lhan cig skyes sbyor.*
544. *Khrid yig 'od dkar phreng ba.*
545. Tsongkhapa Lobzang Drakpa (1357–1419), the founder of the Gelukpa school, on whom see BDRC P64; Treasury of Lives; and the biographical sources listed therein; also Thurman 1982; and Roerich 1949, 1073–79.
546. *Byang chub lam gyi sgron me.*
547. *Gsang ba 'dus pa'i rgyud sde.*
548. Rendawa Zhonu Lodro (1349–1412), a master of the Sakya and Kadam traditions and teacher of Tsongkhapa, was a prolific writer on abhidharma, Madhyamaka, and so forth. See Treasury of Lives and the biographical sources listed therein.
549. Changlungpa Zhonu Lodro of Choding (Spyang lung pa gzhon nu blo gros, 1372–1475) was an important teacher of Śākya Chokden. See the biographical information at BDRC P8966.
550. *dang.* This is marked as uncertain.—Ed.
551. Phyag rgya chen po lnga ldan.
552. Yig bzhi.
553. Bde stong phyag brgya chen po.
554. *Rta mig ma tshul khrims kyi dris bgos pa zhig.*
555. On Sangye Yarjon, the third hierarch of Taklung Upper Plain, see p. 213. On Namgyel Tashi, the fifteenth hierarch, see below, p. 391.
556. *mar gyur.* Translation marked as uncertain.—Ed.
557. The bolded terms, followed by Tibetan transliteration, represent the meaning of the names of the master who is being praised in the verse.—Ed.
558. On the life of Jangchub Tsemo Pelzangpo, see also Tatsak Tse Wangyel 1994, 584–85; and Roerich 1949, 647.
559. These are the fountainheads of the Zhamar line of incarnations. On the latter, see p. 318.
560. On First Zhamar, Drakpa Senge (1283–1349), who was a senior disciple of Third Karmapa Rangjung Dorje, see Roerich 1949, 523–31. On Second Zhamar, Pelden Khacho Wangpo (1350–1405), who was recognized by Fourth Karmapa Rolpei Dorje, see Roerich 1949, 540–45; also BDRC P1413 and the biographical information listed therein.

561. That is to say, Jangchub Gyatso was born two years before the death of Zhamar Khacho Wangpo.
562. The four contradictory circumstances (*'gal rkyen bzhi*) concern obstacles associated with birth (*skye ba*); residence (*gnas pa*); special conditions (*khyad par du gyur pa*) such as being underage; and lack of beauty, including physical disabilities (*mdzes pa*). See Ngawang Zangpo 2014, 249; and Nordrang Orgyen 2008, 552.
563. The five compatible circumstances (*mthun rkyen lnga*) for ordination are those of place (*yul*), mental disposition (*rgyud*), reasoning (*rtags*), reflection (*bsam pa*), and past causes (*sngon gyi rgyu*). See Nordrang Orgyen 2008, 1080.
564. The three transformations of a mendicant (*trividhapartvartana*, *rab byung gi brje ba gsum*) concern transformations of thought, lifestyle, and name. See Nyima and Dorje 2001, 1246.
565. On these four empowerments, see p. 310.
566. This is the threefold structure outlined in *The Hundred and Eight Teaching Manuals of Jonang* (*Jo nang khri brgya*), on which see Gyurme 2020.
567. *Bsre 'pho mtshams sbyor.*
568. *Snyan brgyud yid bzhin gyi nor bu.*
569. *Ting nge 'dzin gyi rgyal po.*
570. *Rang bzhin mnyam pa nyid.*
571. *Nges don phyag rgya chen po lhan cig skyes sbyor.*
572. Roerich 1949, 647.
573. These are the six permissible personal items of a Buddhist monk (*dge slong gi nye ldan gyi yo byad drug*)—namely, the patched outer robe (*saṃghāṭī*, *snam sbyar*), the upper robe (*uttarasaṅgha*, *bla gos*), the inner robe (*antarāvāsa*, *mthang gos*), the mat (*gding ba*), the alms bowl (*lhun bzed*), and the water filter (*chu tshags*). See Nordrang Orgyen 2008, 1332.
574. See Roerich 1949, 647.
575. On Third Zhamar Chophel Yeshe (1406–1452), see Roerich 1949, 546–51. Nyangpo refers to the Nyangchu valley in which Gyantse is located.
576. The text reads iron mouse (*lcags pho byi*).
577. On this term, see Snellgrove 1959, 1:68–69, 2:22–23. On Tsāri, see De Rossi Filibeck 1990, 1–10; and Dorje 2009, 269–72.
578. Kurab Namgyel and Dungkar lie to the north of the Tsāri pilgrimage region, which begins at Chikchar and is here referred to as the Bayo Tashijong (Hidden Land of Good Auspices). See the map of Lhuntse County at www.tibetmap.com.
579. This suggests that he traveled east from Tsāri to Kongpo and then northeast across the Brahmaputra-Salween watershed through Artsa and Pelbar, in the direction of Lhorong.
580. Jangchub Gyatso appears to have been the first hierarch of Taklung Upper Plain to visit Riwoche in person since its founding by Sangye On. On

Lhorong, see Dorje 2009, 492–93; and on Riwoche, see Dorje 2009, 471–74.

581. Choje Miyo Gonpo was the ninth hierarch of Taklung Lower Plain. See below p. 506.

582. Orgyen Gonpo was the second hierarch of Taklung Lower Plain. See p. 486.

583. This is perhaps to be identified with Tashi Gephel monastery, located in Jang Sadam. On the southern region, which extends from present-day Markham County via Gyeltang to Jang Sadam (Lijiang), see Dorje 2009, 508–27.

584. On the trading settlement and modern city of Dartsedo, see Dorje 2009, 552–60.

585. Dentik is an important pilgrimage place in Amdo, containing a revered Padmasambhava cave hermitage. For a brief site description, see Dorje 2009, 714–15.

586. Also known as Ngagi Wangchuk.

587. *Byang chub thugs bskyed.*

588. Unidentified.

589. Zhuntik, like the Yangtik hermitage, would be located in the Dentik area.

590. In this way, Ngawang Namgyel points out that he himself is the collator of the stories surrounding the life of Jangchub Gyatso.

591. See below p. 410.

592. Among them, Go Lo Zhonu Pel (1392–1481) is the author of *The Blue Annals*, translated in Roerich 1949. See also Dudjom Rinpoche 1991, 1:674–75. On Changlungpa Zhonu Lodro, see p. 308.

593. On the life of Fourth Zhamar, Chokyi Drakpa (1453–1525), see Dudjom Rinpoche 1991, 1:675–76.

594. *thar spyod pa.* Translation marked as uncertain.—Ed.

595. Nor 'dzin skyong ba. Translation marked as uncertain.—Ed.

596. On Fifth Zhamar, Konchok Yenlak (1525–1583), who was a disciple of Pawo Tsuklak Trengwa, see BDRC P1426 and the biographical information listed therein. He was ordained as a mendicant by Eighth Karmapa, Mikyo Dorje in 1538 and enthroned at Yangpachen, the seat of the Zhamarpas, in 1539.

597. Sixth Zhamar, Garwang Chokyi Wangchuk (1585–1630) was therefore alive at the time when Ngawang Namgyel compiled this history of Taklung.

598. Fourteenth Zhamar, Mipham Chokyi Lodro, passed away in 2014.

599. The three obscurations (*sgrib gsum*) are with respect to afflicted mental states, the nature of knowable phenomena, and past actions.

600. On Tashi Pel-o Zangpo, see also Roerich 1949, 647.

601. The seven aspects of mystic union (*saptasaṃpuṭa, kha sbyor yan lag bdun*) associated with the buddha body of perfect resource are perfect rapture, mystic union, perfect bliss, insubstantiality, complete compassion, continuity, and non-cessation. See Nyima and Dorje 2001, 262.

602. The three classes of disciples (*rigs can gsum*) are pious attendants, hermit buddhas, and bodhisattvas.

603. *ri mo mngon par gsal ba*. Translation marked as uncertain.—Ed.,
604. The "child of dawn" (*skya rengs kyi bu*) is the mythical bird Jaṭāyu, who was scorched while flying too close to the sun. See Mani 1964, 351.
605. That is to say, he was the younger brother of the previous hierarch, Jangchub Gyatso.
606. The four modes of appropriate physical conduct (*spyod lam rnam pa bzhi*) are walking, standing, sitting, and lying down.
607. These are as follows. (1) His five aggregates became radiant as the five male buddhas—that is the seat of the buddhas (*sangs rgya skyi gdan*). (2) His five elements became radiant as the five female buddhas—that is the seat of the female deities (*lha mo'i gdan*). (3) His sensory activity fields became radiant as the bodhisattvas—that is the seat of the bodhisattvas (*sems dpa'i gdan*). On these three seats (*gdan gsum*), see Nordrang Orgyen 2008, 304.
608. *veṣaparivartana, rtags brje ba.*
609. *aśāyaparivartana, rtags brje ba.*
610. *nāmaparivartana, ming brje ba.*
611. See Nyima and Dorje 2001, 600–601.
612. These seven renunciations (*spong ba bdun*) with respect to physical forms include killing, stealing, sexual misconduct, lying, slandering, abusive language, and nonsensical talk. See Nordrang Oryan 2008, 1667.
613. Nordrang Orgyen 2008, 709–13 includes different listings of fourfold yoga, not those of ground, path, and result.
614. The five certainties (*nges po lnga*) are those of teacher, teaching, retinue, time, and place. See Dorje 2016, 48–53.
615. The four provisional aspects to be purified (*sbyang bya gnas skabs rnam pa bzhi*) within the four cakras are body, speech, mind, and propensities. The four primary doctrines that bring about this purification are those of Inner Heat, Illusory Body, Dream Yoga, and Inner Radiance. The four fruitional buddha bodies are those of essentiality, reality, perfect resource, and emanation.
616. Together these constitute the six doctrines of Nāropā.
617. *Yon tan rin chen sdud pa, Sañcayagāthā* (Toh. 13; KPD 34, 30), chap. 22, v. 2. See Conze 1960, 51. This is also in *The Perfection of Wisdom in Eighteen Thousand Lines* (*Aṣṭādaśasāhasrikāprajñāpāramitā, 'Phags pa shes rab kyi pha rol tu phyin pa khri brgyad stong pa zhes bya ba theg pa chen po'i mdo*; Toh. 10, chap. 84). https://read.84000.co/translation/toh10.html#UT22084-029-001-chapter-84.
618. *Mahāyānasūtrālaṃkārakārikā, Theg pa chen po mdo sde'i rgyan zhes bya ba'i tshig le'ur byas pa* (TPD 70), 860; and Jamspal 2004, 224, v. 10.
619. *Abhisamayālaṃkāranāmaprajñāpāramitopadeśaśāstrakārikā, Shes rab kyi pha rol tu phyin pa'i man ngag gi bstan bcos mngon par rtogs pa'i rgyan* (TPD 49), 7.
620. *Rājaparikathāratnāvalī, Rgyal po la gtam bya ba rin po che'i phreng ba* (TPD 96), 333.

621. Śāntideva, *Bodhicaryāvatāra*, *Byang chub sems pa'i spyod pa la 'jug pa*, chap. 5, v. 102 (TPD 61), 99; see Shantideva 2006, 194.
622. Candragomin, *Bodhisattvasaṃvaraviṃśaka*, *Byang chub sems dpa'i sdom pa nyi shu pa* (TPD 78), 447.
623. The citation is as yet unidentified in Candrakīrti's work (Toh. 3865), though it is quoted by Kunga Namgyel in his *Oral Instructions of the Lineage of Siddhas: The Essence of the Path of Coemergent Mahāmudrā* (*Phyag chen lhan cig skyes sbyor zab don lam gyi snying po grub thob brgyud pa'i zhal lung*).
624. *Āryamūlasarvāstivādiśrāmaṇerakārikāvṛttiprabhāvatī*, *'Phags pa gzhi thams cad yod par smra ba'i dge tshul gyi tshig le'ur byas pa'i 'grel pa* (TPD 93), 194.
625. The first and third lines of this verse are found with slight variants in several canonical works and indigenous commentaries. The second line has not yet been identified.
626. *upasaṃgraha*, *nyer bsdu*.
627. This passage derives from the *Vajrahṛdayālaṃkāratantra*, *Dpal rdo rje snying po rgyan gyi rgyud* (KPD 82), 136–37. Cf. Nordrang Orgyen 2008, 2205–6. See Dorje 2016, 1:26–33.
628. *mandārava*.
629. See pp. 216–18.
630. Sukhāvatī, Bde ldan rnam par bkod pa'i zhing.
631. That is to say, this manuscript version of the Kangyur was inscribed in gold and silver on dark blue paper.
632. See the iconographic description of Kālacakra and Viśvamātā in Hopkins 1985, 80–82.
633. For a description of these eight *śakti* (*nus ma*) goddesses, see Hopkins 1985, 83–84.
634. See Hopkins 1985, 84–86.
635. See Hopkins 1985, 86–87.
636. See Hopkins 1985, 87–90.
637. See Hopkins 1985, 90.
638. See Gray 2007, 55.
639. This is one of the names of Sangye On, founder of Riwoche.
640. Ketaka is a gemstone that can purify turbid water. See Nyima and Dorje 2001, 38.
641. The bolded terms, followed by Tibetan transliteration, represent the meaning of the names of the master who is being praised in the verse.—Ed.
642. On Ngawang Drakpa Pelzangpo (1418–1496), see also Roerich 1949, 647–48. As stated on p. 341, the biography of his early life was written by Minyak Drakdorwa and that of his later life by Tsamla Sonam Zangpo. Other hagiographies in the form of a eulogy were composed by Fourth Zhamar (see p. 318).
643. *Lam sgron*.
644. *Chos spyod thams cad kyi man ngag mngon par rtogs pa'i rgyud*.

645. That is to say, it consecrated a corresponding image of Kākamukha Mahākāla.
646. *rtsi bar ba.* Translation marked as uncertain.—Ed.
647. These were both disciples of Tashi Peltsek. See p. 286.
648. On Bodongpa Chokle Namgyel, see p. 306.
649. This suggests that he traveled to Tsang along the riverside road. Tokar (*thos dkar*) could perhaps be identified with Takar in present-day Chushul County, from where roads to Gyantse, Gongkar, and Lhasa all converge. See Dorje 209, 296.
650. It is clear that he crossed the Yarlung Tsangpo via the Takdruka ferry, south of Oyuk, and approached Rinpung Dzong from the south bank. See Dorje 2009, 286–97, 303–4.
651. The Sakyapa monastery of Jamkhang at Rong Jamchen Chode was founded in 1367 by Zhonu Gyelchok. Nyangto lies south from here, on the main road linking Gyantse with Lhasa. Lhundrubtse would be Gongra Lhundrubding. On these places, including Gyantse, see Akester 2016, 491–97, 529–34; also Dorje 2009, 304–13.
652. This is probably a peripheral temple rather than the Pelkhor Chode, which was built earlier, between 1418 and 1425. See Akester 2016, 491–95; Dorje 2009, 308–13.
653. This would be Rabten Kunzang Pak (1389–1442), the local ruler of Gyantse who built the Pelkhor Chode temple complex, including the renowned Gyantse Kumbum. His silver reliquary is contained within the Royal Chapel on the east wing of the ground floor of the temple.
654. The seat of Pang Lodro Tenpa and Bodongpa, also known as Bodong E, to the west of Shab Geding. See Akester 2016, 631–33.
655. This is most probably Dakchen Lodro Gyeltsen (1444–1495), the twenty-first throne holder of Sakya.
656. These places are all in the Tsibri area, within present-day Dingri county. See Akester 2016, 665–68; Dorje 2009, 359–60.
657. *Ri chos.*
658. *U rgyan bsnyen sgrub.*
659. This would be Jangchub Zangpo of Lhadong, a lineage holder of the Drukpa and Bodongpa traditions. See BDRC P5808.
660. On Dingri Gangkar and Chubar, see Dorje 2009, 365–67, and on Nyenam, also known as Nyalam, 369–71. Chubar is where Mila Repa passed away at the Driche cave hermitage.
661. On the Lapchi area, see Dorje 2009, 367.
662. On the Kyirong area, see Chen 1994, 931–39; and Dorje 2009, 375–78. The sacred image of Phakpa Wati ('Phags pa wa ti) has already been mentioned. See p. 333. The other sites listed here—Drakar Taso (Brag dkar rta so), Rakma Jangchub Dzong (Rag ma byang chub rdzong), Kyangpa Namkha Dzong (Kriang pa nam mkha' rdzong), and Minkhyuk Dribma Dzong (Smin khyug grib ma rdzong) are all associated with Mila Repa.

663. This accords with the secret-practices (*gsang spyod*) system of Bodongpa.
664. Mengab, also written as Menkhab, is a village in the Menchu valley, southwest of Gurtso on the Dingri-Dra highway. See Dorje 2009, 369.
665. On Sakya, see Akester 2016, 577–90; and Dorje 2009, 342–47.
666. Drungchen Norzang of Rinpung seized power from the Phakmodrupa in Tsang in 1435. His son, Donyo Dorje, on whom see p. 342, set in motion the Rinpung administration (1478–1565).
667. On the seat of Ngok Choku Dorje at Zhung Trewuzhing, in present-day Gongkar county, see Akester 2016, 264–67.
668. The Dol (or Drib) valley runs south from the weaving village of Chedezhol in Gongkar county. Yargyab refers to the entire area lying to the east and southeast of Lake Yamdrok. See Dorje 2009, 196–97; and Akester 2016, 270–71.
669. *Trisamayavyūha*, *Dam tshigs gsum bkod.*
670. *Rnam snang mngon byang.*
671. *Rdor dbyings.*
672. *Kun rig.*
673. *Gtsug dgu.*
674. *Gsang 'dus mi bskyod pa.*
675. *'Jam pa'i rdo rje.*
676. *Rdo rje 'jigs byed.*
677. *Bde mchog nag po zhabs lugs.*
678. *Mkha' 'gro rgya mtsho.*
679. *Gur rigs bsdus.*
680. *De nyid 'dus pa.*
681. This is the system of Bodongpa.
682. *Bsnyen sgrub.*
683. On the Lake Yamdrok area, see Dorje 2009, 258–61.
684. See p. 309.
685. The protector deity Tseringma is associated with Mount Everest.
686. On all these protectors, see Nebesky-Wojkowitz 1975, 38–87.
687. Alternatively, this could be Lekden with Three Teeth (Legs ldan mche gsum), on whom see Nebesky-Wojkowitz 1975, 53.
688. On the various spirit lords of the locality (*gzhi bdag*), see Nebesky-Wojkowitz 1975.
689. *Mdo rgyud rnam bshad.*
690. *Ro snyoms rdo rje mgur*
691. *Mahāvairocanābhisambodhitantra*, *Rnam par snang mdzad chen po mngon par rdzogs par byang chub pa rnam par sprul pa byin gyis rlob pa shin tu rgyas pa mdo sde'i dbang po'i rgyal po zhes bya ba'i chos kyi rnam grangs* (Toh. 494; Dg.K. rgyud, *tha*, ff. 151b–260a).
692. These would be the revered subterranean treasures of the Taklung area.
693. See p. 359.

694. Mañjuśrīmitra, **Ekavīrasādhana, 'Jam dpal dpa' bo gcig grub* (Toh. 2571; Dg.T. rgyud, *ngu*, ff. 31a–32a).
695. *Gtsug gtor gdug dkar lha yul che ba.*
696. *Shes rab snying po.*
697. *Rnam rgyal gyi rtog/rtogs pa.*
698. *Sgrol ma'i bstod pa me tog phreng 'dzin.*
699. *Bde mchog gi bstod pa daṇḍaka.*
700. *Shes rab bstod pa.*
701. *Bi varta bye drag tu rtog pa chen po* (*MVT*, Toh. 4346).
702. As yet unidentified.
703. According to Gartse (1999, 337), this is a medicinal compound employed generally in the treatment of fevers, and specifically for chest pains, intestinal colic, muscular spasm, tumors, and animalcule disorders. It contains, *Euphorbia wallichiana* (*thar-nu*), *Euphorbia fischeriana* (*dur byid*), *Rheum emodi* (*chu rtsa*), *Acorus calamus* (*chu dag*), cut meat (*gri sha*), *Stellera chasmaejasme* (*shog shing*), bezoar (*gi wang*), saffron (*gur gum*), bamboo pith (*cu gang*), musk (*gla rtsi*), frankincense (*gu gul*), and aconite (*sman chen*).
704. According to Gartse (1999, 169), the compound of "six white ingredients" (*dkar po drug sbyor*) that is used for alleviating indigestion, low metabolism, and brown phlegm disorder contains natron (*bul tog*), limestone (*cong zhi*), bird's droppings (*bya thal*), *Inula helenium* (*ma nu*), galangale (*sga skya*), and borax (*tshva la*).
705. These are rites pertaining to Sitātapatrā.
706. This is perhaps to be identified with the Tamdo of older maps, located southeast of Urulung in the upper Kyichu (see www.tibetmap.com). Texts speak of *byang lam thang 'brog*, suggesting that it lies on this northern route to Damzhung and Lake Namtso.
707. Amarasiṃha, *Amarakoṣanāma, Mngon brjod kyi bstan bcos 'chi ba med pa'i mdzod ces bya ba skad gnyis sbyar ba* (Toh. 4299; Dg.T. sgra mdo, *se*, ff. 126b–243a).
708. Minyak Drakdorwa is said to have been a contemporary of Taktsang Lotsāwa.
709. Bu ston gyi bka' 'bum.
710. The Trengwachen (Phreng ba can) version of *The Transcendent Perfection of Wisdom in Eight Thousand Lines* is one of three textual traditions, or alternative Tibetan translations, of this sūtra. The three differ in other respects but their most easily identifiable marker lies in how the Sanskrit name *Śreṇika Vatsagotra* is rendered in Tibetan. The three alternatives are *Phreng ba can, Sde can*, and *Bzo sbyangs*. The *Phreng ba can* is the version extant in most Kangyurs.
711. This would be Phodo Lhachu, which is another name for the upper Kyichu, flowing from Damzhung County to Phodo Dzong. See Dorje 2009, 176. There is also a lesser Lhachu—a tributary of the Pachu that flows east from Tolung Dechen county, between Taklung and Drilung. See Dorje 2009, 173–75.

712. *Brtag gnyis kyi bshad pa rngog lugs.*
713. The name of a local estate in the Taklung area.
714. This occurred in the year 1480. On the rise of the house of Rinpung under Drungchen Norzang (d. 1466) and his son Donyo Dorje (1462–1512), see Shakabpa 1984, 86–89. Donyo Dorje founded the monastery of Yangpachen in 1479 and Karma Gonsar Tubten Chokhor in Lhasa in 1503.
715. On Sinpori in Chushul County, see Dorje 2009, 190.
716. Recrossing to the north bank of the Yarlung Tsangpo.
717. This is Tsongdu Tsokpa in the Drachi valley.
718. In other words, on visiting Samye, he paid his respects by avoiding any political association with the Zhamarpa or Karmapa orders.
719. Otherwise known as Nam Tseding (Gnam rtse lding), owing to its location near Lake Namtso in Damzhung County. See Dorje 2009, 164–67.
720. This means that he crossed Zhagong La, which divides Damzhung and Nyemo counties, and then headed into the upper Zhu valley. See Dorje 2009, 296–97.
721. This is an eleventh-century Kadampa monastery founded by Ngok Lotsāwa, which is now in ruins. See Dorje 2009, 297.
722. *Sems 'grel gsum.*
723. *Zhal lung gi bskor.*
724. *'Phags bskor.*
725. *Caryāmelāpakapradīpa, Spyod pa bsdus pa'i sgron ma* (Toh. 1803; Dg.T. rgyud, *ngi*, ff. 57a–106b).
726. *Byams chos sde lnga.*
727. *Rigs tshogs.*
728. *'Jigs byed kyi sku sbra thags.*
729. Gyere Lhakhang in Taktse County, to the north of Yerpa. See Akester 2016, 140.
730. Gzims bsag byang ma.
731. *Mos gus srog 'khor.*
732. *'Gro mgon rin po che'i bka' 'bum.*
733. Kṣemendra, *Avadānakalpalātā, Rtogs brjod dpag bsam khri shing* (Toh. 4155; Dg.T. skyes rab, *ke*, ff. 1b–366a, *khe*, ff. 1b–329a).
734. *Phag mo gzhung drug gi byin rlabs.*
735. That is to say, in the lifetime of Ngawang Namgyel.
736. Choje Kunga Peljor (1428–1476) is revered as the second Drukchen—the reincarnation of Tsangpa Gyare (1161–1211), and the thirteenth preceptor of Ralung Monastery. See BDRC P920; and Treasury of Lives.
737. Drukpa Rinpoche Ngawang Chokyi Gyelpo (1465–1540) was the younger brother of Drukpa Kunlek and teacher of Drukchen Pema Karpo. See BDRC P873.
738. These seven maṇḍalas that Marpa had imparted to Ngok Choku Dorje (see part 1, chap. 7, note 17) are Hevajra (Kye rdo rje lha dgu), Nairātmyā (Yum bdag med lha mo bco lnga), Vajrapañjara (Rdo rje gur rigs bsdus lha zhe

dgu), Caturvajrapīṭha (Rdo rje gdang bzhi), Jñānaḍākinī (De'i yum bka' ye shes mkha' 'gro lha bcu gsum), Mahāmāyā (Sgyu ma chen mo lha lnga), and Mañjuśrīguhyaka according to the Ngok tradition that derives from Smṛtijñānakīrti ('Jam dpal gsangs sngags lha ngo gsum ma). See Nordang Orgyen 2008, 1636.

739. Ngok Jangchub Pel (1360–1446).
740. This is Namgyel Tashi (1524–1563), the fifteenth hierarch of the abbatial succession of Taklung Upper Plain, on whom see p. 391.
741. This is Rinchen Chogyel, the fifteenth hierarch of Drigung. His dates are disputed: 1421–1469, 1448–1504, and 1449–1484 have all been suggested, the last of these being cited in Thupten Phuntsok 2013, 2426.
742. Kunga Rinchen (1475–1527) was the sixteenth hierarch of Drigung. See BDRC P466; and Thupten Phuntsok 2013, 2426.
743. This is the renowned and prolific Sakya scholar Śākya Chokden of Zilung (1428–1507). See BDRC P396.
744. In Penyul.
745. *Bka' brgyud gser phreng.*
746. Lineage prayers refer to him as an emanation of Mañjuśrī.
747. *star gyi pu shud bya.* Translation marked as uncertain.—Ed.
748. *De nyid 'dus pa.*
749. Eighth Karmapa, Mikyo Dorje (1507–1554). See BDRC P385; and Treasury of Lives.
750. *Chos drug gsol 'debs.*
751. Zhalu Lotsāwa Rinchen Chokyong Zangpo (1441–1527). See BDRC P856.
752. *Mgon po'i bstod pa rkang pa brgyad pa.*
753. Sharawa Rabjampa Sangye Senge was a lineage holder of the aural lineage of Rechung. See BDRC P204.
754. *Bde mchog snyan brgyud.*
755. This is Tsangnyon Heruka (Gtsang smyon he ru ka, 1452–1507), illustrious author of the Life of Mila Repa. See BDRC P442; and Treasury of Lives.
756. This is perhaps to be identified with the physician Zurkharwa Nyamnyi Dorje (1439–1475), although the latter's birthplace is said to be in Dakpo rather than Lato.
757. This refers to the astrological determinism (*gza' gtad*) of planetary movements that are said to determine conventional life. Drukpa Kunlek (1455–1529) is famous for his unconventional lifestyle. See Dowman 1980; and Dargye 2001.
758. First Pawo Tulku, Chowang Lhundrub (1440–1503) was the first in the line of the incarnations of Nenang Monastery, near Tsurphu, on which see Akester 2016, 205; and Dorje 2009, 161.
759. *Chos drug gi khrid yig legs bshad khyad par gsum ldan.*
760. Minyak Rabjam Drakpa Dorje (d. c. 1491), was a disciple of Ngorchen Kunga Zangpo and teacher of Sakya Lotsāwa Jampei Dorje (1485–1533).

761. Sangye Nyenpa Tashi Peljor (1457–1525), of Benchen Monastery in Kham, was a teacher of Eighth Karmapa. See BDRC P1012.
762. *Stag lung chos drug nyams khrid.*
763. The text reads *gnam mchod sgrub pa* for *gnam chod sgrub pa.*
764. As yet unidentified.
765. Presently unidentified. This would correspond to the Lijiang area.
766. Unidentified at present.
767. *Stag lung chos drug.*
768. On Kyase Tokden, see BDRC P10358.
769. Unidentified at present.
770. *Pa spom zhva dmar ba'i bzhag thabs.*
771. That is to say, the time of Ngawang Namgyel.
772. The Drungpa Kyilsangwa (Drung pa dkyil srang ba) would control monastic discipline and rectify its breaches.
773. That is to say, in accordance with the Taklungpa tradition itself.
774. *'bur 'dod.* Translation marked as uncertain.—Ed.
775. The distinction between the "brown" community (*smug skyu ba rnams*) and the "striped" community (*khra khyu ba rnams*) is made on the basis of the external decoration of their buildings—the striped walls reflecting the Sakya-Zhalu influence of Buton and the brown walls reflecting the indigenous Taklung tradition.
776. *A Commentary on the Difficult Points of "A Commentary on 'Valid Cognition,'" Tshad ma rnam 'grel gyi dka' 'grel, Pramāṇavārttikapañjikā* (Toh. 4217; Dg.T. tshad ma, *che*, ff. 1b–326b).
777. *An Explanatory Commentary on "A Commentary on 'Valid Cognition,'" Pramāṇavārttikaṭīkā, Tshad ma rnam 'grel gyi 'grel bshad* (Toh. 4220; Dg.T. tshad ma, *je*, ff. 1b–328a, *nye*, ff. 1b–282a).
778. Prajñākaragupta, *An Ornament for "A Commentary on 'Valid Cognition,'" Pramāṇavārttikālaṃkāra, Tshad ma rnam 'grel gyi rgyan* (Toh. 4221; Dg.T. tshad ma, *te*, ff. 1b–308a, *the*, ff. 1b–282a).
779. Chapter three of *The Correct: An Explanatory Commentary on "Ascertainment of Valid Cognition," Pramāṇaviniścayaṭīkā, Tshad ma rnam par nges pa'i 'grel bshad / Tshad ma rnam par nges pa'i ṭī ka 'thad ldan zhes bya ba le'u gsum pa* (Toh. 4227; Dg.T. tshad ma, *tshe*, ff. 1b–178a); chapters one and two of *The Correct: An Explanatory Commentary on "Ascertainment of Valid Cognition," Pramāṇaviniścayaṭīkā, Tshad ma rnam par nges pa'i 'grel bshad / Tshad ma rnam par nges pa'i ṭī ka 'thad ldan zhes bya ba le'u dang po dang gnyis pa* (Toh. 4229; Dg.T. tshad ma, *dze*, ff. 1b–289a); *An Extensive Commentary on "Drop of Reasoning," Nyāyabinduṭīkā, Rigs pa'i thigs pa'i rgya cher 'grel pa* (Toh. 4231; Dg.T. tshad ma, *we*, ff. 36b–92a).
780. *Complete Purity: An Explanatory Commentary on "Ornament for 'A Commentary on Valid Cognition,'" Pramāṇavārttikālaṃkāraṭīkāsupariśuddhānāma,*

Tshad ma rnam 'grel rgyan gyi 'grel bshad shin tu yongs su dag pa zhes bya ba (Toh. 4226; Dg.T. tshad ma, *phe*, ff. 174b–287a, *be*, ff. 1b–261a, *me*, 1b–328a, *tse*, 1b–251a).

781. *Spyod 'jug gi rang 'grel.* This appears to be no longer extant.
782. This passage is also found in Kunga Drolchok's detailed biography (*Rnam thar zhib mo rnam par 'byed pa*) of Zilungpa Śākya Chokden. See his Collected Works (1995), vol. *ma*.
783. See BDRC P5312. He appears to be the author of *A Means for Attainment of Vajrayoginī, Rdo rje rnal 'byor ma'i sgrub thabs* (TPD 42, 1234–37).
784. Tsultrim Chodrub was born during the fifteenth century. See BDRC P7160.
785. Tashi Pelwa is briefly mentioned by Go Lo Zhonu Pel, who was his contemporary. See Roerich 1949, 648. Although allocated to a separate chapter in this book, he was not recognized as a hierarch of the abbatial succession.
786. The fourfold symbolic maṇḍala (*brda can gyi dkyil 'khor rnam pa bzhi*) may correspond to the four ritual procedures of maṇḍala construction (*dkyil 'khor gyi cho ga bzhi*) outlined in Nordang Orgyen 2008, 484.
787. *ye srung.* Translation marked as uncertain.—Ed.
788. The expression "two profound paths" (*zab mo'i lam gnyis*) could differentiate paths that are pure and impure, uncontaminated and contaminated, or supramundane and mundane.
789. The festival of Lhachen Yulgyel Pelbar (Lha chen g.yul rgyal dpal 'bar gyi rab ston) may possibly commemorate the mythological victory of the gods over the antigods, or else it could poetically denote the anniversary of Lhabab Duchen (Lha babs dus chen), on the twenty-second day of the ninth lunar month.
790. The expression "two sciences" (*gtsug lag gnyis*) denotes the spiritual and temporal traditions.
791. Kyormolung Monastery, in Tolung (Akester 2016, 193–95; and Dorje 2009, 169), was founded in the twelfth century by the Kadam master Balti Wangchuk Tsultrim and converted to the Geluk tradition in the fourteenth century. This was where Śākya Chokden began his studies in 1435 at the age of seven. See Komarovski, 2007; and Treasury of Lives.
792. The practice of Vaiśravaṇa in the form Great Yellow One with the Eight Masters of the Horses (Ser chen rta bdag brgyad pa) was prevalent at Taklung, whereas Śākya Chokden held the Kyormolung lineage of Vaiśravaṇa in the form Vaiśravaṇa of the Eight Great Families (rNam sras rigs chen brgyad). See Nebesky-Wojkowitz 1956, 68–81.
793. This is in Daryul.
794. Roasted barley flour.
795. Bde chen ser chen rta bdag brgyad pa.
796. See p. 268.
797. This denotes the fivefold sequence of visualization according to the generation

stage of meditation: (1) emptiness, (2) the lunar throne, (3) the seed-syllable indicative of buddha speech, (4) the hand emblem symbolic of buddha mind, and (5) the fully perfect body of the deity. See Dudjom Rinpoche 1991, 2:140.

798. See Nordrang Orgyen 2008, 2930–31.
799. See Nordrang Orgyen 2008, 1733.
800. See Nordrang Orgyen 2008, 1866.
801. See Nordrang Orgyen 2008, 1746.
802. See Dudjom Rinpoche 1991, 2:158–59.
803. This entire incident is also recounted in the detailed biography of Śākya Chokden (Collected Works, 1995, vol *ma*).
804. See the detailed biography of Śākya Chokden.
805. Presently unidentified.
806. Unidentified at present.
807. Perhaps Tangtong Gyelpo, whose personal name was Tsondru Zangpo.
808. *'jong mo*. Translation marked as uncertain.—Ed.
809. This would be the iron-chain bridge spanning the Phodo Lhachu, constructed by Tangtong Gyelpo. Its remains can still be seen (Dorje 2009, 176).
810. *rta zla,* the first Hor month.
811. *sku gzhan la brten nas*. Translation marked as uncertain.—Ed.
812. That is to say, he was the half brother of Tashi Pelwa. As stated on p. 380, the present biography of Namgyel Drakpa Pelzangpo was composed by his disciple Rinchen Tsultrim Chokdrub. He is also briefly mentioned by name in Pawo Tsuklak Trengwa 1962, 427.
813. Drigung Choje Rinchen Pelzangpo (1429–1469) was the fourteenth hierarch of Drigung. Zholungtso here refers to a meditation hermitage (*ri khrod*) associated with Zholungtso Khapa and Jampel Gyatso, one of the eight attendants of Tsongkhapa. Guṇwa is unidentified at present. On Śavaripā, see p. 75.
814. Chos drug yid bzhin nor bu.
815. Sku rags ma'i chos bskor.
816. *Dus 'khor gyi byed pa'i rtsis*.
817. *Dbyangs char rgyud kyi ri mo*.
818. According to Buddhist phenomenology, the four pahases of an eon of time are those of formation, evolution, dissolution, and vacuity. See Nyima and Dorje 2000, 231.
819. On Tibetan astrology, see Henning 2007; and Schuh 1973. On elemental divination, see Dorje 2001.
820. Śarvavarman, *Kalāpasūtra*, *Sgra ka lā pa* (*Ka lā pa'i mdo*) (Toh. 4282; Dg.T. sgra mdo, *le*, ff. 1b–20a).
821. Candragomin, *Candravyākaraṇasūtranāma*, *Lung ston pa tsandra pa'i mdo* (Toh. 4269; Dg.T. sgra mdo, *re*, ff. 1b–29a).
822. Candragomin, *Uṇ la sogs pa'i 'grel pa* (Toh. 4279; Dg.T. sgra mdo, *re*, ff. 106a–142a).

823. *Pūrṇacandra, *Dhātukāya*, *Byings kyi tshogs* (Toh. 4277; Dg.T. sgra mdo, *re*, ff. 71a–78a).
824. *Syādyantaprakriyā*, *Si la sogs pa'i mtha'i bya ba* (Toh. 4287; Dg.T. sgra mdo, *she*, ff. 1b–54a).
825. Ratnākaraśānti, *Chandoratnākaranāma*, *Sdeb sbyor rin chen 'byung gnas* (Toh. 4304; Dg.T. sgra mdo, *se*, ff. 361a–379a).
826. Daṇḍin, *Kāvyādarśa*, *Snyan ngag me long* (Toh. 4301; Dg.T. sgra mdo, *se*, ff. 318b–341a).
827. On Jamgon Kongtrul's presentation of Sanskrit grammar, see Dorje 2012, 125–38, for prosody, 367–78, for poetics, 359–66, and on synonymics, 379–85.
828. On these non-Tibetan calligraphic scripts, see Dorje 2012, 246–50, and notes 452–66.
829. *De nyid 'dus pa*.
830. *gsang ba byin*. Translation marked as uncertain.—Ed.
831. *Dpal ldan dud sol lha mo*.
832. *Dbang rdo rje phreng ba*.
833. *Sgrub thabs rgya mtsho*.
834. *Sgrub thabs brgya rtsa*.
835. The four attractive qualities of a bodhisattva (*catuḥsaṃgrahavastu*, *bsdu ba'i dngos po/ rnam pa bzhi*), are generosity (*dāna*, *sbyin pa*), pleasant speech (*priyavacana*, *snyan par smra ba*), purposeful activity (*arthacaryā*, *don spyod pa*), and harmony (*samānavihāra*, *don mthun pa*). For the many variants, see Nordrang Orgyen 2008, 695–97.
836. Presently unidentified.
837. Presently unidentified.
838. Gyeltang lies South of Puborang, within the Yangtze basin. On this southern enclave of Kham, see Dorje 2009, 518–23. Dzakhol here must refer to the Mekong areas to the north and west of Gyeltang in present-day Dechen and Markham counties, rather than Dzakhol near Drigung.
839. Saṅghabhadra, *An Exegesis on the Treasury of Phenomenology*, *Abhidharmakośaśāstrakārikābhāṣya*, *Chos mngon pa mdzod kyi bstan bcos kyi tshig le'ur byas pa'i rnam par bshad pa* (TPD 79), 1232.
840. This is the first mention in the narrative of the three large Gelukpa monasteries founded in the Lhasa area by Tsongkhapa and two of his disciples in the first two decades of the fifteenth century. Here they are mentioned alongside the older Kadam, Kagyu, and Sakya establishments.
841. As indicated in Nebesky-Wojkowitz (1956, 46–47), the three primary retainers (*rtsa ba'i 'khor gsum*) of Jñānanātha are Lekyi Gonpo (Las kyi mgon po), Lekden Nakpo (Legs ldan nag po), and Tsandika. There are also eight retainers with different animal faces (*gdong mo brgyad*).
842. Gyad pa. This is marked as uncertain.—Ed.
843. At that time the head of Phakmodru, the Neudzongpa, was Rinchen Dorje (1474–1513).

844. Uruling is located in the upper Kyichu gorge on the road from Phodo Dzong to Damzhung. See www.tibetmap.com.

845. This would have to have occurred between 1509 and his death in 1530. This event would therefore precede the involvement of the Mongols in the usurping of power by Samdrubtse in 1565. It would have coincided with the lifetime of Second Dalai Lama (1475–1542).

846. This work, the *Abridgement of the Lives of the Abbatial Succession* (*Gdan rabs kyi rnam thar snying po nye bar bsdus pa*) would presumably have provided primary source material for Ngawang Namgyel's history of the lineage. It appears to be no longer extant.

847. *Lnga bsdus kyi rtsis gzhi.*

848. *Gtsug lag khang rnams kyi dkar chag.* Three works by him on the *Kālacakra* appear to be extant at BDRC.

849. Rinchen Tsultrim Chokdrub was a disciple of Namgyel Drakpa and teacher of Namgyel Tashi.

850. See p. 381.

851. The nephew mentioned here may in fact have been one of the two sons of Ngawang Chokyi Gyelpo, who were named Ngawang Drakpa (1506–1538) and Ngagi Wangchuk (1517–1554); or else it could possibly refer to the illustrious Fourth Drukchen, Pema Karpo (1527–1592).

852. Yezang Tsepa is one of the names of Go Lo Zhonu Pel (1392–1481), the author of *The Blue Annals*, on whom see chapter 8, note 592. His nephew, Monlam Drakpa Pelzangpo, was an associate of Fourth Zhamar.

853. A master of the Chel (Dpyal) lineage.

854. Kun rig rgyud don gsal ba'i rnam nges. This would not be First Riwoche Jedrung, Tsokye Dorje (1530–1590) who was born the year in which Namgyel Drakpa died. This could refer to the Rinpungpa potentate Tsokye Dorje (1462–1510), who may have been the author of this text.

855. Chokyi Shenyen (1453–1540) was the thirteenth throne holder of Ganden, who held that office from 1516–1521. See BDRC P447; and Treasury of Lives. Our text misreads Chokyi Sherab for Chokyi Shenyen.

856. Perhaps to be identified with Jang Gom Rinchen Zangpo. See BDRC P8LS15428.

857. This would be Unyon Kunga Zangpo (1458–1532). See BDRC P814.

858. Tsultrim Wangchuk (BDRC P3046, b. fifteenth century), was the nephew of Bumrampa Rinchen Chowang (BDRC P2642).

859. Pelkhor Dechen would be Pelkhor Chode Monastery at Gyantse.

860. Langtang Chenga Jeon Śākya Gyeltsen (BDRC P0RK1572) was a disciple of Śākya Chokden.

861. Zurmang Jatang Lodro Gyatso (1479–1540) was a physician renowned for his maṇi pills (*ma ṇi ril sgrub*). See BDRC P5564.

862. This could be First Lhatsun Tulku of Sera Monastery (BDRC P8LS12953).

863. Second Dalai Lama, Gendun Gyatso (1476–1542), tenth throne holder of Drepung. See Treasury of Lives; and BDRC P84.

864. He was also a disciple of Fourth Zhamar. See BDRC P2GS1028.
865. Also known as Yungpa Tsewang Tashi (b. sixteenth century). See BDRC P5837.
866. According to BDRC P2GS993, he was also a patron of Fourth Zhamar. Chongye Taktse is the seat of the family into which Fifth Dalai Lama was born in 1617. See Dorje 2009, 264. The Tibetan is more usually spelled *'phyong rgyas* rather than *'chong rgyas*, as shown here.
867. Probably to be identified with Lingpon Chen Choku Ozer (BDRC P0RK607), who had affiliations with the Ngor tradition.
868. That is to say, Sonam Yeshe Pelzangpo was the younger brother of Namgyel Drakpa and half-brother of Tashi Pelwa.
869. *Rin chen rgyan 'dra.*
870. *Zin bris bklags pas grub pa.* Ngok Chokyi Gyeltsen appears in the Ngok lineage between Ngok Rinchen Zang and Ngok Dondrub Pel.
871. *Śrīkhasamatantrarāja, Dpal nam mkha' dang mnyam pa'i rgyud kyi rgyal po* (Toh. 386; Dg.T. rgyud, *ga*, ff. 199a–202a).
872. *Mchog gzigs rnam pa gnyis kyi zhal lung.*
873. *Grol byed bskyed rim lhan cig skyes ma.*
874. *Rdzogs rim snyan brgyud yid bzhin nor bu.*
875. See p. 272.
876. These instructions denote the particular Taklung lineage.
877. *Chos drug dar khug ma.*
878. *Yid bzhin nor bu.*
879. As stated in *The Golden Garland of the Kamtsang Kagyu* (*Kam tshangs bka' brgyud gser phreng*) of Fifth Karmapa, *The Garland of White Light* (*'Od dkar phreng ba*) was composed by Choje Tashi Peltsek.
880. The white and black vitality channels consist of the nerves and arteries. See Parfionovitch, Dorje, and Meyer 1992.
881. See p. 129.
882. According to Nordrang Orgyen (2008, 329), the three sorts of pure meat (*rnam gsum dag pa'i sha gsum*) exclude the following: (1) meat of an animal that one has seen being killed for one's own sake, (2) meat of an animal that one has reliably heard has been killed for one's own sake, and (3) meat of an animal that one doubts may have been killed for one's own sake.
883. According to Nordrang Orgyen 2008, 175–76, the three kindnesses (*bka' drin gsum ldan*) are the kindnesses of (1) teaching the sacred doctrine, (2) blessing the continuum of consciousness, and (3) nurturing retainers by material means. Alternatively, they are the kindnesses of (1) receiving the vows of individual liberation, (2) receiving the bodhisattva vows, and (3) receiving the vows of the mantras. Or else they may be the kindnesses of (1) receiving empowerment, (2) imparting exegeses of the tantras, and (3) imparting the pith instructions.

884. *gzu yig*. Translation marked as uncertain.—Ed.
885. The text reads water male dragon, but see p. 369. Also, as stated on p. 370, Tashi Pelwa was his half brother.
886. Choje Bum Rabjampa may refer to Yeshe Drakpa, the tenth abbot of Gomang at Drepung.
887. Chime Pelzangpo is probably to be identified with the one who transmitted the Bodongpa teachings to Pawo Tsuklak Trengwa in 1519. See BDRC P5106.
888. Otherwise known as Kongpo Karchen Kunga Drakpa. See BDRC P5595.
889. The four retreat hermitages (*ri khrod rnam pa bzhi*) associated with Taklung are Sengling, Drilung, Tangdrok, and Urulung.
890. *Rtog brjod bka' rgya can*. On Namgyel Tashi (Ngawang Namgyel Tashi Drakpa Gyeltsen Pelzangpo, 1524–1563), see also BDRC P5557. His *Sealed Narrative* (*Rtog brjod bka' rgya can*) has not yet been located.
891. Ārciḥkṣetra, 'Od 'phro'i zhing.
892. See p. 213.
893. See also BDRC P8738.
894. See p. 308.
895. See p. 309.
896. Yet to be identified by name.
897. Tsokye Dorje of Zangzang Neuringpa would be the Rinpungpa potentate Tsokye Dorje (1462–1510), rather than First Jedrung of Riwoche (1530–1590).
898. Rinchen Drak monastery in the vicinity of Lhundrub Dzong. See Akester 2016, 46.
899. *dge ba grub rjes*. Translation marked as uncertain.—Ed.
900. There are seven auspicious conjunctions (*'grub sbyor*) formed by the coincidence of the seven days of the week with specific constellations. See Nyima and Dorje 2001, 680.
901. Presently unidentified. This is possibly the same as Jamyang Ngawang Kunga Rinchen.
902. Gnas lugs phyag rgya chen po lhan cig skyes sbyor.
903. Bde stong phyag rgya chen po.
904. The generation stage entails an external visualization in which the deity appears in front of the meditator (*bdun bskyed*) and an internal visualization when the deity and oneself are identical (*bdag bskyed*). Secretly, the deity then appears as the pure essence of the vital heart mantra (*srog snying dvangs ma*) within the central channel.
905. The expression *mngal dang shol gyi zla ba rtsis pa'i tshigs rdzogs pa* derives from vinaya literature and is an arcane method of calculating the final year of a novice monk prior to receiving full ordination at the age of twenty. That is to say, the novitiate is received at the age of seven, but the full ordination is not permitted until the age of twenty. Once the novice monk has reached the age of nineteen, the final year preceding the full ordination is then calculated

as "nine months of the womb plus the three intercalary months that occur between the ages of seven and nineteen," making a full year of twelve months. See Thupten Phuntsok 2013, 893–94.

906. This was Jamyang Ngawang Kunga Rinchen (1517–1584), the twenty-third throne holder of Sakya, on whom see part 1, chap. 8, note 1045. See also BDRC P460.

907. Kunga Drolchok (1507–1565) was the compiler and author of *The Hundred and Eight Teaching Manuals of Jonang* (*Jo nang khri brgya*). He was the twenty-fourth hierarch of the abbatial succession at Jonang. See BDRC P2387. See also Dorje 2020. On his associations with Taklung, see van der Kuijp and Tuttle 2014, 464–65.

908. Aśvajit ('Phags pa rta thul) was one of Śākyamuni Buddha's five original noble companions.

909. Rāhulabhadra, the son of Śākyamuni Buddha, on whom see p. 28.

910. On Upāli, the original compiler of the vinaya, see p. 28.

911. Yung Rinchen Gonpo (G.yung rin chen mgon po, fl. sixteenth century) appears to have been an eclectic follower of both Second Dalai Lama and Eighth Karmapa. See BDRC P5703.

912. See part 1, chap. 8, note 99.

913. These all refer to the systematic structure of Jetsun Kunga Drolchok's *Hundred and Eight Teaching Manuals of Jonang*. See Dorje 2020.

914. See Nebesky-Wojkowitz 1975, 60–63.

915. On legends associated with the great divine Genyen of Taklung, see Nebesky-Wojkowitz 1956, 161–65.

916. See Nebesky-Wojkowitz 1975, 48–49.

917. *snga ma'i gong gnon gyi tshul du*. Translation marked as uncertain.—Ed.

918. *'khor lo gnyis ma'i man ngag*. This includes the Taklungpa and Drigungpa cycles of Mahākāla in the form Kurakma, exemplified by the *Sku rags ma 'khor lo gnyis ma'i gsang sgrub*.

919. *gzhan snga nas deng sang*. Translation marked as uncertain.—Ed.

920. *khrab khrob*. Translation marked as uncertain.—Ed.

921. That is to say, in the time of Ngawang Namgyel.

922. *Gtor 'bul gyi tshigs bcad*.

923. *Gsol mchod dgyes pa kha skong*. This appears to be no longer extant.

924. Jagaddarpaṇa, *Vajrācāryakriyāsamuccaya*, *Rdo rje slob dpon gyi bya ba kun las btus pa* (Toh. 3305; Dg.T. rgyud, *bu*, ff. 48a–249a).

925. *Rnal 'byor rdzogs phreng*.

926. The author denigrates the shallow approach of those who would shun the elaborate descriptive bases of the generation stage and opt for a simplified generic approach instead.

927. Here the author points out the defects of those who rely exclusively on text-based rituals (*dpe chog*) and those who rely exclusively on mind-based rituals (*blo chog*).

928. Rdor dbyings.
929. Sbas don kun gsal.
930. Chos bzhi.
931. Blo sbyong.
932. Spyan ras gzigs kyi smar khrid.
933. Sgo gnyis.
934. The three sorts of scrutiny (*dpyad pa gsum*) through which gemstones are examined are burning, cutting, and polishing. See Nordrang Orgyen 2008, 332.
935. It seems that these are no longer extant at the present day.
936. *Gsang ba'i rtogs brjod bka' rgya can.*
937. *'Dul ba'i bslab bya dgag sgrub kyi snying po nges par bstan pa.*
938. *Dkyil chog rdo rje phreng ba'i phyag len legs par bshad pa 'jigs med dgongs rgyan.*
939. *Rgyud sde spyi'i rnam par bzhag pa.*
940. *De bzhin gshegs pa'i 'dul ba nges par bstan pa.*
941. *Ting nge 'dzin gyi rgyal po'i mdo don man ngag dang sbyar ba nges don grub pa'i shing rta.*
942. *Stag lung pa'i lugs kyi phyag chen yid bzhin nor bu'i 'chad thabs legs bshad yongs 'du'i ljon pa.*
943. *Phyag chen lhan cig skyes sbyor gyi 'chad thabs rnam dag grub bde'i dga' ston.*
944. *Chos drug yid bzhin nor bu'i khrid yig chen mo ye shes rdo rje'i snying po len pa.*
945. *Ne gu chos drug gi 'chad thabs rnam grangs gsum.*
946. *Sbas don gyi sngon 'gro'i sems bskyed skabs kyi zhal lung.*
947. *Sbas don gyi 'chad thabs 'jam mgon bla ma'i zhal lung mkhas pa'i yid 'phrog.*
948. *Phyag chen lhan cig skyes sbyor / ga'u ma / lnga ldan / chos drug rnam pa gnyis / ro snyoms/ dbu ma lta khrid / rim bzhi / dgyes rdor dag pa gsum / 'jigs byed rva khrid / mgon po'i srog sgrub gnyis rnams kyi dmigs rkang nye bar bsdus pa.*
949. *Sku rags ma'i rgyab skyor bcu chos dang gsum chos kyi gsal byed gnad kyi sgron me.*
950. *Dpal ye shes kyi mgon po'i phyi nang gsang ba'i sgrub bskor ma lus pa gcig tu 'du ba'i khrid yig chen mo dngos grub gnyis kyi 'dod 'jo ba.*
951. *Gsang ba'i rtogs brjod.*
952. *bcu phrag klu yi ming can.* Translation marked as uncertain.—Ed.
953. No longer extant.
954. See p. 514.
955. *Gsang ba'i rtogs brjod bka' rgya ma.*
956. *Rtogs brjod dge legs snye ma.*
957. *Dngul gdung gi dkar chags dang sbrags pa nyung ngu.*
958. *Snyan grags lha'i rnga chen.*
959. *Skye rabs kyi rtogs brjod ngo mtshar tshangs pa'i gaṇḍi.*
960. See Akester 2016, 42.
961. See p. 514.
962. Fourth Drukchen, Pema Karpo (1527–1592), on whom see BDRC P825.

963. Paṇchen Dorje Gyelpo is not yet identified.
964. Kunga Pelzangpo (1513–1595) was a preceptor of Jonang monastery. On his connection with Taklung, see van der Kuijp and Tuttle 2014, 464.
965. Not yet identified.
966. The title Choze (Chos mdzad) denotes a monk who is exempt from manual labor on account of having made special offerings to the monastic community.
967. Not yet identified.
968. Not yet identified.
969. Not yet identified.
970. Not yet identified.
971. The main source for the biography of Namgyel Rinchen Pelzangpo (1532–1599) was the writing of Ngawang Namgyel.
972. As yet unidentified. This would not have been Zhabdrung Ngawang Namgyel (1594–1651) of Bhutan, whose personal name was Dorje Gyelpo (Aris 1979, 203–32).
973. Not yet identified.
974. *gu ru zhi ba'i sman sgrub.*
975. Place not yet identified.
976. *Gu ru thugs sgrub.*
977. Jomo Gang (Jo mo gangs) is the snow peak to the northwest of Zhugu La pass, dividing Yangpachen from Nyemo. See Dorje 2009, 296. On the protector Gangkar Shamema (Gangs dkar sha med ma), see Nebesky-Wojkowitz, 182–87.
978. On Uma Drakar (Dbu ma brag dkar) in present-day Damzhung county, see www.tibetmap.com.
979. Nyelung (Snyed lung) is presently unidentified.
980. *Rdo rje phreng ba.*
981. *Mi tra brgya rtsa.*
982. *Sbyong dkyil bcu gnyis.*
983. *Lnga tshan lnga.*
984. *Sgrub thabs rgya mtsho.*
985. *Sgrub dkyil 'jug pa bde ba.*
986. Lingkar (Gling dkar) is possibly to be identified with Langkor in Damzhung county, on which see www.tibetmap.com.
987. The vase of Vijaya (*rnam rgyal bum pa*) is the buddha's vase (*sangs rgyas kyi bum pa*), one of the five vases employed when empowerment is conferred in the maṇḍala of the vase (*bum pa'i dkyil 'khor*). See Thupten Phuntsok 2013, 1804.
988. See Dorje 2009, 164–65.
989. See Dorje 2009, 302.
990. *Sgyu 'phrul zhi khro.*
991. See Dorje 2009, 302.
992. Meton Chenpo (Mes ston chen po) would be the disciple of Marpa Lotsāwa named Meton Tsonpo of Tsangrong. See p. 119.

993. This would be Buddhajñānapāda, lineage holder of Mahāyoga and of Guhyasamāja in the form Mañjuvajra. See Dudjom Rinpoche 1991, 1:494–96.
994. Perhaps the princess Pemasel, daughter of King Tri Songdetsen. See Dudjom Rinpoche 1991, 1:554–55.
995. See p. 486.
996. This would be Yumo Mikyo Dorje (Yu mo mi bskyod rdo rje, fl. early eleventh century) who maintained the lineage of the Dro tradition ('Bros lugs) of the *Kālacakra Tantra*. See p. 553. His son and successor was Chokyi Wangchuk (Dharmeśvara), on whom see BDRC P2588.
997. Namkha Pelyang was the eighth successor to the abbatial succession of Taklung Upper Plain. See p. 279.
998. The bolded terms, followed by Tibetan transliteration, represent the meaning of the names of the master who is being praised in the verse.—Ed.
999. Ngawang Namgyel shows respect to his immediate predecessor and spiritual mentor. There are two extant biographies of Kunga Tashi—the present one by Ngawang Namgyel and Tāranātha's *Ocean of Enlightened Activity: A Biography of the Glorious Spiritual Mentor* (*Dpal ldan bla ma'i rnam thar 'phrin las rgya mtsho rnam par rgyas pa*; Collected Works of Tāranātha, vol. 38, 72–149). The parts relevant to Kunga Tashi's journey to Amdo and Mongolia have been examined in depth in van der Kuijp and Tuttle 2014.
1000. On the sixteen vital essences (*thig le bcu drug*), see the synopsis of Kunga Drolchok, in Dorje 2020.
1001. Gyelse Ngulchu Chodzongpa Zangpo Pel (Rgyal sras dngul chu chos rdzongs pa bzang po dpal) is otherwise known as Tokme Zangpo (1295–1369).
1002. See p. 355.
1003. Lhundrub Dzong was formerly the administrative capital of Penyul. Its ruins are located to the east of the main road that runs north from Ganden Chokhor to Taklung via Chak La pass. See www.tibetmap.com. It is not to be confused with Phodo Dzong—the present-day capital of Lhundrub county that includes Penyul.
1004. The Sakyapa Dakchen Ngagi Wangchuk mentioned here would probably be Ngakchang Kunga Rinchen (1517–1584), the twenty-third throne holder of Sakya. On Drukpa Ngawang Chogyel (1465–1540), see BDRC P873. On Drigung Rinchen Phuntsok (1509–1557), the seventeenth throne holder of Drigung, see Dudjom Rinpoche 1991, 1:676–77; and BDRC P399.
1005. This is a title of Jetsun Kunga Drolchok (1507–1565) of Jonang.
1006. The year 1542 was also the year that Second Dalai Lama, Gendun Gyatso passed away. His successor, Sonam Gyatso, the first to hold the title Dalai Lama, was born the following year.
1007. On Jonang, see Akester 2016, 615–28, and on Zhalu, 500–507. See also Dorje 2009, 327–30.
1008. Jikdrel Sangwa Jin ('Jigs bral gsang ba byin) is a secret name of Bodongpa Chokle Namgyel, on whom see p. 306.

1009. *dag pa gnyis ldan.*
1010. *Khrid yig chen mo dngos grub kyi 'dod 'jo.*
1011. That is to say, he resembled Śākyamuni Buddha.
1012. This is indicative of the earliest influence of the Geluk tradition at Taklung itself.
1013. The text misreads *phu chu.*
1014. The Qalqa Mongols mostly reside in the present-day republic of Mongolia. Among their diaspora, there are four small banners in China, two in Inner Mongolia, one in Kökenür, and one in Jehol. Those in Kökenür are descended from the subjects of Čogtu Qaγan (Qong Taiji) and his sons, who supported Ligden Qaγan in his patronage of the Kagyu schools, and opposed the rise of the Gelukpa. Later, the Čogtu Qaγan moved to Kökenür with his subjects sometime after 1624, intending to establish with Ligden Qaγan a Mongol kingdom independent of the Manchus. Ligden Qaγan's followers were severely depleted by smallpox en route for Kökenür, and after his death, Čogtu Qaγan began attacking Gelukpa monasteries. His son Arslang was sent to attack Lhasa, but switched sides. Fifth Dalai Lama (1617–1682) summoned the Oirat chieftain Güshi Qaγan Toro-Baiqu, whose fifty thousand men in early 1637 crushed Čogtu Qaγan's thirty thousand at Ulagan Qöśigü. Today, the Oirats of Gushi Qaγan are known as the "Upper Mongols," and they still reside in Qinghai forming twenty-one banners. The remnants of Čogtu Qong Taiji's followers form only one banner and are known as the "Lower Mongols."
1015. This period coincided with the assault of Drigung against the Gelukpa of Olka, sectarian disputes in Lhasa, the decline of Rinpungpa power, and the rise of the kings of Zhigatse. See Shakabpa 1967, 90–92; and Stein 1962, 81–82.
1016. See p. 520.
1017. *rtag bstan/brtan.* Translation marked as uncertain.—Ed.
1018. The hermitage of Cholung Jangtse (Chos lung byang rtse), founded near Jonang Phuntsokling by Jetsun Kunga Drolchok. See van der Kuijp and Tuttle 2014, 465.
1019. Tsewang Pendar is unidentified at present. See the reference in Tāranātha.
1020. Presently unidentified.
1021. That is to say, the officials of the Karmapa and the Zhamarpa.
1022. *grva'i thī.* Translation marked as uncertain.—Ed.
1023. Unidentified at present.
1024. He passed away in 1572. See BDRC P8495.
1025. See Akester 2016, 42.
1026. This would have coincided with the death of Paṇ Sonam Gyatso (1527–1570), the nineteenth hierarch of Drigung.
1027. On Lo Chengapa Ngawang Chokyi Drakpa, see BDRC P7509.
1028. *De nyid 'dus pa'i bskor.*
1029. Tendzin Ngawang Drakpa is presently unidentified.

1030. On Tāranātha's associations with this hermitage, see van der Kuijp and Tuttle 2014, 462.
1031. Akester 2016, 43.
1032. The Tibetan reads *sgo mtshungs* for *sgo mtshams*.
1033. Otherwise known as Taklung Nangso Drakpa Ozer (Stag lung nang so grags pa 'od zer). See van der Kuijp and Tuttle 2014, 472.
1034. Altan Qaγan (1507–1582) was the grandson of Dayan Qaγan (1464–1543), a descendant of Qublai Qaγan and leader of the Tümed Mongols. He invited Sonam Gyatso to Tümed in 1569, and the invitation was eventually accepted in 1577. The monastery of Tekchen Chokhor was built at the place they first met, followed by the Erdeni Juu Monastery in 1586 at Karakorum. He designated Sonam Gyatso as the "Dalai" Lama, and the latter's previous two incarnations were retrospectively accorded that same title. When Sonam Gyatso died in 1588 in Mongolia, his incarnation, Yontan Gyatso, was Altan Qaγan's great-grandson. On the importance of the arrow as an auspicious symbol of longevity, see Gerke 2012, 265–66.
1035. On the region from Dang La pass to the Yangtze, see Dorje 2009, 662–63.
1036. This would be the bridge of salt (*wangzhang*) of the Tsaidam Pendi Range, on which see Dorje 2009, 665, 669.
1037. This is present-day Dulan, on the banks of the Qagan Us River. See Dorje 2009, 667.
1038. Perhaps this is to be identified with the salt lake of Tsaka, on which see Dorje 2009, 669.
1039. Abel (A sbal) appears to have been a younger relative of Altan Qaγan. See van der Kuijp and Tuttle 2014, 473n44. Tselmar (Mtshal dmar) has not yet been identified. It appears (van der Kuijp and Tuttle 2014, 473–74) that Abel also frequented the region extending from Lake Dongi Tsona in Panchen Zhingde through to the lakes Ngoring and Kyaring, southwest of Tsogyenrawa. On that area, see Dorje 2009, 667, 673–754.
1040. Trisho Gyelmo (Khri shog rgyal mo) is the name of the deity presiding over Lake Kökenür (Qinghai hu), on which see Dorje 2009, 674–77.
1041. Washul, or Wanshul, is located in Mangra county. See the references in van der Kuijp and Tuttle 2014, 474n50. On Mangra, see Dorje 2009, 740–42.
1042. The Ordos are a Mongol clan composed of seven traditional banners based in Uushin district, Inner Mongolia. Since 1510, they were ruled by descendants of Batumöngke Dayan Qaγan, one of whom was Altan Qaγan. According to *The Biography of Ninth Karmapa*, both Abel and Bingtu sent gifts and edicts to Karmapa in 1588. See van der Kuijp and Tuttle 2014, 474n51. The Ordos Mongols believed that they were responsible for maintaining the shrine of Chinggis Qaγan, although the mausoleum of Genghis Qaγan is now controlled by the Darqads, who forced the Ordos tribes to settle outside their native grasslands. Nowadays, Ordos is known for its cashmere wool production.

1043. It is unclear whether Karma Lama is to be identified with Ninth Karmapa, Wangchuk Dorje (1556–1603), who was in Mongolia at that time, or as stated in van der Kuijp and Tuttle (2014, 474n53), with Second Dzamtang Choje, Gyelwa Senge (1509–1580). This journey of Kunga Tashi to Mongolia took place the year immediately after Sonam Gyatso had traveled to Mongolia.

1044. On the routes through and around the Amnye Machen Range, see Dorje 2009, 754–57.

1045. *zhaoshu, J̌asaγ, 'ja' sa.*

1046. *gao ming, ka'o ming las.*

1047. Van der Kuijp and Tuttle (2014, 475–78) suggest that these three officials may have been ethnic Monguors holding Ming dynasty titles. Among them, the Jina Nangso (Ji na nang so) and Chinese governor of Ziling Fort were associated with Ziling (Xining), and the Brati Nangso (Bra ti nang so) with Julak in present-day Serkhok county. The Taklung Lasar pass (Stag lung la gsar) appears to be in the upper reaches of the Tsongchu—a tributary of the Yellow River that flows through Dabzhi and Tongkor counties, Ziling and Tsongkha Khar (Pingan), and then through Drotsang (Ledu) and Kamalok (Minhe). On this region and its adjacent valleys, see Dorje 2009, 679–700.

1048. The enclave of Pari in present-day Gansu province has been inhabited by Tibetans since the royal dynastic period. See Dorje 2009, 701–2.

1049. The monasteries of Pari include Chorten Tang, founded by Sakya Paṇḍita in 1274, Taklung Gon Ganden Choling (late fourteenth century), Pari Rabgye Gonpa (Huacangsi), and Gonsar Tosam Dargyeling—the last three being Kagyu establishments before their conversion by the Gelukpa during the seventeenth century. See also the sources listed in van der Kuijp and Tuttle 2014, 478n65.

1050. The Julakchu flows through present-day Mongyon and Kamalok counties, before converging with the Tsongchu.

1051. *qianzhang, mchan chang.* Unidentified by name. On this military title, see van der Kuijp and Tuttle 2014, 476.

1052. *sečen huangtaizi, se chen hong thi'i ji.* The Sečen Qaγan was one of the four qaγans of the Qalqa Mongols, along with Tüśiyetü Qaγan, Jasagtu Qaγan, and Sain Noγan.

1053. *kaṃ chu dus thang.* This is a military title of an official in charge of thirteen myriarchies, employed particularly from the Qing dynasty onward. See van der Kuijp and Tuttle 2014, 478–79.

1054. This was the former palace of Göden, the younger brother of Güyüg Qaγan (1206–1248), a renowned patron of the Sakya school. The location is in Liangzhou.

1055. These four had been established by Sakya Paṇḍita. See the references in van der Kuijp and Tuttle 2014, 478n65.

1056. So far unidentified.

1057. This is the full name of Tāranātha (1575–1634) of Jonang, on whom see BDRC P1428; and Treasury of Lives.
1058. A lama from Cholung, the hermitage of Jetsun Kunga Drolchok, maintaining the Jonang tradition.
1059. An important lineage holder of the Jonang and Shangpa traditions, on whom see BDRC P2788.
1060. A renowned artist of the Menri style, on whom see BDRC P8855.
1061. The text misreads earth bird year for wood female bird.
1062. First Jedrung of Riwoche, otherwise known as Tsokye Dorje (1530–1590), on whom see p. 520; BDRC P3AG45; and Treasury of Lives.
1063. The three hierarchs in this context would be Taklungpa, Kuyalwa Rinchen Gonpo, and Sangye Yarjon. More generally, in the Kagyu tradition, they would include Marpa, Mila Repa, and Gampopa.
1064. This would be Gazi Yeshe Rinchen, a fourteenth-century scion of the Gazi family, from whom the hierarchs of Taklung are often descended. His ancestor Gazi Gongyel was the father of Sangye Yarjon. Namkha Pelyang, the eighth hierarch of the abbatial succession, was the first of the Gazi line to be born in Penyul at Daryul Tengkhang.
1065. On Nangchen and Zurmang, see Dorje 2009, 618–31, and on Karma Gomde, 481–82.
1066. Akester 2016, 43.
1067. On the assembly hall of Reteng, see Akester 2016, 31–33; and Dorje 2009, 176–77.
1068. See Dorje 2009, 662–63.
1069. See Dorje 2009, 667, 753; and Wang Yao 1979.
1070. According to van der Kuijp and Tuttle (2014, 479), *zhongqi* would denote a battalion commander and *daiqing* a Mongol serving the Ming administration.
1071. See BDRC 4250.
1072. *bya chen po*. Translation marked as uncertain.—Ed.
1073. The protector deity of the Amnye Machen Range.
1074. The *tā jus* motif and the *nya jus* inlaid gold-threaded satin motifs of the Mongol and Ming periods are yet to be determined.
1075. Akester 2016, 43.
1076. Kha than bā dur.
1077. His descendants appear to be mentioned by Fifth Dalai Lama, discussing the reincarnation of Choje Jampa Gyatso, throne holder of Ganden, in the family of one Qar Daicing Qadun Bagatur.
1078. Drukpa Rinpoche, Mipham Chokyi Gyelpo (1543–1604), on whom see BDRC P2629.
1079. Mipham Tenpei Nyima (1567–1619), the father of Zhabdrung Ngawang Namgyel of Bhutan, on whom see BDRC P2628.
1080. Bka' 'bum zab bsdus.

1081. Gshin rje char ka'i gdong zor.
1082. This would be Chogyel Rinchen Phuntsok Tashi (1547–1602), the twenty-second hierarch of Drigung, on whom see BDRC P4580.
1083. This is Fourth Dalai Lama, Yonten Gyatso (1589–1616), also known as the thirteenth throne holder of Drepung Assembly Hall. See BDRC P177; and Treasury of Lives.
1084. That is to say, he embraced them, just as he had embraced their predecessors, Konchok Yenlak and Sonam Gyatso.
1085. See Nebesky-Wojkowitz 1975, 469.
1086. Fifth Drukchen, Paksam Wangpo (Dpag bsam dbang po, 1593–1641), on whom see BDRC P877.
1087. That is, Drukpa Mipham Chokyi Gyelpo and Mipham Tenpei Nyima were the forefathers of the founder of the Drukpa Kagyu school in Bhutan.
1088. This is Tāranātha, on whom see part 1, chap. 8, note 1083.
1089. See BDRC P8LS14242.
1090. See BDRC P5829.
1091. Not yet identified by name.
1092. Unidentified.
1093. Unidentified.
1094. Unidentified.
1095. Unidentified.
1096. On this aspect of Mahākāla and the entourage of arrogant spirits (*dregs pa*), see Nebesky-Wojkowitz 1975, 58–59.
1097. *Sku rdzis chos spyod rab gsal.*
1098. *Legs bshad rin po che'i gter.*
1099. *Thams cad mkhyen pa ngag gi dbang po'i rnam thar.*
1100. *Lam zab bla ma'i rnal 'byor.*
1101. *Thar pa rin po che'i rgyan.*
1102. *Sgrub thabs rgya rtsa.*
1103. *Theg pa chen po'i lam gyi rim pa thar pa rin po che'i rgyan.*
1104. The sacred dances (*'cham chen*) of Vajrakīla enact the upper rite (*stod las*), which turns the ritual spike against one's own afflicted mental states, and the lower rite (*smad las*), which wrathfully transmutes the afflicted mental states of others. On this distinction, see Dudjom Rinpoche 1991, 1:710–16.
1105. This translation marked as uncertain, as either green or red.—Ed.
1106. *Lam zab mo bla ma'i rnal 'byor.*
1107. The Lhasa area.
1108. *Rdor dbyings sgar chen.*
1109. *'Jigs byed zhe dgu ma.*
1110. *Rgyud 'bum.*
1111. Snyan brgyud lhan cig skyes ma.
1112. *Mi tra brgya rtsa.*

1113. *Snyan brgyud lhan cig skyes ma.*
1114. Duzhapa Jampa Lhundrub (Dus zhabs pa byams pa lhun grub), a *Kālacakra* master of Jonang, presently unidentified.
1115. As yet unidentified.
1116. Chos drug gi nyams khrid.
1117. *Sbyong dkyil bcu gnyis.*
1118. See Harding 2007, 449n17.
1119. *Lnga tshan lnga.* An anthology of deities and their maṇḍalas associated with Karmapa Dusum Khyenpa, including Cakrasaṃvara.
1120. See part 1, chap. 8, note 441.
1121. Perceptible forms are those of sights, sounds, odors, tastes, and tangibles. Imperceptible forms are those that arise during distracted apperception and those that arise during meditative stability. See Dorje 2012, 543–44.
1122. This place is mentioned in connection with Nyingdrung in *The Testament of Ba Anthology* (*Rba bzhed phyogs bsgrigs*) (Beijing: Mi rigs dpe skrun khang, 2009), 32.
1123. An eight-legged mythological creature, more powerful than a lion or an elephant, possessing the ability to clear a valley in one jump, originally conceived as part-lion and part-bird but in later literature, assuming the form of a deer.
1124. *paṭar 'khyil ba.*
1125. Other references to him in the writings of Fifth Dalai Lama suggest that this governor of the Lhasa area had connections to Ganden.
1126. Khartse (Mkhar rtse) lies below Nalendra Monastery in Penyul. See Akester 2016, 56.
1127. Reference of "this place" is marked as uncertain, either Taklung or Yangpachen.—Ed.
1128. Rngog dkyil bdun.
1129. Mi tra brgya rtsa.
1130. *Brtags gnyis ṭīk chen.*
1131. Bskyed rim bzhi.
1132. Uma Drakar in Damzhung County. See wwww.tibetmap.com.
1133. Lozim Okpa Jampa Chojor (Lo gzims 'og pa 'byams pa chos 'byor) is mentioned by Fifth Dalai Lama under the name Jampa Cholhor ('Byams pa chos lhor).
1134. Unidentified at present.
1135. *Mi tra brgya rtsa.*
1136. *Mdo rtsa.*
1137. *Sgrub thabs brgya rtsa.*
1138. *Sgrol ma nyer gcig.*
1139. *Grub thob brgyad cu.*
1140. See BDRC P8LS14242.
1141. *Sdom pa gsum gyi bslam pa rgya cher bshad pa.*

1142. *Bsdus don.*
1143. Tsib Nesar appears to be listed as a treasure-site of Guru Chowang. See his Collected Works, vol. 13, 483.
1144. Gyabdrak appears to be located in Kongpo, according to the writings of Fifth Dalai Lama.
1145. Tshe dbang brgya rtsa.
1146. Gdugs dkar lha mang.
1147. On Namseling Manor (Rnam sras gling), see Dorje 2009, 207–8.
1148. This would not have been Fourth Drukchen, Pema Karpo who passed away in 1592.
1149. *khra chen mtha' dbus med pa.* Translation marked as uncertain.—Ed.
1150. *Rgyud 'bum.*
1151. *Mdo mangs.*
1152. *Nyi shu lnga pa.*
1153. *Bka' gdams gzhung drug.*
1154. *Rnam thar 'phags lam snang ba.*
1155. *Sngon 'gro bzhi sbyor.*
1156. *Phyag chen chos drug gi dmigs pa'i rtsa tho.*
1157. *Bla ma mchod pa.*
1158. *Bla ma sgrub pa.*
1159. *Chos spyod rab gsal.*
1160. *Bskang gso.*
1161. This could be Chongye, or it could be Tashi Rabten in Menling County, on which see Dorje, 2009, 273.
1162. khā dan bā dur.
1163. *Phag mo gzhung drug.*
1164. *steng hor.* Translation marked as uncertain.—Ed.
1165. This should be the iron female ox, not the earth female ox, as indicated in the text.
1166. Chakhar, the central part of Mongolia.
1167. This refers to the death of his maternal uncle, Chogyel Rinchen Phuntsok Tashi of Drigung. This may be the Drokha chamber at Taklung, or the one near Tangkya, to the north of Meldo Gungkar (see www.tibetmap.com).
1168. Mi g.yo bla med.
1169. *Gu ru zhi drag.*
1170. On Namling in Shang, see Akester 2016, 545–56; and Dorje 2009, 297–302.
1171. This was the fourth Gyeltsab Rinpoche of Tsurphu, Drakpa Dondrub (c. 1550–1617), on whom see BDRC P5684.
1172. The implication is that Ngawang Namgyel had prescient knowledge of the impending civil war between U and Tsang and the eventual eclipse of the Zhamar and Kamtsang factions.
1173. Sixth Zhamar Choktrul, Chokyi Wangchuk (1584–1630), on whom see BDRC P1432.

1174. This may be Jamyang Gyeltsen of Phakmodru.
1175. *Mi tra brgya rtsa.*
1176. As yet unidentified.
1177. On Sera Monastery, see Akester 2016, 115–19; and Dorje 2009, 135–39.
1178. The famous Yongle edition, dated 1410, on which see Dorje 2009, 138.
1179. He appears to be mentioned in the Dukula. See Samten Karmay 2014, 64.
1180. Changlung Choding (Spyang lung chos sdings) lies to the east of Lhundrub Dzong in the upper reaches of the Yulnga valley. See Akester 2016, 47. This is also marked Choding Gonpa at www.tibetmap.com.
1181. *Saṃvaranirdeśaparivarta, Sdom gsum bstan pa* (Toh. 45; Dg.T. dkon brtsegs, *ka*, ff. 1b–45a) and *Ānantamukhapariśodhananirdeśaparivarta, Sgo mtha' yas pa rnam par sbyong ba* (Toh. 46; Dg.T. dkon brtsegs, *ka*, ff. 45b–99b). Both are contained in Pagoda of Precious Gems and the remainder of that collection—that is, Toh. 47–93.
1182. *Mar pa'i shog dril bzhi pa.*
1183. Gu ru zhi ba.
1184. Drag po dmar mthing.
1185. Phur pa spu gri.
1186. Tshe dpag yang gsang.
1187. Phyag rdor gtum po.
1188. *sku rkang gang ma.* Translation marked as uncertain.—Ed.
1189. On this chapel of bronzes, see Akester 2016, 43.
1190. *Gdan bkod.*
1191. Presently unidentified. Yangri is located on the road to Drigung. See Akester 2016, 175–76; and Dorje 2009, 181.
1192. *Yid kyi shing rta.*
1193. On the stone pillars of Tashido, see Dorje 2009, 166–67.
1194. The three Taiji (*thal tshi*), with the status of descendants of Qubilai Qaγan, would perhaps have included Ligden Qaγan (1588–1634). Alternatively, *thal tshi* could be equivalent to the Mongolian title *taishi*, a title reserved for noblemen of non-Borjigit descent who had their own fiefs.
1195. *Skyes rabs kyi rnam thar ngo mtshar tshangs pa'i gaṇḍi.*
1196. *tshoms ka brgyad bkra shis gsar ma.* Translation marked as uncertain.—Ed.
1197. Yang Gon is the name of a hermitage at Sengling. See Akester 2016, 36n26.
1198. *Chos 'byung chen po.*
1199. This would have been Karma Tensung Wangpo (r. 1599–1611), the third ruler (*sde srid*) of the Tsangpa administration based at Samdrubtse (Zhigatse).
1200. The bolded terms, followed by Tibetan transliteration, represent the meaning of the names of the master who is being praised in the verse.—Ed.
1201. He could perhaps be identified as Zhang Lotsāwa Drubpa Pel (b. 1237).
1202. See Tatsak Tse Wangyel 1994, 507.
1203. Tatsak Tse Wangyel (1994, 507) mentions other teachers under whom he also studied, including Sertsun, Gar, Jangla, Tapa, and Khu.

1204. Our text reads *bi dza ya ti*. Tatsak Tse Wangyel (1994, 508) reads *bhi dza ya ma ti*.
1205. The threefold perception (*'du shes gsum ldan*) could suggest either the perception of emancipation, non-harm, and non-injury; or perception of minor, major, and immeasurable scope. See Nordrang Orgyen 2008, 310. Tatsak Tse Wangyel (1994, 508) reads *'dus sde gsum*.
1206. Tatsak Tse Wangyel (1994, 508) adds, "You should shave the hair of the fontanelle, anoint it with perfume, and then engage in sexual intercourse!"
1207. On the life of Sangye On Drakpa Pel (1251–1296), the founder of Riwoche, see also Tatsak Tse Wangyel 1994, 507–35; Roerich 1949, 650–53; and Pawo Tsuklak Trenwa 1961, 426–27.
1208. Dkong mchog sras; Son of the Precious Jewels.
1209. See Tatsak Tse Wangyel 1994, 511.
1210. *Snga ba byang lam ma*.
1211. Our text (590) reads *se ca*, but see Tatsak Tse Wangyel (1994, 512) for the correct spelling.
1212. The source of the following verses has not yet been located.
1213. Recounted in prose in Tatsak Tse Wangyel 1994, 512–13.
1214. According to Tatsak Tse Wangyel (1994, 513), this occurred on the cliff of Phodo (*phod mdo'i brag*).
1215. Cf. Tatsak Tse Wangyel 1994, 513.
1216. The narrative version is found in Tatsak Tse Wangyel 1994, 514.
1217. According to the narrative in Tatsak Tse Wangyel (1994, 514), he did so by parting in two the river's current.
1218. According to Tatsak Tse Wangyel (1994, 514), this happened when the master and his uncle were approached at a river confluence by a vagabond who tried to steal their baggage.
1219. The caragona plant (*bra ma/bru ma*) is used in Tibetan medicine.
1220. *klu sman*. According to Tatsak Tse Wangyel 1994, 514–15, this grove of caragona was growing behind a building known as *so rtsa'i khang*.
1221. A so sras.
1222. See Tatsak Tse Wangyel 1994, 515.
1223. Cf. the narrative in Tatsak Tse Wangyel 1994, 515.
1224. See Tatsak Tse Wangyel 1994, 516. He joked that his strength had increased due to the food and wine provided by Konchok Pel.
1225. According to Tatsak Tse Wangyel (1994, 516), they went there to pick flowers.
1226. See Tatsak Tse Wangyel 1994, 516.
1227. *mi mtho 'tsham 'gyid du 'ongs pa*. This translation marked as uncertain.—Ed.
1228. See Tatsak Tse Wangyel 1994, 516.
1229. See Tatsak Tse Wangyel (1994, 517) adds that consequently they did not have to eat for some days.
1230. Cf. Tatsak Tse Wangyel 1994, 517.

1231. According to Tatsak Tse Wangyel (1994, 517), he asked the eleven playmates to follow later.
1232. See Tatsak Tse Wangyel 1994, 517.
1233. Translation marked as uncertain: torches or posts.—Ed.
1234. See Tatsak Tse Wangyel 1994, 517–18.
1235. According to Tatsak Tse Wangyel (1994, 518) this occurred when he was in his ninth year.
1236. That is, Phakmodrupa Dorje Gyelpo.
1237. *sdigs pa*. Translation marked as uncertain.—Ed.
1238. See Tatsak Tse Wangyel 1994, 518.
1239. According to Tatsak Tse Wangyel (1994, 518), he did so by throwing a stone at a rabbit that had approached the store of unthreshed grain.
1240. *Sgo drug bshags pa*.
1241. Tatsak Tse Wangyel (1994, 518) adds that he did this in order to conceal the corpse of the rabbit with his robe.
1242. See Tatsak Tse Wangyel 1994, 518–19.
1243. *Rten 'brel snying po*.
1244. See Tatsak Tse Wangyel 1994, 519.
1245. See Tatsak Tse Wangyel 1994, 519.
1246. Translation marked as uncertain: turnips or mustard plants.—Ed.
1247. See Tatsak Tse Wangyel 1994, 519.
1248. This could be the Newar (Bal po'i zhabs) Jñānatapa, an accomplished master originally from Siṅghala. See Tatsak Tse Wangyel 1994, 519–20. The location is given as Khargongchen (Mkhar gong can) in Tatsak Tse Wangyel 1994, 519.
1249. *Gshin rje dgra nag*.
1250. *Dgra nag 'dus pa*.
1251. See Tatsak Tse Wangyel 1994, 521–22.
1252. His four teachers, Rinpoche (Sangye Yarjon), Jñānatapa, Kuṇḍalī, and Drojorwa (Drod 'byor ba). See Tatsak Tse Wangyel 1994, 525. The lineage of Nāropā and so forth that he received from Drojorwa is outlined in Tatsak Tse Wangyel 1994, 522–23.
1253. Tatsak Tse Wangyel (1994, 525) recounts this past-life narrative and mentions his revelations recollected from that life.
1254. This narrative concerning Jñānatapa is found in Tatsak Tse Wangyel 1994, 523.
1255. Cf. Tatsak Tse Wangyel 1994, 519–20.
1256. The text misreads *gda' ngag* for *gdams ngag*.
1257. Tatsak Tse Wangyel (1994, 523) adds that he traveled via Purang to Nepal. The narrative of his second visit to Tibet is also recounted in Tatsak Tse Wangyel 1994, 523–24.
1258. Tatsak Tse Wangyel (1994, 524) here remarks that further details can be found in Sangye On's *Record of Teachings Received* (*Gsan yig*) and in his biography (*nges brjod*).

1259. Tatsak Tse Wangyel (1994, 525) lists the successive lineage holders from Nairātmyā, through Lakṣmīnkarā, and so forth, down to Kuṇḍalī.
1260. *me tog mchod zla*.
1261. See Tatsak Tse Wangyel 1994, 522.
1262. Se Chilpuwa (Se spyil phu ba) Chokyi Gyeltsen (1121–1189).
1263. *Gsol 'debs rin chen gter mdzod*.
1264. Our text misreads *ras chog* for *ras mchog*. See Tatsak Tse Wangyel 1994, 525.
1265. Tatsak Tse Wangyel (1994, 525) suggests that he drew a single icon, which he then consecrated one hundred and eight times.
1266. Mok Chokyi Lodro (Rmog chos blo).
1267. See Tatsak Tse Wangyel 1994, 525–26.
1268. Tatsak Tse Wangyel (1994, 526) lists further artifacts, adding that the vajra had been given by Guru Padmākara to Vairotsana.
1269. See Tatsak Tse Wangyel 1994, 526.
1270. See Tatsak Tse Wangyel 1994, 522.
1271. See Tatsak Tse Wangyel 1994, 526.
1272. *chang rjes*. Translation marked as uncertain.—Ed.
1273. *Dbu ma'i 'grel pa chen mo*.
1274. *Gsang ba 'dus pa'i 'grel pa sgron ma gsal ba*.
1275. *dzva ki*. Translation marked as uncertain.—Ed.
1276. Lama Zhang (1122–1193).
1277. *lugs ma 'grim*. Translation marked as uncertain.—Ed.
1278. The form of Mahākāla propitiated by Atiśa, on which see Nebesky-Wojkowitz 1956, 53–54.
1279. See Tatsak Tse Wangyel 1994, 526.
1280. According to Tatsak Tse Wangyel (1994, 527) this was the tooth relic of Mila Repa, and there is no mention of a duplicate.
1281. Cf. Tatsak Tse Wangyel 1994, 527.
1282. See Tatsak Tse Wangyel 1994, 527.
1283. See Tatsak Tse Wangyel 1994, 528.
1284. See Tatsak Tse Wangyel 1994, 528.
1285. See Tatsak Tse Wangyel 1994, 528.
1286. This could be the master Jose (Slob dpon jo sras), to whom Chenga Gyelwa of Drigung wrote an epistle (contained in *Dri gung bka' brgyud chos mdzod chen mo*, vol. 43, 183), and also a lineage successor to Yakdepa Wangchuk Rinchen and Tingedzin Pelzangpo. Alternatively, it may refer to Tashi Lama.
1287. According to Tatsak Tse Wangyel (1994, 529), Chogyel Phakpa encouraged him to return to preside over Taklung in place of Tashi Lama, but he declined. That would perhaps suggest that Phakpa reversed his support for Tashi Lama, affirmed in the Roerich 1949, 651.
1288. See Tatsak Tse Wangyel 1994, 528.
1289. This is the region around Riwoche in Kham, on which see Kaḥtok Situ Chokyi

Gyatso's *A Guide to the Sacred Places of Utsang* (*Dbus gtsang gnas yig*; 1999). See Dorje 2009, 471–74; and Gruschke 2004, 49–54.

1290. *Bkra shis me tog phreng ba.*
1291. See Tatsak Tse Wangyel 1994, 529.
1292. See Tatsak Tse Wangyel 1994, 529–30.
1293. A multiarmed form of Hevajra holding weapons rather than skulls, surrounded by thirteen or nineteen deities, important in the Drukpa tradition.
1294. *yi ge 'bru sdebs dag cha rtsi dras.* Translation marked as uncertain.—Ed.
1295. See Tatsak Tse Wangyel 1994, 530.
1296. See Tatsak Tse Wangyel 1994, 530.
1297. See Tatsak Tse Wangyel 1994, 530–31.
1298. *ser lam chod pa.* Translation marked as uncertain.—Ed.
1299. *Snang ba'i 'khyer so gsum gyi gdam ngag.*
1300. *Dam pa'i hūṃ sgrub.*
1301. That is, until the time of Ngawang Namgyel. These works are for the most part no longer extant.
1302. See Tatsak Tse Wangyel 1994, 531.
1303. As stated earlier, he felt betrayed by Onpo Drakpa, who had broken his commitments, and ensured that the abbatial succession of Riwoche would instead fall to Orgyen Gonpo.
1304. See Tatsak Tse Wangyel 1994, 531–32.
1305. See Tatsak Tse Wangyel 1994, 532.
1306. Our text reads *cho*, but see Tatsak Tse Wangyel 1994, 533: *chos ci zhus.*
1307. See Tatsak Tse Wangyel 1994, 532–33.
1308. See Tatsak Tse Wangyel 1994, 533.
1309. Our text reads *sha ri ba raṃ*, but see Tatsak Tse Wangyel 1994, 535.
1310. See Tatsak Tse Wangyel 1994, 533–35.
1311. Karmapa Rangjung Dorje (1284–1339) would have been in his twelfth year at that time.
1312. See Tatsak Tse Wangyel 1994, 535.
1313. Khu bo lha, Kuzhang.
1314. *Rdzong mgur.*
1315. The insertion of a stalk of grass within the anterior fontanelle (*'jag ma mgor btags*) is considered an indication of success in the practice of consciousness transference. See Patrul Rinpoche 1994, 365.
1316. On the life of Orgyen Gonpo (1293–1366), see also Tatsak Tse Wangyel 1994, 535–42. According to the latter (535), the second son was named Chokyi Gonpo, and the third was Lhadrak Gonpo.
1317. See Tatsak Tse Wangyel 1994, 536.
1318. A cylinder containing a sacred text (*glegs bam*) is tied in the topknot of a yogin to represent liberation by wearing (*btags grol*).
1319. See Tatsak Tse Wangyel 1994, 536.

1320. See Tatsak Tse Wangyel 1994, 536.
1321. Rakshi Tujekyab (Rag shi thugs rje skyabs) was the father of Ratnaguru of Taklung. See BDRC P5516.
1322. See Tatsak Tse Wangyel 1994, 537.
1323. Our text misreads *sgo gyis* for *sgom gyis*. See Tatsak Tse Wangyel 1994, 537, last line.
1324. See Tatsak Tse Wangyel 1994, 537–38.
1325. See Tatsak Tse Wangyel 1994, 538.
1326. *Rgyal ba drod pa'i skye mched kyi rnam thar*. This is from the *Avataṃsaka* (Toh. 44). Tatsak Tse Wangyel (1994, 539) reads *rgyal ba grod skyer gyi rnam thar*.6
1327. *Saddarmapuṇḍarika*.
1328. See Tatsak Tse Wangyel 1994, 538–39.
1329. See Tatsak Tse Wangyel 1994, 539.
1330. *Ye shes snang ba dam pa'i rgyan*.
1331. *Man ngag lung bstan mdzod*. Here these titles denote nonextant works of Sangye On. Tatsak Tse Wangyel (1994, 539) clearly states that Kuzhang Rinpoche received these instructions from Sangye On and offered them all to Orgyen Gonpo.
1332. *Khro bo bcu drug gi 'gros*.
1333. *Rgyal chen sde bzhi'i 'gros*.
1334. These works of Sangye On appear to be no longer extant.
1335. See Tatsak Tse Wangyel 1994, 539–40.
1336. See Kaḥtok Situ Chokyi Gyatso 1999, 20–21.
1337. See Kaḥtok Situ Chokyi Gyatso 1999, 20.
1338. According to Kaḥtok Situ Chokyi Gyatso (1999, 21), Pematso magically wove this saddle blanket in the course of a single day.
1339. See Kaḥtok Situ Chokyi Gyatso 1999, 22.
1340. That is, in the time of Ngawang Namgyel.
1341. See Tatsak Tse Wangyel 1994, 540.
1342. *Zhal gdams brgya rtsa*.
1343. See Tatsak Tse Wangyel 1994, 541.
1344. Gyelwei Tsenchen is generally known by the name of Kungpangwa Lodro Gyeltsen. See Tatsak Tse Wangyel 1994, 541–42.
1345. See Kaḥtok Situ Chokyi Gyatso 1999, 20.
1346. See Kaḥtok Situ Chokyi Gyatso 1999, 22.
1347. *'byig mor*. Translation marked as uncertain.—Ed.
1348. According to Tatsak Tse Wangyel (1994, 542), he became a total renunciant in 1384 (wood male mouse).
1349. On Dzorawa Rinchen Senge, see also Tatsak Tse Wangyel 1994, 541.
1350. See Kaḥtok Situ Chokyi Gyatso 1999, 25.
1351. *Bka' brgyud rin po che'i mgur mtsho*.

1352. The bolded terms, followed by Tibetan transliteration, represent the meaning of the names of the master who is being praised in the verse.—Ed.
1353. The life of Ratnākara of Riwoche is also recounted briefly in Tatsak Tse Wangyel 1994, 542–43.
1354. These were the seats of his half brothers. See Tatsak Tse Wangyel 1994, 542.
1355. *Shes phyin stong phrag brgya pa.*
1356. *'Phags pa brgyad stong pa.*
1357. *Sangs rgyas mtshan 'bum.*
1358. Sakyapa Tekchen Choje Kunga Tashi (1349–1425) was an important teacher of Bodong Paṇchen. See BDRC P3565.
1359. *Sems bskyed mu tig phreng chen.*
1360. *Bka' brgyud bka' 'bum.*
1361. An epithet of Mañjughoṣa.
1362. His silver reliquary is mentioned in Kaḥtok Situ Chokyi Gyatso 1999, 19.
1363. The bolded terms, followed by Tibetan transliteration, represent the meaning of the names of the master who is being praised in the verse.—Ed.
1364. On his life, see also Tatsak Tse Wangyel 1994, 543–44.
1365. *nang rdzong la.*
1366. Perhaps to be identified with the eleventh-century terton Nyemo Zhuye Lekpo (BDRC P7823).
1367. See Tatsak Tse Wangyel 1994, 543–44.
1368. *khang nye.* Translation marked as uncertain: or, "drew near."—Ed.
1369. Tatsak Tse Wangyel (1994, 543) reads HŪṂ.
1370. The bolded terms, followed by Tibetan transliteration, represent the meaning of the names of the master who is being praised in the verse.—Ed.
1371. *mi g.yo gsum.* Perhaps these are identical to the three unmoving states (*mi 'gul ba gsum*)—namely, the posture of the body, the gaze of the eyes, and the unfabricated mind.
1372. A brief account of the life of Miyo Gonpo is also found in Tatsak Tse Wangyel 1994, 544.
1373. The eight qualities of water are coolness, sweetness, lightness, softness, clearness, soothing quality, pleasantness, and wholesomeness. See Dudjom Rinpoche 1991, 2:160–61.
1374. On the artifacts and murals of the middle story, see Kaḥtok Situ Chokyi Gyatso 1999, 23–25.
1375. See Kaḥtok Situ Chokyi Gyatso 1999, 25.
1376. *Kye rdor dznāna lugs kyi brgyud rim gsol 'debs.*
1377. *Phyag rgya chen po lnga ldan.*
1378. *dgon du phebs nas.* Translation marked as uncertain: or "monastery."—Ed.
1379. *Bka' brgyud bka' 'bu.*
1380. On the life of Jangchub Gyatso, see p. 309.
1381. *Ri bo che'i gser phreng.*

1382. *Bla ma'i rnal 'byor byin rlabs dbab pa'i ting ngde 'dzin.*
1383. See Kaḥtok Situ Chokyi Gyatso 1999, 25.
1384. Our text reads earth female pig.
1385. In Nangchen.
1386. This would have been Third Zhamarpa, Choje Chophel Yeshe (1406–1452), and First Situ, Chokyi Gyeltsen (1377–1448).
1387. That is, in the time of the author, Ngawang Namgyel.
1388. The bolded terms, followed by Tibetan transliteration, represent the meaning of the names of the master who is being praised in the verse.—Ed.
1389. According to Kaḥtok Situ Chokyi Gyatso (1999, 19), this image was two arm-spans in size. Its back screen had wood-carved relief images of the thousand buddhas, and its throne ornaments depicted the sixteen elders.
1390. According to Kaḥtok Situ Chokyi Gyatso (1999, 19), this image was fashioned of silver.
1391. Zurmang in Nangchen, on which see Dorje 2009, 620–22.
1392. This journey took him east of the Yangtze and southward through areas presently in Kandze and Dechen prefectures.
1393. According to Kaḥtok Situ Chokyi Gyatso (1999, 23), this image of medicinal clay was commissioned by his successor Jikten Wangchuk.
1394. *Ma thang gi brgyud pa'i rnam thar mu tig phreng ba.* This text is contained in *Dpal ldan stag lung pa'i gsung rnams nor bzhi bang mdzad*, vol. 18, 47–266. BDRC W1PD166109.
1395. *thus btsun.* Translation marked as uncertain.—Ed.
1396. *khyogs shing 'dus pa.* Translation marked as uncertain.—Ed.
1397. See Kaḥtok Situ Chokyi Gyatso 1999, 22.
1398. The text misreads *bdun cu pa*, "seventy."
1399. *Ma thang bka' brgyud kyi chos 'byung.*
1400. This passage is cited in Pawo Tsuklak Trengwa 1962, 358. Its import in this context is to identify Jikten Wangchuk as the secret father of Eighth Karmapa.
1401. *makaradvajin, chu srin rgyal mtshan can.*
1402. *gser zhor bgya ri zer ba.* Translation marked as uncertain.—Ed.
1403. See part 1, chap. 4, note 1.
1404. Rāhulabhadra, son of Śākyamuni Buddha, on whom see p. 28.
1405. This aspect of male-female Cakrasaṃvara is described and illustrated, along with the mantra, in Jikme Chokyi Dorje 2001, 242–43. See also the color illustration in Willson and Brauen 2000, 48.
1406. This was Second Jedrung, Drakpa Gyeltsen (1591–1642).

9. The Biographies of the Diverse Kagyu Traditions

1. The last two lines of this stanza reflect Pawo Tsuklak Trengwa 1962, 376.
2. This term and the related pith instructions are particularly associated with the Drigungpa tradition.

3. This paragraph derives virtually verbatim from Pawo Tsuklak Trengwa 1962, 376.
4. As indicated in part 3, chap. 5, these constitute the four lineages of the oral instructions to Tilopā, those on (1) Dream Yoga from Caryāpā, (2) Illusory Body from Nāgārjuna, (3) Inner Radiance from Kambalapāda, and (4) Inner Heat from the ḍākinī Kusalabhadrī. On the biographies associated with these four lineages, see also Pawo Tsuklak Trengwa 1962, 376–83.
5. These are Tilopā and Nāropā, on whom see part 3, chap. 5; and Pawo Tsuklak Trengwa 1962, 383–93.
6. The lives of Śavaripā and Maitripā are outlined in part 3, chap. 5. See also Pawo Tsuklak Trengwa 1962, 393–94.
7. These four predecessors of Taklungpa the Great were, in succession, Marpa, Mila Repa, Gampopa, and Phakmodrupa. Their lives are presented in chapter 7. See also Pawo Tsuklak Trengwa 1962, 397–419.
8. See Pawo Tsuklak Trengwa 1962, 395; and Roerich 1949, 406.
9. See Roerich 1949, 408.
10. *Btags gnyis kyi zin bris chen mo.*
11. Roerich (1949, 412) remarks that all the descendants of Ngok at Trewu Zhing belonged to the clan of Tsangtsa.
12. His successors are named in Roerich (1949, 414) extending through to the year 1476.
13. On this lineage descended from Ngok Choku Dorje, see Pawo Tsuklak Trengwa 1962, 395–96; and Roerich 1949, 406–14.
14. See Pawo Tsuklak Trengwa 1962, 397; and Roerich 1949, 405–6.
15. *Gsang ba 'dus pa'i rigs lnga.*
16. All names mentioned in this list to here are twelfth-century figures.
17. On the greater and lesser versions of *The Great Exegetical Tantra Titled Nondual Victor* (*bshad brgyud gnyis med rnam rgyal chen mo*; Toh. 453), see Roerich 1949, 417n4. Chak Lotsāwa and Buton Rinchendrub attributed the greater version to Gyapowa Lungpa himself, but this contradicts the evidence of its citations, which are found in earlier works. Our text misreads *bshad brgyud gnyis med rnams rgya chen mo.*
18. This is Nyemdo Sonam Pel (1217–1277).
19. On this lineal succession, see Pawo Tsuklak Trengwa 1962, 396–97; and Roerich 1949, 414–26.
20. Bde mchog mkha' 'gro snyan brgyud.
21. The life of Rechung Dorje Drak (1085–1161) and the activities of his disciples are outlined in Roerich 1949, 438–49.
22. Ngam rdzong snyan brgyud.
23. On the lineage of Namdzong Tonpa Bodhirāja, see Roerich 1949, 449–51.
24. For a description of Daklha Gampo and its historical background, see Akester 2016, 394–401.
25. On this abbatial succession, see also Roerich 1949, 462–68.

26. A brief biography of Barompa Darma Wangchuk can be found in Dungkar Lobzang Trinle 2002, 1544–45.
27. On his life, see Sørensen and Hazod 2007, 102–3, and especially note 123. He is also known as Sherab Senge (1164–1236). Alternative dates (1128–1201) are also found. See Dorje 2009, 623. In decline elsewhere, the Barom tradition is represented by Dzamo Gonpa in Nangchen, which he founded.
28. This is one of the names of First Karmapa Dusum Khyenpa (1110–1193), on whom see Pawo Tsuklak Trengwa 1962, 436–47; and Roerich 1949, 473–80; Tatsak Tse Wangyel 1994, 228–34; Denma Jamyang Tsultrim 1997, 1–65; and Douglas and White 1976, 33–37.
29. The sixth of the thousand buddhas of the Auspicious Eon. See Roerich 1949, 473; and Nordrang Orgyen 2008, 3870.
30. See Roerich 1949, 480–83.
31. See Roerich 1949, 483–85.
32. On the life of Karma Pakshi (1204–1283), see Pawo Tsuklak Trengwa 1962, 448–66; Tatsak Tse Wangyel 1994, 235–38; Roerich 1949, 485–87; Denma Jamyang Tsultrim 1997, 66–80; and Douglas and White 1976, 41–46.
33. See Roerich 1949, 697–702.
34. On the life of Third Karmapa, Rangjung Dorje (1284–1339), see Pawo Tsuklak Trengwa 1962, 466–82; Tatsak Tse Wangyel 1994, 238–43; Roerich 1949, 488–93; Denma Jamyang Tsultrim 1997, 81–95; Douglas and White 1976, 47–52; and Dudjom Rinpoche 1991, 1:572–74.
35. See Roerich 1949, 493; and Dudjom Rinpoche 1991, 1:666–87.
36. On the life of Fourth Karmapa, Rolpei Dorje (1340–1383), see Pawo Tsuklak Trengwa 1962, 483–98; Tatsak Tse Wangyel 1994, 243–50; Roerich 1949, 494–506; Denma Jamyang Tsultrim 1997, 96–114; and Douglas and White 1976, 54–59.
37. See Pawo Tsuklak Trengwa 1962, 488–504; and Roerich 1949, 540–45.
38. On the life of Fifth Karmapa, Dezhin Shekpa (1384–1415), see Pawo Tsuklak Trengwa 1962, 504–20; Tatsak Tse Wangyel 1994, 250–60; Roerich 1949, 507–10; Denma Jamyang Tsultrim 1997, 115–42; and Douglas and White 1976, 61–65.
39. On the life of Sixth Karmapa, Tongwa Donden (1416–1453), see Pawo Tsuklak Trengwa 1962, 522–25; Tatsak Tse Wangyel 1994, 260–70; Roerich 1949, 512–17; Denma Jamyang Tsultrim 1997, 143–44; and Douglas and White 1976, 66–68.
40. On the life of Seventh Karmapa, Chodrak Gyatso (1454–1506), see Pawo Tsuklak Trengwa 1962, 526ff.; Roerich 1949, 517; Denma Jamyang Tsultrim 1997, 145–57; and Douglas and White 1976, 69–71.
41. On the life of Eighth Karmapa, Mikyo Dorje (1507–1554), see Denma Jamyang Tsultrim 1997, 158–68; Douglas and White 1976, 73–78.
42. On the life of Ninth Karmapa, Wangchuk Dorje (1556–1603), see Denma Jamyang Tsultrim 1997, 169–75; and Douglas and White 1976, 79–82.

43. That is to say, in the lifetime of Taklung Ngawang Namgyel.
44. On the life of Tenth Karmapa, Choying Dorje (1604–1674), see Denma Jamyang Tsultrim 1997, 176–88; and Douglas and White 1976, 83–90.
45. See Tatsak Tse Wangyel 1994, 285–88.
46. See Tatsak Tse Wangyel 1994, 301; and Roerich 1949, 540–45.
47. See Roerich 1949, 546–51.
48. See Pawo Tsuklak Trengwa 1962, 528ff.; Dudjom Rinpoche 1991, 1:675–76; and Roerich 1949, 551–52.
49. The late Zhamarpa was the thirteenth in that line of succession, while the present Karmapa is the seventeenth in his line.
50. He was the first of the regents of Tsurphu (*mtshur phu rgyal tshab*), a line that begins during the lifetime of Fifth Karmapa and continues through to the present twelfth incumbent.
51. That is, in the lifetime of Taklung Ngawang Namgyel. The present Tsurphu Gyeltsab is the twelfth in the line.
52. That is, in the lifetime of Taklung Ngawang Namgyel. Second Pawo is the renowned author of *Doctrinal History Titled Scholars' Feast*. The present incumbent, residing at the seat of Nenang, near Tsurphu, is the eleventh in the line of succession.
53. *Sems khrid yid bzhin nor bu.*
54. According to Roerich (1949, 718), this occurred in the year 1316.
55. On this revelatory transmission of Dungtso Repa, see Roerich 1949, 717–24.
56. On his outer, inner, and secret biographies, see Sørensen and Hazod 2007, 74–90; and Roerich 1949, 711–16.
57. On this abbatial succession of Tsel Gungtang, see Sørensen and Hazod 2007, 91–116; and Roerich 1949, 716–17. The former is a major two-volume study of Tsel Gungtang and its heritage.
58. This abbatial succession of Phakmodrupa's seat at Densatil is outlined in Roerich 1949, 571–95; and Pawo Tsuklak Trengwa 1962, 423–24.
59. See Pawo Tsuklak Trengwa (1961, 424) mentions other auspicious circumstances in addition to that one. The background to this aristocratic succession of the Phakmodru dynasty appears to derive from a prophecy found in *The Lang Poti Seru* (*Rlangs po ti ser ru*) and cited in the same source.
60. There were altogether twelve rulers (*sde srid*) of Tibet in the Phakmodru dynasty—namely, Jangchub Gyeltsen (r. 1350–1371), Śākya Gyeltsen (r. 1372–1384), Drakpa Jangchub (r. 1385–1390), Sonam Drakpa (r. 1391–1408), Drakpa Gyeltsen (r. 1409–1434), Sangye Gyeltsen (r. 1435–1439), Drakpa Jungne (r. 1440–1468), Kunga Lekpa (r. 1469–1473), Rinchen Dorje (r. 1474–1513), Chenga Ngagi Wangpo (r. 1514–1564), Ngawang Tashi Drakpa (r. 1565–1578), and Drowei Gonpo (r. 1579–1617). The power of the later rulers was gradually eclipsed by the house of Ringpung in Tsang until, by 1478, the position had little more than nominal or titular significance.
61. On the life of Drigungpa Jikten Gonpo, see Drigung Konchok Gyatso

2004, 283–311; and Pawo Tsuklak Trengwa 1962, 424; and Roerich 1949, 596–608.

62. On his senior disciples, see Drigung Konchok Gyatso 2004, 311–43; and Roerich 1949, 602–8. The former (312) lists not four but twelve Chenga (*spyan snga bcu gnyis*)—namely, Chenga Sherab Jungne, Chenga Drakpa Jungne, Chenga Dakpowa, Chenga Lhodrakpa, Chenga Sonyompa, Chenga On, Chenga Chung, Chenga Jangchub Lingpa, Chenga Namtso Dopa, Chenga Rinchen Zangpo, Chenga Lha Nangpa, and Chenga Gar. The same source (312) also enumerates not twelve but eight Great Glorious Ones (*dpal chen brgyad*)—namely, Pelchen Gurawa, Pelchen Tengphuwa, Pelchen Choye, Pelchen Śrī Pukpa, Pelchen Dorje Yeshe, Pelchen Ngephuwa, Pelchen Tengphuwa, Pelchen Tsonyinpa, and Pelchen Takmapa.
63. Not yet identified.
64. The last mentioned is regarded as either the twenty-second or twenty-first incumbent of Drigung.
65. The abbatial succession of Drigung, from the second incumbent down to the fortieth incumbent, is detailed in Drigung Konchok Gyatso 2004, 343–726. See also Pawo Tsuklak Trengwa 1962, 686–92; and Roerich 1949, 608–10. The dates given in these sources are sometimes at variance.
66. Nyelme Pelriwa Sangye Jagom, Gordongpa Sangye Lhagom, Sertawa Sangye Legom, and Gonsarwa Sangye Gyagom. Roerich 1949, 657.
67. On this line of abbatial succession through to 1476, see Roerich 1949, 653–59.
68. In 1171. See Roerich 1949, 707.
69. Also known as Kusulu the Younger (fl. twelfth century).
70. On the abbatial succession of Trophu, see Pawo Tsuklak Trengwa 1962, 428–29; and Roerich 1949, 705–11.
71. *thun mong ma yin pa'i rnam par thar pa bcu gnyis*. These are enumerated in Pawo Tsuklak Trengwa 1962, 431.
72. Our text, following Pawo Tsuklak (431), omits Namkha Pelzang (1398–1426). See Roerich 1949, 672.
73. The last named, a contemporary of Taklung Ngawang Namgyel, was the father of Zhabdrung Ngawang Namgyel, founder of the Bhutanese state.
74. See Pawo Tsuklak Trengwa 1962, 429–31; Roerich 1949, 659–72; and Drukchen Pema Karpo 1992, 423–64. On Ralung, see Akester 2016, 487–90; and Dorje 2009, 305–6.
75. On the life of Gotsangpa, see Roerich 1949, 680–88; and Pawo Tsuklak Trengwa 1962, 431–33. These meditative commitments of Gotsangpa, also called pledges, are enumerated in the latter (432).
76. See Roerich 1949, 696–702.
77. *Ri chos bskor gsum.*
78. *Gnad kyi khog chen ma drug.*
79. On the life of Yang Gonpa, see Roerich 1949, 688–91; and Pawo Tsuklak Trengwa 1962, 433.

80. This paragraph derives verbatim from Pawo Tsuklak Trengwa 1962, 433.
81. Roerich 1949, 703.
82. Pawo Tsuklak Trengwa 1962, 433–34.
83. These pledges are all enumerated in the life of Lorepa, as found in Pawo Tsuklak Trengwa 1962, 434–35.
84. According to Nordrang Orgyen 2008, these include the capacity of dying in the Great Seal (*phyag rgya chen po 'chi thub*), the capacity of drying cotton clothes through the Inner Heat (*gtum mo ras thub*), the capacity of resorting to secret conduct in the hills (*gsang spyod ri thub*), the capacity of agitating demons who cause ill-health (*nad gdon 'khrugs thub*), and the capacity of applying conditional antidotes (*gnyen po rkyen thub*).
85. The former derive from Onpo Tsāri Rechen and Sangye On, and the latter from Jamyang Gonpo and Tokden Gonpo Yeshe. See Pawo Tsuklak Trengwa 1962, 435.
86. On this Lower Drukpa lineage, see also Roerich 1949, 672–80.
87. Sgam po ba'i ngo bo'i ga dar.
88. This passage derives from Pawo Tsuklak Trengwa 1962.

10. The Origins of Diverse Doctrinal Traditions

1. See Dorje 2017, 243–71.
2. See Dudjom Rinpoche 1991, 1:510–12.
3. See Dudjom Rinpoche 1991, 1:512–21.
4. 'Jam dpal sku.
5. Padma gsung.
6. Yang dag thugs.
7. Bdud rtsi yon tan.
8. Phur ba phrin las.
9. Ma mo sbod gtong.
10. Smod pa drag sngags.
11. 'Jig rten mchod bstod.
12. See Dudjom Rinpoche 1991, 1:283, 1:534–35; and Dorje 2017, 264.
13. On these three classes of the Great Perfection, see Dudjom Rinpoche 1991, 1:311–45, 538–96; and Dorje 2017, 187–226. Our text (694) reads Vairotsana instead of Vimalamitra.
14. *Sgyu 'phrul gsang ba snying po*. On this text and its cycle, see Dorje 2016.
15. See Dorje 1987, 81–83.
16. On this transmission of the oral teachings from Vimalamitra through Nyak to Nub Sangye Yeshe and so on, see Dudjom Rinpoche 1991, 1:601–16.
17. See Dudjom Rinpoche 1991, 1:616.
18. See Dudjom Rinpoche 1991, 1:617–35.
19. See Dudjom Rinpoche 1991, 1:635–45.
20. Our text misreads *me bzhi* for *mes bzhi*.

21. See Dudjom Rinpoche 1991, 1:645–49.
22. On this line of transmission from Cheton Gyanak to Taton Joye, see Dudjom Rinpoche 1991, 1:650–59.
23. See Dudjom Rinpoche 1991, 1:660–63.
24. See Dudjom Rinpoche 1991, 1:663–68.
25. See Dudjom Rinpoche 1991, 1:672–75.
26. According to Pawo Tsuklak Trengwa (1961, 318), Sangye Gonglawa of Dakpo also studied under Pakshi Śākya-o.
27. See Dudjom Rinpoche 1991, 1:701–2; and Cabazon, 2013.
28. See Dudjom Rinpoche 1991, 1:702.
29. See Dudjom Rinpoche 1991, 1:688–99.
30. *'Dus pa'i mdo.*
31. *Rtsa ba'i rgyud kun 'dus rig pa'i mdo.*
32. *Bshad pa'i rgyud mdo dgongs pa 'dus pa.*
33. On *The Sūtra That Gathers All Intentions* and its related Anuyoga literature, see Dudjom Rinpoche 1991, 1:284–89; and Dorje 2017, 264–66. On their transmission, see Dudjom Rinpoche 1991, 1:607–16, 1:717–34.
34. *mdo sgyu sems gsum.*
35. Dudjom Rinpoche 1991, 703–9.
36. These four rivers of textual exegesis, aural instruction, blessing/empowerment, and practical techniques are explained in Dudjom Rinpoche 1:1991, 601.
37. On this transmission, see Dudjom Rinpoche 1991, 1:601–6. Dudjom Rinpoche 1991, 1:612–13, mentions only his five foremost disciples. The seven perspectives of mind according to the class of mind within the Great Perfection are presented in Dudjom Rinpoche 1991, 1:319–26; and Dorje 2017, 197–202. And on their transmission in Tibet, see Dudjom Rinpoche 1991, 1:538ff.
38. See Dudjom Rinpoche 1991, 1:540.
39. *Nam mkha' dang mnyam pa'i rgyud chung ba.*
40. *Ye shes gsang ba.* On these texts and teaching cycles, see Dudjom Rinpoche 1991, 1:326–29; also Dorje 2017, 203–13.
41. The transmission of the class of space in Tibet is outlined in Dudjom Rinpoche 1991, 1:538–52.
42. See Dudjom Rinpoche 1991, 1:552–53.
43. On the class of esoteric instructions, including the Innermost Spirituality (*snying thig*), see Dudjom Rinpoche 1991, 1:329–45; and Dorje 2017, 215–26. On the transmission from Vimalamitra to Nyang Tingdzin Zangpo, see Dudjom Rinpoche 1991, 1:555–56.
44. On Uruzha (*dbu ru zhva'i lha khang*), see Akester 2016, 168–72; and Dorje 2009, 181–83.
45. See Dudjom Rinpoche 1991, 1:556.
46. See Dudjom Rinpoche 1991, 1:556–61.
47. See Dudjom Rinpoche 1991, 1:561–96.
48. See Dudjom Rinpoche 1991, 1:674–75.

49. *Mkha' 'gro snying thig.*
50. See Dudjom Rinpoche 1991, 1:554–55; also 1:572–74.
51. *Pad+ma'i thang yig.*
52. See Dudjom Rinpoche 1991, 1:751ff. See Jamgön Kongtrul Lodrö Tayé 2011, 73–75, on Sangye Lama, and 169–72 on Dechen Lingpa.
53. On the lives of these three figures, see Dudjom Rinpoche 1991, 1:755–70, 1:780–83.
54. *Deb ther sngon po.*
55. Go Lotsāwa's entire chapter on the ancient translations is contained in Roerich 1949, 102–203.
56. See Roerich 1949, 351–52.
57. On Loton Dorje Wangchuk, who founded Gyengong Temple near Zhalu, see Davidson 2007, 96–97.
58. See Davidson 2007, 68–69, 106–7.
59. On the life and works of Drokmi, including these admonitions, see Davidson 2007, 169–209.
60. On Go Khukpa Lhetse's translation of the *Guhyasamāja*, see Roerich 1949, 359–64.
61. See Davidson 2007, 141–48.
62. On the lineage of the Path and Its Fruit and these related cycles, see Davidson 2007, 183–204. On the transmission from Drokmi to Seton Kunrik, see Dhongthog Rinpoche 2016, 56, and on Zhangton Chobar, 97.
63. On these five founders of Sakya, see Dhongthog Rinpoche 2016, 56–68; and Davidson 2007, 291–319, 335–69.
64. He was the son of the eleventh throne holder of Sakya, Zangpo Pel.
65. According to Nordrang Orgyen 2008, 332, the three modes of investigation are correct in terms of direct perception, inference, and conviction that is based on scriptural authority.
66. See Dhongthog Rinpoche 2016, 135–36.
67. See Dhongthog Rinpoche 2016, 125–34.
68. These eighteen traditions are outlined in Dhongthog Rinpoche 2016, 94–95.
69. Ngawang Namgyel's sources include Pawo Tsuklak Trengwa 1962, 694–98; and Roerich 1949, 204–40.
70. On the dissemination of the yoga tantras by Lochen Rinchen Zangpo and Zangkar Lotsāwa, see Roerich 1949, 351–56; and Zangpo 2010, 273–75; and Guarisco and McLeod 2005, 127–40.
71. *pha rgyud gsang ba 'dus pa 'phags lugs.*
72. See Roerich 1949, 358–67. The disciples of Go Lotsāwa are named in Roerich 1949, 364. Distinctions between the traditions of Nāgārjuna and Buddhajñānapāda are discussed in Guarisco and McLeod 2008, 138–48.
73. See Roerich 1949, 364.
74. See Roerich 1949, 365–67.
75. See Roerich 1949, 367–74.

76. The activity of Naktso Lotsāwa in translating these commentaries is mentioned in Roerich 1949, 373; and Zangpo 2010, 291.
77. See Roerich 1949, 374–80. See also Cuevas 2015.
78. See Roerich 1949, 380–82; Zangpo 2010, 286–300; and Guarisco and McLeod 2005, 167–78.
79. See Roerich 1949, 382–88.
80. A royal prince, according to Roerich 1949, 388.
81. See Roerich 1949, 388.
82. See Roerich 1949, 394–97.
83. See Roerich 1949, 390–94; and Zangpo 2010, 297.
84. See Roerich 1949, 389.
85. The various transmissions of the *Kālacakra Tantra* are discussed extensively in Roerich 1949, 753–838; and summarized in Zangpo 2010, 305–8. On its content, see Guarisco and McLeod 2008, 154–61.
86. On the tradition of Dro Lotsāwa (*'bro lugs*), see Roerich 1949, 755–56, and on the detailed biographies of these successive lineage holders, 766–77. The last four are the first incumbents of Jonang Monastery.
87. On the tradition of Ra (*rva lugs*), see Roerich 1949, 789–93; and Zangpo 2010, 305.
88. See Roerich 1949, 793–95.
89. See Roerich 1949, 777–81.
90. See Roerich 1949, 783–88.
91. On this lineage and especially for a detailed account of the life of Trukhang Lotsāwa Sonam Gyatso, see Roerich 1949, 788, 801–37.
92. See Roerich 1949, 779–81.
93. On the tradition of Tsami (*rtsa mi'i lugs*), see Roerich 1949, 699, 760–63, 795–96.
94. *Dus 'khor lhan skyes kyi sgrub thabs.*
95. It appears that these two royal princes of Ngari were both sons of Prince Lhade, the nephew of Lha Lama Yeshe-o. See Eimer 1974.
96. The history of the Kadam lineage is recounted in Pawo Tsuklak Trengwa 1962, 335–75; and Roerich 1949, 241–327. Specifically on the life of Atiśa, fountainhead of the Kadam lineage, see Pawo Tsuklak Trengwa 1962, 335–60; and Roerich 1949, 241–327.
97. See Roerich 1949, 251–64.
98. Roerich (1949, 262) names them as, Mahāpaṇḍita Pitopa, Dharmākaramati, Mitraguhya, Jñānamati, and Kṣitigarbha.
99. Otherwise known as Ame Jangchub Rinchen. See Roerich 1949, 262.
100. See Roerich 1949, 261–62. The last five of these were known as the Five Khampa Brothers.
101. See Roerich 1949, 263–70, 283–84.
102. See Roerich 1949, 265–66, 286.
103. See Roerich (1949, 267) gives his name as Khenpo Shekorwa (*shes skor ba*).

104. See Roerich 1949, 271, 267. The last mentioned is also known as Chim Jampalyang.
105. See Roerich 1949, 269–72.
106. See Roerich 1949, 272–82.
107. See Roerich 1949, 271.
108. See Roerich 1949, 276–82.
109. See Roerich 1949, 282–83.
110. According to Roerich (1949, 292), he was one of the nine outsiders who were "great."
111. Otherwise known as Tsangpa Rinchen Namkha Dorje, the second incumbent of Jayul.
112. See Roerich 1949, 284–305.
113. See Roerich 1949, 305–11.
114. He was the founder of Rinchen Gang. See Roerich 1949, 315.
115. See Roerich 1949, 315–17.
116. See Roerich 1949, 317–20.
117. *Jo bo'i rnam thar.*
118. See Roerich 1949, 321–22,
119. See Roerich 1949, 322.
120. See Roerich 1949, 267–68.
121. See Roerich 1949, 324–26.
122. See Roerich 1949, 326.
123. See Roerich 1949, 328–30.
124. See Roerich 1949, 331–32.
125. These are enumerated in Roerich 1949 (333), with the exception of the last category, here replaced with the "four wise ones" (*shes rab can bzhi*).
126. See Roerich 1949, 330–31.
127. See Roerich 1949, 335.
128. See Roerich 1949, 339–41, 1075–78, 1080–81.
129. See Roerich 1949, 1079–80.
130. See Roerich 1949, 341–44.
131. See Roerich 1949, 344–45.
132. See Roerich 1949, 346.
133. See Roerich 1949, 346–47.
134. See Roerich 1949, 347–50.
135. See Roerich 1949, 341.
136. His life is recounted in Roerich 1949, 867ff.
137. The twelve meditational deities are enumerated in Roerich 1949, 870.
138. According to Roerich 1949, 870–71, he visited Tibet on five occasions—initially in Tsāri, and then in Ngari, Tsang, Nyel, and finally Dingri.
139. Sources for the narrative of the lineage of Pacification (*zhi byed*) include Roerich 1949, 867–979; and the summary in Pawo Tsuklak Trengwa 1962, 693–94.

140. *Zhi byed sgrol ma bskor gsum.*
141. See Roerich 1949, 871–72.
142. Their respective biographies are found in Roerich 1949, 872–74, 876–79, 890–99.
143. See Roerich 1949, 874–76.
144. See Roerich 1949, 890.
145. See Roerich 1949, 879–90.
146. See Roerich 1949, 899ff.
147. See Roerich 1949, 904.
148. See Roerich 1949, 912–13.
149. See Roerich 1949, 920–23.
150. See Roerich 1949, 913–15.
151. The narrative of the twenty-four nuns is found in Roerich 1949, 915–20.
152. *Kun dga'i gdams pa.*
153. See Roerich 1949, 923–29.
154. See Roerich 1949, 929–39.
155. See Roerich 1949, 939–49.
156. See Roerich 1949, 949–55.
157. See Roerich 1949, 955–58.
158. See Roerich 1949, 884–85.
159. Hūṃ sgrub kyi skor.
160. The source for this short description of severance is Pawo Tsuklak Trengwa 1962, 699–700. See also Roerich 1949, 980–99; and Harding 2016.
161. See Roerich 1949, 983–84.
162. See Roerich 1949, 985, and specifically 988–96.
163. See Roerich 1949, 985–86.
164. See Roerich 1949, 986–88.
165. See Pawo Tsuklak Trengwa 1962, 700.
166. The source for this summary of the Shangpa Kagyu lineage is Pawo Tsuklak Trengwa 1962, 700–704. See also Roerich 1949, 728–52.
167. See Roerich 1949, 728–31.
168. See Pawo Tsuklak Trengwa 1962, 701.
169. See Roerich 1949, 733.
170. See Roerich 1949, 733–37.
171. See Roerich 1949, 737–41.
172. See Roerich 1949, 741–43.
173. See Roerich 1949, 743–46.
174. See Roerich 1949, 747–50.
175. The primary source for this section is Pawo Tsuklak Trengwa 1962, 705–32. Also on the royal dynasties of China and Mongolia, see Roerich 1949, 47–60.
176. Sa las nu ma nu. See Emmerick 1967, 17. The prince also goes by the name of Kushtanta.
177. The original capital of Khotan at Yutian, founded. c. 224 B.C.E.

178. Known in Chinese sources as Yuchi Fushizhan (Vijayasambhava I), circa 60 B.C.E.
179. The foregoing account derives from *The Prophecy on Mount Gośṛṅga* (*Gośṛṅgavyākaraṇa, Lang ru lung bstan*; Toh. 357; Dg.K. mdo sde, *aḥ*, ff. 220b–232a). Khotan's influence was enhanced following its conquest of Yarkand in 61 C.E. The country fell under periodic suzerainty of the Han, Tibetans, and Tang, and it was occupied by Tibetan forces from 792–851. The independence of the Buddhist kingdom, in close alliance with Dunhuang, was subsequently maintained until 1006 when Khotan fell to the Islamic Qara-Qanid ruler, Yusuf Kadir (Qadir Qaγan) of Kashgar.
180. Our text misreads "thirty-six."
181. Ci'u dbang.
182. This accords with traditional dating for the appearance of the historical Buddha.
183. Han ga'u dzung.
184. Han ming ti.
185. Dzu ha la, Zhu fa lan.
186. Bai Ma Si.
187. *ching sang*, Ch. *cheng xiang*.
188. Thang ka'u dzung.
189. Thang tha'i dzung.
190. Thang zam tsang.
191. This accords with Roerich 1949, 54. Other sources list twenty-two or twenty-three, taking into account two early emperors (Li Xian and Li Dan) who each had two distinct regnal periods.
192. Nga'i ding.
193. See Roerich 1949, 55, 67.
194. Ci'u tha'i dzung.
195. See Roerich 1949, 55.
196. Cit-tan ta'i gle'u.
197. Spen lyang, M. Bian Liang.
198. Sman rtse, Ch. Manzi. Roerich 1949, 55–56.
199. Hūṃ dbang, Ch. Hudun.
200. See Roerich 1949, 56.
201. See Pawo Tsuklak Trengwa 1962, 721–23.
202. This legend is recounted in Sonam Gyeltsen's *Clear Mirror of Geneology*, on which see Sørensen 1994, 420–21; and Stein 1951, 226. The sacred mountain range, location of the royal tombs of Xixia and temple ruins, lies on the boundary between Ningxia Huizu Autonomous Prefecture and Inner Mongolia Autonomous Prefecture.
203. On the etymology of the name *si hu*, see Stein 1951, 238–60.
204. See Stein 1951, 230n3. This name derives from the regnal title of his father, Li Deming.

205. Emperor Huanzong appears to have been deposed by his cousin, Li Anchuan, in 1206.
206. There were three intervening emperors of Xixia between Huanzong and Mozhu, the last of the imperial Tangut line.
207. The fourth emperor of the Northern Song dynasty.
208. Ten Tangut emperors of Xixia are generally enumerated, commencing with Jingzong (r. 1038–1148) and ending with Mozhu (r. 1226–1227). The stated period of 260 years would extend back to the accession of Li Kerui in 967. Jinzhong's predecessors, including his grandfather Li Jiqian (963–1004) and his father Li Deming (981–1032), were posthumously awarded imperial titles.
209. See Pawo Tsuklak Trengwa 1962, 724–31; and Roerich 1949, 57–60.
210. Mongol sources suggest that he was the twentieth generation in the descent from Borte Chino.
211. See Pawo Tsuklak Trengwa 1962, 732; and Roerich 1949, 59–60.

11. The Origins of the Outer Fields of Classical Learning

1. The author's primary source for this section is Pawo Tsuklak Trengwa 1962, 771–85. The historical and legendary anecdotes concerning the origin and development of the four outer fields of classical learning and their ancillary branches are also presented by Jamgon Kongtrul in Zangpo 2010, 377–430; and their content is analyzed by Jamgon Kongtrul in Dorje 2012.
2. *Sarvajñāvyākaraṇa.* Pawo Tsuklak Trengwa 1962, 773; Zangpo 2010, 379.
3. *Indravyākaraṇa.*
4. See Pawo Tsuklak Trengwa 1962, 773–74; and Zangpo 2010, 379–80.
5. According to Pawo Tsuklak Trengwa (1961, 774), the four restricted days of the month were the eighth, on which teachers are overwhelmed; the fourteenth, on which disciples are overwhelmed; the thirtieth, on which awareness is overwhelmed; and the first, on which all beings are overwhelmed. See also Zangpo 2010, 380.
6. The two prophecies are cited in Pawo Tsuklak Trengwa 1962, 774.
7. Pāṇini, *Pāṇinivyākaraṇa, Brda sprod pa pā ṇi ni'i mdo* (Toh. 4420; Dg.T. sna tshogs, *to*, ff. 1b–27a).
8. *Mahābhāṣya.* The nāga king Vāsuki (Nor rgyas bu), also known as Anantaśeṣa, is said to have emanated as the great grammarian Patañjali to whom *The Great Exposition* (*Mahābhāṣya*) is attributed.
9. The author of *The Kalāpa Grammar* (Toh. 4282) is also known as Śarvavarman, Iśvaravarman, or Rājadeva.
10. **Śiṣyahitākalāpasūtravṛtti, Lung ston pa ka lā pa'i mdo'i 'grel pa slob ma la phan pa zhes* (Toh. 4286; Dg.T. sgra mdo, *le*, ff. 75b–317a).
11. *Rin chen gdugs kyi 'grel pa.*
12. *Si sogs kyi mtha' dpyad.*

13. *Durgasiṃhapañjikā, Spyan gsum 'bangs kyi dur sing.* The latter, though mentioned by Buton, appears to be no longer extant. See Verhagen 1991, 58.
14. On the Kalāpa tradition, see Pawo Tsuklak Trengwa 1962, 774–75; also Zangpo 2010, 383–84.
15. *'Grel pa stong phrag drug pa.*
16. *Vibhaktikārikā, 'Grel pa su bandhu* (*Rnam dbye'i tshig le'ur byas pa*) (Toh. 4274; Dg.T. sgra mdo, *re*, ff. 46a–65a).
17. *Saṃbandhasiddhyabhidhānaprakriyā, 'Brel pa grub pa zhes bya ba'i rab tu byed pa* (Toh. 4278; Dg.T. sgra mdo, *re*, ff. 78b–106a).
18. *Stong phrag drug pa'i 'grel pa.*
19. That is, *The Paradigms of Verbal Roots, Dhātukāya, Byings kyi tshogs* (Toh. 4277).
20. On the Candrapa tradition, see Pawo Tsuklak Trengwa 1962, 775; and Zangpo 2010, 382–83.
21. *Rājaśrīvyākaraṇa.*
22. *prakṛti, rang bzhin.*
23. *pratyaya, rkyen.*
24. *vikāra, rnam 'gyur.* See Dorje 2012, 128–38.
25. Cited in Pawo Tsuklak Trengwa 1962, 775.
26. Subhūticandra, *Amarakoṣaṭīkākāmadhenunāma, 'Chi ba med pa'i mdzod kyi rgya cher 'grel pa 'dod 'jo'i ba mo zhes bya* (Toh. 4300; Dg.T. sgra mdo, *se*, ff. 244b–318a). See Pawo Tsuklak Trengwa 1962, 775; and Dorje 2012, 379–85.
27. *Rtsa ba'i mdo.*
28. *Dper brjod.*
29. Ratnākaraśānti, *Chandoratnākaranāma, Sdeb sbyor rin chen 'byung gnas zhes bya ba* (Toh. 4303; Dg.T. sgra mdo, *se*, ff. 351b–360b) and (Toh. 4304; Dg.T. sgra mdo, *se*, ff. 361a–379a).
30. Cited in Pawo Tsuklak Trengwa 1962, 775; and Zangpo 2010, 428. On prosody, see also Dorje 2012, 367–78.
31. These lists are enumerated in Dorje 2012, 359–66.
32. *Nāgānandanāṭaka, Klu kun du dga' ba zhes bya ba'i zlos gar* (Toh. 4154; Dg.T. skyes rab, *u*, ff. 225a–252a).
33. *Lokānandanāṭaka, 'Jig rten kun du dga' ba'i zlos gar zhes bya ba* (Toh. 4153; Dg.T. skyes rab, *u*, ff. 197b–225a).
34. Gtsug na nor bu. See Pawo Tsuklak Trengwa 1962, 775–76; and Dorje 2012, 387–94.
35. See Pawo Tsuklak Trengwa 1962, 772–73; Dorje 2012, 139–76; and Zangpo 2010, 386–92.
36. Exemplified by the Brahmanical logic of Iśvarasena and Akṣapāda.
37. *Smra ba'i sgrom.*
38. *Pramāṇasamuccaya* (*Pramāṇasūtra*), *Tshad ma kun las btus pa zhes bya ba'i rab tu byed pa* (Toh. 4203; Dg.T. tshad ma, *ce*, ff. 1b–13a).

39. *Pramāṇavārttikakārikā, Tshad ma rnam 'grel gyi tshig le'ur byas pa* (Toh. 4210; Dg.T. tshad ma, *ce*, ff. 94b–151a).
40. *Pramāṇaviniścaya, Tshad ma rnam par nges pa* (Toh. 4211; Dg.T. tshad ma, *ce*, ff. 152b–230a).
41. *Nyāyabindunāmaprakaraṇa, Rigs pa'i thigs pa zhes bya ba'i rab tu byed pa* (Toh. 4212; Dg.T. tshad ma, *ce*, ff. 231b–238a).
42. *Hetubindunāmaprakaraṇa, Gtan tshigs kyi thigs pa zhes bya ba'i rab tu byed pa* (Toh. 4213; Dg.T. tshad ma, *ce*, ff. 238a–255a).
43. *Sambandhaparīkṣāprakaraṇa, 'Brel pa brtag pa'i rab tu byed pa* (Toh. 4214; Dg.T. tshad ma, *ce*, ff. 255a–256a).
44. *Santānāntarasiddhināmaprakaraṇa, Rgyud gzhan grub pa zhes bya ba'i rab tu byed pa* (Toh. 4219; Dg.T. tshad ma, *che*, ff. 355b–359a).
45. *Vādanyāyanāmaprakaraṇa, Rtsod pa'i rigs pa zhes bya ba'i rab tu byed pa* (Toh. 4218; Dg.T. tshad ma, *che*, ff. 326b–355b).
46. *Pramāṇavārttikavṛtti, Tshad ma rnam 'grel gyi 'grel pa* (*Rang don le'u la 'grel pa*) (Toh. 4216; Dg.T. tshad ma, *ce*, ff. 261b–365a).
47. *Pramāṇavārttikapañjikā, Tshad ma rnam 'grel gyi dka' 'grel* (Toh. 4217).
48. As noted in Zangpo 2010 (387), Dharmakīrti had the first two attempts destroyed.
49. *Pramāṇavārttikaṭīkā, Tshad ma rnam 'grel gyi 'grel bshad* (Toh. 4220).
50. *Pramāṇavārttikālaṃkāra, Tshad ma rnam 'grel gyi rgyan* (Toh. 4221).
51. *An Explanatory Commentary on "Ornament for 'A Commentary on Valid Cognition,'" Pramāṇavārttikālaṃkāraṭīkā, Tshad ma rnam 'grel gyi rgyan gyi 'grel bshad* (Toh. 4222; Dg.T. tshad ma, *de*, 1b–365a, *ne*, ff. 1b–312a).
52. *Pramāṇavārttikālaṃkāraṭīkāsupariśuddhānāma, Tshad ma rnam 'grel rgyan gyi 'grel bshad shin tu yongs su dag pa zhes bya ba* (Toh. 4226).
53. *A Commentary on the Third Chapter of "A Commentary on Valid Cognition," *Pramāṇavārttikaṭīkāyāṃtṛtīyaparivarta, Tshad ma rnam 'grel gyi 'grel pa las le'u gsum pa* (Toh. 4225; Dg.T. tshad ma, *phe*, ff. 1b–174a).
54. *Sambandhaparīkṣānusāra, 'Brel pa brtag pa'i rjes su 'brang ba* (Toh. 4237; Dg.T. tshad ma, *zhe*, ff. 21b–35a).
55. *Pramāṇaviniścayaṭīkā, Tshad ma rnam par nges pa'i 'grel bshad / Tshad ma rnam par nges pa'i ṭī ka 'thad ldan zhes bya ba le'u dang po dang gnyis pa* (Toh. 4229).
56. *An Explanatory Commentary on "Ascertainment of Valid Cognition," Pramāṇaviniścayaṭīkā, Tshad ma rnam par nges pa'i 'grel bshad* (Toh. 4228; Dg.T. tshad ma, *tshe*, ff. 178b–295a).
57. This sentence derives verbatim from Pawo Tsuklak Trengwa 1962, 776. On the arts and their historical development in the Buddhist context, see also Dorje 2012, 177–316; and Zangpo 2010, 393–405.
58. These are enumerated in Dorje 2012, 410.
59. This passage derives verbatim from Pawo Tsuklak Trengwa 1962, 776–77. See also Konchog and Davis 2017, 39.

60. *so bdag*. Translation marked as uncertain.—Ed.
61. *Tshangs pa'i tshad yig*.
62. *Characteristics of the Proportions of the Body, Pratibimbamānalakṣaṇa, Sku gzugs kyi tshad kyi mtshan nyid ces bya ba* (Toh. 4316; Dg.T. bzo rig pa/thun mong ba, *ngo*, ff. 11a–15b). See Pawo Tsuklak Trengwa 1962, 777; and Konchog and Davis 2017, 39.
63. See Dorje 2012, 189–93; and Konchog and Davis 2017, 193.
64. On maṇḍala construction and proportions, see Konchog and Davis 2017, 149–92; and Dorje 2012, 234–45.
65. See p. 29.
66. On these diverse styles and their associated motifs, see Dorje 2012, 231–34.
67. On the development of these two indigenous Tibetan styles, exemplified by the paintings of Tashi Lhunpo and Gongkar Chode, respectively, see Konchog and Davis 2017, 48–64; and Dorje 2012, 769n338.
68. See Pawo Tsuklak Trengwa 1962, 777.
69. See Pawo Tsuklak Trengwa 1962, 777–78; and Kilty 2010, 51. This Vedic doxography may include etymology (*nirukta*, *nges tshig*) among the six subjects instead of divine revelations that are heard.
70. On the myths associated with Saraṇyu, including this and other etymologies of the name Nāsatya, see Donniger 2014, 269–80.
71. *arietes beta, gamma*.
72. Our text reads instrumental *kyis* for the genitive *kyi*, as found in Pawo Tsuklak Trengwa 1962, 778.
73. *Gsod dpyad 'bum pa*.
74. The Sanskrit Vīṇajya is suggested elsewhere for *rgyun shes*. There are various enumerations of these seven hermit sages, the earliest probably being that found in the *Jaiminīya Brāhmaṇa*, 2.218–21: Agastya, Atri, Bharadvāja, Gautama, Jamadagni, Vasiṣṭha, and Viśvamitra. For the alternative listing of Atri, Marīci, Pulastya, Aṅgiras, Kaiṭabhajit, or Pulaha, Vasiṣṭha, and Kratu, see Mani 1964, 691; and Kilty 2010, 102.
75. Note that our text reads *rkang gnyis spyod* for *dka' gnyis spyod*. Elsewhere he has been identified as Bharadvāja.
76. Also rendered as Jagannāthauta. See Kilty 2010, 102.
77. Our text reads Haladhara, or Balarāma, and *gzhol 'gro skyes* for Punarvasu. According to Desi Sangye Gyatso, the former is considered to supplement the list of seven. See Kilty 2010, 103. Elsewhere this sage has been tentatively identified with Caraka.
78. These nine are enumerated in Kilty 2010, 103.
79. Elsewhere this person is identified as the teacher of the great physician Jīvaka. As such, he may be identifiable as Piṅgala or Disapamok. See also Zangpo 2010, 406–8.
80. See Pawo Tsuklak Trengwa 1962, 778.
81. This is the twenty-fifth chapter of the *Suvarṇaprabhāsa*, describing the

Buddha's former life as a merchant's son who brings water. See also Kilty 2010, 71–76, 81.

82. See Zangpo 2010, 408–10.

83. Nāgārjuna, *Yogaśataka*, *Sbyor ba brgya pa* (Toh. 4306; Dg.T. gso ba rig pa, *he*, ff. 1b–8b).

84. Nāgārjunagarbha, *Jīvasūtra*, *Sman 'tsho ba'i mdo* (Toh. 4307; Dg.K. gso ba rig pa, *he*, ff. 8b–12a).

85. Nāgārjuna, *Ācāryanāgārjunabhāṣitāvabheṣajakalpa*, *Rtsva a ba'i cho ga* (*Slob dpon klu sgrub kyis bshad pa sman ā ba'i cho ga*) (Toh. 4308; Dg.T. gso ba rig pa, *he*, ff. 12a–13a).

86. Vyāḍipāda. *Rasasiddhiśāstra*. *Dngul chu rin chen phreng ba* (*Dngul chu grub pa'i bstan bcos*) (Toh. 4313; Dg.T. bzo rig pa/thun mong ba, *ngo*, ff. 1b–7a).

87. Anon., *Rasāyanaśāstroddhṛti*, *Gser 'gyur sbyor ba* (*Gser 'gyur gyi bstan bcos bsdus pa*) (Toh. 4314; Dg.T. bzo rig pa/thun mong ba, *ngo*, ff. 7a–8b).

88. Vāgbhaṭa, *Aṣṭāṅgahṛdayanāmavaiḍūryakabhāṣya*, *Yan lag brgyad pa chen po* (*Yan lag brgyad pa'i snying po zhes bya ba'i sman dpyad kyi bshad pa*) (Toh. 4311; Dg.T. gso ba rig pa, *he*, ff. 335b–410a, *e*, ff. 1b–421a).

89. *Yan lag brgyad pa 'jug pa*.

90. Vāgbhaṭa, *Aṣṭāṅgahṛdayasaṃhitā*, *Snying po bsdus pa* (Toh. 4310; Dg.T. gso ba rig pa, *he*, ff. 44b–335a).

91. *Yan lag brgyad pa bsdus pa*.

92. Candranandana, *Padārthacandrikāprabhāsanāmāṣṭāṅgahṛdayavivṛtti*, *Tshig don zla zer* (*Yan lag brgyad pa'i snying po'i rnam par 'grel pa tshig gi don gyi zla zer*) (Toh. 4312; Dg.T. gso ba rig pa, *ko*, ff. 1b–296a, *kho*, ff. 1b–340a, *go*, ff. 1b–304a).

93. Candranandana, **Vaidyāṣṭāṅgahṛdayavṛttibheṣajanāmaparyāya*, *Sman ming zur du bkol ba sgra sbyor nges pa* (*Sman dpyad yan lag brgyad pa'i snying po'i 'grel pa*) (Toh. 4309; Dg.T. gso ba rig pa, *he*, ff. 13b–44a).

94. On these Indian treatises, see Kilty 2010, 123–44; and Zangpo 2010, 410–12.

95. *Sman dpyad chen mo*.

96. *Mi 'jigs pa'i mtshon cha*. See Pawo Tsuklak Trengwa 1962, 780; Kilty 2010, 148–49; and Zangpo 2010, 414.

97. He is not to be confused with the physician Biji, who is said to have reached Tibet from Takṣaśīla during the earlier reign of Lhatotori Nyentsen and who also established his own lineage in Tibet. See Dorje 2017, 514n427. Byzantium here may imply Ferghana or other parts of Central Asia under the nominal suzerainty of Byzantium. On this figure, see also Kilty 2010, 152–56.

98. See Pawo Tsuklak Trengwa 1962, 780.

99. Some of these commitments are enumerated in Pawo Tsuklak Trengwa 1962, 780.

100. These seven admonitions or points of advice are enumerated in Pawo Tsuklak Trengwa 1962, 780.

101. Pawo Tsuklak Trengwa (1961, 780) mentions that he hailed from China. See also Kilty 2010, 164–69; and Zangpo 2010, 415.
102. *Rde'u bskong phyi nang gsang gsum.*
103. The Cheje line appears to be a Bon medical transmission. See also Kilty 2010, 170.
104. See Pawo Tsuklak Trengwa 1962, 780–81; Kilty 2010, 169–71; and Zangpo 2010, 416–17.
105. *Yan lag brgyad pa.*
106. *Dri med gzi brjid rtsa 'grel.*
107. *Gdam pa sum cu pa rtsa 'grel.*
108. See Pawo Tsuklak Trengwa 1962, 780–81; Kilty 2010, 171–73; and Zangpo 2010, 417–18. The nine learned Tibetan physicians are enumerated in the latter (417).
109. See Pawo Tsuklak Trengwa 1962, 781; Kilty 2010, 173; and Zangpo 2010, 418.
110. The hermit sage Manoja (*yid las skyes*) is the recipient of the *Four Tantras*, and the hermit sage Vidyājñāna (*rig pa'i ye shes*), in his various aspects, their expositor.
111. It is interesting that Ngawang Namgyel makes no mention of the development of the *Four Tantras* prior to their final redaction by Yutok Yonten Gonpo and leaves no role for either Yutok the Elder or Drapa Ngonshe. On these figures, see Kilty 2010, 175–205.
112. *Skor tshoms bcu gcig.*
113. See Pawo Tsuklak Trengwa 1962, 781–83; Kilty 2010, 206–60; and Zangpo 2010, 419–21.
114. *Man ngag bye ba ring bsrel.*
115. See Pawo Tsuklak Trengwa 1962, 783; Kilty 2010, 293–318; and Zangpo 2010, 421–22.
116. See Pawo Tsuklak Trengwa 1962, 783–84.

Colophon

1. The four precious substances (*rin chen sna bzhi*) are silver, aquamarine, ruby, and gold.
2. Literally "weapon" (*mtshon*).
3. This likely refers to Taklunga the Great, Tashi Pel.

Part Two: Great Divine Drum of Wondrous Renown

Verses of Homage

1. *bka' sdod ma mgon lcam dral*, an epithet of Mahākāla and Śrīdevī.

Synopsis of the Text

1. The three mysteries (*gsang gsum*) are those of buddha body, speech, and mind. The five wheels of adornment (*rgyan 'khor lo lnga*) additionally include buddha attributes and activities.
2. *Kāvyādarśa*, chap. 1, v. 6. See Ray 2004, 5.
3. Aśvaghoṣa, *Gurupañcaśikhā*, *Bla ma lnga bcu pa* (Toh. 3721; Dg.T. rgyud, *tshu*, ff. 10a–12a).
4. *Bla ma dkon mchog kun 'dus.*

1. The Later Life of Zhabdrung Ngawang Namgyel, the Seventeenth Hierarch

1. That is to say, the wheels of buddha body, speech, mind, attributes, and activities.
2. On this buddha image called Lhachen Pelgyi Lhunpo Dzamling Gyen (Lha chen dpal gyi lhun po 'dzam gling rgyan), see Akester 2016, 42.
3. Paulastya ('Od yangs tsha bo) is an epithet of the wealth-bestowing deity, Kubera.
4. On Yangri Gar, the hermitage of Gyelwang Rinchen Phuntsok, which later became the seat of the Drigung Chungtsang incarnations, see Akester 2016, 175–76. The incumbent in 1609 may have been Drakpa Tsultrim, the third vajra master.
5. This would have been Tenth Karmapa, Choying Dorje (1604–1674).
6. This is possibly to be identified with the geomantic temple of Uru Katsel, on which see Akester 2016, 162–63.
7. Chogyel Rinchen Phuntsok (1547–1602) had recently passed away at this point. On the life of this twenty-second throne holder of Drigung, see also Drigung Konchok Gyatso 2004, 456–65.
8. The text reads *bka' sbod dge bsnyen [tshan] po.*
9. That is to say, they were extant in 1824 at the time when this supplementary narrative was composed.
10. See Akester 2016, 42.
11. *don bskor ba'i slad dang phyogs mthun se gling du phebs.* Translation marked as uncertain.—Ed.
12. *Tshe dbang bde mchog lhan skyes.*
13. Karma Phuntsok Namgyel reigned from 1611 to 1621. He built Zhigatse Castle, which was considered a prototype for the Potala Palace in Lhasa, and sent armies against the Mongols in Lhasa and to Bhutan.
14. *Stag lung lugs tshe dpag dkar po.*
15. *Rta mgrin grub rgyal lugs.*
16. *Smon lam chen mo'i nyin grangs sbar ba.*
17. The main hall within the Great Temple of Lhasa.

18. The text reads *gzhis lan* for *gzhis lag*.
19. *Drag las 'phrin las kyi rno mde'u bka' srung dge bsnyen chen po'i drag las rab gzigs rdo rje me char.*
20. This may be Gyelwang Konchok Rinchen (1590–1654).
21. This is Ngawang Tashi Peldrub (1600–1672), the twentieth hierarch of Taklung Upper Plain, on whom see p. 631.
22. *bka' babs brgyad ldan*. Translation marked as uncertain.—Ed.
23. *Sgrub thabs rgya mtsho.*
24. *Dud sol.*
25. *'Bri gung gser dpe.*
26. *ldog pa ltar*. Translation marked as uncertain.—Ed.
27. This may be Shang Karwa Rinchen Gyeltsen (Shangs dkar ba rin chen rgyal mtshan, 1353–1434). The term "ten difficulties" in Gelukpa circles denotes the five philosophical primary texts and their main commentaries, *dka' bcu pa* being the title of a geshe who has mastered them. The expression does not appear to equate with the *dka' ba spyod ba rnam pa bcu* (Nordrang Orgyen, 2049–50). The expression *rtags brgyad* generally denotes the eight auspicious symbols (*bkra shis rtags brgyad*).
28. *Chos drug yid bzhin nor bu'i nyams khrid.*
29. *Thog mthar rje btsun lhan cig skyes ma.*
30. The name Yar lha mchod may denote the sacred offering shrines at Mount Yarlha Shampo, on which see Aketser 2016, 419–20.
31. *skag grong grong stod*. Translation marked as uncertain.—Ed.
32. *Blo sbyong don bdun ma.*
33. This may possibly have been Drowei Gonpo (1579–c. 1617), the titular king of the Phakmodru dynasty, whose death could have occurred earlier, in 1613.
34. *gdan gnon*. Translation marked as uncertain.—Ed.
35. *Sbad don kun gsal.*
36. *Rgyud sde spyi'i rnam gzhag.*
37. Dingri Namar.
38. At Langtang.
39. This may refer to Sonam Namgyel, a supporter of Fourth Dalai Lama and opponent of the Tsangpa Desi, Karma Phuntsok Namgyel.
40. *Gu ru'i thugs sgrub.*
41. This would have been Fifth Drukchen, Paksam Wangpo (1593–1641).
42. *Dvags po chos bzhi.*
43. *Ston pa'i 'khrungs rabs brgya rtsa.*
44. *chu lho byang*. Translation marked as uncertain.—Ed.
45. *Lam zab bla ma'i sgrub pa.*
46. Our text misreads *dbon tshang sa*.
47. This would have been Sixth Zhamar, Chokyi Wangchuk (1584–1630).
48. This may be Tümenken Čogtu Qong Taiji (1581–1637) or Ligden Qaγan (1588–1634).

49. The Qalqa arrived at the invitation of the Kyisho governor Sonam Namgyel, thereby provoking the involvement of the Tsangpa Desi in Lhasa affairs.
50. *Sdom pa gsum gyi rtsa ba tshigs bcad ma.*
51. With the approval of Sera and Drepung, the monks from Taklung were consequently allocated an equal share of gifts to those received by monks of Sera and Drepung attending the Great Prayer Festival.
52. The text misreads *dpal ldan sa yi tshangs pa sde srid chen po.*
53. This event in 1618 heralded the occupation of Lhasa by the forces of Tsangpa Desi.
54. *Blo sbyong don bdun ma.*
55. Second Jedrung, Drakpa Gyeltsen (1591–1642).
56. Name of a monastery and hamlet near Gyawoding in Tsang.
57. The recognition of Fifth Dalai Lama (1617–1682).
58. Gzhung zhig lha btsun. Translation marked as uncertain.—Ed.
59. *Sgrub thabs brgya rtsa.*
60. *Rdo rje rnal 'byor ma'i lta khrid snyan brgyud yid bzhin nor bu.*
61. According to Tāranātha's *Ocean of Enlightened Activity: A Biography of the Glorious Spiritual Mentor* (*Dpal ldan bla ma'i rnam thar phrin las rgya mtsho rnam par rgyas pa*, Collected Works of Tāranātha, vol. 38, 72–149), Julang is the name of an Oirat chieftain (*o ru ju lang rgyal po*).
62. *Rje stag lung thang pa'i bstod pa rdul bral zhing gi smon lam rnams.*
63. The text misreads *'bri stag dkar gsum.*
64. *De nyid 'dus pa.*
65. Otherwise known as First Dechen Chokhor Yongdzin, Ngawang Zangpo (1546–1615) of Ralung.

2. Choktrul Tashi Peldrub, the Twentieth Hierarch

1. The bolded terms, followed by Tibetan transliteration, represent the meaning of the names of the master who is being praised in the verse.—Ed.
2. *So thar pa rin po che'i rgyan.*
3. *Gsung mgur.*
4. This would have been the twenty-sixth throne holder of Sakya, Ducho Labrangpa Jamyang Sonam Zangpo (1519–1621).
5. *Rgyud sde spyi'i rnam bzhag.*
6. *Sgrub thabs rgya mtsho.*
7. *Bla ma'i rnal 'byor.*
8. *khun phang.* Translation marked as uncertain.—Ed.
9. dbyings na bzhugs shing. Translation marked as uncertain.—Ed.
10. Jama Gon in Nangchen.
11. The text reads *shu 'bib* for *shu 'bubs.*
12. 'Od 'jol phros na. Text marked as uncertain.—Ed.
13. *'khor che ba.* Translation marked as uncertain.—Ed.

14. On Zhabdrung Ngagi Wangchuk, also known as First Taklung Tulku, was the twenty-first incumbent throne holder of Taklung Upper Plain.
15. Zhabdrung Machen at this point becomes the title of the incarnate line at Upper Plain.
16. *Ratnakūṭa.*
17. Also known as Ojo Zhabdrung Tashi Chokyi Gyelpo (1660–1689), he was the twenty-third or twenty-fourth incumbent throne holder of Taklung Upper Plain.
18. *khams che ba'i bsngags brjod ni mi mdzad.* Translation marked as uncertain. —Ed.
19. *Dvags po chos bzhi.*
20. *Blo sbyong don bdun.*
21. *Thugs rje chen po'i dmar khrid.*
22. *Bla ma'i rnal 'byor.*
23. *ma stod smad.* Text marked as uncertain.—Ed.
24. *Thugs sgrub.*
25. *Lam rim chen mo.*
26. Our text reads fire monkey (*me sprel*).
27. The text reads earth dog (*sa khyi*), which would be 1658.
28. This image of Phakmodrupa is mentioned by Tāranātha.
29. *bla ma'i drung.* Translation marked as uncertain.—Ed.
30. *Bka' brgyud bka' 'bum.*
31. *gol ba tsam yong res.* Translation marked as uncertain.—Ed.
32. *Rim lnga snyan brgyud.*
33. *Gsang 'dus lam rim.*
34. *Blo sbyong don bdun ma.*
35. This is Third Jedrung, Drakpa Lekdrub (1646–1708).
36. *Sdom gsum gyi 'grel pa.*
37. This translation marked as uncertain: or "manuscript."—Ed.
38. *Rdo rje'i mgur.*
39. *Rig 'dzin sngags kyi sdom pa.*
40. *Kun spangs zhen pa rang grol.*
41. *Ma thang chos 'byung kha skong.*
42. *Bkra shis dpal grub kyi rnam thar gsol 'debs zhing khams rgya mtsho ma.*
43. *Mkhar thog rdzong btsan gyi gsol mchod.*
44. *Rgyal chen rnam sras gyi bsang.*
45. *'khor bstun.* Translation marked as uncertain.—Ed.

3. Zhabdrung Ngawang Tashi Chogyel, the Twenty-Third Hierarch

1. The bolded terms, followed by Tibetan transliteration, represent the meaning of the names of the master who is being praised in the verse.—Ed.

2. *dbon chos kyi sras.* Translation marked as uncertain.—Ed.
3. *lto sems gang byin gyi dpe ltar.* Translation marked as uncertain.—Ed.
4. *Lha'i dge bsnyen chen po'i gsol mchod srung ma dga' bskyed.*
5. *G.ya' bdud kyi gsol mchod rgyas pa.*

4. Kyabgon Ngawang Trinle Tendzin

1. The bolded terms, followed by Tibetan transliteration, represent the meaning of the names of the master who is being praised in the verse.—Ed.
2. *ma thang gzhung du yod dus.* Translation marked as uncertain.—Ed.
3. *Dregs 'joms rig 'dzin thugs thig.*
4. *Nor rgya ma ma dregs 'dus.*
5. *rig gnas slob mi.* Translation marked as uncertain.—Ed.
6. *Dkon mchog spyi 'dus.*
7. *bu la.* Translation marked as uncertain.—Ed.
8. *lo mtshams zla bas go bcad.* Translation marked as uncertain.—Ed.
9. *Sbyongs dkyil bcu gnyis.*
10. Yan xin jiang jun, Mi hreng ljang 'gi.
11. Jin gan ang bang jiang jun, Rdo rje am pa ljang 'gi.
12. *rtse shod.* Translation marked as uncertain.—Ed.
13. *Gter lung bdun pa.*
14. Mchod khang rtse. Translation marked as uncertain.—Ed.
15. This was Fourth Jedrung (1715–1743).
16. This translation marked as uncertain: or "Mani and Vajraguru."—Ed.
17. *mgur grva.*
18. *Sgrub pa bka' brgyad.*
19. *Rtsa gsum snying thig.*
20. *Zab lam bde gshegs 'dus pa.*
21. *Mkha' 'gro snying thig.*
22. But see Nordrang Orgyen 2008, 807.
23. *Rje ratna na tha'i rnam thar.*

5. Choktrul Tashi Jampel Gyatso and Yangsi Tulku Yizhin Trinle Chokdrub

1. The bolded terms, followed by Tibetan transliteration, represent the meaning of the names of the master who is being praised in the verse.—Ed.
2. *Stag lung pa'i zab chos nor bu bzhi.*
3. *gsar rnying grva gsum.* Translation marked as uncertain.—Ed.
4. *sku rims grul drag mdzad.* Translation marked as uncertain.—Ed.
5. Here the manuscript is corrupted. The text suggests *zhags gzhi sgon gnang.*
6. *mdun du bub pa.* Translation marked as uncertain.—Ed.

7. *Bla mchod.*
8. Kun rig sgrib sel.

6. Tulku Tashi Drakpa Yeshe, a.k.a. Chokyi Nyima

1. The bolded terms, followed by Tibetan transliteration, represent the meaning of the names of the master who is being praised in the verse.—Ed.
2. *yul phu lding dpon.* Translation marked as uncertain.—Ed.
3. *ma zhu.* Translation marked as uncertain.—Ed.
4. This was Kaḥtok Rikdzin Tsewang Norbu (1698–1755). The text misreads *kar gtogs.*
5. *Bla sgrub bde mchog.*
6. *Rin 'byung.*
7. *Bka' brgyad bde 'dus.*
8. *Dbyar than pa shin tu tshabs pa'i bskul ma.*
9. This was Fifth Jedrung, Rinchen Lekdrub (1745–1829).
10. *Bde mchog lhan skyes.*
11. *Zhabs brtan dag snang ma.*
12. *Bla mchod.*
13. Ch. *zha sa*, Mong. *dza sag*
14. *zhe 'dre ba.* Translation marked as uncertain.—Ed.
15. *Sgrub thabs rgya mtsho.*
16. *Tshe sgrub bde mchog yig bdun.*
17. *skyabs brten.* Translation marked as uncertain.—Ed.
18. On the short-length "twenty-finger-width" long poncho or tippet worn by sacred dancers, see Nebesky-Wojkowitz 1997, 94. Our text reads *zor dpangs* for *sor dpangs.*
19. *Yi dam drag khros.*
20. *zhe 'dre ba.* Translation marked as uncertain.—Ed.
21. One dotse equals fifty *sang.*
22. The text reads *bla chos* for *bla mchod.*
23. *sku rdzongs.* Translation marked as uncertain.—Ed.
24. Dre'u lung tshes bcu. Text marked as uncertain.—Ed.
25. *dgung gi blar mtho ba.* Translation marked as uncertain.—Ed.
26. *Bka' thang brgya.*
27. *mdongs mtha'i gar du rtsen.* Translation marked as uncertain, possibly a metaphor.—Ed.
28. *Sbyong dkyil bcu bzhi pa.*
29. *Seng gdong ma'i bzlog pa.*
30. *Thugs rje chen po 'gro 'dul lha lnga.*
31. *Zhi khro dam pa rigs brgya.*

7. Kunkhyen Jikme Gocha, a.k.a. Drakpa Choying Lhundrub

1. The bolded terms, followed by Tibetan transliteration, represent the meaning of the names of the master who is being praised in the verse.—Ed.
2. Literally "like brass pretending to be gold" (*ra gan gser rdzus*).
3. *Gu ru drag khros.*
4. Translation marked as uncertain: the "white and red" possibly refer to wall stripes.—Ed.
5. Rgyal ba dkon mchog spyi 'dus.
6. *Sgrub thabs rin 'byung.*
7. *Tshe dbang 'chi med dpal ster.*

Concluding Verses

1. Readers should note that these Tibetan verses employ verbal repetition (*śabdāvṛtti, tshig bskor ba*), an aspect of the poetic ornament of repetition (*āvṛtti, bskor ba'i rgyan*), in which the initial syllable of each line (*gang*) is repeated. This device is of course lost in translation.
2. These verses employ repetition of the syllable *kun* at the end of the first line and beginning of the second line, of the syllable *du* at the end of the second line and beginning of the third line, and of the syllable *dag* at the end of the third line and beginning of the fourth line.
3. These verses employ repetition of the syllable *yid* at the end of the first line and beginning of the second line, of the syllable *kun* at the end of the second line and beginning of the third line, and of the syllable *sdom* at the end of the third line and beginning of the fourth line.
4. The four gems of the aural lineage (*snyan brgyud nor bu bzhi*) are enumerated as *snyan brgyud bzhi* in Nordrang Orgyen 2008, 612. They are (1) sacred doctrine endowed with transmission, (2) transmission endowed with pith instruction, (3) pith instruction endowed with lineage, and (4) lineage endowed with blessings.
5. These verses employ repetition of the syllable *yang* at the end of the first line and beginning of the second line, of the syllable *che* at the end of the second line and beginning of the third line, and of the syllable *kun* at the end of the third line and beginning of the fourth line.
6. These verses employ repetition of the syllable *ya* at the beginning of each line.
7. The four excellent endowments (*phun tshogs sde bzhi*) are enumerated in Nordrang Orgyen 2008, 726–27. They are (1) the sacred doctrine, (2) the wealth of resoures, (3) the desire for fruitional attainment, and (4) the conclusive attainment of liberation.
8. These verses employ repetition of the syllable *lha* at the beginning of each line.
9. These verses employ repetition of the syllables *bkra shis* at the beginning of each line.

Colophon

1. There are various enumerations of the three kindnesses (*bka' drin gsum ldan*), on which see Nordrang Orgyen 2008, 175–76. One version enumerates (1) the kindness of teaching the sacred doctrine, (2) the kindness of blessing the mindstream, and (3) the kindness of nurturing an assembly with material things. Another refers to the kindnesses of (1) conferring empowerments, (2) explaining the tantras, and (3) granting the pith instructions.
2. *mgrin bzang thig le can*. Translation marked as uncertain.—Ed.

Part Three: A Brief Chronicle of Riwoche

1. Riwoche Monastery

1. A title granted from the time of the Yuan emperors onward, comparable to Tishrī, denoting the respect due to an imperial teacher.

2. The Tulku Successions and Palaces of Riwoche

1. Gong ma ca chin.

3. Jedrung Trinle Jampei Jungne

1. According to Treasury of Lives (Garry 2007), he was born in 1856 (fire dragon) and died in 1922 (water dog). Our text reads 1878 (earth tiger). Barron (2005, 446–47), following Nyoshul Khenpo, offers no dates.
2. According to Barron (2005, 447), his writings including spiritual revelations amount to thirteen volumes.
3. Among them, Dudjom Jikdrel Yeshe Dorje (1904–1987) and Kangyur Rinpoche Longchen Yeshe Dorje (1897–1975).

4. Gara Lama Sonam Rabten

1. According to Treasury of Lives (Gardner 2009), the year of his birth may alternatively have been 1865 (wood ox).
2. According to Treasury of Lives (Gardner 2009), Jedrung Rinpoche and Gara Lama were brothers.

5. The Opening of Pemako

1. On this expedition to Pemako (1903–1909), see Baker 2004, 55–56. Orgyen Wangchuk, the governor of Trongsar Dzong in Bhutan, later became the first Bhutanese king.

6. Chinese Invasions

1. This is following the collapse of the Qing dynasty.

9. The Detention of Jedrung Rinpoche

1. The third point was clearly not upheld since the tulku line of Jedrung Rinpoche is known to have subsequently split into two branches—at Riwoche and in Powo.

10. The Capture and Second Escape of Gara Lama

1. Others report that he reached Shanghai via Nepal. See Treasury of Lives (Gardner 2009).

11. Retribution against Riwoche

1. The author here includes a note stating, "This imperial document with the gold seal was subsequently handed over to Tashi Pelrawa by Dzasak Thubten Wangchuk of Kundeling, and then given to me."
2. Here the author's note states, "At the time when the golden reliquary of the Thirteenth Dalai Lama was constructed, Tashi Pelrawa offered that sword through the secretary of the Potala, (*rtse gzim 'gag*) Tubten Nyinje, for insertion among the sacred contents of the golden reliquary."

Part Four: A Guide to the Sacred Places of Utsang

1. Taklung Upper Plain

1. Otherwise known as Kagyu Domsumling. See Akester 2016, 44.
2. This is the new assembly hall founded in the early nineteenth century by Matrul Tenpei Nyima, on which see Akester 2016, 43–44.
3. The other half was taken by Sangye On to Riwoche.
4. Matrul Tenpei Nyima (1788–1854) was a contemporary of Jamyang Khyentse Wangpo. See Akester 2016, 41.
5. According to Aketser (2016, 41), this Labrang occupied the site of the Old Offering Chapel.
6. According to Akester (2016, 44), this building was founded in 1720 by Tendzin Namgyel.
7. *Mchod khang dmar po'i lo rgyus gnas bshad chen mo*. Situ Chokyi Gyatso derived the following summary of the contents of the Red Offering Chapel from Matrul Tenpei Nyima's *Great Explanation of the Sacred Place: A History*

of the Red Offering Chapel (*Mchod khang dmar po'i lo rgyus gnas bshad chen mo*). This passage is also translated in Aketser 2016, 42–43.

8. This is because he is the author of the inventory.
9. The text here reads *gsang* for *gsar*.
10. *Bde mchog nag po lugs drug cu pa.*
11. *Stag lung thugs sgrub.*

2. Taklung Lower Plain: Riwoche

1. Karma Chakme.
2. See chapter 9, note 39.
3. *Dzi kṣiṃ* (*dzhai kṣyim*) is generally recognized to be a type of dark-red gold that emits rainbow light when smeared with aconite. See Parfionovitch, Dorje, and Meyer 1992, vol. 2, 217.
4. *Ne tso'i g.yu 'bum.*
5. *Mkha' 'gro gsang 'bum.*
6. *Zab bdun phur pa.*
7. *sta bzhi.*
8. *Bde mchog dung bdun.*
9. *rkun bu.* Translation marked as uncertain: or "marmots."—Ed.

Bibliography

1. Source Texts

Kaḥtok Situ Chokyi Gyatso (Kaḥ thog si tu Chos kyi rgya mtsho)
Extracts from *Dbus gtsang gi gnas yig* [A guide to the sacred places of Utsang], 19–29 and 58–68
Lhasa: Bod ljongs bod yig dpe rnying dpe skrun khang, 1999.
BDRC W21611

Jedrung Jampel Gyeltsen (Rje drung 'Jam dpal rgyal mtshan)
A Brief Chronicle of Riwoche, Including Jedrung Tulku Gongma and Gara Lama
Khams ri bo che dgon dang rje drung sprul sku gong ma mgar ra bla ma bcas kyi lo rgyus rags bsdus
In *Selection of Source Materials for the Study of the Culture and History of Tibet* (*Bod kyi rig gnas lo rgyus dpyad gzhi'i rgyu cha bdams bsgrigs*), 208–34
Lhasa: Bod rang skyong ljongs srid gros rig gnas lo rgyus dpyad gzhi'i rgyu cha zhib 'jug u yon lhan khang, 1985.
BDRC WAS19813

Taklung Ngawang Namgyel (also Taklung Zhabdrung Ngawang Namgyel, Stag lung zhabs drung ngag dbang rnam rgyal)
Wondrous Ocean of Eloquence: A Narrative of the Wish-Fulfilling Gem of the Lineage *Brgyud pa yid bzhin nor bu'i rtogs pa brjod pa ngo mtshar rgya mtsho*
In *Chos 'byung ngo mtshar rgya mtsho* [Doctrinal history titled wondrous ocean], 1–723 and 915–29
Lhasa: Bod ljongs bod yig dpe rnying dpe skrun khang, 1992.
BDRC MW17276

Taklung Trirab Ngawang Tenpai Nyima (Stag lung khri rabs Ngag dbang bstan pa'i nyi ma)
Great Divine Drum of Wondrous Renown: An Addendum of Biographies of the Later Abbatial Succession of Upper Taklung, Dorje Den Monastery

Stag lung ya thang rdo rje gdan gyi gdan rabs phyis byon pa dag gi rnam thar kha skong ngo mtshar snyan grags lha yi rnga chen
In *Chos 'byung ngo mtshar rgya mtsho* [Doctrinal history titled wondrous ocean], 761–950.
Lhasa: Bod ljongs bod yig dpe rnying dpe skrun khang, 1992
BDRC MW17276

Kangyur

The Applications of Mindfulness
Smṛtyupasthāna
'Phags pa dam pa'i chos dran pa nye bar gzhag pa
Toh. 287; Dg.K. mdo sde, *ya*, ff. 82a–318a, *ra*, ff. 1b–307a, *la*, ff. 1b–312a, *sha*, ff. 1b–229b.
https://read.84000.co/translation/toh287.html

The Glorious Tantra That Equals Space
Śrīkhasamatantrarāja
Dpal nam mkha' dang mnyam pa'i rgyud kyi rgyal po
Toh. 386; Dg.T. rgyud, *ga*, ff. 199a–202a.
https://read.84000.co/translation/toh386.html

The Great Bounteousness of the Buddhas (also, *The Flower Ornament Sūtra*)
Buddhāvataṃsakasūtra
Sangs rgyas phal po che zhes bya ba shin tu rgyas pa chen po'i mdo
Toh. 44; Dg.K. phal chen, *ka*, ff. 1b–393a, *kha*, ff. 1b–396a, *ga*, ff. 1b–396a, *a*, ff. 1b–363a; KPD 35, 3–1037.
https://read.84000.co/section/O1JC114941JC14666.html

The Gathering of Precious Enlightened Attributes
Sañcayagāthā (Āryaprajñāpāramitāsañcayagāthā)
Yon tan rin chen sdud pa ('Phags pa shes rab kyi pha rol tu phyin pa sdud pa tshigs su bcad pa)
Toh. 13; Dg.K. shes rab sna tshogs, *ka*, ff. 1b–19b; KPD 34, 3–53.

The Great Exegetical Tantra Titled Nondual Victor
Bshad brgyud gnyis med rnam rgyal chen mo (De bzhin gshegs pa thams cad kyi gsang ba rnal 'byor chen po rnam par rgyal ba zhes bya ba mnyam pa nyid gnyis su med pa'i rgyud kyi rgyal po rdo rje dpal mchog chen po brtag pa dang po)
Toh. 453; Dg.K. rgyud, *cha*, ff. 103a–331a; KPD 82, 3–833.

Minor Transmissions of Monastic Disciple
Vinayakṣudrākavastu (also Kṣudrāgama)
'Dul ba phran tshegs kyi gzhi
Toh. 6; Dg.K. 'dul ba, *tha*, ff. 1b–310a, *da*, ff. 1b–333a.

The Ocean of Ḍākas
Ḍākārṇava (Śrīḍākārṇavamahāyoginītantrarājanāma)
Dpal mkha' 'gro rgya mtsho rnal 'byor ma'i rgyud kyi rgyal po chen po zhes bya ba
Toh. 372; Dg.K. rgyud, *kha*, ff. 137a–264b.

The Perfection of Wisdom in Eighteen Thousand Lines
Aṣṭādaśasāhasrikāprajñāpāramitā
'Phags pa shes rab kyi pha rol tu phyin pa khri brgyad stong pa zhes bya ba theg pa chen po'i mdo
Toh. 10; Dg.K. shes phyin, *ka*, ff. 1a–300a, *kha*, ff. 1a–304a, *ga*, ff. 1a–206a.

The Prophecy on Mount Gośṛṅga
Gośṛṅgavyākaraṇa
Lang ru lung bstan
Toh. 357; Dg.K. mdo sde, *aḥ*, ff. 220b–232a.
https://read.84000.co/translation/toh357.html

The Shoulder Bracelet of the Pinnacle of the Victory Banner
Dhvajāgrakeyūranāmadhāraṇī
'Phags pa rgyal mtshan gyi rtse mo'i dpung rgyan ces bya ba'i gzungs
Toh. 612; Dg.K. rgyud, *ba*, ff. 45b–46b; KPD 91, 149–55.

The Sublime Sūtra of the Great Cloud in Twelve Thousand Lines
Āryadvādaśasahasramahāmegha (more commonly, Āryamahāmeghanāmmahāyānasūtra)
'Phags pa sprin chen po stong phrag bcu gnyis pa (more commonly, 'Phags pa sprin chen po zhes bya ba theg pa chen po'i mdo)
Toh. 232; Dg.K. mdo sde, *wa*, ff. 113a–214b.
https://read.84000.co/translation/toh232.html

The Sūtra of Compassion's White Lotus
Karuṇāpuṇḍarikasūtra
'Phags pa snying rje chen po'i pad+ma dkar po zhes bya ba theg pa chen po'i mdo
Toh. 112; Dg.K. mdo sde, *cha*, ff. 129a–297a; KPD 50, 345–777.
https://read.84000.co/translation/toh112.html

The Sūtra of the Cornucopia of Avalokiteśvara's Attributes
Āryakāraṇḍavyūhanāmamahāyānasūtra
'Phags pa za ma tog bkod pa zhes bya ba theg pa chen po'i mdo
Toh. 116; Dg.K. mdo sde, *pa*, ff. 200a–247b.
https://read.84000.co/translation/toh116.html

The Sūtra Demonstrating the Purification of Infinite Approaches
Ānantamukhapariśodhananirdeśaparivarta
Sgo mtha' yas pa rnam par sbyong ba
Toh. 46; Dg.T. dkon brtsegs, *ka*, ff. 45b–99b.
https://read.84000.co/translation/toh46.html

The Sūtra Demonstrating the Three Vows
Saṃvaranirdeśaparivarta
Sdom gsum bstan pa
Toh. 45; Dg.T. dkon brtsegs, *ka*, ff. 1b–45a.

The Sūtra of the Descent to Laṅkā
Āryalaṅkāvatāramahāyānasūtra
'Phags pa lang kar gshegs pa rin po che'i mdo las sangs rgyas thams cad kyi gsung gi snying po'i shes bya ba'i le'u
Toh. 108; Dg.K. mdo sde, *ca*, ff. 192a–284b; KPD 49, 507–729.

The Sūtra of the Hundredfold Homage of Renunciation and Fulfillment
Dpang skong phyag brgya pa
Toh. 267; Dg.K. mdo sde, *ya*, ff. 1b–5b.
https://read.84000.co/translation/toh267.html

The Sūtra of the Prophetic Declaration of the Conqueror Kāśyapa Imparted to King Kṛkī in a Dream
Svapnanirdeśasūtra
Rgyal po kri kri'i rmi lam rgyal ba 'od srung gis lung bstan pa'i mdo (Rmi lam bstan pa'i mdo)
Toh. 48; Dg.K. bkon brtsegs, *ka*, ff. 203b–237b.

The Sūtra Titled King of Meditative Stability
Samādhirājasūtra
'Phags pa chos thams cad kyi rang bzhin mnyam pa nyid rnam par spros pa ting nge 'dzin gyi rgyal po zhes bya ba theg pa chen po'i mdo
Toh. 127; Dg.K. mdo sde, *da*, ff. 1b–170b.
https://read.84000.co/translation/toh127.html

The Sūtra of Youthful Examples
Daharopamasūtra (Kumāradṛṣṭāntasūtra)
Gzhon nu dpe'i mdo
Toh. 296; Dg.K. mdo sde, *sha*, ff. 295b–297a.

The Tantra of the Awakening of Vairocana
Mahāvairocanābhisambodhitantra
Rnam par snang mdzad chen po mngon par rdzogs par byang chub pa rnam par sprul pa byin gyis rlob pa shin tu rgyas pa mdo sde'i dbang po'i rgyal po zhes bya ba'i chos kyi rnam grangs
Toh. 494; Dg.K. rgyud, *tha*, ff. 151b–260a.

The Tantra of the Ornament of the Vajra Essence
Vajrahṛdayālaṃkāratantra
Dpal rdo rje snying po rgyan gyi rgyud
Toh. 451; Dg.K. rgyud, *cha*, ff. 36a–58b; KPD 82, 89–149.

TENGYUR

Abhayadatta
Narrative of the Eighty-Four Great Accomplished Masters
Caturaśītisiddhapravṛtti
Grub thob brgyad cu rtsa bzhi'i lo rgyus
TPD 48, 413–556.

Amarasiṃha
The Treasury of Amarasiṃha
Amarakoṣanāma
Mngon brjod kyi bstan bcos 'chi ba med pa'i mdzod ces bya ba skad gnyis sbyar ba
Toh. 4299; Dg.T. sgra mdo, *se*, ff. 126b–243a.

Anon.
The Alchemical Transformation of Gold
Rasāyanaśāstroddhṛti
Ggser 'gyur sbyor ba (Gser 'gyur gyi bstan bcos bsdus pa)
Toh. 4314; Dg.K. bzo rig pa/thun mong ba, *ngo*, ff. 7a–8b.

Anon.
A Commentary on the "Bhikṣuṇī Pratimokṣa Sūtra" of the Noble Mūlasarvāstivāda
Āryasarvāstivādimūlabhikṣuṇīpratimokṣasūtravṛtti
'Phags pa thams cad yod par smra ba'i rtsa ba'i dge slong ma'i so sor thar pa'i mdo'i 'grel pa
Toh. 4112; Dg.T. 'dul ba, *tsu*, ff. 1b–177a; TPD 87, 3–480.

Anon.
The Narrative of Nandimitra
Nandimitrāvadāna
Dga' ba'i bshes gnyen gyi rtogs brjod
Toh. 4146; Dg.T. 'dul ba, *su*, ff. 240a–44b.

Anon.
Questions of First Year Monks
Bhikṣuvarṣāgrapṛcchā
Dge slong gi dang po'i lo dri ba
Toh. 4133; Dg.T. 'dul ba, *su*, ff. 66a–70b; TPD 93, 911–24.

Āryadeva
The Lamp That Subsumes Conduct
Caryāmelāpakapradīpa
Spyod pa bsdus pa'i sgron ma
Toh. 1803; Dg.T. rgyud, *ngi*, ff. 57a–106b.

Purification of Mental Obscuration
Cittāvaraṇaviśodhananāmaprakaraṇa
Sems kyi sgrib sbyong
Toh. 1804; Dg.T. rgyud, *ngi*, ff. 106b–112a.

Asaṅga
The Compendium of Phenomenology
Abhidharmasamuccaya
Chos mngon pa kun las btus pa
Toh. 4049; Dg.T. sems tsam, *ri*, ff. 44b–120a; TPD 76, 116–313.

Aśvaghoṣa
Fifty Stanzas on the Spiritual Teacher
Gurupañcaśikhā
Bla ma lnga bcu pa
Toh. 3721; Dg.T. rgyud, *tshu*, ff. 10a–12a.

Ātreya
Characteristics of the Proportions of the Body
Pratibimbamānalakṣaṇa
Sku gzugs kyi tshad kyi mtshan nyid ces bya ba
Toh. 4316; Dg.T. bzo rig pa/thun mong ba, *ngo*, ff. 11a–15b.

Candragomin
The Grammar of Candragomin

Candravyākaraṇasūtranāma
Lung ston pa tsandra pa'i mdo
Toh. 4269; Dg.T. sgra mdo, *re*, ff. 1b–29a.

The Treatise on Uṇādi
Uṇ la sogs pa'i 'grel pa
Toh. 4279; Dg.T. sgra mdo, *re*, ff. 106a–142a.

Twenty Verses on the Bodhisattva Vows
Bodhisattvasaṃvaraviṃśaka
Byang chub sems dpa'i sdom pa nyi shu pa
Toh. 4081; Dg.T. sems tsam, *hi*, ff. 166b–167a; TPD 70, 447–450.

Utter Delight of the World
Lokānandanāṭaka
'Jig rten kun du dga' ba'i zlos gar zhes bya ba
Toh. 4153; Dg.T. skyes rab, *u*, ff. 197b–225a.

Candrakīrti
Clear Word Commentary on the Fundamental Stanzas of the Middle Way
Mūlamadhyamakavṛttiprasannapadā
Dbu ma rtsa ba'i 'grel pa tshig gsal ba
Toh. 3860; Dg.T. dbu ma, *'a*, ff. 1b–200a; TPD 60, 4–483.

The Commentary on "The Four Hundred Verses of the Middle Way"
Bodhisattvayogācāracatuḥśatakaṭīkā
Byang chub sems dpa'i rnal 'byor spyod pa bzhi brgya pa'i rgya cher 'grel pa
Toh. 3865; Dg.T. dbu ma, *ya*, ff. 30b–239a; TPD 60, 1008–1496.

The Extensive Commentary Called "Clarifying Lamp"
Pradīpoddyotananāmaṭīkā
Sgron ma gsal bar byed pa zhes bya ba'i rgya cher bshad pa
Toh. 1785; Dg.T. rgyud, *ha*, ff. 1b–201b.

Candranandana
Moonbeams of Word and Meaning: A Commentary on the Concise Essence
Padārthacandrikāprabhāsanāmāṣṭāṅgahṛdayavivṛtti
Tshig don zla zer (Yan lag brgyad pa'i snying po'i rnam par 'grel pa tshig gi don gyi zla zer)
Toh. 4312; Dg.T. gso ba rig pa, *ko*, ff. 1b–296a, *kho*, ff. 1b–340a, *go*, ff. 1b–304a.

Precise Terminology: A Supplement to Materia Medica
*Vaidyāṣṭāṅgahṛdayavṛttibheṣajanāmaparyāya

Sman ming zur du bkol ba sgra sbyor nges pa (Sman dpyad yan lag brgyad pa'i snying po'i 'grel pa)
Toh. 4309; Dg.T. gso ba rig pa, *he*, ff. 13b–44a.

Devākaracandra
Luminosity of Pristine Cognition
Prajñājñānaprakāśa
Shes rab ye shes gsal ba
Toh. 2226; Dg.T. rgyud, *wi*, ff. 79b–92a.

Devendramati (a.k.a. Devendrabuddhi)
A Commentary on the Difficult Points of "A Commentary on 'Valid Cognition'"
Tshad ma rnam 'grel gyi dka' 'grel
Pramāṇavārttikapañjikā
Toh. 4217; Dg.T. tshad ma, *che*, ff. 1b–326b.

Dharmakīrti
The Ascertainment of Valid Cognition
Pramāṇaviniścaya
Tshad ma rnam par nges pa
Toh. 4211; Dg.T. tshad ma, *ce*, ff. 152b–230a.

A Commentary on "A Commentary on 'Valid Cognition'"
Pramāṇavārttikavṛtti
Tshad ma rnam 'grel gyi 'grel pa (Rang don le'u la 'grel pa)
Toh. 4216; Dg.T. tshad ma, *ce*, ff. 261b–365a.

The Exposition of Valid Cognition
Pramāṇavārttikakārikā
Tshad ma rnam 'grel gyi tshig le'ur byas pa
Toh. 4210; Dg.T. tshad ma, *ce*, ff. 94b–151a.

The Inquiry into Relations
Sambandhaparīkṣāprakaraṇa
'Brel pa brtag pa'i rab tu byed pa
Toh. 4214; Dg.T. tshad ma, *ce*, ff. 255a–256a.

The Point of the Axioms
Hetubindunāmaprakaraṇa
Gtan tshigs kyi thigs pa zhes bya ba'i rab tu byed pa
Toh. 4213; Dg.T. tshad ma, *ce*, ff. 238a–255a.

The Point of Reason
Nyāyabindunāmaprakaraṇa
Rigs pa'i thigs pa zhes bya ba'i rab tu byed pa
Toh. 4212; Dg.T. tshad ma, *ce*, ff. 231b–238a.

The Proof of Other Minds
Santānāntarasiddhināmaprakaraṇa
Rgyud gzhan grub pa zhes bya ba'i rab tu byed pa
Toh. 4219; Dg.T. tshad ma, *che*, ff. 355b–359a.

The Reasoning of Polemics
Vādanyāyanāmaprakaraṇa
Rtsod pa'i rigs pa zhes bya ba'i rab tu byed pa
Toh. 4218; Dg.T. tshad ma, *che*, ff. 326b–355b.

Dharmottara
The Correct: An Explanatory Commentary on "Ascertainment of Valid Cognition" (chapter three)
Pramāṇaviniścayaṭīkā
Tshad ma rnam par nges pa'i 'grel bshad / Tshad ma rnam par nges pa'i ṭī ka 'thad ldan zhes bya ba le'u gsum pa
Toh. 4227; Dg.T. tshad ma, *tshe*, ff. 1b–178a.

The Correct: An Explanatory Commentary on "Ascertainment of Valid Cognition" (chapters one and two)
Pramāṇaviniścayaṭīkā
Tshad ma rnam par nges pa'i 'grel bshad / Tshad ma rnam par nges pa'i ṭī ka 'thad ldan zhes bya ba le'u dang po dang gnyis pa
Toh. 4229; Dg.T. tshad ma, *dze*, ff. 1b–289a.

An Extensive Commentary on "Drop of Reasoning"
Nyāyabinduṭīkā
Rigs pa'i thigs pa'i rgya cher 'grel pa
Toh. 4231; Dg.T. tshad ma, *we*, ff. 36b–92a.

Dignāga
The Compendium of Valid Cognition (a.k.a. *The Sūtra of Valid Cognition*)
Pramāṇasamuccaya (Pramāṇasūtra)
Tshad ma kun las btus pa zhes bya ba'i rab tu byed pa
Toh. 4203; Dg.T. tshad ma, *ce*, ff. 1b–13a.

Guṇaprabha

The Root Sūtra of the Vinaya
Vinayasūtra
'Dul ba'i mdo rtsa ba
Toh. 4117; Dg.T. 'dul ba, *wu*, ff. 1b–100a.

Haribhadra

A Treatise on Inflections (*The Subandhu Commentary*)
Vibhaktikārikā
Rnam dbye'i tshig le'ur byas pa ('Grel pa su bandhu)
Toh. 4274; Dg.T. sgra mdo, *re*, ff. 46a–65a.

Harṣadeva

The Drama Titled Utter Delight of the Nāgas
Nāgānandanāṭaka
Klu kun du dga' ba zhes bya ba'i zlos gar
Toh. 4154; Dg.T. skyes rab, *u*, ff. 225a–252a.

Jagaddarpaṇa

The Compendium of Rituals of the Vajra Master
Vajrācāryakriyāsamuccaya
Rdo rje slob dpon gyi bya ba kun las btus pa
Toh. 3305; Dg.T. rgyud, *bu*, ff. 48a–249a.

Jinapāda

An Explanatory Commentary on "Ornament for 'Commentary on Valid Cognition'"
Pramāṇavārttikālaṃkāraṭīkā
Tshad ma rnam 'grel gyi rgyan gyi 'grel bshad
Toh. 4222; Dg.T. tshad ma, *de*, ff. 1b–365a, *ne*, ff. 1b–312a.

Jñānaśrībhadra

A Commentary on the Sūtra of the Descent to Laṅkā
'Phags pa lang kar gshegs pa'i 'grel pa
Āryalaṅkāvatāravṛtti
Toh. 4018; Dg.T. mdo 'grel, *ni*, ff. 1b–262a.

An Explanatory Commentary on "Ascertainment of Valid Cognition"
Pramāṇaviniścayaṭīkā
Tshad ma rnam par nges pa'i 'grel bshad
Toh. 4228; Dg.T. tshad ma, *tshe*, ff. 178b–295a.

Jñānavajra

Ornament of the Heart of the Tathāgata: A Commentary on "The Descent to Laṅkā"
'Phags pa lang kar gshegs pa zhes bya ba theg pa chen po'i mdo'i 'grel pa de bzhin gshegs pa'i snying po'i rgyan zhes bya ba
Āryalaṅkāvatāranāmamahāyānasūtravṛttitathāgatahṛdayālaṃkāranāma
Toh. 4019; Dg.T. mdo 'grel, *pi*, ff. 1b–310a.

Kṛṣṇācārin

A Means for Attainment of Vajrayoginī
Rdo rje rnal 'byor ma'i sgrub thabs
TPD 42, 1234–37.

Kṣemendra

Wish-Fulfilling Vine: Narratives of Bodhisattvas
Bodhisattvāvadānakalpalatā
Byang chub sems dpa'i rtogs pa brjod pa dpag bsam gyi 'khri shing
Toh. 4155; Dg.T. skyes rab, *ke*, ff. 1b–366a, *khe*, ff. 1b–329a.

Kuddālīpāda

The Pith Instructions of the Inconceivable Stage
Acintyakramopadeśanama
Bsam gyis mi khyab pa'i rim pa'i man ngag
Toh. 2228; Dg.T. rgyud, *wi*, ff. 99b–104b.

Mahāvyutpatti

Detailed Inspection [of Terminology]
Bye brag tu rtogs par byed pa
Toh. 4346. Dg.T. sna tshogs, *co*, ff. 1b–131a.
Edited by R. Sakaki. Kyoto, 1916–1925.

Maitreya

The Ornament of Clear Realization
Abhisamayālaṃkāranāmaprajñāpāramitopadeśaśāstrakārikā
Shes rab kyi pha rol tu phyin pa'i man ngag gi bstan bcos mngon par rtogs pa'i rgyan
Toh. 3786; Dg.T. shes phyin, *ka*, ff. 1b–13a; TPD 49, 3–48.

The Ornament of the Sūtras of the Greater Vehicle
Mahāyānasūtrālaṃkārakārikā
Theg pa chen po mdo sde'i rgyan zhes bya ba'i tshig le'ur byas pa
Toh. 4020; Dg.T. sems tsam, *phi*, ff. 1b–39a; TPD 70, 805–901.

The Supreme Continuum of the Great Vehicle
Abhidhānottaratantranāma
Mngon par brjod pa'i rgyud bla ma zhes bya ba
Toh. 369; Dg.T. rgyud, *ka*, ff. 247a–370a.

Mañjuśrīkīrti
Treatise on the Termination Si and Others
Syādyantaprakriyā
Si la sogs pa'i mtha'i bya ba
Toh. 4287; Dg.T. sgra mdo, *she*, ff. 1b–54a.

Mañjuśrīmitra
The Attainment of Mañjuśrī: The Solitary Hero
*Ekavīrasādhana
'Jam dpal dpa' bo gcig grub
Toh. 2571; Dg.T. rgyud, *ngu*, ff. 31a–32a.

Maudgalyāyana
The Designation of Mundane Phenomena
Lokaprajñapti
'Jig rten gzhag pa
Toh. 4086; Dg.T. mngon pa, *i*, ff. 1b–93a.

Nāgārjuna
Discriminative Awareness: The Root Stanzas of the Middle Way
Prajñānāmamūlamadhyamakakārikā
Dbu ma rtsa ba'i tshig le'ur byas pa shes rab ces bya ba
Toh. 3824; Dg.T. dbu ma, *tsa*, ff. 1b–19a.

The Hundred Compounds
Yogaśataka
Sbyor ba brgya pa
Toh. 4306; Dg.T. gso ba rig pa, *he*, ff. 1b–8b.

The Precious Garland
Rājaparikathāratnāvalī
Rgyal po la gtam bya ba rin po che'i phreng ba
Toh. 4158; Dg.T. sprin yig, *ge*, ff. 107a–126a; TPD 96, 288–339.

The Preparation of Ava Grass
Ācāryanāgārjunabhāṣitāvabheṣajakalpa
Rrtsva a ba'i cho ga (Slob dpon klu sgrub kyis bshad pa sman ā ba'i cho ga)
Toh. 4308; Dg.T. gso ba rig pa, *he*, ff. 12a–13a.

Nāgārjunagarbha
The Discourse on Sustenance
Jīvasūtra
Sman 'tsho ba'i mdo
Toh. 4307; Dg.T. gso ba rig pa, *he*, ff. 8b–12a.

The Establishment of the Four Seals
Caturmudrāniścaya
Phyag rgya bzhi gtan la dbab pa
Toh. 2225; Dg.T. rgyud, *wi*, ff. 77a–79b.

Nāropā
The Ultimate Summary: An Explanatory Commentary on "The Summary of Empowerment"
Paramārthasaṃgrahanāmasekoddeśaṭīkā
Dbang mdor bstan pa'i 'grel bshad don dam pa bsdus pa
Toh. 1351; Dg.T. rgyud, *na*, ff. 220b–289a.

Pāṇini
The Grammar of Pāṇini
Pāṇinivyākaraṇa
Brda sprod pa pā ṇi ni'i mdo
Toh. 4420; Dg.T. sna tshogs, *to*, ff. 1b–27a.

Prajñākaragupta
An Ornament for "A Commentary on Valid Cognition"
Pramāṇavārttikālaṃkāra
Tshad ma rnam 'grel gyi rgyan
Toh. 4221; Dg.T. tshad ma, *te*, ff. 1b–308a, *the*, ff. 1b–282a.

*Pūrṇacandra
The Paradigms of Verbal Roots
Dhātukāya
Byings kyi tshogs
Toh. 4277; Dg.T. sgra mdo, *re*, ff. 71a–78a.

Ratnākaraśānti
The Precious Source of Prosody
Chandoratnākaranāma
Sdeb sbyor rin chen 'byung gnas
Toh. 4304; Dg.T. sgra mdo, *se*, ff. 361a–379a.

Sahajavajra
The Synthesis of Abiding
Sthitisamuccaya
Gnas pa bsdus pa
Toh. 2227; Dg.T. rgyud, *wi*, ff. 92a–99b5.

Śākyamati
An Explanatory Commentary on "A Commentary on Valid Cognition"
Pramāṇavārttikaṭīkā
Tshad ma rnam 'grel gyi 'grel bshad
Toh. 4220; Dg.T. tshad ma, *je*, ff. 1b–328a, *nye*, ff. 1b–282a.

Śākyaprabha
Illuminating Commentary on the Monastic Discipline of the Novitiate
Āryamūlasarvāstivādiśrāmaṇerakārikāvṛttiprabhāvatī
'Phags pa gzhi thams cad yod par smra ba'i dge tshul gyi tshig le'ur byas pa'i 'grel pa
Toh. 4125; Dg.T. 'dul ba, *shu*, ff. 74a–162b.

Saṅghabhadra
An Exegesis on "The Treasury of Phenomenology"
Abhidharmakośaśāstrakārikābhāṣya
Chos mngon pa mdzod kyi bstan bcos kyi tshig le'ur byas pa'i rnam par bshad pa
Toh. 4091; Dg.T. mngon pa, *khu*, ff. 95b–266a; TPD 79, 932–1406.

Śāntideva
The Way of the Bodhisattva
Bodhicaryāvatāra
Byang chub sems pa'i spyod pa la 'jug pa
Toh. 3871; Dg.T. dbu ma, *la*, ff. 1b–40a; TPD 61, 951–1048.

Saraha
The Spiritual Songs of the King
Dohākośanāmacaryāgīti
Do ha mdzod ces bya ba spyod pa'i glu (also known as Rgyal po'i do hā)
Toh. 2263; Dg.T. rgyud, *zhi*, ff. 26b–28b; TPD 26, 1013–19.

The Spiritual Songs of the Populace
Dohākośagīti
Do ha mdzod kyi glu (also known as Dmangs kyi do hā)
Toh. 2224; Dg.T. rgyud, *wi*, ff. 70b–77a; TPD 26, 193–208; also in DNZ, 7:7–22.

The Spiritual Songs of the Queen
Dohākośopadeśagīti
Mi zad pa'i gter mdzod man ngag gi glu (also known as Rgyal mo'i do hā and Brtsun mo'i do hā)
Toh. 2264; Dg.T. rgyud, *zhi*, ff. 28b–33b; TPD 26, 1020–34.

Śarvavarman
The Kalāpa Grammar (*The Kalāpa Sūtra*)
Kalāpasūtra
Sgra ka lā pa (Ka lā pa'i mdo)
Toh. 4282; Dg.T. sgra mdo, *le*, ff. 1b–20a.

Śrīdharasena
"Clarifying All Varieties" or "The Garland of Pearls": A Treatise on Expressions
Abhidhānaśāstraviśvalocanamityaparābhidhānamuktāvalīnāma
Mngon brjod kyi bstan bcos sna tshogs gsal ba zhes pa ming gzhan mu tig phreng ba zhes bya ba
Toh. 4453; Dg.T. sna tshogs, *po*, ff. 70b–163b; TPD 120, 1150–1385.

Subhūticandra
The Wish-Granting Cow: An Extensive Commentary on Amarasiṃha's Dictionary (*The Wish-Granting Commentary*)
Amarakoṣaṭīkākāmadhenunāma
'Chi ba med pa'i mdzod kyi rgya cher 'grel pa 'dod 'jo'i ba mo zhes bya
Toh. 4300; Dg.T. sgra mdo, *se*, ff. 244b–318a.

Sūryagarbha
The Accomplished Commentary
Saṃbandhasiddhyabhidhānaprakriyā
'Brel pa grub pa zhes bya ba'i rab tu byed pa
Toh. 4278; Dg.T. sgra mdo, *re*, ff. 78b–106a.

Sūryagupta
A Commentary on the Third Chapter of "A Commentary on 'Valid Cognition'"
*Pramāṇavārttikaṭīkāyāṃtṛtīyaparivarta, Tshad ma rnam 'grel gyi 'grel pa las le'u gsum pa
Toh. 4225; Dg.T. tshad ma, *phe*, ff. 1b–174a.

Vāgbhaṭa
The Great Treatise of the Eight Branches (*The Essence of the Eight Branches: An Explanation of Medical Practices*)
Aṣṭāṅgahṛdayanāmavaiḍūryakabhāṣya

Yan lag brgyad pa chen po (Yan lag brgyad pa'i snying po zhes bya ba'i sman dpyad kyi bshad pa)
Toh. 4311; Dg.T. gso ba rig pa, *he*, ff. 335b–410a7, *e*, ff. 1b–421a.

The Introduction to the Eight Branches
Aṣṭāṅgahṛdayasaṃhitā
Snying po bsdus pa
Toh. 4310; Dg.T. gso ba rig pa, *he*, ff. 44b–335a.

Vajragaṇṭapāda
The Five Stages of Cakrasaṃvara
Śrīcakrasaṃvarapañcakrama
'Khor lo sdom pa'i rim pa lnga pa
Toh. 1433; Dg.T. rgyud, *wa*, ff. 224b–227a.

Vasubandhu
Autocommentary on "The Treasury of Phenomenology"
Abhidharmakośabhāṣya
Chos mngon pa'i mdzod kyi bshad pa
Toh. 4090; Dg.T. mngon pa, *ku*, ff. 26b–258a; TPD 79, 65–630.
Translated from the French in Pruden 1988–90.

The Treasury of Phenomenology
Abhidharmakośakārikā
Chos mngon pa'i mdzod kyi tshig le'ur byas pa chos rjes kra shi
Toh. 4089; Dg.T. mngon pa, *ku*, ff. 1b–25a; TPD 79, 3–59.
Translated from the French in Pruden 1988–90.

Vinītadeva
A Summary of the Different Schools from the Wheel of Chronology of the Different Textual Traditions
Samayabhedoparacanacakrenikāyabhedopadeśanasaṃgrahanāma
Gzhung tha dad pa rim par bklag pa'i 'khor lo las sde pa tha dad pa bstan pa bsdus pa zhes bya ba
Toh. 4140; Dg.T. 'dul ba, *su*, ff. 154b–156b; TPD 93, 1166–73.

Vīraprabhāsvara
The Essence of the Realizations of the Eighty-Four Mahāsiddhas
Caturaśītisiddhisambodhihṛdaya
Grub thob brgyad cu rtsa bzhi'i rtogs pa'i snying po
Toh. 2292; Dg.T. rgyud, *zhi*, ff. 153a–158b; TPD 48, 562–667.

Vyāḍipāda
The Precious Garland of Mercury
Rasasiddhiśāstra
Dngul chu rin chen phreng ba (Dngul chu grub pa'i bstan bcos)
Toh. 4313; Dg.T. bzo rig pa/thun mong ba, *ngo*, ff. 1b–7a.

Yamāri (a.k.a. Jamāri)
Complete Purity: An Explanatory Commentary on "Ornament for 'Commentary on Valid Cognition'"
Pramāṇavārttikālaṃkāraṭīkāsupariśuddhānāma
Tshad ma rnam 'grel rgyan gyi 'grel bshad shin tu yongs su dag pa zhes bya ba
Toh. 4226; Dg.T. tshad ma, *phe*, ff. 174b–287a, *be*, ff. 1b–261a, *me*, ff. 1b–328a, *tse*, ff. 1b–251a.

Yaśobhūti (a.k.a. Rudrabhūti)
The Useful Study Commentary: A Commentary on the Kalāpa Sūtra
*Śiṣyahitākalāpasūtravṛtti
Lung ston pa ka lā pa'i mdo'i 'grel pa slob ma la phan pa
Toh. 4286; Dg.T. sgra mdo, *le*, ff. 75b–317a.

Yaśomitra
The Elucidating Commentary on the "Treasury of Phenomenology"
Abhidharmakośasphuṭārthā
Chos mngon pa'i mdzod kyi 'grel bshad
Toh. 4092; Dg.T. mngon pa, *gu*, ff. 1b–330a, *ngu*, ff. 1b–333a.

5. Tibetan Treatises

Ba Selnang (Sba gsal snang)
The Testament of Ba Anthology
Rba bzhed phyogs bsgrigs
Beijing: Mi rigs dpe skrun khang, 2009.
BDRC MW1KG6259

Buton Rinchendrub (Bu ston rin chen grub)
History of Buddhism Titled Treasury of the Precious Scriptures
Bde bar gshegs pa'i bstan pa'i gsal byed chos kyi 'byung gnas gsung rab rin po che'i mdzod
Beijing: Krung go'i bod kyi shes rig dpe skrun khang, 1988.
BDRC MW1923

Changkya Rolpei Dorje (Lcang skya rol pa'i rdo rje)
A Guide to the Sacred Places of the Pure Land Wutai Shan
Zhing mchog ri bo rtse lnga'i gnas bshad
Xining: Mtsho sngon mi rigs dpe skrun khang, 1993.
BDRC W8LS43784

Choje Jikten Wangchuk (Chos rje 'jigs rten dbang phyug)
Pearl Necklace: Biographies of the Lineage Holders of Taklung Lower Plain
Ma thang gi brgyud pa'i rnam thar mu tig phreng ba
In *Dpal ldan stag lung pa'i gsung rnams nor bzhi bang mdzod* [Treasury of the four jewels: Teachings of the glorious Taklungpa], vol. 18, 47–266.
Khun men: Nor bzhi bstan rgyas tshogs pa, 2007.
BDRC MW1PD166109

Denma Jamyang Tsultrim (Ldan ma 'jam dbyangs tshul khrims)
Biographies of the Successive Lives of the Karmapa
Karmapa sku phreng rim byon mdzad rnam
Lan kru'u: Kan su'u mi rigs dpe skrun khang, 1997.
BDRC MW18133

Drakpa Gyeltsen (Grags pa rgyal mtshan)
The Royal History of Tibet
Bod kyi rgyal rabs
In *Sa skya gong ma rnam lnga'i gsung 'bum dpe bsdur ma las grags pa rgyal mtshan gyi gsung* [The teachings of Drakpa Gyeltsen from the annotated collected works of the five Sakya forefathers]
Beijing: Krung go'i bod rig pa dpe skrun khang, 2007.
BDRC W2DB4569

Drakpa Tsondru (Grags pa brtson 'grus)
Letter to Lopon Jose
Slob dpon jo sras la springs pa
In *'Bri gung bka' brgyud chos mdzod chen mo* [Great Dharma compendium of the Drikung Kagyu], vol. 43, 183.
Lhasa: Bri gung mthil dgon, 2004.
BDRC MW00JW501203

Drigung Konchok Gyatso ('Bri gung dkon mchog rgya mtsho)
Doctrinal History of Drigung
'Bri gung chos 'byung
Beijing: Mi rigs dpe skrun khang, 2004.
BDRC MW27020

Drukchen Pema Karpo ('Brug chen pad+ma dkar po)
Sun of the Fully Bloomed Lotus Revealing the History of Dharma
Chos 'byung bstan pa'i padma rgyas pa'i nyin byed
Lhasa: Bod ljongs bod yig dpe rnying dpe skrun khang, 1992.
BDRC MW10437

Dudjom Jikdrel Yeshe Dorje (Bdud 'joms 'jigs bral ye shes rdo rje)
Concise Political History of Tibet: An Unprecedented Mirror of Clear Crystal
Gangs can bod chen po'i rgyal rabs bsdus gsal du bkod pa sngon med dvangs shel 'phrul gyi me long
In *Collected Works of Dudjom Jikdrel Yeshe Dorje*, vol. 3.
Kalimpong: Dupjung Lama, 1999.

Dungkar Lobzang Trinle (Dung dkar slob bzang phrin las)
The Great Dungkar [Tibetan-Tibetan] Dictionary
Dung dkar tshig mdzod chen mo
Beijing: Krung go'i bod rig pa dge skrun khang, 2002.
BDRC MW26372

Gartse Kalzang Tashi (Mgar rtse skal bzang bkra shis)
Compendium of Terminology in Tibetan Medicine
Bod sman kun 'dus ming mdzod
Xining: Mtsho sngon mi rigs dpe skrun khang, 1999.
BDRC MW20066

Gozhul Drakpa Jungne and Gyelwa Lobzang Khedrub, eds. (Go shul grags pa 'byung gnas, Rgyal ba blo bzang mkhas grub)
Lexicon of the Learned and Accomplished Masters Who Successively Appeared in the Land of Snows
Gangs can mkhas grub rim byon ming mdzod
Lanzhou: Gansu mi rigs dpe skrun khang, 1992.
BDRC MW19801

Jamgon Amezhab Ngawang Kunga Sonam ('Jam mgon A me zhabs Ngag dbang kun dga' bsod nams)
Precious Treasury of the Wondrous Sakya Line of Succession
Sa skya'i gdung rabs ngo mtshar rin po che'i bang mdzod
Beijing: Mi rigs dpe skrun khang, 1986.

Jikme Chokyi Dorje ('Jigs med chos kyi rdo rje)
Great Deities in the Tibetan Tradition
Bod brgyud nang bstan lha tshogs chen mo
Xining: Mtsho sngon mi rigs dpe skrun khang, 2001.
BDRC MW28850

Karmapa Rangjung Dorje (Kar ma pa Rang 'byung rdo rje)
The Black Anthology of the Sacred Songs of Mila Zhepei Dorje, Mighty Lord of Yoga
Rnal 'byor gyi dbang phyug mi la bzhad pa rdo rje'i gsung mgur mdzod nag ma
Chengdu: Si khron mi rigs dpe skrun khang, 2008.
BDRC MW1PD83964

Khagang Tashi Tsering, ed. (Kha sgang bkra shis tshe ring)
Studies on Ancient Tibetan Writing and Orthography
Bod kyi yig rnying zhib 'jug
Beijing: Mi rigs dpe skrun khang, 2003.
BDRC MW24989

Kunga Drolchok (Kun dga' sgrol mchog)
A Detailed Biography of Śākya Chokden
Paṇḍi ta chen po shākya mchog ldan gyi rnam thar zhib mo rnam par 'byed pa
In *Collected Works of Śākya Chokden*, vol. *ma*, ff. 1–233.
New Delhi: Nagwang Topgyel, 1995.
BDRC MW23200_F2AFDB

Kunga Namgyal (Kun dga' rnam rgyal)
Oral Instructions of the Lineage of Siddhas: The Essence of the Path of Coemergent Mahāmudrā
Phyag chen lhan cig skyes sbyor zab don lam gyi snying po grub thob brgyud pa'i zhal lung
Khams nang chen: Zur mang bdud rtsi mthil, n.d.
BDRC W1CZ2485.

Longchenpa (Klong chen pa)
Excellent Wagon: A Commentary on "Finding Rest in Illusion"
Sgyu ma'i ngal gso'i 'grel pa shing rta bzang po
In *Snga 'gyur bka' ma shin tu rgyas pa*
Chengdu: Si khron mi rigs dpe skrun khang, 2009.

Mila Repa (Mi la ras pa)
Biography and Spiritual Songs of Milarepa, the Great Lord of Yogi
Rnal 'byor gyi dbang phyug chen po mi la ras pa'i rnam mgur
Xining: Mtsho sngon mi rigs dpe skrun khang, 1999.
BDRC MW21763

Namkhai Norbu (Nam mkha'i nor bu)
The Radiance of Mount Kailash: A History of Zhang, Tibet
Zhang bod kyi lo rgyus ti se'i 'od

Beijing: Krung go'i bod kyi shes rig dpe skrun khang, 1996.
BDRC MW8LS20269

Nordrang Orgyan (Nor brang o rgyan), ed.
The Great Wondrous Key: A Compendium of Buddhist Numeric Terms, the Hundred Topics of the Land of Snow
Gangs can rig brgya'i chos kyi rnam grangs mthong tshad kun las btus pa ngo mtshar 'phrul gyi lde mig chen po
Beijing: Krung go'i bod rig pa dpe skrun khang, 2008.
BDRC MW1KG2733

Orgyan Lingpa (o rgyan gling pa)
Injunction of the King
Rgyal po'i bka'i thang yig
In *Bka' thang sde lnga* [The five injunctions].
Beijing: Mi rigs dpe skrun khang, 1986.

Pawo Tsuklak Trengwa (Dpa' bo gtsug lag phreng ba)
The Doctrinal History Titled Scholars' Feast
Chos 'byung mkhas pa'i dga' ston
New Delhi: International Academy of Indian Culture, 1962.

The Biography of Venerable Marpa: A Wondrous Description of Attainment
Rje btsun mar pa'i rnam thar grub pa'i ngo mtshar brjod pa dpa' bo gtsug lag phreng ba'i rang rnam 'khrul pa'i bzhin ras 'char ba'i me long
Vārāṇasī: Bidyā dpe mdzod khang, 2010.
BDRC MW1KG6291

Peljor Zangpo (Dpal 'byor bzang po)
Major Chinese and Tibetan Documents
Rgya bod yig tshang chen mo
Chengdu: Si khron mi rigs dpe skrun khang, 1985.
BDRC MW20848

Phakmodrupa Dorje Gyelpo (Phag mo gru pa rdo rje rgyal po)
The Dream Path of Pacification
Zhi byed rmang lam ma
In *Collected Works of Phakmodrupa*, vol. *nga*, ff. 146a–156b.
Kathmandu: Khenpo Shedrub Tenzin and Lama Thinley Namgyal, 2003.
BDRC MW23891

The Great Chronicle of the Past Lives of Glorious Phakmodrupa
Dpal phag mo gru pa'i skyes rabs chen mo

In *Collected Works of Phakmodrupa*, vol. *ka*, ff. 87a–94b.
Kathmandu: Khenpo Shedrub Tenzin and Lama Thinley Namgyal, 2003.
BDRC MW23891

Phuntsok Tseten (Ping Cuo Ci Dan)
A Clear Mirror of History: The Source of the Murals in the Potala
Pho brang po ta la'i ldebs bris ri mo'i 'byung khungs lo rgyus gsal ba'i me long
Beijing: Jiuzhou tushu chubanshe, 2000.

Shedragung Wangchuk Gyelpo (Bshad sgra gung dbang phyug rgyal po)
Bsam yas dkar chag dad pa'i sgo 'byed
Lhasa: Bod ljongs bod yig dpe rnying dpe skrun khang, 2000.
BDRC WAS00KG09682

Sonam Gyeltsen (Bsod nams rgyal mtshan)
Mirror Illuminating Royal Genealogies
Rgyal rabs gsal ba'i me long
Beijing: Mi rigs dpe skrun khang, 2002.
BDRC MW00KG09730

Sonam Kyi (Bsod nams skyid)
An Inventory of Tibetan Obelisk Inscriptions and Bells
Bod kyi rdo ring yi ge dang dril bu'i kha byang
Beijing: Mi rigs dpe skrun khang, 1984.
BDRC MW2CZ9077

Taklung Tangpa, Tashi Pel (Bkra shis dpal)
Springtime of the Excellently Flourishing Cornucopia of Devout Tales
Gtam mos gus kyi snye ma dge legs su mngon par dar ba'i dpyid
In *Stag lung chos mdzod nor bu'i phreng ba* [Taklung jewel garland treasury of dharma of the Taklung].
New Delhi: Stag lung chos mdzod dpe skrun khang, 2011.

Tāranātha, Jestun (Rje btsun tā ra nā tha)
According to the Intention of Marpa: Instructions on the Five Stages of the Noble Tradition of Guhyasamāja, Guiding Instructions to Be Accomplished in One Sitting That Are Free of the Stains of Confusion
Gsang 'dus 'phags lugs rim lnga smar khrid gdan rdzogs kyi khrid yig 'khrul ba'i dri bral zhes bya ba mar pa'i dgongs pa ji lta ba bzhugs
In *Collected Works of Tāranātha*, vol. 9, 194–222.
Beijing: Krung go'i bod rig pa dpe skrun khang, 2008.
BDRC W1PD45495

Ocean of Enlightened Activity: A Biography of the Glorious Spiritual Mentor
Dpal ldan bla ma'i rnam thar 'phrin las rgya mtsho rnam par rgyas pa
In *Collected Works of Tāranātha*, vol. 38, 72–149.
Beijing: Krung go'i bod rig pa dpe skrun khang, 2008.
BDRC W1PD45495

Tatsak Tse Wangyel (Rta tshag tshe dbang rgyal)
The Doctrinal History of Lhorong
Lho rong chos 'byung
Lhasa: Bod ljongs bod yig dpe rnying dpe skrun khang, 1994.
BDRC MW27302

Thupten Phuntsok (Thub bstan phun tshogs)
Treasure Ocean of Tibetan Lexicography
Bod yig tshig gter rgya mtsho
Chengdu: Si khron mi rigs dpe skrun tshogs pa, 2013.

6. Works in Other Languages

Akester, Matthew. 2016. *Jamyang Khyentse Wangpo's Guide to Central Tibet*. Chicago: Serindia.

Aris, Michael. 1978. "A Study on the Historical Foundations of Bhutan with a Critical Edition and Translation of Certain Bhutanese Texts in Tibetan." PhD diss., University of London.

———. 1979. *Bhutan: The Early History of a Himalayan Kingdom*. Warminster, UK: Aris and Phillips.

Baker, Ian. 2004. *The Heart of the World: A Journey to the Last Secret Place*. New York: Penguin.

Barron, Richard trans. 2005. *A Marvelous Garland of Rare Gems: Biographies of Masters of Awareness in the Dzogchen* Lineage. By Nyoshul Khenpo. Junction City, CA: Padma.

Basham, A. L. 1951. *History and Doctrines of the Ājīvikas: A Vanished Indian Religion*. London: Luzac.

Baumer, Christoph. 2011. *China's Holy Mountain: An Illustrated Journey into the Heart of Buddhism*. New York: I. B. Tauris.

Black, Deborah, trans. 1997. *Leaves of the Heaven Tree: The Great Compassion of the Buddha*. Berkeley, CA: Dharma.

Boord Martin J., trans. 2002. *A Bolt of Lightning from the Blue: The Vast Commentary on Vajrakila That Clearly Defines the Essential Points*. Berlin: Edition Khordong.

———, trans. 2010. *Roll of Thunder from the Void: Vajrakila Texts of the Northern Treasures Tradition*. Berlin: Wandel.

Buswell, Robert E. Jr., and Donald S. Lopez Jr. 2014. *The Princeton Dictionary of Buddhism*. Princeton, NJ: Princeton University Press.

Cabezón, José. 2013. *The Buddha's Doctrine and the Nine Vehicles*. New York: Oxford University Press.

Callahan, Elizabeth M., trans. 2007. *The Treasury of Knowledge: Book Six, Part Three: Frameworks of Buddhist Philosophy: A Systematic Presentation of the Cause-Based Philosophical Vehicles*. By Jamgön Kongtrul Lodrö Tayé. Ithaca, NY: Snow Lion.

———, trans. 2014. *The Profound Inner Principles*. By Rangjung Dorje, the third Karmapa. With Jamgön Kongtrul Lodrö Tayé's commentary *Illuminating "The Profound Principles."* Boston: Snow Lion.

Casey, Jane. *Taklung Painting: A Study in Chronology*. 2 vols. Chicago: Serindia, 2023.

Chan, Victor. 1994. *Tibet Handbook*. Chico, CA: Moon.

Chang, Garma C. C. 1977. *The Hundred Thousand Songs of Milarepa*. Boulder: Shambhala.

Chattopadhyaya, Debiprasad, ed. 1970. *Tāranātha's History of Buddhism in India*. Translated by Lama Chimpa and Alaka Chattopadhyaya. Simla: Indian Institute of Advanced Study.

Cleary, Thomas, trans. 1993. *The Flower Ornament Scripture*. Boston: Shambhala.

Clemente, Adriano. 1995. *The Sgra Bla Gods of the Ancestors of Gshen-Rab Mi-Bo according to the Sgra Bla Go Bsang from the Gzi Brjid*. Arcidosso: Shang-Shung Edizioni.

Conze, Edward, and E. Obermiller, eds. 1960. *Prajñā-pāramitā-ratna-guṇa-saṃcaya-gāthā*. Gravenhage: Mouton.

Cuevas, Bryan. 2015. *The All-Pervading Melodious Drumbeat: The Life of Ra Lotsawa*. New York: Penguin Books.

Dargye, Yonten. 2001. *History of the Drukpa Kagyud School in Bhutan: 12th to 17th Century A.D.* Thimphu: Yonten Dargye.

Davidson, Ronald M. 2004. *Tibetan Renaissance: Tantric Buddhism in the Rebirth of Tibetan Culture and the Rise of Sakya*. New York: Columbia University Press.

Dayal, Har. 1932. *The Bodhisattva Doctrine in Buddhist Sanskrit Literature*. London: Kegan Paul, Trench, Trubner.

De Rossi Filibeck, Elena. 1990. "A Guide-Book to Tsari." In *Reflections on Tibetan Culture: Essays in Memory of Turrell V. Wylie*, edited by Lawrence Epstein and Richard F. Sherburne, 1–10. Lewiston, NY: Edwin Mellen.

Decleer, Hubert. 1995. "Atiśa's Journey to Sumatra." In *Buddhism in Practice*, edited by Donald S. Lopez Jr., 532–40. Princeton: Princeton University Press.

———. 1997. "Atiśa's Journey to Tibet." In *Religions of Tibet in Practice*, edited by Donald S. Lopez Jr., 157–77. Princeton: Princeton University Press.

Dharmachakra Translation Committee. 2013–16. *The Noble Great Vehicle Sūtra "The Play in Full." Āryalalitavistaranāmamahāyānasūtra*. 84000: Translating the Words of the Buddha. Last modified 2023. https://read.84000.co/translation/toh95.html.

Dhongthog Rinpoche. 2016. *The Sakya School of Tibetan Buddhism: A History*. Translated by Sam van Schaik. Somerville, MA: Wisdom.

Doniger, Wendy. 2014. *On Hinduism*. New York: Oxford University Press.

Dorje, Gyurme. 1987. "The Guhyagarbhatantra and Its XIVth-Century Tibetan Commentary Phyogs bcu mun sel." 3 vols. PhD diss., University of London.

———, trans. 2005. *The Tibetan Book of the Dead*. New York: Viking.

———. 2009. *Tibet*. 4th ed. Bath: Footprint.

———, trans. 2012. *The Treasury of Knowledge: Book Six, Parts One and Two: Indo-Tibetan Classical Learning and Buddhist Phenomenology*. By Jamgön Kongtrul Lodrö Tayé. Boston: Snow Lion.

———, trans. 2016. *The Complete Nyingma Tradition from Sutra to Tantra, Books 15–17: The Essential Tantras of Mahayoga*. By Choying Tobden Dorje. Boulder: Snow Lion.

———, trans. 2017. *The Complete Nyingma Tradition from Sutra to Tantra, Book 13: Philosophical Systems and Lines of Transmission*. By Choying Tobden Dorje. Boulder: Snow Lion.

———, trans. 2020. *Jonang: The One Hundred and Eight Teaching Manuals*. The Treasury of Precious Instructions, vol. 18. Compiled by Jamgön Kongtrul Lodrö Tayé. Boulder: Snow Lion.

Dorje, Gyurme, Tashi Tsering, Heather Stoddard, and Andre Alexander, eds. 2010. *Jokhang: Tibet's Most Sacred Buddhist Temple*. London: Edition Hansjorg Mayer.

Dotson, Brian. 2007. "Divination and Law in the Tibetan Empire: The Role of Dice in the Legislation of Loans, Interest, Marital Law and Troop Conscription." In *Contributions to the Cultural History of Early Tibet*, edited by Matthew T. Kapstein and Brandon Dotson, 3–77. Leiden: Brill.

Douglas, Kenneth, and Gwendolyn Bays. 1978. *The Life and Liberation of Padmasambhava*. Berkeley, CA: Dharma.

Douglas, Nik, and Meryl White. 1976. *Karmapa: Black Hat Lama of Tibet*. London: Luzac.

Dowman, Keith. 1995. *Power Places of Kathmandu: Hindu and Buddhist Holy Sites in the Sacred Valley of Nepal*. Rochester, VT: Inner Traditions.

Dudjom Rinpoche. 1991. *The Nyingma School of Tibetan Buddhism: Its Fundamentals and History*. Translated and edited by Gyurme Dorje and Matthew Kapstein. 2 vols. Boston: Wisdom.

Dutt, Nalinaksha. 1978. *Buddhist Sects in India*. Delhi: Motilal Banarsidass.

Edgerton, Franklin. 1953. *Buddhist Hybrid Sanskrit*. Delhi: Motilal Banarsidass.

Ehrhard, Franz-Karl. 1989. "A Renovation of Svayambhunath-Stupa in the 18th Century and Its History (according to Tibetan Sources)." *Ancient Nepal: Journal of the Department of Archaeology* 114:1–8.

Eimer, Helmut. 1974–75. "Die Gar log-Episode bei Padma dkar po und ihre Quellen." *Orientalia Suecana* 23–24:182–99.

Ellingson, Ter. 1990. "Tibetan Monastic Constitutions: The Bca' yig." In *Reflections on Tibetan Culture: Essays in Memory of Turrell V. Wylie*, edited Lawrence Epstein and Richard F. Sherburne, 205–29. Lewiston, NY: Edwin Mellen.

Emmerick, R. E. 1967. *Tibetan Texts concerning Khotan*. London: Oxford University Press.

Evans-Wentz, W. Y. 1928. *Tibet's Great Yogi Milarepa: A Biography from the Tibetan being the Jetsün-Kahbum or Biographical History of Jetsün-Milarepa, according to the Late Lama Kazi Dawa-Samdup's English Rendering*. London: Oxford University Press.

Falk, Harry. 2011. "The 'Split' Collection of Kharoṣṭhī Texts." *ARIRIAB* 14: 13–23.

Falk, Harry, and Seishi Karashima. 2012. "A First-Century Prajñāpāramitā Manuscript from Gandhāra, *Parivarta* 1 (Texts from the Split Collection 1)." *ARIRIAB* 15:19–61.

Gardner, Alexander. 2009. "Gara Lama Sonam Rabten." Treasury of Lives. December 2009. https://treasuryoflives.org/biographies/view/Gara-Lama-Sonam-Rapten/13072.

Garry, Ron. 2007. "The Seventh Riwoche Jedrung, Jampa Jungne." Treasury of Lives. August 2007. https://treasuryoflives.org/biographies/view/Riwoche-Jedrung-07-Jampa-Jungne/10315.

Gerke, Barbara. 2012. *Long Lives and Untimely Deaths: Life-Span Concepts and Longevity Practices among Tibetans in the Darjeeling Hills, India*. Leiden: Brill.

Gray, David B., trans. 2007. *The Cakrasaṃvara Tantra*. New York: American Institute of Buddhist Studies.

Grünwedel, Albert. 1933. *Die Legenden des Na ro pa, des Hauptvertreters des Nekromanten- und Hexentums*. Leipzig: Otto Harrassowitz.

Gruschke, Andreas. 2004. *The Cultural Monuments of Tibet's Outer Provinces: Kham*. 2 vols. Thailand: White Lotus.

Guarisco, Elio, and Ingrid McLeod, trans. 2005. *The Treasury of Knowledge: Book Six, Part Four: Systems of Buddhist Tantra*. By Jamgön Kongtrul Lodrö Tayé. Ithaca, NY: Snow Lion.

———, trans. 2008. *The Treasury of Knowledge: Book Eight, Part Three: The Elements of Tantric Practice*. By Jamgön Kongtrul Lodrö Tayé. Ithaca, NY: Snow Lion.

Guenther, Herbert, trans. 1963. *The Life and Teaching of Nāropa*. Oxford: Clarendon.

———. 1971. *Buddhist Philosophy in Theory and Practice*. Boulder: Shambhala.

———. 1993. *Ecstatic Spontaneity: Saraha's Three Cycles of Dohā*. Berkeley, CA: Asian Humanities Press.

Harding, Sarah, trans. 2013. *Machik's Complete Explanation: Clarifying the Meaning of Chöd*. Boston: Snow Lion.

———, trans. 2016. *Chöd: The Sacred Teachings on Severance*. The Treasury of Precious Instructions, vol. 14. Compiled by Jamgön Kongtrul Lodrö Tayé. Boulder: Snow Lion.

Hazod, Guntram, Tsering Gyalbo, and Per K. Sørensen. 2000. *Civilization at the Foot of Mount Sham-po: The Royal House of 1Ha Bug-pa-can and the History of g.Ya'-bzang*. Vienna: Verlag der Österreichischen Akademie der Wissenschaften.

Heimbel, Jörg. 2013. "The Jo gdan tshogs sde bzhi: An Investigation into the History of the Four Monastic Communities in Śākyaśrībhadra's Vinaya Tradition." In *Nepalica-Tibetica: Festgabe for Christoph Cüppers*, vol. 1, edited by Franz-Karl

Ehrhard and Petra Maurer, 187–242. Andiast: International Institute for Tibetan and Buddhist Studies.

Henning, Edward. 2007. *Kālacakra and the Tibetan Calendar*. New York: American Institute of Buddhist Studies.

Higgins, David. 2006. "On the Development of the Non-Mentation (*Amansikāra*) Doctrine in Indo-Tibetan Buddhism." *Journal of the International Association of Buddhist Studies* 29 (2): 255–303.

Hirshberg, Daniel Alexander. 2016. *Remembering the Lotus-Born: Padmasambhava in the History of Tibet's Golden Age*. Somerville, MA: Wisdom.

Hopkins, Jeffrey, trans. 1985. *The Kālachakra Tantra: Rite of Initiation for the Stage of Generation: A Commentary on the Text of Kay-drup-Ge-lek-bēl-sang-bō*. London: Wisdom.

Jackson, David P. 2012. *Mirror of the Buddha: Early Portraits from Tibet*. New York: Rubin Museum of Art.

Jamgön Kongtrul Lodrö Tayé. 1995. *The Treasury of Knowledge: Book One: Myriad Worlds*. Translated by the Kalu Rinpoché Translation Group. Ithaca, NY: Snow Lion.

———. 2011. *The One Hundred Tertöns*. Translated by Yeshe Gyamtso. Woodstock: KTD.

Jamspal, Lobzang, et al., trans. 2004. *The Universal Vehicle Discourse Literature*. New York: American Institute of Buddhist Studies.

Jinpa, Thupten, trans. 2008. *The Book of Kadam: The Core Texts*. Boston: Wisdom.

———, trans. 2013. *Wisdom of the Kadam Masters*. Boston: Wisdom.

Kapstein, Matthew T. 2001. *Reason's Traces: Identity and Interpretation in Indian and Tibetan Buddhist Thought*. Boston: Wisdom.

———. 2006. *The Tibetans*. Oxford: Blackwell.

Karma Thinley. 1980. *The History of the Sixteen Karmapas of Tibet*. Boulder: Prajñā Press.

Karmay, Samten G., trans. 1972. *The Treasury of Good Sayings: A Tibetan History of Bon*. London: Oxford University Press.

Khenpo Könchog Gyaltsen, trans. 1984. *Prayer Flags: The Life and Spiritual Teachings of Jigten Sumgön*. Ithaca, NY: Snow Lion.

———, trans. 1990. *The Great Kagyu Masters: The Golden Lineage Treasury*. Ithaca, NY: Snow Lion.

Kilty, Gavin, trans. 2010. *Mirror of Beryl: A Historical Introduction to Tibetan Buddhism*. By Desi Sangye Gyatso. Boston: Wisdom.

Kloetzli, W. Randolph. 1983. *Buddhist Cosmology: Science and Theology in the Images of Motion and Light*. Delhi: Motilal Banarsidass.

Komarovski, Yaroslav. 2007. "Echoes of Empty Luminosity: Reevaluation and Unique Interpretation of Yogācāra and Niḥsvabhāvavāda Madhyamaka by the Fifteenth Century Tibetan Thinker Śākya Mchog Ldan." PhD diss., University of Virginia.

Konchog Lhadrepa and Charlotte Davis. 2017. *The Art of Awakening: A User's Guide to Tibetan Buddhist Art and Practice*. Boulder: Snow Lion.

Konow, Sten. 1941. *The Two First Chapters of the Daśasāhasrikā Prajñāpāramitā: Restoration of the Sanskrit Text, Analysis, and Index*. Oslo: I kommisjon hos J. Dybwad.

Kossak, Steven M. and Jane Casey Singer. 1997. *Sacred Visions: Paintings from Central Tibet*. New York: Metropolitan Museum of Art.

Kunsang, Erik Pema, trans. 1999. *Light of Wisdom*. Vol. 1. Kathmandu: Rangjung Yeshe.

Lama Kunsang, Lama Pemo, Aubèle Marie, and Maureen Lander. 2012. *History of the Karmapas: The Odyssey of the Tibetan Masters with the Black Crown*. Ithaca, NY: Snow Lion.

Lamotte, Étienne. 1988. *History of Indian Buddhism*. Translated from the French by Sara Boin -Webb. Louvain-la-Neuve: Université catholique de Louvain, Institut orientaliste.

Lessing, Ferdinand D., and Alex Wayman, eds. and trans. 1968. *Mkhas-grub rje's "Fundamentals of the Buddhist Tantras": Rgyud sde spyiḥi rnam par gźag pa rgyas par brjod*. Indo-Iranian Monographs, vol. 8. The Hague: Mouton.

Lhalungpa, Lobsang P. 1992. *The Life of Milarepa*. New York: Viking Penguin.

Mani, Vettam. 1964. *Puranic Encyclopaedia*. Delhi: Motilal Banarsidass.

Martin, Dan. 1994. "Pearls from Bones: Relics, Chortens, Tertons, and the Signs of Saintly Death in Tibet." *Numen* 41, no. 3 (September): 273–324.

———. 2010. "Book-Moving Incident of 1209." In *Edition, Éditions: L'écrit au Tibet, Évolution et Devenir*, edited by Anne Chayet, Cristina Scherrer-Schaub, Françoise Robin, and Jean-Luc Achard, 197–217. Munich: Indus Verlag.

———. 2018. "Art in the Life of Atiśa: Questions about 11th-Century Pāla or Pāla-Inspired Painting in Tibet." Paper presented at The Silk Road and the Art of the Tibetan Plateau Forum: Pāla Art and Its Influence in China, Asia Society, Hong Kong, May 13.

Marullo, Clara. 1995. *The Last Forbidden Kingdom, Mustang: Land of Tibetan Buddhism*. Rutland, VT: Charles E. Tuttle.

Matthiessen, Peter, and Thomas Laird. 1996. *East of Lo Monthang: In the Land of Mustang*. Boston: Shambhala.

Mills, Martin A. 2007. "Reassessing the Supine Demoness: Royal Buddhist Geomancy in the Srong btsan sgam po Mythology." *Journal of the International Association of Tibetan Studies* 3 (December): 15–21.

Nalanda Translation Committee. 1999. *The Life of Marpa the Translator*. Boston: Shambhala.

Namkhai Norbu and Donatella Rossi. 2013. *A History of Zhang Zhung and Tibet*. Berkeley, CA: North Atlantic Books.

Ñāṇamoli, Bhikku, trans. 1979. *The Path of Purification* (*Visuddhimagga*). By Bhadantācariya Buddhaghosa. Kandy, Sri Lanka: Buddhist Publication Society.

Nebesky-Wojkowitz, René. 1975. *Oracles and Demons of Tibet: The Cult and Iconography of the Tibetan Deities*. Graz: Akademische Druck-u.

Ngawang Zangpo, trans. 2010. *The Treasury of Knowledge: Books Two, Three, and Four: Buddhism's Journey to Tibet*. By Jamgön Kongtrul Lodrö Tayé. Ithaca, NY: Snow Lion.

———, trans. 2014. *The Complete Nyingma Tradition from Sutra to Tantra, Books 1–10: Foundations of the Buddhist Path*. By Choying Tobden Dorje. Boston: Snow Lion.

Nyima, Tudeng, and Gyurme Dorje, trans. 2001. *An Encyclopaedic Tibetan-English Dictionary*. Vol. 1. London: Nationalities Publishing House/SOAS.

Padmasambhava. 1998. *Natural Liberation: Padmasambhava's Teachings on the Six Bardos*. Commentary by Gyatrul Rinpoche. Translated by B. Alan Wallace. Somerville, MA: Wisdom.

Parfionovitch, Yuri, Gyurme Dorje, and Fernand Meyer. 1992. *Tibetan Medical Paintings*. London: Serindia.

Patrul Rinpoche. 1994. *The Words of My Perfect Teacher*. Translated by the Padmakara Translation Group. Boston: Shambhala.

———. 2016. *The Nature of Mind: The Dzogchen Instructions of Aro Yeshe Jungne*. Boulder: Shambhala.

Peissel, Michael. 1967. *Mustang: A Lost Tibetan Kingdom*. New Delhi: Faith Books.

Phuntsho, Karma. 2013. The History of Bhutan. London: Haus.

Pruden, Leo M., trans. 1988–90. *Abhidharmakośabhāṣyaṃ*. By Vasubandhu. 4 vols. Berkeley, CA: Asian Humanities Press.

Richardson, Hugh. 1998. *High Peaks, Pure Earth: Collected Writings on Tibetan History and Culture*. London: Serindia.

Roberts, Peter Alan. 2007. *The Biographies of Rechungpa: The Evolution of a Tibetan Hagiography*. London: Routledge.

Robinson, James B. 1979. *Buddha's Lions: The Lives of the Eighty-Four Siddhas*. Berkeley, CA: Dharma.

Roerich, George, trans. 1949. *The Blue Annals*. 1st ed. Delhi: Motilal Banarsidass.

Sangyes Nyenpa. 2014. *Tilopa's Mahamudra Upadesha: The Gangama Instructions with Commentary*. Translated by David Molk. Boston: Snow Lion.

Schaeffer, Kurtis R., Matthew Kapstein, and Gray Tuttle, eds. 2013. *Sources of Tibetan Tradition*. New York: Columbia University Press.

Shantideva. 2006. *The Way of the Bodhisattva*. Translated by the Padmakara Translation Group. Rev. ed. Boulder: Shambhala.

Sherburne, Richard, trans. 2000. *The Complete Works of Atīśa Śrī Dīpaṁkara Jñāna, Jo-bo-rje: The Lamp for the Path and Commentary*. Together with the newly translated twenty-five key texts (Tibetan and English texts). New Delhi: Aditya Prakashan.

Schuh, Dieter. 1973. *Untersuchungen zur Geschichte der tibetischen Kalenderrechnung*. Wiesbaden: F. Steiner.

Schwieger, Peter. 1996. "The Lineage of the Noble House of Ga-Zi in East Tibet." *Kailash: A Journal of Himalayan Studies* 18 (3–4): 115–32.

Shakabpa, Wangchuk D. 1967. *Tibet: A Political History*. New Haven, CT: Yale University Press.

———. 1982. *Lha ldan rwa sa 'phrul-snang gtsug lag khaṅ gi dkar chag* [Catalog and guide to the central temple of Lhasa]. Kalimpong, West Bengal: Shakabpa House.

Slobodník, Martin. 2004. "The Relations between the Chinese Ming Dynasty and the Tibetan Ruling House of Phag-mo-gru in the Years 1368–1434: Political and Religious Aspects." *Asian and African Studies* 13 (2): 155–71.

Snellgrove, David Llewellyn. 1959. *The Hevajra Tantra: A Critical Study*. 2 vols. London: Oxford University Press.

Sørensen, Per K., trans. 1994. *Mirror Illuminating Royal Genealogies: An Annotated Translation of the XIVth Century Tibetan Chronicle rGyal rabs gsal ba'i me long*. Wiesbaden: Harrassowitz Verlag.

Sørensen, Per K., and Guntram Hazod. 2007. *Rulers on the Celestial Plain: Ecclesiastic and Secular Hegemony in Medieval Tibet: A Study of Tshal Gung-Thang*. Vienna: Verlag der Österreichischen Akademie der Wissenschaften.

Sørensen, Per K., Guntram Hazod, and Gyalpo Tsering. 2005. *Thundering Falcon: An Inquiry into the History and Cult of Khra-'Brug, Tibet's First Buddhist Temple*. Vienna: Österreichischen Akademie der Wissenschaften.

Sperling, Elliot. 1980. "The 5th Karmapa and Some Aspects of the Relationship between Tibet and the Early Ming." In *Tibetan Studies in Honour of Hugh Richardson*, edited by Michael Aris and Aung San Suu Kyi, 280–89. Warminster, UK: Aris and Phillips.

———. 1990. "Ming Ch'eng-tsu and the Monk Officials of Glingtshang and Gongyo." In *Reflections on Tibetan Culture: Essays in Memory of Turrell V. Wylie*, edited by Lawrence Epstein and Richard F. Sherburne, 75–90. Lewiston, NY: Edwin Mellen.

Speyer, J. S., trans. 1895. *The Jātakamālā of Āryasūra*. London: The Pali Text Society.

Stein, Rolf. 1951. "Mi-ñag et Si-hia, géographie historique et légendes ancestrales." *Bulletin de l'École française d'Extrême-Orient* 44, no. 1: 223–65.

———. 1962. *La Civilisation Tibétaine*. Paris: Dunod.

Taranatha. 2003. *Le Soleil de la Confiance: La vie du Bouddha*. Translated by Anne Benson. Saint-Léon-sur-Vézère, France: Padmakara.

Tashi Tsering. 2010. "Jowo Śākyamuni." In *Jokhang: Tibet's Most Sacred Buddhist Temple*, edited by Gyurme Dorje et al., 123–58. London: Edition Hansjorg Mayer.

Tate, John. 1989–90. "The Sixteen Arhats in Tibetan Painting." *Oriental Art* 35 (4): 196–206.

Templeman, David, trans. 1983. *Tāranātha's "Bka' Babs Bdun Ldan": The Seven Instruction Lineages*. Dharamsala: Library of Tibetan Works and Archives.

Thartang Tulku. 1984. *Crystal Mirror*. Vol. 6, *Buddha, Dharma, and Sangha: Roots of Transmission*. Berkeley, CA: Dharma.

Thrangu Rinpoche. 2002. *Rechungpa: A Biography of Milarepa's Disciple*. Boulder: Namo Buddha.

Thurman, Robert. 1982. *The Life and Teachings of Tsong-Khapa*. Dharamsala: Library of Tibetan Works and Archives.

Torricelli, Fabrizio, and Sangye T. Naga, trans. 1995. *The Life of the Mahāsiddha Tilopa*. By Mar-pa Chos-kyi blo-gros. Dharamsala: Library of Tibetan Works and Archives.

Tsangyang Heruka. *The Life of Marpa the Translator*. Translated by the Nalanda Translation Committee under the direction of Chögyam Trungpa. Boulder: Shambhala, 2018.

Tucci, Giuseppe. 1999. *Tibetan Painted Scrolls*. Bangkok: SDI Publications.

Uray, Géza. 1972. "The Narrative of Legislation and Organization of the Mkhas-pa'i dga'-ston: The Origins of the Traditions concerning Sron-brcan sgam-po as First legislator and Organizer of Tibet." *Acta Orientalia Academiae Scientiarum Hungaricae* 26 (1): 11–68.

van der Kuijp, Leonard and Gray Tuttle. 2014. "Altan Qaγan (1507–1582) of the Tümed Mongols and the Stag lung Abbot Kun dga' bkra shis rgyal mtshan (1575–1635)." In *Trails of the Tibetan Tradition: Papers for Elliot Sperling*, edited by Roberto Vitali, with assistance from Gedun Rabsel and Nicole Willock, 461–82. Dharamsala: Amnye Machen Institute.

van Schaik, Sam, and Imre Galambos. 2011. *Manuscripts and Travellers: The Sino-Tibetan Documents of a Tenth-Century Buddhist Pilgrim*. Studies in Manuscript Cultures, vol. 2. Boston: De Gruyter.

Verhagen, Peter. 1991. "Sanskrit Grammatical Literature in Tibet: A First Survey." In *Panels of the VIIth World Sanskrit Conference: Kern Institute, Leiden: August 23–29, 1987*, edited by Johannes Bronkhorst, 47–63. Leiden: Brill.

Vitali, Roberto. 1996. *The Kingdoms of Gu.ge Pu.hrang*. Dharamsala: Tho ling dpe med lhun gyis grub pa'i gtsug lag khang lo 1000 'khor ba'i rjes dran mdzad sgo'i sgrig tshogs chung.

Wang Yao. 1979. "Huanghe yuan shang dahu—zhaling, eling mingcheng weizhi kaoshi" [The upper source of the Yellow River—Skya rengs, Sngon rengs] *Shehui kexue zhanxian* 3:163–68.

Willam de Visser, Marinus. 1919. *De Arhats in China en Japan*. Amsterdam: J. Müller.

Williams, Paul. 1989. *Mahayana Buddhism: The Doctrinal Foundations*. London: Routledge.

Yeshe De Project, trans. 1986a. *The Fortunate Aeon: How the Thousand Buddhas become Enlightened*. 4 vols. Berkeley, CA: Dharma.

———. 1986b. *Ancient Tibet*. Berkeley, CA: Dharma.

Index